Bioethics

BLACKWELL PHILOSOPHY ANTHOLOGIES

Each volume in this outstanding series provides an authoritative and comprehensive collection of the essential primary readings from philosophy's main fields of study. Designed to complement the *Blackwell Companions to Philosophy* series, each volume represents an unparalleled resource in its own right, and will provide the ideal platform for course use.

1. Cottingham: *Western Philosophy: An Anthology* (second edition)
2. Cahoone: *From Modernism to Postmodernism: An Anthology* (expanded second edition)
3. LaFollette: *Ethics in Practice: An Anthology* (third edition)
4. Goodin and Pettit: *Contemporary Political Philosophy: An Anthology* (second edition)
5. Eze: *African Philosophy: An Anthology*
6. McNeill and Feldman: *Continental Philosophy: An Anthology*
7. Kim and Sosa: *Metaphysics: An Anthology*
8. Lycan and Prinz: *Mind and Cognition: An Anthology* (third edition)
9. Kuhse and Singer: *Bioethics: An Anthology* (second edition)
10. Cummins and Cummins: *Minds, Brains, and Computers – The Foundations of Cognitive Science: An Anthology*
11. Sosa, Kim, Fantl, and McGrath *Epistemology: An Anthology* (second edition)
12. Kearney and Rasmussen: *Continental Aesthetics – Romanticism to Postmodernism: An Anthology*
13. Martinich and Sosa: *Analytic Philosophy: An Anthology*
14. Jacquette: *Philosophy of Logic: An Anthology*
15. Jacquette: *Philosophy of Mathematics: An Anthology*
16. Harris, Pratt, and Waters: *American Philosophies: An Anthology*
17. Emmanuel and Goold: *Modern Philosophy – From Descartes to Nietzsche: An Anthology*
18. Scharff and Dusek: *Philosophy of Technology – The Technological Condition: An Anthology*
19. Light and Rolston: *Environmental Ethics: An Anthology*
20. Taliaferro and Griffiths: *Philosophy of Religion: An Anthology*
21. Lamarque and Olsen: *Aesthetics and the Philosophy of Art – The Analytic Tradition: An Anthology*
22. John and Lopes: *Philosophy of Literature – Contemporary and Classic Readings: An Anthology*
23. Cudd and Andreasen: *Feminist Theory: A Philosophical Anthology*
24. Carroll and Choi: *Philosophy of Film and Motion Pictures: An Anthology*
25. Lange: *Philosophy of Science: An Anthology*
26. Shafer-Landau and Cuneo: *Foundations of Ethics: An Anthology*
27. Curren: *Philosophy of Education: An Anthology*
28. Shafer-Landau: *Ethical Theory: An Anthology*
29. Cahn and Meskin: *Aesthetics: A Comprehensive Anthology*
30. McGrew, Alspector-Kelly and Allhoff: *The Philosophy of Science: An Historical Anthology*
31. May: *Philosophy of Law: Classic and Contemporary Readings*
32. Rosenberg and Arp: *Philosophy of Biology: An Anthology*
33. Kim, Korman, and Sosa: *Metaphysics: An Anthology* (second edition)
34. Martinich and Sosa: *Analytic Philosophy: An Anthology* (second edition)
35. Shafer-Landau: *Ethical Theory: An Anthology* (second edition)
36. Hetherington: *Metaphysics and Epistemology: A Guided Anthology*
37. Scharff and Dusek: *Philosophy of Technology – The Technological Condition: An Anthology* (second edition)
38. LaFollette: *Ethics in Practice: An Anthology* (fourth edition)
39. Davis: *Contemporary Moral and Social Issues: An Introduction through Original Fiction, Discussion, and Readings*
40. Kuhse, Schüklenk, and Singer: *Bioethics: An Anthology* (third edition)

Bioethics

An Anthology

THIRD EDITION

Edited by

Helga Kuhse, Udo Schüklenk, and Peter Singer

WILEY Blackwell

Contents

Acknowledgments

The editor and publisher gratefully acknowledge the permission granted to reproduce the copyright material in this book:

1 John Finnis, "Abortion and Health Care Ethics," pp. 547–57 from Raanan Gillon (ed.), *Principles of Health Care Ethics*, Chichester: John Wiley, 1994. Reproduced with permission from John Wiley & Sons.

2 Michael Tooley, "Abortion and Infanticide," pp. 37–65 from *Philosophy and Public Affairs* 1 (1972). Reproduced with permission from John Wiley & Sons.

3 Judith Jarvis Thomson, "A Defense of Abortion," pp. 47–66 from *Philosophy and Public Affairs* 1: 1 (1971). Reproduced with permission from John Wiley & Sons.

4 Don Marquis, "Why Abortion Is Immoral," *Journal of Philosophy* 86: 4 (April 1989): 183–202.

5 Gregory Pence, "Multiple Gestation and Damaged Babies: God's Will or Human Choice?" This essay draws on "The McCaughey Septuplets: God's Will or Human Choice," pp. 39–43 from Gregory Pence, *Brave New Bioethics*, Lanham, MD: Rowman & Littlefield, 2002 © Gregory Pence 2002. Courtesy of G. Pence.

6 Dorothy A. Greenfeld and Emre Seli, "Assisted Reproduction in Same Sex Couples," pp. 289–301 from M.V. Sauer (ed.), *Principles of Oocyte and Embryo Donation*, Springer-Verlag, 2013. With kind permission from Springer Science+Business Media.

7 Derek Parfit, "Rights, Interests, and Possible People," pp. 369–75 from Samuel Gorovitz et al. (eds.), *Moral Problems in Medicine*, Englewood Cliffs, NJ: Prentice Hall, 1976. Courtesy of D. Parfit.

8 Ruby Catsanos, Wendy Rogers, and Mianna Lotz, "The Ethics of Uterus Transplantation," pp. 65–73 from *Bioethics* 27: 2 (2013). Reproduced by permission of John Wiley & Sons.

9 Laura M. Purdy, "Genetics and Reproductive Risk: Can Having Children be Immoral?," pp. 39–49 from *Reproducing Persons: Issues in Feminist Bioethics*, Ithaca, NY: Cornell University Press, 1996. Reproduced with permission from Cornell University Press.

10 Adrienne Asch, "Prenatal Diagnosis and Selective Abortion: A Challenge to Practice and Policy," pp. 1649–57 from *American Journal of Public Health* 89: 11 (1999). Reproduced with permission from American Public Health Association.

11 Ruth Chadwick and Mairi Levitt: "Genetic Technology: A Threat to Deafness," pp. 209–15 from *Medicine, Healthcare and Philosophy* 1 (1998). With kind permission from Springer Science+Business Media.

12 The Ethics Committee of the American Society of Reproductive Medicine, "Sex Selection and Preimplantation Genetic Diagnosis," pp. 595–8 from *Fertility and Sterility* 72: 4 (October 1999). Reprinted with permission from Elsevier.

13 Julian Savulescu and Edgar Dahl, "Sex Selection and Preimplantation Diagnosis: A Response to the Ethics Committee of the American Society of Reproductive Medicine," pp. 1879–80 from *Human Reproduction* 15: 9 (2000). By permission of Oxford University Press.

14 John A. Robertson, Jeffrey P. Kahn, and John E. Wagner, "Conception to Obtain Hematopoietic Stem Cells," pp. 34–40 from *Hastings Center Report* 32: 3 (May/June 2002). Reproduced with permission from John Wiley & Sons.

15 David King, "Why We Should Not Permit Embryos to Be Selected as Tissue Donors," pp. 13–16 from *The Bulletin of Medical Ethics* 190 (August 2003). Copyright © RSM Press, 2003. Reproduced by permission of SAGE Publications Ltd., London, Los Angeles, New Delhi, Singapore and Washington DC.

16 Michael Tooley, "The Moral Status of the Cloning of Humans," pp. 67–101 from James M. Humber and Robert I. Almeder (eds.), *Human Cloning*, Totowa, NJ: Humana Press, 1998. With kind permission from Springer Science+Business Media.

17 Jonathan Glover, "Questions about Some Uses of Genetic Engineering," pp. 25–33, 33–6, 42–3, and 45–53 from *What Sort of People Should There Be?* Harmondsworth: Penguin Books, 1984. Reproduced by permission of Penguin Books Ltd.

18 David B. Resnik, "The Moral Significance of the Therapy–Enhancement Distinction in Human Genetics," pp. 365–77 from *Cambridge Quarterly of Healthcare Ethics* 9: 3 (Summer 2000) © Cambridge University Press. Reproduced with permission.

19 Ainsley Newson and Robert Williamson, "Should We Undertake Genetic Research on Intelligence?," pp. 327–42 from *Bioethics* 13: 3/4 (1999). Reproduced with permission from John Wiley & Sons.

20 Nick Bostrom, "In Defense of Posthuman Dignity," pp 202–14 from *Bioethics* 19: 3 (2005). Reproduced with permission from John Wiley & Sons.

21 Jonathan Glover, "The Sanctity of Life," pp. 39–59 from *Causing Death and Lives*, London: Pelican, 1977. Reproduced by permission of Penguin Books Ltd.

22 Sacred Congregation for the Doctrine of the Faith, "Declaration on Euthanasia," Vatican City, 1980.

23 Germain Grisez and Joseph M. Boyle, Jr., "The Morality of Killing: A Traditional View,"

pp. 381–419 from *Life and Death with Liberty and Justice: A Contribution to the Euthanasia Debate*, Notre Dame, IN: University of Notre Dame Press, 1971.

24 James Rachels, "Active and Passive Euthanasia," pp. 78–80 from *New England Journal of Medicine* 292 (1975). Copyright © 1975 Massachusetts Medical Society. Reprinted with permission from Massachusetts Medical Society.

25 Winston Nesbitt, "Is Killing No Worse Than Letting Die?," pp. 101–5 from *Journal of Applied Philosophy* 12: 1 (1995). Reproduced with permission from John Wiley & Sons.

26 Helga Kuhse, "Why Killing Is Not Always Worse – and Sometimes Better – Than Letting Die," pp. 371–4 from *Cambridge Quarterly of Healthcare* 7: 4 (1998). © Cambridge University Press. Reproduced with permission.

27 Franklin G. Miller, Robert D. Truog and Dan W. Brock, "Moral Fictions and Medical Ethics," pp. 453–60 from *Bioethics* 24:9 (2010). Reproduced with permission from John Wiley & Sons.

28 Neil Campbell, "When Care Cannot Cure: Medical Problems in Seriously Ill Babies," pp. 327–44 from F. K. Beller and R. F. Weir (eds.), *The Beginning of Human Life*, Dordrecht: Kluwer Academic Publishers, 1994. With kind permission from Springer Science+Business Media.

29 R. M. Hare, "The Abnormal Child: Moral Dilemmas of Doctors and Parents." Reprinted in *Essays on Bioethics*, Oxford: Clarendon Press, 1993, pp.185–91. Courtesy of the Estate of R. M. Hare.

30 Alison Davis, "Right to Life of Handicapped," p. 181 from *Journal of Medical Ethics* 9 (1983). Reproduced with permission from BMJ Publishing Group.

31 Christine Overall, "Conjoined Twins, Embodied Personhood, and Surgical Separation," pp. 69–84 from L. Tessman (ed.), *Feminist Ethics and Social and Political Philosophy: Theorizing the Non-Ideal*, Springer, 2009. With kind permission from Springer Science+Business Media.

32 Ad Hoc Committee of the Harvard Medical School to Examine the Definition of Brain Death, "'A Definition of Irreversible Coma': Report to Examine the Definition of Brain

Death," pp. 85–8 from *Journal of the American Medical Association* 205:6 (August 1968). Copyright © 1968 American Medical Association. All rights reserved.

33 Ari Joffe, "Are Recent Defences of the Brain Death Concept Adequate?," pp. 47–53 from *Bioethics* 24: 2 (February 2010). Reproduced with permission from John Wiley & Sons.

34 Peter Singer, "Is the Sanctity of Life Ethic Terminally Ill?," pp. 307–43 from *Bioethics* 9: 3/4 (1995). Reproduced with permission from John Wiley & Sons.

35 Ronald Dworkin, "Life Past Reason," pp. 218–29 from *Life's Dominion: An Argument about Abortion, Euthanasia, and Individual Freedom*, New York: Knopf, 1993. Copyright © 1993 by Ronald Dworkin. Used by permission of Alfred A. Knopf, an imprint of the Knopf Doubleday Publishing Group, a division of Random House LLC. All rights reserved.

36 Rebecca Dresser, "Dworkin on Dementia: Elegant Theory, Questionable Policy," pp. 32–8 from *Hastings Center Report* 25: 6 (November/December 1995). Reproduced with permission from John Wiley & Sons.

37 Chris Hill, "The Note," pp. 9–17 from Helga Kuhse (ed.), *Willing to Listen, Wanting to Die*, Ringwood, Australia: Penguin Books, 1994.

38 Daniel Callahan, "When Self-Determination Runs Amok," pp. 52–5 from *Hastings Center Report* 22: 2 (March/April 1992). Reproduced with permission from John Wiley & Sons.

39 John Lachs, "When Abstract Moralizing Runs Amok," pp. 10–13 from *The Journal of Clinical Ethics* 5: 1 (Spring 1994). Copyright, JCE.

40 Bregje D. Onwuteaka-Philipsen et al., "Trends in End-Of-Life Practices Before and After the Enactment of the Euthanasia Law in the Netherlands from 1990 to 2010: A Repeated Cross-Sectional Survey," pp. 908–15 from *The Lancet* 380: 9845 (2012). Reprinted from *The Lancet* with permission from Elsevier.

41 Bernard Lo, "Euthanasia in the Netherlands: What Lessons for Elsewhere?," pp. 869–70 from *The Lancet* 380 (September 8, 2012). Copyright 2012. Reprinted from *The Lancet* with permission from Elsevier.

42 Paul T. Menzel, "Rescuing Lives: Can't We Count?," pp. 22–3 from *Hastings Center Report* 24: 1 (1994). Reproduced with permission from John Wiley & Sons.

43 Alvin H. Moss and Mark Siegler, "Should Alcoholics Compete Equally for Liver Transplantation?," pp. 1295–8 from *Journal of the American Medical Association* 265: 10 (1991). Copyright © 1991 American Medical Association. All rights reserved.

44 John Harris, "The Value of Life," pp. 87–102 from *The Value of Life*, London: Routledge, 1985. Copyright 1985, Routledge. Reproduced by permission of Taylor & Francis Books UK.

45 Nick Beckstead and Toby Ord, "Bubbles under the Wallpaper: Healthcare Rationing and Discrimination," a paper presented to the conference "Valuing Lives" New York University, March 5, 2011, © Nick Beckstead and Toby Ord, reprinted by permission of the authors. This paper is published here for the first time, but draws on Nick Beckstead and Toby Ord, "Rationing and Rationality: The Cost of Avoiding Discrimination," in N. Eyal et al. (eds.), *Inequalities in Health: Concepts, Measures, and Ethics*, Oxford: Oxford University Press, 2013, pp. 232–9. By permission of Oxford University Press.

46 Eike-Henner W. Kluge, "Organ Donation and Retrieval: Whose Body Is It Anyway?" © 1999 by Eike-Henner W. Kluge.

47 Janet Radcliffe-Richards et al., "The Case for Allowing Kidney Sales," pp. 1950–2 from *The Lancet* 351: 9120 (June 27, 1998). Reprinted with permission from Elsevier.

48 Debra Satz, "Ethical Issues in the Supply and Demand of Human Kidneys," pp. 189–206 from *Why Some Things Should Not Be for Sale: The Moral Limits of Markets*, New York: Oxford University Press, 2010, ch. 9, based on an article from *Proceedings of the Aristotelian Society*. Reprinted by courtesy of the Editor of *Proceedings of the Aristotelian Society*: © 2010.

49 John Harris, "The Survival Lottery," pp. 81–7 from *Philosophy* 50 (1975). © Royal Institute of Philosophy, published by Cambridge University Press. Reproduced with permission.

50 Henry K. Beecher, "Ethics and Clinical Research," pp. 1354–60 from *New England Journal of Medicine* 274: 24 (June 1966). Copyright © 1996 Massachusetts Medical Society. Reprinted with permission from Massachusetts Medical Society.

51 Benjamin Freedman, "Equipoise and the Ethics of Clinical Research," pp. 141–5 from *New England Journal of Medicine* 317: 3 (July 1987). Copyright © 1987 Massachusetts Medical Society. Reprinted with permission from Massachusetts Medical Society.

52 Samuel Hellman, "The Patient and the Public Good," pp. 400–2 from *Nature Medicine* 1: 5 (1995). Reprinted by permission from Macmillan Publishers Ltd.

53 John Harris, "Scientific Research Is a Moral Duty," pp. 242–8 from *Journal of Medical Ethics* 31: 4 (2005). Reproduced with permission from BMJ Publishing Group.

54 Sandra Shapshay and Kenneth D. Pimple, "Participation in Research Is an Imperfect Moral Duty: A Response to John Harris," pp. 414–17 from *Journal of Medical Ethics* 33 (2007). Reproduced with permission from BMJ Publishing Group.

55 Peter Lurie and Sidney M. Wolfe, "Unethical Trials of Interventions to Reduce Perinatal Transmission of the Human Immunodeficiency Virus in Developing Countries," pp. 853–6 from *New England Journal of Medicine* 337: 12 (September 1997). Copyright © 1997 Massachusetts Medical Society. Reprinted with permission from Massachusetts Medical Society.

56 Danstan Bageda and Philippa Musoke-Mudido, "We're Trying to Help Our Sickest People, Not Exploit Them," from *The Washington Post*, September 28, 1997. © 1997 Washington Post Company. All rights reserved. Used by permission and protected by the Copyright Laws of the United States. The printing, copying, redistribution, or retransmission of this Content without express written permission is prohibited.

57 Leah Belsky and Henry S. Richardson, "Medical Researchers' Ancillary Clinical Care Responsibilities," pp. 1494–6 from *British Medical Journal* 328 (June, 19, 2004). Reproduced with permission from BMJ Publishing Group.

58 George W. Bush, "President Discusses Stem Cell Research," Office of the Press Secretary, White House, August 9, 2001.

59 Jeff McMahan, "Killing Embryos for Stem Cell Research," pp. 170–89 from *Metaphilosophy* 38: 2/3 (2007). Reproduced with permission from John Wiley & Sons.

60 Immanuel Kant, "Duties towards Animals," pp. 239–41 from *Lectures on Ethics*, trans. Louis Infield, London: Methuen, 1930. Copyright 1930 Methuen, reproduced by permission of Taylor & Francis Books UK.

61 Jeremy Bentham, "A Utilitarian View," section XVIII, IV from *An Introduction to the Principles of Morals and Legislation*, First published c.1820.

62 Peter Singer, "All Animals are Equal," pp. 103–16 from *Philosophic Exchange* 1: 5 (1974). Center for Philosophic Exchange, State University of New York, Brockford, NY, 1974.

63 R. G. Frey and Sir William Paton, "Vivisection, Morals and Medicine: An Exchange," pp. 94–7 and 102–4 from *Journal of Medical Ethics* 9 (1983). Reproduced with permission from BMJ Publishing Group.

64 Michael J. Selgelid: "Ethics and Infectious Disease," pp. 272–89 from *Bioethics* 19: 3 (2005). Reproduced with permission from John Wiley & Sons.

65 Udo Schüklenk and Anita Kleinsmidt, "Rethinking Mandatory HIV Testing during Pregnancy in Areas with High HIV Prevalence Rates: Ethical and Policy Issues," pp. 1179–83 from *American Journal of Public Health* 97: 7 (2007). Reproduced with permission from American Public Health Association.

66 Russell Armstrong, "Mandatory HIV Testing in Pregnancy: Is There Ever a Time?," pp. 1–10 from *Developing World Bioethics* 8: 1 (2008). Reproduced with permission from John Wiley & Sons.

67 Jerome Amir Singh, Ross Upshur, and Nesri Padayatchi, "XDR-TB in South Africa: No Time for Denial or Complacency," *PLoS Med* 4: 1 (2007): e50. doi:10.1371/journal.pmed.0040050. Copyright: © 2007 Singh et al.

68   Mark Siegler, "Confidentiality in Medicine: A Decrepit Concept," pp. 1518–21 from *New England Journal of Medicine* 307: 24 (December 1982). Copyright © 1982 Massachusetts Medical Society. Reprinted with permission from Massachusetts Medical Society.

69   Christian Säfken and Andreas Frewer, "The Duty to Warn and Clinical Ethics: Legal and Ethical Aspects of Confidentiality and HIV/AIDS," pp. 313–326 from *HEC Forum* 19: 4 (2007). With kind permission from Springer Science+Business Media.

70   Immanuel Kant, "On a Supposed Right to Lie from Altruistic Motives," pp. 361–3 from *Critique of Practical Reason and Other Works on the Theory of Ethics*, 6th edition, trans. T. K. Abbott, London, 1909. This essay was first published in a Berlin periodical in 1797.

71   Joseph Collins, "Should Doctors Tell the Truth?," pp. 320–6 from *Harper's Monthly Magazine* 155 (August 1927). Copyright © 1927 Harper's Magazine. All rights reserved. Reproduced from the August issue by special permission.

72   Roger Higgs, "On Telling Patients the Truth," pp. 186–202 and 232–3 from Michael Lockwood (ed.), *Moral Dilemmas in Modern Medicine*, Oxford: Oxford University Press, 1985. By permission of Oxford University Press.

73   John Stuart Mill, "On Liberty," first published in 1859.

74   Justice Benjamin N. Cardozo, Judgment from *Schloendorff v. New York Hospital* (1914), p. 526 from Jay Katz (ed.), *Experimentation with Human Beings: The Authority of the Investigator, Subject, Professions, and State in the Human Experimentation Process*, New York: Russell Sage Foundation, 1972. Reproduced with permission of Russell Sage Foundation.

75   Tom L. Beauchamp, "Informed Consent: Its History, Meaning, and Present Challenges," pp. 515–23 from *Cambridge Quarterly of Health Care Ethics* 20: 4 (2011). © Royal Institute of Philosophy, published by Cambridge University Press. Reproduced with permission from Cambridge University Press and T. Beauchamp.

76   Ruth Macklin, "The Doctor–Patient Relationship in Different Cultures," pp. 86–107 from *Against Relativism: Cultural Diversity and the Search of Ethical Universals in Medicine*, © 1999 by Oxford University Press, Inc. By permission of Oxford University Press, USA.

77   Carl Elliott, "Amputees by Choice," pp. 208–10, 210–15, 219–23, 227–31, 234–6, 323–6 from *Better Than Well: American Medicine Meets the American Dream*, New York and London: W.W. Norton, 2003. Copyright © 2003 by Carl Elliott. Used by permission of W. W. Norton & Company, Inc.

78   Julian Savulescu, "Rational Desires and the Limitation of Life-Sustaining Treatment," pp. 191–222 from *Bioethics* 8: 3 (1994). Reproduced with permission from John Wiley & Sons.

79   Shlomo Cohen, "The Nocebo Effect of Informed Consent," pp. 147–54 from *Bioethics* 28: 3 (2014). Reproduced with permission from John Wiley & Sons.

80   Sarah E. Dock, "The Relation of the Nurse to the Doctor and the Doctor to the Nurse," p. 394 (extract) from *The American Journal of Nursing* 17: 5 (1917).

81   Lisa H. Newton, "In Defense of the Traditional Nurse," pp. 348–54 from *Nursing Outlook* 29: 6 (1981). Copyright Elsevier 1981.

82   Sarah Breier, "Patient Autonomy and Medical Paternity: Can Nurses Help Doctors to Listen to Patients?," pp. 510–21 from *Nursing Ethics* 8: 6 (2001). Reproduced with permission from Sage and S. Breier.

83   Carol Pavlish, Anita Ho, and Ann-Marie Rounkle, "Health and Human Rights Advocacy: Perspectives from a Rwandan Refugee Camp," pp. 538–49 from *Nursing Ethics* 19: 4 (2012). Copyright © 2012 by SAGE Publications. Reprinted by Permission of SAGE.

84   Jonathan D. Moreno, "Neuroethics: An Agenda for Neuroscience and Society," pp. 149–53 from *Nature Reviews* 4 (February 2003). Reprinted by permission from Macmillan Publishers Ltd.

85   Sally Adee, "How Electrical Brain Stimulation Can Change the Way We Think," *The Week*, March 30, 2012.

86   Neil Levy, "Neuroethics: Ethics and the Sciences of the Mind," pp. 69–74 (extract) from *Philosophy*

Compass 4: 10 (2009), pp. 69–81. Reproduced with permission from John Wiley & Sons.

87 Adam Kolber, "Freedom of Memory Today," pp. 145–8 from *Neuroethics* 1 (2008). With kind permission from Springer Science+Business Media.

88 Henry Greely and Colleagues, "Towards Responsible Use of Cognitive-Enhancing Drugs by the Healthy," pp. 702–5 from *Nature* 456 (December 11, 2008). Reprinted by permission from Macmillan Publishers Ltd.

89 Julian Savulescu and Anders Sandberg, "Engineering Love"/"Love Machine: Engineering Lifelong Romance," pp. 28–9 from *New Scientist* 2864. © 2012 Reed Business Information – UK. All rights reserved. Distributed by Tribune Content Agency.

Introduction

The term "bioethics" was coined by Van Rensselaer Potter, who used it to describe his proposal that we need an ethic that can incorporate our obligations, not just to other humans, but to the biosphere as a whole.[1] Although the term is still occasionally used in this sense of an ecological ethic, it is now much more commonly used in the narrower sense of the study of ethical issues arising from the biological and medical sciences. So understood, bioethics has become a specialized, although interdisciplinary, area of study. The essays included in this book give an indication of the range of issues which fall within its scope – but it is only an indication. There are many other issues that we simply have not had the space to cover.

Bioethics can be seen as a branch of ethics, or, more specifically, of applied ethics. For this reason some understanding of the nature of ethics is an essential preliminary to any serious study of bioethics. The remainder of this introduction will seek to provide that understanding.

One question about the nature of ethics is especially relevant to bioethics: to what extent is reasoning or argument possible in ethics? Many people assume without much thought that ethics is subjective. The subjectivist holds that what ethical view we take is a matter of opinion or taste that is not amenable to argument. But if ethics were a matter of taste, why would we even attempt to argue about it? If Helen says "I like my coffee sweetened," whereas Paul says

"I like my coffee unsweetened," there is not much point in Helen and Paul arguing about it. The two statements do not contradict each other. They can both be true. But if Helen says "Doctors should never assist their patients to die" whereas Paul says "Sometimes doctors should assist their patients to die," then Helen and Paul are disagreeing, and there does seem to be a point in their trying to argue about the issue of physician-assisted suicide.

It seems clear that there is some scope for argument in ethics. If I say "It is always wrong to kill a human being" and "Abortion is not always wrong" then I am committed to denying that abortion kills a human being. Otherwise I have contradicted myself, and in doing so I have not stated a coherent position at all. So consistency, at least, is a requirement of any defensible ethical position, and thus sets a limit to the subjectivity of ethical judgments. The requirement of factual accuracy sets another limit. In discussing issues in bioethics, the facts are often complex. But we cannot reach the right ethical decisions unless we are well-informed about the relevant facts. In this respect ethical decisions are unlike decisions of taste. We can enjoy a taste without knowing what we are eating; but if we assume that it is wrong to resuscitate a terminally ill patient against her wishes, then we cannot know whether an instance of resuscitation was morally right or wrong without knowing something about the patient's prognosis and whether the patient

Bioethics: An Anthology, Third Edition. Edited by Helga Kuhse, Udo Schüklenk, and Peter Singer.

has expressed any wishes about being resuscitated. In that sense, there is no equivalent in ethics to the immediacy of taste.

Ethical relativism, sometimes also known as cultural relativism, is one step away from ethical subjectivism, but it also severely limits the scope of ethical argument. The ethical relativist holds that it is not individual attitudes that determine what is right or wrong, but the attitudes of the culture in which one lives. Herodotus tells how Darius, King of Persia, summoned the Greeks from the western shores of his kingdom before him, and asked them how much he would have to pay them to eat their fathers' dead bodies. They were horrified by the idea and said they would not do it for any amount of money, for it was their custom to cremate their dead. Then Darius called upon Indians from the eastern frontiers of his kingdom, and asked them what would make them willing to burn their fathers' bodies. They cried out and asked the King to refrain from mentioning so shocking an act. Herodotus comments that each nation thinks its own customs best. From here it is only a short step to the view that there can be no objective right or wrong, beyond the bounds of one's own culture. This view found increased support in the nineteenth century as Western anthropologists came to know many different cultures, and were impressed by ethical views very different from those that were standardly taken for granted in European society. As a defense against the automatic assumption that Western morality is superior and should be imposed on "savages," many anthropologists argued that, since morality is relative to culture, no culture can have any basis for regarding its morality as superior to any other culture.

Although the motives with which anthropologists put this view forward were admirable, they may not have appreciated the implications of the position they were taking. The ethical relativist maintains that a statement like "It is good to enslave people from another tribe if they are captured in war" means simply "In my society, the custom is to enslave people from another tribe if they are captured in war." Hence if one member of the society were to question whether it really was good to enslave people in these circumstances, she could be

answered simply by demonstrating that this was indeed the custom – for example, by showing that for many generations it had been done after every war in which prisoners were captured. Thus there is no way for moral reformers to say that an accepted custom is wrong – "wrong" just means "in accordance with an accepted custom."

On the other hand, when people from two different cultures disagree about an ethical issue, then according to the ethical relativist there can be no resolution of the disagreement. Indeed, strictly there is no disagreement. If the apparent dispute were over the issue just mentioned, then one person would be saying "In my country it is the custom to enslave people from another tribe if they are captured in war" and the other person would be saying "In my country it is not the custom to allow one human being to enslave another." This is no more a disagreement than such statements as "In my country people greet each other by rubbing noses" and "In my country people greet each other by shaking hands." If ethical relativism is true, then it is impossible to say that one culture is right and the other is wrong. Bearing in mind that some cultures have practiced slavery, or the burning of widows on the funeral pyre of their husbands, this is hard to accept.

A more promising alternative to both ethical subjectivism and cultural relativism is universal prescriptivism, an approach to ethics developed by the Oxford philosopher R. M. Hare. Hare argues that the distinctive property of ethical judgments is that they are universalizable. In saying this, he means that if I make an ethical judgment, I must be prepared to state it in universal terms, and apply it to all relevantly similar situations. By "universal terms" Hare means those terms that do not refer to a particular individual. Thus a proper name cannot be a universal term. If, for example, I were to say "Everyone should do what is in the interests of Mick Jagger" I would not be making a universal judgment, because I have used a proper name. The same would be true if I were to say that everyone must do what is in *my* interests, because the personal pronoun "my" is here used to refer to a particular individual, myself.

It might seem that ruling out particular terms in this way does not take us very far. After all, one can always describe oneself in universal terms. Perhaps

I can't say that everyone should do what is in my interests, but I could say that everyone must do whatever is in the interests of people who ... and then give a minutely detailed description of myself, including the precise location of all my freckles. The effect would be the same as saying that everyone should do what is in my interests, because there would be no one except me who matches that description. But Hare meets this problem very effectively by saying that to prescribe an ethical judgment universally means being prepared to prescribe it for all possible circumstances, including hypothetical ones. So if I were to say that everyone should do what is in the interests of a person with a particular pattern of freckles, I must be prepared to prescribe that in the hypothetical situation in which I do not have this pattern of freckles, but someone else does, I should do what is in the interests of that person. Now of course I may *say* that I should do that, since I am confident that I shall never be in such a situation, but this simply means that I am being dishonest. I am not genuinely prescribing the principle universally.

The effect of saying that an ethical judgment must be universalizable for hypothetical as well as actual circumstances is that whenever I make an ethical judgment, I can be challenged to put myself in the position of the parties affected, and see if I would still be able to accept that judgment. Suppose, for example, that I own a small factory and the cheapest way for me to get rid of some waste is to pour it into a nearby river. I do not take water from this river, but I know that some villagers living downstream do and the waste may make them ill. The requirement that ethical judgments should be universalizable will make it difficult for me to justify my conduct, because if I imagine myself in the hypothetical situation of being one of the villagers, rather than the factory-owner, I would not accept that the profits of the factory-owner should outweigh the risk of adverse effects on my health and that of my children. In this way Hare's approach requires us to take into account the interests and preferences of all others affected by our actions. Hence it allows for an element of reasoning in ethical deliberation.

Since the rightness or wrongness of our actions will, on this view, depend on the way in which they affect others, Hare's universal prescriptivism leads to a form of consequentialism – that is, the view that the rightness of an action depends on its consequences. The best-known form of consequentialism is the classical utilitarianism developed in the late eighteenth century by Jeremy Bentham and popularized in the nineteenth century by John Stuart Mill. They held that an action is right if it leads to a greater surplus of happiness over misery than any possible alternative, and wrong if it does not. By "greater surplus of happiness," the classical utilitarians had in mind the idea of adding up all the pleasure or happiness that resulted from the action and subtracting from that total all the pain or misery to which the action gave rise. Naturally, in some circumstances, it might be possible only to reduce misery, and then the right action should be understood as the one that will result in less misery than any possible alternative.

The utilitarian view is striking in many ways. It puts forward a single principle that it claims can provide the right answer to all ethical dilemmas, if only we can predict what the consequences of our actions will be. It takes ethics out of the mysterious realm of duties and rules, and bases ethical decisions on something that almost everyone understands and values. Moreover, utilitarianism's single principle is applied universally, without fear or favor. Bentham said: "Each to count for one and none for more than one," by which he meant that the happiness of a common tramp counted for as much as that of a noble, and the happiness of an African was no less important than that of a European.

Many contemporary consequentialists agree with Bentham to the extent that they think the rightness or wrongness of an action must depend on its consequences, but they have abandoned the idea that maximizing net happiness is the ultimate goal. Instead they argue that we should seek to bring about whatever will satisfy the greatest number of desires or preference. This variation, which is known as "preference utilitarianism," does not regard anything as good, except in so far as it is wanted or desired. More intense or strongly held preferences would get more weight than weak preferences.

Consequentialism offers one important answer to the question of how we should decide what is right and what is wrong, but many ethicists reject it. The denial of this view was dramatically presented by Dostoevsky in *The Karamazov Brothers*:

> imagine that you are charged with building the edifice of human destiny, the ultimate aim of which is to bring people happiness, to give them peace and contentment at last, but that in order to achieve this it is essential and unavoidable to torture just one little speck of creation, that same little child beating her chest with her little fists, and imagine that this edifice has to be erected on her unexpiated tears. Would you agree to be the architect under those conditions? Tell me honestly![2]

The passage suggests that some things are always wrong, no matter what their consequences. This has, for most of Western history, been the prevailing approach to morality, at least at the level of what has been officially taught and approved by the institutions of Church and State. The ten commandments of the Hebrew scriptures served as a model for much of the Christian era, and the Roman Catholic Church built up an elaborate system of morality based on rules to which no exceptions were allowed.

Another example of an ethic of rules is that of Immanuel Kant. Kant's ethic is based on his "categorical imperative," which he states in several distinct formulations. One is that we must always act so that we can will the maxim of our action to be a universal law. This can be interpreted as a form of Hare's idea of universalizability, which we have already encountered. Another is that we must always treat other people as ends, never as means. While these formulations of the categorical imperative might be applied in various ways, in Kant's hands they lead to inviolable rules, for example, against making promises that we do not intend to keep. Kant also thought that it was always wrong to tell a lie. In response to a critic who suggested that this rule has exceptions, Kant said that it would be wrong to lie even if someone had taken refuge in your house, and a person seeking to murder him came to your door and asked if you knew where he was. Modern Kantians often reject this hard-line approach to rules, and claim that Kant's categorical imperative did not require him to hold so strictly to the rule against lying.

How would a consequentialist – for example, a classical utilitarian – answer Dostoevsky's challenge? If answering honestly – and if one really could be certain

that this was a sure way, and the only way, of bringing lasting happiness to all the people of the world – utilitarians would have to say yes, they would accept the task of being the architect of the happiness of the world at the cost of the child's unexpiated tears. For they would point out that the suffering of that child, wholly undeserved as it is, will be repeated a million-fold over the next century, for other children, just as innocent, who are victims of starvation, disease, and brutality. So if this one child must be sacrificed to stop all this suffering then, terrible as it is, the child must be sacrificed.

Fantasy apart, there can be no architect of the happiness of the world. The world is too big and complex a place for that. But we may attempt to bring about less suffering and more happiness, or satisfaction of preferences, for people or sentient beings in specific places and circumstances. Alternatively, we might follow a set of principles or rules – which could be of varying degrees of rigidity or flexibility. Where would such rules come from? Kant tried to deduce them from his categorical imperative, which in turn he had reached by insisting that the moral law must be based on reason alone, without any content from our wants or desires. But the problem with trying to deduce morality from reason alone has always been that it becomes an empty formalism that cannot tell us what to do. To make it practical, it needs to have some additional content, and Kant's own attempts to deduce rules of conduct from his categorical imperative are unconvincing.

Others, following Aristotle, have tried to draw on human nature as a source of moral rules. What is good, they say, is what is natural to human beings. They then contend that it is natural and right for us to seek certain goods, such as knowledge, friendship, health, love, and procreation, and unnatural and wrong for us to act contrary to these goods. This "natural law" ethic is open to criticism on several points. The word "natural" can be used both descriptively and evaluatively, and the two senses are often mixed together so that value judgments may be smuggled in under the guise of a description. The picture of human nature presented by proponents of natural law ethics usually selects only those characteristics of our nature that the proponent considers desirable. The fact that our species, especially its male members, frequently go to war, and are also prone to commit individual acts of violence against others, is no doubt just as much part of our nature as our desire for knowledge, but no natural law theorist therefore views these activities as good. More generally, natural law theory has its origins in an Aristotelian idea of the cosmos, in which everything has a goal or "end," which can be deduced from its nature. The "end" of a knife is to cut; the assumption is that human beings also have an "end," and we will flourish when we live in accordance with the end for which we are suited. But this is a pre-Darwinian view of nature. Since Darwin, we know that we do not exist for any purpose, but are the result of natural selection operating on random mutations over millions of years. Hence there is no reason to believe that living according to nature will produce a harmonious society, let alone the best possible state of affairs for human beings.

Another way in which it has been claimed that we can come to know what moral principles or rules we should follow is through our intuition. In practice this usually means that we adopt conventionally accepted moral principles or rules, perhaps with some adjustments in order to avoid inconsistency or arbitrariness. On this view, a moral theory should, like a scientific theory, try to match the data; and the data that a moral theory must match is provided by our moral intuitions. As in science, if a plausible theory matches most, but not all, of the data, then the anomalous data might be rejected on the grounds that it is more likely that there was an error in the procedures for gathering that particular set of data than that the theory as a whole is mistaken. But ultimately the test of a theory is its ability to explain the data. The problem with applying this model of scientific justification to ethics is that the "data" of our moral intuitions is unreliable, not just at one or two specific points, but as a whole. Here the facts that cultural relativists draw upon are relevant (even if they do not establish that cultural relativism is the correct response to it). Since we know that our intuitions are strongly influenced by such things as culture and religion, they are ill-suited to serve as the fixed points against which an ethical theory must be tested. Even where there is cross-cultural agreement, there may be some aspects of our intuitions on which *all* cultures unjustifiably favor our own interests over those of others. For

example, simply because we are all human beings, we may have a systematic bias that leads us to give an unjustifiably low moral status to nonhuman animals. Or, because, in virtually all known human societies, men have taken a greater leadership role than women, the moral intuitions of all societies may not adequately reflect the interests of females.

Some philosophers think that it is a mistake to base ethics on principles or rules. Instead they focus on what it is to be a good person – or, in the case of the problems with which this book is concerned, perhaps on what it is to be a good nurse or doctor or researcher. They seek to describe the virtues that a good person, or a good member of the relevant profession, should possess. Moral education then consists of teaching these virtues and discussing how a virtuous person would act in specific situations. The question is, however, whether we can have a notion of what a virtuous person would do in a specific situation without making a prior decision about what it is right to do. After all, in any particular moral dilemma, different virtues may be applicable, and even a particular virtue will not always give unequivocal guidance. For instance, if a terminally ill patient repeatedly asks a nurse or doctor for assistance in dying, what response best exemplifies the virtues of a healthcare professional? There seems no answer to this question, short of an inquiry into whether it is right or wrong to help a patient in such circumstances to die. But in that case we seem bound, in the end, to come back to discussing such issues as whether it is right to follow moral rules or principles, or to do what will have the best consequences.

In the late twentieth century, some feminists offered new criticisms of conventional thought about ethics. They argued that the approaches to ethics taken by the influential philosophers of the past – all of whom have been male – give too much emphasis to abstract principles and the role of reason, and give too little attention to personal relationships and the part played by emotion. One outcome of these criticisms has been the development of an "ethic of care," which is not so much a single ethical theory as a cluster of ways of looking at ethics which put an attitude of caring for others at the center, and seek to avoid reliance on abstract ethical principles. The ethic of care has seemed especially applicable to the work of those involved in direct patient care, and has recently been taken up by a number of nursing theorists as offering a more suitable alternative to other ideas of ethics. Not all feminists, however, support this development. Some worry that the adoption of a "care" approach by nurses may reflect, and even reinforce, stereotypes of women as more emotional and less rational than men. They also fear that it could lead to women continuing to carry a disproportionate burden of caring for others, to the exclusion of adequately caring for themselves.

In this discussion of ethics we have not mentioned anything about religion. This may seem odd, in view of the close connection that has often been made between religion and ethics, but it reflects our belief that, despite this historical connection, ethics and religion are fundamentally independent. Logically, ethics is prior to religion. If religious believers wish to say that a deity is good, or praise her or his creation or deeds, they must have a notion of goodness that is independent of their conception of the deity and what she or he does. Otherwise they will be saying that the deity is good, and when asked what they mean by "good," they will have to refer back to the deity, saying perhaps that "good" means "in accordance with the wishes of the deity." In that case, sentences such as "God is good" would be a meaningless tautology. "God is good" could mean no more than "God is in accordance with God's wishes." As we have already seen, there are ideas of what it is for something to be "good" that are not rooted in any religious belief. While religions typically encourage or instruct their followers to obey a particular ethical code, it is obvious that others who do not follow any religion can also think and act ethically.

To say that ethics is independent of religion is not to deny that theologians or other religious believers may have a role to play in bioethics. Religious traditions often have long histories of dealing with ethical dilemmas, and the accumulation of wisdom and experience that they represent can give us valuable insights into particular problems. But these insights should be subject to criticism in the way that any other proposals would be. If in the end we accept them, it is because we have judged them sound, not because they are the utterances of a pope, a rabbi, a mullah, or a holy person.

Ethics is also independent of the law, in the sense that the rightness or wrongness of an act cannot be settled by its legality or illegality. Whether an act is legal or illegal may often be relevant to whether it is right or wrong, because it is arguably wrong to break the law, other things being equal. Many people have thought that this is especially so in a democracy, in which everyone has a say in making the law. Another reason why the fact that an act is illegal may be a reason against doing it is that the legality of an act may affect the consequences that are likely to flow from it. If active voluntary euthanasia is illegal, then doctors who practice it risk going to jail, which will cause them and their families to suffer, and also mean that they will no longer be able to help other patients. This can be a powerful reason for not practicing voluntary euthanasia when it is against the law, but if there is only a very small chance of the offense becoming known or being proved, then the weight of this consequentialist reason against breaking the law is reduced accordingly. Whether we have an ethical obligation to obey the law, and, if so, how much weight should be given to it, is itself an issue for ethical argument.

Though ethics is independent of the law, in the sense just specified, laws are subject to evaluation from an ethical perspective. Many debates in bioethics focus on questions about what practices should be allowed – for example, should we allow research on stem cells taken from human embryos, sex selection, or cloning? – and committees set up to advise on the ethical, social, and legal aspects of these questions often recommend legislation to prohibit the activity in question, or to allow it to be practiced under some form of regulation. Discussing a question at the level of law and public policy, however, raises somewhat different considerations than a discussion of personal ethics, because the consequences of adopting a public policy generally have much wider ramifications than the consequences of a personal choice. That is why some healthcare professionals feel justified in assisting a terminally ill patient to die, while at the same time opposing the legalization of physician-assisted suicide. Paradoxical as this position may appear – and it is certainly open to criticism – it is not straightforwardly inconsistent.

Naturally, many of the essays we have selected reflect the times in which they were written. Since bioethics often comments on developments in fast-moving areas of medicine and the biological sciences, the factual content of articles in bioethics can become obsolete quite rapidly. In preparing this revised edition, we have taken the opportunity to cover some new issues and to include some more recent writings. We have, for example, included new material on genetic enhancement, as well as on the use of embryonic human stem cells. This edition of the anthology also includes new sections on ethical issues in public health and in the neurosciences. Nevertheless, an article that has dated in regard to its facts often makes ethical points that are still valid, or worth considering, so we have not excluded older articles for this reason.

Other articles are dated in a different way. During the past few decades we have become more sensitive about the ways in which our language may exclude women, or reflect our prejudices regarding race or sexuality. We see no merit in trying to disguise past practices on such matters, so we have not excluded otherwise valuable works in bioethics on these grounds. If they are jarring to the modern reader, that may be a salutary reminder of the extent to which we all are subject to the conventions and prejudices of our times.

Notes

1 See Van Rensselaer Potter, *Bioethics: Bridge to the Future* (Englewood Cliffs, NJ: Prentice-Hall, 1971).

2 *The Karamazov Brothers*, trans. Ignat Avsey (Oxford: Oxford University Press, 1994), vol. I, part 2, bk. 5, ch. 4. First published in 1879.

Part I

Abortion

Introduction

The view that human life has special value is deeply rooted in most people's thinking and no serious ethical theory allows a person to be killed without strong moral justification. Abortions terminate the lives of fetuses. Given that these fetuses are human, and of course innocent of any wrongdoing, it is easy to see why some people consider abortion to be unjustifiable homicide. In some respects fetuses are like persons; but in other respects they are very different. Therefore we need to ask whether they have the same moral status as those human beings we think of as persons.

In the first article in this section, John Finnis ("Abortion and Health Care Ethics") defends what other writers call a conservative view. On this view, personhood begins at conception and "direct abortions," that is, procedures intended to end the life of the fetus, are impermissible, even if the pregnancy is the result of rape, or if an abortion is necessary to save the woman's life.

Finnis defends a position that is consistent with a Roman Catholic perspective, but he maintains that his argument is based not on faith but on reason and hence should be decisive for everyone. He offers a vigorous defense of the view that even the one-cell zygote already has the capacity – found in its genetic structure - for supporting specifically human functions such as self-consciousness, rationality and choice. The earliest human embryo, he says, "*already* has the biological capacity appropriate to supporting the specifically human operations such as self-consciousness,

rationality and choice …" On account of this unexercised, but "active potentiality or capacity," Finnis holds, even the zygote is *already* a person and not merely a potential person.

This does point to an apparent limit to the universality of the prohibition of abortion. If it is the biological capacity to develop "specific human operations" that endows embryos and fetuses with personhood, this leaves some embryos and fetuses – those that are damaged and lack the capacity to develop the requisite human operations - outside the circle of protection. At the very least, defenders of a position like Finnis's need to explain why this is not the case. With these exceptions, however, if Finnis's argument does establish that zygotes, embryos and fetuses are persons, killing a one-cell human organism is killing a person. It would therefore have the same moral significance as killing an adult person.

Finnis is aware that "our imagination balks at equating the intelligent adult with a one-cell zygote smaller than a full stop," but holds that "*reason* can find no event or principle or criterion by which to judge that the typical adult or newborn child … is anything other than one and the same individual human being – human person – as the one-cell 46-chromosome zygote whose emergence was the beginning of the personal history of that same child and adult."

Michael Tooley provided a challenge to the conservative view that fetuses are persons. In his 1972 landmark article "Abortion and Infanticide," included

Bioethics: An Anthology, Third Edition. Edited by Helga Kuhse, Udo Schüklenk, and Peter Singer.
© 2016 John Wiley & Sons, Inc. Published 2016 by John Wiley & Sons, Inc.

here as the second reading, he seeks to articulate and defend an ethically significant criterion that confers personhood and a right to life. To have a right to life, Tooley argues, an entity needs to possess a concept of self, that is, be "capable of desiring to continue existing as a subject of experiences and other mental states." An entity that has this capability is a person, whereas one that lacks it is not. This view has implications that enable us to defend abortion, but also challenge the moral views of most people who accept abortion; for on this view neither fetuses nor newborn infants are persons, whereas some nonhuman animals, such as chimpanzees and elephants, do seem to be persons.

In opposition to Finnis, Tooley thus holds that the *potential* – even in Finnis's sense of active potential or capacity - to become a person is not sufficient to give fetuses a right to life. Here it is important to take a closer look at the notions of potentiality and capacity. Sleeping persons – unable to exercise the capacity to desire their own continued existence while asleep – are, according to Tooley, still persons because they *possess* the relevant capacity in a sense in which fetuses do not. A person who is asleep was self-conscious before she went to sleep and will be the same self-conscious person when she wakes up; a fetus, on the other hand, has never been awake and self-conscious.

As we have seen, both Finnis and Tooley take the issue of personhood to be central. Judith Jarvis Thomson, in "A Defense of Abortion," takes a very different approach. For the purposes of her argument, Thomson accepts the conservative position that the fetus is a person, but argues that *even if* one grants this premise, the conclusion that every person has a right to life – in the sense that would make abortion wrong – does not follow. She then uses an ingenious analogy to support her view that one person's right to life does not always outweigh another person's rights to something less than life. This general view applies, Thomson holds, in the case of pregnancy and abortion. A woman has a right to control her body, and a fetus only has the right to use a woman's body if she has implicitly given it that right. This would be the case if the woman is responsible, in some sense of the term, for its presence in her body. In many cases – certainly in the case of a pregnancy resulting from rape, and arguably, if more doubtfully, when contraception has failed – the woman bears little or no responsibility for

the presence of the fetus in her body and would thus, according to Thomson, be justified in having an abortion. She would not be killing the fetus unjustly.

Thomson reminds us that any complete assessment of the ethics of abortion must focus not only on the purported rights or interests of fetuses, but also on the rights of women. But her argument has been criticized as incomplete. One of the strongest objections focuses on her narrow understanding of the right to life. It has, for example, been argued that a right to life, properly understood, also entails the provision of positive aid. If this is correct, then Thomson's argument on abortion is inconclusive, as long as the conservative view that the fetus is a person is accepted.

In the final article of Part I, Don Marquis adopts yet another approach to explain, as the title of his article indicates, "Why Abortion Is Immoral." Like Finnis and Tooley, he assumes that the morality of abortion depends on whether or not the fetus is the kind of being whose life it is seriously wrong to end. According to Marquis, abortion is immoral for the same reason that it is wrong to kill you or me – not because the fetus is a person or a potential person, but rather because killing the fetus deprives it of its future. The loss of one's life is one of the greatest losses one can suffer; it deprives the victim of all the projects, experiences, enjoyments and so on that would otherwise have constituted that individual's future. This, Marquis holds, is what makes killing, other things being equal, wrong – regardless of whether one is a fetus, child, or adult.

Marquis argues that his position must not be confused with a conservative or sanctity of human life view. It does not, for example, rule out euthanasia. Killing a person who wants to die when she is seriously ill and faces a life of pain and suffering does not deprive that person of a valuable future. Nor is his theory, he claims, speciesist (see Peter Singer in Part VIII). The view that killing is wrong because it is the loss to the victim of the victim's future is, Marquis points out, straightforwardly incompatible with the view that it is wrong to kill only beings that are biologically human. It would be equally wrong to kill nonhuman animals and species from other planets, if these beings have futures relevantly like ours. Similarly, it would not be wrong to kill a human fetus with a genetic abnormality that precludes any possibility of a life that is worth living.

These features of his theory, Marquis claims, avoid some of the problems faced both by proponents of a conservative view, and by adherents of a personhood view. Those who deny that fetuses are persons find themselves in the embarrassing position of having to accept that their theory will, in principle, not only allow the killing of fetuses, but also the killing of infants. Conservatives, on the other hand, often rely on what Marquis calls the "invalid inference" that it is wrong to kill fetuses because they are potential persons. But is Marquis's own account really so different from the argument from potential? Does it, like that argument, face the further criticism that such accounts make abortion and contraception equally wrong: if it is wrong to kill a one-cell zygote because doing so deprives the zygote of a valuable future, why is it not equally wrong to deprive an egg and a sperm, still separate but considered jointly, of a valuable future?

1

Abortion and Health Care Ethics

John Finnis

If the unborn are human persons, the principles of justice and non-maleficence (rightly understood) prohibit every abortion; that is, every procedure or technical process carried out with the intention of killing an unborn child or terminating its development. In the first part of this chapter I argue that the only reasonable judgement is that the unborn are indeed human persons. In the second I explore the ways in which the principles of justice and non-maleficence bear on various actions and procedures which harm or may well harm the unborn. The right understanding of those principles, in the context of 'the four principles' [i.e. autonomy, beneficence, non-maleficence and justice], is sketched in an earlier chapter, 'Theology and the Four Principles: A Roman Catholic View I' but the considerations which I set out in the present chapter in no way depend on Catholic faith; they are philosophical and natural-scientific considerations valid and, in my view, properly decisive for everyone, quite independently of any religious premises.

Most People Begin at Fertilization

Leaving aside real or supposed divine, angelic and extraterrestrial beings, the one thing common to all who, in common thought and speech, are regarded as *persons* is that they are *living human individuals*. This being so, anyone who claims that some set of living, whole, bodily human individuals are not persons, and ought not to be regarded and treated as persons, must demonstrate that the ordinary notion of a person is misguided and should be replaced by a different notion. Otherwise the claim will be mere arbitrary discrimination. But no such demonstration has ever been provided, and none is in prospect.

Among the most serious attempts to provide a demonstration is Michael Tooley's argument that personhood is gradually acquired by development; it concludes that not only the unborn but also newborn babies are not persons.[1]

But Tooley's argument begs the question by simply *assuming* two basic but unargued premises: (a) that abortion is morally acceptable, and (b) that an active potentiality or capacity which is not being actually exercised cannot be the defining property of personhood even when it is a capacity really possessed by an individual.[2-4]

Some contemporary neo-Aristotelians, notably Joseph Donceel, have argued that personhood is dependent on sense organs and a brain, and that the early embryo, though a living human individual, is only a pre-personal entity which changes into a person (is 'ensouled'), not gradually but by a sudden,

Original publication details: John Finnis, "Abortion and Health Care Ethics," pp. 547–57 from Raanan Gillon (ed.), *Principles of Health Care Ethics*, Chichester: John Wiley, 1994. Reproduced with permission from John Wiley & Sons.

Bioethics: An Anthology, Third Edition. Edited by Helga Kuhse, Udo Schüklenk, and Peter Singer.

substantial change that occurs when the brain first begins to develop; *thereafter*, the personal soul shapes the development of the whole entity.[5] (By 'substantial change' is meant the change which occurs when an individual entity of one kind changes into an individual entity of a different kind, as typically occurs, for example, in a chemical reaction.) But Donceel's view, like its mediaeval predecessors, is inconsistent with the biological data and with itself.[3, 6, 7] The beginning of the brain's development does not yet provide a bodily basis for intellectual activities, but provides only the precursor of such a basis; so if this precursor is sufficient for 'ensoulment', there is no reason why earlier precursors should fail to suffice. In fact each embryonic human individual has from the outset a specific developmental tendency (involving a high degree of organization) which includes the epigenetic primordia of all its organs. The hypothesis of a substantial change by ensoulment at some time after the forming of the zygote is an unnecessary multiplication of entities, to be eliminated by Occam's razor, i.e. the scientific principle of economy in explanations.

The biological basis for the mediaeval view that specifically human ensoulment takes place some weeks after conception has completely disappeared. Mediaeval Aristotelians such as Thomas Aquinas depended upon the biology then current, which taught that life originates from semen and menstrual blood, that neither of these is alive, and that the very limited active instrumental power in the semen organizes the blood into a body which can begin to grow and nourish itself first in a plant-like way and then in an animal-like way. If the mediaeval Aristotelians had known about the organic life which organizes the roughly one billion items of molecular information in the one-cell conceptus with a self-directing dynamic integration that will remain continuously and identifiably identical until death, they would have concurred with the view of their successors (and almost everyone else) since the eighteenth century.[8] On this later view the fertilized human ovum is specifically human (not merely vegetable), and even the youngest human embryo already has a body which in its already specified (but quite undeveloped) capacities, its epigenetic primordia, is apt for understanding, knowing and

choosing. Rather as you or I have the capacity to speak Tibetan or Icelandic, though we lack the ability to do so, so even the youngest human embryo *already* has the biological capacity appropriate to supporting specifically human operations such as self-consciousness, rationality and choice (given only time and metabolic transformations of air, water and other sustenance). The active potential which he or she already has includes the very capacities which are distinctive of persons.[9] So he or she is a human being and human person with potential, not a merely potential human person or potential human being.

The most serious contemporary effort to show that there is no lasting human *individual* (and therefore no person) until about two weeks after conception, is by Norman Ford.[10] Unlike Tooley and Donceel, Ford holds that personhood begins when an individual with a truly human nature emerges. But the conclusions of his argument are so radically opposed to any biological understanding of human development that they turn out to offer no serious alternative to the standard view: an individual with a truly human nature begins at fertilization. (For detailed analysis, refutations and bibliography, see references 3, 11–13.) Still, Ford's argument is worth tracing, because it attempts to take seriously certain claims often unreflectively uttered, such as that until implantation, or the formation of the primitive streak, or the loss of toti- or pluri-potentiality among the embryo's cells, or the end of the period during which twinning may naturally occur, the conceptus is 'not individuated'.

Ford proposes that at fertilization an ontologically individual and biologically human entity, the zygote, begins, but that (whatever biologists may think) this is never the same individual as the one which (with the same genetic constitution and gender) will begin about 16 days later and will thereafter survive as one and the same individual until death perhaps many decades later. For, according to Ford, the ontologically individual and human zygote is replaced at the first mitotic division by two ontologically individual beings, which in turn are replaced by four, the four by eight, the eight by 12 and 16, these by 32 and 64, and so forth, until by day 14 there are many thousands of ontologically entirely distinct individual human beings (even though all biologists think there is still, unless there has been twinning, only one individual human being). Then these thousands of individuals all suddenly cease to exist when God forms them into 'one living body'.

What drives Ford towards this remarkable conclusion is, on the one hand, his imagination, which finds nothing that looks human in shape until the spatial axes of future somatic development emerge around day 15, and on the other hand the classic puzzle about twinning and mosaics (hypothetical combination of two embryos into one). However, his own theory makes twinning unintelligible, since it occurs at a time, around day six or seven, when, on his view, there is not one individual to become two, but hundreds to become... how many? (Ford does not even try to apply his theory to the facts about twinning, facts which he has earlier treated as decisive against the standard view.)

What, then, should be said about twinning, and about the assumed possibility of human mosaics? Simply that, biologically, one always finds just individuals. If these split, or combine to form a mosaic, one then simply finds one or more different individuals. Twinning is an unusual way of being generated; the relationship between the earlier and the later generated individuals is an unusual form of parentage. Being absorbed into a mosaic would presumably be an unusual way of dying. Common thought and language has not had to categorize these events, but there is little or no intrinsic difficulty in doing so.

Nor should one here substitute one's imagination for one's reason. Domination of thought and argument by imagination and conventional associations occurs at various places in the debate. Many people, for example, allow themselves to be dominated by the assumption that no single organ can be larger than all the other organs of an animal, and/or that no major organ can be transient and disposable; they therefore refuse to take seriously the biological data and philosophical considerations which establish that the placenta is an organ of the embryo. Or again, many people (not least some theologians) argue that personhood or ensoulment cannot begin at conception, because they feel it intolerable to suppose that a high proportion of human persons never get beyond the earliest stage of existence as persons. Now that supposition may indeed challenge the imagination. But it is not intolerable to reason, for (a) in every era hitherto, *infant* mortality has been very high, often as

high as the rate of pregnancy losses in modern western society; (b) many pregnancy losses are due to chromosomal defects so severe that the losses are not of human beings, but only of beings which (like hydatidiform moles) had a human genome but lacked the epigenetic primordia of a human body normal enough to be the organic basis of at least some intellectual act; and (c) as Ford himself reflects[11] (p. 181), it is presumptuous to suppose that we know how God provides for those who never have any intellectual life, and what are the limits of his provision.

Any entity which, remaining the same individual, will develop into a paradigmatic instance of a substantial kind already is an instance of that kind. The one-cell human organism originating with the substantial change which occurs upon the penetration of a human ovum by a human sperm typically develops, as one and the same individual, into a paradigmatic instance of the rational bodily person, the human person; in every such case, therefore, it is already an actual instance of the human person. In the atypical case where a *genetically* human zygote lacks the epigenetic primordia needed to develop any brain, there is no human being and so no human person, no unborn child.[14] And there is another atypical range of cases: some people, including some or all identical twins, were never activated ova, because their life began during the two or three weeks after fertilization, by others dividing or perhaps also others combining.

In all this, what is decisive is not the possession of a unique human genome, but rather the organic integration of a single, whole bodily individual organism. That organic integration, whether the developing organism has one cell or many and whether those cells are toti-potential, pluri-potential or fully specialized, is found from the inception of fertilization. On all biologically and philosophically pertinent criteria that event marks substantial change (in the sense explained above), and no subsequent development or event can be identified plausibly as a genuine substantial change. If there remain biologically and/or philosophically unresolved questions about identity (individuation) in the exceptional cases of embryos which are about to twin, this no more affects the identity of the remaining 97 per cent of embryos than the puzzles about the identity of some adult Siamese twins affect the identity of the rest of us.

Of course, our imagination balks at equating the intelligent adult with a one-cell zygote smaller than a full stop and weighing only 2 mg. But imagination also balks at differentiating between a full-term child just before and just after birth. And *reason* can find no event or principle or criterion by which to judge that the typical adult or newborn child or full-term or mid-term unborn child is anything other than one and the same individual human being – human person – as the one-cell, 46-chromosome zygote whose emergence was the beginning of the personal history of that same child and adult.

In short, science and philosophy concur in the conclusion: every living human individual must be regarded as a person.

Justice, Beneficence and Non-maleficence for Mother and Child

Every attempt to harm an innocent human person violates the principles of non-maleficence and justice, and is always wrong. Every procedure adopted with the intention of killing an unborn child, or of terminating its development, is an attempt to harm, even if it is adopted only as a means to some beneficent end (purpose) and even if it is carried out with very great reluctance and regret. Such procedures are often called 'direct abortions'. But here 'direct' does not refer to physical or temporal immediacy, but to the reasons for the procedure: whatever is chosen as an end or (however reluctantly) as a means is 'directly' willed.[15–17] What is only an unintended side-effect is 'indirectly' willed. Using this terminology, one can rightly say that 'direct abortion' is always wrong, while 'indirect abortion' is not always wrong. But it would be clearer to reserve the word 'abortion' (or 'induced abortion' or 'therapeutic abortion') for procedures adopted with the intent to kill or terminate the development of the fetus, and to call by their own proper names any therapeutic procedures which have amongst their foreseen but unintended results the termination of pregnancy and death of the fetus.

The ethics governing therapeutic procedures which impact fatally on the unborn can be summarized as follows:

1. The direct killing of the innocent – that is, killing either as an end or as a chosen means to some other end – is always gravely wrong. This moral norm excludes even the choice to kill one innocent person as a means of saving another or others, or even as a means of preventing the murder of another or others.

2. Every living human individual is equal to every other human person in respect of the right to life. Since universal propositions are true equally of every instance which falls under them, *equality in right to life* is entailed by the truth of two universal propositions: (a) every living human individual must be regarded and treated as a person, and (b) every innocent human person has the right never to be directly killed.

3. The unborn can never be considered as aggressors, still less as unjust aggressors. For the concept of aggression involves action. But it is only the very existence and the vegetative functioning of the unborn (and not its animal activities, its movements, its sensitive reactions to pain, etc., real as these are) that can give rise to problems for the life or health of the mother. So the concept of aggression extends only by metaphor to the unborn. Moreover, the unborn child, being in its natural place through no initiative and no breach of duty of its own, cannot be reasonably regarded as intruder, predator or aggressor; its relation to its mother is just that: mother and child.[18]

4. Provided that bringing about death or injury is not chosen as a means of preserving life, an action which is necessary to preserve the life of one person can be permissible even if it is certain also to bring about the death or injury of another or others.

5. Not every indirect killing is permissible; sometimes, though indirect, it is unjust, e.g. because there is a non-deadly alternative to the deadly procedure which could be used for preserving life.

A just law and a decent medical ethic forbidding the killing of the unborn cannot admit an exception 'to save the life of the mother'. Many of the laws in Christian nations used to include exactly that exception (and no others), but there are two decisive reasons why a fully just law and medical ethic cannot include a provision formulated in that sort of way.

First, that sort of formulation implies that, in this case at least, killing may rightly be chosen as a means to an end. Second, by referring only to the mother, any such formulation implies that her life should *always* be preferred, which is unfair.

However, a just law and a decent medical ethic cannot delimit permissible killing by limiting its prohibition to 'direct killing' (or 'direct abortion'). For this would leave unprohibited the cases where indirect killing is unjust (e.g. because it could have been delayed until the time when the unborn child would survive the operation; or because it was done to relieve the mother of a condition which did not threaten her life).

Where the life of mother or of the unborn child is at stake, the requirements both of a decent medical ethic (including the four principles) and of just law can be expressed in the following proposition:

If the life of either the mother or the child can be saved only by some medical procedure which will adversely affect the other, then it is permissible to undertake such a procedure with the intention of saving life, provided that the procedure is the most effective available to increase the overall probability that one or the other (or both) will survive, i.e. to increase the *average probability* of their survival.

This proposition does not say or imply that killing as a means can be permissible. It does not give an unfair priority to either the mother or the child. It excludes any indirect killing which would be unfair.

Nevertheless, it may seem at first glance that the proposition would admit direct abortion in certain cases. For people often assume, and many Catholic theologians argue, that any procedure is direct abortion if in the process of cause and effect it *at once* or *first* brings about the damage to the unborn child.

But even amongst Catholic theologians who reject every kind of compromise with secular consequentialism and proportionalism, there are some who propose an alternative understanding of direct killing, using the framework of Thomas Aquinas's analysis of acts with two effects and of Pope Pius XII's interpretation of 'direct killing' as an action which aims at the destruction of an innocent human life either as an end or as a means.[19, 20] The directness which is in choosing a means is to be understood,

according to these theologians, not by reference to immediacy or priority in the process of cause and effect, as such, but by reference to the intelligible content of a choice to do something inherently suited to bring about intended benefit.

The proposition I have set out above requires that any procedure which adversely affects the life of either the mother or the unborn child be intended *and inherently suited* to preserving life (both lives) so far as is possible. It thus falls within an acceptable understanding of Catholic teaching on direct abortion. At the same time it demands that any such procedure satisfy the requirements of justice (fairness) which are conditions for the moral permissibility of indirect abortion. The most obvious and likely application of the proposition is in cases where four conditions are satisfied: some pathology threatens the lives of both the pregnant woman and her child; it is not safe to wait, or waiting will very probably result in the death of both; there is no way to save the child; and an operation that can save the mother's life will result in the child's death. Of these cases the example most likely to be met in modern health care is that of ectopic pregnancy (assuming that the embryo cannot be successfully transplanted from the tube to the uterus).

Abortion to 'save the life of the mother' because she is threatening to commit suicide (or because her relatives are threatening to kill her) obviously falls outside the proposition and is a case of direct, impermissible killing. It is neither the only means of saving her life (guarding or restraining her or her relatives is another means), nor is it a means suited of its nature to saving life; of itself, indeed, the abortion in such a case does nothing but kill.

Rape

A woman who is the victim of rape is entitled to defend herself against the continuing effects of such an attack and to seek immediate medical assistance with a view to preventing conception.[21] (Such efforts to prevent conception are not necessarily acts of contraception, for they seek to prevent conception not *as* the coming to be of a new human life but rather *as* the invasion of her ovum as a final incident in the invasion of her body by her assailant's bodily substances.)

But the possible presence of an unborn child changes the moral situation notably. Even if a procedure for terminating pregnancy were undertaken without any intention, even partly, to terminate the development and life of the unborn child, but *solely* to relieve the mother of the continued bodily effects of the rape, that procedure would be unjust to the unborn child, who is wholly innocent of the father's wrongdoing. For people are generally willing to accept, and expect their close friends and relatives to accept, grave burdens short of loss of life or moral integrity in order to avert certain death. So imposing certain or even probable death on the unborn child in these circumstances is an unfair discrimination against the child.

However, if a procedure such as the administration of the 'post-coital pill' is undertaken for the purpose only of *preventing* conception after rape but involves some *risk* of causing abortion *as a side-effect* (because it is not known at what stage of her cycle the woman is), there can be no universal judgement that the adoption of such a procedure is unjust to the unborn. For there are many legitimate activities which foreseeably cause some risk of serious or even fatal harm, a risk which in many cases is rightly accepted by upright and informed people as a possible side-effect of their choices to engage in those activities.[22, 23]

Prenatal Screening and Genetic Counselling

Examinations and tests done with the intention of, if need be, treating the unborn or preparing for a safe pregnancy and delivery are desirable and right when undertaken on the same criteria as other medical procedures. Examinations and tests done to allay anxiety or curiosity are justifiable only if they involve no significant risk to the child. But anyone who does or accepts a test or examination with the thought of perhaps suggesting or arranging or carrying out an abortion if the results show something undesirable, is already willing, conditionally, abortion, and so is already making himself or herself into a violator of the principles of non-maleficence and justice.

Health care personnel who respect those principles have a responsibility not only to refrain from recommending or conducting tests or examinations with a view to seeing whether or not abortion is 'medically indicated', but also the responsibility of telling a woman within their care which of the various tests she may be offered by others are done only or mainly for that immoral (but widely accepted) purpose and which are done to safeguard the health of the unborn child.[24]

Participation

Anyone who commands, directs, advises, encourages, prescribes, approves, or actively defends doing something immoral is a cooperator in it if it is done and, even if it is not in the event done, has already willed it to be done and thus already participates in its immorality. So a doctor who does not perform abortions but refers pregnant women to consultant obstetricians with a view to abortion wills the immorality of abortion.

On the other hand, some people whose activity contributes to the carrying out of an immoral act need not will the accomplishment of the immoral act; their cooperation in the evil is not a participation in the immorality as such. Their cooperation is often called 'material', to distinguish it from the so-called 'formal' (intended) cooperation of those who (for whatever reason and with whatever enthusiasm or reluctance) will the successful doing of the immoral act. Formal cooperation in immoral acts is always wrong; material cooperation is not always wrong, but will be wrong if it is unfair or a needless failure to witness to the truth about the immorality or a needless giving of a bad example. So a nurse in a general hospital who is unwilling to participate in abortions but is required by the terms of her employment to prepare patients for surgical operations (cleaning, shaving, etc.) may prepare patients for abortion without ever willing the killing or harming of the unborn child; she does only whatever she does towards any morally good operation; so her cooperation can be morally permissible *if* in all the circumstances it is not unfair and a needless occasion of scandal (morally corrupting example to others). The surgeon, on the other hand, must will the harm to the unborn, since that is the point of the immoral abortion and he or she must will the operation's success; so he or she is a participant, indeed a primary participant, in immorality, even if he or she too is doing so only in order to retain employment or gain medical qualifications.[25] Hospital managers who want every patient to give written and full consent to operations must want women who come to the hospital for abortions to consent precisely to abortion; so these managers willy-nilly encourage the women's immoral willing of abortion; indeed, the managers' immoral commitment of will may well be greater than that of women whose consent is given in a state of emotional upheaval and distress.

All health care personnel have a moral right (and duty) of non-participation in wrongdoing. This right is not in essence one of 'conscientious objection', since it is founded not on the sheer fact of having made a good-faith judgement of conscience – which might be mistaken – but on the basic human duty and corresponding right not to participate in what really is a moral evil. But where the state recognizes a legal right of 'conscientious objection' to participation in abortion, health care personnel have the moral right and duty to avail themselves of that legal right wherever they would otherwise incur any kind of legal obligation or institutional responsibility to cooperate 'formally' (i.e. intentionally) in abortion. They should take the appropriate steps in good time (but even if they have culpably failed to take those steps, should still refuse all formal cooperation in any of the immoral activities now so widespread in the practice of health care).

Embryo Experimentation

What has been said above about abortion applies, of course to embryos living *in vitro* – understanding by 'embryo' any human individual from the beginning of fertilization. Any form of experimentation on or observation of an embryo which is likely to damage that embryo (or any other embryo which it might engender by twinning), or to endanger it by delaying the time of its transfer and implantation, is maleficent or unjust or both, unless the procedures are intended to benefit that individual itself. Any form of freezing or other storage done without genuine and definite prospect of a subsequent transfer, unimpaired, to the proper mother is unjust unless done as a measure to save the embryo in an unexpected emergency. Any procedure whereby embryos are brought into being with a view to selecting among them the fittest or most desirable for transfer and implantation involves a radically unjust and maleficent intention, however good its further motivations.[26-28]

Benevolence and Autonomy

The open acceptance of abortion into reputable medical practice during the past quarter of a century – an ethical and civilization collapse of historic magnitude and far-reaching effects – creates a profound challenge for all who remain willing to adhere to the proper meaning of non-maleficence and justice. They need a proper sense of their own autonomy, as upright moral subjects who preserve and respect the truth amid a social fabric of untruths and rationalizations. They also need to retain and live out a full respect for the principle of beneficence. By refusing their participation in abortion they show beneficence to the unborn (even though these will almost certainly be killed by others); and to the mothers of the unborn (however little they appreciate it at the time); and to all whose lives are endangered by the spread of an ethos of 'ethical killing' in the name of compassion or autonomy. They retain a full responsibility for the compassionate care of pregnant women and for women whose pregnancy was terminated by abortion, no less than of women threatened by or suffering in or after miscarriage or stillbirth. They should be aware of the very real special needs and vulnerabilities of those who have had an induced abortion, even though those needs and sequelae are widely denied by those who promote abortion and produce rationalizations for doing and undergoing it.

References

1 Tooley, M. 1983. *Abortion and Infanticide*. Oxford: Clarendon Press.
2 Hurst, G. 1977. *Beginning Lives*, pp. 107–11. Oxford: Basil Blackwell/Open University.
3 Grisez, G. 1989. When do people begin? *Proceedings of the American Catholic Philosophical Association*, 63: 27–47.
4 Atkinson, G. M. 1977. Persons in the whole sense. *American Journal of Jurisprudence*, 22: 86–117.

5   Donceel, J. F. 1970. Immediate animation and delayed hominization. *Theological Studies*, 31: 76–105.

6   Ashley, B. 1976. A critique of the theory of delayed hominization, pp. 113–33, *in* McCarthy, D. G. and Moraczewski, A. S. (eds), *An Ethical Evaluation of Fetal Experimentation: an interdisciplinary study*. Pope John XXIII Medical-Moral Research and Education Center, St Louis, MO.

7   Gallagher, J. 1985. Is the human embryo a person? *Human Life Institute Reports*, No. 4, pp. 22–6. Human Life Research Institute, Toronto.

8   Heaney, S. J. 1992. Aquinas and the presence of the human rational soul in the early embryo. *Thomist*, 56: 19–48.

9   Wade, F. C. 1975. Potentiality in the abortion discussion. *Review of Metaphysics*, 29: 239–55.

10   Ford, N. M. 1988. *When did I begin?* Cambridge: Cambridge University Press.

11   Fisher, A. O. P. 1991. Individuogenesis and a recent book by Fr. Norman Ford. *Rivista di Studi sulla Persona e la Famiglia Anthropotes*, 2: 199–244.

12   Fisher, A. 1991. 'When did I begin?' revisited. Linacre Quarterly, August, pp. 59–68.

13   Tonti-Filippini, N. 1989. A critical note. *Linacre Quarterly*, 56: 36–50.

14   Suarez, A. 1990. Hydatidiform moles and teratomas confirm the human identity of the preimplantation embryo. *Journal of Medicine and Philosophy*, 15: 627–35.

15   Pius XII, Pope. 1944. Address of 12 November 1944. *Discorsi & Radiomessaggi*, 6: 191–2.

16   Congregation for the Doctrine of the Faith. 1974. *De abortu procurato*, para. 7. Declaration on Abortion of 18 November. London: Catholic Truth Society.

17   Finnis, J. 1991. *Moral Absolutes*, pp. 40, 67–77. Washington, DC: Catholic University of America Press.

18   Finnis, J. 1973. The rights and wrongs of abortion: a reply to Judith Thomson. *Philosophy and Public Affairs*, 2: 117 at 138–43; reprinted in Dworkin, R. 1977. *The Philosophy of Law*. Oxford: Clarendon Press.

19   Zalba, M. 1977. 'Nihil prohibet unius actus esse duos effectus' (Summa theologica 2-2, q.64, a.7) Numquid applicari potest principium in abortu therapeutico? Atti del Congresso Internazionale (Roma-Napoli, 17/24 Aprile 1974), *Tommaso d'Aquino nel suo Settimo Centenario, vol. 5, L'Agire Morale*, pp. 557–68, esp. 567–8. Naples: Edizioni Domenicane Italiane.

20   Grisez, G. and Boyle, J. M. 1979. *Life and Death with Liberty and Justice*, pp. 404–7. South Bend, IN, and London: Notre Dame University Press.

21   Catholic Archbishops of Great Britain. 1980. *Abortion and the Right to Live*, para. 21. London: Catholic Truth Society.

22   Catholic Bishops' Joint Committee on Bio-ethical Issues. 1986. The morning-after pill: some practical and moral questions about post-coital 'contraception'. *Briefing*, 16: 33–9.

23   Catholic Bishops' Joint Committee on Bio-ethical Issues. 1986. The morning-after pill – a reply. *Briefing*, 16: 254–5.

24   Sutton, A. 1990. *Prenatal Diagnosis: Confronting the Ethical Issues*, pp. 1–188. London: Linacre Centre.

25   Grisez, G. 1984. *Christian Moral Principles*, pp. 300–3. Chicago, IL: Franciscan Herald Press.

26   Fisher, A. O. P. 1989. *IVF: The Critical Issues*. Melbourne: Collins Dove.

27   Catholic Bishops' Joint Committee on Bioethical Issues. 1983. *In Vitro Fertilisation: Morality and Public Policy*, part II. Abingdon: Joint Committee on Bioethical Issues.

28   Congregation for the Doctrine of the Faith. 1987. *Donum Vitae. Instruction on respect for human life in its origin and the dignity of procreation*. London: Catholic Truth Society.

2

Abortion and Infanticide

Michael Tooley[1]

This essay deals with the question of the morality of abortion and infanticide. The fundamental ethical objection traditionally advanced against these practices rests on the contention that human fetuses and infants have a right to life. It is this claim which will be the focus of attention here. The basic issue to be discussed, then, is what properties a thing must possess in order to have a serious right to life. My approach will be to set out and defend a basic moral principle specifying a condition an organism must satisfy if it is to have a serious right to life. It will be seen that this condition is not satisfied by human fetuses and infants, and thus that they do not have a right to life. So unless there are other substantial objections to abortion and infanticide, one is forced to conclude that these practices are morally acceptable ones. In contrast, it may turn out that our treatment of adult members of other species – cats, dogs, polar bears – is morally indefensible. For it is quite possible that such animals do possess properties that endow them with a right to life.

I Abortion and Infanticide

One reason the question of the morality of infanticide is worth examining is that it seems very difficult to formulate a completely satisfactory liberal position on abortion without coming to grips with the infanticide issue. The problem the liberal encounters is essentially that of specifying a cutoff point which is not arbitrary: at what stage in the development of a human being does it cease to be morally permissible to destroy it? It is important to be clear about the difficulty here. The conservative's objection is not that since there is a continuous line of development from a zygote to a newborn baby, one must conclude that if it is seriously wrong to destroy a newborn baby it is also seriously wrong to destroy a zygote or any intermediate stage in the development of a human being. His point is rather that if one says it is wrong to destroy a newborn baby but not a zygote or some intermediate stage in the development of a human being, one should be prepared to point to a *morally relevant* difference between a newborn baby and the earlier stage in the development of a human being.

Precisely the same difficulty can, of course, be raised for a person who holds that infanticide is morally permissible. The conservative will ask what morally relevant differences there are between an adult human being and a newborn baby. What makes it morally permissible to destroy a baby, but wrong to kill an adult? So the challenge remains. But I will argue that in this case there is an extremely plausible answer.

Original publication details: Michael Tooley, "Abortion and Infanticide," pp. 37–65 from *Philosophy and Public Affairs* 1 (1972). Reproduced with permission from John Wiley & Sons.

Reflecting on the morality of infanticide forces one to face up to this challenge. In the case of abortion a number of events – quickening or viability, for instance – might be taken as cutoff points, and it is easy to overlook the fact that none of these events involves any morally significant change in the developing human. In contrast, if one is going to defend infanticide, one has to get very clear about what makes something a person, what gives something a right to life.

One of the interesting ways in which the abortion issue differs from most other moral issues is that the plausible positions on abortion appear to be extreme positions. For if a human fetus is a person, one is inclined to say that, in general, one would be justified in killing it only to save the life of the mother.[2] Such is the extreme conservative position.[3] On the other hand, if the fetus is not a person, how can it be seriously wrong to destroy it? Why would one need to point to special circumstances to justify such action? The upshot is that there is no room for a moderate position on the issue of abortion such as one finds, for example, in the Model Penal Code recommendations.[4]

Aside from the light it may shed on the abortion question, the issue of infanticide is both interesting and important in its own right. The theoretical interest has been mentioned: it forces one to face up to the question of what makes something a person. The practical importance need not be labored. Most people would prefer to raise children who do not suffer from gross deformities or from severe physical, emotional, or intellectual handicaps. If it could be shown that there is no moral objection to infanticide the happiness of society could be significantly and justifiably increased.

Infanticide is also of interest because of the strong emotions it arouses. The typical reaction to infanticide is like the reaction to incest or cannibalism, or the reaction of previous generations to masturbation or oral sex. The response, rather than appealing to carefully formulated moral principles, is primarily visceral. When philosophers themselves respond in this way, offering no arguments, and dismissing infanticide out of hand it is reasonable to suspect that one is dealing with a taboo rather than with a rational prohibition.[5] I shall attempt to show that this is in fact the case.

II Terminology: "Person" versus "Human Being"

How is the term "person" to be interpreted? I shall treat the concept of a person as a purely moral concept, free of all descriptive content. Specifically, in my usage the sentence "X is a person" will be synonymous with the sentence "X has a (serious) moral right to life."

This usage diverges slightly from what is perhaps the more common way of interpreting the term "person" when it is employed as a purely moral term, where to say that X is a person is to say that X has rights. If everything that had rights had a right to life, these interpretations would be extensionally equivalent. But I am inclined to think that it does not follow from acceptable moral principles that whatever has any rights at all has a right to life. My reason is this. Given the choice between being killed and being tortured for an hour, most adult humans would surely choose the latter. So it seems plausible to say it is worse to kill an adult human being than it is to torture him for an hour. In contrast, it seems to me that while it is not seriously wrong to kill a newborn kitten, it is seriously wrong to torture one for an hour. This *suggests* that newborn kittens may have a right not to be tortured without having a serious right to life. For it seems to be true that an individual has a right to something whenever it is the case that, if he wants that thing, it would be wrong for others to deprive him of it. Then if it is wrong to inflict a certain sensation upon a kitten if it doesn't want to experience that sensation, it will follow that the kitten has a right not to have sensation inflicted upon it.[6] I shall return to this example later. My point here is merely that it provides some reason for holding that it does not follow from acceptable moral principles that if something has any rights at all, it has a serious right to life.

There has been a tendency in recent discussions of abortion to use expressions such as "person" and "human being" interchangeably. B. A. Brody, for example, refers to the difficulty of determining "whether destroying the foetus constitutes the taking of a human life," and suggests it is very plausible that "the taking of a human life is an action that has bad consequences for him whose life is being taken."[7]

When Brody refers to something as a human life he apparently construes this as entailing that the thing is a person. For if every living organism belonging to the species *Homo sapiens* counted as a human life, there would be no difficulty in determining whether a fetus inside a human mother was a human life.

The same tendency is found in Judith Jarvis Thomson's article, which opens with the statement: "Most opposition to abortion relies on the premise that the fetus is a human being, a person, from the moment of conception."[8] The same is true of Roger Wertheimer, who explicitly says: "First off I should note that the expressions 'a human life,' 'a human being,' 'a person' are virtually interchangeable in this context."[9]

The tendency to use expressions like "person" and "human being" interchangeably is an unfortunate one. For one thing, it tends to lend covert support to antiabortionist positions. Given such usage, one who holds a liberal view of abortion is put in the position of maintaining that fetuses, at least up to a certain point, are not human beings. Even philosophers are led astray by this usage. Thus Wertheimer says that "except for monstrosities, every member of our species is indubitably a person, a human being, at the very latest at birth."[10] Is it really *indubitable* that newborn babies are persons? Surely this is a wild contention. Wertheimer is falling prey to the confusion naturally engendered by the practice of using "person" and "human being" interchangeably. Another example of this is provided by Thomson: "I am inclined to think also that we shall probably have to agree that the fetus has already become a human person well before birth. Indeed, it comes as a surprise when one first learns how early in its life it begins to acquire human characteristics. By the tenth week, for example, it already has a face, arms and legs, fingers and toes; it has internal organs, and brain activity is detectable."[11] But what do such physiological characteristics have to do with the question of whether the organism is a person? Thomson, partly, I think, because of the unfortunate use of terminology, does not even raise this question. As a result she virtually takes it for granted that there are some cases in which abortion is "positively indecent."[12]

There is a second reason why using "person" and "human being" interchangeably is unhappy

philosophically. If one says that the dispute between pro- and anti-abortionists centers on whether the fetus is a human, it is natural to conclude that it is essentially a disagreement about certain facts, a disagreement about what properties a fetus possesses. Thus Wertheimer says that "if one insists on using the raggy fact–value distinction, then one ought to say that the dispute is over a matter of fact in the sense in which it is a fact that the Negro slaves were human beings."[13] I shall argue that the two cases are not parallel, and that in the case of abortion what is primarily at stake is what moral principles one should accept. If one says that the central issue between conservatives and liberals in the abortion question is whether the fetus is a person, it is clear that the dispute may be either about what properties a thing must have in order to be a person, in order to have a right to life – a moral question – or about whether a fetus at a given stage of development as a matter of fact possesses the properties in question. The temptation to suppose that the disagreement must be a factual one is removed.

It should now be clear why the common practice of using expressions such as "person" and "human being" interchangeably in discussions of abortion is unfortunate. It would perhaps be best to avoid the term "human" altogether, employing instead some expression that is more naturally interpreted as referring to a certain type of biological organism characterized in physiological terms, such as "member of the species *Homo sapiens*." My own approach will be to use the term "human" only in contexts where it is not philosophically dangerous.

III The Basic Issue: When is a Member of the Species *Homo sapiens* a Person?

Settling the issue of the morality of abortion and infanticide will involve answering the following questions: What properties must something have to be a person, i.e., to have a serious right to life? At what point in the development of a member of the species *Homo sapiens* does the organism possess the properties that make it a person? The first question raises a moral issue. To answer it is to decide what basic[14] moral principles involving the ascription of a right to life one ought to accept. The second question raises a purely factual issue, since the properties in question are properties of a purely descriptive sort.

Some writers seem quite pessimistic about the possibility of resolving the question of the morality of abortion. Indeed, some have gone so far as to suggest that the question of whether the fetus is a person is in principle unanswerable: "we seem to be stuck with the indeterminateness of the fetus' humanity."[15] An understanding of some of the sources of this pessimism will, I think, help us to tackle the problem. Let us begin by considering the similarity a number of people have noted between the issue of abortion and the issue of Negro slavery. The question here is why it should be more difficult to decide whether abortion and infanticide are acceptable than it was to decide whether slavery was acceptable. The answer seems to be that in the case of slavery there are moral principles of a quite uncontroversial sort that settle the issue. Thus most people would agree to some such principle as the following: No organism that has experiences, that is capable of thought and of using language, and that has harmed no one, should be made a slave. In the case of abortion, on the other hand, conditions that are generally agreed to be sufficient grounds for ascribing a right to life to something do not suffice to settle the issue. It is easy to specify other, purportedly sufficient conditions that will settle the issue, but no one has been successful in putting forward considerations that will convince others to accept those additional moral principles.

I do not share the general pessimism about the possibility of resolving the issue of abortion and infanticide because I believe it is possible to point to a very plausible moral principle dealing with the question of *necessary* conditions for something's having a right to life, where the conditions in question will provide an answer to the question of the permissibility of abortion and infanticide.

There is a second cause of pessimism that should be noted before proceeding. It is tied up with the fact that the development of an organism is one of gradual and continuous change. Given this continuity, how is one to draw a line at one point and declare it permissible to destroy a member of *Homo sapiens* up to, but not beyond, that point? Won't there be an arbitrariness

about any point that is chosen? I will return to this worry shortly. It does not present a serious difficulty once the basic moral principles relevant to the ascription of a right to life to an individual are established.

Let us turn now to the first and most fundamental question: What properties must something have in order to be a person, i.e., to have a serious right to life? The claim I wish to defend is this: An organism possesses a serious right to life only if it possesses the concept of a self as a continuing subject of experiences and other mental states, and believes that it is itself such a continuing entity.

My basic argument in support of this claim, which I will call the self-consciousness requirement, will be clearest, I think, if I first offer a simplified version of the argument, and then consider a modification that seems desirable. The simplified version of my argument is this. To ascribe a right to an individual is to assert something about the prima facie obligations of other individuals to act, or to refrain from acting, in certain ways. However, the obligations in question are conditional ones, being dependent upon the existence of certain desires of the individual to whom the right is ascribed. Thus if an individual asks one to destroy something to which he has a right, one does not violate his right to that thing if one proceeds to destroy it. This suggests the following analysis: "A has a right to X" is roughly synonymous with "If A desires X, then others are under a prima facie obligation to refrain from actions that would deprive him of it."[16]

Although this analysis is initially plausible, there are reasons for thinking it not entirely correct. I will consider these later. Even here, however, some expansion is necessary, since there are features of the concept of a right that are important in the present context, and that ought to be dealt with more explicitly. In particular, it seems to be a conceptual truth that things that lack consciousness, such as ordinary machines, cannot have rights. Does this conceptual truth follow from the above analysis of the concept of a right? The answer depends on how the term "desire" is interpreted. If one adopts a completely behavioristic interpretation of "desire," so that a machine that searches for an electrical outlet in order to get its batteries recharged is described as having a desire to be recharged, then it will not follow from this analysis that objects that lack consciousness cannot have rights.

On the other hand, if "desire" is interpreted in such a way that desires are states necessarily standing in some sort of relationship to states of consciousness, it will follow from the analysis that a machine that is not capable of being conscious, and consequently of having desires, cannot have any rights. I think those who defend analyses of the concept of a right along the lines of this one do have in mind an interpretation of the term "desire" that involves reference to something more than behavioral dispositions. However, rather than relying on this, it seems preferable to make such an interpretation explicit. The following analysis is a natural way of doing that: "A has a right to X" is roughly synonymous with "A is the sort of thing that is a subject of experiences and other mental states, A is capable of desiring X, and if A does desire X, then others are under a prima facie obligation to refrain from actions that would deprive him of it."

The next step in the argument is basically a matter of applying this analysis to the concept of a right to life. Unfortunately the expression "right to life" is not entirely a happy one, since it suggests that the right in question concerns the continued existence of a biological organism. That this is incorrect can be brought out by considering possible ways of violating an individual's right to life. Suppose, for example, that by some technology of the future the brain of an adult human were to be completely reprogrammed, so that the organism wound up with memories (or rather, apparent memories), beliefs, attitudes, and personality traits completely different from those associated with it before it was subjected to reprogramming. In such a case one would surely say that an individual had been destroyed, that an adult human's right to life had been violated, even though no biological organism had been killed. This example shows that the expression "right to life" is misleading, since what one is really concerned about is not just the continued existence of a biological organism, but the right of a subject of experiences and other mental states to continue to exist.

Given this more precise description of the right with which we are here concerned, we are now in a position to apply the analysis of the concept of a right stated above. When we do so we find that the statement "A has a right to continue to exist as a subject of experiences and other mental states" is roughly synonymous with the statement "A is a subject of experiences and other

mental states, A is capable of desiring to continue to exist as a subject of experiences and other mental states, and if A does desire to continue to exist as such an entity, then others are under a prima facie obligation not to prevent him from doing so."

The final stage in the argument is simply a matter of asking what must be the case if something is to be capable of having a desire to continue existing as a subject of experiences and other mental states. The basic point here is that the desires a thing can have are limited by the concepts it possesses. For the fundamental way of describing a given desire is as a desire that a certain proposition be true.[17] Then, since one cannot desire that a certain proposition be true unless one understands it, and since one cannot understand it without possessing the concepts involved in it, it follows that the desires one can have are limited by the concepts one possesses. Applying this to the present case results in the conclusion that an entity cannot be the sort of thing that can desire that a subject of experiences and other mental states exist unless it possesses the concept of such a subject. Moreover, an entity cannot desire that it itself *continue* existing as a subject of experiences and other mental states unless it believes that it is now such a subject. This completes the justification of the claim that it is a necessary condition of something's having a serious right to life that it possess the concept of a self as a continuing subject of experiences, and that it believe that it is itself such an entity.

Let us now consider a modification in the above argument that seems desirable. This modification concerns the crucial conceptual claim advanced about the relationship between ascription of rights and ascription of the corresponding desires. Certain situations suggest that there may be exceptions to the claim that if a person doesn't desire something, one cannot violate his right to it. There are three types of situations that call this claim into question: (i) situations in which an individual's desires reflect a state of emotional disturbance; (ii) situations in which a previously conscious individual is temporarily unconscious; (iii) situations in which an individual's desires have been distorted by conditioning or by indoctrination.

As an example of the first, consider a case in which an adult human falls into a state of depression which his psychiatrist recognizes as temporary. While in the state he tells people he wishes he were dead. His psychiatrist, accepting the view that there can be no violation of an individual's right to life unless the individual has a desire to live, decides to let his patient have his way and kills him. Or consider a related case in which one person gives another a drug that produces a state of temporary depression; the recipient expresses a wish that he were dead. The person who administered the drug then kills him. Doesn't one want to say in both these cases that the agent did something seriously wrong in killing the other person? And isn't the reason the action was seriously wrong in each case the fact that it violated the individual's right to life? If so, the right to life cannot be linked with a desire to live in the way claimed above.

The second set of situations are ones in which an individual is unconscious for some reason – that is, he is sleeping, or drugged, or in a temporary coma. Does an individual in such a state have any desires? People do sometimes say that an unconscious individual wants something, but it might be argued that if such talk is not to be simply false it must be interpreted as actually referring to the desires the individual *would* have if he were now conscious. Consequently, if the analysis of the concept of a right proposed above were correct, it would follow that one does not violate an individual's right if one takes his car, or kills him, while he is asleep.

Finally, consider situations in which an individual's desires have been distorted, either by inculcation of irrational beliefs or by direct conditioning. Thus an individual may permit someone to kill him because he has been convinced that if he allows himself to be sacrificed to the gods he will be gloriously rewarded in a life to come. Or an individual may be enslaved after first having been conditioned to desire a life of slavery. Doesn't one want to say that in the former case an individual's right to life has been violated, and in the latter his right to freedom?

Situations such as these strongly suggest that even if an individual doesn't want something, it is still possible to violate his right to it. Some modification of the earlier account of the concept of a right thus seems in order. The analysis given covers, I believe, the paradigmatic cases of violation of an individual's rights, but there are other, secondary cases where one also wants to say that someone's right has been violated which are not included.

Precisely how the revised analysis should be formulated is unclear. Here it will be sufficient merely to say that, in view of the above, an individual's right to X can be violated not only when he desires X, but also when he *would* now desire X were it not for one of the following: (i) he is in an emotionally unbalanced state; (ii) he is temporarily unconscious; (iii) he has been conditioned to desire the absence of X.

The critical point now is that, even given this extension of the conditions under which an individual's right to something can be violated, it is still true that one's right to something can be violated only when one has the conceptual capability of desiring the thing in question. For example, an individual who would now desire not to be a slave if he weren't emotionally unbalanced, or if he weren't temporarily unconscious, or if he hadn't previously been conditioned to want to be a slave, must possess the concepts involved in the desire not to be a slave. Since it is really only the conceptual capability presupposed by the desire to continue existing as a subject of experiences and other mental states, and not the desire itself, that enters into the above argument, the modification required in the account of the conditions under which an individual's rights can be violated does not undercut my defense of the self-consciousness requirement.[18]

To sum up, my argument has been that having a right to life presupposes that one is capable of desiring to continue existing as a subject of experiences and other mental states. This in turn presupposes both that one has the concept of such a continuing entity and that one believes that one is oneself such an entity. So an entity that lacks such a consciousness of itself as a continuing subject of mental states does not have a right to life.

It would be natural to ask at this point whether satisfaction of this requirement is not only necessary but also sufficient to ensure that a thing has a right to life. I am inclined to an affirmative answer. However, the issue is not urgent in the present context, since as long as the requirement is in fact a necessary one we have the basis of an adequate defense of abortion and infanticide. If an organism must satisfy some other condition before it has a serious right to life, the result will merely be that the interval during which infanticide is morally permissible may be somewhat longer.

Although the point at which an organism first achieves self-consciousness and hence the capacity of desiring to continue existing as a subject of experiences and other mental states may be a theoretically incorrect cutoff point, it is at least a morally safe one: any error it involves is on the side of caution.

IV   Some Critical Comments on Alternative Proposals

I now want to compare the line of demarcation I am proposing with the cutoff points traditionally advanced in discussions of abortion. My fundamental claim will be that none of these cutoff points can be defended by appeal to plausible, basic moral principles. The main suggestions as to the point past which it is seriously wrong to destroy something that will develop into an adult member of the species *Homo sapiens* are these: (a) conception; (b) the attainment of human form; (c) the achievement of the ability to move about spontaneously; (d) viability; (e) birth.[19] The corresponding moral principles suggested by these cutoff points are as follows. (1) It is seriously wrong to kill an organism, from a zygote on, that belongs to the species *Homo sapiens*. (2) It is seriously wrong to kill an organism that belongs to *Homo sapiens* and that has achieved human form. (3) It is seriously wrong to kill an organism that is a member of *Homo sapiens* and that is capable of spontaneous movement. (4) It is seriously wrong to kill an organism that belongs to *Homo sapiens* and that is capable of existing outside the womb. (5) It is seriously wrong to kill an organism that is a member of *Homo sapiens* that is no longer in the womb.

My first comment is that it would not do *simply* to omit the reference to membership in the species *Homo sapiens* from the above principles, with the exception of principle (2). For then the principles would be applicable to animals in general, and one would be forced to conclude that it was seriously wrong to abort a cat fetus, or that it was seriously wrong to abort a motile cat fetus, and so on.

The second and crucial comment is that none of the five principles given above can plausibly be viewed as a *basic* moral principle. To accept any of them as such would be akin to accepting as a basic moral principle the proposition that it is morally permissible to enslave black members of the species *Homo sapiens* but not white members. Why should it be seriously wrong to kill an unborn member of the species *Homo sapiens* but not seriously wrong to kill an unborn kitten? Difference in species is not per se a morally relevant difference. If one holds that it is seriously wrong to kill an unborn member of the species *Homo sapiens* but not an unborn kitten, one should be prepared to point to some property that is morally significant and that is possessed by unborn members of *Homo sapiens* but not by unborn kittens. Similarly, such a property must be identified if one believes it seriously wrong to kill unborn members of *Homo sapiens* that have achieved viability but not seriously wrong to kill unborn kittens that have achieved that state.

What property might account for such a difference? That is to say, what *basic* moral principles might a person who accepts one of these five principles appeal to in support of his secondary moral judgment? Why should events such as the achievement of human form, or the achievement of the ability to move about, or the achievement of viability, or birth serve to endow something with a right to life? What the liberal must do is to show that these events involve changes, or are associated with changes, that are morally relevant.

Let us now consider reasons why the events involved in cutoff points (b) through (e) are not morally relevant, beginning with the last two: viability and birth. The fact that an organism is not physiologically dependent upon another organism, or is capable of such physiological independence, is surely irrelevant to whether the organism has a right to life. In defense of this contention, consider a speculative case where a fetus is able to learn a language while in the womb. One would surely not say that the fetus had no right to life until it emerged from the womb, or until it was capable of existing outside the womb. A less speculative example is the case of Siamese twins who have learned to speak. One doesn't want to say that since one of the twins would die were the two to be separated, it therefore has no right to life. Consequently it seems difficult to disagree with the conservative's claim that an organism which lacks a right to life before birth or before becoming viable cannot acquire this right immediately upon birth or upon becoming viable.

This does not, however, completely rule out viability as a line of demarcation. For instead of defending viability as a cutoff point on the ground that only then does a fetus acquire a right to life, it is possible to argue rather that when one organism is physiologically dependent upon another, the former's right to life may conflict with the latter's right to use its body as it will, and moreover, that the latter's right to do what it wants with its body may often take precedence over the other organism's right to life. Thomson has defended this view: "I am arguing only that having a right to life does not guarantee having either a right to the use of or a right to be allowed continued use of another person's body – even if one needs it for life itself. So the right to life will not serve the opponents of abortion in the very simple and clear way in which they seem to have thought it would."[20] I believe that Thomson is right in contending that philosophers have been altogether too casual in assuming that if one grants the fetus a serious right to life, one must accept a conservative position on abortion.[21] I also think the only defense of viability as a cutoff point which has any hope of success at all is one based on the considerations she advances. I doubt very much, however, that this defense of abortion is ultimately tenable. I think that one can grant even stronger assumptions than those made by Thomson and still argue persuasively for a semiconservative view. What I have in mind is this. Let it be granted, for the sake of argument, that a woman's right to free her body of parasites which will inhibit her freedom of action and possibly impair her health is stronger than the parasite's right to life, and is so even if the parasite has as much right to life as an adult human. One can still argue that abortion ought not to be permitted. For if A's right is stronger than B's, and it is impossible to satisfy both, it does not follow that A's should be satisfied rather than B's. It may be possible to compensate A if his right isn't satisfied, but impossible to compensate B if his right isn't satisfied. In such a case the best thing to do may be to satisfy B's claim and to compensate A. Abortion may be a case in point. If the fetus has a right to life and the right is not satisfied, there is certainly no way the fetus can be compensated. On the other hand, if the woman's right to rid her body of harmful and annoying parasites is not satisfied, she can be compensated. Thus it would seem that the just

thing to do would be to prohibit abortion, but to compensate women for the burden of carrying a parasite to term. Then, however, we are back at a (modified) conservative position.[22] Our conclusion must be that it appears unlikely there is any satisfactory defense either of viability or of birth as cutoff points.

Let us now consider the third suggested line of demarcation, the achievement of the power to move about spontaneously. It might be argued that acquiring this power is a morally relevant event on the grounds that there is a connection between the concept of an agent and the concept of a person, and being motile is an indication that a thing is an agent.[23]

It is difficult to respond to this suggestion unless it is made more specific. Given that one's interest here is in defending a certain cutoff point, it is natural to interpret the proposal as suggesting that motility is a necessary condition of an organism's having a right to life. But this won't do, because one certainly wants to ascribe a right to life to adult humans who are completely paralyzed. Maybe the suggestion is rather that motility is a sufficient condition of something's having a right to life. However, it is clear that motility alone is not sufficient, since this would imply that all animals, and also certain machines, have a right to life. Perhaps, then, the most reasonable interpretation of the claim is that motility together with some other property is a sufficient condition of something's having a right to life, where the other property will have to be a property possessed by unborn members of the species *Homo sapiens* but not by unborn members of other familiar species.

The central question, then, is what this other property is. Until one is told, it is very difficult to evaluate either the moral claim that motility together with that property is a sufficient basis for ascribing to an organism a right to life or the factual claim that a motile human fetus possesses that property while a motile fetus belonging to some other species does not. A conservative would presumably reject motility as a cutoff point by arguing that whether an organism has a right to life depends only upon its potentialities, which are of course not changed by its becoming motile. If, on the other hand, one favors a liberal view of abortion, I think that one can attack this third suggested cutoff point, in its unspecified form, only by determining what properties are necessary, or what properties sufficient, for an individual to have a right to life. Thus I would base my rejection of motility as a cutoff point on my claim, defended above, that a necessary condition of an organism's possessing a right to life is that it conceive of itself as a continuing subject of experiences and other mental states.

The second suggested cutoff point – the development of a recognizably human form – can be dismissed fairly quickly. I have already remarked that membership in a particular species is not itself a morally relevant property. For it is obvious that if we encountered other "rational animals," such as Martians, the fact that their physiological makeup was very different from our own would not be grounds for denying them a right to life.[24] Similarly, it is clear that the development of human form is not in itself a morally relevant event. Nor do there seem to be any grounds for holding that there is some other change, associated with this event, that is morally relevant. The appeal of this second cutoff point is, I think, purely emotional.

The overall conclusion seems to be that it is very difficult to defend the cutoff points traditionally advanced by those who advocate either a moderate or a liberal position on abortion. The reason is that there do not seem to be any basic moral principles one can appeal to in support of the cutoff points in question. We must now consider whether the conservative is any better off.

V   Refutation of the Conservative Position

Many have felt that the conservative's position is more defensible than the liberal's because the conservative can point to the gradual and continuous development of an organism as it changes from a zygote to an adult human being. He is then in a position to argue that it is morally arbitrary for the liberal to draw a line at some point in this continuous process and to say that abortion is permissible before, but not after, that particular point. The liberal's reply would presumably be that the emphasis upon the continuity of the process is misleading. What the conservative is really doing is simply challenging the liberal to specify the properties a thing must have in order to be a person, and to show that the developing organism does acquire the properties at the point selected by the lib-

eral. The liberal may then reply that the difficulty he has meeting this challenge should not be taken as grounds for rejecting his position. For the conservative cannot meet this challenge either; the conservative is equally unable to say what properties something must have if it is to have a right to life.

Although this rejoinder does not dispose of the conservative's argument, it is not without bite. For defenders of the view that abortion is always wrong have failed to face up to the question of the basic moral principles on which their position rests. They have been content to assert the wrongness of killing any organism, from a zygote on, if that organism is a member of the species *Homo sapiens*. But they have overlooked the point that this cannot be an acceptable *basic* moral principle, since difference in species is not in itself a morally relevant difference. The conservative can reply, however, that it is possible to defend his position – but not the liberal's – *without* getting clear about the properties a thing must possess if it is to have a right to life. The conservative's defense will rest upon the following two claims: first, that there is a property, even if one is unable to specify what it is, that (i) is possessed by adult humans, and (ii) endows any organism possessing it with a serious right to life. Second, that if there are properties which satisfy (i) and (ii) above, at least one of those properties will be such that any organism potentially possessing that property has a serious right to life even now, simply by virtue of that potentiality, where an organism possesses a property potentially if it will come to have that property in the normal course of its development. The second claim – which I shall refer to as the potentiality principle – is critical to the conservative's defense. Because of it he is able to defend his position without deciding what properties a thing must possess in order to have a right to life. It is enough to know that adult members of *Homo sapiens* do have such a right. For then one can conclude that any organism which belongs to the species *Homo sapiens*, from a zygote on, must also have a right to life by virtue of the potentiality principle.

The liberal, by contrast, cannot mount a comparable argument. He cannot defend his position without offering at least a partial answer to the question of what properties a thing must possess in order to have a right to life.

The importance of the potentiality principle, however, goes beyond the fact that it provides support for the conservative's position. If the principle is unacceptable, then so is his position. For if the conservative cannot defend the view that an organism's having certain potentialities is sufficient grounds for ascribing to it a right to life, his claim that a fetus which is a member of *Homo sapiens* has a right to life can be attacked as follows. The reason an adult member of *Homo sapiens* has a right to life, but an infant ape does not, is that there are certain psychological properties which the former possesses and the latter lacks. Now, even if one is unsure exactly what these psychological properties are, it is clear that an organism in the early stages of development from a zygote into an adult member of *Homo sapiens* does not possess these properties. One need merely compare a human fetus with an ape fetus. What mental states does the former enjoy that the latter does not? Surely it is reasonable to hold that there are no significant differences in their respective mental lives – assuming that one wishes to ascribe any mental states at all to such organisms. (Does a zygote have a mental life? Does it have experiences? Or beliefs? Or desires?) There are, of course, physiological differences, but these are not in themselves morally significant. *If* one held that potentialities were relevant to the ascription of a right to life, one could argue that the physiological differences, though not morally significant in themselves, are morally significant by virtue of their causal consequences: they will lead to later psychological differences that are morally relevant, and for this reason the physiological differences are themselves morally significant. But if the potentiality principle is not available, this line of argument cannot be used, and there will then be no differences between a human fetus and an ape fetus that the conservative can use as grounds for ascribing a serious right to life to the former but not to the latter.

It is therefore tempting to conclude that the conservative view of abortion is acceptable if and only if the potentiality principle is acceptable. But to say that the conservative position can be defended if the potentiality principle is acceptable is to assume that the argument is over once it is granted that the fetus has a right to life, and, as was noted above, Thomson has shown that there are serious grounds for questioning this assumption. In any case, the important point here is that the conservative position on abortion is acceptable *only if* the potentiality principle is sound.

One way to attack the potentiality principle is simply to argue in support of the self-consciousness requirement – the claim that only an organism that conceives of itself as a continuing subject of experiences has a right to life. For this requirement, when taken together with the claim that there is at least one property, possessed by adult humans, such that any organism possessing it has a serious right to life, entails the denial of the potentiality principle. Or at least this is so if we add the uncontroversial empirical claim that an organism that will in the normal course of events develop into an adult human does not from the very beginning of its existence possess a concept of a continuing subject of experiences together with a belief that it is itself such an entity.

I think it best, however, to scrutinize the potentiality principle itself, and not to base one's case against it simply on the self-consciousness requirement. Perhaps the first point to note is that the potentiality principle should not be confused with principles such as the following: the value of an object is related to the value of the things into which it can develop. This "valuation principle" is rather vague. There are ways of making it more precise, but we need not consider these here. Suppose now that one were to speak not of a right to life, but of the value of life. It would then be easy to make the mistake of thinking that the valuation principle was relevant to the potentiality principle – indeed, that it entailed it. But an individual's right to life is not based on the value of his life. To say that the world would be better off if it contained fewer people is not to say that it would be right to achieve such a better world by killing some of the present inhabitants. *If* having a right to life were a matter of a thing's value, then a thing's potentialities, being connected with its expected value, would clearly be relevant to the question of what rights it had. Conversely, once one realizes that a thing's rights are not a matter of its value, I think it becomes clear that an organism's potentialities are irrelevant to the question of whether it has a right to life.

But let us now turn to the task of finding a direct refutation of the potentiality principle. The basic issue is this. Is there any property J which satisfies the following conditions: (1) There is a property K such that any individual possessing property K has a right to life, and there is a scientific law L to the effect that any organism possessing property J will in the normal course of events come to possess property K at some later time. (2) Given the relationship between property J and property K just described, anything possessing property J has a right to life. (3) If property J were not related to property K in the way indicated, it would not be the case that anything possessing property J thereby had a right to life. In short, the question is whether there is a property J that bestows a right to life on an organism *only because* J stands in a certain causal relationship to a second property K, which is such that anything possessing that property *ipso facto* has a right to life.

My argument turns upon the following critical principle: Let C be a causal process that normally leads to outcome E. Let A be an action that initiates process C, and B be an action involving a minimal expenditure of energy that stops process C before outcome E occurs. Assume further that actions A and B do not have any other consequences, and that E is the only morally significant outcome of process C. Then there is no moral difference between intentionally performing action B and intentionally refraining from performing action A, assuming identical motivation in both cases. This principle, which I shall refer to as the moral symmetry principle with respect to action and inaction, would be rejected by some philosophers. They would argue that there is an important distinction to be drawn between "what we owe people in the form of aid and what we owe them in the way of non-interference,"[25] and that the latter, "negative duties," are duties that it is more serious to neglect than the former, "positive" ones. This view arises from an intuitive response to examples such as the following. Even if it is wrong not to send food to starving people in other parts of the world, it is more wrong still to kill someone. And isn't the conclusion, then, that one's obligation to refrain from killing someone is a more serious obligation than one's obligation to save lives?

I want to argue that this is not the correct conclusion. I think it is tempting to draw this conclusion if one fails to consider the motivation that is likely to be associated with the respective actions. If someone performs an action he knows will kill someone else, this will usually be grounds for concluding that he

wanted to kill the person in question. In contrast, failing to help someone may indicate only apathy, laziness, selfishness, or an amoral outlook: the fact that a person knowingly allows another to die will not normally be grounds for concluding that he desired that person's death. Someone who knowingly kills another is more likely to be seriously defective from a moral point of view than someone who fails to save another's life.

If we are not to be led to false conclusions by our intuitions about certain cases, we must explicitly assume identical motivations in the two situations. Compare, for example, the following: (1) Jones sees that Smith will be killed by a bomb unless he warns him. Jones's reaction is: "How lucky, it will save me the trouble of killing Smith myself." So Jones allows Smith to be killed by the bomb, even though he could easily have warned him. (2) Jones wants Smith dead, and therefore shoots him. Is one to say there is a significant difference between the wrongness of Jones's behavior in these two cases? Surely not. This shows the mistake of drawing a distinction between positive duties and negative duties and holding that the latter impose stricter obligations than the former. The difference in our intuitions about situations that involve giving aid to others and corresponding situations that involve not interfering with others is to be explained by reference to probable differences in the motivations operating in the two situations, and not by reference to a distinction between positive and negative duties. For once it is specified that the motivation is the same in the two situations, we realize that inaction is as wrong in the one case as action is in the other.

There is another point that may be relevant. Action involves effort, while inaction usually does not. It usually does not require any effort on my part to refrain from killing someone, but saving someone's life will require an expenditure of energy. One must then ask how large a sacrifice a person is morally required to make to save the life of another. If the sacrifice of time and energy is quite large it may be that one is not morally obliged to save the life of another in that situation. Superficial reflection upon such cases might easily lead us to introduce the distinction between positive and negative duties, but again it is clear that this would be a mistake. The point is not that one has a greater duty to refrain from killing others than to perform positive actions that will save them. It is rather that positive actions require effort, and this means that in deciding what to do a person has to take into account his own right to do what he wants with his life, and not only the other person's right to life. To avoid this confusion, we should confine ourselves to comparisons between situations in which the positive action involves minimal effort.

The moral symmetry principle, as formulated above, explicitly takes these two factors into account. It applies only to pairs of situations in which the motivations are identical and the positive action involves minimal effort. Without these restrictions, the principle would be open to serious objection; with them, it seems perfectly acceptable. For the central objection to it rests on the claim that we must distinguish positive from negative duties and recognize that negative duties impose stronger obligations than positive ones. I have tried to show how this claim derives from an unsound account of our moral intuitions about certain situations.

My argument against the potentiality principle can now be stated. Suppose at some future time a chemical were to be discovered which when injected into the brain of a kitten would cause the kitten to develop into a cat possessing a brain of the sort possessed by humans, and consequently into a cat having all the psychological capabilities characteristic of adult humans. Such cats would be able to think, to use language, and so on. Now it would surely be morally indefensible in such a situation to ascribe a serious right to life to members of the species *Homo sapiens* without also ascribing it to cats that have undergone such a process of development: there would be no morally significant differences.

Secondly, it would not be seriously wrong to refrain from injecting a newborn kitten with the special chemical, and to kill it instead. The fact that one could initiate a causal process that would transform a kitten into an entity that would eventually possess properties such that anything possessing them *ipso facto* has a serious right to life does not mean that the kitten has a serious right to life even before it has been subjected to the process of injection and transformation. The possibility of transforming kittens into persons will not make it any more wrong to kill newborn kittens than it is now.

Thirdly, in view of the symmetry principle, if it is not seriously wrong to refrain from initiating such a causal process, neither is it seriously wrong to interfere with such a process. Suppose a kitten is accidentally injected with the chemical. As long as it has not yet developed those properties that in themselves endow something with a right to life, there cannot be anything wrong with interfering with the causal process and preventing the development of the properties in question. Such interference might be accomplished either by injecting the kitten with some "neutralizing" chemical or simply by killing it.

But if it is not seriously wrong to destroy an injected kitten which will naturally develop the properties that bestow a right to life, neither can it be seriously wrong to destroy a member of *Homo sapiens* which lacks such properties, but will naturally come to have them. The potentialities are the same in both cases. The only difference is that in the case of a human fetus the potentialities have been present from the beginning of the organism's development, while in the case of the kitten they have been present only from the time it was injected with the special chemical. This difference in the time at which the potentialities were acquired is a morally irrelevant difference.

It should be emphasized that I am not here assuming that a human fetus does not possess properties which in themselves, and irrespective of their causal relationships to other properties, provide grounds for ascribing a right to life to whatever possesses them. The point is merely that if it is seriously wrong to kill something, the reason cannot be that the thing will later acquire properties that in themselves provide something with a right to life.

Finally, it is reasonable to believe that there are properties possessed by adult members of *Homo sapiens* which establish their right to life, and also that any normal human fetus will come to possess those properties shared by adult humans. But it has just been shown that if it is wrong to kill a human fetus, it cannot be because of its potentialities. One is therefore forced to conclude that the conservative's potentiality principle is false.

In short, anyone who wants to defend the potentiality principle must either argue against the moral symmetry principle or hold that in a world in which kittens could be transformed into "rational animals" it would be seriously wrong to kill newborn kittens. It is hard to believe there is much to be said for the latter moral claim. Consequently one expects the conservative's rejoinder to be directed against the symmetry principle. While I have not attempted to provide a thorough defense of that principle, I have tried to show that what seems to be the most important objection to it – the one that appeals to a distinction between positive and negative duties – is based on a superficial analysis of our moral intuitions. I believe that a more thorough examination of the symmetry principle would show it to be sound. If so, we should reject the potentiality principle, and the conservative position on abortion as well.

VI   Summary and Conclusions

Let us return now to my basic claim, the self-consciousness requirement: An organism possesses a serious right to life only if it possesses the concept of a self as a continuing subject of experiences and other mental states, and believes that it is itself such a continuing entity. My defense of this claim has been twofold. I have offered a direct argument in support of it, and I have tried to show that traditional conservative and liberal views on abortion and infanticide, which involve a rejection of it, are unsound. I now want to mention one final reason why my claim should be accepted. Consider the example mentioned in section II – that of killing, as opposed to torturing, newborn kittens. I suggested there that while in the case of adult humans most people would consider it worse to kill an individual than to torture him for an hour, we do not usually view the killing of a newborn kitten as morally outrageous, although we would regard someone who tortured a newborn kitten for an hour as heinously evil. I pointed out that a possible conclusion that might be drawn from this is that newborn kittens have a right not to be tortured, but do not have a serious right to life. If this is the correct conclusion, how is one to explain it? One merit of the self-consciousness requirement is that it provides an explanation of this situation. The reason a newborn kitten does not have a right to life is explained by the fact that it does not possess the concept of a self. But how is one to explain the kitten's having a right not

to be tortured? The answer is that a desire not to suffer pain can be ascribed to something without assuming that it has any concept of a continuing self. For while something that lacks the concept of a self cannot desire that a self not suffer, it can desire that a given sensation not exist. The state desired – the absence of a particular sensation, or of sensations of a certain sort – can be described in a purely phenomenalistic language, and hence without the concept of a continuing self. So long as the newborn kitten possesses the relevant phenomenal concepts, it can truly be said to desire that a certain sensation not exist. So we can ascribe to it a right not to be tortured even though, since it lacks the concept of a continuing self, we cannot ascribe to it a right to life.

This completes my discussion of the basic moral principles involved in the issue of abortion and infanticide. But I want to comment upon an important factual question, namely, at what point an organism comes to possess the concept of a self as a continuing subject of experiences and other mental states, together with the belief that it is itself such a continuing entity. This is obviously a matter for detailed psychological investigation, but everyday observation makes it perfectly clear, I believe, that a newborn baby does not possess the concept of a continuing self, any more than a newborn kitten possesses such a concept. If so, infanticide during a time interval shortly after birth must be morally acceptable.

But where is the line to be drawn? What is the cutoff point? If one maintained, as some philosophers have, that an individual possesses concepts only if he can express these concepts in language, it would be a matter of everyday observation whether or not a given organism possessed the concept of a continuing self. Infanticide would then be permissible up to the time an organism learned how to use certain expressions. However, I think the claim that acquisition of concepts is dependent on acquisition of language is mistaken. For example, one wants to ascribe mental states of a conceptual sort – such as beliefs and desires – to organisms that are incapable of learning a language. This issue of prelinguistic understanding is clearly outside the scope of this discussion. My point is simply that *if* an organism can acquire concepts without thereby acquiring a way of expressing those concepts linguistically, the question of whether a given organism possesses the concept of a self as a continuing subject of experiences and other mental states, together with the belief that it is itself such a continuing entity, may be a question that requires fairly subtle experimental techniques to answer.

If this view of the matter is roughly correct, there are two worries one is left with at the level of practical moral decisions, one of which may turn out to be deeply disturbing. The lesser worry is where the line is to be drawn in the case of infanticide. It is not troubling because there is no serious need to know the exact point at which a human infant acquires a right to life. For in the vast majority of cases in which infanticide is desirable, its desirability will be apparent within a short time after birth. Since it is virtually certain that an infant at such a stage of its development does not possess the concept of a continuing self, and thus does not possess a serious right to life, there is excellent reason to believe that infanticide is morally permissible in most cases where it is otherwise desirable. The practical moral problem can thus be satisfactorily handled by choosing some period of time, such as a week after birth, as the interval during which infanticide will be permitted. This interval could then be modified once psychologists have established the point at which a human organism comes to believe that it is a continuing subject of experiences and other mental states.

The troubling worry is whether adult animals belonging to species other than *Homo sapiens* may not also possess a serious right to life. For once one says that an organism can possess the concept of a continuing self, together with the belief that it is itself such an entity, without having any way of expressing that concept and that belief linguistically, one has to face up to the question of whether animals may not possess properties that bestow a serious right to life upon them. The suggestion itself is a familiar one, and one that most of us are accustomed to dismiss very casually. The line of thought advanced here suggests that this attitude may turn out to be tragically mistaken. Once one reflects upon the question of the *basic* moral principles involved in the ascription of a right to life to organisms, one may find himself driven to conclude that our everyday treatment of animals is morally indefensible, and that we are in fact murdering innocent persons.

Notes

1 I am grateful to a number of people, particularly the editors of *Philosophy & Public Affairs*, Rodelia Hapke and Walter Kaufmann, for their helpful comments. It should not, of course, be inferred that they share the views expressed in this paper.

2 Judith Jarvis Thomson, in her article "A Defense of Abortion," *Philosophy & Public Affairs*, I, no. I (Fall 1971): 47–66 [see chapter 3 in this volume], has argued with great force and ingenuity that this conclusion is mistaken. I will comment on her argument later in this paper.

3 While this is the position conservatives tend to hold, it is not clear that it is the position they ought to hold. For if the fetus is a person it is far from clear that it is permissible to destroy it to save the mother. Two moral principles lend support to the view that it is the fetus which should live. First, other things being equal, should not one give something to a person who has had less rather than to a person who has had more? The mother has had a chance to live, while the fetus has not. The choice is thus between giving the mother more of an opportunity to enjoy life while giving the fetus none at all and giving the fetus an opportunity to enjoy life while not giving the mother a further opportunity to do so. Surely fairness requires the latter. Secondly, since the fetus has a greater life expectancy than the mother, one is in effect distributing more goods by choosing the life of the fetus over the life of the mother.

The position I am here recommending to the conservative should not be confused with the official Catholic position. The Catholic Church holds that it is seriously wrong to kill a fetus directly even if failure to do so will result in the death of *both* the mother and the fetus. This perverse value judgment is not part of the conservative's position.

4 Section 230.3 of the American Law Institute's *Model Penal Code* (Philadelphia, 1962). There is some interesting, though at times confused, discussion of the proposed code in *Model Penal Code – Tentative Draft No. 9* (Philadelphia, 1959), pp. 146–62.

5 A clear example of such an unwillingness to entertain seriously the possibility that moral judgments widely accepted in one's own society may nevertheless be incorrect is provided by Roger Wertheimer's superficial dismissal of infanticide on pages 69–70 of his article "Understanding the Abortion Argument," *Philosophy & Public Affairs*, I, no. I (Fall 1971): 67–95.

6 Compare the discussion of the concept of a right offered by Richard B. Brandt in his *Ethical Theory* (Englewood Cliffs, NJ, 1959), pp. 434–41. As Brandt points out, some philosophers have maintained that only things that can *claim* rights can have rights. I agree with Brandt's view that "inability to claim does not destroy the right" (p. 440).

7 B. A. Brody, "Abortion and the Law," *Journal of Philosophy*, LXVIII, no. 12 (17 June 1971): 357–69. See pp. 357–8.

8 Thomson, "A Defense of Abortion," p. 47.

9 Wertheimer, "Understanding the Abortion Argument," p. 69.

10 Ibid.

11 Thomson, "A Defense of Abortion," pp. 47–48.

12 Ibid., p. 65.

13 Wertheimer, "Understanding the Abortion Argument," p. 78.

14 A moral principle accepted by a person is *basic for him* if and only if his acceptance of it is not dependent upon any of his (nonmoral) factual beliefs. That is, no change in his factual beliefs would cause him to abandon the principle in question.

15 Wertheimer, "Understanding the Abortion Argument," p. 88.

16 Again, compare the analysis defended by Brandt in *Ethical Theory*, pp. 434–41.

17 In everyday life one often speaks of desiring things, such as an apple or a newspaper. Such talk is elliptical, the context together with one's ordinary beliefs serving to make it clear that one wants to eat the apple and read the newspaper. To say that what one desires is that a certain proposition be true should not be construed as involving any particular ontological commitment. The point is merely that it is sentences such as "John wants it to be the case that he is eating an apple in the next few minutes" that provide a completely explicit description of a person's desires. If one fails to use such sentences one can be badly misled about what concepts are presupposed by a particular desire.

18 There are, however, situations other than those discussed here which might seem to count against the claim that a person cannot have a right unless he is conceptually capable of having the corresponding desire. Can't a young child, for example, have a right to an estate, even though he may not be conceptually capable of wanting the estate? It is clear that such situations have to be carefully considered if one is to arrive at a satisfactory account of the concept of a right. My inclination is to say that the correct description is not that the child now has a right to the estate, but that he will come to have such a right when he is mature, and that in the meantime no one else has a right to the estate. My reason for saying that the child does not now have a right to the estate is that he cannot now do things with the estate, such as selling it or giving it away that he will be able to do later on.

19 Another frequent suggestion as to the cutoff point not listed here is quickening. I omit it because it seems clear that if abortion after quickening is wrong, its wrongness must be tied up with the motility of the fetus, not with the mother's awareness of the fetus' ability to move about.

20 Thomson, "A Defense of Abortion," p. 56.

21 A good example of a failure to probe this issue is provided by Brody's "Abortion and the Law."

22 Admittedly the modification is a substantial one, since given a society that refused to compensate women, a woman who had an abortion would not be doing anything wrong.

23 Compare Wertheimer's remarks, "Understanding the Abortion Argument," p. 79.

24 This requires qualification. If their central nervous systems were radically different from ours, it might be thought that one would not be justified in ascribing to them mental states of an experiential sort. And then, since it seems to be a conceptual truth that only things having experiential states can have rights, one would be forced to conclude that one was not justified in ascribing any rights to them.

25 Philippa Foot, "The Problem of Abortion and the Doctrine of the Double Effect," *Oxford Review*, 5 (1967): 5–15. See the discussion on pp. 11ff.

3

A Defense of Abortion

Judith Jarvis Thomson[1]

Most opposition to abortion relies on the premise that the fetus is a human being, a person, from the moment of conception. The premise is argued for, but, as I think, not well. Take, for example, the most common argument. We are asked to notice that the development of a human being from conception through birth into childhood is continuous; then it is said that to draw a line, to choose a point in this development and say "before this point the thing is not a person, after this point it is a person" is to make an arbitrary choice, a choice for which in the nature of things no good reason can be given. It is concluded that the fetus is, or anyway that we had better say it is, a person from the moment of conception. But this conclusion does not follow. Similar things might be said about the development of an acorn into an oak tree, and it does not follow that acorns are oak trees, or that we had better say they are. Arguments of this form are sometimes called "slippery slope arguments" – the phrase is perhaps self-explanatory – and it is dismaying that opponents of abortion rely on them so heavily and uncritically.

I am inclined to agree, however, that the prospects for "drawing a line" in the development of the fetus look dim. I am inclined to think also that we shall probably have to agree that the fetus has already become a human person well before birth. Indeed, it comes as a surprise when one first learns how early

in its life it begins to acquire human characteristics. By the tenth week, for example, it already has a face, arms and legs, fingers and toes; it has internal organs, and brain activity is detectable.[2] On the other hand, I think that the premise is false, that the fetus is not a person from the moment of conception. A newly fertilized ovum, a newly implanted clump of cells, is no more a person than an acorn is an oak tree. But I shall not discuss any of this. For it seems to me to be of great interest to ask what happens if, for the sake of argument, we allow the premise. How, precisely, are we supposed to get from there to the conclusion that abortion is morally impermissible? Opponents of abortion commonly spend most of their time establishing that the fetus is a person, and hardly any time explaining the step from there to the impermissibility of abortion. Perhaps they think the step too simple and obvious to require much comment. Or perhaps instead they are simply being economical in argument. Many of those who defend abortion rely on the premise that the fetus is not a person, but only a bit of tissue that will become a person at birth; and why pay out more arguments than you have to? Whatever the explanation, I suggest that the step they take is neither easy nor obvious, that it calls for closer examination than it is commonly given, and that when we do give it this closer examination we shall feel inclined to reject it.

Original publication details: Judith Jarvis Thomson, "A Defense of Abortion," pp. 47–66 from *Philosophy and Public Affairs* 1: 1 (1971). Reproduced with permission from John Wiley & Sons.

Bioethics: An Anthology, Third Edition. Edited by Helga Kuhse, Udo Schüklenk, and Peter Singer.

I propose, then, that we grant that the fetus is a person from the moment of conception. How does the argument go from here? Something like this, I take it. Every person has a right to life. So the fetus has a right to life. No doubt the mother has a right to decide what shall happen in and to her body; everyone would grant that. But surely a person's right to life is stronger and more stringent than the mother's right to decide what happens in and to her body, and so outweighs it. So the fetus may not be killed; an abortion may not be performed.

It sounds plausible. But now let me ask you to imagine this. You wake up in the morning and find yourself back to back in bed with an unconscious violinist. A famous unconscious violinist. He has been found to have a fatal kidney ailment, and the Society of Music Lovers has canvassed all the available medical records and found that you alone have the right blood type to help. They have therefore kidnapped you, and last night the violinist's circulatory system was plugged into yours, so that your kidneys can be used to extract poisons from his blood as well as your own. The director of the hospital now tells you, "Look, we're sorry the Society of Music Lovers did this to you – we would never have permitted it if we had known. But still, they did it, and the violinist now is plugged into you. To unplug you would be to kill him. But never mind, it's only for nine months. By then he will have recovered from his ailment, and can safely be unplugged from you." Is it morally incumbent on you to accede to this situation? No doubt it would be very nice of you if you did, a great kindness. But do you *have* to accede to it? What if it were not nine months, but nine years? Or longer still? What if the director of the hospital says, "Tough luck, I agree, but you've now got to stay in bed, with the violinist plugged into you, for the rest of your life. Because remember this. All persons have a right to life, and violinists are persons. Granted you have a right to decide what happens in and to your body, but a person's right to life outweighs your right to decide what happens in and to your body. So you cannot ever be unplugged from him." I imagine you would regard this as outrageous, which suggests that something really is wrong with that plausible-sounding argument I mentioned a moment ago.

In this case, of course, you were kidnapped; you didn't volunteer for the operation that plugged the violinist into your kidneys. Can those who oppose abortion on the ground I mentioned make an exception for a pregnancy due to rape? Certainly. They can say that persons have a right to life only if they didn't come into existence because of rape; or they can say that all persons have a right to life, but that some have less of a right to life than others, in particular, that those who came into existence because of rape have less. But these statements have a rather unpleasant sound. Surely the question of whether you have a right to life at all, or how much of it you have, shouldn't turn on the question of whether or not you are the product of a rape. And in fact the people who oppose abortion on the ground I mentioned do not make this distinction, and hence do not make an exception in the case of rape.

Nor do they make an exception for a case in which the mother has to spend the nine months of her pregnancy in bed. They would agree that would be a great pity, and hard on the mother; but all the same, all persons have a right to life, the fetus is a person, and so on. I suspect, in fact, that they would not make an exception for a case in which, miraculously enough, the pregnancy went on for nine years, or even the rest of the mother's life.

Some won't even make an exception for a case in which continuation of the pregnancy is likely to shorten the mother's life; they regard abortion as impermissible even to save the mother's life. Such cases are nowadays very rare, and many opponents of abortion do not accept this extreme view. All the same, it is a good place to begin: a number of points of interest come out in respect to it.

1. Let us call the view that abortion is impermissible even to save the mother's life "the extreme view." I want to suggest first that it does not issue from the argument I mentioned earlier without the addition of some fairly powerful premises. Suppose a woman has become pregnant, and now learns that she has a cardiac condition such that she will die if she carries the baby to term. What may be done for her? The fetus, being a person, has a right to life, but as the mother is a person too, so has she a right to life. Presumably they have an equal right to life. How is it supposed to come out that an abortion may not be performed? If mother and child have an equal right to life, shouldn't we perhaps flip a coin? Or should we add to the mother's

right to life her right to decide what happens in and to her body, which everybody seems to be ready to grant – the sum of her rights now outweighing the fetus' right to life?

The most familiar argument here is the following. We are told that performing the abortion would be directly killing[3] the child, whereas doing nothing would not be killing the mother, but only letting her die. Moreover, in killing the child, one would be killing an innocent person, for the child has committed no crime, and is not aiming at his mother's death. And then there are a variety of ways in which this might be continued. (1) But as directly killing an innocent person is always and absolutely impermissible, an abortion may not be performed. Or, (2) as directly killing an innocent person is murder, and murder is always and absolutely impermissible, an abortion may not be performed.[4] Or, (3) as one's duty to refrain from directly killing an innocent person is more stringent than one's duty to keep a person from dying, an abortion may not be performed. Or, (4) if one's only options are directly killing an innocent person or letting a person die, one must prefer letting the person die, and thus an abortion may not be performed.[5]

Some people seem to have thought that these are not further premises which must be added if the conclusion is to be reached, but that they follow from the very fact that an innocent person has a right to life.[6] But this seems to me to be a mistake, and perhaps the simplest way to show this is to bring out that while we must certainly grant that innocent persons have a right to life, the theses in (1) through (4) are all false. Take (2), for example. If directly killing an innocent person is murder, and thus is impermissible, then the mother's directly killing the innocent person inside her is murder, and thus is impermissible. But it cannot seriously be thought to be murder if the mother performs an abortion on herself to save her life. It cannot seriously be said that she *must* refrain, that she *must* sit passively by and wait for her death. Let us look again at the case of you and the violinist. There you are, in bed with the violinist, and the director of the hospital says to you, "It's all most distressing, and I deeply sympathize, but you see this is putting an additional strain on your kidneys, and you'll be dead within the month. But you *have* to stay where you are all the same.

Because unplugging you would be directly killing an innocent violinist, and that's murder, and that's impermissible." If anything in the world is true, it is that you do not commit murder, you do not do what is impermissible, if you reach around to your back and unplug yourself from that violinist to save your life.

The main focus of attention in writings on abortion has been on what a third party may or may not do in answer to a request from a woman for an abortion. This is in a way understandable. Things being as they are, there isn't much a woman can safely do to abort herself. So the question asked is what a third party may do, and what the mother may do, if it is mentioned at all, is deduced, almost as an afterthought, from what it is concluded that third parties may do. But it seems to me that to treat the matter in this way is to refuse to grant to the mother that very status of person which is so firmly insisted on for the fetus. For we cannot simply read off what a person may do from what a third party may do. Suppose you find yourself trapped in a tiny house with a growing child. I mean a very tiny house, and a rapidly growing child – you are already up against the wall of the house and in a few minutes you'll be crushed to death. The child on the other hand won't be crushed to death; if nothing is done to stop him from growing he'll be hurt, but in the end he'll simply burst open the house and walk out a free man. Now I could well understand it if a bystander were to say, "There's nothing we can do for you. We cannot choose between your life and his, we cannot be the ones to decide who is to live, we cannot intervene." But it cannot be concluded that you too can do nothing, that you cannot attack it to save your life. However innocent the child may be, you do not have to wait passively while it crushes you to death. Perhaps a pregnant woman is vaguely felt to have the status of house, to which we don't allow the right of self-defense. But if the woman houses the child, it should be remembered that she is a person who houses it.

I should perhaps stop to say explicitly that I am not claiming that people have a right to do anything whatever to save their lives. I think, rather, that there are drastic limits to the right of self-defense. If someone threatens you with death unless you torture someone else to death, I think you have not the right, even to save your life, to do so. But the case under consideration here is very different. In our case there are only two people involved, one whose life is threatened, and one who threatens it. Both are innocent: the one who is threatened is not threatened because of any fault, the one who threatens does not threaten because of any fault. For this reason we may feel that we bystanders cannot intervene. But the person threatened can.

In sum, a woman surely can defend her life against the threat to it posed by the unborn child, even if doing so involves its death. And this shows not merely that the theses in (1) through (4) are false; it shows also that the extreme view of abortion is false, and so we need not canvass any other possible ways of arriving at it from the argument I mentioned at the outset.

2. The extreme view could of course be weakened to say that while abortion is permissible to save the mother's life, it may not be performed by a third party, but only by the mother herself. But this cannot be right either. For what we have to keep in mind is that the mother and the unborn child are not like two tenants in a small house which has, by an unfortunate mistake, been rented to both: the mother *owns* the house. The fact that she does adds to the offensiveness of deducing that the mother can do nothing from the supposition that third parties can do nothing. But it does more than this: it casts a bright light on the supposition that third parties can do nothing. Certainly it lets us see that a third party who says "I cannot choose between you" is fooling himself if he thinks this is impartiality. If Jones has found and fastened on a certain coat, which he needs to keep him from freezing, but which Smith also needs to keep him from freezing, then it is not impartiality that says "I cannot choose between you" when Smith owns the coat. Women have said again and again "This body is *my* body!" and they have reason to feel angry, reason to feel that it has been like shouting into the wind. Smith, after all, is hardly likely to bless us if we say to him, "Of course it's your coat, anybody would grant that it is. But no one may choose between you and Jones who is to have it."

We should really ask what it is that says "no one may choose" in the face of the fact that the body that houses the child is the mother's body. It may be simply a failure to appreciate this fact. But it may be something more interesting, namely the sense that

one has a right to refuse to lay hands on people, even where it would be just and fair to do so, even where justice seems to require that somebody do so. Thus justice might call for somebody to get Smith's coat back from Jones, and yet you have a right to refuse to be the one to lay hands on Jones, a right to refuse to do physical violence to him. This, I think, must be granted. But then what should be said is not "no one may choose," but only "*I* cannot choose," and indeed not even this, but "*I* will not *act*," leaving it open that somebody else can or should, and in particular that anyone in a position of authority, with the job of securing people's rights, both can and should. So this is no difficulty. I have not been arguing that any given third party must accede to the mother's request that he perform an abortion to save her life, but only that he may.

I suppose that in some views of human life the mother's body is only on loan to her, the loan not being one which gives her any prior claim to it. One who held this view might well think it impartiality to say "I cannot choose." But I shall simply ignore this possibility. My own view is that if a human being has any just, prior claim to anything at all, he has a just, prior claim to his own body. And perhaps this needn't be argued for here anyway, since, as I mentioned, the arguments against abortion we are looking at do grant that the woman has a right to decide what happens in and to her body.

But although they do grant it, I have tried to show that they do not take seriously what is done in granting it. I suggest the same thing will reappear even more clearly when we turn away from cases in which the mother's life is at stake, and attend, as I propose we now do, to the vastly more common cases in which a woman wants an abortion for some less weighty reason than preserving her own life.

3. Where the mother's life is not at stake, the argument I mentioned at the outset seems to have a much stronger pull. "Everyone has a right to life, so the unborn person has a right to life." And isn't the child's right to life weightier than anything other than the mother's own right to life, which she might put forward as ground for an abortion?

This argument treats the right to life as if it were unproblematic. It is not, and this seems to me to be precisely the source of the mistake.

For we should now, at long last, ask what it comes to, to have a right to life. In some views having a right to life includes having a right to be given at least the bare minimum one needs for continued life. But suppose that what in fact *is* the bare minimum a man needs for continued life is something he has no right at all to be given? If I am sick unto death, and the only thing that will save my life is the touch of Henry Fonda's cool hand on my fevered brow, then all the same, I have no right to be given the touch of Henry Fonda's cool hand on my fevered brow. It would be frightfully nice of him to fly in from the West Coast to provide it. It would be less nice, though no doubt well meant, if my friends flew out to the West Coast and carried Henry Fonda back with them. But I have no right at all against anybody that he should do this for me. Or again, to return to the story I told earlier, the fact that for continued life that violinist needs the continued use of your kidneys does not establish that he has a right to be given the continued use of your kidneys. He certainly has no right against you that *you* should give him continued use of your kidneys. For nobody has any right to use your kidneys unless you give him such a right; and nobody has the right against you that you shall give him this right – if you do allow him to do on using your kidneys, this is a kindness on your part, and not something he can claim from you as his due. Nor has he any right against anybody else that *they* should give him continued use of your kidneys. Certainly he had no right against the Society of Music Lovers that they should plug him into you in the first place. And if you now start to unplug yourself, having learned that you will otherwise have to spend nine years in bed with him, there is nobody in the world who must try to prevent you, in order to see to it that he is given something he has a right to be given.

Some people are rather stricter about the right to life. In their view, it does not include the right to be given anything, but amounts to, and only to, the right not to be killed by anybody. But here a related difficulty arises. If everybody is to refrain from killing that violinist, then everybody must refrain from doing a great many different sorts of things. Everybody must refrain from slitting his throat, everybody must refrain from shooting him – and everybody must refrain from unplugging you from him. But does he have a right against everybody that they shall refrain from unplugging you from him? To refrain from doing this is to allow him to continue to use your kidneys. It could be argued that he has a right against us that *we* should allow him to continue to use your kidneys. That is, while he had no right against us that we should give him the use of your kidneys, it might be argued that he anyway has a right against us that we shall not now intervene and deprive him of the use of your kidneys. I shall come back to third-party interventions later. But certainly the violinist has no right against you that *you* shall allow him to continue to use your kidneys. As I said, if you do allow him to use them, it is a kindness on your part, and not something you owe him.

The difficulty I point to here is not peculiar to the right to life. It reappears in connection with all the other natural rights; and it is something which an adequate account of rights must deal with. For present purposes it is enough just to draw attention to it. But I would stress that I am not arguing that people do not have a right to life – quite to the contrary, it seems to me that the primary control we must place on the acceptability of an account of rights is that it should turn out in that account to be a truth that all persons have a right to life. I am arguing only that having a right to life does not guarantee having either a right to be given the use of or a right to be allowed continued use of another person's body – even if one needs it for life itself. So the right to life will not serve the opponents of abortion in the very simple and clear way in which they seem to have thought it would.

4. There is another way to bring out the difficulty. In the most ordinary sort of case, to deprive someone of what he has a right to is to treat him unjustly. Suppose a boy and his small brother are jointly given a box of chocolates for Christmas. If the older boy takes the box and refuses to give his brother any of the chocolates, he is unjust to him, for the brother has been given a right to half of them. But suppose that, having learned that otherwise it means nine years in bed with that violinist, you unplug yourself from him. You surely are not being unjust to him, for you gave him no right to use your kidneys, and no one else can have given him any such right. But we have to notice that in unplugging yourself, you are killing him; and violinists, like everybody else, have a right to life, and

thus in the view we were considering just now, the right not to be killed. So here you do what he supposedly has a right you shall not do, but you do not act unjustly to him in doing it.

The emendation which may be made at this point is this: the right to life consists not in the right not to be killed, but rather in the right not to be killed unjustly. This runs a risk of circularity, but never mind: it would enable us to square the fact that the violinist has a right to life with the fact that you do not act unjustly toward him in unplugging yourself, thereby killing him. For if you do not kill him unjustly, you do not violate his right to life, and so it is no wonder you do him no injustice.

But if this emendation is accepted, the gap in the argument against abortion stares us plainly in the face: it is by no means enough to show that the fetus is a person, and to remind us that all persons have a right to life – we need to be shown also that killing the fetus violates its right to life, i.e., that abortion is unjust killing. And is it?

I suppose we may take it as a datum that in a case of pregnancy due to rape the mother has not given the unborn person a right to the use of her body for food and shelter. Indeed, in what pregnancy could it be supposed that the mother has given the unborn person such a right? It is not as if there were unborn persons drifting about the world, to whom a woman who wants a child says "I invite you in."

But it might be argued that there are other ways one can have acquired a right to the use of another person's body than by having been invited to use it by that person. Suppose a woman voluntarily indulges in intercourse, knowing of the chance it will issue in pregnancy, and then she does become pregnant; is she not in part responsible for the presence, in fact the very existence, of the unborn person inside her? No doubt she did not invite it in. But doesn't her partial responsibility for its being there itself give it a right to the use of her body?[7] If so, then her aborting it would be more like the boy's taking away the chocolates, and less like your unplugging yourself from the violinist – doing so would be depriving it of what it does have a right to, and thus would be doing it an injustice.

And then, too, it might be asked whether or not she can kill it even to save her own life: If she voluntarily called it into existence, how can she now kill it, even in self-defense?

The first thing to be said about this is that it is something new. Opponents of abortion have been so concerned to make out the independence of the fetus, in order to establish that it has a right to life, just as its mother does, that they have tended to overlook the possible support they might gain from making out that the fetus is *dependent* on the mother, in order to establish that she has a special kind of responsibility for it, a responsibility that gives it rights against her which are not possessed by any independent person – such as an ailing violinist who is a stranger to her.

On the other hand, this argument would give the unborn person a right to its mother's body only if her pregnancy resulted from a voluntary act, undertaken in full knowledge of the chance a pregnancy might result from it. It would leave out entirely the unborn person whose existence is due to rape. Pending the availability of some further argument, then, we would be left with the conclusion that unborn persons whose existence is due to rape have no right to the use of their mothers' bodies, and thus that aborting them is not depriving them of anything they have a right to and hence is not unjust killing.

And we should also notice that it is not at all plain that this argument really does go even as far as it purports to. For there are cases and cases, and the details make a difference. If the room is stuffy, and I therefore open a window to air it, and a burglar climbs in, it would be absurd to say, "Ah, now he can stay, she's given him a right to the use of her house – for she is partially responsible for his presence there, having voluntarily done what enabled him to get in, in full knowledge that there are such things as burglars, and that burglars burgle." It would be still more absurd to say this if I had had bars installed outside my windows, precisely to prevent burglars from getting in, and a burglar got in only because of a defect in the bars. It remains equally absurd if we imagine it is not a burglar who climbs in, but an innocent person who blunders or falls in. Again, suppose it were like this: people-seeds drift about in the air like pollen, and if you open your windows, one may drift in and take root in your carpets or upholstery. You don't want children, so you fix up your windows with fine mesh screens, the very best you can buy. As can happen, however, and on very, very rare occasions does happen, one of the screens is defective; and a seed drifts in and takes root. Does the person-plant who now develops have a right to the use of your house? Surely not – despite the fact that you voluntarily opened your windows, you knowingly kept carpets and upholstered furniture, and you knew that screens were sometimes defective. Someone may argue that you are responsible for its rooting, that it does have a right to your house, because after all you *could* have lived out your life with bare floors and furniture, or with sealed windows and doors. But this won't do – for by the same token anyone can avoid a pregnancy due to rape by having a hysterectomy, or anyway by never leaving home without a (reliable!) army.

It seems to me that the argument we are looking at can establish at most that there are *some* cases in which the unborn person has a right to the use of its mother's body, and therefore *some* cases in which abortion is unjust killing. There is room for much discussion and argument as to precisely which, if any. But I think we should sidestep this issue and leave it open, for at any rate the argument certainly does not establish that all abortion is unjust killing.

5. There is room for yet another argument here, however. We surely must all grant that there may be cases in which it would be morally indecent to detach a person from your body at the cost of his life. Suppose you learn that what the violinist needs is not nine years of your life, but only one hour: all you need do to save his life is to spend one hour in that bed with him. Suppose also that letting him use your kidneys for that one hour would not affect your health in the slightest. Admittedly you were kidnapped. Admittedly you did not give anyone permission to plug him into you. Nevertheless it seems to me plain you *ought* to allow him to use your kidneys for that hour – it would be indecent to refuse.

Again, suppose pregnancy lasted only an hour, and constituted no threat to life or health. And suppose that a woman becomes pregnant as a result of rape. Admittedly she did not voluntarily do anything to bring about the existence of a child. Admittedly she did nothing at all which would give the unborn person a right to the use of her body. All the same it might well be said, as in the newly emended violinist story, that she *ought* to allow it to remain for that hour – that it would be indecent in her to refuse.

Now some people are inclined to use the term "right" in such a way that it follows from the fact that you ought to allow a person to use your body for the hour he needs, that he has a right to use your body for the hour he needs, even though he has not been given that right by any person or act. They may say that it follows also that if you refuse, you act unjustly toward him. This use of the term is perhaps so common that it cannot be called wrong; nevertheless it seems to me to be an unfortunate loosening of what we would do better to keep a tight rein on. Suppose that box of chocolates I mentioned earlier had not been given to both boys jointly, but was given only to the older boy. There he sits, stolidly eating his way through the box, his small brother watching enviously. Here we are likely to say "You ought not to be so mean. You ought to give your brother some of those chocolates." My own view is that it just does not follow from the truth of this that the brother has any right to any of the chocolates. If the boy refuses to give his brother any, he is greedy, stingy, callous – but not unjust. I suppose that the people I have in mind will say it does follow that the brother has a right to some of the chocolates, and thus that the boy does act unjustly if he refuses to give his brother any. But the effect of saying this is to obscure what we should keep distinct, namely the difference between the boy's refusal in this case and the boy's refusal in the earlier case, in which the box was given to both boys jointly, and in which the small brother thus had what was from any point of view clear title to half.

A further objection to so using the term "right" that from the fact that A ought to do a thing for B, it follows that B has a right against A that A do it for him, is that it is going to make the question of whether or not a man has a right to a thing turn on how easy it is to provide him with it; and this seems not merely unfortunate, but morally unacceptable. Take the case of Henry Fonda again. I said earlier that I had no right to the touch of his cool hand on my fevered brow, even though I needed it to save my life. I said it would be frightfully nice of him to fly in from the West Coast to provide me with it, but that I had no right against him that he should do so. But suppose he isn't on the West Coast. Suppose he has only to walk across the room, place a hand briefly on my brow – and lo, my life is saved. Then surely he ought to do it, it would be indecent to refuse. Is it to be said "Ah, well, it follows that in this case she has a right to the touch of his hand on her brow, and so it would be an injustice in him to refuse"? So that I have a right to it when it is easy for him to provide it, though no right when it's hard? It's rather a shocking idea that anyone's rights should fade away and disappear as it gets harder and harder to accord them to him.

So my own view is that even though you ought to let the violinist use your kidneys for the one hour he needs, we should not conclude that he has a right to do so – we should say that if you refuse, you are, like the boy who owns all the chocolates and will give none away, self-centered and callous, indecent in fact, but not unjust. And similarly, that even supposing a case in which a woman pregnant due to rape ought to allow the unborn person to use her body for the hour he needs, we should not conclude that he has a right to do so; we should conclude that she is self-centered, callous, indecent, but not unjust, if she refuses. The complaints are no less grave; they are just different. However, there is no need to insist on this point. If anyone does wish to deduce "he has a right" from "you ought," then all the same he must surely grant that there are cases in which it is not morally required of you that you allow that violinist to use your kidneys, and in which he does not have a right to use them, and in which you do not do him an injustice if you refuse. And so also for mother and unborn child. Except in such cases as the unborn person has a right to demand it – and we were leaving open the possibility that there may be such cases – nobody is morally *required* to make large sacrifices, of health, of all other interests and concerns, of all other duties and commitments, for nine years, or even for nine months, in order to keep another person alive.

6. We have in fact to distinguish between two kinds of Samaritan: the Good Samaritan and what we might call the Minimally Decent Samaritan. The story of the Good Samaritan, you will remember, goes like this:

A certain man went down from Jerusalem to Jericho, and fell among thieves, which stripped him of his raiment, and wounded him, and departed, leaving him half dead.

And by chance there came down a certain priest that way; and when he saw him, he passed by on the other side.

And likewise a Levite, when he was at the place, came and looked on him, and passed by on the other side.

But a certain Samaritan, as he journeyed, came where he was; and when he saw him he had compassion on him.

And went to him, and bound up his wounds, pouring in oil and wine, and set him on his own beast, and brought him to an inn, and took care of him.

And on the morrow, when he departed, he took out two pence, and gave them to the host, and said unto him, "Take care of him; and whatsoever thou spendest more, when I come again, I will repay thee." (Luke 10: 30–35)

The Good Samaritan went out of his way, at some cost to himself, to help one in need of it. We are not told what the options were, that is, whether or not the priest and the Levite could have helped by doing less than the Good Samaritan did, but assuming they could have, then the fact they did nothing at all shows they were not even Minimally Decent Samaritans, not because they were not Samaritans, but because they were not even minimally decent.

These things are a matter of degree, of course, but there is a difference, and it comes out perhaps most clearly in the story of Kitty Genovese, who, as you will remember, was murdered while thirty-eight people watched or listened, and did nothing at all to help her. A Good Samaritan would have rushed out to give direct assistance against the murderer. Or perhaps we had better allow that it would have been a Splendid Samaritan who did this, on the ground that it would have involved a risk of death for himself. But the thirty-eight not only did not do this, they did not even trouble to pick up a phone to call the police. Minimally Decent Samaritanism would call for doing at least that, and their not having done it was monstrous.

After telling the story of the Good Samaritan, Jesus said "Go, and do thou likewise." Perhaps he meant that we are morally required to act as the Good Samaritan did. Perhaps he was urging people to do more than is morally required of them. At all events it seems plain that it was not morally required of any of the thirty-eight that he rush out to give direct assistance at the risk of his own life, and that it is not morally required of anyone that he give long stretches of his life – nine years or nine months – to sustaining the life of a person who has no special right (we were leaving open the possibility of this) to demand it.

Indeed, with one rather striking class of exceptions, no one in any country in the world is *legally* required to do anywhere near as much as this for anyone else. The class of exceptions is obvious. My main concern here is not the state of the law in respect to abortion, but it is worth drawing attention to the fact that in no state in this country is any man compelled by law to be even a Minimally Decent Samaritan to any person; there is no law under which charges could be brought against the thirty-eight who stood by while Kitty Genovese died. By contrast, in most states in this country women are compelled by law to be not merely Minimally Decent Samaritans, but Good Samaritans to unborn persons inside them. This doesn't by itself settle anything one way or the other, because it may well be argued that there should be laws in this country – as there are in many European countries – compelling at least Minimally Decent Samaritanism.[8] But it does show that there is a gross injustice in the existing state of the law. And it shows also that the groups currently working against liberalization of abortion laws, in fact working toward having it declared unconstitutional for a state to permit abortion, had better start working for the adoption of Good Samaritan laws generally, or earn the charge that they are acting in bad faith.

I should think, myself, that Minimally Decent Samaritan laws would be one thing, Good Samaritan laws quite another, and in fact highly improper. But we are not here concerned with the law. What we should ask is not whether anybody should be compelled by law to be a Good Samaritan, but whether we must accede to a situation in which somebody is being compelled – by nature, perhaps – to be a Good Samaritan. We have, in other words, to look now at third-party interventions. I have been arguing that no person is morally required to make large sacrifices to sustain the life of another who has no right to demand them, and this even where the sacrifices do not include life itself; we are not morally required to be Good Samaritans or anyway Very Good Samaritans to one another. But what if a man cannot extricate himself from such a situation? What if he appeals to us to extricate him? It seems to me plain that there are

cases in which we can, cases in which a Good Samaritan would extricate him. There you are, you were kidnapped, and nine years in bed with that violinist lie ahead of you. You have your own life to lead. You are sorry, but you simply cannot see giving up so much of your life to the sustaining of his. You cannot extricate yourself, and ask us to do so. I should have thought that – in light of his having no right to the use of your body – it was obvious that we do not have to accede to your being forced to give up so much. We can do what you ask. There is no injustice to the violinist in our doing so.

7.   Following the lead of the opponents of abortion, I have throughout been speaking of the fetus merely as a person, and what I have been asking is whether or not the argument we began with, which proceeds only from the fetus being a person, really does establish its conclusion. I have argued that it does not.

But of course there are arguments and arguments, and it may be said that I have simply fastened on the wrong one. It may be said that what is important is not merely the fact that the fetus is a person, but that it is a person for whom the woman has a special kind of responsibility issuing from the fact that she is its mother. And it might be argued that all my analogies are therefore irrelevant – for you do not have that special kind of responsibility for that violinist, Henry Fonda does not have that special kind of responsibility for me. And our attention might be drawn to the fact that men and women both *are* compelled by law to provide support for their children.

I have in effect dealt (briefly) with this argument in section 4 above; but a (still briefer) recapitulation now may be in order. Surely we do not have any such "special responsibility" for a person unless we have assumed it, explicitly or implicitly. If a set of parents do not try to prevent pregnancy, do not obtain an abortion, and then at the time of birth of the child do not put it out for adoption, but rather take it home with them, then they have assumed responsibility for it, they have given it rights, and they cannot *now* withdraw support from it at the cost of its life because they now find it difficult to go on providing for it. But if they have taken all reasonable precautions against having a child, they do not simply by virtue of their biological relationship to the child who comes into existence have a special responsibility for it. They may wish to assume responsibility for it, or they may not wish to. And I am suggesting that if assuming responsibility for it would require large sacrifices, then they may refuse. A Good Samaritan would not refuse – or anyway, a Splendid Samaritan, if the sacrifices that had to be made were enormous. But then so would a Good Samaritan assume responsibility for that violinist; so would Henry Fonda, if he is a Good Samaritan, fly in from the West Coast and assume responsibility for me.

8. My argument will be found unsatisfactory on two counts by many of those who want to regard abortion as morally permissible. First, while I do argue that abortion is not impermissible, I do not argue that it is always permissible. There may well be cases in which carrying the child to term requires only Minimally Decent Samaritanism of the mother, and this is a standard we must not fall below. I am inclined to think it a merit of my account precisely that it does *not* give a general yes or a general no. It allows for and supports our sense that, for example, a sick and desperately frightened fourteen-year-old schoolgirl, pregnant due to rape, may of *course* choose abortion, and that any law which rules this out is an insane law. And it also allows for and supports our sense that in other cases resort to abortion is even positively indecent. It would be indecent in the woman to request an abortion, and indecent in a doctor to perform it, if she is in her seventh month, and wants the abortion just to avoid the nuisance of postponing a trip abroad. The very fact that the arguments I have been drawing attention to treat all cases of abortion, or even all cases of abortion in which the mother's life is not at stake, as morally on a par ought to have made them suspect at the outset.

Secondly, while I am arguing for the permissibility of abortion in some cases, I am not arguing for the right to secure the death of the unborn child. It is easy to confuse these two things in that up to a certain point in the life of the fetus it is not able to survive outside the mother's body; hence removing it from her body guarantees its death. But they are importantly different. I have argued that you are not morally required to spend nine months in bed, sustaining the life of that violinist; but to say this is by no means to say that if, when you unplug yourself, there is a miracle and he survives, you then have a right to turn round and slit his throat. You may detach yourself even if this costs him his life; you have no right to be guaranteed his death, by some other means, if unplugging yourself does not kill him. There are some people who will feel dissatisfied by this feature of my argument. A woman may be utterly devastated by the thought of a child, a bit of herself, put out for adoption and never seen or heard of again. She may therefore want not merely that the child be detached from her, but more, that it die. Some opponents of abortion are inclined to regard this as beneath contempt – thereby showing insensitivity to what is surely a powerful source of despair. All the same, I agree that the desire for the child's death is not one which anybody may gratify, should it turn out to be possible to detach the child alive.

At this place, however, it should be remembered that we have only been pretending throughout that the fetus is a human being from the moment of conception. A very early abortion is surely not the killing of a person, and so is not dealt with by anything I have said here.

Notes

1 I am very much indebted to James Thomson for discussion, criticism, and many helpful suggestions.

2 Daniel Callahan, *Abortion: Law, Choice and Morality* (New York, 1970), p. 373. This book gives a fascinating survey of the available information on abortion. The Jewish tradition is surveyed in David M. Feldman, *Birth Control in Jewish Law* (New York, 1968), Part 5, the Catholic tradition in John T. Noonan, Jr., "An Almost Absolute Value in History," in *The Morality of Abortion*, ed. John T. Noonan, Jr. (Cambridge, Mass., 1970).

3 The term "direct" in the arguments I refer to is a technical one. Roughly, what is meant by "direct killing" is either killing as an end in itself, or killing as a means to some end, for example, the end of saving someone else's life. See note 6, below, for an example of its use.

4 Cf. *Encyclical Letter of Pope Pius XI on Christian Marriage*, St. Paul Editions (Boston, n.d.), p. 32: "however much we may pity the mother whose health and even life is gravely imperiled in the performance of the duty allotted to her by nature, nevertheless what could ever

be a sufficient reason for excusing in any way the direct murder of the innocent? This is precisely what we are dealing with here." Noonan (*The Morality of Abortion*, p. 43) reads this as follows: "What cause can ever avail to excuse in any way the direct killing of the innocent? For it is a question of that."

5   The thesis in (4) is in an interesting way weaker than those in (1), (2), and (3): they rule out abortion even in cases in which both mother *and* child will die if the abortion is not performed. By contrast, one who held the view expressed in (4) could consistently say that one needn't prefer letting two persons die to killing one.

6   Cf. the following passage from Pius XII, *Address to the Italian Catholic Society of Midwives:* "The baby in the maternal breast has the right to life immediately from God – Hence there is no man, no human authority, no science, no medical, eugenic, social, economic or moral 'indication' which can establish or grant a valid juridical ground for a direct deliberate disposition of an innocent human life, that is a disposition which looks to its destruction either as an end or as a means to another end perhaps in itself not illicit. – The baby, still not born, is a man in the same degree and for the same reason as the mother" (quoted in Noonan, *The Morality of Abortion*, p. 45).

7   The need for a discussion of this argument was brought home to me by members of the Society for Ethical and Legal Philosophy, to whom this paper was originally presented.

8   For a discussion of the difficulties involved, and a survey of the European experience with such laws, see *The Good Samaritan and the Law*, ed. James M. Ratcliffe (New York, 1966).

4

Why Abortion Is Immoral

Don Marquis

The view that abortion is, with rare exceptions, seriously immoral has received little support in the recent philosophical literature. No doubt most philosophers affiliated with secular institutions of higher education believe that the anti-abortion position is either a symptom of irrational religious dogma or a conclusion generated by seriously confused philosophical argument. The purpose of this essay is to undermine this general belief. This essay sets out an argument that purports to show, as well as any argument in ethics can show, that abortion is, except possibly in rare cases, seriously immoral, that it is in the same moral category as killing an innocent adult human being.

The argument is based on a major assumption. Many of the most insightful and careful writers on the ethics of abortion – such as Joel Feinberg, Michael Tooley, Mary Anne Warren, H. Tristram Engelhardt, Jr, L. W. Sumner, John T. Noonan, Jr, and Philip Devine[1] – believe that whether or not abortion is morally permissible stands or falls on whether or not a fetus is the sort of being whose life it is seriously wrong to end. The argument of this essay will assume, but not argue, that they are correct.

Also, this essay will neglect issues of great importance to a complete ethics of abortion. Some anti-abortionists will allow that certain abortions, such as abortion before implantation or abortion when the life of a woman is threatened by a pregnancy or abortion after rape, may be morally permissible. This essay will not explore the casuistry of these hard cases. The purpose of this essay is to develop a general argument for the claim that the overwhelming majority of deliberate abortions are seriously immoral.

I

A sketch of standard anti-abortion and pro-choice arguments exhibits how those arguments possess certain symmetries that explain why partisans of those positions are so convinced of the correctness of their own positions, why they are not successful in convincing their opponents, and why, to others, this issue seems to be unresolvable. An analysis of the nature of this standoff suggests a strategy for surmounting it.

Consider the way a typical anti-abortionist argues. She will argue or assert that life is present from the moment of conception or that fetuses look like babies or that fetuses possess a characteristic such as a genetic code that is both necessary and sufficient for being human. Anti-abortionists seem to believe that (1) the truth of all of these claims is quite obvious, and (2) establishing any of these claims is sufficient to show that abortion is morally akin to murder.

A standard pro-choice strategy exhibits similarities. The pro-choicer will argue or assert that fetuses are not

Original publication details: Don Marquis, "Why Abortion Is Immoral," *Journal of Philosophy* 86: 4 (April 1989): 183–202.

Bioethics: An Anthology, Third Edition. Edited by Helga Kuhse, Udo Schüklenk, and Peter Singer.

persons or that fetuses are not rational agents or that fetuses are not social beings. Pro-choicers seem to believe that (1) the truth of any of these claims is quite obvious, and (2) establishing any of these claims is sufficient to show that an abortion is not a wrongful killing.

In fact, both the pro-choice and the anti-abortion claims do seem to be true, although the "it looks like a baby" claim is more difficult to establish the earlier the pregnancy. We seem to have a standoff. How can it be resolved?

As everyone who has taken a bit of logic knows, if any of these arguments concerning abortion is a good argument, it requires not only some claim characterizing fetuses, but also some general moral principle that ties a characteristic of fetuses to having or not having the right to life or to some other moral characteristic that will generate the obligation or the lack of obligation not to end the life of a fetus. Accordingly, the arguments of the anti-abortionist and the pro-choicer need a bit of filling in to be regarded as adequate.

Note what each partisan will say. The anti-abortionist will claim that her position is supported by such generally accepted moral principles as "It is always prima facie seriously wrong to take a human life" or "It is always prima facie seriously wrong to end the life of a baby." Since these are generally accepted moral principles, her position is certainly not obviously wrong. The pro-choicer will claim that her position is supported by such plausible moral principles as "Being a person is what gives an individual intrinsic moral worth" or "It is only seriously prima facie wrong to take the life of a member of the human community." Since these are generally accepted moral principles, the pro-choice position is certainly not obviously wrong. Unfortunately, we have again arrived at a standoff.

Now, how might one deal with this standoff? The standard approach is to try to show how the moral principles of one's opponent lose their plausibility under analysis. It is easy to see how this is possible. On the one hand, the anti-abortionist will defend a moral principle concerning the wrongness of killing which tends to be broad in scope in order that even fetuses at an early stage of pregnancy will fall under it. The problem with broad principles is that they often embrace too much. In this particular instance, the principle "It is always prima facie wrong to take a human life" seems to entail that it is wrong to end the existence of a living human cancer-cell culture, on the grounds that the culture is both living and human. Therefore, it seems that the anti-abortionist's favored principle is too broad.

On the other hand, the pro-choicer wants to find a moral principle concerning the wrongness of killing which tends to be narrow in scope in order that fetuses will *not* fall under it. The problem with narrow principles is that they often do not embrace enough. Hence, the needed principles such as "It is prima facie seriously wrong to kill only persons" or "It is prima facie wrong to kill only rational agents" do not explain why it is wrong to kill infants or young children or the severely retarded or even perhaps the severely mentally ill. Therefore, we seem again to have a standoff. The anti-abortionist charges, not unreasonably, that pro-choice principles concerning killing are too narrow to be acceptable; the pro-choicer charges, not unreasonably, that anti-abortionist principles concerning killing are too broad to be acceptable.

Attempts by both sides to patch up the difficulties in their positions run into further difficulties. The anti-abortionist will try to remove the problem in her position by reformulating her principle concerning killing in terms of human beings. Now we end up with: "It is always prima facie seriously wrong to end the life of a human being." This principle has the advantage of avoiding the problem of the human cancer-cell culture counterexample. But this advantage is purchased at a high price. For although it is clear that a fetus is both human and alive, it is not at all clear that a fetus is a human *being*. There is at least something to be said for the view that something becomes a human being only after a process of development, and that therefore first trimester fetuses and perhaps all fetuses are not yet human beings. Hence, the anti-abortionist, by this move, has merely exchanged one problem for another.[2]

The pro-choicer fares no better. She may attempt to find reasons why killing infants, young children, and the severely retarded is wrong which are independent of her major principle that is supposed to explain the wrongness of taking human life, but which will not also make abortion immoral. This is no easy task. Appeals to social utility will seem satisfactory only to those who resolve not to think of the enormous difficulties with a utilitarian account of the wrongness of killing and the significant social costs of preserving the lives of the unproductive.[3] A pro-choice strategy that extends the definition of "person" to infants or even to young children seems just as arbitrary as an anti-abortion strategy that extends the definition of "human being" to fetuses. Again, we find symmetries in the two positions and we arrive at a standoff.

There are even further problems that reflect symmetries in the two positions. In addition to counterexample problems, or the arbitrary application problems that can be exchanged for them, the standard anti-abortionist principle "It is prima facie seriously wrong to kill a human being," or one of its variants, can be objected to on the grounds of ambiguity. If "human being" is taken to be a *biological* category, then the anti-abortionist is left with the problem of explaining why a merely biological category should make a moral difference. Why, it is asked, is it any more reasonable to base a moral conclusion on the number of chromosomes in one's cells than on the color of one's skin?[4] If "human being," on the other hand, is taken to be a *moral* category, then the claim that a fetus is a human being cannot be taken to be a premise in the anti-abortion argument, for it is precisely what needs to be established. Hence, either the anti-abortionist's main category is a morally irrelevant, merely biological category, or it is of no use to the anti-abortionist in establishing (noncircularly, of course) that abortion is wrong.

Although this problem with the anti-abortionist position is often noticed, it is less often noticed that the pro-choice position suffers from an analogous problem. The principle "Only persons have the right to life" also suffers from an ambiguity. The term "person" is typically defined in terms of psychological characteristics, although there will certainly be disagreement concerning which characteristics are most important. Supposing that this matter can be settled, the pro-choicer is left with the problem of explaining why *psychological* characteristics should make a *moral* difference. If the pro-choicer should attempt to deal with this problem by claiming that an explanation is not necessary, that in fact we do treat such a cluster of psychological properties as having moral significance, the sharp-witted anti-abortionist should have a ready response. We do treat being both living and human as having moral significance. If it is legitimate for the

pro-choicer to demand that the anti-abortionist provide an explanation of the connection between the biological character of being a human being and the wrongness of being killed (even though people accept this connection), then it is legitimate for the anti-abortionist to demand that the pro-choicer provide an explanation of the connection between psychological criteria for being a person and the wrongness of being killed (even though that connection is accepted).[5]

Feinberg has attempted to meet this objection (he calls psychological personhood "commonsense personhood"):

> The characteristics that confer commonsense personhood are not arbitrary bases for rights and duties, such as race, sex or species membership; rather they are traits that make sense out of rights and duties and without which those moral attributes would have no point or function. It is because people are conscious; have a sense of their personal identities; have plans, goals, and projects; experience emotions; are liable to pains, anxieties, and frustrations; can reason and bargain, and so on — it is because of these attributes that people have values and interests, desires and expectations of their own, including a stake in their own futures, and a personal well-being of a sort we cannot ascribe to unconscious or nonrational beings. Because of their developed capacities they can assume duties and responsibilities and can have and make claims on one another. Only because of their sense of self, their life plans, their value hierarchies, and their stakes in their own futures can they be ascribed fundamental rights. There is nothing arbitrary about these linkages. ("Abortion," p. 270)

The plausible aspects of this attempt should not be taken to obscure its implausible features. There is a great deal to be said for the view that being a psychological person under some description is a necessary condition for having duties. One cannot have a duty unless one is capable of behaving morally, and a being's capability of behaving morally will require having a certain psychology. It is far from obvious, however, that having rights entails consciousness or rationality, as Feinberg suggests. We speak of the rights of the severely retarded or the severely mentally ill, yet some of these persons are not rational. We speak of the rights of the temporarily unconscious. The New Jersey Supreme Court based their decision in the Quinlan case on Karen Ann Quinlan's right to privacy, and she was known to be permanently unconscious at that time. Hence, Feinberg's claim that having rights entails being conscious is, on its face, obviously false.

Of course, it might not make sense to attribute rights to a being that would never in its natural history have certain psychological traits. This modest connection between psychological personhood and moral personhood will create a place for Karen Ann Quinlan and the temporarily unconscious. But then it makes a place for fetuses also. Hence, it does not serve Feinberg's pro-choice purposes. Accordingly, it seems that the pro-choicer will have as much difficulty bridging the gap between psychological personhood and personhood in the moral sense as the anti-abortionist has bridging the gap between being a biological human being and being a human being in the moral sense.

Furthermore, the pro-choicer cannot any more escape her problem by making person a purely moral category than the anti-abortionist could escape by the analogous move. For if person is a moral category, then the pro-choicer is left without the resources for establishing (noncircularly, of course) the claim that a fetus is not a person, which is an essential premise in her argument. Again, we have both a symmetry and a standoff between pro-choice and anti-abortion views.

Passions in the abortion debate run high. There are both plausibilities and difficulties with the standard positions. Accordingly, it is hardly surprising that partisans of either side embrace with fervor the moral generalizations that support the conclusions they preanalytically favor, and reject with disdain the moral generalizations of their opponents as being subject to inescapable difficulties. It is easy to believe that the counterexamples to one's own moral principles are merely temporary difficulties that will dissolve in the wake of further philosophical research, and that the counterexamples to the principles of one's opponents are as straightforward as the contradiction between A and O propositions in traditional logic. This might suggest to an impartial observer (if there are any) that the abortion issue is unresolvable.

There is a way out of this apparent dialectical quandary. The moral generalizations of both sides are not quite correct. The generalizations hold for the most part, for the usual cases. This suggests that they are all *accidental* generalizations, that the moral claims made by those on both sides of the dispute do not touch on the *essence* of the matter.

This use of the distinction between essence and accident is not meant to invoke obscure metaphysical categories. Rather, it is intended to reflect the rather atheoretical nature of the abortion discussion. If the generalization a partisan in the abortion dispute adopts were derived from the reason why ending the life of a human being is wrong, then there could not be exceptions to that generalization unless some special case obtains in which there are even more powerful countervailing reasons. Such generalizations would not be merely accidental generalizations; they would point to, or be based upon, the essence of the wrongness of killing, what it is that makes killing wrong. All this suggests that a necessary condition of resolving the abortion controversy is a more theoretical account of the wrongness of killing. After all, if we merely believe, but do not understand, why killing adult human beings such as ourselves is wrong, how could we conceivably show that abortion is either immoral or permissible?

II

In order to develop such an account, we can start from the following unproblematic assumption concerning our own case: it is wrong to kill *us*. Why is it wrong? Some answers can be easily eliminated. It might be said that what makes killing us wrong is that a killing brutalizes the one who kills. But the brutalization consists of being inured to the performance of an act that is hideously immoral; hence, the brutalization does not explain the immorality. It might be said that what makes killing us wrong is the great loss others would experience due to our absence. Although such hubris is understandable, such an explanation does not account for the wrongness of killing hermits, or those whose lives are relatively independent and whose friends find it easy to make new friends.

A more obvious answer is better. What primarily makes killing wrong is neither its effect on the murderer nor its effect on the victim's friends and relatives, but its effect on the victim. The loss of one's life is one of the greatest losses one can suffer. The loss of one's life deprives one of all the experiences, activities, projects, and enjoyments that would otherwise have constituted one's future. Therefore, killing someone is wrong, primarily because the killing inflicts (one of) the greatest possible losses on the victim. To describe this as the loss of life can be misleading, however. The change in my biological state does not by itself make killing me wrong. The effect of the loss of my biological life is the loss to me of all those activities, projects, experiences, and enjoyments which would otherwise have constituted my future personal life. These activities, projects, experiences, and enjoyments are either valuable for their own sakes or are means to something else that is valuable for its own sake. Some parts of my future are not valued by me now, but will come to be valued by me as I grow older and as my values and capacities change. When I am killed, I am deprived both of what I now value which would have been part of my future personal life, but also what I would come to value. Therefore, when I die, I am deprived of all of the value of my future. Inflicting this loss on me is ultimately what makes killing me wrong. This being the case, it would seem that what makes killing *any* adult human being prima facie seriously wrong is the loss of his or her future.[6]

How should this rudimentary theory of the wrongness of killing be evaluated? It cannot be faulted for deriving an 'ought' from an 'is', for it does not. The analysis assumes that killing me (or you, reader) is prima facie seriously wrong. The point of the analysis is to establish which natural property ultimately explains the wrongness of the killing, given that it is wrong. A natural property will ultimately explain the wrongness of killing, only if (1) the explanation fits with our intuitions about the matter and (2) there is no other natural property that provides the basis for a better explanation of the wrongness of killing. This analysis rests on the intuition that what makes killing a particular human or animal wrong is what it does to that particular human or animal. What makes killing wrong is some natural effect or other of the killing. Some would deny this. For instance, a divine-command theorist in ethics would deny it. Surely this denial is, however, one of those features of divine-command theory which renders it so implausible.

The claim that what makes killing wrong is the loss of the victim's future is directly supported by two considerations. In the first place, this theory explains why we regard killing as one of the worst of crimes. Killing is especially wrong, because it deprives the victim of more than perhaps any other crime. In the second place, people with AIDS or cancer who know they are dying believe, of course, that dying is a very bad thing for them. They believe that the loss of a future to them that they would otherwise have experienced is what makes their premature death a very bad thing for them. A better theory of the wrongness of killing would require a different natural property associated with killing which better fits with the attitudes of the dying. What could it be?

The view that what makes killing wrong is the loss to the victim of the value of the victim's future gains additional support when some of its implications are examined. In the first place, it is incompatible with the view that it is wrong to kill only beings who are biologically human. It is possible that there exists a different species from another planet whose members have a future like ours. Since having a future like that is what makes killing someone wrong, this theory entails that it would be wrong to kill members of such a species. Hence, this theory is opposed to the claim that only life that is biologically human has great moral worth, a claim which many anti-abortionists have seemed to adopt. This opposition, which this theory has in common with personhood theories, seems to be a merit of the theory.

In the second place, the claim that the loss of one's future is the wrong-making feature of one's being killed entails the possibility that the futures of some actual nonhuman mammals on our own planet are sufficiently like ours that it is seriously wrong to kill them also. Whether some animals do have the same right to life as human beings depends on adding to the account of the wrongness of killing some additional account of just what it is about my future or the futures of other adult human beings which makes it wrong to kill us. No such additional account will be offered in this essay. Undoubtedly, the provision of such an account would be a very difficult matter. Undoubtedly, any such account would be quite controversial. Hence, it surely should not reflect badly on this sketch of an elementary theory of the wrongness of killing that it is indeterminate with respect to some very difficult issues regarding animal rights.

In the third place, the claim that the loss of one's future is the wrong-making feature of one's being killed does not entail, as sanctity of human life theories do, that active euthanasia is wrong. Persons who are severely and incurably ill, who face a future of pain and despair, and who wish to die will not have suffered a loss if they are killed. It is, strictly speaking, the value of a human's future which makes killing wrong in this theory. This being so, killing does not necessarily wrong some persons who are sick and dying. Of course, there may be other reasons for a prohibition of active euthanasia, but that is another matter. Sanctity-of-human-life theories seem to hold that active euthanasia is seriously wrong even in an individual case where there seems to be good reason for it independently of public policy considerations. This consequence is most implausible, and it is a plus for the claim that the loss of a future of value is what makes killing wrong that it does not share this consequence.

In the fourth place, the account of the wrongness of killing defended in this essay does straight-forwardly entail that it is prima facie seriously wrong to kill children and infants, for we do presume that they have futures of value. Since we do believe that it is wrong to kill defenseless little babies, it is important that a theory of the wrongness of killing easily account for this. Personhood theories of the wrongness of killing, on the other hand, cannot straightforwardly account for the wrongness of killing infants and young children.[7] Hence, such theories must add special ad hoc accounts of the wrongness of killing the young. The plausibility of such ad hoc theories seems to be a function of how desperately one wants such theories to work. The claim that the primary wrong-making feature of a killing is the loss to the victim of the value of its future accounts for the wrongness of killing young children and infants directly; it makes the wrongness of such acts as obvious as we actually think it is. This is a further merit of this theory. Accordingly, it seems that this value of a future-like-ours theory of the wrongness of killing shares strengths of both sanctity-of-life and personhood accounts while avoiding weaknesses of both. In addition, it meshes with a central intuition concerning what makes killing wrong.

The claim that the primary wrong-making feature of a killing is the loss to the victim of the value of its future has obvious consequences for the ethics of abortion. The future of a standard fetus includes a set of experiences, projects, activities, and such which are identical with the futures of adult human beings and are identical with the futures of young children. Since the reason that is sufficient to explain why it is wrong to kill human beings after the time of birth is a reason that also applies to fetuses, it follows that abortion is prima facie seriously morally wrong.

This argument does not rely on the invalid inference that, since it is wrong to kill persons, it is wrong to kill potential persons also. The category that is morally central to this analysis is the category of having a valuable future like ours; it is not the category of personhood. The argument to the conclusion that abortion is prima facie seriously morally wrong proceeded independently of the notion of person or potential person or any equivalent. Someone may wish to start with this analysis in terms of the value of a human future, conclude that abortion is, except perhaps in rare circumstances, seriously morally wrong, infer that fetuses have the right to life, and then call fetuses "persons" as a result of their having the right to life. Clearly, in this case, the category of person is being used to state the *conclusion* of the analysis rather than to generate the *argument* of the analysis.

The structure of this anti-abortion argument can be both illuminated and defended by comparing it to what appears to be the best argument for the wrongness of the wanton infliction of pain on animals. This latter argument is based on the assumption that it is prima facie wrong to inflict pain on me (or you, reader). What is the natural property associated with the infliction of pain which makes such infliction wrong? The obvious answer seems to be that the infliction of pain causes suffering and that suffering is a misfortune. The suffering caused by the infliction of pain is what makes the wanton infliction of pain on me wrong. The wanton infliction of pain on other adult humans causes suffering. The wanton infliction of pain on animals causes suffering. Since causing suffering is what makes the wanton infliction of pain wrong and since the wanton infliction of pain on animals causes suffering, it follows that the wanton infliction of pain on animals is wrong.

This argument for the wrongness of the wanton infliction of pain on animals shares a number of structural features with the argument for the serious prima facie wrongness of abortion. Both arguments start with an obvious assumption concerning what it is wrong to do to me (or you, reader). Both then look for the characteristic or the consequence of the wrong action which makes the action wrong. Both recognize that the wrong-making feature of these immoral actions is a property of actions sometimes directed at individuals other than postnatal human beings. If the structure of the argument for the wrongness of the wanton infliction of pain on animals is sound, then the structure of the argument for the prima facie serious wrongness of abortion is also sound, for the structure of the two arguments is the same. The structure common to both is the key to the explanation of how the wrongness of abortion can be demonstrated without recourse to the category of person. In neither argument is that category crucial.

This defense of an argument for the wrongness of abortion in terms of a structurally similar argument for the wrongness of the wanton infliction of pain on animals succeeds only if the account regarding animals is the correct account. Is it? In the first place, it seems plausible. In the second place, its major competition is Kant's account. Kant believed that we do not have direct duties to animals at all, because they are not persons. Hence, Kant had to explain and justify the wrongness of inflicting pain on animals on the grounds that "he who is hard in his dealings with animals becomes hard also in his dealing with men."[8] The problem with Kant's account is that there seems to be no reason for accepting this latter claim unless Kant's account is rejected. If the alternative to Kant's account is accepted, then it is easy to understand why someone who is indifferent to inflicting pain on animals is also indifferent to inflicting pain on humans, for one is indifferent to what makes inflicting pain wrong in both cases. But, if Kant's account is accepted, there is no intelligible reason why one who is hard in his dealings with animals (or crabgrass or stones) should also be hard in his dealings with men. After all, men are persons: animals are no more persons than crabgrass or stones. Persons are Kant's crucial moral category. Why, in short, should a Kantian accept the basic claim in Kant's argument?

Hence, Kant's argument for the wrongness of inflicting pain on animals rests on a claim that, in a world of Kantian moral agents, is demonstrably false.

Therefore, the alternative analysis, being more plausible anyway, should be accepted. Since this alternative analysis has the same structure as the anti-abortion argument being defended here, we have further support for the argument for the immorality of abortion being defended in this essay.

Of course, this value of a future-like-ours argument, if sound, shows only that abortion is prima facie wrong, not that it is wrong in any and all circumstances. Since the loss of the future to a standard fetus, if killed, is, however, at least as great a loss as the loss of the future to a standard adult human being who is killed, abortion, like ordinary killing, could be justified only by the most compelling reasons. The loss of one's life is almost the greatest misfortune that can happen to one. Presumably abortion could be justified in some circumstances, only if the loss consequent on failing to abort would be at least as great. Accordingly, morally permissible abortions will be rare indeed unless, perhaps, they occur so early in pregnancy that a fetus is not yet definitely an individual. Hence, this argument should be taken as showing that abortion is presumptively very seriously wrong, where the presumption is very strong – as strong as the presumption that killing another adult human being is wrong.

III

How complete an account of the wrongness of killing does the value of a future-like-ours account have to be in order that the wrongness of abortion is a consequence? This account does not have to be an account of the necessary conditions for the wrongness of killing. Some persons in nursing homes may lack valuable human futures, yet it may be wrong to kill them for other reasons. Furthermore, this account does not obviously have to be the sole reason killing is wrong where the victim did have a valuable future. This analysis claims only that, for any killing where the victim did have a valuable future like ours, having that future by itself is sufficient to create the strong presumption that the killing is seriously wrong.

One way to overturn the value of a future-like-ours argument would be to find some account of the wrongness of killing which is at least as intelligible and which has different implications for the ethics of abortion. Two rival accounts possess at least some degree of plausibility. One account is based on the obvious fact that people value the experience of living and wish for that valuable experience to continue. Therefore, it might be said, what makes killing wrong is the discontinuation of that experience for the victim. Let us call this the *discontinuation account*.[9] Another rival account is based upon the obvious fact that people strongly desire to continue to live. This suggests that what makes killing us so wrong is that it interferes with the fulfillment of a strong and fundamental desire, the fulfillment of which is necessary for the fulfillment of any other desires we might have. Let us call this the *desire account*.[10]

Consider first the desire account as a rival account of the ethics of killing which would provide the basis for rejecting the anti-abortion position. Such an account will have to be stronger than the value of a future-like-ours account of the wrongness of abortion if it is to do the job expected of it. To entail the wrongness of abortion, the value of a future-like-ours account has only to provide a sufficient, but not a necessary, condition for the wrongness of killing. The desire account, on the other hand, must provide us also with a necessary condition for the wrongness of killing in order to generate a pro-choice conclusion on abortion. The reason for this is that presumably the argument from the desire account moves from the claim that what makes killing wrong is interference with a very strong desire to the claim that abortion is not wrong because the fetus lacks a strong desire to live. Obviously, this inference fails if someone's having the desire to live is not a necessary condition of its being wrong to kill that individual.

One problem with the desire account is that we do regard it as seriously wrong to kill persons who have little desire to live or who have no desire to live or, indeed, have a desire not to live. We believe it is seriously wrong to kill the unconscious, the sleeping, those who are tired of life, and those who are suicidal. The value-of-a-human-future account renders standard morality intelligible in these cases; these cases appear to be incompatible with the desire account.

The desire account is subject to a deeper difficulty. We desire life, because we value the goods of this life. The goodness of life is not secondary to our desire for it. If this were not so, the pain of one's own premature death could be done away with merely by an appropriate alteration in the configuration of one's desires. This is absurd. Hence, it would seem that it is the loss of the goods of one's future, not the interference with the fulfillment of a strong desire to live, which accounts ultimately for the wrongness of killing.

It is worth noting that, if the desire account is modified so that it does not provide a necessary, but only a sufficient, condition for the wrongness of killing, the desire account is compatible with the value of a future-like-ours account. The combined accounts will yield an anti-abortion ethic. This suggests that one can retain what is intuitively plausible about the desire account without a challenge to the basic argument of this paper.

It is also worth noting that, if future desires have moral force in a modified desire account of the wrongness of killing, one can find support for an anti-abortion ethic even in the absence of a value of a future-like-ours account. If one decides that a morally relevant property, the possession of which is sufficient to make it wrong to kill some individual, is the desire at some future time to live – one might decide to justify one's refusal to kill suicidal teenagers on these grounds, for example – then, since typical fetuses will have the desire in the future to live, it is wrong to kill typical fetuses. Accordingly, it does not seem that a desire account of the wrongness of killing can provide a justification of a pro-choice ethic of abortion which is nearly as adequate as the value of a human-future justification of an anti-abortion ethic.

The discontinuation account looks more promising as an account of the wrongness of killing. It seems just as intelligible as the value of a future-like-ours account, but it does not justify an anti-abortion position. Obviously, if it is the continuation of one's activities, experiences, and projects, the loss of which makes killing wrong, then it is not wrong to kill fetuses for that reason, for fetuses do not have experiences, activities, and projects to be continued or discontinued. Accordingly, the discontinuation account does not have the anti-abortion consequences that the value of a future-like-ours account has. Yet, it seems as intelligible as the value of a future-like-ours account, for when we think of what would be wrong with our being killed, it does seem as if it is the discontinuation of what makes our lives worthwhile which makes killing us wrong.

Is the discontinuation account just as good an account as the value of a future-like-ours account? The discontinuation account will not be adequate at all, if it does not refer to the *value* of the experience that may be discontinued. One does not want the discontinuation account to make it wrong to kill a patient who begs for death and who is in severe pain that cannot be relieved short of killing. (I leave open the question of whether it is wrong for other reasons.) Accordingly, the discontinuation account must be more than a bare discontinuation account. It must make some reference to the positive value of the patient's experiences. But, by the same token, the value of a future-like-ours account cannot be a bare future account either. Just having a future surely does not itself rule out killing the above patient. This account must make some reference to the value of the patient's future experiences and projects also. Hence, both accounts involve the value of experiences, projects, and activities. So far we still have symmetry between the accounts.

The symmetry fades, however, when we focus on the time period of the value of the experiences, etc., which has moral consequences. Although both accounts leave open the possibility that the patient in our example may be killed, this possibility is left open only in virtue of the utterly bleak future for the patient. It makes no difference whether the patient's immediate past contains intolerable pain, or consists in being in a coma (which we can imagine is a situation of indifference), or consists in a life of value. If the patient's future is a future of value, we want our account to make it wrong to kill the patient. If the patient's future is intolerable, whatever his or her immediate past, we want our account to allow killing the patient. Obviously, then, it is the value of that patient's future which is doing the work in rendering the morality of killing the patient intelligible.

This being the case, it seems clear that whether one has immediate past experiences or not does no work in the explanation of what makes killing wrong. The addition the discontinuation account makes to the value of a human future account is otiose. Its addition to the value-of-a-future account plays no role at all in rendering intelligible the wrongness of killing. Therefore, it can be discarded with the discontinuation account of which it is a part.

IV

The analysis of the previous section suggests that alternative general accounts of the wrongness of killing are either inadequate or unsuccessful in getting around the anti-abortion consequences of the value of a future-like-ours argument. A different strategy for avoiding these anti-abortion consequences involves limiting the scope of the value of a future argument. More precisely, the strategy involves arguing that fetuses lack a property that is essential for the value-of-a-future argument (or for any anti-abortion argument) to apply to them.

One move of this sort is based upon the claim that a necessary condition of one's future being valuable is that one values it. Value implies a valuer. Given this one might argue that, since fetuses cannot value their futures, their futures are not valuable to them. Hence, it does not seriously wrong them deliberately to end their lives.

This move fails, however, because of some ambiguities. Let us assume that something cannot be of value unless it is valued by someone. This does not entail that my life is of no value unless it is valued by me. I may think, in a period of despair, that my future is of no worth whatsoever, but I may be wrong because others rightly see value – even great value – in it. Furthermore, my future can be valuable to me even if I do not value it. This is the case when a young person attempts suicide, but is rescued and goes on to significant human achievements. Such young people's futures are ultimately valuable to them, even though such futures do not seem to be valuable to them at the moment of attempted suicide. A fetus's future can be valuable to it in the same way. Accordingly, this attempt to limit the anti-abortion argument fails.

Another similar attempt to reject the anti-abortion position is based on Tooley's claim that an entity cannot possess the right to life unless it has the capacity to desire its continued existence. It follows that, since fetuses lack the conceptual capacity to desire to continue to live, they lack the right to life. Accordingly, Tooley concludes that abortion cannot be seriously prima facie wrong ("Abortion and Infanticide," pp. 46–7 [see chapter 2 in this volume]).

What could be the evidence for Tooley's basic claim? Tooley once argued that individuals have a prima facie right to what they desire and that the lack of the capacity to desire something undercuts the basis of one's right to it (pp. 44–5). This argument plainly will not succeed in the context of the analysis of this essay, however, since the point here is to establish the fetus's right to life on other grounds. Tooley's argument assumes that the right to life cannot be established in general on some basis other than the desire for life. This position was considered and rejected in the preceding section of this paper.

One might attempt to defend Tooley's basic claim on the grounds that, because a fetus cannot apprehend continued life as a benefit, its continued life cannot be a benefit or cannot be something it has a right to or cannot be something that is in its interest. This might be defended in terms of the general proposition that, if an individual is literally incapable of caring about or taking an interest in some X, then one does not have a right to X or X is not a benefit or X is not something that is in one's interest.[11]

Each member of this family of claims seems to be open to objections. As John C. Stevens[12] has pointed out, one may have a right to be treated with a certain medical procedure (because of a health insurance policy one has purchased), even though one cannot conceive of the nature of the procedure. And, as Tooley himself has pointed out, persons who have been indoctrinated, or drugged, or rendered temporarily unconscious may be literally incapable of caring about or taking an interest in something that is in their interest or is something to which they have a right, or is something that benefits them. Hence, the Tooley claim that would restrict the scope of the value of a future-like-ours argument is undermined by counterexamples.[13]

Finally, Paul Bassen[14] has argued that, even though the prospects of an embryo might seem to be a basis for the wrongness of abortion, an embryo cannot be a victim and therefore cannot be wronged. An embryo cannot be a victim, he says, because it lacks sentience. His central argument for this seems to be that, even though plants and the permanently unconscious are alive, they clearly cannot be victims. What is the explanation of this? Bassen claims that the explanation is that their lives consist of mere metabolism and mere metabolism is not enough to ground victimizability. Mentation is required.

The problem with this attempt to establish the absence of victimizability is that both plants and the permanently unconscious clearly lack what Bassen calls "prospects" or what I have called "a future life like ours." Hence, it is surely open to one to argue that the real reason we believe plants and the permanently unconscious cannot be victims is that killing them cannot deprive them of a future life like ours; the real reason is not their absence of present mentation.

Bassen recognizes that his view is subject to this difficulty, and he recognizes that the case of children seems to support this difficulty, for "much of what we do for children is based on prospects." He argues, however, that, in the case of children and in other such cases, "potentiality comes into play only where victimizability has been secured on other grounds" (p. 333).

Bassen's defense of his view is patently question-begging, since what is adequate to secure victimizability is exactly what is at issue. His examples do not support his own view against the thesis of this essay. Of course, embryos can be victims: when their lives are deliberately terminated, they are deprived of their futures of value, their prospects. This makes them victims, for it directly wrongs them.

The seeming plausibility of Bassen's view stems from the fact that paradigmatic cases of imagining someone as a victim involve empathy, and empathy requires mentation of the victim. The victims of flood, famine, rape, or child abuse are all persons with whom we can empathize. That empathy seems to be part of seeing them as victims.[15]

In spite of the strength of these examples, the attractive intuition that a situation in which there is victimization requires the possibility of empathy is subject to counterexamples. Consider a case that Bassen himself offers: "Posthumous obliteration of an author's work constitutes a misfortune for him only if he had wished his work to endure" (p. 318). The conditions Bassen wishes to impose upon the possibility of being victimized here seem far too strong. Perhaps this author, due to his unrealistic standards of excellence and his low self-esteem, regarded his work as unworthy of survival, even though it possessed genuine literary merit. Destruction of such work would surely victimize its author. In such a case, empathy with the victim concerning the loss is clearly impossible.

Of course, Bassen does not make the possibility of empathy a necessary condition of victimizability; he requires only mentation. Hence, on Bassen's actual view, this author, as I have described him, can be a victim. The problem is that the basic intuition that renders Bassen's view plausible is missing in the author's case. In order to attempt to avoid counterexamples, Bassen has made his thesis too weak to be supported by the intuitions that suggested it.

Even so, the mentation requirement on victimizability is still subject to counterexamples. Suppose a severe accident renders me totally unconscious for a month, after which I recover. Surely killing me while I am unconscious victimizes me, even though I am incapable of mentation during that time. It follows that Bassen's thesis fails. Apparently, attempts to restrict the value of a future-like-ours argument so that fetuses do not fall within its scope do not succeed.

V

In this essay, it has been argued that the correct ethic of the wrongness of killing can be extended to fetal life and used to show that there is a strong presumption that any abortion is morally impermissible. If the ethic of killing adopted here entails, however, that contraception is also seriously immoral, then there would appear to be a difficulty with the analysis of this essay.

But this analysis does not entail that contraception is wrong. Of course, contraception prevents the actualization of a possible future of value. Hence, it follows from the claim that if futures of value should be maximized that contraception is prima facie immoral. This obligation to maximize does not exist, however; furthermore, nothing in the ethics of killing in this paper entails that it does. The ethics of killing in this essay would entail that contraception is wrong only if something were denied a human future of value by contraception. Nothing at all is denied such a future by contraception, however.

Candidates for a subject of harm by contraception fall into four categories: (1) some sperm or other, (2) some ovum or other, (3) a sperm and an ovum separately, and (4) a sperm and an ovum together. Assigning the harm to some sperm is utterly arbitrary, for no reason can be given for making a sperm the subject of harm rather than an ovum. Assigning the harm to some ovum is utterly arbitrary, for no reason

can be given for making an ovum the subject of harm rather than a sperm. One might attempt to avoid these problems by insisting that contraception deprives both the sperm and the ovum separately of a valuable future like ours. On this alternative, too many futures are lost. Contraception was supposed to be wrong, because it deprived us of one future of value, not two. One might attempt to avoid this problem by holding that contraception deprives the combination of sperm and ovum of a valuable future like ours. But here the definite article misleads. At the time of contraception, there are hundreds of millions of sperm, one (released) ovum and millions of possible combinations of all of these. There is no actual combination at all. Is the subject of the loss to be a merely possible combination? Which one? This alternative does not yield an actual subject of harm either. Accordingly, the immorality of contraception is not entailed by the loss of a future-like-ours argument simply because there is no nonarbitrarily identifiable subject of the loss in the case of contraception.

VI

The purpose of this essay has been to set out an argument for the serious presumptive wrongness of abortion subject to the assumption that the moral permissibility of abortion stands or falls on the moral status of the fetus. Since a fetus possesses a property, the possession of which in adult human beings is sufficient to make killing an adult human being wrong, abortion is wrong. This way of dealing with the problem of abortion seems superior to other approaches to the ethics of abortion, because it rests on an ethics of killing which is close to self-evident, because the crucial morally relevant property clearly applies to fetuses, and because the argument avoids the usual equivocations on "human life," "human being," or "person." The argument rests neither on religious claims nor on Papal dogma. It is not subject to the objection of "speciesism." Its soundness is compatible with the moral permissibility of euthanasia and contraception. It deals with our intuitions concerning young children.

Finally, this analysis can be viewed as resolving a standard problem – indeed, *the* standard problem – concerning the ethics of abortion. Clearly, it is wrong to kill adult human beings. Clearly, it is not wrong to end the life of some arbitrarily chosen single human cell. Fetuses seem to be like arbitrarily chosen human cells in some respects and like adult humans in other respects.

The problem of the ethics of abortion is the problem of determining the fetal property that settles this moral controversy. The thesis of this essay is that the problem of the ethics of abortion, so understood, is solvable.

Notes

1 Feinberg, "Abortion," in *Matters of Life and Death: New Introductory Essays in Moral Philosophy*, Tom Regan, ed. (New York: Random House, 1986), pp. 256–93; Tooley, "*Abortion and Infanticide*," *Philosophy and Public Affairs*, II, 1 (1972): 37–65 [see chapter 2 in this volume], Tooley, *Abortion and Infanticide* (New York: Oxford, 1984); Warren, "*On the Moral and Legal Status of Abortion*," *The Monist*, 1.VII, 1 (1973): 43–61; Engelhardt, "*The Ontology of Abortion*," *Ethics*, I. XXXIV, 3 (1974): 217–34; Sumner, *Abortion and Moral Theory* (Princeton: University Press, 1981); Noonan, "An Almost Absolute Value in History," in *The Morality of Abortion: Legal and Historical Perspectives*, Noonan, ed. (Cambridge: Harvard, 1970); and Devine, *The Ethics of Homicide* (Ithaca: Cornell, 1978).

2 For interesting discussions of this issue, see Warren Quinn, "*Abortion: Identity and Loss*," *Philosophy and Public Affairs*, XIII, 1 (1984): 24–54; and Lawrence C. Becker, "*Human Being: The Boundaries of the Concept*," *Philosophy and Public Affairs*, IV, 4 (1975): 334–59.

3 For example, see my "Ethics and the Elderly: Some Problems," in Stuart Spicker, Kathleen Woodward, and David Van Tassel, eds., *Aging and the Elderly: Humanistic Perspectives in Gerontology* (Atlantic Highlands, NJ: Humanities, 1978), pp. 341–55.

4 See Warren, "On the Moral and Legal Status of Abortion," and Tooley, "Abortion and Infanticide."

5 This seems to be the fatal flaw in Warren's treatment of this issue.

6 I have been most influenced on this matter by Jonathan Glover, *Causing Death and Saving Lives* (New York: Penguin, 1977), ch. 3; and Robert Young, "*What Is So Wrong with Killing People?*" *Philosophy*, LIV, 210 (1979): 515–28.

7 Feinberg, Tooley, Warren, and Engelhardt have all dealt with this problem.

8 Kant, "Duties to Animals and Spirits," in *Lectures on Ethics*, trans. Louis Infeld (New York: Harper, 1963), p. 239.

9 I am indebted to Jack Bricke for raising this objection.

10 Presumably a preference utilitarian would press such an objection. Tooley once suggested that his account has such a theoretical underpinning. See his "Abortion and Infanticide," pp. 44–5.

11 Donald VanDeVeer seems to think this is self-evident. See his "Whither Baby Doe?" in *Matters of Life and Death*, p. 233.

12 "Must the Bearer of a Right Have the Concept of That to Which He Has a Right?" *Ethics*, XCV, 1 (1984): 68–74.

13 See Tooley again in "Abortion and Infanticide," pp. 47–9.

14 "Present Sakes and Future Prospects: The Status of Early Abortion," *Philosophy and Public Affairs*, XI, 4 (1982): 322–6.

15 Note carefully the reasons he gives on the bottom of p. 316.

Part II

Issues in Reproduction

Introduction

Developments in reproductive medicine have, over the past 50 years, presented us with remarkable new options, giving us increasing control over our fertility. Effective contraception and sterilization procedures have separated sex from reproduction, while various infertility treatments, such as in vitro fertilization, have dramatically increased the possibilities for reproduction without sex. Fertile couples are now able to limit and space the number of children they are going to have, while those who were once considered infertile are able to have children.

There are also new opportunities to decide what our children will be like. Prenatal diagnosis of fetuses and testing of in vitro embryos allows prospective parents to decide not to bring a disabled child into the world, even without the use of abortion. (Those who accept the view defended by John Finnis in Part I of this anthology will not be mollified by a procedure that still involves the discarding of a viable human embryo.) The same techniques allow parents to select the sex of their child. Cloning and genetic modification of offspring are now possible for several species of mammals, and some think that it is only a matter of time before they take place in humans as well.

A wide range of different issues are covered in this part of the anthology. Two interrelated clusters of questions, while by no means exhaustive of the ethical issues raised, are central to many of the discussions presented here: the limits, if any, to reproductive freedom, and the rights or interests of future children.

Assisted Reproduction

Being unable to have children can be a source of profound grief and great unhappiness. But some widely accepted technologies and procedures for overcoming infertility continue to raise troubling ethical issues. Fertility drugs given to women to enhance the production of eggs can lead to multiple pregnancies. When a woman carries more than one fetus, infants are frequently born prematurely and, if not stillborn, may have to spend long periods in neonatal intensive care. There is also an increased risk of brain damage and other serious disabilities.

In the first article in Part II, Greg Pence ("Multiple Gestation and Damaged Babies: God's Will or Human Choice?") describes the case of 29-year-old Bobbi McCaughey, whose use of a fertility drug led to her giving birth, in 1996, to seven infants. All survived, but with a range of different disabilities. While aware of the risks, the couple had rejected the idea of selectively aborting a number of the fetuses, saying that whatever happened was "God's will." But, writes Pence, it is difficult to hold God responsible for any children turning out disabled or dead: "If God was clear about anything in this case, it was that the

Bioethics: An Anthology, Third Edition. Edited by Helga Kuhse, Udo Schüklenk, and Peter Singer.

McCaugheys should not have had kids. Otherwise, why did He make them infertile?" Rather than being able to claim that God is responsible, Pence argues, those who take fertility drugs should, if necessary, be willing to reduce the number of fetuses "for the good of your unborn-children."

One outcome of the new reproductive techniques is that they make it easier for same sex couples to have children who are genetically related to at least one of them. A few years ago, to discuss the provision of assisted reproduction to same sex couples would have been pushing the frontiers of what was socially acceptable. With increasing acceptance of marriage equality, and of the rights of same sex couples to have children, however, the use of assisted reproduction by same sex couples is increasing, and no longer seems as shocking as it once did. In "Assisted Reproduction in Same Sex Couples," Dorothy Greenfeld and Emre Seli present some data on same sex child-rearing and offer recommendations for protecting what they see as the rights of same sex couples to have children, including the right to use assisted reproduction where it is available for heterosexual couples.

When controversial new reproductive possibilities are first mooted, those opposed to the innovation often argue that the children produced by it will be harmed in some way. This argument was used against the introduction of in vitro fertilization, and it was also used against same sex couples being allowed to have children. So far, such arguments have generally lacked evidence, and as Greenfeld and Seli have shown, this is the case with children reared by same sex couples. But in any case, should we accept the assumption that *if* children produced by a new reproductive technique were in some way less well-off than other children, this would be a ground for not permitting the new technique? Derek Parfit offers an argument against this assumption in his article "Rights, Interests, and Possible People." He asks readers to consider the case of a woman who wants to stop taking contraceptive pills in order to have another child. She is told by her doctor that she is suffering from a temporary condition that will result in any child she conceives now having a handicap – although one that is still compatible with living a worthwhile life. If she waits three months, on the other hand, she will conceive a normal child. Many people think that

if the woman decides not to wait, she will be harming her child. But, Parfit argues, this conclusion does not follow. If the woman were to wait, she would not be having *this* child, but a different child – a child conceived three months later from a different egg and a different sperm. Based on the assumption that the first child, while handicapped, has a life worth living, it would thus be difficult to claim that the handicapped child has been harmed by having been brought into existence. His life is still better than no life at all.

If Parfit is correct on this point, could it still be claimed that single women and lesbian couples should be denied access to infertility services for the sake of their as-yet-unconceived children? On the face of it, this could be argued only if these children were going to have lives so devoid of happiness and whatever else makes a life worth living that nonexistence is preferable to existence. Given that this is an implausible supposition, denying access to infertility services to same sex couples would prevent the existence of children who would very probably have lived worthwhile lives. We can hardly justify a prohibition on the use of assisted reproduction on the grounds that the prohibition is in the best interests of the children who would be born as a result of that use, if the children would have worthwhile lives, and without the availability of the technique, would not be born at all.

With assisted reproduction, no sooner does one frontier zone become accepted as part of normal medical services than a new one appears. In "The Ethics of Uterus Transplantation," Ruby Catsanos, Wendy Rogers and Mianna Lotz discuss the possibility of offering a uterus transplant to a woman who is infertile because she lacks a functioning uterus. Such women can have their own genetic children by using in vitro fertilization to produce an embryo, and then using a surrogate to bear the child. Medically, this is much more straightforward than a uterus transplant, although it can give rise to its own ethical, legal and social problems. What some women want, however, is not only to have their own genetic child, but to bear and give birth to that child. If there is a right to assisted reproduction, does that extend to the satisfaction of the desire to bear and give birth to one's child? Catsanos, Rogers, and Lotz recognize the importance of this desire, for some women, but are also well aware of the difficulties, both technical and ethical, of uterus transplants. The topic offers the opportunity to explore the limits of a putative right to assisted reproduction.

Prenatal Screening, Sex Selection, and Cloning

As our knowledge of genetics expands, prospective parents are increasingly given the opportunity to make use of this knowledge to prevent the birth of genetically compromised children. Here it is important to note that prevention need not involve abortion or the destruction of preimplantation embryos. At-risk parents can avoid having a disabled child by deciding not to have children, by adopting children, or by using donor gametes or embryos.

Is it wrong to bring severely disabled children into the world, if one could avoid doing so? Laura Purdy ("Genetics and Reproductive Risks: Can Having Children Be Immoral?") gives an affirmative answer. Rejecting the view "that it is morally permissible to conceive individuals so long as we do not expect them to be so miserable that they wish they were dead," she argues that parents ought to ensure that any children they are going to have possess "normal health." While she acknowledges that the notion is vague, she takes it to be sufficient to mark out as wrong the bringing into the world of children who are at risk of having serious genetic afflictions, such as Huntington's Disease.

Not everybody accepts, however, that "normal health" is a necessary prerequisite for leading a satisfying life. Adrienne Asch argues, in "Prenatal Diagnosis and Selective Abortion: A Challenge of Practice and Policy," that severely disabled people can have satisfying lives. While acknowledging that biological disability can have a negative impact on people's lives, she holds that the main cause of suffering for people with a disability is "discriminatory social arrangements." In her view, healthcare professionals need to critically examine their attitudes to disability, and public policies and procedures ought to be changed, so that prospective parents can make truly informed choices.

It may well be the case, as Asch and many other disability rights advocates contend, that even very

serious disabilities and diseases are, other things being equal, compatible with a worthwhile life. Indeed, as long as the focus is solely on the quality of life of the possible or potential child (what Derek Parfit, in his article, calls "the person-affecting" view), it may be difficult to argue that parents ought to refrain from reproduction *for the child's sake*, unless the child's life is likely to be so bad that it would be better for the child not to be born. But should prospective parents act on the person-affecting view, or should they perhaps also take the interests of an alternative, healthy child, into account – the child they might have instead of the disabled one? R. M. Hare argues that they should, in his article "The Abnormal Child: Moral Dilemmas of Doctors and Parents" in Part IV of this anthology.

Setting the above set of questions to one side, another problem presents itself: Given that at least some genetic testing is now widely accepted, which conditions should be tested for? It is, for example, now possible to test during pregnancy for some kinds of deafness, if the gene causing deafness in the family is known. It seems likely that further genetic tests will become available, identifying more fetuses and embryos that will not be able to hear. But is deafness really the undesirable condition it is often thought to be? As Ruth Chadwick and Mairi Levitt point out in "Genetic Technology: A Threat To Deafness," some deaf people see deafness not as a disability, but rather as an essential component underlying a culture – Deaf culture – with its own language, values, customs, and so on. From a disability perspective, attempts to eliminate deafness might thus be seen not as a benefit but as a threat to deafness and to Deaf culture.

This is contentious. But even if we accept that it is no better to have the ability to hear than to lack that ability, and that Deaf culture is threatened by attempts to eliminate deafness, does it follow that parents should have deaf children? After examining a range of complex philosophical and ethical issues about the nature of disease and disability, about culture and community, and parental responsibilities, Chadwick and Levitt reach the conclusion that parental choice, or reproductive liberty, must also be accorded moral weight. Parents should be free to refuse an abortion and to bring a deaf child into the world, but reproductive liberty does not necessarily require that the state provide medical services such as preimplantation diagnosis to enable prospective parts to select for deafness.

The notion that there ought to be a sphere of liberty within which prospective parents are free to make reproductive choices is widely accepted. There is, however, disagreement as to whether reproductive liberty has limits, and if it does, where these limits ought to be drawn. Take sex selection. Many jurisdictions allow parents to prevent the birth of children affected by certain genetic diseases, but do not allow them to do this for nonmedical reasons, such as wanting to balance the sex ratio of their children. In a statement entitled "Sex Selection and Preimplantation Genetic Diagnosis," the Ethics Committee of the American Society of Reproductive Medicine indicates the extent to which it shares the concerns behind such laws. The Committee itself does not believe that nonmedical sex selection is so clearly and seriously wrong that it favors the use of the law to prohibit it. Instead, the Committee would stop at discouraging sex selection for nonmedical reasons.

Julian Savulescu and Edgar Dahl respond to the Committee's statement in their essay "Sex Selection and Preimplantation Diagnosis." They find its arguments unpersuasive, particularly given that, in Western societies, most people seeking to use sex selection do so not because they value one sex more than the other, but to balance the number of boys and girls in their family.

There is another reason, apart from avoiding disability or selecting for sex, why parents might want to employ medical technologies to bring one child rather than another into the world. Hematopoietic stem cells from umbilical cord blood or bone marrow have the potential to save the lives of children suffering from diseases affecting the blood or immune system. When compatible cells are not available from other sources, parents of a child threatened by death may want to conceive another child who can serve as the donor of those cells. Would it be wrong for the parents to do so? John A. Robertson, Jeffrey P. Kahn, and John E. Wagner examine a range of objections in "Conception to Obtain Hematopoietic Stem Cells" and reach the conclusion that they are unconvincing. Parents committed to loving and nurturing the second child should, they argue, have access to preimplantation testing of embryos in order to be able to ensure

that the child is a suitable match for the already existing child.

Those opposing preimplantation genetic diagnosis for the above purpose may, however, have concerns that go beyond the welfare interests of the future child. David King explains "Why We Should Not Permit Embryos to Be Selected as Tissue Donors." He believes that the practice objectifies the child and turns it into a mere tool. This contradicts, he says, the basic Kantian ethical principle that human beings must always be treated as ends, and never merely as a means to an end. Even if the future child will be a much-loved member of the family, we ought to resist the temptation to allow the selection of embryos as tissue donors because it is yet another step in the objectification of humans and "and the consequences of doing so are … disastrous."

But is the maxim that we must never regard others solely as a means to an end infringed if the tissue-matched child is loved and cherished in its own right, as an end? Kant's maxim provides, as King correctly notes, a plausible account of what is wrong with slavery, but its implication in the present context are far less clear. People generally have children for a variety of reasons: they want a sister for "Ann," a companion for their old age, a son to continue the bloodline, and so on. If tissue matching of embryos to save another child were ruled out by the Kantian maxim, would this not also perhaps rule out many other widely accepted reasons for having children as well?

In allowing tissue matching of embryos, we are, King holds, proceeding down a slippery slope toward some very bad societal consequences. Critics of this kind of argument might question, however, whether the bad consequences at the bottom of the slope are truly bad, or as bad as they are made out to be. They may also ask whether the slope is really so slippery and if sound laws and public policies would not arrest any possible slide.

For many people reproductive human cloning is one of the bad consequences that lie at the bottom of the slippery slope. When the existence of the sheep called Dolly (the first mammal to owe its existence to somatic cell nuclear transfer, or cloning) was announced in 1997, there was swift worldwide reaction. People feared that the cloning of humans would not be far away. Only 24 hours after the world knew of Dolly's existence, a bill outlawing human cloning was announced in New York State, and a few days later, US President Clinton banned federal funding for research into it.

Michael Tooley examines this issue in "The Moral Status of the Cloning of Humans." He distinguishes between the questions of whether reproductive human cloning is *in principle* morally acceptable and whether it is acceptable *at the present time*, given current scientific knowledge and understanding, and reaches the conclusion that the practice is currently morally problematic, but that once it is perfected it might offer some benefits, and be acceptable.

Assisted Reproduction

5

Multiple Gestation and Damaged Babies
God's Will or Human Choice?

Gregory Pence

The media rejoiced in 1996 at the apparently healthy birth of the McCaughey septuplets. Cable television glamorized the Gosselins on "Jon & Kate Plus 8." Rarely did the darker side emerge in the media's coverage. Call me a curmudgeon, but something stinks here.

Humans too often generalize from a few well-publicized cases (witness the ban on commercial surrogacy after the Baby M case). In France – where the French zealously pursue pregnancy because the government financially awards the birth of each new baby – use of fertility drugs has led to a tenfold increase in the number of triplets and thirtyfold increase in the number of quadruplets since 1982.

With so many babies delivered during one birth, some complain about the costs to society, and gestation and birth of the septuplets probably cost a cool million dollars. Others complain that the human uterus did not evolve to bear litters, making multiplets unnatural. Still others wonder how Bobbi McCaughey's body and health will be affected.

Although these complaints matter, they are morally secondary. Costs can be spread over millions of payers, and unnatural in one era becomes normal in the next (witness anesthesia). Also, if Mrs. McCaughey made an informed choice, she is free to risk injuring her body in childbirth as she sees fit.

My real worry concerns the children's wellbeing. The McCaugheys took Pergonal, a fertility drug, conceived seven embryos, and refused to terminate any because any terrible results were "God's will." In doing so, they risked the health and lives of their babies.

Why? Multiple-birth babies are: usually premature (each may weigh less than two pounds); three times as likely to be severely handicapped at birth; and often spend months in neonatal intensive care units. During gestation, nutrients and oxygenated blood in the womb are scarce (a uterine lifeboat, if you will); thus, not all of seven fetuses will likely emerge healthy. To prevent disabilities resulting from uterine deprivation, physicians recommend "selective reduction" of all but 1 or 2 embryos.

At their fourth birthday in 2001, the McCaughey septuplets lagged in development and were not all potty trained. Joel suffered seizures; Nathan had spastic diplegia, a form of cerebral palsy requiring botox injections (to paralyze spastic muscles) and orthopedic braces. Alexis had hypotonic quadriplegia, a cerebral palsy that causes muscle weakness.

After two major orthopaedic surgeries, Nathan still could not walk at age seven. Alexis had an indwelling feeding tube for four years. Although the McCaugheys homeschool, they sent Nathan and Alexis in 2006

Original publication details: Gregory Pence, "Multiple Gestation and Damaged Babies: God's Will or Human Choice?" This essay draws on "The McCaughey Septuplets: God's Will or Human Choice," pp. 39–43 from Gregory Pence, *Brave New Bioethics*, Lanham, MD: Rowman & Littlefield, 2002 © Gregory Pence 2002. Courtesy of G. Pence.

Bioethics: An Anthology, Third Edition. Edited by Helga Kuhse, Udo Schüklenk, and Peter Singer.
© 2016 John Wiley & Sons, Inc. Published 2016 by John Wiley & Sons, Inc.

to a school for developmentally challenged children financed by taxpayers.[1]

It is irresponsible to say, as the McCaugheys did, that it was God's will that two of their children now have cerebral palsy. If God was clear about anything in this case, it was that the McCaugheys should not have had kids. Otherwise, why did He make them infertile?

If you take a fertility drug and conceive too many embryos, you should reduce the embryos for the good of your unborn-children. You shouldn't create severely-disabled kids and attribute it to "God's will." You should take responsibility for creating damaged kids.

NBC News once featured the quintuplets of Denise Amen and her husband, who were offered the chance to reduce and did not. One of her babies was born blind and others are developmentally challenged.

In 1985, a Mormon couple, Patti and Sam Frustaci, conceived septuplets. Informed of the risks and urged to reduce, they refused. Four of their seven babies died, and the three survivors had severe disabilities, including cerebral palsy. The Frustacis then sued their physicians.

And in a 1996 case in England, Mandy Allwood conceived seven or eight embryos at once. Offered a large cash bonus by a tabloid for exclusive rights if all made it to term, Mandy announced she would not reduce. As a result, all of them died.

In a case of a multiple pregnancy in West Virginia, a mother refused selective reduction, but only one child survived; it was blind, paraplegic, and severely retarded. Her infertility-physician said that he would no longer accept women who rejected selective reduction because he couldn't stand creating disabled babies.

Not too many people are interested in long-term follow-up, yet it is important to do it.

Of the five Canadian Dionne quintuplets in 1934, although all seemed healthy at birth, only three lived to old age (one died at age 20 of an epileptic seizure). Nor did they lead happy lives, because their parents exploited their fame.

Nadya Suleman had six embryos left over from previous in-vitro fertilization treatments and underwent another cycle of IVF to implant all. Nadya already had children from previous cycles of IVF, two of whom were disabled. Two of her six implanted embryos split into twins, resulting in eight embryos. When first-trimester sonograms revealed many fetuses, Suleman refused reduction, and physicians later delivered eight babies. She later raised all the children on public assistance, and exhausted her own mother and father (who felt compelled to help her raise their grandchildren).

Kate and Jon Gosselin had twin girls, born from insemination of Jon's sperm in 2000. They wanted more, so fertility doctors injected Kate with drugs to stimulate her ovaries to release more than one egg (as in the McCaughey case) before introducing Jon's sperm. Six embryos resulted, and the Gosselins chose not to reduce. In 2004, physicians delivered eight babies by caesarean. A 2007 television series glamorized the controlled chaos of this family of ten children. A plastic surgeon did free plastic surgery on Kate's stomach to correct the damage from carrying six babies.

In 2009, after both Gosselins had extra-marital affairs, they divorced. Thereafter, Jon seemed to abandon his interest in the children. The Gosselins and Nadya Suleman seemed immature, self-absorbed, and not focused on the best interests of their children.

New York City Mayor Rudy Giuliani was on a call-in radio show in 2001 when a suicidal, Orthodox Jewish woman with five little babies (three of them identical triplets) said that five babies made her crazy. Although the Mayor got her help, what about others? The same year, Jacqueline Thompson and her husband Linden, parents of sextuplets, were living exhausted on the edge in Washington, D.C. until a radio-caller publicized their plight.

What about the two-year-old sister of the McCaughey septuplets? Will her role in childhood be only to help her mother raise the famous septuplets? Moreover, will the two McCaughey parents be able to give each child the nurturing and one-on-one parenting that is ideal? Would you want to grow up with one-seventh of the attention you got from your dad? I wonder if the McCaugheys will have the time, energy, and money to allow each child to develop to his full potential.

The United States is a long way from a philosophically consistent policy on fetal rights and reproductive responsibility. The Supreme Court of South Carolina recently ruled that a mother can be prosecuted for using cocaine in her pregnancy because the usage harms her fetus. In 2002, the President's Council on

Bioethics said that there should be a federal law against originating a child by cloning because of possible harm to the baby. Yet when McCaugheys, Gosselins, and Sulemans create disabled children, they are glamorized. Something seems akilter here.

Note

1 Ann Curry, "After 10 Years, New Adventures for Septuplets," Dateline, December 12, 2007; http://www.nbcnews.com/id/22223331/#.USAS0hzB-AE.

6

Assisted Reproduction in Same Sex Couples

Dorothy A. Greenfeld and Emre Seli

In recent years a growing recognition of same sex unions as culturally and socially acceptable has led inevitably to a parallel acceptance of such unions as a foundation for family. Advances in gay rights, the liberalization of legal restraints, and the increasing availability of assisted reproduction have led to more men and women being open about their homosexuality, open about their relationships, and open about their desire to become parents within the context of a same sex relationship.[1,2] As a result, fertility programs have experienced a growing demand for service from same sex couples seeking parenthood through alternative reproductive techniques. This movement has culminated in a phenomenon commonly referred to as the "gay baby boom".[3]

Conception for same sex couples requires assisted reproduction by definition. As such, gay men and women considering parenthood through these means face a decision-making process not common to heterosexual couples. For example, lesbian couples entering fertility treatment need to give consideration as to who will carry the pregnancy and how to choose a sperm donor. Gay male couples need to give consideration as to who will provide the sperm as well as how to choose an egg donor and a surrogate.

This chapter will address the increasing numbers of planned lesbian and gay families resulting from assisted reproductive technology (ART) and the decision-making process unique to gay couples when planning such families. A discussion of the historical significance of the contribution that the gay civil rights movement has made toward this new openness, a review of the literature on same sex parents and their children, and medical, social, and psychological issues unique to this population will be included. Clinical considerations in treating gay men and women and recommendations for inclusion of same sex couples in the fertility setting also will be described.

Historical Overview of Same Sex Reproduction in the USA

It is currently estimated that in the USA there are between 6 and 14 million children with at least one gay parent.[1] According to the US Census report of 2010, same sex couples live in every state in the union, and one in five same sex couples is raising children.[4] Many of these children were adopted (4% of all adopted children in the USA live with a gay parent).[5] Others were conceived in a heterosexual relationship that resulted in divorce when one parent came out as gay. Increasingly, however,

Original publication details: Dorothy A. Greenfeld and Emre Seli, "Assisted Reproduction in Same Sex Couples," pp. 289–301 from M.V. Sauer (ed.), *Principles of Oocyte and Embryo Donation*, Springer-Verlag, 2013. With kind permission from Springer Science+Business Media.

children are born to gay parents and conceived through assisted reproduction. As noted above, this ongoing phenomenon is due in part to a new openness and a growing determination among same sex couples to marry and have children. Currently, same sex marriage is legal in eight countries around the world: Argentina, Belgium, Canada, Iceland, the Netherlands, Norway, Portugal, South Africa, Spain, and Sweden, In the USA, same sex marriage is legal in six states: Connecticut, Iowa, Massachusetts, New Hampshire, New York, and Vermont. It is also legal in the District of Columbia.[6]

Of course, the growing numbers of gay couples choosing to become parents together didn't happen overnight or in a vacuum. In fact, the movement toward social acceptance and the openness exhibited by gay men and women have evolved considerably in the past 40 years with a somewhat tumultuous history.

In the 1950s in the USA it was dangerous to be admittedly gay or "out." At the time homosexuality was viewed as criminally deviant as well as medically psychopathological. For example, in 1953 President Eisenhower issued executive order 10,405 which banned gays from being employed by the federal government.[7] Others were threatened and afraid of losing their jobs as well. Gay men and women could be legally prosecuted and, on occasion, end up in jail or a mental institution. In the psychiatric community it was believed that both gay men and lesbians were "curable," but lesbians were regarded as more likely to respond to "treatment." Lesbianism was described as a form of neurosis that involved narcissistic gratification and sexual immaturity, while gay males were generally depicted as predatory hypersexual loners.[8]

Events occurred in the following decades that served as a catalyst to the gay civil rights movement toward greater equality. The first, the so-called Stonewall Rebellion is usually cited as the event which triggered the start of the gay rights movement in America. The Stonewall Inn, a gay bar in the Greenwich Village neighborhood of Manhattan, was the site of a routine police raid on June 28, 1969. Such raids were common at the time, an expression of society's intolerance and prejudice toward gays, but on that particular night the patrons fought back, leading to a riot, which continued for several days. Over the next weeks and months gays and lesbians formed activist groups to mount what became the beginning of a national campaign for gay rights.[7, 8]

Another significant source of gay pride happened in 1973 when the American Psychiatric Association, in what was described as a contentious meeting, voted to remove homosexuality as a psychopathological syndrome from its Diagnostic and Statistical Manual (DSM), the official list of psychiatric disorders.[9] To appreciate the significance of such an event, it is important to remember that this represented a dramatic conceptual shift by the most important national organization of the American psychiatric profession.[7] Similarly, the American Psychological Association, the national organ of American psychologists, voted to eliminate homosexuality as a psychiatric diagnosis in 1975, and since then several organizations have called for nondiscrimination for gay men and women and their children. These organizations include the American Academy of Family Physicians, the American Academy of Pediatrics, the American Bar Association, the Child Welfare League, and the National Association of Social Workers.[10]

The Emergence of Assisted Reproduction for Lesbians and Gay Men

As gay men and women became more confident and candid about being gay and about their same sex relationships, they grew in determination and confidence about planning families and becoming parents within the context of their same sex relationships. The movement toward gay men and women seeking parenthood through reproductive assistance began in the lesbian community and had its inception in California. In 1979, health activists seeking to provide medical care to lesbian and single heterosexual women opened the Lyon-Martin Health Center in San Francisco. One of the founders, Sherron Mills, wanted to start an insemination service for lesbian and single heterosexual women who wanted to start a family, but the Board of Directors balked at such an idea. In 1983,

Mills left the Lyon–Martin clinic and opened the first lesbian-owned sperm bank offering insemination services to lesbians.[11]

At that time the initial ethical arguments against such treatment were that it was a waste of medical resources because the patients were not technically infertile and that such treatment was not in the best interest of the children who would be stigmatized and needed both a mother and a father.[12,13] Interestingly, these concerns applied not only to women who were gay but to all women who were single (gay or heterosexual). Dunstan, for example, stated, "If, as we must assume, the dominant inescapable interest must he of the child and his enjoying a normal upbringing ... then deliberately to contrive its birth into a lesbian union or to a single woman would be to deny it justice".[12]

In recent years the inclusion of same sex female couples seeking parenthood together has become quite common in fertility treatment centers. Lesbians seek parenthood through intrauterine insemination (IUI) or in vitro fertilization (IVF), sometimes with donor egg as well as donor sperm, and, increasingly, through a process referred to as "reciprocal IVF" where one partner provides the eggs and the other partner carries the pregnancy, in effect one is the biological mother and one is the birth mother.[14]

In the late 1970s a few agencies in the USA began to offer surrogacy as an option for parenthood to infertile couples, but gay men were not part of that first wave of intended parents. At that time the commonly used treatment was "traditional surrogacy," which meant that the woman legally contracted to carry the pregnancy was artificially inseminated by the intended father. She relinquished the baby to the intended parents when it was born, and the intended mother adopted the baby. By the 1980s gay male couples began to actively pursue this form of parenthood.[15]

Gestational surrogacy is where the woman carrying the pregnancy goes through IVF and embryo(s) implanted which are not genetically related to her. In 1984, the first birth through "gestational surrogacy" was achieved in the USA.[16] Since that time increasing numbers of gay men seek fatherhood through IVF using an egg donor and a gestational surrogate. Typically, one partner provides the sperm but in some cases, the eggs are divided and each partner's sperm fertilizes half of the oocytes retrieved. Many times the couples choose to transfer an embryo from each partner, often resulting in twins who are in fact half siblings.[17]

Barriers to Assisted Reproduction for Gay Couples

ART is not for everyone, and barriers to treatment are a very real factor to many couples, gay or straight. For example, the financial costs associated with treatment often running to thousands of dollars are prohibitive to many. Another prohibitive factor for many is their geographical location, where information about how to proceed with such a parental quest may be lacking and, worse yet, access to treatment and treatment centers may not exist, especially in some very rural parts of the country.[18]

Perhaps the most egregious barrier for gay couples seeking ART is when there is access to treatment, but it is not available to gay couples. For example, while lesbians commonly are welcomed by fertility treatment centers, the issue is often quite different for gay men. Gay men seeking parenthood through ART using an egg donor and a gestational surrogate [15,19] are not always welcomed by fertility treatment centers. For example, a survey of 369 fertility centers in 2005 revealed that most programs (79%) routinely accept lesbians for treatment but are less likely to accept gay men.[20] In 2006, the Ethics Committee of the American Society for Reproductive Medicine (ASRM) issued a statement with the following recommendation: "Unmarried persons, gays and lesbians have interests in having and rearing children. There is not persuasive evidence that children raised by single parents and or by gays and lesbians are harmed or disadvantaged, and by that fact alone programs should treat all requests for assisted reproduction equally and without regard to marital status or sexual orientation".[21]

Despite the obstacles, gay men and women remain determined to move forward and choose to have families. A study in 2006 of 133 lesbian and gay youth between 15 and 22 years of age determined that the majority expected to be partnered and married and to be raising children as adults.[22]

Key Issues Regarding Same Sex Reproduction: Review of the Literature

Historically, gay men and women have been denied custody or visitation with their children following divorce because of "judicial and legislative assumptions about adverse effects of parental homosexuality on children".[23] Research on gay men and lesbians and their children began to appear in the literature in the 1980s, initiated by researchers looking at whether there was sufficient data to support some of the assumptions about children of gay parents. These assumptions included the expectation that such children would experience stigmatization, poor peer relationships, emotional problems, and/or abnormal psychosexual development.[23,24] Since then the body of literature has grown substantially and has focused on the attitudes and behavior of gay and lesbian parents and the psychosexual development, social experience, and emotional status of their children.[25]

Motivations for Parenthood

In a study of the association between motivation for parenthood and its impact on the parent child relationship, Bos et al. compared 100 lesbian two-mother families planning parenthood through insemination with 100 heterosexual families with no history of infertility treatment. Both groups were in the process of making the transition to parenthood. Investigators compared parenthood motives, reflection (how often subjects thought about the reasons for having children), and strength of the desire to have children. Results were that while both groups rank their parenthood similarly, lesbian mothers had spent more time thinking about having children and their desire to have a child was stronger compared to heterosexual mothers.[27] A study looking at parental motivations among gay and heterosexual fathers found that fathers from both groups were motivated by the same thing: the desire to nurture children, to have the constancy of children in their lives, to achieve a sense of family that children provide, and to have a sense of immortality through having children.[28]

Family Relationships, Attitudes, and Behaviors

In the 1980s several studies compared parenting behaviors of divorced lesbian mothers to divorced heterosexual mothers. In both groups mothers had custody of the children.[29-31] The studies were in agreement that there were no significant differences in the quality of family relationships between groups. More recently, studies have looked at planned lesbian families – where children were conceived through donor insemination and compared them to heterosexual-led families and found that measures of self-esteem, psychological adjustment, parental stress, anxiety, depression, and attitudes toward child-rearing revealed no significant differences between groups.[30, 32, 33]

Several studies also compared divorced gay fathers with divorced heterosexual fathers (neither group had custody of the children); no differences were found in terms of nurturance and parental roles. Fathers in both groups were involved with their children and were equally nurturing, although gay fathers were found to adhere to stricter disciplinary guidelines, to place greater emphasis on guidance and cognitive skills, and to be more involved in children's activities.[28, 34, 35] Gay fathers were more cautious about displaying physical affection toward their partners in front of the children than were their heterosexual counterparts.[35]

Other studies considered the partnership status of divorced gay fathers and its effect on the quality of parenting. Crosbie-Burnett et al. reported that family satisfaction was reported to be highest by gay fathers, their partners, and the children when the partner was well integrated into the family.[36,37] Another study found that gay fathers who had a partner and especially those who lived with a partner gave themselves higher marks for managing parental challenges than did single gay fathers.[38]

Gender Identity and Sexual Orientation of Children of Gay Parents

A long held myth about gay parenting is that children of gay parents would likely be confused about their gender identity and would more likely be gay. This assumption has been explored in several studies. Studies of young children of lesbian mothers reveal no differences in their choices of toys, dress, activity, or choice of friends from those children raised by heterosexual mothers.[25] Studies of adolescents revealed no differences as well. Huggins looked at 36 adolescents between the ages of 13 and 19 half of whom had divorced heterosexual mothers and half of whom had divorced lesbian mothers. Only one subject, a son of a heterosexual mother, identified himself as gay.[39] Three studies examined the sexual preferences of children of gay fathers. Bailey et al. queried 43 men between the ages of 17 and 43 who were conceived in a heterosexual relationship, but whose fathers divorced or separated and became openly gay. Thirty-seven subjects were heterosexual.[40] Another study described 19 sons and daughters of gay men who were between the ages of 14 and 35 years of age. Sixteen reported a heterosexual preference.[41] Miller studied 14 sons and daughters of gay fathers. Of that group of children, who were between the ages of 14 and 33 years of age, two described themselves as lesbian or gay.[42]

The sexual orientation of adults raised by gay parents has also been studied. Tasker and Golombok compared young adults raised by lesbian mothers to young adults raised by single heterosexual mothers and found no differences between groups in rates of reported same sex attraction.[43] In general, studies suggest that children raised by gay parents do not identify as gay in significantly higher rates than do children raised by heterosexual parents.[18]

The Social and Psychological Adjustment of Children of Gay Parents

The social and psychological well-being of children of gay and lesbian parents has long been an area of consideration by researchers based on the following concerns: that children in gay households may be at risk for psychopathology because they lack a live-in male or female role model; that such children may be exposed to a higher level of stress by virtue of the fact that they are growing up in a gay household: and that children with gay parents will likely suffer stigmatization and peer victimization leading to lower self-esteem.[17]

Studies looking at young children of lesbian two-mother families found that they were no more likely to be rated as having psychological difficulties than children raised in two parent heterosexual households.[3,31] In studies of older children Gartrell et al. found that 10-year-olds with lesbian mothers did not differ from population-based norms in rates of emotional and behavioral problems.[44] Another study compared 12–16-year-olds from lesbian-led and heterosexual-led families and found no differences in rates of depression, anxiety, and overall psychological functioning.[45]

Wainwright et al. examined the psychosocial adjustment of adolescents living with female same sex parents and compared them to adolescents living in opposite-sex parents and found that in terms of self-esteem, psychological adjustment, academic achievement, and parental warmth, there were no significant differences between groups. What the authors determined was that the teenagers' adjustment was not based on their parents' sexual orientation but rather on their relationship with their parents. Those who had closer relationships with their parents did better overall regardless of sexual orientation.[46]

A study addressing stigma and peer relationships looked at 8–12-year-olds in planned lesbian mother households and found that though reports of stigmatization by peers was low overall, those children who did perceive higher levels of stigma experienced lower levels of psychological well-being.[47] Gartrell et al. reported similar results when interviewing 10-year-olds raised in lesbian-led households. Though few reported experiencing homophobia, those who did experience homophobia suffered more emotional and behavioral problems.[44]

Gay Fatherhood through Assisted Reproduction

As gay men increasingly choose fatherhood through surrogacy and egg donation, there are as yet no studies on the well-being of children resulting from these procedures. However, two recent studies have begun to explore the demographic, medical, and psychological aspects of gay men seeking fatherhood through ART. Greenfeld and Seli medically and psychologically assessed the first 30 gay men seeking ART in their program (15 couples) and reported their findings. All subjects met medical and psychological criteria for acceptance into the program. All of the couples were in a committed relationship and had been together for at least 6 years. Subjects had given the decision as to who would provide the sperm a great deal of careful thought. Most of the subjects (80%) chose one partner to be the sperm donor. He was the elder, the one with "better genes," or the one who cared most about being biologically related to the resulting offspring. Three couples chose to transfer an embryo from each partner.[17]

Bergman et al. looked at the transition to parenthood for gay fathers whose children were conceived through surrogacy. Through structured interviews with one of the partners of 40 gay male couples, the authors described demographic and psychological changes in the lives of gay males as a result of parenthood. Fathers were predominantly Caucasian and socioeconomically well-off (mean income was $270,000). Subjects reported changes in lifestyle with friends more likely to be other parents, changes in job with one partner often opting to be the stay-at-home father, greater closeness with families of origin, and increased self-esteem as a result of becoming fathers.[48]

Medical Aspects of Reproduction for Same Sex Couples

Medical screening of same sex couples follows ASRM guidelines for medical screening of heterosexual couples entering ART programs with the obvious qualification that, in the case of lesbian couples, two women are involved in the screening and, in the case of gay males, it is two men. While both partners are part of the initial screening, typically, the partner providing the gametes ultimately becomes the identified patient.

Lesbian Couples

Medical screening for lesbian couples entering an ART program includes a meeting with the primary physician who takes a careful medical history of both partners and discusses the options for treatment. These include intrauterine insemination with donor sperm,

IVF with donor sperm, and so-called reciprocal IVF where one partner provides the oocytes and the other carries the pregnancy. This medical consultation includes the couple's plans for proceeding. Who, for example, will carry the pregnancy? Who will provide the sperm?

Gay Male Couples

Medical screening of gay male couples entering an ART program includes a meeting with the primary physician who takes a careful medical history of both partners and provides an explanation of the procedures involved in ART using oocyte donation and gestational surrogacy. The partner providing the sperm also undergoes a semen analysis and communicable disease testing mandated by the US Food and Drug Administration (FDA).

Social and Psychological Aspects of Same Sex Reproduction

The transition to parenthood for most couples, heterosexual or gay, involves decision-making and thoughtfulness and raises a number of concerns. Is this the right time to have a child? Will we be good parents? Can we afford to have children? Is this a world we want to bring a child into? For the gay couple, however, the process can be much more complicated.[49] Gay men and women choosing parenthood through assisted reproduction often struggle with homophobic attitudes in society, questionable family and social support, legal issues, and the decisions they must make in order to achieve conception. Who will provide the sperm and the egg? Who will carry the pregnancy?

Homophobia

Homophobia is described as negative feelings toward homosexuals and those thought to be homosexual. These feelings include antipathy, contempt, prejudice, aversion, and irrational fear. Homophobia can lead to discrimination and in the worst cases is state sponsored and can lead to criminalization and prosecution of homosexual behaviors. Eighty countries around the world consider homosexuality illegal, and five countries carry out the death penalty for homosexual behavior (Iran, Mauritania, Saudi Arabia, Sudan, and Yemen).[18]

Internalized homophobia refers to negative feelings toward oneself because of one's homosexuality. Those who experience internalized homophobia display lower levels of self-esteem, lower levels of disclosure about being gay, decreased family and social support, and greater psychological distress.[49]

Gay couples contemplating parenthood, especially those who have themselves been the victims of discrimination and homophobia, may be concerned that their offspring may be discriminated against for having gay parents. Those who experience internalized homophobia may struggle with their own beliefs that homosexuality is wrong and/or that gay persons are indeed less fit to be parents than heterosexual persons. They may subscribe to the belief that every child needs both a mother and a father and that growing up in a gay household is therefore harmful to children.

Family and Social Support

When contemplating parenthood, heterosexual couples may take for granted social and family support for their decision to have a child, but such is often not the case for same sex couples. Gay men and women often face family dissolution, social isolation, and even violence as a result of coming out. Even family and friends who have shown support for their gay friend or family member may recoil at the idea of gay parenthood. Thus, same sex couples may face non-support and even moral condemnation from family and friends when announcing their intention to become parents at the very time they could use that support the most.[18] The act of parenting may raise hostility and the old mythology that children may be stigmatized or that gay men and women are psychologically unfit to parent.

On the other hand, studies report that the very act of having children brings some gay couples closer to their families. Bergman et al. found that the gay men in their study reported feeling closer to family once they had children.[49] Gartrell et al. in a longitudinal study of the transition to parenthood among lesbian couples found that post childbirth 69% of the 84 lesbian mothers reported that having a child did indeed enhance the quality of their relationship with their family.[44] Gay couples who become parents often find great changes in their social life. They may shift from having gay friends who are childless and have no desire to have children to spending more time with other parents, gay or heterosexual.

Legal Issues

Despite the fact that same sex marriage is legal in some parts of the USA (and some other parts of the world), same sex couples continue to be denied the same legal protections that are provided to heterosexual couples.[18] For the most part, heterosexuals who are planning to become parents do not start the process with a legal consultation as is so often the case for same sex couples. Typically, when same sex couples become parents together, even though they share an equal commitment to parenting, the partner who is biologically related to the offspring is generally regarded as the "legal parent." In some cases the nonbiological parent gains legal parenthood through a process known as second-parent adoption. Unfortunately, fewer than half the states allow second-parent adoption leaving couples to seek legal rights through wills or powers of attorney. Many states solve such issues through the courts on a "case by case basis."

In an article promoting the importance of second-parent adoption for gay families, the American Academy of Pediatrics argues that denying legal parent status through adoption for second (nonbiological) parents prevents "these children from enjoying the psychological and legal security that comes from having two willing, capable, and loving parents".[50] The legal sanction provided by second-parent adoption accomplishes the following: second-parent custody rights are protected should the legal parent die; protects second-parent rights to custody should the couple separate; establishes the requirement for child support from both if the couple separates, ensures child's eligibility for health benefits from both parents; gives both parents the legal right to make medical decisions for their children; and creates the basis for financial security in the case of the death of either parent.[50]

Also legally complex is the subject of surrogacy. A legal contract between surrogate and the intended parents is required in all cases, but when the intended parents are of the same sex, the issues may be more difficult. For example, Wald presents the scenario of a gay male couple who live in New York and contract with a gestational surrogate who lives in Ohio. Because the birth certificate is based on where the surrogate delivers, and in this case it would be Ohio, second-parent adoption does not apply in Ohio for same sex couples, so only one of the fathers would legally be the parent.[51]

Decision-Making for Prospective Gay Parents

Same sex couples planning parenthood often give consideration to the question of whether to adopt or to choose assisted reproduction. Lesbians who choose the latter often do so for one or more of the following reasons: because of one partner's desire to experience pregnancy and childbirth, because they wish to raise a child from birth, and/or because they believe that the biological connection is more likely to elicit family support.[18] Gay men choosing surrogacy over adoption do so because they may want the biological connection to the child, they desire to raise the child from birth, and/or because they believe the surrogacy process may be easier and will allow them more control over the intrauterine life of their future children. In addition, some gay men are concerned about the possible emotional difficulties a child may experience later in life when they learn they were relinquished by birth parents.[52]

Lesbians: Who Will Carry the Pregnancy?

Lesbians choosing assisted reproduction need to give consideration as to who will carry the pregnancy, whether to use a known or unknown sperm donor, and what donor characteristics they regard as most important. For some, the issue of who will carry the pregnancy is an easy decision if one partner very much wants to be pregnant and the other does not. Among lesbian couples who both want to carry a pregnancy, they typically decide that each should have the opportunity to do so, and hence the decision becomes about who will go first. That decision usually is based on the age of the intended mothers, their work schedules, and sometimes about which partner has the greater sense of urgency.[2] Goldberg looked at the transition to parenthood in 29 lesbian couples and how they made the decision about the carrying the pregnancy. In 41% of the couples the birth mother was the one who had the greatest desire to experience pregnancy and birth. For 14% the reason was primarily determined by difficulties in fertility, where the partner who had initially opted to carry the pregnancy had not gotten pregnant and the other partner subsequently became the birth mother. Forty-five percent made the decision based on practicality – who had the better job? The better insurance? Who was more able to take maternity leave? While most couples in the study found that the decisions they made really worked for them, those who chose for fertility reasons often had significant difficulty with the decision, especially when it involved choosing the partner who had least wanted to carry.[53]

Lesbians: Decisions about the Donor

Once couples have made a decision about who will carry the pregnancy, they need to think about the sperm donor. Part of the decision-making process is whether to use an anonymous donor or one who is known to them (such as a friend). Previous studies of heterosexual couples who need a donor sperm found that they overwhelmingly choose anonymous donors.[54] but for lesbians who weigh the pros and the cons of known versus anonymous carefully, the decision is mixed. Goldberg studied pregnant lesbians and their partners and found that 59% chose an anonymous donor, 31% chose a known donor, and 10% chose an "identity release" donor who is willing to be contacted when the offspring reach 18 (increasingly, sperm banks are offering a category of sperm donors who are willing to have their identity released to offspring).[53]

Some women choose anonymous donors because they do not know anyone who would be willing to donate or anyone they would be willing to ask to donate, but others are very clear about why they want to choose an anonymous donor. Some cite legal concerns about the possibility that a biological father might want to claim custody and, in any case, that they want to raise a child together without interference from another person. Sometimes it is the nonbiological mother who feels most strongly about using an anonymous donor because of concern that using someone known would complicate and potentially interfere with the security of a two-mother family and that a third party could even potentially threaten her position as a co-parent.[18]

Lesbian couples who choose a known donor want their children to have information about who their biological father is, though they typically do not want him to serve in the role of father. These couples often make the decision out of concern for the offspring, feeling that they may want information about their biological and genetic history. Finally, some lesbian couples use known donors because they desire to complete the insemination process in private (either with home insemination or through sexual intercourse with the donor) without interference from the medical establishment. Another issue for lesbian couples when considering using a donor is to determine the characteristics they consider most important about the donor. Just as heterosexual couples seeking donor sperm often select a donor who physically resembles the intended father, so too do lesbians often choose physical characteristics such as eye color, hair color, height, and race which are physically comparable to the nonbiological mother. These commonalities may include interests, hobbies, talents, education, and occupation. Couples often feel that this matching is important to help create a more cohesive family link based on shared traits common to both mothers.[18]

Gay Male Couples: Who Will Provide the Sperm?

In their study of gay male couples seeking fatherhood through ART, Greenfeld and Seli found that participants typically had given the question of who would provide the sperm a great deal of thought and were very clear about their decision. Most chose only one of the partners to donate, but their reasons for choosing him were varied. Sometimes it was because he was the one who cared more about the biological connection or because he had "better genes." In other instances one partner was chosen because he was older and both agreed that he should "go first," or in some cases, one partner had children from a previous heterosexual relationship and the other partner wanted a chance to be biologically related to a child. The few couples that had equal desire for biological fatherhood chose to inseminate equal numbers of oocytes to transfer one embryo from each partner to the carrier.[17] Because there are so few studies on gay men and ART, we do not know whether the nonbiological father feels in any way left out of the process or less connected to the offspring than the biological father.

Gay Male Couples: Decisions about Donors and Surrogates

Gay men also face the decision of whether to use a known egg donor or an anonymous donor. Those who seek a known donor or an agency "identity release" donor often have in mind the idea that they want to provide offspring information about their genetic heritage. One study found that gay males who used anonymous donors looked for these characteristics: the donor should be tall, attractive, educated, and bearing a resemblance to the non-inseminating partner.[17]

Typically, gay couples do not choose donors with whom they and their offspring will have ongoing relationships, but the same is not always true for the surrogates. Couples usually contract with a surrogate who is recruited through an agency. During the treatment process and subsequent pregnancy, gay men often have a close relationship with the surrogate and appreciate her input, defer to her on aspects of the pregnancy, and value her female presence.[17] In fact gay men often form ongoing relationships with the surrogate because "she is necessarily part of the pregnancy for the duration".[54] Another issue of importance for gay men when choosing a surrogate is to determine that she resides and will deliver in a state where surrogacy is legal and where both fathers can be on the birth certificate.

Psychological Evaluation of Same Sex Couples Entering ART

The psychological consultation with same sex couples entering ART programs is both informational and evaluative. Pretreatment preparation and information provides couples with a clear understanding of the physical, financial, legal, and emotional demands of the treatment. Gay men and women do not typically enter these ART after a history of infertility and thus are not familiar with the medical treatment and the emotional ups and downs that can accompany it. The consultation is evaluative in that it is important to determine that couples are psychologically prepared for this treatment. Specifically, it is important to determine that they share a close and supportive relationship and are equally committed to the process, and that they do not have complicated social and psychiatric problems that could interfere with the treatment or their ability to become or function as parents. The consultation follows the recommended guidelines of the American Society for Reproductive Medicine as well as the guidelines of the American Psychological Association for counseling same sex couples.[55, 56]

Summary and Conclusions

Gay men and women increasingly seek assistance from fertility programs in order to achieve parenthood. Because same sex couples do not get pregnant accidentally, they enter these programs after careful consideration and thought.[52] Fertility programs offering ART to same sex couples need to be respectful of couples' relationships and demonstrate an appreciation of the challenges unique to same sex couples participating in their programs. Clinicians and staff members need to work toward providing a "gay-friendly" environment that is gender neutral and sensitive to all matters homophobic.

The literature on gay men and women and their children conceived through assisted reproduction has some limitations. Most of the studies have small sample size and their subjects are predominantly white, urban, well educated, middle to upper class, and lesbian. In fact, in a review of 23 studies published between 1978 and 2003, only three addressed gay fathers.[26] Despite these limitations the consensus is that these families are doing well and that there are no significant differences in the psychological development in children raised by gay families compared to children raised by heterosexual parents.[23, 25, 26]

References

1 Gates G, Ost J. *The Gay and Lesbian Atlas.* Washington DC: The Urban Institute; 2004.

2 Johnson SM, O'Connor E. *The Gay Baby Boom: The Psychology of Gay Parenthood.* New York: New York University Press; 2002.

3 Patterson CJ. Families of the lesbian baby boom: parent's division of labor and children's adjustment. *Dev Psychol.* 1995:31:115–23.

4 United States Census 2010. 2010 census demographic profiles. See http://www.census.gov/2010census/news/press-kits/demographic-profiles.html.

5 Gates G, Badgett CN, Macombe JE, Chambers K. *Adoption and Foster Care by Lesbians and Gay Parents in the United States.* Washington DC: The Urban Institute; 2007.

6 Deprez EE. State-by-state laws on gay marriage produce patchwork quilt. Bloomberg News, February 10, 2012.

7 Adam B. *The Rise of a Gay and Lesbian Movement.* New York: Twayne; 1995.

8 Carter D. *Stonewall: The Riots That Sparked the Gay Revolution.* New York: St. Martin's Press; 2005.

9 Bayer R. *Homosexuality and American Psychiatry: The Politics of Diagnosis.* Princeton: Princeton University Press; 1987.

10 Cooper L., Cates P. *Too High a Price: The Case against Restricting Gay Parenting.* New York: American Civil Liberties Union Foundation; 2006.

11 "Founder of lesbian sperm bank named a 'top innovator'" Jan 29, 2009 PRWeb http://www.prweb.com/releases/lesbian/spermbank/prweb1863014.htm. Accessed 11 Aug 2011.

12 Dunstan GR. Ethical aspects of donor insemination. *J Med Ethics.* 1975;1(1):42–4.

13 Fletcher JC. Artificial insemination for lesbians: ethical considerations. *Arch Intern Med.* 1985;31:105–14.

14 Marina S, Marina D, Marina F, Fosas N, Galiana N, Jove I. Sharing motherhood: biological lesbian co-mothers, a new IVF indication. *Hum Reprod.* 2010;25: 938–41.

15 Hanafin H. Surrogacy and gestational carrier participants. In Covington SN, Burns LH, editors, *Infertility Counseling: A Comprehensive Handbook for Clinicians*. 2nd ed. New York: Cambridge University Press; 2006, pp. 370–86.

16 Utian WH, Sheean L, Goldfarb JM, Kiwi R. Successful pregnancy after in vitro fertilization embryo transfer from an infertile woman to a surrogate. *N Engl J Med*. 1985;313(21):1351–2.

17 Greenfeld DA, Seli E. Gay men choosing parenthood through assisted reproduction: medical and psychological considerations. *Fertil Steril*. 2011;95: 225–9.

18 Goldberg AE. *Lesbian and Gay Parents and Their Children: Research on the Family Life Style*. Washington DC: American Psychological Association; 2010.

19 Greenfeld DA. Gay male couples and assisted reproduction: should we assist? *Fertil Steril*. 2007;88: 18–20.

20 Gumankind AD, Caplan AL, Braverman AM. Screening practices and beliefs of assisted reproductive technology programs. *Fertil Steril*. 2005;83: 61–7.

21 Ethics Committee of the American Society for Reproductive Medicine. Access to fertility treatment by gays, lesbians, and unmarried persons. *Fertil Steril*. 2006;86:1333–5.

22 D'Augelli AR, Rendina HJ, Sinclair KO, Grossman AH. Lesbian and gay youth's aspirations for marriage and raising children. *J LGBT Issues Counsel*. 2006/2007;12:77–91.

23 Tasker F. Lesbian mothers, gay fathers, and their children: a review. *J Dev Behav Pediatr*. 2005:26:224–40.

24 Patterson CJ. Children of lesbian and gay parents. *Child Dev*. 1992;63(5):1025–42.

25 Perrin EC. Committee on Psychosocial Aspects of Child and Family Health. Technical report: co parent or second parent adoption by it sex parents. *Pediatrics*. 2002;109:341–4.

26 Anderssen N, Amlie C, Ytteroy EA. Outcomes of children with lesbian or gay parents: a review of studies from 1978 to 2000. *Scand J Psychol*. 2002;43: 335–51.

27 Bos HMW, van Balen F, van den Boom DC. Planned lesbian families: their desire and motivation to have children. *Hum Reprod*. 2003;18:2216–24.

28 Bigner JJ, Jacobsen RB. Parenting behaviors of homosexual and heterosexual fathers. *J Homosex*. 1989;18:163–72.

29 Kirkpatrick M, Smith C, Roy R. Lesbian mothers and their children: a comparative study. *Am J Orthopsychiatry*. 1981;51:545–51.

30 Golombok S, Spencer A, Rutter M. Children in lesbian and single parent households: psychosexual and psychiatric appraisal. *J Child Psychol Psychiatry*. 1983;24:551–72.

31 Green R, Mandel JB, Hotvedt ME, Gray J, Smith L. Lesbian mothers and their children: a comparison with solo parent heterosexual mothers and their children. *Arch Sex Behav*. 1986;15:167–84.

32 Flaks DK, Ficher I, Masterpasqua F, Joseph G. Lesbians choosing motherhood: a comparative study of lesbian and heterosexual parents and their children. *Dev Psychol*. 1995;31:105–14.

33 Golombok S, Tasker F, Murray C. Children raised in fatherless families from infancy: family relationships and the socioemotional development of children of lesbian and single heterosexual mothers. *J Child Psychol Psychiatry*. 1997;38:783–91.

34 Turner PH, Scadden L, Harris MB. Parenting in gay and lesbian families. *J Gay Lesbian Psychother*. 1990;1:55–66.

35 Harris MB, Turner PH. Gay and lesbian parents. *J Homosex*. 1985;12:101–13.

36 Bigner JJ, Jacobsen RB. The value of children to gay and heterosexual fathers. *J Homosex*. 1989;18: 163–72.

37 Bigner JJ, Jacobsen RB. Adult responses to child behavior and attitudes toward fathering: gay and non-gay fathers. *J Homosex*. 1992;23:99–112.

38 Crosbie-Burnett M, Helbrecht L. A descriptive empirical study of gay male stepfamilies. *Fam Relat*. 1993;42:256–62.

39 Huggins SL. A comparative study of self-esteem of adolescent children of divorced lesbian mothers and divorced heterosexual mothers. In Bozett FW, editor, *Homosexuality and the Family*. New York: Harrington Park Press; 1989.

40 Bailey JM, Bobrow D, Wolfe M, Mikach S. Sexual orientation of adult sons of gay fathers. *Dev Psychol*. 1995;31:124–9.

41 Bozett FW. Gay fathers: how and why they disclose their homosexuality to their children. *Fam Relat*. 1980;29:173–9.

42 Miller B. Gay fathers and their children. *Fam Coord*. 1979;28:544–52.

43 Golombok S, Tasker F. Do parents influence the sexual orientation of their children: findings from a longitudinal study of lesbian families. *Develop Psychol*. 1996;32:3–11

44 Gartrell N, Deck A, Rodas C, Peyser H, Banks A. The national lesbian family study: 4. Interviews with the 10-year-old children. *Am J Orthopsychiatry*. 2005;75:518–24.

45 Rivers I, Poteat VP, Noret N. Victimization, social support, and psychosocial functioning in same-sex and opposite-sex couples in the United States. *Dev Psychol.* 2008;44:127–34.

46 Wainwright J, Russell S, Patterson C. Psychosocial adjustment, school outcomes, and romantic relationships of adolescents with same-sex parents. *Child Dev.* 2004;75:1886–98.

47 Bos HMW, van Balen F. Children in planned lesbian families: stigmatization, psychological adjustment, and protective factors. *Cult Health Sex.* 2008;10:221–36.

48 Bergman K, Rubio RJ, Green RJ, Padros E. Gay men who become fathers via surrogacy: the transition to parenthood. *J GLBT Fam Stud.* 2010;6:111–41.

49 Newcomb M. Internalized homophobia and internalizing mental health problems: a meta-analytical review. *Clin Psychol Rev.* 2010;30: 1019–29.

50 American Academy of Pediatrics. Coparent or second-parent adoption. *Pediatrics.* 2002;109:339–40.

51 Wald D. Gay surrogacy: a legal perspective. 2007.

52 Lev AI. Gay dads: choosing surrogacy. *Lesbian Gay Psychol Rev.* 2006;7:73–7.

53 Goldberg AE, Sayer AG. Lesbian couples' relationship quality across the transition to parenthood. *J Marriage Fam.* 2006;68:87–100.

54 Mitchell V, Green RJ. Different storks for different folks: gay and lesbian parents' experiences with alternative insemination and surrogacy. *J GLBT Stud.* 2007;3:81–104.

55 American Society for Reproductive Medicine. Psychological assessment of gamete donors and recipients. *Fertil Steril.* 2007;77 Suppl 5:S6–8.

56 Division 44/Committee on Lesbian, Gay and Bisexual Clients. Guidelines for psychotherapy with lesbian, gay and bisexual clients. *Am Psychol.* 2000;55: 1440–51.

7

Rights, Interests, and Possible People

Derek Parfit

Do possible people have rights and interests? Professor Hare has argued that they do. I shall claim that, even if they don't, we should often act *as if* they do.

We can start with future people. Suppose that the testing of a nuclear weapon would, through radiation, cause a number of deformities in the people who are born within the next ten years. This would be against the interests of these future people. These people will exist whether or not the weapon is tested, and, if it is, they will be affected for the worse – they will be worse off than they would otherwise have been. We can harm these people though they don't live *now*, just as we can harm foreigners though they don't live *here*.

What about *possible* people? The difference between these and future people can be defined as follows. Suppose that we must act in one of two ways. "Future people" are the people who will exist whichever way we act. "Possible people" are the people who will exist if we act in one way, but who won't exist if we act in the other way. To give the simplest case: if we are wondering whether to have children, the children that we *could* have are possible people.

Do they have rights and interests? Suppose, first, that we decide to have these children. Can this affect their interests? We can obviously rephrase this question so that it no longer asks about possible people. We can ask: can it be in, or be against, an *actual* person's interests to have been conceived? I shall return to this.

Suppose, next, that we decide not to have children. Then these possible people never get conceived. Can *this* affect their interests? Can it, for instance, harm these children?

The normal answer would be "No." Professor Hare takes a different view. We can simplify the example he discussed. We suppose that a child is born with some serious handicap or abnormality, which is incurable, and would probably make the child's life, though still worth living, less so than a normal life. We next suppose that unless we perform some operation the child will die; and that, if it does, the parents will have another normal child, whom they wouldn't have if this child lives. The question is, should we operate?

Hare suggests that we should not. He first assumes that we ought to do what is in the best interests of all the people concerned. He then claims that among these people is "the next child in the queue" – the normal child whom the parents would later have only if the handicapped child dies. The interests of this possible child may, he thinks, "tip the balance." The possible child, unlike the actual child, "has a high prospect of a normal and happy life"; Hare would therefore claim that we do *less* harm to the actual child by failing to save his life than we do to the possible child "by stopping him from being conceived and born."

In this particular case, many would agree with Hare that we shouldn't operate, but for different reasons.

Original publication details: Derek Parfit, "Rights, Interests, and Possible People," pp. 369–75 from Samuel Gorovitz et al. (eds.), *Moral Problems in Medicine*, Englewood Cliffs, NJ: Prentice Hall, 1976. Courtesy of D. Parfit.

They may think that a new-born child is not yet a full person, with rights and interests;[1] or they may doubt whether life with a serious handicap would be worth living.

The implications of Hare's view can be better seen in another case. Take a couple who – we assume – live in an age before the world was over-populated, and who are wondering whether to have children. Suppose next that, if they do, their children's lives would probably be well worth living. Then, on Hare's view, if the couple choose not to have these children they would be doing them serious harm. Since there is no over-population, it would seem to follow that their choice is morally wrong. Most of us, I think, would deny this. We believe that there can be nothing wrong in deciding to remain childless. And if we also ask what Hare would count as over-population, his conclusion would again be widely disputed. This is another subject to which I shall return.

What I have called "Hare's view" is that we can harm people by preventing their conception. There are precedents for this view. The Talmud says that when Amram decided not to beget children, he was admonished for denying them the World to Come.[2] But, as Hare admits, his view is unusual. He would argue that it can be justified by an appeal to the logic of moral reasoning.[3] I shall not discuss whether this is so; but instead take a complementary path. I shall assume that we cannot harm those we don't conceive. Even so, I shall argue, it is hard to avoid Hare's conclusions.

The principle with which Hare works is that we should do what is in the best interests of those concerned. Most of us accept some principle of this kind. We may believe that other principles are often more important; but we accept, as one of our principles, something to do with interests, with preferences, or with happiness and misery. As this list suggests, such a principle can take different forms. We need only look at a single difference. The principle can take what I call an "impersonal" form: for example, it can run

(1) We should do what most reduces misery and increases happiness.

It can instead take a "person-affecting" form: for example

(2) We should do what harms people the least and benefits them most.

When we can only affect actual people, those who do or will exist, the difference between these forms of the principle makes, in practice, no difference. But when we can affect *who* exists, it can make a great difference.

Return, for instance, to the childless couple in the uncrowded world. According to principle (1) – the "impersonal" principle – they should do what most increases happiness. One of the most effective ways of increasing the quality of happiness is to increase the number of happy people. So the couple ought to have children; their failure to do so is, according to (1), morally wrong.

Most of us would say: "This just shows the absurdity of the impersonal principle. What we ought to do is make people happy, not make happy people. The right principle is (2), the 'person-affecting' principle. If the couple don't have children, there is no-one whom they've harmed, or failed to benefit. That is why they have done nothing wrong."

This reply involves the rejection of Hare's view. It assumes that we cannot harm people by preventing their conception. If we *can*, the childless couple would be doing wrong even on the person-affecting principle.

We can generalize from this example. Most of us hold a person-affecting, not an impersonal, principle. If we reject Hare's view, there are cases where this makes a great practical difference. But if we accept Hare's view, it makes no difference. The person-affecting principle, when combined with Hare's view, leads to the same conclusions as the impersonal principle.

Some of these conclusions are, as I said, striking. I shall now begin to argue towards them. We can avoid these conclusions only if we *both* accept what I shall call "the restriction of our principles to acts which affect people" *and* claim that our acts cannot affect possible people. Hare denies the latter; I shall be denying the former. The person-affecting restriction seems to me, at least in any natural form, unacceptable.

We can start with one of the two questions that I postponed. Can it be in our interests to have been conceived? Can we benefit from receiving life?

If we can, the childless couple are again at fault, even on person-affecting grounds – for if they have children they will be benefitting people, as principle (2) tells them to do.

We might say: "But we can only benefit if we are made better off than we would otherwise have been. This couple's children wouldn't otherwise have been – so they cannot benefit from receiving life." I have doubts about this reasoning. For one thing, it implies that we cannot benefit people if we *save* their lives, for here too they wouldn't otherwise have been. True, there are problems in comparing life with non-existence. But if we assume that a person's life has been well worth living, should we not agree that to have saved this person's life many years ago would be to have done this person a great benefit? And if it can be in a person's interests to have had his life prolonged, even, say, just after it started, why can it not be in his interests to have had it started?

Here is a second problem. If we cannot benefit a person by conceiving him, then we cannot harm him either. But suppose we know that any child whom we could conceive will have an abnormality so severe that it will live for only a few years, will never develop, and will suffer fairly frequent pain. It would seem to be clearly wrong to go ahead, knowingly, and conceive such a child.[4] And the main reason why it would be wrong is that the child will suffer. But if we cannot *harm* a child by giving it a life of this kind, then this reason why the act is wrong cannot be stated in "person-affecting" terms. We shall have to say, "It is wrong because it increases suffering." We should then be back with half of the impersonal principle; and it will be hard, in consistency, to avoid the other half. (We might perhaps claim that only suffering matters morally – that happiness is morally trivial. But this position, though superficially attractive, collapses when we think it through.)

We have been asking whether the act of conceiving a child can affect this child, for better or worse. If we answer "Yes," the person-affecting restriction makes no difference; principle (2) leads to the same conclusions as principle (1). We may therefore wish to answer "No" – but to this we have found objections.

The problem here can, I think, be solved. We can state the person-affecting principle in a different form:

(3) It is wrong to do what, of the alternatives, affects people for the worse.

We interpret (3) so that if people fail to receive possible benefits, they count as affected for the worse. If we adopt principle (3), we can afford to allow that conceiving someone is a case of affecting him. Since failing to receive benefits counts as being affected for the worse, principle (3) still tells us – like principle (2) – to do what benefits people most. But there is one exception. To the one benefit of receiving life (3) – unlike (2) – gives no weight. For when we fail to give this benefit, there isn't an actual person who fails to receive it – who is thus affected for the worse. (I am now assuming, you remember, that we cannot affect possible people.)

Most of us, I claimed, think there is nothing wrong in *not* having children, even if they would have been very happy. But we think that having children who are bound to suffer is wrong. Principle (3) supports this asymmetrical pair of judgments. It supports our view that the Childless Couple did no wrong; but it also supports our view about "wrongful conception" – for the child here is an actual person affected for the worse.

In the move from (2) to (3), a natural principle is revised in a somewhat artificial way. But this revision does not seem to drain the principle of its plausibility. All the revision does is this. When we are choosing what to do, we are told to aim, not to achieve the outcome where people are better off, but to avoid the outcome where they are worse off. This procedure, adding up the "minuses," seems to be just as general and as plausible as the other, adding up the "pluses." So we are not, in moving to (3), "tailoring" our principles in an *ad-hoc* way. And the justification for the move is that only principle (3) (combined with the assumption that conceiving is affecting) gives support to the asymmetrical judgments that we find plausible.[5]

So far, so good. But I shall now argue that the person-affecting principle needs to be more drastically revised. This *may* drain it of its plausibility.

Consider the following case, which involves two women. The first is one month pregnant, and is told by her doctor that, unless she takes a simple treatment, the child she is carrying will develop a certain handicap.

We suppose again that life with this handicap would probably be worth living, but less so than a normal life. It would obviously be wrong for the mother not to take the treatment, for this will handicap her child. And the person-affecting principle tells us that this would be wrong. (Note that we need not assume that a one-month-old foetus is a person, for there *will be* a person whom the woman has affected for the worse.)

We next suppose that there is a second woman, who is about to stop taking contraceptive pills so that she can have another child. She is told that she has a temporary condition such that any child she conceives now will have just the same handicap; but that if she waits three months she will then conceive a normal child. It seems clear that it would be wrong for this second woman, by not waiting, to deliberately have a handicapped rather than a normal child. And it seems (at least to me) clear that this would be just *as* wrong as it would be for the first woman to deliberately handicap her child.

But if the second woman does deliberately have a handicapped child, has she harmed him – affected him for the worse? We must first ask: "Could he truly claim, when he grows up, 'If my mother had waited, I would have been born three months later, as a normal child'?" The answer is, "No." If his mother had waited, he would not have been born at all; she would have had a different child. When I claim this, I need not assume that the time of one's conception, or the particular cells from which one grew, are essential to one's identity. *Perhaps* we can suppose that I might have been conceived a year later, if we are supposing that my parents had no child when they in fact had me, but a year later had a child who was exactly or very much *like* me. But in our case the child the woman would have if she waits would be as unlike the child she would have now as any two of her actual children would be likely to be. Given this, we cannot claim that they would have been the same child. (To argue this in another way. Suppose that I am in fact my mother's first child and eldest son. And suppose that things had gone like this: she had no child when I was in fact born, then had a girl, then a boy. Can I claim that I, her first child, would have been that girl? Why not claim that I, her eldest son, would have been that boy? Both claims are equally good, and so, since they cannot both be true, equally bad. So, if she *had*

waited before having children, I would not have been born at all.)[6]

The second woman's handicapped child is, then, not worse off than he would otherwise have been, for he wouldn't otherwise have been. Might we still claim that in deliberately conceiving a handicapped child, the woman harms this child? We might perhaps claim this if the child's life would be not worth living – would be worse than nothing; but we have assumed that it would be worth living. And in this case being handicapped is the only way in which this child can receive life. So the case is like that in which a doctor removes a person's limb to save his life. It would not be true, at least in a morally relevant sense, that the doctor harmed this person, or affected him for the worse. We seem bound to say the same about my second woman.

I conclude, then, that if the second woman deliberately conceives a handicapped rather than a normal child, she would not be harming this child. The first woman, if she deliberately neglects the treatment, would be harming her child. Notice next that in every other way the two acts are exactly similar. The side-effects on other people should be much the same. These side-effects would provide *some* person-affecting grounds for the claim that the second woman's act would be wrong. But it is obvious that if we judge the two acts on person-affecting principles, the first woman's act must be considerably *more* wrong. In her case, there are not just side-effects – her child is seriously harmed. The second woman's child is *not* harmed. Since this is the only difference between the two acts, the case provides a test for person-affecting principles. The impersonal principle tells us to reduce misery and increase happiness, whether or not people are affected for better or worse. If there is any plausibility in the restriction to acts which affect people, it must be worse to *harm* someone than to cause equivalent unhappiness in a way which harms no-one. The second woman's act must, in other words, be less wrong than the first's. If we think that it is not less wrong, we cannot accept the restriction to acts which affect people.

The acts which I have described are of course unusual. But this does not make them a worse test for the person-affecting restriction. On the contrary, they are unusual because they are designed as a test. The two women's acts are designed to be as similar as they could be, except in one respect. Each woman deliberately brings it about that she has a handicapped rather than a normal child. The only difference is that in one case the handicapped and the normal child are the same child, while in the other they are not. This is precisely the difference which, on the person-affecting principle, matters. If we think that the two acts would be just as wrong, we cannot believe that it does matter.

Some of you may think that the person-affecting principle survives this test. You may think: "Since the second woman doesn't harm her child, what she does *is* less wrong." But there are other cases where such implications seem harder to accept. Take genetic counseling. We could not advise the dominant carriers of diseases to accept genetic counseling *for the sake* of their children, for if they reject this counseling, and marry other dominant carriers, it will not be true that their children will

have been harmed, or affected for the worse. Or again, Dr. Kass has argued that it would be wrong to use certain kinds of artificial fertilization, on the ground that if children are conceived in these ways, rather than in normal ways, they run greater risks of certain deformities.[7] But these particular children cannot be conceived in normal ways. For them, the alternatives are artificial fertilization, or nothing. So we can only claim that we would be harming them, or affecting them for the worse, if the risks of deformities were so great that their lives would probably be not worth living.

When we turn to population policy, the implications become much harder to accept....

[Editorial note: the rest of Parfit's talk is not reprinted here. His more recent thoughts about the problems discussed in this talk, and the larger problems of population policy, will appear in a future issue of the journal, *Philosophy & Public Affairs*, under the title "Overpopulation."]

Notes

1 Cf. Michael Tooley, "Abortion and Infanticide," *Philosophy and Public Affairs*, 2, No. 1 (Fall 1972) [see chapter 2 in this volume].

2 Quoted in G. Tedeschi, "On Tort Liability for 'Wrongful Life,'" *Israel Law Review*, October 1966, p. 514, footnote 3.

3 The logic he describes in his books, *The Language of Morals*, O.U.P. 1952, and *Freedom and Reason*, O.U.P. 1963.

4 For a legal discussion of related issues, see "A Cause of Action for 'Wrongful Life,'" *Minnesota Law Review*, 55, No. 1 (November 1970).

5 This asymmetry is discussed in Jan Narveson's two articles: "Utilitarianism and New Generations," *Mind*, January 1967, and "Moral Problems of Population," *The Monist*, January 1973. I have learned much from both of these.

6 For a different view, take a remark in Gwen Raverat's *Period Piece*, Faber and Faber 1952, "It is always a fascinating problem to consider who we would have been if our mother (or our father) had married another person."

7 "Making babies—the new biology and the 'old' morality," Leon Kass, *The Public Interest*, Winter, 1972.

8

The Ethics of Uterus Transplantation

Ruby Catsanos, Wendy Rogers, and Mianna Lotz

Introduction

Infertility can be devastating for many women. For some the cause is uterine infertility, that is, dysfunction or absence of the uterus. At present, women suffering from uterine infertility who wish to have children have two options: adoption or gestational surrogacy. Uterus transplantation (hereafter 'UTx') creates a third option: to conceive *and gestate* a pregnancy, thereby fulfilling what some women describe as a desire not just for 'my own child' but for 'my own pregnancy'.

UTx is currently the subject of research in a number of centres in the US and Europe. Transplants have been attempted in mice, rabbits, sheep and non-human primates with varying degrees of success.[1] One human uterus transplant has been performed to date, in Saudi Arabia in 2000.[2] In early 2007 a team of US doctors led by Dr Giuseppe Del Priore from New York Downtown Hospital received approval from its Institutional Review Board to undertake a staged human uterine transplantation study.[3]

Although technically a development in the field of organ (or more precisely, composite tissue) transplantation, the ultimate goal of UTx in humans is to cure uterine infertility, making it also a form of assisted reproduction. Consequently, the ethical issues associated with uterus transplantation arise at the intersection of two bioethical debates: expansion of the field of organ transplantation, and developments in assisted reproduction technologies (ART).

In this paper we map out some of the main areas for ethical investigation in respect of uterine transplantation. Our purpose here is relatively modest. We aim only to highlight the as-yet-undiscussed areas of potential ethical concern that will require further investigation and analysis in relation to uterine transplants in women. Arriving at an overall ethical conclusion about the moral acceptability of UTx and proposing possible resolutions, must await a future discussion.

Ethical Foundation of Transplantation

Organ and tissue transplants have become an accepted part of modern medical practice over the past fifty years. Transplants offer improvements in mortality and morbidity through replacement of diseased organs with healthy ones from either living or cadaveric donors. The earliest organ transplants were reserved for patients facing imminent death, and post-transplant survival rates were low. In the fifty-plus years since then, advances in both surgical techniques and immunosuppressive therapies have led to significant

Original publication details: Ruby Catsanos, Wendy Rogers, and Mianna Lotz, "The Ethics of Uterus Transplantation," pp. 65–73 from *Bioethics* 27: 2 (2013). Reproduced by permission of John Wiley & Sons.

Bioethics: An Anthology, Third Edition. Edited by Helga Kuhse, Udo Schüklenk, and Peter Singer.
© 2016 John Wiley & Sons, Inc. Published 2016 by John Wiley & Sons, Inc.

improvements in post-transplant morbidity and mortality. Despite these developments, organ transplantation remains an invasive procedure with potentially significant risks related to the surgical procedure itself, problems with the graft (infection, rejection) and the effects of long-term immunosuppressive therapy (including cancer and increased risk of infection). For these reasons, transplants of organs such as the heart, liver and lungs are predominantly reserved for patients with end-stage organ failure for whom there are no other treatment options. Transplants in these patients are ethically justified by appeals to beneficence, as the potential risks of transplant are (or are considered to be) outweighed by the benefits of decreased symptoms and prolonged life.

Not all organ transplants, however, are clearly life-saving. The commonest and most successful solid organ transplants are kidney transplants. While kidney transplants do lead to improvements in morbidity and mortality compared with dialysis,[4] it is possible to live for many years on dialysis. We can therefore contrast organ transplants without which the patient would die (e.g. heart or liver) with those that lead to improvements in the quality and/or length of life but which are not immediately life-saving. Historically this latter group of quality of life transplants has included kidney and eye transplants. These are relatively uncontentious as the alternatives (impaired vision, long-term dialysis) are burdensome and can impact severely on patients' choices and lifestyles. Once again, these transplants are justified by considerations of beneficence.

More recent expansions in the field of transplantation challenge this ethical balance. Transplants such as limb allografts (hand transplants) and face transplants call for ethical justification beyond that required in the more standard transplant cases.[5] If we consider hand transplants, the balance of risks and benefits is quite complicated. In terms of physical dexterity, hand transplants do not compare well to bionic hand alternatives, especially in the short-to-medium term.[6] However, for at least some recipients, function as measured by dexterity is not the most important feature of a replacement upper limb. The first double hand transplant recipient in the US had previously lived for ten years with prosthetic hooks, undertaking many activities of daily life including working and driving a car.[7] Prior to surgery in 2009, he indicated that he was motivated, at least in part, by a desire to experience tactile sensations, with their associated emotional dimensions. He stated: 'I'll be able to reach out and touch and hug. That'll be a big deal. It will be great to hold my wife's hands again.'[8] The desire to regain feeling in his upper limbs was sufficiently strong to motivate his decision for transplant, despite the risks of surgery and his existing level of function with his prostheses. Initial predictions were for the transplanted hands to achieve their functional potential within two years.[9] Yet twelve months on this recipient has achieved very little function and the revised prognosis, even with many more years of daily therapy, remains uncertain.[10] This example is not atypical, but despite the guarded prognosis, over fifty hand transplants have taken place worldwide, including sixteen double hand transplants.[11]

Examples such as these require us to be explicit about the benefits and risks at stake with transplants that aim to improve quality of life for recipients. Once we move away from evident improvements in function such as occur with eye and kidney transplants, we must take careful account of what it is that motivates patients to undertake the risks of transplantation when the outcome is uncertain, and the side-effects of long-term immunosuppression onerous. As we have seen from the hand transplant example, factors such as regaining sensation may outweigh purely functional parameters such as dexterity for individual patients. For patients undertaking face transplants, motivating factors do include functional improvement to breathing, swallowing and speaking, which are often compromised in cases of severe facial deformity. However, by far the most significant motivating factor expressed by recipients and candidates who have spoken publicly has been the chance of having a socially acceptable face, of being able to move about unnoticed in public.[12]

Matters become more complex still in relation to uterine transplantation. Women who lack a functioning uterus do not have compromised health in terms of impaired day-to-day physiological function; nor is their lack of a uterus visible or socially inhibiting in the way that prosthetic upper limbs or facial deformities typically are. Furthermore, access to adoption and surrogacy would allow such women to become mothers; their children may even be genetically related to them. However, it would seem that a key motivating factor for UTx is the desire to actually *bear* genetically-related children.[13]

The strength of this desire may stem from a number of factors. For many women, experiencing pregnancy is a central aspect of their identity as women.[14] The uterus represents a symbol of femininity, of women's biological difference from men. Pregnancy and child-birth is a unique physical and emotional experience shared only by women.[15] Many women facing the removal of their uterus through hysterectomy undergo feelings of loss and damage to their gender identity;[16] like the heart, the uterus is an organ with symbolic significance. The psychological and emotional aspects of pregnancy, the contribution of gender roles to personal identity, and societal expectations regarding procreation are difficult things to measure and weigh in relation to its risks, thereby raising questions about the ethical justification for UTx.

What Can UTx Deliver?

To date uterine transplantation research has focused on addressing the technical issues associated with transplant surgery via experimental transplantation in animal models. The success of these transplants is measured in terms of the ability of the transplanted uterus to survive, and then to gestate a pregnancy. From a medical research perspective, the justification for UTx appears to rely upon estimates of the numbers of women with uterine infertility that are likely to 'be interested in conceiving', based on statistical analysis of fecundity rates in the general population.[17] This 'interest in conceiving' is construed as a medical need, thereby justifying UTx research and planned treatment.[18] Given this medical view of UTx as a way of treating a particular kind of infertility, it is pertinent to consider whether it is likely to succeed even on these terms, before considering the issues that women might take to be significant in desiring a pregnancy of their own and whether UTx is likely to satisfy these.

There have been some successes with UTx in animals; these include live births in auto-transplanted uteri (i.e. removal and reattachment of the same uterus) in sheep and dogs, and live births with transplants in genetically identical mice.[19] The relevance of these studies for humans is questionable, however, due to differences in anatomy, graft size and tissue resistance in humans compared with non-human animals.[20] Attempts to transplant uteri in higher primates (e.g. rhesus monkeys) have not been promising. Auto-transplanted uteri functioned normally, but no pregnancies resulted; and transplants with donor uteri failed.[21]

If the transplant is initially successful, questions then arise about the health of the transplanted uterus during pregnancy. Studies of pregnancy in women after kidney transplantation show that a small number of pregnancies are complicated by rejection and graft deterioration in the transplanted organ.[22] Although small, this risk assumes greater significance when the transplanted organ is the uterus, as rejection will not only compromise the graft, but also any existing pregnancy. It is possible that the risk of rejection during pregnancy will be higher in UTx compared with other transplanted organs, given that with UTx, it is the transplanted organ itself which bears the direct stress of the pregnancy.

Based on the above, a number of concerns arise. First, there is currently little experimental ground for regarding UTx to be close to success in terms of establishing menstruation in the graft. Second, the likelihood of establishing a pregnancy in a transplanted uterus is low. And third, should a pregnancy develop, there are significant risks of rejection and other complications incompatible with the medical goal of treating infertility by securing a live birth.

The situation is further complicated if we consider the aims of UTx from the perspective of potential recipients, women who want to have a pregnancy of their own rather than pursue the current options of surrogacy or adoption. As yet, there is little or no published research dealing with this aspect. However the response from women with uterine infertility to media reports of potential human uterine transplantation was overwhelming, with a large proportion citing 'experiencing pregnancy' as the factor motivating them to request consideration for UTx.[23] There are other possible reasons underlying the willingness to undergo UTx. These might include the desire to have a child for the father, inferred from statements such as 'I've always felt that I couldn't give him kids, now there's hope'.[24] This sentiment reflects the sense of ownership ascribed to gestation, and hence the notion that the mother 'gives' the father a child, despite the fact that the foetus is created equally from the gametes of both parents. This desire could not be fulfilled and, in fact, would be usurped, in a surrogate pregnancy. Another motivating factor is the opportunity to have greater control, viz-a-viz surrogacy arrangements, over aspects of the gestational process such as lifestyle and medical decisions affecting the foetus.

The importance of the actual pregnancy experience will depend on the expectations and motivations of individual women. For some the experience of pregnancy may be of little importance compared with achieving a live birth; but responses in the media suggest that the desire for the affective experience of gestating a foetus is a significant motivating factor.[25] This makes it important to note that the pregnancy experienced by a UTx recipient will be very different from that of a woman gestating a foetus in her own uterus.

First, physical differences will inevitably exist. As the medical aim of UTx is to secure a uterine graft robust enough to sustain a pregnancy, the transplant procedure will focus upon adequate blood supply.[26] Importantly, descriptions of the proposed surgical procedure do not include connection of nerves to the transplanted uterus. It is not presently feasible to do this, and innervation is not essential for the uterus to perform its gestational function.[27] Yet this will result in the absence of sensation in the uterus, thereby substantially altering precisely the *experience* of pregnancy.[28] Hormonally mediated effects such as morning sickness and fatigue will be preserved, but the recipients of UTx will not be able to feel foetal movements, or any kind of contractions. In addition, the function of the vagina may be compromised, requiring a caesarean delivery.[29] Even if vaginal function is preserved, Del Priore's team proposes, at least initially, to undertake prophylactic caesarean delivery as a precaution, thereby ruling out the possibility of experiencing labour and vaginal delivery. These differences are not insignificant; for some potential recipients the lack of sensation and normal delivery could undermine their desire to experience pregnancy.

Emotionally, the experience may also be significantly different. Transplant patients commonly react to their transplanted organ with some degree of estrangement.[30] Thus potential feelings of alienation from the transplanted uterus, exacerbated by its lack

of innervation, may be anticipated. Experience from heart transplantations yields insight as to possible psychological reactions of UTx recipients. Studies of post-operative reactions of heart transplant recipients suggest that symbolic attribution of the heart as the seat of the emotions complicates recipients' acceptance of its replacement.[31] Despite being counselled pre-surgery to think of the heart as merely a pump, many recipients reported concerns that having another person's heart presented a threat to their sense of bodily integrity. These concerns interfered with psychological integration of the transplanted heart.[32] It may be appropriate to counsel heart transplant patients to think of their heart simply as a pump since, in reality, our attribution of emotions to our heart is figurative and we know this. However, adopting the analogy that the uterus is merely an incubator may not be quite so straightforward. The uterus is a physical and emotional bridge between the woman and her foetus. Any feelings of alienation towards the uterus may compromise the woman's relationship not only with her uterus but, more importantly, with the growing foetus.

The recipient's emotional response to the experience of UTx pregnancy may also be complicated by the fact that the donor uterus not only belonged to someone else but also gestated that woman's children and formed part of that woman's reproductive identity.[33] We know from hand and face transplants that personal qualities from the donor may be attributed to transplanted organs, leading to a sense of estrangement for the recipient.[34] Clearly, hands and faces are visible and expressive parts of the body, making them more readily associated with a person's sense of identity than an internal organ. However, the fact that the transplanted uterus once gestated another woman's pregnancies may interfere with the recipient's ability to accept it as her own.

The post-operative course of organ transplants can be stormy, with episodes of acute rejection not uncommon. Emotional responses are intimately linked to the physical aspects of transplantation, such that even temporary episodes of physiological rejection can compromise psychological acceptance of the organ.[35] In the case of life-preserving transplantations, recipients have no choice but to live with the transplanted organ, but with transplantation of non-vital organs, removal is an option. Indeed, this occurred with the first hand transplant patient whose graft was eventually amputated after pockets of rejection developed and slowed recovery. The recipient was widely quoted as desiring removal of the transplanted hand because he felt alienated from it.[36] Such a reaction could have serious repercussions in the case of a transplanted uterus intended to, or already gestating a foetus.

Finally, at least in the early stages of UTx, conception and implantation will be achieved by IVF rather than occurring naturally. This is despite the fact that women will be considered for UTx only if they are otherwise fertile. Potential recipients will be required to undergo IVF prior to transplantation to increase the chances of successful implantation and to decrease exposure of the embryo to immunosuppressant medication.[37] This is another significant respect in which UTx pregnancy will differ from typical pregnancy.

We can see therefore that UTx offers an as yet remote chance of being medically successful in terms of achieving a healthy pregnancy. Further, even if this should occur, the experience of pregnancy in a transplanted uterus, which is key to reported desires to undertake the procedure, will be compromised through lack of sensation, medicalisation of the process, and potential emotional alienation arising from a number of sources.

UTx, Medical Harms and Risk of Pregnancy

As well as considering the desired outcomes of UTx, we must also consider potential harms. UTx recipients will incur the same surgical risks and drug regimen as other transplant patients. These include risks from surgery itself, ancillary risks such as infection or infarction, potential loss of function in the graft, and side-effects associated with immunosuppressive medication. In the case of UTx, the foetus, as well as the recipient, will be exposed to immunosuppressive drugs, and subject to the consequences should complications occur post implantation.

Very little data is available with which to predict how pregnancy would affect a transplanted uterus. A number of studies have been conducted of women who fall pregnant after heart, liver, lung and kidney transplants. These show that immunosuppressants cause increased maternal morbidity during pregnancy and are associated with a higher incidence of premature births.[38] Immunosuppressants also increase a recipient's vulnerability to infection, some of which are known to pose risks to the developing foetus. These side-effects cannot be avoided as immunosuppressive medication is necessary to prevent rejection. Notably however, UTx provides the unique opportunity to avoid long term exposure to immunosuppressants, as the uterus can be removed after successful pregnancy.[39]

In general, women are not barred from proceeding with pregnancies that involve some risk to their health as long as the decision to do so is made autonomously. A presumption in favour of reproductive autonomy would *prima facie* suggest that in the context of uterus transplants, the relevant test for risk should be no more demanding than that confronted by a woman with her own uterus choosing to undertake a risky pregnancy. Unfortunately, as with all innovative procedures, there are unknown risks that undermine the legitimacy of any such comparison. The paucity of comparative data in animal models, and the novel characteristics of the uterus as a transplantable organ, mean the first UTx recipients will unavoidably be human 'guinea pigs' in a procedure that is essentially experimental.

Questions Concerning Informed Consent to UTx

Informed consent constitutes a basic ethical requirement in delivering health care. While the conditions for consent (i.e. competent patient, provision and understanding of relevant information, lack of coercion) are well recognised, there are features of innovative procedures such as UTx that may compromise valid consent. Research indicates that patients seeking innovative surgery typically focus on the perceived benefits rather than the possibility of complications or failure, particularly when the stakes are high.[40] This general tendency to be optimistic about innovative procedures may be exacerbated by the emotional factors surrounding UTx. As noted earlier, the responses of women with uterine infertility to media reports about UTx, support this concern. Women recounted stories of medically necessary hysterectomies, and expressed regret that they were no longer able to carry a child. Emotive terms such as 'desperate' and 'unbearable' were used frequently, untempered by discussion of the risks.[41] In this highly charged emotional atmosphere, it will be both essential and difficult to ensure fully informed and voluntary consent for UTx.

Amongst the many potential challenges for meeting appropriate consent requirements for UTx, a few stand out as likely to be particularly vexatious. Unlike other assisted reproduction techniques that focus on ways to help an otherwise infertile couple have a genetically related child, the objective of uterus transplantation is also to allow a woman to *gestate* her own foetus. For that reason it is crucial that potential recipients be fully apprised of what they can reasonably expect from a pregnancy and birth following UTx, in order to make a fully informed decision. As discussed earlier, the pregnancy experience may not meet recipients' expectations, due to the need for IVF, reduced sensations of pregnancy, absent labour and a caesarean delivery. It is quite possible that these physiological differences may prevent recipients from fully realizing psychological and emotional goals of pregnancy, including ante-natal bonding to the foetus. Explaining and understanding these factors will be challenging if women have already made an emotional commitment to receiving a transplant.

A very real question also exists as to what early candidates are consenting to. It is highly unlikely, all things considered, that the first human uterus transplants will result in pregnancies. In the 2000 Saudi Arabian living donor case, the transplant was initially successful in that the recipient had two menstrual cycles; however, after approximately three months, the uterus died suddenly secondary to clotting in the connecting blood vessels, necessitating its removal.[42] Inevitably the first transplants will be experimental. Whether or not early recipients are formally enrolled in a research trial, it would seem appropriate that the standard for informed consent be closer to that of consent to *research* by healthy volunteers, than to that of patients consenting to *treatment*. This is because early recipients will be undertaking the risks of transplantation with great uncertainty in regards to obtaining any personal benefit, yet while also incurring significant risks. Thus their case is similar to that of healthy volunteers in that

they undertake the risks of research absent any immediate health risk: infertility is not a life-threatening condition. Unlike patients with end-stage cancer who may enter research trials in the hope of prolonging their lives, infertile women who undergo UTx will risk their health with very uncertain prospects of compensating benefit.

Donor Issues

At present, the protocol of the New York UTx team specifies use only of cadaveric donors, in which case the usual consent procedures for post mortem organ donation will obtain. However, uterus transplant from *live* donors is a possibility, and indeed is the option preferred by the leader of a competing team.[43] Distinct donor consent issues therefore arise. Living donors may be altruistic volunteers, friends or relatives. As with living related kidney donation, donation from matched relatives may minimise the need for immunosuppressant medication, thereby reducing risks to recipients and their pregnancies. However, related donors would potentially face emotional pressures akin to those experienced by related kidney donors. Altruistic donations by strangers can reduce concerns over coerced consent, but without the benefit of closer immunological matching.

A third potential source of uteri is from women undertaking simultaneous removal of a healthy uterus as part of a larger gynaecological procedure. This would create an organ pool not available in other forms of transplantation. There is, however, a risk for uterus donors in that a uterus is only expendable if the potential donor is unequivocally certain that she will not now nor in the future desire another pregnancy herself. Interestingly, some of the women responding to news of UTx research had chosen hysterectomy as the solution to a medical problem, thinking they had completed their families, only to find themselves in a new relationship and desirous of having children with their new partner. This is a potential risk for living donors. In addition, and as we have discussed, the uterus is an organ invested with emotional and psychological significance, a fact that must be impressed upon potential living donors. What can be said, therefore, is that UTx donorship will raise both familiar and novel challenges for meeting the appropriately stringent ethical requirements of informed consent.

Having canvassed the challenges of UTx, we next consider the alternatives.

Alternatives to UTx?

To determine whether UTx is justified, *in light of the available alternatives*, those alternatives must be meaningful. At present a woman suffering from uterine infertility who wants a genetically related child has one option: gestational surrogacy. Although a technically straightforward solution to uterine infertility, gestational surrogacy is not without emotional, social and legal complications.

First, it is only a theoretical alternative for many women, given that gestational surrogacy is opposed by some religions and is illegal in some countries. More commonly, gestational surrogacy has not been considered by legislators and the laws of many countries are silent on the issue. Even in jurisdictions where specific legislation exists, gestational surrogacy is dealt with inconsistently. Most jurisdictions recognise the gestational mother as the legal mother, requiring adoption by the commissioning parents; but some give legal priority to the genetic mother. In still other jurisdictions, whilst surrogacy is technically permitted, surrogacy agreements are unenforceable.[44] This situation may be due simply to legal frameworks lagging behind advances in medical technology, rather than reflecting opposition to gestational surrogacy.[45] If this is the case, however, one could argue that the main objective ought to be to develop the law around gestational surrogacy, rather than to develop reproductive alternatives.

For the present, the uncertainty of the relative legal positions of the parties to a surrogacy arrangement adds to the risks of gestational surrogacy, with significant attention given in the media to legal battles ensuing when surrogacy arrangements break down, as occurs when the surrogate changes her mind about relinquishing the baby, or when the commissioning parents attempt to renege on the agreement.[46]

Legal uncertainties aside, gestational surrogacy is commonly represented as a 'risky' alternative. Questions of who has control and decision-making rights in matters affecting the pregnancy; issues arising from the gestational surrogate's intimate relationship with the foetus; and concerns about the motives and emotional stability of gestational surrogates, remain vexed.[47] The genetic mother can attempt to control the pregnancy by stipulating in the surrogacy agreement the conduct required of the surrogate. However, in practical terms, she has no physical control over the manner in which the surrogate cares for herself or the foetus during the pregnancy and ultimately the surrogate is entitled to continue or terminate her pregnancy in the same circumstances as any other pregnant woman.

Additionally, whatever the surrogate's motive for entering into the arrangement, the reality is that she has an intimate physical, if not psychological, relationship with the foetus throughout the pregnancy. Ultimately, the risk (even if small) of the surrogate developing an attachment to the foetus cannot be ignored, nor its consequences over-estimated.

As this brief consideration shows, gestational surrogacy offers a far from unproblematic remedy for women with uterine infertility. Surrogacy ultimately requires the existence of a relationship of trust between all parties concerned. At present, the precarious legal nature of gestational surrogacy agreements, combined with the negative public perception of surrogates, all-too-easily undermine the trust required for such arrangements. However, these are contingent matters; accordingly the viability of surrogacy as an alternative to UTx is subject to change. Thus there is a limited extent to which current negative perceptions and unaccommodating laws around gestational surrogacy can legitimately be invoked as a basis for advocating UTx as the 'better' reproductive alternative.

Reproductive Autonomy and Uterus Transplantation as ART

Arguably, women wanting uterus transplants are exercising their right to a form of assisted reproductive technology (ART) that is no different in principle from currently used and accepted procedures. As such, it is important to closely examine the notion of reproductive autonomy in an analysis of the ethics of UTx. The justification for UTx is grounded in women's alleged intense desire for pregnancy, with little questioning of the foundation of such a desire. To be sure, the social pressure to parent is complex. Yet parenting is essentially a *social* activity not necessarily requiring a genetic relationship between parent and child. Nor is child-*bearing* an essential prerequisite for parenting. Additionally, in the scheme of the overall parental relationship, pregnancy plays at most a transient role in the relationship between mother and child. More fundamentally, some feminist critics of reproductive technology argue that our pronatal society fosters an expectation that childbearing is an essential part of a woman's social role which, in turn, leads women to undertake risky procedures to remedy reproductive deficiencies that would not otherwise have troubled them.[48] This raises the question of whether uterus transplants (and indeed most forms of ART) should be promoted at all.

The rights of the fertile to make reproductive choices without interference is frequently asserted as a basic human right, often supported with references to Articles in Conventions and Charters of Human Rights. However, reproductive autonomy has long been extended beyond the negative right of non-interference in relation to reproductive choices, to include the provision of assistance to those who want but are unable to reproduce. Conventional ART – including pro-fertility medications, artificial insemination, in vitro fertilisation, oocyte donation, sperm donation, gestational surrogacy, and the like – has been a part of reproductive medicine for decades. Thus it might be argued that women wanting uterus transplants are simply exercising their presumptive right to reproductive freedom or 'procreative liberty'.

Yet the question must be asked: how far ought we to go in order to allow – even encourage – the 'otherwise infertile' to have a genetically related child? The question raises two further inter-related issues: the extent to which the desire to have children is socially engendered; and the availability of a moral justification for the desire to bear genetically related offspring. As stated earlier, critics of ART argue that societal expectations about childbearing as a fundamental part of women's life plans potentially compromises aspects of women's reproductive freedoms. Women may feel compelled to use ART as a result of pressure from society, family members and others to have a child of 'their own'.[49] However, in a society in which child-rearing is perceived as the norm and those who choose not to have children often feel alienated, or are perceived as selfish, it is understandable that the infertile will feel a sense of loss on discovering they cannot naturally conceive. If the pressure of societal expectations contributes to a woman's belief that she must have children, it is perhaps not unreasonable to suggest that society incurs an obligation to assist her in that pursuit.

Assuming that parenting is a morally acceptable pursuit within a person's life plan, the second issue concerns our preference for genetically related offspring. Generally, a desire for genetically related offspring is assumed to be morally justified on the basis that genetics creates some connection or bond between parent and child which enhances their relationship. That we as a matter of fact tend to prefer a genetic link with our children is clear. However, in the face of increasingly controversial technologies, the assumptions underlying this preference may be questioned.[50] Parenting itself is essentially a social activity not necessarily requiring a genetic relationship between parent and child; and non-biological explanations (context, socialisation and learning) readily account for parent-child psychological similarity.[51]

Notwithstanding the challenges of justifying unlimited expansion of and access to ART, the provision of other forms of ART for more than thirty years places a heavy burden of justification on anyone who would curtail the extension of reproductive rights to UTx. Although UTx does considerably extend the scope of current medical practice, this is not in itself an argument against similarly extending the boundaries of reproductive autonomy, so as to encompass it. There will almost certainly be infertile women who desire to be genetic, social and gestational mothers. Where a woman does not have a functioning uterus, it is far from clear how we might legitimately encourage use of a surrogate (with all its attendant difficulties) but withhold the opportunity to employ an (in principle) established surgical technique – namely, organ transplantation – in order to allow her to achieve a pregnancy 'of her own'. While it lies outside the scope of this paper to fully explore the arguments, it can at least be said that there exist no obvious *prima facie* grounds for not extending existing reproductive rights to ART to encompass uterine transplantation.

Conclusion

In standard contexts, a decision to undertake a quality of life transplant rests on an assumption that the benefits outweigh the risks, coupled with the knowledge that the recipient is fully informed of those risks prior to consenting to surgery. At its simplest, the benefits involved amount to restoration of physiological function. However, as we have shown in this paper, the possibility of transplantation of the uterus constitutes one case in which potential recipients' expectations may extend well beyond physiological function restoration. This suggests the need for further examination of the ethics of transplants that have motivations beyond restoration of function alone.

As we have indicated, UTx research to date has focused entirely on the technical viability of the surgical transplant procedure. Researchers have proceeded on the assumption that there is a medical need to be met by UTx. This assumption may be warranted given prevailing societal expectations about the provision of ART to infertile couples. However, we would suggest that the eagerness of women to subject themselves to ever more painful, debilitating, risky and uncertain procedures – into which category UTx most certainly falls – surely provides cause to question the foundation of that particular reproductive aspiration. A more definitive answer to the question of the ethical justifiability of UTx must await such an examination.

Notes

1 M. Brännström, C. Wranning and A. Altchek. Experimental Uterus Transplantation. *Hum Reprod Update* 2010; 16: 329–345: 339; A. Nair et al. Uterus Transplant. *Annals NY Academy of Sciences* 2008; 1127: 83–91: 85.

2 W. Fageeh et al. Transplantation of the Human Uterus. *Int Journal of Gynecology and Obstetrics* 2002; 76: 245–251.

3 New York Downtown Hospital IRB Approved Protocols 2004–2006. This is an 'in principle' approval of a staged study. To date, specific approvals have been received to test procurement procedures of deceased donor uteri; to carry out a statistical analysis of uterine infertility to estimate the minimum number of potential candidates in the USA; and to distribute questionnaires, consent forms and associated material to assemble a potential recipient cohort.

4 R.A. Wolfe et al. Comparison of Mortality in All Patients on Dialysis, Patients on Dialysis Awaiting Transplantation, and Recipients of a First Cadaveric Transplant. *N Engl J Med* 1999; 341: 1725–1730; F.K. Port et al. Comparison of Survival Probabilities for Dialysis Patients vs Cadaveric Renal Transplant Recipients. *JAMA* 1993; 270: 1339–1343; 1342.

5 D. Dickenson and G. Widdershoven. Ethical Issues in Limb Transplants. *Bioethics* 2001; 15: 110–124; R. Huxtable and J. Woodley. Gaining Face or Losing Face? Framing the Debate on Face Transplants. *Bioethics* 2005; 19: 505–522.

6 R.C. Johnson. Smarter Bionic Hands Could Restore Sense of Touch. *Smarter Technology*, 26 Oct. 2009;

M. Costandi. The World's Most Advanced Bionic Hand. Neurophilosophy, 21 Dec. 2006. Available at: http://neurophilosophy.wordpress.com/2006/12/21/the-worlds-most-advanced-bionic-hand/ [Accessed 17 Dec 2010].

7 Jeff Kepner's homepage. Available at: http://www.newhandsforjeff.com/ [Accessed 17 Dec 2010].

8 MailOnline. Mail Foreign Service. Double Hand Transplant Patient Dreams of Feeling Wife's Touch and Cooking Again. 17 July 2009. London. Available at: http://www.dailymail.co.uk/health/article-1200283/Double-hand-transplant-patient-dreams-feeling-wifes-touch-cooking-again.html [Accessed 17 Dec 2010].

9 Ibid.

10 M. Park. One Year after Double Hand Transplant, Progress Elusive. 30 Aug 2010. CNN International Edition. Available at: http://edition.cnn.com/2010/HEALTH/08/26/double.hand.transplant/index.html [Accessed 17 Dec 2010].

11 P. Wysong. Advances in Hand and Face Transplantation: An Expert Interview with Dr. Jean-Michel Dubernard. 29 Sept 2010. New York. Available at: http://www.medscape.com/viewarticle/729305 [Accessed 17 Dec 2010].

12 J. Follain. Face Transplant Patient Isabelle Dinoire Reveals Her New Life. *Sunday Times*, 17 Jan 2010. London; N. Hines. American Face Transplant Patient James Maki Recalls Hermit-like Existence before Operation. *Sunday Times*, 22 May 2009. London; S. Jacobson. Fort Worth Man Awaits Doctors'

Decision on Face Transplant. *Dallas Morning News*, 5 July 2010. Dallas.

13 R. Stein. First U.S. Uterus Transplant Planned. *Washington Post*, 15 Jan 2007. Available at: http://www.washingtonpost.com/wp-dyn/content/article/2007/01/14/AR2007011401091.html [Accessed 17 Dec 2010]; R. Rabin. Prospect of Womb Transplant Raises Hopes and Red Flags. *New York Times*, 30 Jan 2007. Available at: http://www.nytimes.com/2007/01/30/health/30womb.html?pagewanted=print [Accessed 17 Dec 2010]; L. Fayed. Uterus Transplants for Women Unable to Have Children. About.com: Cancer. Comments. 15 Jan 2007.

14 R. Landau. Artificial Womb versus Natural Birth: An Exploratory Study of Women's Views. *J Reprod Infant Psychol* 2007; 25: 4–17.

15 Ibid: 7–8, 10.

16 J. Elson. *Am I Still a Woman? Hysterectomy and Gender Identity*. Philadelphia, PA: Temple University Press, 2004.

17 Nair et al. Potential Candidates for Uterine Transplantation: An Assessment of Need. *Fertil Steril* 2007; 88, Suppl 1: S224–225.

18 Nair. Experimental Uterus Transplantation, pp. 84–85.

19 Brännström et al. Experimental Uterus Transplantation, p. 339.

20 M.A. Bedaiwy, A. Shahin and T. Falcone. Reproductive Organ Transplantation: Advances and Controversies. *Fertil Steril* 2008; 90: 2031–2055: 2042.

21 A. Altchek. Uterus Transplantation. *Mt Sinai J Med* 2003; 70: 154–162: 158.

22 V.T. Armenti et al. Immunosuppression in Pregnancy: Choices for Infant and Maternal Health. *Drugs* 2002; 62: 2361–2375: 2372; Bedaiwy et al. Reproductive Organ Transplantation, pp. 2043–2049.

23 See note 13.

24 C. Nordqvist. Uterus Transplant Planned, visitor opinions. *Medical News Today*, 16 Jan 2007. Available at: http://www.medicalnewstoday.com/articles/60904.php [Accessed 17 Dec 2010].

25 See note 13.

26 Brännström et al., Experimental Uterus Transplantation, p. 335.

27 Altchek. Uterus Transplantation, p. 159.

28 Ibid.

29 Ibid.

30 R. Fox and J.P. Swazey. *Spare Parts: Organ Replacement in American Society*. New York: Oxford University Press, 1992: 36.

31 E. Kaba et al. Somebody Else's Heart Inside Me: A Descriptive Study of Psychological Problems after a Heart Transplantation. *Issues in Medical Health Nursing* 2005; 26: 611–625: 620.

32 Ibid: 617.

33 Brännström's team propose 'previous successful pregnancy' as a criterion for uterus donation. See Brännström et al. Experimental Uterus Transplantation, p. 332.

34 R. Ellis. It Was Grotesque – Hand Transplant Recipient Warns of Mental Trauma. *Daily Telegraph (Sydney)*, 19 Dec 2005; Foreign Hand Not Wanted. *The Australian*, 28 Oct 2000; Doctors Amputate First Transplanted Human Hand. *Sunday Times*, 4 Feb 2001.

35 Kaba et al. Somebody Else's Heart Inside Me, p. 620.

36 BBC News Online: World: Europe. Surgeons Sever Transplant Hand. 3 Feb 2001. Available at: http://news.bbc.co.uk/2/low/europe/1151553.stm [Accessed 17 Dec 2010].

37 Brännström et al. Experimental Uterus Transplantation, p. 339.

38 These studies show a higher incidence of premature birth – less than 37 weeks gestation (on average 50% of births are premature) – and low birth weight, with many pregnancies complicated by maternal hypertension (a sharp rise in blood pressure in the mother) and preeclampsia (high blood pressure coupled with protein in the urine and swelling of the hands and feet), which puts the lives of the mother and foetus at risk if left untreated. See Armenti et al. Immunosuppression in Pregnancy, p. 2372; Bedaiwy et al. Reproductive Organ Transplantation, p. 2046; Altchek. Uterus Transplantation, p. 154.

39 Removal after 1–2 successful pregnancies is the currently expressed intention of those contemplating UTx. See Brännström et al. Experimental Uterus Transplantation, p. 338.

40 F.D. Moore. Ethical Problems Special to Surgery: Surgical Teaching, Surgical Innovation, and the Surgeon in Managed Care. *Arch Surg* 2000; 135: 14–16.

41 See references for note 13; also C. Gayle. World's First Uterus Transplant on the Horizon – But Is It a Good Idea? Blogger News Network. 10 Nov 2006. Available at: http://www.bloggernews.net/11942 [Accessed 17 Dec 2010].

42 Fageeh et al. Transplantation of the Human Uterus.

43 M. Brännström, C. Wranning and R. Racho El-Akouri. Transplantation of the Uterus. *Mol Cell Endocrinol* 2003; 202: 177–184: 182; Brännström et al. Experimental Uterus Transplantation, p. 332.

44 Surrogacy Arrangements Act 1985, UK s1A; Human Fertilisation and Embryology Act 2008, UK s33; Adoption of Children Act 1965 (NSW) s26; R. Ber.

Ethical Issues in Gestational Surrogacy. *Theoretical Medicine and Bioethics: Philosophy of Medical Research and Practice* 2000; 21: 153–169:159; *Johnson v. Calvert* (1993) 5 Cal.4th 84, 19 Cal. Rptr.2d 494.

45 J.K. Ciccarelli and J.C. Ciccarelli. The Legal Aspects of Parental Rights in Assisted Reproductive Technology. *J Soc Iss* 2005; 61: 127–137.

46 *Johnson v. Calvert*; *In the Matter of Baby M*, 537 A.2d 1227 (NJ 1988); S. Sidner. Surrogate Baby Stuck in Legal Limbo. 12 Aug 2008. CNN World.

47 Ber, Ethical Issues in Gestational Surrogacy, pp. 153–169.

48 L.M. Purdy. Assisted Reproduction. Ch17 in H. Kuhse

and P. Singer, eds., A Companion to Bioethics. Oxford: Blackwell, 2001: 164.

49 S.-V. Brakman and S.J. Scholz. Adoption, ART, and a Re-conception of the Maternal Body: Toward Embodied Maternity. *Hypatia* 2006; 21: 54–73: 63.

50 M. Lotz. Overstating the Biological: Geneticism and Essentialism in Social Cloning and Social Sex Selection. In L. Skene and J. Thompson, eds., The Sorting Society: The Ethics of Genetic Screening and Therapy. Cambridge: Cambridge University Press, 2008: 133–148: 133–140.

51 Ibid: 136.

Prenatal Screening, Sex Selection, and Cloning

9

Genetics and Reproductive Risk
Can Having Children Be Immoral?

Laura M. Purdy

Is it morally permissible for me to have children? A decision to procreate is surely one of the most significant decisions a person can make. So it would seem that it ought not be made without some moral soul-searching.

There are many reasons why one might hesitate to bring children into this world if one is concerned about their welfare. Some are rather general, such as the deteriorating environment or the prospect of poverty. Others have a narrower focus, such as continuing civil war in one's country or the lack of essential social support for child-rearing in the United States. Still others may be relevant only to individuals at risk of passing harmful diseases to their offspring.

There are many causes of misery in this world, and most of them are unrelated to genetic disease. In the general scheme of things, human misery is most efficiently reduced by concentrating on noxious social and political arrangements. Nonetheless, we should not ignore preventable harm just because it is confined to a relatively small corner of life. So the question arises, Can it be wrong to have a child because of genetic risk factors?[1]

Unsurprisingly, most of the debate about this issue has focused on prenatal screening and abortion: much useful information about a given fetus can be made available by recourse to prenatal testing. This fact has meant that moral questions about reproduction have become entwined with abortion politics, to the detriment of both. The abortion connection has made it especially difficult to think about whether it is wrong to prevent a child from coming into being, because doing so might involve what many people see as wrongful killing; yet there is no necessary link between the two. Clearly, the existence of genetically compromised children can be prevented not only by aborting already existing fetuses but also by preventing conception in the first place.

Worse yet, many discussions simply assume a particular view of abortion without recognizing other possible positions and the difference they make in how people understand the issues. For example, those who object to aborting fetuses with genetic problems often argue that doing so would undermine our conviction that all humans are in some important sense equal.[2] However, this position rests on the assumption that conception marks the point at which humans are endowed with a right to life. So aborting fetuses with genetic problems looks morally the same as killing "imperfect" people without their consent.

This position raises two separate issues. One pertains to the legitimacy of different views on abortion. Despite the conviction of many abortion activists to the contrary, I believe that ethically respectable views

Original publication details: Laura M. Purdy, "Genetics and Reproductive Risk: Can Having Children be Immoral?," pp. 39–49 from *Reproducing Persons: Issues in Feminist Bioethics,* Ithaca, NY: Cornell University Press, 1996. Reproduced with permission from Cornell University Press.

Bioethics: An Anthology, Third Edition. Edited by Helga Kuhse, Udo Schüklenk, and Peter Singer.

can be found on different sides of the debate, including one that sees fetuses as developing humans without any serious moral claim on continued life. There is no space here to address the details, and doing so would be once again to fall into the trap of letting the abortion question swallow up all others. However, opponents of abortion need to face the fact that many thoughtful individuals do *not* see fetuses as moral persons. It follows that their reasoning process, and hence the implications of their decisions, are radically different from those envisioned by opponents of prenatal screening and abortion. So where the latter see genetic abortion as murdering people who just don't measure up, the former see it as a way to prevent the development of persons who are more likely to live miserable lives, a position consistent with a world-view that values persons equally and holds that each deserves a high-quality life. Some of those who object to genetic abortion appear to be oblivious to these psychological and logical facts. It follows that the nightmare scenarios they paint for us are beside the point: many people simply do not share the assumptions that make them plausible.

How are these points relevant to my discussion? My primary concern here is to argue that conception can sometimes be morally wrong on grounds of genetic risk, although this judgment will not apply to those who accept the moral legitimacy of abortion and are willing to employ prenatal screening and selective abortion. If my case is solid, then those who oppose abortion must be especially careful not to conceive in certain cases, as they are, of course, free to follow their conscience about abortion. Those like myself who do not see abortion as murder have more ways to prevent birth.

Huntington's Disease

There is always some possibility that reproduction will result in a child with a serious disease or handicap. Genetic counselors can help individuals determine whether they are at unusual risk and, as the Human Genome Project rolls on, their knowledge will increase by quantum leaps. As this knowledge becomes available, I believe we ought to use it to determine whether possible children are at risk *before* they are conceived.

In this chapter I want to defend the thesis that it is morally wrong to reproduce when we know there is a high risk of transmitting a serious disease or defect. This thesis holds that some reproductive acts are wrong, and my argument puts the burden of proof on those who disagree with it to show why its conclusions can be overridden. Hence it denies that people should be free to reproduce mindless of the consequences.[3] However, as moral argument, it should be taken as a proposal for further debate and discussion. It is not, by itself, an argument in favor of legal prohibitions of reproduction.[4]

There is a huge range of genetic diseases. Some are quickly lethal; others kill more slowly, if at all. Some are mainly physical, some mainly mental; others impair both kinds of function. Some interfere tremendously with normal functioning, others less. Some are painful, some are not. There seems to be considerable agreement that rapidly lethal diseases, especially those, such as Tay-Sachs, accompanied by painful deterioration, should be prevented even at the cost of abortion. Conversely, there seems to be substantial agreement that relatively trivial problems, especially cosmetic ones, would not be legitimate grounds for abortion.[5] In short, there are cases ranging from low risk of mild disease or disability to high risk of serious disease or disability. Although it is difficult to decide where the duty to refrain from procreation becomes compelling, I believe that there are some clear cases. I have chosen to focus on Huntington's Disease to illustrate the kinds of concrete issues such decisions entail. However, the arguments are also relevant to many other genetic diseases.[6]

The symptoms of Huntington's Disease usually begin between the ages of 30 and 50:

> Onset is insidious. Personality changes (obstinacy, moodiness, lack of initiative) frequently antedate or accompany the involuntary choreic movements. These usually appear first in the face, neck, and arms, and are jerky, irregular, and stretching in character. Contradictions of the facial muscles result in grimaces; those of the respiratory muscles, lips, and tongue lead to hesitating, explosive speech. Irregular movements of the trunk are present; the gait is shuffling and dancing. Tendon reflexes are increased...Some patients display a fatuous euphoria; others are spiteful, irascible, destructive, and violent. Paranoid reactions are common. Poverty of thought and

impairment of attention, memory, and judgment occur. As the disease progresses, walking becomes impossible, swallowing difficult, and dementia profound. Suicide is not uncommon.[7]

The illness lasts about fifteen years, terminating in death.

Huntington's Disease is an autosomal dominant disease, meaning it is caused by a single defective gene located on a non-sex chromosome. It is passed from one generation to the next via affected individuals. Each child of such an affected person has a 50 percent risk of inheriting the gene and thus of eventually developing the disease, even if he or she was born before the parent's disease was evident.[8]

Until recently, Huntington's Disease was especially problematic because most affected individuals did not know whether they had the gene for the disease until well into their child-bearing years. So they had to decide about child-bearing before knowing whether they could transmit the disease or not. If, in time, they did not develop symptoms of the disease, then their children could know they were not at risk for the disease. If unfortunately they did develop symptoms, then each of their children could know there was a 50 percent chance that they too had inherited the gene. In both cases, the children faced a period of prolonged anxiety as to whether they would develop the disease. Then, in the 1980s, thanks in part to an energetic campaign by Nancy Wexler, a genetic marker was found that, in certain circumstances, could tell people with a relatively high degree of probability whether or not they had the gene for the disease.[9] Finally, in March 1993, the defective gene itself was discovered.[10] Now individuals can find out whether they carry the gene for the disease, and prenatal screening can tell us whether a given fetus has inherited it. These technological developments change the moral scene substantially.

How serious are the risks involved in Huntington's Disease? Geneticists often think a 10 percent risk is high.[11] But risk assessment also depends on what is at stake: the worse the possible outcome, the more undesirable an otherwise small risk seems. In medicine, as elsewhere, people may regard the same result quite differently. But for devastating diseases such as Huntington's this part of the judgment should be

unproblematic: no one wants a loved one to suffer in this way.[12]

There may still be considerable disagreement about the acceptability of a given risk. So it would be difficult in many circumstances to say how we should respond to a particular risk. Nevertheless, there are good grounds for a conservative approach, for it is reasonable to take special precautions to avoid very bad consequences, even if the risk is small. But the possible consequences here *are* very bad: a child who may inherit Huntington's Disease has a much greater than average chance of being subjected to severe and prolonged suffering. And it is one thing to risk one's own welfare, but quite another to do so for others and without their consent.

Is this judgment about Huntington's Disease really defensible? People appear to have quite different opinions. Optimists argue that a child born into a family afflicted with Huntington's Disease has a reasonable chance of living a satisfactory life. After all, even children born of an afflicted parent still have a 50 percent chance of escaping the disease. And even if afflicted themselves, such people will probably enjoy some thirty years of healthy life before symptoms appear. It is also possible, although not at all likely, that some might not mind the symptoms caused by the disease. Optimists can point to diseased persons who have lived fruitful lives, as well as those who seem genuinely glad to be alive. One is Rick Donohue, a sufferer from the Joseph family disease: "You know, if my mom hadn't had me, I wouldn't be here for the life I have had. So there is a good possibility I will have children."[13] Optimists therefore conclude that it would be a shame if these persons had not lived.

Pessimists concede some of these facts but take a less sanguine view of them. They think a 50 percent risk of serious disease such as Huntington's is appallingly high. They suspect that many children born into afflicted families are liable to spend their youth in dreadful anticipation and fear of the disease. They expect that the disease, if it appears, will be perceived as a tragic and painful end to a blighted life. They point out that Rick Donohue is still young and has not experienced the full horror of his sickness. It is also well-known that some young persons have such a dilated sense of time that they can hardly envision themselves at 30 or 40, so the prospect of pain at that age is unreal to them.[14]

More empirical research on the psychology and life history of suffers and potential sufferers is clearly needed to decide whether optimists or pessimists have a more accurate picture of the experiences of individuals at risk. But given that some will surely realize pessimists' worst fears, it seems unfair to conclude that the pleasures of those who deal best with the situation simply cancel out the suffering of those others when that suffering could be avoided altogether.

I think that these points indicate that the morality of procreation in such situations demands further investigation. I propose to do this by looking first at the position of the possible child, then at that of the potential parent.

Possible Children and Potential Parents

The first task in treating the problem from the child's point of view is to find a way of referring to possible future offspring without seeming to confer some sort of morally significant existence on them. I follow the convention of calling children who might be born in the future but who are not now conceived "possible" children, offspring, individuals, or persons.

Now, what claims about children or possible children are relevant to the morality of child-bearing in the circumstances being considered? Of primary importance is the judgment that we ought to try to provide every child with something like a minimally satisfying life. I am not altogether sure how best to formulate this standard, but I want clearly to reject the view that it is morally permissible to conceive individuals so long as we do not expect them to be so miserable that they wish they were dead.[15] I believe that this kind of moral minimalism is thoroughly unsatisfactory and that not many people would really want to live in a world where it was the prevailing standard. Its lure is that it puts few demands on us, but its price is the scant attention it pays to human well-being.

How might the judgment that we have a duty to try to provide a minimally satisfying life for our children be justified? It could, I think, be derived fairly straightforwardly from either utilitarian or contractarian theories of justice, although there is no space here for discussion of the details. The net result of such analysis would be to conclude that neglecting this duty would create unnecessary unhappiness or unfair disadvantage for some persons.

Of course, this line of reasoning confronts us with the need to spell out what is meant by "minimally satisfying" and what a standard based on this concept would require of us. Conceptions of a minimally satisfying life vary tremendously among societies and also within them. *De rigueur* in some circles are private music lessons and trips to Europe, whereas in others providing eight years of schooling is a major accomplishment. But there is no need to consider this complication at length here because we are concerned only with health as a prerequisite for a minimally satisfying life. Thus, as we draw out what such a standard might require of us, it seems reasonable to retreat to the more limited claim that parents should try to ensure something like normal health for their children. It might be thought that even this moderate claim is unsatisfactory as in some places debilitating conditions are the norm, but one could circumvent this objection by saying that parents ought to try to provide for their children health normal for that culture, even though it may be inadequate if measured by some outside standard.[16] This conservative position would still justify efforts to avoid the birth of children at risk for Huntington's Disease and other serious genetic diseases in virtually all societies.[17]

This view is reinforced by the following considerations. Given that possible children do not presently exist as actual individuals, they do not have a right to be brought into existence, and hence no one is maltreated by measures to avoid the conception of a possible person. Therefore, the conservative course that avoids the conception of those who would not be expected to enjoy a minimally satisfying life is at present the only fair course of action. The alternative is a *laissez-faire* approach that brings into existence the lucky, but only at the expense of the unlucky. Notice that attempting to avoid the creation of the unlucky does not necessarily lead to *fewer* people being brought into being; the question boils down to taking steps to bring those with better prospects into existence, instead of those with worse ones.

I have so far argued that if people with Huntington's Disease are unlikely to live minimally satisfying lives, then those who might pass it on should not have genetically related children. This is consonant with the principle that the greater the danger of serious problems, the stronger the duty to avoid them. But this principle is in conflict with what people think of as the right to reproduce. How might one decide which should take precedence?

Expecting people to forgo having genetically related children might seem to demand too great a sacrifice of them. But before reaching that conclusion we need to ask what is really at stake. One reason for wanting children is to experience family life, including love, companionship, watching kids grow, sharing their pains and triumphs, and helping to form members of the next generation. Other reasons emphasize the validation of parents as individuals within a continuous family line, children as a source of immortality, or perhaps even the gratification of producing partial replicas of oneself. Children may also be desired in an effort to prove that one is an adult, to try to cement a marriage, or to benefit parents economically.

Are there alternative ways of satisfying these desires? Adoption or new reproductive technologies can fulfill many of them without passing on known genetic defects. Sperm replacement has been available for many years via artificial insemination by donor. More recently, egg donation, sometimes in combination with contract pregnancy,[18] has been used to provide eggs for women who prefer not to use their own. Eventually it may be possible to clone individual humans, although that now seems a long way off. All of these approaches to avoiding the use of particular genetic material are controversial and have generated much debate. I believe that tenable moral versions of each do exist.[19]

None of these methods permits people to extend both genetic lines or realize the desire for immortality or for children who resemble both parents; nor is it clear that such alternatives will necessarily succeed in proving that one is an adult, cementing a marriage, or providing economic benefits. Yet, many people feel these desires strongly. Now, I am sympathetic to William James's dictum regarding desires: "Take any demand, however slight, which any creature, however weak, may make. Ought it not, for its own sole sake be satisfied? If not, prove why not."[20] Thus a world where more desires are satisfied is generally better than one where fewer are. However, not all desires can be legitimately satisfied, because as James suggests, there may be good reasons, such as the conflict of duty and desire, why some should be overruled.

Fortunately, further scrutiny of the situation reveals that there are good reasons why people should attempt with appropriate social support to talk themselves out of the desires in question or to consider novel ways of fulfilling them. Wanting to see the genetic line continued is not particularly rational when it brings a sinister legacy of illness and death. The desire for immortality cannot really be satisfied anyway, and people need to face the fact that what really matters is how they behave in their own lifetimes. And finally, the desire for children who physically resemble one is understandable, but basically narcissistic, and its fulfillment cannot be guaranteed even by normal reproduction. There are other ways of proving one is an adult, and other ways of cementing marriages – and children don't necessarily do either. Children, especially prematurely ill children, may not provide the expected economic benefits anyway. Nongenetically related children may also provide benefits similar to those that would have been provided by genetically related ones, and expected economic benefit is, in many cases, a morally questionable reason for having children.

Before the advent of reliable genetic testing, the options of people in Huntington's families were cruelly limited. On the one hand, they could have children, but at the risk of eventual crippling illness and death for them. On the other, they could refrain from child-bearing, sparing their possible children from significant risk of inheriting this disease, perhaps frustrating intense desires to procreate – only to discover, in some cases, that their sacrifice was unnecessary because they did not develop the disease. Or they could attempt to adopt or try new reproductive approaches.

Reliable genetic testing has opened up new possibilities. Those at risk who wish to have children can get tested. If they test positive, they know their possible children are at risk. Those who are opposed to abortion must be especially careful to avoid conception if they are to behave responsibly. Those not opposed to abortion can responsibly conceive children, but only if they are willing to test each fetus and abort those who carry the gene. If individuals at risk test negative, they are home free.

What about those who cannot face the test for themselves? They can do prenatal testing and abort fetuses who carry the defective gene. A clearly positive test also implies that the parent is affected, although negative tests do not rule out that possibility. Prenatal testing can thus bring knowledge that enables one to avoid passing the disease to others, but only, in some cases, at the cost of coming to know with certainty that one will indeed develop the disease. This situation raises with peculiar force the question of whether parental responsibility requires people to get tested.

Some people think that we should recognize a right "not to know." It seems to me that such a right could be defended only where ignorance does not put others at serious risk. So if people are prepared to forgo genetically related children, they need not get tested. But if they want genetically related children, then they must do whatever is necessary to ensure that affected babies are not the result. There is, after all, something inconsistent about the claim that one has a right to be shielded from the truth, even if the price is to risk inflicting on one's children the same dread disease one cannot even face in oneself.

In sum, until we can be assured that Huntington's Disease does not prevent people from living a minimally satisfying life, individuals at risk for the disease have a moral duty to try not to bring affected babies into this world. There are now enough options available so that this duty needn't frustrate their reasonable desires. Society has a corresponding duty to facilitate moral behavior on the part of individuals. Such support ranges from the narrow and concrete (such as making sure that medical testing and counseling is available to all) to the more general social environment that guarantees that all pregnancies are voluntary, that pronatalism is eradicated, and that women are treated with respect regardless of the reproductive options they choose.

Notes

1 I focus on genetic considerations, although with the advent of AIDS the scope of the general question here could be expanded. There are two reasons for sticking to this relatively narrow formulation. One is that dealing with a smaller chunk of the problem may help us to think more clearly, while realizing that some conclusions may nonetheless be relevant to the larger problem. The other is the peculiar capacity of some genetic problems to affect ever more individuals in the future.

2 For example, see Leon Kass, "Implications of Prenatal Diagnosis for the Human Right to Life," in *Ethical Issues in Human Genetics*, ed. Bruce Hilton et al. (New York: Plenum, 1973).

3 This is, of course, a very broad thesis. I defend an even broader version in ch. 2 of *Reproducing Persons*, "Loving Future People."

4 Why would we want to resist legal enforcement of every moral conclusion? First, legal action has many costs, costs not necessarily worth paying in particular cases. Second, legal enforcement tends to take the matter out of the realm of debate and treat it as settled. But in many cases, especially where mores or technology are rapidly evolving, we don't want that to happen. Third, legal enforcement would undermine individual freedom and decision-making capacity. In some cases, the ends envisioned are important enough to warrant putting up with these disadvantages.

5 Those who do not see fetuses as moral persons with a right to life may nonetheless hold that abortion is justifiable in these cases. I argue at some length elsewhere that lesser defects can cause great suffering. Once we are clear that there is nothing discriminatory about failing to conceive particular possible individuals, it makes sense, other things being equal, to avoid the prospect of such pain if we can. Naturally, other things rarely are equal. In the first place, many problems go undiscovered until a baby is born. Second, there are often substantial costs associated with screening programs. Third, although women should be encouraged to consider the moral dimensions of routine pregnancy, we do not want it to be so fraught with tension that it becomes a miserable experience. (See ch. 2 of *Reproducing Persons*, "Loving Future People.")

6 It should be noted that failing to conceive a single individual can affect many lives: in 1916, 962 cases could be traced from six seventeenth-century arrivals in America. See Gordon Rattray Taylor, *The Biological Time Bomb* (New York: Penguin, 1968), p. 176.

7   *The Merck Manual* (Rahway, NJ: Merck, 1972), pp. 1363, 1346. We now know that the age of onset and severity of the disease are related to the number of abnormal replications of the glutamine code on the abnormal gene. See Andrew Revkin, "Hunting Down Huntington's," *Discover* (December 1993): 108.

8   Hymie Gordon, "Genetic Counseling," *JAMA*, 217, no. 9 (August 30, 1971): 1346.

9   See Revkin, "Hunting Down Huntington's," 99–108.

10 "Gene for Huntington's Disease Discovered," *Human Genome News*, no. 1 (May 1993): 5.

11 Charles Smith, Susan Holloway, and Alan E. H. Emery, "Individuals at Risk in Families – Genetic Disease," *Journal of Medical Genetics*, 8 (1971): 453.

12 To try to separate the issue of the gravity of the disease from the existence of a given individual, compare this situation with how we would assess a parent who neglected to vaccinate an existing child against a hypothetical viral version of Huntington's.

13 *The New York Times* (September 30, 1975), p. 1. The Joseph family disease is similar to Huntington's Disease except that symptoms start appearing in the twenties. Rick Donohue was in his early twenties at the time he made this statement.

14 I have talked to college students who believe that they will have lived fully and be ready to die at those ages. It is astonishing how one's perspective changes over time and how ages that one once associated with senility and physical collapse come to seem the prime of human life.

15 The view I am rejecting has been forcefully articulated by Derek Parfit, *Reasons and Persons* (Oxford: Clarendon, 1984). For more discussion, see ch. 2 of *Reproducing Persons*, "Loving Future People."

16 I have some qualms about this response, because I fear that some human groups are so badly off that it might still be wrong for them to procreate, even if that would mean great changes in their cultures. But this is a complicated issue that needs to be investigated on its own.

17 Again, a troubling exception might be the isolated Venezuelan group Nancy Wexler found, where, because of inbreeding, a large proportion of the population is affected by Huntington's. See Revkin, "Hunting Down Huntington's."

18 Or surrogacy, as it has been popularly known. I think that "contract pregnancy" is more accurate and more respectful of women. Eggs can be provided either by a woman who also gestates the fetus or by a third party.

19 The most powerful objections to new reproductive technologies and arrangements concern possible bad consequences for women. However, I do not think that the arguments against them on these grounds have yet shown the dangers to be as great as some believe. So although it is perhaps true that new reproductive technologies and arrangements should not be used lightly, avoiding the conceptions discussed here is well worth the risk. For a series of viewpoints on this issue, including my own "Another Look at Contract Pregnancy" (ch. 12 of *Reproducing Persons*), see Helen B. Holmes, *Issues in Reproductive Technology I: An Anthology* (New York: Garland, 1992).

20 William James, *Essays in Pragmatism*, ed. A. Castell (New York: Hafner, 1948), p. 73.

10

Prenatal Diagnosis and Selective Abortion

A Challenge to Practice and Policy

Adrienne Asch

> Although sex selection might ameliorate the situation of some individuals, it lowers the status of women in general and only perpetuates the situation that gave rise to it....If we believe that sexual equality is necessary for a just society, then we should oppose sex selection.
>
> Wertz and Fletcher[1(pp242–243)]

> The very motivation for seeking an "origin" of homosexuality reveals homophobia. Moreover, such research may lead to prenatal tests that claim to predict for homosexuality. For homosexual people who live in countries with no legal protections these dangers are particularly serious.
>
> Schüklenk et al.[2(p6)]

The tenor of the preceding statements may spark relatively little comment in the world of health policy, the medical profession, or the readers of this journal, because many recognize the dangers of using the technology of prenatal testing followed by selective abortion for the characteristic of fetal sex. Similarly, the medical and psychiatric professions, and the world of public health, have aided in the civil rights struggle of gays and lesbians by insisting that homosexuality is not a disease. Consequently, many readers would concur with those who question the motives behind searching for the causes of homosexuality that might lead scientists to develop a prenatal test for that characteristic. Many in our society, however, have no such misgivings about prenatal testing for characteristics regarded as genetic or chromosomal diseases, abnormalities, or disabilities:

Human mating that proceeds without the use of genetic data about the risks of transmitting diseases will produce greater mortality and medical costs than if carriers of potentially deleterious genes are alerted to their carrier status and *encouraged* to mate with noncarriers or to use other reproductive strategies [emphasis added].[3(p84)]

Attitudes toward congenital disability per se have not changed markedly. Both premodern as well as contemporary societies have regarded disability as undesirable and to be avoided. Not only have parents recognized the birth of a disabled child as a potentially divisive, destructive force in the family unit, but the larger society has seen disability as unfortunate (p89)…. Our society still does not countenance the elimination of diseased/disabled people; but it does urge the termination of diseased/disabled fetuses. The urging is not explicit, but implicit (p90).[4]

Original publication details: Adrienne Asch, "Prenatal Diagnosis and Selective Abortion: A Challenge to Practice and Policy," pp. 1649–57 from *American Journal of Public Health* 89: 11 (1999). Reproduced with permission from American Public Health Association.

Writing in the *American Journal of Human Genetics* about screening programs for cystic fibrosis, A. L. Beaudet acknowledged the tension between the goals of enhancing reproductive choice and preventing the births of children who would have disabilities:

> Although some would argue that the success of the program should be judged solely by the effectiveness of the educational programs (i.e., whether screenees understood the information), it is clear that prevention of [cystic fibrosis] is also, at some level, a measure of a screening program, since few would advocate expanding the substantial resources involved if very few families wish to avoid the disease.[5(p603)]

Prenatal tests designed to detect the condition of the fetus include ultrasound, maternal serum α-fetoprotein screening, chorionic villus sampling, and amniocentesis. Some (ultrasound screenings) are routinely performed regardless of the mother's age and provide information that she may use to guide her care throughout pregnancy; others, such as chorionic villus sampling or amniocentesis, do not influence the woman's care during pregnancy but provide information intended to help her decide whether to continue the pregnancy if fetal impairment is detected. Amniocentesis, the test that detects the greatest variety of fetal impairments, is typically offered to women who will be 35 years or older at the time they are due to deliver, but recently commentators have urged that the age threshold be removed and that the test be available to women regardless of age.[6] Such testing is increasingly considered a standard component of prenatal care for women whose insurance covers these procedures, including women using publicly financed clinics in some jurisdictions.

These tests, which are widely accepted in the field of bioethics and by clinicians, public health professionals, and the general public, have nonetheless occasioned some apprehension and concern among students of women's reproductive experiences, who find that women do not uniformly welcome the expectation that they will undergo prenatal testing or the prospect of making decisions depending on the test results.[7] Less often discussed by clinicians is the view, expressed by a growing number of individuals, that the technology is itself based on erroneous assumptions about the adverse impact of disability on life. Argument from this perspective focuses on what is communicated about societal and familial acceptance of diversity in general and disability in particular.[8-17] Like other women-centered critiques of prenatal testing, this article assumes a pro-choice perspective but suggests that unreflective uses of testing could diminish, rather than expand, women's choices. Like critiques stemming from concerns about the continued acceptance of human differences within the society and the family, this critique challenges the view of disability that lies behind social endorsement of such testing and the conviction that women will, or should, end their pregnancies if they discover that the fetus has a disabling trait.

If public health frowns on efforts to select for or against girls or boys and would oppose future efforts to select for or against those who would have a particular sexual orientation, but promotes people's efforts to avoid having children who would have disabilities, it is because medicine and public health view disability as extremely different from and worse than these other forms of human variation. At first blush this view may strike one as self-evident. To challenge it might even appear to be questioning our professional mission. Characteristics such as chronic illnesses and disabilities (discussed together throughout this article) do not resemble traits such as sex, sexual orientation, or race, because the latter are not in themselves perceived as inimical to a rewarding life. Disability is thought to be just that – to be incompatible with life satisfaction. When public health considers matters of sex, sexual orientation, or race, it examines how factors in social and economic life pose obstacles to health and to health care, and it champions actions to improve the well-being of those disadvantaged by the discrimination that attends minority status. By contrast, public health fights to eradicate disease and disability or to treat, ameliorate, or cure these when they occur. For medicine and public health, disease and disability is the problem to solve, and so it appears natural to use prenatal testing and abortion as one more means of minimizing the incidence of disability.

In the remainder of this article I argue, first, that most of the problems associated with having a disability stem from discriminatory social arrangements that are changeable, just as much of what has in the past made the lives of women or gays difficult has been the set of social arrangements they have faced (and which they have begun to dismantle). After discussing ways in which the characteristic of disability resembles and differs from other characteristics, I discuss why I believe the technology of prenatal testing followed by selective abortion is unique among means of preventing or ameliorating disability, and why it offends many people who are untroubled by other disease prevention and health promotion activities. I conclude by recommending ways in which health practitioners and policymakers could offer this technology so that it promotes genuine reproductive choice and helps families and society to flourish.

Contrasting Medical and Social Paradigms of Disability

The definitions of terms such as "health," "normality," and "disability" are not clear, objective, and universal across time and place. Individual physical characteristics are evaluated with reference to a standard of normality, health, and what some commentators term "species-typical functioning."[18, 19] These commentators point out that within a society at a particular time, there is a shared perception of what is typical physical functioning and role performance for a girl or boy, woman or man. Boorse's definition of an undesirable departure from species-typicality focuses on the functioning of the person rather than the cause of the problem: "[A] condition of a part or process in an organism is pathological when the ability of the part or process to perform one or more of its species-typical biological functions falls below some central range of the statistical distribution for that ability."[18(p370)] Daniels writes, "Impairments of normal species functioning reduce the range of opportunity open to the individual in which he may construct his plan of life or conception of the good."[19(p27)]

Chronic illness, traumatic injury, and congenital disability may indeed occasion departures from "species-typical functioning," and thus these conditions do constitute differences from both a statistical average and a desired norm of well-being. Certainly society prizes some characteristics, such as intelligence, athleticism, and musical or artistic skill, and rewards

people with more than the statistical norm of these attributes; I will return to this point later. Norms on many health-related attributes change over time; as the life span for people in the United States and Canada increases, conditions that often lead to death before 40 years of age (e.g., cystic fibrosis) may become even more dreaded than they are today. The expectation that males will be taller than females and that adults will stand more than 5 feet in height leads to a perception that departures from these norms are not only unusual but undesirable and unhealthy. Not surprisingly, professionals who have committed themselves to preventing illness and injury, or to ameliorating and curing people of illnesses and injuries, are especially attuned to the problems and hardships that affect the lives of their patients. Such professionals, aware of the physical pain or weakness and the psychological and social disruption caused by acute illness or sudden injury, devote their lives to easing the problems that these events impose.

What many scholars, policymakers, and activists in the area of disability contend is that medically oriented understandings of the impact of disability on life contain 2 erroneous assumptions with serious adverse consequences: first, that the life of a person with a chronic illness or disability is forever disrupted, as one's life might be temporarily disrupted as a result of a back spasm, an episode of pneumonia, or a broken leg; second, that if a disabled person experiences isolation, powerlessness, unemployment, poverty, or low social status, these are inevitable consequences of biological limitation. Body, psyche, and social life do change immediately following an occurrence of disease, accident, or injury, and medicine, public health, and bioethics all correctly appreciate the psychological and physical vulnerability of patients and their families and friends during immediate medical crises. These professions fail people with disabilities, however, by concluding that because there may never be full physical recovery, there is never a regrouping of physical, cognitive, and psychological resources with which to participate in a rewarding life. Chronic illness and disability are not equivalent to acute illness or sudden injury, in which an active disease process or unexpected change in physical function disrupts life's routines. Most people with conditions such as spina bifida, achondroplasia, Down syndrome, and many other mobility and sensory impairments perceive themselves as healthy, not sick, and describe their conditions as givens of their lives – the equipment with which they meet the world. The same is true for people with chronic conditions such as cystic fibrosis, diabetes, hemophilia, and muscular dystrophy. These conditions include intermittent flare-ups requiring medical care and adjustments in daily living, but they do not render the person as unhealthy as most of the public – and members of the health profession – imagine.

People with disabilities are thinking about a traffic jam, a disagreement with a friend, which movie to attend, or which team will win the World Series – not just about their diagnosis. Having a disability can intrude into a person's consciousness if events bring it to the fore: if 2 lift-equipped buses in a row fail to stop for a man using a wheelchair; if the theater ticket agent insults a patron with Down syndrome by refusing to take money for her ticket; if a hearing-impaired person misses a train connection because he did not know that a track change had been announced.

The second way in which medicine, bioethics, and public health typically err is in viewing all problems that occur to people with disabilities as attributable to the condition itself, rather than to external factors. When ethicists, public health professionals, and policymakers discuss the importance of health care, urge accident prevention, or promote healthy lifestyles, they do so because they perceive a certain level of health not only as intrinsically desirable but as a prerequisite for an acceptable life. One commentator describes such a consensual view of types of life in terms of a "normal opportunity range": "The normal opportunity range for a given society is the array of life plans reasonable persons in it are likely to construct for themselves."[19(p33)] Health care includes that which is intended to "maintain, restore, or provide functional equivalents where possible, to normal species functioning."[19(p32)]

The paradigm of medicine concludes that the gaps in education, employment, and income that persist between adults with disabilities and those without disabilities are inevitable because the impairment precludes study or limits work. The alternative paradigm, which views people with disabilities in social, minority-group terms, examines how societal arrangements – rules, laws, means of communication, characteristics of buildings and transit systems, the typical 8-hour workday – exclude some people from participating in school, work, civic, or social life. This newer paradigm is expressed by enactment of the Individuals with Disabilities Education Act and the Americans with Disabilities Act and is behind the drive to ensure that employed disabled people will keep their access to health care through Medicaid or Medicare. This paradigm – still more accepted by people outside medicine, public health, and bioethics than by those within these fields – questions whether there is an inevitable, unmodifiable gap between people with disabilities and people without disabilities. Learning that in 1999, nine years after the passage of laws to end employment discrimination, millions of people with disabilities are still out of the work force, despite their readiness to work,[20] the social paradigm asks what remaining institutional factors bar people from the goal of productive work. Ethical and policy questions arise in regard to the connection that does or should exist between health and the range of opportunities open to people in the population.

Commitments to alleviate the difficulties arising from chronic illness and disability and efforts to promote healthy lifestyles throughout the population need not lead to a devaluation of the members of society who do not meet our typical understanding of health, but people with disabilities have indeed been subject to systematic segregation and second-class treatment in all areas of life. It is possible to appreciate the norm of 2 arms without being repelled by a woman with 1 arm; yet social science, autobiography, legislation, and case law reveal that people with both visible and "invisible" disabilities lose opportunities to study, work, live where and with whom they choose, attend religious services, and even vote.[21-27]

The Americans with Disabilities Act, signed into law in 1990, is a ringing indictment of the nation's history with regard to people with disabilities:

Congress finds that…(3) discrimination against individuals with disabilities persists in such critical areas as employment,…education, recreation,…health services,…and access to public services; (7) individuals with disabilities are a discrete and insular minority who have been faced with restrictions and limitations, subjected to a history of purposeful unequal treatment, and relegated to a position of political powerlessness in our society, based on characteristics that are beyond the control of such individuals and resulting from stereotypic assumptions not truly indicative of the individual ability of such individuals to participate in, and contribute to, society.[28]

Eight years after the passage of the Americans with Disabilities Act, disabled people reported some improvements in access to public facilities and that things are getting better in some areas of life, but major gaps between the disabled and the nondisabled still exist in income, employment, and social participation. To dramatically underscore the prevalence of social stigma and discrimination: "fewer than half (45%) of adults with disabilities say that people generally treat them as an equal after they learn they have a disability."[20]

It is estimated that 54 million people in the United States have disabilities, of which impairments of mobility, hearing, vision, and learning; arthritis; cystic fibrosis; diabetes; heart conditions; and back problems are some of the most well-known.[20] Thus, in discussing discrimination, stigma, and unequal treatment for people with disabilities, we are considering a population that is larger than the known gay and lesbian population or the African American population. These numbers take on new significance when we assess the rationale behind prenatal diagnosis and selective abortion as a desirable strategy to deal with disability.

Prenatal diagnosis for disability prevention

If some forms of disability prevention are legitimate medical and public health activities, and if people with disabilities use the health system to improve and maintain their own health, there is an acknowledgment that the characteristic of disability may not be desirable. Although many within the disability rights movement challenge prenatal diagnosis as a means of disability prevention, no one objects to public health efforts to clean up the environment, encourage seatbelt use, reduce tobacco and alcohol consumption, and provide prenatal care to all pregnant women. All these activities deal with the health of existing human beings (or fetuses expected to come to term) and seek

to ensure their well-being. What differentiates prenatal testing followed by abortion from other forms of disability prevention and medical treatment is that prenatal testing followed by abortion is intended not to prevent the disability or illness of a born or future human being but to prevent the birth of a human being who will have one of these undesired characteristics. In reminding proponents of the Human Genome Project that gene therapy will not soon be able to cure disability, James Watson declared,

> [W]e place most of our hopes for genetics on the use of antenatal diagnostic procedures, which increasingly will let us know whether a fetus is carrying a mutant gene that will seriously proscribe its eventual development into a functional human being. By terminating such pregnancies, the threat of horrific disease genes contributing to blight many family's prospects for future success can be erased.[29(p19)]

But Watson errs in assuming that tragedy is inevitable for the child or for the family. When physicians, public health experts, and bioethicists promote prenatal diagnosis to prevent future disability, they let disability become the only relevant characteristic and suggest that it is such a problematic characteristic that people eagerly awaiting a new baby should terminate the pregnancy and "try again" for a healthy child. Professionals fail to recognize that along with whatever impairment may be diagnosed come all the characteristics of any other future child. The health professions suggest that once a prospective parent knows of the likely disability of a future child, there is nothing else to know or imagine about who the child might become: disability subverts parental dreams.

The focus of my concern here is not on the decision made by the pregnant woman or by the woman and her partner. I focus on the view of life with disability that is communicated by society's efforts to develop prenatal testing and urge it on every pregnant woman. If public health espouses goals of social justice and equality for people with disabilities, as it has worked to improve the status of women, gays and lesbians, and members of racial and ethnic minorities, it should reconsider whether it wishes to continue endorsing the technology of prenatal diagnosis. If there is an unshakable commitment to the technology in the name of reproductive choice, public health should work with practitioners to change the way in which information about impairments detected in the fetus is delivered.

Rationales for prenatal testing

The medical professions justify prenatal diagnosis and selective abortion on the grounds of the *costs* of childhood disability – the costs to the child, to the family, and to the society. Some proponents of the Human Genome Project from the fields of science and bioethics argue that in a world of limited resources, we can reduce disability-related expenditures if all diagnoses of fetal impairment are followed by abortion.[30]

On both empirical and moral grounds, endorsing prenatal diagnosis for societal reasons is dangerous. Only a small fraction of total disability can now be detected prenatally, and even if future technology enables the detection of predisposition to diabetes, forms of depression, Alzheimer disease, heart disease, arthritis, or back problems – all more prevalent in the population than many of the currently detectable conditions – we will never manage to detect and prevent most disability. Rates of disability increase markedly with age, and the gains in life span guarantee that most people will deal with disability in themselves or someone close to them. Laws and services to support people with disabilities will still be necessary, unless society chooses a campaign of eliminating disabled people in addition to preventing the births of those who would be disabled. Thus, there is small cost-saving in money or in human resources to be achieved by even the vigorous determination to test every pregnant woman and abort every fetus found to exhibit disabling traits.

My moral opposition to prenatal testing and selective abortion flows from the conviction that life with disability is worthwhile and the belief that a just society must appreciate and nurture the lives of all people, whatever the endowments they receive in the natural lottery. I hold these beliefs because – as I show throughout this article – there is abundant evidence that people with disabilities can thrive even in this less than welcoming society. Moreover, people with disabilities do not merely take from others, they contribute as well – to families, to friends, to the economy. They contribute neither in spite of nor because of their disabilities, but because along with their disabilities come other characteristics of personality, talent, and humanity that render people with disabilities full members of the human and moral community.

Implications for People with Disabilities

Implications for children and adults with disabilities, and for their families, warrant more consideration. Several prominent bioethicists claim that to knowingly bring into the world a child who will live with an impairment (whether it be a "withered arm," cystic fibrosis, deafness, or Down syndrome) is unfair to the child because it deprives the child of the "right to an open future" by limiting some options.[31] Green's words represent a significant strand of professional thinking: "In the absence of adequate justifying reasons, a child is morally wronged when he/she is knowingly, deliberately, or negligently brought into being with a health status likely to result in significantly greater disability or suffering, or significantly reduced life options relative to the other children with whom he/she will grow up."[32(p10)] Green is not alone in his view that it is irresponsible to bring a child into the world with a disability.[33, 34]

The biology of disability can affect people's lives, and not every feature of life with a disability is socially determined or mediated. People with cystic fibrosis cannot now expect to live to age 70. People with type I diabetes can expect to have to use insulin and to have to think carefully and continuously about what and how much they eat and about their rest and exercise, perhaps more than typical sedentary people who are casual about the nutritional content of their food. People who use a wheelchair for mobility will not climb mountains; people with the intellectual disabilities of Down syndrome or fragile X chromosome are not likely to read this article and engage in debate about its merits and shortcomings. Yet, as disability scholars point out, such limitations do not preclude a whole class of experiences, but only certain instances in which these experiences might occur. People who move through the world in wheelchairs may not be able to climb mountains, but they can and do participate in other athletic activities that are challenging and exhilarating and call for stamina, alertness, and teamwork. Similarly, people who have Down syndrome or fragile X chromosome are able to have other experiences of thinking hard about important questions and making distinctions and decisions. Thus, they exercise capacities for reflection and judgment, even if not in the rarified world of abstract verbal argument (P. Ferguson, e-mail, March 5, 1999).

The child who will have a disability may have fewer options for the so-called open future that philosophers and parents dream of for children. Yet I suspect that disability precludes far fewer life possibilities than members of the bioethics community claim. That many people with disabilities find their lives satisfying has been documented. For example, more than half of people with spinal cord injury (paraplegia) reported feeling more positively about themselves since becoming disabled.[35(p83)] Similarly, Canadian teenagers who had been extremely-low-birthweight infants were compared with nondisabled teens and found to resemble them in terms of their own subjective ratings of quality of life. "Adolescents who were [extremely-low-birthweight] infants suffer from a greater burden of morbidity, and rate their healthrelated quality of life as significantly lower than control teenagers. Nevertheless, the vast majority of the [extremely-low-birthweight] respondents view their health-related quality of life as quite satisfactory and are difficult to distinguish from controls."[36(p453)]

Interestingly, professionals faced with such information often dismiss it and insist that happy disabled people are the exceptions.[37] Here again, James Watson expresses a common view when he says,

> Is it more likely for such children to fall behind in society or will they through such afflictions develop the strengths of character and fortitude that lead…to the head of their packs? Here I'm afraid that the word handicap cannot escape its true definition – being placed at a disadvantage. From this perspective seeing the bright side of being handicapped is like praising the virtues of extreme poverty. To be sure, there are many individuals who rise out of its inherently degrading states. But we perhaps most realistically should see it as the major origin of asocial behavior. [29(p19)]

I return to the points made earlier regarding how many of the supposed limits and problems associated with disability are socially, rather than biologically, imposed. The 1998 survey of disabled people in the United States conducted by Louis Harris Associates found gaps in education, employment, income, and social participation between people with disabilities and people without disabilities and noted that fewer disabled than nondisabled people were "extremely satisfied" with their lives. The reasons for dissatisfaction did not stem from anything inherent in the impairments; they stemmed from disparities in attainments and activities that are not inevitable in a society that takes into account the needs of one sixth of its members.[20] Only 29% of people with disabilities work full- or part-time, yet of disabled working-age people surveyed who were unemployed, more than 70% would prefer to work, and most did not perceive their disability as precluding them from productive employment. Unemployment, and thus inadequate income, coupled with problems in obtaining health insurance or in having that insurance pay for actual disability-related expenses, accounts for the problems most commonly described by disabled people as diminishing life satisfaction.[20]

For children whose disabling conditions do not cause early degeneration, intractable pain, and early death, life offers a host of interactions with the physical and social world in which people can be involved to their and others' satisfaction. Autobiographical writings and family narratives testify eloquently to the rich lives and the even richer futures that are possible for people with disabilities today[22,38] (also P. Ferguson, e-mail, March 5, 1999).

Nonetheless, I do not deny that disability can entail physical pain, phychic anguish, and social isolation – even if much of the psychological and social pain can be attributed to human cruelty rather than to biological givens. In order to imagine bringing a child with a disability into the world when abortion is possible, prospective parents must be able to imagine saying to a child, "I wanted you enough and believed enough in who you could be that I felt you could have a life you would appreciate even with the difficulties your disability causes." If parents and siblings, family members and friends can genuinely love and enjoy the child for who he or she is and not lament what he or she is not; if child care centers, schools, and youth groups routinely include disabled children; if television programs, children's books, and toys take children with disabilities into account by including them naturally in programs and products, the child may not live with the anguish and isolation that have marred life for generations of disabled children.

Implications for Family Life

Many who are willing to concede that people with disabilities could have lives they themselves would enjoy nonetheless argue that the cost to families of raising them justifies abortion. Women are seen to carry the greatest load for the least return in caring for such a child. Proponents of using the technology to avoid the births of children with disabilities insist that the disabled child epitomizes what women have fought to change about their lives as mothers: unending labor, the sacrifice of their work and other adult interests, loss of time and attention for the other children in the family as they juggle resources to give this disabled child the best available support, and uncertain recompense in terms of the mother's relationship with the child.[39]

Writing in 1995 on justifications for prenatal testing, Botkin proposed that only conditions that impose "burdens" on parents equivalent to those of an unwanted child warrant society-supported testing.

> The parent's harms are different in many respects from the child's, but include emotional pain and suffering, loss of a child, loss of opportunities, loss of freedom, isolation, loneliness, fear, guilt, stigmatization, and financial expenses....Some conditions that are often considered severe may not be associated with any experience of harm for the child. Down syndrome is a prime example. Parents in this circumstance are not harmed by the suffering of a child...but rather by their time, efforts, and expenses to support the special needs of an individual with Down syndrome....It might also be added that parents are harmed by their unfulfilled expectations with the birth of an impaired child. In general terms, the claim is that parents suffer a sufficient harm to justify prenatal testing or screening when the severity of a child's condition raises problems for the parents of a similar magnitude to the birth of an unwanted child....

> [P]arents of a child with unwanted disability have their interests impinged upon by the efforts, time, emotional burdens, and expenses added by the disability that they would not have otherwise experienced with the birth of a healthy child.[40(pp36–37)]

I believe the characterizations found in the writings of Wertz and Fletcher[39] and Botkin[40] are at the heart of professionals' support for prenatal testing and deserve careful scrutiny. Neither Wertz and Fletcher nor Botkin offer citations to literature to support their claims of family burden, changed lifestyle, disappointed expectations, or additional expenses, perhaps because they believe these are indisputable. Evaluating the claims, however, requires recognizing an assumption implied in them: that there is no benefit to offset the "burden," in the way that parents can expect rewards of many kinds in their relationship with children who do not have disabilities. This assumption, which permeates much of the medical, social science, and bioethics literature on disability and family life and disability in general, rests on a mistaken notion. As rehabilitation psychologist Beatrice Wright has long maintained,[41,42] people imagine that incapacity in one arena spreads to incapacity in all – the child with cystic fibrosis is always sick and can never play; the child who cannot walk cannot join classmates in word games, parties, or sleepovers; someone who is blind is also unable to hear or speak. Someone who needs assistance with one activity is perceived to need assistance in all areas and to contribute nothing to the social, emotional, or instrumental aspects of family life.

Assuming for a moment that there are "extra burdens" associated with certain aspects of raising children with disabilities, consider the "extra burdens" associated with raising other children: those with extraordinary (above statistical norm) aptitude for athletics, art, music, or mathematics. In a book on gifted children, Ellen Winner writes,

> [A]ll the family's energy becomes focused on this child....Families focus in two ways on the gifted child's development: either one or both parents spend a great deal of time stimulating and teaching the child themselves, or parents make sacrifices so that the child gets high-level training from the best available teachers. In both cases, family life is totally arranged around the

child's needs. Parents channel their interests into their child's talent area and become enormously invested in their child's progress.[43(p187)]

Parents, professionals working with the family, and the larger society all value the gift of the violin prodigy, the talent of the future Olympic figure skater, the aptitude of a child who excels in science and who might one day discover the cure for cancer. They perceive that all the extra work and rearrangement associated with raising such children will provide what people seek in parenthood: the opportunity to give ourselves to a new being who starts out with the best we can give, who will enrich us, gladden others, contribute to the world, and make us proud.

If professionals and parents believed that children with disabilities could indeed provide their parents many of the same satisfactions as any other child in terms of stimulation, love, companionship, pride, and pleasure in influencing the growth and development of another, they might reexamine their belief that in psychological, material, and social terms, the burdens of raising disabled children outweigh the benefits. A vast array of literature, both parental narrative and social science quantitative and qualitative research, powerfully testifies to the rewards – typical and atypical – of raising children with many of the conditions for which prenatal testing is considered de rigeur and abortion is expected (Down syndrome, hemophilia, cystic fibrosis, to name only some).[44–50] Yet bioethics, public health, and genetics remain woefully – scandalously – oblivious, ignorant, or dismissive of any information that challenges the conviction that disability dooms families.

Two years before the gene mutation responsible for much cystic fibrosis was identified, Walker et al. published their findings about the effects of cystic fibrosis on family life. They found that mothers of children with cystic fibrosis did not differ from mothers of children without the condition on measures of

> …Child Dependency and Management Difficulty, Limits on Family Opportunity, Family Disharmony, and Financial Stress. The difference between the two groups of mothers almost reached statistical significance on a fifth subscale, Personal Burden, which measured the mother's feeling of burden in her caretaking role.… The similarities between mothers of children with cystic

fibrosis and those with healthy children were more apparent than the differences. Mothers of children with cystic fibrosis did not report significantly higher levels of stress than did the control group mothers of healthy children. Contrary to suggestions that mothers of children with cystic fibrosis feel guilty and inadequate as parents, the mothers in this study reported levels of parenting competence equal to those reported by the mothers of healthy children.[50(pp242–243)]

The literature on how disability affects family life is, to be sure, replete with discussions of stress; anger at unsupportive members of the helping professions; distress caused by hostility from extended family, neighbors, and strangers; and frustration that many disability-related expenses are not covered by health insurance.[44–51] And it is a literature that increasingly tries to distinguish why – under what conditions – some families of disabled children founder and others thrive. Contrary to the beliefs still much abroad in medicine, bioethics, and public health, recent literature does not suggest that, on balance, families raising children who have disabilities experience more stress and disruption than any other family.[52]

Implications for Professional Practice

Reporting in 1997 on a 5-year study of how families affected by cystic fibrosis and sickle cell anemia viewed genetic testing technologies, Duster and Beeson learned to their surprise that the closer the relationship between the family member and the affected individual, the more uncomfortable the family member was with the technology.

> [The] closer people are to someone with genetic disease the more problematic and usually unacceptable genetic testing is as a strategy for dealing with the issues.… The experience of emotional closeness to someone with a genetic disease reduces, rather than increases, the acceptability of selective abortion. A close relationship with an affected person appears to make it more difficult to evaluate the meaning or worth of that person's existence solely in terms of their genetic disease. Family members consistently affirm the value of the person's life in spite of the disorders, and see value for their family in their

experiences with [and] of this member, and in meeting the challenges the disease poses.[53(p43)]

This finding is consistent with other reports that parents of children with disabilities generally reject the idea of prenatal testing and abortion of subsequent fetuses, even if those fetuses are found to carry the same disabling trait.[54, 55]

Professionals charged with developing technologies, offering tests, and interpreting results should assess their current assumptions and practice on the basis of the literature on disability and family life generally and data about how such families perceive selective abortion. Of the many implications of such data, the first is that familiarity with disability as one characteristic of a child one loves changes the meaning of disability for parents contemplating a subsequent birth. The disability, instead of being the child's sole, or most salient, characteristic, becomes only one of the child's characteristics, along with appearance, aptitudes, temperament, interests, and quirks. The typical woman or couple discussing prenatal testing and possible pregnancy termination knows very little about the conditions for which testing is available, much less what these conditions might mean for the daily life of the child and the family. People who do not already have a child with a disability and who are contemplating prenatal testing must learn considerably more than the names of some typical impairments and the odds of their child's having one.

To provide ethical and responsible clinical care for anyone concerned about reproduction, professionals themselves must know far more than they now do about life with disability; they must convey more information, and different information, than they now typically provide. Shown a film about the lives of families raising children with Down syndrome, nurses and genetic counselors – but not parents – described the film as unrealistic and too positive a portrayal of family life.[56] Whether the clinician is a genetics professional or (as is increasingly the case) an obstetrician promoting prenatal diagnosis as routine care for pregnant women, the tone, timing, and content of the counseling process cry out for drastic overhaul.

Many discussions of genetic counseling suggest that counselors (even graduates of master's-level genetic counseling programs, who now provide a minority of the information that surrounds the testing process and the decisions following results) are ill equipped by their own training and norms of practice to provide any insights into disability in today's society. Most graduate programs in genetic counseling do not include courses in the social implications of life with disability for children and families; do not include contact between counselor trainees and disabled children and adults outside clinical settings; and do not expose counselors to the laws, disability rights organizations, and peer support groups that constitute what is described as the disability rights and independent living movement. Often, if providers seek a "consumer" perspective on genetic issues, they consult the Alliance of Genetic Support Groups. This organization, however, has focused on genetic research and cure and has not concentrated on improving life for people with genetic disabilities; it is not currently allied in activity or ideology with the disabled community and the social paradigm of disability. Reviews of medical school curricula suggest that medical students do not receive formal instruction on life with disability, which would remind them that the people with disabilities they see in their offices have lives outside those offices.

Until their own education is revamped, obstetricians, midwives, nurses, and genetics professionals cannot properly counsel prospective parents. With broader exposure themselves, they would be far more likely to engage in discussions with their patients that would avoid problems such as those noted by Lippman and Wilfond in a survey of genetic counselors. These researchers found that counselors provided far more positive information about Down syndrome and cystic fibrosis to parents already raising children diagnosed with those conditions than they did to prospective parents deciding whether to continue pregnancies in which the fetus had been found to have the condition.

> At the least, we must recognize that every description of a genetic disorder is a story that contains a message. The story is the vehicle through which complex and voluminous information is reduced for the purposes of communication between health-care provider and health-care seeker. The message is shaped as the storyteller selects what to include and what to exclude to reduce the amount of information.... Should we strive to tell the same story to families considering

carrier testing and prenatal diagnosis and to families who receive a postnatal diagnosis?...Is telling the same story required if we are to provide sufficiently balanced information to allow potential parents to make fully informed family-planning decisions?[57]

Lippman and Wilfond question the disparity in information provided; I call for change to ensure that everyone obtaining testing or seeking information about genetic or prenatally diagnosable disability receives sufficient information about predictable difficulties, supports, and life events associated with a disabling condition to enable them to consider how a child's disability would fit into their own hopes for parenthood. Such information for all prospective parents should include, at a minimum, a detailed description of the biological, cognitive, or psychological impairments associated with specific disabilities, and what those impairments imply for day-to-day functioning; a discussion of the laws governing education, entitlements to family support services, access to buildings and transportation, and financial assistance to disabled children and their families; and literature by family members of disabled children and by disabled people themselves.

If prenatal testing indicates a disabling condition in the fetus, the following disability-specific information should be given to the prospective parents: information about services to benefit children with specific disabilities in a particular area, and about which of these a child and family are likely to need immediately after birth; contact information for a parent-group representative; and contact information for a member of a disability rights group or independent living center. In addition, the parents should be offered a visit with both a child and family and an adult living with the diagnosed disability.

Although some prospective parents will reject some or all of this information and these contacts, responsible practice that is concerned with genuine informed decision making and true reproductive choice must include access to this information, timed so that prospective parents can assimilate general ideas about life with disability before testing and obtain particular disability-relevant information if they discover that their fetus carries a disabling trait. These ideas may appear unrealistic or unfeasible, but a growing number of diverse voices support similar versions of these reforms to encourage wise decision making. Statements by Little People of America, the National Down Syndrome Congress, the National Institutes of Health workshop, and the Hastings Center Project on Prenatal Testing for Genetic Disability all urge versions of these changes in the process of helping people make childbearing decisions.[58–61]

These proposals may be startling in the context of counseling for genetically transmitted or prenatally diagnosable disability, but they resonate with the recent discussion about childbearing for women infected with the HIV virus:

> The primary task of the provider would be to engage the client in a meaningful discussion of the implications of having a child and of not having a child for herself, for the client's family and for the child who would be born....Providers would assist clients in examining what childbearing means to them....Providers also would assist clients in gaining an understanding of the factual information relevant to decisions about childbearing... however, the conversation would cover a range of topics that go far beyond what can be understood as the relevant *medical* facts, and the direction of the conversation would vary depending on each person's life circumstances and priorities [emphasis added].[62(pp453–454)]

This counseling process for women with HIV who are considering motherhood demonstrates that information in itself is not sufficient. As Mary White, Arthur Caplan, and other commentators on genetic counseling have noted, the norm of nondirectiveness, even when followed, may leave people who are seeking help with difficult decisions feeling bewildered and abandoned.[63,64] Along with others who have expressed growing concern about needed reforms in the conduct of prenatal testing and counseling, I urge a serious conversation between prospective parents and clinicians about what the parents seek in childrearing and how a disabling condition in general or a specific type of impairment would affect their hopes and expectations for the rewards of parenthood. For some people, any mobility, sensory, cognitive, or health impairment may indeed lead to disappointment of parental hopes; for others, it may be far easier to imagine incorporating disability into family life without believing that the rest of their lives will be blighted.

Ideally, such discussions will include mention of the fact that every child inevitably differs from parental dreams, and that successful parenting requires a mix of shaping and influencing children and ruefully appreciating the ways they pick and choose from what parents offer, sometimes rejecting tastes, activities, or values dear to the parents. If prospective parents cannot envision appreciating the child who will depart in particular, known ways from the parents' fantasy, are they truly ready to raise would-be athletes when they hate sports, classical violinists when they delight in the Grateful Dead? Testing and abortion guarantee little about the child and the life parents create and nurture, and all parents and children will be harmed by inflated notions of what parenting in an age of genetic knowledge can bring in terms of fulfilled expectations.

Public health professionals must do more than they have been doing to change the climate in which prenatal tests are offered. Think about what people would say if prenatal clinics contained pamphlets telling poor women or African American women that they should consider refraining from childbearing because their children could be similarly poor and could endure discrimination or because they could be less healthy and more likely to find themselves imprisoned than members of the middle class or than Whites. Public health is committed to ending such inequities, not to endorsing them, tolerating them, or asking prospective parents to live with them. Yet the current promotion of prenatal testing condones just such an approach to life with disability.

Practitioners and policymakers can increase women's and couples' reproductive choice through testing and counseling, and they can expend energy and resources on changing the society in which families consider raising disabled children. If families that include children with disabilities now spend more money and ingenuity on after-school care for those children because they are denied entrance into existing programs attended by their peers and siblings,[65] public health can join with others to ensure that existing programs include *all* children. The principle of education for all, which is reforming public education for disabled children, must spread to incorporate those same children into the network of services and supports that parents count on for other children. Such programs, like other institutions, must change to

fit the people who exist in the world, not claim that some people should not exist because society is not prepared for them. We can fight to reform insurance practices that deny reimbursement for diabetes test strips; special diets for people with disabilities; household modifications that give disabled children freedom to explore their environment; and modifications of equipment, games, and toys that enable disabled children to participate in activities comparable to those of their peers. Public health can fight to end the catch-22 that removes subsidies for life-sustaining personal assistance services once disabled people enter the workforce, a policy that acts as a powerful disincentive to productivity and needlessly perpetuates poverty and dependence.

Laws such as the Individuals with Disabilities Education Act and the Americans with Disabilities Act chart a course of inclusion for disabled people of all ages. In 1980, Gliedman and Roth, who pioneered the development of the minority-group paradigm that infuses much of the critique of current genetic technology, wrote a blueprint for the inclusive society that public health should strive to create:

> Suppose that somewhere in the world an advanced industrial society genuinely respected the needs and the humanity of handicapped people. What would a visitor from this country make of the position of the disabled individual in American life?...To begin with, the traveler would take for granted that a market of millions of children and tens of millions of adults would not be ignored. He would assume that many industries catered to the special needs of the handicapped. Some of these needs would be purely medical...but many would not be medical. The visitor would expect to find industries producing everyday household and domestic appliances designed for the use of people with poor motor coordination....He would anticipate a profusion of specialized and sometimes quite simple gadgets designed to enhance control of a handicapped person over his physical world – special hand tools, office supplies, can openers, eating utensils, and the like....
>
> As he examined our newspapers, magazines, journals and books, as he watched our movies, television shows, and went to our theaters, he would look for many reports about handicap,... cartoon figures on children's TV programs, and many characters in children's stories who are handicapped. He would expect constantly to come across advertisements aimed at handicapped people. He

would expect to find many handicapped people appearing in advertisements not specifically aimed at them.

The traveler would explore our factories, believing that handicapped people were employed in proportion to their vast numbers....He would walk the streets of our towns and cities. And everywhere he went he would expect to see multitudes of handicapped people going about their business, taking a holiday, passing an hour with able-bodied or handicapped friends, or simply being alone....

He would explore our manmade environment, anticipating that provision was made for the handicapped in our cities and towns....He would expect the tiniest minutiae of our dwellings to reflect the vast numbers of disabled people....

He would assume that disabled individuals had their share of elected and appointive offices. He would expect to find that the role played by the disabled as a special interest group at the local and national levels was fully commensurate with their great numbers.[66(pp13–15)]

Despite the strides of the past few decades, our current society is far from the ideal described by Gliedman and Roth, an ideal toward which the disability community strives. Medicine, bioethics, and public health can put their efforts toward promoting such a society; with such efforts, disability could become nearly as easy to incorporate into the familial and social landscape as the other differences these professions respect and affirm as ordinary parts of the human condition. Given that more than 50 million people in the US population have disabling traits and that prenatal tests may become increasingly available to detect more of them, we are confronting the fact that tests may soon be available for characteristics that we have until now considered inevitable facts of human life, such as heart disease.

In order to make testing and selecting for or against disability consonant with improving life for those who will inevitably be born with or acquire disabilities, our clinical and policy establishments must communicate that it is as acceptable to live with a disability as it is to live without one and that society will support and appreciate everyone with the inevitable variety of traits. We can assure prospective parents that they and their future child will be welcomed whether or not the child has a disability. If that professional message is conveyed, more prospective parents may envision that their lives can be rewarding, whatever the characteristics of the child they are raising. When our professions can envision such communication and the reality of incorporation and appreciation of people with disabilities, prenatal technology can help people to make decisions without implying that only one decision is right. If the child with a disability is not a problem for the world, and the world is not a problem for the child, perhaps we can diminish our desire for prenatal testing and selective abortion and can comfortably welcome and support children of all characteristics.

Acknowledgments

This article benefited from my involvement with the project on Prenatal Testing for Genetic Disability of The Hastings Center. Many thanks go to Betty Wolder Levin for giving me the opportunity to present these views. Daniel Goldstein, Alison MacIntyre, Lili Schwan-Rosenwald, Maggie Starr, Caroline Moon, Deborah Kent, Rosemary Agnew, Simone Davion, and Taran Jeffries provided invaluable help in several phases of the work on this article under exceptionally difficult circumstances.

References

1 Wertz DC, Fletcher JC. Sex selection through prenatal diagnosis. In: Holmes HB, Purdy LM, eds. *Feminist Perspectives in Medical Ethics*. Bloomington: Indiana University Press; 1992:240–253.

2 Schüklenk U, Stein E, Kerin J, Byne W. The ethics of genetic research on sexual orientation. *Hastings Center Rep.* 1997;27(4):6–13.

3 *Mapping Our Genes*. Washington, DC: US Congress, Office of Technology Assessment; 1988.

4 Retsinas J. Impact of prenatal technology on attitudes toward disabled infants. In: Wertz D. *Research in the Sociology of Healthcare*. Westport, Conn: JAI Press; 1991:75–102.

5 Beaudet AL. Carrier screening for cystic fibrosis. *Am J Hum Genet.* 1990;47:603–605.

6 Kuppermann M, Goldberg JD, Nease RF, Washington AE. Who should be offered prenatal diagnosis? The thirty-five-year-old question. *Am J Public Health.* 1999; 89:160–163.

7 Rothenberg KH, Thompson EJ, eds. *Women and Prenatal Testing: Facing the Challenges of Genetic Technology*. Columbus: Ohio State University Press; 1994.

8 Miringoff ML. *The Social Costs of Genetic Welfare*. New Brunswick, NJ: Rutgers University Press; 1991.

9 Hubbard R. *The Politics of Women's Biology*. New Brunswick, NJ: Rutgers University Press; 1990:chap 12–14.

10 Lippman A. Prenatal genetic testing and screening: constructing needs and reinforcing inequities. *Am J Law Med*. 1991;17(1–2):15–50.

11 Field MA. Killing "the handicapped" – before and after birth. *Harvard Womens Law J*. 1993;16:79–138.

12 Fine M, Asch A. The question of disability: no easy answers for the women's movement. *Reproductive Rights Newsletter*. 1982;4(3):19–20.

13 Minden S. Born and unborn: the implications of reproductive technologies for people with disabilities. In: Arditti R, Duelli-Klein R, Mindin S, eds. *Test-Tube Women: What Future for Motherhood?* Boston, Mass: Pandora Press; 1984:298–312.

14 Finger, A. *Past Due: Disability, Pregnancy and Birth*. Seattle, Wash: Seal Press; 1987.

15 Kaplan D. Prenatal screening and diagnosis: the impact on persons with disabilities. In: Rothenberg KH, Thompson EJ, eds. *Women and Prenatal Testing: Facing the Challenges of Genetic Technology*. Columbus: Ohio State University Press; 1994:49–61.

16 Asch A. Reproductive technology and disability. In: Cohen S, Taub N. *Reproductive Laws for the 1990s*. Clifton, NJ: Humana Press; 1989:69–124.

17 Asch A, Geller G. Feminism, bioethics and genetics. In: Wolf S, ed. *Feminism and Bioethics: Beyond Reproduction*. New York, NY: Oxford University Press; 1996: 318–350.

18 Boorse C. Concepts of health. In: Van de Veer D, Regan T, eds. *Health Care Ethics*. Philadelphia, Pa: Temple University Press; 1987:359–393.

19 Daniels NL. *Just Health Care: Studies in Philosophy and Health Policy*. Cambridge, England: Cambridge University Press; 1985.

20 National Organization on Disability's 1998 Harris Survey of Americans With Disabilities. See http://nod.org/research_publications/surveys_research and http://www.socio.com/rad43.php.

21 Schneider J, Conrad P. *Having Epilepsy: The Experience and Control of Illness*. Philadelphia, Pa: Temple University Press; 1983.

22 Brightman AJ. *Ordinary Moments: The Disabled Experience*. Baltimore, Md: Paul H. Brookes Publishing Co; 1984.

23 Goffman E. *Stigma: Notes on the Management of Spoiled Identity*. Englewood Cliffs, NJ: Prentice-Hall; 1963.

24 Gartner A, Joe T. *Images of the Disabled, Disabling Images*. New York, NY: Praeger; 1987.

25 Hockenberry J. *Moving Violations: War Zones, Wheelchairs, and Declarations of Independence*. New York, NY: Hyperion; 1996.

26 Russel M. *Beyond Ramps: Disability at the End of the Social Contract*. Monroe, Me: Common Courage Press; 1998.

27 Bickenbach JE. *Physical Disability and Social Policy*. Toronto, Ontario: University of Toronto Press; 1993.

28 Americans with Disabilities Act (Pub L No. 101–336, 1990, § 2).

29 Watson JD. President's essay: genes and politics. *Annual Report Cold Springs Harbor*. 1996:1–20.

30 Shaw MW. Presidential address: to be or not to be, that is the question. *Am J Human Genetics*. 1984; 36:1–9.

31 Feinberg J. The child's right to an open future. In: Aiken W, LaFollette H, eds. *Whose Child? Children's Rights, Parental Authority, and State Power*. Totowa, NJ: Rowman & Littlefield; 1980:124–153.

32 Green R. Prenatal autonomy and the obligation not to harm one's child genetically. *J Law Med Ethics*. 1996;25(1):5–16.

33 Davis DS. Genetic dilemmas and the child's right to an open future. *Hastings Cent Rep*. 1997;27(2):7–15.

34 Purdy L. Loving future people. In: Callahan J, ed. *Reproduction, Ethics and the Law*. Bloomington: Indiana University Press; 1995:300–327.

35 Ray C, West J. Social, sexual and personal implications of paraplegia. *Paraplegia*. 1984;22:75–86.

36 Saigal S, Feeny D, Rosenbaum P, Furlong W, Burrows E, Stoskopf B. Self-perceived health status and health-related quality of life of extremely low-birth-weight infants at adolescence. *JAMA*. 1996; 276:453–459.

37 Tyson JE, Broyles RS. Progress in assessing the long-term outcome of extremely low-birth-weight infants. *JAMA*. 1996;276:492–493.

38 Turnbull HR, Turnbull AP, eds. *Parents Speak Out: Then and Now*. Columbus, Ohio: Charles E. Merrill Publishing Co; 1985.

39 Wertz DC, Fletcher JC. A critique of some feminist challenges to prenatal diagnosis. *J Womens Health*. 1993; 2:173–188.

40 Botkin J. Fetal privacy and confidentiality. *Hastings Cent Rep*. 1995;25(3):32–39.

41 Wright BA. Attitudes and the fundamental negative bias: conditions and correlates. In: Yuker HE, ed. *Attitudes Toward Persons With Disabilities*. New York, NY: Springer; 1988:3–21.

42   Wright BA. *Physical Disability: A Pyscho-Social Approach.* New York, NY: Harper & Row; 1983.

43   Winner E. *Gifted Children: Myths and Realities.* New York, NY: Basic Books; 1996.

44   Massie R, Massie S. *Journey.* New York, NY: Alfred A. Knopf; 1975.

45   Berube M. *Life As We Know It: A Father, a Family and an Exceptional Child.* New York, NY: Pantheon; 1996.

46   Beck M. *Expecting Adam: A True Story of Birth, Rebirth and Everyday Magic.* New York, NY: Times Books/ Random House; 1999.

47   Turnbull AP, Patterson JM, Behr SK, Murphy DL, Marquis JG, Blue-Banning J, eds. *Cognitive Coping, Families, and Disability.* Baltimore, Md: Paul H. Brookes Publishing Co; 1993.

48   Taanila A, Kokkonen J, Jarvelin MK. The long-term effects of children's early-onset disability on marital relationships. *Dev Med Child Neurol.* 1996;38:567–577.

49   Van Riper M, Ryff C, Pridham K. Parental and family well-being in families of children with Down syndrome: a comparative study. *Res Nurs Health.* 1992; 15:227–235.

50   Walker LS, Ford MB, Donald WD. Cystic fibrosis and family stress: effects of age and severity of illness. *Pediatrics.* 1987;79:239–246.

51   Lipsky DK. A parental perspective on stress and coping. *Am J. Orthopsychiatry.* 1985;55:614–617.

52   Ferguson P, Gartner A, Lipsky DK. The experience of disabilities in families: a synthesis of research and parent narratives. In Parens E, Asch A, eds. *Prenatal Testing and Disability Rights.* Washington, DC: Georgetown University Press; 2000.

53   Duster T, Beeson D. *Pathways and Barriers to Genetic Testing and Screening: Molecular Genetics Meets the "High Risk" Family.* Final report. Washington, DC: US Dept of Energy; October 1997.

54   Wertz DC. How parents of affected children view selective abortion. In: Holmes HB, ed. *Issues in Reproductive Technology.* New York, NY: New York University Press; 1992:161–189.

55   Evers-Kiebooms G, Denayer L, van den Berghe H. A child with cystic fibrosis, II: subsequent family planning decisions, reproduction and use of prenatal diagnosis. *Clin Genet.* 1990;37:207–215.

56   Cooley WC, Graham ES, Moeschler JB, Graham JM. Reactions of mothers and medical professionals to a film about Down syndrome. *Am J Dis Child.* 1990; 144:1112–1116.

57   Lippman A, Wilfond B. Twice-told tales: stories about genetic disorders. *Am J Human Genet.* 1992;51: 936–937.

58   Little People of America, Position Statement on Genetic Discoveries in Dwarfism. See http://www. lpaonline.org/.

59   National Down Syndrome Congress. *Position Statement on Prenatal Testing and Eugenics: Families' Rights and Needs.* Prepared for and approved by the Professional Advisory Committee. August 1994. See http://www.ndsccenter. org/issue-position-statements/.

60   Appendix: Reproductive genetic testing: impact on women. National Institutes of Health workshop statement. In: Rothenberg KH, Thompson EJ, eds. *Women and Prenatal Testing: Facing the Challenges of Genetic Technology.* Columbus: Ohio State University Press; 1994:295–300.

61   Parens E, Asch A. The disability rights critique of prenatal genetic testing: reflections and recommendations. *Hastings Cent Rep.* 1999;29(5, suppl): S1–S22.

62   Faden RR, Kass NE, Acuff KL, et al. HIV infection and childbearing: a proposal for public policy and clinical practice. In: Faden R, Kass N, eds. *HIV, Aids and Childbearing: Public Policy, Private Lives.* New York, NY: Oxford University Press; 1996:447–461.

63   Caplan AL. Neutrality is not morality. In: Bartels D, Leroy B, Caplan AL, eds. *Prescribing Our Futures: Ethical Challenges in Genetic Counseling.* New York, NY: Aldine De Gruyter; 1993.

64   White MT. Making responsible decisions: an interpretive ethic for genetic decisionmaking. *Hastings Cent Rep.* 1999;29:14–21.

65   Freedman RI, Lichfield L, Warfield ME. Balancing work and family: perspectives of parents of the children with developmental disabilities. *Fam Soc J Contemp Hum Serv.* October 1995:507–514.

66   Gliedman J, Roth W. *The Unexpected Minority: Handicapped Children in America.* New York, NY: Harcourt Brace Jovanovich; 1980.

11

Genetic Technology
A Threat to Deafness

Ruth Chadwick and Mairi Levitt

Introduction

The Human Genome Project is providing information on the role of genes in all sorts of diseases and
conditions and seems to offer the potential for
unlimited medical benefits: to relieve human beings
of the burden of genetic disease. The need for
research into progressive, terminal diseases like Tay-
Sachs and Huntington's is obvious and sufferers and
their families hope for a means of prevention and
ultimately a cure. But as it becomes possible to
detect a condition before birth questions are raised
as to whether such tests should be carried out.
Deafness is just one condition which cannot be
assumed to be undesirable. Some deaf people consider themselves to be members of deaf culture, with
its own language, customs and values and see genetic
technology as a potential threat to their minority
culture. Others, particularly those who become deaf
in later life, would welcome any 'cure'. This paper is
in two parts; the first part looks at the likely outcomes of work in deaf genetics and their social
impact. The second part examines the philosophical
arguments surrounding genetic intervention in the
case of deafness.

Work in Genetics and Its Social Impact

To what extent does deafness have a genetic basis?

There is thought to be a genetic cause in over half the
children born with a hearing impairment in developed countries (Petit, 1996, p. 386). The proportion is
increasing as other causes, such as infection, decrease.
The genes responsible may cause only hearing loss or
one of the 200 syndromes which cause hearing loss
with other conditions – the chromosomes for two
of the most common (Usher syndrome types 1 & 2
and Waardenburg syndrome) have been identified
(Kimberling, 1992). Most cases of non-syndromic
hereditary deafness are autosomal recessive and therefore may not be obviously 'in the family' (Petit, 1996,
p. 387). This is relevant to discussion of ethical and
social implications of deaf genetics because most parents of born-deaf children will themselves be hearing.
Other causes of deafness at birth are maternal rubella
infection (numbers declined) and premature birth
(numbers increased, perhaps because more of these
babies survive). In the population as a whole most

Original publication details: Ruth Chadwick and Mairi Levitt: "Genetic Technology: A Threat to Deafness," pp. 209–15 from
Medicine, Healthcare and Philosophy 1 (1998). With kind permission from Springer Science+Business Media.

hearing loss is not genetic but the result of damage to the hair cells which line the cochlea. Hair cells die from aging, infection or noise damage.

In the conclusion of a study of the causes of deafness among children in Manchester, Dr Das from the Centre of Audiology commented:

> Genetic causes are now a majority and further improvement in this field will facilitate genetic counselling and possible reduction in the numbers (Das, 1996, p. 12).

Here he makes the point that once we discover the genes responsible for different types of deafness we have to decide what to do with this knowledge. He expects people with the genes to receive counselling before they plan to have children and anticipates a 'possible reduction in numbers'. Such comments have been seen as a threat by members of the deaf community. Although Das is careful not to assume that a reduction in numbers will necessarily be the result of counselling, a programme would not be set up unless it was accepted that some sort of 'treatment' would be offered.

Attitudes to deafness will affect an individual's willingness to take part in linkage studies which attempt to identify the genes affecting hearing. A study by Grundfast and Rosen identified three groups who might be approached to join a study, each with different attitudes to the research. Firstly, those with normal hearing tend to be willing from altruistic motives to take part, secondly, the hearing impaired, who use speech as their main means of communication, are usually eager to take part and finally, the deaf who communicate in sign language and are ambivalent about such research. They conclude that:

> scientific investigators should avoid the assumption that deafness is undesired by all who are affected (Grundfast and Rosen, 1992, p. 978).

Using genetic knowledge

Once genes are located and cloned then there is the possibility of developing genetic tests to be used in prenatal diagnosis and preimplantation screening with IVF (in-vitro fertilisation). A reduction in numbers would only come about if the embryos with the disorder were to be discarded or a mother carrying a fetus with the disorder accepted the offer of a termination. Some parents might feel that they wanted the knowledge so that they could prepare for a baby with hearing loss rather than terminate the pregnancy. The average age for finding hearing loss is decreasing in the UK and although there is scope for earlier diagnosis the effects are uncertain (Fortnum et al., 1996, p. 7). If parents had earlier diagnosis would they prepare by making contact with the deaf community and beginning to learn sign language or might it adversely effect their early communication and interaction with the baby if they knew it was deaf?

The future – gene therapy

Patients have been treated but not yet cured by gene therapy. The type of gene therapy currently being tried out delivers copies of the gene to cells, targeting the parts of the body where the genetic disorder is affecting a function. For example if the lungs are affected, as they are in a person with cystic fibrosis, then patients have used an inhaler to deliver the DNA contained in a vector (an inactivated virus) to their lungs. Germline gene therapy would add the gene at the beginning, in the embryo/pre-embryo. This has been done in animals but is controversial for use in humans, even if it was technically possible, because the changes would be inherited by the next generation.

There are possibilities of gene therapy for the deafened as well. Studies of reptiles and birds show that the hair cells lining the cochlea can regenerate (Johns, 1993, p. 23). If the gene which switches on the mechanism of cell division was found then in the future it could be possible to introduce a copy of the gene and stimulate the growth of new hair cells.

One objection to this discussion might be that prenatal testing for deafness is only possible in a few cases of syndromic deafness and there is not yet any proven gene therapy for deafness. The reason for thinking about future possibilities is that there is a tendency for research to be done and then ethical problems discussed only when the technology makes something possible, as in the ethical debate sparked by the birth of Dolly, the cloned sheep.

When beginning to look at the uses of genetic technology with deaf children there seem to be several important points to be considered about the child and family. First, most born-deaf children, around 90%, will have hearing parents. Secondly, if preimplantation screening or prenatal screening for deaf genes is available the decision to have it will be taken by the usually hearing mother, or parents. Likewise, decisions about gene therapy, if it were to become available, will be taken by the (usually hearing) parents.

Three questions that will be considered are:

1. Is deafness a condition that should be eliminated or cured?
2. Should parents decide for children?
3. What would be the effect on the deaf community?

1. Is deafness a condition that should be eliminated or cured?

The fact is that for many hearing people and those who are deafened it is. Those who view the deaf as disabled emphasise the physical condition, the degree of hearing loss. The deaf are seen as inevitably restricted and handicapped by the hearing impairment. To quote a hearing parent: 'Her deafness…is a loss; a risk to safety as she walks along a busy street, a barricade to the world of music' (Blackmore, 1996). In this view deafness is an objective condition, independent of the way other people perceive and react to it. Genetic testing for deafness supports this view because deafness becomes both a medical and an individual problem. It is the individual woman who has the test and she who must decide what to do about it. Genetic technology is offered with the focus on individual choice (Bailey, 1997, p. 19).

An alternative view is to acknowledge that the condition of deafness is present but what this means for anyone depends on the society in which they live. To quote from the opinion of a deaf person in *See Hear!*, a magazine for the deaf and deafened, 'It is not a question of curing my deafness but of curing society's attitude toward deafness' (*See Hear!*, June 1993, p. 8). This conveys the feelings of deaf (not deafened) adults and many of those who work with deaf people and write about deafness. In this view, conditions like deafness are made into handicaps by social, economic and political policies: the problem is social not individual. The priority to genetic approaches leaves the 'conditions that create social disadvantage or handicap…largely unchallenged' (McDonough quoted in Lippman, 1994, p. 162).

While a middle path between these two versions of deafness is possible, advances in understanding the genetics of deafness and any possibilities of therapy emphasise the medical rather than the social version. There are parallels here with the arguments about cochlear implants in young children. At the moment the technology cannot eliminate deafness. Those who are opposed to the implantation of young children argue that cochlear implants will not make a prelingually deaf child into a hearing child who will acquire oral language as he/she grows up. Instead s/he will be an outsider in the hearing world and, if oral language replaces sign language, an outsider in the deaf world too. The child will grow up disabled in terms of the hearing world rather than as an insider in the deaf community. So it is wrong to implant young children because

a. implants don't work in the sense of making the child into a hearing child

and

b. implants threaten deaf culture.

Leaving aside the question of how effective cochlear implants are, what if gene therapy could make a fetus, unborn or newborn child into a hearing child who would grow up as a full member of hearing society, so demolishing argument (a)? Is the second objection (b) a sufficiently strong one as to prevent gene therapy being carried out?

If it were available for some forms of adult deafness, many deafened adults would want gene therapy to make them hearing again. To quote from an alternative opinion in *See Hear!*, 'A cure that returns operas and symphonies to me? Yes, please' (*See Hear!*, June 1993, p. 8). Probably gene therapy would be uncontroversial ethically for deafened adults but there would be problems of cost. Many of the deafened would be elderly; would treatment be rationed in some way? Gene therapy can only benefit a few and drain resources from all kinds of public health and conventional treatments that would benefit many. Which leads to the second question:

2. Should parents decide for their children?

In the case of gene technology and deafness parents, or other adults, will usually have to decide for the embryo, fetus or child, if a decision is to be made at all.

There are likely to be pressures on parents to 'do the best for their child' and, for those who are hearing; which geneticists, doctors and counsellors are likely to be, this means making it hearing. What is likely to come first is prenatal screening and decisions over termination. Prenatal screening is becoming an accepted part of pregnancy and mothers often feel that they must accept whatever tests are offered to make sure their baby is all right – they are then in a vulnerable position if the test shows that the baby has any sort of genetic condition as they have to make a decision over what to do next.

The principle of informed consent is paramount in genetic counselling. Parents are to be given the information that will enable them to make up their own minds. However, the argument from members of the deaf community is that parents receive biased information in the sense that they are not informed by those who know what it is like to be deaf or to have deaf children. To illustrate this point Murray Holmes, from the British Deaf Association, approached 18 hearing mothers of deaf schoolchildren (age 8–16) and asked them two questions:

'If told your child would be born deaf and you had the choice of gene implantation, termination or to continue with a natural birth and face the consequences, which would you choose?' 89% would have opted for gene implantation and all the rest for termination. Thus all would have wanted one of the 'treatments' offered. They were then asked, with hindsight what would your choice be now? 78% would have the deaf child, 22% would have gene implantation (Holmes, 1997, p. 13). This was not a large scale research project, nor was there a random sample but the results illustrate the point that members of the Deaf Community stress; that hearing parents (in this case mothers) see deafness as a handicap and do not know about Deaf Culture. If they did then some might make different decisions.

Once parents have a child with a genetic disorder you would expect them to be reluctant to say, 'I would not have had this child if I had known', because it would be like saying he/she should not exist. However, the question Murray Holmes asked was different because the choice was not between the child existing or an abortion but between the child existing as a deaf child or, with gene therapy, as a hearing child. Parents would still have their child but he/she would not be deaf.

If gene therapy was developed for some types of deafness most hearing parents would want it because they would be making the decision before they had experience of having a deaf child and would want a child who could be part of their world. On the other hand there are the ten per cent of deaf children born to deaf parents who will also have decisions made on their behalf. Do deaf parents have the right to keep their child deaf like them? Do hearing parents have the right to make their child hearing like them?

3.   What would be the effect on the deaf community?

Some of the worries of the deaf community are: the fear of a revival of eugenics, they refer to a shared history of the programmes of sterilisation and murder of deaf people under Nazism; the fear that there will be a decrease in resources for the deaf if numbers dwindle and the feeling of threat that however the offer of genetic counselling is made 'you are saying that people like me ought not to exist' (Buchanan, 1996). When medical resources are needed the example of thalassemia in Cyprus suggests that a decline in numbers might improve treatment for those with the condition. The same could apply to technological facilities for deaf people but if numbers were very small it is less likely that signed programmes on television or theatre performances, for example, would become more widely available. The parallel is with a shrinking cultural and linguistic minority rather than with a shrinking number of sick or disabled people. There comes a point at which a culture is no longer viable as the numbers who know the language and shared history decline. The feeling of threat expressed by members of the deaf community ('you are saying that people like me should not exist') implies that nothing should be done to reduce the number of born-deaf people who are potential members of the deaf community. Is it possible to want to cure deafness without saying deaf people are not valued?

A debate over what genetic conditions it is desirable to eliminate begins only when prenatal testing becomes available. Deafness is not unique, as some have suggested, in being seen positively by adults who have grown up with the condition, and negatively by the general public and some parents of babies and young children with the condition. The availability of preimplantation and prenatal testing would probably reduce the numbers of children born and therefore reduce, at least to some extent, the numbers in the deaf community. Parents will make decisions on an individual basis rather than consider the effect reducing the numbers of deaf children will have on the deaf community.

A Philosophical Response

It is important to make some clarifications and distinctions. In the literature a distinction is sometimes drawn between two senses of deaf, which we might call deaf1 and deaf2, where deaf1 denotes non-hearing and deaf2 refers to membership of deaf culture. In what follows, however, although we shall be referring to the deaf culture argument, we shall use 'deaf' simply to mean non-hearing. Members of deaf culture reject the label of disability. There is the related issue of how disability should be defined, as we have indicated in the first part of this paper. One kind of definition makes functional limitation an essential feature of disability; another defines it in terms of social justice (Hull, 1998). Hull argues persuasively that the better course is to acknowledge that disability involves a complex mixture of functional and social factors. Disability can be equated with disadvantage, where either functional limitations or social structures can be the major factors producing the disadvantage.

As Hull and others have recognised, it is important to recognise the social contribution to disability (cf. Edwards, 1998), to acknowledge that there are issues of social justice involved. To attempt to solve the moral issues surrounding deafness1 and deafness2 via a definition of disability is not helpful, because moral issues cannot be settled by definition alone, just as the question whether infertility counts as a 'disease' cannot by itself settle the moral question of whether reproductive technologies should be made available at public expense. So the question 'Is deafness a condition that should be eliminated or cured?' incorporates several aspects. First, there is the issue that deafness is not *a* condition. Again, 'elimination' and 'cure' are not only different concepts but their interpretation may depend on the means to be employed. Thirdly, the

moral issue will turn on questions such as whether people do wrong if they knowingly produce a child who is deaf; or whether people should be *free* to choose to have a child who is deaf.

More distinctions are in order. Above we have drawn attention to different kinds of intervention that might be envisaged. Now we want to focus on means that might be employed *in order to* bring about the birth of a deaf child. These include:

1. choosing to continue to term with deaf fetus
2. preimplantation diagnosis and selection of deaf embryo
3. use of techniques of gene 'therapy' to introduce deafness

How are we to address the issue from a moral point of view? We want to consider three approaches: the child-centred approach, the adult-centred approach and the community-centred approach.

Child–Centred Approach

Suppose a parent decides to have a child who is deaf when this could be avoided. Is the child wronged? If an adult implemented her wish to have a deaf child by injuring a hearing child after birth this would count as wronging the child. This would be the case even if it were not done by an external injury but by a pain-less method such as a pill. So why might it be different in the case of genetic choice? One argument is that if *this* child had not been born deaf it would not have existed at all: so as long as the child does not have a life that it is not worth living it has not been wronged. (It is important to note that this line of argument cuts both ways – a representative of deaf culture could not claim that a child had been wronged by being born as a hearing child either). This is what distinguishes the case from the external injury case. This would be one way of looking at the preimplantation diagnosis example. If, however, what is at issue is the introduction of deafness by gene therapy then the question arises as to whether personal identity is changed by genetic manipulation (cf. Chadwick, 1998).

Let us suppose that it *does* have identity-changing effects. Then, on the reasoning above, the resulting person cannot claim to have been wronged because she could not have existed had it not been for the identity change. On the other hand if it does not have identity-changing effects then it is at least conceivable that the resulting person could claim to have been wronged. But in what might the wrong consist?

There are two main approaches to this: the welfare argument and the 'open future' argument.

The welfare argument

From the point of view of biomedical functioning there is the introduction of a limitation: a hearing system which does not work. Being deaf denies one a range of human experience – one of the five senses available to human beings. Further, statistical evidence suggests that deaf people have less access to opportunities to work than hearing people and that their average income is less (cf. Tucker, 1998).

It does not follow from this that deaf people will have a less worthwhile or less happy life. The above points can be countered by the addition of special circumstances obtaining in relation to membership of the deaf community, bringing with it a sense of belonging. In fact, it can be argued, as Levitt has shown, that hearing children born to deaf parents would be less well off, in welfare terms, because they would be outsiders in both the hearing and deaf communities. Because of this difference of perspective, it is difficult to resolve the welfare question, and some commentators have turned to an autonomy-based argument (e.g. Davis, 1997).

The open future argument

Following Joel Feinberg's open future argument, Dena Davis has argued that bringing about the birth of a deaf child is wrong in so far as it denies the child an open future (Davis, 1997). The problem with this argument is first a general point. In so far as the claim is that a particular genetic inheritance can inhibit an open future, to what extent can any of us claim to have an open future? The argument seems to rely on genetic determinism. In the case of deafness, however, there is a specific point to the argument, namely that it should be up to the child to decide whether or not he or she wants to be deaf (where it is assumed that there is no

identity change involved), but by the time the child is capable of making a choice it will be too late, if born deaf, to acquire hearing and spoken language.

The child-centred approach, then, is fraught with problems, in so far as there is a fundamental disagreement over what counts as the welfare of the child, and it is not possible to wait for the child to decide. This leads to the consideration of the adult-centred approach, which Mairi Levitt discussed as her second issue, 'Should parents decide for their children?'

The Adult-Centred Approach

'Choice' has played a prominent role in the debate surrounding the Human Genome Project but it has also been subject to criticism from those who point to the context in which choices are made, which may be one hostile to disability. Again there are a number of issues at stake. First there are theoretical issues as to whether there should be any constraints on choice. Jonathan Glover, in talking about parental choices, has suggested that some parental choices might be 'disturbing'. He says:

> If parents chose characteristics likely to make their children unhappy, or likely to reduce their abilities, we might feel that the children should be protected against this. (Imagine parents belonging to some religious sect who wanted their children to have a religious symbol as a physical mark on their face, and who wanted them to be unable to read, as a protection against their faith being corrupted.) (Glover, 1984, p. 48)

For him the argument that parents might want to identify with their children has something in it but is indecisive. Otherwise it would not be acceptable to introduce literacy to a generation whose parents were illiterate.

A similar type of choice, however, has been upheld by American courts in the decision about the Amish's right to withdraw their children from education after the eighth grade because that would undermine their right to maintain their religious and cultural identity (Davis, 1997). In order to argue against this, Davis uses the open future argument, but as we have seen both that and the welfare argument are fraught with difficulties.

Another criticism of the choice argument is that where choice is exercised in favour of deafness this amounts to 'elective disability' (Tucker, 1998), the implication being that society may not have an obligation to provide facilities. There are problems with this response, however. First, the phrase 'elective disability' assumes that the content of the choice *is* disability, but in the light of the disagreement over the definition of disability that description of the content of the choice might be disputed. Despite this, however, Tucker argues that "the Deaf cultural community are strong activists for the promulgation of laws protecting people with disabilities" (Tucker, 1998, p. 10), so perhaps the criticism is strengthened if those who make the choice then *do* define themselves as having a disability in order to benefit from social facilities provided to cope with disability. A possible response to this might be that since from the opposing view disability is socially constructed there is no inconsistency in taking advantages of facilities to redress the balance of this socially constructed phenomenon.

The second problem with the 'elective disability' argument is that in the case of parents choosing for their children, the people who are chosen to be deaf are not in fact the *same* people as those who are making the choice. Thus it would not be fair to describe them as being in a state of elective disability.

The third point about the elective disability argument is that it lends credence to those who argue that the attempt to justify the advances associated with the Human Genome Project in the name of choice is simply rhetoric; if the 'right' choices are not made then those who 'choose' disability will suffer loss of social support.

This leads to consideration of the context in which choices are made, which may exert pressure in favour of certain choices, or be less facilitative of choice. While there has been consensus that if a woman found that her fetus has a condition such as deafness she should be free to choose to continue the pregnancy, where preimplantation diagnosis is at stake the issues are rather different. As Draper and Chadwick have argued (1999), this development may be construed as taking choice out of the hands of patients and in particular of women. Where choosing the introduction of a gene might be involved the co-operation of others would be involved to a greater degree still.

The fact that co-operation of others may be involved to a greater or lesser degree in some choices is a practical issue but it also has moral implications. To what extent is it morally acceptable for representatives of particular cultures to request the use of the services of others to maintain that culture?

The Deaf Community Argument

There is of course a question as to the status of the deaf community and its claim to a distinctive culture, as compared with other linguistic communities. This might be challenged in so far as it is a response to a particular functional limitation, from a biomedical point of view, but we shall put that on one side and look at the moral issue of maintaining the community. The point about the maintenance of a particular culture cannot be *assumed* to be an overriding consideration without further investigation, just as the maintenance of certain cultural traditions like female genital mutilation and footbinding cannot be assumed to be overriding considerations.

So how do we resolve the issues? If we imagine two possible worlds, A and B, in one of which (A) deafness has been eliminated while in the other it has not, and assume the same number of people in each, which is preferable? What are the criteria on which to judge? The question to ask is not whether A is happier, overall, than B. Just as the welfare argument was not very helpful in addressing the child, it is not very helpful here either. The question, rather, is one of social justice. What are the burdens and costs of getting to either of these worlds and *on whom do they fall?* There is an issue about the effects on people currently alive feeling they are not valued in so far as they identify with their condition. There are persuasive arguments for the view that people can experience as constitutive of their identities what are regarded by some as disabilities (cf. Edwards, 1998) and that the attempt to 'eradicate' genetic handicap can amount to discrimination (Holland, 1998). It is not clear that the appropriate response to this is to *choose* deafness for their children. What these arguments *do* justify are policies which counter discrimination in society and an environment hostile to certain conditions. It would require further argument, however, to justify the use of medical technology to *maintain* these conditions. It is far from clear what the argument would be to suggest that it is an appropriate use of medical expertise to maintain a particular community of culture, *for that reason*. The deaf community argument cannot settle the argument of whether people should be free to choose deafness for their children, unless we know more about what that choice implies. It is not *sufficient* by itself to justify assistance of medical (genetic) technology; nor is it *necessary* to justify *non*-interference, e.g. in termination decisions, because the individual choice argument can do the work required.

Conclusion

What has emerged from the above discussion is the complexity of the issues involved in the questions raised earlier, with regard to whether deafness is a condition that should be eliminated or cured, whether parents should choose for their children and the effect on the deaf community. I have focused on the freedom to choose deafness, rather than the issues on whether choosing against deafness is discriminatory. The discrimination argument has been well handled elsewhere (e.g. Holland, 1998). In thinking about the freedom to choose deafness it does seem, however, that both the child-centred approach and the community-centred approach are insufficient, and this leaves us with the adult-centred approach, where much depends on the context in which choices are made and the type of means to be employed in implementing choice. In so far as individuals should be free to reject a termination, choice can support the freedom to choose a pregnancy where the fetus is deaf, but of itself cannot provide an argument for the assistance of medical technology to favour deafness (or any other characteristic): that depends on what is an appropriate use of medical expertise and whether that too should guided by individual preferences or other considerations.

References

Bailey, R.: 1997, 'Who needs curing and from what? A response from a Disability Rights Perspective', *Deaf Worlds. Deaf People, Community and Society* 13(2), pp. 16–21.

Blackmore, W.: 1996, 'I don't want to be deaf, mummy', *The Times*, Thursday, June 6th, p. 18.

Buchanan, A.: 1996, 'Choosing who will be disabled: genetic intervention and the morality of inclusion', *Social Philosophy and Policy Foundation* 13(2), pp. 18–46.

Chadwick, R.: 1998, 'Gene therapy'. In: H. Kuhse and P. Singer (eds.), *A Companion to Bioethics*. Oxford: Blackwell, pp. 189–197.

Das, J.: 1996, 'Aetiology of bilateral sensorineural hearing impairment in children: a 10 year study', *Archives of Disease in Childhood* 74, pp. 8–12.

Davis, D.S.: 1997, 'Genetic dilemmas and the child's right to an open future', *Rutgers Law Journal* 28(3), pp. 549–592.

Draper, H. and R. Chadwick: 1999, 'Beware! Preimplantation genetic diagnosis may solve some old problems but it also raises new ones', *Journal of Medical Ethics* 25(2), pp. 114–120.

Edwards, S.D.: 1998, 'Nordenfelt's theory of diability', *Theoretical Medicine and Bioethics* 19(1), pp. 89–100.

Fortnum H., A. Davis, A. Butler and J. Stevens: 1996, *Health Service Implications of Changes in Aetiology and Referral Patterns of Hearing-impaired Children in Trent 1985–1993*. Nottingham: MRC Institute of Hearing Research.

Glover, J.: 1984, *What Sort of People Should There Be?* Harmondsworth: Penguin.

Grundfast, K. and J. Rosen: 1992, 'Ethical and cultural considerations in research on hereditary deafness', *Molecular Biology and Genetics* 25(5), pp. 973–978.

Holland, A.: 1998, 'Genetically based handicap', *Journal of Applied Philosophy* 15(2), pp. 119–132.

Holmes, A.M.: 1997, 'Reply to Foundation Paper 2 – The British Deaf Association', *Deaf Worlds. Deaf People, Community and Society* 13(2), pp. 13–15.

Hull, R.: 1998, 'Defining disability – a philosophical approach', *Res Publica* 5(2), pp. 199–210.

Johns, N.: 1993(April), 'Genetic research – "Ear – repair thyself"', *See HEAR!* pp. 22–23.

Kimberling, W.J.: 1992, *Current Progress in Finding Genes Involved in Hearing Impairment*. National Institute for the Deaf and Other Communication Disorders NIDCD. Boyes Town National Research Hospital, 555 N. 30th St, Omaha, NE68131 paper available on the Internet.

Leon, P.E., H. Raventos, E. Lynch, J. Morrow and M.C. King: 1992, 'The gene for an inherited form of deafness maps to chromosome 5 q31', *Proceedings of the National Academy of Sciences of the United States of America* 89(11), pp. 5181–5184.

Lippman, A.: 1994, 'Prenatal genetic testing and screening: constructing needs and reinforcing inequalities'. In: Angus

Clarke (ed.), *Genetic Counselling. Practice and Principles.* London and New York: Routledge.

Moores, D.: 1994, 'Eugenics revisited: heredity deafness and genetic technology', *American Annals of the Deaf* 139(4), p. 393.

Petit, C.: 1996, 'Genes responsible for human hereditary deafness: symphony of a thousand', *Nature Genetics* 14, 14/12/96, pp. 385–391.

Tucker, B.P.: 1998, 'Deaf culture, cochlear implants, and elective disability', *Hastings Center Report* 28(4), pp. 6–14.

12

Sex Selection and Preimplantation Genetic Diagnosis

The Ethics Committee of the American Society
of Reproductive Medicine

In 1994, the Ethics Committee of the American Society of Reproductive Medicine concluded, although not unanimously, that whereas preimplantation sex selection is appropriate to avoid the birth of children with genetic disorders, it is not acceptable when used solely for nonmedical reasons. Since 1994, the further development of less burdensome and invasive medical technologies for sex selection suggests a need to revisit the complex ethical questions involved.

Background

Interest in sex selection has a long history dating to ancient cultures. Methods have varied from special modes and timing of coitus to the practice of infanticide. Only recently have medical technologies made it possible to attempt sex selection of children before their conception or birth. For example, screening for carriers of X-linked genetic diseases allows potential parents not only to decide whether to have children but also to select the sex of their offspring before pregnancy or before birth.

Among the methods now available for prepregnancy and prebirth sex selection are [1] prefertilization separation of X-bearing from Y-bearing spermatozoa

(through a technique that is now available although still investigational for humans), with subsequent selection for artificial insemination or for IVF; [2] preimplantation genetic diagnosis (PGD), followed by the sex selection of embryos for transfer; and [3] prenatal genetic diagnosis, followed by sex-selective abortion. The primary focus of this document is on the second method, sex selection through PGD, although the issues particular to this method overlap with the issues relevant to the others. Preimplantation genetic diagnosis is used with assisted reproductive technologies such as IVF to identify genetic disorders, but it also can provide information regarding the sex of embryos either as a by-product of testing for genetic disorders or when it is done purely for sex selection (Table 12.1).

As the methods of sex selection have varied throughout history, so have the motivations for it. Among the most prominent of motivations historically have been simple desires to bear and raise children of the culturally preferred gender, to ensure the economic usefulness of offspring within a family, to achieve gender balance among children in a given family, and to determine a gendered birth order. New technologies also have served these aims, but they have raised to prominence the goal of avoiding the birth of children with sex-related genetic disorders.

Original publication details: The Ethics Committee of the American Society of Reproductive Medicine, "Sex Selection and Preimplantation Genetic Diagnosis," pp. 595–8 from *Fertility and Sterility* 72: 4 (October 1999). Reprinted with permission from Elsevier.

Bioethics: An Anthology, Third Edition. Edited by Helga Kuhse, Udo Schüklenk, and Peter Singer.

Table 12.1 Embryo sex identification by preimplantation genetic diagnosis for nonmedical reasons

(a) Patient is undergoing IVF and PGD.
     Patient learns sex identification of embryo as *part of*, or as *a by-product of*, PGD done for other medical reasons.
(b) Patient is undergoing IVF and PGD.
     Patient requests that sex identification be *added to* PGD being done for other medical reasons.
(c) Patient is undergoing IVF, but PGD is not necessary to treatment.
     Patient *requests PGD* solely for the purpose of sex identification.
(d) Patient is not undergoing either IVF or PGD (for the treatment of infertility or any other medical reason).
     Patient *requests IVF and PGD* solely for the purpose of sex identification.

Whatever its methods or its reasons, sex selection has encountered significant ethical objections throughout its history. Religious traditions and societies in general have responded with concerns varying from moral outrage at infanticide to moral reservations regarding the use of some prebirth methods of diagnosis for the sole purpose of sex selection. More recently, concerns have focused on the dangers of gender discrimination and the perpetuation of gender oppression in contemporary societies.

This document's focus on PGD for sex selection is prompted by the increasing attractiveness of prepregnancy sex selection over prenatal diagnosis and sex-selective abortion, and by the current limited availability of methods of prefertilization sex selection techniques that are both reliable and safe. Although the actual use of PGD for sex selection is still infrequent, its potential use continues to raise important ethical questions.

Central to the controversies over the use of PGD for sex selection, particularly for nonmedical reasons, are issues of gender discrimination, the appropriateness of expanding control over nonessential characteristics of offspring, and the relative importance of sex selection when weighed against medical and financial burdens to parents and against multiple demands for limited medical resources. In western societies, these concerns inevitably encounter what has become a strong presumption in favor of reproductive choice.

The General Ethical Debate

Arguments for PGD and sex selection make two primary appeals. The first is to the right to reproductive choice on the part of the person or persons who seek to bear a child. Sex selection, it is argued, is a logical extension of this right. The second is an appeal to the important goods to be achieved through this technique and the choices it allows – above all, the medical good of preventing the transmission of sex-linked genetic disorders such as hemophilia A and B, Lesch-Nyhan syndrome, Duchenne-Becker muscular dystrophy, and Hunter syndrome. There also are perceived individual and social goods such as gender balance or distribution in a family with more than one child, parental companionship with a child of one's own gender, and a preferred gender order among one's children. More remotely, it sometimes is argued that PGD and sex selection of embryos for transfer is a lesser evil (medically and ethically) than the alternative of prenatal diagnosis and sex-selected abortion, and even that PGD and sex selection can contribute indirectly to population limitation (i.e., with this technique, parents no longer are compelled to continue to reproduce until they achieve a child of the preferred gender).

Arguments against PGD used for sex selection appeal either to what is considered inherently wrong with sex selection or to the bad consequences that are likely to outweigh the good consequences of its use. Suspicion of sex selection as wrong is lodged in the concerns identified earlier: the potential for inherent gender discrimination, inappropriate control over nonessential characteristics of children, unnecessary medical burdens and costs for parents, and inappropriate and potentially unfair use of limited medical resources for sex selection rather than for more genuine and urgent medical needs. These concerns are closely connected with predictions of negative consequences, such as risk of psychological harm to sex-selected offspring (i.e., by placing on them too high expectations), increased marital conflict over sex-selective decisions, and reinforcement of gender bias in society as a whole. Sometimes the predictions reach to dire consequences such as an overall change in the human sex ratio detrimental to the future of a particular society.

Preimplantation Genetic Diagnosis and Sex Selection: Joining the Particular Issues

The right to reproductive freedom has never been considered an absolute right, certainly not if it is extended to include every sort of decision about reproduction or every demand for positive support in individuals' reproductive decisions. Still, serious reasons (e.g., the likelihood of seriously harmful consequences or the presence of a competing stronger right) must be provided if a limitation on reproductive freedom is to be justified. Hence, the weighing of opposing positions regarding PGD and sex selection depends on an assessment of the strength of the reasons given for and against it.

Preimplantation genetic diagnosis has the potential for serving sex selection in varying categories of cases, each of which raises different medical and ethical questions. Preimplantation genetic diagnosis may be done for disease prevention, or it may be done for any of the other motivations individuals have for determining the sex of their offspring. Moreover, information about the sex of an embryo may be obtained (a) as an essential part of or by-product of PGD performed for other (medical) reasons or (b) through a test for sex identification that is added to PGD performed for medical reasons. Further, (c) a patient who is undergoing IVF procedures as part of fertility treatment (but whose treatment does not require PGD for medical reasons) may request PGD solely for the purpose of sex selection, and (d) a patient who is fertile (hence, not undergoing IVF as part of treatment) may request IVF and PGD, both solely for the purpose of sex selection. Each of these situations calls for a distinct medical and ethical assessment (Table 12.1).

There presently is little debate over the ethical validity of PGD for sex selection when its aim is to prevent the transmission of sex-linked genetic disease. In this case, sex selection does not prefer one sex over the other for its own supposed value; it does not, therefore, have the potential to contribute as such to gender bias. And when the genetic disorder is severe, efforts to prevent it can hardly be placed in a category of trivializing or instrumentalizing human reproduction. Moreover, prepregnancy sex-selective techniques used for this purpose appear to have a clear claim on limited resources along with other medical procedures that are performed with the goal of eliminating disease and suffering.

It is less easy to eliminate concerns regarding PGD and sex selection when it is aimed at serving social and psychological goals not related to the prevention of disease. It must be recognized, of course, that individuals and couples have wide discretion and liberty in making reproductive choices, even if others object. Yet ethical arguments against sex selection appear to gain strength as the categories of potential cases descend from (a) to (d). For example, desires for family gender balance or birth order, companionship, family economic welfare, and the ready acceptance of offspring who are more "wanted" because their gender is selected may not in every case deserve the charge of unjustified gender bias, but they are vulnerable to it.

Whatever they may mean for an individual or family choice, they also, if fulfilled on a large scale through PGD for sex selection, may contribute to a society's gender stereotyping and overall gender discrimination. On the other hand, if they are expressed and fulfilled only on a small scale and sporadically (as is presently the case), their social implications will be correspondingly limited. Still, they remain vulnerable to the judgment that no matter what their basis, they identify gender as a reason to value one person over another, and they support socially constructed stereotypes of what gender means. In doing so, they not only reinforce possibilities of unfair discrimination, but they may trivialize human reproduction by making it depend on the selection of nonessential features of offspring.

Desired potential social benefits of sex selection also may appear insufficiently significant when weighed against unnecessary bodily burdens and risks for women, and when contrasted with other needs for and claims on medical resources. In particular, many would judge it unreasonable for individuals who do not otherwise need IVF (for the treatment of infertility or prevention of genetic disease) to undertake its burdens and expense solely to select the gender of their offspring. Although individuals may be free to accept such burdens, and although costs may be borne in a way that does not directly violate the rights of others, to encourage PGD for sex selection when it is not medically indicated presents ethical problems.

More remote sorts of consequences of PGD and sex selection, both good and bad, remain too speculative to place seriously in the balance of ethical assessments of the techniques. That is, potential good consequences such as population control, and potential bad consequences such as imbalance in a society's sex ratio, seem too uncertain in their prediction to be determinative of the issues of sex selection. Even if, for example, the current rise in sex selection of offspring in a few countries suggests a correlation between the availability of sex selection methods and the concrete expression of son-preference, there can be no easy transfer of these data to other societies. This does not mean, however, that all concerns for the general social consequences of sex selection techniques regarding general gender discrimination can be dismissed.

The United States is not likely to connect sex selection practices with severe needs to limit population (as may be the case in other countries). Moreover, gender discrimination is not as deeply intertwined with economic structures in the United States as it may be elsewhere. Nonetheless, ongoing problems with the status of women in the United States make it necessary to take account of concerns for the impact of sex selection on goals of gender equality.

Moreover, the issue of controlling offspring characteristics that are perceived as nonessential cannot be summarily dismissed. Those who argue that offering parental choices of sex selection is taking a major step toward "designing" offspring present concerns that are not unreasonable in a highly technologic culture. Yet it appears precipitous to assume that the possibility of gender choices will lead to a feared radical transformation of the meaning of human reproduction. A "slippery slope" argument seems overdrawn when it is used here. The desire to have some control over the gender of offspring is older than the new technologies that make this possible. This, however, suggests that should otherwise permissible technologies for sex selection be actively promoted for nonmedical reasons – as in (b), (c), and (d) above – their threat to widely valued meanings of human reproduction may call for more serious concern than other speculative and remote negative consequences of PGD and sex selection.

Objections to PGD and sex selection on the grounds of misallocation of resources are more difficult to sustain. Questions of this sort are not so obviously relevant to systems of medical care like the one in the United States. If an individual is able and willing to pay for desired (and medically reasonable) services, there is no direct, easy way to show how any particular set of choices takes away from the right of others to basic care. Yet even here, individual and group decisions do have an impact on the overall deployment of resources for medical care and on the availability of reproductive services.

Although, as already noted, there is little controversy about the seriousness of the need to prevent genetic diseases, it is doubtful that gender preference on the basis of other social and psychological desires should be given as high a priority. The distinction between medical needs and nonmedical desires is particularly relevant if PGD is done solely for sex selection based on nonmedical preferences. The greater the demand on medical resources to achieve PGD for no other reason than sex selection, as in descending order in (b) through (d) above, the more questions surround it regarding its appropriateness for medical practice. If, on the other hand, PGD is done as part of infertility treatment, and the information that allows sex selection is not gained through the additional use of medical resources, it presumably is free of more serious problems of fairness in the allocation of scarce resources and appropriateness to the practice of medicine.

The ethical issues that have emerged in this document's concern for PGD and sex selection are in some ways particular to the uses and consequences of a specific reproductive technology. Their general significance is broader than this, however. For example, the concerns raised here provide at least a framework for an ethical assessment of new techniques for selecting X-bearing or Y-bearing sperm for IUI or IVF (ongoing clinical trial reports of which appeared while this document was being developed). Here, too, sex selection for the purposes of preventing the transmission of genetic diseases does not appear to present ethical problems. However, here also, sex selection for nonmedical reasons, especially if facilitated on a large scale, has the potential to reinforce gender bias in a society, and it may constitute inappropriate use and allocation of medical resources. Finally, although sperm sorting and IUI can entail less burden for parents, questions of the risk to offspring from techniques that involve staining and the use of a laser on sperm DNA remain under investigation.

Recommendations

Of the arguments in favor of PGD and sex selection, only the one based on the prevention of transmittable genetic diseases is strong enough to clearly avoid or override concerns regarding gender equality, acceptance of offspring for themselves and not their inessential characteristics, health risks and burdens for individuals attempting to achieve pregnancy, and equitable use and distribution of medical resources. These concerns remain for PGD and sex selection when it is used to fulfill nonmedical preferences or social and psychological needs. However, because it is not clear in every case that the use of PGD and sex selection for nonmedical reasons entails certainly grave wrongs or sufficiently predictable grave negative consequences, the Committee does not favor its legal prohibition. Nonetheless, the cumulative weight of the arguments against nonmedically motivated sex selection gives cause for serious ethical caution. The Committee's recommendations therefore follow from an effort to respect and to weigh ethical concerns that are sometimes in conflict – namely, the right to reproductive freedom, genuine medical needs and goals, gender equality, and justice in the distribution of medical resources. On the basis of its foregoing ethical analysis, the Committee recommends the following:

1. Preimplantation genetic diagnosis used for sex selection to prevent the transmission of serious genetic disease is ethically acceptable. It is not inherently gender biased, bears little risk of consequences detrimental to individuals or to society, and represents a use of medical resources for reasons of human health.

2. In patients undergoing IVF, PGD used for sex selection for nonmedical reasons – as in (a) through (c) above – holds some risk of gender bias, harm to individuals and society, and inappropriateness in the use and allocation of limited medical resources. Although these risks are lower when sex identification is already part of a by-product of PGD being done for medical reasons (a), they increase when sex identification is added to PGD solely for purposes of sex selection (b) and when PGD is itself initiated solely for sex selection (c). They remain a concern whenever sex selection is done for nonmedical reasons. Such use of PGD therefore should not be encouraged.

3. The initiation of IVF with PGD solely for sex selection (d) holds even greater risk of unwarranted gender bias, social harm, and the diversion of medical resources from genuine medical need. It therefore should be discouraged.

4. Ethical caution regarding PGD for sex selection calls for study of the consequences of this practice. Such study should include cross-cultural as well as intracultural patterns, ongoing assessment of competing claims for medical resources, and reasonable efforts to discern changes in the level of social responsibility and respect for future generations.

13

Sex Selection and Preimplantation Diagnosis
A Response to the Ethics Committee of the American Society of Reproductive Medicine

Julian Savulescu and Edgar Dahl

Introduction

In its recent statement 'Sex Selection and Preimplantation Genetic Diagnosis', the Ethics Committee of the American Society of Reproductive Medicine concluded that it is ethically appropriate to employ these new reproductive technologies to avoid the birth of children suffering from X-linked genetic disorders (Ethics Committee of the American Society of Reproductive Medicine, 1999 [see chapter 12 in this volume]). However, to use preimplantation genetic diagnosis and sex selection solely for non-medical reasons, the Committee claims, is morally inappropriate. The Committee 'does not favour its legal prohibition', but it strongly advises that sex selection and preimplantation genetic diagnosis for non-medical reasons 'should be discouraged'.

Why does the Ethics Committee think that sex selection and preimplantation genetic diagnosis for non-medical reasons is ethically inappropriate and ought to be discouraged? Although the Committee acknowledges that individuals enjoy procreative liberty and that 'serious reasons must be provided if a limitation on reproductive freedom is to be justified', it claims that the social risks of sex selection outweigh the social benefits. What are these 'social risks' supposed to be?

The reservation against sex selection for non-medical reasons is often based on the assumption that it will invariably lead to a serious distortion of the sex ratio. The Committee has certainly been wise not to rely on this highly speculative objection. According to the available empirical evidence, individuals in Western societies do not have a preference for a particular sex. Most couples still wish to leave the sex of their children 'up to fate'. And those few who would want some control over the gender of their children desire to have a 'balanced family', that is a family with both daughters and sons, most often one daughter and one son (Stratham *et al.*, 1993).

While sex selection in the West is unlikely to disturb the sex ratio (Simpson and Carson, 1999), more openly available sex selection would further distort the sex ratio in Asia. The male to female ratio is nearly 1.2 in China and some parts of India. In 1990, there were 100 million women 'missing' as a

Original publication details: Julian Savulescu and Edgar Dahl, "Sex Selection and Preimplantation Diagnosis: A Response to the Ethics Committee of the American Society of Reproductive Medicine," pp. 1879–80 from *Human Reproduction* 15: 9 (2000). By permission of Oxford University Press.

result of various forms of discrimination (Benagiano and Bianchi, 1999). But some have argued that disturbed sex ratios may not be detrimental to women. Advantages which have been postulated include increase in influence of the rarer gender, reduced population growth and interbreeding of different populations (Sureau, 1999). In a practical sense, sex selection employing preimplantation genetic diagnosis may be preferable to the alternatives. It would be morally preferable to many people to termination of 'wrong sex' pregnancies or female infanticide (Sureau, 1999) and is preferable to increasing population burdens in an attempt to have a child of the desired sex (Simpson and Carson, 1999).

The Committee also does not base its reservation about sex selection on vague 'slippery slope' arguments. The Committee is well aware that it is perfectly possible to draw a legal line between the selection for sex and the selection for other characteristics, such as eye colour, height or intelligence. Thus, if there is consensus that selection for sex is morally acceptable but selection for, let us say, intelligence is not, professional or legislative controls can be employed to allow the former but not the latter. Arguments claiming that sex selection is the initial step down a road that will inevitably lead to the creation of 'designer babies' or a 'new eugenics' are simply invalid.

However, if it is not the fear of a distorted sex ratio or a slide towards eugenics, then, what are the social risks the Committee is referring to? The Committee rests its case against sex selection for non-medical reasons upon four claims. Firstly, sex selection is to be opposed because it identifies 'gender as a reason to value one person over another'. Secondly, it may 'contribute to a society's gender stereotyping and gender discrimination'. Thirdly, because it is 'unreasonable for individuals who do not otherwise need IVF to undertake its burdens and expense solely to select the gender of their offspring'. And fourthly, because it represents a 'misallocation of limited medical resources'.

Consider the first objection. The claim that couples requesting sex selection 'identify gender as a reason to value one person over another' is simply unsound. Couples seeking the service of Gender Clinics are typically in their mid-thirties, have two or three children of the same sex and wish to have at least one child of the opposite sex. Their choice for a child of a particular sex depends entirely upon the sex of the children they already have. If they already have two or three boys they tend to choose a girl, if they already have two or three girls they tend to choose a boy (Fugger et al., 1998). Since their choice is simply based on the gender of already existing children, and not on the absurd assumption that one sex is 'superior' to another, the claim that these couples are making a sexist choice is an unjustified accusation.

The existing data of Gender Clinics also undermine the second objection of the Committee that sex selection for non-medical reasons may 'reinforce gender bias in a society'. Since couples seeking sex selection are almost exclusively motivated by the desire to balance their family and choose girls with the same frequency as boys, it is hard to see how their choices are supposed to contribute to a society's gender discrimination (Khatamee et al., 1989; Liu and Rose, 1995). If these were real concerns, sex selection could be limited to balancing family sex, and only after the first child.

The third objection that it is 'unreasonable' for a woman to undergo a burdensome IVF treatment solely to select the sex of her child smacks suspiciously of medical paternalism. The Committee seems to be aware of this as it tones down its statement in the following sentence, saying that 'individuals may be free to accept such burdens'. Yet, it insists, 'to encourage preimplantation genetic diagnosis for sex selection when it is not medically indicated presents ethical problems.' What ethical problems does it present? Unfortunately, we are not told. More importantly, the issue is not whether preimplantation genetic diagnosis for sex selection is to be 'encouraged', but whether the mere fact that an IVF treatment cycle imposes a burden on a woman is a sufficient reason to 'discourage' her. If a woman is aware of the physical and psychological costs to herself but thinks having a child of a certain sex is worth the trouble, it is an autonomous decision that needs to be respected. After all it is her life and her body. The Committee seems blind to the importance of gender to parents, and that parents are best left to themselves to make decisions about the constitution of their family (Savulescu, 1999).

The Committee did not focus on the physical risks of preimplantation diagnosis to children born and these clearly need to be evaluated in any sex selection procedure (Benagiano and Bianchi, 1999; Simpson and Carson, 1999). Experience so far is encouraging, with several hundred children being born after PGD without apparent detriment. Systematic review is continuing (ESHRE PGD Consortium Steering Committee, 1999).

The fourth and last objection of the Committee is that preimplantation genetic diagnosis for sex selection constitutes 'inappropriate use and allocation of medical resources'. To our knowledge, no-one has so far seriously advocated that the state, i.e. the tax-payer, should subsidize sex selection for non-medical reasons. Again, the Committee seems to be aware of this when it continues: 'If an individual is able and willing to pay for desired services, there is no direct, easy way to show how any particular set of choices takes away from the right of others to basic care.' Nonetheless, it claims: 'Yet even here, individual and group decisions do have an impact on the overall deployment of resources for medical care and on the availability of reproductive services.' The Committee is relentless in its claim that allowing sex selection is a misallocation of resources, repeating itself at least four times on this issue. Since this objection seems to be the most compelling, it would have been helpful to show how a privately paid service for sex selection can possibly deprive the community of its scarce medical resources. If people are permitted to spend their own money on cosmetic surgery without being accused of violating 'the right of others to basic care', it is hard to see why couples willing to spend their own money on sex selection should be treated differently. Moreover, given the burdens, the expense and the low success rate of IVF, it is highly unlikely that preimplantation genetic diagnosis for sex selection will ever become so widespread as to have an 'impact on the overall deployment of resources for medical care and on the availability of reproductive services'.

Thus, when the Committee concludes that preimplantation genetic diagnosis for sex selection poses a 'risk of unwarranted gender bias, social harm, the diversion of medical resources from genuine medical need and should therefore be discouraged', it seems that the boldness of its statement is in conspicuous contrast to the weakness of its arguments.

References

Benagiano, G. and Bianchi, P. (1999) Sex preselection: an aid to couples or a threat to humanity? *Hum. Reprod.*, 14: 868–870.

ESHRE PGD Consortium Steering Committee (1999) ESHRE Preimplantation Genetic Diagnosis (PGD) Consortium: preliminary assessment of data from January 1997 to September 1998. *Hum. Reprod.*, 14: 3138–3148.

Ethics Committee of the American Society of Reproductive Medicine (1999) Sex selection and preimplantation genetic diagnosis. *Fertil. Steril.*, 72: 595–598.

Fugger, E.F., Black, S.H., Keyvanfar, K. *et al.* (1998) Births of normal daughters after Microsort sperm separation and intrauterine insemination, in-vitro fertilization, or intracytoplasmic sperm injection. *Hum. Reprod.*, 13: 2367–2370.

Khatamee, M.A., Leinberger-Sica, A., Matos, P. *et al.* (1989) Sex preselection in New York City: who chooses which sex and why. *Int. J. Fertil.*, 34: 353–354.

Liu, P. and Rose, A. (1995) Social aspects of >800 couples coming forward for gender selection of their children. *Hum. Reprod.*, 10: 968–971.

Savulescu, J. (1999) Sex selection – the case for. *Med. J. Australia*, 171: 373–375.

Simpson, J.L. and Carson, S.A. (1999) The reproductive option of sex selection. *Hum. Reprod.*, 14: 870–872.

Statham, H., Green, J., Snowdon, C. and France-Dawson, M. (1993) Choice of baby's sex. *Lancet*, 341: 564–565.

Sureau, G. (1999) Gender selection: a crime against humanity or the exercise of a fundamental right? *Hum. Reprod.*, 14: 867–868.

14

Conception to Obtain Hematopoietic Stem Cells

John A. Robertson, Jeffrey P. Kahn, and John E. Wagner

Parents with children who have diseases affecting the blood or immune system often face a difficult dilemma. Hematopoietic stem cells from umbilical cord blood or bone marrow may cure or alleviate their child's disease, but there may be no histo-compatible cells available for transplant. Some parents then decide to have another child, hoping that this child will be a suitable match for bone marrow or umbilical cord blood stem cells for the existing child. If a prenatal test for the primary disease is available, they may request prenatal diagnosis, both to make sure that the fetus is not affected by disease and to ascertain whether the second child will be a suitable match for the first. More recently, some couples have used preimplantation genetic diagnosis to allow them to transfer only HLA-matched embryos to the uterus.

Conceiving a child in order to serve as a hematopoietic stem cell donor raises difficult medical, ethical, and legal issues. An overarching ethical issue is whether it is ethically acceptable to conceive a child in part to be an organ or tissue donor for an existing child. If so, ethical and legal questions then arise about the different methods available for testing whether the child will be a suitable stem cell donor. If the parents opt for testing, they must use either prenatal diagnosis followed by selective abortion (if the fetus is not one they want to bring to term), or preimplantation genetic diagnosis and selective transfer of embryos (to

ensure that they have a fetus they want to bring to term). Finally, society as a whole must take up questions about whether and how to restrict, regulate, or provide support for these practices.

The Need for Transplants

Hematopoietic stem cell transplants have become the treatment of choice for many malignant and nonmalignant diseases, including leukemia, Hodgkin's disease, sickle cell disease, thalassemia, and congenital hematopoietic disorders such as Fanconi anemia.[1] Unfortunately, it often is not easy to obtain suitable cells.

The best results are obtained when the cells are from sibling donors.[2] Patients who do not have access to cells from a closely matched relative can face a long and often unsuccessful search to find a compatible donor. The National Marrow Donor Program lists 6.5 million names, leaving a roughly one in four hundred chance, depending on the patient's ethnic group, that an unrelated individual will be an acceptable match. Finding a donor is especially hard for people not of Northern European descent because they have a smaller pool from which to draw.[3] If the parents find an unrelated donor, their child still faces serious immunologic risks of infection and graft versus host

Original publication details: John A. Robertson, Jeffrey P. Kahn, and John E. Wagner, "Conception to Obtain Hematopoietic Stem Cells," pp. 34–40 from *Hastings Center Report* 32: 3 (May/June 2002). Reproduced with permission from John Wiley & Sons.

disease, in which the transplanted white blood cells attack their host.

The use of umbilical cord blood from an unrelated donor has ameliorated some of the problems associated with marrow donation. The HLA matching need not be as precise, for example. Also, the interval between beginning a search and finding a donor is shorter, and the risk of acute and chronic graft versus host disease is lower.[4] There is still a high risk of opportunistic infection, however. Also, because of the smaller quantities of stem cells in the cord blood, the rate of graft failure increases and fewer neutrophils, essential to the immune system, are recovered.[5]

It is these limitations that have led some parents to consider conceiving another child to serve as a stem cell donor. Parents would have a one in four chance of naturally conceiving an HLA-matched child. If the disease for which the transplant is sought is autosomal recessive, as with Fanconi anemia, then there is only a three in sixteen chance of conceiving a child who is both disease free and HLA matched. Prenatal diagnosis can inform parents both whether the fetus has the disease and whether the child will be HLA matched. Preimplantation genetic diagnosis can ensure that only disease free and perfectly matched embryos are transferred to the woman's uterus.[6]

Creating a Child

The central ethical issues that arise with conceiving a child to be a hematopoietic stem cell donor concern the child's rights and welfare. Might the interests of the child be compromised for the sake of the existing child? Even if the child's interests are not directly harmed, do the parents and physicians risk violating the Kantian imperative that we treat other persons as ends and never as "mere means"?[7]

The circumstances in which parents face such choices strongly suggest that these concerns can be overcome, however. If the parents were already planning another child, then their existing child's needs may have spurred them to reproduce earlier than they intended, but advancing the reproductive calendar seems to pose little risk to the second child. Nor is the second child likely to be harmed, or have her interests ignored, even if her sibling's needs

motivated her conception. The birth of a child creates a powerful bond regardless of the circumstances of conception. Indeed, the fact that the parents are willing to conceive another child to protect the first suggests that they are highly committed to the well-being of their children, and that they will value the second child for its own sake as well.

Because the hematopoietic stem cells will usually be obtained from umbilical cord blood, no physical intrusions on the child to obtain the stem cells need ordinarily occur. In any event, bone marrow donations from infants and minors to siblings have been ethically and legally acceptable for many years. The burdens of bone marrow aspiration are held to be minor enough, given the benefits to the child from having a sibling survive, to fall within the discretion of parents to have such a procedure done on their child.[8]

Nor should either failure or success in saving the older child affect the welfare of the new child. The children may end up having a very special bond with each other regardless of whether a transplant occurs or succeeds. If a transplant cures the existing child, the second child will have made a huge contribution to household welfare. Yet if the stem cell transplant fails, the second child is not likely to be blamed for an attempt that would have been impossible without its birth. Although the parents will have suffered a grievous loss, they will be left with a healthy second child, who had helped them try to save the first.

Because conceiving a child to provide cord blood donation does not harm or misuse the child, it falls squarely within the parents' discretion to reproduce as they choose.[9] Decisions to have children have long been entwined with narcissistic or utilitarian purposes, from continuing one's lineage to seeking companionship, replacing a dead or dying child, adding additional workers to the household, and providing a "defence 'gainst time's scythe." Although the need for hematopoietic stem cells might make the purposeful nature of most reproduction more transparent than it usually is, aiding an existing child is as valid as many other reasons that motivate people to reproduce. Indeed, it is a choice that doubles the parents' chance of having surviving children, for it may save the life of an older child while enabling another to be born.

A more serious ethical problem would arise if parents sought to have a child *merely* to serve as a stem cell donor, with no intention to rear the child after its birth. This might occur, for example, if they gave the child up for adoption because she was not a good match, or because they had obtained the umbilical cord blood and were not interested in rearing her. Such a crassly instrumental approach would appear to use the child as a "mere means." It also seems to conflict with standard conceptions of the parents' role as involving a commitment to nurture and care for their children.

As objectionable as such an action seems, however, it is not clear that the parents have actually harmed the child, nor that they should legally be stopped from doing so. If the parents had not decided to conceive the child, the child would never have existed, and life as an adopted child is usually as meaningful and fulfilling as other lives.[10] Although we may judge harshly people who embark on reproduction without intending to care for their offspring, the interests of such children have been advanced *once they are born*, for this motivation has enabled them to exist.

Despite such arguments, however, the practice is sufficiently counter to prevailing conceptions of parental commitments that few physicians would be comfortable participating in it, and many might try to discourage it. They should stick to their position even if the couple makes giving the child up for adoption a condition of conception. Further, clinics should find out whether parents are committed to rearing a child conceived to donate stem cells. Although they may not be able to stop the parents from conceiving, and should not necessarily refuse to use hematopoietic stem cells that become available as a result, they can and should discourage the practice.

If parents may ethically conceive a child in order to provide stem cells to an older child, then the question also arises whether they are *obligated* to do so. But this question can be put swiftly to rest. While parents often make sacrifices for their children, they have no legal obligations to provide blood, tissue, or organs for them, much less obligations to have another child for its sake. Nor are they morally obligated to undertake the onerous task of conceiving and gestating a child to obtain cord blood cells for an existing child. The burdens of producing and rearing the new child are substantial, and are not implicitly assumed in the decision to have the first child. These choices are sufficiently personal that they should be left to individual discretion. Likewise, if they have tried once to produce a child with compatible stem cells and have not succeeded, they are not morally or legally obligated to continue trying.

Assuring a Match

There are different methods for assuring a close HLA match, and they raise different issues.

Coital conception followed by gestation without prenatal testing offers the least certainty, for one cannot tell in advance whether the second child will be the one in four that is HLA matched, much less satisfy the three in sixteen chance that the child will be both HLA matched and free of autosomal recessive disease. Of course, it can happen. In the well-publicized Ayala case in 1993, a couple underwent a vasectomy reversal and then gave birth to a naturally conceived daughter who was an exact match for a daughter with chronic myelogenous leukemia.[11] Parents who embark on coital conception for this purpose should understand the relatively low probability of success and commit themselves to rearing a child regardless of the closeness of a match.

Much greater certainty that the child will be a close HLA match is possible with prenatal diagnosis, perhaps followed by selective abortion, and preimplantation genetic diagnosis followed by selective transfer. Each method has advantages and disadvantages.

Prenatal Diagnosis

For many blood disorders, prenatal diagnosis can inform parents both whether a fetus has the disease and, if it does not, whether it would be a close HLA match for the child they already have. If the match is not close, the parents will be better prepared to pursue other therapeutic alternatives. Alternatively, they could decide to terminate the pregnancy and try again, although most parents in this situation continue the pregnancy to term. Arlene Auerbach, for example, studied thirty-two couples who underwent prenatal testing after conception of a child they hoped would serve as a stem cell donor to an earlier child afflicted with Fanconi anemia. All but two of the twenty-six fetuses that were poor HLA matches were nonetheless carried to term.[12]

The question of abortion is particularly troubling. In theory, parents could even use abortion not only to screen out affected or poorly matched fetuses but even to obtain matched fetal tissue *after* abortion. Those who are pro-life would strongly condemn all of these uses of abortion, of course. Those who are pro-choice might accept the termination of affected fetuses, but they might be more conflicted about the abortion of unaffected fetuses that are not a good HLA match, and they might object outright to obtaining matched fetal tissue after abortion.

Somebody who is pro-choice cannot consistently object to the latter choices on the ground that fetuses have rights or interests in themselves, because they deny that premise in their acceptance of a woman's choice of abortion for unwanted pregnancy. Their objection would appear to rest on symbolic or expressive grounds: that is, they do not want to sanction a practice that treats fetuses as resources to serve the needs of others. They might, for example, think that although previable fetuses are not persons or moral subjects, it is disrespectful of human life generally to create and then destroy a healthy fetus merely because it lacks a genetic trait – HLA-matching genes – useful to another person.[13] Such a view is similar to the reluctance that some have to permit the creation of embryos for research, even though they readily accept research on embryos left over from infertility treatments.

Parents faced with getting compatible tissue to save one of their children might disagree that great symbolic importance should be attached to abortion in these circumstances. If the fetus is too undeveloped to have rights or inherent moral status, and abortion is otherwise generally permissible, then arguably no additional disrespect for human life flows from aborting an otherwise healthy fetus that is not a close HLA match. If the parents are not interested in rearing a child who is a poor HLA match, their lack of interest may be enough to make continuing the pregnancy a

great difficulty for them – even though they are willing to rear a child who is a close match. Auerbach has reassuringly shown that few parents in this situation have actually chosen to abort.[14] But it would clearly be within a woman's constitutional rights to abort an unaffected, ill-matched fetus, since motivation is not generally a relevant criterion in limiting reproductive rights.[15]

The logic of this position would extend even to aborting when the fetus is a good match and sufficient hematopoietic stem cells for transplant could be retrieved from fetal remains. On the pro-choice premises, the parents are not harming or wronging the fetus in either case, since it lacks inherent rights and the abortion is occurring as early as possible prior to viability. If parents are not ready to have another child, conception and abortion to obtain fetal tissue will enable them to obtain the stem cells while avoiding the later stages of pregnancy and the birth of a child they are not prepared to rear. For them, these are sufficiently worthy concerns to outweigh the negative symbolism of aborting in order to obtain fetal tissue for transplant.

Current federal law prohibits this course of action. Aborting for the purpose of obtaining fetal tissue for a designated recipient is a felony punishable by up to five years in prison.[16] This ban may be unconstitutional, however, for it appears to violate a woman's right to decide when to get pregnant and when prior to viability to terminate a pregnancy.[17] If the prohibition did significantly burden a woman's decisions about conception and abortion, then its validity would turn on whether the state's interest in not commodifying women and fetuses, or in maintaining a particular view of respect for life, justifies the infringement of liberty. However, because those interests do not justify state restrictions on abortion in nontransplant cases, they may not justify restrictions on abortion to obtain stem cells for transplant.

Preimplantation Genetic Diagnosis

Preimplantation genetic diagnosis, like prenatal diagnosis, provides advance certainty about whether a child is affected by the disease and would be a good HLA match. Its main advantage is that it provides this information prior to implantation and pregnancy, thus making it possible to select embryos rather than fetuses. Several couples with children with Fanconi anemia and other disorders have sought PGD for this purpose. In one well-publicized case, a family with a child with Fanconi anemia was able to use this technique to give birth to an unaffected, HLA-matched sibling whose cord blood was then used for a stem cell transplant to his older sister.[18] Other couples, however, have not been so successful.[19] If PGD proves to be safe, effective, and easily accessible for HLA selection of embryos, it could become the preferred technique for parents in this situation.

The likelihood of success

PGD has both practical and ethical disadvantages, however. The practical barriers are its efficacy and cost. For women under thirty-five, in vitro fertilization has a take-home-baby success rate of 30 percent or higher, and the success rate is likely to be higher if the woman is fertile, as she likely would be if she is seeking PGD for stem cell donations.[20] However, couples who undergo IVF and PGD in order to obtain HLA-matched stem cells are likely to face a much lower success rate. Since only 75 percent of oocytes retrieved in a stimulated cycle are successfully fertilized, and only 60 percent of them reach the blastocyst stage in vitro, there would probably be considerably fewer viable embryos that meet the three in sixteen chance of being both an identical match and free of autosomal recessive disease. Since not all such embryos will implant and go to term, a couple using PGD to get matched stem cells might have to undergo several IVF cycles to achieve their goal, if they are successful at all.

Regardless of its success rates, many couples lack access to this technique. Few centers provide PGD for any purpose, much less for HLA matching.[21] In addition, the cost of IVF and PGD is prohibitive for many couples. Since health insurance does not now cover IVF and PGD, only couples who can spend $15,000 to $20,000 per cycle, probably for several cycles, will be able to use this method. Although those who can pay for the opportunity should not be denied it just because others cannot pay for it, ensuring access to IVF and PGD for all those whose children need hematopoietic stem cell transplants remains a problem.

Embryo status

Because the use of IVF and PGD permits the transfer of only the selected embryos, it also involves the intentional creation of embryos that will not be transferred to the uterus. Positions on this aspect of the procedure reflect differing views of the moral status of embryos and the likelihood that using PGD for HLA matching will lead to using PGD for other nonmedical indications. The issue of the embryo's status is sharpest for those who view embryos as having the same moral status and rights that people have after birth. For example, those who hold strong right-to-life views will object to PGD because of the deliberate nontransfer or destruction of embryos that it entails. Those who think the preimplantation human embryo lacks inherent moral status would be more willing to accept the procedure, and indeed would find it less disrespectful of human life than abortion for the same purpose at a later stage of development.

The creation of unneeded embryos poses a much more difficult question for those who, while believing that embryos have symbolic but not inherent value, do not approve of creating embryos solely for research. Although distinguishing the two cases is difficult, creating embryos that are likely to be discarded is for the parents seeking these transplants a necessary part of a medical intervention, with an intended life-enhancing benefit, and so may be more justifiable than creating embryos for medical research. In addition, permitting the procedure might prevent parents from employing prenatal diagnosis and selective abortion to obtain matched tissue.

It is important to bear in mind that even in basic IVF, as performed to help infertile couples have children, it is common practice to create more embryos than can safely be transferred to the uterus and to store or eventually discard the rest. This practice is accepted by most people (those with right-to-life views excepted) because it serves the important purpose of promoting pregnancy for infertile persons. Although PGD for HLA-matching targets a trait that does not threaten a child's health, it does serve an important, life-affirming social purpose – that of saving the life of a child, reassuring parents that compatible stem cells are available, and preventing abortion. Many couples in this situation would find PGD for HLA selection ethically justified.

The slippery slope

Some worry that using this procedure to obtain stem cell transplants makes it easier to use reproductive technology for negative selection or eugenic purposes. When PGD is used to obtain stem cells, embryos would be rejected either because they have a serious genetic disease or because they do not provide a specific HLA match. If unaffected embryos can be created and then excluded because they lack a genotype that makes them useful tissue donors, then embryos could be created and discarded for other utilitarian or preferential reasons – because they are of the wrong gender or have other physical traits that might be ascertainable by PGD. Although PGD operates negatively by screening and exclusion, its use for HLA matching might set a precedent for *positive* alteration and gene targeting, as might occur in germline gene therapy, nuclear transfer cloning, enhancement, or other nonmedical purposes. The fear is that these steps will lead to widespread use of PGD and genetic technology to choose, exclude, or alter genomes of offspring as parents choose.

This slippery slope argument assumes both that future genetic alteration and manipulation will be unmitigatedly horrible, and that accepting the procedure now in question – HLA typing of embryos prior to transfer – will lead inexorably to abusive and uncontrollable genetic engineering of humans, if only by changing attitudes that would make the next step toward genetic engineering easier to take. Both premises are flawed. First, some cases of genetic alteration might turn out to be medically desirable and ethically acceptable; one example might be germline gene therapy to remove genes that cause major congenital malformations. It is simply too soon to say that all genetic alterations we might someday be able to perform on embryos are so unacceptable that anything that might somehow lead to such practices should be prohibited, whatever its benefits.

Second, even if all positive genetic alteration of embryos were to be deemed unacceptable, those practices could be banned without also stopping otherwise justifiable forms of negative genetic selection, such as screening embryos for HLA type. Given the clear line between negative selection and positive alteration of embryos, it is not necessary to bar cases of highly beneficial negative selection in order to prevent future positive selection.

Embryonic Stem Cells

An alternative that may someday be available is producing hematopoietic stem cells directly from *embryonic* stem cells, thus avoiding the birth of a child in order to obtain hematopoietic stem cells. This option would require skill in directing embryonic stem cells to produce the hematopoietic stem cells needed, and the ability to ensure that those stem cells are HLA-matched to the recipient.

Although research on turning embryonic stem cells into the replacement cells needed for therapy has just begun, if it were successful, unlimited supplies of hematopoietic stem cells could become available for therapy. The problem of ensuring a close HLA match may be more daunting, however. Unless libraries of embryonic stem cells corresponding to most HLA types existed, histocompatible stem cells for the recipient would have to be directly fashioned for each patient.

One way of fashioning them would be through therapeutic cloning. If the transplant recipient's own nuclear DNA were transferred into an enucleated egg from the mother, the resulting embryo would be perfectly histocompatible with the recipient. This method would be fruitless if the disease being treated is inborn and genetic, as is likely the case with many childhood diseases. In those cases, disease would very likely recur.

Another way of producing embryonic stem cells would be to create embryos using the parents' gametes and derive the stem cells only from those with a close HLA match. This method would entail creating embryos that would not be transferred to the uterus, and would raise many of the same issues as preimplantation genetic diagnosis to obtain HLA-matched stem cells. In this scenario, however, pregnancy and childbirth would not be necessary to realize the intended benefits. Some couples would clearly prefer such an option. There are as yet no laws banning the creation of embryos for use or destruction in therapy.

Policy and Practice

If the reasoning offered here is sound, a couple may have a child to provide stem cells for another child, and they may also use preimplantation testing to ensure a close tissue match. The use of prenatal testing and abortion is more troubling, but may fall within a woman's rights. Interestingly, a similar conclusion has recently been reached by the Human Fertilisation and Embryology Authority in the United Kingdom, after extensive public consultation.[22]

We close with a few observations about policy and practice. First, it should be clear that, except for the possibility of aborting a fetus to obtain from it tissue for transplant, there are few legal barriers preventing parents and physicians from using prenatal testing and PGD to produce HLA-matched stem cells for transplant. The federal government does not fund PGD for HLA selection, nor any other practices surrounding conception to obtain hematopoietic stem cells for transplant, but public funding restrictions do not prevent private funding of conception, prenatal, and embryo selection practices. Of course, future laws against creating embryos for research or therapeutic purposes, if constitutional, could limit some preimplantation methods for ensuring a close match.

Second, parents are not morally or legally obligated to conceive another child to benefit an existing child. Indeed, parents should go forward with conception to obtain stem cells only if they are prepared to nurture, care for, and love any child they have as a result. If they do decide to have a child to obtain stem cells, they may do so without resorting to prenatal diagnosis or PGD. They may also stop after any unsuccessful IVF cycle for this purpose, or after the birth of a child who was not an appropriate match. Given the relative burdens and benefits of conceiving for donation purposes, the decision to conceive a child to serve as a donor for an existing child is quintessentially an individual one to be made or not as the parents choose.

Third, physicians and patient groups should inform parents of these options for obtaining matched stem cells, so that they may choose what is best for them and their child, including where they may receive safe and effective IVF and PGD or prenatal services. Physicians and patient groups should also provide counseling to couples who are considering conception to obtain matched stem cells.

In some instances, the best alternative for parents who have a child with a life-threatening disease may be to conceive another child. The parents' commitment to loving and nurturing the second child is the key factor in determining whether such a decision would be acceptable.

Parents considering this course may also wish to explore options for prenatal and preimplantation testing that will assure that the child is free of autosomal recessive disease and is HLA-matched to the child they already have. Such practices may be controversial, but they will often reflect deep concern for *both* children, and should be available for parents who have no other good therapeutic alternatives.

References

1 M.M. Horowitz, "Use and Growth of Hematopoietic Cell Transplantation," in *Hematopoietic Cell Transplantation*, second edition, ed. S.J. Forman et al. (Malden, Mass.: Blackwell Science Inc., 1999), 12–17; and J.E. Wagner et al., "Hematopoietic Stem Cell Transplantation in the Treatment of Fanconi Anemia," in *Hematopoietic Cell Transplantation*, second edition, ed. S.J. Forman et al. (Malden, Mass.: Blackwell Science Inc., 1999), 1204–19.

2 D.I. Marks et al., "Allogeneic Bone Marrow Transplantation for Chronic Myeloid Leukemia Using Sibling and Volunteer Unrelated Donors: A Comparison of Complications in the First Two Years," *Annals of Internal Medicine* 119 (1993): 207–214.

3 D.L. Confer, "Unrelated Marrow Donor Registries," *Current Opinions in Hematology* 4 (1997): 408–412.

4 J.E. Wagner, "Placental and Umbilical Cord Blood Transplantation," in *Hematology: Basic Principles and Practice*, third edition, ed. R. Hoffman et al. (New York: Churchhill Livingston, 1999); V. Rocha et al., "Graft versus Host Disease in Children Transplanted with HLA Identical Sibling Umbilical Cord Blood versus Bone Marrow Hematopoietic Stem Cells," *NEJM* 342 (2000): 1846–54.

5   J. Wagner, personal communication.

6   Y. Verlansky et al., "Preimplantation Diagnosis for Fanconi Anemia Combined with HLA Matching," *JAMA* 285 (2001): 3130; L. Belkin, "The Made-to-Order Savior," *The New York Times Magazine*, 1 July 2001.

7   I. Kant, *Grounding for the Metaphysic of Morals*, second edition, tr. James W. Ellington (Indianapolis, Ind.: Hackett Publishing, 1981), 42, 66–67.

8   C.H. Baron et al., "Live Organ and Tissue Transplants from Minor Donors in Massachusetts," *Boston University Law Review* 55 (1975): 159–93, at 159.

9   J.A. Robertson, *Children of Choice: Freedom and the New Reproductive Technologies* (Princeton, N.J.: Princeton University Press, 1994), 28–40.

10 D. Heyd *Genethics: Moral Issues in the Creation of People* (Berkeley, Calif.: University of California Press, 1992), 59–62; Robertson, *Children of Choice*, 75–78; and D. Brock, "The Non-identity Problem and Genetic Harms – The Case of Wrongful Handicaps," *Bioethics* 9 (1995), 69–85.

11 Robertson, *Children of Choice*, 214–17.

12 A.D. Auerbach, "Umbilical Cord Blood Transplants for Genetic Disease: Diagnostic and Ethical Issues in Fetal Studies," *Blood Cells* 20 (1994): 303–309.

13 N.W. Danis, "Fetal Tissue Transplants: Restricting Recipient Designation," *Hastings Law Journal* 39 (1988): 1079–85.

14 Auerbach, "Umbilical Cord Blood Transplants for Genetic Disease."

15 Roe v. Wade, 410 U.S. 113 (1973).

16 National Institutes of Health Revitalization Act of 1993, Pub.L.No. 103–43, Sect. 111, 107 Stat. 129 (codified at 42 U.S.C. Sec. 498A).

17 J.A. Robertson, "Abortion to Obtain Tissue for Transplant," *Suffolk Law Review* 27 (1994): 1359–89.

18 D. Grady, "Son Conceived to Provide Blood Cells for Daughter," *New York Times*, 4 October 2000.

19 L. Belkin, "The Made-to-Order Savior."

20 U.S. Department of Health and Human Services, Centers for Disease Control and Prevention, *1996 Assisted Reproductive Technology Success Rates: National Summary and Fertility Clinic Reports* (Washington, D.C.: U.S. Department of Health and Human Services, 1998).

21 J.C. Harper, "Preimplantation Diagnosis of Inherited Disease by Embryo Biopsy: An Update of the World Figures," *Journal of Assisted Reproduction and Genetics* 13 (1996): 90–95.

22 Ethics Committee of the Human Fertilisation and Embryology Authority, "Ethical Issues in the Creation and Selection of Preimplantation Embryos to Produce Tissue Donors," 22 November 2001. http://www.hfea.gov.uk (2002)

15

Why We Should Not Permit Embryos to Be Selected as Tissue Donors

David King

The announcement of the birth of a son to the Whitaker family, who was selected as an embryo to be a tissue-matched donor for his sick brother, has sparked the usual massive media interest. It seems that the Whitaker family have great public sympathy and support for their use of the technique. As usual, the main voices opposing the use of this technique have been those of the pro-lifers. The predominant view, summarised as: 'What can be wrong with saving the life of a sick child?' demands a proper response, which is not grounded in the belief that embryos possess a right to life.

Children as Things

The main objection to the use of pre-implantation genetic diagnosis (PGD) for this purpose is that it objectifies the child by turning it into a mere tool, and so contradicts the basic ethical principle that we should never use human beings merely as a means to an end (however good that end may be), because they should also be treated as ends in themselves. That is the basic ethical objection to slavery, for example. In response to this, it is often said that the new child will

be loved for himself, and will not be treated by his parents as a mere tool, and this is no doubt true. However, the Whitakers have made it very clear that their primary purpose for conceiving Jamie was to save their other son: this will nearly always be the case for couples in their position. The case against this use of PGD does not depend on fine analysis of each couple's motivations and emotional states, or on how much they succeed in loving their new child despite the reasons for his/her conception, but on the consequences of breaking the ethical rule.

While most people would agree with the ethical principle, many seem to feel that it is a case of abstract principles versus real individual suffering; and because, as is typical in our public discourse, the case is discussed without considering the context, ie. the overall trends promoted by reproductive and biomedical technology, the reasons for concern about objectification seem remote and theoretical. However, I would argue that these cases, far from being special examples, in which we should allow exceptions to our principles, are in fact typical examples of the way that reproductive and biomedical technologies objectify human beings. That is why it is so important that we resist the selection of embryos as tissue donors: because these

Original publication details: David King, "Why We Should Not Permit Embryos to Be Selected as Tissue Donors," pp. 13–16 from *The Bulletin of Medical Ethics* 190 (August 2003). Copyright © RSM Press, 2003. Reproduced by permission of SAGE Publications Ltd., London, Los Angeles, New Delhi, Singapore and Washington DC.

cases significantly advance the objectifying trend, and the consequences of doing so are, in the not-so-long term, disastrous.

Selection of embryos as tissue donors falls squarely into the objectifying trend in two senses: the literal and the ethical. What makes many people very uncomfortable about biomedical technology in general is the way that the relentless march of reductionist science continually turns human beings, at various stages of development, into human organisms, useful sources of biological raw material for spare parts. As science discovers more and more about the workings of the human body, our bodies are seen as no more than machines, with no special moral meaning or dignity, and the pressure to extract various components in order to benefit others becomes ever greater. The problem is the way that this pressure leads to rewriting of ethical rules. Whether it is at the beginning of the lifecycle, with the envisioned creation of cloned embryos purely as sources of stem cells and the proposed extraction of eggs from aborted fetuses for use in IVF, or at the end, with the constant shifting of definitions of death to facilitate 'harvesting' of organs for transplantation, the integrity of human organisms and the ethical rules protecting them seem everywhere under siege from the enthusiasm of biomedical technicians. Only able-bodied post-natal humans seem, for the moment, to be safe.

The creation of babies as sources of tissue, and, as shocking, the co-option of reproduction for reasons other than procreation, push instrumentalisation of human life one step further, and dispose of one more ethical principle. They also set the stage for further steps: how long before we will be told that saving a child this way is the best reason for cloning? And if we can create embryos and children as sources of cells, if it proves necessary, (perhaps because it proves impossible to create the required organs from embryonic stem cells), why not allow the embryos to grow into fetuses and 'harvest' tissues at that stage?

Leaving aside these next steps, many people could benefit medically from matched tissue donation – there is nothing unique about Charlie Whitaker's disease. How will we feel when the tissue recipient is not another child, but an adult, maybe a parent or a more remote family member?

In the reproductive context, objectification has a particular ethical meaning, often summed up in the term 'designer babies'. The increasing technologisation of reproduction, and the use of technology to choose our children's characteristics, tend to make reproduction just another process for producing consumer goods. Although the outputs of this process are undeniably human beings, by choosing their characteristics we turn them into things, just human-designed objects. Conversely, by taking this new power of selection/design over a key part of what constitutes those individuals, we elevate ourselves above them. This is part of what people mean when they talk about playing God. The parent–child relationship becomes a designer–object relationship, rather than one between two fundamentally equal human subjects.

The selection of children as tissue donors is an example of the objectifying trend in techno-reproduction, albeit not a typical one. Here, the child is not selected for characteristics that will 'improve' it, but to benefit another child. In one sense this is more acceptable, since the aim of the procedure is undoubtedly good, and is not motivated by consumerist desires for 'enhancement'. But in another sense it is a more extreme example of objectification, because the primary reason for the child's being is not even to be a child as such, but to be a source of spare parts for another.

As the discussions about how Jamie is likely to feel and be treated have shown, there are immediate consequences of breaking the ethical rule: it is not a matter of 'real suffering versus abstract ethical principles'. Despite all the love that his parents will no doubt give him, how will Jamie feel as he grows up, knowing that he was wanted first for his genes, and only secondly for himself? What if the transplant fails? There is a considerable chance that the cord blood transplant will fail: the next step is bone marrow extraction, which is painful and has risks. It is not hard to see that, having conceived Jamie to save his brother, his parents will feel impelled to submit him to this procedure, and the doctors who might otherwise have counselled them against submitting a young child to this, will feel weakened.

In response to these points, it is suggested that people often have children for bad reasons, and we do nothing about that, so why object to this? In my view this is intellectual laziness of the worst sort. First, two wrongs do not make a right. Secondly, it is precisely this kind of argumentation which always drives us down slippery slopes: 'You've accepted X in the past, so there's no reason for not accepting Y, the next step'. Often the very bioethicists who reject slippery slopes as non-existent, and insist we can always draw a line, are the same people who, when the time for linedrawing arrives, tell us it would be inconsistent to do so. More importantly, we must realise that the availability of technology to change chance and hope into certainty and expectation completely transforms the situation, and the nature of reproduction. While parents may have children for various more or less acceptable social reasons, this use of PGD wrenches procreation from its biological purpose and its social context in a way which objectifies the child in a qualitatively new way – now we have children as medical aids.

In summary, when we look at these cases in their proper context, it is clear that the rule not to use people as mere means to an end (instrumentalising them) is not just a remote theoretical principle. Objectification and instrumentalisation are an inherent feature of reproductive biomedicine, not something that just crops up in occasional cases. Thus we can be quite certain that, if we abandon the principle now, we will see more and worse to follow.

What Kind of Ethics Do We Need?

It is apparent that cases like these pose a challenge not only to our mechanisms for discussion and decision, but to the kind of ethics that underlie the mainstream of debates.

First, it should be clear that the kind of ethics purveyed by the HFEA is not merely grossly inadequate but positively misleading. It is not only that the HFEA is dominated by a philosophy that allows no critique of science itself, or of the direction of medicine. Nor is it that the ethics employed are abstract and have to conform to the discourse rules of bioethics, which forbid historical analysis of social processes, such as the trend of objectification and the forces driving it. The problem is worse: the HFEA cannot even articulate the basic ethical issues at the centre of public concern.

Surveying the HFEA's public statements on the Whitaker case we find two arguments: the potential

psychological effect for Jamie, and the risk of PGD to the embryo, which can only be justified if there is benefit to that embryo, i.e. being assured of not suffering from a genetic disorder. The latter argument is the basis of the HFEA's permitting the Hashmi family to undergo embryo selection. Their child Zain suffers from thalassemia, a genetic disease, so they could argue that their primary purpose for PGD was to prevent the new child having thalassemia, and that tissue type selection would add no extra risk to the embryo. The HFEA turned down the Whitakers last year because their son was suffering from a disorder which is not genetic, and there is therefore no case for using PGD to avoid it.

These arguments are pathetically weak and seem almost designed not to stand the test of time and the pressure of public opinion. While it is true that Jamie may be psychologically harmed by the conditions of his coming into being, that harm, of itself (i.e. understood without reference to the objectification inherent in reproductive biomedicine), seems paltry in comparison to the good involved in saving a child. As for the distinction based on whether the child has a genetic or sporadic condition, it is not surprising the public finds it incomprehensible for the HFEA to support publicly the Hashmis one week and turn down the Whitakers the next. The distinction, in a common sense view of the world, is meaningless: to hang the different decisions on it is silly. There is no firm evidence that PGD is harmful and, again, such a risk seems small in comparison to the saving of a life. Either the use of the technique is acceptable in both cases, or in neither.

More importantly, nowhere in the HFEA's public pronouncements can we find any clear reference to the point, which has been at the centre of the public debate, about the Kantian ethical principle of non-instrumentalisation/objectification. Now even the rules of liberal ethics cannot be publicly mentioned. How can this be? The answer is that the HFEA is, by virtue of its own institutional nature, not allowed to use the sort of ethical principles that ordinary people use. It can consider medical benefit and risk and, because it is written into the relevant legislation, the welfare of the child. But for the HFEA, which has legal responsibilities, and exists in a controversial and litigious climate, it is impossible to base its decision even on ethical principles as universally accepted as Kant's, because to do so makes it vulnerable: only benefit, risk and welfare considerations, on a strictly individual case-by-case basis, are legally defensible. (The Whitaker/Hashmi distinction, for example, is not based on any real moral difference between the cases; in the Whitaker case the HFEA overruled its own ethics committee, which wanted to be consistent with its decision on the Hashmis. What dictated the HFEA decision in these cases was the need to stay within the letter of the law, which appears to forbid selection of embryos to benefit another individual. Its calculation was correct, and allowed it to defend its decision in the High Court against a pro-life group's challenge. In effect they made the right decision for the wrong reasons. This is one more example of sensible policy and decision making being tripped up by accidents of drafting of the 1990 HFE Act: it has been comprehensively overtaken by developments in science and technology and needs amending.)

So the result of the HFEA's institutional status is that the key ethical decision-making body in this area is forced to behave as an ethical illiterate, and to operate ethically on the basis of political pragmatism. This will never lead to decisions that are either principled or in the public interest.

What is happening is strikingly reminiscent of the history of genetically modified organisms (GMOs): that experience should be a warning to the government. Throughout the 1990s critics complained that the Advisory Committee on Release to the Environment (ACRE) based judgements about the environmental risk of GMOs on narrow, case-by-case analyses of the direct environmental impact of small-scale experimental trials, without considering wider issues. It did so because of the narrow definition of environmental harm in the 1990 Environmental Protection Act. ACRE was not permitted to consider the impact of GMOs in farming (eg. changes in patterns of pesticide use created by GMO use) which might have large environmental impacts, let alone the wider implications of GMOs. Its members had a narrow range of scientific expertise, with no sociologist, economist or expert in farming and the

environment. So it could not address many concerns of environmentalists and other critics, yet it was the main venue of regulatory decisions which, by government dogma, must be 'science-based'. These concerns eventually exploded into direct action and public furore. ACRE was completely overhauled, European law was rewritten, and the government was forced to delay while it mounted farm-scale trials of the impact of GMOs.

The HFEA is in essentially the same position as ACRE in the 1990s. Its legal responsibilities stop it from addressing the public's real concerns, about the trends of objectification, consumerism and eugenics, and where these technologies, step by step, are taking us. As long as HFEA continues to work this way, the head of steam will continue to build, and who knows how it will be released.

Clearly what is needed is an ethical discourse that can articulate and discuss people's real, long-term concerns, and can balance them against the demands of individual cases. Here we see a key distinction from the debate over GMOs, where the pressure for 'progress' was driven by the cold and unsympathetic imperatives of science and the market, with no clear benefit to people. With reproductive technology we risk being overwhelmed by a tidal wave of sentiment about sick children, blinding us to where these decisions are leading. In public discussion of the Whitaker case, many parents said they would do anything to save their sick child. God preserve us from people who will do anything! We must not make public policy, with profound long-term consequences, on the basis of individual families' desperation, however much we may empathise with them.

Ultimately, an adequate ethical discourse needs to reassess the dominant imperative to eliminate all disease and suffering, and the moral blackmail which is wielded at those who dare to suggest that other concerns might have equal importance. For if we fail to do so, we will find, not so far in the future, that the consequences of abandoning principle after principle will be felt not only in terms of a moral vacuum, but in the profound suffering of real human beings, in ways that we can now only begin to imagine.

16

The Moral Status of the Cloning of Humans

Michael Tooley

Introduction

Is the cloning of humans beings morally acceptable, or not? If it is acceptable, are there any significant benefits that might result from it? In this essay, I shall begin by distinguishing between two radically different cases in which a human being might be cloned, one in which the aim is to produce a mindless human organism that would serve as a living organ bank, and another in which the aim is to produce a person. I shall then go on to discuss the moral status of each.

My discussion of the first sort of case will be very brief, for the moral issues that arise in that case are precisely those that arise in connection with abortion. The second sort of case, on the other hand, raises very different issues, and it will be the main focus of my discussion. I shall argue that cloning of this second sort is in principle morally unobjectionable, and that, in addition, there are a number of ways in which such cloning would be beneficial.

Cloning: Persons, Human Beings, Organs, and Tissue

Cloning, in the broad sense, can be applied to very different things. One might, for example, clone a person's bone marrow, in order to use it in a transplant operation to treat a disease from which the person in question is suffering. Or one might, perhaps, clone some organ, though whether this is really possible in the case of structurally complex organs, such as the heart, is far from clear. In any case, such uses of cloning are both morally unproblematic, and obviously beneficial.

Most people would also think, I believe, that the cloning of nonhuman animals is not in itself problematic. Whether this is true for all animals is, however, not entirely clear. If, as some philosophers have argued, some nonhuman animals are persons, with a capacity, say, for thought and self-consciousness, then the moral status of cloning in the case of such animals would, presumably, be very closely related to the status of cloning in the case of humans.

Let us focus, however, upon humans. Here it is crucial to distinguish two different cases of cloning, since they give rise to very different moral issues. First, there is the case in which a human being is cloned to produce another human with the same genetic makeup as the original individual, and in which the human being thus produced is to serve as an organ bank, so that if the original individual loses an arm in an accident, or winds up with cancer of the liver, appropriate spare parts will be available. If the second human being were a person, it would, of course, be wrong to take parts from him or her to repair the damage to the original individual. The idea, however, is that something

Original publication details: Michael Tooley, "The Moral Status of the Cloning of Humans," pp. 67–101 from James M. Humber and Robert I. Almeder (eds.), *Human Cloning*, Totowa, NJ: Humana Press, 1998. With kind permission from Springer Science+Business Media.

will be done to the brain of the human that is produced so that the human organism in question never acquires the capacity for consciousness, let alone the capacities that make something a person, such as the capacity for thought and self-consciousness.

Second, there is the case of cloning in which the goal is to produce a person, not a mindless organ bank. It is this latter type of cloning that is going to be the main focus of my discussion. Before turning to it, however, let me briefly touch on the former sort.

What objections might be directed against cloning that is done with the goal of producing an organ bank for some person? One objection might be that if one were to use those organs, one would be using what belonged to someone else. Or, depending on what organs one was harvesting, one might even be bringing about the death of a human being. But here it is natural to reply that there is no person to whom the organs belong, or who is destroyed if the organism in question is killed. So no one's property is being taken from him or her, and no person is being killed.

How might one support this reply? The most familiar way of doing so is by appealing to cases in which a normal adult suffers brain damage that ensures that there will never again be any mental states at all associated with the human organism in question. Perhaps there is complete destruction of the upper brain, or perhaps all of the individual's brain has been destroyed, and the organism in question is now being maintained on a life support system. In such cases, would it be seriously wrong to terminate life processes in the organism in question? The vast majority of people seem to think that it would not be. But if that view is right, then it would seem that one needs to distinguish between something like the death of a person, the death of an individual who enjoys a certain sort of mental life, and the death of a human organism.

It is possible to maintain, of course, that the intuitions in question rest on an unsound view of human nature. Perhaps humans have immaterial, immortal souls that are the basis both of all their mental capacities, and of the states that make for personal identity. In that case, upper brain death, or even whole brain death, would not necessarily mean that there was no longer any person associated with the human body in question.

This is one possible view. But it is also a deeply implausible one, since there are facts about human

beings, and other animals, that provide strong evidence for the hypothesis that the basis for all mental capacities lies in the brain. Thus, in the first place, there are extensive correlations between the behavioral capacities of different animals and the neural structures present in their brains. Second, the gradual maturation of the brain of a human being is accompanied by a corresponding increase in his or her intellectual capabilities. Third, damage to the brain, caused either by external trauma, or by stroke, results in impairment of one's cognitive capacities, and the nature of the impairment is correlated with the part of the brain that was damaged. These facts, and others, receive a very straightforward explanation, given the hypothesis that mental capacities have as their basis appropriate neural circuitry, whereas they would both be unexplained, and deeply puzzling, if mental capacities had their basis, not in the brain, but in some immaterial substance.

In addition, it is worth remarking, as a number of Catholic writers such as Karl Rahner and Joseph Donceel have pointed out,[1] that the hypothesis that an immaterial soul is added at the point of conception has, at least within Christianity, a very problematic implication, since most conceptions result, it seems, not in live births, but in miscarriages, and so the theological question arises as to the fate of those human beings who are never born. It seems unfair that they should wind up in hell. But equally, if they automatically went to heaven, that would seem unfair to humans who are born, and who, according to the New Testament, are more likely to wind up in hell than in heaven.[2] The traditional solution involves postulating a third after-life destiny – limbo – which, though originally rather unattractive, subsequently came to be conceived of as a place of perfect natural happiness. Even so, the idea that the majority of the human race never have a chance for eternal life in heaven seems ethically rather troubling.

How do things stand if one sets aside, as implausible, the idea that an immaterial, immortal soul enters the body at conception? The answer is that, first, the distinction between a human organism and a person then becomes a very important one. But, secondly, that distinction does not in itself suffice to show that there is nothing problematic about cloning that is aimed at producing a mindless organ bank, since this still leaves the possibility of arguing that what is seriously wrong here is not the killing of a mindless human being, but the earlier act of permanently preventing the organism in question from developing a functioning brain.

What reasons might be offered for holding that the latter act is morally wrong? One possibility would be to appeal to an idea just considered, and rejected as implausible, namely, the idea that every human organism involves an immaterial immortal soul. For if that were so, then there would be someone whose interests might well be harmed, depending on exactly what happens to a soul in such a body, by the act of preventing the development of the brain of the organism in question. There is, however, a very different line of argument that one can offer, and one that does not involve the implausible assumption that humans involve immaterial souls, since one can claim instead that what is wrong about ensuring that a human organism can never develop a functioning brain is not that one is harming a person, but that one is thereby destroying a potentiality for personhood.

But is it morally wrong to destroy a potentiality for personhood? The following argument shows, I believe, that it is not. Compare the following two actions, the first of which involves two steps: One modifies an unfertilized human egg cell, or else a spermatozoon, or both, in such a way that, if the egg cell is fertilized by the spermatozoon, the result will be a member of our species that lacks an upper brain, and, thus, which will never enjoy any mental states whatsoever; one then brings about fertilization, and implants the resulting embryo. What about the second action? It involves taking a fertilized human egg cell, and changing it in such a way that it suffers from precisely the same defect as the fertilized egg cell that results from the first action. The argument now proceeds as follows. The person who holds that it is wrong to destroy a potentiality for personhood will certainly claim that the second action possesses a wrongmaking property – that of being an act of destroying a potentiality for personhood – which the first action does not possess. In response, it might be claimed that one is, in a sense, destroying a potentiality for personhood in the case of the first action as well as the second, and, thus, that, since the first action is not morally wrong, neither is the second. To this, however, one can reply that one needs to distinguish between active potentialities and

merely passive potentialities: One has a passive potentiality for personhood when one has a situation that, if acted upon in appropriate ways, will give rise to a person; one has an active potentiality for personhood if one has a situation that will give rise to a person as long as it is not interfered with. The conclusion will then be that the first action involves the destruction of only a passive potentiality for personhood, but the second action involves the destruction of an active potentiality for personhood, and that it is only the latter that is wrong.

It may seem, then, that the defender of the view that it is wrong to destroy a potentiality for personhood has escaped the objection by reformulating the claim in terms of active potentiality. It turns out, however, that this response will not really do. In the first place, a fertilized human egg cell, on its own, does not involve an active potentiality for personhood: if left alone, it will simply die. If it is to develop into a person, it needs to be placed in an environment that will supply it with warmth, nutrients, and so on.

But, second, even if one waived this point, the above response still could not provide a satisfactory response to the above argument. The reason is that one can bring in a third sort of action, which is as follows. Suppose that artificial wombs have been perfected, and that there is a device that contains an unfertilized human egg cell, and a human spermatozoon, and in which the device is such that, if is not interfered with, it will bring about fertilization, and then transfer the fertilized human egg cell to an artificial womb, from which will emerge, in nine months' time, a healthy newborn human. Now one has a situation that involves not merely an almost active potentiality for personhood, as in the case of the fertilized human egg cell on its own, but, rather, a fully active potentiality for personhood. To turn off this device, then, and to allow the unfertilized egg cell to die, would involve the destruction of an active potentiality for personhood, and so that action would have to be wrong if the above, active potentiality principle were correct. But the action of turning off the device is not morally wrong, and so it follows that it is not wrong to destroy an active potentiality for personhood.

This argument could be countered if one had reasons for holding that human mental capacities, rather than being based on structures present in the brain, were dependent on the existence of an immaterial soul that God adds to a fertilized human egg cell, since, then, one could hold that it was really only after the addition of such an immaterial entity that an active potentiality for personhood was present. However, as we have seen, there is very strong evidence against the view that mental capacities have their basis, not in neural circuitry in the brain, but, instead, in some immaterial substance.

The terrain that we have just traversed, rather quickly, is very familiar, of course, from discussions of the moral status of abortion. Thus, discussions of abortion, or at least popular discussions, often begin with the claim that abortion is wrong, because it involves the killing of an innocent member of our species. The objection is then that there are cases in which an innocent member of our species is killed, but in which no injustice is done, namely, cases in which either the upper brain, or the brain as a whole, has already been destroyed. And so it is suggested that what is really wrong about killing, when it is wrong, is that a person is being destroyed. But if this is right, then one can argue that abortion is not wrong because the human that is killed by abortion has not developed to the point in which one has a person. This, then, typically leads, at least in the case of philosophically informed opponents of abortion, to the response that, while it is wrong to kill innocent persons, it is also wrong to destroy an active potentiality for personhood. And then, finally, one can reply, as above, that the potentiality principle in question cannot be correct, since it is exposed to counterexamples. For there are cases in which the destruction of an active potentiality for personhood is not morally wrong.

To conclude: The creation of mindless human organisms would be wrong if it harmed a person who inhabited, at some point, the human body in question, or if the destruction of an active potentiality for personhood were wrong. But there are good reasons for thinking that neither of these things is the case. In the absence of some other line of argument, then, one is justified in concluding that there is no sound moral argument against the use of cloning to produce mindless human organisms to serve as organ banks.

Cloning in the Present Context

Let us now turn to the question of the moral status of cloning when the objective is that of producing a person. I shall be arguing that cloning with that goal in mind is in principle morally acceptable. This, however, is not to say that such cloning would be morally unproblematic at the present time. And, indeed, I believe that there are good reasons why cloning, aimed at producing persons, should not be done at present.

To see why, let us begin by considering what was involved in the successful attempt by Ian Wilmut and his coworkers to clone a sheep from the cell of an adult animal:

> The investigators started their experiments with 434 sheep oocytes. Of those, 157 failed to fuse with the transplanted donor cells and had to be discarded. The 277 successfully fused cells were grown in culture, but only twenty-nine embryos lived long enough to be transferred to surrogate mothers. During gestation the investigators detected twenty-one fetuses with ultrasound scanning, but gradually all were lost except Dolly.[3]

Given these statistics, it seems clear that the idea of producing persons via cloning would not be a rational undertaking at present. What is irrational need not, of course, be morally problematic. But in the present case, one is considering an action that affects other people, and so one needs to ask whether it would be acceptable to encourage more than 200 women to be surrogate mothers in a situation in which it is likely that very few, if any, will have a successful pregnancy. And the situation is even worse if one is proposing cloning as a way of treating infertility: Given the present state of technology, the result will, in all probability, be enormous frustration and emotional suffering.

In response, it might be said that you pay your money, and you take your chances: If an infertile couple desperately wants a child that will be a clone of someone, how can it be immoral to allow them to try? But this argument could also be used in other cases, such as in that of providing those who are depressed, and who would like to commit suicide, with the means to do so. What I want to say, accordingly, is that if some course of action is very irrational, as, it seems to me, the attempt to have a child by cloning would be at present, then one may very well be acting immorally if one provides a person with the opportunity of performing that action.

But there are also other reasons for holding that the attempt to clone persons at the present time is morally objectionable – reasons that concern the individual who may result, if the attempt is successful. In the first place, the fact that only one of 277 pregnancies was successful in the case of the sheep suggests that something is seriously wrong with the procedure at present, and that, in turn, raises the question of whether there may not be a very significant chance, in the case of humans, that the outcome might be a seriously defective child, possibly born premature, but saved via intensive care. The attempt to clone a person, given the present state of the art, would seem to be wrong, therefore, because of the impaired quality of life that may be enjoyed by the resulting person.

Second, there is the unanswered question of how cloned individuals will fare when it comes to aging, because there is an important theory of aging that suggests that Dolly may very well have a significantly reduced life expectancy, as a result of having developed from the nucleus of a six-year-old sheep. Here is the basis of the worry:

> As early as the 1930s investigators took note of pieces of noncoding DNA – DNA that does not give rise to protein – at the ends of each chromosome, which they called telomeres (from the Greek words for "end" and "part"). When the differentiated cells of higher organisms undergo mitosis, the ordinary process of cell division, not all of the DNA in their nuclei is replicated. The enzyme that copies DNA misses a small piece at the ends of each chromosome, and so the chromosomes get slightly shorter each time a cell divides. As long as each telomere remains to buffer its chromosome against the shortening process, mitosis does not bite into any genes (remember that the telomeres are noncoding, much like the leaders at the ends of a reel of film). Eventually, however, the telomeres get so short that they can no longer protect the vital parts of the chromosome. At that point the cell usually stops dividing and dies.[4]

The question, accordingly, is whether Dolly started life with cells whose chromosomes have telomeres whose length is comparable to those in the cells of a six-year-old sheep. Perhaps not, since it may be that, once a nucleus has been transplanted into an egg from which the nucleus has been removed, there is some mechanism that will produce an enzyme, called telomerase, that can create full-length telomeres. But the risk is surely a very serious one, and this provides strong grounds, I suggest, for holding that one should not at this point attempt to produce people by cloning.

The last two reasons also support a stronger conclusion, namely, that there are grounds for a temporary, legal prohibition on the cloning of humans when the goal is to produce persons. The risk that is involved in such cloning is that one will bring into existence a person who will age prematurely, or who will suffer from other defects. What is at stake are potential violations of an individual's rights, and thus something that justifies the introduction of appropriate legislation.

The qualification here perhaps needs to be emphasized: This conclusion applies only to cloning that is directed at producing a person, since, if one's goal were instead to produce a mindless human organism to serve as an organ bank, the above considerations would not apply.

Is It Intrinsically Wrong to Produce a Person by Cloning?

Let us now turn to the question of whether the use of cloning to produce a person is, in principle, morally acceptable or not. In this section, I shall focus on the question of whether cloning, so used, is intrinsically wrong. Then, in a later section, I shall consider whether cloning to produce persons necessarily has consequences that render it morally wrong.

How might one attempt to argue that the production of persons via cloning is intrinsically wrong? Here it seems to me that Dan Brock is right when he suggests that there are basically two lines of argument that deserve examination.[5] First, there is an argument that appeals to what might initially be described as the right of a person to be a unique individual, but which, in the end, must be characterized instead as the right of a person to a genetically unique nature. Second, there is an argument that appeals to the idea that a person has a right to a future that is, in a certain sense, open.

Does a person have a right to a genetically unique nature?

Many people feel that being a unique individual is important, and the basic thrust of this first attempt to show that cloning is intrinsically wrong involves the idea that the uniqueness of individuals would be in some way impaired by cloning. In response, I think that one might very well question whether uniqueness is important. If, for example, it turned out that there was, perhaps on some distant planet, an individual that was qualitatively identical to oneself, down to the last detail, both physical and psychological, would that really make one's own life less valuable, less worth living?

In thinking about this issue, it may be important to distinguish two different cases: first, the case in which the two lives are qualitatively identical because of the operation of deterministic causal laws; second, the case in which it just happens that both individuals are always in similar situations in which they freely decide upon the same actions, have the same thoughts and feelings, and so on. The second of these scenarios, I suggest, is not troubling. The first, on the other hand, may be. But if it is, is it because there is a person who is qualitatively indistinguishable from oneself, or, rather, because one's life is totally determined?

I am inclined to question, accordingly, the perhaps rather widely held view that uniqueness is an important part of the value of one's life. Fortunately, however, one need not settle that issue in the present context, since cloning does not, of course, produce a person who is qualitatively indistinguishable from the individual who has been cloned, for, as is shown by the case of identical twins, two individuals with the same genetic makeup, even if raised within the same family at the same time, will differ in many respects, because of the different events that make up their life histories.

How great are those differences? The result of one study was as follows:

> On average, our questionnaires show that the personality traits of identical twins have a 50 percent correlation. The traits of fraternal twins, by contrast, have a correlation of 25 percent, non-twin siblings a correlation of 11 percent and strangers a correlation of close to zero.[6]

Consequently, the personality traits of an individual and his or her clone should, on average, exhibit no more than a 50 percent correlation, and, presumably, the correlation will generally be even less, given that an individual and his or her clone will typically be raised at different times, and in generations that may differ quite substantially in terms of basic beliefs and fundamental values.

The present argument, accordingly, if it is to have any chance, must shift from an appeal to the claim that a person has a right to absolute uniqueness to an appeal to the very different claim that a person has a right to a genetically unique nature. How, then, does the argument fare when reformulated in that way?

An initial point worth noticing is that any appeal to a claimed right to a genetically unique nature poses a difficulty for a theist: if there is such a right, why has God created a world where identical twins can arise? But there are, of course, many features of the world that are rather surprising, if our world is one that was created by an omnipotent, omniscient, and morally perfect person, and so the theist who appeals to a right to a genetically unique nature may simply reply that the presence of twins is just another facet of the general problem of evil.

How can one approach the question of whether persons have a right to a genetically unique nature? Some writers, I think, are content to rest with a burden of proof approach. Here the idea is that, although it may be the case that many people do think that being a unique individual, in the sense of not being qualitatively identical with anyone else, is an important part of what is valuable about being a person, the idea that persons have a right to a genetically unique identity is one that, by contrast, has been introduced only recently, and so those who advance the latter claim really need to offer some reason for thinking that it is true.

There are, however, other ways of approaching this question that involve offering positive arguments against the claim. One possibility, for example, is to appeal to the intuitions that one has upon reflection. Thus, one can consider the case of identical twins, and ask oneself whether, upon reflection, one thinks that it would be prima facie wrong to reproduce if one somehow knew that doing so would result in identical twins. I think it would be surprising if many people felt that this was so.

Another way of approaching the issue is by appealing to some plausible general theory of rights. Thus, for example, I am inclined to think that rights exist when there are serious, self-regarding interests that deserve to be protected. If some such view is correct, then one can approach the question of whether persons have a right to a genetically unique nature by asking whether one has some serious, self-regarding interest that would be impaired if one were a clone. Is the latter the case? The initial reason for thinking that it is not is that the existence of a clone does not seem to impinge on a person in the same way in which being prevented from performing some action that harms no one, or being tortured, or being killed, does: A distant clone might have no impact at all upon one's life.

In response, it might be argued that, while the mere existence of a clone need have no impact on, and so need not impair in any way, one's self-regarding interests, the situation might be very different if one knew of the existence of the clone, since that knowledge might, for example, be damaging to one's sense of individuality. But why should this be so, given that individuals can differ greatly, although sharing the same genetic makeup? It seems to me that if the knowledge that a clone of oneself exists were disturbing to one, this would probably be because of the presence of some relevant, false belief, such as a belief in genetic determinism. But if this is so, then the question arises as to whether rights exist when the interests that they protect are ones that will be harmed only if the potential subjects of the harm have certain false, and presumably irrational, beliefs. My own feeling is that the responsibility for such harm is properly assigned to the individual who has acquired the irrational beliefs whose presence is necessary if there is to be any harm. Consequently, it seems to me that the actions of others should not be constrained in order to prevent such harm from occurring, and thus that there is no right that is violated in such a case.

A third way of thinking about this question of whether there is a right to a genetically unique nature is to consider a scenario in which individuals with the same genetic makeup are very common indeed, and to consider whether such a world would, for example,

be inferior to the present world. Imagine, for example, that it is the year 4004 BC, and that God is contemplating creating human beings. He has already considered the idea of letting humans come into being via evolution, but has rejected that plan on the grounds that a lottery approach to such a vital matter as bringing humans into existence hardly seems appropriate. He also considers creating an original human pair that are genetically distinct, and who will then give rise to humans who will be genetically quite diverse. Upon reflection, however, that idea also seems flawed, since the random shuffling of genes will result in individuals who may be physically impaired, or disposed to unpleasant diseases, such as cancer, that will cause them enormous suffering and lead to premature deaths. In the end, accordingly, the Creator decides upon a genetic constitution with the following two properties. First, it will not lead to serious physical handicaps and diseases, and it will allow an individual, who makes wise choices, to grow in mind and spirit. Second, all of the genes involve identical alleles. God then creates one person with that genetic makeup – call her Eve – and a second individual, Adam, whose only genetic difference is that he has one X chromosome, and one Y chromosome, where Eve has two X chromosomes. The upshot will then be that when Adam and Eve reproduce, they will breed true, because of the fact that they have, aside from the one difference, the same genetic makeup, with identical alleles for every inherited character, and so all of their descendants will be genetically identical to either Adam or Eve.

How would such a world compare with the actual world? If one were choosing from behind the Rawlsian veil of ignorance, would it be rational to prefer the actual world, or the alternative world? This is not, perhaps, an easy question. But it is clear that there would be some significant pluses associated with the alternative world. First, unlike the actual world, one would be assured of a genetic makeup that would be free of dispositions to various unwelcome and life-shortening diseases, or to other debilitating conditions such as depression, schizophrenia, and so on. Secondly, inherited traits would be distributed in a perfectly equitable fashion, and no one would start out, as is the case in the actual world, severely disadvantaged, and facing an enormous uphill battle. Third, aside from the differences between men and women, everyone would be physically the same, and so people would differ only with regard to the quality of their "souls," and thus one would have a world in which judgments of people might well have a less superficial basis than is often the case in the actual world. So there would seem to be some serious reasons for preferring the alternative world over the actual world.

The third advantage just mentioned also points, of course, to an obvious practical drawback of the alternative world: knowing who was who would be a rather more difficult matter than it is in the actual world. But this problem can be dealt with by variants on the above scenario. One variant, for example, would involve having identity of genetic makeup, except regarding the genes that determine the appearance of face and hair. Then one would be able to identify individuals in just the way that one typically does in the actual world. This change would mean, of course, that one was no longer considering an alternative world in which there was widespread identity with respect to genetic makeup. Nevertheless, if this other alternative world would be preferable to the actual world, I think that it still provides an argument against the view that individuals have a right to a unique genetic makeup. For, first of all, the preferability of this other alternative world strongly suggests that genetic difference, rather than being desirable in itself, is valuable only to the extent that it is needed to facilitate the easy identification of people. Second, is it plausible to hold that, although genetic uniqueness is crucial, a very high degree of genetic similarity is not? But in the alternative world we are considering here, the degree of genetic similarity between any two individuals would be extraordinarily high. Third, the alternative world is one in which the genes that determine the initial structure of one's brain are not merely very similar, but absolutely the same in all individuals. But, then, can one plausibly hold that genetic uniqueness is morally crucial, while conceding that a world in which individuals do not differ regarding the genes that determine the initial nature of their brains might be better than the actual world?

These three considerations, I suggest, provide good reasons for holding that one cannot plausibly maintain that individuals have a right to a genetically unique nature, without also holding that the actual world is to

be preferred to the alternative world just described. The identification problem can, however, also be addressed without shifting to a world where people differ genetically, since one could instead suppose that a different mechanism for identifying other people is built into human beings. God could, for example, incorporate special circuitry into the human brain, which broadcasts both one's name and appropriate identifying information about one, and which picks up the information that is broadcast by other humans within one's perceptual field. The information is then checked against a memory bank containing information about everyone one knows, and if it turns out that one is in perceptual contact with some person with whom one is acquainted, and if one would like to know who the person in question is, one would automatically find oneself in possession of the relevant information.

The result would be a world where all individuals will have exactly the same genetic makeup, aside from an X and a Y chromosome, and all of the attractive features of the original alternative world would be present, without there being any problem of determining who was who. One can then ask how this world compares with the actual world, and whether, in particular, the fact that all people in this alternative world would have essentially the same genetic makeup really seems to be, upon reflection, a reason for preferring the actual world.

The open future argument

Dan Brock mentions a second argument for the view that cloning that aims at producing persons is intrinsically wrong.[7] The argument, which is based upon ideas put forward by Joel Feinberg, who speaks of a right to an open future,[8] and by Hans Jonas, who refers to a right to ignorance of a certain sort,[9] is essentially as follows. One's genetic makeup may very well determine to some extent the possibilities that lie open to one, and so it may constrain the course of one's future life. If there is no one with the same genetic makeup, or if there is such a person, but one is unaware of the fact, or, finally, if there is such a person, but the person is either one's contemporary, or someone who is younger, then one will not be able to observe the course of the life of someone with the same genetic makeup as oneself. But what if one does know of a genetically identical person whose life precedes one's own? Then one could have knowledge that one might well view as showing that certain possibilities were not really open to one, and so one would have less of a sense of being able to choose the course of one's life.

To see why this argument is unsound, one needs to ask about the reasoning that might be involved if someone, observing the earlier life of someone with the same genetic makeup, concludes that his or her own life is subject to certain constraints. One possibility is that one may have observed someone striving very hard, over a long period of time, to achieve some goal and failing to get anywhere near it. Perhaps the earlier, genetically identical individual wanted to be the first person to run the marathon in under two hours, and after several years of intense and well-designed training, attention to diet, and so on, never got below two and one-half hours. One would then surely be justified in viewing that particular goal as not really open to one. But would that knowledge be a bad thing, as Jonas seems to be suggesting? I would think that, on the contrary, such knowledge would be valuable, since it would make it easier for one to choose goals that one could successfully pursue.

A very different possibility is that one might observe the course of the life of the genetically identical individual, and conclude that no life significantly different from that life could really be open to one. Then one would certainly feel that one's life was constrained to a very unwelcome extent. But in drawing the conclusion that one's life could not be significantly different from that of the other individual, one would be drawing a conclusion for which there is not only no evidence, but one that there is excellent evidence against: The lives of identical twins demonstrate that very different lives indeed are possible, given the same genetic makeup.

In short, the idea that information about the life of a person genetically identical to oneself would provide grounds for concluding that only a narrow range of alternatives was open to one would only be justified if genetic determinism, or a close approximation thereto, was correct. But nothing like genetic determinism is true. This second argument for the view that cloning with the goal of producing persons is intrinsically wrong is, accordingly, unsound.

Considerations in Support of the Cloning of Persons

Whether it is desirable to produce persons by cloning depends, as we noticed earlier, upon the outcome of an issue that is not yet decided: the aging question. Here, however, I shall simply assume that it will become possible to clone an adult individual in such a way that one winds up with a cell whose chromosomes have full-length telomeres, so that the individual who results will have a normal life expectancy. Given that assumption, I want to argue that there are a number of important benefits that may result from the cloning of humans that is done with the goal of producing persons.

In setting out what I take to be benefits of cloning, I shall not address possible objections. These will be discussed, instead, under "Objections to the Cloning of Humans."

Scientific knowledge: psychology and the heredity-vs-environment issue

A crucial theoretical task for psychology is the construction of a satisfactory theory that will explain the acquisition of traits of character, and central to the development of such a theory is information about the extent to which various traits are inherited, or, alternatively, dependent on aspects of the environment that are controllable, or, finally, dependent on factors, either in the brain or in the environment, that have a chancy quality. But such knowledge is not just theoretically crucial to psychology. Knowledge of the contributions that are, and are not, made to the individual's development by his or her genetic makeup, by the environment in which he or she is raised, and by chance events, will enable one to develop approaches to childrearing that will increase the likelihood that one can raise people with desirable traits, people who will have a better chance of realizing their potentials, and of leading happy and satisfying lives. So this knowledge is not merely of great theoretical interest: it is also potentially very beneficial to society.

In the attempt to construct an adequate theory of human development, the study of identical twins has been very important, and has generated considerable information on the nature/nurture issue. But adequate theories still seem rather remote. Cloning would provide a powerful way of speeding up scientific progress in this area, since society could produce a number of individuals with the same genetic makeup, and then choose adoptive parents who would provide those individuals with good, but significantly different environments, in which to mature.

Cloning to benefit society

One very familiar suggestion is that one might benefit mankind by cloning individuals who have made very significant contributions to society. In the form in which it is usually put, when it is assumed that, if, for example, one had been able to clone Albert Einstein, the result would be an individual who would also make some very significant contribution to science, the suggestion is surely unsound. In the first place, whether an individual will do highly creative work surely depends on traits whose acquisition is a matter of the environment in which the individual is raised, rather than on being determined simply by his or her genetic makeup. But could it not be argued in response that one could control the environment as well, raising a clone of Einstein, for example, in an environment that was as close as possible to the sort of environment in which Einstein was raised? That, of course, might prove difficult. But even if it could be done, it is not clear that it would be sufficient, because there is a second point that can be made here, namely, that great creative achievements may depend on things that are to some extent accidental, and whose occurrence is not ensured by the combination of a certain genetic makeup and a certain general sort of environment. Many great mathematicians, for example, have developed an intense interest in numbers at an early age. Is there good reason to think that, had one been able to clone Carl Friedrich Gauss, and reared that person in an environment similar to Gauss's, that person would have developed a similar interest in numbers, and gone on to achieve great things in mathematics? Or is it likely that a clone of Einstein, raised in an environment similar to that in which Einstein was raised, would have wondered, as Einstein did, what the world would look like if one could travel as fast as light, and then gone on to reflect on the issues that fascinated

Einstein, and that led ultimately to the development of revolutionary theories in physics?

I think that there are, then, some serious problems with the present suggestion in the form in which it is usually put. On the other hand, I am not convinced that a slightly more modest version cannot be sustained. Consider, for example, the Polgar sisters. There we have a case in which the father of three girls succeeded in creating an environment in which all three of his daughters became very strong chess players, and one of them, Judit Polgar, is now the strongest female chess player who has ever lived. Is it not reasonable to think that if one were to make a number of clones of Judit Polgar, and then raise them in an environment very similar to that in which the Polgar sisters were raised, the result would be a number of very strong chess players?

More generally, I think it is clear that there is a strong hereditary basis for intelligence,[10] and I also believe that there is good reason for thinking that other traits that may play a crucial role in creativity, such as extreme persistence, determination, and confidence in one's own abilities, are such as are likely to be produced by the right combination of heredity and environment. So, although the chance that the clone of an outstandingly creative individual will also achieve very great things is perhaps, at least in many areas, not especially high, I think that there is reason for thinking that, given an appropriate environment, the result will be an individual who is likely to accomplish things that may benefit society in significant ways.

Happier and healthier individuals

A third benefit of cloning is that it should make it possible to increase the likelihood that the person that one is bringing into existence will enjoy a healthy and happy life. For, to the extent that one's genetic constitution has a bearing on how long one is likely to live, on what diseases, both physical and mental, one is likely to suffer from, and on whether one will have traits of character or temperament that make for happiness, or for unhappiness, by cloning a person who has enjoyed a very long life, who has remained mentally alert, and not fallen prey to Alzheimer's disease, who has not suffered from cancer, arthritis, heart attacks, stroke, high blood pressure, and so on, and who has exhibited no tendencies to depression, or schizophrenia, and so on, one is increasing the chances that the individual that one is producing will also enjoy a healthy and happy life.

More satisfying childrearing: individuals with desired traits

Many couples would prefer to raise children who possess certain traits. In some cases they may want children who have a certain physical appearance. In other cases, they might like to have children who have the physical abilities that would enable them to have a better chance of performing at a high level in certain physical activities. Or they might prefer to have children who would have the intellectual capabilities that would enable them to enjoy mathematics or science. Or they might prefer to have children who possess traits that would enable them to engage in, and enjoy, various aesthetic pursuits. Some of the traits that people might like their children to have presumably have a very strong hereditary basis; others are such as a child, given both the relevant genes, and the right environment, would be very likely to acquire. To the extent that the traits in question fall into either of these categories, the production of children via cloning would enable more couples to raise children with traits that they judge to be desirable.

More satisfying childrearing: using self-knowledge

There is a second way in which cloning could make childrearing more satisfying, and it emerges if one looks back on one's own childhood. Most people, when they do this, remember things that they think were good, and other things that they think would have been better if they had been different. In some cases, of course, one's views may be unsound, and it may be that some of the things that one's parents did, and which one did not like, actually had good effects on one's development. On the whole, however, it seems plausible that most people have reasonably sound views on which features of the way in which they were raised had good effects overall, and which did not.

The idea, then, is that if a couple raises a child who is a clone of one of the parents, the knowledge that the relevant parent has of the way in which he or she was raised can be used to bring up the child in a way that fits better with the individual psychology of the child. In addition, given the greater psychological similarity that will exist between the child and one of his parents in such a case, the relevant parent will better be able, at any point, to appreciate how things look from the child's point of view. So it would seem that there is a good chance both that such a couple will find childrearing a more rewarding experience, and that the child will have a happier childhood through being better understood.

Infertility

Since the successful cloning that resulted in Dolly, at least one person has expressed the intention of pushing ahead with the idea of using cloning to help infertile couples. For reasons that emerged under the second heading, "Cloning in the Present Context," the idea that cloning should be so used in the near future seems morally very problematic. In principle, however, the general idea would seem to have considerable merit. One advantage, for example, as Dan Brock and others have pointed out, is that "cloning would allow women who have no ova or men who have no sperm to produce an offspring that is biologically related to them."[11] Another advantage, also noted by Brock, is that "embryos might be cloned, either by nuclear transfer or embryo splitting, in order to increase the number of embryos for implantation and improve the chances of successful conception."[12]

Children for homosexual couples

Many people, especially in the United States, believe that homosexuality is deeply wrong, and that homosexuals should not be allowed either to marry or to raise children. These opinions, however, would be rejected, I think, by most philosophers, who would hold, on the contrary, that homosexuality is not morally wrong, and that homosexuals should be allowed both to marry, and to raise children. Assume, for the sake of the present discussion, that the latter views are correct. Then, as Philip Kitcher and others have noted, cloning would seem to be a promising method of providing a homosexual couple with children that they could raise, since, in the case of a gay couple, each child could be a clone of one person; in the case of a lesbian couple, every child could, in a sense, be biologically connected with both people:

> A lesbian couple wishes to have a child. Because they would like the child to be biologically connected to each of them, they request that a cell nucleus from one of them be inserted into an egg from the other, and that the embryo be implanted in the uterus of the woman who donated the egg.[13]

Cloning to save lives

A final possibility is suggested by the well-known case of the Ayala parents in California, who decided to have another child in the hope, which turned out to be justified, that the resulting child would be able to donate bone marrow for a transplant operation that would save the life of their teenage daughter, who was suffering from leukemia. If cloning had been possible at the time, a course of action would have been available to them that, unlike having another child in the normal way, would not have been chancy: If they could have cloned the child who was ill, a tissue match would have been certain.

Objections to the Cloning of Humans

The cloning of mindless organ banks

Certain objections to the cloning of humans to produce mindless human organisms that would serve as a source of organs for others are perfectly intelligible. If someone objects to this idea on the grounds that one is destroying a person, the concern that is being expressed here is both completely clear and serious. The same is true if the objection is, instead, that such cloning is seriously wrong, since, in preventing a human organism from developing a functioning brain, one is depriving an immaterial soul associated with the organism in question of the possibility of experiencing life in this world. And, finally, the same is also true if someone holds that such cloning would be wrong, because it involves the destruction of an active potentiality for personhood.

The problem with these objections, accordingly, is not that they are in any way incoherent. Nor is it the case that the points raised are unimportant. The problem is simply that all of these objections are, in the end, unsound, for reasons that emerged earlier. Thus, the problem with the first objection is that there are excellent reasons for holding that human embryos do not possess those capacities, such as the capacity for thought and self-consciousness, that something must have, at some point, if it is to be a person. The problem with the second objection is that there are strong reasons for holding that the ontological basis for the capacities involved in consciousness, self-consciousness, thought, and other mental processes resides in the human brain, and not in any immaterial soul. Finally, the problem with the third objection lies in the assumption that the destruction of an active potentiality for personhood is morally wrong, for that claim is, on the one hand, unsupported by any satisfactory argument, and, on the other, exposed to decisive objections, one of which was set out earlier.

Often, however, it seems that people who would agree that the above objections are unsound, and who, moreover, do not view abortion as morally problematic, still express uneasiness about the idea of producing mindless human organ banks. Such uneasiness is rarely articulated, however, and it usually takes the form simply of describing the idea of mindless organ banks as a ghoulish scenario. This sort of dismissal of the use of cloning to produce organ banks is very puzzling. For what we are considering here is a way in which lives can be saved, and so, if one rejects this use of cloning, one is urging a course of action that will result in the deaths of innocent people. To do this on the grounds that mindless organ banks strike one as ghoulish seems morally irresponsible in the extreme: If this use of cloning is to be rejected, serious moral argument is called for.

The cloning of humans to produce persons

Violation of rights objections

Some people oppose cloning that is done with the goal of producing a person, on the grounds that such cloning involves a violation of some right of the person who is produced. The most important versions of this first sort of objection are those considered earlier, namely, that there is a violation either of a person's right to be a unique individual, or, more accurately, to be a genetically unique individual, or, alternatively, of a person's right to enjoy an open future that is not constrained by knowledge of the course of the life of some individual with the same genetic makeup. But for the reasons set out earlier, neither of these objections is sound.

Brave new world style objections
Next, there is a type of objection that is not frequently encountered in scholarly discussions, but which is rather common in the popular press, and which involves scenarios in which human beings are cloned in large numbers to serve as slaves, or as enthusiastic soldiers in a dictator's army. Such scenarios, however, do not seem very plausible. Is it really at all likely that, were cloning to become available, society would decide that its rejection of slavery had really been a mistake? Or that a dictator who was unable to conscript a satisfactory army from the existing citizens would be able to induce people to undertake a massive cloning program, in order that, 18 years or so down the line, he would finally have the army he had always wanted?

Psychological distress
This objection is closely related to the earlier, violation of rights objections, because the idea is that, even if cloning does not violate a person's right to be a unique individual, or to have a unique genetic makeup, or to have an open and unconstrained future, nevertheless, people who are clones may feel that their uniqueness is compromised, or that their future is constrained, and this may cause substantial psychological harm and suffering.

There are two reasons for rejecting this objection as unsound. The first arises once one asks what one is to say about the beliefs in question, that is, the belief that one's uniqueness is compromised by the existence of a clone, and the belief that one's future is constrained if one has knowledge of the existence of a clone. Both beliefs are, as we have seen, false. But, in addition, it also seems clear that such beliefs would be, in general, irrational, since it is hard to see what grounds one

could have for accepting either belief, other than something like genetic determinism, against which, as we saw earlier, there is conclusive evidence.

Once it is noted that the feelings that may give rise to psychological distress are irrational, one can appeal to the point that I made earlier, when we considered the question of whether knowledge of the existence of a clone might, for example, be damaging to one's sense of individuality, and whether, if this were so, such damage would be grounds for holding that there was a corresponding right that would be violated by cloning. What I argued at that point was that harm to an individual that arises because the individual has an irrational belief has a different moral status from harm that is not dependent on the presence of an irrational belief, and that, in particular, the possibility of the former sort of harm should not be taken as morally constraining others. The responsibility for such harm should, instead, be assigned to the individual who has the irrational belief, and the only obligation that falls on others is to point out to the person in question why the belief is an irrational one.

The second reason why the present objection cannot be sustained is also connected with the fact that the feelings in question are irrational, since the irrationality of the feelings means that they would not be likely to persist for very long, once cloning had become a familiar occurrence. For example, suppose that John feels that he is no longer a unique individual, or that his future is constrained, given that he is a clone of some other individual. Mary may also be a clone of some individual, and she may point out to John that she is very different from the person with whom she is genetically identical, and that she has not been constrained by the way the other person lived her life. Will John then persist in his irrational belief? This does not really seem very likely. If so, any distress that is produced will not be such as is likely to persist for any significant period of time.

Failing to treat individuals as ends in themselves
A fourth objection is directed, not against the cloning of persons in general, but against certain cases, such as those in which parents clone a child who is suffering from some life-threatening condition, in order to produce another child who will be able to save the

first child's life. The thrust of this objection is that such cases involve a failure to view individuals as ends in themselves. Thus Philip Kitcher, referring to such cases, says that "a lingering concern remains," and he goes on to ask whether such scenarios "can be reconciled with Kant's injunction to 'treat humanity, whether in your own person or in the person of another, always at the same time as an end and never simply as a means.'"[14]

What is one to say about this objection? It may be important to be explicit about what sacrifices the child who is being produced is going to have to make to save his or her sibling. When I set out this sort of case under the subheading "Cloning to Save Lives," I assumed that what was involved was a bone marrow transplant. Kitcher, in his formulation, assumes that it will be a kidney transplant. I think that one might well be inclined to take different views of these two cases, given that, in the kidney donation case, but not the bone marrow case, the donor is making a sacrifice that may have unhappy consequences for that person in the future.

To avoid this complicating factor, let us concentrate, then, on the bone marrow case. In such a case, would there be a violation of Kant's injunction? There could be, if the parents were to abandon, or not really to care for the one child, once he or she had provided bone marrow to save the life of the other child. But this, surely, would be a very unlikely occurrence. After all, the history of the human race is mostly the history of unplanned children, often born into situations in which the parents were anything but well off, and yet, typically, those children were deeply loved by their parents.

In short, though this sort of case is, by hypothesis, one in which the parents decide to have a child with a goal in mind that has nothing to do with the well being of that child, this is no reason for supposing that they are therefore likely to treat that child merely as a means, and not also as an end in itself. Indeed, surely there is good reason to think, on the contrary, that such a child will be raised in no less loving a way than is normally the case.

Interfering with personal autonomy
The final objection that I shall consider is also one that has been advanced by Philip Kitcher, and he puts it as follows: "If the cloning of human beings is

undertaken in the hope of generating a particular kind of person, then cloning is morally repugnant. The repugnance arises not because cloning involves biological tinkering but because it interferes with human autonomy."[15]

This objection would not apply to all of the cases that I mentioned in "Considerations in Support of the Cloning of Persons" as ones in which the cloning of a person would be justified. It does, however, apply to many of them. Is the objection sound? I cannot see that it is. First, notice that, in some cases, when one's goal is to produce "a particular kind of person," what one is aiming at is simply a person who will have certain potentialities. Parents might, for example, want to have children who are capable of enjoying intellectual pursuits. The possession of the relevant capacities does not force the children to spend their lives engaged in such pursuits, and so it is hard to see how cloning that is directed at that goal would interfere with human autonomy.

Second, consider cases in which the goal is not to produce a person who will be *capable* of doing a wider range of things, but an individual who will be *disposed* in certain directions. Perhaps it is this sort of case that Kitcher has in mind when he speaks of interfering with human autonomy. But is it really morally problematic to attempt to create persons who will be disposed in certain directions, and not in others? To answer this question, one needs to consider concrete cases, such as the sorts of cases that I mentioned earlier. Is it morally wrong, for example, to attempt to produce, via cloning, individuals who will, because of their genetic makeup, be disposed not to suffer from conditions that may cause considerable pain, such as arthritis, or from life-threatening diseases, such as cancer, high blood pressure, strokes, and heart attacks? Or to attempt to produce individuals who will have a cheerful temperament, or who will not be disposed to depression, to anxiety, to schizophrenia, or to Alzheimer's disease?

It seems unlikely that Kitcher, or others, would want to say that attempting to produce individuals who will be constitutionally disposed in the ways just indicated is a case of interfering with human autonomy. But then, what are the traits that are such that attempting to create a person with those traits is a case of interfering with human autonomy? Perhaps

Kitcher, when he speaks about creating a particular kind of person, is thinking not just of any properties that persons have, but, more narrowly, of such things as personality traits, or traits of character, or having certain interests? But again one can ask whether there is anything morally problematic about attempting to create persons with such properties. Some personality traits are desirable, and parents typically encourage their children to develop those traits. Some character traits are virtues, and others are vices, and both parents and society attempt to encourage the acquisition of the former, and to discourage the acquisition of the latter. Finally, many interests, such as music, art, mathematics, science, games, physical activities, can add greatly to the quality of one's life, and once again, parents typically expose their children to relevant activities, and help their children to achieve levels of proficiency that will enable them to enjoy those pursuits.

The upshot is that, if cloning that aimed at producing people who would be more likely to possess various personality traits, or traits of character, or who would be more likely to have certain interests, was wrong because it was a case of interfering with personal autonomy, then the childrearing practices of almost all parents would stand condemned on precisely the same grounds. But such a claim, surely, is deeply counterintuitive.

In addition, however, one need not rest content with an appeal to intuitions here. The same conclusion follows on many high-order moral theories. Suppose, for example, that one is once again behind the Rawlsian veil of ignorance, and that one is deciding among societies that differ regarding their approaches to the rearing of children. Would it be rational to choose a society in which parents did not attempt to encourage their children to develop personality traits that would contribute to the latters' happiness? Or a society in which parents did not attempt to instill in their children a disposition to act in ways that are morally right? Or one in which parents made no attempt to develop various interests in their children? It is, I suggest, hard to see how such a choice could be a rational one, given that one would

be opting, it would seem, for a society in which one would be likely to have a life that, on average, would be less worth living.

I conclude, therefore, that, contrary to what Philip Kitcher has claimed, it is not true that most cloning scenarios are morally repugnant, and that, in particular, there is, in general, nothing morally problematic about aiming at creating a child with specific attributes.

Conclusion

In this essay, I have distinguished between two very different cases involving the cloning of a human being – one that aims at the production of mindless human organisms that are to serve as organ banks for the people who are cloned, and another that aims at the creation of persons. Regarding the former, the objections that can be advanced are just the objections that can be directed against abortion, and, for reasons that I briefly outlined above, those objections can be shown to be unsound.

Very different objections arise in the case of cloning whose aim is the production of persons. Concerning this second sort of cloning, I argued that it is important to distinguish between the question of whether such cloning is, in principle, morally acceptable, and whether it is acceptable at the present time. Regarding the latter question, I argued that the present use of cloning to produce persons would be morally problematic. By contrast, concerning the question of whether such cloning is in principle morally acceptable, I argued, first, that such cloning is not intrinsically wrong; second, that there are a number of reasons why the cloning of persons would be desirable; and, third, that the objections that have been directed against such cloning cannot be sustained.

My overall conclusion, in short, is that the cloning of human beings, both to produce mindless organ banks, and to produce persons, is both morally acceptable, in principle, and potentially very beneficial for society.

Notes and References

1 Donceel, J. F. (1970) Immediate animation and delayed hominization. *Theological Stud.* 31, 76–105. Donceel refers to Rahner, K. (1967) *Schriften zur Theologie* 8, 287.

2 *See*, for example, Matthew 7:13–14 and 22:13–14.

3 Di Berardino, M. A. and McKinnell, R. G. (1997) Backward compatible. *The Sciences* 37, 32–37.

4 Hart, R., Turturro, A., and Leakey, J. (1997) Born again. *The Sciences* 37, 47–51.

5 Brock, D. W. (1998) Cloning human beings: an assessment of the ethical issues pro and con, in *Clones and Clones*, Nussbaum, M. C. and Sunstein, C. R., eds., Norton, New York. *See* the section entitled "Would the use of human cloning violate important human rights?"

6 Bouchard, T. J., Jr. (1997) Whenever the twain shall meet. *The Sciences* 37, 52–57.

7 Brock, D., in the section entitled "Would the use of human cloning violate important human rights?"

8 Feinberg, J. (1980) The child's right to an open future, in *Whose Child? Children's Rights, Parental Authority, and*

State Power, Aiken, W. and LaFollette, H., eds., Rowan and Littlefield, Totowa, NJ.

9 Jonas, H. (1974) *Philosophical Essay: From Ancient Creed to Technological Man*, Prentice-Hall, Englewood Cliffs, NJ.

10 *See*, for example, the discussion of this issue in Bouchard, pp. 55, 56.

11 Brock, D., in the subsection entitled "Human cloning would be a new means to relieve the infertility some persons now experience."

12 Ibid.

13 Kitcher, P. (1998) Whose self is it, anyway? *The Sciences* 37, 58–62. It should be noted that, although Kitcher mentions this idea as initially attractive, in the end he concludes that it is problematic, for a reason that will be considered in the subsection "The Cloning of Humans to Produce Persons."

14 Ibid., p. 61.

15 Ibid., p. 61.

Bibliography

Bilger, B. (1997) Cell block. *The Sciences* 37, 17–19.

Bouchard, T. J., Jr. (1997) Whenever the twain shall meet. *The Sciences* 37, 52–57.

Brock, D.W. (1998) Cloning human beings: an assessment of the ethical issues pro and con, in *Clones and Clones*, Nussbaum, M. C. and Sunstein, C. R., eds., Norton, New York.

Callahan, D. (1993) Perspective on cloning: a threat to individual uniqueness. *Los Angeles Times, November* 12, B7.

Di Berardino, M.A., and McKinnell, R. G. (1997) Backward compatible. *The Sciences* 37, 32–37.

Donceel, J. F. (1970) Immediate animation and delayed hominization. *Theological Stud.* 31, 76–105.

Feinberg, J. (1980) The child's right to an open future, in *Whose Child? Children's Rights, Parental Authority, and State Power*, Aiken, W. and LaFollette, H., eds., Rowan and Littlefield, Totowa, NJ.

Fletcher, J. (1974) *The Ethics of Genetic Control*, Anchor Books, Garden City, NY.

Gurdon, J. B. (1997) The birth of cloning. *The Sciences* 37, 26–31.

Hart, R., Turturro, A., and Leakey, J. (1997) Born again? *The Sciences* 37, 47–51.

Jonas, H. (1974) *Philosophical Essay: From Ancient Creed to Technological Man*, Prentice-Hall, Englewood Cliffs, NJ.

Kitcher, P. (1997) Whose self is it, anyway? *The Sciences* 37, 58–62.

Macklin, R. (1994) Splitting embryos on the slippery slope: ethics and public policy. *Kennedy Inst. Ethics J.* 4, 209–226.

Meade, H. M. (1997) Dairy gene. *The Sciences* 37, 20–25.

Robertson, J. A. (1994) *Children of Choice: Freedom and the New Reproductive Technologies*, Princeton University Press, Princeton, NJ.

Robertson, J. A. (1994) The question of human cloning. *Hastings Center Report* 24, 6–14.

Wilmut, I. (1996) Sheep cloned by nuclear transfer from a cultured cell line. *Nature* 380, 64–66.

Part III

Genetic Manipulation

Introduction

Our genes play an important role in what kind of people we are – whether we are, for example, short or tall, healthy or sick, mentally slow or bright; and while there is debate about the extent to which certain characteristics are inherited or the product of our environment, it is difficult to deny that some characteristics at least have a genetic basis. To deny this would, as Jonathan Glover points out in "Questions about Some Uses of Genetic Engineering," amount to thinking "that it is only living in kennels which makes dogs different from cats."

Genetic manipulation, sometimes also referred to as genetic engineering, involves intervening at the genetic level in order to eliminate, modify or enhance certain genetic traits or conditions. Recent scientific breakthroughs, including the mapping of the human genome, have added significantly to our understanding of our genes, and provide increasing and unprecedented possibilities for control over our genetic destiny. Should we make use of this knowledge, and to which ends? Should we, for example, use genetic manipulation only to prevent serious genetic disorders, or should we also use it for the enhancement of certain traits and characteristics?

The distinction between gene therapy and gene enhancement is not clear-cut. While it might be agreed that increasing the height a boy is expected to reach at maturity from 170 cm to 190 cm is a form of enhancement, what if we are seeking to increase his expected height from 150 cm to 170 cm? The same

appears to be true when we are looking at a trait such as intelligence. Increasing a person's IQ by 20 points from 110 to 130 would generally be considered enhancement, but would raising her IQ from 90 to 110 be a form of therapy or of enhancement? The answer ultimately depends, David Resnik argues in "The Moral Significance of the Therapy–Enhancement Distinction in Human Genetics," on contested philosophical distinctions, such as the distinction between health and disease, and normality and abnormality.

Despite some fuzziness at the margins, we do, however, often have a plausible understanding of where the boundary between therapy and enhancement should be drawn. The next question is whether this boundary is morally significant. Again, many people think the answer is "yes." They take the view that gene therapy, as an extension of the conventional goals of medicine, is morally acceptable, while enhancement is morally problematic. But are the arguments in support of the ethical significance of these distinctions sound?

Some people reject positive genetic engineering on the grounds of risk; but is risk – even significant risk – a sufficient reason to rule out all genetic interventions? Jonathan Glover argues that the fact that a practice involves risks is not sufficient to show that it is morally wrong, or should be banned. In some cases, the dangers of not proceeding might be greater than the dangers of proceeding selectively and cautiously. Moreover, would considerations of risk be a reason

Bioethics: An Anthology, Third Edition. Edited by Helga Kuhse, Udo Schüklenk, and Peter Singer.
© 2016 John Wiley & Sons, Inc. Published 2016 by John Wiley & Sons, Inc.

against all positive interventions, or against only some of them? And would it be a reason against positive or enhancing genetic interventions only, or also a reason against therapeutic or negative interventions?

Arguments about risk are important, but do not go to the heart of the objections to genetic engineering. Even if gene therapy could be shown to be relatively safe, one oft-heard objection – that it involves "playing God" – would remain. But this objection, as Glover and others argue, is unpersuasive. Taken literally, it obviously will not appeal to nonbelievers; and, if understood metaphorically as a prohibition on interfering with "God's creation," that is, with nature, it would seem to rule out not only all genetic engineering (whether positive or negative), but all other medical interventions as well.

A more plausible way of understanding the "playing God" argument might be to see it as an objection to eugenic schemes, where, as Glover puts it, necessarily fallible people with limited horizons are making God-like decisions to improve the human race. Past eugenic programs in continental Europe (and particularly in Nazi Germany), Great Britain and the United States continue to cast a dark shadow over contemporary genetics. These programs were widely associated with a variety of often highly questionable coercive government schemes intended to "improve" the gene pool. The question of whether positive genetic engineering is morally acceptable must, however, Glover argues, be separated from the question of whether particular state-controlled eugenic programs are acceptable. One might think that it is wrong for state authorities to decide who should and should not be able to have children, and what these children should be like, but not wrong if individual parents were to make these kinds of reproductive decisions themselves.

One day, Glover continues, preimplantation selection procedures might also be able to be applied to more complex genetic traits, such as intelligence, imaginativeness or generosity. Would it be wrong to employ genetic engineering to achieve such ends? The rejection of some positive genetic interventions is difficult to reconcile with our acceptance of various other environmental measures that seek to encourage children to develop in particular ways. As Glover puts it:

> We act environmentally to influence people in ways that go far beyond the elimination of medical defects. Homes and schools would be impoverished by attempting to restrict their influence on children to the mere prevention of physical and mental disorder. And if we are right here to cross the positive–negative boundary, encouraging children to ask questions, or to be generous and imaginative, why should crossing the same boundary for the same reasons be ruled out absolutely when the means are genetic?

In their article "Should We Undertake Genetic Research on Intelligence?" Ainsley Newson and Robert Williamson give a partial answer to the type of questions posed by Glover. As far as intelligence is concerned, they argue, enhancement is not only morally permissible, but, other things being equal, "morally demanded in Western Society."

Those who are most enthusiastic about genetic enhancement call themselves transhumanists to signify that they think it desirable to move beyond the human nature that we have inherited from the long and blind process of evolutionary selection. In the last essay in Part III, Nick Bostrom defends transhumanism against the criticism that if we change our nature, we will lose our human dignity. Though the idea of human dignity is often invoked, the values behind it are rarely made explicit. Bostrom distinguishes different things that we might mean by "human dignity." He then defends – as the title of his essay, "In Defense of Posthuman Dignity," indicates – the concept of "posthuman" dignity, that is, the idea that there is moral worth in seeing human nature as dynamic and changing, and in seeking to make moral progress by improving it.

17

Questions about Some Uses of Genetic Engineering

Jonathan Glover

There is a widespread view that any project for the genetic improvement of the human race ought to be ruled out: that there are fundamental objections of principle. The aim of this discussion is to sort out some of the main objections. It will be argued that our resistance is based on a complex of different values and reasons, none of which is, when examined, adequate to rule out in principle this use of genetic engineering. The debate on human genetic engineering should become like the debate on nuclear power: one in which large possible benefits have to be weighed against big problems and the risk of great disasters. The discussion has not reached this point, partly because the techniques have not yet been developed. But it is also partly because of the blurred vision which fuses together many separate risks and doubts into a fuzzy-outlined opposition in principle.

Avoiding the Debate about Genes and the Environment

In discussing the question of genetic engineering, there is everything to be said for not muddling the issue up with the debate over the relative importance of genes and environment in the development of such characteristics as intelligence. One reason for avoiding that debate is that it arouses even stronger passions than genetic engineering, and so is filled with as much acrimony as argument. But, apart from this fastidiousness, there are other reasons.

The nature–nurture dispute is generally seen as an argument about the relative weight the two factors have in causing differences within the human species: 'IQ is 80 per cent hereditary and 20 per cent environmental' versus 'IQ is 80 per cent environmental and 20 per cent hereditary'. No doubt there is some approximate truth of this type to be found if we consider variations within a given population at a particular time. But it is highly unlikely that there is any such statement which is simply true of human nature regardless of context. To take the extreme case, if we could iron out all environmental differences, any residual variations would be 100 per cent genetic. It is only if we make the highly artificial assumption that different groups at different times all have an identical spread of relevant environmental differences that we can expect to find statements of this kind applying to human nature in general. To say this is not to argue that studies on the question should not be conducted, or are bound to fail. It may well be possible, and useful, to find out the relative weights of the two kinds of factor for a given characteristic among a certain group at a particular time. The point is that any such conclusions lose relevance, not only when

Original publication details: Jonathan Glover, "Questions about Some Uses of Genetic Engineering," pp. 25–33, 33–6, 42–3, and 45–53 from *What Sort of People Should There Be?* Harmondsworth: Penguin Books, 1984. Reproduced by permission of Penguin Books Ltd.

environmental differences are stretched out or compressed, but also when genetic differences are. And this last case is what we are considering.

We can avoid this dispute because of its irrelevance. Suppose the genetic engineering proposal were to try to make people less aggressive. On a superficial view, the proposal might be shown to be unrealistic if there were evidence to show that variation in aggressiveness is hardly genetic at all: that it is 95 per cent environmental. (Let us grant, most implausibly, that such a figure turned out to be true for the whole of humanity, regardless of social context.) But all this would show is that, within our species, the distribution of genes relevant to aggression is very uniform. It would show nothing about the likely effects on aggression if we use genetic engineering to give people a different set of genes from those they now have.

In other words, to take genetic engineering seriously, we need take no stand on the relative importance or unimportance of genetic factors in the explanation of the present range of individual differences found in people. We need only the minimal assumption that different genes could give us different characteristics. To deny *that* assumption you need to be the sort of person who thinks it is only living in kennels which makes dogs different from cats.

Methods of Changing the Genetic Composition of Future Generations

There are essentially three ways of altering the genetic composition of future generations. The first is by environmental changes. Discoveries in medicine, the institution of a National Health Service, schemes for poverty relief, agricultural changes, or alterations in the tax position of large families, all alter the selective pressures on genes.[1] It is hard to think of any social change which does not make some difference to who survives or who is born.

The second method is to use eugenic policies aimed at altering breeding patterns or patterns of survival of people with different genes. Eugenic methods are 'environmental' too: the difference is only that the genetic impact is intended. Possible strategies range from various kinds of compulsion (to have more children, fewer children, or no children, or even compulsion over the choice of sexual partner) to the completely voluntary (our present genetic counselling practice of giving prospective parents information about probabilities of their children having various abnormalities).

The third method is genetic engineering: using enzymes to add to or subtract from a stretch of DNA.

Most people are unworried by the fact that a side-effect of an environmental change is to alter the gene pool, at least where the alteration is not for the worse. And even in cases where environmental factors increase the proportion of undesirable genes in the pool, we often accept this. Few people oppose the National Health Service, although setting it up meant that some people with genetic defects, who would have died, have had treatment enabling them to survive and reproduce. On the whole, we accept without qualms that much of what we do has genetic impact. Controversy starts when we think of aiming deliberately at genetic changes, by eugenics or genetic engineering. I want to make some brief remarks about eugenic policies, before suggesting that policies of deliberate intervention are best considered in the context of genetic engineering.

Scepticism has been expressed about whether eugenic policies have any practical chance of success. Medawar has pointed out the importance of genetic polymorphism: the persistence of genetically different types in a population.[2] (Our different blood groups are a familiar example.) For many characteristics, people get a different gene from each parent. So children do not simply repeat parental characteristics. Any simple picture of producing an improved type of person, and then letting the improvement be passed on unchanged, collapses.

But, although polymorphism is a problem for this crudely utopian form of eugenics, it does not show that more modest schemes of improvement must fail. Suppose the best individuals for some quality (say, colour vision) are heterozygous, so that they inherit a gene A from one parent, and a gene B from the other. These ABs will have AAs and BBs among their children, who will be less good than they are. But AAs and BBs may still be better than ACs or ADs, and perhaps much better than CCs or CDs. If this were so, overall improvement could still be brought about by encouraging people whose genes included an A or a B to have more children than those who had only Cs or Ds. The point of taking a quality like colour vision is that it may be genetically fairly simple. Qualities like kindness or intelligence are more likely to depend on the interaction of many genes, but a similar point can be made at a higher level of complexity.

Polymorphism raises a doubt about whether the offspring of the three 'exceptionally intelligent women' fertilized by Dr Shockley or other Nobel prize-winners will have the same IQ as the parents, even apart from environmental variation. But it does not show the inevitable failure of any large-scale attempts to alter human characteristics by varying the relative numbers of children different kinds of people have. Yet any attempt, say, to raise the level of intelligence, would be a very slow affair, taking many generations to make much of an impact. This is one reason for preferring to discuss genetic engineering. For the genetic engineering of human improvements, if it becomes possible, will have an immediate effect, so we will not be guessing which qualities will be desirable dozens of generations later.

There is the view that the genetic-engineering techniques required will not become a practical possibility. Sir Macfarlane Burnet, writing in 1971 about using genetic engineering to cure disorders in people already born, dismissed the possibility of using a virus to carry a new gene to replace a faulty one in cells throughout the body: 'I should be willing to state in any company that the chance of doing this will remain infinitely small to the last syllable of recorded time.'[3] Unless engineering at the stage of sperm cell and egg is easier, this seems a confident dismissal of the topic to be discussed here. More recent work casts doubt on this confidence.[4] So, having mentioned this scepticism, I shall disregard it. We will assume that genetic engineering of people may become possible, and that it is worth discussing. (Sir Macfarlane Burnet's view has not yet been falsified as totally as Rutherford's view about atomic energy. But I hope that the last syllable of recorded time is still some way off.)

The main reason for casting the discussion in terms of genetic engineering rather than eugenics is not a practical one. Many eugenic policies are open to fairly straightforward moral objections, which hide the deeper theoretical issues. Such policies as compulsory sterilization, compulsory abortion, compelling people to pair off in certain ways, or compelling people to have more or fewer children than they would otherwise have, are all open to objection on grounds of overriding people's autonomy. Some are open to objection on grounds of damage to the institution of the family. And the use of discriminatory tax- and child-benefit policies is an intolerable step towards a society of different genetic castes.

Genetic engineering need not involve overriding anyone's autonomy. It need not be forced on parents against their wishes, and the future person being engineered has no views to be overridden. (The view that despite this, it is still objectionable to have one's genetic characteristics decided by others, will be considered later.) Genetic engineering will not damage the family in the obvious ways that compulsory eugenic policies would. Nor need it be encouraged by incentives which create inequalities. Because it avoids these highly visible moral objections, genetic engineering allows us to focus more clearly on other values that are involved.

(To avoid a possible misunderstanding, one point should be added before leaving the topic of eugenics. Saying that some eugenic policies are open to obvious moral objections does not commit me to disapproval of all eugenic policies. In particular, I do not want to be taken to be opposing two kinds of policy. One is genetic counselling: warning people of risks in having children, and perhaps advising them against having them. The other is the introduction of screening-programmes to detect foetal abnormalities, followed by giving the mother the option of abortion where serious defects emerge.)

Let us now turn to the question of what, if anything, we should do in the field of human genetic engineering.

The Positive–Negative Distinction

We are not yet able to cure disorders by genetic engineering. But we do sometimes respond to disorders by adopting eugenic policies, at least in voluntary form. Genetic counselling is one instance, as applied to those thought likely to have such disorders as

Huntington's chorea. This is a particularly appalling inherited disorder, involving brain degeneration, leading to mental decline and lack of control over movement. It does not normally come on until middle age, by which time many of its victims would in the normal course of things have had children. Huntington's chorea is caused by a dominant gene, so those who find that one of their parents has it have themselves a 50 per cent chance of developing it. If they do have it, each of their children will in turn have a 50 per cent chance of the disease. The risks are so high and the disorder so bad that the potential parents often decide not to have children, and are often given advice to this effect by doctors and others.

Another eugenic response to disorders is involved in screening-programmes for pregnant women. When tests pick up such defects as Down's syndrome (mongolism) or spina bifida, the mother is given the possibility of an abortion. The screening-programmes are eugenic because part of their point is to reduce the incidence of severe genetic abnormality in the population.

These two eugenic policies come in at different stages: before conception and during pregnancy. For this reason the screening-programme is more controversial, because it raises the issue of abortion. Those who are sympathetic to abortion, and who think it would be good to eliminate these disorders will be sympathetic to the programme. Those who think abortion is no different from killing a fully developed human are obviously likely to oppose the programme. But they are likely to feel that elimination of the disorders would be a good thing, even if not an adequate justification for killing. Unless they also disapprove of contraception, they are likely to support the genetic-counselling policy in the case of Huntington's chorea.

Few people object to the use of eugenic policies to eliminate disorders, unless those policies have additional features which are objectionable. Most of us are resistant to the use of compulsion, and those who oppose abortion will object to screening-programmes. But apart from these other moral objections, we do not object to the use of eugenic policies against disease. We do not object to advising those likely to have Huntington's chorea not to have children, as neither compulsion nor killing is involved.

Those of us who take this view have no objection to altering the genetic composition of the next generation, where this alteration consists in reducing the incidence of defects.

If it were possible to use genetic engineering to correct defects, say at the foetal stage, it is hard to see how those of us who are prepared to use the eugenic measures just mentioned could object. In both cases, it would be pure gain. The couple, one of whom may develop Huntington's chorea, can have a child if they want, knowing that any abnormality will be eliminated. Those sympathetic to abortion will agree that cure is preferable. And those opposed to abortion prefer babies to be born without handicap. It is hard to think of any objection to using genetic engineering to eliminate defects, and there is a clear and strong case for its use.

But accepting the case for eliminating genetic mistakes does not entail accepting other uses of genetic engineering. The elimination of defects is often called 'negative' genetic engineering. Going beyond this, to bring about improvements in normal people, is by contrast 'positive' engineering. (The same distinction can be made for eugenics.)

The positive–negative distinction is not in all cases completely sharp. Some conditions are genetic disorders whose identification raises little problem. Huntington's chorea or spina bifida are genetic 'mistakes' in a way that cannot seriously be disputed. But with other conditions, the boundary between a defective state and normality may be more blurred. If there is a genetic disposition towards depressive illness, this seems a defect, whose elimination would be part of negative genetic engineering. Suppose the genetic disposition to depression involves the production of lower levels of an enzyme than are produced in normal people. The negative programme is to correct the genetic fault so that the enzyme level is within the range found in normal people. But suppose that within 'normal' people also there are variations in the enzyme level, which correlate with ordinary differences in tendency to be cheerful or depressed. Is there a sharp boundary between 'clinical' depression and the depression sometimes felt by those diagnosed as 'normal'? Is it clear that a sharp distinction can be drawn between raising someone's enzyme level so that it falls within the normal range and raising someone else's level from the bottom of the normal range to the top?

The positive–negative distinction is sometimes a blurred one, but often we can at least roughly see where it should be drawn. If there is a rough and ready distinction, the question is: how important is it? Should we go on from accepting negative engineering to accepting positive programmes, or should we say that the line between the two is the limit of what is morally acceptable?

There is no doubt that positive programmes arouse the strongest feelings on both sides. On the one hand, many respond to positive genetic engineering or positive eugenics with Professor Tinbergen's thought: 'I find it morally reprehensible and presumptuous for anybody to put himself forward as a judge of the qualities for which we should breed.'

But other people have held just as strongly that positive policies are the way to make the future of mankind better than the past. Many years ago H. J. Muller expressed this hope:

> And so we foresee the history of life divided into three main phases. In the long preparatory phase it was the helpless creature of its environment, and natural selection gradually ground it into human shape. In the second – our own short transitional phase – it reaches out at the immediate environment, shaking, shaping and grinding to suit the form, the requirements, the wishes, and the whims of man. And in the long third phase, it will reach down into the secret places of the great universe of its own nature, and by aid of its ever growing intelligence and co-operation, shape itself into an increasingly sublime creation – a being beside which the mythical divinities of the past will seem more and more ridiculous, and which setting its own marvellous inner powers against the brute Goliath of the suns and the planets, challenges them to contest.[5]

The case for positive engineering is not helped by adopting the tones of the mad scientist in a horror film. But behind the rhetoric is a serious point. If we decide on a positive programme to change our nature, this will be a central moment in our history, and the transformation might be beneficial to a degree we can now scarcely imagine. The question is: how are we to weigh this possibility against Tinbergen's objection, and against other objections and doubts?

For the rest of this discussion, I shall assume that, subject to adequate safeguards against things going wrong, negative genetic engineering is acceptable. The issue is positive engineering. I shall also assume that we can ignore problems about whether positive engineering will be technically possible. Suppose we have the power to choose people's genetic characteristics. Once we have eliminated genetic defects, what, if anything, should we do with this power? [...]

The View That Overall Improvement Is Unlikely or Impossible

There is one doubt about the workability of schemes of genetic improvement which is so widespread that it would be perverse to ignore it. This is the view that, in any genetic alteration, there are no gains without compensating losses. On this view, if we bring about a genetically based improvement, such as higher intelligence, we are bound to pay a price somewhere else: perhaps the more intelligent people will have less resistance to disease, or will be less physically agile. If correct, this might so undermine the practicability of applying eugenics or genetic engineering that it would be hardly worth discussing the values involved in such programmes.

This view perhaps depends on some idea that natural selection is so efficient that, in terms of gene survival, we must already be as efficient as it is possible to be. If it were possible to push up intelligence without weakening some other part of the system, natural selection would already have done so. But this is a naive version of evolutionary theory. In real evolutionary theory, far from the genetic status quo always being the best possible for a given environment, some mutations turn out to be advantageous. and this is the origin of evolutionary progress. If natural mutations can be beneficial without a compensating loss, why should artificially induced ones not be so too?

It should also be noticed that there are two different ideas of what counts as a gain or a loss. From the point of view of evolutionary progress, gains and losses are simply advantages and disadvantages from the point of view of gene survival. But we are not compelled to take this view. If we could engineer a genetic change in some people which would have the effect of making them musical prodigies but also sterile, this would be a hopeless gene in terms of survival, but this need not force us, or the musical prodigies themselves, to think of the change as for the worse. It depends on how we rate musical ability as against having children, and evolutionary survival does not dictate priorities here.

The view that gains and losses are tied up with each other need not depend on the dogma that natural selection *must* have created the best of all possible sets of genes. A more cautiously empirical version of the claim says there is a tendency for gains to be accompanied by losses. John Maynard Smith, in his paper on 'Eugenics and Utopia',[6] takes this kind of 'broad balance' view and runs it the other way, suggesting, as an argument in defence of medicine, that any loss of genetic resistance to disease is likely to be a good thing: 'The reason for this is that in evolution, as in other fields, one seldom gets something for nothing. Genes which confer disease-resistance are likely to have harmful effects in other ways: this is certainly true of the gene for sickle-cell anaemia and may be a general rule. If so, absence of selection in favour of disease resistance may be eugenic.'

It is important that different characteristics may turn out to be genetically linked in ways we do not yet realize. In our present state of knowledge, engineering for some improvement might easily bring some unpredicted but genetically linked disadvantage. But we do not have to accept that there will in general be a broad balance, so that there is a presumption that any gain will be accompanied by a compensating loss (or Maynard Smith's version that we can expect a compensating gain for any loss). The reason is that what counts as a gain or loss varies in different contexts. Take Maynard Smith's example of sickle-cell anaemia. The reason why sickle-cell anaemia is widespread in Africa is that it is genetically linked with resistance to malaria. Those who are heterozygous (who inherit one sickle-cell gene and one normal gene) are resistant to malaria, while those who are homozygous (whose genes are both sickle-cell) get sickle-cell anaemia. If we use genetic engineering to knock out sickle-cell anaemia where malaria is common, we will pay the price of having more malaria.

But when we eradicate malaria, the gain will not involve this loss. Because losses are relative to context, any generalization about the impossibility of overall improvements is dubious.

The Family and Our Descendants

Unlike various compulsory eugenic policies, genetic engineering need not involve any interference with decisions by couples to have children together, or with their decisions about how many children to have. And let us suppose that genetically engineered babies grow in the mother's womb in the normal way, so that her relationship to the child is not threatened in the way it might be if the laboratory or the hospital were substituted for the womb. The cruder threats to family relationships are eliminated.

It may be suggested that there is a more subtle threat. Parents like to identify with their children. We are often pleased to see some of our own characteristics in our children. Perhaps this is partly a kind of vanity, and no doubt sometimes we project on to our children similarities that are not really there. But, when the similarities do exist, they help the parents and children to understand and sympathize with each other. If genetic engineering resulted in children fairly different from their parents, this might make their relationship have problems.

There is something to this objection, but it is easy to exaggerate. Obviously, children who were like Midwich cuckoos, or comic-book Martians, would not be easy to identify with. But genetic engineering need not move in such sudden jerks. The changes would have to be detectable to be worth bringing about, but there seems no reason why large changes in appearance, or an unbridgeable psychological gulf, should be created in any one generation. We bring about environmental changes which make children different from their parents, as when the first generation of children in a remote place are given schooling and made literate. This may cause some problems in families, but it is not usually thought a decisive objection. It is not clear that genetically induced changes of similar magnitude are any more objectionable.

A related objection concerns our attitude to our remoter descendants. We like to think of our descendants stretching on for many generations. Perhaps this is in part an immortality substitute. We hope they will to some extent be like us, and that, if they think of us, they will do so with sympathy and approval. Perhaps these hopes about the future of mankind are relatively unimportant to us. But, even if we mind about them a lot, they are unrealistic in the very long term. Genetic engineering would make our descendants less like us, but this would only speed up the natural rate of change. Natural mutations and selective pressures make it unlikely that in a few million years our descendants will be physically or mentally much like us. So what genetic engineering threatens here is probably doomed anyway. [...]

Risks and Mistakes

[...] One of the objections [to genetic engineering] is that serious risks may be involved.

Some of the risks are already part of the public debate because of current work on recombinant DNA. The danger is of producing harmful organisms that would escape from our control. The work obviously should take place, if at all, only with adequate safeguards against such a disaster. The problem is deciding what we should count as adequate safeguards. I have nothing to contribute to this problem here. If it can be dealt with satisfactorily, we will perhaps move on to genetic engineering of people. And this introduces another dimension of risk. We may produce unintended results, either because our techniques turn out to be less finely tuned than we thought, or because different characteristics are found to be genetically linked in unexpected ways.

If we produce a group of people who turn out worse than expected, we will have to live with them. Perhaps we would aim for producing people who were especially imaginative and creative, and only too late find we had produced people who were also very violent and aggressive. This kind of mistake might not only be disastrous, but also very hard to 'correct' in subsequent generations. For when we suggested sterilization to the people we had produced, or else corrective genetic engineering for *their* offspring, we might find them hard to persuade. They might like the way they were, and reject, in characteristically violent fashion, our explanation that they were a mistake.

The possibility of an irreversible disaster is a strong deterrent. It is enough to make some people think we should rule out genetic engineering altogether, and to make others think that, while negative engineering is perhaps acceptable, we should rule out positive engineering. The thought behind this second position is that the benefits from negative engineering are clearer, and that, because its aims are more modest, disastrous mistakes are less likely.

The risk of disasters provides at least a reason for saying that, if we do adopt a policy of human genetic engineering, we ought to do so with extreme caution. We should alter genes only where we have strong reasons for thinking the risk of disaster is very small, and where the benefit is great enough to justify the risk. (The problems of deciding when this is so are familiar from the nuclear power debate.) This 'principle of caution' is less strong than one ruling out all positive engineering, and allows room for the possibility that the dangers may turn out to be very remote, or that greater risks of a different kind are involved in *not* using positive engineering. These possibilities correspond to one view of the facts in the nuclear power debate. Unless with genetic engineering we think we can already rule out such possibilities, the argument from risk provides more justification for the principle of caution than for the stronger ban on all positive engineering. [...]

Not Playing God

Suppose we could use genetic engineering to raise the average IQ by fifteen points. (I mention, only to ignore, the boring objection that the average IQ is always by definition 100.) Should we do this? Objectors to positive engineering say we should not. This is not because the present average is preferable to a higher one. We do not think that, if it were naturally fifteen points higher, we ought to bring it down to the present level. The objection is to our playing God by deciding what the level should be.

On one view of the world, the objection is relatively straightforward. On this view, there really is a God, who has a plan for the world which will be disrupted if we stray outside the boundaries assigned to us. (It is *relatively* straightforward: there would still be the problem of knowing where the boundaries came. If genetic engineering disrupts the programme, how do we know that medicine and education do not?)

The objection to playing God has a much wider appeal than to those who literally believe in a divine plan. But, outside such a context, it is unclear what the objection comes to. If we have a Darwinian view, according to which features of our nature have been selected for their contribution to gene survival, it is not blasphemous, or obviously disastrous, to start to control the process in the light of our own values. We may value other qualities in people, in preference to those which have been most conducive to gene survival.

The prohibition on playing God is obscure. If it tells us not to interfere with natural selection at all, this rules out medicine, and most other environmental and social changes. If it only forbids interference with natural selection by the direct alteration of genes, this rules out negative as well as positive genetic engineering. If these interpretations are too restrictive, the ban on positive engineering seems to need some explanation. If we can make positive changes at the environmental level, and negative changes at the genetic level, why should we not make positive changes at the genetic level? What makes this policy, but not the others, objectionably God-like?

Perhaps the most plausible reply to these questions rests on a general objection to any group of people trying to plan too closely what human life should be like. Even if it is hard to distinguish in principle between the use of genetic and environmental means, genetic changes are likely to differ in degree from most environmental ones. Genetic alterations may be more drastic or less reversible, and so they can be seen as the extreme case of an objectionably God-like policy by which some people set out to plan the lives of others.

This objection can be reinforced by imagining the possible results of a programme of positive engineering, where the decisions about the desired improvements were taken by scientists. Judging by the literature written by scientists on this topic, great prominence would be given to intelligence. But can we be sure that enough weight would be given to other desirable qualities? And do things seem better if for scientists we substitute doctors, politicians or civil servants? Or some committee containing businessmen, trade unionists, academics, lawyers and a clergyman?

What seems worrying here is the circumscribing of potential human development. The present genetic lottery throws up a vast range of characteristics, good and bad, in all sorts of combinations. The group of people controlling a positive engineering policy would inevitably have limited horizons, and we are right to worry that the limitations of their outlook might become the boundaries of human variety. The drawbacks would be like those of town-planning or dog-breeding, but with more important consequences.

When the objection to playing God is separated from the idea that intervening in this aspect of the natural world is a kind of blasphemy, it is a protest against a particular group of people, necessarily fallible and limited, taking decisions so important to our future. This protest may be on grounds of the bad consequences, such as loss of variety of people, that would come from the imaginative limits of those taking the decisions. Or it may be an expression of opposition to such concentration of power, perhaps with the thought: 'What right have *they* to decide what kinds of people there should be?' Can these problems be side-stepped?

The Genetic Supermarket

Robert Nozick is critical of the assumption that positive engineering has to involve any centralized decision about desirable qualities: 'Many biologists tend to think the problem is one of *design*, of specifying the best types of persons so that biologists can proceed to produce them. Thus they worry over what sort(s) of person there is to be and who will control this process. They do not tend to think, perhaps because it diminishes the importance of their role, of a system in which they run a "genetic supermarket", meeting the individual specifications (within certain moral limits) of prospective parents. Nor do they think of seeing what limited number of types of persons people's choices would converge upon, if indeed there would be any such convergence. This supermarket system has the great virtue that it involves no centralized decision fixing the future human type(s).'[7]

This idea of letting parents choose their children's characteristics is in many ways an improvement on decisions being taken by some centralized body. It seems less likely to reduce human variety, and could even increase it, if genetic engineering makes new combinations of characteristics available. (But we should be cautious here. Parental choice is not a guarantee of genetic variety, as the influence of fashion or of shared values might make for a small number of types on which choices would converge.)

To those sympathetic to one kind of liberalism, Nozick's proposal will seem more attractive than centralized decisions. On this approach to politics, it is wrong for the authorities to institutionalize any religious or other outlook as the official one of the society. To a liberal of this kind, a good society is one which tolerates and encourages a wide diversity of ideals of the good life. Anyone with these sympathies will be suspicious of centralized decisons about what sort of people should form the next generation. But some parental decisons would be disturbing. If parents chose characteristics likely to make their children unhappy, or likely to reduce their abilities, we might feel that the children should be protected against this. (Imagine parents belonging to some extreme religious sect, who wanted their children to have a religious symbol as a physical mark on their face, and who wanted them to be unable to read, as a protection against their faith being corrupted.) Those of us who support restrictions protecting children from parental harm after birth (laws against cruelty, and compulsion on parents to allow their children to be educated and to have necessary medical treatment) are likely to support protecting children from being harmed by their parents' genetic choices.

No doubt the boundaries here will be difficult to draw. We already find it difficult to strike a satisfactory balance between protection of children and parental freedom to choose the kind of upbringing their children should have. But it is hard to accept that society should set no limits to the genetic choices parents can make for their children. Nozick recognizes this when he says the genetic supermarket should meet the specifications of parents 'within certain moral limits'. So, if the supermarket came into existence, some centralized policy, even if only the restrictive one of ruling out certain choices harmful to the children, should exist. It would be a political decision where the limits should be set.

There may also be a case for other centralized restrictions on parental choice, as well as those aimed at preventing harm to the individual people being designed. The genetic supermarket might have more oblique bad effects. An imbalance in the ratio between the sexes could result. Or parents might think their children would be more successful if they were more thrusting, competitive and selfish. If enough parents acted on this thought, other parents with different values might feel forced into making similar choices to prevent their own children being too greatly disadvantaged. Unregulated individual decisions could lead to shifts of this kind, with outcomes unwanted by most of those who contribute to them. If a majority favour a roughly equal ratio between the sexes, or a population of relatively uncompetitive people, they may feel justified in supporting restrictions on what parents can choose. (This is an application to the case of genetic engineering of a point familiar in other contexts, that unrestricted individual choices can add up to a total outcome which most people think worse than what would result from some regulation.)

Nozick recognizes that there may be cases of this sort. He considers the case of avoiding a sexual imbalance and says that 'a government could require that genetic manipulation be carried on so as to fit a certain ratio'.[8] He clearly prefers to avoid governmental intervention of this kind, and, while admitting that the desired result would be harder to obtain in a purely libertarian system, suggests possible strategies for doing so. He says: 'Either parents would subscribe to an information service monitoring the recent births and so know which sex was in shorter supply (and hence would be more in demand in later life), thus adjusting their activities, or interested individuals would contribute to a charity that offers bonuses to maintain the ratios, or the ratio would leave 1:1, with new family and social patterns developing.' The proposals for avoiding the sexual imbalance without central regulation are not reassuring. Information about likely prospects for marriage or sexual partnership might not be decisive for parents' choices. And, since those most likely to be 'interested individuals' would be in the age group being genetically engineered, it is not clear that the charity would be given donations adequate for its job.[9]

If the libertarian methods failed, we would have the choice between allowing a sexual imbalance or imposing some system of social regulation. Those who dislike central decisions favouring one sort of person over others might accept regulation here, on the grounds that neither sex is being given preference: the aim is rough equality of numbers.

But what about the other sort of case, where the working of the genetic supermarket leads to a general change unwelcome to those who contribute to it? Can we defend regulation to prevent a shift towards a more selfish and competitive population as merely being the preservation of a certain ratio between characteristics? Or have we crossed the boundary, and allowed a centralized decision favouring some characteristics over others? The location of the boundary is obscure. One view would be that the sex-ratio case is acceptable because the desired ratio is equality of numbers. On another view, the acceptability derives from the fact that the present ratio is to be preserved. (In this second view, preserving altruism would be acceptable, so long as no attempt was made to raise the proportion of altruistic people in the population. But is *this* boundary an easy one to defend?)

If positive genetic engineering does become a reality, we may be unable to avoid some of the decisions being taken at a social level. Or rather, we could avoid this, but only at what seems an unacceptable cost, either to the particular people being designed, or to their generation as a whole. And, even if the social decisions are only restrictive, it is implausible to claim that they are all quite free of any taint of preference for some characteristics over others. But, although this suggests that we should not be doctrinaire in our support of the liberal view, it does not show that the view has to be abandoned altogether. We may still think that social decisions in favour of one type of person rather than another should be few, even if the consequences of excluding them altogether are unacceptable. A genetic supermarket, modified by some central regulation, may still be better than a system of purely central decisions. The liberal value is not obliterated because it may sometimes be compromised for the sake of other things we care about.

A Mixed System

The genetic supermarket provides a partial answer to the objection about the limited outlook of those who would take the decisions. The choices need not be concentrated in the hands of a small number of people. The genetic supermarket should not operate in a completely unregulated way, and so some centralized decisions would have to be taken about the restrictions that should be imposed. One system that would answer many of the anxieties about centralized decision-making would be to limit the power of the decision-makers to one of veto. They would then only check departures from the natural genetic lottery, and so the power to bring about changes would not be given to them, but spread through the whole population of potential parents. Let us call this combination of parental initiative and central veto a 'mixed system'. If positive genetic engineering does come about, we can imagine the argument between supporters of a mixed system and supporters of other decision-making systems being central to the political theory of the twenty-first century, parallel to the place occupied in the nineteenth and twentieth centuries by the debate over control of the economy.[10]

My own sympathies are with the view that, if positive genetic engineering is introduced, this mixed system is in general likely to be the best one for taking decisions. I do not want to argue for an absolutely inviolable commitment to this, as it could be that some centralized decision for genetic change was the only way of securing a huge benefit or avoiding a great catastrophe. But, subject to this reservation, the dangers of concentrating the decision-making create a strong presumption in favour of a mixed system rather than one in which initiatives come from the centre. And, if a mixed system was introduced, there would have to be a great deal of political argument over what kinds of restrictions on the supermarket should be imposed. Twenty-first-century elections may be about issues rather deeper than economics.

If this mixed system eliminates the anxiety about genetic changes being introduced by a few powerful people with limited horizons, there is a more general unease which it does not remove. May not the limitations of one generation of parents also prove disastrous? And, underlying this, is the problem of what values parents should appeal to in making their choices. How can we be confident that it is better for one sort of person to be born than another?

Values

The dangers of such decisions, even spread through all prospective parents, seem to me very real. We are swayed by fashion. We do not know the limitations of our own outlook. There are human qualities whose value we may not appreciate. A generation of parents might opt heavily for their children having physical or intellectual abilities and skills. We might leave out a sense of humour. Or we might not notice how important to us is some other quality, such as emotional warmth. So we might not be disturbed in advance by the possible impact of the genetic changes on such a quality. And, without really wanting to do so, we might stumble into producing people with a deep coldness. This possibility seems one of the worst imaginable. It is just one of the many horrors that could be blundered into by our lack of foresight in operating the mixed system. Because such disasters are a real danger, there is a case against positive genetic engineering, even when the changes do not result from centralized decisions. But this case, resting as it does on the risk of disaster, supports a principle of caution rather than a total ban. We have to ask the question whether there are benefits sufficiently great and sufficiently probable to outweigh the risks.

But perhaps the deepest resistance, even to a mixed system, is not based on risks, but on a more general problem about values. Could the parents ever be justified in choosing, according to some set of values, to create one sort of person rather than another?

Is it sometimes better for us to create one sort of person rather than another? We say 'yes' when it is a question of eliminating genetic defects. And we say 'yes' if we think that encouraging some qualities rather than others should be an aim of the upbringing and education we give our children. Any inclination to say 'no' in the context of positive genetic engineering must lay great stress on the two relevant boundaries. The positive–negative boundary is needed to mark off the supposedly unacceptable positive policies from the acceptable elimination of defects. And the genes–environment boundary is needed to mark off positive engineering from acceptable positive aims of educational policies. But it is not clear that confidence in the importance of these boundaries is justified.

The positive–negative boundary may seem a way of avoiding objectionably God-like decisions, on the basis of our own values, as to what sort of people there should be. Saving someone from spina bifida is a lot less controversial than deciding he shall be a good athlete. But the distinction, clear in some cases, is less sharp in others. With emotional states or intellectual functioning, there is an element of convention in where the boundaries of normality are drawn. And, apart from this, there is the problem of explaining why the positive–negative boundary is so much more important with genetic intervention than with environmental methods. We act environmentally to influence people in ways that go far beyond the elimination of medical defects. Homes and schools would be impoverished by attempting to restrict their influence on children to the mere prevention of physical and mental disorder. And if we are right here to cross the positive–negative boundary, encouraging children to ask questions, or to be generous and imaginative, why should crossing the same boundary for the same reasons be ruled out absolutely when the means are genetic?

Notes

1   Chris Graham has suggested to me that it is misleading to say this without emphasizing the painful slowness of this way of changing gene frequencies.

2   *The Future of Man* (The Reith Lectures, 1959), London, 1960, chapter 3; and in 'The Genetic Improvement of Man', in *The Hope of Progress*, London, 1972.

3 *Genes. Dreams and Realities*, London, 1971, p. 81.

4 'Already they have pushed Cline's results further, obtaining transfer between rabbit and mouse, for example, and good expression of the foreign gene in its new host. Some, by transferring the genes into the developing eggs, have managed to get the new genes into every cell in the mouse, including the sex cells; those mice have fathered offspring who also contain the foreign gene.' Jeremy Cherfas: *Man Made Life*, Oxford, 1982, pp. 229–30.

5 *Out of the Night*, New York. 1935. To find a distinguished geneticist talking like this after the Nazi period is not easy.

6 John Maynard Smith: *On Evolution*, Edinburgh, 1972; the article is reprinted from the issue on 'Utopia' of *Daedalus, Journal of the American Academy of Arts and Sciences*, 1965.

7 *Anarchy, State and Utopia*, New York, 1974, p. 315.

8 *Anarchy, State and Utopia,* p. 315.

9 This kind of unworldly innocence is part of the engaging charm of Nozick's dotty and brilliant book.

10 Decision-taking by a central committee (perhaps of a dozen elderly men) can be thought of as a 'Russian' model. The genetic supermarket (perhaps with genotypes being sold by TV commercials) can be thought of as an 'American' model. The mixed system may appeal to Western European social democrats.

18

The Moral Significance of the Therapy–Enhancement Distinction in Human Genetics

David B. Resnik

Introduction

The therapy–enhancement distinction occupies a central place in contemporary discussions of human genetics and has been the subject of much debate.[1-7] At a recent conference on gene therapy policy, scientists predicted that within a few years researchers will develop techniques that can be used to enhance human traits.[8] In thinking about the morality of genetic interventions, many writers have defended somatic gene therapy,[9,10] and some have defended germline gene therapy,[11,12] but only a handful of writers defend genetic enhancement,[13] or even give it a fair hearing.[14-16] The mere mention of genetic enhancement makes many people cringe and brings to mind the Nazi eugenics programs, Aldous Huxley's *Brave New World*, "The X-Files," or the recent movie "Gattaca." Although many people believe that gene therapy has morally legitimate medical uses,[17,18] others regard genetic enhancement as morally problematic or decidedly evil.[19-21]

The purpose of this essay is to examine the moral significance of the therapy–enhancement distinction in human genetics. Is genetic enhancement inherently unethical? Is genetic therapy inherently ethical? I will argue that the distinction does not mark a firm boundary between moral and immoral genetic interventions, and that genetic enhancement is not inherently immoral. To evaluate the acceptability of any particular genetic intervention, one needs to examine the relevant facts in light of moral principles. Some types of genetic therapy are morally acceptable while some types of genetic enhancement are unacceptable. In defending this view, I will discuss and evaluate several different ways of attempting to draw a solid moral line between therapy and enhancement.[22]

Somatic versus Germline Interventions

Before discussing the therapy–enhancement distinction, it is important that we understand another distinction that should inform our discussion, viz. the distinction between somatic and germline interventions.[23,24] Somatic interventions attempt to modify somatic cells, while germline interventions attempt to modify germ cells. The gene therapy clinical trials that have been performed thus far have been on somatic cells. If we combine these two distinctions, we obtain four types of genetic interventions:

1. Somatic genetic therapy (SGT)
2. Germline genetic therapy (GLGT)
3. Somatic genetic enhancement (SGE)
4. Germline genetic enhancement (GLGE)

Original publication details: David B. Resnik, "The Moral Significance of the Therapy–Enhancement Distinction in Human Genetics," pp. 365–77 from *Cambridge Quarterly of Healthcare Ethics* 9: 3 (Summer 2000) © Cambridge University Press. Reproduced with permission.

Bioethics: An Anthology, Third Edition. Edited by Helga Kuhse, Udo Schüklenk, and Peter Singer.
© 2016 John Wiley & Sons, Inc. Published 2016 by John Wiley & Sons, Inc.

While I accept the distinction between somatic and germline interventions, it is important to note that even interventions designed to affect somatic cells can also affect germ cells: current SGT trials carry a slight risk of altering germ cells.[25] Even so, one might argue that this is a morally significant distinction because somatic interventions usually affect only the patient, while germline interventions are likely to affect future generations.[26] In any case, the therapy–enhancement distinction encompasses somatic as well as germline interventions, and my discussion of this distinction will include both somatic as well as germline interventions.

The Concepts of Health and Disease

Perhaps the most popular way of thinking about the moral significance of the therapy–enhancement distinction is to argue that the aim of genetic therapy is to treat human diseases while the aim of genetic enhancement is to perform other kinds of interventions, such as altering or "improving" the human body.[27–29] Since genetic therapy serves morally legitimate goals, genetic therapy is morally acceptable; but since genetic enhancement serves morally questionable or illicit goals, genetic enhancement is not morally acceptable.[30–33] I suspect that many people view the distinction and its moral significance in precisely these terms. W. French Anderson states a clear case for the moral significance of genetic enhancement:

> On medical and ethical grounds we should draw a line excluding any form of genetic engineering. We should not step over the line that delineates treatment from enhancement.[34]

However, this way of thinking of medical genetics makes at least two questionable assumptions: (1) that we have a clear and uncontroversial account of health and disease, and (2) that the goal of treating diseases is morally legitimate, while other goals are not. To examine these assumptions, we need to take a quick look at discussions about the concepts of health and disease.

The bioethics literature contains a thoughtful debate about the definitions of health and disease and

it is not my aim to survey that terrain here.[35,36] However, I will distinguish between two basic approaches to the definition of health, a value-neutral (or descriptive) approach and a value-laden (or normative) one.[37] According to the value-neutral approach, health and disease are descriptive concepts that have an empirical, factual basis in human biology. Boorse defended one of the most influential descriptive approaches to health and disease: a diseased organism lacks the functional abilities of a normal member of its species.[38] To keep his approach value-neutral, Boorse interprets "normal" in statistical terms, i.e., "normal" = "typical." Daniels expands on Boorse's account of disease by suggesting that natural selection can provide an account of species-typical functions: functional abilities are traits that exist in populations because they have contributed to the reproduction and survival of organisms that possessed them.[39] Thus a human with healthy lungs has specific respiratory capacities that are normal in our species, and these capacities have been "designed" by natural selection. A human who lacks these capacities, such as someone with cystic fibrosis or emphysema, has a disease.

According to the value-laden approach, our concepts of health and disease are based on social, moral, and cultural norms. A healthy person is someone who falls within these norms; a diseased person deviates from them. Someone who deviates from species-typical functions could be considered healthy in a society that views that deviation as healthy: although schizophrenia has a biological basis, in some cultures schizophrenics are viewed as "gifted" or "sacred," while in other cultures they are viewed as "mentally ill." Likewise, some cultures view homosexuality as a disease, while others do not.[40–42]

Many different writers have tried to work out variants on these two basic approaches to health and disease, and some have tried to develop compromise views,[43,44] but suffice it to say that the first assumption mentioned above – i.e., that we have a clear and uncontroversial account of health and disease – is questionable.

Even if we lack an uncontroversial account of disease, we could still ask whether either of the two basic approaches would condemn genetic enhancement unconditionally. Consider the descriptive approach first. If statements about disease merely describe deviations from species-typical traits, does it follow that we may perform genetic interventions to treat diseases but not to enhance otherwise healthy people? Since we regard the concept of disease as descriptive, we cannot answer this question without making some normative assumptions. Saying that someone has a disease is like saying that he or she has red hair, is five feet tall, or was born in New York City. These descriptions of that person carry no normative import. Hence the descriptive account of disease, by itself, does not provide us with a way of drawing a solid moral line between therapy and enhancement. For this approach to disease to draw moral boundaries between therapy and enhancement, it needs to be supplemented by a normatively rich account of the rightness of therapy and wrongness of enhancement.

Perhaps the normative approach fares better than the descriptive one. If we accept this view, it follows that therapy has some positive moral value, since therapy is an attempt to treat diseases, which are defined as traits or abilities that do not fall within social or cultural norms. If it is "bad" to have a disease, then we are morally justified in performing interventions that attempt to treat or prevent diseases, since these procedures impart "good" states of being. Thus this normative approach implies that therapy is morally right. But does it imply that enhancement is morally wrong? The answer to this question depends, in large part, on the scope of the concepts of health and disease. If we hold that the concept of health defines a set of traits and abilities that should be possessed by all members of society and that any deviations are diseases, then any intervention that results in a deviation from these norms would be viewed as immoral. Hence, enhancement would be inherently immoral. But this account of health and disease is way too broad; there must be some morally neutral traits and abilities. If there are no morally neutral traits and abilities, then any person that deviates from health norms is "sick." This view would leave very little room for individual variation, to say nothing of the freedom to choose to deviate from health norms. If we accept a narrower account of health and disease, then we will open up some room for morally acceptable deviations from health norms. But this interpretation implies that enhancement interventions could be morally acceptable, provided that they do not violate other moral norms, such as nonmaleficence, autonomy, utility, and so on. Enhancement would not be inherently wrong, on

this view, but the rightness or wrongness of any enhancement procedure would depend on its various factual and normative aspects.

The upshot of this discussion is that neither of the two main approaches to health and disease provides us with solid moral boundaries between genetic enhancement and genetic therapy. One might suggest that we examine alternative approaches, but I doubt that other, more refined theories of health and disease will provide us with a way of drawing sharp moral boundaries between genetic enhancement and genetic therapy. Perhaps we should look at other ways of endowing the distinction with moral significance.

The Goals of Medicine

A slightly different approach to these issues asserts that genetic therapy is on solid moral ground because it promotes the goals of medicine, while genetic enhancement promotes other, morally questionable goals. But what are the goals of medicine? This is not an easy question to answer, since medicine seems to serve a variety of purposes, such as the treatment of disease, the prevention of disease, the promotion of human health and well-being, and the relief of suffering. Many of the so-called goals of medicine, such as the prevention of disease and the promotion of human health, may also be promoted by procedures that we would classify as forms of enhancement.[45] For example, some writers have suggested that we might be able to perform genetic interventions that enhance the human immune system by making it better able to fight diseases, including cancer.[46] Most people would accept the idea that providing children with immunizations against the measles, mumps, and rubella promotes the goals of medicine. If we accept the notion that ordinary, nongenetic enhancement of the immune system promotes the goals of medicine, then shouldn't we also agree that genetic enhancements of the immune system serve the same goals? And what about other forms of healthcare, such as rhinoplasty, liposuction, orthodontics, breast augmentation, hair removal, and hair transplants? If these cosmetic procedures serve medical goals, then cosmetic uses of genetic technology, such as somatic gene therapy for baldness, and germline gene therapy for straight teeth, would also seem to serve medical goals. Finally, consider the procedures that are designed to relieve suffering, such as pain control and anesthesia. If we can develop drugs to promote these goals, then why not develop genetic procedures to meet similar objectives? It is not beyond the realm of possibility that we could use genetic therapy to induce the body to produce endorphins. Many forms of enhancement may serve medical goals. Once again, the therapy–enhancement distinction appears not to set any firm moral boundaries in genetic medicine.

One might attempt to avoid this problem by narrowly construing the goals of medicine: the goals of medicine are to treat and prevent diseases in human beings. Other uses of medical technology do not serve the goals of medicine. There are two problems with this response. First, it assumes that we agree on the goals of medicine and the definitions of health and disease. Second, even if we could agree that medicine's goals are to treat and prevent diseases and we can define "health" and "disease," why would it be immoral to use medical technology and science for nonmedical purposes? If a medical procedure, such as mastectomy, is developed for therapeutic purposes, what is wrong with using that procedure for "non-medical" purposes, such as breast reduction surgery in men with overdeveloped breasts? Admittedly, there are many morally troubling nonmedical uses of medical science and technology, such as the use of steroids by athletes and the use of laxatives by anorexics, but these morally troubling uses of medicine are morally troubling because they violate various moral principles or values, such as fairness and nonmaleficence, not because they are nonmedical uses of medicine.

One might argue that those who use medical science and technology for nonmedical purposes violate medicine's professional norms, but this point only applies to those who consider themselves to be medical professionals. If a procedure violates medical norms, it is medically unethical, but this does not mean that the procedure is unethical outside of the context of medical care. For example, the American Medical Association holds that it is unethical for physicians to assist the state in executions, but this policy does not constitute an unconditional argument against capital punishment. To make the case against capital punishment, one must appeal to wider moral and political norms. Hence the goals of medicine also do not set a morally sharp dividing line between genetic therapy and enhancement.

Our Humanness

One might try to draw moral boundaries between genetic therapy and genetic enhancement by arguing that genetic enhancement is inherently immoral because it changes the human form. Genetic therapy only attempts to restore or safeguard our humanness, while enhancement changes those very features that make us human. Although GLGE and GLGT can more profoundly change human traits than SGE and SGT, both technologies can alter our humanness (or our humanity). To explore these issues in depth, we need to answer two questions: (1) What traits or abilities make us human? and (2) Why would it be wrong to change those traits or abilities? Philosophers have proposed answers to the first question ever since Aristotle defined man as "the rational animal." A thorough answer to the question of defining our humanness takes us way beyond the scope of this essay, but I will offer the reader a brief perspective.[47]

If we have learned anything from the abortion debate, we have learned that it is not at all easy to specify necessary and sufficient conditions for a thing to be human. Humanness is best understood as a cluster concept in that it can be equated with a list of characteristics but not with a set of necessary and sufficient conditions.[48] Some of these characteristics include:

a. physical traits and abilities, such as an opposable thumb, bipedalism, etc.
b. psychosocial traits and abilities, such as cognition, language, emotional responses, sociality, etc.
c. phylogenetic traits, such as membership in the biological species *Homo sapiens*.

The beings that we call "human" possess many of these traits and abilities, even though some humans have more of these traits and abilities than others. For example, a newborn and an adult have many of the same physical and phylogenetic traits and abilities, even though the adult has more psychosocial traits and abilities. For my purposes, I do not need to say which of these traits and abilities are more "central" to the concept of humanness, since I am not defending a definition that provides necessary or sufficient conditions.

The question I would like to explore in more depth concerns the wrongness of changing those traits that make us human. Would it be inherently wrong to alter the human form? This question presupposes the pragmatically prior question, Can we alter the human form? The answer to this question depends on two factors: (1) the definition of our humanness; and (2) our scientific and technological abilities. According to the definition I assume in this essay, it is possible to alter the human form, since the human form consists of a collection of physiological, psychosocial, and phylogenetic traits and abilities, which can be changed in principle.[49] Although we lacked the ability to change the traits that constitute our humanness at one time, advances in science and technology have given us the ability to change human traits. Since we have good reasons to believe that we can change our humanness, we can now ask whether we should do so.

Most moral theories, with the notable exception of the natural law approach, imply that there is nothing inherently wrong with changing the human form. For the purposes of this essay, I will not examine all of these moral theories here but will only briefly mention two very different perspectives on morality that reach similar conclusions. According to utilitarianism, an action or policy that alters our humanness could be morally right or it could be morally wrong, depending on the consequences of that action or policy. If genetic enhancement produces a greater balance of good/bad consequences, then enhancement would be morally acceptable. For example, genetic interventions that enhance the human immune system might be morally acceptable, but interventions that result in harmful mutations would be unacceptable. Kantians would object to attempts to alter our humanness if those attempts violate human dignity and autonomy. Some, but not all, genetic interventions could threaten our dignity and autonomy. For example, using SGT to promote hair growth should pose no threat to human dignity and autonomy (if informed consent is not violated), but using GLGE to create a race of "slaves" or "freaks" would pose a dire threat to dignity and autonomy. The main point here is that most moral theories would hold that there is nothing inherently wrong with changing our humanness; the moral rightness or wrongness of such attempts depends on their relation to other moral concerns, such as utility, autonomy, natural rights, virtue, etc.[50]

However, the natural law approach to morality could be interpreted as implying that tampering with the human form is inherently wrong. This argument assumes that the human form has inherent worth and that any changes to that form defile or destroy its worth. The human form is morally sacred and should not be altered.[51] For example, one might hold that a great painting, such as the "Mona Lisa," has inherent worth and it should therefore be left as it is; to change the "Mona Lisa" is to destroy it. Or perhaps one might argue that it would be wrong to change the formula for "Coke" or the plot of "Hamlet." But what is inherently wrong with changing the human form?

One argument that changing the human form is inherently wrong is that natural selection has "designed" us to have specific traits, and that any attempt to change those traits would be a foolhardy and vain intervention in nature's wisdom. It has taken thousands of years of adaptation for the human species to evolve into its present form. How can we possibly improve on nature's perfection? We are more likely to make a major blunder or mistake with human genetic engineering than to make an important advance.[52] Human genetic engineering is likely to produce harmful mutations, gross abnormalities, Frankenstein monsters, etc.[53] There are two problems with this neo-Darwinian view. First, it is Panglossian and naïve: natural selection is not perfect – nature makes mistakes all the time. We possess many traits, such as the appendix, that serve no useful function. There are some traits that we could add, such as enhancements to the immune system, that could be very useful. Though we should not underestimate nature's wisdom and our ignorance, it is simply false that nature has made us perfect with no room for change or improvement.[54] Second, the argument overestimates human ignorance and carelessness. The history of medical technology allows us to see that while we have had many failures in altering the human form, such as Nazi eugenics programs, we have also had some successes, such as artificial limbs and eyeglasses. Although we should exhibit extreme care, discretion, and circumspection in all genetic interventions, not all changes we make in the human form will result in natural disasters.

A second argument approaches the issue from a theological perspective. According to this view, God, not natural selection, has designed us to have specific traits. Hence any human attempt to change those traits would be a foolish (and arrogant) challenge to God's wisdom. Those who attempt to "play God" by changing human nature commit the mortal sin of hubris. One obvious difficulty with this argument is that it is not likely to convince nonbelievers, but let us set aside that problem and engage in some speculative theology. The question we need to ask in response to this argument is, Would God not want us to change human traits? Changes we can now make to human traits could promote human welfare and justice. Why would God allow us to have this power and not use it? Of course, God would not want us to use our power to increase human suffering or injustice, but why would He not want us to use this power for good purposes? Although several well-known theologians have taken a strong stance against human genetic engineering,[55] religious denominations are not united in their opposition to genetic engineering.[56] For example, the National Council of Churches adopted a resolution that the effort to use genetics to improve on nature is not inherently wrong, and the Council later stated that God has given men and women powers of co-creation, though these powers should be used with care.[57,58]

Regardless of whether one accepts the views of a particular church, it is not at all clear that a theologically based natural law theory provides us with good reasons for thinking that it is inherently wrong to change the human form. One could accept a theologically based approach to morality that leaves some room for human beings to alter the human form, provided that we exhibit wisdom, care, and restraint in changing our form.[59] Some changes (e.g., those that result in suffering or injustice) are morally wrong, but other changes (e.g., those that promote happiness or justice) are morally acceptable.

The Rights of the Unborn

Another way of arguing that at least some forms of genetic enhancement are inherently wrong is to claim that GLGE and GLGT violate the rights of unborn children.[60] These procedures are often said to violate the rights of unborn children because they:

a. are experimental procedures that violate the informed consent of unborn children;[61]
b. deny unborn children the right to have a germline that has not been genetically manipulated;[62] or
c. deny unborn children a right to an open future.[63]

All of these arguments make the morally controversial assumption that unborn children have rights. I will not challenge this assertion here.[64] Even if one assumes that unborn children have rights, it still does not follow that GLGE or GLGT violate those rights.

Let's consider (a) first. GLGT and GLGE do not violate the unborn child's right to informed consent because this right can be exercised by competent adults acting in the child's best interests. We allow proxy consent as a legitimate way of exercising informed consent for many procedures that can profoundly affect the welfare of children, such as fetal surgery and experimental surgery on newborns to repair congenital defects. If it makes sense to use proxy consent in these kinds of experiments, then it should also make sense to use proxy consent for other types of experiments, such as GLGT or GLGE, provided that these experiments can be shown to be in the best interests of unborn children.[65]

(b) is a very esoteric position. What kind of right is the "right to have a genome that has not been genetically manipulated"? Most writers conceive of rights in terms of interests: rights function to protect the interests of individuals.[66] Interests are needs and benefits that most people require to have a fulfilling life, such as freedom, health, education, self-esteem, and so on. So do unborn children have an interest in being born with a genome that has not been manipulated? If such an interest exists, then it is highly unusual and certainly not universal. Children whose parents hold specific religious or philosophical doctrines that forbid germline manipulation may have an interest in being born with an unadulterated genome, but other children will not have this interest. For most children, being born with a genome that predisposes them to health and a wide range of opportunities is more important than being born with a genome that has not been manipulated.

This bring us to argument (c). A right to an "open future" is a right to make one's own choices and life plans on reaching adulthood.[67] Parents who excessively impose their own choices, values, and life plans on their children may violate this right. For example, parents who decide to have a son castrated in order to make sure that he becomes a good singer close off many choices and plans that he could have made as an adult, e.g., having children through natural means. The right to an open future is by no means an unusual or esoteric right, since almost all children have the interests that this right protects, e.g., freedom of choice, freedom of opportunity, etc. But even if we admit this much, does it follow that GLGT or GLGE constitute an inherent violation of this right? I don't think so. While some uses of genetic technology could be regarded as an overbearing imposition of parental values on children, other uses of GLGT and GLGE may augment a child's right to an open future. If parents use GLGE to enhance a child's immune system, then they could be increasing his opportunities to an open future by helping him fight diseases, which can limit opportunities. On the other hand, parents who attempt to produce an eight-foot-tall child in order to make her into a basketball player probably are violating her right to an open future by imposing their choices on her life.

However, there is not a sharp distinction between violating a child's right to an open future and being a responsible parent.[68] We readily accept the idea that parents should try to raise children who are healthy, intelligent, responsible, and happy, and we endorse various parental attempts to promote these values, such as private education, athletics, SAT preparation, and so on. Parents that act in the best interests of the children and have hope for their future are simply being good parents. But when does this healthy and responsible concern for a child's future interfere with the child's right to choose his own values and life plans? This is not an easy question to answer. In any case, this quandary supports my claim that GLGT and GLGE do not inherently violate a child's right to an open future. Some uses of these technologies might have this effect; others might not. The upshot of this section is that we have once again debunked several arguments that might be construed as proving that genetic enhancement is inherently wrong. It may be wrong under some circumstances, but not in others.

Eugenics

Some have attacked GLGT and GLGE on the grounds that they constitute a form of eugenics, an attempt to control the human gene pool.[69] Is eugenics inherently wrong? To understand this question, we can distinguish between positive and negative eugenics: positive eugenics attempts to increase the number of favorable or desirable genes in the human gene pool, while negative eugenics attempts to reduce the number of undesirable or harmful genes, e.g., genes that cause genetic diseases. We should also distinguish between state-sponsored and parental eugenics: under state-sponsored eugenics programs the government attempts to control the human gene pool; in parental eugenics parents exert control over the gene pool through their reproductive choices.[70]

Parental eugenics occurs every time people select mates or sperm or egg donors. Most people do not find this kind of eugenics to be as troubling as the state-sponsored eugenics programs envisioned by Aldous Huxley or implemented by Nazi Germany. Indeed, one might argue that this kind of eugenics is a morally acceptable exercise of parental rights.[71] Moreover, most parents do not make their reproductive choices with the sole aim of controlling the human gene pool; any effects these choices have on the gene pool are unintended consequences of parental actions. As long as we accept the idea that parents should be allowed to make some choices that affect the composition of the human gene pool, then parental eugenics is not inherently wrong.

But what about state-sponsored eugenics? One might argue that state-sponsored eugenics programs, such as involuntary sterilization of the mentally disabled or mandatory genetic screening, are morally wrong because they:

a. constitute unjustifiable violations of individual liberty and privacy;
b. are a form of genetic discrimination;
c. can have adverse evolutionary consequences by reducing genetic diversity; and
d. can lead us down a slippery slope toward increased racial and ethnic hatred, bias, and genocide.

Although these arguments do not prove that all forms of state-sponsored eugenics are morally wrong, they place a strong burden of proof on those who defend these programs. It is not my aim to explore state-sponsored eugenics in depth here.[72] However, even if we assume that state-sponsored eugenics is inherently wrong, this still only proves that some forms of GLGE or GLGT are inherently wrong. There is nothing inherently wrong with parental choices to use GLGE or GLGT to help children achieve health, freedom, and other values. Thus arguments that appeal to our concerns about eugenics do not prove that genetic enhancement is inherently wrong. Some forms of genetic enhancement, e.g., state-sponsored eugenics, are wrong, others are not.

Conclusion: The Significance of the Distinction

Two decades ago, James Rachels challenged the moral significance of the active–passive euthanasia distinction in a widely anthologized essay.[73] This paper has attempted to perform a similar debunking of the therapy–enhancement distinction in human genetics. It has considered and rejected a variety of different ways of arguing that the therapy–enhancement distinction in human genetics marks a solid, moral boundary. Genetic enhancement is not inherently immoral nor is genetic therapy inherently moral. Some forms of enhancement are immoral, others are not; likewise, some types of therapy are immoral, others are not. The implication of this view is that we should not use the therapy–enhancement distinction as our moral compass in human genetics. In evaluating the ethical aspects of any particular genetic intervention, we should ask not whether it is therapy or enhancement but whether the intervention poses significant risks, offers significant benefits, violates or promotes human dignity, is just or unjust, and so on.

Having said this much, I think some forms of enhancement can be morally justified, provided that

they can be shown to be safe and effective. For example, using genetic technology to protect people against diseases could be justified on the grounds that it benefits patients. I think one can even justify the use of genetics for cosmetic purposes in terms of benefits to patients. We can also view some forms of genetic therapy as unacceptable (at present) because they pose unjustifiable risks to patients or future generations. For example, all forms of GLGT and some types of SGT, such as a procedure for fighting cancer at the genetic level, are too risky, given our current scientific and technical limitations. In any case, the moral assessment of these procedures depends on considerations of probable benefits and harms (as well as other moral qualities), not on their classification as "therapy" or "enhancement."

So what is the significance of the therapy–enhancement distinction? What role should it play in thinking about the ethics of human genetics? Can it guide public policy? The most I can say in favor of the distinction is that it defines moral zones without any sharp boundaries. The significance of the distinction may lie in its ability to address our fears and hopes: we hope that genetic therapy will help us treat diseases and improve human health, but we fear that genetic enhancement will lead us down a slippery slope toward a variety of undesirable consequences, such as discrimination, bias, eugenics, injustice, biomedical harms, and so on.[74] Genetic enhancement will probably always dwell in the shadow of the slippery slope argument, while genetic therapy will probably always bask in the glory of modern medicine. Our hopes and fears may or may not be warranted; only time will tell. In the meantime, even if the therapy–enhancement distinction does not draw any solid moral boundaries, we need to be aware of the distinction in public dialogues about genetics. In these dialogues, it may be useful to address the fears of enhancement and the hopes of therapy while attempting to grapple with the realities of the genetic revolution.

Notes

1   Juengst E. Can enhancement be distinguished from prevention in genetic medicine? *Journal of Medicine and Philosophy* 1997;22:125–42.

2   Holtug N. Altering humans – the case for and against human gene therapy. *Cambridge Quarterly of Healthcare Ethics* 1997;6:157–74.

3   Berger E, Gert B. Genetic disorders and the ethical status of germ-line gene therapy. *Journal of Medicine and Philosophy* 1991;16:667–83.

4   Anderson W. Human gene therapy: scientific and ethical considerations. *Journal of Medicine and Philosophy* 1985;10:275–91.

5   Anderson W. Human gene therapy: why draw a line? *Journal of Medicine and Philosophy* 1989;14:81–93.

6   Anderson W. Genetics and human malleability. *Hastings Center Report* 1990;20(1):21–4.

7   McGee G. *The Perfect Baby*. Lanham, Md.: Rowman and Littlefield, 1997.

8   Vogel G. Genetic enhancement: from science fiction to ethics quandary. *Science* 1997;277:1753–4.

9   See note 4, Anderson 1985.

10 Fowler G, Juengst E, and Zimmerman B. Germ-line gene therapy and the clinical ethos of medical genetics. *Theoretical Medicine* 1989;19:151–7.

11 See note 3, Berger, Gert 1991.

12 Zimmerman B. Human germ-line gene therapy: the case for its development and use. *Journal of Medicine and Philosophy* 1991;16:593–612.

13 Glover J. *What Sort of People Should There Be*? New York: Penguin Books, 1984.

14 See note 7, McGee 1997.

15 Resnik D. Debunking the slippery slope argument against human germ line gene therapy. *Journal of Medicine and Philosophy* 1993;19:23–40.

16 Resnik D. Genetic engineering and social justice: a Rawlsian approach. *Social Theory and Practice* 1997; 23(3):427–48.

17 See note 3, Berger, Gert 1991.

18 See note 4, Anderson 1985.

19 See note 6, Anderson 1990.

20 Rifkin J. *Algeny*. New York: Viking Press, 1983.

21 Ramsey P. *Fabricated Man: The Ethics of Genetic Control*. New Haven: Yale University Press, 1970.

22 It is not my aim in this essay to argue that there is no distinction between therapy and enhancement; I am only attempting to question the moral significance of the distinction. If it turns out that there is not a tenable distinction between therapy and enhancement, so much the worse for the moral significance of this distinction. For the purpose of this essay I will define "enhancement" as a medical intervention that has goals other than therapeutic ones. There may be many types of enhancement on this view. Some forms of enhancement, such as a circumcision, can have therapeutic aims as well, e.g., preventing urinary tract infections. Some forms of therapy, such as heart transplantation, could have enhancement effects, e.g., a

person could acquire an above average heart. Some interventions, such as preventative medicine, could straddle the line between enhancement and therapy. For further discussion, see note 1, Juengst 1997.

23 See note 4, Anderson 1985.

24 Suzuki D, Knudtson P. *Genethics*. Cambridge, Mass.: Harvard University Press, 1989.

25 Resnik D, Langer P, Steinkraus H. *Human Germ-line Gene Therapy: Scientific, Ethical, and Political Issues*. Austin, Texas: RG Landes, 1999.

26 See note 24, Suzuki, Knudtson 1989.

27 See note 5, Anderson 1989.

28 See note 6, Anderson 1990.

29 Baird P. Altering human genes: social, ethical, and legal implications. *Perspectives in Biology and Medicine* 1994;37:566–75.

30 In the current debate in bioethics, several writers have attempted to use the concepts of health and disease to distinguish between genetic therapy and genetic enhancement.

31 See note 1, Juengst 1997.

32 See note 3, Berger, Gert 1991.

33 See note 5, Anderson 1989.

34 See note 6, Anderson 1990:24.

35 Caplan A. The concepts of health, illness, and disease. In: Veatch R, ed. *Medical Ethics*, 2nd ed. Sudbury, Mass.: Jones and Bartlett, 1997:57–74.

36 Khushf G. Expanding the horizon of reflection on health and disease. *Journal of Medicine and Philosophy* 1995;1–4.

37 Some writers distinguish between relativist and nonrelativist accounts; some others distinguish between biological and social accounts. But the basic insight is the same: the concepts of health and disease are normative or descriptive.

38 Boorse C. Health as a theoretical concept. *Philosophy of Science* 1977;44:542–73.

39 Daniels N. *Just Health Care*. Cambridge: Cambridge University Press, 1985.

40 Sigerist H. *Civilization and Disease*. Chicago: University of Chicago Press, 1943.

41 Pellegrino, ED, Thomasma, DC. *For the Patient's Good*. New York: Oxford University Press, 1988.

42 For an overview of the normative approach, see Caplan A. *Moral Matters*. New York: John Wiley and Sons, 1995.

43 Culver C, Gert B. *Philosophy in Medicine*. New York: Oxford University Press, 1982.

44 Lennox J. Health as an objective value. *Journal of Medicine and Philosophy* 1995;20:501–11.

45 See note 44, Lennox 1995.

46   Culver K. The current status of gene therapy research. *The Genetic Resource* 1993;7:5–10.

47   See note 25, Resnik, Langer, Steinkraus 1999.

48   English J. Abortion and the concept of a person. *Canadian Journal of Philosophy* 1975;5(2):233–43.

49   It is possible to define "human" in such a way that it is logically impossible to change our humanness. If we stipulate that possession of a single property is a necessary and sufficient condition for being human, then any changes we make in that property would result in people that are not human. For example, we can define "triangle" = "three-sided object." If me make an object that has four sides, it is not an altered triangle; it is not a triangle at all. For a definition of humanness that would seem to imply that it is difficult (though not impossible) to alter our humanness, see Anderson W. Genetic engineering and our humanness. *Human Gene Therapy* 1994;5:755–60.

50   See note 25, Resnik, Langer, Steinkraus 1999.

51   For the purposes of this essay, I will not attribute this view to any particular author, since I think it deserves consideration on its own merit. For writers who come close to defending this view, see note 8, Vogel 1997, as well as Kass L. *Toward a More Natural Science.* New York: Free Press, 1985.

52   See note 20, Rifkin 1983.

53   These arguments do not address genetic enhancement per se, since they also apply to GLGT and they do not apply to SGT or SGE.

54   See note 25, Resnik, Langer, Steinkraus 1999.

55   See note 21, Ramsey 1970.

56   Cole-Turner, R. Genes, religion, and society: the developing views of the churches. *Science and Engineering Ethics* 1997;3(3):273–88.

57   National Council of Churches. *Human Life and the New Genetics.* New York: National Council of Churches of Christ in the U.S.A., 1980.

58   National Council of Churches. *Genetic Engineering: Social and Ethical Consequences.* New York: National Council of Churches of Christ in the U.S.A., 1983.

59   Peters, T. *Playing God?: Genetic Determinism and Human Freedom.* New York: Routledge, 1997.

60   For further discussion see Buchanan A, Brock D. *Deciding for Others.* Cambridge: Cambridge University Press, 1989.

61   Lappé, M. Ethical issues in manipulating the human germ line. *Journal of Medicine and Philosophy* 1991;16: 621–39.

62   Commission of the European Community. *Adopting a Specific Research and Technological Development Programme in the Field of Health.* Brussels: Commission of the European Community, 1989.

63   Davis D. Genetic dilemmas and the child's right to an open future. *Hastings Center Report* 1997;27(2): 7–15.

64   These arguments do not constitute an objection to SGT or SGE.

65   See note 25, Resnik, Langer, Steinkraus 1999.

66   Feinberg J. *Social Philosophy.* Englewood Cliffs, N.J.: Prentice-Hall, 1973.

67   Feinberg J. The child's right to an open future. In: Aiken W and Lafollette H, eds. *Whose Child? Children's Rights, Parental Authority, and State Power.* Totowa, N.J.: Littlefield, Adam, 1980:124–53.

68   See note 7, McGee 1997.

69   For further discussion of eugenics, see Paul D. *Controlling Human Heredity: 1865 to the Present.* Atlantic Highlands, N.J.: Humanities Press International, 1995.

70   Kitcher P. *The Lives to Come.* New York: Simon and Schuster, 1997.

71   Robertson J. *Children of Choice.* Princeton, N.J.: Princeton University Press, 1994.

72   For further discussion, see Parens E. Taking behavioral genetics seriously. *Hastings Center Report* 1996;26(4): 13–18.

73   Rachels J. Active and passive euthanasia. *New England Journal of Medicine* 1975;292(2):78–80.

74   See note 15, Resnik 1993.

19

Should We Undertake Genetic Research on Intelligence?

Ainsley Newson and Robert Williamson

Introduction

Throughout this century, intelligence has been the subject of intense debate, including the extent to which it is inherited, the significance that differences in social, educational and economic environments contribute to a person's intelligence, and whether the differences in intelligence levels between ethnic groups are genetically determined. This debate surrounding intelligence has sharpened in the light of emerging efforts to identify genes for high intelligence.

The First Hurdle – What Is Intelligence?

Although intelligence is held in high regard by both individuals and societies, and is clearly an inherent part of the conception we have of ourselves, a succinct description of intelligence is not easy to enunciate. The intangibility of intelligence has generated intense controversy, which occurs at three broad levels: general debate surrounding its definition, debate about the measurement and quantification of intelligence,[1] and debate surrounding the existence of a general intelligence factor.[2] The argument around these issues has increased opposition to the determination of the genetic basis of intelligence.

For the purposes of this discussion the following definition of intelligence will be accepted:

> [intelligence is] a very general mental capability that, among other things, involves the ability to reason, plan, solve problems, think abstractly, comprehend complex ideas, learn quickly and learn from experience…it reflects a broader and deeper capability for comprehending our surroundings.[3]

From this definition, it is important to note that 'intelligent' behaviour will vary to some extent with the environment, and that intelligence will not necessarily remain constant throughout life for a given individual.

What Is Currently Known about the Genetics of Intelligence?

Francis Galton first suggested that intelligence was heritable in his 1869 study *Hereditary Genius*, in which he developed the first statistical tools of behavioural genetics. Galton held the determinist belief that intelligence was dependent completely on chromosomal inheritance. He is now referred to as 'the father of eugenics', as he advocated selective breeding programs to increase the quality of human 'stock'.

Original publication details: Ainsley Newson and Robert Williamson, "Should We Undertake Genetic Research on Intelligence?," pp. 327–42 from *Bioethics* 13: 3/4 (1999). Reproduced with permission from John Wiley & Sons.

After the atrocities in Nazi Germany, environmentalism emerged to declare that all people, irrespective of class, race or gender were genetically equal with respect to intelligence. However, the doctrine of determinism again emerged with the advent of behavioural genetic studies in the 1950s, which aimed to investigate the heritable aspect of intelligence statistically. The continuing debate between determinism and environmentalism has been termed the 'Nature–Nurture' controversy.

Most observers would now agree that both genes and the environment have an effect on intelligence, although the relative contributions of these (if it is possible to separate them) have not been conclusively determined. The current model for intelligence proposes that within a particular population there will be many intelligence genes, and a significant environmental impact. Different 'versions' of each of these intelligence genes (termed alleles) will contribute either to raising or lowering the intelligence levels of individuals within that population. We expect different people with average IQ scores to have different combinations of these alleles. Persons with mental retardation might have disastrous

mutations causing dysfunction of one of the genes (as for the liver cholesterol receptor in the case of coronary artery disease). This model predicts the classic 'bell curve' distribution of intelligence seen in populations (Figure 19.1), and implies that the inheritance of intelligence is *probabilistic*, with any single gene involved neither necessary nor sufficient to determine intelligence. Genes determine only the *likelihood* of a particular intelligence level, they do not pre-determine intelligence.[4]

Behavioural Genetic Studies of Intelligence

Formal behavioural genetic (quantitative) studies of intelligence have been used for over 40 years to attempt to demonstrate that intelligence has a heritable component. Although subjected to harsh criticism,[5] these studies statistically apportion the contribution of genes and environment to differences in intelligence (as measured by psychometric tests). The genetic contribution within a particular population at a particular time is termed 'heritability'.

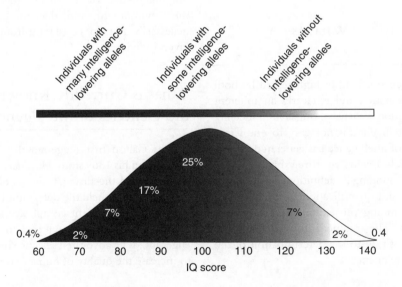

Figure 19.1 The Normative Distribution of IQ scores within a large population. IQ scores are shown, and it can be seen that most of the population is of average intelligence, with few people having very low or very high intelligence. Clearly a single gene cannot provide this distribution. Source: Diagram adapted from Plomin, R., and J. C. Defries. The Genetics of Cognitive Abilities and Disabilities. *Scientific American* 278.5 (1998): 62–69.

Heritability expresses the genetic contribution to intelligence as a percentage of the overall population variation in intelligence. The behavioural genetic approach does not identify specific genes involved in intelligence, nor does it stipulate the contribution of genes to an individual's intelligence.

The combined results of behavioural genetic studies state the heritability of intelligence in a particular population as approximately or somewhat greater than 50%.[6] This technique quantifies differences between people (and therefore indicates that 50% of the differences *between people* are due to genetic differences); the intrinsic contribution of genetics to intelligence in an individual might be more or less than 50%.

Molecular Genetic Studies of Intelligence

As behavioural techniques have been unable to determine categorically the aetiology of intelligence, researchers are now using molecular genetic approaches to attempt to identify and characterise genes that underlie the biological mechanisms of intelligence.[7] The project is attempting to localise several Quantitative Trait Loci (QTLs) for high intelligence.

The technique being used to identify intelligence QTLs is 'allelic association', a statistical tool that tests whether one of a number of alleles of a particular DNA sequence (marker) occurs at a higher frequency in children with high intelligence than low intelligence. A difference in the allele frequency of a DNA marker between the two populations could indicate the presence of an intelligence gene in the region of the marker. Presently this approach is being used to examine markers on human chromosomes 6 and 4. Although this technique is based on DNA sequence analysis, any association found will rely on a statistical correlation for the particular group under investigation, and will have limited applicability to individuals within that population, or to other populations.

The first DNA sequence associated with high intelligence was announced in 1998,[8] and codes for the hormone receptor gene *Igf2r*. The gene has been predicted to have a small effect, contributing to about 2% (or 4 IQ points) to the total variation in intelligence. However this is still a preliminary result and requires further research.

Molecular genetic studies of intelligence have been criticised because researchers are seeking genes for high intelligence, rather than low intelligence (which is thought to have a higher heritability[9]). Researchers have defended this position by stating that by studying high intelligence, there is a greater chance of a bona fide discovery, as there will be less chance of other factors such as detrimental environment interfering with results.

The identification of intelligence genes is still in its initial stages. However, the scientists involved believe that this research will lead to the identification of genes for intelligence, an understanding of the significance of each gene to intelligence in the population under investigation, and a more general understanding of cognitive pathways.

Should Genetic Research into Intelligence Be Done?

Although the scientists involved in this research believe that ethical issues can be overcome,[10] the research has been subjected to ethical criticisms. Here we unpack the arguments that have been raised against the research. We argue that they are inconsistent with social and legal norms concerning individual rights, and we show that the force of many can be diminished by an analysis of scientific misconceptions that are made. Furthermore, if justifications by the researchers are addressed, a claim for the moral requirement of this research can be made out.

Objections to the development of genetic testing

The overriding claim in the ethical criticisms of this research is that the genetic information obtained will be used to divide, disadvantage and disempower people, through the development of genetic tests.[11] Is this potential consequence of genetic testing for intelligence of enough concern to prevent genetic research of intelligence?

The objections to genetic testing for intelligence can be grouped into two broad classes. The first is that of claims relative to individual harm and the second concerns social harm to groups. The objection to genetic testing of intelligence based on individual harm claims that genetic information about intelligence will cause psychological injury. As genetic information has an important role in a person's self-perception, people will use this 'genetic label' as an indication of their capabilities. This information could alter intellectual performance, as has been shown with psychological studies involving negative reinforcement of intellectual ability.[12]

This objection falls because genetic tests, if it were possible to apply them, would be *less efficient* at predicting intelligence than current IQ tests. The only difference between these two is that genetic tests may be used predictively. However, currently the best way to predict IQ is to average the IQ of the parents.[13] Therefore if genetic testing should be banned, we would also have to ban IQ testing. Although we are not claiming here that IQ tests are not controversial, most educators would pronounce this a counter-intuitive action. IQ tests were developed to help those who most need educational intervention, and their benefits are well documented.

Objections to the development of genetic testing on the basis of social harm claim that genetic testing will cause 'geneticism',[14] the judging of people exclusively as products of their genes, with a consequential limitation on group opportunity and the creation of a new 'eugenics'. We classify these potential harms into four overlapping classes: family harm, harm to individuals in a social context, group harm and eugenic harm.

Firstly the claim that genetic information about intelligence will harm a supportive family environment states that this information will detrimentally influence parental expectations of their children and allow for 'genetic blame' in parenting.

Secondly in addition to the proposed psychological harm resulting from genetic information, individuals could also suffer discrimination within a societal context. Obvious cases where this may occur are in the educational (in the case of children) and workplace (in the case of adults) arenas, where those with no alleles for high intelligence may be denied opportunities.

Thirdly, genetic information generated from testing different racial or socioeconomic groups could be used in assessments of individual and group potential, at the expense of considerations of other important social factors. Genetic information concerning intelligence could also be used to assert the 'supremacy' of one ethnic or socioeconomic group over another.[15]

Perhaps a more fundamental objection to this research (and in fact much behavioural genetic research) is that the availability of genetic information will justify the creation of a new 'eugenics', where people are not allowed to be born on the basis of predictive genetic tests, or are subject to compulsory treatment.[16] This will be a particularly cogent objection if research defines genetic causes leading to an IQ of less than 80 (used to define mild mental retardation), a group who are not currently subject to discrimination.

These objections do have some significance, but we do not consider that these claims warrant the prohibition of genetic research into intelligence.

Primarily it is the role of the State to protect the rights of individuals and groups from discrimination. The State accepts this responsibility and has enacted many anti-discrimination statutes, which would apply in this situation. In addition, it can reasonably be assumed that testing would not be compulsory, and would only be used if it held some benefit for the person concerned.

Furthermore, the critics overstate the potential for the development of predictive genetic tests for intelligence. Due to the large number of genes involved, and a significant environmental impact, any single gene will have only a small contribution to overall intelligence, rendering the development of genetic tests improbable.[17] Moreover, the scientists claim that this research is not designed to replace existing intelligence testing and educational procedures.[18]

Additionally, the claims about genetic testing for intelligence perpetuate some misconceptions about behavioural genetics research. The first of these is the application of genetic information between groups. Genetic research will identify genes that contribute to differences within a particular group. These genes may not affect the differences between groups, and the same gene may have an altered significance in a different population. Therefore the applicability of results outside the group from which they were obtained (whether it be different in socioeconomic status, race, age or gender) will be difficult.

A second misconception concerns the application of group measurements to individuals. Just as behavioural genetic information cannot be applied between groups, neither can it be applied directly to any individual. A gene that functions to determine the range of intelligence for a group may have no significance for an individual within that group.

Thirdly, several of the objections assume that intelligence will be genetically determined or immutable. That intelligence has a genetic component does not imply genetic determinism. The genetic effect may be altered by other genes, or environmental interventions.

Objections concerning the allocation of resources to this research

This objection contends that valuable public research funding should not be allocated to determine the genetic basis of a non-pathogenic entity such as intelligence. The information from the study has a limited potential for beneficence (as many of the results will be population-specific) and the potential for individual and group harm should preclude this.

We accept that objections of this nature do have some force within a distributive justice framework. However, these claims do not override the prerogative to perform this research, and their significance can be diminished by two counter-claims. Firstly, the amount of funding for this research has to be compared with the costs that learning disabilities generate for taxpayers; in America alone this is more than $5 billion annually. The potential for this research to limit this large cost must be considered.

Secondly, even in the absence of tangible benefits from the initial research results, it could be claimed that it would be better to obtain information about our intelligence than to defer to pseudo-biology or speculation for information. Indeed, some have claimed that we have a duty to impart this knowledge,[19] which can then be used to inform social policy fairly and honestly.

Therefore, we argue that the force of the objections made against genetic research on intelligence is lessened in light of the protection of rights, the potential value of the information and the improbability of genetic tests of high accuracy being developed. We claim that this research is ethically permissible. Moreover, this research may be morally required, in light of the potential to delineate how genes interact with neural, psychological and environmental processes during cognitive development. This will allow the creation of significant interventions to optimise the potential of all children.

What Should We Do with the Results of This Research?

Once genes and pathways involved in cognitive ability are delineated, therapeutic interventions to increase intelligence may be developed. One such intervention could use gene therapy technologies to alter the DNA of existing or future people. This will require knowledge of the major alleles for high intelligence, as well as precise DNA recombination tools. The technology may be utilised to prevent and treat low intellectual capacity,[20] but the same therapies could be given to those with 'normal' intellectual function.

In this final section, we will discuss the issue of enhancement of intelligence of future people, and will claim that a categorical rejection of this technology will be very difficult. We will highlight the problems in several objections raised thus far, and suggest that there is no intrinsic difference between different means of increasing intelligence. Therefore genetic enhancement does not require a higher ethical standard than that which is currently used in distributing medical treatments or goods within a just society. However, we are not advocating that this technology should replace traditional interventions to optimise intelligence, nor that this genetic technology should take precedence over other important medical procedures.

This discussion makes the assumption that the enhancement procedure will not entail any risk greater than that encountered with minor medical procedures. We will also assume that the motivation of parents behind the use of this technology is to improve the quality of life for their children, and is not motivated by overbearingness or calculativeness.[21] However, we recognise that the ethical acceptability of genetic enhancement technology may in fact be different between a framework managed by the State and one where the technology is available in a free market.

There are several general objections to genetic enhancement. The first is that genetic enhancement is *against nature*.[22] This claims that we should not use unnatural means to achieve natural ends. A related objection is that genetic enhancement is *playing God*,[23] which contends that actions that are playing God can lead to unpredictable and disastrous circumstances. However, every medical intervention is 'against nature', and all serious interventions involving life and death, or reproduction, can be regarded as 'playing God'; there is no reason to single out genetic enhancement.

Genetic enhancement might be construed as an extension of pre-implantation screening. Here, if all other things are equal, if a sub-set of embryos had a higher genetic intellectual potential than others, the logical choice would be to choose these embryos for implantation.[24] Surely this is justified, because it would be unethical to choose to implant embryos which are known to be of lower genetic intellectual potential?

Genetic enhancements are also discounted by appeals to a *treatment/enhancement distinction*,[25] which states that gene therapy which alleviates disease can be distinguished from that which enhances, and that the 'line' between them should not be crossed. However, there are many contexts where this distinction is already blurred, such as plastic surgery for a disfigurement or growth hormone treatment for genetic dwarfism. Mothers are already urged to forgo alcohol and tobacco during pregnancy because of adverse effects on the fetus, including future intelligence. We will not discuss these objections further, as they have been well reviewed in the literature.

Following is a discussion of other potential ethical problems in genetic enhancement. We have classified them into two groups – the genetic enhancement of individuals, and the potential social effects of genetic enhancement.

The genetic enhancement of individuals

There are two main arguments against the genetic enhancement of the intellectual potential of future individuals. The first is that genetic enhancement will adversely affect the sense of personal identity of future persons, causing them psychological harm. This does not concern the traditional philosophical questions of identity, as they 'may not be the questions that trouble an individual who discovers that her parents had an extra gene or genes added. [Rather,] she may suffer from…an "identity crisis", concerned with who she is, where she's coming from, and where she is going'.[26]

However, can it seriously be claimed that children will regret that parents had made them more intelligent? Increasing the intellectual potential of the future person will actually offer the future child the opportunity for an enhanced quality of life. Moreover, by studying a parallel case such as the psychological outcome of children from donor insemination clinics, where the parents can choose certain traits for their future children, there is no evidence that the children have suffered adverse psychological harm.[27] The child chosen in this way appears to have no altered feelings of self-worth, and there is no substantial reason to suggest that genetic enhancement will be any different.

The second objection is that the genetic enhancement of intelligence will force parental preconceptions onto the child, thus reducing their autonomy.

A response to this objection is that the genetic direction of a capacity such as intelligence is not morally different to other commonly acceptable child-rearing methods. Parents consistently influence their children (both before and after they are born) and make decisions for them in their best interests.[28] The genetic enhancement of intelligence will not undermine autonomy any more than current methods of child rearing, including parental choice of a child's school, hobbies or sports. A child with enhanced intelligence will still be free to form their own life plan, at least to the same extent that they can as children being reared without genetic enhancement.

The potential social effects of enhancement

The objections to genetic enhancement of intelligence in a social context can be grouped into three classes. The first is the claim that genetic enhancement creates unfairness in society.[29] It states that genetic enhancement will give some people or groups of people an unfair advantage over others, because some groups may wish to use the technology but be unable to afford it. This will deny future people fair equality of opportunity, and will increase the division between privileged and underprivileged groups in society.

A response to this claim is that we have been achieving the goal of optimising intelligence,[30] but by using other morally acceptable means (such as a private education[31]), for centuries. Those who object to enhancement would also have to object to private education, which few do. Interventions into a person's environment can cause as profound an alteration to that person's life as a genetic alteration. Why should there be a higher ethical standard for genetic enhancement than other intelligence optimisation methods? Moreover, delineating a difference between changing a person's genes and changing their environment will be very difficult, given the large interaction between them.

The second claim is that genetic enhancement of intelligence will justify or exacerbate negative value judgements about the quality of life of existing people with learning disabilities or mental retardation, and will devalue them as persons.[32]

We accept that it cannot be categorically demonstrated that having a learning disability is objectively bad. However, psychological studies have shown that people with learning disabilities *in general* suffer more psychological harm than those without disability,[33] and we believe that this would still occur even in the absence of negative societal judgements. Additionally, wanting to prevent learning disabilities and mental retardation does not entail that people with these conditions have less moral status than those who do not; many persons with disability are active in attempting to prevent disability occurring in others.

The third and most compelling claim is that genetic enhancement will create a Prisoner's Dilemma, where, despite the individual advantages of genetic enhancement, a large social cost will result, and genetic enhancement should therefore not be performed by anyone. Assuming that everyone can have access to this technology, what could be the social costs of being more intelligent?

Gregory Kavka[34] has raised four general claims about the social costs of enhancement. Two of his claims have significance for this discussion.

The first of these claims is that genetic enhancement will cause an imbalance of the desirable distribution of the characteristic in the population, thus upsetting delicate social balances.

However, arguably society would benefit from having more people who are more intelligent – everyone would be functioning at a higher level and productivity would increase. This is a favourable situation when compared to a society where people are worse off than they could be.

Kavka's second concern is that if everyone were to be enhanced, competitiveness will also increase, such that no-one will be better off than they were prior to enhancement. The distribution of goods (such as a place at University) will become more difficult, as more people will be aiming to utilise the same amount of resources.

This claim does not show that collectively we will be *worse off* if enhancement is introduced. If intelligence were to be optimised by using genetic means in addition to current means, it is likely that productivity will increase and resource generation will result, to make society better off collectively.

Another potential claim is that if genetic enhancement of intelligence were introduced, the value of intelligence as a competitive good would decrease. The paradigm of enhancement of intelligence would be viewed in much the same way as that of drug use in sport,[35] whereby acts by people who have enhanced their performance are devalued.

Can we extrapolate from sport to intelligence? Intelligence is arguably an unconditional good for the life of a person, and, unlike sport, is not an entity where one person's 'win' implies loss for others. Rather, we can appeal to a situation such as an artist's colony, composed of a large group of people with similar talents.[36] Here art flourishes. Each individual can pursue their own end, and new techniques prosper.

Overall, the optimisation of intelligence is ethically acceptable, and indeed morally demanded in Western society, as long as the processes to achieve this do not impose social harms. Providing that a genetic means to optimise intelligence of individuals and social groups is not viewed as a deterministic and singular mechanism with which to optimise intelligence, it will not be ethically problematic. However, in the process of optimising intelligence, we must ensure that the value of different intelligent behaviours in different contexts is respected, and that intelligence is not the only means employed in valuing people.

merely a different means (equivalent to that of environmental enhancements) to achieving a socially required goal – that of optimising intelligence within the community.

Conclusion

In this paper we have reviewed the debate surrounding genetic research on intelligence, and have argued that the objections raised to date do not serve to reject it categorically. We have appealed to the current practices of IQ testing and the State protection of rights and interests, as well as outlining some of the misconceptions the objections make about the research.

We have then argued that genetic enhancement cannot be categorically defeated within a system of fair allocation, by arguing that genetic enhancement is

Acknowledgments

The authors would like to acknowledge Associate Professor Julian Savulescu, for advice on earlier drafts of this manuscript and for beneficial discussions. Numerous ideas concerning genetic enhancement emerged from discussions with Dr David McCarthy. Additionally, the authors would like to thank Dr Darren Shickle and Dr Daniel Wikler for comments resulting from the presentation of this paper at the IAB4 conference.

Notes

1　The validity of intelligence tests is often questioned. For examples of criticisms, see: Maddox, J., 'Genetics and hereditable IQ', *Nature*, 309 (1984), p. 579, and Gould, S.J., *The mismeasure of man* (New York, Norton, 1996).

2　See, for example, Gardner, H., *Frames of mind: the theory of multiple intelligences*, 2nd edn (London, Fontana, 1993).

3　Gottfredson, L.S., 'Mainstream Science on Intelligence: An Editorial with 52 Signatories, History and Bibliography', *Intelligence*, 24 (1997), pp. 13–23. For a general review see Sternberg, R.J., 'The Concept of Intelligence and Its Role in Lifelong Learning and Success', *Am Psych*, 52 (1997), pp. 1030–1037.

4　Plomin, R., 'Identifying genes for cognitive abilities and disabilities', in *Intelligence, heredity and environment*, ed R.J. Sternberg and E. Grigorenko (Cambridge, Cambridge University Press, 1997), pp. 89–104, p. 95.

5　For criticism, see Bailey, R.C., 'Hereditarian scientific fallacies', *Genetica*, 99 (1997), pp. 125–33.

6　Chipeur, H.M., M.J. Rovine, and R. Plomin, 'LISREL modelling: Genetic and environmental influences on IQ revisited', *Intelligence*, 14 (1990), pp. 11–29.

7　Plomin, R., et al, 'DNA markers associated with high versus low IQ: the IQ Quantitative Trait Loci (QTL) Project', *Behav Genet*, 24 (1994), pp. 107–18.

8　Chorney, M.J., et al, 'A Quantitative Trait Locus associated with Cognitive Ability in Children', *Psychological Science*, 9 (1998), pp. 159–166.

9　Bailey, J.M., and W. Revelle, 'Increased heritability for lower IQ levels?', *Behav Genet* 21 (1991), pp. 397–404; and Detterman, D.K., L.A. Thompson, and R. Plomin, 'Differences in heritability across groups differing in ability', *Behav Genet*, 20 (1990), pp. 369–384.

10　Daniels, J., P. McGuffin, and M. Owen, 'Molecular genetic research on IQ: can it be done? Should it be done?', *J Biosoc Sci*, 28 (1996), pp. 491–507, and Vines, G., 'The search for the clever stuff', *The Guardian* (1996 Feb 1), pp. 2–3.

11　Dr John Kihlstrom, a prominent American psychologist, has already suggested the development of a genetic test in light of the recent research findings. See Ewing, T., 'Brilliant Genes are Showing', *The Age (Melbourne)* (1998, May 21), p. 21.

12　See Sutherland, A., and M.L. Goldschmid, 'Negative Teacher Expectation and IQ Change in Children with Superior Intellectual Potential', *Child Dev*, 45 (1974), pp. 852–856; and Steele, C.M., 'A Threat in the Air – How Stereotypes Shape Intellectual Identity and Performance', *Am Psychol*, 52 (1997), pp. 613–629.

13　Plomin, R., et al., 'Variability and stability in cognitive abilities are largely genetic later in life', *Behav Genet*, 24 (1994), pp. 207–15.

14　Chadwick, R.F., 'The Perfect Baby: An Introduction', in *Ethics, Reproduction and Genetic Control*, ed Chadwick, R.F. (London, Routledge, 1992), pp. 93–135 esp pp. 105–107.

15 Differences in IQ scores between ethnic groups have been used as a premise for the domination of one ethnic group by another. See Herrnstein, R.J., and C. Murray, *The bell curve: intelligence and class structure in American life* (New York, Free Press, 1994).

16 Goodey, C., 'Genetic Markers for Intelligence', *Bulletin of Medical Ethics*, 126 (1996, Aug), pp. 13–16.

17 Plomin, R., 'Identifying genes for cognitive abilities and disabilities', p. 100.

18 Plomin, R., and I. Craig, 'Human behavioural genetics of cognitive abilities and disabilities', *Bioessays* 19 (1997), pp. 1117–24.

19 Eysenck, H.J, 'The Intelligence Controversy: The Ethical Problem', in *Ethical Issues in Scientific Research: An Anthology*, ed E. Erwin, S. Gendin and L. Kleinman (New York, Garland, 1994), pp. 371–375.

20 Indeed, this has been offered as a justification of the research, to prevent those with genetic risk (say, for example, for a learning disability) from suffering. See Plomin and Craig, 'Human behavioural genetics of cognitive abilities and disabilities'.

21 For a discussion of questionable motivations of parents behind genetic interventions, see McGee, G., 'Parenting in an Era of Genetics', *The Hastings Center Report*, 27.2 (1997), pp. 16–22.

22 Reviewed in Engelhardt, H.T. Jr., 'Human Nature Technologically Revisited', *Social Philosophy and Policy* 8 (1990), pp. 180–191; and Häyry, M., 'Categorical Objections to genetic engineering – a critique', in *Ethics and Biotechnology*, ed A. Dyson and J. Harris (London, Routledge, 1994), pp. 202–215.

23 See, for example, Chadwick, R.F., 'Playing God', *Bioethics News*, 9.4 (1990), pp. 38–46.

24 This has been discussed by John Harris with respect to disability – see Harris, J., 'Is gene therapy a form of eugenics?', *Bioethics*, 7 (1993), pp. 178–187, esp p. 179.

25 For a critique, see Jeungst, E., 'Can Enhancement Be Distinguished from Prevention in Genetic Medicine?', *J Med Philos*, 22 (1997), pp. 125–42.

26 Chadwick, R.F., 'The Perfect Baby: An Introduction', p. 126.

27 See, for example, Brewaeys, A., 'Donor insemination, the impact on family and child development', *J Psychosom Obstet Gynaecol* 17 (1996), pp. 1–13, and Golombok, R.S., et al., 'Families created by the new reproductive technologies: quality of parenting and social and emotional development of the children', *Child Dev*, 66 (1995), pp. 285–98, and Kovaks, G.T., et al., 'A controlled study of the psycho-social development of children conceived following insemination with donor semen', *Hum Reprod*, 8 (1993), pp. 788–90.

28 See, for example, McGee, G., 'Parenting in an Era of Genetics'.

29 See, for example, Kavka, G.S., 'Upside Risks – social consequences of beneficial biotechnology', in *Are genes us?: the social consequences of the new genetics*, ed. C.F. Cranor (New Brunswick, Rutgers University Press, 1994), pp. 155–179, and Holm, S., 'Genetic engineering and the north–south divide', *Ethics and Biotechnology*, ed. Dyson, A. and Harris, J. (London, Routledge, 1994), pp. 47–63.

30 Which we assume is a moral requirement of society.

31 Harris, J., *Wonderwoman and Superman – the ethics of human biotechnology* (Oxford, Oxford University Press, 1992), pp. 140–142.

32 Goodey, C., 'Genetic Markers for Intelligence'.

33 See, for example, Konstantareas, M.M., and S. Homatidis., 'Self-image and people with learning disabilities', *Br J Nurs*, 6 (1997), pp. 99–102.

34 Kavka, G.S., 'Upside Risks – social consequences of beneficial biotechnology'.

35 Parens, E., 'The goodness of fragility: on the prospect of genetic technologies aimed at the enhancement of human capabilities', *Kennedy Institute of Ethics Journal*, 5 (1995), pp. 141–153.

36 Savulescu, J. Personal Communication, October 28, 1998.

20

In Defense of Posthuman Dignity

Nick Bostrom

Transhumanists vs. Bioconservatives

Transhumanism is a loosely defined movement that has developed gradually over the past two decades, and can be viewed as an outgrowth of secular humanism and the Enlightenment. It holds that current human nature is improvable through the use of applied science and other rational methods, which may make it possible to increase human health-span, extend our intellectual and physical capacities, and give us increased control over our own mental states and moods.[1] Technologies of concern include not only current ones, like genetic engineering and information technology, but also anticipated future developments such as fully immersive virtual reality, machine-phase nanotechnology, and artificial intelligence.

Transhumanists promote the view that human enhancement technologies should be made widely available, and that individuals should have broad discretion over which of these technologies to apply to themselves (morphological freedom), and that parents should normally get to decide which reproductive technologies to use when having children (reproductive freedom).[2] Transhumanists believe that, while there are hazards that need to be identified and avoided, human enhancement technologies will offer enormous potential for deeply valuable and humanly beneficial uses. Ultimately, it is possible that such enhancements may make us, or our descendants, 'posthuman', beings who may have indefinite health-spans, much greater intellectual faculties than any current human being – and perhaps entirely new sensibilities or modalities – as well as the ability to control their own emotions. The wisest approach *vis-à-vis* these prospects, argue transhumanists, is to embrace technological progress, while strongly defending human rights and individual choice, and taking action specifically against concrete threats, such as military or terrorist abuse of bioweapons, and against unwanted environmental or social side-effects.

In opposition to this transhumanist view stands a bioconservative camp that argues against the use of technology to modify human nature. Prominent bioconservative writers include Leon Kass, Francis Fukuyama, George Annas, Wesley Smith, Jeremy Rifkin, and Bill McKibben. One of the central concerns of the bioconservatives is that human enhancement technologies might be 'dehumanizing'. The worry, which has been variously expressed, is that these technologies might undermine our human dignity or inadvertently erode something that is deeply valuable about being human but that is difficult to put into words or to factor into a cost-benefit analysis. In some cases (for example, Leon Kass) the unease seems

Original publication details: Nick Bostrom, "In Defense of Posthuman Dignity," pp 202–14 from *Bioethics* 19: 3 (2005).
Reproduced with permission from John Wiley & Sons.

Bioethics: An Anthology, Third Edition. Edited by Helga Kuhse, Udo Schüklenk, and Peter Singer.

to derive from religious or crypto-religious sentiments, whereas for others (for example, Francis Fukuyama) it stems from secular grounds. The best approach, these bioconservatives argue, is to implement global bans on swathes of promising human enhancement technologies to forestall a slide down a slippery slope towards an ultimately debased, posthuman state.

While any brief description necessarily skirts significant nuances that differentiate between the writers within the two camps, I believe the above characterization nevertheless highlights a principal fault line in one of the great debates of our times: how we should look at the future of humankind and whether we should attempt to use technology to make ourselves 'more than human'. This paper will distinguish two common fears about the posthuman and argue that they are partly unfounded and that, to the extent that they correspond to real risks, there are better responses than trying to implement broad bans on technology. I will make some remarks on the concept of dignity, which bioconservatives believe to be imperiled by coming human enhancement technologies, and suggest that we need to recognize that not only humans in their current form, but posthumans too could have dignity.

Two Fears about the Posthuman

The prospect of posthumanity is feared for at least two reasons. One is that the state of being posthuman might in itself be degrading, so that by becoming posthuman we might be harming ourselves. Another is that posthumans might pose a threat to 'ordinary' humans. (I shall set aside a third possible reason, that the development of posthumans might offend some supernatural being.)

The most prominent bioethicist to focus on the first fear is Leon Kass:

> Most of the given bestowals of nature have their given species-specified natures: they are each and all of a given *sort*. Cockroaches and humans are equally bestowed but differently natured. To turn a man into a cockroach – as we don't need Kafka to show us – would be dehumanizing. To try to turn a man into more than a man might be so as well. We need more than generalized appreciation for nature's gifts. We need a particular regard and respect for the special gift that is our own given nature ...[3]

Transhumanists counter that nature's gifts are sometimes poisoned and should not always be accepted. Cancer, malaria, dementia, aging, starvation, unnecessary suffering, and cognitive shortcomings are all among the presents that we would wisely refuse. Our own species-specified natures are a rich source of much of the thoroughly unrespectable and unacceptable – susceptibility for disease, murder, rape, genocide, cheating, torture, racism. The horrors of nature in general, and of our own nature in particular, are so well documented[4] that it is astonishing that somebody as distinguished as Leon Kass should still in this day and age be tempted to rely on the natural as a guide as to what is desirable or normatively right. We should be grateful that our ancestors were not swept away by the Kassian sentiment, or we would still be picking lice off each other's backs. Rather than deferring to the natural order, transhumanists maintain that we can legitimately reform ourselves and our natures in accordance with humane values and personal aspirations.

If one rejects nature as a general criterion of the good, as most thoughtful people nowadays do, one can of course still acknowledge that particular ways of modifying human nature would be debasing. Not all change is progress. Not even all well-intentioned technological intervention in human nature would be on balance beneficial. Kass goes far beyond these truisms, however, when he declares that utter dehumanization lies in store for us as the inevitable result of our obtaining technical mastery over our own nature:

> The final technical conquest of his own nature would almost certainly leave mankind utterly enfeebled. This form of mastery would be identical with utter dehumanization. Read Huxley's *Brave New World*, read C. S. Lewis's *Abolition of Man*, read Nietzsche's account of the last man, and then read the newspapers. Homogenization, mediocrity, pacification, drug-induced contentment, debasement of taste, souls without loves and longings – these are the inevitable results of making the essence of human nature the last project of technical mastery. In his moment of triumph, Promethean man will become a contented cow.[5]

The fictional inhabitants of *Brave New World*, to pick the best known of Kass's examples, are admittedly short on dignity (in at least one sense of the word). But the claim that this is the *inevitable* consequence of our obtaining technological mastery over human nature is exceedingly pessimistic – and unsupported – if understood as a futuristic prediction, and false if construed as a claim about metaphysical necessity.

There are many things wrong with the fictional society that Huxley described. It is static, totalitarian, caste-bound; its culture is a wasteland. The brave new worlders themselves are a dehumanized and undignified lot. Yet posthumans they are not. Their capacities are not super-human but in many respects substantially inferior to our own. Their life expectancy and physique are quite normal, but their intellectual, emotional, moral, and spiritual faculties are stunted. The majority of the brave new worlders have various degrees of engineered mental retardation. And everyone, save the ten world controllers (along with a miscellany of primitives and social outcasts who are confined to fenced preservations or isolated islands), are barred or discouraged from developing individuality, independent thinking, and initiative, and are conditioned not to desire these traits in the first place. *Brave New World* is not a tale of human enhancement gone amok, but is rather a tragedy of technology and social engineering being deliberately used to cripple moral and intellectual capacities – the exact antithesis of the transhumanist proposal.

Transhumanists argue that the best way to avoid a *Brave New World* is by vigorously defending morphological and reproductive freedoms against any would-be world controllers. History has shown the dangers in letting governments curtail these freedoms. The last century's government-sponsored coercive eugenics programs, once favored by both the left and the right, have been thoroughly discredited. Because people are likely to differ profoundly in their attitudes towards human enhancement technologies, it is crucial that no single solution be imposed on everyone from above, but that individuals get to consult their own consciences as to what is right for themselves and their families. Information, public debate, and education are the appropriate means by which to encourage others to make wise choices, not a global ban on a broad range of potentially beneficial medical and other enhancement options.

The second fear is that there might be an eruption of violence between unaugmented humans and post-humans. George Annas, Lori Andrews, and Rosario

Isasi have argued that we should view human cloning and all inheritable genetic modifications as 'crimes against humanity' in order to reduce the probability that a posthuman species will arise, on grounds that such a species would pose an existential threat to the old human species:

> The new species, or 'posthuman,' will likely view the old 'normal' humans as inferior, even savages, and fit for slavery or slaughter. The normals, on the other hand, may see the post-humans as a threat and if they can, may engage in a preemptive strike by killing the posthumans before they themselves are killed or enslaved by them. It is ultimately this predictable potential for genocide that makes species-altering experiments potential weapons of mass destruction, and makes the unaccountable genetic engineer a potential bioterrorist.[6]

There is no denying that bioterrorism and unaccountable genetic engineers developing increasingly potent weapons of mass destruction pose a serious threat to our civilization. But using the rhetoric of bioterrorism and weapons of mass destruction to cast aspersions on therapeutic uses of biotechnology to improve health, longevity, and other human capacities is unhelpful. The issues are quite distinct. Reasonable people can be in favor of strict regulation of bioweapons, while promoting beneficial medical uses of genetics and other human enhancement technologies, including inheritable and 'species-altering' modifications.

Human society is always at risk of some group deciding to view another group of humans as being fit for slavery or slaughter. To counteract such tendencies, modern societies have created laws and institutions, and endowed them with powers of enforcement, that act to prevent groups of citizens from enslaving or slaughtering one another. The efficacy of these institutions does not depend on all citizens having equal capacities. Modern, peaceful societies can have large numbers of people with diminished physical or mental capacities along with many other people who may be exceptionally physically strong or healthy or intellectually talented in various ways. Adding people with technologically enhanced capacities to this already broad distribution of ability would not need to rip society apart or trigger genocide or enslavement.

The assumption that inheritable genetic modifications or other human enhancement technologies would lead to two distinct and separate species should also be questioned. It seems much more likely that there would be a continuum of differently modified or enhanced individuals, which would overlap with the continuum of as-yet unenhanced humans. The scenario in which 'the enhanced' form a pact and then attack 'the naturals' makes for exciting science fiction, but is not necessarily the most plausible outcome. Even today, the segment containing the tallest ninety percent of the population could, in principle, get together and kill or enslave the shorter decile. That this does not happen suggests that a well-organized society can hold together even if it contains many possible coalitions of people sharing some attribute such that, if they ganged up, they would be capable of exterminating the rest.

To note that the extreme case of a war between humans and posthumans is not the most likely scenario is not to say that there are no legitimate social concerns about the steps that may take us closer to posthumanity. Inequity, discrimination, and stigmatization – against, or on behalf of, modified people – could become serious issues. Transhumanists would argue that these (potential) social problems call for social remedies. One example of how contemporary technology can change important aspects of someone's identity is sex reassignment. The experiences of transsexuals show that Western culture still has work to do in becoming more accepting of diversity. This is a task that we can begin to tackle today by fostering a climate of tolerance and acceptance towards those who are different from ourselves. Painting alarmist pictures of the threat from future technologically modified people, or hurling preemptive condemnations of their necessarily debased nature, is not the best way to go about it.

What about the hypothetical case in which someone intends to create, or turn themselves into, a being of such radically enhanced capacities that a single one or a small group of such individuals would be capable of taking over the planet? This is clearly not a situation that is likely to arise in the imminent future, but one can imagine that, perhaps in a few decades, the prospective creation of superintelligent machines could raise this kind of concern. The would-be creator of a new life form with such surpassing capabilities would have an obligation to ensure that the proposed being is free from psychopathic tendencies and, more generally, that it has humane inclinations. For example, a future artificial intelligence programmer should be required to make a strong case that launching a purportedly human-friendly superintelligence would be safer than the alternative. Again, however, this (currently) science fiction scenario must be clearly distinguished from our present situation and our more immediate concern with taking effective steps towards incrementally improving human capacities and health-span.

Is Human Dignity Incompatible with Posthuman Dignity?

Human dignity is sometimes invoked as a polemical substitute for clear ideas. This is not to say that there are no important moral issues relating to dignity, but it does mean that there is a need to define what one has in mind when one uses the term. Here, we shall consider two different senses of dignity:

1. Dignity as moral status, in particular the inalienable right to be treated with a basic level of respect.
2. Dignity as the quality of being worthy or honorable; worthiness, worth, nobleness, excellence.[7]

On both these definitions, dignity is something that a posthuman could possess. Francis Fukuyama, however, seems to deny this and warns that giving up on the idea that dignity is unique to human beings – defined as those possessing a mysterious essential human quality he calls 'Factor X'[8] – would invite disaster:

> Denial of the concept of human dignity – that is, of the idea that there is something unique about the human race that entitles every member of the species to a higher moral status than the rest of the natural world – leads us down a very perilous path. We may be compelled ultimately to take this path, but we should do so only with our eyes open. Nietzsche is a much better guide to what lies down that road than the legions of bioethicists and casual academic Darwinians that today are prone to give us moral advice on this subject.[9]

What appears to worry Fukuyama is that introducing new kinds of enhanced person into the world might cause some individuals (perhaps infants, or the mentally handicapped, or unenhanced humans in general) to lose some of the moral status that they currently possess, and that a fundamental precondition of liberal democracy, the principle of equal dignity for all, would be destroyed.

The underlying intuition seems to be that instead of the famed 'expanding moral circle', what we have is more like an oval, whose shape we can change but whose area must remain constant. Thankfully, this purported conservation law of moral recognition lacks empirical support. The set of individuals accorded full moral status by Western societies has actually increased, to include men without property or noble descent, women, and non-white peoples. It would seem feasible to extend this set further to include future posthumans, or, for that matter, some of the higher primates or human–animal chimaeras, should such be created – and to do so without causing any compensating shrinkage in another direction. (The moral status of problematic borderline cases, such as foetuses or late-stage Alzheimer patients, or the brain-dead, should perhaps be decided separately from the issue of technologically modified humans or novel artificial life forms.) Our own role in this process need not be that of passive bystanders. We can work to create more inclusive social structures that accord appropriate moral recognition and legal rights to all who need them, be they male or female, black or white, flesh or silicon.

Dignity in the second sense, as referring to a special excellence or moral worthiness, is something that current human beings possess to widely differing degrees. Some excel far more than others do. Some are morally admirable; others are base and vicious. There is no reason for supposing that posthuman beings could not also have dignity in this second sense. They may even be able to attain higher levels of moral and other excellence than any of us humans. The fictional brave new worlders, who were subhuman rather than posthuman, would have scored low on this kind of dignity, and partly for that reason they would be awful role models for us to emulate. But surely we can create more uplifting and appealing visions of what we may aspire to become. There may be some who would

transform themselves into degraded posthumans – but then some people today do not live very worthy human lives. This is regrettable, but the fact that some people make bad choices is not generally a sufficient ground for rescinding people's right to choose. And legitimate countermeasures are available: education, encouragement, persuasion, social and cultural reform. These, not a blanket prohibition of all posthuman ways of being, are the measures to which those bothered by the prospect of debased posthumans should resort. A liberal democracy should normally permit incursions into morphological and reproductive freedoms only in cases where somebody is abusing these freedoms to harm another person.

The principle that parents should have broad discretion to decide on genetic enhancements for their children has been attacked on the grounds that this form of reproductive freedom would constitute a kind of parental tyranny that would undermine the child's dignity and capacity for autonomous choice; for instance, by Hans Jonas:

> Technological mastered nature now again includes man who (up to now) had, in technology, set himself against it as its master … But whose power is this – and over whom or over what? Obviously the power of those living today over those coming after them, who will be the defenseless other side of prior choices made by the planners of today. The other side of the power of today is the future bondage of the living to the dead.[10]

Jonas is relying on the assumption that our descendants, who will presumably be far more technologically advanced than we are, would nevertheless be defenseless against our machinations to expand their capacities. This is almost certainly incorrect. If, for some inscrutable reason, they decided that they would prefer to be less intelligent, less healthy, and lead shorter lives, they would not lack the means to achieve these objectives and frustrate our designs.

In any case, if the alternative to parental choice in determining the basic capacities of new people is entrusting the child's welfare to nature, that is blind chance, then the decision should be easy. Had Mother Nature been a real parent, she would have been in jail for child abuse and murder. And transhumanists can accept, of course, that just as society may in exceptional circumstances override parental autonomy, such as in cases of neglect or abuse, so too may society impose regulations to protect the child-to-be from genuinely harmful genetic interventions – but not because they represent choice rather than chance.

Jürgen Habermas, in a recent work, echoes Jonas' concern and worries that even the mere *knowledge* of having been intentionally made by another could have ruinous consequences:

> We cannot rule out that knowledge of one's own hereditary features as programmed may prove to restrict the choice of an individual's life, and to undermine the essentially symmetrical relations between free and equal human beings.[11]

A transhumanist could reply that it would be a mistake for an individual to believe that she has no choice over her own life just because some (or all) of her genes were selected by her parents. She would, in fact, have as much choice as if her genetic constitution had been selected by chance. It could even be that she would enjoy significantly *more* choice and autonomy in her life, if the modifications were such as to expand her basic capability set. Being healthy, smarter, having a wide range of talents, or possessing greater powers of self-control are blessings that tend to open more life paths than they block.

Even if there were a possibility that some genetically-modified individuals might fail to grasp these points and thus might feel oppressed by their knowledge of their origin, that would be a risk to be weighed against the risks incurred by having an unmodified genome, risks that can be extremely grave. If safe and effective alternatives were available, it would be irresponsible to risk starting someone off in life with the misfortune of congenitally diminished basic capacities or an elevated susceptibility to disease.

Why We Need Posthuman Dignity

Similarly ominous forecasts were made in the seventies about the severe psychological damage that children conceived through *in vitro* fertilization would suffer upon learning that they originated from a test tube – a prediction that turned out to be entirely false. It is hard to avoid the impression that some bias or philosophical prejudice is responsible for the readiness with which many bioconservatives seize on even the flimsiest of empirical justifications for banning human enhancement technologies of certain types but not others. Suppose it turned out that playing Mozart to pregnant mothers improved the child's subsequent musical talent. Nobody would argue for a ban on Mozart-in-the-womb on grounds that we cannot rule out that some psychological woe might befall the child once she discovers that her facility with the violin had been prenatally 'programmed' by her parents. Yet when, for example, it comes to genetic enhancements, eminent bioconservative writers often put forward arguments that are not so very different from this parody as weighty, if not conclusive, objections. To transhumanists, this looks like doublethink. How can it be that to bioconservatives almost any anticipated downside, predicted perhaps on the basis of the shakiest pop-psychological theory, so readily achieves that status of deep philosophical insight and knockdown objection against the transhumanist project?

Perhaps a part of the answer can be found in the different attitudes that transhumanists and bioconservatives have towards posthuman dignity. Bioconservatives tend to deny posthuman dignity and view posthumanity as a threat to human dignity. They are therefore tempted to look for ways to denigrate interventions that are thought to be pointing in the direction of more radical future modifications that may eventually lead to the emergence of those detestable posthumans. But unless this fundamental opposition to the posthuman is openly declared as a premise of their argument, this then forces them to use a double standard of assessment whenever particular cases are considered in isolation: for example, one standard for germ-line genetic interventions and another for improvements in maternal nutrition (an intervention presumably not seen as heralding a posthuman era).

Transhumanists, by contrast, see human and posthuman dignity as compatible and complementary. They insist that dignity, in its modern sense, consists in what we are and what we have the potential to become, not in our pedigree or our causal origin. What we are is not a function solely of our DNA but also of our technological and social context. Human nature in this broader sense is dynamic, partially human-made, and improvable. Our current extended phenotypes (and the lives that we lead) are markedly different from those of our hunter-gatherer ancestors. We read and write, we wear clothes, we live in cities, we earn money and buy food from the supermarket, we call people on the telephone, watch television, read newspapers, drive cars, file taxes, vote in national elections, women give birth in hospitals, life-expectancy is three times longer than in the Pleistocene, we know that the Earth is round and that stars are large gas clouds lit from inside by nuclear fusion, and that the universe is approximately 13.7 billion years old and enormously big. In the eyes of a hunter-gatherer, we might already appear 'posthuman'. Yet these radical extensions of human capabilities – some of them biological, others external – have not divested us of moral status or dehumanized us in the sense of making us generally unworthy and base. Similarly, should we or our descendants one day succeed in becoming what relative to current standards we may refer to as posthuman, this need not entail a loss dignity either.

From the transhumanist standpoint, there is no need to behave as if there were a deep moral difference between technological and other means of enhancing human lives. By defending posthuman dignity we promote a more inclusive and humane ethics, one that will embrace future technologically modified people as well as humans of the contemporary kind. We also remove a distortive double standard from the field of our moral vision, allowing us to perceive more clearly the opportunities that exist for further human progress.[12]

Notes

1   N. Bostrom. 2003. The Transhumanist FAQ, v. 2.1. *World Transhumanist Association*.

2   N. Bostrom. Human Genetic Enhancements: A Transhumanist Perspective. *Journal of Value Inquiry*, Vol. 37, No. 4, pp. 493–506.

3   L. Kass. Ageless Bodies, Happy Souls: Biotechnology and the Pursuit of Perfection. *The New Atlantis* 2003; 1.

4   See e.g. J. Glover. 2001. *Humanity: A Moral History of the Twentieth Century*. New Haven. Yale University Press.

5   L. Kass. 2002. *Life, Liberty, and Defense of Dignity: The Challenge for Bioethics*. San Francisco. Encounter Books: p. 48.

6   G. Annas, L. Andrews and R. Isasi. Protecting the Endangered Human: Toward an International Treaty Prohibiting Cloning and Inheritable Alterations. *American Journal of Law and Medicine* 2002; 28, 2&3: p. 162.

7   J. A. Simpson and E. Weiner, eds. 1989. *The Oxford English Dictionary, 2nd ed*. Oxford. Oxford University Press.

8   F. Fukuyama. 2002. *Our Posthuman Future: Consequences of the Biotechnology Revolution*. New York. Farrar, Strauss and Giroux: p. 149.

9   Fukuyama, *Our Posthuman Future*, p. 160.

10 H. Jonas. 1985. *Technik, Medizin und Ethik: Zur Praxis des Prinzips Verantwortung*. Frankfurt am Main. Suhrkamp.

11 J. Habermas. 2003. *The Future of Human Nature*. Oxford. Blackwell: p. 23.

12 For their comments I am grateful to Heather Bradshaw, John Brooke, Aubrey de Grey, Robin Hanson, Matthew Liao, Julian Savulescu, Eliezer Yudkowsky, Nick Zangwill, and to the audiences at the Ian Ramsey Center seminar of June 6th in Oxford 2003, the Transvision 2003 conference at Yale, and the 2003 European Science Foundation Workshop on Science and Human Values, where earlier versions of this paper were presented, and to two anonymous referees.

Part IV

Life and Death Issues

Introduction

It is widely believed that it is wrong to kill an innocent person, but there are great variations in people's
beliefs as to whether this rule is absolute, without any
exceptions, or if not, what those exceptions are. This
diversity of views also characterizes the contributions
to this anthology.

When discussing issues related to the wrongness of
killing, two clusters of questions immediately present
themselves:

1. To *whom* does the prohibition of killing apply? To
   all human beings? *Only* to human beings? An
   answer to these questions is central to discussions
   of abortion (see Part I), the ethics of experimenting on human embryos and nonhuman animals
   (see Parts VII and VIII) and, in the present Part IV,
   to the ethical issues raised by the birth of seriously ill or premature infants, by the concept of
   brain death, and by the use of advance directives.
2. When is a decision that leads to death wrong? Is
   there, for example, a morally relevant difference
   between killing a person and deliberately not saving her? Is it morally wrong to kill a person when
   the person is suffering from an incurable disease,
   and asks for help in dying? Must doctors always
   prolong their patients' lives by all possible means, or
   are there times when the quality of a patient's life
   is so poor that it would be wrong for doctors not
   to allow, or perhaps even help, the patient to die?

Jonathan Glover sets the scene in "The Sanctity of
Life" by asking when and why killing is directly
wrong. He rejects the view that all human life has
sanctity, or is intrinsically or absolutely valuable, and
instead develops the concept of a "life worth living."
What makes killing directly wrong, he holds, is that
it destroys a life that is worth living. Views based on
the concept of a "life worth living" do not rule out
all killings; they would in principle permit the taking
of lives that are *not* worth living. This might, for
example, be the case when a terminally ill and suffering patient asks his doctor to end his life, or when
a patient has irreversibly lost all consciousness.

The idea that we may be justified in ending the lives
of some human beings because the quality of their
lives is so poor is contrary to the traditional Roman
Catholic position, espoused in the "Declaration on
Euthanasia." On this view, *all* innocent human lives,
regardless of their quality or kind, have sanctity and
must never intentionally be cut short. As the
Declaration states: "nothing and no one can in any way
permit the killing of an innocent human being,
whether a fetus or an embryo, an infant or an adult, an
old person, or one suffering from an incurable disease,
or a person who is dying."

While the Declaration thus absolutely prohibits
killing, it does not impose an absolute duty to prevent
the death of innocent human beings. This applies also
to the practice of medicine. While doctors must not

Bioethics: An Anthology, Third Edition. Edited by Helga Kuhse, Udo Schüklenk, and Peter Singer.
© 2016 John Wiley & Sons, Inc. Published 2016 by John Wiley & Sons, Inc.

practice "euthanasia," they are, under certain circumstances, permitted to allow their patients to die. But is there a conceptually and morally sound way of distinguishing between killing and letting die, and between doctors practicing "euthanasia" and making deliberate decisions not to keep patients alive despite the ready availability of the means to do so?

Killing and Letting Die

In attempting to draw a distinction between killing and allowing to die (often also referred to as the distinction between "active" and "passive euthanasia"), writers typically invoke a number of further distinctions, such as those between

- acts and omissions;
- ordinary and extraordinary (or burdensome) means of treatment; and
- intending death and merely foreseeing death.

In his influential 1975 article "Active and Passive Euthanasia," James Rachels argues that, other things being equal, there is no moral difference between active and passive euthanasia, or between doing something that leads to death and doing nothing to prevent death. To show this, Rachels asks readers to consider two cases that are identical in all relevant respects, except that one is a case of killing and one a case of letting die. Rachels argues that the two cases are morally on a par, and that the same is true of active and passive euthanasia in the practice of medicine: the mere difference between killing a patient and letting a patient die is in itself morally irrelevant.

Not everyone accepts Rachels's implicit assumption that the killing/letting die distinction rests on the distinction between actions and omissions, or between "doing something" and "doing nothing." Germain Grisez and Joseph M. Boyle ("The Morality of Killing: A Traditional View") hold that what distinguishes killing from letting die is the agent's intention. An agent kills, they argue, when she directly intends death; she allows to die when she merely foresees that the patient will die as a consequence of another morally permissible action or omission. On this view, then, some omissions intended to lead to

death can amount to killings. If one *aims* at death, that is, if one commits oneself to a project that includes a person's death, then one kills, even if the project is carried out by way of an omission. If, on the other hand, one does not aim at death, but rather commits oneself to some other morally good or at least morally indifferent project, then a foreseen death could be a case of letting die, and not a case of impermissible killing.

On this view all intentional killings of innocent human beings are wrong; but not every case in which death is an outcome of someone's action or omission involves moral wrongdoing. Just as martyrs may lay down their lives for a higher good, so patients may reasonably reject "extraordinary treatment" (treatment that is experimental, risky, or unduly burdensome or costly, or disproportionate to the benefit it brings), without thereby committing an act of suicide; and doctors may withdraw or withhold life-prolonging treatment, or administer life-shortening palliative care, without thereby intending to kill these patients.

Winston Nesbitt asks "Is Killing No Worse Than Letting Die?" and agrees with both Grisez and Boyle, and with Rachels, that some omissions that result in death are the moral equivalent of killings. But, he argues, a person who is prepared to kill someone for personal gain poses a greater threat to other members of society than a person who is merely prepared, for the same reason, to let someone die. The person who is prepared to "let die" may not save me when my life is in danger, but "is no more dangerous than an incapacitated person, or for that matter, a rock or tree." If a person is prepared to kill, however, I must also fear some positive attempts on my life. This shows, Nesbitt concludes, that killing is indeed worse than letting die.

Helga Kuhse, in "Why Killing Is Not Always Worse – and Sometimes Better – Than Letting Die," grants, for the sake of the argument, that we should be more concerned by the presence of people who are prepared to kill for personal gain than by the presence of people who are merely prepared to let die for personal gain. But, she argues, it does not follow from this that killing is always worse than letting die. That judgment should be reversed when agents are not seeking to benefit themselves, but to benefit others, as would be the case in euthanasia. Doctors sometimes allow their patients to die because death is assumed to be a benefit, from the patient's point of view. And if death is, in these cases, a benefit rather than a harm, then active euthanasia will not be worse, and might be better, than passive euthanasia. Should we feel threatened by doctors who are not only prepared to let die, but also prepared to kill? No, says Kuhse: "We should be comforted by their presence."

In the final contribution on the killing/letting die distinction, Franklin Miller, Robert Truog, and Dan Brock explore the role of moral fictions in sustaining the idea that a physician who brings about a patient's death by withdrawing a ventilator, at the patient's request, acts both legally and ethically, whereas a physician who gives a lethal injection, again at the request of the patient, acts contrary both to ethics and to the law (in almost all countries). These fictions operate in regard to such central issues as the nature of the act, the causal role played by the physician, and the physician's intention. Exposing these fictions shows, according to Miller, Truog, and Brock, that on the issue of killing and letting die, conventional medical ethics is "radically mistaken."

Severely Disabled Newborns

Some infants are born with severe disabilities; others are born prematurely, at the margin of viability. Should the lives of these babies always be prolonged, or are there grounds – such as the baby's best interests – for sometimes allowing or helping an infant to die?

In "When Care Cannot Cure: Medical Problems in Seriously Ill Babies," the Australian pediatrician Neil Campbell notes that in cases in which infants suffer from various disabilities, such as mental deficiency, paralysis, blindness and deafness, lack of self-awareness, and so on, doctors will often withhold or withdraw treatments, believing that it is in the infant's best interest to do so. During a two-year period at the Royal Children's Hospital in Melbourne, 76.5 percent of all deaths occurred following the withdrawal of life-supporting treatment. In these cases, feeding and fluids were sometimes withheld, and infants received sufficiently high doses of analgesics, such as morphine, to alleviate pain and distress. While it is sometimes denied that this kind of treatment amounts to active

euthanasia, Campbell observes that such arguments "appear, to some bedside attendants, casuistic."

R. M. Hare, in "The Abnormal Child: Modern Dilemmas of Doctors and Parents," asks us to give equal consideration to all the interests involved when deciding to sustain or not sustain the life of a seriously disabled infant. One of the often forgotten interests is, he holds, that of "the next child in the queue." To make this interest vivid, Hare asks us to imagine a dialogue between a disabled fetus and an as-yet-unconceived brother, Andrew. Assuming that the parents of the disabled fetus will not have another child if the fetus survives, but will do so if the fetus dies, the fetus and Andrew try to find a solution based on equal consideration of their interests in having a happy existence. They agree on a proposal that gives the best possible chance of a healthy baby – even if, under some circumstances, it may mean ending the life of a baby with a disability. (Derek Parfit's article "Rights, Interests, and Possible People," in Part II, is relevant again here.)

Alison Davis in "Right to Life of Handicapped" disagrees with Hare and defends the right to life of disabled people. She suffers from severe disabilities herself, but applauds the fact that her parents neither aborted nor abandoned her: "My parents were encouraged to leave me in the hospital and 'go home and have another,' and I owe my life to the fact that they refused to accept the advice of the experts." The idea that newborn infants are not person, she writes, "denies the right of handicapped people to be recognized as equal human beings ..."

Considerable publicity has been given, in recent years, to efforts to separate conjoined twins. Such operations often involve a large team of surgeons, working for many hours, and a substantial investment of hospital resources. These efforts are typically regarded as laudable and even heroic, despite the fact that in some cases the foreseen "best" outcome involves the death of one of the conjoined twins so that the other may live free of a conjoined sibling. Why is this not a case of killing, or even of murder? Christine Overall in "Conjoined Twins, Embodied Personhood, and Surgical Separation" shows that asking such questions leads us more deeply into the relationship between being a person and being embodied. The outcome of her investigation is that, at least sometimes, to separate conjoined twins, even if both twins survive, may do a wrong to the conjoined persons that they were.

Brain Death

Before the development of sophisticated means of life-support, the definition of death seemed uncontroversial. It was widely understood as the cessation of life, defined by doctors as the stoppage of the circulation of the blood and other vital functions, such as respiration and pulsation. In short, people were assumed to be dead when they stopped breathing and their hearts had stopped beating. The advent of respirators complicated matters. With the help of these machines, breathing and heartbeat can be sustained indefinitely, even if the patient is completely unresponsive and all electrical activity of the brain has ceased. This raised questions about the adequacy of the traditional understanding of death and, following the publication of the report by the Ad Hoc Committee of the Harvard Medical School to Examine the Definition of Brain Death in 1968, led to the widespread acceptance of brain death – that is, the permanent loss of all brain function – as an additional criterion of death. This acceptance meant, as Peter Singer notes in "Is the Sanctity of Life Ethic Terminally Ill?" "that warm, breathing, pulsating human beings are not given further medical support" and that "their hearts and other organs can be cut out of their bodies and given to strangers."

As Ari Joffe points out in "Are Recent Defences of the Brain Death Concept Adequate?" every year thousands of patients are pronounced dead on the basis of the concept of brain death. One would therefore hope that this concept has a strong and clear rationale; but when Joffe examines the rationales put forward in recent expert defenses of brain death, he finds them surprisingly weak. Yet if brain death is not really death, the implications of this conclusion are, as Joffe says, "enormously significant." He ends by suggesting that it may be time to consider the suggestion that even though brain death is not death, it is such a devastating state to be in that taking organs, including hearts, from those in this state could be acceptable. Since one can hardly remove the heart of a living human being without killing that human, to accept this suggestion would mean abandoning the idea that it is always wrong to kill an innocent human being.

In "Is the Sanctity of Life Ethic Terminally Ill?" Singer accepts this implication. He argues that the brain death criterion is a convenient fiction, readily accepted, because of its practical benefits for organ transplantation and for making the best use of our limited medical resources. (The discussion of moral fictions in the article by Miller, Truog, and Brock is relevant here.) Once we see through the fiction that brain death is the death of the human organism, we realize that by accepting "brain death," we have abandoned the traditional ethic of the sanctity of human life. It is therefore, Singer suggests, time to adopt a new and more honest approach to the handling, not only of those whose brains have irreversibly ceased to function, but also of people who can be shown beyond doubt to have irreversibly lost consciousness.

Advance Directives

Today there is widespread agreement that competent and informed patients have the right to refuse unwanted medical treatment, including life-sustaining treatment. Many people also assume that this right can be extended into the future by way of advance directives, such as "living wills" or proxy directives. Living wills allow people, while they are still competent, to stipulate that, should they one day become incompetent, they do not wish to receive certain treatments; and proxy directives allow for the appointment of an agent or "proxy" to make treatment decisions for the incompetent patient, should this situation occur.

Advance directives seem attractive. Medicine is continually increasing its capacity to prolong life, but cannot always restore functioning and well-being. Many people regard such diminished lives as undesirable. Moreover, given that death is often preceded by a period of mental incapacity, advance directives seem to offer a relatively simple and, many people think, morally defensible way of guiding medical decision-making, in accordance with the formerly competent person's values and beliefs.

But, as Ronald Dworkin points out in "Life Past Reason," there is a possible problem: the interests of the formerly competent person may not be identical with the interests of the now incompetent patient. Dworkin focuses his discussion on the case of "Margo," who was suffering from advanced Alzheimer's disease. Although Margo was no longer able to make medical decisions for herself, she was in the words of one of her carers "one of the happiest people" he had ever known. If Margo, while still competent, had stipulated that her life should not be sustained (or that it should be actively terminated) should she ever become permanently incompetent, then, Dworkin argues, a seemingly happy life would be lost if her carers complied with her wishes. This raises the question of whether decision-making should (always) be based on a person's earlier decision, or whether it should be based on the interests of the incompetent patient she has become.

Dworkin argues for the "precedence of autonomy" – that is, the view that a competent or autonomous person's interest in controlling her life ought to take precedence over any interests the future incompetent individual might have. Rebecca Dresser responds, in "Dworkin on Dementia: Elegant Theory, Questionable Policy," that the precedence Dworkin urges we give to autonomy must face a philosophical challenge posed by the psychological view of personal identity. On this view, psychological continuity is a *necessary* condition of personal identity. This presupposes that for Margo at 70, say, to be the same person as Margo at 80, there must be sufficient psychological continuity (exemplified by memories, intentions, beliefs, desires, and so on) between the formerly competent person and the now incompetent patient. If these psychological links become very weak or are absent, as often will be the case in advanced Alzheimer's disease, there are grounds for claiming that the severely demented patient is not the same person as the author of the advance directive. Why then should the earlier Margo have the moral authority to control what happens to the demented Margo later on?

Voluntary Euthanasia and Medically Assisted Suicide

Few topics in bioethics have received as much consistent public attention during the last two decades as voluntary euthanasia and medically assisted suicide.

Does a person who is incurably ill, who suffers much and wants to die, have the right to bring her life to an end, and is it proper for others to help her in this quest?

Different philosophers and cultures have given very different answers to this question. Some have condemned suicide and voluntary euthanasia – even in the face of great suffering – as cowardly and wrong, while others have praised a self-chosen death as courageous and as an expression of our ultimate freedom and dignity. The pre-Christian philosopher Seneca, for example, was among those who thought it was better to choose one's own death than to live with vastly diminished capacities. As he put it:

> I will not abandon old age, if old age preserves me intact as regards the better part of myself; but if old age begins to shatter my mind, and to pull its various faculties to pieces, if it leaves me not life, but only the breath of life, I shall rush out of a house that is crumbling and tottering. I shall not avoid illness by seeking death, as long as the illness is curable and does not impede my soul. I shall not lay violent hands upon myself just because I am in pain; for death under such circumstances is defeat. But if I find out that the pain must always be endured, I shall depart, not because of the pain, but because it will be a hindrance to me as regards all my reasons for living.[1]

Today, incurable illness, the loss of one's faculties, and unrelievable pain and suffering are still the basis of many requests for voluntary euthanasia and medically assisted suicide. But since the advent of Christianity, suicide has widely been regarded as intrinsically wrong. Life began to be seen not as our own to be disposed of when we choose, but as a gift from God, which only He has the right to reclaim.

While this has been the prevailing attitude in Western societies for hundreds of years, it is not universally shared. Many people – Christians and non-Christians alike – take the view that in the face of incurable illness and suffering, assisted suicide and voluntary euthanasia can be rational and morally defensible choices. Chris Hill took this view after he became a paraplegic. As he describes in "The Note," before his accident he had been a great traveler and adventurer, who loved skiing, diving, dancing, and sex. After his accident, he was paralyzed from the chest down, doubly incontinent, sexless, "a talking head mounted on a bloody wheelchair." His unwillingness to involve others in an act that might cause them to be charged with the criminal offense of assisting suicide meant that, as his doctor later wrote, he died alone in a deserted parking lot.[2]

Some people accept that suicide, without the assistance of others, can sometimes be a morally defensible choice, but, they argue, voluntary euthanasia is quite a different matter because it involves others in the life-ending act. Daniel Callahan appears to share this view. In "When Self-Determination Runs Amok," he writes that euthanasia requires two people to make it possible, and "a complicit society to make it acceptable." To counter the argument that doctors are already providing euthanasia when they discontinue life-support, Callahan argues that there is a moral difference between stopping life-support, on the one hand, and "more active forms of killing, such as lethal injection," on the other. In stopping life-support, doctors are not causing death, he holds; they are not killing the patient; rather it is the disease that kills the patient. This issue is, of course, more thoroughly discussed in the essays we have grouped under the heading "Killing and Letting Die."

Callahan holds that the provision of voluntary euthanasia is incompatible with the aims of medicine. Often people will commit suicide or request euthanasia not only because they are ill, but also and predominantly because they find life oppressive, empty or meaningless. But, he argues, it is "not medicine's place" to deal with the anguish we may feel when contemplating the human condition.

John Lachs disagrees. In "When Abstract Morality Runs Amok" he accuses Callahan of relying more on intuitional guideposts than on argument. But, Lachs holds, intuitions are inherently problematical. Rather than constituting an expression of eternal moral truths, they may simply echo traditional views that have not been subjected to much critical scrutiny.

Callahan also makes a slippery slope argument against the acceptance of voluntary euthanasia and supports this argument by referring to what he believed to be happening in the Netherlands. When Callahan wrote his article, in 1992, Dutch courts had ruled that doctors who carried out euthanasia in accordance with guidelines set by the Royal Dutch Medical Association should not be convicted of a crime; nevertheless the statute law that made euthanasia a crime still existed, and there were little data available to throw light on the consequences

of permitting or prohibiting voluntary euthanasia. The Dutch Parliament legalized voluntary euthanasia in 2002. The situation in the Netherlands has now been studied thoroughly, and there are also studies from Belgium (which has also legalized voluntary euthanasia) and the US states of Oregon and Washington, which have legalized physician assistance in dying. Other studies in countries like Australia and New Zealand, where euthanasia and physician assistance in dying remain illegal, allow comparisons of medical practice under different legal situations. These studies provide a good basis for assessing factual claims about the consequences of legalizing or not legalizing voluntary euthanasia and physician assistance in dying.[3]

One of these studies is included in this anthology: "Trends in End-Of-Life Practices Before and After the Enactment of the Euthanasia Law in the Netherlands from 1990 to 2010: A Repeated Cross-Sectional Survey." Bregje Onwuteaka-Philipsen and her colleagues found that the rate of euthanasia in the Netherlands has been fairly stable since 1995, before euthanasia became legal, and they found no evidence of widespread abuse, or of a disproportionate use of euthanasia among vulnerable populations, such as older people or incompetent patients. This study, and others that have come to similar conclusions, show that the evidence does not support the factual claims about the situation in the Netherlands made by Callahan and some other critics of the legalization of voluntary euthanasia.

It remains true that, as Bernard Lo comments in "Euthanasia in the Netherlands: What Lessons for Elsewhere?" there are some issues that raise concerns. One of these is the practice – which appears to be increasing both in the Netherlands and in countries where euthanasia remains illegal – of what is sometimes called "terminal sedation" – in effect, putting patients into a state of deep sedation until they die. Obviously, this is a way of relieving all suffering, but the ground for concern is that, as compared with the practice of euthanasia in the Netherlands, terminal sedation is more likely to take place without the patient explicitly asking for it. Perhaps that is because doctors who put their patients into terminal sedation are invoking another moral fiction – that terminal sedation is not euthanasia.

Notes

1   Seneca, "58th Letter to Lucilius," trans. R. M. Gummere, in T. E. Page et al. (eds.), *Seneca: Ad Lucilium Epistulae Morales*, vol. 1 (London: Heinemann, 1961), p. 409.

2   George Quittner, "Some Thoughts on the Life and Death of Chris Hill," in Helga Kuhse (ed.), *Willing to Listen, Wanting to Die* (Ringwood, Australia: Penguin, 1994), p. 20.

3   See, e.g., P. J. van der Maas et al., "Euthanasia, Physician Assisted Suicide, and Other Medical Practices Involving the End of Life in the Netherlands, 1990–1995," *New England Journal of Medicine*, 335 (1996): 1699–1705; H. Kuhse et al., "End-of-Life Decisions in Australian Medical Practice," *Medical Journal of Australia*, 166 (1997): 191–6; Luc Deliens et al., "End-of-Life Decisions in Medical Practice in Flanders, Belgium: A Nationwide Survey," *The Lancet*, 356 (2000): 1806–11; Kay Mitchell and R. Glynn Owens, "National Survey of Medical Decisions at End of Life Made by New Zealand General Practitioners," *British Medical Journal*, 327 (2003): 202–3; B. D. Onwuteaka-Philipsen et al., "Euthanasia and Other End-of-Life Decisions in the Netherlands in 1990, 1995, and 2001," *The Lancet*, 362 (2003): 395–9. For official reports on the application of Oregon's Death with Dignity Act, see http://public.health.oregon.gov/ProviderPartnerResources/EvaluationResearch/DeathwithDignityAct (accessed June 2015).

21

The Sanctity of Life

Jonathan Glover

I cannot but have reverence for all that is called life. I cannot avoid compassion for all that is called life. That is the beginning and foundation of morality.

Albert Schweitzer, *Reverence for Life*

To persons who are not murderers, concentration camp administrators, or dreamers of sadistic fantasies, the inviolability of human life seems to be so self-evident that it might appear pointless to inquire into it. To inquire into it is embarrassing as well because, once raised, the question seems to commit us to beliefs we do not wish to espouse and to confront us with contradictions which seem to deny what is self-evident.

Edward Shils, 'The Sanctity of Life', in D. H. Labby, *Life or Death: Ethics and Options*, 1968

Most of us think it is wrong to kill people. Some think it is wrong in all circumstances, while others think that in special circumstances (say, in a just war or in self-defence) some killing may be justified. But even those who do not think killing is always wrong normally think that a special justification is needed. The assumption is that killing can at best only be justified to avoid a greater evil.

It is not obvious to many people what the answer is to the question '*Why* is killing wrong?' It is not clear whether the wrongness of killing should be treated as a kind of moral axiom, or whether it can be explained by appealing to some more fundamental principle or set of principles. One very common view is that some principle of the sanctity of life has

to be included among the ultimate principles of any acceptable moral system.

In order to evaluate the view that life is sacred, it is necessary to distinguish between two different kinds of objection to killing: direct objections and those based on side-effects.

1 Direct Objections and Side-Effects

Direct objections to killing are those that relate solely to the person killed. Side-effects of killings are effects on people other than the one killed. Many of the possible reasons for not killing someone appeal to

Original publication details: Jonathan Glover, "The Sanctity of Life," pp. 39–59 from *Causing Death and Lives,* London: Pelican, 1977. Reproduced by permission of Penguin Books Ltd.

Bioethics: An Anthology, Third Edition. Edited by Helga Kuhse, Udo Schüklenk, and Peter Singer.

side-effects. (To call them 'side-effects' is not to imply that they must be less important than the direct objections.) When a man dies or is killed, his parents, wife, children or friends may be made sad. His family may always have a less happy atmosphere and very likely less money to spend. The fatherless children may grow up to be less secure and confident than they would have been. The community loses whatever good contribution the man might otherwise have made to it. Also, an act of killing may help weaken the general reluctance to take life or else be thought to do so. Either way, it may do a bit to undermine everyone's sense of security.

Most people would probably give some weight to these side-effects in explaining the wrongness of killing, but would say that they are not the whole story, or even the main part of it. People who say this hold that there are direct objections to killing, independent of effects on others. This view can be brought out by an imaginary case in which an act of killing would have no harmful side-effects.

Suppose I am in prison, and have an incurable disease from which I shall very soon die. The man who shares my cell is bound to stay in prison for the rest of his life, as society thinks he is too dangerous to let out. He has no friends, and all his relations are dead. I have a poison that I could put in his food without him knowing it and that would kill him without being detectable. Everyone else would think he died from natural causes.

In this case, the objections to killing that are based on side-effects collapse. No one will be sad or deprived. The community will not miss his contribution. People will not feel insecure, as no one will know a murder has been committed. And even the possible argument based on one murder possibly weakening my own reluctance to take life in future carries no weight here, since I shall die before having opportunity for further killing. It might even be argued that consideration of side-effects tips the balance positively in favour of killing this man, since the cost of his food and shelter is a net loss to the community.

Those of us who feel that in this case we cannot accept that killing the man would be either morally right or morally neutral must hold that killing is at least sometimes wrong for reasons independent of side-effects. One version of this view that killing is directly wrong is the doctrine of the sanctity of life. To state this doctrine in an acceptable way is harder than it might at first seem.

2 Stating the Principle of the Sanctity of Life

The first difficulty is a minor one. We do not want to state the principle in such a way that it must have overriding authority over other considerations. To say 'taking life is always wrong' commits us to absolute pacifism. But clearly a pacifist and a non-pacifist can share the view that killing is in itself an evil. They need only differ over when, if ever, killing is permissible to avoid other evils. A better approximation is 'taking life is directly wrong', where the word 'directly' simply indicates that the wrongness is independent of effects on other people. But even this will not quite do. For, while someone who believes in the sanctity of life must hold that killing is directly wrong, not everyone who thinks that killing is sometimes or always directly wrong has to hold that life is sacred. (It is possible to believe that killing is directly wrong only where the person does not want to die or where the years of which he is deprived would have been happy ones. These objections to killing have nothing to do with side-effects and yet do not place value on life merely for its own sake.) The best formulation seems to be 'taking life is intrinsically wrong'.

There is another problem about what counts as 'life'. Does this include animals? When we think of higher animals, we may want to say 'yes', even if we want to give animal life less weight than human life. But do we want to count it wrong to tread on an ant or kill a mosquito? And, even if we are prepared to treat all animal life as sacred, there are problems about plant life. Plants are living things. Is weeding the garden wrong? Let us avoid these difficulties for the moment by stating the principle in terms of human life. When we have become clearer about the reasons for thinking it wrong to kill people, we will be better placed to see whether the same reasons should make us respect animal or plant life as well. So, to start with, we have the principle: 'taking human life is intrinsically wrong'.

Can any explanation be given of the belief that taking human life is intrinsically wrong? Someone who simply says that this principle is an axiom of his moral system, and refuses to give any further explanation, cannot be 'refuted' unless his system is made inconsistent by the inclusion of this principle. (And, even then, he might choose to give up other beliefs rather than this one.) The strategy of this chapter will be to try to cast doubt on the acceptability of this principle by looking at the sort of explanation that might be given by a supporter who was prepared to enter into some discussion of it. My aim will be to suggest that the doctrine of the sanctity of life is not acceptable, but that there is embedded in it a moral view we should retain. We should reject the view that taking human life is *intrinsically* wrong, but retain the view that it is normally *directly* wrong: that most acts of killing people would be wrong in the absence of harmful side-effects.

The concept of human life itself raises notorious boundary problems. When does it begin? Is an eight-month fetus already a living human being? How about a newly fertilized egg? These questions need discussing, but it seems preferable to decide first on the central problem of why we value human life, and on that basis to draw its exact boundaries, rather than to stipulate the boundaries arbitrarily in advance. But there is another boundary problem that can be discussed first, as it leads us straight into the central issue about the sanctity of life. This boundary problem is about someone fallen irreversibly into a coma: does he still count as a living human being? (It may be said that what is important is not the status of 'human being', but of 'person'. In this chapter I write as though human beings are automatically persons. In the later discussion of abortion, there will be some attention given to those who say of a fetus that, while it is certainly a member of species *Homo sapiens*, it is not yet a person.)

3   The Boundary between Life and Death

It was once common to decide that someone was dead because, among other things, his heart had stopped beating. But now it is well known that people can sometimes be revived from this state, so some other criterion has to be used. Two candidates sometimes proposed are that 'death' should be defined in terms of the irreversible loss of all electrical activity in the brain or that it should be defined in terms of irreversible loss of consciousness.

Of these two definitions, the one in terms of irreversible loss of consciousness is preferable. There is no point in considering the electrical activity unless one holds the (surely correct) view that it is a necessary condition of the person being conscious. It seems better to define 'death' in terms of irreversible loss of consciousness itself, since it is from this alone that our interest in the electrical activity derives. This is reinforced by the fact that, while loss of all brain activity guarantees loss of consciousness, the converse does not hold. People incurably in a vegetable state normally have some electrical activity in some parts of the brain. To define 'death' in terms of irreversible loss of consciousness is not to deny that our best evidence for this may often be continued absence of electrical activity. And, when we understand more about the neurophysiological basis of consciousness, we may reach the stage of being able to judge conclusively from the state of his brain whether or not someone has irreversibly lost consciousness.

An argument sometimes used in favour of the definition in terms of irreversible loss of consciousness is that it avoids some of the problems that nowadays arise for adherents of more traditional criteria. Glanville Williams[1] has discussed a hypothetical case that might raise legal difficulties. Suppose a man's heart stops beating and, just as the doctor is about to revive him, the man's heir plunges a dagger into his breast. Glanville Williams wonders if this would count as murder or merely as illegal interference with a corpse. If, to avoid complications, we assume that there was a reasonable expectation that the man would otherwise have been revived, the question is one of the boundary between life and death. Making irreversible loss of consciousness the boundary has the advantage, over more traditional criteria, of making the heir's act one of murder.

It may be objected that, in ordinary language, it makes sense to say of someone that he is irreversibly comatose but still alive. This must be admitted. The proposed account of death is a piece of conceptual revision, motivated by the belief that, for such purposes as deciding whether or not to switch off a respirator, the irreversibly comatose and the traditionally 'dead' are on a par. Those who reject this belief will want to reject the 'irreversible loss of consciousness' account of death. And, if they do reject it, they are not forced to revert to traditional views that give a paradoxical answer to the Glanville Williams case. It would be possible to have two tests that must be passed before someone is counted as dead, involving respiratory and circulatory activities stopping *and* brain damage sufficient to make loss of consciousness irreversible. Let us call this the 'double-test' view.

In giving an account of 'death', how should we choose between irreversible loss of consciousness and the double-test view? If we are worried about doctors being wrong in their diagnosis of irreversible loss of consciousness, the double-test view would in practice give an additional safeguard against the respirator being switched off too early. But that is a rather oblique reason, even if of some practical importance. If detecting irreversible loss of consciousness posed no practical problem, how would we then choose between the two views? Appeals to traditional usage are of no value, for what is in question is a proposal for conceptual reform. The only way of choosing is to decide whether or not we attach any value to the preservation of someone irreversibly comatose. Do we value 'life' even if unconscious, or do we value life only as a vehicle for consciousness? Our attitude to the doctrine of the sanctity of life very much depends on our answer to this question.

4 'Being Alive Is Intrinsically Valuable'

Someone who thinks that taking life is intrinsically wrong may explain this by saying that the state of being alive is itself intrinsically valuable. This claim barely rises to the level of an argument for the sanctity of life, for it simply asserts that there is value in what the taking of life takes away.

Against such a view, cases are sometimes cited of people who are either very miserable or in great pain, without any hope of cure. Might such people not be better off dead? But this could be admitted without

giving up the view that life is intrinsically valuable. We could say that life has value, but that not being desperately miserable can have even more value.

I have no way of refuting someone who holds that being alive, even though unconscious, is intrinsically valuable. But it is a view that will seem unattractive to those of us who, in our own case, see a life of permanent coma as in no way preferable to death. From the subjective point of view, there is nothing to choose between the two. Schopenhauer saw this clearly when he said of the destruction of the body:

> But actually we feel this destruction only in the evils of illness or of old age; on the other hand, for the *subject*, death itself consists merely in the moment when consciousness vanishes, since the activity of the brain ceases. The extension of the stoppage to all the other parts of the organism which follows this is really already an event after death. Therefore, in a subjective respect, death concerns only consciousness.[2]

Those of us who think that the direct objections to killing have to do with death considered from the standpoint of the person killed will find it natural to regard life as being of value only as a necessary condition of consciousness. For permanently comatose existence is subjectively indistinguishable from death, and unlikely often to be thought intrinsically preferable to it by people thinking of their own future.

5 'Being Conscious Is Intrinsically Valuable'

The believer in the sanctity of life may accept that being alive is only of instrumental value and say that it is consciousness that is intrinsically valuable. In making this claim, he still differs from someone who only values consciousness because it is necessary for happiness. Before we can assess this belief in the intrinsic value of being conscious, it is necessary to distinguish between two different ways in which we may talk about consciousness. Sometimes we talk about 'mere' consciousness and sometimes we talk about what might be called 'a high level of consciousness'.

'Mere' consciousness consists simply in awareness or the having of experiences. When I am awake, I am aware of my environment. I have a stream of consciousness that comes abruptly to a halt if I faint or fades out when I go to sleep (until I have dreams). There are large philosophical problems about the meaning of claims of this kind, which need not be discussed here. I shall assume that we all at some level understand what it is to have experiences, or a stream of consciousness.

But this use of 'consciousness' should be distinguished from another, perhaps metaphorical, use of the word. We sometimes say that men are at a higher level of consciousness than animals, or else that few, if any, peasants are likely to have as highly developed a consciousness as Proust. It is not clear exactly what these claims come to, nor that the comparison between men and animals is of the same sort as the comparison between peasants and Proust. But perhaps what underlies such comparisons is an attempt to talk about a person's experiences in terms of the extent to which they are rich, varied, complex or subtle, or the extent to which they involve emotional responses, as well as various kind of awareness. Again, it is not necessary to discuss here the analysis of the meaning of these claims. It is enough if it is clear that to place value on 'mere' consciousness is different from valuing it for its richness and variety. I shall assume that the claim that being conscious is intrinsically good is a claim about 'mere' consciousness, rather than about a high level of consciousness.

If one is sceptical about the intrinsic value of 'mere' consciousness, as against that of a high level of consciousness, it is hard to see what consideration can be mentioned in its favour. The advocate of this view might ask us to perform a thought experiment of a kind that G. E. Moore would perhaps have liked. We might be asked to imagine two universes, identical except that one contained a being aware of its environment and the other did not. It may be suggested that the universe containing the conscious being would be intrinsically better.

But such a thought experiment seems unconvincing. There is the familiar difficulty that, confronted with a choice so abstract and remote, it may be hard to feel any preference at all. And, since we are dealing with 'mere' consciousness rather than with a high level of consciousness, it is necessary to postulate that the conscious being has no emotional responses. It cannot be pleased or sorry or in pain; it cannot be interested or bored; it is merely aware of its environment. Views may well differ here, but, if I could be brought to take part in this thought experiment at all, I should probably express indifference between the two universes. The only grounds I might have for preferring the universe with the conscious being would be some hope that it might evolve into some more interesting level of consciousness. But to choose on these grounds is not to assign any intrinsic value to 'mere' consciousness.

The belief that the sole reason why it is directly wrong to take human life is the intrinsic value of 'mere' consciousness runs into a problem concerning animals. Many of us place a special value on human life as against animal life. Yet animals, or at least the higher ones, seem no less aware of their surroundings than we are. Suppose there is a flood and I am faced with the choice of either saving a man's life or else saving the life of a cow. Even if all side-effects were left out of account, failure to save the man seems worse than failure to save the cow. The person who believes that the sanctity of life rests solely on the value of 'mere' consciousness is faced with a dilemma. Either he must accept that the life of the cow and the life of the man are in themselves of equal value, or he must give reasons for thinking that cows are less conscious than men or else not conscious at all.

It is hard to defend the view that, while I have good grounds for thinking that other people are conscious, I do not have adequate reasons for thinking that animals are conscious. Humans and animals in many ways respond similarly to their surroundings. Humans have abilities that other animals do not, such as the ability to speak or to do highly abstract reasoning, but it is not only in virtue of these abilities that we say people are conscious. And there is no neurophysiological evidence that suggests that humans alone can have experiences.

The alternative claim is that animals are less conscious than we are. The view that 'mere' consciousness is a matter of degree is attractive when considered in relation to animals. The philosophical literature about our knowledge of other minds is strikingly silent and unhelpful about the animal boundaries of consciousness. How far back down the evolutionary scale does consciousness extend? What kind and degree of complexity must a nervous system exhibit to be the vehicle of experiences? What kind and degree of complexity of behaviour counts as the manifestation of consciousness? At least with our present ignorance of the physiological basis of human consciousness, any clear-cut boundaries of consciousness, drawn between one kind of animal and another, have an air of arbitrariness. For this reason it is attractive to suggest that consciousness is a matter of degree, not stopping abruptly, but fading away slowly as one descends the evolutionary scale.

But the belief that 'mere' consciousness is a matter of degree is obscure as well as attractive. Is it even an intelligible view?

There are two ways in which talk of degrees of consciousness can be made clearer. One is by explaining it in terms of the presence or absence of whole 'dimensions' of consciousness. This is the way in which a blind man is less conscious of his environment than a normal man. (Though, if his other senses have developed unusual acuity, he will in other respects be more conscious than a normal man.) But if a lower degree of consciousness consists either in the absence of a whole dimension such as sight, or in senses with lower acuity than those of men, it is not plausible to say that animals are all less conscious than we are. Dogs seem to have all the dimensions of consciousness that we do. It is true that they often see less well, but on the other hand their sense of smell is better than ours. If the sanctity of life were solely dependent on degree of consciousness interpreted this way, we often could not justify giving human life priority over animal life. We might also be committed to giving the life of a normal dog priority over the life of a blind man.

The other way in which we talk of degrees of 'mere' consciousness comes up in such contexts as waking up and falling asleep. There is a sleepy state in which we can be unaware of words that are softly spoken, but aware of any noise that is loud or sharp. But this again fails to separate men from animals. For animals are often alert in a way that is quite unlike the drowsiness of a man not fully awake.

Whether or not 'mere' consciousness fades away lower down on the evolutionary scale (and the idea of a sharp boundary *does* seem implausible), there seems at least no reason to regard the 'higher' animals as less aware of the environment than ourselves. (It is not being suggested that animals are only at the level of 'mere' consciousness, though no doubt they are less far above it than most of us.) If the whole basis of the ban on killing were the intrinsic value of mere consciousness, killing higher animals would be as bad as killing humans.

It would be possible to continue to hold mere consciousness to be of intrinsic value, and either to supplement this principle with others or else to abandon the priority given to human life. But when the principle is distinguished from different ones that would place a value on higher levels of consciousness, it has so little intuitive appeal that we may suspect its attractiveness to depend on the distinction not being made. If, in your own case, you would opt for a state never rising above mere consciousness, in preference to death, have you purged the illegitimate assumption that you would take an interest in what you would be aware of?

6 'Being Human Is Intrinsically Valuable'

It is worth mentioning that the objection to taking human life should not rest on what is sometimes called 'speciesism': human life being treated as having a special priority over animal life *simply* because it is human. The analogy is with racism, in its purest form, according to which people of a certain race ought to be treated differently *simply* because of their membership of that race, without any argument referring to special features of that race being given. This is objectionable partly because of its moral arbitrariness: unless some relevant empirical characteristics can be cited, there can be no argument for such discrimination. Those concerned to reform our treatment of animals point out that speciesism exhibits the same arbitrariness. It is not in itself sufficient argument for treating a creature less well to say simply that it is not a member of our species. An adequate justification must cite relevant differences between the species. We still have the question of what features of a life are of intrinsic value.

7 The Concept of a 'Life Worth Living'

I have suggested that, in destroying life or mere consciousness, we are not destroying anything intrinsically valuable. These states only matter because they are necessary for other things that matter in themselves. If a list could be made of all the things that are valuable for their own sake, these things would be the ingredients of a 'life worth living'.

One objection to the idea of judging that a life is worth living is that this seems to imply the possibility of comparing being alive and being dead. And, as Wittgenstein said, 'Death is not an event in life: we do not live to experience death.'

But we can have a preference for being alive over being dead, or for being conscious over being unconscious, without needing to make any 'comparisons' between these states. We prefer to be anaesthetized for a painful operation; queuing for a bus in the rain at midnight, we wish we were at home asleep; but for the most part we prefer to be awake and experience our life as it goes by. These preferences do not depend on any view about 'what it is like' being unconscious, and our preference for life does not depend on beliefs about 'what it is like' being dead. It is rather that we treat being dead or unconscious as nothing, and then decide whether a stretch of experience is better or worse than nothing. And this claim, that life of a certain sort is better than nothing, is an expression of our preference.

Any list of the ingredients of a worthwhile life would obviously be disputable. Most people might agree on many items, but many others could be endlessly argued over. It might be agreed that a happy life is worth living, but people do not agree on what happiness is. And some things that make life worth living may only debatably be to do with happiness. (Aristotle:[3] 'And so they tell us that Anaxagoras answered a man who was raising problems of this sort and asking why one should choose rather to be born

than not – "for the sake of viewing the heavens and the whole order of the universe".')

A life worth living should not be confused with a morally virtuous life. Moral virtues such as honesty or a sense of fairness can belong to someone whose life is relatively bleak and empty. Music may enrich someone's life, or the death of a friend impoverish it, without him growing more or less virtuous.

I shall not try to say what sorts of things do make life worth living. (Temporary loss of a sense of the absurd led me to try to do so. But, apart from the disputability of any such list, I found that the ideal life suggested always sounded ridiculous.) I shall assume that a life worth living has more to it than mere consciousness. It should be possible to explain the wrongness of killing partly in terms of the destruction of a life worth living, without presupposing more than minimal agreement as to exactly what makes life worthwhile.

I shall assume that, where someone's life is worth living, this is a good reason for holding that it would be directly wrong to kill him. This is what can be extracted from the doctrine of the sanctity of life by someone who accepts the criticisms made here of that view. If life is worth preserving only because it is the vehicle for consciousness, and consciousness is of value only because it is necessary for something else, then that 'something else' is the heart of this particular objection to killing. It is what is meant by a 'life worth living' or a 'worthwhile life'.

The idea of dividing people's lives into ones that are worth living and ones that are not is likely to seem both presumptuous and dangerous. As well as seeming to indicate an arrogant willingness to pass godlike judgements on other people's lives, it may remind people of the Nazi policy of killing patients in mental hospitals. But there is really nothing godlike in such a judgement. It is not a moral judgement we are making, if we think that someone's life is so empty and unhappy as to be not worth living. It results from an attempt (obviously an extremely fallible one) to see his life from his own point of view and to see what he gets out of it. It must also be stressed that no suggestion is being made that it automatically becomes right to kill people whose lives we think are not worth living. It is only being argued that, if someone's life is worth living, this is *one* reason why it is directly wrong to kill him.

8   Is the Desire to Live the Criterion of a Worthwhile Life?

It might be thought that a conclusive test of whether or not someone's life is worth living is whether or not he wants to go on living. The attractiveness of this idea comes partly from the fact that the question whether someone has a worthwhile life involves thinking from his point of view, rather than thinking of his contribution to the lives of other people.

This proposal would commit us to believing that a person cannot want to end his life if it is worth living, and that he cannot want to prolong his life where it is not worth living. But these beliefs are both doubtful. In a passing mood of depression, someone who normally gets a lot out of life may want to kill himself. And someone who thinks he will go to hell may wish to prolong his present life, however miserable he is. The frying pan may be worse than nothing but better than the fire. And some people, while not believing in hell, simply fear death. They may wish they had never been born, but still not want to die.

For these reasons, someone's own desire to live or die is not a conclusive indication of whether or not he has a life worth living. And, equally obviously, with people who clearly do have lives worth living, the relative strength of their desires to live is not a reliable indicator of how worthwhile they find their lives. Someone whose hopes are often disappointed may cling to life as tenaciously as the happiest person in the world.

If we are to make these judgements, we cannot escape appealing to our own independent beliefs about what sorts of things enrich or impoverish people's lives. But, when this has been said, it should be emphasized that, when the question arises whether someone's life is worth living at all, his own views will normally be evidence of an overwhelmingly powerful kind. Our assessments of what other people get out of their lives are so fallible that only a monster of self-confidence would feel no qualms about correcting the judgement of the person whose life is in question.

9   Length of Life

The upshot of this discussion is that one reason why it is wrong to kill is that it is wrong to destroy a life which is worth living.

This can be seen in a slightly different perspective when we remember that we must all die one day, so that killing and life-saving are interventions that alter length of life by bringing forward or postponing the date of death. An extreme statement of this perspective is to be found in St Augustine's *City of God*:

> There is no one, it goes without saying, who is not nearer to death this year than he was last year, nearer tomorrow than today, today than yesterday, who will not by and by be nearer than he is at the moment, or is not nearer at the present time than he was a little while ago. Any space of time that we live through leaves us with so much less time to live, and the remainder decreases with every passing day; so that the whole of our lifetime is nothing but a race towards death, in which no one is allowed the slightest pause or any slackening of the pace. All are driven on at the same speed, and hurried along the same road to the same goal. The man whose life was short passed his days as swiftly as the longer-lived; moments of equal length rushed by for both of them at equal speed, though one was farther than the other from the goal to which both were hastening at the same rate.

The objection to killing made here is that it is wrong to shorten a worthwhile life. Why is a longer-lasting worthwhile life a better thing than an equally worthwhile but briefer life? Some people, thinking about their own lives, consider length of life very desirable, while others consider the number of years they have is of no importance at all, the quality of their lives being all that matters.

There is an argument (echoed in Sartre's short story *Le Mur*) used by Marcus Aurelius in support of the view that length of life is unimportant:

> If a god were to tell you 'Tomorrow, or at least the day after, you will be dead', you would not, unless the most abject of men, be greatly solicitous whether it was to be the later day rather than the morrow, for what is the difference between them? In the same way, do not reckon if of great moment whether it will come years and years hence, or tomorrow.[4]

This argument is unconvincing. From the fact that some small differences are below the threshold of mattering to us, it does not follow that all differences are insignificant. If someone steals all your money except either a penny or twopence, you will not mind much which he has left you with. It does not follow that the difference between riches and poverty is trivial.

There are at least two good reasons why a longer life can be thought better than a short one. One is that the quality of life is not altogether independent of its length: many plans and projects would not be worth undertaking without a good chance of time for their fulfilment. The other reason is that, other things being equal, more of a good thing is always better than less of it. This does not entail such absurd consequences as that an enjoyable play gets better as it gets longer, without limit. The point of the phrase 'other things being equal' is to allow for waning of interest and for the claims of other activities. So, unless life begins to pall, it is not in any way unreasonable to want more of it and to place a value on the prolonging of other people's worthwhile lives.

This suggests an answer to a traditional scepticism about whether people are harmed by being killed. This scepticism is stated in its most extreme form by Socrates in the *Apology*: 'Now if there is no consciousness, but only a dreamless sleep, death must be a marvellous gain.' There is clearly some exaggeration here. Death is not a dreamless sleep, but something we can treat as on a par with it. There is the doubtful suggestion that people would normally prefer a dreamless sleep to their waking lives. But, stripped of these exaggerations, there remains the valid point that being dead is not a state we experience, and so cannot be unpleasant. It was this that led Lucretius to think that the fear of death was confused:

> If the future holds travail and anguish in store, the self must be in existence, when that time comes, in order to experience it. But from this fate we are redeemed by death, which denies existence to the self that might have suffered these tribulations.

He reinforced this by a comparison with the time before birth:

> Look back at the eternity that passed before we were born, and mark how utterly it counts to us as nothing. This is a mirror that nature holds up to us, in which

we may see the time that shall be after we are dead. Is there anything terrifying in the sight – anything depressing...?[5]

Lucretius is right that being dead is not itself a misfortune, but this does not show that it is irrational to want not to die, nor that killing someone does him no harm. For, while I will not be miserable when dead, I am happy while alive, and it is not confused to want more of a good thing rather than less of it.

Bernard Williams has suggested that a reply to Lucretius of this kind does not commit us to wanting to be immortal.[6] He argues that immortality is either inconceivable or terrible. Either desires and satisfactions change so much that it is not clear that the immortal person will still be *me*, or else they are limited by my character and will start to seem pointlessly boring: 'A man at arms can get cramp from standing too long at his post, but sentry-duty can after all be necessary. But the threat of monotony in eternal activities could not be dealt with in that way, by regarding immortal boredom as an unavoidable ache derived from standing ceaselessly at one's post.' It is true that the reply to Lucretius does not commit us to desiring immortality. But I am not convinced that someone with a fairly constant character *need* eventually become intolerably bored, so long as they can watch the world continue to unfold and go on asking new questions and thinking, and so long as there are other people to share their feelings and thoughts with. Given the company of the right people, I would be glad of the chance to sample a few million years and see how it went.

10   The 'No Trade-Off' View

In stating the principle of the sanctity of life, it seemed important not to suggest that it always took priority over other values: 'taking human life is intrinsically wrong', not 'taking human life is always wrong'. The same point holds for the acceptable principle that we have tried to extract from the sanctity of life view: 'it is wrong to destroy a life which is worth living'. There is a tacit 'other things being equal' clause. For we can hold this view while thinking that the avoidance of other things even worse may sometimes have to take priority. We can have this objection to killing without being absolute pacifists.

The alternative, which may be called the 'no trade-off' view, gives an infinite value to not killing people (whose lives are worthwhile) compared to anything else. This may be because the *act* of killing seems infinitely appalling, which is an implausible view when we think of other horrendous acts, such as torturing. Or it may be because infinite value is set on worthwhile life itself. If this second alternative is chosen, it commits us to giving the saving of life overriding priority over all other social objectives. A piece of life-saving equipment is to be preferred to any amount of better housing, better schools or higher standard of living. Neither of these versions of the no trade-off view seems particularly attractive when the implications are clear.

11   The Social Effects of Abandoning the Sanctity of Life

Sometimes the doctrine of the sanctity of life is defended in an oblique way. The social implications of widespread abandonment of the view that taking human life is intrinsically wrong are said to be so appalling that, whatever its defects, the doctrine should not be criticized.

It must be faced that there is always a real possibility of producing a society where an indifference to the lives of at least some groups of people has terrible results. The sort of attitude is exhibited clearly in some passages from letters sent by the I.G. Farben chemical trust to the camp at Auschwitz.[7]

> In contemplation of experiments with a new soporific drug, we would appreciate your procuring for us a number of women...We received your answer but consider the price of 200 marks a woman excessive. We propose to pay not more than 170 marks a head. If agreeable, we will take possession of the women. We need approximately 150...Received the order of 150 women. Despite their emaciated condition, they were found satisfactory. We shall keep you posted on developments concerning this experiment...The tests were made. All subjects died. We shall contact you shortly on the subject of a new load.

If criticism of the doctrine of the sanctity of life made even a small contribution to developing such attitudes, that would be an overwhelming reason for not making any criticism. But the views to be argued for here in no way give support to these attitudes. (It is the first and most elementary test to be passed by an adequate account of the morality of killing that it should not fail to condemn them.) It is a thesis of this book that conventional moral views about killing are often intellectually unsatisfactory. The attempt to replace the unsatisfactory parts of a moral outlook may even result in something less likely to be eroded.

References

1   Glanville Williams: *The Sanctity of Life and the Criminal Law* (London, 1958), ch. 1.
2   A. Schopenhauer, *The World as Will and Representation*, translated by E. J. F. Payne (New York, 1969), Book 4, section 54.
3   *Eudemian Ethics*, 1216 a 11.
4   Marcus Aurelius, *Meditations*, trans. M. Staniforth (Harmondsworth, 1964).
5   Lucretius, *The Nature of the Universe*, trans. R. E. Latham (Harmondsworth, 1951).
6   Bernard Williams, 'The Makropulos Case', in *Problems of the Self* (Cambridge, 1973).
7   Bruno Bettelheim, *The Informed Heart* (London, 1961), ch. 6.

22

Declaration on Euthanasia

Sacred Congregation for the Doctrine of the Faith

The Congregation considers it opportune to set forth the Church's teaching on euthanasia.

It is indeed true that, in this sphere of teaching, the recent popes have explained the principles, and these retain their full force;[1] but the progress of medical science in recent years has brought to the fore new aspects of the question of euthanasia, and these aspects call for further elucidation on the ethical level.

In modern society, in which even the fundamental values of human life are often called into question, cultural change exercises an influence upon the way of looking at suffering and death; moreover, medicine has increased its capacity to cure and to prolong life in particular circumstances, which sometimes give rise to moral problems. Thus people living in this situation experience no little anxiety about the meaning of advanced old age and death. They also begin to wonder whether they have the right to obtain for themselves or their fellowmen an "easy death", which would shorten suffering and which seems to them more in harmony with human dignity.

A number of Episcopal Conferences have raised questions on this subject with the Sacred Congregation for the Doctrine of the Faith. The Congregation, having sought the opinion of experts on the various aspects of euthanasia, now wishes to respond to the Bishops' questions with the present Declaration, in order to help them to give correct teaching to the faithful entrusted to their care, and to offer them elements for reflection that they can present to the civil authorities with regard to this very serious matter...

It is hoped that this Declaration will meet with the approval of many people of good will, who, philosophical or ideological differences notwithstanding, have nevertheless a lively awareness of the rights of the human person. These rights have often in fact been proclaimed in recent years through declarations issued by International Congresses;[2] and since it is a question here of fundamental rights inherent in every human person, it is obviously wrong to have recourse to arguments from political pluralism or religious freedom in order to deny the universal value of those rights.

I The Value of Human Life

Human life is the basis of all goods, and is the necessary source and condition of every human activity and of all society. Most people regard life as something sacred and hold that no one may dispose of it at will, but believers see in life something greater, namely a gift of God's love, which they are called upon to preserve and make fruitful. And it is this latter consideration that gives rise to the following consequences:

1. No one can make an attempt on the life of an innocent person without opposing God's love for that person, without violating a fundamental

Original publication details: Sacred Congregation for the Doctrine of the Faith, "Declaration on Euthanasia," Vatican City, 1980.

right, and therefore without committing a crime of the utmost gravity.[3]

2. Everyone has the duty to lead his or her life in accordance with God's plan. That life is entrusted to the individual as a good that must bear fruit already here on earth, but that finds its full perfection only in eternal life.

3. Intentionally causing one's own death, or suicide, is therefore equally as wrong as murder; such an action on the part of a person is to be considered as a rejection of God's sovereignty and loving plan. Furthermore, suicide is also often a refusal of love for self, the denial of the natural instinct to live, a flight from the duties of justice and charity owed to one's neighbour, to various communities or to the whole of society – although, as is generally recognized, at times there are psychological factors present that can diminish responsibility or even completely remove it.

However, one must clearly distinguish suicide from that sacrifice of one's life whereby for a higher cause, such as God's glory, the salvation of souls or the service of one's brethren, a person offers his or her own life or puts it in danger (cf. *Jn* 15: 14).

II   Euthanasia

In order that the question of euthanasia can be properly dealt with, it is first necessary to define the words used.

Etymologically speaking, in ancient times *euthanasia* meant an *easy death* without severe suffering. Today one no longer thinks of this original meaning of the word, but rather of some intervention of medicine whereby the sufferings of sickness or of the final agony are reduced, sometimes also with the danger of suppressing life prematurely. Ultimately, the word *euthanasia* is used in a more particular sense to mean "mercy killing", for the purpose of putting an end to extreme suffering, or saving abnormal babies, the mentally ill or the incurably sick from the prolongation, perhaps for many years, of a miserable life, which could impose too heavy a burden on their families or on society.

It is therefore necessary to state clearly in what sense the word is used in the present document.

By euthanasia is understood an action or an omission which of itself or by intention causes death, in order that all suffering may in this way be eliminated. Euthanasia's terms of reference, therefore, are to be found in the intention of the will and in the methods used.

It is necessary to state firmly once more that nothing and no one can in any way permit the killing of an innocent human being, whether a fetus or an embryo, an infant or an adult, an old person, or one suffering from an incurable disease, or a person who is dying. Furthermore, no one is permitted to ask for this act of killing, either for himself or herself or for another person entrusted to his or her care, nor can he or she consent to it, either explicitly or implicitly. Nor can any authority legitimately recommend or permit such an action. For it is a question of the violation of the divine law, an offence against the dignity of the human person, a crime against life, and an attack on humanity.

It may happen that, by reason of prolonged and barely tolerable pain, for deeply personal or other reasons, people may be led to believe that they can legitimately ask for death or obtain it for others. Although in these cases the guilt of the individual may be reduced or completely absent, nevertheless the error of judgement into which the conscience falls, perhaps in good faith, does not change the nature of this act of killing, which will always be in itself something to be rejected. The pleas of gravely ill people who sometimes ask for death are not to be understood as implying a true desire for euthanasia; in fact it is almost always a case of an anguished plea for help and love. What a sick person needs, besides medical care, is love, the human and supernatural warmth with which the sick person can and ought to be surrounded by all those close to him or her, parents and children, doctors and nurses.

III   The Meaning of Suffering for Christians and the Use of Painkillers

Death does not always come in dramatic circumstances after barely tolerable sufferings. Nor do we have to think only of extreme cases. Numerous testimonies which confirm one another lead one to the conclusion that nature itself has made provision to render more bearable at the moment of death separations that would be terribly painful to a person in full health. Hence it is that a prolonged illness, advanced old age, or a state of loneliness or neglect can bring about psychological conditions that facilitate the acceptance of death.

Nevertheless the fact remains that death, often preceded or accompanied by severe and prolonged suffering, is something which naturally causes people anguish.

Physical suffering is certainly an unavoidable element of the human condition; on the biological level, it constitutes a warning of which no one denies the usefulness; but, since it affects the human psychological makeup, it often exceeds its own biological usefulness and so can become so severe as to cause the desire to remove it at any cost.

According to Christian teaching, however, suffering, especially suffering during the last moments of life, has a special place in God's saving plan; it is in fact a sharing in Christ's Passion and a union with the redeeming sacrifice which he offered in obedience to the Father's will. Therefore one must not be surprised if some Christians prefer to moderate their use of painkillers, in order to accept voluntarily at least a part of their sufferings and thus associate themselves in a conscious way with the sufferings of Christ crucified (cf. *Mt* 27: 34). Nevertheless it would be imprudent to impose a heroic way of acting as a general rule. On the contrary, human and Christian prudence suggest for the majority of sick people the use of medicines capable of alleviating or suppressing pain, even though these may cause as a secondary effect semiconsciousness and reduced lucidity. As for those who are not in a state to express themselves, one can reasonably presume that they wish to take these painkillers, and have them administered according to the doctor's advice.

But the intensive use of painkillers is not without difficulties, because the phenomenon of habituation generally makes it necessary to increase their dosage in order to maintain their efficacy. At this point it is fitting to recall a declaration by Pius XII, which retains its full force; in answer to a group of doctors who had put the question: "Is the suppression of pain and consciousness by the use of narcotics…permitted by religion and morality to the doctor and the patient (even at the approach of death and if one foresees that the use of narcotics will shorten life)?" the Pope said: "If no other means exist, and if, in the given circumstances, this does not prevent the carrying out of other religious and moral duties: Yes."[4] In this case, of course, death is in no way intended or sought, even if the risk of it is reasonably taken; the intention is simply to relieve pain effectively, using for this purpose painkillers available to medicine.

However, painkillers that cause unconsciousness need special consideration. For a person not only has to be able to satisfy his or her moral duties and family obligations; he or she also has to prepare himself or herself with full consciousness for meeting Christ. Thus Pius XII warns: "It is not right to deprive the dying person of consciousness without a serious reason."[5]

IV Due Proportion in the Use of Remedies

Today it is very important to protect, at the moment of death, both the dignity of the human person and the Christian concept of life, against a technological attitude that threatens to become an abuse. Thus, some people speak of a "right to die", which is an expression that does not mean the right to procure death either by one's own hand or by means of someone else, as one pleases, but rather the right to die peacefully with human and Christian dignity. From this point of view, the use of therapeutic means can sometimes pose problems.

In numerous cases, the complexity of the situation can be such as to cause doubts about the way ethical principles should be applied. In the final analysis, it pertains to the conscience either of the sick person, or of those qualified to speak in the sick person's name, or of the doctors, to decide, in the light of moral obligations and of the various aspects of the case.

Everyone has the duty to care for his or her own health or to seek such care from others. Those whose task it is to care for the sick must do so conscientiously and administer the remedies that seem necessary or useful.

However, is it necessary in all circumstances to have recourse to all possible remedies?

In the past, moralists replied that one is never obliged to use "extraordinary" means. This reply, which as a principle still holds good, is perhaps less clear today, by reason of the imprecision of the term and the rapid progress made in the treatment of sickness. Thus some people prefer to speak of "proportionate" and "disproportionate" means. In any case, it will be possible to make a correct judgement as to the means by studying the type of treatment to be used, its degree of complexity or risk, its cost and the possibilities of using it, and comparing these elements with the result that can be expected, taking into account the state of the sick person and his or her physical and moral resources.

In order to facilitate the application of these general principles, the following clarifications can be added:

– If there are no other sufficient remedies, it is permitted, with the patient's consent, to have recourse to the means provided by the most advanced medical techniques, even if these means are still at the experimental stage and are not without a certain risk. By accepting them, the patient can even show generosity in the service of humanity.

– It is also permitted, with the patient's consent, to interrupt these means, where the results fall short of expectations. But for such a decision to be made, account will have to be taken of the reasonable wishes of the patient and the patient's family, as also of the advice of the doctors who are specially competent in the matter. The latter may in particular judge that the investment in instruments and personnel is disproportionate to the results foreseen; they may also judge that the techniques applied impose on the patient strain or suffering out of proportion with the benefits which he or she may gain from such techniques.

– It is also permissible to make do with the normal means that medicine can offer. Therefore one cannot impose on anyone the obligation to have recourse to a technique which is already in use but which carries a risk or is burdensome. Such a refusal is not the equivalent of suicide; on the contrary, it should be considered as an acceptance of the human condition, or a wish to avoid the application of a medical procedure disproportionate to the results that can be expected, or a desire not to impose excessive expense on the family or the community.

– When inevitable death is imminent in spite of the means used, it is permitted in conscience to take the decision to refuse forms of treatment that would only secure a precarious and burdensome prolongation of life, so long as the normal care due to the sick person in similar cases is not interrupted. In such circumstances the doctor has no reason to reproach himself with failing to help the person in danger.

Conclusion

The norms contained in the present Declaration are inspired by a profound desire to serve people in accordance with the plan of the Creator. Life is a gift of God, and on the other hand death is unavoidable; it is necessary therefore that we, without in any way hastening the hour of death, should be able to accept it with full responsibility and dignity. It is true that death marks the end of our earthly existence, but at the same time it opens the door to immortal life. Therefore all must prepare themselves for this event in the light of human values, and Christians even more so in the light of faith.

As for those who work in the medical profession, they ought to neglect no means of making all their skill available to the sick and the dying; but they should also remember how much more necessary it is to provide them with the comfort of boundless kindness and heartfelt charity. Such service to people is also service to Christ the Lord, who said: "As you did it to one of the least of these my brethren, you did it to me" (Mt 25: 40).

At the audience granted to the undersigned Prefect, His Holiness Pope John Paul II approved this Declaration, adopted at the ordinary meeting of the Sacred Congregation for the Doctrine of the Faith, and ordered its publication.

Rome, the Sacred Congregation for the Doctrine of the Faith, 5 May 1980.

FRANJO Card. ŠEPER
Prefect

✠ Jérôme Hamer, O. P.
Tit. Archbishop of Lorium
Secretary

Notes

1 Pius XII, *Address to those attending the Congress of the International Union of Catholic Women's Leagues*, 11 September 1947: *AAS* 39 (1947), p. 483; *Address to the Italian Catholic Union of Midwives*, 29 October 1951: *AAS* 43 (1951), pp. 835–54; *Speech to the members of the International Office of military medicine documentation*, 19 October 1953: *AAS* 45 (1953), pp. 744–54; *Address to those taking part in the IXth Congress of the Italian Anaesthesiological Society*, 24 February 1957: *AAS* 49 (1957), pp. 146; cf. also *Address on "reanimation"*, 24 November 1957: *AAS* 49 (1957), pp. 1027–33; Paul.VI, *Address to the members of the United Nations Special Committee on Apartheid*, 22 May 1974: *AAS* 66 (1974), p. 346; John Paul. II: *Address to the Bishops of the United States of America*, 5 October 1979: *AAS* 71 (1979), p. 1225.

2 One thinks especially of Recommendation 779 (1976) on the rights of the sick and dying, of the Parliamentary Assembly of the Council of Europe at its XXVIIth Ordinary Session; cf. Sipeca, no. 1 (March 1977), pp. 14–15.

3 We leave aside completely the problems of the death penalty and of war, which involve specific considerations that do not concern the present subject.

4 Pius XII, *Address of 24 February 1957*: *AAS* 49 (1957), p. 147.

5 Pius XII, ibid., p. 145; cf. *Address of 9 September 1958*: *AAS* 50 (1958), p. 694.

Killing and Letting Die

23

The Morality of Killing
A Traditional View

Germain Grisez and Joseph M. Boyle, Jr.

The Morality of Killing

In the strict sense one kills a person when, having considered bringing about a person's death as something one could do, one commits oneself to doing it by adopting this proposal instead of some alternative and by undertaking to execute it. By definition killing in the strict sense is an action contrary to the good of life. The adoption of a proposal to bring about someone's death is incompatible with respect for this good. Thus every act which is an act of killing in the strict sense is immoral. No additional circumstance or condition can remove this immorality.

This definition and moral characterization of killing in the strict sense make no distinction between intent to kill, attempt to kill, and the consummation of the undertaking by successful execution. These distinctions, which are legally significant, are morally irrelevant. If one commits oneself to realizing a certain state of affairs, by the commitment one constitutes oneself as a certain type of person. If one commits oneself to killing a person, one constitutes oneself a murderer. This remains true even if one is prevented from attempting to execute one's purpose – for example, if someone else kills the intended victim first. Even more obviously it remains true if one attempts to execute one's purpose but fails – for example, if one shoots to kill but misses the intended victim.

Although everything which is an act of killing in the strict sense is immoral, not every deadly deed is an act of killing in this sense. As we have explained, some deadly deeds carry out a consciously projected design, but the performance is not the execution of a proposal adopted by the actor's choice to bring about the death of a human individual. The examples of the enraged wife and the dutiful soldier belong here. In what follows we call this type of performance a "deadly deed" to distinguish it from a killing in the strict sense.

Finally, there are other cases of causing death, such as some killing in self-defense, which are neither killing in the strict sense nor deadly deeds as here defined. The proposal adopted or the consciously projected design carried out by persons defending themselves might not extend beyond incapacitating the attacker, but this can result in the attacker's death if the only available and adequate means to incapacitate the attacker also will result in mortal wounds…

We turn now to the consideration of cases in which one brings about one's own death. Even in ordinary language some ethically significant distinctions are made in speaking of this, for one does not call "suicide" all cases in which someone causes his or her own death. Most people who consider suicide immoral do not class martyrs and heroes as suicides, since "suicide" sug-

Original publication details: Germain Grisez and Joseph M. Boyle, Jr., "The Morality of Killing: A Traditional View," pp. 381–419 from *Life and Death with Liberty and Justice: A Contribution to the Euthanasia Debate,* Notre Dame, IN: University of Notre Dame Press, 1971.

gests an act of killing oneself. Yet not all who commit suicide do a moral act of killing in the strict sense.

In cases in which suicide is an act of killing in the strict sense the proposal to kill oneself is among the proposals one considers in deliberation, and this proposal is adopted by choice as preferable to alternatives. For example, a person who for some reason is suffering greatly might think: "I wish I no longer had to suffer as I am suffering. If I were dead, my suffering would be at an end. But I am not likely to die soon. I could kill myself. But I fear death and what might follow after it. I could put up with my misery and perhaps find some other way out." One thinking in this way is deliberating. In saying "I could kill myself" suicide is proposed. If this proposal is adopted, one's moral act is killing in the strict sense. As in other instances this act is incompatible with the basic good of human life, and it cannot morally be justified, regardless of what else might be the case.

One can propose to kill oneself without saying to oneself "I could kill myself." One might say something which one would accept as equivalent in meaning: "I could destroy myself," "I could rub myself out," or something of the sort. Again, one might say something which one would admit amounts to "I could kill myself" although not equivalent in meaning to it, such as "I could shoot myself," when what one has in mind is shooting oneself in the head and thereby causing death, not merely shooting oneself to cause a wound…

There are still other cases in which individuals contribute to the causation of their own deaths by acts which are morally significant but which in no way execute proposals which are properly suicidal. Typical martyrs lay down their lives. The death could be avoided if the martyr were willing to do something believed wrong or to leave unfulfilled some duty which is accepted as compelling. But the martyr refuses to avoid death by compromise or evasion of duty. Such persons do only what they believe to be morally required; the consequent loss of their own lives is willingly accepted by martyrs, neither sought nor chosen as a means to anything.

The martyr reasons somewhat as follows: "I would like to please everyone and to stay alive. But they are demanding of me that I do what I believe to be wrong or that I omit doing what I believe to be my sacred mission. They threaten me with death if I do not meet their demands. But if I were to comply with their threat, I would be doing evil in order that the good of saving my life might follow from it. This I may not do. Therefore, I must stand as long as I can in accord with my conscience, even though they are likely to kill me or torture me into submission."

Someone who does not understand the martyr's reasoning is likely to consider the martyr a suicide. But martyrs who reason thus do not propose to bring about their own deaths. The martyr bears witness to a profound commitment, first of all before the persecutors themselves. The latter can and in the martyr's view should accept this testimony and approve the rightness of the commitment. The martyr's refusal to give in does not bring about the persecutor's act of killing; the martyr only fails to win over the persecutor and to forestall the deadly deed…

Of course, we hold that suicide which is killing in the strict sense is necessarily immoral simply because it violates the basic good of human life. One who deliberately chooses to end his or her own life constitutes by this commitment a self-murderous self. But considerations which tell against even nonsuicidal acts which bring about a person's own death also argue against the moral justifiability of suicidal acts, which execute a proposal to destroy one's own life.

Considering matters from a moral point of view and from the side of the one whose life is to be ended, voluntary euthanasia is not significantly different from other cases of suicide. The proposal is to bring about death as a means to ending suffering. This proposal, if adopted and executed, is an instance of killing in the strict sense. It can never be morally justified.

Of course, a person who is in severe pain and who seeks death to escape it is likely to have mitigated responsibility or even to be drawn into acceptance without a deliberate choice, just as is the case with others whose suffering drives them to a deadly deed against themselves.

However, if an individual plans to seek euthanasia and arranges for it well in advance of the time of suffering, then the possibility that the demand for death is not an expression of deliberate choice is greatly lessened. The conditions which from the point of view of proponents of euthanasia are optimum for making a decision about the matter are precisely the conditions in which the decision is likely to be a morally unjustifiable act of killing in the strict sense.

Considering voluntary euthanasia from the point of view of the person who would carry out the killing, matters seem no better from a moral viewpoint. The performance can hardly fail to be an execution of a deliberate choice; the one carrying out the killing can hardly be driven to it, nor can anyone in the present culture accept the duty unquestioningly...

Nonvoluntary euthanasia also clearly proposes death as a treatment of choice. The act hardly can fail to be killing in the strict sense. And in addition to the violation of the good of life, the rights of those to be killed also will be violated – for example, by denial to them of equal protection of the laws. Nonvoluntary euthanasia would violate both life and justice...

The preceding treatment has been concerned with instances in which people bring about death by an outward performance. We now turn to a consideration of cases in which individuals refuse treatment for themselves or others, or withhold treatment, or fail or neglect to give it. To apply the moral theory which we articulated to such cases we must first say something about omissions.

If people act when they carry out a proposal which they have adopted by choice, certain cases of outward nonperformance must count as human actions. One can adopt a proposal and carry it out by deliberately not causing or preventing something which one could cause or prevent. One's choice not to cause or prevent something can be a way of realizing a state of affairs one considers somehow desirable. For example, one might adopt the proposal to protest against a government policy permitting the use of public funds for abortion by not paying certain taxes. In this case one aims to realize a desired state of affairs by means of nonconformance with the demands of the law. The nonconformance need involve no outward performance at all.

Omissions of this type – those in which one undertakes to realize a proposed state of affairs by not causing or preventing something – are very important for understanding the morality of withholding treatment from dying patients, refusing treatment proposed for oneself, and in general letting people die.

It clearly is possible to kill in the strict sense by deliberately letting someone die. If one adopts the proposal to bring about a person's death and realizes this proposal by not behaving as one otherwise would behave, then one is committed to the state of affairs which includes the person's death. This commitment, although carried out by a nonperformance, is morally speaking an act of killing. It involves the adoption and execution of a proposal contrary to the basic good of human life. Thus, any case in which one chooses the proposal that a person die and on this basis allows the person to die is necessarily immoral.

For example, if a child is born suffering from various defects and if the physicians and parents decide that the child, the family, and society will all be better off if the burdens entailed by the child's continued life are forestalled by its death, and if they therefore adopt the proposal not to perform a simple operation, which otherwise would be done, so that the child will die, then the parents and physicians morally speaking kill the child – "kill" in the strict sense clarified at the beginning of this chapter. The fact that there is no blood spilled, no poison injected, that the death certificate can honestly show that the child has died from complications arising from its defective condition – none of this is morally relevant. The moral act is no different from any other moral act of murder.

The same thing will be true in every instance in which a judgement is made that someone – whether oneself or another – would be better off dead, the proposal to bring about death by not causing or preventing something is considered and adopted, and this proposal is executed by outward nonperformance of behavior which one otherwise might have attempted...

Michael Tooley and others also have criticized those who hold that there is a significant moral difference between killing a person and letting the person die. Their criticism is that if one considers a case of killing and a case of letting die between which there is no difference except that in the one the death is brought about by a performance which causes it while in the other it is brought about by not causing or preventing something, then there is no moral difference between the two cases.

We agree. Both actions are killing in the strict sense; neither can ever be moral. However, not every instance in which someone deliberately lets another die is an action shaped by the proposal that the person whose death is accepted should die or die sooner than would otherwise be the case. We turn now to the consideration of such deliberate omissions which, considered from a moral point of view, are not acts of killing.

The fundamental point about these omissions is that one can omit to do some good or prevent some evil without adopting any proposal which either is opposed to the good or embraces (as means) the evil whose occurrence one accepts. This possibility is most obviously instantiated when one must forgo doing a certain good or preventing a certain evil because one has a duty, incompatible with doing the good or preventing the evil, to do some other good or prevent some other evil.

For example, in an emergency situation in which many people are seriously injured and the medical resources – including time and personnel – are limited, those making decisions must choose to treat some and put off the treatment of others, perhaps with fatal consequences to those not treated first. The nontreatment of those who are not treated is deliberate; even their deaths might be foreseen as an inevitable consequence and knowingly accepted when the decision to treat others is made. Yet plainly the nontreatment of those who are not treated need involve no proposal that these people should die or die more quickly than they otherwise would. Provided there is no partiality or other breach of faith with those not treated, the execution of a proposal to save others does not embrace the death of those who die, and no immorality is done…

There is another type of reason for forgoing doing good which involves no disrespect for the good which would be realized by the action. One might notice that doing the action good in itself will in fact bring about many undesirable consequences. And one might choose not to adopt the proposal to do the good in order to avoid accepting these various bad consequences. This situation is exemplified in a very important way in many instances in which potentially life-prolonging treatment is refused, withheld, or withdrawn – even in the case of a patient who is not dying – because of the expected disadvantages of accepting, carrying out, or continuing treatment…

We have articulated grounds on which someone might reasonably consider treatment undesirable: if the treatment is experimental or risky, if it would be painful or otherwise experienced negatively, if it would interfere with activities or experiences the patient might otherwise enjoy, if it would conflict with some moral or religious principle to which the patient adheres, if it would be psychologically repugnant to the patient, or if the financial or other impact of the treatment upon other persons would constitute a compelling reason to refuse treatment.

The moral legitimacy of refusing treatment in some cases on some such grounds certainly was part of what Pius XII was indicating by his famous distinction between ordinary and extraordinary means of treatment. The Pope defined "extraordinary means" as ones which involve a "great burden," and he allowed that one could morally forgo the use of extraordinary means. The conception of extraordinary means clearly is abused, however, when the proposal is to bring about death by the omission of treatment, and the difficulties of the treatment are pointed to by way of rationalizing the murderous act. If it is decided that a person would be better off dead and that treatment which would be given to another will be withheld because of the poor quality of the life to be preserved, then the focus in decision is not upon the means and its disadvantageous consequences. Rather, what is feared is that the means would be effective, that life would be preserved, and that the life itself and its consequences would be a burden.

Moreover, even when treatment is refused, withheld, or withdrawn because of an objection to the means – and without the adopting of a proposal to bring about death – there still can be a serious moral failing.

A person who refuses lifesaving or life-prolonging treatment, not on a suicidal proposal but because of great repugnance for the treatment itself, might have an obligation to maintain life longer in order to fulfill duties toward others.

For example, someone on dialysis might wish to give up the treatment because of the difficulties it involves, and some persons in this situation could discontinue treatment and accept death without moral fault. But a parent with children in need of continued care, a professional person with grave responsibilities, and many other persons who can prolong their lives at considerable sacrifice to themselves are morally bound to do so, even by this extraordinary means, because they have accepted duties which others are entitled to have fulfilled, and persons who love the goods as one ought will faithfully fulfill duties toward others at considerable cost to themselves.

Similarly, if one refuses, withholds, or withdraws lifesaving or life-prolonging treatment for another because of the grave burdens entailed by such treatment, the burdens must be grave indeed. This is especially clear in cases in which the patient is not dying – for example, cases of defective infants. One must be quite sure, at the least, that with no suicidal proposal one would in the patient's place not wish the treatment. Otherwise, one accepts moral responsibility for a very grave wrong toward the patient.

24

Active and Passive Euthanasia

James Rachels

The traditional distinction between active and passive euthanasia requires critical analysis. The conventional doctrine is that there is such an important moral difference between the two that, although the latter is sometimes permissible, the former is always forbidden. This doctrine may be challenged for several reasons. First of all, active euthanasia is in many cases more humane than passive euthanasia. Secondly, the conventional doctrine leads to decisions concerning life and death on irrelevant grounds. Thirdly, the doctrine rests on a distinction between killing and letting die that itself has no moral importance. Fourthly, the most common arguments in favor of the doctrine are invalid. I therefore suggest that the American Medical Association policy statement that endorses this doctrine is unsound.

The distinction between active and passive euthanasia is thought to be crucial for medical ethics. The idea is that it is permissible, at least in some cases, to withhold treatment and allow a patient to die, but it is never permissible to take any direct action designed to kill the patient. This doctrine seems to be accepted by most doctors, and it is endorsed in a statement adopted by the House of Delegates of the American Medical Association on December 4, 1973.

The intentional termination of the life of one human being by another – mercy killing – is contrary to that for which the medical profession stands and is contrary to the policy of the American Medical Association.

The cessation of the employment of extraordinary means to prolong the life of the body when there is irrefutable evidence that biological death is imminent is the decision of the patient and/or his immediate family. The advice and judgment of the physician should be freely available to the patient and/or his immediate family.

However, a strong case can be made against this doctrine. In what follows I will set out some of the relevant arguments, and urge doctors to reconsider their views on this matter.

To begin with a familiar type of situation, a patient who is dying of incurable cancer of the throat is in terrible pain, which can no longer be satisfactorily alleviated. He is certain to die within a few days, even if present treatment is continued, but he does not want to go on living for those days since the pain is unbearable. So he asks the doctor for an end to it, and his family joins in the request.

Suppose the doctor agrees to withhold treatment, as the conventional doctrine says he may. The justification for his doing so is that the patient is in terrible agony, and since he is going to die anyway, it would be wrong to prolong his suffering needlessly. But now notice this. If one simply withholds treatment, it may take the patient longer to die, and so he may suffer more than he would if more direct action were taken and a

Original publication details: James Rachels, "Active and Passive Euthanasia," pp. 78–80 from *New England Journal of Medicine* 292 (1975). Copyright © 1975 Massachusetts Medical Society. Reprinted with permission from Massachusetts Medical Society.

Bioethics: An Anthology, Third Edition. Edited by Helga Kuhse, Udo Schüklenk, and Peter Singer.
© 2016 John Wiley & Sons, Inc. Published 2016 by John Wiley & Sons, Inc.

lethal injection given. This fact provides strong reason for thinking that, once the initial decision not to pro-long his agony has been made, active euthanasia is actually preferable to passive euthanasia, rather than the reverse. To say otherwise is to endorse the option that leads to more suffering rather than less, and is contrary to the humanitarian impulse that prompts the decision not to prolong his life in the first place.

Part of my point is that the process of being "allowed to die" can be relatively slow and painful, whereas being given a lethal injection is relatively quick and painless. Let me give a different sort of example. In the United States about one in 600 babies is born with Down's syndrome. Most of these babies are otherwise healthy – that is, with only the usual pediatric care, they will proceed to an otherwise normal infancy. Some, however, are born with congenital defects such as intestinal obstructions that require operations if they are to live. Sometimes, the parents and the doctor will decide not to operate, and let the infant die. Anthony Shaw describes what happens then:

> When surgery is denied [the doctor] must try to keep the infant from suffering while natural forces sap the baby's life away. As a surgeon whose natural inclination is to use the scalpel to fight off death, standing by and watching a salvageable baby die is the most emotionally exhausting experience I know. It is easy at a conference, in a theoretical discussion, to decide that such infants should be allowed to die. It is altogether different to stand by in the nursery and watch as dehydration and infection wither a tiny being over hours and days. This is a terrible ordeal for me and the hospital staff – much more so than for the parents who never set foot in the nursery.[1]

I can understand why some people are opposed to all euthanasia, and insist that such infants must be allowed to live. I think I can also understand why other people favor destroying these babies quickly and painlessly. But why should anyone favor letting "dehydration and infection wither a tiny being over hours and days?" The doctrine that says that a baby may be allowed to dehydrate and wither, but may not be given an injection that would end its life without suffering, seems so patently cruel as to require no further refutation. The strong language is not intended to offend, but only to put the point in the clearest possible way.

My second argument is that the conventional doctrine leads to decisions concerning life and death made on irrelevant grounds.

Consider again the case of the infants with Down's syndrome who need operations for congenital defects unrelated to the syndrome to live. Sometimes, there is no operation, and the baby dies, but when there is no such defect, the baby lives on. Now, an operation such as that to remove an intestinal obstruction is not prohibitively difficult. The reason why such operations are not performed in these cases is, clearly, that the child has Down's syndrome and the parents and doctor judge that because of that fact it is better for the child to die.

But notice that this situation is absurd, no matter what view one takes of the lives and potentials of such babies. If the life of such an infant is worth preserving, what does it matter if it needs a simple operation? Or, if one thinks it better that such a baby should not live on, what difference does it make that it happens to have an unobstructed intestinal tract? In either case, the matter of life and death is being decided on irrelevant grounds. It is the Down's syndrome, and not the intestines, that is the issue. The matter should be decided, if at all, on that basis, and not be allowed to depend on the essentially irrelevant question of whether the intestinal tract is blocked.

What makes this situation possible, of course, is the idea that when there is an intestinal blockage, one can "let the baby die," but when there is no such defect there is nothing that can be done, for one must not "kill" it. The fact that this idea leads to such results as deciding life or death on irrelevant grounds is another good reason why the doctrine should be rejected.

One reason why so many people think that there is an important moral difference between active and passive euthanasia is that they think killing someone is morally worse than letting someone die. But is it? Is killing, in itself, worse than letting die? To investigate this issue, two cases may be considered that are exactly alike except that one involves killing whereas the other involves letting someone die. Then, it can be asked whether this difference makes any difference to the moral assessments. It is important that the cases be exactly alike, except for this one difference, since otherwise one cannot be confident that it is this difference and not some other that accounts for any variation in the assessments of the two cases. So, let us consider this pair of cases:

In the first. Smith stands to gain a large inheritance if anything should happen to his six-year-old cousin. One evening while the child is taking his bath. Smith sneaks into the bathroom and drowns the child, and then arranges things so that it will look like an accident.

In the second. Jones also stands to gain if anything should happen to his six-year-old cousin. Like Smith, Jones sneaks in planning to drown the child in his bath. However, just as he enters the bathroom Jones sees the child slip and hit his head, and fall face down in the water. Jones is delighted: he stands by, ready to push the child's head back under if it is necessary, but it is not necessary. With only a little thrashing about, the child drowns all by himself, "accidentally," as Jones watches and does nothing.

Now Smith killed the child, whereas Jones "merely" let the child die. That is the only difference between them. Did either man behave better, from a moral point of view? If the difference between killing and letting die were in itself a morally important matter, one should say that Jones's behavior was less reprehensible than Smith's. But does one really want to say that? I think not. In the first place, both men acted from the same motive, personal gain, and both had exactly the same end in view when they acted. It may be inferred from Smith's conduct that he is a bad man, although that judgment may be withdrawn or modified if certain further facts are learned about him – for example, that he is mentally deranged. But would not the very same thing be inferred about Jones from his conduct? And would not the same further considerations also be relevant to any modification of this judgement? Moreover, suppose Jones pleaded, in his own defense. "After all, I didn't do anything except just stand there and watch the child drown. I didn't kill him: I only let him die." Again, if letting die were in itself less bad than killing, this defense should have at least some weight. But it does not. Such a "defense" can only be regarded as a grotesque perversion of moral reasoning. Morally speaking, it is no defense at all.

Now, it may be pointed out, quite properly, that the cases of euthanasia with which doctors are concerned are not like this at all. They do not involve personal gain or the destruction of normal healthy children. Doctors are concerned only with cases in which the patient's life is of no further use to him, or in which

the patient's life has become or will soon become a terrible burden. However, the point is the same in these cases: the bare difference between killing and letting die does not, in itself, make a moral difference. If a doctor lets a patient die, for humane reasons, he is in the same moral position as if he had given the patient a lethal injection for humane reasons. If his decision was wrong – if, for example, the patient's illness was in fact curable – the decision would be equally regrettable no matter which method was used to carry it out. And if the doctor's decision was the right one, the method used is not in itself important.

The AMA policy statement isolates the crucial issue very well: the crucial issue is "the intentional termination of the life of one human being by another." But after identifying this issue, and forbidding "mercy killing," the statement goes on to deny that the cessation of treatment is the intentional termination of a life. This is where the mistake comes in, for what is the cessation of treatment, in these circumstances, if it is not "the intentional termination of the life of one human being by another?" Of course it is exactly that, and if it were not, there would be no point to it.

Many people will find this judgment hard to accept. One reason, I think, is that it is very easy to conflate the question of whether killing is, in itself, worse than letting die, with the very different question of whether most actual cases of killing are more reprehensible than most actual cases of letting die. Most actual cases of killing are clearly terrible (think, for example, of all the murders reported in the newspapers), and one hears of such cases every day. On the other hand, one hardly ever hears of a case of letting die, except for the actions of doctors who are motivated by humanitarian reasons. So one learns to think of killing in a much worse light than of letting die. But this does not mean that there is something about killing that makes it in itself worse than letting die, for it is not the bare difference between killing and letting die that makes the difference in these cases. Rather, the other factors – the murderer's motive of personal gain, for example, contrasted with the doctor's humanitarian motivation – account for different reactions to the different cases.

I have argued that killing is not in itself any worse than letting die: if my contention is right, it follows that active euthanasia is not any worse than passive euthanasia. What arguments can be given on the other side? The most common. I believe, is the following:

"The important difference between active and passive euthanasia is that, in passive euthanasia, the doctor does not do anything to bring about the patient's death. The doctor does nothing, and the patient dies of whatever ills already afflict him. In active euthanasia, however, the doctor does something to bring about the patient's death: he kills him. The doctor who gives the patient with cancer a lethal injection has himself caused his patient's death: whereas if he merely ceases treatment, the cancer is the cause of the death."

A number of points need to be made here. The first is that it is not exactly correct to say that in passive euthanasia the doctor does nothing, for he does do one thing that is very important: he lets the patient die. "Letting someone die" is certainly different, in some respects, from other types of action – mainly in that it is a kind of action that one may perform by way of not performing certain other actions. For example, one may let a patient die by way of not giving medication, just as one may insult someone by way of not shaking his hand. But for any purpose of moral assessment, it is a type of action nonetheless. The decision to let a patient die is subject to moral appraisal in the same way that a decision to kill him would be subject to moral appraisal: it may be assessed as wise or unwise, compassionate or sadistic, right or wrong. If a doctor deliberately let a patient die who was suffering from a routinely curable illness, the doctor would certainly be to blame for what he had done, just as he would be to blame if he had needlessly killed the patient. Charges against him would then be appropriate. If so, it would be no defense at all for him to insist that he didn't "do anything." He would have done something very serious indeed, for he let his patient die.

Fixing the cause of death may be very important from a legal point of view, for it may determine whether criminal charges are brought against the doctor. But I do not think that this notion can be used to show a moral difference between active and passive euthanasia. The reason why it is considered bad to be the cause of someone's death is that death is regarded as a great evil – and so it is. However, if it has been decided that euthanasia – even passive euthanasia – is desirable in a given case, it has also been decided that in this instance death is no greater an evil than the patient's continued existence. And if this is true, the usual reason for not wanting to be the cause of someone's death simply does not apply.

Finally, doctors may think that all of this is only of academic interest – the sort of thing that philosophers may worry about but that has no practical bearing on their own work. After all, doctors must be concerned about the legal consequences of what they do, and active euthanasia is clearly forbidden by the law. But even so, doctors should also be concerned with the fact that the law is forcing upon them a moral doctrine that may well be indefensible, and has a considerable effect on their practices. Of course, most doctors are not now in the position of being coerced in this matter, for they do not regard themselves as merely going along with what the law requires. Rather, in statements such as the AMA policy statement that I have quoted, they are endorsing this doctrine as a central point of medical ethics. In that statement, active euthanasia is condemned not merely as illegal but as "contrary to that for which the medical profession stands," whereas passive euthanasia is approved. However, the preceding considerations suggest that there is really no moral difference between the two, considered in themselves (there may be important moral differences in some cases in their *consequences*, but, as I pointed out, these differences may make active euthanasia, and not passive euthanasia, the morally preferable option). So, whereas doctors may have to discriminate between active and passive euthanasia to satisfy the law, they should not do any more than that. In particular, they should not give the distinction any added authority and weight by writing it into official statements of medical ethics.

Reference

1   A. Shaw 'Doctor, Do We Have a Choice?' *New York Times Magazine*. January 30, 1972, p. 54.

25

Is Killing No Worse Than Letting Die?

Winston Nesbitt

I want in this paper to consider a kind of argument sometimes produced against the thesis that it is worse to kill someone (that is, to deliberately take action that results in another's death) than merely to allow someone to die (that is, deliberately to fail to take steps which were available and which would have saved another's life). Let us, for brevity's sake, refer to this as the 'difference thesis', since it implies that there is a moral difference between killing and letting die.

One approach commonly taken by opponents of the difference thesis is to produce examples of cases in which an agent does not kill, but merely lets someone die, and yet would be generally agreed to be just as morally reprehensible as if he had killed. This kind of appeal to common intuitions might seem an unsatisfactory way of approaching the issue. It has been argued[1] that what stance one takes concerning the difference thesis will depend on the ethical theory one holds, so that we cannot decide what stance is correct independently of deciding what is the correct moral theory. I do not, however, wish to object to the approach in question on these grounds. It may be true that different moral theories dictate different stances concerning the difference thesis, so that a theoretically satisfactory defence or refutation of the thesis requires a satisfactory defence of a theory which entails its soundness or unsoundness. However, the issue of its soundness or otherwise is a vital one in the

attempt to decide some pressing moral questions,[2] and we cannot wait for a demonstration of the correct moral theory before taking up any kind of position with regard to it. Moreover, decisions on moral questions directly affecting practice are rarely derived from ethical first principles, but are usually based at some level on common intuitions, and it is arguable that at least where the question is one of public policy, this is as it should be.

2

It might seem at first glance a simple matter to show at least that common moral intuitions favour the difference thesis. Compare, to take an example of John Ladd's,[3] the case in which I push someone who I know cannot swim into a river, thereby killing her, with that in which I come across someone drowning and fail to rescue her, although I am able to do so, thereby letting her die. Wouldn't most of us agree that my behaviour is morally worse in the first case?

However, it would be generally agreed by those involved in the debate that nothing of importance for our issue, not even concerning common opinion, can be learned through considering such an example. As Ladd points out, without being told any more about the cases mentioned, we are inclined to assume that

Original publication details: Winston Nesbitt, "Is Killing No Worse Than Letting Die?," pp. 101–5 from *Journal of Applied Philosophy* 12: 1 (1995). Reproduced with permission from John Wiley & Sons.

there are other morally relevant differences between them, because there usually would be. We assume, for example, some malicious motive in the case of killing, but perhaps only fear or indifference in the case of failing to save. James Rachels and Michael Tooley, both of whom argue against the difference thesis, make similar points,[4] as does Raziel Abelson, in a paper defending the thesis.[5] Tooley, for example, notes that as well as differences in motives, there are also certain other morally relevant differences between typical acts of killing and typical acts of failing to save which may make us judge them differently. Typically, saving someone requires more effort than refraining from killing someone. Again, an act of killing necessarily results in someone's death, but an act of failing to save does not – someone else may come to the rescue. Factors such as these, it is suggested, may account for our tendency to judge failure to save (i.e., letting die) less harshly than killing. Tooley concludes that if one wishes to appeal to intuitions here, 'one must be careful to confine one's attention to pairs of cases that do not differ in these, or other significant respects.'[6]

Accordingly, efforts are made by opponents of the difference thesis to produce pairs of cases which do not differ in morally significant respects (other than in one being a case of killing while the other is a case of letting die or failing to save). In fact, at least the major part of the case mounted by Rachels and Tooley against the difference thesis consists of the production of such examples. It is suggested that when we compare a case of killing with one which differs from it *only* in being a case of letting die, we will agree that either agent is as culpable as the other; and this is then taken to show that any inclination we ordinarily have to think killing worse than letting die is attributable to our tending, illegitimately, to think of typical cases of killing and of letting die, which differ in other morally relevant respects. I want now to examine the kind of example usually produced in these contexts.

3

I will begin with the examples produced by James Rachels in the article mentioned earlier, which is fast becoming one of the most frequently reprinted articles

in the area.[7] Although the article has been the subject of a good deal of discussion, as far as I know the points which I will make concerning it have not been previously made. Rachels asks us to compare the following two cases. The first is that of Smith, who will gain a large inheritance should his six-year-old nephew die. With this in mind, Smith one evening sneaks into the bathroom where his nephew is taking a bath, and drowns him. The other case, that of Jones, is identical, except that as Jones is about to drown his nephew, the child slips, hits his head, and falls, face down and unconscious, into the bath-water. Jones, delighted at his good fortune, watches as his nephew drowns.

Rachels assumes that we will readily agree that Smith, who kills his nephew, is no worse, morally speaking, than Jones, who merely lets his nephew die. Do we really want to say, he asks, that either behaves better from the moral point of view than the other? It would, he suggests, be a 'grotesque perversion of moral reasoning' for Jones to argue, 'After all, I didn't do anything except just stand and watch the child drown. I didn't kill him; I only let him die.'[8] Yet, Rachels says, if letting die were in itself less bad than killing, this defence would carry some weight.

There is little doubt that Rachels is correct in taking it that we will agree that Smith behaves no worse in his examples than does Jones. Before we are persuaded by this that killing someone is in itself morally no worse than letting someone die, though, we need to consider the examples more closely. We concede that Jones, who merely let his nephew die, is just as reprehensible as Smith, who killed his nephew. Let us ask, however, just what is the ground of our judgement of the agent in each case. In the case of Smith, this seems to be adequately captured by saying that Smith drowned his nephew for motives of personal gain. But can we say that the grounds on which we judge Jones to be reprehensible, and just as reprehensible as Smith, are that he let his nephew drown for motives of personal gain? I suggest not – for this neglects to mention a crucial fact about Jones, namely that he was fully prepared to kill his nephew, and would have done so had it proved necessary. It would be generally accepted, I think, quite independently of the present debate, that someone who is fully prepared to perform a reprehensible action, in the expectation of certain circumstances, but does not do so because the expected circumstances do not eventuate, is just as reprehensible as someone who actually performs that action in those circumstances. Now this alone is sufficient to account for our judging Jones as harshly as Smith. He was fully prepared to do what Smith did, and would have done so if circumstances had not turned out differently from those in Smith's case. Thus, though we may agree that he is just as reprehensible as Smith, this cannot be taken as showing that his letting his nephew die is as reprehensible as Smith's killing his nephew – for we would have judged him just as harshly, given what he was prepared to do, even if he had not let his nephew die. To make this clear, suppose that we modify Jones' story along the following lines – as before, he sneaks into the bathroom while his nephew is bathing, with the intention of drowning the child in his bath. This time, however, just before he can seize the child, *he* slips and hits his head on the bath, knocking himself unconscious. By the time he regains consciousness, the child, unaware of his intentions, has called his parents, and the opportunity is gone. Here, Jones neither kills his nephew *nor* lets him die – yet I think it would be agreed that given his preparedness to kill the child for personal gain, he is as reprehensible as Smith.

The examples produced by Michael Tooley, in the book referred to earlier, suffer the same defect as those produced by Rachels. Tooley asks us to consider the following pair of scenarios, as it happens also featuring Smith and Jones. In the first, Jones is about to shoot Smith when he sees that Smith will be killed by a bomb unless Jones warns him, as he easily can. Jones does not warn him, and he is killed by the bomb – i.e., Jones lets Smith die. In the other, Jones wants Smith dead, and shoots him – i.e., he kills Smith.

Tooley elsewhere[9] produces this further example: two sons are looking forward to the death of their wealthy father, and decide independently to poison him. One puts poison in his father's whiskey, and is discovered doing so by the other, who was just about to do the same. The latter then allows his father to drink the poisoned whiskey, and refrains from giving him the antidote, which he happens to possess.

Tooley is confident that we will agree that in each pair of cases, the agent who kills is morally no worse than the one who lets die. It will be clear, however, that his examples are open to criticisms parallel to those just produced against Rachels. To take first the case where Jones is saved the trouble of killing Smith by the fortunate circumstance of a bomb's being about to explode near the latter: it is true that we judge Jones to be just as reprehensible as if he had killed Smith, but since he was fully prepared to kill him had he not been saved the trouble by the bomb, we would make the same judgement even if he had neither killed Smith nor let him die (even if, say, no bomb had been present, but Smith suffered a massive and timely heart attack). As for the example of the like-minded sons, here too the son who didn't kill was prepared to do so, and given this, would be as reprehensible as the other even if he had not let his father die (if, say, he did not happen to possess the antidote, and so was powerless to save him).

Let us try to spell out more clearly just where the examples produced by Rachels and Tooley fail. What both writers overlook is that what determines whether someone is reprehensible or not is not simply what he in fact does, but what he is prepared to do, perhaps as revealed by what he in fact does. Thus, while Rachels is correct in taking it that we will be inclined to judge Smith and Jones in his examples equally harshly, this is not surprising, since both are judged reprehensible for precisely the same reason, namely that they were fully prepared to kill for motives of personal gain. The same, of course, is true of Tooley's examples. In each example he gives of an agent who lets another die, the agent is fully prepared to kill (though in the event, he is spared the necessity). In their efforts to ensure that the members of each pair of cases they produce do not differ in any morally relevant respect (except that one is a case of killing and the other of letting die), Rachels and Tooley make them *too* similar – not only do Rachels' Smith and Jones, for example, have identical motives, but both are guilty of the same moral offence.

4

Given the foregoing account of the failings of the examples produced by Rachels and Tooley, what modifications do they require if they are to be legitimately used to gauge our attitudes towards killing and letting die, respectively? Let us again concentrate on Rachels' examples. Clearly, if his argument is to avoid the defect pointed out, we must stipulate that though Jones was prepared to let his nephew die once he saw that this would happen unless he intervened, he was not prepared to kill the child. The story will now go something like this: Jones stands to gain considerably from his nephew's death, as before, but he is not prepared to kill him for this reason. However, he happens to be on hand when his nephew slips, hits his head, and falls face down in the bath. Remembering that he will profit from the child's death, he allows him to drown. We need, however, to make a further stipulation, regarding the explanation of Jones' not being prepared to kill his nephew. It cannot be that he fears untoward consequences for himself, such as detection and punishment, or that he is too lazy to choose such an active course, or that the idea simply had not occurred to him. I think it would be common ground in the debate that if the only explanation of his not being prepared to kill his nephew was one of these kinds, he would be morally no better than Smith, who differed only in being more daring, or more energetic, whether or not fate then happened to offer him the opportunity to let his nephew die instead. In that case, we must suppose that the reason Jones is prepared to let his nephew die, but not to kill him, is a moral one – not intervening to save the child, he holds, is one thing, but actually bringing about his death is another, and altogether beyond the pale.

I suggest, then, that the case with which we must compare that of Smith is this: Jones happens to be on hand when his nephew slips, hits his head, and falls unconscious into his bath-water. It is clear to Jones that the child will drown if he does not intervene. He remembers that the child's death would be greatly to his advantage, and does not intervene. Though he is prepared to let the child die, however, and in fact does so, he would not have been prepared to kill him,

because, as he might put it, wicked though he is, he draws the line at killing for gain.

I am not entirely sure what the general opinion would be here as to the relative reprehensibility of Smith and Jones. I can only report my own, which is that Smith's behaviour is indeed morally worse than that of Jones. What I do want to insist on, however, is that, for the reasons I have given, we cannot take our reactions to the examples provided by Rachels and Tooley as an indication of our intuitions concerning the relative heinousness of killing and of letting die.

So far, we have restricted ourselves to discussion of common intuitions on our question, and made no attempt to argue for any particular answer. I will conclude by pointing out that, given the fairly common view that the *raison d'être* of morality is to make it possible for people to live together in reasonable peace and security, it is not difficult to provide a rationale for the intuition that in our modified version of Rachels' examples, Jones is less reprehensible than Smith. For it is clearly preferable to have Jones-like persons around rather than Smith-like ones. We are not threatened by the former – such a person will not save me if my life should be in danger, but in this he is no more dangerous than an incapacitated person, or for that matter, a rock or tree (in fact he may be better, for he *might* save me as long as he doesn't think he will profit from my death). Smith-like persons, however, *are* a threat – if such a person should come to believe that she will benefit sufficiently from my death, then not only must I expect no help from her if my life happens to be in danger, but I must fear positive attempts on my life. In that case, given the view mentioned of the point of morality, people prepared to behave as Smith does are clearly of greater concern from the moral point of view than those prepared only to behave as Jones does; which is to say that killing is indeed morally worse than letting die.

Notes

1 See, for example, John Chandler (1990), 'Killing and letting die – putting the debate in context', *Australasian Journal of Philosophy*, 68, no. 4, pp. 420–31.

2 It underlies, or is often claimed to underlie, for example, the Roman Catholic position on certain issues in the abortion debate, and the view that while 'passive' euthanasia may sometimes be permissible, 'active' euthanasia never is. It also seems involved in the common view that even if it is wrong to fail to give aid to the starving of the world, thereby letting them die, it is not as wrong as dropping bombs on them, thereby killing them.

3   John Ladd (1985), 'Positive and negative euthanasia' in
    James E. White (ed.), *Contemporary Moral Problems*
    (St Paul: West Publishing Co), pp. 58–68.

4   James Rachels (1979), 'Active and passive euthanasia' in
    James Rachels (ed.), *Moral Problems* (New York: Harper
    and Row), pp. 490–7; Michael Tooley (1983), *Abortion
    and Infanticide* (Oxford: Clarendon Press), pp. 187–8.

5   Raziel Abelson (1982), 'There is a moral difference,' in
    Raziel Abelson and Marie-Louise Friquegnon (eds),

    Ethics for Modern Life (New York: St Martin's Press),
    pp. 73–83.

6   Tooley, *Abortion and Infanticide*, p. 189.

7   Rachels, 'Active and passive euthanasia'.

8   Ibid., p. 494.

9   Michael Tooley (1980), 'An irrelevant consideration:
    killing and letting die' in Bonnie Steinbeck (ed.), *Killing
    and Letting Die* (Englewood Cliffs, NJ: Prentice-Hall),
    pp. 56–62.

26

Why Killing is Not Always Worse – and Sometimes Better – Than Letting Die

Helga Kuhse

I

The conventional assumption is that killing a person is worse than allowing her to die. Beginning with James Rachels' famous article "Active and Passive Euthanasia", first published in the *New England Journal of Medicine* in 1975[1] this "difference thesis"[2] has been challenged by producing pairs of cases in which an agent who lets someone die would generally be judged to be no less reprehensible than an agent who kills. In a recent article, Winston Nesbitt argues that these pairs of cases typically contain a crucial common feature which will indeed make *these* cases of letting die the same as killing.[3] Once this crucial feature is removed, he holds, these cases will support, rather than undermine, the difference view.

Winston Nesbitt's argument in support of the difference thesis rests on a number of contestable assumptions. In briefly retracing his argument, I shall leave these assumptions unchallenged, to show then that *even if* we accept these assumptions, Nesbitt's conclusion – that killing is worse than letting die – does not follow.

It will be adequate, for our purposes, to focus on just one of the paired examples discussed by Nesbitt: James Rachels' case of the "nasty uncles".[4] The first case involves Smith, who will gain a large inheritance should his six-year-old nephew die. One evening, Smith sneaks into the bathroom where his nephew is taking a bath, and drowns him. The second case, that of Jones, is exactly like the first case, except that as Jones is about to drown his nephew, the child slips, hits his head, and falls, face down and unconscious, into the water. Jones is delighted, and stands by as his nephew drowns.

In these examples, both men were motivated by personal gain, and both were aiming at the child's death. The only relevant difference between the cases is that Smith killed the child, whereas Jones allowed the child to die. But that difference, Rachels claims, is not morally relevant in itself, and the difference thesis is false.

Nesbitt agrees with Rachels that these examples support the common intuition that Jones is no less reprehensible than Smith, and that there is, in these cases, no difference between killing and allowing to die. The reason is, Nesbitt holds, that both agents were prepared to kill, for the sake of personal gain. After all, Jones was no less prepared to kill than Smith was – except that an accident (the child slipping, hitting his head and falling face down in the water) obviated the need for Jones to act on his intention. "[W]hat determines whether someone is reprehensible or not", Nesbitt holds, "is not what he in fact does but what he is prepared to do, perhaps as revealed by what he in fact does" (p. 104).

Original publication details: Helga Kuhse, "Why Killing Is Not Always Worse – and Sometimes Better – Than Letting Die," pp. 371–4 from *Cambridge Quarterly of Healthcare* 7: 4 (1998). © Cambridge University Press. Reproduced with permission.

Bioethics: An Anthology, Third Edition. Edited by Helga Kuhse, Udo Schüklenk, and Peter Singer.

This entails, Nesbitt continues, that Rachels' examples cannot show that the difference thesis is false. Both cases contain the morally relevant feature that the agent was *prepared* to kill. To test the difference thesis, this common feature must be removed. We must assume that Jones believes the difference thesis to be true, and that he was prepared to let his nephew die, but, unlike Smith, was not prepared to kill the child (p. 104). In this case, Nesbitt holds, we might indeed want to judge Smith more reprehensible than Jones.

It is this difference, the difference between an agent being prepared to kill and an agent merely being prepared to let die, that is, according to Nesbitt, morally significant – at least if we accept the widely held view that "the *raison d'être* of morality is to make it possible for people to live together in reasonable peace and security" (p. 105).

We are not threatened, Nesbitt concludes his argument, if a person is prepared to allow another to die, but is not prepared to kill. Such a person "will not save me if my life should be in danger, but in this he is no more dangerous than an incapacitated person, or for that matter, a rock or a tree". A person who is prepared to kill, on the other hand, *is* a threat.

> If such a person should come to believe that she will benefit sufficiently from my death, then not only must I expect no help from her if my life happens to be in danger, but I must fear positive attempts on my life. In that case, given the view mentioned of the point of morality, people prepared to behave as Smith does are clearly of greater concern from the moral point of view than those prepared only to behave as Jones does; which is to say that killing is indeed morally worse than letting die. (p. 105)

II

Let us accept that Nesbitt is correct and that we should indeed be more concerned by the presence of Smith-type persons than by Jones-type persons. But what does this show? Does it show, as Nesbitt holds, that "killing is indeed morally worse than letting die", or does it show that it is worse if agents, who are motivated by personal gain, are not merely content to stand by as "nature" bestows some good on them, but are also prepared to intervene in the course of nature, to achieve their ends?

There is an illegitimate conflation in Winston Nesbitt's argument between the rightness and wrongness of actions, and the goodness and badness of agents.[5] We might thus agree that it is a bad thing for individuals to be motivated by personal gain, rather than by, say, the common good, and that it is *worse*, other things being equal, if such an agent is not only prepared to "let death happen", but to "make death happen".[6] But this is not, of course, the same as showing that killing is worse than letting die. Killing may be worse than letting die in these cases, and better than letting die in others.

Consider the following case, similar to a case that came before the Swedish courts some years ago:

> A truck driver and his co-driver had an accident on a lonely stretch of road. The truck caught fire and the driver was trapped in the wreckage of the cabin. The co-driver struggled to free him, but could not do so. The driver, by now burning, pleaded with his colleague – an experienced shooter – to take a rifle, which was stowed in a box on the back of the truck, and shoot him. The co-driver took the rifle and shot his colleague.

Was what the co-driver did morally reprehensible? Did he act wrongly? Students who are presented with this case will generally answer both questions in the negative. The reason for their intuitions is not hard to find. In this case, the agent was not motivated by personal gain, but by compassion. He acted not to benefit himself, but to benefit another. Should we feel threatened by such agents? Hardly. We should be comforted by their presence. Conversely, however, we should feel threatened, or at least abandoned, if we were surrounded by agents who believed in the difference thesis and behaved like "an incapacitated person, or…a rock or a tree", who would "let us die" when we sincerely wanted someone "to make us die".

Not only does Nesbitt conflate the distinction between agents and actions, he also implicitly assumes that death is always and everywhere an evil. If this view is already challenged by the above example, it has been utterly rejected in the practice of medicine by patients and doctors alike. Patients and doctors do not believe that life is always a good and will, in many cases, deliberately choose a shorter life over a longer one. Terminally or incurably ill patients standardly refuse life-sustaining treatment, and doctors allow these patients to die, for the patients' good. To put it slightly differently, while death is normally an evil, and to kill a person (or to let her die when we could save her) is harming her, this is not the case when continued life presents an intolerable burden to the person whose life it is. In short, then, doctors who are "letting" a patient die, for the patient's good, are benefiting rather than harming the patient – they are practising what is often called "passive euthanasia".

If patients can, however, be benefited by being "let die", because death is a good, then they can also be benefited by being killed – by the doctor practising "active euthanasia". Indeed, in some cases, active euthanasia will be preferable, from the patient's point of view, to passive euthanasia: being "let die" may involve unwanted protracted pain and suffering for the patient, and fail to give her the dignified death she wants. Moreover, there are patients for whom death would be a good, but who do not need life support, and whom the doctor cannot let die. This means that a doctor who is merely prepared to "let die", but not to "make die", is, once again, like an incapacitated person, a rock or a tree, who, while not preventing good befalling some patients, will merely stand by and do nothing to make the good happen for others.[7]

If the *raison d'être* of morality is to allow people to live together in relative peace and security, what kind of motivation would we like doctors to have, and what kinds of action would we like them to perform? Clearly, we would like them to be motivated to primarily seek *our* good, rather than their own; to keep us alive, if this is in our best interests, and to "let" us die, or to "make" us die, when either one of these actions serves us best. If this is correct, the difference thesis is false. Killing is not always worse than letting die. Sometimes it is morally better.

III

James Rachels had devised the case of "the nasty uncles" to demonstrate that there is no intrinsic moral difference between killing and letting die, or active and passive euthanasia. Now, if Nesbitt is right, Rachels' example of the "nasty uncles" fails to show that the difference thesis is false. If I am right, however, Nesbitt in turn fails to establish the truth of the difference thesis. While he has shown that killing is sometimes worse than letting die, I have shown that killing is sometimes better than letting die.

This has clear implications for the public debate over (voluntary) euthanasia. Nesbitt accepts that the truth or falsity of the difference thesis may ultimately depend on the truth of the moral theory that underpins it. But, he says, "we cannot wait for a demonstration of the correct moral theory" before we attempt to make decisions on pressing moral questions, such as "active" or "passive" euthanasia (or killing a patient and letting her die). Rather, answers to practical public-policy questions are rarely derived from first ethical principles, but are, quite properly, based on common intuitions (p. 101, n. 2).

Acceptance of Nesbitt's "common intuition" view would lead one to question the contemporary blanket public-policy distinction between active and passive euthanasia: while doctors are typically permitted, by law, to "let" patients die, at the patients' request, they are almost everywhere prohibited from "making" them die. In countries like Australia, Britain and the United States, recognition of people's common intuitions would, however, lead one to the view that not only passive, but also active voluntary euthanasia should be allowed.[8]

Far from establishing the truth of the difference thesis, Winston Nesbitt has undermined the very thesis he set out support. Not only is active euthanasia no worse than passive euthanasia, and sometimes morally better; his argument also lends support to the view that public policies should allow some forms of active euthanasia.

Notes

1 Rachels, J. 'Active and Passive Euthanasia', *New England Journal of Medicine* (9 January, 1975): 78–80.

2 See note 3; Nesbitt, p. 101.

3 Nesbitt, W. 'Is Killing No Worse Than Letting Die?' *Journal of Applied Philosophy*, 12 (1) (1995): 101–6.

4 See note 2.

5 Kuhse, H. *The Sanctity of Life Doctrine in Medicine – A Critique* (Oxford: Clarendon Press, 1987), pp. 88–90, 142, 148, 158–63. See also 'Frankena W. McCormick and the Traditional Distinction' in R. McCormick and

P. Ramsey (eds), *Doing Evil to Achieve Good* (Chicago: Loyola University Press, 1978).

6   Walton, D. *On Defining Death* (Montreal: McGill–Queens University Press, 1979), pp. 118–20; Kuhse (see note 5), pp. 79–81.

7   Here it is, of course, important to not confuse the distinction between killing and letting die, or between "making happen" and "letting happen" with the distinction between actions and omissions. In distinction from a tree or a rock, an agent may act to "let happen" – for example, by telling the nurse not to attach the patient to a respirator, or by turning the respirator off. See note 5, Kuhse, chs 2 and 3.

8   Opinion polls in these countries have consistently shown strong public support for active voluntary euthanasia. For the opinions of some groups of health-care professionals see, for example, Heilig, S., 'The SFMS Euthanasia Survey: Results and Analyses', *San Francisco Medicine* (May, 1988): 24–6, 34; Ward, B. J., 'Attitudes among NHS Doctors to Requests for Euthanasia', *BMJ*, 308 (1995): 1332–4; Baume P. and O'Malley, E., 'Euthanasia: Attitudes and Practices of Medical Practitioners', *Medical Journal of Australia*, 161 (1994): 137–44; Kuhse, H. and Singer, P., 'Voluntary Euthanasia and the Nurse: an Australian Survey', *International Journal of Nursing Studies*, 30(4) (1993): 311–22.

27

Moral Fictions and Medical Ethics

Franklin G. Miller, Robert D. Truog, and Dan W. Brock

John and Sam are motorcycle enthusiasts. At age 50 both of them have serious accidents that leave them quadriplegic and dependent on a ventilator to breathe. Two years after the accident John remains ventilator-dependent, whereas Sam has regained the capacity to breathe spontaneously and has been weaned off his ventilator. During the third year after their accidents, both John and Sam find their lives intolerable; they don't want to go on living because of their complete dependence on others for the activities of daily life and the associated absence of privacy. John requests to be admitted to the hospital where he was treated after the accident, in order to have his home ventilator withdrawn and receive the palliative care he needs to die peacefully. Hospital clinicians are initially reluctant to honor John's request but agree to do so after being persuaded that he is a competent decision-maker who has thought carefully about his situation. Sam requests his physician to administer a lethal dose of medication so that he can die a swift and dignified death. Although Sam's physician is sympathetic to his request, he refuses to comply with it because active euthanasia, even with consent, is contrary to the law and medical ethics.

Why are the normative responses to these two patient requests so different within the prevailing stance of medical ethics? John's decision to die by stopping treatment is not considered suicide, despite the fact that he is not terminally ill and has the potential to live at least 10 years while being maintained on a ventilator. Rather, it is understood as a refusal of burdensome or unwanted treatment. Because it is not suicide, the assistance of physicians and nurses in agreeing to withdraw the ventilator is not assisted suicide. In stopping the ventilator they are omitting to continue life-sustaining treatment; they are not performing voluntary active euthanasia. Instead, their conduct is sometimes described as 'passive euthanasia.' They do not kill John, but merely allow him to die from his underlying spinal cord injury and inability to breathe spontaneously. They do not (and must not) intend to cause John's death, but do and must respect his right to refuse treatment. John's medical condition, not the ventilator withdrawal, is considered the cause of death. Accordingly, the clinicians agreeing to stop John's ventilator are not morally responsible for a death-causing act. Their conduct is morally permissible; indeed, it is (arguably) morally obligatory, as competent patients have a right to refuse unwanted medical treatment. Refusing to honor patients' refusals of medical treatment amounts to battery under the common law; and patients have a constitutional right to refuse medical treatment, endorsed by the US Supreme Court in the Cruzan case.[1]

Original publication details: Franklin G. Miller, Robert D. Truog and Dan W. Brock, "Moral Fictions and Medical Ethics," pp. 453–60 from *Bioethics* 24: 9 (2010). Reproduced with permission from John Wiley & Sons.

In contrast, Sam is asking for help in causing his death; hence, his request can be understood as suicidal. If what he does is not committing suicide, it is because the final act that causes death, when a physician accedes to Sam's request, is performed by the physician. This act is characterized as (voluntary) active euthanasia. Clearly, a physician deliberately administering a known lethal dose of medication would be intending to cause the patient's death, and thus would be morally responsible for killing the patient. Such conduct is morally forbidden in prevailing medical ethics throughout the world and is treated legally as criminal homicide, except in the Netherlands and Belgium.

In this article we challenge the standard assessment within medical ethics of withdrawing life-sustaining treatment [WLST] and voluntary active euthanasia [VAE]. The major points in our ethical analysis are not original, as both we and other commentators have made similar points about the lack of a cogent basis for treating withdrawing life-sustaining treatment as fundamentally different from assisted suicide and active euthanasia, from an ethical perspective.[2] Yet standard medical ethics and the law have remained impervious to this critique. We suggest that the concept of *moral fictions*, as applied to the contrasting characterization of the cases of John and Sam, can help exhibit concretely how and why the conventional moral conceptualization is radically mistaken.

The Concept of Moral Fictions

Fictions are commonplace in the law, but they have received scant attention in medical ethics. Fictions are false statements; but not all false statements are fictions. Fictions are *motivated* false statements, endorsed in order to uphold a position felt to be important.[3] (By stressing the motivated character of moral fictions, we do not suggest that the motivation to endorse false beliefs is always conscious.) For those critics who do not share the motivation – the commitment to the position in question – fictions appear to be patently false or confused. Moral fictions are false statements endorsed to uphold cherished or entrenched moral positions in the face of conduct that is in tension with these established moral positions. Professionals are uncomfortable with the thought that they may be practising unethically. Especially when routine practices, viewed candidly,

appear to conflict with established norms, there is a strong incentive to construe these practices in a way that removes the conflict. Moral fictions serve this purpose. In other words, moral fictions can be understood as a tool for counteracting a form of cognitive dissonance[4] – specifically, the cognitive dissonance constituted by the inconsistency between routine practices and prevailing norms.

Viewed without the confabulations of moral fictions, accepted end-of-life practices patently conflict with standard medical ethics. The moral fictions relating to end-of-life decisions are motivated to make morally challenging medical practices, such as withdrawing life-sustaining treatment and providing pain-relieving medication at the risk of hastening death, consistent with the norm that doctors must not kill, or assist in killing, patients. We shall argue that the underlying fault that the moral fictions conceal lies not in accepted practices, which are justified, but in established norms that cannot withstand critical scrutiny.

Two types of moral fictions are on display in the standard assessment of John's request to withdraw life-sustaining treatment (see Table 27.1). First, as we demonstrate below, the description of withdrawing life-sustaining treatment involves a series of motivated false factual statements. These include false statements about the nature of the patient's request, the nature of the act that clinicians are asked to perform in this case, the causal relationship between the act of treatment withdrawal and the patient's death, and the intention of physicians who accede to such requests. Second, there are erroneous moral judgments based on these mistaken factual claims: judgments about moral responsibility and moral permissibility. When shorn of these moral fictions, the differential moral assessment of complying with the patient requests of John and Sam is undermined.

Appeal to fictions in moral discourse does not entail deliberate fabrication, lying, or deception. Most people who espouse moral fictions believe them (in good faith) to be true. Moreover, because these fictions are culturally entrenched, even when their falsity or invalidity is exposed, not everyone will agree that a given proposition counts as a moral fiction. Moral fictions, according to our analysis, differ from legal fictions in that the latter are never believed to be literally true propositions. For example, the legal doctrines that a corporation is a person, or that persons who are absent

Table 27.1 Comparing end-of-life decisions

Consider two cases: (1) ventilator-dependent quadriplegic requests withdrawal of ventilator (WLST); (2) quadriplegic, who has regained spontaneous breathing and weaning from ventilator, requests lethal dose of medication (VAE).

Status quo		
	WLST	*VAE*
Is the doctor causing death?	No	Yes
Is it an active intervention?	No	Yes
Is the doctor intending death?	No	Yes
Does the doctor kill the patient?	No	Yes
Is it suicide?	No	Maybe
Is it assisted suicide	No	Maybe
Is the doctor morally responsible for death?	No	Yes
Is it permitted morally?	Yes	No
Is it legal?	Yes	No

Without moral fictions		
	WLST	*VAE*
Is the doctor causing death?	Yes	Yes
Is it an active intervention?	Yes	Yes
Is the doctor intending death?	Sometimes Yes, sometimes No	Yes
Does the doctor kill the patient?	Yes	Yes
Is it suicide?	Yes	Yes
Is it assisted suicide?	Yes	Yes
Is the doctor morally responsible for death?	Yes	Yes
Is it permitted morally?	Yes	Yes
Is/should it be legal?	Yes	Open question

and unaccounted for are considered dead after a period of seven years, are not taken as true statements of fact. Rather, the law treats corporations *as if* they are persons and missing persons as if they are dead. Those who appeal to moral fictions, however, typically assert them with confidence as literally true.

Exposing the Moral Fictions

Suicide

If we think of suicide literally as aiming at and causing one's own death, then both John and Sam are making suicidal requests. There is a difference between the situations of John and Sam, which might be thought relevant to whether their respective requests are suicidal. John has a burdensome life-sustaining treatment and Sam does not. Might John's aim be to stop the burden of the ventilator but not to end his life? Assuming, however, that it is the pervasive paralysis and

associated burdens that are driving John's judgment that his life is not worth living, then his decision to seek withdrawal of life-sustaining treatment does not stem from the mere fact that he needs the assistance of a burdensome mechanical ventilator to breathe. For the sake of this analysis, we make the reasonable supposition that he would be no less interested in ending his life if he were in the same condition as Sam, who is able to breathe spontaneously.

To be sure, the description of suicide for these two cases might be resisted because neither patient is directly capable of causing his own death and each is seeking the help of others to do so. Yet both John and Sam are aiming at death, for only death in their eyes will free them from a condition that they find intolerable; and it is their request for help in dying that sets in motion the causal chain leading to death when clinicians comply with their requests.

Another reason to resist the use of 'suicide' in these cases is that suicide is thought typically to reflect irrational conduct, driven by depression or psychosis.

Both John and Sam find their lives no longer worth living in the light of the disabilities caused by spinal cord injury. Some may disagree with their personal quality-of-life assessments, but it is difficult to see their aim to end their lives as irrational, especially in the case of individuals who have completed rehabilitation and had ample time to adjust to a life with paralysis below the neck. The concept of rational suicide is not incoherent, unless one stipulates dogmatically (thus begging the question) that it is always irrational to opt for death, no matter what the circumstances. Hence, we conclude that it is a moral fiction to assert that the requests of either John or Sam are not suicidal.

Suppose we concede that John and Sam are seeking suicide. It would seem natural to infer that both are requesting assisted suicide; for they need the help of someone else to realize their wish to die. Nevertheless, from a conceptual perspective it might be insisted that regardless of the suicidal nature of the requests of John and Sam, clinicians who accede to these requests are not engaging in assisted suicide because the immediate death-causing act is performed by the physician, not the patient. As a matter of linguistic stipulation there is no objection to this stance. Yet we see no reason why some life-terminating acts (including the cases of John and Sam) cannot be legitimately described as both assisted suicide and active euthanasia; even though others can only be described as one or the other: prescribing a lethal dose of medication ingested by a patient is assisted suicide, not active euthanasia; whereas giving a lethal dose of medication to an incompetent patient, who has not voluntarily requested to end her life, is active non-voluntary euthanasia, not assisted suicide. In any case, the standard assessment in medical ethics of compliance with John's request rejects the label of 'assisted suicide' because of moral fictions concerning causation and intention that we discuss below.

Causation

How should we think about the act of an attending physician who complies with John's request to stop his ventilator? According to conventional medical ethics, the withdrawal of life-sustaining therapy allows the patient to die from his underlying spinal cord injury and inability to breathe spontaneously; it is an omission of treatment, not an act that causes the patient's death.[5] We contend that this familiar account flies in the face of a candid look at the facts. Now at 50 years of age, John has the potential to live for a decade or more supported by continued mechanical ventilation and personal care. What explains his death following withdrawal of mechanical ventilation is not the course of his spinal cord injury but the act of turning off the ventilator. It is the proximate cause of death. Moreover, disconnecting the ventilator without his consent would be homicide. The very same act of stopping treatment that causes death in the latter case of homicide is performed by a clinician with John's consent.[6] The consent makes the difference between homicide and legitimate treatment withdrawal, but this ethical and legal difference has nothing to do with the cause of the patient's death, which is the same in both cases.

Withdrawing life-sustaining treatment, when followed shortly by the patient's death, is a life-terminating intervention. Indeed, the very fact that mechanical ventilation can sustain life for those patients incapable of breathing on their own implies that stopping mechanical ventilation will end the life of these patients. In other words, the power to sustain life by technological means goes hand-in-hand with the power to end life when these means are withheld or withdrawn. This characterization of medical practice in the case of life-sustaining therapy is an obvious application of our common sense understanding of causation,[7] which is obscured by the moral fictions embraced by conventional medical ethics. To be sure, John's inability to breathe on his own is part of the causal explanation for why he dies after his ventilator is stopped. If Sam happened to be attached temporarily to a ventilator, he most likely would not die if the ventilator were stopped. But in John's case, the withdrawal of the ventilator contributes causally to his death precisely because had it not been withdrawn he would continue living, probably for a substantial period of time. The withdrawal of the ventilator is what results in John's dying at the time and in the manner that he does. Hence, we conclude that it is a fiction to describe John's death following withdrawal of the ventilator as merely allowing him to die and not causing his death.

This fiction about causation is closely tied to another fiction about killing. The ordinary common sense notion of A killing B is that A performs an action that causes B's death. The moral fiction that John's physician does not cause his death by removing the ventilator seems also to imply that he does not kill John. And if he does not kill John, then what he must do is allow John to die of his underlying disease. The conceptual picture in this view is that John has a lethal condition, his inability to breathe on his own, that the ventilator is keeping that lethal condition from proceeding to John's death, and so when the physician removes the ventilator in doing so he merely allows John's lethal disease process to proceed unimpeded to his death. The moral fiction about causation is thus closely related to another moral fiction about the difference between killing and allowing to die and, more specifically, about whether stopping the ventilator is killing or allowing to die.

It is important to correct a widespread misconception about the use of 'killing' to describe the death-causing act of withdrawing life-sustaining treatment. In the medical context, 'killing' is commonly understood as meaning the unjustified taking of life, despite the fact that we recognize that in other contexts, such as self-defence, killing can be justified. Accordingly, it seems jarring to describe withdrawing life support as killing. We understand 'killing' in medicine, however, to mean causing death, which may or may not be morally justified, depending on the circumstances.

Intention

Withdrawing life-sustaining treatment is considered legally permitted and ethically justified when it is based on a valid refusal of treatment by a competent patient or by an authorized surrogate decision-maker, based on the prior preferences of the patient or a sound judgment about the patient's best interest. In medical ethics, however, according to the conventional view, it is unethical for physicians to intend to cause death. To square these two potentially conflicting positions, the moral fiction is endorsed that whenever clinicians justifiably withdraw life support, they do not intend to cause death. We have argued above that withdrawal of a ventilator, as in the case of John,

causes death. Is it credible that physicians never do, nor should, intend to cause death when they justifiably withdraw life support? In John's case, his plan is to end his life by withdrawing the ventilator, as he has decided that it is no longer worth continuing to live with the profound disability caused by his spinal cord injury. A clinician who views John's plan as reasonable given his circumstances, values, and preferences and is prepared to help by withdrawing his ventilator, intends not only to respect John's autonomous choice but to cause death in order to realize his plan. If this account is resisted, it is owing to the moral fiction that it is always unethical for clinicians to intend the death of their patients.

Recent empirical evidence indicates that many physicians, at least in Europe, acknowledge an intention to cause death when withdrawing life support. A large-scale survey of end-of-life decisions in six European countries (Belgium, Denmark, Italy, the Netherlands, Sweden, and Switzerland) demonstrated that a majority of physicians reported an explicit intention to hasten death when mechanical respiration (66%) and dialysis (69%) were withdrawn.[8] (Intending to hasten death is the same as intending to cause death, as hastening death causes death to occur earlier than it otherwise would.) Discussing their findings, the authors state that '[t]he data presented in this paper clearly show that the view that withholding or withdrawing treatment means allowing patients to die, even though not intending them to do so, is untenable from an empirical point of view.' Additionally, they observe that 'in the context of withholding and withdrawing treatment there is a great divergence between the traditional moral rule and today's medical practice'.

We do not claim, however, that whenever life-sustaining treatment is withdrawn clinicians necessarily intend to cause death. Certainly, if the intention is to determine whether the patient can be weaned from a ventilator, as in the earlier care of Sam, there is no such intent. Additionally, in the case of imminently dying patients who are likely to die in a short period of time regardless of continued life-sustaining treatment, the intention of clinicians often may be to remove a burdensome and unwanted impediment to a peaceful death, foreseeing that doing so is likely to hasten death.

Moral responsibility

Once the fictions are exposed, underlying conventional descriptions of causality and intention with respect to withdrawing life-sustaining treatment, it becomes clear that denying the moral responsibility of clinicians for the death of the patient in John's case is also a fiction. It is important to understand what is meant by 'moral responsibility'. We are morally responsible for acts that can be attributed to us, whether right or wrong.[9] Specifically, a clinician is morally responsible for causing a patient's death by withdrawing a ventilator when this life-terminating act can be attributed from a moral perspective to the clinician. Is causing the death something that the physician did voluntarily and knowingly, so that it can be attributed to him? We are morally responsible for what we intend to do, or do knowingly, or do negligently. It follows that clinicians are responsible for causing the death of patients by withdrawing life support, regardless of whether one agrees with our claim that death is intended in many, but not necessarily all, of these cases. Moral responsibility for causing death does not equate to culpability for wrong-doing, unless it is presumed that it is always wrong to do so. Death-causing treatment withdrawals can be right or wrong acts depending on the circumstances, including critically the informed consent of competent patients or legally authorized surrogate decision-makers.

In withdrawing life-sustaining treatment, responsibility for causing death is shared by patients or surrogates and clinicians. Indeed, the primary responsibility rests with the patient, or surrogate deciding on behalf of the patient. This prior authorization for treatment withdrawal is a morally necessary condition for clinicians (justifiably) taking responsibility for withdrawing life support and thus for causing the death that ensues.

Differential moral assessment

Finally, we come to the differential moral evaluation of voluntary active euthanasia by means of a requested lethal injection in the case of Sam and a withdrawal of mechanical ventilation in response to the request/treatment refusal of John. If these cases don't vary with respect to the physician's role in the causation of death,

intention to cause death, and moral responsibility for causing death, and the patients provide valid consent, then it is puzzling to regard physician conduct in acceding to John's request as morally permissible but morally forbidden in the case of Sam. This differential judgment presupposes that there is some morally relevant characteristic that makes withdrawing life-sustaining treatment permissible but administering a lethal dose of medication impermissible, which also constitutes a moral fiction.

To reject this differential moral judgment does not imply that there are no morally significant differences, either in evaluating the acts themselves or for public policy, between withdrawing life-sustaining treatment from a competent patient and voluntary active euthanasia by means of injecting patients with a lethal dose of medication.[10] Patients have both a moral and a legal claim-right to stop unwanted life-sustaining treatment, which physicians and health care institutions are obligated to respect. The validity of this right is not contingent on clinicians endorsing the patient's reasons for treatment refusal. The right to refuse treatment, however, is not the same as the right to receive whatever treatment is demanded by a patient or a surrogate. Even if voluntary euthanasia is regarded as ethically legitimate, as in the Netherlands and Belgium, a physician may legitimately refuse a competent patient's request for a lethal dose of medication in some circumstances. However, the moral judgment that we are concerned with here is whether it is legitimate ethically in some circumstances (setting aside issues of legality) for a physician to comply willingly with a competent patient's voluntary and resolute request for a lethal injection. Voluntary active euthanasia is akin to abortion in this respect. Patients arguably have a moral liberty-right of noninterference by others with their physician's voluntary compliance with a valid request for abortion or active euthanasia, not a claim-right to receive an abortion or lethal injection upon demand from an objecting and unwilling physician.[11]

There are psychological differences between stopping life-sustaining treatment and administering a lethal injection, just as there are psychological differences between withholding and withdrawing life-sustaining treatment. When the moral fictions surrounding withdrawal of life-sustaining treatment are exposed, it doesn't follow that the psychological differences vanish.

Giving a patient a lethal injection feels different from turning off a ventilator. The absence of any necessary difference in intention, causation of death, and moral responsibility doesn't make this feeling go away. Some commentators argue that there is a difference in the impact on professional integrity between these two ways of causing a patient's death.[12] Active euthanasia uses the ordinary tools of medicine – a syringe filled with drugs – to cause a patient's death. Stopping life-sustaining treatment withdraws the technological tools of medicine, resulting in a patient's death. We fail to see how this amounts to any meaningful difference in what it is permitted for a physician to do.

It might be objected that the reluctance of physicians to perform active euthanasia should be respected because there is no need for patients who choose to end their lives to receive physician assistance. Instead they can find other ways to kill themselves, including stopping eating and drinking.[13] Of course, the fact that there is a permissible alternative to active euthanasia does not show that active euthanasia is in itself morally wrong. The major difficulty with stopping eating and drinking is that it can take a considerable period of time to die in this way, lasting up to two weeks or more. Moreover, the option of stopping eating and drinking is not only open to someone like Sam who is not on life support, but also to John, who is. If it is problematic for physicians to assist Sam in requesting death by lethal injection, why is it not problematic to assist John by stopping his ventilator? In both cases patients are seeking a swift and peaceful death with physician assistance, and there is no relevant difference between these means of assisted death with respect to causation and moral responsibility for the patient's death. When the moral fictions underlying the stance of prevailing medical ethics to withdrawing life-sustaining treatment are exposed, the difference in attitudes of clinicians with respect to these two ways of complying with patient requests for assisted death is seen to lack rational support.

The Moral Work of Moral Fictions

Moral fictions, being motivated beliefs, serve a purpose. The moral fictions we have reviewed here uphold the traditional norm of medical ethics that

doctors must not kill or intend their patients' deaths; and they are needed to square medical practice with the prevailing law, which treats intentional causing of death as criminal homicide, with exceptions such as self-defence, capital punishment, and just war. Bioethics scholars can expose and decry these moral fictions, as sins against commitment to the truth and as grounding erroneous moral judgments. But clinicians, ethics consultants, and teachers of clinical ethics cannot so easily escape the grip of these moral fictions. For the legitimate practice of withdrawing life-sustaining treatment *appears* to depend on upholding these moral fictions in view of the law and prevailing medical ethics.

With respect to the law, it is relatively easy to see these moral fictions as fictions that need to be endorsed in order to make medical practice consistent with the law. They can be understood essentially as legal fictions. We can look at withdrawing life-sustaining treatment *as if* it is not suicide or assisted suicide; as if it is passive euthanasia and merely allowing to die; as if it does not cause death; as if death necessarily is not intended. Therefore, physicians are not legally responsible for causing the death of their patients and not guilty of homicide when they withdraw life-sustaining treatment. Furthermore, the fiction about suicide permits the families of patients who decide to stop life-sustaining treatment to receive life insurance payments, which may be precluded if the death is officially denominated as suicide. Perhaps more important, it permits patients and families who are morally opposed to suicide to accept the withdrawal of life-sustaining treatment.

From a moral perspective, however, embracing these moral fictions is problematic. The *as if* approach doesn't work comfortably with respect to bona fide moral judgments. The teacher of medical ethics can attempt to teach end-of-life decision-making without moral fictions, pointing out how a candid appraisal of the facts and associated moral judgments conflict with prevailing medical ethics, and why it is better from a moral perspective (and in an ideal world) to abandon the fictions. But what message does this send to clinicians and trainees who have been socialized into a profession that owes allegiance to the norm that doctors must not kill patients? There is a risk that physicians will balk at medical ethics without moral fictions, becoming reluctant to engage patients and family members in conversations about stopping life-sustaining treatment and resistant to patient or family requests to do so. The moral progress with respect to the use of life-sustaining treatment that has developed since the 1970s might be imperiled. On the other hand, the extent to which patients, families, and/or clinicians already recognize these beliefs to be fictions – even if not fully consciously and explicitly – may contribute to unease or reluctance about withdrawing life-sustaining treatment, which could be reduced by greater clarity.

Abandoning the Moral Fictions

We do not claim that there is an easy response to this quandary, in part because of uncertainty about what the effects would be of abandoning these moral fictions. One way to reduce the tension between exposing moral fictions and practising ethically within the prevailing legal and moral status quo is to emphasize the principles that justify compliance with requests to withdraw life-sustaining treatment and the provision of needed palliative care: respecting patient self-determination and promoting patient well-being.[14] It must be emphasized that causing death is not necessarily harmful and can be good for patients, depending on their situation. The intentions of patients and physicians with respect to causing death and what counts as causing death have nothing to do, in themselves, with whether withdrawing of life-sustaining treatment can be justified by appeal to these principles. The entrenched but ethically dubious norm that doctors must not kill can be surrendered without abandoning the traditional norm of doing no harm to patients (that is not compensated by proportional patient benefit). More specifically, the unqualified prohibition on doctors killing patients (i.e. intentionally causing the death of patients) should be replaced by the norm that doctors should not kill without valid consent, either from competent patients or authorized surrogate decision-makers. There is no way, however, to adopt this strategy of eschewing moral fictions without giving up the differential moral judgment that withdrawing life-sustaining treatment, but not voluntary active euthanasia, is permissible.

It remains an open question, which we do not attempt to address here, whether there are legitimate grounds as a matter of policy and law for continuing to prohibit assisted suicide and active euthanasia. It is possible that the potential for abuse that accompanies legalization of physician-assisted death justifies continuing to prohibit these practices. In one respect, there is an inherently greater potential for abuse in active euthanasia, because any person can be killed by lethal injection, whereas withdrawing life-sustaining treatment can only kill those who are on life support and need it to continue living. Although careful oversight of decisions to undertake active euthanasia can minimize abuses, the absence of abuse can never be guaranteed.[15] To put this in perspective, however, we need to recognize that our currently accepted practices of withdrawing life-sustaining treatment also have the potential for abuse, especially in the case of incompetent patients. With the rare exception of disputed cases reviewed by the courts, decisions to withdraw life support are made without standard procedures to assess the decisions of patients and surrogate decision-makers and without formal oversight. Hence, there is no way to know the extent of abuse that our society has been prepared to tolerate in recognizing the right to refuse life-sustaining treatment. It is an empirical issue, on which there is little evidence, whether expanding the scope of legitimate, legally permissible death-causing acts by clinicians would foster intolerable abuses that could not be obviated by reasonable regulatory procedures.

In view of moral discomfort with the idea of doctors killing patients, is it clear that we should give up the moral fictions that permeate conventional medical ethics relating to end-of-life decisions? Perhaps the truth is unbearable and facing it will produce worse consequences than indulging in fictions about our accepted end-of-life practices.[16] If we knew that facing the truth about these practices would create a backlash, with the result that suffering patients are made worse off, then tolerating these moral fictions would seem desirable. A problem, however, is that once a moral fiction is seen for what it is, it is difficult to continue to pass the fiction off as the truth. Moreover, we don't know that abandoning these moral fictions will set back moral progress or plunge us down the slippery slope. It may be best to proceed gradually in abandoning the moral fictions relating to end-of-life practices, tolerating some measure of obfuscation along the way. However, medical ethics that is shot through with fictions is unstable and likely to be transformed over time as the reality of end-of-life practices is exposed.

In theory, the moral work done by the moral fictions in the ethics of end-of-life decisions is expendable.

Nothing need be lost from a moral perspective in abandoning these moral fictions, and much is to be gained in honesty, moral clarity, and professional integrity. The transition, however, from the moral status quo to a landscape of medical ethics without moral fictions will demand a cultural transformation within the practice of medicine and medical ethics.

Notes

1 A. Meisel. The Legal Consensus about Forgoing Life-Sustaining Treatment: Its Status and Prospects. *Kennedy Inst Ethics J* 1992; 2: 309–345; N.L. Cantor. Twenty-Five Years after *Quinlan*: A Review of the Jurisprudence of Death and Dying. *J Law Med Ethics* 2001; 29: 182–196.

2 J. Rachels. 1986. *The End of Life*. New York: Oxford University Press; P. Singer. 1994. *Rethinking Life and Death: The Collapse of Our Traditional Ethics*. New York: St. Martin's Press; D. Brock. 1993. *Life and Death*. New York: Cambridge University Press.

3 G. Calabresi and P. Bobbitt. 1978. *Tragic Choices*. New York: W.W. Norton.

4 C. Tavris and E. Aronson. 2007. *Mistakes Were Made: (But Not by Me)*. Orlando, FL: Harcourt: 13–20.

5 E.D. Pellegrino. Doctors Must Not Kill. *J Clin Ethics* 1992; 3: 95–102; D. Callahan. 1993. *The Troubled Dream of Life*. Washington DC: Georgetown University Press: 158–172; B. Brody. 2003. *Taking Issue*. Washington DC: Georgetown University Press: 158–172.

6 Brock, *Life and Death*, pp. 208–213.

7 H.L.A. Hart and T. Honore. 1985. *Causation in the Law*, 2nd edn. New York: Oxford University Press.

8 G. Bosshard et al. Intentionally Hastening Death by Withholding or Withdrawing Treatment. *Wiener Klinische Wochenschrift* 2006; 118: 322–326.

9 T. Scanlon. 1998. *What We Owe to Each Other*. Cambridge, MA: Harvard University Press: 248–251.

10 F.G. Miller, J.J. Fins and L. Snyder. Assisted Suicide Compared with Refusal of Treatment: A Valid Distinction? *Ann Intern Med* 2000; 132: 470–475.

11 R. Dworkin et al. 1998. The philosopher's brief. In *Physician-Assisted Suicide*. M.P. Battin, R. Rhodes and A. Silvers, eds. New York: Routledge.

12 W. Gaylin et al. Doctors Must Not Kill. *JAMA* 1988; 259: 2139–2140; L.R. Kass. Neither for Love nor Money: Why Doctors Must Not Kill. *Public Interest* 1989; 94: 25–46.

13 J.L. Bernat, B. Gert and R.P. Mogielnicki. Patient Refusal of Hydration and Nutrition: An Alternative to Physician-Assisted Suicide or Voluntary Active Euthanasia. *Arch Intern Med* 1993; 153: 2723–2728.

14 Brock, *Life and Death*, pp. 205–208.

15 F.G. Miller et al. Regulating Physician-Assisted Death. *N Engl J Med* 1994; 331: 119–123.

16 D. Brock. Truth or Consequences: The Role of Philosophers in Policy-Making. In Brock, *Life and Death*, pp. 408–416.

Severely Disabled Newborns

Severely Troubled Newborns

28

When Care Cannot Cure
Medical Problems in Seriously Ill Babies

Neil Campbell

Thankfully, most babies are born intact and healthy after a normal pregnancy, and thereafter they thrive. But a few, around 4–6%, are born seriously ill or become ill after birth.[1]

Illnesses in babies have two important characteristics: they are often life-threatening, and they can cause serious handicaps or chronic ill health (morbidity) in babies who survive. Advances in knowledge, organization of newborn health services, and technology are achieving cures or amelioration of many illnesses that in the past resulted in death or permanent severe handicap. With mechanical ventilators and other complex life-supporting treatment most extremely premature babies now survive. In the past most died. Complex surgery can now ensure survival of most babies with severe malformations, even those considered "monstrous".

We can take over the function of most organs, for days or weeks, when they temporarily fail. Mechanical ventilators and extra-corporeal membrane oxygenators can assume the functions of failing hearts and lungs. Hemo-filtration and dialysis can take over the functions of failing livers and kidneys, and transfusions of red blood cells, white blood cells, and blood platelets, the functions of failing bone marrow. Intravenous nutrition can take over the functions of the diseased bowel. The only major organs we cannot yet transplant are brain and bowel, given donors.

However there are still many babies for whom modern techniques are less than successful. In some, new treatments achieve little more than delaying death. In others death is averted but survival results in permanent severe handicaps or lifelong ill health. When treatment falls far short of complete success, ethical questions arise. Are such treatments in babies' and families' best interests? How can costs be justified?

This paper describes a number of newborn illnesses to show how they create ethical problems. First, however, two caveats: It is conventional to describe newborn intensive care activities in medical-technical language, implying scientific objectivity, but this language does not accurately reflect reality. Many things we do in newborn intensive care involve value judgements and some of these have ethical content. Second, medical-technical language speaks of pathology and physiology, mechanical ventilators and blood gases, drug doses and brain functions. Such language can obscure the deeper context – that of hopes and fears, joys and grief, pleasures and pains, and life and death. Scientific objectivity has its place in newborn intensive care, but much is lost if it overshadows the human values and goals it is meant to serve.

Original publication details: Neil Campbell, "When Care Cannot Cure: Medical Problems in Seriously Ill Babies," pp. 327–44 from F. K. Beller and R. F. Weir (eds.), *The Beginning of Human Life,* Dordrecht: Kluwer Academic Publishers, 1994. With kind permission from Springer Science+Business Media.

Illnesses in newborn babies can be classified into three main diagnostic groups: extreme prematurity (babies born 8–17 weeks early); birth defects, including malformations, chromosomal disorders, intrauterine infections, and inborn errors of metabolism; and acquired diseases (babies normal at the end of pregnancy, but becoming ill during or after delivery: the most important acquired diseases are birth asphyxia and bacterial infections).

This paper concentrates on aspects of extreme prematurity and representative birth defects. These illustrate well the ways in which newborn illnesses create ethical problems. There are many areas of ethical concern in newborn care – informed consent, "standard" versus "experimental" treatments, pain, withdrawal of treatment, costs and resource allocation, and duties to impaired survivors. This paper confines itself to placing in context the ethical questions of withdrawal of treatment and resource allocation.

Extreme Prematurity

Normal babies are born after 38 to 42 weeks of pregnancy (gestation) and average around 3400 grams in birthweight. A few babies (about 1.2%) are born far too early, and have a characteristic set of problems resulting from immaturity of organ and tissue functions. Very low birthweight (VLBW) babies are those of birthweight less than 1500 g (usually less than 32 weeks' gestation). Within this group are the tiniest babies, the extremely low birthweight (ELBW) group, less than 1000 g and usually less than 28 weeks' gestation. Live-born ELBW babies represent 0.3–0.4% of all live births. There are 11,000–14,000 in the US each year.[2]

ELBW babies are usually critically ill in the hours and days after birth. Although they have a strange beauty to those experienced in their care, their skin is thin and leaks body fluids; the flesh is jellyish and bruises easily. Liver, kidneys, heart, and glands perform poorly: the babies have great difficulty even maintaining normal body warmth. They experience a variety of complex problems in the early weeks of life. Three will be described: respiratory distress syndrome (RDS), intracerebral hemorrhage, and necrotizing enterocolitis (NEC).

Respiratory distress syndrome (RDS)

Most ELBW babies develop lung disease, respiratory distress syndrome (RDS), within minutes, and their lungs are simply too immature and delicate to function normally. The baby's breathing in distressed and labored. Most affected babies must be placed on mechanical ventilators, and given extra oxygen and other life-sustaining treatments. The disease usually gets progressively worse in the first three days. Many babies die during this time. Their lungs are so affected the ventilator cannot support them, and other complications pile up. In some babies it is obvious hours in advance that they will die. In such situations, how long should care continue? Until the baby is moribund? Until the heart stops? Continuing maximal, intrusive, expensive therapies in babies who are dying is, to some, obscene. And yet, how can caregivers be sure death will occur? How much certainty is required?

In surviving babies RDS starts improving on the fourth day, but the lungs will have been injured to some extent by the physical effect of the pressure produced by the ventilator (barotrauma) and the toxic chemical effect of oxygen (oxygen toxicity). These iatrogenic injuries to the lung are called bronchopulmonary dysplasia (BPD). BPD slows the rate of recovery from RDS. In a few babies BPD gets progressively worse over many days, and a vicious cycle is set up: the baby must remain on the ventilator and oxygen because of his/her damaged lungs, but the ventilator and oxygen, while keeping the baby alive, exacerbate the lung damage.

BPD keeps some babies on the ventilator for weeks or months. Occasional babies become respiratory cripples: they never get off the ventilator.

When it becomes clear – at a month, or six months, or a year of age – that a baby will never get off the ventilator, parents and caregivers are faced with caring for a baby with poor quality of life and a dismal long-term outlook. A point may be reached where maximal therapy cannot keep the baby comfortable. Should therapy be withdrawn? If months of ventilator dependency have gone by, should caregivers withdraw *before* the point of failing maximal therapy has been reached? Does the presence of other complications which further reduce quality of life – for example, moderate brain damage – have relevance?

Ethical problems arising from the use of mechanical ventilators are well illustrated by the example of RDS in the ELBW baby, but similar problems arise in many other serious diseases of newborn babies. A mechanical ventilator is used to assist a baby's breathing when it is inadequate. Breathing may be inadequate because the lungs are severely diseased, or because the brain is diseased or injured in such a way that it no longer drives the lungs to breathe.

The ventilator pumps oxygen into the lungs many times per minute, hour after hour, day after day. It can keep a baby alive for weeks or months, even if most of the brain is dead or the lungs hopelessly damaged and incapable of healing. Ventilators achieve excellent results in babies with diseases which *temporarily* prevent their breathing adequately: the ventilator maintains life until treatment and nature allow the baby to cope alone. Dilemmas arise if babies are kept alive by ventilators when they have no hope of eventually recovering sufficiently to cope alone. Being on a ventilator involves many painful or frightening experiences throughout each day, only partially ameliorated by sedation or analgesia. Babies on ventilators are socially and emotionally isolated: it is difficult to pick them up for feeds and cuddles, and the necessary sedation depresses their awareness.

Intracerebral hemorrhage

During the first week of life 40–50% of ELBW babies suffer bleeding of varying severity into the brain (intraventricular hemorrhage, IVH). Blood flow to the brain fluctuates widely during the unstable states ELBW babies experience in the first days after birth. During unstable episodes brain blood flow may temporarily cease, injuring areas of the brain (cerebral ischemia). Injured areas may die. When brain blood flow improves again, bleeding may occur into injured or dead areas of brain.

Small hemorrhages (small areas of ischemia) have little immediate or long-term effect on the baby. Large hemorrhages can cause sudden deterioration and, occasionally, death. When babies survive large hemorrhages, permanent serious intellectual and physical handicaps are common. Between 75% and 100% of babies with extensive intracerebral hemorrhages or ischemia have severe permanent handicaps.

The presence of areas of ischemia or hemorrhage in the brain can be seen by ultrasound or CAT scanners; ultrasound scans are usually performed daily or more often in sick ELBW babies. However, extensive ischemic areas may not be obvious to scanners in the first few days of life. Their effects may be detected only several weeks later, as the injured areas of brain dissolve or shrivel away. This process is called periventricular leukomalacia (PVL). Thus ischemic brain injuries occurring in the first few days, which will result in severe handicaps, may only be detected at several weeks of age.

Sometimes clotted blood from hemorrhagic areas of brain block the circulation of the brain's cerebrospinal fluid. The blocked fluid builds up within the spaces in the brain called the ventricles, producing hydrocephalus. The ventricles distend, further injuring the surrounding brain. Some ELBW babies with hydrocephalus need a surgical operation to insert a plastic tube into the distended ventricles, to drain the fluid blockage (ventriculoperitoneal shunt; V-P shunt).

When an ELBW baby suddenly deteriorates in the first few days with a massive intracerebral hemorrhage, should life-supporting measures be discontinued? If so, what degree of risk of severe handicap should suffice for decision making? Only certainty? Fifty percent? When, at several weeks of age, a baby thought to have had only moderate cerebral ischemia in the first week is found to be developing extensive periventricular leukomalacia, with large areas of brain dissolving away, should life-sustaining treatment continue? At this stage the baby may be off the ventilator and other intensive life-supporting treatment. The only life-sustaining treatment the baby may be getting is scheduled feeding via a stomach tube, as he or she cannot suck or swallow. Should this scheduled feeding continue? Is it not life-supporting in the same way as is a mechanical ventilator?

The term "scheduled feeding," introduced above, requires explanation. Healthy normal babies are "demand" fed – that is, fed from breast or bottle whenever they show signs of hunger or thirst, rather than to a formal timetable or schedule. Ill babies may have no sense of hunger, nor be able to suck and swallow. For example, ELBW babies cannot suck or swallow effectively, as the brain mechanisms controlling these functions are immature and uncoordinated. Babies unconscious from brain diseases or medications do not demand feed. Also, major brain abnormalities often disturb the swallowing and sucking mechanisms. Babies with malformations of the mouth or throat also may not be able to suck and swallow. Babies with very distressed breathing from lung diseases or heart failure may be too short of breath to demand feed, or to swallow feed safely without breathing it into their lungs (aspiration).

To ensure effective nutrition in such babies, carefully planned feeding schedules, delivered by artificial means such as stomach tubes, must be prescribed. Waking and demanding, thirst and appetite, and sucking and swallowing, are replaced by scheduled feeding. For ill babies, such regimes are lifesaving. They ensure survival until the baby's recovery allows normal demand feeding. If it is acceptable to withdraw life-sustaining treatments such as mechanical ventilation from babies in whom hope for survival or meaningful life is gone, is it not also acceptable to withdraw scheduled feeding?

Necrotizing enterocolitis (NEC)

After the first week of life 2–5% of ELBW babies develop a severe inflammation of the bowel, necrotizing enterocolitis (NEC). The inflammation may be so severe that it destroys varying lengths of the bowel – from a few centimetres to the entire bowel. Some babies are overwhelmed by the inflammation and quickly die. In survivors, when parts of the bowel have been destroyed, surgical operations are required to remove them. Loss of short lengths of bowel at operation have little practical consequence, but if greater lengths of bowel are lost, the baby may be left with insufficient bowel for normal digestion.

In mild cases of NEC the inflamed bowel is rested for 2–3 weeks by stopping milk feeds. The babies' nutritional requirements are provided with intravenous nutrition. When milk feeds are recommenced, they usually succeed. In worse cases, when substantial bowel has been lost, reintroduction of feeds results in diarrhea. It may take weeks or months for the shortened bowel to recover sufficiently for normal milk feeding to succeed. During the recovery period the baby's health and growth rely on intravenous nutrition.

Occasionally babies lose so much bowel at operation that they can never recover sufficient bowel function to see them through life. Such babies will always be dependent on intravenous nutrition. In some it is obvious at the surgical operation that there is insufficient bowel for life. In others it becomes apparent only after months of intravenous nutrition and repeated failures of milk feeding.

When it is found at surgery that too much bowel has died, what should caregivers do? The baby can survive only if she is given lifelong intravenous nutrition. She will never be able to be fed normally. She is usually critically ill, on a mechanical ventilator and other life-sustaining treatments. Should they be discontinued? When it becomes apparent only after months of intravenous nutrition that the bowel will never work successfully, what should caregivers do? Once again, the baby is faced with a life of total intravenous nutrition. By this time the baby is off the ventilator, but will have developed complications of intravenous nutrition.

Intravenous nutrition is a complex, expensive procedure in which all nutrition is administered through a catheter in a vein. IV nutrition can keep a baby healthy and growing for weeks, months, or years without oral feeds, yet life-threatening infections of the intravenous catheter are common. IV nutrition also causes liver damage, worst in the most immature babies, which can cause progressive failure of the liver over several months. Thus a baby being kept alive by intravenous nutrition because his bowel does not work can die of liver failure at 6–12 months of age, a complication of the intravenous nutrition. Liver failure is a distressing condition: the baby swells up all over (edema), the abdomen becomes tense with fluid (ascites), the blood fails to clot, and frequent, distressing hemorrhages result.

When a baby develops liver failure after months of intravenous nutrition, what should caregivers do? There is little hope of recovery of either the liver or the bowel. Life with progressive liver failure is very unpleasant. Should intravenous nutrition be withdrawn? IV nutrition achieves wonderful results when babies have bowel diseases which prevent normal milk feeding for weeks or months, but which eventually get better. It creates dilemmas when it keeps babies alive with bowel diseases which will never ameliorate sufficiently for the baby to feed naturally.

Given these complex problems, what is the overall outcome for VLBW and ELBW babies? Tables 28.1 and 28.2 show typical outcome figures for all babies from a single region (Victoria, Australia). Similar figures are reported from regions in North America and Europe.

Live-born ELBW babies constitute only 0.3% of all births, but 34% of all baby deaths. Care is nowadays offered at 23 weeks' gestation (around 600 g, 17 weeks early). Few survive. By 24–25 weeks' gestation (700–799 g) around 30% survive: around 25% of survivors have severe handicaps; the chances of surviving without handicap are about 10%. By 26–27 weeks' gestation (900–999 g) 75% survive: around 10% have severe handicaps; the chances of surviving without handicap are around 40%. As organization of care and methods of treatment improve, outcomes improve. Current extremely premature babies are likely to do better than babies born five or ten years ago.

What of costs and resources? In our state (Victoria, Australia) VLBW babies constitute 0.6% of all live-born babies, and yet they make up 53% of all admissions to neonatal intensive care units, and 83% of patient ventilator days. Thus a tiny population is responsible for a substantial workload. Estimates of costs vary from country to country and with the methods of costing used. Typical costs for ELBW babies in intensive care units are around $A1,000 per day, and average hospitalization costs around $A50,000–$A80,000 per baby. The earlier the gestation, the higher the cost. To achieve a survivor at 24 weeks in our region costs around $A300,000.

Such cost estimates include only initial hospitalization after birth. They do not include costs for subsequent hospitalization, nor lifetime costs of care for handicaps. ELBW costs compare badly with costs of other patient populations. They are more expensive than VLBW babies and mature babies needing treatment for malformations: they are far more expensive than children needing intensive care for life-threatening conditions beyond the first year of life. The care of ELBW babies diverts scarce resources from other babies, children, and adults with better potential outcomes. Should costs be taken into account in treatment decisions?

Care is nowadays often offered at 23 weeks' gestation, when the chances of survival are less than 10%, the chances of serious handicap in survivors around 30%, and the cost for each survivor between $300,000 and $400,000. Caregivers know that termination of pregnancy for serious fetal defects is performed as late as 28 weeks' gestation, legal or not. Given all these considerations, many people ask whether there is a gestation and birth size below which care should not be offered. Do caregivers really have a mandate from their society to use such large resources when returns are so poor?

Severe handicaps

In this discussion of VLBW and ELBW babies frequent reference has been made to severe handicaps (and there are many other serious illnesses in babies which also result in handicaps). Severe handicaps involve various combinations of mental deficiency, body paralysis, blindness, and deafness. Mental deficiency means varying degrees of reduced intelligence;

Table 28.1 VLBW and ELBW outcomes

Birth weight, grams	Gestational age, weeks	Survival rate	Severe handicap	Normal survivor
1250–1500	29–31	> 95%	< 10%	60%
1000–1250	27–29	85%		
900–999	26–27	75%	10–15%	35–40%
800–899	25–26	45%		
700–799	24–25	30%	15–25%	5–15%
600–699	23–24	<10%		

Table 28.2 VLBW and ELBW babies

	Victoria 1987		Live births 61,000		Neonatal deaths 292	
Birth weight	Total births	Live births		Percentage of all births	Neonatal deaths		Percentage of all deaths
< 1500 g (VLBW)	627	467	=	0.76%	139	=	47%
< 1000 g (ELBW)	294	177	=	0.3%	100	=	34%

lack of awareness of self, others, and "the meaning of life"; and lack of ability to interact socially and emotionally. Body paralysis means varying degrees of lack of control of muscles, body, and limbs, with resulting immobility and dependence on others for feeding, toileting, and other aspects of life's basics.

Survival of a baby with severe handicaps has a serious effect on his or her family. Marital breakdown is frequent, and when it occurs the mother is often left to cope as a single parent. There is a high incidence of psychiatric disturbances in affected families. Other children in the family can suffer emotional hardship and deprivation as a result. For some families, though, the care of a severely handicapped child can be an experience of moral growth and enrichment. Many parents, especially mothers, develop an extraordinary bond of love for a handicapped child, even when the child's existence leads to so much hardship. Indeed, to the outsider, the loving sacrifice by parents of self and family interests to the handicapped child is a central part of the tragedy.

It is widely held that when withdrawal of treatment is being considered, the best interests of the baby should prevail. Does a baby have interests which can be viewed in isolation, as separate from those of the family?

Birth Defects: Conditions That Can Be Fixed

The list of birth defects is very long.[3] Major categories include malformations of one or more major organs or body structures, the rest of the baby being normal; chromosome abnormalities, in which every tissue of the baby is abnormal; inborn errors of metabolism, in which there are malfunctions in one or more of the body's chemical processes; and intrauterine infections, which usually affect most of the fetus's developing tissues, causing abnormal tissue function and in some cases malformations.

To illustrate ethical dilemmas, birth defects are best classified according to prognosis – what effects they have on survival and function – rather than diagnosis.

Prognostically, birth defects can be divided into those conditions which can be fixed, and those which cannot. In the former conditions, there is a very high chance of survival if all available treatment is offered.

With survival there is a normal or "acceptable" life span, with no handicaps, or an "acceptable" level of handicap and no chronic ill health, or an "acceptable" level of chronicity. Obviously, much hinges on the definition of "acceptable."

More, and more serious, newborn illnesses are moving into this category. Although outcomes in this group are good, treatment is often long and arduous for the baby. Intrusive, distressing treatments are often needed, and hospitalization may continue for months. Costs can be very high, especially in babies needing prolonged mechanical ventilation, surgical operations, or intravenous nutrition. On the other hand, the average stay in hospital for mature babies with esophageal atresia (failure of the gullet to form normally), who require major chest surgery on the first day of life, is nine days. Most babies requiring bypass cardiac surgery are home within three weeks.

Birth Defects: Conditions That Cannot Be Fixed

Those conditions which cannot be fixed can be categorized as follows: (1) conditions in which death is inevitable, despite all available care. Active treatment only lengthens the period before death occurs; (2) conditions in which active treatment will ensure survival, but with severe handicaps, chronic ill health, or shortened life span; and (3) conditions in which survival *might* be achieved with prolonged, intrusive, distressing treatments, but with serious handicaps, chronic ill health or shortened life span. (Classification according to prognosis is helpful in ethical discussions about *all* baby illnesses – the ELBW baby, babies with birth asphyxia or infections – not just birth defects.)

Conditions in which death is inevitable

This group includes such conditions as Potter's syndrome and its variants (renal agenesis or dysplasia with pulmonary hypoplasia), anencephaly, chromosomal abnormalities such as trisomy 18, and some complex heart malformations.

Potter's syndrome and its variants   In this condition, for unknown reasons, the fetus's kidneys fail to form (renal agenesis). Fetal lung growth depends on the development of normal fetal kidneys. When the fetal kidneys fail to form, the fetal lungs fail to grow adequately. At birth Potter's syndrome babies look abnormal. They have very distressed breathing and cannot cope unless given oxygen and placed on a ventilator. These treatments are often started if the baby's condition is not recognized. Some die quickly despite ventilation and oxygen; in others survival is prolonged, but never beyond a day or so.

It is generally assumed that the lungs will never work satisfactorily, so that temporarily taking over their function with ventilators, oxygen, or extracorporeal membrane oxygenation (ECMO) is inappropriate. Babies cannot survive long-term without kidneys. It is generally assumed that it is inappropriate to temporarily take over kidney functions with renal dialysis or hemofiltration, although renal transplantation might be technically possible if donors are available. Given all of these assumptions, death is inevitable.

Are these assumptions morally sound? If a Potter's syndrome baby is placed on a ventilator before the condition is recognized, is there an ethical problem in stopping? What should be done with the baby if ventilation is withdrawn? Such babies may be conscious and aware, and death from hypoxia is frightening until unconsciousness is reached.

Potter's syndrome occurs in about 1 in 10,000 births. There are therefore approximately 370 Potter's syndrome babies born in the US each year.

Anencephaly   In anencephaly there is failure of development of most of the brain (the cerebral hemispheres and much of the midbrain) together with the covering skull and scalp. Two-thirds are born dead. Most born alive die within minutes or hours; a few live for days or months. It is generally assumed that the babies have no conscious awareness and that death is inevitable. They may, however, suck, cry, grimace, and even smile.

Because death is assumed to be inevitable, most caregivers withhold treatment likely to prolong life. However, recently anencephalic infants have been placed on mechanical ventilation and other life-supporting treatments, with a view to using them as sources of organs for transplantation. These babies have done better than expected. So, are assumptions about the inevitability of death soundly based? No one can say with certainty, since in the past no one has really tried to achieve survival.

Anencephaly occurs in about 3 in 10,000 births: there are about 1,100 born each year in the US, 350 of these alive at birth.

Trisomy 18   There are several chromosomal disorders, including trisomy 18, which result in profound mental insufficiency and a shortened life span. In trisomy 18 every cell in the developing fetus, from conception, has additional genetic material (an extra chromosome). This results in abnormality of all the developing tissues. The babies have an abnormal appearance. Their consciousness is depressed and it is assumed they are never aware of themselves, others, or their environment. Some have life-threatening malformations, especially of the heart or esophagus (esophageal atresia). The brain is so abnormal that its reflex nerve mechanisms controlling sucking, swallowing, and coughing do not function adequately. In some babies this results in frequent choking episodes, or blockages of the breathing passages with saliva or other secretions. Attempts at feeding often result in choking. Feeds may be breathed into the lungs (aspiration), causing pneumonia.

Half die in the first month; fewer than 10% survive the first year. It is assumed that death is inevitable from choking episodes, feeding difficulties, or pneumonia. Treatment for life-threatening malformations is therefore usually withheld. No one really knows how long life might continue if all available treatment were offered — ventilator support for poor breathing or pneumonia; surgery for life-threatening malformations; antibiotics for infections; and careful attention to nutrition. The view that death is inevitable may thus be a self-fulfilling prophesy.

What treatment should be offered to babies with trisomy 18 or other similar chromosomal abnormalities? Scheduled feeds by stomach tube, or intravenous fluids, will prolong life in some of them. In others, with choking episodes or a malformed heart, feeds and fluids may hasten death. Should caregivers clear out the throat with suction catheters when choking episodes occur? These episodes are distressing to watch, but it is assumed the baby is unaware and does not suffer. Regular sucking out of the airways can be lifesaving, but is this beneficial to the baby? Trisomy 18 occurs in about 3 in 10,000 births. There are about 1,000 per year in the US.

When death is "inevitable" It will be seen from these descriptions of conditions in which death is considered inevitable that "inevitable" is a relative term. It is not known how long such babies might live if all available treatment were given. Technically, the only major organs not currently transplantable are brain and bowel: if donors were available, and ECMO tried, an occasional Potter's syndrome baby might be salvageable. If mechanical ventilation and other active treatment were offered, anencephalics might live weeks or months. If surgery and other forms of active intervention were offered, babies with trisomy 18 might live for years. Even when active treatment is not offered, some babies with "inevitably" lethal conditions survive for weeks or months.

Nevertheless most caregivers believe that life-sustaining treatments should be withheld from these categories. Given that survival prospects are not accurately known, since no one really tries for survival, are decisions in these babies based on the "inevitability" of death, or are they rather based on "quality of life" judgements? Caregivers who view quality-of-life judgements as unacceptable criteria for deciding to withdraw treatment usually accept that life-sustaining treatments are not morally mandatory in babies for whom death is "inevitable." Perhaps these are quality of life judgements after all.

Survival with severe handicaps

This category includes conditions in which active treatment will ensure survival but with severe handicaps, shortened life span, and chronic ill health. Diagnoses included in this group are severe spina bifida and a range of chromosomal abnormalities less severe in their effects than trisomy 18.

Severe spina bifida Spina bifida (high meningomyelocoele with congenital hydrocephalus) results from failure of the brain and spinal cord to develop normally in the fetus (neural tube defect). The spinal cord carries all the nerves from the brain to all the other body structures. It is contained within the spinal column. In spina bifida one section of the spinal cord, together with the surrounding spinal column, fails to form properly. The backbone lies open with the malformed spinal cord exposed. This lesion is called a meningomyelocoele. All functions below the level of the lesion are severely abnormal, since they are normally controlled by the spinal cord nerves. Below the lesion there is no sensation: the muscles are paralyzed; organs such as urinary bladder, genitals, and lower bowel function abnormally. If the lesion is low on the back, the handicaps which result are mild. High lesions, midway up the back, result in a child who will never walk, may not be able to sit upright normally; and will have no feeling below the waist, marked disturbances (incontinence) of urine and bowel functions, and abnormal sexual function.

Most babies with meningomyelocoele also have brain malformations, i.e., hydrocephalus. In mild cases (the majority) this may require surgical operations (ventriculo-peritoneal shunts), but has no serious effects on the baby's future. In severe cases hydrocephalus can result in significant mental deficiency not correctable by surgery.

The child with a high meningomyelocoele and severe hydrocephalus has a difficult life. Surgery on the back lesion, to prevent infection, and on the head to prevent worse mental deficiency, and scheduled feeding in the early weeks of life, will ensure survival. Without these most die after weeks or months, depending on how they are cared for. Survivors spend much of their childhood in the hospital with complications. They are confined to bed or wheelchair. Their lives may be shortened by such complications as infections in the hydrocephalus shunt or kidney failure from the urinary bladder dysfunction.

The incidence of spina bifida varies from place to place, between 1 in 1,000 and 5 in 1,000 births. About one-quarter have high back lesions and serious hydrocephalus. Given the potentially poor quality of life, many caregivers practice selective treatment, withholding surgery or other lifesaving procedures from severely affected babies. However, not all such babies die: occasional babies survive, with worse handicaps than if they had been offered surgery at the beginning.

Can withholding treatment that would ensure survival be justified on the grounds of poor future quality of life? If an occasional baby might survive despite surgery's being withheld, can scheduled feeding, antibiotics, and other forms of life-prolonging care be withheld?

More than 95% of spina bifida fetuses can be detected in the womb. Termination of pregnancy can be performed if parents wish. Although this is seen by many as the answer to the ethical problems arising in babies with severe spina bifida, it is really only a shift in the ethical framework, from the ethics of withholding treatment from babies to the ethics of abortion.

Babies whose outcome is uncertain

These babies might survive after long, complex, intrusive treatment, but they might not. Survival may result in a lifetime of chronic ill health or severe handicaps. Diagnoses in this group include multiple malformation syndromes not due to chromosomal disorders, and hypoplastic left heart syndrome.

Multiple malformation syndromes There are many conditions in which babies have several major malformations. Consider a baby who has esophageal atresia (failure of the gullet to form); a major heart malformation; major abnormalities of the kidneys; and major malformations of the spine, arms, hands, and legs (Vater syndrome).

The esophagus can usually be easily repaired, but there may be annoying complications throughout childhood. Most heart defects can now be cured or improved by surgery, although some need more than one operation. The kidney abnormalities may be correctable, but there may be a risk of progressive kidney failure in childhood, with poor health and eventual need for transplantation. The spinal deformity may be correctable, but may result in a permanent marked twisting of the back. The arm, hand, and leg deformities may be improved but not corrected: walking without aids such as calipers or crutches may be difficult or impossible; the arm and hand abnormalities may make this and other functions harder. Brain function and intelligence will be normal unless diseases of the brain such as meningitis are acquired during treatment of the other conditions.

At best, such a baby will need lengthy hospitalization, with a number of surgical operations and other arduous treatments. If everything goes well, only the back, arm, hand, and leg deformities will persist as lifetime problems. At worst, complications of treatment of any of the malformations could result in death; partial success in these treatments could result in chronic ill health; kidney failure could lead to the need for transplantation; and complications of treatment causing brain damage could cause mental deficiency. Given the certainty of physical handicaps from arms, hands, legs and back, the uncertainty of survival despite months of arduous treatment, and the possibility of progressive kidney failure, could a case be made not to embark on any lifesaving treatment at the outset?

If life-threatening complications develop after weeks or months of care, how far should arduous treatment such as mechanical ventilation and surgical operations be pushed? Is a point reached where it is appropriate to say, "Enough is enough"?

Hypoplastic left heart syndrome (HLHS) This is a relatively common malformation of the heart in which the left half of the heart, the parts responsible for pumping blood around the body, fail to form properly. Babies with HLHS are usually beautiful babies. In the past they all died, most in the first week of life. Now a number of centers around the world offer surgery. Instead of dying, babies are placed on mechanical ventilators, given other complex, arduous treatment, and then have surgery to make the heart sufficiently functional to sustain life for the first year or two. If this first stage is successful, a second operation must be performed to improve long-term survival. An alternative to this two-stage treatment, advocated by some, is cardiac transplantation soon after birth.

Death rates after the first operation in various centers around the world vary from 50% to 95%, babies die hours, weeks, or months after surgery. Not many babies live to the second operation. It is too early to know how many babies will live, or for how long, after the second operation. No one knows the long-term outcome of cardiac transplantation in the first year of life, and finding donors is difficult.[4]

Before surgery was offered for HLHS, death was inevitable, but happened quickly and peacefully. With surgery, most babies still die (perhaps all will die in childhood – who knows?), but after hours, weeks, or months of intrusive, arduous treatments. Should babies and families be offered such treatment in the (so far) small hope of eventual survival? Or should it be accepted that, in some conditions, it may be better not to try? HLHS babies consume huge resources in health care systems where resources are finite. Is it fair on all that resources are used in this way? And yet, if surgeons do not try, how will advances ever be made?

Withholding Treatment

So far this paper has described a number of serious newborn illnesses to illustrate how ethical dilemmas arise, especially in relation to decisions for or against lifesaving treatment.

What happens in practice? Ways in which these problems are resolved vary around the world. In 1973 neonatologists at the Yale–New Haven Hospital (US) reported that 14% of deaths in babies followed withdrawal of treatment.[5] In 1986 Hammersmith (UK) reported a figure of 30%.[6] Our own practices are outlined below. Discussions with neonatologists in several countries lead us to believe our practices are not unusual.

We believe that withdrawal of treatment should be considered when there is little hope of survival despite all care, or when quality of life may be unacceptably poor. When such is the case, the doctor in charge must inform parents about all relevant aspects of diagnosis and prognosis and give a clear view of what he or she thinks is best.

In the context of near-certainty of death or very poor quality of life, after all necessary advice and guidance has been given, the decision whether to continue or to stop active treatment belongs to the parents. If parents decide that treatment should be continued, contrary to caregivers' views, all measures should be continued in good faith, but the doctor in charge should tactfully continue to advocate his/her views.

The baby's interests are of central importance, but we do not believe they should (or can) be separated from the interests of the family. It is appropriate for the parents and their advisers to take into account the effects of the baby's continuing defects on the rest of the family, should the baby survive.

When everyone agrees it is best to withdraw treatment, no measures likely to prolong life inappropriately should be continued. This includes oxygen, antibiotics, intravenous fluids, and scheduled feeding. When all life-sustaining treatments are withdrawn, attention to the baby's comfort is paramount. Ensuring the baby's comfort will often require analgesics and sedatives which may as a side effect shorten the baby's life.

Withdrawal of treatment at Royal Children's Hospital, Melbourne, Australia

We have studied all deaths in our unit in a recent two-year period. There were 1,362 babies admitted with complex problems during the period studied. Of these 132 (9.7%) died. Thirty-one (23.5%) of the deaths occurred despite all efforts to ensure the babies' survivals. The remaining 101 deaths (76.5%) occurred following withdrawal of life-supporting treatment.

Babies from whom treatment was withdrawn were classified in the three prognostic categories previously mentioned.

Babies in whom death was inevitable   There were 42 babies in this group (41.6%). They were almost certain to die despite all available treatment; withdrawal of treatment shortened the time to the babies' deaths. In this group were extremely low birthweight babies with RDS, and lungs hopelessly disrupted by high-pressure mechanical ventilation or massive brain hemorrhages; babies born without kidneys and with lungs too small to support life (Potter's syndrome); babies with chromosomal disorders such as trisomies 18 and 13. The ELBW babies would have died within hours, as would those with Potter's syndrome. Some of the babies with chromosomal abnormalities might have lived weeks or months. The medical and ethical assumptions guiding their care were that death was inevitable and so life-prolonging treatment was burdensome and not serving their interests.

Babies who would almost certainly have survived with life-sustaining treatment but with severe handicaps and chronic ill health   There were 17 babies in this group (16.8%). Diagnoses included babies with severe birth asphyxia, spina bifida with hydrocephalus, and Down's syndrome with lifethreatening malformations. The medical and ethical decisions for these babies were based on judgements of the future quality of life of the babies and their families.

Babies in whom prognosis for survival was uncertain   With active, prolonged, and potentially distressing treatment they might have survived, but more likely would have died. If they had survived it would have been with serious handicaps and chronic ill health. Diagnoses in this group included severe birth asphyxia, ELBW babies with serious intracerebral hemorrhages, and various serious chromosomal abnormalities.

It can be seen that withdrawal decisions were based on prognosis – whether or not babies could survive, and what the quality of survival would be – rather than diagnosis. Many forms of treatment were withdrawn. Those essential to survival were as follows: Of the 101 babies who had active treatment withdrawn, 40 (39.6%) had withdrawal of mechanical ventilation. Forty-eight babies (47.%) had scheduled feeding withheld. These were babies unable to feed from breast or bottle, so that immediate survival depended on scheduled gavage (stomach tube) feeding, gastrostomy feeding, or other special techniques. Oral feeding was not withheld from babies who "demanded" feeding and in whom oral feeding would not itself be life-threatening. Feeding was not withheld; it was simply not imposed.

Eight babies not on mechanical ventilators had oxygen therapy withdrawn. Five babies had intravenous nutrition withdrawn.

It will be clear from what has been said so far that not all babies who are going to die, or to survive with severe handicaps, are extremely tiny or immature, or "monstrous" or malformed. Some are of normal size and pleasing to look at. Not all are brain-damaged or in coma: some are conscious, aware, and responsive. Even when most of the brain is malformed or injured, babies can exhibit "normal" baby behaviors such as gazing, feeding, crying, and smiling, since these are brainstem functions.

Not all are on mechanical ventilators or other complex high-technology support. Some are breathing unaided, in ordinary baby cots, receiving no life-support treatment except oxygen or scheduled feeding and fluids, or suctioning of secretions from the throat to prevent choking. Not all are desperately ill and in the first days or weeks of life: some are stable and several months of age.

Palliative care: fluids and feeds

When life-supporting treatment is withdrawn from babies, palliative care to relieve pain or distress is essential. For many babies palliative care is straightforward: analgesics and sedatives are given even though they often incidentally shorten life. Many caregivers have ethical difficulties withholding feeds and fluids. To them feeding babies is a fundamental part of human nurturing, and seeing babies fade away dehydrated and starving seems morally repugnant.

In our experience, continuing feeds and fluids makes many dying babies worse. The dying process is prolonged. Babies who are breathless and distressed from lung disease, heart failure, or kidney failure remain distressed if fluids are continued, but symptoms improve as fluids are withdrawn and dehydration develops. Babies with abnormalities of brain or airway, which cause choking episodes and labored breathing, improve as dehydration develops and saliva and other secretions diminish. Babies with malformations of the mouth or throat, or brain abnormalities preventing them from sucking, swallowing, or coughing effectively, are made worse by feeding attempts. They may vomit and choke, or if feed is aspirated into the lungs it may cause death. Withholding feeds and fluids is sound palliative care for many dying babies.

When treatments directly supporting life, such as mechanical ventilation, oxygen, or drugs maintaining blood pressure or heart function, are withdrawn, death may follow in minutes or hours. Babies who are aware or in pain pose special problems. The symptoms resulting from withdrawal are distressing until consciousness is lost. Doses of analgesics such as morphine, sufficient to make relief of distress certain, may kill them – that is, cause immediate cessation of breathing and consciousness, whereas without analgesia they might breathe for hours. Arguments that such analgesia is not active euthanasia appear, to some bedside attendants, casuistic.

Slippery-slope arguments against euthanasia in such cases appear to many to be especially unjust. Such arguments appear to say to the baby, "As far as your interests are concerned it would be morally best if we induced a quick and painless death. But if we do, it will launch the rest of us down a slippery slope. So put up with your distress, and save us all from slippery slopes."

I have emphasized earlier that most babies with serious illnesses have good outcomes. It is these who make neonatology such a rewarding endeavor. As methods of treatment improve, further good outcomes should result, but that is not guaranteed. Unless sophisticated high-technology medicine is balanced by imagination (allowing us insight into other people's worlds), compassion, and forbearance (accepting that there are valid views other than our own), outcomes may well be worse.

Notes

1 For a brief account of medical problems in the newborn see Marshal H. Klaus and Avroy A. Fanaroff, *Care of the High-risk Neonate*, 3rd ed (Philadelphia: W. B. Saunders, 1986). For a comprehensive account see Avroy A. Fanaroff and Richard J. Martin (eds), *Neonatal–Perinatal Medicine*, 4th ed (St Louis: C.V. Mosby, 1987).

2 For comprehensive accounts of VLBW and ELBW babies see David Harvey (ed.), *The Baby under 1,000 g* (London: Wright, 1989); and Dharmapuri Vidyasagar (ed.), *The Tiny Baby* (Philadelphia: W. B. Saunders, 1986).

3 For outlines of the majority of birth defects see Kenneth Jones, *Smith's Recognizable Patterns of Human Malformations*, 4th ed (Philadelphia: W. B. Saunders, 1988).

4 James H. Moller and William A. Neal (eds), *Fetal, Neonatal, and Infant Cardiac Disease* (Norwalk: Appleton and Lange, 1990) 35: 723–43.

5 R. S. Duff and A. G. M. Campbell, "Moral and ethical dilemmas in the special care nursery." *New England Journal of Medicine*, 289 (1973) 890–4.

6 Andrew Whitelaw, "Death as an option in neonatal intensive care." *Lancet* (1986: ii): 328–31.

29

The Abnormal Child
Moral Dilemmas of Doctors and Parents

R. M. Hare

I was asked to make a philosophical contribution to our discussions; and any philosopher who tries to do this sort of thing is up against a serious difficulty. If he is content to act merely as a kind of logical policeman and pick up bad arguments that are put forward by other people, he will be unpopular, but may (if he is competent at his trade) establish for himself a fairly strong negative position. But if he wants to do something more constructive than that, and is going to rely on something more solid than his own intuitions and more stable than the received opinions on the subject, he will have to start from some general theory about how one argues on questions like this; and then at once he is on much shakier ground, because there is no general theory about moral argument that is universally accepted. All I can do in this situation is to tell you in outline the theory that I accept myself and then argue from that.

However, I have perhaps made my position sound shakier than it actually is; for the theory that I shall be using is one which ought to be acceptable to most of the main schools of ethics, because it relies only on certain formal characteristics of the moral words or concepts which we use in these arguments. I *think* (though obviously I shall have no time to argue) that this theory is consonant with the Christian principles that we should do to others as we wish that they should do to us, and that we should love our neighbour as

ourselves; with the Kantian principle that we should act in such a way that we can will the maxim of our action to be a universal law; and with the utilitarian principle that everybody is to count as one and nobody as more than one (that is to say, that their interests are to be equally regarded). Other approaches to the theory of moral argument which lead to the same kind of principle are the so-called Ideal Observer theory, according to which what we ought to do is what a person would prescribe who was fully acquainted with the facts and impartially benevolent to all those affected; and the so-called Rational Contractor theory which says that the principles we ought to follow are those which a rational self-interested person would agree to if he did not know which end of the stick *he* was going to receive in any of the situations to be adjudicated by the principles.

All these methods come really to the same thing, that when faced with a decision which affects the interests of different people, we should treat the interests of all these people (including ourselves if we are affected) as of equal weight, and do the best we can for them. This is the fundamental principle. There are a great many other principles, some of them of great importance, which occupy a different level from this fundamental principle, and may appear to conflict with it, as they certainly do conflict on occasion with one another. I mean principles like those which forbid

Original publication details: R. M. Hare, "The Abnormal Child: Moral Dilemmas of Doctors and Parents." Reprinted in *Essays on Bioethics*, Oxford: Clarendon Press, 1993, pp.185–91. Courtesy of the Estate of R. M. Hare.

Bioethics: An Anthology, Third Edition. Edited by Helga Kuhse, Udo Schüklenk, and Peter Singer.

lying or promise-breaking or murder; or that (very important to doctors) which demands loyalty to those to whom one is under some special obligation owing to a particular relation one stands in to them (for example one's wife or one's child or one's patient).

However, I think it is right to subordinate all these principles to the fundamental one, because in cases of conflict between these different principles, it is only the fundamental principle that can give us any secure answer as to what we should do. The fundamental principle is the law and the prophets; although particular laws (and particular prophecies for that matter) are no doubt very important, they take their origin from the need to preserve and to do justice between the interests of people (that is, to secure to them their rights); and when there is a conflict between the principles – or even some doubt about the application of a particular principle – it is this fundamental principle which has to be brought in to resolve it.

An example that may occur to you after having heard what has been said is this: granted that the obstetrician has a special duty to his patient, the mother, and that the pediatrician has a special duty to *his* patient, the child, surely what they ought all in all to do when the interests of mother and child conflict should be governed by equal consideration for these interests and not by what branch of the profession each of them happens to have specialized in.

I am going therefore, in the hope of shedding some light on the dilemmas of doctors and parents, to ask, first of all, what are the different interests involved in the sort of case we are considering. There is first the interest of the child; but what *is* this? We can perhaps illuminate this question by asking "What if it were ourselves in that child's position – what do we prescribe for *that* case?" On the one hand it may be presumed to be in the child's interest to live, if this is possible; but if the life is going to be a severely handicapped one, it is possible that this interest in living may be at least greatly diminished. Then there is the interest of the mother, in whose interest also it is to live, and whose life may be in danger; and it is also in her interest not to have an abnormal child, which might prevent or severely impair the normal development of the rest of the family. The other members of the family have a similar interest. Against this, it is said that good sometimes comes to a family through

having to bring up an abnormal child; and I can believe that this is so in some cases.

Then there are the interests (not so great individually but globally very great) which belong to those outside the family: first of all those of doctors and nurses who are concerned; then those of the rest of the staffs of hospitals, homes and other services which will be involved in looking after the child and the family. There are also the interests of all those people who *would* be looked after, or looked after better, by all these services if they did not already have too much on their hands; and there are the interests of the taxpayers who pay for it all. And lastly, there is another interest which is commonly ignored in these discussions, and which is so important that it often, I think, ought to tip the balance; but what this other interest is I shall not reveal until I have talked about those I have mentioned so far.

When I said that equal consideration ought to be given to all the interests affected, I did not mean that we should treat as equal the interest of the mother in continuing to live and that of the doctor in not being got out of bed in the middle of the night. As individuals, these people are entitled to equal consideration; but because life matters more to one than sleep to the other, that makes it right for the doctor to get out of bed and go and look after the mother. If the doctor had a car smash outside the mother's front door and she could save *his* life by getting out of bed in the middle of the night, then by the same principle she should do so. As individuals, they are equipollent; the difference is introduced by the differing importance to each of them of the various outcomes.

The number of those affected can also be important; if a GP can save a patient from a sleepless and distressful night by going along in the evening and providing a pain-killer, he will often do it, even in these days; but if a pill were not enough, and it were necessary for a whole team of nurses and an ambulance to turn out, he might decide to wait till the morning unless there were a real danger of a grave deterioration in the patient's condition. A very large number of people each of whom is affected to a small degree may outweigh one person who is affected to a greater degree. So even the fact that 60 million taxpayers will have to pay an average of 20 pence extra each a year to improve or extend the Health

Service is of some moral, as well as political, importance. But I agree on the whole with those who ask us not to attach too much importance to these economic arguments; although I totally failed recently to get from an economist a straight answer to the question of the order of size of the sums involved in looking after handicapped children, I am prepared to accept for the sake of argument that they are relatively small. So let us leave the taxpayer out of it, and the rival claimants for care, and just consider the interests of the immediate family.

Here, however, we must notice the other important interest that I mentioned just now – that of the next child in the queue. For some reason that I cannot understand this is seldom considered. But try looking at the problem with hindsight. The example I am going to use is over-simplified, and I am deliberately not specifying any particular medical condition, because if I do I shall get my facts wrong. Suppose the child with the abnormality was not operated on. It had a substantial chance of survival, and, if it survived, it had a large chance of being severely handicapped. So they didn't operate, and what we now have is not that child, but young Andrew who was born two years later, perfectly normal, and leaves school next summer. Though not brilliant, he is going probably to have a reasonably happy life and make a reasonably useful contribution to the happiness of others. The choice facing the doctors and the family was really a choice between (if they didn't operate) a very high probability of having Andrew (who would not have been contemplated if they had a paralysed child in the family) and on the other hand (if they did operate) a combination of probabilities depending on the precise prognosis (shall we say a 10 per cent chance of a living normal child, a 40 per cent chance of a living but more or less seriously handicapped child, and a 50 per cent chance of a dead child plus the possibility of Andrew in the future).

If we agree with most people that family planning is right, and that therefore this family is justified in limiting its children to a predetermined number (however large), then that is the kind of choice it will be faced with, and in the situation I have imagined *was* faced with. We should try discussing with Andrew himself whether they made the right choice.

If I have characterized the choice correctly, then nearly everything is going to depend on what the prognosis was, and on our estimates of the value *to the persons concerned* of being alive and normal, and, by contrast, of being alive and defective or handicapped in some specified way. In making these value-judgements I do not see that we can do better than put ourselves imaginatively in the places of those affected, and judge as if it were our own future that was at stake. Since a sensitive doctor is bound constantly, in the course of his practice, to make this sort of imaginative judgement about what is for the best for other people, looking at it from their point of view, I do not think that it can be said that it raises any difficulties of principle; but it obviously raises very great difficulties in practice, which the sensitive and experienced doctor is as likely as anybody to be able to overcome in consultation with parents and others affected.

But the problems mostly arise from the difficulty of prognosis. That is why the work reported by Professor Smithells is so crucial. In principle it might be possible to put a numerical value upon the probabilities of the various outcomes, and having estimated how the various outcomes for the people involved affect their interests, to make a utilitarian calculation and choose the course that gives the best prospect of good and the least prospect of harm for those concerned, all in all. In practice we are bound to rely a lot on guesswork; but when guessing, it is an advantage to have a clear idea of what you are guessing *at*, and I have suggested that what we should be guessing at is what is for the best for all the parties taken together.

The prognosis, however, is always going to be pretty uncertain, and the question therefore arises of *when* the decision should be made. I suppose that it would be agreed that if there is doubt in the very early stages of pregnancy, it might be advisable to wait until the fetus had developed sufficiently to make the prognosis more certain. A hard-headed utilitarian might try to extend this principle and say that in cases of suspected abnormality we should let the child be born, operate if appropriate, and then kill the child if the operation resulted in a very severe handicap, and have another child instead. In this way we should maximize the chances of bringing into the world a human being with a high prospect of happiness. If the medical profession finds this suggestion repugnant, as it almost certainly does, and does not *want* the law changed; or if it is thought (perhaps rightly) to inflict too much mental suffering on the mother, then we shall have to be content with a far less certain procedure – that of either terminating or, if we don't terminate and then the child is born, estimating the chances *before* deciding whether to operate, and (if we do decide to operate) taking the risk, however small, of being left with a dreadfully handicapped child.

If we imagine our possible Andrew and his possible brother (the former existing only as a possible combination of sperm and ovum, the latter already existing as a fetus) – if, I say, we imagine them carrying out a prenatal dialogue in some noumenal world (and of course the supposition is just as fantastic in one case as it is in the other) and trying to arrive at a solution which will give them, taken together, the best chance of happy existence, the dialogue might go like this. Andrew points out that if the fetus is not born there is a high probability that he, Andrew, will be born and will have a normal and reasonably happy life. There is of course a possibility that the parents will change their minds about having any more children, or that one of them will die; but let us suppose that this is rather unlikely, and that there is no particular fear that the next child will be abnormal.

To this the fetus might reply, "At least I have got this far; why not give me a chance?" But a chance of what? They then do the prognosis as best they can and work out the chances of the various outcomes if the present pregnancy is not terminated. It turns out that there is a slim chance, but only a slim chance, that the fetus will, if born and operated on, turn into a normal and, let us hope, happy child; that there is a considerable chance on the other hand that it will perish in spite of the operation; and that there is a far from negligible chance of its surviving severely handicapped. In that case, I think Andrew, the later possible child, can claim that he is the best bet, because the chance of the parents dying or changing their minds before he is born is pretty small, and certainly far less than the chance that the present fetus, if born, will be very seriously handicapped.

In order for the fetus to prevent Andrew winning the argument in this way, there is one move it can make. It can say, "All right, we'll make a bargain. We will say that I am to be born and operated on, in the hope of restoring me to normality. If the operation is successful, well and good. If it isn't, then I agree that I should be scrapped and make way for Andrew." I think you will see if you look at the probabilities that this compromise gives the best possible chance of having a healthy baby, and at the same time gives the fetus all the chance that it ever had of itself being that baby. But it does this at the cost of abolishing the substantial chance that there was of having this particular child, albeit in a seriously handicapped condition. I call this a *cost*, because many will argue (though I am not sure that I want to follow them) that life with a severe handicap is preferable, for the person who has it, to no life at all. Of course it depends on the severity of the handicap. And of course this policy involves so much distress for the mother that we might rule it out on that score alone, and terminate instead.

Perhaps I should end by removing what might be an obstacle to understanding. In order to expound the argument, I asked you to imagine Andrew and the fetus having a discussion in some noumenal world (and, by the way, it needn't bother you if you don't know what "noumenal" means; I only used it in order to keep my philosophical end up in the face of all your no doubt necessary medical jargon). This way of dramatizing the argument is perhaps useful though not necessary; and it carries with it one danger. We have to imagine the two possible children conducting this very rational discussion, and therefore we think of them being in a sense already grown up enough to conduct it; and that may lead us to suppose that, for either of them, to be deprived of the possibility of adulthood *after* having had this taste of it would be a very great evil. People (most of them) cling tenaciously to life (though it is a matter for argument, at what age they start to do this); and therefore to deprive a person of life is thought of as *normally* an evil. This certainly does not apply to Andrew, since he is not alive yet and so cannot be *deprived* of life in the relevant sense, though it can be *withheld* from him. I do not think it applies to the fetus as such, since it has as yet no conscious life (which is what we are talking about) and therefore cannot feel the loss of it or even the fear of that loss. If anybody thinks that fetuses *do* have conscious feelings sufficient to be put in this balance, I ask him to agree at least that their intensity is relatively small, and likewise of those of the newborn infant. So I do not think that the harm you are doing to the fetus or the unsuccessfully operated upon newborn infant by killing them is greater than that which you are doing to Andrew by stopping him from being conceived and born. In fact I think it is much less, because Andrew, unlike them, has a high prospect of a normal and happy life.

In my view as a philosopher, these are the sorts of considerations that doctors, surgeons and parents ought to be looking at when they are faced with these dilemmas.

30

Right to Life of Handicapped

Alison Davis

In reference to your items on the bill drafted by Mr and Mrs Brahams permitting doctors to withhold treatment from newborn handicapped babies, I would like to make the following points.

I am 28 years old, and suffer from a severe physical disability which is irreversible, as defined by the bill. I was born with myelomeningocele spina bifida. Mr and Mrs Brahams suggest several criteria for predicting the potential quality of life of people like me, and I note that I fail to fulfil most of them.

I have suffered considerable and prolonged pain from time to time, and have undergone over 20 operations, thus far, some of them essential to save my life. Even now my health is at best uncertain. I am doubly incontinent and confined to a wheelchair and thus, according to the bill, I should have 'no worthwhile quality of life'.

However, because I was fortunately born in rather more tolerant times, I was given the chance to defy the odds and live, which is now being denied to handicapped newborns. Even so, my parents were encouraged to leave me in the hospital and 'go home and have another' and I owe my life to the fact that they refused to accept the advice of the experts.

Despite my disability I went to an ordinary school and then to university, where I gained an honours degree in sociology. I now work full-time defending the right to life of handicapped people. I have been married eight years to an able-bodied man, and over the years we have travelled widely in Europe, the Soviet Union and the United States. This year we plan to visit the Far East.

Who could say I have 'no worthwhile quality of life'? I am sure though that no doctor could have predicted when I was 28 days old (and incidentally had received no operation at all) that despite my physical problems I would lead such a full and happy life. I do not doubt that they were 'acting in good faith' when they advised my parents to abandon me, but that does not mean that their advice was correct.

I was pleased to see that Dr Havard considered legislation was not the right way to solve the problem, though I suspect his disquiet was rather over an infringement of the liberty of doctors than out of any concern for the rights of the handicapped. Whatever his motives, though, I feel the medical profession could go a lot farther than it has to condemn the constant undermining of the rights of handicapped people at progressively later stages in their lives. There is nothing magical about the age of 28 days after all. It is simply the currently accepted boundary of 'non-personhood' for babies with congenital defects.

This notion of 'non-personhood' denies the right of handicapped people to be recognized as equal human beings in a caring society, and it makes a mockery of the goodwill which seemingly abounded in the International Year of Disabled People.

Original publication details: Alison Davis, "Right to Life of Handicapped," p. 181 from *Journal of Medical Ethics* 9 (1983). Reproduced with permission from BMJ Publishing Group.

Bioethics: An Anthology, Third Edition. Edited by Helga Kuhse, Udo Schüklenk, and Peter Singer.

Legislation of the type proposed could well also lead to the *de facto* decriminalization of the act of killing a handicapped person of any age, just as it did in Hitler's Germany. And if it does, woe betide any handicapped people who are too ill to defend their right to life by protesting that they are in fact happy. And woe betide us all, when we get too old to be considered 'useful' and all the friends who could have spoken in our defence have already been oh so lovingly 'allowed to die'.

31

Conjoined Twins, Embodied Personhood, and Surgical Separation

Christine Overall

Both as liberation movement and as theory, feminism has always had a special concern with embodiment. Gender, sexuality and reproduction, often the defining conditions for women's lives, make the feminist focus on the body essential. In addition, health, illness, and disability, race, age, size, and appearance challenge us to consider the ways in which various kinds of bodies are treated as sites for empowerment or pretexts for oppression.[1] Feminist theory raises important questions about embodiment: Are some bodies more valuable than others? What is the relationship between different types of bodies and different types of power? Is there a genuine difference between what is natural and what is not natural for human bodies? Feminists are interested in the political meanings and uses of bodies, and how they both reflect and reinforce the culture in which they are located (Weitz 2003). But human bodies are not inherently endowed with meaning and significance, and many of the socially-significant characteristics and values of bodies are attributed or misattributed to them as part of the process of trying to understand, manipulate, and change our embodiment.

Moreover, we human beings do not merely inhabit our bodies, like a pilot in a ship, a ghost in a machine, or a divine soul in an earthly casement. We *are* our bodies. Yet we are also more than our bodies. Human beings, I suggest, are embodied persons. Rather than idealizing human beings as non-material minds, spirits, or souls, it is essential to recognize how our embodiment defines and constitutes our personhood.

However, embodied personhood is not the same for all human beings. Feminists have given a great deal of attention to the ways in which racial, sexed, disabled, and aged embodiments have been constituted, and the significance, to the maintenance of systems of hierarchy and oppression, of being racialized, sexed, disabled, or aged. Yet one fundamental form of embodiment is seldom subjected to feminist analysis and critique: the state of what I shall call singletonhood.

The state of singletonhood is defined by two main properties. First, there is the property of being fundamentally *unattached* to any other human body. Second, there is the property of having a *one-to-one relationship* between a single human body and consciousness. This relationship includes three characteristics: the individual's physical independence, the individual's ownership of and authority over her body, and the

Original publication details: Christine Overall, "Conjoined Twins, Embodied Personhood, and Surgical Separation," pp. 69–84 from L. Tessman (ed.), *Feminist Ethics and Social and Political Philosophy: Theorizing the Non-Ideal*, Springer, 2009. With kind permission from Springer Science+Business Media.

individual's self-awareness as a single body and sense of privacy with respect to her body. Together, these particular properties of embodiment are so taken-for-granted as to be virtually unrecognized, unarticulated, and unanalyzed, whether by feminist or by non-feminist philosophers.

Conjoined twins, however, provide material evidence both that singletonhood is not universal and that the properties of singletonhood ought not to be taken for granted as unexceptional or as ideal. For, as this paper will demonstrate, the history of attitudes toward and treatments of conjoined twins reflects one or both of the following errors: The erroneous attribution to conjoined twins of the properties that constitute singletonhood, or the assumption that these properties are inevitably the only or at least the best way of experiencing embodied personhood.

These errors fail to take account of the characteristics that make conjoined twins ontologically unique and their embodied personhood valuable. Recognizing these errors is therefore important for at least two reasons. First, it is certainly worthwhile for its own sake to understand the varieties and value of human embodiment. Second, and more pragmatically, we know from other cases that failing to understand the varieties of human embodiment, over-generalizing from one type of embodiment to another, or valuing some forms of embodiment more than others, can lead to unjustified ethical attitudes, inappropriate social policies, and even dangerous medical treatments. Sexist societies, for example, are notorious for taking male bodies as the norm for human embodiment and either ignoring female embodiment or inappropriately generalizing from the characteristics and needs of male bodies to the characteristics and needs of female bodies. The result has been the failure to attend and respond to the specific procreative, sexual, and medical needs of female human beings (e.g., Sherwin 1992). Ableist societies are notorious for taking temporarily able-bodied bodies as the norm for embodiment and either ignoring the varieties of disabled embodiment or inappropriately generalizing from the characteristics and needs of temporarily able-bodied bodies to the characteristics and needs of disabled bodies. The result has been the failure to attend and respond to the specific medical, environmental, and social needs of disabled human beings (e.g., Wendell 1996).

Similarly, I will argue, societies that take singletonhood not just as the norm but as the ideal for human embodiment and inappropriately generalize from the characteristics and needs of singletons to the characteristics and needs of conjoined twins have for centuries failed to recognize and respond to the unique medical, social, and environmental needs of those who are conjoined. Hence, an examination of the unique embodiment of conjoined twins demonstrates and reinforces the importance of refusing to assimilate all human beings to an ideal or taken-for-granted type of embodiment, and a compelling example of the need for non-idealizing approaches to ethical decision-making.

1 Conjoined Twins

The birth in British Columba on October 25, 2006 of conjoined twins Tatiana and Krista Simms immediately prompted media discussions, fuelled by medical speculation, of whether or not the twins could be surgically separated. Since surgical separation often results in the death or severe disability of one or both twins, the question whether separation is justified for any given pair of conjoined twins is inevitably controversial. I argue that the debate remains unsettled because of insufficient attention to the actual metaphysical status of conjoined twins, in particular, attention to their embodied personhood.

Conjoined twins are caused by the delayed division of the fertilized egg, resulting in genetically identical siblings who are physically connected. They are very rare, occurring in maybe one in 50,000 or one in 100,000 births (Segal 1999, 297). Twins may be joined at a variety of different locations, including the chest, the back, the lower trunk, and the head. Sometimes they are so joined as to share a common lower body and only two legs. They are always monozygotic (that is, the product of one fertilized egg, unlike fraternal twins), always of the same sex, always share one placenta and one amnionic membrane, and always have identical chromosomal patterns (Bondeson 2000, 151). Yet there are both equal and symmetrical forms, and unequal and asymmetrical forms (Segal 1999, 298), the latter being cases in which one twin is smaller and/or less developed than the other, or one twin suffers from a congenital disease that the other does not share.[2] Forty to sixty percent of conjoined twins are delivered stillborn, and only 35% survive longer than a single day (Quigley 2003, 161). The overall survival rate is between 2 and 25%, with about 600 sets surviving over the past 500 years. The majority, about two-thirds, are female (Dreger 2004, 31).

Within bioethics there has been extensive discussion of particular cases of conjoined twins and whether or not it is justified to attempt to separate them via surgery (e.g., Annas 1987, Wasserman 2001). 'Nearly two hundred surgical separations of conjoined twins have been attempted, with approximately 90% occurring after 1950. Survival of one or both twins has occurred in close to 150 cases' (Segal 1999, 306). Given these odds, is the surgical separation of these twins morally justified? Many discussions, especially by physicians, make the error of supposing that embodied personhood means the same thing for conjoined twins as it does for singletons.[3] In what follows, I first discuss the issue of surgical separation and attitudes toward it. I describe the history of metaphysical assumptions about conjoined twins and the debates about separating them. I then discuss embodied personhood and the crucial ways in which it is different for conjoined twins than it is for singletons, including non-conjoined twins.

2   The Issue of Separation

There are three types of cases in which surgery to separate conjoined twins may be contemplated. First, there are those for whom the continued bodily configuration, in the absence of surgery, is life-threatening for one or both twins. Such was the case for Gracie and Rosie Attard of Malta, thoracopagus twins who were joined extensively at the base of the torso. Failure to operate would eventually mean death for both children, since Rosie was said to be entirely dependent on Gracie for crucial life functions, including the circulation of blood. Second, there are those for whom the continued bodily configuration is not life-threatening for either twin and therefore surgery is medically unnecessary. This group includes Chang and Eng Bunker, the original so-called 'Siamese twins,' who were joined via a band of tissue at their mid-section,

and nineteenth century twins Millie and Christine McKoy, joined at the base of the spine. Both pairs of twins were otherwise entirely functional and lived full lives. It also includes contemporary children like Kendra and Maliya Herrin, joined at the abdomen and pelvis, who appeared to be healthy before separation but who lacked sufficient organs (including a liver and large intestine) and limbs (legs) for each to have a complete set after separation ('Kendra and Maliya Herrin' 2009). Within this second group, there are those for whom elective surgery for separation is not life-threatening for either twin, and those for whom surgery is life-threatening for one or both twins. For example, it is speculated that surgery would not have been life-threatening for the Bunker brothers, even during the nineteenth century when they lived, although they always refused to consider the possibility. By contrast, Reba and Lori Schappell, adult twins joined near the top of the head, are healthy while conjoined, but their separation is deemed impossible because of the entwinement of their brains. The moral debate among bioethicists about separation is primarily focused upon three groups: first, those like Rosie and Gracie Attard, where at least one twin is likely to die without surgery; second, pairs like Reba and Lori Schappell, where separation could be gravely dangerous or fatal to both; and third, pairs like Kendra and Maliya Herrin, where separation results in severe impairments for one or both twins.

Surgeons who routinely favour the separation of conjoined twins speak of 'freeing them from one another' (surgeon quoted in Quigley 2003, 5). Heinz Röde, a pediatric surgeon at Cape Town Children's Hospital where many separations are performed, says, 'My own philosophy and that of our department is that Siamese twins are born to be separated' (BBC 2000). Neurosurgeon Jonathan Peter adds, 'I think the ethical decision about separating twins is … quite established and I think it is the right thing to do, so the risks are worth taking.' He claims, '[T]o live a life joined together at the waist is no life to live at all' (BBC 2000).

The separation is regarded as particularly urgent when one twin is partly or wholly dependent upon the other for life processes such as the circulation of blood. Dena Davis says, 'Nobody, certainly not a child, can be required to act as permanent life support for another person' (Dena S. Davis, quoted in Quigley 2003, 12). The dependent child, in these cases, is sometimes thought of as a 'parasite'. Simon Edge remarks, in regard to Gracie and Rosie Attard,

> Where the egg has not divided symmetrically, the lesser half is not a human being. It is more logical to think of it as a tumor, a growth which is sapping life. By giving it a name, these poor parents [of conjoined twins] have created a situation where they think they are killing a baby by having the operation. But what they are calling Mary [Rosie][4] is really a tumor, and all that is being proposed is the removal of a tumor. (Simon Edge, quoted in Quigley 2003, 13)

Yet even in cases where the conjoinment is not life-threatening, that is, where neither twin will die without surgery, there is pressure to 'normalize' such twins (Quigley 2003, 5). Such was the case with male conjoined twins Lin and Win Htut. Between them they had only one set of genitalia. Nonetheless, the Canadian surgeon who separated them thought the operation 'worth a whirl' (Wong 2005, F4). Lin was 'allowed to keep the male genitals' (Quigley 2003, 89) because the nurse who attended the twins thought he was 'more dominant' (Wong 2005, F4). Win's sex was reassigned to female because he was thought to 'have the nature of a little girl, so clean and tidy' (Wong 2005, F4). 'A vagina was constructed from a section of colon for Win, but it was acknowledged that the child would never be able to have a full sexual response and would of course be unable to bear children. She would have to begin taking female hormones at puberty' (Quigley 2003, 89).[5]

By contrast, those who mostly oppose the separation of conjoined twins point out that, in the words of author Christine Quigley, '[F]rom an early age, many [conjoined twins] state – and most of them emphatically – that they would not want to be separated' (Quigley 2003, 4). Alice Dreger, a medical historian whose goal is justice for conjoined twins, says, 'Most people who are conjoined, given the opportunity to do so, accept and embrace a life of two minds in one packaging of skin' (Dreger 2004, 43). She adds, '[C]onjoinment becomes so essential to these twins – to their sense of who they are – that they cannot readily conceive of living in a different mode' (Dreger 2004, 47).

Opponents of separation have been especially critical when the separation results in the death of one twin. Quigley states, 'Edward Kiely [a surgeon] of Great Ormond Street Hospital agrees that separation is an extremely difficult problem, particularly when there is no overriding medical indication to operate: "You've got two healthy children. You can't make them better than they are if they're healthy. You can certainly make them an awful lot worse and you may kill one or both in the attempt to separate them"' (Quigley 2003, 151). In the case of Rosie and Gracie Attard, 'It was the first time a British court had been asked to accelerate the death of one person in order to offer the chance of life to another' (Laura King, quoted in Quigley 2003, 12). Dreger remarks, 'The sacrifice separation of conjoined twins is the only instance in which physicians are sometimes given permission by legal authorities and ethics committees to intentionally kill a child who is not clinically brain-dead' (Alice Dreger, quoted in Quigley 2003, 149).[6] George Annas refers to it as 'selective infanticide' (Annas 1987, 27), and Michael Barilan points out that if one of two non-conjoined identical twins was terribly ill, she would not be killed in order to provide organs to enhance the life of the other one (Barilan 2003, 32).

3 The History of Metaphysical Assumptions about Conjoined Twins

Historically, conjoined twins were regarded collectively, as a monster or freak of nature, and as being one individual, not two.[7] For example, Millie McKoy and Christine McKoy, born into slavery in 1851 and exhibited in public for most of their lives, were encouraged to think of themselves as one entity. They were consistently talked about and addressed as if they were one person, despite having between them two heads, four arms, and four legs, and being joined only at the lower part of the spine. They were called, and referred to themselves as, 'Millie-Christine'. This phenomenon may not have been a mere artefact of the dehumanization caused by slavery – though it may have been a wise show-business decision. For even after being emancipated, they chose to bill themselves in their exhibitions as the 'Double-Headed Girl' (Smith 1988, 63).[8] People who met them spoke of conversing with the two heads of a single entity (Martell 2000, 169), and published descriptions of the twins would mix singular and plural, saying both that *they* danced well, and that '*she* was talking to herself – that is, the two mouths were engaged in speaking' (Martell 2000, 201, my emphasis). Theologians debated whether the two women would be resurrected joined as in life or separated (Martell 2000, 119) – a debate that reflected ambivalence as to whether Millie and Christine had two souls or only one.[9]

Thinking of the McKoy twins as just one person, not two, is an approach that was even, rather surprisingly, adopted by a recent biographer of the women. Writing in 2000, Joanne Martell refers to the twins as 'Millie-Christine,' just as did the various circuses that exhibited the twins. Martell writes,

> Whether to speak of Millie-Christine as 'she' or 'they' posed a problem. Monemia McKoy [the twins' mother] said 'my baby' or 'my child.' Family members called her 'Sister.' But most people outside the family looked at Millie-Christine and saw twins. 'They had the nicest personalities,' a neighbor recalled. Millie-Christine herself was ambiguous on the subject. 'Although we speak of ourselves in the plural, we feel as *one person*,' she wrote.
>
> I handled the problem the same way Millie-Christine and people who knew her did – by using either form, as seemed appropriate to the context. (Martell 2000, viii, emphasis in original)

Similarly, writing about the Attard twins, philosopher Michael Barilan refers to them as 'the Maltese,' a term that he claims is neither plural nor singular, but which mostly sounds singular to me (Barilan 2003, 29). Significantly, he also remarks, 'Does the fact that many conjoined twins develop diverse personalities persuade us that conjoined twins are two distinct persons? Not necessarily' (Barilan 2003, 36).

Likewise, philosopher David Hershenov refers to dicephalus ('two-headed') twins as '*a* dicephalus,' and defines them as having 'two cerebrums but otherwise no more organs than the average reader'. He is wrong about this statement, if it's taken literally, since dicephalus twins *each* have the normal number of everything else (eyes, nose, etc.) that goes along with having a head. Consider the contemporary adolescent sisters Abigail Hensel and Brittany Hensel. They are dicephalous twins who between them have two heads and a partially doubled upper torso, but only two arms, one lower torso, and two legs. Yet Hershenov claims that dicephalus twins are 'one organism, not two conjoined organisms. ... [T]he dicephalus is just one person cut off from himself' (Hershenov 2004, 448). George Annas, normally a progressive and empathic writer, suggests with apparent approval that judges might conclude 'that a child with one body and two heads is just *one* child, and that removing one of the heads would be similar to removing an extra arm or leg' (Annas 1987, 28).

Despite this persistence of the idea that conjoined twins are only one individual, the more common viewpoint in the late twentieth and early twenty-first centuries is that conjoined twins are two persons, not one, no matter how much they are conjoined. For example, Dreger assumes that with conjoined twins there are two individuals, two persons, whose anatomy just happens not to be the norm. She notes, 'It seems to be typical for each [conjoined twin] to think of him- or herself as a unique, individual being' (Dreger 2004, 41).[10] Indeed, in the last fifty years or so there has been a lot of emphasis on how different each twin (supposedly) is (e.g., Smith 1988).

I suspect this emphasis is the outcome of a more general change in attitude toward non-conjoined identical twins. The tendency, manifest in the twentieth century until the 1970s (Klein 2003, 20), to think of non-conjoined twins as a unit, 'the twins,' is no longer in vogue. An expert in non-conjoined identical twins, Nancy Segal, writes, 'identical twins are sometimes referred to as "one". ... But the twins' differences [are] obvious to them and to their families. Surprisingly, many identical twins say that they don't look alike, probably because they see small differences between themselves that others don't see. It's wrong to think that identical twins' nearly identical looks and behaviors mean that they have identical selves' (Segal 2005, 252).[11]

Some writers have gone so far as to claim that conjoined twins are likely to be *more* different from each other than un-conjoined identical twins, and that this difference might occur because the embryonic cell mass splits at a point when the mass is beginning to develop a right and a left side; hence conjoined twins are physical 'opposites' or mirror images, at least in terms of handedness and the direction of their hair whorls and fingerprints (Horatio Newman, in Smith 1988, 116).

Even the Hensel twins, more extensively joined than almost any others, have always been strongly encouraged by their parents to think of themselves as two people, and they seem to think of themselves that way (Quigley 2003, 77–79). Their mother remarks, 'I just want people to know that they're two separate kids with their own personalities' (Patty Hensel, quoted in Quigley 2003, 79), and she supports their duality by, for example, ensuring that every shirt they wear has two separate necks.[12]

The Hensels' approach of regarding conjoined twins as two persons appears, at least *prima facie*, more enlightened than Millie-Christine's self-description as one. There is something morally significant about the presence of a functioning head, no matter what the nature of the body to which it is attached. It is likely that most people's moral intuitions will revolt against George Annas's suggestion that a supposedly extra head can simply be removed. I don't think that removing a functioning head is just like removing a functioning arm or leg. There is something uniquely significant about each head, since each one is the locus of visual, auditory, kinaesthetic, olfactory, and gustatory sensations, and each is, actually or potentially, capable of thought, emotion, and action.

It seems entirely reasonable to conclude that, where there are two functioning heads, there are two persons, even – or especially – in a case like that of the Hensels where the body is otherwise mostly unitary. I therefore assume that conjoined twins are almost always two persons and that counting heads offers a basic but accurate way of assessing the number of persons present. This assumption, with its criterion, also suits those rare cases of conjoined twins where there are not two heads. Consider Myrtle Cobin, born in the nineteenth century, who was 'double-bodied from the waist down' [the technical term is 'dipygus'] (Quigley 2003, 52). Although she is classified among conjoined twins, it makes good sense to see her as just one person with extra body parts, and she was viewed as such by her contemporaries.

4   Embodied Personhood in Singletons, Non-Conjoined Twins, and Conjoined Twins

Still, there is something inadequate about thinking of conjoined twins as simply two ordinary persons, full-stop – like identical twins, but ones who just happen to be closely linked. There are several reasons for this inadequacy, and they all have to do, I suggest, with the differences between embodied personhood for singletons (as well as non-conjoined twins) and embodied personhood for conjoined twins.

First, in singletons embodied personhood means a one-to-one relationship between one person and one body. Each person has one and only one distinct physical body, with which she has a unique relationship, and which is separate from the body of anyone else. My being the person I am is inseparable from my having, or being, the one body that is mine (cf. Barilan 2003, 41, endnote 10). As Stephen Jay Gould remarks, 'physical separation is the essence of our vernacular definition of individuality' (Stephen Jay Gould, quoted in Smith 1988, 115), and Dreger concurs: 'psychosocial individuality [conventionally requires] anatomical individuality' (Dreger 2004, 7).[13]

In singletons, embodied personhood also involves the idea of ownership of, rights to, and authority over one's various bodily parts. I think and speak of 'my' arm, 'my' toes, 'my' lungs, and so on. Although I do not own them in the way that I own my books and my clothes, they are intimately a part of me, and no one else has any entitlement to them or authority over them. I have the exclusive use and disposition of my own body parts. I may seek the advice of others, but if I donate an organ, permit the removal or amputation of a body part, undergo surgery, engage in physical training, or move to another province, it is my decision and mine alone. I have both authority and power over only one body.

Finally, embodied personhood in singletons also includes ideas about self-awareness and privacy. A singleton person is aware of herself as an individual separate from other individuals, and understands physical privacy in terms of the protection of her unique body from the gaze and the interference of others.

What about non-conjoined twins? Is their embodied personhood different from that of singletons? Experts on non-conjoined twins indicate that, in their infancy, non-conjoined twins may be less clear about the boundaries of their own bodies than singletons are. Elizabeth M. Bryan writes, 'When most babies are beginning to explore their own bodies, twins may spend as much time in discovering that of their twin. Initially they seem to make no distinction between the two. It is not uncommon to see twins peacefully sucking each other's thumbs' (Bryan 1984, 113). Some twins, when very young, call themselves by the name of their twin. The situation may be more complex for identical non-conjoined twins than for fraternal twins, who usually do not look more alike than any other pair of siblings. Indeed, fraternal twins learn to identify their mirror-images several months before identical twins master the task (Bryan 1984, 113).

According to Elizabeth A. Stewart, whereas infant singletons must only learn to differentiate themselves from their mother, infant non-conjoined twins have the challenge of separating psychologically both from their mother and from each other, thereby developing a bodily identity that recognizes that they are not one with their twin (Stewart 2000, 66). Sometimes non-conjoined twins continue to be heavily dependent, psychologically, on each other, even into adulthood (Stewart 2000, 71ff; 165–167). However, there is no evidence that, as they mature, non-conjoined twins do not recognize that they are *physically* separate from each other, just like other singletons. Indeed, one expert writes,

> It used to be thought that twins sucking each other's thumbs were bound to grow up with a confused idea of where their own body ended and where their twin's began, but it has been pointed out that a sharp bite or kick will very quickly define which bits belong to whom. 'Getting to know you' through physical contact is actually an effective way of 'getting to know me' too. Far from being confused, infant twins are probably more aware of their own physical outline much earlier than single children at the same stage. (Rosambeau 1987, 43)

Hence, at maturity, non-conjoined twins are like singletons as regards their embodied personhood: There is a one-to-one relationship between one person and one body; each twin has ownership of, rights to, and authority over her/his various bodily parts; and each twin possesses self-awareness as a separate individual, understanding physical privacy in terms of the protection of her/his unique body from the gaze and the interference of others.

Conjoined twins are inherently different from singletons and non-conjoined twins in all of these respects.

First, because the twins are not physically separate, each one is in a one-to-one relationship not with just one body but with two. Thus, whatever food or drink a conjoined twin takes into her mouth inevitably reaches her twin's body. She is not simply nourishing herself; she is nourishing her twin. So, also, if one drinks a lot of alcohol and the other does not, both twins will experience the effects and endure the consequences. Conjoined twins do not always have the same medical conditions, but if one takes prescription medication, the other will be affected. The same is true for cigarette smoking and the use of illegal drugs. In addition, if one twin has a sexual relationship, necessarily the other twin is implicated in the relationship.[14] Moreover, health care for one twin is inevitably health care for both twins. If one twin undergoes surgery, the other must also lie on the operating table and feel the effects of the anaesthetic. And although there are cases where each twin takes a different job (Reba and Lori Schappell are one example), it is impossible for one to travel without the other, or to take physical risks without the other (Barilan 2003, 34). Finally, if one commits suicide, the other will die. So for conjoined twins, who they are is partly constituted by the relationship of each one to two bodies.

Second, for conjoined twins the idea of ownership of and authority over organs and limbs is inevitably different from what it is in the case of singletons. We might be inclined to say that the hand on the right side of twin A, closest to A's head, is A's hand; it belongs to A.[15] But her use of that hand inevitably has great potential either to increase or to infringe upon the wellbeing and rights of twin B. We should say, therefore, that A's ownership of and authority over the hand is both more powerful and more constrained than a singleton person's ownership of and control over her hand.

But we might want to say something even stronger. Consider the fact that for a conjoined twin, organ donation, limb amputation, surgery, physical training, and travel inherently involve the person to whom she is conjoined. No unilateral decision about these activities can be made; or if it is made, either through duplicity or because one twin is incompetent or even unconscious, the activities still inevitably happen to two persons, not just to one. Or imagine that one twin wants to commit suicide, and that her death will cause the death of the other twin, who nonetheless wants to live. In such a case the suicidal twin does not have a right to dispose of her body as she sees fit. Hence in contrast to singletons, it is not reasonable to say that the body parts, organs, and limbs of conjoined twins belong to only one of the twins, or that only one twin has authority over them. All body parts, organs, and limbs are a part of the whole entity that is twin A and twin B. Thus, in regard to conjoined twins Rosie and Gracie Attard, David Wasserman argues that

> the organs in Jodie's [Gracie's] body ... belong[] to Mary [Rosie] as well. On this understanding of their embodiment, [Rosie] and [Gracie] share a single, asymmetrical body, and each has an equal interest in every part of it (except, perhaps, each other's brains, heads, and necks). The surgery [that separated them] is like a forced and unequal partition of jointly-owned property, that transfers [Rosie's] half interest in the working heart and lungs to [Gracie]. (Wasserman 2001, 10)

Therefore, says Wasserman, we should see the twins as 'fellow victim[s] of an embodiment inadequate to sustain them both,' rather than seeing Rosie as a parasitic and deadly threat to Gracie (Wasserman 2001, 9).

I believe we should see all conjoined twins as *each* having a joint interest in, ownership of, and authority over their unseparated physical being. Body parts do not belong exclusively to just one twin (Himma 1999, 430). In effect, the twins share one body, many of whose parts are doubled, rather than having two bodies that are merely contingently joined.

Third, self-awareness, privacy, and bodily integrity are inevitably different for conjoined twins than for singletons. From the earliest time of consciousness, each twin has a sense of embodied personhood that includes the other twin. Each is a permanent feature of the physical gestalt of the other. Thus, for each one, bodily privacy means the privacy of their shared

physicality. Now according to physician Heinz Röde, the result of this condition is that 'They will always have to share whatever they do. That is defecation they will share, it's a practical example, they will share mobility, they will share sleeping, they will share the ups and downs of life. ... I think for the rest of the world it's unacceptable to live in close proximity to somebody else if the chance had been for a successful separation early on' (BBC 2000).

Röde's description is resonant with the horror *he* feels for such a condition. And he's right in one respect: for most of the rest of the world, that is, singletons, it is unacceptable to have to experience what feels like unremitting violations of privacy throughout their entire lives. But conjoined twins see their situation differently. For them, having the other twin present at a particular activity could, most of the time, be no more a violation of one's privacy than having one's arm present at an activity. When necessary, and primarily for the sake of romance with singletons, conjoined twins also have developed methods of handling conventional matters of privacy. Take, for example, twentieth-century show-business twins Daisy and Violet Hilton. Each one had romantic relationships, although Daisy was repeatedly denied, in a number of American states, a license to marry her boyfriend on grounds of 'morality and decency' (Quigley 2003, 84). Clearly, the state inappropriately applied singleton standards of privacy to conjoined twins. But Violet Hilton explained that when necessary, they learned 'to get rid of each other. ... [W]e get rid of each other mentally. ... We ... learned how not to know what the other was doing unless it was our business to know it' (quoted in Smith 1988, 74).[16] This is, of course, not how most contemporary singletons seek out privacy, but it works for conjoined twins.

5 Some Conclusions

Embodied personhood is not the same for all human beings, and arguably there is still much to figure out about the nature and value of certain variations.[17] The examination of the ontological status of conjoined twins reinforces the importance that feminists have placed upon understanding the true range of variations of human embodiment. It both demonstrates and reinforces the value of refusing to assimilate all human beings to an ideal or taken-for-granted type of embodiment, and is a compelling example of the need for non-idealizing approaches to ethical decision-making. Failing to understand the varieties of embodiment, and over-generalizing from one type of embodiment to another, can lead to the imposition of inappropriate treatments that presume that one form of embodiment is ideal. By contrast, an accurate understanding of the nature of human beings' embodied personhood is the essential ontological basis for making ethical and political decisions about fairness to and the wellbeing of human beings.

As I have shown, until at least the twentieth century, conjoined twins were frequently regarded not as two persons but as one, and were treated as freaks and objects of exhibition. Since that time, conjoined twins are more readily recognized as being two persons. Yet it is also assumed that their conjoinment is merely contingent to, rather than constitutive of, their personhood. Surgery, to create for each of them an embodiment as a singleton (even at the risk of severe physical trauma and even death for one or both), is usually regarded as the most appropriate medical and ethical response to their deviance. They continue to be seen as being inherently impaired and therefore in need of *re*pair via surgical separation, regardless of whether or not the conjoinment itself is life-threatening. Thus, Richard Hull and Stephen Wilkinson, for example, use 'normal species functioning' (Hull and Wilkinson 2006, 117) as the standard by which they decide that all conjoined twins are impaired. 'Normal species functioning' refers, in their account, only to the situation of singletons.[18]

To be sure, having an unusual embodiment may indeed *be* an impairment within a social context that renders persons with that anatomy disabled. An unusual embodiment may be constituted as an impairment within a social context that takes one form of embodiment as the norm and fails to attend and respond to other forms of embodiment. But merely having an unusual anatomy is not necessarily an impairment in itself. Being conjoined is neither an unavoidable weakness or problem, nor an inevitable reason for pity on the part of singletons. Indeed, it can even be an enhancement.

According to Dreger, for example, Chang and Eng Bunker's conjoinment 'actually may have *accentuated* each man's individuality and *increased* many of his freedoms,' including travel and earning an income (Dreger 2004, 18, her emphasis).[19] Likewise, Millie and Christine McKoy, born into slavery, had much greater freedom than singleton slaves because of being conjoined twins, for their condition enabled them to earn money, travel, purchase property, and eventually buy their freedom and live as emancipated women. Today, when viewing the films of Abigail and Brittany Hensel, it is hard not to believe that the life of each the two adolescents is immeasurably enriched by the constant conjunction with her sister. The girls make jokes, do homework together, and share a rich social and athletic life (Figure 8 Films 2006).

Nonetheless, conjoined twins have almost always been the target of a good deal of ableist fear and oppression. Throughout recorded history it has probably been the extraordinarily small number of conjoined twins who have survived birth and infancy that has led to the social constitution of their version of embodied personhood as an impairment. They are a tiny minority who deviate from the norm of singletonhood. Yet what is genuinely 'impaired' is conjoined twins' capacity to function in just the way singletons do. And if it is assumed that singleton existence is the *only* acceptable form of life then conjoined twins are inevitably rendered impaired.

Unfortunately, unjustified assumptions about conjoined twins' embodied personhood may also result in inappropriate decisions about their medical treatment. For singletons, the preservation of bodily integrity and autonomy means the protection of the one body that is one's own from non-consensual contact of any sort by another person. But for conjoined twins, the preservation of bodily integrity and autonomy often means the protection of their *shared* anatomy. For them, embodied personhood inevitably departs from singleton norms with respect to physical independence, bodily ownership and authority, and self-awareness and privacy. Each twin is a permanent part of the 'environment' of the other (Smith 1988, 107). Each twin is, in effect, an 'integral part' of the other (suggested by George Annas, quoted in Dreger 2004, 104).

From this perspective, the separation of conjoined twins is not a matter of simply freeing one person from another. Nor is it a matter of making each twin into what she already is: a distinct person. *Pace* Barilan (who argues that in some cases there are *no* persons present until after separation [Barilan 2003]), it is also not a matter of *creating* persons through the process of separation.

Instead, the separation of conjoined twins should be recognized for what it is: the creation of a new type of embodied personhood for each of the twins.[20] It is an embodied personhood that is constituted by a radically different body, a body that may obtain some new powers and certainly acquires the standard properties of singlehood, but thereby also loses the advantages, born of conjoinment, that it formerly had.[21] As Barilan remarks, 'what some take to be "corrective" or "rehabilitative" surgery is actually a distortion of a unique inter-human world' (Barilan 2003, 39). The embodied personhood that is experienced by conjoined twins who are surgically separated is replaced by a new experience of embodied personhood: the experience of singletonhood, and along with it, all the pain and trauma that accompany major surgery. Whether that replacement is an improvement is a judgment that only former conjoined twins can make. It cannot be assumed,

a priori, to be an improvement by lifetime singletons who have never experienced conjoinment.

Hence, the implication of the reflections in this paper is not that the surgical separation of conjoined twins is never justified, but rather that surgical separation must be evaluated within the context of a non-idealized, non-ableist understanding of conjoined twins' actual embodied personhood. For as feminists emphasize, the body is never merely incidental in defining who we are, whether we are singletons or conjoined.

Acknowledgments

I am grateful for comments on an earlier version of this paper that were offered by audience members at the Annual Meeting of the Canadian Society for Women in Philosophy, Trent University, Peterborough, Ontario, October 28, 2006; the Department of Philosophy Colloquium Series, Dalhousie University, Halifax, Nova Scotia, January 12, 2007; and the Department of Philosophy Colloquium Series, Memorial University, St. John's, Newfoundland, January 18, 2007. I was also assisted by helpful comments from Lisa Tessman.

Notes

1   See, for example, Davis 2003; Miedema et al. 2000; Price and Shildrick 1999; Shildrik and Mykitiuk 2005.

2   For example, in the case of conjoined twins Lori Schappell and Reba Schappell, Reba has spina bifida and can't walk, while Lori does not have spina bifida and can walk (BBC 2000).

3   Michael Barilan, however, argues that in some cases there are *no* persons present until after separation (Barilan 2003).

4   'Mary' and 'Jodie' were the pseudonyms for Rosie and Gracie respectively, which used in legal debates about the twins.

5   This choice was a recipe for potential disaster. The evidence suggests that sex reassignment for a genetic boy can be disorienting and even destructive (e.g., Colapinto 2002), and that raising a child as a girl in such a case may be wildly inappropriate. Indeed, Win Htut says that, having learned at age five that he had been born a boy, he decided by age ten that he was still a boy

and told his mother he would always remain one. He now lives as a man (Wong 2005, F4).

6   I have not been able to find any studies that explore the long-term psychological or physical effects on the surviving twin after surgery that killed the other but I believe they deserve to be investigated.

7   Oddly, however, in the past, an entirely parasitic twin, lacking many organs and a head, was sometimes given its own name (Bondeson 2000, 155) and thought of as a true sibling.

8   Cf. the comment of the father of Pakistani twins Hira and Nida: 'I see them as one life that God has given to two children.' The Canadian surgeon who operated on them said, 'There's a possibility of cutting *this* into two children' (Shildrick 2001, 397).

9   In the 1930s, conjoined twins Mary Gibb and Margaret Gibb tried to take advantage of the ambiguity of their personhood by arguing that they should travel on a single ticket by train or ship. The White Star Line, a

passenger ship company, responded that meals for two individuals would be needed, so they had to have two tickets (Smith 1988, 76).

10 Margrit Shildrick suggests that this view may be a response to the threat of union: 'the much-repeated claim that despite appearances such twins are essentially autonomous – as though concorporation were merely a surface effect – acts almost as a necessary strategy of ontological reassurance' (Shildrick 2001, 392–393).

11 Segal also says, 'We have travelled full circle in our thinking about keeping twins together or apart, first leaning toward inseparability, then pushing toward individuality, and now easing toward a happy balance in which two people enjoy themselves and each other' (Segal 1999, 69).

12 In a recent video, one of their teachers comments that one twin, Abigail, is more assertive and outspoken than the other, Brittany.

13 'In the United States, conjoinment might be especially challenging because American culture equates individualism with independence, and interdependence with weakness' (Dreger 2004, 31).

14 The degree of involvement depends to some extent on the nature of the conjoinment. In the case of twins Chang Bunker and Eng Bunker, both of whom married, each was, at the very least, in the same bed when the other had sexual intercourse with his wife. In the case of dicephalous twins, with two heads but mostly one body, a sexual relationship by one twin with another person is possible only if both have the relationship.

15 In the case of the twins Gracie and Rosie Attard, David Wasserman points out that physicians and members of the media tended to think that the one heart in the twins' body 'really' belonged to one twin in particular, simply because it was on that twin's 'side' of the body mass. The 'side,' I suggest, could only be defined by reference to nearness to the head.

16 They claimed that they learned this trick from Harry Houdini.

17 One important example is pregnant embodiment. Although it is very different from conjoined embodiment, there may be something to be learned about pregnancy from the analysis of conjoinment and its differences from singletonhood. To anyone who has experienced pregnancy it will be evident that while the pregnant woman remains a single person, her state of singletonhood is both similar to and different from that of non-pregnant singletons. The pregnant woman is not merely attached to but contains, or is possessed by, or simply relates intimately and physically to another living being of the species homo sapiens. (See, for example, the discussions in Whitbeck 1983, 1984.) She thereby constitutes, and is constituted by, a physical relationship with a future embodied person. This relationship, I suggest, redefines, at the very least, the physical independence and the self-awareness that help to constitute her embodied personhood when non-pregnant.

18 See Hull and Wilkinson 2006 for an extended argument that conjoined twins are impaired. This claim is related to Hull and Wilkinson's second argument that, contrary to the theme of this paper, conjoined twins do not have an ontological status that is different from that of singletons.

19 When troubles arose in their relationships with their wives, they made a plan of 'alternating autonomy,' three days and three days (Smith 1988, 31). That is, each twin determined their joint activities three days of each week.

20 Dreger goes so far as to say, '[W]hen one's identity is grounded in the experience of one's anatomy – as it is for virtually all of us – the elimination of that experience can legitimately be equated with the elimination of self' (Dreger 2004, 124). There is no evidence to suggest that surgical separation eliminates formerly conjoined persons' sense of self. But at the very least, by radically altering their bodies such surgery does transform them as persons.

21 Given these advantages, I predict that it is only a matter of time before pairs of individuals will be seeking surgery to conjoin their bodies.

References

Annas, G. 1987. 'Siamese Twins: Killing One to Save the Other'. Hastings Center Report 17 (2): 27–29.

Barilan, Y.M. 2003. 'One or Two: An Examination of the Recent Case of the Conjoined Twins from Malta'. Journal of Medicine and Philosophy 28 (1): 27–44.

BBC. 2000. 'Conjoined Twins'. Transcript of a BBC programme, http://www.bbc.co.uk/science/horizon/2000/conjoined_twins_transcript.shtml (accessed on January 5, 2003).

Bondeson, J. 2000. The Two-Headed Boy, and Other Medical Marvels (Ithaca, New York: Cornell University Press).

Bryan, E.M. 1984. Twins in the Family (London: Constable).

Colapinto, J. 2002. As Nature Made Him: The Boy Who Was Raised as a Girl (New York: HarperCollins).

Davis, K. 2003. Dubious Equalities and Embodied Differences: Cultural Studies on Cosmetic Surgery (Lanham, Maryland: Rowman & Littlefield).

Dreger, A.D. 2004. *One of Us: Conjoined Twins and the Future of Normal* (Cambridge, MA: Harvard University Press).

Figure 8 Films. 2006. 'Joined for Life: Abby and Brittany Turn Sixteen'. Synopsis at http://www.figure8films.tv/site/shows/jfl_abby_brittany_turn_16.php.

Hershenov, D. 2004. 'Countering the Appeal of the Psychological Approach to Personal Identity'. *Philosophy* 79: 447–474.

Himma, K.E. 1999. 'Thomson's Violinist and Conjoined Twins'. *Cambridge Quarterly of Healthcare Ethics* 8: 428–439.

Hull, R. and S. Wilkinson. 2006. 'Separating Conjoined Twins: Disability, Ontology, and Moral Status'. In D. Benatar, ed., *Cutting to the Core: Exploring the Ethics of Contested Surgeries* (Lanham, Maryland: Rowman & Littlefield), 113–126.

'Kendra and Maliya Herrin'. 2009. At http://www.herrintwins.com/about.shtml.

Klein, B.S. 2003. *Not All Twins Are Alike: Psychological Profiles of Twinship* (Westport, Connecticut: Praeger).

Martell, J. 2000. *Millie-Christine: Fearfully and Wonderfully Made* (Winston-Salem, North Carolina: John F. Blair).

Miedema, B., J.M. Stoppard, and V. Anderson, eds. 2000. *Women's Bodies, Women's Lives: Health, Well-Being, and Body Image* (Toronto: Sumach Press).

Price, J. and M. Shildrick, eds. 1999. *Feminist Theory and the Body: A Reader* (New York: Routledge).

Quigley, C. 2003. *An Historical, Biological and Ethical Issues Encyclopedia* (Jefferson, North Carolina: McFarland).

Rosambeau, M. 1987. *How Twins Grow Up* (London: Bodley Head).

Segal, N.L. 1999. *Entwined Lives: Twins and What They Tell Us about Human Behavior* (New York: Dutton).

Segal, N.L. 2005. *Indivisible by Two: Lives of Extraordinary Twins* (Cambridge, MA: Harvard University Press).

Sherwin, S. 1992. *No Longer Patient: Feminist Ethics and Health Care* (Philadelphia: Temple University Press).

Shildrick, M. 2001. 'Some Speculations on Matters of Touch'. *Journal of Medicine and Philosophy* 26 (4): 387–404.

Shildrick, M. and R. Mykitiuk, eds. 2005. *Ethics of the Body: Postconventional Challenges* (Boston: MIT Press).

Smith, J.D. 1988. *Psychological Profiles of Conjoined Twins: Heredity, Environment, and Identity* (New York: Praeger).

Stewart, E.A. 2000. *Exploring Twins: Towards a Social Analysis of Twinship* (New York: St. Martin's Press).

Wasserman, D. 2001. 'Killing Mary to Save Jodie: Conjoined Twins and Individual Rights'. *Philosophy and Public Policy Quarterly* 21 (1): 9–14.

Weitz, R., ed. 2003. *The Politics of Women's Bodies: Sexuality, Appearance, and Behavior* (New York: Oxford University Press, second edition).

Wendell, S. 1996. *The Rejected Body: Feminist Philosophical Reflections on Disability* (New York: Routledge).

Whitbeck, C. 1983. 'A Different Reality: Feminist Ontology'. In C. Gould, ed., *Beyond Domination: New Perspectives on Women and Philosophy* (Totowa, New Jersey: Rowman & Allanheld), 64–88.

Whitbeck, C. 1984. 'The Maternal Instinct'. In J. Trebilcot, ed., *Mothering: Essays in Feminist Theory* (Totowa, New Jersey: Rowman & Allanheld), 185–198.

Wong, J. 2005. 'Twin Peaks'. *The Globe and Mail* (Saturday, June 25): F1, F3, F4–5.

Brain Death

32

A Definition of Irreversible Coma

Report of the Ad Hoc Committee of the Harvard Medical School to Examine the Definition of Brain Death

Our primary purpose is to define irreversible coma as a new criterion for death. There are two reasons why there is need for a definition: (1) Improvements in resuscitative and supportive measures have led to increased efforts to save those who are desperately injured. Sometimes these efforts have only partial success so that the result is an individual whose heart continues to beat but whose brain is irreversibly damaged. The burden is great on patients who suffer permanent loss of intellect, on their families, on the hospitals, and on those in need of hospital beds already occupied by these comatose patients. (2) Obsolete criteria for the definition of death can lead to controversy in obtaining organs for transplantation.

Irreversible coma has many causes, but *we are concerned here only with those comatose individuals who have no discernible central nervous system activity*. If the characteristics can be defined in satisfactory terms, translatable into action – and we believe this is possible – then several problems will either disappear or will become more readily soluble.

More than medical problems are present. There are moral, ethical, religious, and legal issues. Adequate definition here will prepare the way for better insight into all of these matters as well as for better law than is currently applicable.

Characteristics of Irreversible Coma

An organ, brain or other, that no longer functions and has no possibility of functioning again is for all practical purposes dead. Our first problem is to determine the characteristics of a *permanently* nonfunctioning brain.

A patient in this state appears to be in deep coma. The condition can be satisfactorily diagnosed by points 1, 2, and 3 to follow. The electroencephalogram (point 4) provides confirmatory data, and when available it should be utilized. In situations where for one reason or another electro-encephalographic monitoring is not available, the absence of cerebral function has to be determined by purely clinical signs, to be described, or by absence of circulation as judged by standstill of blood in the retinal vessels, or by absence of cardiac activity.

1. *Unreceptivity and Unresponsivity*. – There is a total unawareness to externally applied stimuli and inner need and complete unresponsiveness – our definition of irreversible coma. Even the most intensely painful stimuli evoke no vocal or other response, not even a groan, withdrawal of a limb, or quickening of respiration.

Original publication details: Ad Hoc Committee of the Harvard Medical School to Examine the Definition of Brain Death, "'A Definition of Irreversible Coma': Report to Examine the Definition of Brain Death," pp. 85–8 from *Journal of the American Medical Association* 205: 6 (August 1968). Copyright © 1968 American Medical Association. All rights reserved.

2. *No Movements or Breathing.* – Observations covering a period of at least one hour by physicians is adequate to satisfy the criteria of no spontaneous muscular movements or spontaneous respiration or response to stimuli such as pain, touch, sound, or light. After the patient is on a mechanical respirator, the total absence of spontaneous breathing may be established by turning off the respirator for three minutes and observing whether there is any effort on the part of the subject to breathe spontaneously. (The respirator may be turned off for this time provided that at the start of the trial period the patient's carbon dioxide tension is within the normal range, and provided also that the patient had been breathing room air for at least 10 minutes prior to the trial.)

3. *No Reflexes.* – Irreversible coma with abolition of central nervous system activity is evidenced in part by the absence of elicitable reflexes. The pupil will be fixed and dilated and will not respond to a direct source of bright light. Since the establishment of a fixed, dilated pupil is clear-cut in clinical practice, there should be no uncertainty as to its presence. Ocular movement (to head turning and to irrigation of the ears with ice water) and blinking are absent. There is no evidence of postural activity (decerebrate or other). Swallowing, yawning, vocalization are in abeyance. Corneal and pharyngeal reflexes are absent.

As a rule the stretch of tendon reflexes cannot be elicited; i.e., tapping the tendons of the biceps, triceps, and pronator muscles, quadriceps and gastrocnemius muscles with the reflex hammer elicits no contraction of the respective muscles. Plantar or noxious stimulation gives no response.

4. *Flat Electroencephalogram.* – Of great confirmatory value is the flat or isoelectric EEG. We must assume that the electrodes have been properly applied, that the apparatus is functioning normally, and that the personnel in charge is competent. We consider it prudent to have one channel of the apparatus used for an electrocardiogram. This channel will monitor the ECG so that, if it appears in the electroencephalographic leads because of high resistance, it can be readily identified. It also establishes the presence of the active heart in the absence of the EEG. We recommend that another channel be used for a noncephalic lead. This will pick up space-borne or vibration-borne artifacts and identify them. The simplest form of such a monitoring noncephalic electrode has two leads over the dorsum of the hand, preferably the right hand, so the ECG will be minimal or absent. Since one of the requirements of this state is that there be no muscle activity, these two dorsal hand electrodes will not be bothered by muscle artifact. The apparatus should be run at standard gains $10\mu v/mm$, $50\mu v/5mm$. Also it should be isoelectric at double this standard gain which is $5\mu v/mm$ or $25\mu v/5$ mm. At least ten full minutes of recording are desirable, but twice that would be better.

It is also suggested that the gains at some point be opened to their full amplitude for a brief period (5 to 100 seconds) to see what is going on. Usually in an intensive care unit artifacts will dominate the picture, but these are readily identifiable. There shall be no electroencephalographic response to noise or to pinch.

All of the above tests shall be repeated at least 24 hours later with no change.

The validity of such data as indications of irreversible cerebral damage depends on the exclusion of two conditions: hypothermia (temperature below 90°F [32.2°C]) or central nervous system depressants, such as barbiturates.

Other Procedures

The patient's condition can be determined only by a physician. When the patient is hopelessly damaged as defined above, the family and all colleagues who have participated in major decisions concerning the patient, and all nurses involved, should be so informed. Death is to be declared and *then* the respirator turned off. The decision to do this and the responsibility for it are to be taken by the physician-in-charge, in consultation with one or more physicians who have been directly involved in the case. It is unsound and undesirable to force the family to make the decision.

Legal commentary

The legal system of the United States is greatly in need of the kind of analysis and recommendations for medical procedures in cases of irreversible brain damage as described. At present, the law of the United States, in all 50 states and in the federal courts, treats the question of human death as a question of fact to be decided in every case. When any doubt exists, the courts seek medical expert testimony concerning the time of death of the particular individual involved. However, the law makes the assumption that the medical criteria for determining death are settled and not in doubt among physicians. Furthermore, the law assumes that the traditional method among physicians for determination of death is to ascertain the absence of all vital signs. To this extent, *Black's Law Dictionary* (4th edition, 1951) defines death as

> The cessation of life; the ceasing to exist; *defined by physicians* as a total stoppage of the circulation of the blood, and a cessation of the animal and vital functions consequent thereupon, such as respiration, pulsation, etc. [italics added]

In the few modern court decisions involving a definition of death, the courts have used the concept of the total cessation of all vital signs. Two cases are worthy of examination. Both involved the issue of which one of two persons died first.

In *Thomas vs Anderson* (96 Cal App 2d 371, 211 P 2d 478) a California District Court of Appeal in 1950 said, "In the instant case the question as to which of the two men died first was a question of fact for the determination of the trial court…"

The appellate court cited and quoted in full the definition of death from *Black's Law Dictionary* and concluded, "death occurs precisely when life ceases and does not occur until the heart stops beating and respiration ends. Death is not a continuous event and is an event that takes place at a precise time."

The other case is *Smith vs Smith* (229 Ark, 579, 317 SW 2d 275) decided in 1958 by the Supreme Court of Arkansas. In this case the two people were husband and wife involved in an auto accident. The husband was found dead at the scene of the accident. The wife was taken to the hospital unconscious. It is alleged that she "remained in coma due to brain injury" and died at the hospital 17 days later. The petitioner in court tried to argue that the two people died simultaneously. The judge writing the opinion said the petition contained a "quite unusual and unique allegation." It was quoted as follows:

> That the said Hugh Smith and his wife, Lucy Coleman Smith, were in an automobile accident on the 19th day of April, 1957, said accident being instantly fatal to each of them at the same time, although the doctors maintained a vain hope of survival and made every effort to revive and resuscitate said Lucy Coleman Smith until May 6th, 1957, when it was finally determined by the attending physicians that their hope of resuscitation and possible restoration of human life to the said Lucy Coleman Smith was entirely vain, and
>
> That as a matter of modern medical science, your petitioner alleges and states, and will offer the Court competent proof that the said Hugh Smith, deceased, and said Lucy Coleman Smith, deceased, lost their power to will at the same instant, and that their demise as earthly human beings occurred at the same time in said automobile accident, neither of them ever regaining any consciousness whatsoever.

The court dismissed the petition as a *matter of law*. The court quoted *Black's* definition of death and concluded,

> Admittedly, this condition did not exist, and as a matter of fact, it would be too much of a strain of credulity for us to believe any evidence offered to the effect that Mrs. Smith was dead, scientifically or otherwise, unless the conditions set out in the definition existed.

Later in the opinion the court said, "Likewise, we take judicial notice that one breathing, though unconscious, is not dead."

"Judicial notice" of this definition of death means that the court did not consider that definition open to serious controversy; it considered the question as settled in responsible scientific and medical circles. The judge thus makes proof of uncontroverted facts unnecessary so as to prevent prolonging the trial with unnecessary proof and also to prevent fraud being committed upon the court by quasi "scientists" being called into court to controvert settled scientific principles at a price. Here, the Arkansas Supreme Court considered the definition of death to be a settled, scientific, biological fact. It refused to consider the plaintiff's offer of evidence that "modern medical science" might say otherwise. In simplified form, the above is the state of the law in the United States concerning the definition of death.

In this report, however, we suggest that responsible medical opinion is ready to adopt new criteria for pronouncing death to have occurred in an individual sustaining irreversible coma as a result of permanent brain damage. If this position is adopted by the medical community, it can form the basis for change in the current legal concept of death. No statutory change in the law should be necessary since the law treats this question essentially as one of fact to be determined by physicians. The only circumstance in which it would be necessary that legislation be offered in the various states to define "death" by law would be in the event that great controversy were engendered surrounding the subject and physicians were unable to agree on the new medical criteria.

It is recommended as a part of these procedures that judgement of the existence of these criteria is solely a medical issue. It is suggested that the physician in charge of the patient consult with one or more other physicians directly involved in the case before the patient is declared dead on the basis of these criteria. In this way, the responsibility is shared over a wider range of medical opinion, thus providing an important degree of protection against later questions which might be raised about the particular case. It is further suggested that the decision to declare the person dead, and then to turn off the respirator, be made by physicians not involved in any later effort to transplant organs or tissue from the deceased individual. This is advisable in order to avoid any appearance of self-interest by the physicians involved.

It should be emphasized that we recommend the patient be declared dead before any effort is made to take him off a respirator, if he is then on a respirator. This declaration should not be delayed until he has been taken off the respirator and all artificially stimulated signs have ceased. The reason for this recommendation is that in our judgement it will provide a greater degree of legal protection to those involved. Otherwise, the physicians would be turning off the respirator on a person who is, under the present strict, technical application of law, still alive.

Comment

Irreversible coma can have various causes: cardiac arrest; asphyxia with respiratory arrest; massive brain damage; intracranial lesions, neoplastic or vascular. It can be produced by other encephalopathic states such as the metabolic derangements associated, for example, with uremia. Respiratory failure and impaired circulation underlie all of these conditions. They result in hypoxia and ischemia of the brain.

From ancient times down to the recent past it was clear that, when the respiration and heart stopped, the brain would die in a few minutes; so the obvious criterion of no heart beat as synonymous with death was sufficiently accurate. In those times the heart was considered to be the central organ of the body; it is not surprising that its failure marked the onset of death. This is no longer valid when modern resuscitative and supportive measures are used. These improved activities can now restore "life" as judged by the ancient standards of persistent respiration and continuing heart beat. This can be the case even when there is not the remotest possibility of an individual recovering consciousness following massive brain damage. In other situations "life" can be maintained only by means of artificial respiration and electrical stimulation of the heart beat, or in temporarily bypassing the heart, or, in conjunction with these things, reducing with cold the body's oxygen requirement.

In an address, "The Prolongation of Life," (1957),[1] Pope Pius XII raised many questions; some conclusions stand out: (1) In a deeply unconscious individual vital functions may be maintained over a prolonged period only by extraordinary means. Verification of the moment of death can be determined, if at all, only by a physician. Some have suggested that the moment of death is the moment when irreparable and overwhelming brain damage occurs. Pius XII acknowledged that it is not "within the competence of the Church" to determine this. (2) It is incumbent on the physician to take all reasonable, ordinary means of restoring the spontaneous vital functions and consciousness, and to employ such extraordinary means as are available to him to this end. It is not obligatory, however, to continue to use extraordinary means indefinitely in hopeless cases. "But normally one is held to use only ordinary means – according to circumstances of persons, places, times, and cultures – that is to say, means that do not involve any grave burden for oneself or another." It is the church's view that a time comes when resuscitative efforts should stop and death be unopposed.

Summary

The neurological impairment to which the terms "brain death syndrome" and "irreversible coma" have become attached indicates diffuse disease. Function is abolished at cerebral, brain-stem, and often spinal levels. This should be evident in all cases from clinical examination alone. Cerebral, cortical, and thalamic involvement are indicated by a complete absence of receptivity of all forms of sensory stimulation and a lack of response to stimuli and to inner need. The term "coma" is used to designate this state of unreceptivity and unresponsivity. But there is always coincident paralysis of brain-stem and basal ganglionic mechanisms as manifested by an abolition of all postural reflexes, including induced decerebrate postures; a complete paralysis of respiration; widely dilated, fixed pupils; paralysis of ocular movements; swallowing; phonation; face and tongue muscles. Involvement of spinal cord, which is less constant, is reflected usually in loss of tendon reflex and all flexor withdrawal or nocifensive reflexes. Of the brain-stem–spinal mechanisms which are conserved for a time, the vasomotor reflexes are the most persistent, and they are responsible in part for the paradoxical state of retained cardiovascular function, which is to some extent independent of nervous control, in the face of widespread disorder of cerebrum, brain stem, and spinal cord.

Neurological assessment gains in reliability if the aforementioned neurological signs persist over a period of time, with the additional safeguards that there is no accompanying hypothermia or evidence of drug intoxication. If either of the latter two conditions exist, interpretation of the neurological state should await the return of body temperature to normal level and elimination of the intoxicating agent. Under any other circumstances, repeated examinations over a period of 24 hours or longer should be required in order to obtain evidence of the irreversibility of the condition.

Reference

1   Pius XII: The Prolongation of Life. *Pope Speaks*, 4 (1958): 393–8.

33

Are Recent Defences of the Brain Death Concept Adequate?

Ari Joffe

Brain death or brainstem death (BD) is accepted in most developed countries around the world as being the death of the patient.[1] Brain death is said to occur when several tests are fulfilled: there is a known cause compatible with irreversible loss of brain function, there are no factors confounding the examination of brain function, there is loss of consciousness, there is loss of brainstem reflexes including spontaneous breathing, and these are diagnosed as irreversible.[2] When one examines the rationale for BD being death itself, it is surprisingly hard to justify. Here I will briefly examine the flaws in the arguments in support of BD being death. Then I will critique recent writings by expert proponents of the BD concept that, ironically, show that a clear and defensible conceptual rationale to support BD being death has not been articulated. This is important because thousands of patients are pronounced with BD every year, and this has been the main way to obtain organs for transplantation without violating the so-called dead donor rule.

Flaws in the BD Concept and Criterion

It is said that BD is a criterion for death because it fulfils the definition (concept) of death, that is, the irreversible loss of integration of the organism as a whole, with resulting dis-integration and progression of entropy in the now dead organism.[3] This is why it is said that cardiac arrest is inevitable within a very short period of time in the now non-integrated corpse. The flaw is that there are known to be many cases of correctly diagnosed BD where 'survival' has lasted for weeks, months, and even years.[4] Ongoing integrated functioning of the organism, including growth, assimilation of nutrients, excretion of wastes, gestation of a fetus to viability, fighting of infections, fluid and electrolyte regulation, and other functions continued in these patients without a cardiac arrest.[5] These cases show that during brain death, with irreversible loss of all functions of the entire brain, there is ongoing

Original publication details: Ari Joffe, "Are Recent Defences of the Brain Death Concept Adequate?," pp. 47–53 from *Bioethics* 24: 2 (February 2010). Reproduced with permission from John Wiley & Sons.

Table 33.1 Conceptual rationales used to justify brain death as death itself

Criterion of brain death	Rationale for why it is death	Flaws in rationale
Whole brain death: irreversible loss of all critical functions of the entire brain.[1]	Death is the loss of integrative unity of the organism.[2]	– many with prolonged survival shows that integrative unity is not lost.[3]
		– many integrative functions continue, showing that the brain is a modulator and not the central regulator of integrative unity.[4] – high cervical spine injury patients lack the same degree of integrative unity as the brain dead patient.[5]
	The prognosis is for imminent cardiac arrest, and for an unacceptable quality of life.	– prognosis of death or unacceptable quality of life is not death itself. Prognosis of death is not a diagnosis of death
	There is loss of all function of the brain (including brainstem).	– this does not explain why this loss of function is death. This confuses a criterion of death (loss of brain function) with a concept of death.
	There is loss of all brain structure (infraction of brain).	– this does not explain why this loss of structure is death. This confuses a criterion of death (loss of brain structure) with a concept of death.
Higher brain death: irreversible loss of the function of the cerebrum.	Death is the loss of the capacity for consciousness.	– this implies person essentialism; that we are essentially persons, and were never a fetus or newborn.[6]
		– this means that a patient in a permanent vegetative state, with movement, wake cycles, and breathing, can be buried or cremated in that state.[7]
Brainstem death: irreversible loss of the capacity for consciousness and the ability to breathe.	Death is the loss of the capacity for consciousness and the loss of the ability to breathe.	– this does not explain why the loss of these functions is death. This confuses a criterion of death (loss of consciousness and breathing) with a concept of death.
		– the capacity for consciousness may not be lost. The cerebral hemispheres may be relatively spared, leaving the substrate required for the capacity for consciousness still present.[8] – loss of the 'conscious soul' suggests Cartesian dualism, implies we can know when this soul departs the body, and that the soul departs when the ability to demonstrate consciousness is lost. – loss of the 'breath of life' suggests that the patient with a cervical spinal cord injury and no ability to breathe is dead while alert and ventilated.

[1] President's Commission for the Study of Ethical Problems in Medicine and Biomedical and Behavioral Research. 1981. *Defining Death: Medical, Legal and Ethical Issues in the Determination of Death*. Washington, DC: US Government Printing Office.. See also J.L. Bernat, C.M. Culver and B. Gert. On the definition and criterion of death. *Ann Intern Med* 1981; 94: 389–394; J.L. Bernat. A defense of the whole brain concept of death. *Hastings Center Report* 1998; 28: 14–23; S.D. Shemie et al., Severe brain injury to neurological determination of death: Canadian forum recommendations. *CMAJ* 2006; 174: S1–S12.

[2] President's Commission, *Defining Death*. See also Bernat et al., On the definition and criterion of death. In Table 33.1 I have used the term 'rationale' instead of 'concept'. The standard way of justifying BD is to consider the concept of death, the criterion of death, and the tests of death. In this formulation the concept of death is what the criterion must satisfy, and the tests are to confirm the criterion is met. For example, the tests at the bedside for BD confirm the criterion is met (loss of function of the entire brain); in turn, this state of loss of function of the entire brain must satisfy a concept of death, usually said to be the loss of integrative unity of the organism.

[3] D.A. Shewmon, Chronic 'brain death': meta-analysis and conceptual consequences. *Neurology* 1998; 51: 1538–1545. See also D.J. Powner and I.M. Bernstein, Extended somatic support for pregnant women after brain death. *Crit Care Med* 2003; 31: 1241–1249.

[4] D.A. Shewmon, The brain and somatic integration: insights into the standard biological rationale for equating brain death with death. *J Med Philos* 2001; 26: 457–478.

[5] D.A. Shewmon. Hypothesis: spinal shock and 'brain death': somatic pathophysiological equivalence and implications for the integrative-
(Continued)

Table 33.1 *(Continued)*

unity rationale. *Spinal Cord* 1999; 37: 313–324. In this paper Shewmon makes a convincing argument that, from an integrative unity perspective, the high spinal cord injury patient who is clearly alive is physiologically identical to the BD patient.

[6] D. DeGrazia. Identity, killing, and the boundaries of our existence. *Philos Public Aff* 2003; 31: 413–442. See also D. DeGrazia. Are we essentially persons? Olson, Baker, and a reply. *The Philosophical Forum* 2002; 33: 101–120.

[7] R.D. Truog. Is it time to abandon brain death? *Hastings Cent Rep* 1997; 27: 29–37. This higher brain death criterion is not accepted as death in any country in the world.

[8] M.M. Grigg et al. Electroencephalographic activity after brain death. *Arch Neurol* 1987; 44: 948–954. See also E. Rodin et al. Brain-stem death. *Clinical Electroencephalography* 1985; 16: 63–71; D.A. Shewmon. Brainstem death, brain death and death: a critical re-evaluation of the purported equivalence. *Issues in Law and Medicine* 1998; 14: 125–145; A. Ferbert et al. Isolated brain-stem death: case report with demonstration of preserved visual evoked potentials. *Electroenceph Clin Neurophysiol* 1986; 65: 157–160; S. Kaukinen et al. Significance of electrical brain activity in brain-stem death. *Intensive Care Med* 1995; 21: 76–78; J. Ogata et al. Primary brainstem death: a clinico-pathological study. *J Neurol Neurosurg Psychiatry* 1988; 51: 646–650; H.P. Schlake et al. Determination of cerebral perfusion by means of planar brain scintigraphy and 99mTc-HMPAO in brain death, persistent vegetative state and severe coma. *Intensive Care Med* 1992; 18: 76–81; M.J. Zwarts. Clinical brainstem death with preserved electroencephalographic activity and visual evoked response. *Arch-Neurol* 2001; 58: 1010.

integration of the organism as a whole; the concept of death (loss of integration of the organism as a whole) has not been met. Other rationales for why BD is death have been offered, but have been less well accepted and easier to counter than the integration hypothesis (Table 33.1).

It is also said that BD is the loss of functions in the entire brain including the brainstem (brain death) or only in the brainstem (brainstem death).[6] However, it is now known that functions and structure of the brain continue in many patients correctly diagnosed as BD (Table 33.2). It is argued that the remaining functions are not critical to the organism's integrative unity.[7] No rationale for this argument has been offered. Specifically, why, for example, pupillary reaction to light or an oculovestibular reflex is more critical to integrative unity than ongoing electroencephalogram activity, auditory brainstem evoked potentials, hypothalamic function, cerebral blood flow, or lack of pathologic brain destruction is not clear.[8]

Recent Expert Explanations and Defences of the BD Concept

Brain death

Laureys recently stated that 'brain death signifies death not because it is invariably imminently followed by asystole, but because it is accompanied by irreversible loss of critical *cerebral* functions' (emphasis added).[9]

I agree with Laureys that many are 'intuitively attracted to the brain death formulation', and probably for the reason that there is loss of *cerebral* functions.[10] However, loss of cerebral functions is not BD, and would suggest that patients in an irreversible vegetative state with ongoing breathing and movement are dead and, if this is true, then they can be buried or cremated in their current state.[11] Laureys goes on to state that the long 'survivals [in BD] merely indicates that their bodily decomposition has been delayed until their circulation has ceased.'[12] Of course, this shows that the body has not lost integrative unity, and is not decomposing until circulation has ceased. It turns out that Laureys was unable to provide a rationale for BD being death.

Bernat recently wrote that the BD concept's:

> shortcomings are relatively inconsequential. Those scholars attacking the established whole brain death formulation have a duty to show that their proposed alternative formulations not only more accurately represent biological reality, but also can be translated into successful public policy that is intuitively acceptable and maintains public confidence in physician's accuracy in death determination and in the integrity of the organ procurement process.'[13]

This is a problematic defence of the BD concept. The suggestion is that BD can be a 'compromise' or an 'approximation' in order to maintain public confidence and organ procurement.[14] In effect, this is admitting that there is not a satisfactory rationale for BD being equivalent to death, only a compromise

Table 33.2 Brain structure and function that continue after brain death

Brain function or structure	Proportion with continued function or structure
Electroencephalogram activity	20%[1]
Brainstem auditory and/or somatosensory evoked potentials	5%[2]
Hypothalamic functions: ongoing antidiuretic hormone regulation, ongoing temperature regulation, etc	50%[3]
Hemodynamic response to incision for organ procurement (rise in heart rate and blood pressure)	>20%[4]
Ability to breathe at a pCO2 >80 mmHg	Case reports[5]
Cerebral blood flow by radionuclide angiography	5–20%[6]
Lack of extensive brain pathologic destruction	>10%[7]

[1] M.M. Grigg et al. Electroencephalographic activity after brain death. *Arch Neurol* 1987; 44: 948–954. See also A. Paolin et al. Reliability in diagnosis of brain death. *Intensive Care Med* 1995; 21: 657–662.

[2] M. Ruiz-Garcia et al. Brain death in children: clinical, neurophysiological and radioisotopic angiography findings in 125 patients. *Childs Nerv Syst* 2000; 16: 40–46; E. Facco et al. Role of short latency evoked potentials in the diagnosis of brain death. *Clinical Neurophysiology* 2002; 113: 1855–1866.

[3] R.D. Truog. Is it time to abandon brain death? *Hastings Cent Rep* 1997; 27: 29–37. See also D. Staworn et al. Brain death in pediatric intensive care unit patients: incidence, primary diagnosis, and the clinical occurrence of Turner's triad. *Crit Care Med* 1994; 22: 1301–1305; J.C. Fackler, J.C. Troncoso and F.R. Gioia. Age-specific characteristics of brain death in children. *AJDC* 1988; 142: 999–1003.

[4] H.J. Gramm et al. Hemodynamic responses to noxious stimuli in brain-dead organ donors. *Intensive Care Med* 1992; 18: 493–495; R.C. Wetzel et al. Hemodynamic responses in brain dead organ donor patients. *Anesth Analg* 1985; 64: 125–128.

[5] R.J. Brilli and D. Bigos. Apnea threshold and pediatric brain death *Crit Care Med* 2000; 28: 1257; R.V. Vardis and M.M. Pollack. Increased apnea threshold in a pediatric patient with suspected brain death. *Crit Care Med* 1998; 26: 1917–1919.

[6] R.W. Kurtek et al. Tc-99m Hexamethylpropylene Amine Oxime scintigraphy in the diagnosis of brain death and its implications for the harvesting of organs used for transplantation. *Clin Nucl Med* 2000; 25: 7–10; W.M. Flowers and B.R. Patel. Persistence of cerebral blood flow after brain death. *Southern Medical Journal* 2000; 93: 364–370.

[7] Fackler et al., Age-specific characteristics of brain death in children. See also P.M. Black. Brain death (First and second parts). *N Engl J Med* 1978; 299: 338–344 and 393–401; A.E. Walker, E.L. Diamond and J. Moseley. The neuropathological findings in irreversible coma: a critique of the 'respirator brain'. *J Neuropathol Exp Neurol* 1975; 34: 295–323; R. Schroder. Later changes in brain death. Signs of partial recirculation. *Acta Neuropathol (Berl)* 1983; 62: 15–23; A. Mohandas and S.N. Chou. Brain death: a clinical and pathological study. *J Neurosurg* 1971; 35: 211–218; B. Drake, S. Ashwal and S. Schneider. Determination of cerebral death in the pediatric intensive care unit. *Pediatrics* 1986; 78: 107–112.

that has allowed the utilitarian goal of organ donation.

Shemie recently suggested that BD is 'better understood as "brain arrest" [BA] – the complete loss of clinical brain function.'[15] Whether the state is named 'BD' or 'BA' does not provide a rationale for why this state is death. Shemie writes: 'mechanical ventilation merely interrupts the way brain failure *leads to death*' (emphasis added).[16] By the same reasoning, if we label infarction of the colon 'colon arrest', we could write that 'surgery merely interrupts the way colon arrest leads to death'; but this does not mean we consider 'colon arrest' death. Shemie also writes: the 'basic physiological mechanism of death [in BA occurs] ... via interruption of airway control and respiratory drive caus[ing] a secondary respiratory arrest and then cardiac arrest ... [BA] *threaten[s] life* in this manner' (emphasis added).[17] In another publication Shemie again makes this clear: '... primary brain arrest, which

via interruption of airway control and respiratory drive, causes a secondary respiratory then cardiac arrest. Regardless of initial disease state, all critical illnesses *threaten life* in this way.'[18] Thus, 'BA' leads to death when it is allowed to result in irreversible loss of circulation. If 'BA' threatens life, and leads to death, it cannot *be* death itself.

Shemie further writes 'intensive care does not replace any functions of the brain ... any degree of brain failure, including BD, can be sustained indefinitely with mechanical ventilation and vigilant care.'[19] If death is the loss of integrative unity of the organism due to 'BA', then the 'BA' patient 'sustained indefinitely' by intensive care must have integrative unity, and must have had the brain-stem functions (such as breathing) taken over by intensive care. This must mean that intensive care does indeed replace some functions of the brain. If 'BA' is death, there must be some other concept of death that it satisfies; however, what this is has not been clarified, in my view because BA is *not* death.

Perhaps intensive care cannot replace consciousness. Irreversible loss of the capacity for consciousness may be a concept of death, as Shemie suggests when arguing that in resuscitation 'cerebral blood flow is the primary issue ... poor outcomes do not distinguish between death and vegetative survival.'[20] If this is true, then breathing has nothing to do with death, and as mentioned above, we should bury or cremate patients in an irreversible vegetative state.[21] Shemie makes this clear when he writes: 'Death is the point in time when concrete consequences occur, including ... potential for organ donation and autopsy, ... and disposition of the body by burial or cremation.'[22] Interestingly, this would imply that the patient with BD, while ventilated with ongoing circulation, could at that time have their autopsy or cremation (before breathing and circulation stop).

Brainstem death

Shemie writes that BD may be from 'isolated brainstem injury.'[23] However, BD requires that the capacity for consciousness be lost. In brainstem death it is not necessarily true that the capacity for consciousness is lost, as the cerebrum may be relatively spared. If there is some cerebral integrity, then the presumed site for consciousness to occur is preserved. There are many cases of brainstem death without cerebral death[24] and in one series this occurred in 3.6% of BD cases.[25] Rodin et al. state that the EEG in these cases 'would suggest that if there was cognition at all it would probably have been in the realm of dream type rather than waking reality ... it is advisable that we do not confuse quality of life with presence of life.'[26]

Pallis has offered the rationale that brainstem death is death because it marks the time when the 'conscious soul' has departed, and the 'breath of life' is gone.[27] This is a problematic defence of the BD concept. As Shewmon suggests, 'this is poetry, not physiology.'[28] Specifically, this suggests Cartesian dualism, implies we can know when the soul has departed, and further, that this is coincident with the time that the capacity for *demonstrating* consciousness has irreversibly been lost. Similarly, by this rationale the patient in a permanent

vegetative state has also lost the 'conscious soul.' The 'breath of life' rationale would suggest that the patient with a high cervical-spine injury, with permanent loss of the ability to initiate respiration, has likewise lost the 'breath of life' and is dead while fully aware on a ventilator. Moreover, the BD patient may not have lost the 'breath of life' as it is unclear why *spontaneous* breathing is necessary when no other life supporting functions are required to be spontaneous.[29] Finally, why one must lose both abilities is unclear.

Recent surveys of physicians' understanding of BD

The expert clinicians at the bedside, who diagnose BD and send patients for organ procurement, also seem to evidence questioning of the validity of BD being death. A recent American survey asked 25 pediatric critical care attending physicians if they agree with the statement 'life supports should be withdrawn from a child who is legally BD even if the parents do not agree'; 34% responded that they disagree or are uncertain.[30] In recent surveys of neurosurgeons and pediatric intensivists in Canada, when faced with a BD patient who has no cerebral blood flow yet whose family insists on continued 'life support', 31% and 37% respectively would continue life support.[31] If similar life support would not be continued on a patient after circulatory death (which is highly likely), this suggests that BD is thought to be different from death. Whether life support in either circumstance is continued because of doubting the diagnosis of death, or fear of litigation, the results demonstrate that BD and circulatory death are not considered the singular state of death. Remarkably, when the Canadian neurosurgeons were asked 'are BD and cardiac death the same state (i.e. are both death of the patient)?' 45% answered 'no'.[32] The President's Commission, in *Defining Death*, pointed out that the unitary death standard is the loss of all brain functions, and BD and circulatory death are each death because they each satisfy this single standard; Canadian neurosurgeons do not seem to agree.[33]

These surveys in Canada also showed the following: when asked to choose a conceptual reason to explain why BD is equivalent to death, only a minority chose a loss of integration of the organism concept, and many chose a higher brain or prognosis concept; most answered that BD is not compatible with EEG activity or brainstem evoked potential activity; and over one third answered that BD is not compatible with some cerebral blood flow or with minimal microscopic brainstem damage.[34] These responses not only suggest lack of a rationale to justify the BD criterion of death but, also, lack of an understanding of the BD criterion itself (see Tables 33.1 and 33.2). These findings also suggest that the recent Canadian consensus forum that clarified the definition and testing for BD may have been based on both an insufficient consideration of the concept of death, and of the actual empirical clinical state of those declared brain dead.[35]

Older surveys have had similar findings (Table 33.3). Youngner et al. showed that one third of physicians and nurses involved in the management of BD considered the patient dead because they had irreversible loss of *cortical* function, and another third because they had an unacceptable *quality of life* or were irreversibly *dying*.[36] Tomlinson found that physicians 'use BD as a criterion for death, but they have ready to hand no clear concept of death which underlies their use of the BD criterion.'[37] In interviews with intensivists, Lock found that 'they are more ambivalent than many of them care to admit, however, about the status of a living cadaver. While they agree that brain death is irreversible, they do not believe that brain death individuals are dead.'[38] Some anesthetists feel that the BD patient should be given anesthesia during organ harvest, due to doubts about possible pain in the donor.[39]

Implications

It could be argued that the failure of recent authors successfully to defend the BD concept only shows flaws in their argumentation, and not that the concept of BD itself is flawed.[40] The problem with this interpretation is that these authors are attempting to

Table 33.3 Representative statements by physicians regarding brain death found in previous reports

Study	Selected physician quotations
Lock[1]	'I believe that a "humanistic" death happens at the same time as brain death … For me the child has gone to heaven or wherever, and I'm dealing with an organism, respectfully, of course, but that child's soul, or whatever you want to call it, is no longer there.'
	'… an in-between thing. It's neither a cadaver nor a person …'
	'I guess I equate the death of a person with the death of the spirit because I don't really know about anything else, like a hereafter … I guess one would have to take it as meaning that part of a person which is different, sort of not in the physical realm … won't ever be the person they used to know.'
	'The body wants to die, you can sense that when it becomes difficult to keep the blood pressure stable and so on … We don't want this patient to expire before we can harvest the organs, so it's important to keep them stable and alive …'
	'It's not death, but it is an irreversible diagnosis, which I accept.'
Tomlinson[2]	'The machine is the way he would have to live the rest of his life.'
	'The machine is basically what's keeping him alive.'
	'If kept on the ventilator, the patient will die of sepsis.'
	'… have no consciousness or have no thought processes; the spirit has left …'
Young and Matta[3]	'Faced with the knowledge of the persistence of higher brain and spinal function in some donors, the inability to test the reticular formation directly and the dramatic preoperative haemodynamic changes that occur, sedation and analgesia should be given with muscle relaxation for organ donation.'
Keep[4]	'The ethical question we have to ask ourselves therefore is this: would we be content to cremate the body of a loved one in the knowledge that it would withdraw its limbs and that there would be a sharp rise in heart rate and blood pressure when it entered the furnace? If we would not, then we have no right to inflict a similar fate on an un-anaesthetized organ donor.'

[1] M. Lock, Inventing a new death and making it believable. *Anthropology and Medicine* 2002; 9: 97–115, at pp. 108, 109, 110.

[2] T. Tomlinson, Misunderstanding death on a respirator. *Bioethics* 1990; 4: 253–264, at pp. 257, 259.

[3] P.J. Young and B.F. Matta, Anaesthesia for organ donation in the brainstem dead – why bother? *Anaesthesia* 2000; 55: 105–106, at p. 106.

[4] P.J. Keep, Anaesthesia for organ donation in the brainstem dead. *Anaesthesia* 2000; 55: 590.

address the recent critiques of the BD concept. The flaws in the BD concept are well argued in the literature (Table 33.1). Thus far, I submit, the experts defending the BD concept against these flaws have not been successful. Unless a successful defence can be offered, the flaws of the BD concept remain.

If BD is not death, the implications for society in general, and medicine in particular, may be enormously significant. The practice of organ donation is said to be based on a medical and societal consensus that BD is death, and non-paired vital organs are only donated by the dead (the so-called 'dead donor rule').[41] To suggest otherwise may result in a breakdown of the societal consensus and organ donation. However, this is not an argument to clarify why BD may be death. As this paper argues, the medical and societal consensus was based on flawed concepts, and therefore BD being legally accepted as death is a legal fiction.[42] I suggest that it may be more appropriate to argue that the state of BD is such a profoundly devastating condition that it may suffice to allow organ donation (with consent), even though the donor is not dead until after organ harvest, discontinuation of ventilation, and irreversible loss of circulation. Several other authors have argued along the same lines.[43]

Some suggest that cerebral function is an integral and vital part of human beings, making them members of the human moral community, the kind of being who warrants certain kinds of treatment.[44] This may be true; but I do not consider this an acceptable argument to clarify why BD may be death. Consciousness, the mind ('mind essentialism'),[45] or personhood ('person essentialism'),[46] when meant in a *non-dualistic* sense, has not been accepted by any

society as death. As argued above, a person in a permanently unconscious state (vegetative) is not considered dead in any society; burial, cremation, or organ donation without anesthetic in these patients has been unthinkable. This suggests that loss of cerebral function and consciousness is not *what we mean* by the word death. It may be, however, that many would consent to organ donation with anesthetic in the state of BD because they consider the donor to have lost a critical or essential part of what makes them human. This is similar to the suggestion above that BD may be a sufficiently devastating condition to morally allow consent to organ donation. Nevertheless, this remains problematic, because the rationale is based on a higher brain consciousness concept.

Conclusion

Over time, it has become clear that the BD criterion does not fulfill an accepted definition of death, and that the tests used to confirm BD do not fulfill the accepted criterion of BD. Recent defences of the BD concept against these claims have been unsuccessful. I suggest that it is far from clear that the patient with BD, brainstem death, or 'BA' is actually dead. *If* BD *is* death, an acceptable conceptual rationale for BD being equivalent to death should be clarified, and this should be done urgently. Otherwise, it may be time to consider the argument that BD, although not death, is a sufficiently devastating state that it would allow consent to organ donation. The implications of this suggestion require much discussion.

Notes

1   E.F.M. Wijdicks. Brain death worldwide: accepted fact but no global consensus in diagnostic criteria. *Neurology* 2002; 58: 20–25.

2   S.D. Shemie et al. Severe brain injury to neurological determination of death: Canadian forum recommendations. *CMAJ* 2006; 174: S1–S12.

3   President's Commission for the Study of Ethical Problems in Medicine and Biomedical and Behavioral Research. 1981. *Defining Death: Medical, Legal and Ethical Issues in the Determination of Death*. Washington, DC: US

Government Printing Office. See also J.L. Bernat, C.M. Culver and B. Gert. On the definition and criterion of death. *Ann Intern Med* 1981; 94: 389–394.

4   D.A. Shewmon. Chronic 'brain death': meta-analysis and conceptual consequences. *Neurology* 1998; 51: 1538–1545. See also D.J. Powner and I.M. Bernstein. Extended somatic support for pregnant women after brain death. *Crit Care Med* 2003; 31: 1241–1249.

5   D.A. Shewmon. The brain and somatic integration: insights into the standard biological rationale for

equating brain death with death. *J Med Philos* 2001; 26: 457–478.

6   President's Commission, *Defining Death*. See also Shemie et al., Severe brain injury to neurological determination of death.

7   J.L. Bernat. A defense of the whole brain concept of death. *Hastings Center Report* 1998; 28: 14–23.

8   R.D. Truog. Is it time to abandon brain death? *Hastings Cent Rep* 1997; 27: 29–37.

9   S. Laureys. Death, unconsciousness, and the brain. *Nature Rev Neurosci* 2005; 6: 899–908, see esp. p. 901.

10   Laureys, Death, unconsciousness, and the brain, p. 901.

11   Truog, Is it time to abandon brain death?

12   Laureys, Death, unconsciousness, and the brain, p. 900.

13   J.L. Bernat. The whole-brain concept of death remains optimum public policy. *J Law Med Ethics* 2006; 34: 35–43, see esp. p. 41.

14   Bernat, The whole-brain concept of death remains optimum public policy, p. 41. Here Bernat writes: 'I acknowledge that the whole-brain formulation, although coherent, is imperfect, and that my attempts to defend it have not adequately addressed all valid criticisms … In the real world of public policy on biological issues, we must frequently make compromises or approximations to achieve acceptable practices and laws … while I am willing to acknowledge that whole-brain death formulation remains imperfect, I continue to support it because on the public policy level its shortcomings are relatively inconsequential.' Similarly, when referring to the problems with donation after cardiac death defining death as occurring after two minutes of absent circulation, Bernat writes: 'The good accruing to the organ recipient, the donor patient, and the donor family resulting from organ donation justified overlooking the biological shortcoming because, although the difference in the death criteria was real, it was inconsequential'; meaning, he explains, that 'there would be no difference whatsoever in their outcomes.'

15   S. Shemie. Diagnosis of brain death in children: technology and the inadequate lexicon of death. *Lancet Neurology* 2007; 6: 87–88, see esp. p. 88. See also S. Shemie. Brain arrest, cardiac arrest and uncertainties in defining death. *Journal de Pediatria* 2007; 83: 102–104, esp. p. 103; Shemie et al., Severe brain injury to neurological determination of death.

16   Shemie, Diagnosis of brain death in children, p. 87; Shemie, Brain arrest, cardiac arrest and uncertainties in defining death, p. 103.

17   Shemie, Diagnosis of brain death in children, p. 87.

18   Shemie, Brain arrest, cardiac arrest and uncertainties in defining death, pp. 102–103.

19   Shemie, Brain arrest, cardiac arrest and uncertainties in defining death, p. 103.

20   Shemie, Diagnosis of brain death in children, p. 87.

21   Truog, Is it time to abandon brain death?

22   Shemie, Brain arrest, cardiac arrest and uncertainties in defining death, p. 102.

23   Shemie, Diagnosis of brain death in children, p. 87.

24   M.M. Grigg et al., Electroencephalographic activity after brain death. *Arch Neurol* 1987; 44: 948–954. See also M.A. Kelly et al. Electroen-cephalographic activity after brain death. *Arch Neurol* 1987; 44: 948–954; E. Rodin et al., Brain-stem death. *Clinical Electroencephalography* 1985; 16: 63–71; A. Ferbert et al., Isolated brain-stem death: case report with demonstration of preserved visual evoked potentials. *Electroenceph Clin Neurophysiol* 1986; 65: 157–160; S. Kaukinen et al., Significance of electrical brain activity in brain-stem death. *Intensive Care Med* 1995; 21: 76–78; J. Ogata et al., Primary brainstem death: a clinico-pathological study. *J Neurol Neurosurg Psychiatry* 1988; 51: 646–650; H.P. Schlake et al., Determination of cerebral perfusion by means of planar brain scintigraphy and 99mTc-HMPAO in brain death, persistent vegetative state and severe coma. *Intensive Care Med* 1992; M.J. Zwarts, Clinical brainstem death with preserved electroencephalographic activity and visual evoked response. *Arch-Neurol* 2001; 58: 1010.

25   Grigg et al., Electroencephalographic activity after brain death.

26   Rodin et al., Brain-stem death, p. 70.

27   C. Pallis. 1999. On the brainstem criterion of death. In *The Definition of Death: Contemporary Controversies.* S.J. Youngner, R.M. Arnold and R. Schapiro, eds. Baltimore, Maryland: The Johns Hopkins University Press: 93–100, see esp. p. 96. Here Pallis writes: 'The single matrix in which my definition is embedded is a sociological one, namely Judeo-Christian culture. Inasmuch as Western civilization retains any moral or ethical standards, they are still influenced by the culture in question. It is important, in my opinion, that, even if we today express our views in modern physiological and secular terms, we recognize their cultural roots. The "loss of the capacity for consciousness" is much the same as the "departure of the conscious soul from the body," just as the "loss of the capacity to breathe" is much the same as the "loss of the breath of life." … For those interested in philology, I have described the widespread identity, in various languages, of terms denoting soul and breath. I think it is legitimate to look at words – and ideas – in relation to the company they keep.'

28   D.A. Shewmon, Brainstem death, brain death and death: a critical re-evaluation of the purported equivalence. *Issues in Law and Medicine* 1998; 14: 125–145, at p. 130.

29   F.M. Kamm. Brain death and spontaneous breathing. *Philos Public Aff* 2002; 30: 297–320.

30   M.Z. Solomon et al. New and lingering controversies in pediatric end-of-life care. *Pediatrics* 2005; 116: 872–883.

31   A.R. Joffe and N. Anton. Brain death: understanding of the conceptual basis by pediatric intensivists in Canada *Arch Pediatr Adol Med* 2006; 160: 747–752; A.R. Joffe, N. Anton, and V. Mehta. A survey to determine the understanding of the conceptual basis and diagnostic tests used for brain death by neurosurgeons in Canada. *Neurosurgery* 2007; 61: 1039–1047.

32   Joffe et al., A survey.

33   President's Commission, *Defining Death*.

34   Joffe and Anton, Brain death; Joffe et al., A survey.

35   Shemie et al., Severe brain injury to neurological determination of death.

36   S.J. Youngner et al. 'Brain death' and organ retrieval: a cross-sectional survey of knowledge and concepts among health professionals. *JAMA* 1989; 261: 2205–2210.

37   T. Tomlinson. Misunderstanding death on a respirator. *Bioethics* 1990; 4: 253–264.

38   M. Lock. Inventing a new death and making it believable. *Anthropology and Medicine* 2002; 9: 97–115.

39   P.J. Young and B.F. Matta. Anaesthesia for organ donation in the brainstem dead – why bother? *Anaesthesia* 2000; 55: 105–106; P.J. Keep. Anaesthesia for organ donation in the brainstem dead. *Anaesthesia* 2000; 55: 590.

40   This was suggested to me by an anonymous reviewer.

41   R.M. Arnold and S.J. Youngner. The dead donor rule: should we stretch it, bend it, or abandon it? *Kennedy Inst Ethics J* 1993; 3: 263–278.

42   See the discussion in: R.A. Charo. 1999. Dusk, dawn, and defining death: legal classifications and biological categories. In *The Definition of Death: Contemporary Controversies*, Youngner et al., eds: 277–292; D.W. Brock. The role of the public in public policy on the definition of death. In *The Definition of Death*: 293–307.

43   See the discussion in: R.D. Truog and V.M. Robinson. Role of brain death and the dead-donor rule in the ethics of organ transplantation. *Crit Care Med* 2003; 31: 2391–2396 (the authors argue that brain death is not death, rather, a state where the patient is not harmed by organ donation); R.M. Veatch. Abandon the dead donor rule or change the definition of death? *Kennedy Inst Ethics J* 2004; 14: 261–276 (the author argues that death should *be defined* by when it is morally acceptable to treat a patient as if they were dead); G. Boniolo. Death and transplantation: let's try to get things methodologically straight. *Bioethics* 2007; 21: 32–40 (the author argues for using a pragmatic, explicit, stipulative, conditional definition of an 'explantability window' when it would be ethical, as a matter of judgement of value, to donate organs, even though the patient may not be dead). All these proposals require much more discussion as to whether the patient, if not dead, is harmed in any way by organ donation being the proximate cause of death.

44   An anonymous reviewer suggested this line of argument. This is similar to the argument in R.M. Veatch. The death of whole-brain death: the plague of the disaggregators, somaticists, and mentalists. *J Med Phil* 2005; 30: 353–378. See esp. p. 370, where Veatch writes: 'full moral standing – life, in this morally significant sense – is the characteristic of all humans with "embodied capacity for consciousness" … Embodied consciousness takes a stand about both capacities for both the minimal somatic functions and the minimal mental functions that are necessary for full moral standing to be present. When, and only when, these are jointly present, then the sufficient conditions for full moral standing are present.'

45   Veatch, The death of whole-brain death; J. McMahan. An alternative to brain death. *J Law Med Ethics* 2006; 34: 44–48. See esp. pp. 47–48, where McMahan writes: 'What it is important to be able to determine is when we die in the nonbiological sense – that is, when we cease to exist. If we are embodied minds, we die or cease to exist when we irreversibly lose the capacity for consciousness … Note that when I say the right criterion of death is a higher-brain criterion, I am not claiming that a human organism in a persistent vegetative state is dead. If persistent vegetative state involves the loss of the capacity for consciousness, then neither you nor I could ever exist in a persistent vegetative state. But you could be survived by your organism, which could remain biologically alive in a persistent vegetative state even though you were dead (that is, had ceased to exist) … I believe that the treatment of a living but unoccupied human organism is governed morally by principles similar to those that govern the treatment of a corpse'.

46   D. DeGrazia, Identity, killing, and the boundaries of our existence. *Philos Public Aff* 2003; 31: 413–442, at p. 437: 'Because minds are not living substances distinct from the animals that have minds, the passing of a mind is not literally a form of death. It is rather the loss of a form of functioning that we typically treasure as, inter alia, a source of our self-narratives'.

34

Is the Sanctity of Life Ethic Terminally Ill?

Peter Singer

I   Introduction

It is surely no secret to anyone at this Congress that I have for a long time been a critic of the traditional sanctity of life ethic. So if I say that I believe that, after ruling our thoughts and our decisions about life and death for nearly two thousand years, the traditional sanctity of life ethic is at the point of collapse, some of you may think this is mere wishful thinking on my part. Consider, however, the following three signs of this impending collapse, which have taken place – coincidentally but perhaps appropriately enough – during the past two years in which I have had the honour of holding the office of President of the International Association of Bioethics.

- On February 4, 1993, in deciding the fate of a young man named Anthony Bland, Britain's highest court threw out many centuries of traditional law and medical ethics regarding the value of human life and the lawfulness of intentionally ending it.
- On November 30, 1993, the Netherlands parliament finally put into law the guidelines under which Dutch doctors have for some years been openly giving lethal injections to patients who suffer unbearably without hope of improvement, and who ask to be helped to die.
- On May 2, 1994, twelve Michigan jurors acquitted Dr Jack Kevorkian of a charge of assisting Thomas Hyde to commit suicide. Their refusal to convict Kevorkian was a major victory for the cause of physician-assisted suicide, for it is hard to imagine a clearer case of assisting suicide than this one. Kevorkian freely admitted supplying the carbon monoxide gas, tubing and a mask to Hyde, who had then used them to end a life made unbearable by the rapidly progressing nerve disorder ALS.

These three events are the surface tremors resulting from major shifts deep in the bedrock of Western ethics. We are going through a period of transition in our attitude to the sanctity of human life. Such transitions cause confusion and division. Many factors are involved in this shift, but today I shall focus on ways in which our growing technical capacity to keep human beings alive has brought out some implications of the sanctity of life ethic that – once we are forced to face them squarely – we cannot accept. This will lead me to suggest a way forward.

Original publication details: Peter Singer, "Is the Sanctity of Life Ethic Terminally Ill?," pp. 307–43 from *Bioethics* 9: 3/4 (1995). Reproduced with permission from John Wiley & Sons.

II   Revolution by Stealth: The Redefinition of Death

The acceptance of brain death – that is, the permanent loss of all brain function – as a criterion of death has been widely regarded as one of the great achievements of bioethics. It is one of the few issues on which there has been virtual consensus; and it has made an important difference in the way we treat people whose brains have ceased to function. This change in the definition of death has meant that warm, breathing, pulsating human beings are not given further medical support. If their relatives consent (or in some countries, as long as they have not registered a refusal of consent), their hearts and other organs can be cut out of their bodies and given to strangers. The change in our conception of death that excluded these human beings from the moral community was among the first in a series of dramatic changes in our view of life and death. Yet, in sharp contrast to other changes in this area, it met with virtually no opposition. How did this happen?

Everyone knows that the story of our modern definition of death begins with "The Ad Hoc Committee of the Harvard Medical School to Examine the Definition of Brain Death" (see the previous chapter). What is not so well known is the link between the work of this committee and Dr Christiaan Barnard's famous first transplantation of a human heart, in December 1967. Even before Barnard's sensational operation, Henry Beecher, chairman of a Harvard University committee that oversaw the ethics of experimentation on human beings, had written to Robert Ebert, Dean of the Harvard Medical School, suggesting that the committee should consider some new questions. He had, he told the Dean, been speaking with Dr Joseph Murray, a surgeon at Massachusetts General Hospital and a pioneer in kidney transplantation. "Both Dr Murray and I," Beecher wrote, "think the time has come for a further consideration of the definition of death. Every major hospital has patients stacked up waiting for suitable donors."[1] Ebert did not respond immediately; but within a month of the news of the South African heart transplant, he set up, under Beecher's chairmanship, the group that was soon to become known as the Harvard Brain Death Committee.

The committee was made up mostly of members of the medical profession – ten of them, supplemented by a lawyer, a historian, and a theologian. It did its work rapidly, and published its report in the *Journal of the American Medical Association* in August 1968. The report was soon recognized as an authoritative document, and its criteria for the determination of death were adopted rapidly and widely, not only in the United States but, with some modification of the technical details, in most countries of the world. The report began with a remarkably clear statement of what the committee was doing and why it needed to be done:

> Our primary purpose is to define irreversible coma as a new criterion for death. There are two reasons why there is a need for a definition: (1) Improvements in resuscitative and supportive measures have led to increased efforts to save those who are desperately injured. Sometimes these efforts have only a partial success so that the result is an individual whose heart continues to beat but whose brain is irreversibly damaged. The burden is great on patients who suffer permanent loss of intellect, on their families, on the hospitals, and on those in need of hospital beds already occupied by these comatose patients. (2) Obsolete criteria for the definition of death can lead to controversy in obtaining organs for transplantation.

To a reader familiar with bioethics in the 1990s, there are two striking aspects of this opening paragraph. The first is that the Harvard committee does not even attempt to argue that there is a need for a new definition of death because hospitals have a lot of patients in their wards who are really dead, but are being kept attached to respirators because the law does not recognize them as dead. Instead, with unusual frankness, the committee said that a new definition was needed because irreversibly comatose patients were a great burden, not only on themselves (why to be in an irreversible coma is a burden to the patient, the committee did not say), but also to their families, hospitals, and patients waiting for beds. And then there was the problem of "controversy" about obtaining organs for transplantation.

In fact, frank as the statement seems, in presenting its concern about this controversy, the committee was still not being entirely candid. An earlier draft had been more open in stating that one reason for changing the definition of death was the "great need for tissues and organs of, among others, the patient whose cerebrum has been hopelessly destroyed, in order to restore those who are salvageable". When this draft was sent to Ebert, he advised Beecher to tone it down because of its "unfortunate" connotation "that you wish to redefine death in order to make viable organs more readily available to persons requiring transplants".[2] The Harvard Brain Death Committee took Ebert's advice: it was doubtless more politic not to put things so bluntly. But Beecher himself made no secret of his own views. He was later to say, in an address to the American Association for the Advancement of Science:

> There is indeed a life-saving potential in the new definition, for, when accepted, it will lead to greater availability than formerly of essential organs in viable condition, for transplantation, and thus countless lives now inevitably lost will be saved.[3]

The second striking aspect of the Harvard committee's report is that it keeps referring to "irreversible coma" as the condition that it wishes to define as death. The committee also speaks of "permanent loss of intellect" and even says "we suggest that responsible medical opinion is ready to adopt new criteria for pronouncing death to have occurred in an individual sustaining irreversible coma as a result of permanent brain damage." Now "irreversible coma as a result of permanent brain damage" is by no means identical with the death of the whole brain. Permanent damage to the parts of the brain responsible for consciousness can also mean that a patient is in a "persistent vegetative state", a condition in which the brain stem and the central nervous system continue to function, but consciousness has been irreversibly lost. Even today, no legal system regards those in a persistent vegetative state as dead.

Admittedly, the Harvard committee report does go on to say, immediately following the paragraph quoted above: "*we are concerned here only with those comatose individuals who have no discernible central nervous system*

activity." But the reasons given by the committee for redefining death – the great burden on the patients, their families, the hospitals and the community, as well as the waste of organs needed for transplation – apply in every respect to *all* those who are irreversibly comatose, not only to those whose entire brain is dead. So it is worth asking: why did the committee limit its concern to those with no brain activity at all? One reason could be that there was at the time no reliable way of telling whether a coma was irreversible, unless the brain damage was so severe that there was no brain activity at all. Another could be that people whose whole brain is dead will stop breathing after they are taken off a respirator, and so will soon be dead by anyone's standard. People in a persistent vegetative state, on the other hand, may continue to breathe without mechanical assistance. To call for the undertakers to bury a "dead" patient who is still breathing would be a bit too much for anyone to swallow.

We all know that the redefinition of death proposed by the Harvard Brain Death Committee triumphed. By 1981, when the United States President's Commission for the Study of Ethical Problems in Medicine examined the issue, it could write of "the emergence of a medical consensus" around criteria very like those proposed by the Harvard committee.[4] Already, people whose brains had irreversibly ceased to function were considered legally dead in at least fifteen countries, and in more than half of the states of the United States. In some countries, including Britain, Parliament had not even been involved in the change: the medical profession had simply adopted a new set of criteria on the basis of which doctors certified a patient dead.[5] This was truly a revolution without opposition.

The redefinition of death in terms of brain death went through so smoothly because it did not harm the brain-dead patients and it benefited everyone else: the families of brain-dead patients, the hospitals, the transplant surgeons, people needing transplants, people who worried that they might one day need a transplant, people who feared that they might one day be kept on a respirator after their brain had died, taxpayers, and the government. The general public understood that if the brain has been destroyed, there can be no recovery of consciousness, and so there is no point in maintaining the body. Defining such people as dead was a convenient way around the problems of making their organs available for transplantation, and withdrawing treatment from them.

But does this way round the problems really work? On one level, it does. By the early 1990s as Sweden and Denmark, the last European nations to cling to the traditional standard, adopted brain death definitions of death, this verdict appeared to be confirmed. Among developed nations, only Japan was still holding out. But do people really think of the brain dead as *dead*? The Harvard Brain Death Committee itself couldn't quite swallow the implications of what it was recommending. As we have seen, it described patients whose brains have ceased to function as in an "irreversible coma" and said that being kept on a respirator was a burden to them. Dead people are not in a coma, they are dead, and nothing can be a burden to them any more.

Perhaps the lapses in the thinking of the Harvard committee can be pardoned because the concept of brain death was then so new. But twenty-five years later, little has changed. Only last year the *Miami Herald* ran a story headlined "Brain-Dead Woman Kept Alive in Hopes She'll Bear Child"; while after the same woman did bear her child, the *San Francisco Chronicle* reported: "Brain-Dead Woman Gives Birth, then Dies". Nor can we blame this entirely on the lamentable ignorance of the popular press. A study of doctors and nurses who work with brain-dead patients at hospitals in Cleveland, Ohio, showed that one in three of them thought that people whose brains had died could be classified as dead because they were "irreversibly dying" or because they had an "unacceptable quality of life".[6]

Why do both journalists and members of the health care professions talk in a way that denies that brain death is really death? One possible explanation is that, even though people know that the brain dead are dead, it is just too difficult for them to abandon obsolete ways of thinking about death. Another possible explanation is that people have enough common sense to see that the brain dead are not really dead. I favour this second explanation. The brain death criterion of death is nothing other than a convenient fiction. It was proposed and accepted because it makes it possible for us to salvage organs that would

otherwise be wasted, and to withdraw medical treatment when it is doing no good. On this basis, it might seem that, despite some fundamental weaknesses, the survival prospects of the concept of brain death are good. But there are two reasons why our present understanding of brain death is not stable. Advances in medical knowledge and technology are the driving factors.

To understand the first problem with the present concept of brain death, we have to recall that brain death is generally defined as the irreversible cessation of all functions of the brain.[7] In accordance with this definition, a standard set of tests are used by doctors to establish that all functions of the brain have irreversibly ceased. These tests are broadly in line with those recommended in 1968 by the Harvard Brain Death Committee, but they have been further refined and updated over the years in various countries. In the past ten years, however, as doctors have sought ways of managing brain-dead patients, so that their organs (or in some cases, their pregnancies) could be sustained for a longer time, it has become apparent that, even when the usual tests show that brain death has occurred, *some brain functions continue*. We think of the brain primarily as concerned with processing information through the senses and the nervous system, but the brain has other functions as well. One of these is to supply various hormones that help to regulate several bodily functions. We now know that some of these hormones continue to be supplied by the brains of most patients who, by the standard tests, are brain dead. Moreover, when brain-dead patients are cut open in order to remove organs, their blood pressure may rise and their heartbeat quicken. These reactions mean that the brain is still carrying out some of its functions, regulating the responses of the body in various ways. As a result, the legal definition of brain death, and current medical practice in certifying brain-dead people as dead, have come apart.[8]

It would be possible to bring medical practice into line with the current definition of death in terms of the irreversible cessation of *all* brain function. Doctors would then have to test for all brain functions, including hormonal functions, before declaring someone dead. This would mean that some people who are now declared brain dead would be considered alive, and therefore would have to continue to be supported on a respirator, at significant cost, both financially and in terms of the extended distress of the family. Since the tests are expensive to carry out and time-consuming in themselves, continued support would be necessary during the period in which they are carried out, even if in the end the results showed that the person had no brain function at all. In addition, during this period, the person's organs would deteriorate, and may therefore not be usable for transplantation. What gains would there be to balance against these serious disadvantages? From the perspective of an adherent of the sanctity of life ethic, of course, the gain is that we are no longer killing people by cutting out their hearts while they are still alive. If one really believed that the quality of a human life makes no difference to the wrongness of ending that life, this would end the discussion. There would be no ethical alternative. But it would still be true that not a single person who was kept longer on a respirator because of the need to test for hormonal brain functioning would ever return to consciousness.

So if it is life with consciousness, rather than life itself, that we value, then bringing medical practice into line with the definition of death does not seem a good idea. It would be better to bring the definition of brain death into line with current medical practice. But once we move away from the idea of brain death as the irreversible cessation of *all* brain functioning, what are we to put in its place? Which functions of the brain will we take as marking the difference between life and death, and why?

The most plausible answer is that the brain functions that really matter are those related to consciousness. On this view, what we really care about – and ought to care about – is *the person* rather than the body. Accordingly, it is the permanent cessation of function of the cerebral cortex, not of the whole brain, that should be taken as the criterion of death. Several reasons could be offered to justify this step. First, although the Harvard Brain Death Committee specified that its recommendations applied only to those who have "no discernible central nervous system activity", the arguments it put forward for its redefinition of death applied in every respect to patients who are permanently without any awareness, whether or not they have some brainstem function. This seems to have been no accident, for it reflected the view of

the committee's chairman, Henry Beecher, who in his address to the American Association for the Advancement of Science, from which I have already quoted, said that what is essential to human nature is:

> the individual's personality, his conscious life, his uniqueness, his capacity for remembering, judging, reasoning, acting, enjoying, worrying, and so on …[9]

As I have already said, when the Harvard Committee issued its report, the irreversible destruction of the parts of the brain associated with consciousness could not reliably be diagnosed if the brainstem was alive. Since then, however, the technology for obtaining images of soft tissues within the body has made enormous progress. Hence a major stumbling block to the acceptance of a higher brain definition of death has already been greatly diminished in its scope, and will soon disappear altogether.

Now that medical certainty on the irreversibility of loss of higher brain functions can be established in at least some cases, the inherent logic of pushing the definition of death one step further has already led, in the United States, to one Supreme Court judge suggesting that the law could consider a person who has irreversibly lost consciousness to be no longer alive. Here is Mr Justice Stevens, giving his judgement in the case of Nancy Cruzan, a woman who had been unconscious for eight years and whose guardians sought court permission to withdraw tube feeding of food and fluids so that she could die:

> But for patients like Nancy Cruzan, who have no consciousness and no chance of recovery, there is a serious question as to whether the mere persistence of their bodies is "life", as that word is commonly understood… The State's unflagging determination to perpetuate Nancy Cruzan's physical existence is comprehensible only as an effort to define life's meaning, not as an attempt to preserve its sanctity…In any event, absent some theological abstraction, the idea of life is not conceived separately from the idea of a living person.[10]

Admittedly, this was a dissenting judgement; the majority decided the case on narrow constitutional grounds that are not relevant to our concerns here, and what Stevens said has not become part of the law of the United States. Nevertheless, dissenting judgements are often a way of floating an idea that is "in the air" and may become part of the majority view in a later decision. As medical opinion increasingly comes to accept that we can reliably establish when consciousness has been irreversibly lost, the pressure will become more intense for medical practice to move to a definition of death based on the death of the higher brain.

Yet there is a very fundamental flaw in the idea of moving to a higher brain definition of death. If, as we have seen, people already have difficulty in accepting that a warm body with a beating heart on a respirator is really dead, how much more difficult would it be to bury a "corpse" that is still breathing while the lid of the coffin is nailed down? That is simply an absurdity. Something has gone wrong. But what?

In my view, the trouble began with the move to brain death. The Harvard Brain Death Committee was faced with two serious problems. Patients in an utterly hopeless condition were attached to respirators, and no one dared to turn them off; and organs that could be used to save lives were rendered useless by the delays caused by waiting for the circulation of the blood in potential donors to stop. The committee tried to solve both these problems by the bold expedient of classifying as dead those whose brains had ceased to have any discernible activity. The consequences of the redefinition of death were so evidently desirable that it met with scarcely any opposition, and was accepted almost universally. Nevertheless, it was unsound from the start. Solving problems by redefinition rarely works, and this case was no exception. We need to begin again, with a different approach to the original problems, one which will break out of the intellectual strait-jacket of the traditional belief that all human life is of equal value. Until last year, it seemed difficult to imagine how a different approach could ever be accepted. But last year Britain's highest court took a major step toward just such a new approach.

III   Revolution by the Law Lords: The Case of Anthony Bland

The revolution in British law regarding the sanctity of human life grew out of the tragedy at Hillsborough Football Stadium in Sheffield, in April 1989. Liverpool was playing Nottingham Forest in an FA Cup semi-final. As the match started, thousands of supporters were still trying to get into the ground. A fatal crush occurred against some fencing that had been erected to stop fans getting onto the playing field. Before order could be restored and the pressure relieved, 95 people had died in the worst disaster in British sporting history. Tony Bland, a 17-year-old Liverpool fan, was not killed, but his lungs were crushed by the pressure of the crowd around him, and his brain was deprived of oxygen. Taken to hospital, it was found that only his brain-stem had survived. His cortex had been destroyed. Here is how Lord Justice Hoffmann was later to describe his condition:

> Since April 15 1989 Anthony Bland has been in persistent vegetative state. He lies in Airedale General Hospital in Keighley, fed liquid food by a pump through a tube passing through his nose and down the back of his throat into the stomach. His bladder is emptied through a catheter inserted through his penis, which from time to time has caused infections requiring dressing and antibiotic treatment. His stiffened joints have caused his limbs to be rigidly contracted so that his arms are tightly flexed across his chest and his legs unnaturally contorted. Reflex movements in the throat cause him to vomit and dribble. Of all this, and the presence of members of his family who take turns to visit him, Anthony Bland has no consciousness at all. The parts of his brain which provided him with consciousness have turned to fluid. The darkness and oblivion which descended at Hillsborough will never depart. His body is alive, but he has no life in the sense that even the most pitifully handicapped but conscious human being has a life. But the advances of modern medicine permit him to be kept in this state for years, even perhaps for decades.[11]

Whatever the advances of modern medicine might permit, neither Tony Bland's family nor his doctors could see any benefit to him or to anyone else, in keeping him alive for decades. In Britain, as in many other countries, when everyone is in agreement in these situations it is quite common for the doctors simply to withdraw artificial feeding. The patient then dies within a week or two. In this case, however, the coroner in Sheffield was inquiring into the deaths caused by the Hillsborough disaster, and Dr Howe decided that he should notify the coroner of what he was intending to do. The coroner, while agreeing that

Bland's continued existence could well be seen as entirely pointless, warned Dr Howe that he was running the risk of criminal charges – possibly even a charge of murder – if he intentionally ended Bland's life.

After the coroner's warning, the administrator of the hospital in which Bland was a patient applied to the Family Division of the High Court for declarations that the hospital might lawfully discontinue all life-sustaining treatment, including ventilation, and the provision of food and water by artificial means, and discontinue all medical treatment to Bland "except for the sole purpose of enabling Anthony Bland to end his life and to die peacefully with the greatest dignity and the least distress".

At the Family Division hearing a public law officer called the Official Solicitor was appointed guardian for Bland for the purposes of the hearing. The Official Solicitor did not deny that Bland had no awareness at all, and could never recover, but he nevertheless opposed what Dr Howe was planning to do, arguing that, legally, it was murder. Sir Stephen Brown, President of the Family Division, did not accept this view, and he made the requested declarations to the effect that all treatment might lawfully be stopped. The Official Solicitor appealed, but Brown's decision was upheld by the Court of Appeal. The Official Solicitor then appealed again, thus bringing the case before the House of Lords.

We can best appreciate the significance of what the House of Lords did in the case of Tony Bland by looking at what the United States Supreme Court would not do in the similar case of Nancy Cruzan. Like Bland, Cruzan was in a persistent vegetative state, without hope of recovery. Her parents went to court to get permission to remove her feeding tube. The Missouri Supreme Court refused, saying that since Nancy Cruzan was not competent to refuse life-sustaining treatment herself, and the state has an interest in preserving life, the court could only give permission for the withdrawal of life-sustaining treatment if there were clear and convincing evidence that this was what Cruzan would have wanted. No such evidence had been presented to the court. On appeal the United States Supreme Court upheld this judgement, ruling that the state of Missouri had a right to require clear and convincing evidence that

Cruzan would have wanted to be allowed to die, before permitting doctors to take that step. (By a curious coincidence, that evidence was produced in court shortly after the Supreme Court decision, and Cruzan was allowed to die.)

The essential point here is that in America the courts have so far taken it for granted that life-support must be continued, *unless* there is evidence indicating that the patient would not have wished to be kept alive in the circumstances in which she now is. In contrast, the British courts were quite untroubled by the absence of any information about what Bland's wishes might have been. As Sir Thomas Bingham, Master of the Rolls of the Court of Appeal, said in delivering his judgement:

> At no time before the disaster did Mr Bland give any indication of his wishes should he find himself in such a condition. It is not a topic most adolescents address.[12]

But the British courts did not therefore conclude that Bland must be treated until he died of old age. Instead, the British judges asked a different question: what is in the best interests of the patient?[13] In answer, they referred to the unanimous medical opinion that Bland was not aware of anything, and that there was no prospect of any improvement in his condition. Hence the treatment that was sustaining Bland's life brought him, as Sir Stephen Brown put it in the initial judgement in the case, "no therapeutical, medical, or other benefit".[14] In essence, the British courts held that when a patient is incapable of consenting to medical treatment, doctors are under no legal duty to continue treatment that does not benefit a patient. In addition, the judges agreed that the mere continuation of biological life is not, in the absence of any awareness or any hope of ever again becoming aware, a benefit to the patient.

On one level, the British approach is straight-forward common sense. But it is common sense that breaks new legal ground. To see this, consider the following quotation from John Keown:

> Traditional medical ethics...never asks whether the patient's *life* is worthwhile, for the notion of a worthless life is as alien to the Hippocratic tradition as it is to English criminal law, both of which subscribe to the

principle of the sanctity of human life which holds that, because all lives are intrinsically valuable, it is always wrong intentionally to kill an innocent human being.[15]

As a statement of traditional medical ethics and traditional English criminal law, this is right. The significance of the *Bland* decision is that it openly embraces the previously alien idea of a worthless life. Sir Thomas Bingham, for example, said:

> Looking at the matter as objectively as I can, and doing my best to look at the matter through Mr Bland's eyes and not my own, I cannot conceive what benefit his continued existence could be thought to give him…[16]

When the case came before the House of Lords, Their Lordships took the same view. Lord Keith of Kinkel discussed the difficulties of making a value judgement about the life of a "permanently insensate" being, and concluded cautiously that:

> It is, however, perhaps permissible to say that to an individual with no cognitive capacity whatever, and no prospect of ever recovering any such capacity in this world, it must be a matter of complete indifference whether he lives or dies.[17]

In a similar vein, Lord Mustill concluded that to withdraw life-support is not only legally, but also ethically justified, "since the continued treatment of Anthony Bland can no longer serve to maintain that combination of manifold characteristics which we call a personality".[18]

There can therefore be no doubt that, with the decision in the Bland case, British law has abandoned the idea that life itself is a benefit to the person living it, irrespective of its quality. But that is not all that Their Lordships did in deciding Tony Bland's fate. The second novel aspect of their decision is that it was as plain as anything can be that the proposal to discontinue tube feeding was *intended* to bring about Bland's death. A majority of the judges in the House of Lords referred to the administrator's intention in very direct terms. Lord Browne-Wilkinson said:

> What is proposed in the present case is to adopt a course with the intention of bringing about Anthony Bland's

death…the whole purpose of stopping artificial feeding is to bring about the death of Anthony Bland.[19]

Lord Mustill was equally explicit:

> the proposed conduct has the aim for…humane reasons of terminating the life of Anthony Bland by withholding from him the basic necessities of life.[20]

This marks a sharp contrast to what for many years was considered the definitive view of what a doctor may permissibly intend. Traditionally the law had held that while a doctor may knowingly do something that has the effect of shortening life, this must always be a mere side-effect of an action with a different purpose, for example, relieving pain. As Justice (later Lord) Devlin said in the celebrated trial of Dr John Bodkin Adams:

> it remains the fact, and it remains the law, that no doctor, nor any man, no more in the case of the dying than of the healthy, has the right deliberately to cut the thread of human life.[21]

In rewriting the law of murder regarding the question of intention, the British law lords have shown a clarity and forthrightness that should serve as a model to many others who try to muddle through difficult questions by having a little bit of both sides. There is no talk here of ordinary and extraordinary means of treatment, nor of what is directly intended and what is merely foreseen. Instead the judges declared that Bland's doctors were entitled to take a course of action that had Bland's death as its "whole purpose"; and they made this declaration on the basis of a judgement that prolonging Bland's life did not benefit him.

Granted, this very clarity forces on us a further question: does the decision allow doctors to kill their patients? On the basis of what we have seen so far, this conclusion seems inescapable. Their Lordships, however, did not think they were legalizing euthanasia. They drew a distinction between ending life by actively doing something, and ending life by not providing treatment needed to sustain life. That distinction has long been discussed by philosophers and bioethicists, who debate whether it can make good sense to accept passive euthanasia while rejecting active euthanasia. In the *Bland* case, it is significant that, while the law lords insist that in distinguishing between acts and omissions they are merely applying the law as it stands, they explicitly recognize that at this point law and ethics have come apart, and something needs to be done about it. Lord Browne-Wilkinson, for example, expressed the hope that Parliament would review the law. He then ended his judgement by admitting that he could not provide a moral basis for the legal decision he had reached! Lord Mustill was just as frank and even more uncomfortable about the state of the law, saying that the judgement, in which he had shared, "may only emphasize the distortions of a legal structure which is already both morally and intellectually misshapen".[22]

The law lords' problem was that they had inherited a legal framework that allowed them some room to manoeuvre, but not a great deal. Within that framework, they did what they could to reach a sensible decision in the case of Anthony Bland, and to point the law in a new direction that other judges could follow. In doing so, they recognized the moral incoherence of the position they were taking, but found themselves unable to do anything about it, beyond drawing the problem to the attention of Parliament. They could hardly have done more to show clearly the need for a new approach to life-and-death decisions.

IV Conclusion

What is the link between the problems we face in regard to the concept of brain death, and the decision reached by Their Lordships in the case of Tony Bland? The link becomes clearer once we distinguish between three separate questions, often muddled in discussions of brain death and related issues:

1. When does a human being die?
2. When is it permissible for doctors intentionally to end the life of a patient?

3. When is it permissible to remove organs such as the heart from a human being for the purpose of transplantation to another human being?

Before 1968, in accordance with the traditional concept of death, the answer to the first question would have been: when the circulation of the blood stops permanently, with the consequent cessation of breathing, of a pulse, and so on.[23] The answer to the second question would then have been very simple: never. And the answer to the third question would have been equally plain: when the human being is dead.

The acceptance of the concept of brain death enabled us to hold constant the straightforward answers to questions 2 and 3, while making what was presented as no more than a scientific updating of a concept of death rendered obsolete by technological advances in medicine. Thus no ethical question appeared to be at issue, but suddenly hearts could be removed from, and machines turned off on, a whole new group of human beings.

The *Bland* decision says nothing about questions 1 and 3, but dramatically changes the answer that British law gives to question 2. The simple "never" now becomes "when the patient's continued life is of no benefit to her": and if we ask when a patient's life is of no benefit to her, the answer is: "when the patient is irreversibly unconscious". If we accept this as a sound answer to question 2, however, we may well wish to give the same answer to question 3. Why not, after all? And if we now have answered both question 2 and question 3 by reference not to the death of the patient, but to the impossibility of the patient regaining consciousness, then question 1 suddenly becomes much less relevant to the concerns that the Harvard Brain Death Committee was trying to address. We could therefore abandon the redefinition of death that it pioneered, with all the problems that have now arisen for the brain death criterion. Nor would we feel any pressure to move a step further, to defining death in terms of the death of the higher brain, or cerebral cortex. Instead, we could, without causing any problems in the procurement of organs or the withdrawal of life-support, go back to the traditional conception of death in terms of the irreversible cessation of the circulation of the blood.[24]

Notes

1   Henry Beecher to Robert Ebert, 30 October 1967. The letter is in the Henry Beecher Manuscripts at the Francis A. Countway Library of Medicine, Harvard University, and is quoted by David Rothman, *Strangers at the Bedside* (New York: Basic Books, 1991), pp. 160–1.

2   The first draft and Ebert's comment on it are both quoted by Rothman, *Strangers at the Bedside*, pp. 162–4. The documents are in the Beecher Manuscript collection.

3   Henry Beecher, "The New Definition of Death, Some Opposing Viewpoints", *International Journal of Clinical Pharmacology*, 5 (1971), pp. 120–1 (italics in original).

4   President's Commission for the Study of Ethical Problems in Medicine, *Defining Death: A Report on the Medical, Legal and Ethical Issues in the Determination of Death* (Washington, DC: US, Government Printing Office, 1981), pp. 24, 25.

5   *Defining Death*, pp. 67, 72.

6   Stuart Youngner et al., "'Brain Death' and Organ Retrieval: A Cross-sectional Survey of Knowledge and Concepts Among Health Professionals", *Journal of the American Medical Association*, 261 (1990), 2209.

7   See, for example, the United States Uniform Determination of Death Act. Note that the Harvard committee had referred to the absence of central nervous system "activity" rather than function. The use of the term "function" rather than "activity" makes the definition of brain death more permissive, because, as the United States President's Commission recognized (*Defining Death*, p. 74), electrical and metabolic activity may continue in cells or groups of cells after the organ has ceased to function. The Commission did not think that the continuation of this activity should prevent a declaration of death.

8   Robert Truog, "Rethinking brain death", in K. Sanders and B. Moore (eds), *Anencephalics, Infants and Brain Death Treatment Options and the Issue of Organ Donation* (Law Reform Commission of Victoria, Melbourne, 1991), pp. 62–74; Amir Halevy and Baruch

Brody, "Brain Death: Reconciling Definitions, Criteria and Tests", *Annals of Internal Medicine*, 119 6 (1993), 519–25; Robert Veatch, "The Impending Collapse of the Whole-Brain Definition of Death", *Hastings Center Report*, 23 4 (1993), 18–24.

9   Henry Beecher, "The New Definition of Death, Some Opposing Views", unpublished paper presented at the meeting of the American Association for the Advancement of Science, December 1970, p. 4, quoted from Robert Veatch, *Death, Dying and the Biological Revolution* (New Haven: Yale University Press, 1976), p. 39.

10 *Cruzan v. Director, Missouri Department of Health* (1990) 110 S. Ct. pp. 2886–7.

11 *Airedale NHS, Trust v. Bland (C.A)* (19 February 1993) 2 Weekly Law Reports, p. 350.

12 Ibid., p. 333; the passage was quoted again by Lord Goff of Chieveley in his judgement in the House of Lords, p. 364.

13 Ibid., pp. 374, 386.

14 Ibid., p. 331.

15 John Keown, "Courting Euthanasia? Tony Bland and the Law Lords", *Ethics & Medicine*, 9 3 (1993), 36.

16 *Airedale NHS Trust v Bland*, p. 339.

17 Ibid., p. 361.

18 Ibid., p. 400.

19 Ibid., p. 383.

20 Ibid., p. 388.

21 *R. v. Adams* (1959), quoted by Derek Morgan, "Letting babies die legally", *Institute of Medical Ethics Bulletin* (May 1989), p. 13. See also Patrick Devlin, *Easing the Passing: The Trial of Dr John Bodkin Adams* (London: Faber and Faber, 1986), pp. 171, 209.

22 *Aircdale NHS Trust v. Bland*, pp. 388–9.

23 For a statement of the traditional definition, see, for example, *Blacks Law Dictionary*, 4th edn (West Publishing Company, 1968).

24 This address incorporates material subsequently published in my book *Rethinking Life and Death* (Melbourne: Text, 1994; St Martin's Press, 1995).

Advance Directives

35

Life Past Reason

Ronald Dworkin

We turn finally to what might be the saddest of the tragedies we have been reviewing. We must consider the autonomy and best interests of people who suffer from serious and permanent dementia, and what the proper respect for the intrinsic value of *their* lives requires. The most important cause of dementia is Alzheimer's disease, a progressive disease of the brain named after a German psychiatrist and neuropathologist, Alois Alzheimer, who first identified and described it in 1906. Patients in the late stages of this disease have lost substantially all memory of their earlier lives and cannot, except perodically and in only a fragmented way, recognize or respond to other people, even those to whom they were formerly close. They may be incapable of saying more than a word or two. They are often incontinent, fall frequently, or are unable to walk at all. They are incapable of sustaining plans or projects or desires of even a very simple structure. They express wishes and desires, but these change rapidly and often show very little continuity even over periods of days or hours.

Alzheimer's is a disease of physiological deterioration. Nerve terminals of the brain degenerate into a matted plaque of fibrous material. Though researchers have expressed some hope that treatment can be developed to slow that degeneration,[1] no such treatment has yet been established, and there is apparently little prospect of dramatically reversing very advanced brain deterioration. A specialist describes the degeneration as occurring "gradually and inexorably, usually leading to death in a severely debilitated, immobile state between four and twelve years after onset."[2] But according to the US Office of Technology Assessment, death may be delayed for as long as twenty-five years.[3]

Our discussion will focus only on the disease's late stages. I shall not consider, except in passing, the present structure of legal rights and other provisions for demented or mentally incapacitated people, or the present practices of doctors and other custodians or officials who are charged with their care. Nor shall I attempt any report of the recent research into genetic and other features of such diseases, or into their diagnosis, prognosis, or treatment. All these are the subjects of a full literature.[4] I will concentrate on the question of what moral rights people in the late stages of dementia have or retain, and of what is best for them. Is some minimum level of mental competence essential to having any rights at all? Do mentally incapacitated people have the same rights as normally competent people, or are their rights altered or diminished or extended in some way in virtue of their disease? Do they, for example, have the same rights to autonomy, to the care of their custodians, to dignity, and to a minimum level of resources as sick people of normal mental competence?

Original publication details: Ronald Dworkin, "Life Past Reason," pp. 218–29 from *Life's Dominion: An Argument about Abortion, Euthanasia, and Individual Freedom*, New York: Knopf, 1993. Copyright © 1993 by Ronald Dworkin. Used by permission of Alfred A. Knopf, an imprint of the Knopf Doubleday Publishing Group, a division of Random House LLC. All rights reserved.

Bioethics: An Anthology, Third Edition. Edited by Helga Kuhse, Udo Schüklenk, and Peter Singer.
© 2016 John Wiley & Sons, Inc. Published 2016 by John Wiley & Sons, Inc.

These are questions of great and growing importance. In 1990, the Alzheimer's Association estimated that four million Americans had the disease, and as Alzheimer's is a disease of the elderly, the number is expected to increase as the population continues to age. In 1989, a Harvard Medical School study estimated that 11.3 percent of the American population sixty-five or over probably had Alzheimer's. The estimated prevalence increased sharply with age: 16.4 percent of people between seventy-five and eighty-four were estimated to have Alzheimer's, and a stunning 47.55 percent of those over eighty-five.[5] (Other studies, using a narrower definition of the disease, suggest a significantly lesser but still alarming prevalence.[6]) The incidence of the disease is comparable in other countries. According to the Alzheimer's Disease Society in Britain, for example, 20 percent of people over eighty are afflicted, more than half a million people have the disease, and that figure will rise to three-quarters of a million in thirty years.[7] Alzheimer's cost is staggering, both for the community and for individuals. Dennis Selkoe, a leading expert on the disease, said in 1991, "The cost to American society for diagnosing and managing Alzheimer's disease, primarily for custodial care, is currently estimated at more than $80 billion annually."[8] In 1992, the annual cost of nursing home care in the United States for one individual with Alzheimer's ranged from $35,000 to $52,000.[9]

Each of the millions of Alzheimer's cases is horrible, for the victims and for those who love and care for them. A recent book dedicated "to everyone who gives a '36-hour day' to the care of a person with a dementing illness" describes the lives of some of these patients in chilling detail, not just in the final, immobile last stages, but along the way.

> Often, Mary was afraid, a nameless shapeless fear.... People came, memories came, and then they slipped away. She could not tell what was reality and what was memory of things past.... The tub was a mystery. From day to day she could not remember how to manage the water: sometimes it all ran away, sometimes it kept rising and rising so that she could not stop it.... Mary was glad when her family came to visit. Sometimes she remembered their names, more often she did not.... She liked it best when they just held her and loved her.

> Even though Miss Ramirez had told her sister over and over that today was the day to visit the doctor, her sister would not get into the car until she was dragged in, screaming, by two neighbors. All the way to the doctor's office she shouted for help and when she got there she tried to run away.

> Mr. Lewis suddenly burst into tears as he tried to tie his shoelaces. He threw the shoes in the wastebasket and locked himself, sobbing, in the bathroom.[10]

When Andrew Firlik was a medical student, he met a fifty-four-year-old Alzheimer's victim whom he called Margo, and he began to visit her daily in her apartment, where she was cared for by an attendant. The apartment had many locks to keep Margo from slipping out at night and wandering in the park in a nightgown, which she had done before. Margo said she knew who Firlik was each time he arrived, but she never used his name, and he suspected that this was just politeness. She said she was reading mysteries, but Firlik "noticed that her place in the book jumps randomly from day to day; dozens of pages are dog-eared at any given moment.... Maybe she feels good just sitting and humming to herself, rocking back and forth slowly, nodding off liberally, occasionally turning to a fresh page." Margo attended an art class for Alzheimer's victims – they all, including her, painted pretty much the same picture every time, except near the end, just before death, when the pictures became more primitive. Firlik was confused, he said, by the fact that "despite her illness, or maybe somehow because of it, Margo is undeniably one of the happiest people I have ever known." He reports, particularly, her pleasure at eating peanut-butter-and-jelly sandwiches. But, he asks, "When a person can no longer accumulate new memories as the old rapidly fade, what remains? Who is Margo?"[11]

I must now repeat an observation that I have made before: we are considering the rights and interests not of someone who has always been demented, but of someone who was competent in the past. We may therefore think of that person, in considering his rights and interests, in two different ways: as a *demented* person, emphasizing his present situation and capacities, or as a person who has *become* demented, having an eye to the course of his whole life. Does a competent person's right to autonomy include, for example, the power to dictate that life-prolonging treatment be denied him later, or that funds not be spent on maintaining him in great comfort, even if he, when demented, pleads for it? Should what is done for him then be in his contemporary best interests, to make the rest of his life as pleasant and comfortable as possible, or in the best interests of the person he has been? Suppose a demented patient insists on remaining at home, rather than living in an institution, though this would impose very great burdens on his family, and that we all agree that people lead critically better lives when they are not a serious burden to others. Is it really in his best interests, overall, to allow him to become such a burden?

A person's dignity is normally connected to his capacity for self-respect. Should we care about the dignity of a dementia patient if he himself has no sense of it? That seems to depend on whether his past dignity, as a competent person, is in some way still implicated. If it is, then we may take his former capacity for self-respect as requiring that he be treated with dignity now; we may say that dignity now is necessary to show respect for his life as a whole. Many prominent issues about the rights of the demented, then, depend on how their interests now relate to those of their past, competent selves.[12]

Autonomy

It is generally agreed that adult citizens of normal competence have a right to autonomy, that is, a right to make important decisions defining their own lives for themselves. Competent adults are free to make poor investments, provided others do not deceive or withhold information from them, and smokers are allowed to smoke in private, though cigarette advertising must warn them of the dangers of doing so. This autonomy is often at stake in medical contexts.[13] A Jehovah's Witness, for example, may refuse blood transfusions necessary to save his life because transfusions offend his religious convictions. A patient whose life can be saved only if his legs are amputated but who prefers to die soon than to live a life without legs is allowed to refuse the operation. American law generally recognizes a patient's right to

autonomy in circumstances like those.[14] But when is that right lost? How far, for example, do mentally incapacitated people have a right to make decisions for themselves that others would deem not in their best interests?[15] Should Mary, the woman who couldn't recognize relatives or manage a tub, be allowed to spend or give away her money as she wishes, or to choose her own doctors, or to refuse prescribed medical treatment, or to decide which relative is appointed as her guardian? Should she be allowed to insist that she be cared for at home, in spite of her family's opinion that she would get better care in an institution?

There may, of course, be some other reason, beyond autonomy, for allowing Mary and other demented people to do as they please. For example, if they are prevented from doing as they wish, they may become so agitated that we do them more harm than good by opposing them, even though the decision they make is not itself in their interests. But do we have reason to respect their decision even when this is not so, even when we think it would be in their best interests, all things considered, to take some decision out of their hands?

We cannot answer that question without reflecting on the point of autonomy, that is, on the question of why we should ever respect the decisions people make when we believe that these are not in their interests. One popular answer might be called the *evidentiary* view: it holds that we should respect the decisions people make for themselves, even when we regard these decisions as imprudent, because each person generally knows what is in his own best interests better than anyone else.[16] Though we often think that someone has made a mistake in judging what is in his own interests, experience teaches us that in most cases we are wrong to think this. So we do better, in the long run, to recognize a general right to autonomy, which we always respect, than by reserving the right to interfere with other people's lives whenever we think they have made a mistake.

If we accepted this evidentiary account of autonomy, we would not extend the right of autonomy to decisions made by the seriously demented, who, having altogether lost the power to appreciate and engage in reasoning and argument, cannot possibly know what is in their own best interests as well as trained specialists, like doctors, can. In some cases, any presumption that demented people know their own interests best would be incoherent: when, for example, as is often the case, their wishes and decisions change radically from one bout of lucidity to another.

But in fact the evidentiary view of autonomy is very far from compelling. For autonomy requires us to allow someone to run his own life even when he behaves in a way that he himself would accept as not at all in his interests.[17] This is sometimes a matter of what philosophers call "weakness of the will." Many people who smoke know that smoking, all things considered, is not in their best interests, but they smoke anyway. If we believe, as we do, that respecting their autonomy means allowing them to act in this way, we cannot accept that the point of autonomy is to protect an agent's welfare. And there are more admirable reasons for acting against what one believes to be in one's own best interests. Some people refuse needed medical treatment because they believe that other people, who would then have to go without it, need it more. Such people act out of convictions we admire, even if we do not act the same way, and autonomy requires us to respect their decisions. Once again, the supposed explanation of the right to autonomy — that it promotes the welfare of people making apparently imprudent decisions — fails to account for our convictions about when people have that right. All this suggests that the point of autonomy must be, at least to some degree, independent of the claim that a person generally knows his own best interests better than anyone else. And then it would not follow, just because a demented person may well be mistaken about his own best interests, that others are entitled to decide for him. Perhaps the demented have a right to autonomy after all.

But we must try to find another, more plausible account of the point of autonomy, and ask whether the demented would have a right to autonomy according to it. The most plausible alternative emphasizes the integrity rather than the welfare of the choosing agent; the value of autonomy, on this view, derives from the capacity it protects: the capacity to express one's own character — values, commitments, convictions, and critical as well as experiential interests — in the life one leads. Recognizing an individual right of autonomy makes self-creation possible. It allows each of us to be responsible for shaping our lives according to our own coherent or incoherent — but, in any case, distinctive — personality. It allows us to lead our own lives rather than be led along them, so that each of us can be, to the extent a scheme of rights can make this possible, what we have made of ourselves. We allow someone to choose death over radical amputation or a blood transfusion, if that is his informed wish, because we acknowledge his right to a life structured by his own values.

The integrity view of autonomy does not assume that competent people have consistent values or always make consistent choices, or that they always lead structured, reflective lives. It recognizes that people often make choices that reflect weakness, indecision, caprice, or plain irrationality — that some people otherwise fanatical about their health continue to smoke, for example. Any plausible integrity-based theory of autonomy must distinguish between the general point or value of autonomy and its consequences for a particular person on a particular occasion. Autonomy encourages and protects people's general capacity to lead their lives out of a distinctive sense of their own character, a sense of what is important to and for them. Perhaps one principal value of that capacity is realized only when a life does in fact display a general, overall integrity and authenticity. But the right to autonomy protects and encourages the capacity in any event, by allowing people who have it to choose how far and in what form they will seek to realize that aim.

If we accept this integrity-based view of the importance of autonomy, our judgement about whether incapacitated patients have a right to autonomy will turn on the degree of their general capacity to lead a life in that sense. When a mildly demented person's choices are reasonably stable, reasonably continuous with the general character of his prior life, and inconsistent and self-defeating only to the rough degree that the choices of fully competent people are, he can be seen as still in charge of his life, and he has a right to autonomy for that reason. But if his choices and demands, no matter how firmly expressed, systematically or randomly contradict one another, reflecting no coherent sense of self and no discernible even short-term aims, then he has presumably lost the capacity that it is the point of autonomy to protect.

Recognizing a continuing right to autonomy for him would be pointless. He has no right that his choices about a guardian (or the use of his property, or his medical treatment, or whether he remains at home) be respected for reasons of autonomy. He still has the right to beneficence, the right that decisions on these matters be made in his best interests; and his preferences may, for different reasons, be important in deciding what his best interests are. But he no longer has the right, as competent people do, himself to decide contrary to those interests.

"Competence" is sometimes used in a task-specific sense, to refer to the ability to grasp and manipulate information bearing on a given problem. Competence in that sense varies, sometimes greatly, even among ordinary, nondemented people; I may be more competent than you at making some decisions and less competent at others. The medical literature concerning surrogate decision making for the demented points out, properly, that competence in this task-specific sense is relative to the character and complexity of the decision in question.[18] A patient who is not competent to administer his complex business affairs may nevertheless be able to grasp and appreciate information bearing on whether he should remain at home or enter an institution, for example.

But competence in the sense in which it is presupposed by the right to autonomy is a very different matter. It means the more diffuse and general ability I described: the ability to act out of genuine preference or character or conviction or a sense of self. There will, of course, be hard cases in which we cannot know with any confidence whether a particular dementia patient is competent in that sense. But we must make that overall judgement, not some combination of judgements about specific task capability, in order to decide whether some mentally incapacitated patient has a right to autonomy.[19] Patients like Mary have no right that *any* decision be respected just out of concern for their autonomy. That may sound harsh, but it is no kindness to allow a person to take decisions against his own interests in order to protect a capacity he does not and cannot have.

So neither the evidentiary view of autonomy nor the more plausible integrity view recommends any right to autonomy for the seriously demented. But what about a patient's *precedent* autonomy? Suppose a patient is incompetent in the general, overall sense but that years ago, when perfectly competent, he executed a living will providing for what he plainly does not want now. Suppose, for example, that years ago, when fully competent, Margo had executed a formal document directing that if she should develop Alzheimer's disease, all her property should be given to a designated charity so that none of it could be spent on her own care. Or that in that event she should not receive treatment for any other serious, life-threatening disease she might contract. Or even that in that event she should be killed as soon and as painlessly as possible? If Margo had expressed any of those wishes when she was competent, would autonomy then require that they be respected now by those in charge of her care, even though she seems perfectly happy with her dog-eared mysteries, the single painting she repaints, and her peanut-butter-and-jelly sandwiches?

If we had accepted the evidentiary view of autonomy, we would find the case for respecting Margo's past directions very weak. People are not the best judges of what their own best interests would be under circumstances they have never encountered and in which their preferences and desires may drastically have changed. But if we accept the integrity view, we will be drawn to the view that Margo's past wishes must be respected. A competent person making a living will providing for his treatment if he becomes demented is making exactly the kind of judgement that autonomy, on the integrity view, most respects: a judgement about the overall shape of the kind of life he wants to have led.

This conclusion is troubling, however, even shocking, and someone might want to resist it by insisting that the right to autonomy is *necessarily* contemporary: that a person's right to autonomy is only a right that his present decisions, not past ones that he has since disowned, be respected. Certainly that is the normal force of recognizing autonomy. Suppose that a Jehovah's Witness has signed a formal document stipulating that he is not to receive blood transfusions even if out of weakness of will he requests one when he would otherwise die. He wants, like Ulysses, to be tied to the mast of his faith. But when the moment comes, and he needs a transfusion, he pleads for it. We would not think ourselves required, out of respect for his autonomy, to disregard his contemporary plea.

We can interpret that example in different ways, though, and the difference is crucial for our present problem. We might say, first, that the Witness's later plea countermanded his original decision because it expressed a more contemporary desire. That presumes that it is only right to defer to past decisions when we have reason to believe that the agent still wishes what he wanted then. On that view, precedent autonomy is an illusion: we treat a person's past decision as important only because it is normally evidence of his present wishes, and we disregard it entirely when we know that it is not. On the other hand, we might say that the Witness's later plea countermanded his original decision because it was a fresh exercise of his autonomy, and that disregarding it would be treating him as no longer in charge of his own life. The difference between these two views about the force of precedent autonomy is crucial when someone changes his mind *after* he has become incompetent – that is, when the conditions of autonomy no longer hold. Suppose that the same accident that made a transfusion medically necessary for the Witness also deranged him, and that while still plainly deranged he demands the transfusion. On the first view, we would not violate his autonomy by administering it, but on the second, we would.

Which of the two views about the force of past decisions is more persuasive? Suppose we were confident that the deranged Witness, were he to receive the transfusion and live, would become competent again and be appalled at having had a treatment he believed worse for him than dying. In those circumstances, I believe, we would violate his autonomy by giving him the transfusion. That argues for the second view about the force of past decisions, the view that endorses precedent autonomy as genuine. We refuse to give the deranged Witness a transfusion not because we think he really continues to want what he wanted before – this is not like a case in which someone who objects to a given treatment is unconscious when he needs it – but because he lacks the necessary capacity for a fresh exercise of autonomy. His former decision remains in force because no new decision by a person capable of autonomy has annulled it.

Someone might say that we are justified in withholding the transfusion only because we know that the Witness would regret the transfusion if he recovered.

But that prediction would make no difference if he was fully competent when he asked for the transfusion and desperate to live at that moment, though very likely to change his mind again and be appalled tomorrow at what he has done. Surely we should accede to his request in those circumstances. What makes the difference, when we are deciding whether to honor someone's plea even though it contradicts his past deep convictions, is whether he is now competent to make a decision of that character, not whether he will regret making it later.

Our argument for the integrity view, then, supports a genuine doctrine of precedent autonomy. A competent person's right to autonomy requires that his past decisions about how he is to be treated if he becomes demented be respected even if they contradict the desires he has at that later point. If we refuse to respect Margo's precedent autonomy – if we refuse to respect her past decisions, though made when she was competent, because they do not match her present, incompetent wishes – then we are violating her autonomy on the integrity view. This conclusion has great practical importance. Competent people who are concerned about the end of their lives will naturally worry about how they might be treated if they become demented. Someone anxious to ensure that his life is not then prolonged by medical treatment is worried precisely because he thinks that the character of his whole life would be compromised if it were. He is in the same position as people who sign living wills asking not to be kept alive in a hopeless medical condition or when permanently vegetative. If we respect *their* past requests, as the Supreme Court has decided American states must do, then we have the same reasons for respecting the wishes not to be kept alive of someone who dreads not unconsciousness but dementia.

The argument has very troubling consequences, however. The medical student who observed Margo said that her life was the happiest he knew. Should we really deny a person like that the routine medical care needed to keep her alive? Could we ever conceivably *kill* her? We might consider it morally unforgivable not to try to save the life of someone who plainly enjoys her life, no matter how demented she is, and we might think it beyond imagining that we should actually kill her. We might hate living in a community whose officials might make or license either of those decisions. We might have other good reasons for treating Margo as she now wishes, rather than as, in my imaginary case, she once asked. But still, that violates rather than respects her autonomy.

Notes

1 Doctors are now investigating treatments that include reducing the presence in the brain of toxic substances that may play a role in neurodegeneration, enhancing the supply of trophic factors (which facilitate neuronal repair and growth) and neurotransmitters that are missing or deficient in Alzheimer's patients, and controlling diet-related factors such as blood glucose levels that appear to affect mental functioning in the elderly. See Dennis J. Selkoe, "Aging Brain, Aging Mind," *Scientific American*, 135 (September 1992); Robert J. Joynt, "Neurology," *Journal of the American Medical Association*, 268 (1992), 380; and Andrew A. Skolnick, "Brain Researchers Bullish on Prospects for Preserving Mental Functioning in the Elderly," *Journal of the American Medical Association*, 267 (1992), 2154.

2 Selkoe, "Amyloid Protein and Alzheimer's Disease," *Scientific American* (November 1991), 68.

3 OTA document, "Losing a Million Minds," OTA-BA-323 (1987), 14.

4 Legal provision and practices of custodial care are discussed in several of the papers contained in the OTA document, "Losing a Million Minds." For discussions of clinical diagnosis and histopathology, see, for example, Guy McKhann et al., "Clinical Diagnosis of Alzheimer's Disease: Report of the NINCDS-ADRDA Work Group Under the Auspices of Department of Health and Human Services Task Force on Alzheimer's Disease," *Neurology*, 34 (1984), 939; Christine M. Hulette et al., "Evaluation of Cerebral Biopsies for the Diagnosis of Dementia," *Archives of Neurology*, 49 (1992), 28; Selkoe, "Amyloid Protein and Alzheimer's Disease"; and M. Farlow et al., "Low Cerebrospinal-fluid Concentrations of Soluble Amyloid β-protein Precursor in Hereditary Alzheimer's Disease," *The Lancet*, 340 (1992), 453.

5 Evans et al., "Estimated Prevalence of Alzheimer's Disease in the United States," *Milbank Quarterly*, 68 (1990), 267.

6 In 1992, the continuing Framingham Study determined the prevalence of dementia in its study cohort as 23.8 percent from ages eighty-five to ninety-three. See Bachman et al., "Prevalence of Dementia and Probable Senile Dementia of the Alzheimer Type in the Framingham Study," *Neurology*, 42 (January 1992), 42. For a discussion of the differences between the studies cited in this and the preceding note, see Selkoe, "Aging Brain, Aging Mind."

7 See "UK: Dementia Condition Alzheimer's Disease Will Hit 750,000 in 30 Years," *The Guardian*, July 6, 1992.

8 Selkoe, "Amyloid Protein and Alzheimer's Disease," 68.

9 See Abstract, *Journal of the American Medical Association*, 267 (May 27, 1992), 2809 (summarizing Welch et al., "The Cost of Institutional Care in Alzheimer's Disease," *Journal of the American Geriatric Society*, 40 [1992], 221).

10 Nancy L. Mace and Peter V. Rabins, *The 36-Hour Day: A Family Guide to Caring for Persons with Alzheimer's Disease, Related Dementing Illnesses, and Memory Loss in Later Life* (Baltimore: Johns Hopkins University Press, 1981, 1991).

11 See Andrew D. Firlik, "Margo's Logo," *Journal of the American Medical Association*, 265 (1991), 201.

12 I should mention another great practical problem about the relationship between a demented person and the competent person he once was. Should the resources available to a demented patient depend on what he actually put aside when he was competent, by way of insurance for his own care in that event? Insurance schemes, both private schemes and mandated public schemes, play an important part in the way we provide resources for catastrophes of different sorts. But is the insurance approach the proper model to use in thinking about provision for the demented? That must depend on whether we believe that a competent person has the appropriate prudential concern for the incompetent person he might become, and that in turn depends on knotty philosophical problems about the concept of personal identity. I cannot discuss, in this book, either that philosophical problem or any of the other serious problems about the justice of financing the extraordinarily expensive care of demented patients in different ways. I have discussed both at some length, however, in a report, "Philosophical Problems of Senile Dementia," written for the United States Congress Office of Technology Assessment in Washington, DC, and available from that office.

13 See discussion in Allen E. Buchanan et al., "Surrogate Decision-Making for Elderly Individuals Who Are Incompetent or of Questionable Competence," November 1985, a report prepared for the Office of Technology Assessment.

14 See George J. Annas and Leonard H. Glantz, "With-
    holding and Withdrawing of Life-Sustaining Treatment
    for Elderly Incompetent Patients: A Review of Appellate
    Court Decisions," September 16, 1985, a report prepared
    for the Office of Technology Assessment.

15 I am assuming, in this discussion, that it can be in a
    person's overall best interests, at least sometimes, to
    force him to act otherwise than as he wants – that it
    can be in a person's overall best interests, for example,
    to be made not to smoke, even if we acknowledge that
    his autonomy is to some degree compromised,
    considered in itself, as against his interests.

16 Buchanan et al., "Surrogate Decision-Making."

17 There is an important debate in the economic literature
    on the question whether it can be rational to act
    against one's own best interests. The better view is that
    it can. See, for example, Amartya Sen, "Rational Fools:
    A Critique of the Behavioural Foundations
    of Economic Theory," *Philosophy and Public Affairs*, 6,
    no. 4 (Summer 1977).

18 See Buchanan et al., "Surrogate Decision-Making."
    Questions of task-sensitive competence are plainly
    relevant to the issues considered in the Buchanan report.
    But when the argument against surrogate decision
    making relies on the autonomy of the demented person
    affected by these decisions, the overall, non-task-sensitive
    sense of competence is also relevant.

19 Problems are presented for this judgement of overall
    integrity capacity when a patient appears only
    periodically capable of organizing his life around a
    system of desires and wishes. He seems able to take
    command of his life sometimes, and then lapses into a
    more serious stage of dementia, becoming lucid again
    only after a substantial intervening period, at which
    time the desires and interests he expresses are very
    different, or even contradictory. It would be a mistake
    to say that such a patient has the capacity for autonomy
    "periodically." The capacity autonomy presupposes is
    of necessity a temporally extended capacity: it is the
    capacity to have and act out of a personality.

36

Dworkin on Dementia

Elegant Theory, Questionable Policy

Rebecca Dresser

In his most recent book, *Life's Dominion: An Argument about Abortion, Euthanasia, and Individual Freedom,*[1] Ronald Dworkin offers a new way of interpreting disagreements over abortion and euthanasia. In doing so, he enriches and refines our understanding of three fundamental bioethical concepts: autonomy, beneficence, and sanctity of life. It is exciting that this eminent legal philosopher has turned his attention to bioethical issues. *Life's Dominion* is beautifully and persuasively written; its clear language and well-constructed arguments are especially welcome in this age of inaccessible, jargon-laden academic writing. *Life's Dominion* also is full of rich and provocative ideas; in this article, I address only Dworkin's remarks on euthanasia, although I will refer to his views on abortion when they are relevant to my analysis.

Professor Dworkin considers decisions to hasten death with respect to three groups: (1) competent and seriously ill people; (2) permanently unconscious people; and (3) conscious, but incompetent people, specifically, those with progressive and incurable dementia. My remarks focus on the third group, which I have addressed in previous work,[2] and which in my view poses the most difficult challenge for policymakers.

I present Dworkin's and my views as a debate over how we should think about Margo. Margo is described by Andrew Firlik, a medical student, in a *Journal of the American Medical Association* column called "A Piece of My Mind."[3] Firlik met Margo, who has Alzheimer disease, when he was enrolled in a gerontology elective. He began visiting her each day, and came to know something about her life with dementia.

Upon arriving at Margo's apartment (she lived at home with the help of an attendant), Firlik often found Margo reading; she told him she especially enjoyed mysteries, but he noticed that "her place in the book jump[ed] randomly from day to day." "For Margo," Firlik wonders, "is reading always a mystery?" Margo never called her new friend by name, though she claimed she knew who he was and always seemed pleased to see him. She liked listening to music and was happy listening to the same song repeatedly, apparently relishing it as if hearing it for the first time. Whenever she heard a certain song, however, she smiled and told Firlik that it reminded her of her deceased husband. She painted, too, but like the other Alzheimer patients in her art therapy class, she created

Original publication details: Rebecca Dresser, "Dworkin on Dementia: Elegant Theory, Questionable Policy," pp. 32–8 from *Hastings Center Report* 25: 6 (November/December 1995). Reproduced with permission from John Wiley & Sons.

the same image day after day: "a drawing of four circles, in soft rosy colors, one inside the other."

The drawing enabled Firlik to understand something that previously had mystified him:

> Despite her illness, or maybe somehow because of it, Margo is undeniably one of the happiest people I have known. There is something graceful about the degeneration her mind is undergoing, leaving her carefree, always cheerful. Do her problems, whatever she may perceive them to be, simply fail to make it to the worry centers of her brain? How does Margo maintain her sense of self? When a person can no longer accumulate new memories as the old rapidly fade, what remains? Who is Margo?

Firlik surmises that the drawing represented Margo's expression of her mind, her identity, and that by repeating the drawing, she was reminding herself and others of that identity. The painting was Margo, "plain and contained, smiling in her peaceful, demented state."

In *Life's Dominion*, Dworkin considers Margo as a potential subject of his approach. In one variation, he asks us to suppose that

> years ago, when fully competent, Margo had executed a formal document directing that if she should develop Alzheimer's disease…she should not receive treatment for any other serious, life-threatening disease she might contract. Or even that in that event she should be killed as soon and as painlessly as possible. (p. 226)

He presents an elegant and philosophically sophisticated argument for giving effect to her prior wishes, despite the value she appears to obtain from her life as an individual with dementia.

Dworkin's position emerges from his inquiry into the values of autonomy, beneficence, and sanctity of life. To understand their relevance to a case such as Margo's, he writes, we must first think about why we care about how we die. And to understand that phenomenon, we must understand why we care about how we live. Dworkin believes our lives are guided by the desire to advance two kinds of interests. *Experiential* interests are those we share to some degree with all sentient creatures. In Dworkin's words:

> We all do things because we like the experience of doing them: playing softball, perhaps, or cooking and eating well, or watching football, or seeing *Casablanca* for the twelfth time, or walking in the woods in October, or listening to *The Marriage of Figaro*, or sailing fast just off the wind, or just working hard at something. Pleasures like these are essential to a good life – a life with nothing that is marvelous only because of how it feels would be not pure but preposterous. (p. 201)

But Dworkin deems these interests less important than the second sort of interests we possess. Dworkin argues that we also seek to satisfy our *critical* interests, which are the hopes and aims that lend genuine meaning and coherence to our lives. We pursue projects such as establishing close friendships, achieving competence in our work, and raising children, not simply because we want the positive experiences they offer, but also because we believe we should want them, because our lives as a whole will be better if we take up these endeavors.

Dworkin admits that not everyone has a conscious sense of the interests they deem critical to their lives, but he thinks that "even people whose lives feel unplanned are nevertheless often guided by a sense of the general style of life they think appropriate, of what choices strike them as not only good at the moment but in character for them" (p. 202). In this tendency, Dworkin sees us aiming for the ideal of integrity, seeking to create a coherent narrative structure for the lives we lead.

Our critical interests explain why many of us care about how the final chapter of our lives turns out. Although some of this concern originates in the desire to avoid experiential burdens, as well as burdens on our families, much of it reflects the desire to escape dying under circumstances that are out of character with the prior stages of our lives. For most people, Dworkin writes, death has a "special, symbolic importance: they want their deaths, if possible, to express and in that way vividly to confirm the values they believe most important to their lives" (p. 211). And because critical interests are so personal and widely varied among individuals, each person must have the right to control the manner in which life reaches its conclusion. Accordingly, the state should refrain from imposing a "uniform, general view [of appropriate end-of-life-care] by way of sovereign law" (p. 213).

Dworkin builds on this hierarchy of human interests to defend his ideas about how autonomy and beneficence should apply to someone like Margo. First, he examines the generally accepted principle that we should in most circumstances honor the competent person's autonomous choice. One way to justify this principle is to claim that people generally know better than anyone else what best serves their interests; thus, their own choices are the best evidence we have of the decision that would most protect their welfare. Dworkin labels this the *evidentiary* view of autonomy. But Dworkin believes the better explanation for the respect we accord to individual choice lies in what he calls the *integrity* view of autonomy. In many instances, he contends, we grant freedom to people to act in ways that clearly conflict with their own best interests. We do this, he argues, because we want to let people "lead their lives out of a distinctive sense of their own character, a sense of what is important to them" (p. 224). The model once again assigns the greatest moral significance to the individual's critical interests, as opposed to the less important experiential interests that also contribute to a person's having a good life.

The integrity view of autonomy partially accounts for Dworkin's claim that we should honor Margo's prior choice to end her life if she developed Alzheimer disease. In making this choice, she was exercising, in Dworkin's phrase, her "precedent autonomy" (p. 226). The evidentiary view of autonomy fails to supply support for deferring to the earlier decision, Dworkin observes, because "[p]eople are not the best judges of what their own best interests would be under circumstances they have never encountered and in which their preferences and desires may drastically have changed" (p. 226). He readily admits that Andrew Firlik and others evaluating Margo's life with dementia would perceive a conflict between her prior instructions and her current welfare. But the integrity view of autonomy furnishes compelling support for honoring Margo's advance directives. Margo's interest in living her life in character includes an interest in controlling the circumstances in which others should permit her life as an Alzheimer patient to continue. Limiting that control would in Dworkin's view be "an unacceptable form of moral paternalism" (p. 231).

Dworkin finds additional support for assigning priority to Margo's former instructions in the moral principle of beneficence. People who are incompetent to exercise autonomy have a right to beneficence

from those entrusted to decide on their behalf. The best interests standard typically has been understood to require the decision that would best protect the incompetent individual's current welfare.[4] On this view, the standard would support some (though not necessarily all) life-extending decisions that depart from Margo's prior directives. But Dworkin invokes his concept of critical interests to construct a different best interests standard. Dworkin argues that Margo's critical interests persist, despite her current inability to appreciate them. Because critical interests have greater moral significance than the experiential interests Margo remains able to appreciate, and because "we must judge Margo's critical interests as she did when competent to do so" (p. 231), beneficence requires us to honor Margo's prior preferences for death. In Dworkin's view, far from providing a reason to override Margo's directives, compassion counsels us to follow them, for it is compassion "toward the whole person" that underlies the duty of beneficence (p. 232).

To honor the narrative that is Margo's life, then, we must honor her earlier choices. A decision to disregard them would constitute unjustified paternalism and would lack mercy as well. Dworkin concedes that such a decision might be made for other reasons – because we "find ourselves unable to deny medical help to anyone who is conscious and does not reject it" (p. 232), or deem it "morally unforgiveable not to try to save the life of someone who plainly enjoys her life" (p. 228), or find it "beyond imagining that we should actually kill her" (p. 228), or "hate living in a community whose officials might make or license either of [Margo's] decisions" (pp. 228–9). Dworkin does not explicitly address whether these or other aspects of the state's interest in protecting life should influence legal policy governing how people like Margo are treated.

Dworkin pays much briefer attention to Margo's fate in the event that she did not explicitly register her preferences about future treatment. Most incompetent patients are currently in this category, for relatively few people complete formal advance treatment directives.[5] In this scenario, the competent Margo failed to declare her explicit wishes, and her family is asked to determine her fate. Dworkin suggests that her relatives may give voice to Margo's autonomy by judging what her choice would have been if she had thought about it, based on her character and personality. Moreover, similar evidence enables them to determine her best interests, for it is her critical interests that matter most in reaching this determination. If Margo's dementia set in before she explicitly indicated her preferences about future care, "the law should so far as possible leave decisions in the hands of [her] relatives or other people close to [her] whose sense of [her] best interests…is likely to be much sounder than some universal, theoretical, abstract judgement" produced through the political process (p. 213).

Life's Dominion helps to explain why the "death with dignity" movement has attracted such strong support in the United States. I have no doubt that many people share Dworkin's conviction that they ought to have the power to choose death over life in Margo's state. But I am far from convinced of the wisdom or morality of these proposals for dementia patients.

Advance Directives and Precedent Autonomy

First, an observation. Dworkin makes an impressive case that the power to control one's future as an incompetent patient is a precious freedom that our society should go to great lengths to protect. But how strongly do people actually value this freedom? Surveys show that a relatively small percentage of the US population engages in end-of-life planning, and that many in that group simply designate a trusted relative or friend to make future treatment decisions, choosing not to issue specific instructions on future care.[6] Though this widespread failure to take advantage of the freedom to exercise precedent autonomy may be attributed to a lack of publicity or inadequate policy support for advance planning, it could also indicate that issuing explicit instructions to govern the final chapter of one's life is not a major priority for most people. If it is not, then we may question whether precedent autonomy and the critical interests it protects should be the dominant model for our policies on euthanasia for incompetent people. Dworkin constructs a moral argument for giving effect to Margo's directives, but does not indicate

how his position could be translated into policy. Consider how we might approach this task. We would want to devise procedures to ensure that people issuing such directives were competent, their actions voluntary, and their decisions informed. In other medical settings, we believe that a person's adequate understanding of the information relevant to treatment decision-making is a prerequisite to the exercise of true self-determination. We should take the same view of Margo's advance planning.

What would we want the competent Margo to understand before she chose death over life in the event of dementia? At a minimum, we would want her to understand that the experience of dementia differs among individuals, that for some it appears to be a persistently frightening and unhappy existence, but that most people with dementia do not exhibit the distress and misery we competent people tend to associate with the condition. I make no claims to expertise in this area, but my reading and discussions with clinicians, caregivers, and patients themselves suggest that the subjective experience of dementia is more positive than most of us would expect. Some caregivers and other commentators also note that patients' quality of life is substantially dependent on their social and physical environments, as opposed to the neurological condition itself.[7] Thus, the "tragedy" and "horror" of dementia is partially attributable to the ways in which others respond to people with this condition.

We also would want Margo to understand that Alzheimer disease is a progressive condition, and that options for forgoing life-sustaining interventions will arise at different points in the process. Dworkin writes that his ideas apply only to the late stages of Alzheimer disease, but he makes implementation of Margo's former wishes contingent on the mere development of the condition (pp. 219, 226). If we were designing policy, we would want to ensure that competent individuals making directives knew something about the general course of the illness and the points at which various capacities are lost. We would want them to be precise about the behavioral indications that should trigger the directive's implementation. We would want them to think about what their lives could be like at different stages of the disease, and about how invasive and effective various possible interventions might be. We would want to give them the opportunity to talk with physicians, caregivers, and individuals diagnosed with Alzheimer disease, and perhaps, to discuss their potential choices with a counselor.

The concern for education is one that applies to advance treatment directives generally, but one that is not widely recognized or addressed at the policy level. People complete advance directives in private, perhaps after discussion with relatives, physicians, or attorneys, but often with little understanding of the meaning or implications of their decisions. In one study of dialysis patients who had issued instructions on treatment in the event of advanced Alzheimer disease, a subsequent inquiry revealed that almost two-thirds of them wanted families and physicians to have some freedom to override the directives to protect their subsequent best interests.[8] The patients' failure to include this statement in their directives indicates that the instructions they recorded did not reflect their actual preferences. A survey of twenty-nine people participating in an advance care planning workshop found ten agreeing with both of the following inconsistent statements: "I would never want to be on a respirator in an intensive care unit"; and "If a short period of extremely intensive medical care could return me to near-normal condition, I would want it."[9] Meanwhile, some promoters of advance care planning have claimed that subjects can complete directives during interviews lasting fifteen minutes.[10]

We do not advance people's autonomy by giving effect to choices that originate in insufficient or mistaken information. Indeed, interference in such choices is often considered a form of justified paternalism. Moreover, advance planning for future dementia treatment is more complex than planning for other conditions, such as permanent unconsciousness. Before implementing directives to hasten death in the event of dementia, we should require people to exhibit a reasonable understanding of the choices they are making.[11]

Some shortcomings of advance planning are insurmountable, however. People exercising advance planning are denied knowledge of treatments and other relevant information that may emerge during the time between making a directive and giving it effect. Opportunities for clarifying misunderstandings are truncated, and decision-makers are not asked to explain or defend their choices to the clinicians, relatives, and friends whose care and concern may lead depressed or imprudent individuals to alter their wishes.[12] Moreover, the rigid adherence to advance planning Dworkin endorses leaves no room for the changes of heart that can lead us to deviate from our earlier choices. All of us are familiar with decisions we have later come to recognize as ill-suited to our subsequent situations. As Dworkin acknowledges, people may be mistaken about their future experiential interests as incompetent individuals. A policy of absolute adherence to advance directives means that we deny people like Margo the freedom we enjoy as competent people to change our decisions that conflict with our subsequent experiential interests.[13]

Personal identity theory, which addresses criteria for the persistence of a particular person over time, provides another basis for questioning precedent autonomy's proper moral and legal authority. In *Life's Dominion*, Dworkin assumes that Margo the dementia patient is the same person who issued the earlier requests to die, despite the drastic psychological alteration that has occurred. Indeed, the legitimacy of the precedent autonomy model absolutely depends on this view of personal identity. Another approach to personal identity would challenge this judgement, however. On this view, substantial memory loss and other psychological changes may produce a new person, whose connection to the earlier one could be less strong, indeed, could be no stronger than that between you and me.[14] Subscribers to this view of personal identity can argue that Margo's earlier choices lack moral authority to control what happens to Margo the dementia patient.

These shortcomings of the advance decision-making process are reasons to assign less moral authority to precedent autonomy than to contemporaneous autonomy. I note that Dworkin himself may believe in at least one limit on precedent autonomy in medical decision-making. He writes that people "who are repelled by the idea of living demented, totally dependent lives, speaking gibberish," ought to be permitted to issue advance directives "stipulating that if they become permanently and seriously demented, and then develop a serious illness, they should not be given medical treatment except to avoid pain" (p. 231). Would he oppose honoring a request to avoid all medical treatment, including pain-relieving measures, that was motivated by religious or philosophical concerns? The above remark suggests that he might give priority to Margo's existing experiential interests in avoiding pain over her prior exercise of precedent autonomy. In my view, this would be a justified limit on precedent autonomy, but I would add others as well.

Critical and Experiential Interests: Problems with the Model

What if Margo, like most other people, failed to exercise her precedent autonomy through making an advance directive? In this situation, her surrogate decision-makers are to apply Dworkin's version of the best interests standard. Should they consider, first and foremost, the critical interests she had as a competent person? I believe not, for several reasons. First, Dworkin's approach to the best interests standard rests partially on the claim that people want their lives to have narrative coherence. Dworkin omits empirical support for this claim, and my own observations lead me to wonder about its accuracy. The people of the United States are a diverse group, holding many different world views. Do most people actually think as Dworkin says they do? If I were to play psychologist, my guess would be that many people take life one day at a time. The goal of establishing a coherent narrative may be a less common life theme than the simple effort to accept and adjust to the changing natural and social circumstances that characterize a person's life. It also seems possible that people generally fail to draw a sharp line between experiential and critical interests, often choosing the critical projects Dworkin describes substantially because of the rewarding experiences they provide.

Suppose Margo left no indication of her prior wishes, but that people close to her believe it would be in her critical interests to die rather than live on in her current condition. Dworkin notes, but fails to address, the argument that "in the circumstances of dementia, critical interests become less important and experiential interests more so, so that fiduciaries may rightly ignore the former and concentrate on the latter" (p. 232). Happy and contented Margo will experience clear harm from the decision that purports to advance the critical interests she no longer cares about. This seems to me justification for a policy against active killing or withholding effective, non-burdensome treatments, such as antibiotics, from dementia patients whose lives offer them the sorts of pleasures and satisfactions Margo enjoys. Moreover, if clear evidence is lacking on Margo's own view of her critical interests, a decision to hasten her death might actually conflict with the life narrative she envisioned for herself. Many empirical studies have shown that families often do not have a very good sense of their relatives' treatment preferences.[15] How will Margo's life narrative be improved by her family's decision to hasten death, if there is no clear indication that she herself once took that view?

I also wonder about how to apply a best interests standard that assigns priority to the individual's critical interests. Dworkin writes that family members and other intimates applying this standard should decide based on their knowledge of "the shape and character of [the patient's] life and his own sense of integrity and critical interests" (p. 213). What sorts of life narratives would support a decision to end Margo's life? What picture of her critical interests might her family cite as justification for ending her life now? Perhaps Margo had been a famous legal philosopher whose intellectual pursuits were of utmost importance to her. This fact might tilt toward a decision to spare her from an existence in which she can only pretend to read. But what if she were also the mother of a mentally retarded child, whom she had cared for at home? What if she had enjoyed and valued this child's simple, experiential life, doing everything she could to protect and enhance it? How would this information affect the interpretation of her critical interests as they bear on her own life with dementia?

I am not sure whether Dworkin means to suggest that Margo's relatives should have complete discretion in evaluating considerations such as these. Would he permit anyone to challenge the legitimacy of a narrative outcome chosen by her family? What if her closest friends believed that a different conclusion would be more consistent with the way she had constructed her life? And is there any room in Dworkin's scheme for surprise endings? Some of our greatest fictional characters evolve into figures having little resemblance to the persons we met in the novels' opening chapters. Are real-life characters such as the fiercely independent intellectual permitted to become people who appreciate simple experiential pleasures and accept their dependence on others?

Finally, is the goal of respecting individual differences actually met by Dworkin's best interests standard? Although Dworkin recognizes that some people believe their critical interests would be served by a decision to extend their lives as long as is medically possible (based on their pro-life values), at times he implies that such individuals are mistaken about their genuine critical interests, that in actuality no one's critical interests could be served by such a decision. For example, he writes that after the onset of dementia, nothing of value can be added to a person's life, because the person is no longer capable of engaging in the activities necessary to advance her critical interests (p. 230). A similar judgement is also evident in his discussion of an actual case of a brain-damaged patient who "did not seem to be in pain or unhappy," and "recognized familiar faces with apparent pleasure" (p. 233). A court-appointed guardian sought to have the patient's life-prolonging medication withheld, but the family was strongly opposed to this outcome, and a judge denied the guardian's request. In a remark that seems to conflict with his earlier support for family decision-making, Dworkin questions whether the family's choice was in the patient's best interests (p. 233). These comments lead me to wonder whether Dworkin's real aim is to defend an objective nontreatment standard that should be applied to all individuals with significant mental impairment, not just those whose advance directives or relatives support a decision to hasten death. If so, then he needs to provide additional argument for this more controversial position.

The State's Interest in Margo's Life

My final thoughts concern Dworkin's argument that the state has no legitimate reason to interfere with Margo's directives or her family's best interests judgement to end her life. A great deal of *Life's Dominion* addresses the intrinsic value of human life and the nature of the state's interest in protecting that value.

Early in the book, Dworkin defends the familiar view that only conscious individuals can possess interests in not being destroyed or otherwise harmed. On this view, until the advent of sentience and other capacities, human fetuses lack interests of their own that would support a state policy restricting abortion. A policy that restricted abortion prior to this point would rest on what Dworkin calls a *detached* state interest in protecting human life. Conversely, a policy that restricts abortion after fetal sentience (which coincides roughly with viability) is supported by the state's *derivative* interest in valuing life, so called because it derives from the fetus's own interests (pp. 10–24, 168–70). Dworkin believes that detached state interests in ensuring respect for the value of life justify state prohibitions on abortion only after pregnant women are given a reasonable opportunity to terminate an unwanted pregnancy. Prior to this point, the law should permit women to make decisions about pregnancy according to their own views on how best to respect the value of life. After viability, however, when fetal neurological development is sufficiently advanced to make sentience possible, the state may severely limit access to abortion, based on its legitimate role in protecting creatures capable of having interests of their own (pp. 168–70).

Dworkin's analysis of abortion provides support, in my view, for a policy in which the state acts to protect the interests of conscious dementia patients like Margo. Although substantially impaired, Margo retains capacities for pleasure, enjoyment, interaction, relationships, and so forth. I believe her continued ability to participate in the life she is living furnishes a defensible basis for state limitations on the scope of her precedent autonomy, as well as on the choices her intimates make on her behalf. Contrary to Dworkin, I believe that such moral paternalism is justified when dementia patients have a quality of life comparable to Margo's. I am not arguing that all directives regarding dementia care should be overridden, nor that family choices should always be disregarded. I think directives and family choices should control in the vast majority of cases, for such decisions rarely are in clear conflict with the patient's contemporaneous interests. But I believe that state restriction is justified when a systematic evaluation by clinicians and others involved in patient care produces agreement that a minimally intrusive life-sustaining intervention is likely to preserve the life of someone as contented and active as Margo.

Many dementia patients do not fit Margo's profile. Some are barely conscious, others appear frightened, miserable, and unresponsive to efforts to mitigate their pain. Sometimes a proposed life-sustaining treatment will be invasive and immobilizing, inflicting extreme terror on patients unable to understand the reasons for their burdens. In such cases, it is entirely appropriate to question the justification for treatment, and often to withhold it, as long as the patient can be kept comfortable in its absence. This approach assumes that observers can accurately assess the experiential benefits and burdens of patients with neurological impairments and decreased ability to communicate. I believe that such assessments are often possible, and that there is room for a great deal of improvement in meeting this challenge.

I also believe that the special problems inherent in making an advance decision about active euthanasia justify a policy of refusing to implement such decisions, at the very least until we achieve legalization for competent patients without unacceptable rates of error and abuse.[16] I note as well the likely scarcity of health care professionals who would be willing to participate in decisions to withhold simple and effective treatments from someone in Margo's condition, much less to give her a lethal injection, even if this were permitted by law. Would Dworkin support a system that required physicians and nurses to compromise their own values and integrity so that Margo's precedent autonomy and critical interests could be advanced? I seriously doubt that many health professionals would agree to implement his proposals regarding dementia patients whose lives are as happy as Margo's.

We need community reflection on how we should think about people with dementia, including our possible future selves. Dworkin's model reflects a common response to the condition: tragic, horrible, degrading, humiliating, to be avoided at all costs. But how much do social factors account for this tragedy? Two British scholars argue that though we regard dementia patients as "the problem," the patients

are rather less of a problem than *we*. *They* are generally more authentic about what they are feeling and doing; many of the polite veneers of earlier life have been stripped away. *They* are clearly dependent on others, and usually come to accept that dependence; whereas many "normal" people, living under an ideology of extreme individualism, strenuously deny their dependency needs. *They* live largely in the present, because certain parts of their memory function have failed. *We* often find it very difficult to live in the present, suffering constant distraction; the sense of the present is often contaminated by regrets about the past and fears about the future.[17]

If we were to adopt an alternative to the common vision of dementia, we might ask ourselves what we could do, how we could alter our own responses so that people with dementia may find that life among us need not be so terrifying and frustrating. We might ask ourselves what sorts of environments, interactions, and relationships would enhance their lives.

Such a "disability perspective" on dementia offers a more compassionate, less rejecting approach to people with the condition than a model insisting that we should be permitted to order ourselves killed if this "saddest of the tragedies" (p. 218) should befall us. It supports as well a care and treatment policy centered on the conscious incompetent patient's subjective reality; one that permits death when the experiential burdens of continued life are too heavy or the benefits too minimal, but seeks to delay death when the patient's subjective existence is as positive as Margo's appears to be. Their loss of higher-level intellectual capacities ought not to exclude people like Margo from the moral community nor from the law's protective reach, even when the threats to their well-being emanate from their own former preferences. Margo's connections to us remain sufficiently strong that we owe her our concern and respect in the present. Eventually, the decision to allow her to die will be morally defensible. It is too soon, however, to exclude her from our midst.

Acknowledgment

I presented an earlier version of this essay at the annual meeting of the Society for Health and Human Values, 8 October 1994, in Pittsburgh. I would like to thank Ronald Dworkin and Eric Rakowski for their comments on my analysis.

Notes

1 Ronald Dworkin, *Life's Dominion: An Argument about Abortion, Euthanasia, and Individual Freedom* (New York: Knopf, 1993;Vintage, 1994).

2 See, for example, Rebecca Dresser, "Missing Persons: Legal Perceptions of Incompetent Patients," *Rutgers Law Review*, 609 (1994): 636–47; Rebecca Dresser and Peter J. Whitehouse, "The Incompetent Patient on the Slippery Slope," *Hastings Center Report*, 24, no. 4 (1994): 6–12; Rebecca Dresser, "Autonomy Revisited: The Limits of Anticipatory Choices," in *Dementia and Aging: Ethics, Values, and Policy Choices*, ed. Robert H. Binstock, Stephen G. Post, and Peter J. Whitehouse (Baltimore, MD: Johns Hopkins University Press, 1992), pp. 71–85.

3 Andrew D. Firlik, "Margo's Logo," *JAMA*, 265 (1991): 201.

4 See generally Dresser, "Missing Persons."

5 For a recent survey of the state of advance treatment decision-making in the US, see "Advance Care Planning: Priorities for Ethical and Empirical Research," Special Supplement, *Hastings Center Report* 24, no. 6 (1994).

6 See generally "Advance Care Planning." The failure of most persons to engage in formal end-of-life planning does not in itself contradict Dworkin's point that most people care about how they die. It does suggest, however, that people do not find the formal exercise of precedent autonomy to be a helpful or practical means of expressing their concerns about future life-sustaining treatment.

7 See generally Dresser, "Missing Persons," 681–91; Tom Kitwood and Kathleen Bredin, "Towards a Theory of Dementia Care: Personhood and Well Being," *Ageing and Society*, 12 (1992): 269–87.

8 Ashwini Sehgal et al., "How Strictly Do Dialysis Patients Want Their Advance Directives Followed?" *JAMA*, 267 (1992): 59–63.

9 Lachlan Forrow, Edward Gogel, and Elizabeth Thomas, "Advance Directives for Medical Care" (letter), *New England Journal of Medicine*, 325 (1991): 1255.

10 Linda L. Emanuel et al., "Advance Directives for Medical Care – A Case for Greater Use," *New England Journal of Medicine*, 324 (1991): 889–95.

11 See Eric Rakowski, "The Sanctity of Human Life," *Yale Law Journal*, 103 (1994): 2049, 2110–11.

12 See Allen Buchanan and Dan Brock, "Deciding for Others," in *The Ethics of Surrogate Decisionmaking* (Cambridge: Cambridge University Press, 1989), at 101–7 for discussion of these and other shortcomings of advance treatment decision-making.

13 See generally Rebecca Dresser and John A. Robertson, "Quality-of-Life and Non-Treatment Decisions for Incompetent Patients: A Critique of the Orthodox Approach," *Law, Medicine & Health Care*, 17 (1989): 234–44.

14 See Derek Parfit, *Reasons and Persons* (New York: Oxford University Press, 1985), pp. 199–379.

15 See, e.g., Allison B. Seckler et al., "Substituted Judgment: How Accurate Are Proxy Predictions?" *Annals of Internal Medicine*, 115 (1992): 92–8.

16 See generally Leslie P. Francis, "Advance Directives for Voluntary Euthanasia: A Volatile Combination?" *Journal of Medicine & Philosophy*, 18 (1993): 297–322.

17 Kitwood and Bredin, "Towards a Theory of Dementia Care," 273–4.

Voluntary Euthanasia and Medically Assisted Suicide

37

The Note

Chris Hill

An open letter to anyone who wants to understand why I've checked out. It's very personal, pretty horrible and perhaps a bit shocking. I hope that those of you who knew me well enough find it unnecessary to read this.

Well, this is it – perhaps the hardest thing you've ever had to read, easily the most difficult thing I've ever attempted to write. To understand my over-whelming sense of loss and why I chose to take my own life, you need to know a bit about my life before and after my accident. Let's take a closer look.

I was born at one of the best times in one of the world's best countries – Australia. I had more than the proverbial happy childhood. Great parents, world travel, a good education and fabulous experiences like Disneyland, swimming with a wild dolphin in the turquoise waters of the Bahamas, riding across the desert sands around the Egyptian pyramids and much more.

Later, after the travel bug had bitten good and hard, I set out on my own adventures. I can remember only a fraction of them, but many rich images come flooding back. I stood on the lip of a live volcano in Vanuatu and stared down into the vision of hell in its throat; I watched the morning sun ignite Himalayan peaks in a blaze of incandescent glory; smoked hashish with a leper in an ancient Hindu temple; danced naked under the stars with the woman I love on a tropical beach that left a trail of phosphorescent blue footsteps

behind us; skied waist-deep powder snow in untracked Coloradon glades; soared thermals to 8000 feet in a hang-glider and have literally flown with the eagles. In Maryland, on midsummer nights redolent with the smell of freshly ploughed earth, I rode past fields lit by the twinkling light of a billion fireflies. I've ridden a motorcycle at 265 km/h on a Japanese racetrack and up to the 5000 metre snowline on an Ecuadorian volcano. And speaking of riding, what haven't I seen from behind the bars of a motorcycle? More than 200 000 kilometres in over a dozen countries embracing everything from some of the world's most spectacular wilderness areas to its greatest cities and vast slums containing millions of impoverished souls.

Along the way I picked up a decent education, including two university degrees, and learnt another language. All this and so much more – more than most people would experience in several lifetimes.

Perhaps most importantly of all, everywhere I've been I enjoyed the support of a caring family, the company of good friends and, more than once, the rewards of being involved in a caring relationship. They – you, if you're reading – are ultimately what made my life as rich as it was, and I thank you.

I was lucky enough to know love, and I indulged in lust. I enjoyed exotic erotica with perhaps more than a hundred women of many different nationalities in places that ranged from the bedroom to a crowded

Original publication details: Chris Hill, "The Note," pp. 9–17 from Helga Kuhse (ed.), *Willing to Listen, Wanting to Die*, Ringwood, Australia: Penguin Books, 1994.

ship's deck on the Aegean Sea, fields, rivers, trees, beaches, cars and motorcycles. There's been a *ménage à trois* in various combinations and even a few outright orgies. How wonderful to have been sexually active in the pre-AIDS era. I record this not as an exercise in testosterone-fuelled chest-beating, but to point out that sex was an important part of my life, and so that you can better understand my sense of loss.

In short, I once lived life to the max, always grateful that I had the opportunity to do just that, and always mindful to live for today because there may be no tomorrow.

Just as well, it seems. After my hang-gliding accident – how ironic that something I loved so much could destroy me so cruelly – tomorrows were nothing but a grey void of bleak despair. I was paralysed from the chest down, more than three-quarters dead. A talking head mounted on a bloody wheelchair. No more of the simple pleasures I once took for granted. No walking, running, swimming, riding motorcycles, the wonderful feel of grass, sand or mud underfoot, nothing. The simplest of everyday tasks – getting up, having a shower, getting dressed – became an enormous hassle and the source of endless frustration. That in itself was completely shattering physically and emotionally, but I lost so much more than mobility. I lost my dignity and self-respect. I would forever be a burden on those around me and I didn't want that no matter how willingly and unthinkingly family and friends assumed that burden. Every time I had to ask someone to do something for me, every time I was dragged up a damn step, was like thrusting a hot blade into the place where my pride used to be.

All that was bad enough, but there was so much more. No balance. My every action was as graceless as a toy dog nodding in the back of some beat-up car. No ability to regulate my body temperature properly – in a sense I was cold-blooded, more like a lizard than a human being. And without abdominal muscles I couldn't cough, sneeze, shout, blow out a candle or even fart.

Worse still, I couldn't shit or piss. Those body functions had to be performed manually, which meant sticking a 30-centimetre-long silicon tube up my willie four times a day so I could drain myself into a plastic bag, and sticking a finger up my arse every second day to dig out the shit. Sometimes both procedures drew blood. They always made me shudder with revulsion,

but I had a powerful incentive to persevere. Autonomic dysreflexia it's called, the potentially fatal rise in blood pressure and excruciating headache that occurs if body waste isn't properly removed and backs up. I had a taste of it in hospital once, and that was enough.

Despite this regimen, there was no guarantee I wouldn't shit or piss my pants in public or wake up wallowing in it. Can you imagine living with that uncertainty? Can you imagine the shame and humiliation when it actually happened? Unbearable abominations that made me feel less than human. For me, it was no way to live.

There's more. I wept every morning when I saw myself in the mirror. I'd become a hunchback with a bloated pot belly above withered legs with muscles as soft and useless as marshmallow. It was an unbearable sight for someone who was once so grateful for being blessed with such an athletic and healthy body. Paraplegia meant that I also had to live with the constant possibility of pressure sores, ugly ulcers that can require months of hospitalization to cure. They're common. So are urinary tract infections and haemorrhoids. I suffer from both, and they also usually lead back to hospital sooner or later. I would rather die than return to hospital.

Then there was the pain in my shoulder. A damaged nerve meant that two muscles in my left shoulder didn't work and they wasted away, leaving the others to compensate and me with a pain that frequently made simple actions difficult. Then there were swollen ankles, which once meant sleeping with pillows under my feet so they could drain overnight. My chest became hypersensitive, which may sound like fun but meant that I felt like I was wearing an unbearably scratchy woollen jumper over bare skin. And after sitting in the chair for a few hours my bum, which shouldn't have had any sensation, felt like it was on fire. There were also tinea, crutch rot, headaches…The list of horrors was endless, and I haven't even mentioned some of the worst ones.

While at Moorong [Spinal Unit] I began to wake with pins and needles – loss of sensation – in my hands and arms. Sometimes it took hours to pass, and I began to fear losing what little I had left. That was unbearable. Tethering, nerves pinched by the scar tissue formed around the broken bones in my neck, I was told. The doctors talked about tests and surgery on my neck, wrists. Forget it. There was no way I'd return to hospital, let alone for such delicate, radical and debilitating surgery.

All my many pleasures had been stripped from me and replaced by a hellish living nightmare. The mere sight of someone standing up, a child skipping, a bicyclist's flexing leg muscles, were enough to reduce me to tears. Everything I saw and did was a stinging reminder of my condition and I cried constantly, even behind the jokes and smiles. I was so tired of crying. I never imagined that anyone could hurt so bad and cry so much. I guarantee that anybody who thinks it can't have been too bad would change their mind if they lived in my body for a day.

People kill animals to put them out of their misery if they're suffering even a tiny part of what I had to put up with, but I was never given the choice of a dignified death and I was very bitter about that. I could accept that accidents happen and rarely asked 'why me?', but I felt that the legislature's and the medical profession's attitude of life at any cost was an inhumane presumption that amounted to arrogance. And what of the dollar cost? My enforced recovery and rehabilitation cost taxpayers at least $150,000 by my rough count, money that wouldn't have been wasted had anybody bothered to ask me how I felt about the whole thing and what I'd like to do.

I had one good reason for living, of course, and her name is Lee-Ann, the best thing that ever happened to me. Wonderful Lee-Ann, without whom I would have gone insane long before now. But I wept whenever I thought of us together. What future could we have? No matter how hard I worked and how much I achieved, she would inevitably be a nursemaid in a million different ways, and I hated that, no matter that she so willingly and lovingly assumed the burden.

Nor would I condemn her to spend her nights sleeping with a sexless wooden lump twitching with spasm. That's right, sexless — impotent. Stripped of my sexuality, I felt that I'd lost part of my essence, the very core of my masculinity. I was even denied the sensual pleasure of embrace, because from the chest down I couldn't feel warmth, didn't even know if someone was touching me. I love Lee-Ann, but she deserves better than the pointless life I could offer, and I believe that I'm giving her another chance at happiness no matter how much pain I cause in the short term.

Someone so desirable — open, honest, natural, loyal, with a great sense of humour and a figure the desire of men and envy of women — has a better chance than most of finding the happiness she deserves, and I hope with all my heart she finds it.

I had other reasons for living, of course — my family and friends. I remember, many years ago, lying on the verandah roof of a colonial mansion in the mountains of northern Burma. A shooting star streaked through the clear night sky and I made a wish. I wished for health, wealth and happiness for all those I loved and cared about. I repeated that wish several times in the following years and was enormously gratified to gradually see it come to pass for most of my family and friends. I'm not suggesting that my wishes had anything to do with their various successes — that was largely the result of their own efforts and the occasional dash of good fortune. But after my accident, even the joy I derived from seeing the happiness of those I cared about went sour for me. Seeing others get on with their lives, doing what I no longer could, was terribly distressing for me. I couldn't live my life vicariously through other people's satisfactions and achievements. I was a self-centred person and I'd always done what I wanted, had my own reasons for living.

Mum and Dad, you often said that you didn't care what I did as long as I was happy. I expect that many of my friends felt the same way. Well, I was terminally, unbearably unhappy with no way out — except death. I know others have come to terms with paraplegia, or even quadriplegia, and managed to lead successful, apparently normal and happy lives. I've met and been encouraged by some of them. I tips me hat to them, for they have done what I cannot. Then again, perhaps I have done what they could not. Four attempts taught me that it takes an enormous amount of courage to commit suicide. Unfortunately, I didn't find the examples of others in my position motivating or inspirational. For me, life as a para was so far from the minimum I considered acceptable that it just didn't matter. It's quality of life, not quantity, that's important.

It's a challenge, many of you said. Bullshit. My life was just a miserable existence, an awful parody of normalcy. What's a challenge without some reward to make it worthwhile?

Despite that, I gave it a go. I worked hard – harder than I ever have at anything – to try and rebuild my life. I tried picking up the threads and doing whatever I was still capable of. I went out to shops, theatres and restaurants, even a concert. I learnt to drive again, and worked. I hated every second of it with a passion I'd never felt before. What good is a picnic when you can't play with the kids and dogs and throw a frisbee? What's the point of going to a gig if you can't dance when the music grips you? I used to be a player, not a spectator, and my new existence (life seems too strong a word) was painful, frustrating and completely unsatisfying.

At least you can still work, some said. Great. I liked my job, the caring, talented and generous people I worked with and especially where we worked. But it was still just a job, and as you all know, I worked to live, not lived to work. Work was never a reason for living for me. And what of the future? Where would I go, what would I do? There's no future for a wheelchair-bound journalist, not one with my interests anyway. I'd never be able to do any of the things, like travel and adventure, that drew me to journalism in the first place and ultimately made the long office hours worth-while.

I accepted death – embraced it eagerly, in fact, after so many months of the nightmare – without fear or regret. I had a full, rewarding and successful life by any measure, and in my last weeks I couldn't think of a single thing I'd always wanted to do but hadn't yet done. Well, actually, I guess I can think of a few things, but they don't amount to much. I'd always wanted to ride a Harley or drive a convertible Porsche, and I would have loved to have been 'stoked in the green room' – ridden a tube. Surfing would definitely have been the next sport I would have taken up. I've got a pretty good idea of the buzz it offers, and I think I would have liked it. Anyway, death is the last great adventure, and I was ready for it. I wasn't religious – how could anyone believe in a just, compassionate and almighty God after seeing and experiencing what

I have? – but I felt quietly confident that whatever lay beyond had to be something more, something better, if anything.

I had one enormous regret, of course. I didn't want to hurt anyone the way I know I have.

I wish it didn't have to be this way. I didn't want to make those I love suffer, and the knowledge that I would bring awful grief to those I least wanted to hurt in the world compounded my own misery unbelievably. I'm so sorry. I hope you can find it in your hearts to forgive me. I wish you could see death as I did, as a release, something to celebrate, and be happy for me. I would rather have thrown a raging party and simply have disappeared at dawn with your blessings and understanding. Of course, it could never have happened that way. At any rate, I thank you all for making my last months as happy as they were, for your optimism and support, for the rays of light with which you pierced my gloom. My condition was permanent; I can only hope your grief fades quickly with the healing passage of time.

Chris Hill
10 February 1993

Statement

I have decided to take my own life for reasons detailed in the accompanying note. It is a fully considered decision made in a normal, rational state of mind and I have not been influenced or assisted by anyone else. Suicide is not a crime and I have the right not to be handled or treated against my will, so I absolutely forbid anyone to resuscitate or interfere with me while I continue to live, unless it is to end my suffering. Anyone who disregards this notice will be committing a civil and criminal offence against me.

In the event that I do not die, I wish to be placed under the care of Dr George Quittner at Mosman Hospital.

Chris Hill

38

When Self-Determination Runs Amok

Daniel Callahan

The euthanasia debate is not just another moral debate, one in a long list of arguments in our pluralistic society. It is profoundly emblematic of three important turning points in Western thought. The first is that of the legitimate conditions under which one person can kill another. The acceptance of voluntary active euthanasia would morally sanction what can only be called "consenting adult killing." By that term I mean the killing of one person by another in the name of their mutual right to be killer and killed if they freely agree to play those roles. This turn flies in the face of a long-standing effort to limit the circumstances under which one person can take the life of another, from efforts to control the free flow of guns and arms, to abolish capital punishment, and to more tightly control warfare. Euthanasia would add a whole new category of killing to a society that already has too many excuses to indulge itself in that way.

The second turning point lies in the meaning and limits of self-determination. The acceptance of euthanasia would sanction a view of autonomy holding that individuals may, in the name of their own private, idiosyncratic view of the good life, call upon others, including such institutions as medicine, to help them pursue that life, even at the risk of harm to the common good. This works against the idea that the meaning and scope of our own right to lead our own lives must be conditioned by, and be compatible with, the good of the community, which is more than an aggregate of self-directing individuals.

The third turning point is to be found in the claim being made upon medicine: it should be prepared to make its skills available to individuals to help them achieve their private vision of the good life. This puts medicine in the business of promoting the individualistic pursuit of general human happiness and well-being. It would overturn the traditional belief that medicine should limit its domain to promoting and preserving human health, redirecting it instead to the relief of that suffering which stems from life itself, not merely from a sick body.

I believe that, at each of these three turning points, proponents of euthanasia push us in the wrong direction. Arguments in favor of euthanasia fall into four general categories, which I will take up in turn: (1) the moral claim of individual self-determination and well-being; (2) the moral irrelevance of the difference between killing and allowing to die; (3) the supposed paucity of evidence to show likely harmful consequences of legalized euthanasia; and (4) the compatibility of euthanasia and medical practice.

Original publication details: Daniel Callahan, "When Self-Determination Runs Amok," pp. 52–5 from *Hastings Center Report* 22: 2 (March/April 1992). Reproduced with permission from John Wiley & Sons.

Self-Determination

Central to most arguments for euthanasia is the principle of self-determination. People are presumed to have an interest in deciding for themselves, according to their own beliefs about what makes life good, how they will conduct their lives. That is an important value, but the question in the euthanasia context is, What does it mean and how far should it extend? If it were a question of suicide, where a person takes her own life without assistance from another, that principle might be pertinent, at least for debate. But euthanasia is not that limited a matter. The self-determination in that case can only be effected by the moral and physical assistance of another. Euthanasia is thus no longer a matter only of self-determination, but of a mutual, social decision between two people, the one to be killed and the other to do the killing.

How are we to make the moral move from my right of self-determination to some doctor's right to kill me – from *my* right to *his* right? Where does the doctor's moral warrant to kill come from? Ought doctors to be able to kill anyone they want as long as permission is given by competent persons? Is our right to life just like a piece of property, to be given away or alienated if the price (happiness, relief of suffering) is right? And then to be destroyed with our permission once alienated?

In answer to all those questions, I will say this: I have yet to hear a plausible argument why it should be permissible for us to put this kind of power in the hands of another, whether a doctor or anyone else. The idea that we can waive our right to life, and then give to another the power to take that life, requires a justification yet to be provided by anyone.

Slavery was long ago outlawed on the ground that one person should not have the right to own another, even with the other's permission. Why? Because it is a fundamental moral wrong for one person to give over his life and fate to another, whatever the good consequences, and no less a wrong for another person to have that kind of total, final power. Like slavery, dueling was long ago banned on similar grounds: even free, competent individuals should not have the power to kill each other, whatever their motives, whatever the circumstances. Consenting adult killing, like consenting adult slavery or degradation, is a strange route to human dignity.

There is another problem as well. If doctors, once sanctioned to carry out euthanasia, are to be themselves responsible moral agents – not simply hired hands with lethal injections at the ready – then they must have their own *independent* moral grounds to kill those who request such services. What do I mean? As those who favor euthanasia are quick to point out, some people want it because their life has become so burdensome it no longer seems worth living.

The doctor will have a difficulty at this point. The degree and intensity to which people suffer from their diseases and their dying, and whether they find life more of a burden than a benefit, has very little directly to do with the nature or extent of their actual physical condition. Three people can have the same condition, but only one will find the suffering unbearable. People suffer, but suffering is as much a function of the values of individuals as it is of the physical causes of that suffering. Inevitably in those circumstances, the doctor will in effect be treating the patient's values. To be responsible, the doctor would have to share those values. The doctor would have to decide, on her own, whether the patient's life was "no longer worth living."

But how could a doctor possibly know that or make such a judgement? Just because the patient said so? I raise this question because, while in Holland at a euthanasia conference, the doctors present agreed that there is no objective way of measuring or judging the claims of patients that their suffering is unbearable. And if it is difficult to measure suffering, how much more difficult to determine the value of a patient's statement that her life is not worth living?

However one might want to answer such questions, the very need to ask them, to inquire into the physician's responsibility and grounds for medical and moral judgement, points out the social nature of the decision. Euthanasia is not a private matter of self-determination. It is an act that requires two people to make it possible, and a complicit society to make it acceptable.

Killing and Allowing to Die

Against common opinion, the argument is sometimes made that there is no moral difference between stopping life-sustaining treatment and more active forms of killing, such as lethal injection. Instead I would contend that the notion that there is no morally significant difference between omission and commission is just wrong. Consider in its broad implications what the eradication of the distinction implies: that death from disease has been banished, leaving only the actions of physicians in terminating treatment as the cause of death. Biology, which used to bring about death, has apparently been displaced by human agency. Doctors have finally, I suppose, thus genuinely become gods, now doing what nature and the deities once did.

What is the mistake here? It lies in confusing causality and culpability, and in failing to note the way in which human societies have overlaid natural causes with moral rules and interpretations. Causality (by which I mean the direct physical causes of death) and culpability (by which I mean our attribution of moral responsibility to human actions) are confused under three circumstances.

They are confused, first, when the action of a physician in stopping treatment of a patient with an underlying lethal disease is construed as *causing* death. On the contrary, the physician's omission can only bring about death on the condition that the patient's disease will kill him in the absence of treatment. We may hold the physician morally responsible for the death, if we have morally judged such actions wrongful omissions. But it confuses reality and moral judgement to see an omitted action as having the same causal status as one that directly kills. A lethal injection will kill both a healthy person and a sick person. A physician's omitted treatment will have no effect on a healthy person. Turn off the machine on me, a healthy person, and nothing will happen. It will only, in contrast, bring the life of a sick person to an end because of an underlying fatal disease.

Causality and culpability are confused, second, when we fail to note that judgements of moral responsibility and culpability are human constructs. By that I mean that we human beings, after moral reflection, have decided to call some actions right or wrong, and to devise moral rules to deal with them. When physicians could do nothing to stop death, they were not held responsible for it. When, with medical progress, they began to have some power over death – but only its timing and circumstances, not its ultimate inevitability – moral rules were devised to set forth their obligations. Natural causes of death were not

thereby banished. They were, instead, overlaid with a medical ethics designed to determine moral culpability in deploying medical power.

To confuse the judgements of this ethics with the physical causes of death – which is the connotation of the word *kill* – is to confuse nature and human action. People will, one way or another, die of some disease; death will have dominion over all of us. To say that a doctor "kills" a patient by allowing this to happen should only be understood as a moral judgement about the licitness of his omission, nothing more. We can, as a fashion of speech only, talk about a doctor *killing* a patient by omitting treatment he should have provided. It is a fashion of speech precisely because it is the underlying disease that brings death when treatment is omitted; that is its cause, not the physician's omission. It is a misuse of the word *killing* to use it when a doctor stops a treatment he believes will no longer benefit the patient – when, that is, he steps aside to allow an eventually inevitable death to occur now rather than later. The only deaths that human beings invented are those that come from direct killing – when, with a lethal injection, we both cause death and are morally responsible for it. In the case of omissions, we do not cause death even if we may be judged morally responsible for it.

This difference between causality and culpability also helps us see why a doctor who has omitted a treatment he should have provided has "killed" that patient while another doctor – performing precisely the same act of omission on another patient in different circumstances – does not kill her, but only allows her to die. The difference is that we have come, by moral convention and conviction, to classify unauthorized or illegitimate omissions as acts of "killing." We call them "killing" in the expanded sense of the term: a culpable action that permits the real cause of death, the underlying disease, to proceed to its lethal conclusion. By contrast, the doctor who, at the patient's request, omits or terminates unwanted treatment does not kill at all. Her underlying disease, not his action, is the physical cause of death; and we have agreed to consider actions of that kind to be morally licit. He thus can truly be said to have "allowed" her to die.

If we fail to maintain the distinction between killing and allowing to die, moreover, there are some disturbing possibilities. The first would be to confirm many physicians in their already too-powerful belief that, when patients die or when physicians stop treatment because of the futility of continuing it, they are somehow both morally and physically responsible for the deaths that follow. That notion needs to be abolished, not strengthened. It needlessly and wrongly burdens the physician, to whom should not be attributed the powers of the gods. The second possibility would be that, in every case where a doctor judges medical treatment no longer effective in prolonging life, a quick and direct killing of the patient would be seen as the next, most reasonable step, on grounds of both humaneness and economics. I do not see how that logic could easily be rejected.

Calculating the Consequences

When concerns about the adverse social consequences of permitting euthanasia are raised, its advocates tend to dismiss them as unfounded and overly speculative. On the contrary, recent data about the Dutch experience suggests that such concerns are right on target. From my own discussions in Holland, and from articles on that subject, I believe we can now fully see most of the *likely* consequences of legal euthanasia.

Three consequences seem almost certain, in this or any other country: the inevitability of some abuse of the law; the difficulty of precisely writing, and then enforcing, the law; and the inherent slipperiness of the moral reasons for legalizing euthanasia in the first place.

Why is abuse inevitable? One reason is that almost all laws on delicate, controversial matters are to some extent abused. This happens because not everyone will agree with the law as written and will bend it, or ignore it, if they can get away with it. From explicit admissions to me by Dutch proponents of euthanasia, and from the corroborating information provided by the Remmelink Report and the outside studies of Carlos Gomez and John Keown, I am convinced that in the Netherlands there are a substantial number of cases of nonvoluntary euthanasia, that is, euthanasia undertaken without the explicit permission of the person being killed. The other reason abuse is inevitable is that the law is likely to have a low enforcement priority in the criminal justice system. Like other laws of similar status, unless there is an unrelenting and harsh willingness to pursue abuse, violations will

ordinarily be tolerated. The worst thing to me about my experience in Holland was the casual, seemingly indifferent attitude toward abuse. I think that would happen everywhere.

Why would it be hard to precisely write, and then enforce, the law? The Dutch speak about the requirement of "unbearable" suffering, but admit that such a term is just about indefinable, a highly subjective matter admitting of no objective standards. A requirement for outside opinion is nice, but it is easy to find complaisant colleagues. A requirement that a medical condition be "terminal" will run aground on the notorious difficulties of knowing when an illness is actually terminal.

Apart from those technical problems there is a more profound worry. I see no way, even in principle, to write or enforce a meaningful law that can guarantee effective procedural safeguards. The reason is obvious yet almost always overlooked. The euthanasia transaction will ordinarily take place within the boundaries of the private and confidential doctor–patient relationship. No one can possibly know what takes place in that context unless the doctor chooses to reveal it. In Holland, less than 10 percent of the physicians report their acts of euthanasia and do so with almost complete legal impunity. There is no reason why the situation should be any better elsewhere. Doctors will have their own reasons for keeping euthanasia secret, and some patients will have no less a motive for wanting it concealed.

I would mention, finally, that the moral logic of the motives for euthanasia contain within them the ingredients of abuse. The two standard motives for euthanasia and assisted suicide are said to be our right of self-determination, and our claim upon the mercy of others, especially doctors, to relieve our suffering. These two motives are typically spliced together and presented as a single justification. Yet if they are considered independently – and there is no inherent reason why they must be linked – they reveal serious problems. It is said that a competent, adult person should have a right to euthanasia for the relief of suffering. But why must the person be suffering? Does not that stipulation already compromise the principle of self-determination? How can self-determination have any limits? Whatever the person's motives may be, why are they not sufficient?

Consider next the person who is suffering but not competent, who is perhaps demented or mentally retarded. The standard argument would deny euthanasia to that person. But why? If a person is suffering but not competent, then it would seem grossly unfair to deny relief solely on the grounds of incompetence. Are the incompetent less entitled to relief from suffering than the competent? Will it only be affluent, middle-class people, mentally fit and savvy about working the medical system, who can qualify? Do the incompetent suffer less because of their incompetence?

Considered from these angles, there are no good moral reasons to limit euthanasia once the principle of taking life for that purpose has been legitimated. If we really believe in self-determination, then any competent person should have a right to be killed by a doctor for any reason that suits him. If we believe in the relief of suffering, then it seems cruel and capricious to deny it to the incompetent. There is, in short, no reasonable or logical stopping point once the turn has been made down the road to euthanasia, which could soon turn into a convenient and commodious expressway.

Euthanasia and Medical Practice

A fourth kind of argument one often hears both in the Netherlands and in this country is that euthanasia and assisted suicide are perfectly compatible with the aims of medicine. I would note at the very outset that a physician who participates in another person's suicide already abuses medicine. Apart from depression (the main statistical cause of suicide), people commit suicide because they find life empty, oppressive, or meaningless. Their judgement is a judgement about the value of continued life, not only about health (even if they are sick). Are doctors now to be given the right to make judgements about the kinds of life worth living and to give their blessing to suicide for those they judge wanting? What conceivable competence, technical or moral, could doctors claim to play such a role? Are we to medicalize suicide, turning judgements about its worth and value into one more clinical issue? Yes, those are rhetorical questions.

Yet they bring us to the core of the problem of euthanasia and medicine. The great temptation of modern medicine, not always resisted, is to move beyond the promotion and preservation of health into the boundless realm of general human happiness and well-being. The root problem of illness and mortality is both medical and philosophical or religious. "Why must I die?" can be asked as a technical, biological question or as a question about the meaning of life. When medicine tries to respond to the latter, which it is always under pressure to do, it moves beyond its proper role.

It is not medicine's place to lift from us the burden of that suffering which turns on the meaning we assign to the decay of the body and its eventual death. It is not medicine's place to determine when lives are not worth living or when the burden of life is too great to be borne. Doctors have no conceivable way of evaluating such claims on the part of patients, and they should have no right to act in response to them. Medicine should try to relieve human suffering, but only that suffering which is brought on by illness and dying as biological phenomena, not that suffering which comes from anguish or despair at the human condition.

Doctors ought to relieve those forms of suffering that medically accompany serious illness and the threat of death. They should relieve pain, do what they can to allay anxiety and uncertainty, and be a comforting presence. As sensitive human beings, doctors should be prepared to respond to patients who ask why they must die, or die in pain. But here the doctor and the patient are at the same level. The doctor may have no better answer to those old questions than anyone else; and certainly no special insight from his training as a physician. It would be terrible for physicians to forget this, and to think that in a swift, lethal injection, medicine has found its own answer to the riddle of life. It would be a false answer, given by the wrong people. It would be no less a false answer for patients. They should neither ask medicine to put its own vocation at risk to serve their private interests, nor think that the answer to suffering is to be killed by another. The problem is precisely that, too often in human history, killing has seemed the quick, efficient way to put aside that which burdens us. It rarely helps, and too often simply adds to one evil still another. That is what I believe euthanasia would accomplish. It is self-determination run amok.

39

When Abstract Moralizing Runs Amok

John Lachs

Moral reasoning is more objectionable when it is abstract than when it is merely wrong. For abstractness all but guarantees error by missing the human predicament that needs to be addressed, and worse, it is a sign that thought has failed to keep faith with its mission. The function of moral reflection is to shed light on the difficult problems we face; it cannot perform its job without a clear understanding of how and why certain of our practices come to seem no longer satisfactory.

It is just this grasp of the problem that is conspicuously lacking in Daniel Callahan's assault on euthanasia in "Self-Determination Run Amok"[1] [*sic*]. The rhetoric Callahan unleashes gives not even a hint of the grave contemporary moral problems that euthanasia and assisted suicide, a growing number of people now think, promise to resolve.

Instead, we are offered a set of abstract distinctions calculated to discredit euthanasia rather than to contribute to a sound assessment of it. Thus, Callahan informs us that suffering "brought on by illness and dying as biological phenomena"[2] is to be contrasted with suffering that comes from "anguish or despair at the human condition." The former constitutes the proper concern of medicine (so much for psychiatry!), the latter of religion and philosophy. Medication is the answer to physical pain; euthanasia can, therefore, be only a misconceived response to worries about the meaning of existence. Those who believe in it offer a "swift lethal injection" as the "answer to the riddle of life."

This way of putting the matter will come as a surprise to those who suffer from terrible diseases and who no longer find life worth living. It is grotesque to suppose that such individuals are looking for the meaning of existence and find it, absurdly, in a lethal injection. Their predicament is not intellectual but existential. They are not interested in the meaning of life but in acting on their belief that their own continued existence is, on balance, of no further benefit to them.

Those who advocate the legalization of euthanasia and the practice of assisted suicide propose them as answers to a serious and growing social problem. We now have the power to sustain the biological existence of large numbers of very sick people, and we use this power freely. Accordingly, individuals suffering from painful terminal diseases, Alzheimer's patients, and those in a persistent vegetative state are routinely kept alive long past the point where they can function as human beings. They must bear the pain of existence without the ability to perform the activities that give life meaning. Some of these people feel intensely that they are a burden to others, as well as to themselves, and that their speedy and relatively dignified departure would be a relief to all concerned. Many observers of no more than average sensitivity agree that the plight of these patients is severe enough to justify such desires.

Original publication details: John Lachs, "When Abstract Moralizing Runs Amok," pp. 10–13 from *The Journal of Clinical Ethics* 5: 1 (Spring 1994). Copyright, JCE.

Bioethics: An Anthology, Third Edition. Edited by Helga Kuhse, Udo Schüklenk, and Peter Singer.

Some of these sufferers are physically not in a position to end their lives. Others could do so if they had the necessary instruments. In our culture, however, few have a taste for blowing out their brains or jumping from high places. That leaves drugs, which almost everyone is accustomed to taking, and which everyone knows can ease one peacefully to the other side.

The medical profession has, however, acquired monopoly power over drugs. And the danger of legal entanglement has made physicians wary of helping patients hasten their deaths in the discreet, humane way that has been customary for centuries. The result is that people who want to die and for whom death has long ceased to be an evil can find no way out of their misery. Current and growing pressures on the medical profession to help such sufferers are, therefore, due at least partly to medicine itself. People want physicians to aid in their suicides because, without such help, they cannot end their lives. This restriction of human autonomy is due to the social power of medicine; it is neither surprising nor morally wrong, therefore, to ask those responsible for this limitation to undo some of its most noxious effects. If the medical profession relinquished its hold on drugs, people could make effective choices about their future without the assistance of physicians. Even limited access to deadly drugs, restricted to single doses for those who desire them and who are certified to be of sound mind and near the end of life, would keep physicians away from dealing in death.

Unfortunately, however, there is little sensible public discussion of such policy alternatives. And these policy alternatives may, in any case, not satisfy Callahan, who appears to believe that there is something radically wrong with anyone terminating a human life. Because he plays coy, his actual beliefs are difficult to make out. He says the notion that self-determination extends to suicide "might be pertinent, at least for debate."[3] But his argument against euthanasia sidesteps this issue: he maintains that even if there is a right to kill oneself, it is not one that can be transferred. The reason for this is that doing so would lead to "a fundamental moral wrong" – that of one person giving over "his life and fate to another."

One might wonder how we know that transferring power over oneself is "a fundamental moral wrong." Callahan appears to entertain the idea with intuitive certainty, which gives him the moral and the logical high ground and entitles him to demand a justification from whoever disagrees. But such intuitions are problematic themselves: is fervent embrace of them enough to guarantee their truth? Morality would be very distant from the concerns of life if it depended on such guideposts placed here and there in the desert of facts, unrelated to each other or to anything else. Their message, moreover, makes the guide posts suspect: it comes closer to being an echo of tradition or an expression of current views than a revelation of eternal moral truths.

Most important, the very idea of a right that intrinsically *cannot* be handed on is difficult to grasp. Under normal circumstances, to have a right is to be free or to be entitled to have or to do something. I have a right, for example, to clean my teeth. No one else has the right to do that without my consent. But I can authorize another, say my sweetheart or my dental hygienist, to do it for me. Similarly, I can assign my right to my house, to my left kidney, to raising my children, to deciding when I rise, when I go to sleep, and what I do in between (by joining the Army), and by a power of attorney even to pursuing my own interest.

To be sure, the transfer of rights is not without limits. My wife and I can, for example, give over our right to our children, though we cannot do so for money. I can contract to slave away for ten hours a day cooking hamburgers, but I cannot sell myself to be, once and for all, a slave. This does not mean, however, that some rights are intrinsically nontransferable. If my right to my left kidney were nontransferable, I could neither sell it nor give it away. But I can give it away, and the only reason I cannot sell it is because sales of this sort were declared, at some point, to be against public policy. We cannot sell ourselves into slavery for the same reason: human societies set limits to this transfer of rights on account of its unacceptable costs.

The case is no different with respect to authorizing another to end my life. If I have a right to one of my kidneys, I have a right to both. And if I can tell a needy person to take one of them, I can tell two needy people to take one each. There is nothing *intrinsically* immoral about this, even though when the second helps himself I die. Yet, by dying too soon, I may leave opportunities unexplored and obligations unmet. Unscrupulous operators may take advantage of my goodwill or naiveté. The very possibility of such acts invites abuse. For these or similar reasons, we may decide that giving the first kidney is morally accept-able, but giving the second is not. The difference between the two acts, however, is not that the first is generous while the second is "a fundamental moral wrong," but that the second occurs in a context and has consequences and costs that the first does not.

Only in terms of context and cost, therefore, can we sensibly consider the issue of the morality of euthana-sia. Moving on the level of abstract maxims, Callahan misses this point altogether. He declares: "There are no good moral reasons to limit euthanasia once the prin-ciple of taking life…has been legitimated."[4] Serious moral reflection, though it takes principles into account, is little interested in legitimating *them*. Its focus is on determining the moral acceptability of certain sorts of actions performed in complex con-texts of life. Consideration of the circumstances is always essential: it is fatuous, therefore, to argue that if euthanasia is ever permissible, then "any competent person should have a right to be killed by a doctor for any reason that suits him."[5]

We can achieve little progress in moral philosophy without the ability and readiness to make relevant dis-tinctions. Why, then, does Callahan refuse to acknowl-edge that there are important differences between the situation of a terminally ill patient in grave pain who wants to die and that of a young father in the dental chair who wishes, for a moment, that he were dead? Callahan's reason is that he thinks all judgments about the unbearability of suffering and the worthlessness of one's existence are subjective and, as such, parts of a "private, idiosyncratic view of the good life."[6] The amount of our suffering "has very little directly to do" with our physical condition, and so the desire to end life is capricious and unreliable. If medicine honored such desires, it would "put its own vocation at risk" by serving "the private interests" of individuals.

I cannot imagine what the vocation of medicine might be if it is not to serve the private interests of individuals. It is, after all, my vision of the good life that accounts for my wish not to perish in a diabetic coma. And surgeons certainly pursue the private interests of their patients in removing cancerous growths and in providing face-lifts. Medicine does not surrender its vocation in serving the desires of indi-viduals: since health and continued life are among our primary wishes, its career consists in just this service.

Nevertheless, Callahan is right that our judgments about the quality of our lives and about the level of our suffering have a subjective component. But so do the opinions of patients about their health and illness, yet physicians have little difficulty in placing these percep-tions in a broader, objective context. Similarly, it is both possible and proper to take into account the objective circumstances that surround desires to terminate life. Physicians have developed considerable skill in relating subjective complaints to objective conditions; only by absurd exaggeration can we say that the doctor must accept either all or none of the patient's claims. The context of the young father in the dental chair makes it clear that only a madman would think of switching from novocaine to cyanide when he moans that he wants to be dead. Even people of ordinary sensitivity understand that the situation of an old person whose friends have all died and who now suffers the excruci-ating pain of terminal cancer is morally different.

The question of the justifiability of euthanasia, as all difficult moral questions, cannot be asked with-out specifying the details of context. Dire warnings of slippery slopes and of future large-scale, quietly conducted exterminations trade on overlooking dif-ferences of circumstance. They insult our sensitivity by the suggestion that a society of individuals of good will cannot recognize situations in which their fellows want and need help and cannot distinguish such situations from those in which the desire for death is rhetorical, misguided, temporary, or idiotic. It would indeed be tragic if medicine were to leap to the aid of lovelorn teenagers whenever they feel life is too much to bear. But it is just as lamentable to stand idly by and watch unwanted lives fill up with unproductive pain.

Callahan is correct in pointing out that, in euthana-sia and in assisted suicide, the physician and the patient must have separate justifications for action. The patient's wish is defensible if it is the outcome of a sound reflective judgment. Such judgments take into account the current condition, pending projects, and long-term prospects of the individual and relate them to his or her permanent interests and established values. As all assessments, these can be in error. For this reason, persons soliciting help in dying must be ready to demonstrate that they are of sound mind and thus capable of making such choices, that their desire is enduring, and that both their subjective and their objective condition makes their wish sensible.

Physicians must first decide whether their personal values permit them to participate in such activities. If they do, they must diligently examine the justifiability of the patient's desire to die. Diagnosis and prognosis are often relatively easy to ascertain. But we are not without resources for a sound determination of the internal condition of individuals either: extensive questioning on multiple occasions, interviews with friends and loved ones, and exploration of the life history and values of people contribute mightily to understanding their state of mind. Physicians who are prepared to aid individuals with this last need of their lives are not, therefore, in a position where they have to believe everything they hear and act on every request. They must make independent judgments instead of subordinating themselves as unthinking tools to the passing desires of those they wish to help. This does not attribute to doctors "the powers of the gods." It only requires that they be flexible in how they aid their patients and that they do so with due caution and on the basis of sound evaluation.

Callahan is once again right to be concerned that, if allowed, euthanasia will "take place within the boundaries of the private and confidential doctor-patient relationship."[7] This does, indeed, invite abuse and permit callous physicians to take a casual attitude to a momentous decision. Callahan is wrong, however, in supposing that this constitutes an argument against euthanasia. It is only a reason not to keep euthanasia secret, but to shed on it the wholesome light of publicity. Though the decision to terminate life is intensely private, no moral consideration demands that it be kept the confidential possession of two individuals. To the contrary, the only way we can minimize wrong decisions and abuse is to require scrutiny of the decision, prior to action on it, by a suitable social body.

Such examination, including at least one personal interview with the patient, should go a long distance toward relieving Callahan's concern that any law governing euthanasia would have "a low enforcement priority in the criminal justice system."[8] With formal social controls in place, there should be very little need for the involvement of courts and prosecutors.

To suppose, as Callahan does, that the principle of autonomy calls for us to stand idly by, or even to assist, whenever and for whatever reason people want to end their lives is calculated to discredit both euthanasia and autonomy. No serious moralist has ever argued that self-determination must be absolute. It cannot hold unlimited sway, as Mill and other advocates of the principle readily admit, if humans are to live in a society. And morally, it would cut no ice if murderers and rapists argued for the legitimacy of their actions by claiming that they flow naturally and solely from who they are.

The function of the principle of autonomy is to affirm *a* value and to shift the burden of justifying infringements of individual liberty to established social and governmental powers. The value it affirms is that of individual agency expressed in the belief that, through action and suffering and death, the life of each person enjoys a sort of private integrity. This means that, in the end, our lives belong to no one but ourselves. The limits to such self-determination or self-possession are set by the demands of social life. They can be discovered or decided upon in the process of moral reflection. A sensible approach to euthanasia can disclose how much weight autonomy carries in that context and how it can be balanced against other, equally legitimate but competing values.

In the hands of its friends, the principle of self-determination does not run amok. What runs amok in Callahan's version of autonomy and euthanasia is the sort of abstract moralizing that forgets the problem it sets out to address and shuts its eye to need and suffering.

Notes

1 D. Callahan, "Self-Determination Run Amok," *Hastings Center Report* 22 (March–April 1992): 52–55.
2 Ibid., 55.
3 Ibid., 52.
4 Ibid., 54.
5 Ibid.
6 Ibid., 52.
7 Ibid., 54.
8 Ibid.

40

Trends in End-of-Life Practices Before and After the Enactment of the Euthanasia Law in the Netherlands from 1990 to 2010

A Repeated Cross-Sectional Survey

Bregje D. Onwuteaka-Philipsen, Arianne Brinkman-Stoppelenburg, Corine Penning, Gwen J. F. de Jong-Krul, Johannes J. M. van Delden, and Agnes van der Heide

Introduction

At the end of life, many patients need comfort-oriented care. Such care might include end-of-life decision making (eg, on forgoing burdensome treatment or intensifying alleviation of pain or other symptoms). During this period, people can even develop a death wish, when suffering becomes overwhelming.[1,2] Patients might then ask their physician to end their life. In most countries physicians are not allowed to grant such a request, but there is much debate on this issue.[3–6] Concerns expressed include the fear of an expanding practice of euthanasia (eg, among vulnerable groups such as older people or incompetent patients). It is not known to what extent refused requests for euthanasia result in patients ending their own life.

Since 2002, the Netherlands has been one of the few countries where euthanasia and physician-assisted suicide are, under strict conditions, regulated by law. Comparable laws exist in Belgium and Luxembourg; Oregon, Montana, Washington (USA), and Switzerland have legally regulated assistance in suicide.[7,8] In the Netherlands, euthanasia is defined as the administering of lethal drugs by a physician with the explicit intention to end a patient's life on the patient's explicit request. In physician-assisted suicide the patient self-administers medication that was prescribed intentionally by a physician. In the Netherlands, the enactment of the euthanasia law was preceded by several decades of debate among medical practitioners, lawyers, ethicists, politicians, and the general public in which a reporting procedure was developed.[7] This debate has been informed by nationwide studies on end-of-life decision making that were done in 1990, before the first reporting procedure, 1995, 2001, and 2005.[9–13] These studies

Original publication details: Bregje D. Onwuteaka-Philipsen et al., "Trends in End-Of-Life Practices Before and After the Enactment of the Euthanasia Law in the Netherlands from 1990 to 2010: A Repeated Cross-Sectional Survey," pp. 908–15 from *The Lancet* 380: 9845 (2012). Reprinted from *The Lancet* with permission from Elsevier.

have allowed monitoring of the practice of end-of-life decision making in relation to development of the regulatory system. In 2005, 3 years after enactment of the euthanasia law, the euthanasia rate had decreased significantly, from 2·6% of all deaths in 2001, to 1·7% in 2005, which was a reversal of the trend from 1990 to 2001. Ending of life without an explicit request of the patient had decreased, albeit not significantly (0·7% in 2001 and 0·4% in 2005).[9] In 2010, 8 years after enactment of the euthanasia law, we investigated how end-of-life decision making practices have further developed.

Methods

Study design

In 2010, we undertook a nationwide death-certificate study that was largely similar to earlier studies done in 1990, 1995, 2001, and 2005.[9–13] We drew a random sample from the central death registry of Statistics Netherlands, to which all deaths and causes were reported. The period studied was Aug 1, through Nov 1, in all studied years. All deaths that occurred in that period were assigned to one of five strata. When the cause of death clearly precluded end-of-life decision making (eg, instant death in a traffic accident), cases were assigned to stratum one. These cases were retained in the sample, but no questionnaires were sent out to the physician. On the basis of cause of death, cases were assigned to one of the other strata looking at the likelihood that an end-of-life decision had preceded death: when this decision was unlikely (eg, acute myocardial infarction or aneurysm) cause of death was allocated to stratum two, when this decision was possible (eg, heart failure or Parkinson's disease) to stratum three, and when this decision was more probable (eg, cancer) to stratum four. Cases were assigned to stratum five when the physician had noted on the death certificate that they had actively ended the life of the patient. The final sampling contained 50% of the cases of stratum five, 25% of the cases in stratum four, 13% of those in stratum three, 8% of those in stratum one and two. To ensure that children younger than 17 years of age and nonwestern immigrants, two small groups in death statistics, were represented well in the sample all deaths in which an end-of-life decision could not be precluded in these groups were sampled.

All attending physicians of the sampled cases in strata two to five received a questionnaire. The data collection procedure precluded identification of physician and patient. The Ministry of Justice gave a guarantee that no physician could be prosecuted on the basis of information given to the researchers. According to Dutch policy, the study did not require review by an ethics committee.

Questionnaire

The questionnaire focused on end-of-life decision making that might have preceded the death of the patient involved. The four key questions addressed the following factors: (1) whether the respondent had withheld or withdrawn medical treatment while taking into account the possible hastening of death; (2) whether the respondent had intensified measures to alleviate pain or other symptoms while taking into account or partly intending the possible hastening of death; (3) whether the respondent had withheld or withdrawn medical treatment with the explicit intention of hastening death; or (4) whether the respondent had administered, supplied, or prescribed drugs with the explicit intention of hastening death, resulting in the patient's death. These questions were validated in the 1990 and 1995 study, and were kept identical in all years studied. If more than one of the key questions was answered affirmatively, the act that involved the most explicit intention was used to classify the case. If the intention was similar, the administration of drugs prevailed over the withholding or withdrawing of treatment. If question four was answered affirmatively and if the act was done in response to an explicit request by the patient, the act was classified as euthanasia or assisted suicide (depending on whether or not the patients had taken the drugs themselves). If question four was answered affirmatively and the act was not done in response to an explicit request by the patient, the act was classified as ending of life without explicit request.

Details about the decision-making process, the type of drugs that had been used, and the degree to which death had been hastened as estimated by the physician, were asked for the most important end-of-life decision, if any. Physicians were further asked to choose the term that they thought best described their end-of-life decision: "forgoing treatment", "alleviation of symptoms", "palliative or terminal sedation", "ending of life", "assisted suicide", or "euthanasia". Finally, we asked whether the patient had been "deeply and continuously sedated until death", whether the patient had made a request for euthanasia or physician-assisted suicide that was not granted, and whether patients had purposely ended their life by stopping eating and drinking.

Statistical analyses

All cases were weighted to adjust for the stratification procedure and for differences in response rates in relation to age, sex, marital status, region of residence, and cause and place of death. The results were then extrapolated to 2010, to reflect all deaths in 2010 in the Netherlands (n=136 058). This weighting procedure was done in all years studied (1990, 1995, 2001, 2005, and 2010). As a result of this weighting procedure the percentages presented cannot be derived from the absolute unweighted numbers presented. 95% CIs were calculated. This procedure took into account the weighting by standardising the weighting factors to the actual number of cases.

Role of funding source

The sponsor of the study had no role in study design, data collection, data analysis, data interpretation, or writing of the report. The corresponding author had full access to all the data in the study and had final responsibility for the decision to submit for publication.

Results

Of the 8496 questionnaires that were mailed, 6263 were returned and eligible for analysis (response rate 74%). Response rates in the different strata ranged between 64% and 84%, with response being higher in strata in which the likelihood of an end-of-life decision was higher. Response rates in 1990, 1995,

2001, and 2005 were comparable (range 74% to 78%). The frequency of euthanasia increased between 2005 and 2010 (table 40.1). The frequency of physician-assisted suicide remained low over the years. Figure 40.1 shows that the increase in the number of instances of euthanasia is related to both an increase in the number of explicit requests for euthanasia (from 4·8% [95% CI 4·4–5·2; 503 of 9965] of all deaths surveyed in 2005 to 6·7% [6·1–7.3; 766 of 6861] in 2010) and the proportion of requests that were granted (from 37% [252 of 503] to 45% [496 of 766] of requests). The frequency of ending of life without an explicit patient request decreased over the years (from 0·8% [95% CI 0·6–1·1; 45 of 5197] of all deaths in 1990 to 0·2% [0·1–0·3%; 13 of 6861] in 2010). While the frequency of forgoing of life-prolonging treatment was relatively stable over the years, the frequency of intensified alleviation of symptoms increased, especially between 2005 and 2010. The percentage of all cases in which physicians intensified alleviation of symptoms, rather than only cases in which that action was most important, was 30% (29–31; 1832 of 5617) in 2005 and 45% (44–46; 2777 of 6861) in 2010. For forgoing treatment, the percentage of all cases in which treatment was forgone, thus also when this factor was not the most important, was 28% (95% CI 27–29; 1434 of 5617) in 2005 and 37% (36–39; 2103 of 6861) in 2010 (data not shown).

We also saw an increase of continuous deep sedation until death. A small proportion of patients in 2010 had intentionally hastened death by stopping eating and drinking (table 40.1). Further analysis showed that in 0·2% (seven of 6861) of all deaths patients had intentionally stopped eating and drinking after an ungranted euthanasia request. Another 0·04% (13 of 6861) had committed suicide with drugs or another method after an ungranted euthanasia request. Thus, in 7% (20 of 270) of deaths in which the patient had made a ungranted euthanasia request the patient hastened death him or herself (data not shown).

Euthanasia and physician-assisted suicide most often concern younger people, cancer patients, and patients attended by general practitioners (table 40.2). The decreased frequency of ending of life without explicit patient request is most pronounced in people younger than 65 years of age, where it decreased

Table 40.1 Frequency of euthanasia, assisted suicide, and other end-of-life practices in the Netherlands in 1990, 1995, 2001, 2005, and 2010

	1990	1995	2001	2005	2010
Number of deaths in the Netherlands	128 824	135 675	140 377	136 402	136 056
Number of studied cases	5197	5146	5617	9965	6861
Most important end-of-life decision					
Euthanasia	141 (1·7% [1·4–2·1])	257 (2·4% [2·1–2·6])	310 (2·6% [2·3–2·8])	294 (1·7% [1·5–1·8])	475 (2·8% [2·5–3·2])
Assisted suicide	18 (0·2% [0·1–0·3])	25 (0·2% [0·1–0·3])	25 (0·2% [0·1–0·3])	17 (0·1% [<0·1–0·1])	21 (0·1% [0·1–0·2])
Ending of life without explicit patient request	45 (0·8% [0·6–1·1])	64 (0·7% [0·5–0·9])	42 (0·7% [0·5–0·9])	24 (0·4% [0·2–0·6])	13 (0·2% [0·1–0·3])
Intensified alleviation of symptoms	1166 (18·8% [17·9–19·9])	1161 (19·1% [18·1–20·1])	1312 (20·1% [19·1–21·1])	1478 (24·7% [23·5–26·0])	2202 (36·4% [35·2–37·6])
Forgoing of life-prolonging treatment	991 (17·9% [17·0–18·9])	1097 (20·2% [19·1–21·3])	1210 (20·2% [19·1–21·3])	767 (15·6% [15·0–16·2])	974 (18·2% [17·3–19·1])
Total	2361 (39·4% [38·1–40·7])	2604 (42·6% [41·3–43·9])	2899 (43·8% [42·6–45·0])	2570 (42·5% [41·1–43·9])	3685 (57·8% [56·7–59·0])
Continuous deep sedation[†][†]	NA	NA	–	521 (8·2% [7·8–8·6])	789 (12·3% [11·6–13·1])
Patient deciding to end life by stopping eating and drinking	NA	NA	NA	NA	18 (0·4% [0·3–0·6])

Data are absolute number or number of patients (weighted % [95% CI]). All percentages are weighted for sampling fractions, non-response, and random sampling deviations, to make them representative for all deaths in the year studied. Therefore, the percentages presented cannot be derived from the unweighted absolute numbers presented. NA=not available.
*Continuous deep sedation might have been provided in conjunction with practices that possibly hastened death.
[†]In 2001, continuous deep sedation was only studied when it occurred in conjunction with an end-of-life decision; the frequency was 5·6%; corresponding numbers are 7·1% in 2005 and 11% in 2010.

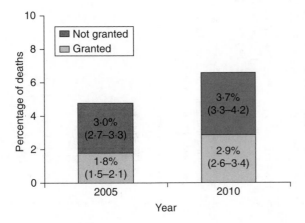

Figure 40.1 Weighted percentage (95% CI) of all deaths preceded by a granted or ungranted request for euthanasia or physician-assisted suicide

A request can be ungranted for different reasons, among which a refusal of the physician, or the patient dying before the physician could decide on granting the request. There were 9965 deaths in 2005 and 6861 deaths in 2010. Absolute unweighted numbers: 252 granted requests and 251 ungranted for euthanasia in 2005; and 496 granted requests and 270 ungranted requests in 2010.

between 2001 and 2010, and among clinical specialists (table 40.2). For intensified alleviation of symptoms the increase was consistently seen in all patient groups.

The most important reasons for the physician to grant the euthanasia requests that were mentioned most often in 2010 were the wish of the patient (85% [420 of 496]; 82% [219 of 262] in 2005), no prospect of improvement (82% [405 of 496]; 85% [223 of 262] in 2005), no more options for treatment (73% [370 of 496]; not asked in 2005), and loss of dignity (61% [311 of 496]; 60% [164 of 262] in 2005). Between 2005 and 2010, no clear differences were seen in the percentage of cases in which physician discussed end-of-life decisions with the patient, relatives, and other physicians. Both in 2005 and 2010, most cases of euthanasia and physician-assisted suicide were undertaken with neuromuscular relaxants and barbiturates. A non-significant decrease occurred in use of these drugs for ending of life without explicit request (from 29·4% [95% CI 14·9–49·4; seven of 24] to 1·6% [0·1–31·0; one of 13]). Intensified alleviation of symptoms was more commonly done with a combination of benzodiazepines and opioids in 2010 than in 2005

(table 40.3). No clear differences were seen between the years in the estimated degree to which end-of-life decisions had shortened life. In 2010, euthanasia and physician-assisted suicide were estimated to have shortened the patient's life by a week or more in 58% (322 of 496) of cases, compared with 9% (one of 13) for ending of life without explicit request and 3% (61 of 2202) for intensified alleviation of symptoms. In over half of all cases of intensified alleviation of symptoms, the physician estimated that life had not been shortened; this is a small increase compared with 2005 (table 40.3). Finally, in 2010, of all physicians who had indicated in the questionnaire to have made an end-of-life decision that was classified as euthanasia or physician-assisted suicide, most classed "euthanasia", "assisted suicide", or "ending of life" the most appropriate term for their act, followed by "palliative or terminal sedation"; these classifications are comparable with 2005. In 2010, ending of life without explicit patient request was never labelled as "ending of life" (in 2005 about a fifth of cases were classed as "ending of life"); it was mostly labelled as "palliative or terminal sedation" or "alleviation of symptoms" (table 40.3).

The absolute number of cases of euthanasia or physician-assisted suicide in 2010 was about 4050. In 2010, 3136 (77%) cases of euthanasia or physician-assisted suicide were reported to euthanasia review committees in the Netherlands.[14] In our questionnaire we also asked whether physicians had reported their act to a euthanasia review committee. With these data a similar reporting rate was calculated (table 40.4). The reporting rate in 2010 is comparable with the reporting rate of 2005 (80%; 1933 of 2425), and higher than the reporting rate before enactment of the law (18% [486 of 2700] in 1990; 41% [1466 of 3600] in 1995, and 54% [2054 of 3800] in 2001). In the unreported cases the drugs used were hardly ever neuromuscular relaxants or barbiturates and the most appropriate term according to the physician was never "euthanasia" or "assisted suicide" (table 40.4). Furthermore, in cases in which the physician had reported to a euthanasia review committee the estimated shortening of life was more often a week or more than in unreported cases (table 40.4). Finally general practitioners were more inclined to report whereas clinical specialists were less inclined to report.

Table 40.2 Frequencies of euthanasia or physician-assisted suicide, ending of life without explicit request, and intensified alleviation of symptoms in 2001, 2005 and 2010, according to patient characteristics

	All deaths in 2010 (%)	Euthanasia and physician-assisted suicide			Ending of life without explicit request			Intensified alleviation of symptoms		
		2001	2005	2010	2001	2005	2010	2001	2005	2010
Age (years)										
0–64 (n=2079)	19%	139 (5·0% [4·1–6·0])	131 (3·5% [2·7–4·4])	191 (5·6% [4·6–6·7])	11 (1·0% [0·7–1·5])	13 (1·0% [0·7–1·5])	4 (0·2% [0·1–0·5])	303 (18·9% [17·3–20·7])	384 (21·4% [19·7–23·2])	533 (30·5% [28·5–32·5])
65–79 (n=2156)	31%	134 (3·3% [2·6–4·1])	126 (2·1% [1·5–2·8])	191 (4·0% [3·2–4·9])	11 (0·4% [0·2–0·8])	5 (0·3 % [0·1–0·6])	4 (0·3% [0·1–0·6])	456 (20·8% [19·1–23·5])	536 (25·4% [23·4–26·7])	721 (35·3% [33·3–37·3])
≥80 (n=2626)	51%	58 (1·4 % [1·0–1·9])	54 (0·8% [0·5–1·2])	114 (1·4% [1·0–1·9])	20 (0·7% [0·4–1·1])	6 (0·2% [0·1–0·4])	5 (0·2% [0·1–0·4])	553 (20·2% [18·6–21·7])	558 (25·6% [24·2–27·6])	948 (39·2% [37·1–40·8])
Sex										
Male (n=3538)	49%	175 (3·1% [2·6–3·7])	181 (2·0% [1·6–2·5])	281 (3·5% [2·9–4·2])	19 (0·7% [0·5–1·0])	11 (0·4 % [0·2–0·7])	7 (0·2% [0·1–0·4])	591 (19·1% [17·7–20·3])	731 (23·7% [22·4–25·2])	1101 (34·5% [33·4–36·5])
Female (n=3278)	52%	156 (2·5% [2·0–3·1])	130 (1·5% [1·1–2·0])	215 (2·5% [1·9–3·0])	23 (0·7% [0·4–1·0])	13 (0·4% [0·2–0·7])	6 (0·2% [0·1–0·4])	721 (21·1% [19·6–22·4])	747 (25·7% [24·5–27·5])	1101 (38·2% [36·4–39·6])
Cause of death										
Cancer (n=3055)	31%	280 (7·4% [6·5–8·4])	269 (5·1% [4·4–6·0])	415 (7·6% [6·7–8·6])	24 (1·0% [0·7–1·4])	9 (0·3% [0·1–0·6])	6 (0·2% [0·1–0·4])	709 (33·4% [31·2–34·6])	989 (37·1% [35·1–38·7])	1369 (47·7% [46·2–49·8])
Cardiovascular disease (n=931)	22%	6 (0·4% [0·1–1·0])	7 (0·3% [0·1–0·9])	15 (0·5% [0·2–1·3])	4 (0·6% [0·2–1·4])	2 (0·2% [0·1–0·8])	0	128 (11·1% [9·0–13·0])	175 (14·3% [11·8–16·3])	193 (21·5% [18·7–24·5])
Other or unknown (n=2875)	47%	45 (1·2% [0·8–1·7])	35 (0·4% [0·2–0·7])	66 (1·1% [0·8–1·6])	14 (0·5% [0·3–0·8])	13 (0·6% [0·3–0·9])	7 (0·3% [0·1–0·6])	475 (17·1% [15·6–18·4])	314 (24·1% [22·4–25·6])	640 (36·0% [34·2–37·8])
Type of physician*										
General practitioner (n=3424)	45%	274 (5·8% [5·1–6·7])	272 (3·7% [3·1–4·4])	456 (5·8% [5·1–6·7])	20 (0·6% [0·4–0·9])	6 (0·2% [0·1–0·4])	5 (0·2% [0·1–0·4])	609 (20·9% [19·6–22·4])	686 (23·9% [22·5–25·3])	1152 (34·3% [32·4–35·6])
Clinical specialist (n=1248)	26%	48 (1·8% [1·1–2·7])	22 (0·5% [0·2–1·0])	16 (0·9% [0·4–1·6])	18 (1·2% [0·7–2·0])	7 (0·7% [0·3–1·4])	2 (0·4% [0·1–0·9])	300 (18·2% [15·9–20·2])	352 (22·7% [20·5–25·1])	546 (32·1% [29·4–34·6])
Elderly care physician (n=1588)	29%	9 (0·4% [0·1–0·8])	12 (0·2% [0·1–0·6])	29 (0·4% [0·1–0·8])	4 (0·4% [0·1–0·7])	4 (0·3% [0·1–0·7])	6 (0·2% [0·1–0·6])	403 (31·7% [29·7–34·3])	410 (35·7% [33·6–38·3])	504 (45·8% [43·5–48·4])
Total (n=6861)	100%	331 (2·8% [2·4–3·2])	311 (1·8% [1·5–2·1])	496 (3·0% [2·5–3·3])	42 (0·7% [0·5–0·9])	24 (0·4% [0·2–0·6])	13 (0·2% [0·1–0·3])	1312 (20·1% [19·1–21·1])	1478 (24·7% [23·5–26·0])	2202 (36·4% [35·2–37·6])

Data are percentage or absolute number of patients (weighted % [95% CI]). Percentages are weighted for sampling fractions, non-response, and random sampling deviations, to make them representative of all deaths in the year studied. Therefore, the percentages presented cannot be derived from the unweighted absolute numbers presented.

*Missing observations for 2005: five for euthanasia and physician-assisted suicide, six for ending of life without explicit request, and 30 for intensified alleviation of symptoms.

Table 40.3 Characteristics of euthanasia or physician-assisted suicide, ending of life without explicit request, and intensified alleviation of symptoms, in 2005 and 2010

	Euthanasia and physician-assisted suicide		Ending of life without explicit request		Intensified alleviation of symptoms	
	2005 (n=262)	2010 (n=496)	2005 (n=24)	2010 (n=13)	2005 (n=1478)	2010 (n=2202)
Discussion						
Discussion with or previous wish of patient	262 (100·0%)	496 (100·0%)	10 (60·0% [36·6–77·9])	6 (59·1% [31·6–86·1])	554 (35·3% [32·5–37·4])	760 (32·9% [31·1–35·0])
Discussion with relative(s)	200 (75·5% [70·0–80·4])	346 (70·5% [67·0–75·0])	13 (80·9% [57·8–92·9])	7 (72·2% [38·6–90·9])	724 (54·0% [51·5–56·5])	962 (48·6% [46·9–51·1])
Discussion with other physician(s)	230 (87·7% [84·3–92·1])	459 (93·8% [91·5–95·9])	15 (65·3% [44·7–84·4])	5 (53·4% [25·1–80·8])	411 (29·5% [27·6–32·3])	596 (27·9% [26·1–29·9])
No discussion with any of the above	0	0	4 (19·1% [7·1–42·2])	5 (24·9% [5·0–53·8])	613 (38·2% [35·5–40·5])	994 (41·2% [39·0–43·1])
Drugs*						
Neuromuscular relaxants†	197 (67·0% [61·5–72·9])	392 (72·2% [68·0–75·9])	5 (23·4% [9·7–46·7])	1 (1·6% [0·1–36·0])	..	..
Barbiturates†	10 (8·5% [6·0–13·3])	37 (7·9% [5·8–10·8])	2 (6·0% [0·2–21·5])	0	..	..
Benzodiazepines and opioids	9 (6·7% [4·1–10·6])	28 (13·3% [10·0–15·9])	5 (22·4% [7·1–42·2])	4 (26·1% [5·2–54·1])	384 (23·7% [21·8–26·6])	853 (37·1% [35·0–39·0])
Benzodiazepines	7 (7·0% [4·1–10·6])	7 (3·0% [10·0–15·9])	1 (3·3% [0·1–21·1])	1 (9·0% [0·1–36·3])	71 (3·5% [3·1–5·1])	119 (4·8% [4·1–6·0])
Opioids	13 (10·5% [7·3–14·9])	5 (3·1% [1·7–4·9])	7 (40·2% [22·1–63·4])	7 (63·3% [32·2–86·4])	947 (69·4% [66·7–71·4])	1134 (56·4% [53·9–58·1])
Other	1 (0·3%)	2 (0·5% [0·3–2·3])	3 (4·7% [0·2–21·3])	0	58 (3·4% [2·2–4·0])	37 (1·7% [1·2–2·3])
Shortening of life						
Probably no life shortening	2 (0·7% [0·2–3·3])	1 (0·4%)	3 (17·2% [4·7–37·4])	1 (9·4% [0·1–36·3])	778 (54·2% [51·5–56·5])	1275 (58·6% [56·9–61·0])
Less than a week	101 (44·1% [37·9–49·9])	166 (40·3% [35·6–44·2])	14 (68·3% [44·7–84·4])	10 (76·1% [46·2–95·0])	397 (26·8% [24·7–29·3])	587 (26·9% [25·2–28·9])
A week or more	153 (53·9% [47·8–59·9])	322 (58·0% [53·7–62·4])	6 (11·6% [2·7–32·3])	1 (9·1% [0·1–36·3])	47 (3·4% [2·2–4·0])	61 (3·1% [2·3–3·8])
Unknown	6 (1·3% [0·2–0·3])	7 (1·3% [0·3–2·3])	1 (2·9% [0·1–21])	1 (5·4% [0·1–36·3])	256 (15·6% [14·1–17·8])	279 (11·4% [9·7–12·3])
Most appropriate term for decision according to physician						
Euthanasia or assisted suicide	225 (82·8% [78·3–87·4])	412 (76·7% [73·3–80·7])	0	0	0	1 (<0·1%)
Ending of life	5 (0·5% [0·2–3·3])	9 (2·0% [1·0–3·7])	4 (17·2% [4·7–37·4])	0	0	1 (<0·1%)
Alleviation of symptoms	7 (3·6% [1·9–6·9])	2 (1·5% [1·0–3·7])	8 (33·3% [15·6–55·3])	4 (40·6% [13·9–68·4])	849 (57·5% [54·4–59·5])	1201 (57·5% [55·9–60·1])
Non-treatment decision	1 (0·2%)	0	1 (3·9% [0·1–21])	1 (1·7% [0·0–36])	79 (5·5% [4·0–6·2])	625 (8·3% [6·9–9·2])
Palliative or terminal sedation	22 (12·2% [7·9–15·7])	44 (18·1% [14·6–21·3])	10 (41·8% [22·1–63·4])	7 (52·2% [25·1–80·8])	281 (19·2% [17·0–21·0])	486 (20·3% [18·3–21·7])
Unknown	2 (0·7% [0·1–2·7])	8 (1·7% [1·0–3·7])	1 (3·8% [0·1–21·1])	1 (5·5% [0·1–36·3])	269 (17·8% [16·0–20·0])	355 (13·9% [12·5–15·4])

Data are absolute number of patients (weighted % [95% CI]). Percentages are weighted for sampling fractions, non-response and random sampling deviations, to make them representative for all deaths in the year studied. Therefore the percentages presented cannot be derived from the unweighted absolute numbers presented.

*Drugs could have been neuromuscular relaxants, in any combination; barbiturates, alone or in combination with other drugs except neuromuscular relaxants; the combination of benzodiazepines and opioids possibly in combination with other drugs except neuromuscular relaxants or barbiturates; benzodiazepines alone or in combination with other drugs except neuromuscular relaxants, barbiturates, and opioids; or other drugs than the ones mentioned above.

†Not asked separately for intensified alleviation of symptoms.

Table 40.4 Characteristics of reported and unreported cases of euthanasia and physician-assisted suicide

	Not reported (n=45)	Reported (n=443)	Total (n=496)*
Age (years)			
0–64	14 (20·5% [9·5–34·6])	174 (38·1% [33·4–42·4])	191 (34·8% [30·9–39·3])
65–79	18 (47·3% [31·7–62·1])	170 (39·4% [34·5–43·6])	191 (40·7% [36·6–45·3])
≥80	13 (32·2% [18·2–46·6])	99 (22·5% [18·0–25·7])	114 (24·5% [21·2–28·8])
Sex			
Male	24 (53·7% [37·9–68·3])	254 (58·1% [53·4–62·6])	281 (57·2% [52·7–61·4])
Female	21 (46·3% [31·7–62·1])	189 (41·9% [37·4–46·6])	215 (42·8% [38·6–47·3])
Cause of death			
Cancer	36 (63·4% [46·5–76·2])	371 (83·1% [79·6–86·6])	415 (79·1% [75·4–82·6)
Cardiovascular disease	2 (9·8% [3·7–24·1])	13 (2·5% [1·6–5·0])	15 (4·0% [2·5–6·2])
Other/unknown	7 (26·8% [14·6–41·9])	59 (14·4% [10·8–17·2])	66 (16·9% [13·6–20·2])
Type of physician			
General practitioner	36 (71·4% [55·7–83·6])	408 (92·5% [90·2–95·2])	269 (88·1% [85·0–90·8])
Clinical specialist	2 (23·8% [12·9–39·5])	14 (4·4% [2·4–6·3])	7 (8·4% [5·8–10·8])
Elderly care physicians	7 (4·8% [0·5–15·2])	21 (3·1% [1·6–5·0])	35 (3·5% [2·5–6·2])
Drugs			
Neuromuscular relaxants	1 (<0·1%)	386 (90·2% [86·9–92·7])	392 (72·2% [68·0–75·9])
Barbiturates	1 (<0·1%)	36 (9·8% [7·3–13·1])	37 (7·9% [5·8–10·8])
Benzodiazapines and opioids	28 (66·7% [51·0–80·0])	0	28 (13·3% [10·0–15·9])
Benzodiazepines	7 (15·4% [6·5–29·4])	0	7 (3·0% [1·7–4·9])
Opioids	5 (15·4% [6·5–29·4])	0	5 (3·1% [1·7–4·9])
Other	1 (2·5% [0·1–11·8])	1 (<0·1%)	2 (0·5% [0·3–2·3])
Shortening of life			
Probably no life shortening	1 (2·6% [0·1–11·8])	0	1 (0·4%)
Less than a week	39 (87·0% [73·2–94·9])	126 (28·2% [23·8–32·2])	166 (40·3% [35·6–44·2])
A week or more	5 (10·4% [3·7–24·1])	315 (71·3% [66·9–75·3])	322 (58·0% [53·7–62·4])
Unknown	0	2 (0·6% [0·3–2·3])	7 (1·3% [0·3–2·3])
Most appropriate term for the act according to physician			
Euthanasia or assisted suicide	0	432 (97·4% [95·0–98·4])	412 (76·7% [73·3–80·7])
Ending of life	1 (2·5% [0·1–11·8])	8 (1·6% [0·9–3·8])	9 (2·0% [1·0–3·7])
Alleviation of symptoms	2 (7·5% [2·5–21])	0	2 (1·5% [1·0–3·7])
Palliative or terminal sedation	4 (90·0% [2·5–21·2])	2 (0·7% [0·3–2·3])	44 (18·1% [14·6–21·3])

Data are absolute number of patients (weighted % [95% CI]). All percentages are weighted for sampling fractions, non-response, and random sampling deviations, to make them representative of all deaths in the Netherlands in 2010. Therefore the percentages presented cannot be derived from the unweighted absolute numbers presented.

*For eight cases, it was not known whether the physician had reported the case to a euthanasia review committee.

Discussion

After the modest decrease in euthanasia frequency 3 years after enactment of the euthanasia law, we saw an increase 8 years after the enactment. A rise in the number of patients requesting euthanasia explains this increase partly. While more than half of these requests were not granted, physicians granted requests more often in 2010 than in 2005. As no differences occurred in patient characteristics of cases of euthanasia and physician-assisted suicide, the increase seems not to be due to expansion to other patient groups.

Euthanasia is still mostly undertaken in younger people, cancer patients, and in general practice rather than in hospitals or nursing homes. As the rate of euthanasia and physician-assisted suicide in 2010 was comparable with the rate before enactment of the law in 2001, some physicians might have been unsure about how the law would work in practice, in 2005, shortly after the enactment of the law, making them more reluctant to undertake euthanasia. In Belgium, the euthanasia rate decreased from 1·1% in 1998 to 0·3% in 2001, shortly before enactment of a euthanasia law in 2002, increasing again to 1·9% in 2007.[15]

Although, in Belgium the increase occurred just before the enactment of the law, this trend might represent a similar phenomenon as in the Netherlands because in Belgium the euthanasia law was heavily debated before its enactment.[16]

After publication of the Dutch 1990 study,[13] the subject that raised the most international debate was the number of cases of ending of life without an explicit patient request (panel).[18, 19] The frequency of this practice has been decreasing since. One reason for this decrease might be the increased attention for palliative care over the last decade,[20, 21] Additionally, this decrease might be related to the regulation of euthanasia and physician-assisted suicide, through enabling patients and physicians to openly discuss end-of-life preferences. In Belgium, where a euthanasia law was enacted in 2002, the rate of ending of life without request was higher in 1998 (3·2%) than in 2001 (1·5%) and 2007 (1·8%).[15] In the UK the rate ending life without request was stable between 2004 and 2008 (0·3%).[22] While there is debate in the UK about regulation of assisted dying, no law exists on euthanasia or physician-assisted suicide in the UK. Notwithstanding the decrease of ending of life without explicit request, information on characteristics of these cases is important to assess this practice. Although the absolute numbers are small, in half of these cases the decision has been discussed with the patient and in a quarter of cases the physician did not discuss the decision with either patient, relative, or other physicians.

The frequency of intensified alleviation of symptoms has risen, especially between 2005 and 2010. This finding is unexpected because evidence shows that the life-shortening effects of opioids are often overestimated.[23–25] Yet, in over half of the cases in which symptoms were alleviated while taking into account a possible life-shortening effect, the physician thought that life had actually not been shortened. Knowledge about the limited life-shortening potential of opioids thus might have taken away reluctance in physicians and patients to use opioids. This effect is probably related to increased attention for palliative care in the Netherlands, which could also explain the rising use of continuous deep sedation until death.[20, 21] This finding is in line with results of a study in Dutch nursing homes showing an increase in the use of pain relief and no change in treatment with anti-

Panel: **Research in context**

Systematic review

The Netherlands, Belgium, and Luxembourg are the only countries in the world where the ending of a patient's life by a physician on the patient's explicit request is legally allowed, if strict criteria are met. Physician assistance in a patient's suicide is, also under strict conditions, legally allowed in Switzerland, and some states in the USA. We searched PubMed and Medline databases for reports on the frequency of the use of euthanasia and physician-assisted suicide and the main background characteristics of these practices. We used the search terms "euthanasia", "assisted suicide", "epidemiology", "incidence", and "frequency". Our search was limited to articles that were published in English during the past 10 years, which presented studies about physician-assistance in dying in adults.

Interpretation

Studies from countries where euthanasia and physician-assisted suicide are not legal mainly focus on health-care professionals' attitudes towards end-of-life decision making and physician assistance in dying. In these studies, the term euthanasia is not always referring to the practice of a physician ending a patient's life on his or her explicit request. The frequencies and main background characteristics of physicians' involvement in ending their patients' lives on their explicit request during the past 10 years have been studied in the Netherlands, USA, UK, Belgium, Germany, and in one international study that included Sweden, Denmark, the Netherlands, Belgium, Switzerland, Italy, and Australia (the Eureld study).[17] The frequency of this practice varies between countries, with the highest rates in countries where it is legal. In all countries, this practice mainly involves patients with incurable cancer who are in the end stage of their disease. Whereas in the Netherlands euthanasia and physician-assisted suicide are mainly done by general practitioners in patients who are dying at home, physician assistance in dying is a more hospital-based practice in other countries. The frequency of physicians ending a patient's life in the absence of an explicit request does not seem to be increased in countries where euthanasia is legalised.

biotics of dementia patients with pneumonia over a decade.[26] In Belgium, an increase in intensified alleviation of pain and symptoms and in continuous deep sedation also coincided with increased attention for palliative care.[15] In the UK, a decrease in the use of intensified alleviation of symptoms was noted, from 30% in 2004 to 22% in 2008. However, whether these rates are comparable is debatable because in 2004 wording in the questionnaires was similar to the wording in our studies (taking into account possible life-shortening effect), whereas in 2008 the wording was different (knowledge of probable or certain hastening of life).[20]

We noted that in 2010, according to their physician, in 0·4% (18 of 6861) of all deaths the patient intentionally had stopped eating and drinking. This is substantially lower than the rate recorded in a proxy-report in a Dutch population-based survey in 2009.[27] Physicians are not always aware of patients intentionally stopping eating and drinking. The survey showed that in 72% of cases the person stopping eating and drinking had a disease diagnosis. However, a sample of deceased people might yield more accurate estimates of end-of-life practices than a population-based sample of proxies. We noted that in almost half of patients who intentionally stopped eating and drinking, they had made a euthanasia request that was not granted, which is a similar percentage as reported in the proxy survey. While this proportion is substantial, it is a minority of all deceased patients whose request did not result in euthanasia. An even smaller group committed suicide after their euthanasia request was not granted. We are not aware of studies of patients intentionally ending their life in the course of a serious illness in other countries. Whether the legal option of euthanasia or physician-assisted suicide influences these rates would be interesting to know.

Eight years after enactment of the euthanasia law the percentage of cases that were reported to the review committees, which is a legal obligation, stabilised. In unreported cases virtually all physicians labelled their decision themselves as "palliative or terminal sedation" or as "alleviation of symptoms", and none of them used neuromuscular relaxants or barbiturates. By contrast, in reported cases virtually all physicians labelled their act as "euthanasia" or "assisted suicide", and all used neuromuscular relaxants or barbiturates, the drugs advised for undertaking euthanasia or physician-assisted suicide by the Royal Dutch Association for Pharmacy and by the Euthanasia Review Committees. These characteristics of unreported cases have led some to argue that cases of

euthanasia in which opioids were used should not be included in the euthanasia rate.[28] Excluding unreported cases would make for a reporting rate of about 100%, both in 2005 and 2010. However, use of opioids was only classified as euthanasia when physicians affirmed that death was caused by administering this drug with the intention to end life. Hastening of death by administration of opioids in these cases cannot be ruled out. Obviously, the classification scheme used in our studies is more likely to result in an overestimation than in an underestimation of the euthanasia frequency. In any case, our finding that about 100% of the cases in which the advised drugs were used were reported suggests that non-reporting by physicians is not related to unwillingness to report cases of euthanasia. This finding seems more related to lack of clarity about or discrepancy between effects of drugs and intention with regard to hastening death. Further education seems the most appropriate way to further increase the reporting rate.

Together with the high response rates and the availability of data for over two decades, an important strength of the study is the substantial sample of deaths that is representative for all deaths in all settings nationwide. A limitation is that information is derived from physicians, making us rely on the physicians' assessment of the situation. While this approach is the best source for information on the physicians' experiences, such as the physician's intention or the most appropriate term for the decision according to the physician, it can be more difficult for physicians to assess the life-shortening effect of drugs. Additionally, physicians might give socially desirable answers. However, we noted a similar reporting rate when comparing reporting based on information given by our respondents with the actual number of cases of euthanasia and physician-assisted suicide reported to Euthanasia Review Committees in 2010.[14] Finally, our study does not enable the assessment of quality of care or decision making on the patient level. For instance, to assess whether symptom control was sufficient is not possible. Our study's strength lies in providing population-level information relevant to health policy.

In conclusion, 8 years after the enactment of the Dutch euthanasia law, the incidence of euthanasia and physician-assisted suicide is comparable with that in the period before the law. The reporting rate seems to have stabilised at about eight out of ten cases. Euthanasia and physician-assisted suicide did not shift to different patient groups and the frequency of ending of life without explicit request continued to fall. Although translating these results to other countries is not straightforward, they can inform the debate on legalisation of euthanasia or physician-assisted suicide in other countries.

References

1 Rodin G, Zimmermann C, Rydall A, et al. The desire for hastened death in patients with metastatic cancer. *J Pain Symptom Manage* 2007; 33: 661–75.

2 Breitbart W, Rosenfeld B, Pessin H, et al. Depression, hopelessness, and desire for hastened death in terminally ill patients with cancer. *JAMA* 2000; 284: 2907–11.

3 Finlay I, Wheatley V, Izdebski C. The proposed assisted dying bill in the UK: a response to Lord Joffe. *Palliat Med* 2006; 20: 115–16.

4 Pereira J. Legalizing euthanasia or assisted suicide: the illusion of safeguards and controls. *Curr Oncol* 2011; 18: e38–45.

5 Ferrand E, Rondeau E, Lemaire F, Fischler M. Requests for euthanasia and palliative care in France. *Lancet* 2011; 377: 467–68.

6 Levene IR. Legislation protects the vulnerable? *CMAJ* 2010; 182: 1330.

7 Bosshard G, Broeckaert B, Clark D, Materstvedt LJ, Gordijn B, Müller-Busch HC. A role for doctors in assisted dying? An analysis of legal regulations and medical professional positions in six European countries. *J Med Ethics* 2008; 34: 28–32.

8 Delbeke E. The way assisted suicide is legalised: balancing a medical framework against a demedicalised model. *Eur J Health Law* 2011; 18: 149–62.

9 van der Heide A, Onwuteaka-Philipsen BD, Rurup ML, et al. End-of-life practices in the Netherlands under the Euthanasia Act. *N Engl J Med* 2007; 356: 1957–65.

10 Onwuteaka-Philipsen BD, van der Heide A, Koper D, et al. Euthanasia and other end-of-life decisions in the Netherlands in 1990, 1995, and 2001. *Lancet* 2003; 362: 395–99.

11 van der Wal G, van der Maas PJ, Bosma JM, et al. Evaluation of the notification procedure for physician-assisted death in the Netherlands. *N Engl J Med* 1996; 335: 1706–11.

12 van der Maas PJ, van der Wal G, Haverkate I, et al. Euthanasia and other end-of-life decisions in the Netherlands 1990–1995. *N Engl J Med* 1996; 335: 1699–705.

13 Van Der Maas PJ, Van Delden JJM, Pijnenborg L, Looman CWN. Euthanasia and other medical decisions concerning the end of life. *Lancet* 1991; 338: 669–74.

14 Regional Euthanasia Review Committees. Annual report 2010. The Hague: Regional Euthanasia Review Committees, 2011 [in Dutch].

15 Bilsen J, Cohen J, Chambaere K, et al. Medical end-of-life practices under the euthanasia law in Belgium. *N Engl J Med* 2009; 361: 1119–21.

16 Deliens L, van der Wal G. The euthanasia law in Belgium and the Netherlands. *Lancet* 2003; 362: 1239–40.

17 van der Heide A, Deliens L, Faisst K, et al, on behalf of the EURELD consortium. End-of-life decision-making in six European countries: descriptive study. *Lancet* 2003; 362: 345–50.

18 ten Have HA, Welie JVM. Euthanasia: normal medical practice? *Hastings Cent Rep* 1992; 22: 34–38.

19 Fleming JI. Euthanasia, the Netherlands and slippery slopes. *Bioeth Res Notes* 1992; 4: 1–4.

20 Gordijn B, Janssens R. Euthanasia and palliative care in The Netherlands: an analysis of the latest developments. *Health Care Anal* 2004; 12: 195–207.

21 Dyer C. Legalisation of assisted dying does not harm palliative care, study concludes. *BMJ* 2011; 343: d6779.

22 Seale C. End-of-life decisions in the UK involving medical practitioners. *Palliat Med* 2009; 23: 198–204.

23 Morita T, Tsunoda J, Inoue S, Chihara S. Effects of high dose opioids and sedatives on survival in terminally ill cancer patients. *J Pain Symptom Manage* 2001; 21: 282–89.

24 Sykes N, Thorns A. The use of opioids and sedatives at the end of life. *Lancet Oncol* 2003; 4: 312–18.

25 Good PD, Ravenscroft PJ, Cavenagh J. Effects of opioids and sedatives on survival in an Australian inpatient palliative care population. *Intern Med J* 2005; 35: 512–17.

26 van der Steen JT, Meuleman-Peperkamp I, Ribbe MW. Trends in treatment of pneumonia among Dutch nursing home patients with dementia. *J Palliat Med* 2009; 12: 789–95.

27 Chabot BE, Goedhart A. A survey of self-directed dying attended by proxies in the Dutch population. *Soc Sci Med* 2009; 68: 1745–51.

28 den Hartogh G. Mysterious data: the reporting rate cannot increase further. *Med Contact (Bussum)* 2003; 58: 1063–66.

41

Euthanasia in the Netherlands

What Lessons for Elsewhere?

Bernard Lo

The Netherlands is one of the few places in the world where euthanasia and physician-assisted suicide are legal under specific circumstances. In *The Lancet*, Bregje Onwuteaka-Philipsen and colleagues present the findings from their analysis of trends in euthanasia and physician-assisted suicide before and after the 2002 enactment of the euthanasia law in the Netherlands [see chapter 40 in this volume][1] – the most recent rigorously designed, empirical study done in the country to date. By sampling all deaths in the Netherlands, the investigators were able to analyse trends and report some reassuring findings, but they also identified cases that raise ethical concerns.

After a decrease shortly after the legislation was passed in 2002, the frequency of euthanasia in the Netherlands has increased to 2·8% of all deaths in 2010 (95% CI 2·5–3·2), slightly above the 2001 level. The frequency of physician-assisted suicide has been stable (at 0·1% [0·1–0·2] of all deaths in 2010). Abuse has not been widespread, and there is no apparent disproportionate use in vulnerable populations. Physicians do not substitute hastening death for the provision of palliative care. Instead, they intensify the alleviation of symptoms (in 36·4% [35·2–37·6] of patients in 2010) much more often than they undertake euthanasia or physician-assisted suicide, and the increase in the

alleviation of symptoms is also much steeper than the increase in euthanasia. Physicians grant fewer than half of euthanasia requests from patients. These findings, together with other reports,[2] provide reassurance to individuals who do not oppose euthanasia and physician-assisted suicide as violations of their religious beliefs or professional ethics. However, the effect of these data on euthanasia debates elsewhere might be limited, because countries differ greatly in demography, culture, and organisation of medical care.

The cases that raise ethical concerns merit attention from all physicians, irrespective of their views on euthanasia and physician-assisted suicide. Physicians have a professional responsibility for quality improvement,[3] which should include end-of-life care. Improvement in the overall quality of end-of-life care would benefit a much larger number of patients than those who request euthanasia. First, the line between euthanasia and the less controversial, much more common practice of palliative sedation can be blurred in clinical practice. Even when euthanasia and physician-assisted suicide are illegal, patients might request them, and on occasion physicians oblige.[4-6] In about 20% of cases the investigators classified as euthanasia or physician-assisted suicide, the physicians viewed the case as alleviation of symptoms (1·5%

Original publication details: Bernard Lo, "Euthanasia in the Netherlands: What Lessons for Elsewhere?," pp. 869–70 from *The Lancet* 380 (September 8, 2012). Copyright 2012. Reprinted from *The Lancet* with permission from Elsevier.

[1·0–3·7]) or palliative or terminal sedation (18·1% [14·6–21·3]). In other studies, physicians also misclassify some cases of euthanasia.[7, 8] The goal of palliative sedation is to relieve a patient's refractory symptoms, to the point of unconsciousness if necessary. All physicians, even opponents of euthanasia, should support proportionate palliative sedation, which uses the least sedation needed to control refractory symptoms.[9] But physicians who say they are undertaking palliative sedation sometimes cross the line to euthanasia. One reason for this happening might be confusion regarding intention. The physician's intention to hasten the patient's death is crucial in the Dutch definition of euthanasia and assisted suicide. Intention should be judged not only by physicians' statements but also by actions.[10, 11] If a physician increases the dose of opioids or sedatives in an unresponsive patient in the absence of clinical signs or symptoms that could reasonably be interpreted as distress – such as restlessness, grimacing, withdrawal from stimuli, hypertension, or tachycardia[12, 13] – these actions could be inferred as intention to hasten death.

Second, decisions about palliative sedation, especially continuous deep sedation until death, should be discussed with patients or families. Ethically, these practices might involve a trade-off between awareness and comfort. Patients vary in how they want to set this balance, and physicians are unlikely to know a patient's preferences without explicitly asking them. However, in 41·2% of cases (39·0–43·1) classified by the investigators as intensified alleviation of symptoms, the physician did not discuss the decision with the patient, relatives, or another physician. Knowing why such discussions do not occur, especially in cases of palliative or terminal sedation, would be a first step towards facilitating and improving these important conversations.

Third, physicians' failure to report cases of euthanasia and physician-assisted suicide, as required by Dutch law, in about 20% of cases raises concerns. More detailed information about non-reported cases would be useful. How did physicians explain how they characterised their actions and their intentions with regard to hastening death? Did they discuss these decisions with patients and families? Was there an association between failure to report and failure to discuss these decisions with patients and families? Such additional information might identify unresolved ethical or clinical issues and suggest how to improve the reporting of euthanasia in the Netherlands.

Finally, cases of euthanasia without the explicit request of the patient are contrary to Dutch law and ethically problematic, especially when the physician did not discuss euthanasia with the patient, family, or another physician. Some readers will be reassured that the frequency of this rare practice has decreased over time. However, an in-depth analysis of these cases might reveal more widespread conceptual confusions or flaws in practice.

We commend Onwuteaka-Philipsen and colleagues for their careful, rigorous study, but additional information from in-depth interviews in ethically problematic cases is needed. How do physicians think through these difficult situations? What key concepts are uncertain, misunderstood, or might need modification? How do doctors talk with patients and families about these practices, and are there missed opportunities to improve such discussions? By answering these questions, physicians can improve the quality of care for dying patients and their families, irrespective of their views on euthanasia and physician-assisted suicide.

References

1 Onwuteaka-Philipsen BD, Brinkman-Stoppelenburg A, Penning C, de Jong-Krul GJF, van Delden JJM, van der Heide A. Trends in end-of life practices before and after the enactment of the euthanasia law in the Netherlands from 1990 to 2010: a repeated cross-sectional survey. *Lancet* 2012; published online July 11. doi:10.1016/S0140-6736(12)61034–4.

2 Regional Euthanasia Review Committees. Annual report 2010. At http://www.euthanasiecommissie. nl/overdetoetsingscommissies/jaarverslag [in Dutch] (accessed June 29, 2012).

3 Medical Professionalism Project. Medical professionalism in the new millennium: a physicians' charter. *Lancet* 2002; 359: 520–22.

4 Meier DE, Emmons CA, Wallenstein S, Quill T, Morrison RS, Cassel CK. Physician-assisted death in the United States: a national prevalence survey. *N Engl J Med* 1998; 338: 1193–201.

5 van der Heide A, Deliens L, Faisst K, et al. End-of-life decision-making in six European countries: descriptive study. *Lancet* 2003; 362: 345–50.

6 Cohen J, van Delden J, Mortier F, et al. Influence of physicians' life stances on attitudes to end-of-life decisions and actual end-of-life decision-making in six countries. *J Med Ethics* 2008; 34: 247–53.

7 Smets T, Cohen J, Bilsen J, Van Wesemael Y, Rurup ML, Deliens L. The labelling and reporting of euthanasia by Belgian physicians: a study of hypothetical cases. *Eur J Public Health* 2012; 22: 19–26.

8 Buiting HM, van der Heide A, Onwuteaka-Philipsen BD, et al. Physicians' labelling of end-of-life practices: a hypothetical case study. *J Med Ethics* 2010; 36: 24–29.

9 Quill TE, Lo B, Brock DW, Meisel A. Last-resort options for palliative sedation. *Ann Intern Med* 2009; 151: 421–24.

10 Lo B, Rubenfeld G. Palliative sedation in dying patients: "we turn to it when everything else hasn't worked". *JAMA* 2005; 294: 1810–16.

11 Alpers A, Lo B. The Supreme Court addresses physician-assisted suicide: can its decisions improve palliative care. *Arch Fam Pract* 1999; 8: 200–05.

12 Schweickert WD, Kress JP. Strategies to optimize analgesia and sedation. *Crit Care* 2008; 12 (suppl 3): S6.

13 Li D, Puntillo K, Miaskowski C. A review of objective pain measures for use with critical care adult patients unable to self-report. *J Pain* 2008; 9: 2–10.

Part V

Resource Allocation

Introduction

Needs, wants and desires have no limits, but resources are finite. This is true also of healthcare resources. As a consequence not all healthcare needs and wants can be satisfied. Even if a society greatly increased its healthcare budget to meet more healthcare needs, it would still be the case that even more healthcare needs could be met, and more lives saved, if only even more money and resources were available. But money spent on healthcare cannot be spent on other things we value and want – better schools and roads, clean water, national parks, public housing, and so on.

Given the finiteness of healthcare resources, we thus need to find some ethically defensible way of allocating these resources.

It is sometimes suggested that these decisions be left to the market, or the ability of consumers to pay. But most developed countries have adopted public policies – guided by social welfare and justice considerations – that provide some basic level of healthcare to the poor and other vulnerable groups, people who would otherwise die because they cannot afford to pay for private health insurance or care. This means that a market-oriented way of allocating healthcare resources is at best inadequate and that the problem of finding another ethically defensible way of allocating scarce healthcare resources still awaits an answer.

Allocation questions arise at different levels of decision-making and, depending on their level, are commonly referred to as "macro" or "micro" allocation decisions. Questions such as these arise when resource allocation decisions need to be made on macro or micro levels:

1. How much of the national budget should be devoted to healthcare as opposed to, say, schools, roads, public housing, defense, and so on?
2. How much of the healthcare budget should be spent on different areas within healthcare – say, on maternal healthcare vis-à-vis neonatal intensive care, dialysis, heart transplants, and so on?
3. If not enough resources are available to treat or save everyone within particular areas of medicine, who should have access to the last intensive care bed, or be the recipient of a scarce donor heart?

Questions (1) and (2) are generally regarded as macro-allocation issues, and the kinds of questions raised by (3) are regarded as micro-allocation issues. Contributions to this Part V of the anthology focus mainly on questions (2) and (3), and leave mute most of the issues raised by question (1).

Resource allocation poses some of the most challenging and perplexing ethical questions in the field of bioethics. In this brief introduction to the field, we can do no more than raise a small number of issues.

Decisions that affect directly who will or will not have access to a particular scarce healthcare resource arise in many areas of medicine, but are perhaps nowhere more keenly felt than in the area of organ transplantation. It is now possible to successfully

Bioethics: An Anthology, Third Edition. Edited by Helga Kuhse, Udo Schüklenk, and Peter Singer.
© 2016 John Wiley & Sons, Inc. Published 2016 by John Wiley & Sons, Inc.

transplant organs such as kidneys, livers, hearts, lungs, and pancreases. Organ transplants can save or prolong lives. But organs for transplant are scarce (see also Part VI, "Obtaining Organs"), and many potential recipients will die while on waiting lists for a suitable organ.

The allocation of scarce organs and other life-saving technologies involve life-and-death decisions – choosing from among a number of different individuals a few who will be given a chance to live, while those not chosen are likely to die. Some people think it is inappropriate for humans to make these "God-like" decisions. Rather than develop and defend particular selection criteria, they say that we should rely on a random strategy such as drawing lots, tossing a coin, or the natural lottery of the principle "first come, first served."

In "Rescuing Lives: Can't We Count?" Paul Menzel focuses on multiple organ transplants – where a patient needs more than one organ – and argues against the use of the "first come, first served" strategy in this context. Instead, Menzel urges us to "count before we cut," that is, distribute organs in a way that will save more lives rather than fewer. Menzel directs his argument only against the transplant of multiple organs on a first-come-first-served basis and does not say what allocation principle or principles should be employed over and above the principle that we should save more rather than fewer lives. He does not say, for example, whether considerations such as the length and/or quality of a life saved should count, or whether factors such as the patient's age or her "social worth" are morally relevant.

Is responsibility for one's own ill-health a morally relevant consideration? Alvin Moss and Mark Siegler ask "Should Alcoholics Compete Equally for Liver Transplantation?" and therefore raise this question regarding alcoholism. Alcohol-related end-stage liver disease is the principal cause of liver failure and avoiding alcohol abuse prevents it. Alcoholics who do not change their lifestyle are therefore responsible for their liver failure in a way in which nonalcoholics are not. Given this, nonalcoholic patients who develop liver failure due to no fault of their own should, the authors conclude, have priority over alcoholics.

Is this view defensible, or is it undermined by the recognition that social and genetic factors predispose some people to certain lifestyles and diseases? Public policies do not generally attempt to distinguish between those who are and those who are not responsible for their diseases; bypass surgery, for example, is generally provided not only to lean joggers, but also to overweight hamburger-consuming "couch potatoes" – and perhaps for good reasons. After all, who would ultimately determine whether a patient is or is not (fully) responsible for her condition? A distant bureaucrat, a busy doctor, or a committee? One might thus take the view that even though it is not, in some sense of the term, "fair" that those who are responsible for their disease should have the same access to a scarce resource, it would be undesirable to write this principle into transplant protocols, public policies or laws.

Should age play a role in healthcare resource allocation decisions? This issue is considered by John Harris in "The Value of Life." He holds that age is – in all situations bar one – morally irrelevant as long as we don't know when we will die, and have a fervent wish to live. The only time when age might become relevant, Harris argues, is when one person has had a reasonable lifespan or a "fair innings" (traditionally thought to consist of three score and ten years), and the other person has not. In this case, Harris holds, even though both might fervently wish to live, only the younger person could claim that she has been deprived of a fair innings (which the other person has had), over and above the loss of life itself.

Economists typically hold that public resources should be spent so as to maximize the satisfaction of human needs, wants, or preferences. Healthcare economists have developed the idea of the QALY (Quality Adjusted Life Year) as a unit of measure of the benefits gained by various ways of using health-care resources. The idea behind the QALY is that years of good quality are better than years of poor quality, and as long as the quality is positive, more years of life are better than fewer. On this basis we can compare the benefits gained by spending our dollars on different forms of treatment or prevention of ill-health. One common objection to the use of the QALY is that it seems to imply that, other things beings being equal, it is better to prolong the lives of those who are healthy rather than of those who are disabled. This seems to put people with disabilities under a kind of double jeopardy – first they are disabled, and then for that reason when they need scarce healthcare resources in order to survive, they are less likely to get them. Nick Beckstead and Toby Ord confront this objection in "Bubbles under the Wallpaper: Healthcare Rationing and Discrimination." They argue that, unpalatable as this implication of the use of QALYs may seem, it may well be better than any alternative method of allocating healthcare resources.

42

Rescuing Lives

Can't We Count?

Paul T. Menzel

On 16 September 1993, five-year-old Laura Davies of Manchester, England, received small and large intestines, stomach, pancreas, liver, and two kidneys in a fifteen-hour transplant operation at Children's Hospital of Pittsburgh. The National Health Service paid for little of her care, but scores of private donors responded to newspaper publicity and her parents' appeals to provide the half-million pounds and more required for her various operations. In this case, where was medical technology taking us?

Laura died on 11 November. According to her Manchester physician at the time of the operation, however, Laura had a "better than 50–50 chance." After all, the three previous child recipients of multiple organs at Pittsburgh since the advent of a new antirejection drug in 1992 are still alive. It is thus difficult to dismiss the willingness of Laura's parents and physicians to proceed as using her for their own emotional or scientific purposes. Though surely "experimental," the surgery was the only chance Laura had.

And if anyone, either then or now in light of her death, claims that the 50–50 odds were inflated, a straightforward reply is available: maybe you're right, but let us employ this procedure, now and at other times, to see. Plucky Laura herself seemed to put the "guinea pig" charge to rest. "I'm not worried," she told reporters at a press conference. Then she ended the session with a song.

A standard objection to high expense-per-benefit care also does not apply: funded privately by response to special appeal, Laura's care does not come at the expense of anyone else whom limited funds might have saved. With a child like this and the money pouring in from donations, why should we dispute her parents' and physicians' decision? On a medical mission? Sure. Carried away? In the circumstances, seemingly not.

Still, something has been missed that is very problematic about Laura's aggressive care: in the attempt to save her, a greater number of other lives were sacrificed. It's a straightforward function of the marked scarcity of organs. Nearly half the children now on organ transplant waiting lists die before they get them. We should all be able to see the big picture: if one person at the head of the queue gets four scarce organs instead of one, four others somewhere down the queue, not one, never get any.

Both the British and the US publics seem reluctant to recognize this. Take Pennsylvania's Governor Casey last spring. At first his waiting only a few days before receiving a heart–liver transplant met with skepticism: had he been allowed to jump the queue because of his political status? The Pittsburgh transplant center

Original publication details: Paul T. Menzel, "Rescuing Lives: Can't We Count?," pp. 22–3 from *Hastings Center Report* 24: 1 (1994). Reproduced with permission from John Wiley & Sons.

quickly replied: absolutely not, he was treated as any other multiple organ failure patient would have been. Because of the multiple failure, his need was more urgent. With the political queue-jumping charge rebuffed, the critics backed off.

But if organs are scarce, and those used in multiple scarce organ transplants could virtually always have saved more lives if used on others, what can possibly justify any multiple organ transplant candidate's elevation to the top of the queue? Except in the event of an extremely rare match, only two readily understandable explanations seem available, and neither justifies what was done.

One is pushing outward the medical frontier: carry out Casey's and Davies's more challenging operations despite the current sacrifice of a greater number of others' lives, and we will eventually develop new, effective forms of lifesaving. But this sort of argument represents the most extreme kind of medical adventurism. With the scarcity of organs virtually certain to continue – especially for children and infants, where we are already getting close to maximum contribution – what is the likelihood that multiple organ transplants will *ever* cease to use up on one person what could have saved several? A totally Pollyannaish view of future organ supply drives the "experimental development" argument. We should experiment with multiple scarce organ transplants only if we have good reason to believe that sometime in the future we will have ample supply. But there is every reason to think we will *never* have that!

The other readily understandable explanation is an odd view of "urgency." The Pittsburgh surgeons appear to regard the failure of both a heart and a liver as constituting more urgent need. This too falls apart upon examination. Certainly I am as close to death's door if "just" my heart fails as I am if my heart and liver both fail. Where, in "only heart failure," is there any lack of real urgency?

To say that Governor Casey or Laura Davies have greater medical need because they require two or seven organs instead of one betrays, I suppose, a kind of "Dunkirk Syndrome": thinking that the more *difficult* the rescue was, the greater was the need at the time. Admittedly, nations and doctors understandably feel in such circumstances that they have pulled off something more *miraculous* – in fact they have! But

where in that pride in greater effort or thankfulness for greater luck is hidden any more urgent *need?*

So advancement of medical technology and urgent medical need utterly fail to justify multiple scarce-organ transplants. Their defense would have to invoke either of two much more difficult explanations. One is a direct, jolting challenge to the moral relevance of numbers at all in these kinds of acute care situations: there simply is no obligation to save the greater number. Such a position gets a foothold in our thinking through the claim that each and every individual deserves an equal chance of being saved; we should therefore flip coins to determine whether we will save the one or the four, not save the four right off because they are the greater number. Regardless of the merits of this view in academic philosophical terms,[1] however, it hardly fits the transplant setting. We continually strive to expand the organ pool. Why? To save more lives, obviously. If with that expanded supply we end up saving no more people than before because we use up enough of our organ bank on multiple organ recipients, what has been the point of our supply expansion efforts?

A second difficult explanation is at least anchored in some actual social reactions. Little objection to the occasional practice of using up multiple scarce organs on one recipient comes from competing single-organ patients, patients' families, or their representatives. The reason, I suspect, is that the context of waiting together on a queue is already transparently and pervasively infused with luck – the luck of the right organ and a good match arriving at the right time for one candidate, but not for another. Living continually with such grave unknowns may lead people to celebrate unselfishly when anyone gets saved. No patient begrudges another's sheer luck; all understand that there is no rhyme, reason, or desert in the outcome anyhow. Once in that laudable mindset, people may not even attend to the numbers. The many cast no challenging glance into the eyes of the few. Challenge, defense, claim – here, all are out of court. It's as if the many even consent to their own lack of rescue as long as someone is saved.

I am intrigued by this possibility of consent,[2] but I suspect that our surmisals here about the empathetic consent of organ failure patients who wait unsuccessfully on the queue are romantic and quite distort their actual feelings. Most of the real competitor potential recipients out there somewhere on the queue do not sit together in a transplant center's waiting room, directly sharing one another's fortune. In any case, why should those in the society who manage the process of organ procural and disbursement not empathize sequentially with *all* who might be saved, thereby letting the numbers of real, equally invaluable rescuable persons build up to turn their decision? Again, in terms of persuasive justifications, multiple scarce-organ transplants strike out.

Surgeons, the press, and the public need to face up to these considerations in cases like Laura Davies. How can transplant centers justify ultimately letting two or more persons somewhere down the queue likely die because they have drawn so much out of the organ bank to save one? And why should the press play along with this lifesaving delusion and publicize appeals to unknowing financial donors without telling them the morally relevant facts? If donors knew, why should they feel good about having contributed to a net *non*-lifesaving project? In the whole situation, only Laura Davies's parents, in their attachment to their child, come out clean.

Worse yet, the essential problem in the multiple scarce organ cases portends bigger trouble. It has ominous implications for the distribution of other scarce health care resources. If in multiple organ transplants we are blind to the real lives of competing potential beneficiaries, where they, too, are acutely ill, how much more blind will we be in typical contexts of distributing scarce monies where the competing beneficiaries are more distant, and certainly not on any queue of named individuals?

Let's count before we cut.

Notes

1   Frances M. Kamm, *Morality, Mortality: Death and Whom to Save From It*, vol. 1 (New York: Oxford University Press, 1993), pp. 75–122. See also J. Taurek, "Should the Numbers Count?" *Philosophy and Public Affairs*, 6, no. 4 (1977): 293–316; and Derek Parfit, "Innumerate Ethics," *Philosophy and Public Affairs*, 7, no. 4 (1978): 285–301.

2   The attempt to discern the implications of consent to risk drove most of this author's reasoning in *Strong Medicine: The Ethical Rationing of Health Care* (New York: Oxford University Press, 1990).

43

Should Alcoholics Compete Equally for Liver Transplantation?

Alvin H. Moss and Mark Siegler

Until recently, liver transplantation for patients with alcohol-related end-stage liver disease (ARESLD) was not considered a treatment option. Most physicians in the transplant community did not recommend it because of initial poor results in this population[1] and because of a predicted high recidivism rate that would preclude long-term survival.[2] In 1988, however, Starzl and colleagues[3] reported 1-year survival rates for patients with ARESLD comparable to results in patients with other causes of end-stage liver disease (ESLD). Although the patients in the Pittsburgh series may represent a carefully selected population,[3,4] the question is no longer Can we perform transplants in patients with alcoholic liver disease and obtain acceptable results? but Should we? This question is particularly timely since the Health Care Financing Administration (HCFA) has recommended that Medicare coverage for liver transplantation be offered to patients with alcoholic cirrhosis who are abstinent. The HCFA proposes that the same eligibility criteria be used for patients with ARESLD as are used for patients with other causes of ESLD, such as primary biliary cirrhosis and sclerosing cholangitis.[5]

Should Patients with ARESLD Receive Transplants?

At first glance, this question seems simple to answer. Generally, in medicine, a therapy is used if it works and saves lives. But the circumstances of liver transplantation differ from those of most other lifesaving therapies, including long-term mechanical ventilation and dialysis, in three important respects:

Nonrenewable resource

First, although most lifesaving therapies are expensive, liver transplantation uses a nonrenewable, absolutely scarce resource – a donor liver. In contrast to patients with end-stage renal disease, who may receive either a transplant or dialysis therapy, every patient with ESLD who does not receive a liver transplant will die. This dire, absolute scarcity of donor livers would be greatly exacerbated by including patients with ARESLD as potential candidates for liver transplantation. In 1985, 63 737 deaths due to hepatic disease occurred in the United States, at

Original publication details: Alvin H. Moss and Mark Siegler, "Should Alcoholics Compete Equally for Liver Transplantation?," pp. 1295–8 from *Journal of the American Medical Association* 265: 10 (1991).

Bioethics: An Anthology, Third Edition. Edited by Helga Kuhse, Udo Schüklenk, and Peter Singer.

least 36 000 of which were related to alcoholism, but fewer than 1000 liver transplants were performed.[6] Although patients with ARESLD represent more than 50% of the patients with ESLD, patients with ARESLD account for less than 10% of those receiving transplants (*New York Times*. April 3, 1990:B6[col 1]). If patients with ARESLD were accepted for liver transplantation on an equal basis, as suggested by the HCFA, there would potentially be more than 30 000 additional candidates each year. (No data exist to indicate how many patients in the late stages of ARESLD would meet transplantation eligibility criteria.) In 1987, only 1182 liver transplants were performed; in 1989, fewer than 2000 were done.[6] Even if all donor livers available were given to patients with ARESLD, it would not be feasible to provide transplants for even a small fraction of them. Thus, the dire, absolute nature of donor liver scarcity mandates that distribution be based on unusually rigorous standards – standards not required for the allocation of most other resources such as dialysis machines and ventilators, both of which are only *relatively* scarce.

Comparison with cardiac transplantation

Second, although a similar dire, absolute scarcity of donor hearts exists for cardiac transplantation, the allocational decisions for cardiac transplantation differ from those for liver transplantation. In liver transplantation, ARESLD causes more than 50% of the cases of ESLD; in cardiac transplantation, however, no one predominant disease or contributory factor is responsible. Even for patients with end-stage ischemic heart disease who smoked or who failed to adhere to dietary regimens, it is rarely clear that one particular behavior caused the disease. Also, unlike our proposed consideration for liver transplantation, a history of alcohol abuse is considered a contraindication and is a common reason for a patient with heart disease to be denied cardiac transplantation.[7,8] Thus, the allocational decisions for heart transplantation differ from those for liver transplantation in two ways: determining a cause for end-stage heart disease is less certain, and patients with a history of alcoholism are usually rejected from heart transplant programs.

Expensive technology

Third, a unique aspect of liver transplantation is that it is an expensive technology that has become a target of cost containment in health care.[9] It is, therefore, essential to maintain the approbation and support of the public so that organs continue to be donated under appropriate clinical circumstances – even in spite of the high cost of transplantation.

General guideline proposed

In view of the distinctive circumstances surrounding liver transplantation, we propose as a general guideline that patients with ARESLD should not compete equally with other candidates for liver transplantation. We are *not* suggesting that patients with ARESLD should *never* receive liver transplants. Rather, we propose that a priority ranking be established for the use of this dire, absolutely scarce societal resource and that patients with ARESLD be lower on the list than others with ESLD.

Objections to Proposal

We realize that our proposal may meet with two immediate objections: (1) Some may argue that since alcoholism is a disease, patients with ARESLD should be considered equally for liver transplantation.[10] (2) Some will question why patients with ARESLD should be singled out for discrimination, when the medical profession treats many patients who engage in behavior that causes their diseases.[11] We will discuss these objections in turn.

Alcoholism: How is it similar to and different from other diseases?

We do not dispute the reclassification of alcoholism as a disease.[12] Both hereditary and environmental factors contribute to alcoholism, and physiological, biochemical, and genetic markers have been associated with increased susceptibility.[13] Identifying alcoholism as a disease enables physicians to approach it as they do other medical problems and to differentiate it from bad habits, crimes, or moral weaknesses. More important, identifying alcoholism as a disease also legitimizes medical interventions to treat it.[14]

Alcoholism is a chronic disease,[12,15] for which treatment is available and effective. More than 1.43 million patients were treated in 5586 alcohol treatment units in the 12-month period ending October 30, 1987.[16] One comprehensive review concluded that more than two thirds of patients who accept therapy improve.[17] Another cited four studies in which at least 54% of patients were abstinent a minimum of 1 year after treatment.[18] A recent study of alcohol-impaired physicians reported a 100% abstinence rate an average of 33.4 months after therapy was initiated. In this study, physician-patients rated Alcoholics Anonymous, the largest organization of recovering alcoholics in the world, as the most important component of their therapy.[19]

Like other chronic diseases – such as type I diabetes mellitus, which requires the patient to administer insulin over a lifetime – alcoholism requires the patient to assume responsibility for participating in continuous treatment. Two key elements are required to successfully treat alcoholism: the patient must accept his or her diagnosis and must assume responsibility for treatment.[20,21] The high success rates of some alcoholism treatment programs indicate that many patients can accept responsibility for their treatment. ARESLD, one of the sequelae of alcoholism, results from 10 to 20 years of heavy alcohol consumption. The risk of ARESLD increases with the amount of alcohol consumed and with the duration of heavy consumption.[22] In view of the quantity of alcohol consumed, the years, even decades, required to develop ARESLD, and the availability of effective alcohol treatment, attributing personal responsibility for ARESLD to the patient seems all the more justified. We believe, therefore, that even though alcoholism is a chronic disease, alcoholics should be held responsible for seeking and obtaining treatment that could prevent the development of late-stage complications such as ARESLD. Our view is consistent with that of Alcoholics Anonymous: alcoholics are responsible for undertaking a program for recovery that will keep their disease of alcoholism in remission.[23]

Are we discriminating against alcoholics?

Why should patients with ARESLD be singled out when a large number of patients have health problems that can be attributed to so-called voluntary health-risk behavior? Such patients include smokers with chronic lung disease; obese people who develop type II diabetes; some individuals who test positive for the human immunodeficiency virus; individuals with multiple behavioral risk factors (inattention to blood pressure, cholesterol, diet, and exercise) who develop coronary artery disease; and people such as skiers, motor-cyclists, and football players who sustain activity-related injuries. We believe that the health care system should respond based on the actual medical needs of patients rather than on the factors (eg, genetic, infectious, or behavioral) that cause the problem. We also believe that individuals should bear some responsibility – such as increased insurance premiums – for medical problems associated with voluntary choices. The critical distinguishing factor for treatment of ARESLD is the scarcity of the resource needed to treat it. The resources needed to treat most of these other conditions are only moderately or relatively scarce, and patients with these diseases or injuries can receive a share of the resources (ie, money, personnel, and medication) roughly equivalent to their need. In contrast, there are insufficient donor livers to sustain the lives of all with ESLD who are in need.[24] This difference permits us to make some discriminating choices – or to establish priorities – in selecting candidates for liver transplantation based on notions of fairness. In addition, this reasoning enables us to offer patients with alcohol-related medical and surgical problems their fair share of relatively scarce resources, such as blood products, surgical care, and intensive care beds, while still maintaining that their claim on donor livers is less compelling than the claims of others.

Reasons Patients with ARESLD Should Have a Lower Priority on Transplant Waiting Lists

Two arguments support our proposal. The first argument is a moral one based on considerations of fairness. The second one is based on policy considerations and examines whether public support of liver transplantation can be maintained if, as a result of a first-come, first-served approach, patients with ARESLD receive more than half the available donor livers. Finally, we will consider further research necessary to determine which patients with ARESLD should be candidates for transplantation, albeit with a lower priority.

Fairness

Given a tragic shortage of donor livers, what is the fair or just way to allocate them? We suggest that patients who develop ESLD through no fault of their own (eg, those with congenital biliary atresia or primary biliary cirrhosis) should have a higher priority in receiving a liver transplant than those whose liver disease results from failure to obtain treatment for alcoholism. In view of the dire, absolute scarcity of donor livers, we believe it is fair to hold people responsible for their choices, including decisions to refuse alcoholism treatment, and to allocate organs on this basis.

It is unfortunate but not unfair is make this distinction.[25] When not enough donor livers are available for all who need one, choices have to be made, and they should be founded on one or more proposed principles of fairness for distributing scarce resources.[26,27] We shall consider four that are particularly relevant:

- *To each, an equal share of treatment.*
- *To each, similar treatment for similar cases.*
- *To each, treatment according to personal effort.*
- *To each, treatment according to ability to pay.*

It is not possible to give each patient with ESLD an *equal share*, or, in this case, a functioning liver. The problem created by the absolute scarcity of donor livers is that of inequality; some receive livers while others do not. But what is fair need not be equal. Although a first-come, first-served approach has been suggested to provide each patient with an equal chance, we believe it is fairer to give a child dying of biliary atresia an opportunity for a *first* normal liver than it is to give a patient with ARESLD who was born with a normal liver a *second* one.

Because the goal of providing each person with an equal share of health care sometimes collides with the realities of finite medical resources, the principle of *similar treatment for similar cases* has been found to be helpful. Outka[26] stated it this way: "If we accept the case for equal access, but if we simply cannot,

physically cannot, treat all who are in need, it seems more just to discriminate by virtue of categories of illness, rather than between rich ill and poor ill." This principle is derived from the principle of formal justice, which, roughly stated, says that people who are equal in relevant respects should be treated equally and that people who are unequal in relevant respects should be treated differently.[27] We believe that patients with ARESLD are unequal in a relevant respect to others with ESLD, since their liver failure was preventable; therefore, it is acceptable to treat them differently.

Our view also relies on the principle of *To each, treatment according to personal effort.* Although alcoholics cannot be held responsible for their disease, once their condition has been diagnosed they can be held responsible for seeking treatment and for preventing the complication of ARESLD. The standard of personal effort and responsibility we propose for alcoholics is the same as that held by Alcoholics Anonymous. We are not suggesting that some lives and behaviors have greater value than others – an approach used and appropriately repudiated when dialysis machines were in short supply.[26–30] But we are holding people responsible for their personal effort.

Health policymakers have predicted that this principle will assume greater importance in the future. In the context of scarce health care resources, Blank[31] foresees a reevaluation of our health care priorities, with a shift toward individual responsibility and a renewed emphasis on the individual's obligation to society to maximize one's health. Similarly, more than a decade ago, Knowles[32] observed that prevention of disease requires effort. He envisioned that the next major advances in the health of the American people would be determined by what individuals are willing to do for themselves.

To each, treatment according to ability to pay has also been used as a principle of distributive justice. Since alcoholism is prevalent in all socioeconomic strata, it is not discrimination against the poor to deny liver transplantation to patients with alcoholic liver disease.[33] In fact, we believe that poor patients with ARESLD have a stronger claim for a donor liver than rich patients, precisely because many alcohol treatment programs are not available to patients lacking in substantial private resources or health insurance. Ironically, it is precisely this group of poor and uninsured patients who are most likely not to be eligible to receive a liver transplant because of their inability to pay. We agree with Outka's view of fairness that would discriminate according to categories of illness rather than according to wealth.

Policy considerations regarding public support for liver transplantation

Today, the main health policy concerns involve issues of financing, distributive justice, and rationing medical care.[34–37] Because of the many deficiencies in the US health care system – in maternal and child health, in the unmet needs of the elderly, and in the millions of Americans without health insurance – an increasing number of commentators and drawing attention to the trade-offs between basic health care for the many and expensive, albeit lifesaving care for the few.[9,25,38,39]

Because of its high unit cost, liver transplantation is often at the center of these discussions, as it has been in Oregon, where the legislature voted to eliminate Medicaid reimbursement for all transplants except kidneys and corneas.[9] In this era of health care cost containment, a sense of limits is emerging and allocational choices are being made. Oregon has already shown that elected officials and the public are prepared to face these issues.

In our democracy, it is appropriate that community mores and values be regarded seriously when deciding the most appropriate use of a scarce and nonrenewable organ symbolized as a "Gift of Life." As if to underscore this point, the report of the Task Force on Organ Transplantation recommended that each donated organ be considered a national resource for the public good and that the public must participate in decisions on how to use this resource to best serve the public's interests.[40]

Much of the initial success in securing public and political approval for liver transplantation was achieved by focusing media and political attention not on adults but on children dying of ESLD. The public may not support transplantation for patients with ARESLD in the same way that they have endorsed this procedure for babies born with biliary atresia. This assertion is bolstered not only by the events in Oregon but also by the results of a Louis Harris and Associates[41] national survey, which showed that lifesaving therapy for premature infants or for patients with cancer was given the highest health care priority by the public and that lifesaving therapy for patients with alcoholic liver disease was given the lowest. In this poll, the public's view of health care priorities was shared by leadership groups also polled: physicians, nurses, employers, and politicians.

Just because a majority of the public holds these views does not mean that they are right, but the moral intuition of the public, which is also shared by its leaders, reflects community values that must be seriously considered. Also indicative of community values are organizations such as Mothers Against Drunk Driving, Students Against Drunk Driving, corporate employee assistance programs, and school student assistance programs. Their existence signals that many believe that a person's behavior can be modified so that the consequences of behavior such as alcoholism can be prevented.[42] Thus, giving donor livers to patients with ARESLD on an equal basis with other patients who have ESLD might lead to a decline in public support for liver transplantation.

Should Any Alcoholics Be Considered for Transplantation? Need for Further Research

Our proposal for giving lower priority for liver transplantation to patients with ARESLD does not completely rule out transplantation for this group. Patients with ARESLD who had not previously been offered therapy and who are now abstinent could be acceptable candidates. In addition, patients lower on the waiting list, such as patients with ARESLD who have been treated and are now abstinent, might be eligible for a donor liver in some regions because of the increased availability of donor organs there. Even if only because of these possible conditions for transplantation, further research is needed to determine which patients with ARESLD would have the best outcomes after liver transplantation.

Transplant programs have been reluctant to provide transplants to alcoholics because of concern about one unfavorable outcome: a high recidivism rate. Although the overall recidivism rate for the Pittsburgh patients was only 11.5%, in the patients who had been abstinent less than 6 months it was 43%.[2] Also, compared with the entire group in which 1-year survival was 74%, the survival rate in this subgroup was lower, at 64%.[2]

In the recently proposed Medicare criteria for coverage of liver transplantation, the HCFA acknowledged that the decision to insure patients with alcoholic cirrhosis "may be considered controversial by some."[5] As if to counter possible objections, the HCFA listed requirements for patients with alcoholic cirrhosis: patients must meet the transplant center's requirement for abstinence prior to liver transplantation and have documented evidence of sufficient social support to ensure both recovery from alcoholism and compliance with the regimen of immunosuppressive medication.

Further research should answer lingering questions about liver transplantation for ARESLD patients: Which characteristics of a patient with ARESLD can predict a successful outcome? How long is abstinence necessary to qualify for transplantation? What type of a social support system must a patient have to ensure good results? These questions are being addressed.[43] Until the answers are known, we propose that further transplantation for patients with ARESLD be limited to abstinent patients who had not previously been offered alcoholism treatment and to abstinent treated patients in regions of increased donor liver availability and that it be carried out as part of prospective research protocols at a few centers skilled in transplantation and alcohol research.

Comment

Should patients with ARESLD compete equally for liver transplants? In a setting in which there is a dire, absolute scarcity of donor livers, we believe the answer is no. Considerations of fairness suggest that a first-come, first-served approach for liver transplantation is not the most just approach. Although this decision is difficult, it is only fair that patients who have not assumed equal responsibility for maintaining their health or for accepting treatment for a chronic disease should be treated differently. Considerations of public values and mores suggest that the public may not support liver transplantation if patients with ARESLD routinely receive more than half of the available donor livers. We conclude that since not all can live, priorities must be established and that patients with ARESLD should be given a lower priority for liver transplantation than others with ESLD.

References

1 Scharschmidt BF. Human liver transplantation: analysis of data on 540 patients from four centers. *Hepatology*. 1984;4:95S–101S.

2 Kumar S, Stauber RE, Gavaler JS, et al. Orthotopic liver transplantation for alcoholic liver disease. *Hepatology*. 1990;11:159–164.

3 Starzl TE, Van Thiel D, Tzakis AG, et al. Orthotopic liver transplantation for alcoholic cirrhosis. *JAMA*. 1988;260:2542–2544.

4 Olbrisch ME, Levenson JL. Liver transplantation for alcoholic cirrhosis. *JAMA*. 1989;261:2958.

5 Health Care Financing Administration. Medicare program: criteria for Medicare coverage of adult liver transplants. *Federal Register*. 1990; 55:3545–3553.

6 Office of Health Technology Assessment, Agency for Health Care Policy Research. *Assessment of Liver Transplantation*. Rockville, Md: US Dept of Health and Human Services; 1990:3, 25.

7 Schroeder JS, Hunt S. Cardiac transplantation update 1987. *JAMA*. 1987;258:3142–3145.

8 Surman OS. Psychiatric aspects of organ transplantation. *Am J Psychiatry*. 1989;146:972–982.

9 Welch HG, Larson EB. Dealing with limited resources: the Oregon decision to curtail funding for organ transplantation. *N Engl J Med*. 1988; 319:171–173.

10 Flavin DK, Niven RG, Kelsey JE. Alcoholism and orthotopic liver transplantation. *JAMA*. 1988;259:1546–1547.

11 Atterbury CE. The alcoholic in the lifeboat: should drinkers be candidates for liver transplantation? *J Clin Gastroenterol*. 1986;8:1–4.

12 Mendelson JH, Mello NK. *The Diagnosis and Treatment of Alcoholism*. 2nd ed. New York, NY: McGraw-Hill International Book Co; 1985:1–20.

13 Blum K, Noble EP, Sheridan PJ, et al. Allelic association of human dopamine D_2 receptor gene in alcoholism. *JAMA*. 1990;263:2055–2060.

14 Aronson MD. Definition of alcoholism. In: Barnes HN, Aronson MD, Delbanco TL, eds. *Alcoholism: A Guide for the Primary Care Physician.* New York, NY: Springer-Verlag NY Inc; 1987:9–15.

15 Klerman GL. Treatment of alcoholism. *N Engl J Med.* 1989:320:394–395.

16 *Seventh Special Report to the US Congress on Alcohol and Health.* Washington, DC: US Dept. Health and Human Services; 1990. Publication 90– 1656.

17 Saxe L. *The Effectiveness and Costs of Alcoholism Treatment: Health Technology Case Study No. 22.* Washington, DC: Congress of the United States, Office of Technology Assessment; 1983:3–6.

18 Nace EP. *The Treatment of Alcoholism.* New York, NY: Brunner/Mazel Publishers; 1987:43–46.

19 Galanter M, Talbott D, Gallegos K, Ruberstone E. Combined Alcoholics Anonymous and professional care for addicted physicians. *Am J Psychiatry.* 1990;147:64–68.

20 Johnson B, Clark W. Alcoholism: a challenging physician–patient encounter. *J Gen Intern Med.* 1989;4:445–452.

21 Bigby JA. Negotiating treatment and monitoring recovery. In: Barnes HN, Aronson MD, Delbanco TL, eds. *Alcoholism: A Guide for the Primary Care Physician.* New York, NY: Springer Verlag NY Inc; 1987:66–72.

22 Grant BF, Dufour MC, Harford TC. Epidemiology of alcoholic liver disease. *Sem Liver Dis.* 1988;8:12–25.

23 Thoreson RW, Budd FC. Self-help groups and other group procedures for treating alcohol problems. In: Cox WM, ed. *Treatment and Prevention of Alcohol Problems: A Resource Manual.* Orlando, Fla: Academic Press Inc; 1987:157–181.

24 Winslow GR. *Triage and Justice.* Berkeley: University of California Press; 1982:39–44, 133–150.

25 Engelhardt HT Jr. Shattuck Lecture: allocating scarce medical resources and the availability of organ transplantation. *N Engl J Med.* 1984;311: 66–71.

26 Outka G. Social justice and equal access to health care. *J Religious Ethics.* 1974;2:11–32.

27 Beauchamp TL, Childress JF. *Principles of Biomedical Ethics.* 3rd ed. New York, NY: Oxford University Press; 1989:256–306.

28 Ramsey P. *The Patient as Person.* New Haven, Conn: Yale University Press; 1970:242–252.

29 Fox RC, Swazey JP. *The Courage to Fail.* 2nd ed. Chicago, Ill: University of Chicago Press, 1978: 226–265.

30 Annas GJ. The prostitute, the playboy, and the poet: rationing schemes for organ transplantation. *Am J Public Health.* 1985;75:187–189.

31 Blank RH. *Rationing Medicine.* New York, NY: Columbia University Press; 1988:1–37, 189–252.

32 Knowles JH. Responsibility for health. *Science.* 1977;198:1103.

33 Moore RD, Bone LR, Geller G, Marmon JA, Stokes EJ, Levine DM. Prevalence, detection, and treatment of alcoholism in hospitalized patients. *JAMA.* 1989; 261:403–407.

34 Fuchs VR. The 'rationing' of medical care. *N Engl J Med.* 1984;311:1572–1573.

35 Daniels N. Why saying no to patients in the United States is so hard: cost containment, justice, and provider autonomy. *N Engl J Med.* 1986;314:1380–1383.

36 Callahan D. Allocating health resources. *Hastings Cent Rep.* 1988;18:14–20.

37 Evans RW. Health care technology and the inevitability of resource allocation and rationing decisions. *JAMA.* 1983;249:2047–2053, 2208–2219.

38 Thurow LC. Learning to say no. *N Engl J Med.* 1984;311:1569–1572.

39 Caper P. Solving the medical care dilemma. *N Engl J Med.* 1988;318:1535–1536.

40 Task Force on Organ Transplantation. *Organ Transplantation: Issues and Recommendations.* Washington, DC: US Dept of Health and Human Services; 1986:9.

41 Louis Harris and Associates. *Making Difficult Health Care Decisions.* Boston, Mass: The LORAN Commission; 1987:73–89.

42 Fishman R. *Alcohol and Alcoholism.* New York, NY: Chelsea House Publishers; 1986:27–34.

43 Beresford TP, Turcotte JG, Merion R, et al. A rational approach to liver transplantation for the alcoholic patient. *Psychosomatics.* 1990;31:241–254.

44

The Value of Life

John Harris

Suppose that only one place is available on a renal dialysis programme or that only one bed is vacant in a vital transplantation unit or that resuscitation could be given in the time and with the resources available to only one patient. Suppose further that of the two patients requiring any of these resources, one is a 70-year-old widower, friendless and living alone, and the other a 40-year-old mother of three young children with a husband and a career.

Or suppose that following a major disaster medical resources were available to save the lives of only half those for whom medical care was vital for life. Or, less dramatically, suppose that in the next two years, only half of 200 patients waiting for surgery that will alleviate severe discomfort can be accommodated in the only available hospital. Suppose further and finally that all candidates stand an equal chance of maximum benefit from any of the available treatments. Whom should we treat and what justifies our decision?

Many will think that in the first case preference should be given to the young mother rather than the old friendless widower, that this is obviously the right choice. There might be a number of grounds for such a decision. Two of these grounds have to do with age. One indicates a preference for the young on the grounds that they have a greater expectation of life if they are restored to health. The other favours the young simply because their life is likely to be fuller

and hence more valuable than that of the older person. Another consideration to which many will want to give some weight is that of the number of people dependent on or even caring about a potential victim. It is sometimes also considered relevant to give weight to the patient's probable usefulness to the community or even their moral character before a final decision is made. And of course these considerations may be taken together in various combinations.

In the case of a major disaster related problems arise. If say a policy of triage[1] has identified the only group of victims to be treated, those for whom medical intervention will make the difference between life and death, but there are still not enough resources to help all such persons, then, again, many will hold that the right thing to do is help the young or those with dependants and so on first.

Those who believe that they ought to select the patient or patients to be saved on any of the above criteria will believe that they must show preference for some types or conditions of person over others. Another available strategy is of course to decline to choose between people in any way that involves preferring one patient, or one sort of person, to another. Perhaps the easiest way of declining to show such a preference is to toss a coin or draw lots to decide who shall be helped. I want to consider what might count as a good reason for preferring to help

Original publication details: John Harris, "The Value of Life," pp. 87–102 from *The Value of Life*, London: Routledge, 1985. Copyright 1985, Routledge. Reproduced by permission of Taylor & Francis Books UK.

Bioethics: An Anthology, Third Edition. Edited by Helga Kuhse, Udo Schüklenk, and Peter Singer.
© 2016 John Wiley & Sons, Inc. Published 2016 by John Wiley & Sons, Inc.

some patients rather than others where all cannot be helped and also whether our intuitive preference for saving the younger and more useful members of society can be sustained.

I   The Moral Significance of Age

Many, perhaps most, people feel that, in cases like the one with which we began, there is some moral reason to save the 40-year-old mother rather than the 70-year-old widower. A smaller, but perhaps growing, group of people would see this as a sort of 'ageist' prejudice which, in a number of important areas of resource allocation and care, involves giving the old a much worse deal than the younger members of society. This is an exceptionally difficult issue to resolve. A number of the ways of thinking about the issue of the moral relevance of age yield opposed conclusions or seem to tug in opposite directions.

I want first to look at an argument which denies that we should prefer the young mother in our opening example. It is an anti-ageist argument so that is what I will call it, but it is not perhaps the usual sort of argument used to defend the rights of the old.

The anti-ageist argument

All of us who wish to go on living have something that each of us values equally although for each it is different in character, for some a much richer prize than for others, and we none of us know its true extent. This thing is of course 'the rest of our lives'. So long as we do not know the date of our deaths then for each of us the 'rest of our lives' is of indefinite duration. Whether we are 17 or 70, in perfect health or suffering from a terminal disease, we each have the rest of our lives to lead. So long as we each fervently wish to live out the rest of our lives, however long that turns out to be, then if we do not deserve to die, we each suffer the same injustice if our wishes are deliberately frustrated and we are cut off prematurely. Indeed there may well be a double injustice in deciding that those whose life expectation is short should not benefit from rescue or resuscitation. Suppose I am told today that I have terminal cancer with only approximately six months or so to live, but I want to

live until I die, or at least until I decide that life is no longer worth living. Suppose I am then involved in an accident and, because my condition is known to my potential rescuers and there are not enough resources to treat all who could immediately be saved, I am marked among those who will not be helped. I am then the victim of a double tragedy and a double injustice. I am stricken first by cancer and the knowledge that I have only a short time to live and I'm then stricken again when I'm told that because of my first tragedy a second and more immediate one is to be visited upon me. Because I have once been unlucky I'm now no longer worth saving.

The point is a simple but powerful one. However short or long my life will be, so long as I want to go on living it then I suffer a terrible injustice when that life is prematurely cut short. Imagine a group of people all of an age, say a class of students all in their mid-twenties. If fire trapped all in the lecture theatre and only twenty could be rescued in time, should the rescuers shout 'youngest first!'? Suppose they had time to debate the question or had been debating it 'academically' before the fire? It would surely seem invidious to deny some what all value so dearly merely because of an accident of birth? It might be argued that age here provides no criterion precisely because although the lifespans of such a group might be expected to vary widely, there would be no way of knowing who was most likely to live longest. But suppose a reliable astrologer could make very realistic estimates or, what amounts to the same thing, suppose the age range of the students to be much greater, say 17 to 55. Does not the invidiousness of selecting by birth-date remain? Should a 17-year-old be saved before a 29-year-old or she before the 45-year-old and should the 55-year-old clearly be the last to be saved or the first to be sacrificed?

Our normal intuitions would share this sense of the invidiousness of choosing between our imaginary students by reason of their respective ages, but would start to want to make age relevant at some extremes, say if there were a 2-day-old baby and a 90-year-old grandmother. We will be returning to discuss a possible basis for this intuition in a moment. However, it is important to be clear that the anti-ageist argument denies the relevance of age or life expectancy as a criterion absolutely. It argues that even if I know for certain that I have only a little space to live, that space, however short, may be very precious to me. Precious, precisely because it is all the time I have left, and just as precious to me on that account as all the time you have left is precious to you, however much those two time spans differ in length. So that where we both want, equally strongly, to go on living, then we each suffer the same injustice[2] when our lives are cut short or are cut further short.[3]

It might seem that someone who would insist on living out the last few months of his life when by 'going quietly' someone else might have the chance to live for a much longer time would be a very selfish person. But this would be true only if the anti-ageist argument is false. It will be true only if it is not plausible to claim that living out the rest of one's life could be equally valuable to the individual whose life it is irrespective of the amount of unelapsed time that is left. And this is of course precisely the usual situation when individuals do not normally have anything but the haziest of ideas as to how long it is that they might have left.

I think the anti-ageist argument has much plausibility. It locates the wrongness of ending an individual's life in the evil of thwarting that person's desire to go on living and argues that it is profoundly unjust to frustrate that desire merely because some of those who have exactly the same desire, held no more strongly, also have a longer life expectancy than the others. However, there are a number of arguments that pull in the opposite direction and these we must now consider.

The fair innings argument

One problem with the anti-ageist argument is our feeling that there is something unfair about a person who has lived a long and happy life hanging on grimly at the end, while someone who has not been so fortunate suffers a related double misfortune, of losing out in a lottery in which his life happened to be in the balance with that of the grim octogenarian. It might be argued that we could accept the part of the anti-ageist argument which focuses on the equal value of unelapsed time, if this could be tempered in some way. How can it be just that someone who has already had more than her fair share of life and its delights should

be preferred or even given an equal chance of continued survival with the young person who has not been so favoured? One strategy that seems to take account of our feeling that there is something wrong with taking steps to prolong the lives of the very old at the expense of those much younger is the fair innings argument.

The fair innings argument takes the view that there is some span of years that we consider a reasonable life, a fair innings. Let's say that a fair share of life is the traditional three score and ten, seventy years. Anyone who does not reach 70 suffers, on this view, the injustice of being cut off in their prime. They have missed out on a reasonable share of life; they have been short-changed. Those, however, who do make 70 suffer no such injustice, they have not lost out but rather must consider any additional years a sort of bonus beyond that which could reasonably be hoped for. The fair innings argument requires that everyone be given an equal chance to have a fair innings, to reach the appropriate threshold but, having reached it, they have received their entitlement. The rest of their life is the sort of bonus which may be cancelled when this is necessary to help others reach the threshold.

The attraction of the fair innings argument is that it preserves and incorporates many of the features that made the anti-ageist argument plausible, but allows us to preserve our feeling that the old who have had a good run for their money should not be endlessly propped up at the expense of those who have not had the same chance. We can preserve the conclusion of the anti-ageist argument, that so long as life is equally valued by the person whose life it is, it should be given an equal chance of preservation, and we can go on taking this view until the people in question have reached a fair innings.

There is, however, an important difficulty with the fair innings argument. It is that the very arguments which support the setting of the threshold at an age which might plausibly be considered to be a reasonable lifespan equally support the setting of the threshold at any age at all, so long as an argument from fairness can be used to support so doing. Suppose that there is only one place available on the dialysis programme and two patients are in competition for it. One is 30 and the other 40 years of age. The fair innings argument requires that neither be preferred on the grounds of age since both are below the threshold and are entitled to an equal chance of reaching it. If there is no other reason to choose between them we should do something like toss a coin. However, the 30-year-old can argue that the considerations which support the fair innings argument require that she be given the place. After all, what's fair about the fair innings argument is precisely that each individual should have an equal chance of enjoying the benefits of a reasonable lifespan. The younger patient can argue that, from where she's standing, the age of 40 looks much more reasonable a span than that of 30, and that she should be given the chance to benefit from those ten extra years.

This argument generalized becomes a reason for always preferring to save younger rather than older people, whatever the age difference, and makes the original anti-ageist argument begin to look again the more attractive line to take. For the younger person can always argue that the older has had a fairer innings, and should now give way. It is difficult to stop whatever span is taken to be a fair innings collapsing towards zero under pressure from those younger candidates who see their innings as less fair than that of those with a larger share.

But perhaps this objection to the fair innings argument is mistaken? If seventy years is a fair innings it does not follow that the nearer a span of life approaches seventy years, the fairer an innings it is. This may be revealed by considering a different sort of threshold. Suppose that most people can run a mile in seven minutes, and that two people are given the opportunity to show that they can run a mile in that time. They both expect to be given seven minutes. However, if one is in fact given only three minutes and the other only four, it's not true that the latter is given a fairer running time: for people with average abilities four minutes is no more realistic a time in which to run a mile than is three. Four minutes is neither a fair threshold in itself, nor a fairer one than three minutes would be.

Nor does the argument that establishes seven minutes as an appropriate threshold lend itself to variation downwards. For that argument just is that seven is the number of minutes that an average adult takes to run a mile. Why then is it different for lifespans? If three score and ten is the number of years available to most people for getting what life has to offer, and is also the number of years people can reasonably expect to have, then it is a misfortune to be allowed anything less however much less one is allowed, if nothing less than the full span normally suffices for getting what can be got out of life. It's true that the 40-year-old gets more time than the 30-year-old, but the frame of reference is not time only, but time normally required for a full life.[4]

This objection has some force, but its failure to be a good analogy reveals that two sorts of considerations go to make an innings fair. For while living a full or complete life, just in the sense of experiencing all the ages of man,[5] is one mark of a fair innings, there is also value in living through as many ages as possible. Just as completing the mile is one value, it is not the only one. Runners in the race of life also value ground covered, and generally judge success in terms of distance run.

What the fair innings argument needs to do is to capture and express in a workable form the truth that while it is always a *misfortune* to die when one wants to go on living, it is not a *tragedy* to die in old age; but it is, on the other hand, both a tragedy and a misfortune to be cut off prematurely. Of course ideas like 'old age' and 'premature death' are inescapably vague, and may vary from society to society, and over time as techniques for postponing death improve. We must also remember that, while it may be invidious to choose between a 30- and a 40-year-old on the grounds that one has had a fairer innings than the other, it may not be invidious to choose between the 30- and the 65-year-old on those grounds.

If we remember, too, that it will remain wrong to end the life of someone who wants to live or to fail to save them, and that the fair innings argument will only operate as a principle of selection where we are forced to choose between lives, then something workable might well be salvaged.

While 'old age' is irredeemably vague, we can tell the old from the young, and even the old from the middle-aged, so that, without attempting precise formulation, a reasonable form of the fair innings argument might hold; and might hold that people who had achieved old age or who were closely approaching it would not have their lives further prolonged when this could only be achieved at the cost of the lives of those who were not nearing old age. These categories could be left vague, the idea being that it would be morally defensible to prefer to save the lives of those who 'still had their lives before them' rather than those who had 'already lived full lives'. The criterion to be employed in each case would simply be what reasonable people would say about whether someone had had a fair innings. Where reasonable people would be in no doubt that a particular individual was nearing old age *and* that that person's life could only be further prolonged at the expense of the life of someone that no reasonable person would classify as nearing old age, then the fair innings argument would apply, and it would be justifiable to save the younger candidate.

In cases where reasonable people differed or it seemed likely that they would differ as to whether people fell into one category or the other, then the anti-ageist argument would apply and the inescapable choice would have to be made arbitrarily.

But again it must be emphasized that the fair innings argument would only operate as a counsel of despair, when it was clearly impossible to postpone the deaths of all those who wanted to go on living. In all other circumstances the anti-ageist argument would apply.

So far so good. There are, however, further problems in the path of the anti-ageist argument and some of them are also problems for the fair innings argument.

Numbers of lives and numbers of years

One immediate problem is that, although living as long as possible, however long that turns out to be, will normally be very important to each individual, it seems a bad basis for planning health care or justifying the distribution of resources.

Suppose a particular disease, cancer, kills 120,000 people a year. Suppose further that a drug is developed which would prolong the lives of all cancer victims by one month but no more. Would it be worth putting such a drug into production? What if, for the same cost, a different drug would give ten years' complete remission, but would only operate on a form of cancer that affects 1,000 people? If we cannot afford both, which should we invest in? Or what if there is only one place on a renal dialysis programme and two

patients who could benefit, but one will die immediately without dialysis but in six months in any event. The other will also die immediately without dialysis but with such help will survive for ten years. Although each wants the extra span of life equally badly, many would think that we ought to save the one with the longer life expectancy, that she is the 'better bet'.

All of these cases are an embarrassment for the anti-ageist argument, for our reaction to them implies that we do value extra years more. But how much more?

Extra life-time versus extra lives

> If we choose to save one person for a predicted span of sixty years, rather than saving five people each for a predicted span of ten years, we have gained ten extra life years at the cost of overriding the desires of four extra people.[6]

So far we have looked at the issue of whether we should count length of life or desire to live as the most important factor when deciding which of two people should be saved. If all things are equal, there can be no reason to prefer one to the other and so we should choose in a way that does not display preference, by lot, for example. The question that seems so difficult is what, if any, difference should length of life make to such choices?

The anti-ageist argument says that it should make no difference, but the cases we have just been examining seem to pull the other way. And if we are persuaded by such cases this seems to imply that we do think length of life or life expectancy gives additional value to lives and so constitutes a factor which must be given some weight. One consequence of this is that we should think it more important to save one 10-year-old rather than five 60-year-olds (if we take 70 as an arbitrary maximum).[7] Equally, it would be better to save one 20-year-old rather than two 50-year-old people, for we would again save ten life years by so doing. Or one 15-year-old rather than two 45-year-olds (a saving of five life years) and so on.

It is just at this point that the anti-ageist argument seems to require resuscitation, for there is surely something invidious about sacrificing two 45-year-olds to one 15-year-old. To take the 'life years' view seems to discount entirely the desires and hopes and life plans of people in middle age, whenever an importunate youngster can place herself in the balance against them. But we do not normally think it better to save a 15-year-old rather than a 45-year-old when we cannot save both, so why should we think it better to save a 15-year-old rather than *two* 45-year olds?

For those who do favour saving one 15-year-old rather than two 45-year-olds, there is another difficulty. The life-time view seems to commit us to favouring total life-time saved rather than total number of people saved, with bizarre consequences. Suppose I could prolong the lives of 121,000 people for one month? This would yield a saving of 121,000 life months. Alternatively I could develop a drug which would give ten more years of life to 1,000 people. This would yield a saving of 120,000 life months. Thus, on the time-span view, we should choose to extend the lives of 121,000 people by one month rather than 1,000 people by ten years each. So, what started out by looking as though it constituted an objection to the anti-ageist argument actually supports it in some circumstances. For, while we should favour length of life, where numbers of lives balanced against one another are equal, we should favour numbers of lives where, summed together, they yield a greater contribution to the total amount of life-time saved.

Unfortunately the force of the comparison between extending the lives of 120,000 people for one month or 1,000 for ten years was to encourage us to think that life-time saved was more important than numbers of lives saved. Its support for this conclusion now seems less decisive. What it seems to indicate is a very complicated calculus in which allocation of resources would be dependent on the amount of life-time such allocation could save. It would also lead to some bizarre orderings of priority, and not necessarily to those envisaged by enthusiasts of such a scheme.

One such enthusiast, Dr Donald Gould, produced the following scenario:

> Calculations are based on the assumption that all who survive their first perilous year ought then to live on to the age of 70…In Denmark for example, there are 50,000 deaths a year, but only 20,000 among citizens in the 1–70 bracket. These are the ones that count. The annual number

of life years lost in this group totals 264,000. Of these 80,000 are lost because of accidents and suicides, 40,000 because of coronary heart disease, and 20,000 are due to lung disease. On the basis of these figures, a large proportion of the 'health' budget ought to be spent on preventing accidents and suicides and a lesser…amount on attempting to prevent and cure heart and lung disease. Much less would be spent on cancer which is predominantly a disease of the latter half of life, and which therefore contributes relatively little to the total sum of life years lost…No money at all would be available for trying to prolong the life of a sick old man of 82.[8]

The first thing to note about Gould's scenario is, that while deaths before the age of 70 may be the only life years *considered to have been lost*,[9] it does not follow that there is no reason to attempt to *gain* life years by prolonging the lives of the over-seventies if that seems feasible. For example, if a reasonable prognosis is that the life of the 70-year-old could be prolonged for five years by some intervention, then that is still a gain of five life years. This can have important consequences, for it means that it would be quite wrong to write off all care for the over-seventies. Suppose a simple procedure would add one year to the lives of all septuagenarians. This would yield a huge gain in life years spread over a whole population. Suppose, as is perhaps likely, the number of septuagenarians in Denmark was over 260,000, then the number of life years saved by adding a further year to their lives would exceed the total to be gained by all the measures to prevent accidents, suicides, heart disease and so on. This would then become the chief priority for health care spending.

Gould starts his calculations after 'the first perilous year' but this cut-off point would require justification. We might well conclude, persuaded by his general line of argument, that neonatal and postnatal care would have the first priority for resources.

The life-time position then can support a wide variety of practices and may lead to a policy of achieving small gains in lifespan for large numbers of people rather than to the sorts of substantial gains for those individuals with most to lose that its supporters seem to have principally in mind.

Threshold of discrimination   It is tempting to think that we might be able to get over some of the problems of the life-time position by arguing that we can discount small gains in time as below the level of discrimination, in the sense that the benefit to the individual which accrued from living for a comparatively short period of extra time was nugatory. This might solve a few of the problems for the life-time position which arise from the necessity it imposes of favouring one group of people over another, wherever and whenever they are sufficiently numerous that the total life-time saved by rescuing them, even for a negligibly short period, exceeds that which might be saved by rescuing another smaller group who would live longer individually, but shorter collectively. However, the problem will remain wherever the amount of life-time to be saved is just enough to be worth having (or is thought so to be by those whose time it is) but seems a poor return on the investment required to procure it or in terms of other savings, including savings of longer individual life-time, that might be made instead.

People versus policies We are strongly inclined to believe that where, for example, we can prolong the lives of 120,000 people by one month or 1,000 people by ten years that we should do the latter and that it is better to use a scarce resource to save the life of someone who is likely to live on for at least ten years rather than that of someone who will die in six months in any event. This inclination makes it look as though what we must in fact value is length of life-time rather than simply saving lives. But valuing life-time can be as dangerous to our moral intuitions as is the anti-ageist argument. Again, it might be tempting to believe that a policy of devoting resources to saving individual lives for as long as possible was better than simply maximizing life-time saved. There might be a number of different grounds for such a belief. One such ground would be the expectation that procedures which could prolong individual lives by a substantial period would lead to a greater saving of life-time in the long term than would procedures which merely postponed death for a month or so. But in the absence of any strong evidence for such a conclusion this expectation would be at best an act of faith and at worse a pious hope. Is there any way out?

The fallacy of life-time views

Suppose various medical research teams to be in competition for all research funds available and that one team could demonstrate that it was capable of producing an elixir of life that would make anyone taking it immortal. Suppose further that the entire world medical research budget, if applied to this end, would produce just enough elixir for one dose, and that nothing less than a full dose would have any effect at all. The life-time view suggests that all the money should go to making one person immortal rather than, say, to an alternative project by which another team could make everyone on earth live to a flourishing 80![10]

But there is an obvious fallacy in this argument which reveals a defect in the whole life-time approach. Making one person immortal will produce a saving of no more life years than would the alternative of making everyone on earth live to a flourishing 80. So long as the world itself and its population lasts as long as the immortal (and how – and where – could he last longer?) there would be no net increase in life years lived. Indeed, so long as there is either a stable or an increasing world population, from the life years point of view, it matters not at all who lives and who dies, nor does it matter how many years anyone survives. For, so long as those who die are replaced on a one-for-one or better than a one-for-one basis, there will be no loss of life years. Nor will there be any gain in life years when particular individuals live for longer. For if the overall world population is stable then prolonging the life of particular individuals does not increase the total number of life years the world contains. And if the world population is increasing then it is highly unlikely that prolonging the lives of particular people will fuel that increase. Indeed the reverse is more likely to be the case with the survival of people beyond child-bearing age having a retarding effect on the rate of increase.

In the context of a stable or of an increasing world population, any idea that any policy which did not have the effect of increasing the population in fact made any contribution to the amount of life-time saved would be an illusion.

We do not then have always to calculate the probable net saving in life-time of any particular policy or therapy, before knowing what to do, and can revert to the more customary consideration of the numbers of lives that might be saved or lost. This, however, highlights once again the problems of whether lives that can only be saved for relatively short periods of time (that can only be prolonged by a few months say) are as worth saving as those for whom the prognosis in terms of life expectancy is much longer. A manoeuvre that seems to capture our intuitions here involves modifying the life-time view into a worthwhile life-time view.

Worthwhile life-time

While to many just staying alive may be the most important consideration, and while they may even wish to continue to live even at appalling cost in terms of pain, disability and so on even, as we have seen,[11] where their lives are hardly worth living, they of course prefer to live worthwhile lives. So that, while any life might be better than no life, people generally expect medical care to concern itself not simply with preventing death but with restoring worthwhile existence.

Many sorts of thing will go to diminish the worth of life just as many and various considerations go to make life valuable and these will differ from individual to individual. For the moment we are just concerned with the question of how life expectancy operates as one of these.

If someone were sentenced to death and told that the execution would take place at dawn the next day, they would not, I imagine, be excessively overjoyed if they were then informed that the execution had been postponed for one month. Similarly if the prognosis for a particular disease were very accurate indeed, to be told that one had only seven months to live would not be dramatically less terrible than to be told one had six months to live. There are two related reasons for this. The first is simply that the prospect of imminent death colours, or rather discolours, existence and leaves it joyless. The second is that an almost necessary condition for valuing life is its open-endedness. The fact that we do not normally know how long we have to live liberates the present and leaves us apparently free to plan the future without having to be constantly aware of the futility of so doing.[12] If life had a short

and finite (rather than indefinite) future, most things would not seem to be worth doing and the whole sense of the worth of life as an enterprise would evaporate.[13]

In the light of these considerations many people would not much value such short periods of remission, and support for policies which could at best produce such small gains might well be slight. However, some might well value highly the chance of even a small share of extra time. So far from emptying their life of meaning, it might enable them to 'round it off' or complete some important task or settle or better arrange their affairs. It might, so far from being of no value, be just what they needed to sort their life out and make some sort of final sense of it.

We have frequently noted the extreme difficulty involved in discounting the value of someone's life where we and they disagree about whether or not it is worth living, and we have also noted the injustice of preferring our assessment to theirs when so much is at stake for them. In view of all this it would be hard to prefer our judgement to theirs here.

Perhaps the problem would in reality be a small one. These dilemmas only arise where we cannot both help some people to live for relatively short periods *and* at the same time help others to live for much longer ones. Where there is no such conflict there is no question that we should go on helping people to stay alive for just so long as they want us to. However, the fact that hard cases are rare does not mean that we can turn our backs on them.

Fair innings or no ageism?

We have then two principles which can in hard cases pull in opposite directions. What should we do in the sorts of hard cases we have been considering? First, we should be clear that while the very old and those with terminal conditions are alike, in that they both have a short life expectancy, they may well differ with respect to whether or not they have had a fair innings. I do not believe that this issue is at all clear-cut but I am inclined to believe that where two individuals both equally wish to go on living for as long as possible our duty to respect this wish is paramount. It is, as I have suggested, the most important part of what is involved in valuing the lives of others. Each person's desire to stay alive should be regarded as of the same importance and as deserving the same respect as that of anyone else, irrespective of the quality of their life or its expected duration.

This would hold good in all cases in which we have to choose between lives, except one. And that is where one individual has had a fair innings and the other not. In this case, while both equally wish to have their lives further prolonged one, but not the other, has had a fair innings. In this case, although there is nothing to choose between the two candidates from the point of view of their respective will to live and both would suffer the injustice of having their life cut short when it might continue, only one would suffer the further injustice of being deprived of a fair innings – a benefit that the other has received.

It is sometimes said that it is a misfortune to grow old, but it is not nearly so great a misfortune as not to grow old. Growing old when you don't want to is not half the misfortune that is not growing old when you do want to. It is this truth that the fair innings argument captures. So that while it remains true, as the anti-ageist argument asserts, that the value of the unelapsed possible lifespan of each person who wants to go on living is equally valuable however long that span may be, the question of which person's premature death involves the greater injustice can be important. The fair innings argument points to the fact that the injustice done to someone who has not had a fair innings when they lose out to someone who has is significantly greater than in the reverse circumstances. It is for this reason that in the hopefully rare cases where we have to choose between candidates who differ only in this respect that we should choose to give as many people as possible the chance of a fair innings.

Notes

1 Triage is a policy for coping with disasters where resources are insufficient to provide the normal standard of care for all. It involves dividing survivors into three groups: those who will die in any event, those who will live in any event, and those for whom care will make the difference between life and death. Care is then given only to this last group. The argument is that this is the most economical use of resources where resources are insufficient to help all.

2 This may be a rash assumption because of the voluntary nature of many risks.

3 Of course if I don't value it because it is so short as to be scarcely worth having then the point does not apply in such a case.

4 I owe this objection to Tom Sorrel and am greatly in his debt here and elsewhere in this chapter for his generous and penetrating criticisms and comments.

5 No non-sexist form is available here, nor is one desirable since a different formulation would lose the resonance of the phrase.

6 Jonathan Glover, *Causing Death and Saving Lives* (Harmondsworth: Penguin, 1977), p. 221.

7 I'm assuming 70 as the full measure of life expectancy of healthy people and that all candidates are healthy in the sense that there is no reason to regard their life expectancy as less than average.

8 Quoted by Jonathan Glover (see note 6), p. 221. I am indebted here and elsewhere to Glover's stimulating discussion of these matters.

9 Because any figure of life expectancy will be arbitrary and one has to be taken.

10 The elixir of life example which prompted this argument about the fallacy of life-time views in stable or increasing populations I owe to Tom Sorrel, whose formulation of it I largely use.

11 See chapter 2 in *The Value of Life* (1985), from which this extract is taken.

12 Many people have argued of course that it is always futile to plan for the future because the inevitability of our world's ultimate destruction makes everything futile.

13 For the record we should note that small gains in life-time will only seem to be worthless to those who gain them if it is known that they will be short. If the potential beneficiaries are kept in ignorance of the fact that they can be granted only a short remission then the extra time will not be clouded by the futility deriving from its short duration and the gain, though small, will be as worthwhile as any other segment of their lives of comparable duration. Of course the deception may not be justified.

45

Bubbles under the Wallpaper
Healthcare Rationing and Discrimination

Nick Beckstead and Toby Ord

The ethics of priority setting in public health is both difficult and crucial. It involves hard questions about life and death on a scale that ranges from choices for individual patients to health strategies for the entire world's population. The problems arise because we simply do not have enough resources to provide everyone with all the medical care they need. We must therefore make seemingly impossible choices.

Over the last forty years, a standard has emerged for facing such choices: the QALY approach. A Quality Adjusted Life Year (QALY) is a unit for measuring the gains from medical interventions and is designed to be equivalent to the health gained by saving a year of life at full health. To determine how many QALYs are gained by a medical intervention, one looks at the length and (health-related) quality of a person's remaining lifespan, both with and without the intervention. The length is measured in years, and the quality at a given time is assigned a weight between 0 and 1, where 1 is full health and 0 is a quality of life equivalent to death. The length of life is multiplied by the weight, so that (for example) ten years of life at full health is worth 10 QALYs, as is 20 years of life with a condition that has a quality of life

weighting of 0.5 (a weighting commonly assigned to blindness). Once a QALY value is assigned to the person's future with the intervention and to their future without it, the difference between these is the gain due to the intervention. This method can thus measure benefits gained through the extension of life, as well as through the improvement of one's quality of life, or combinations of the two.

The QALY approach to priority setting is, roughly speaking, to rank all possible health interventions in terms of the ratio of QALYs gained to dollars spent and then to fund these interventions in order of their cost-effectiveness. This approach has a clear and important rationale: given a fixed health budget, it leads to the largest possible health gains. As such, it has been very successful in terms of promoting aggregate health.[1]

However, some ethicists and policy makers are concerned that the QALY approach achieves these gains in health at the expense of justice. For while it is uncontroversial that one gains in health by extending one's life, or by raising the health-related quality of a given period of one's life, the QALY approach also produces a seemingly unsatisfactory conclusion: since

Original publication details: Nick Beckstead and Toby Ord, "Bubbles under the Wallpaper: Healthcare Rationing and Discrimination," a paper presented to the conference "Valuing Lives" New York University, March 5, 2011, © Nick Beckstead and Toby Ord, reprinted by permission of the authors. This paper is published here for the first time, but draws on Nick Beckstead and Toby Ord, "Rationing and Rationality: The Cost of Avoiding Discrimination," in N. Eyal et al. (eds.), *Inequalities in Health: Concepts, Measures, and Ethics*, Oxford: Oxford University Press, 2013, pp. 232–9. By permission of Oxford University Press.

a healthy person gains more QALYs from having their life extended than does a person with a disability, other things being equal, we should save the life of a healthy person over that of a disabled person. This objection has been forcibly made by John Harris (who described it as 'double jeopardy' for the disabled),[2] and it rose to national prominence in the United States after attempts to use the QALY approach in the state of Oregon were overturned on anti-discrimination grounds.[3]

The status of this objection is thus of key importance with respect to priority setting in healthcare. Is the current approach unjust? If so, should we make large sacrifices in terms of aggregate health in order to remedy it? Or does the objection rest on a mistake, in which case these large sacrifices would be in vain?

Bubbles under the Wallpaper

Attempts to resolve this problem have not met with great success. A solution favoured by Erik Nord and others involves ignoring quality-weights when deciding to whom we should give a life-saving treatment, provided the people to be saved regard their lives as worth living.[4] As Magnus Johannesson has pointed out,[5] Nord's proposal would sometimes conflict with individual preferences: it would sometimes rank one treatment higher than another, though this would be worse for someone and better for no one. Johannesson offers his own proposal, which also faces devastating objections.[6] In looking at such proposals, one gets the feeling that the task may be like trying to get a bubble out from behind the wallpaper; pushing down in one place simply moves the bubble elsewhere.

In this paper, we confirm this intuition by showing that *any* attempt to set priorities in health will face a highly counter-intuitive conclusion, often one of the counter-intuitive conclusions that people have tried to avoid in the above cases.[7] To see how this works, consider the following simplified case:[8]

Example

Alice and Beth were both perfectly healthy 20-year-olds, but have recently contracted an unusual disease. This disease will kill them very soon unless treated,

and even then they will suffer from serious complications, such as blindness and/or a reduced lifespan. To make matters worse, there are not enough resources to treat them both. There are, however three possible treatment options outlined in the table:

	Option X	Option Y	Option Z
Alice	45 years (blind)	–	–
Beth	–	60 years (blind)	35 years (full health)

In X, Alice is treated and will live for 45 years but will lose her sight. Because Beth was infected by a slightly weaker strain, there are two treatment options available to her: in Y, she will live for 60 years but will lose her sight, in Z she will live for only 35 years, but will retain her sight. Beth has been asked which of options Y and Z she prefers, and (after considerable research and reflection) she arrived at a strong preference for 35 years of life with full health over 60 years of life with blindness (this is in line with most people's preferences and with the commonly used QALY ratings).

Which of these options should we choose? Let us first consider them pair-wise: in other words, which would we choose if it were a choice between only X and Y, only Y and Z, or only X and Z. We will then see that there are three problems that we would like to avoid:

1. *Preference for smaller benefits* X produces a smaller benefit for Alice than Y does for Beth. Since there is nothing else to distinguish between the two people, choosing X over Y demonstrates a morally perverse preference for producing smaller benefits rather than larger ones.

2. *Pointless violation of autonomy* Y is worse than Z for Beth and they are equally bad for Alice. Choosing Y over Z thus involves violating Beth's autonomy for no gain at all (in fact, to produce what she and experts both regard as a worse outcome).

3. *Disability discrimination* Z provides fewer years of life for Beth than X provides for Alice. The only thing Z has in its favour is that Beth would be at full health, whereas X would leave Alice with a disability. Thus, choosing Z over X involves discriminating on the grounds of disability.

We are thus left with a cycle of preferences: we must choose Y over X in order to avoid *Preference for smaller benefits*, we must choose Z over Y to avoid *Pointless violation of autonomy*, and we must choose X over Z to avoid *Disability discrimination*.[9] However, this puts us in a very precarious position. Having cyclic preferences opens one up to so-called 'money pump' arguments. For example, consider the following. If you think it is important to choose Y over X given a choice between the two, then presumably you would be prepared to sacrifice something – at least a single penny – to choose Y in such a case. Similarly if you think the same thing between Y and Z, and between Z and X then you would be prepared to pay a penny to transfer in each of these cases. But this would leave you back where you began: with option X and slightly less money. Moreover, you would still be prepared to trade a penny to move from X to Y and could be made to go around this cycle until you had very little money remaining. Of course it is not just money that can be 'pumped' but anything of value.[10]

We could thus add a fourth problem:

4. *Cyclic preferences* Choosing Y over X, Z over Y, and X over Z, is an example of cyclic preferences, which violate the conditions of rational choice theory and leave one open to irrational behaviour such as money pumping.

It can be easily seen that any way of ranking health outcomes will therefore satisfy one of these four undesirable conditions. Given this conclusion, we must give up on producing a system of priority setting that avoids these problems and learn to live with the least of the evils, whichever it may be.

A Rights–Based Approach?

When confronted with this problem, it may seem natural to reach for a certain kind of rights-based approach. On this approach, when we have equally expensive treatments but can save only one person's life, the person who stands to gain the most life-years (ignoring any quality adjustments) is awarded the right to treatment. The person may then select the treatment that she most prefers to receive, under the advisement of her doctor.

Thus, if the choices are X and Z, Alice would be awarded the right to treatment and we would choose option X. Whereas if option Y were also available, Beth would receive the right to treatment, and since she prefers option Z to option Y, we would choose option Z.

In this section, we show that this approach faces considerable difficulties. These difficulties arise because the approach suffers from *Cyclic preferences*. Objections of this kind can be extended to other theories that suffer from *Cyclic preferences*, so the section can also be viewed as a way of illustrating the problems associated with embracing *Cyclic preferences*.

To see that this approach suffers from *Cyclic preferences* but avoids 1–3, note that in pairwise cases, it chooses Y over X, Z over Y, and X over Z. The rights-based approach therefore cannot be applied across all individual cases without leaving the decision maker open to being money pumped. This is unlikely to arise in practice, but casts doubt upon the rationality of the approach.

Cyclic preferences also lead to another strange problem for the rights-based approach. Note that the rights-based approach chooses X out of the options X and Z, but when Y is added to the set of options, it switches its choice to Z. In decision theory, this is known as violating the *Independence of irrelevant alternatives*.[11] This violation may not seem like a deep defect: after all, it emerges naturally from a seemingly reasonable system of rights, and partially as a result of the autonomous choice of individuals. However, if we extend the example, we can see cases where this violation of the *Independence of irrelevant alternatives* seems particularly unreasonable.

First, let us add a few details to the Alice and Beth case. Suppose that for each treatment (X, Y, or Z) that could be delivered, there is a corresponding vial of medicine which must be administered. After this, the patient must receive a very uncommon medicine, of which the clinic has only a single dose. Following the rights-based approach, the doctor decides on option Z, so he walks over to the table and selects vial Z, then fills a syringe with it. Just as he is about to inject Beth with this medicine, he hears a small crash: vial Y has just fallen off the table and shattered, making treatment Y unavailable. The doctor then realises that it would now be wrong to give treatment Z, as it has become a choice between only X and Z, so he goes back to the table and fills a syringe from vial X to give to Alice instead.

There is something very odd about this behaviour. This example brings the dependence on irrelevant alternatives to the fore and casts doubt upon whether the rights-based approach is a reasonable protocol.

Alternatively, consider a case in which the doctor knows that they have treatment X and Z available, but can't remember whether they have any of treatment Y. In this case, the doctor is uncertain of which is the right treatment to deliver. If Y is available, he must administer treatment Z to Beth (to avoid a *Pointless violation of autonomy*), but if it is not, then he must administer X to Alice (to avoid *Disability discrimination*). Since these are both weighty problems that adherents to the rights-based approach want to avoid, it is thus imperative for the doctor to spend some time searching the clinic to see if Y is available, or perhaps telephoning suppliers, even though he will not actually use it. More extreme examples could be constructed if the doctor would need to run moderately expensive tests in order to see if option Y was available or not.

Finally, consider a case in which we can help either Charles or Dan. They are both healthy 20-year-olds who were struck by a similar disease to Alice and Beth. To begin with, suppose that there are two options, P and Q, where P involves giving Charles 10 more years to live at full health and Q involves giving Dan 12 more years to live, but he would lose his sight. In this case, the rights-based approach would suggest treating Dan.

	Option P	Option Q	Option R	Option S	...
Charles	10 years (full health)	–	14 years (blind)	–	...
Dan	–	12 years (blind)	–	16 years (blind & deaf)	...

But now suppose that there was a third option, R, in which Charles could live for 14 years at the expense of being blind. Like most people, Charles does not prefer this to 10 years at full health, but if option R is available, then the rights-based approach recommends treating Charles. Now suppose there is a fourth option, S, where Dan could live for 16 years but would be both blind

and deaf. Dan does not prefer this to 12 years with blindness and hearing, but now the rights-based approach would recommend treating Dan. Notice that we are now deciding between P and Q (which are the only options that will conceivably be chosen) on the basis of R and S. One could imagine a long sequence of increasingly irrelevant alternatives, the existence of which keeps swinging the balance between P and Q. Moreover, as it is very important on this view whether such options exist, we would often be required to spend some time and money investigating whether such options exist before making our decisions.

We thus find that the rights-based approach looks increasingly unreasonable. As noted above, these examples can be extended to other theories that possess *Cyclic preferences*, thereby demonstrating how important it is for a theory to avoid this problem.

Randomness to the Rescue?

Many philosophers are convinced on independent grounds that fairness requires us to leave some of our most important decisions up to chance, so it is natural to wonder whether a move to lotteries could resolve the present problem. The purpose of a lottery system is to give each person a fair chance of being treated – where this may be an equal chance or a chance weighted by how much the person involved stands to gain.[12]

Although lotteries may seem like a sensible solution in a case where we must allocate treatments to a small number of individuals in the same hospital, they seem less sensible as a general approach to priority setting. Given the numbers of people affected, we are most concerned with getting global priorities right. On that note, it is hard to believe that the government should draw numbers in order to decide which kinds of medical research to fund, which kinds of doctors to hire, or which kinds of treatments are worth funding. We won't pretend to have established that lotteries are unreasonable in this setting, but we note that randomness does not look promising as a solution to our problem, at least on the most important level.

However, even in its most plausible application, a lottery approach affords no traction on our problem. To defend this claim, we can give an argument that is highly analogous to the one given earlier. The first step is simply to use analogues of 1–3 that apply to gambles. In this case, we'd like to avoid policies that have any of the following three undesirable properties:

1★ *Preference for smaller benefits*★ When the potential treatments are X and Y, the policy allows Alice at least as great a chance as Beth even though Alice and Beth are equally healthy and Beth would live for an additional 15 years.[13]

2★ *Pointless violation of autonomy*★ When the potential treatments include Y and Z, the policy allocates a non-zero probability to Y, even though Beth prefers treatment Z and Beth's favoured treatment would come at no one else's expense.

3★ *Disability discrimination*★ When the potential treatments are X and Z, the policy demands a lottery over X and Z that gives Beth at least a great a chance as Alice, even though (i) Beth stands to gain fewer years of life and (ii) we would favour Alice if she were not disabled.[14]

In the previous section, avoiding 1–3 required having cyclic preferences over X, Y, and Z. Here, we replace that cyclic ranking with another. In this case the relation 'A merits more probability than B, when the choices are A and B' turns out to be cyclic. To avoid *Preference for smaller benefits*★, we must give Y more probability than X. To avoid *Pointless violation of autonomy*★, we must give Z more probability than Y. To avoid *Disability discrimination*★, we must give X more probability than Z. That this relation could be cyclic is strange in itself. More importantly, it seems that we are dealing with the same problem all over again. Intuitively, treatment A should get more probability than treatment B only if we should prefer that treatment A be given rather than that treatment B be given. And, for the reasons noted above, we should not have cyclic preferences.

In case it seems that the problem just noted can somehow be avoided, note that it is impossible to satisfy 1★–3★ if we want to avoid a policy with the following undesirable (disjunctive) property:

4★ *Dependence on irrelevant treatments*★

a. The policy allows that adding a potential treatment for one person could decrease her odds of being treated. Intuitively, it would be unfair (and bizarre) to decrease a person's odds of being treated on the grounds that additional possible ways of curing that person (and no one else) were discovered, or

b. The policy allows that adding a potential treatment for one person could decrease another person's chances of being treated, even though the first person prefers an alternative treatment that is already available. Intuitively, the person whose chances decrease could complain that she was being given a lesser chance for irrelevant reasons.

We relegate the proof that it is impossible to avoid all of 1★–4★ to a note, since the argument is slightly more technical than the previous one.[15] The basic problem is that any lottery system that avoids *Preference for smaller benefits*★, *Pointless violation of autonomy*★, and *Dependence on irrelevant treatments*★ will give more probability to Z than X when the choices are X, Y, and Z. On the other hand, any lottery system that avoids *Disability discrimination*★ and *Dependence on irrelevant treatments*★ will give at least as much probability to X as it does to Z. It is not possible to have both.

This result about lotteries can be viewed as a generalization of our original argument. Whatever the merits of randomization elsewhere, a move to lotteries cannot solve the present problem.

Conclusion

We have shown that it is impossible for a moral theory to provide guidance in multi-person trade-offs between length of life and quality of life without facing one of four very challenging conclusions. Of these, we think that the ones most likely to be accepted are *Disability discrimination* and *Cyclic preferences*. Thus, while we have not explicitly argued in favour of the QALY approach and its controversial applications in situations with respect to life-saving treatment for the disabled, we have shown it to be substantially more plausible in light of the challenges faced by all of its competitors. This makes it a lot less clear that we should change the QALY system and thereby throw away the great health gains it has achieved.

We should also note, in passing, that the specific issues addressed here are part of a wider problem in the discourse on ethical theories. Some systems, such as the QALY approach, make their consequences clearly known in advance, making them easy targets for attack by intuitive counterexample. A single, confidently held, pre-theoretic judgment is often regarded as enough to reject such a position. Incomplete competitors frequently avoid this challenge because it is usually hard to

see what problems an incomplete alternative will face.. In the present case we were able to produce an argument that applies to *all* competitors to the QALY approach, getting around the issue of underspecification, but unfortunately this is not always possible. Proponents of highly incomplete ethical positions must be careful when challenging more systematic competitors; the next impossibility argument may be around the corner, even if no one has been clever enough to discover it yet.

Notes

1   Here we are setting aside some important issues. For example, the QALY system will only maximize health gains if the weights are appropriately chosen. In practice, this can be difficult. But this is orthogonal to the issues that we discuss here. For the sake of argument, we assume that we are dealing with a system with reasonably chosen weights.

2   Harris (1987). See Singer et al. (1995) for a response to Harris.

3   For more on the Oregon cost-setting exercise, see Hadorn (1991).

4   Nord et al. (1999).

5   Johannesson (2001).

6   Nord et al. (2003).

7   In an economist's vocabulary, we do this by establishing an *impossibility theorem*. We show that certain intuitively inevitable constraints on a fair system for prioritizing health are impossible to meet.

8   Note that in this case there is no pre-existing disability. In such cases, prioritarian and egalitarian adjustments to the QALY framework make no significant difference to which option is chosen. Some might argue that, in this kind of case, there is nothing wrong with favouring the healthy over the blind. To address this point, we could change the case so that Alice became blind five years ago. Our analysis of the revised case would remain the same.

9   Note that we are using the term 'cyclic preferences' in a broad sense, referring both to cycles of preferences within a given set of options, and cycles of preferences across sets of options (such as the present case).

10   The status of money pump arguments is somewhat controversial. Sometimes they are used to argue that rational people do not have cyclic preferences. In that context, it is assumed that rational people always choose A over B when they prefer A to B. But someone

who believes in the rationality of cyclic preferences may deny this, pointing to cases of strategic reasoning that appear to be counterexamples to this generalization. We need not settle this issue here. What's true is that if policy-makers want to set healthcare priorities using a ranking system that they can follow in general, the ranking system will be susceptible to a money pump if the ranking is cyclic.

11   This strange feature arises directly from the *Cyclic preferences*: one cannot stabilise a cyclic system of preferences in the case where all three options are presented at once without violating the *Independence of irrelevant alternatives*.

12   Broome (1984).

13   Some people may be tempted to think that it isn't so bad to satisfy *Preference for smaller benefits*★ on the grounds that a fair coin toss is the appropriate response to this case. We think that a difference of 15 years should be enough to make this implausible. We could adjust the case by choosing a more debilitating condition and allowing an even larger gap in years. For this solution to work in general, one must be willing to do fair coin tosses even when the difference in benefits could be very great. We find this idea absurd; it is anathema to the very idea of priority setting in health care.

14   To avoid *Disability discrimination*★ one must give Alice a greater chance of being treated when the choices are X and Z (equal chances would not be allowed). We can run a version of our argument using another version of this requirement that allows giving each person an equal chance in this situation. To see this, note that we make use of a weak inequality rather than a strict one in line 6 of the proof in note 15.

15   We proceed by assuming the four conditions do not hold and deriving a contradiction. For some simplifying notation, let $\Pr(A:ABC)$ be the probability assigned by

a lottery to A when the alternatives are A, B, and C. Likewise, $\text{Pr}(B{:}BC)$ is the probability assigned to B when the alternatives are B and C. Then we can argue as follows:

1	$\text{Pr}(Y{:}XY) >$ $\quad\text{Pr}(X{:}XY)$	to avoid *Preference for smaller benefits**
2	$\text{Pr}(Y \text{ or } Z{:}XYZ) >$ $\quad\text{Pr}(X{:}XYZ)$	to avoid *Dependence on irrelevant treatments** and satisfy 1
3	$\text{Pr}(Y{:}XYZ) = 0$	to avoid *Pointless violation of autonomy**
4	$\text{Pr}(Z{:}XYZ) = \text{Pr}(Y$ $\quad\text{or } Z{:}XYZ)$	from 3 and probability theory
5	$\text{Pr}(Z{:}XYZ) >$ $\quad\text{Pr}(X{:}XYZ)$	from 2 and 4
6	$\text{Pr}(X{:}XZ) \geq$ $\quad\text{Pr}(Z{:}XZ)$	to avoid *Disability discrimination**
7	$\text{Pr}(X{:}XYZ) \geq$ $\quad\text{Pr}(Z{:}XYZ)$	to avoid *Dependence on irrelevant treatments** and to satisfy 6
8	contradiction!	from 5 and 7

References

Broome, John. 1984. Selecting people randomly. *Ethics* 95:38–55.

Hadorn, David C. 1991. The Oregon priority-setting exercise: quality of life and public policy. *Hastings Center Report* 21(3):11–16.

Harris, John. 1987. QALYfying the value of life. *Journal of Medical Ethics* 13:117–123.

Johannesson, Magnus. 2001. Should we aggregate relative or absolute changes in QALYs? *Health Economics* 10: 573–577.

Nord, Erik, et al. 1999. Incorporating societal concerns for fairness in numerical valuations of health programs. *Health Economics* 8:25–39.

Nord, Erik, Paul Menzel and Jeff Richardson. 2003. The value of life: individual preferences and social choice. A comment to Magnus Johannesson. *Health Economics* 12: 873–877.

Singer, Peter, et al. 1995. Double jeopardy and the use of QALYs in health care allocation. *Journal of Medical Ethics* 21:144–150.

Part VI

Obtaining Organs

Introduction

In organ transplantation, solid organs and tissues – as distinct from blood or cells – are removed from the body of one individual (the organ donor) and placed into the body of another. Organs can be taken from living or from dead donors. Solid organs available for transplantation are scarce, and some of the difficult ethical issues raised by the problem of scarcity are discussed in Part V on Resource Allocation. When distributing scarce resources, the primary focus is on the criteria that determine who should have access to the resource – given that the resource cannot be made available to everyone. The essays in the present Part VI of the anthology, on the other hand, focus primarily on those from whom the organs are obtained, and on some of the important ethical issues raised by different approaches to the procurement of organs, and attempts to increase their supply.

In "Organ Donation and Retrieval: Whose Body Is It, Anyway?" Eike-Henner W. Kluge starts by presenting the widely shared view that a paid organ procurement system would do little for the poor. Unable to afford the organs, they would, Kluge writes, "become the walking organ banks of the well-to-do." Kluge then proceeds to address the question of how organ shortages might be alleviated.

While most countries have rejected commercial systems – opting instead for an approach that limits the freedom of individuals to decide what will happen to their bodies during their lifetime and after death – there are great variations between the different approaches taken by different countries and states. Countries like Australia, Canada and Britain, for example, have "opting in" systems of organ donation. Under an "opting in" system people can volunteer to donate organs after their death. Some European countries, including Belgium, Spain and France, have adopted "opting out" systems. Here the assumption is that all citizens are potential organ donors, unless they opt out of the system, that is, withdraw their presumed consent.

Kluge supports various steps, including the adoption of presumed-consent legislation, to alleviate the shortage of organs for transplantation. In the absence of such laws, he also advocates making use of another source of organs that can become available without a change in the law, but merely a change in the way in which transplant societies work. At present, the protocols of transplant societies in countries with "opting in" legislation typically require the consent of the next of kin, even when the prior wishes of the deceased person are clear. Organ retrieval will not proceed without the next of kin's consent. The fact that the wishes of relatives can thus trump the wishes of deceased family members runs counter, Kluge argues, to contemporary consent laws, which state that a competent person's consent to organ donation is "full" and "binding."

Violation of consent is, however, not – in Kluge's further argument – the only or most important consequence of transplant societies insisting on

Bioethics: An Anthology, Third Edition. Edited by Helga Kuhse, Udo Schüklenk, and Peter Singer.
© 2016 John Wiley & Sons, Inc. Published 2016 by John Wiley & Sons, Inc.

next-of-kin consent: this insistence also entails that the organ shortage is greater than it needs to be and people are dying while waiting for an organ. As Kluge concludes, "not only does that violate the autonomous decision of the donor, it also costs lives."

It is common ground between Kluge and Janet Radcliffe-Richards and her colleagues ("The Case for Allowing Kidney Sales") that the shortage of organs for transplantation causes suffering and death and that this tragic toll could be reduced if more organs were available. Unfortunately, in that respect there has been little change since these articles were published in 1998–9. As Debra Satz reports in "Ethical Issues in the Supply and Demand of Human Kidneys," several new techniques have been employed in attempts to increase the supply of kidneys (including some that Kluge suggests) but it remains true that many people are suffering and dying because of the shortage of kidneys for transplantation. Satz indicates that in the United States alone, several thousand patients on the waiting list for a kidney die every year, some of whom would not have died if a kidney had been available.

For most commodities, a shortage leads to an increase in price which in turn provides a greater incentive to potential sellers, thus increasing the supply and overcoming, or at least reducing, the shortage. At present (2015) the sale of organs is illegal everywhere except in Iran, and international bodies like the United Nations and the World Health Organization support an international ban on organ sales. This has not put a stop to the international black market in kidneys.

The suggestion that it should be possible to buy and sell organs usually receives an extremely hostile reception both in the popular media and among members of professional organizations involved with organ transplantation. Radcliffe-Richards et al. urge professionals to reconsider the issue with a more open mind. The usual arguments against the sale of kidneys are, they contend, surprisingly weak, and the best

explanation of their acceptance is that they are a way to justify our almost automatic feeling of repugnance at the idea of buying and selling human body parts. But the burden of justifying a prohibition that causes a great deal of avoidable death and suffering is heavy, and feelings of disgust are not sufficient to discharge it.

Debra Satz's discussion of the ethical issues in the supply and demand of human kidneys – a chapter of her book *Why Some Things Should Not Be for Sale: The Moral Limits of Markets* – responds to the voices that have recently been raised in support of reexamining the ban on kidney sales. Drawing on recent research, she casts doubt on the claim that offering payment for kidneys would increase the supply, noting that it might cause altruistic donations to decline. Still, she acknowledges that at some price, the offer of payment will no doubt increase the net supply of kidneys. Would selling kidneys be wrong even if it did increase the supply, and thus save lives? Would it, for instance, be wrong because people in desperate poverty are not in a position to give their free consent to the sale of their bodily organs? Do we want a world in which the poor survive by selling their organs to the rich? Satz carefully considers these and other objections to a market for organs, and asks whether various forms of regulation could help to overcome them. Whatever else one might think about her reasoning, she has certainly moved the discussion well beyond rationalizations for a feeling of repugnance.

In the last essay in Part VI, John Harris puts forward an ingenious proposal to increase the supply of organs, and to give each of us as long and healthy a life as is possible. On the face of it, his proposed "survival lottery" appears to be an eminently sensible scheme that has the potential to save large numbers of lives, and of increasing everybody's chances of reaching a ripe old age. But is Harris making a serious proposal, or inviting us to reexamine our assumptions about the extent to which it would be desirable to pool our risks in order to save lives?

46

Organ Donation and Retrieval

Whose Body Is It Anyway?

Eike-Henner W. Kluge

One of the most important advances in acute care medicine over the last thirty years has been the development of organ transplantation. In many instances, such as end-stage liver and heart disease, organ transplantation saves lives. In others, such as kidney disease, organ transplantation frees patients from dependence on expensive medical technology and allows them to resume an almost normal mode of existence. From a humane perspective, this makes organ transplantation very attractive.

The benefits of organ transplantation are not confined to patients. Kidney transplantation is economically more cost-effective than continued renal dialysis of patients; and as transplantation techniques become more sophisticated for other organs, similar cost savings will be realized in other areas as well. Therefore, as health-care resources are increasingly being diminished, transplantation emerges as an appealing health-care modality.

However, organ transplantation depends on the availability of organs. All countries are experiencing an acute shortage of human organs for transplantation. At any given time and in any jurisdiction, there are hundreds of people waiting for transplants.[1] Quite literally, they are waiting for a new lease on life. That is why transplant societies in all countries are doing their best to raise organ donor awareness so that more people will donate their organs; and why medical establishments and surgical teams are working to improve their techniques of organ recovery and transplantation. When the lack of a suitable organ may mean death, every organ counts and no organ may be wasted.

The responses to this organ shortage have been varied. Some countries treat human organs and bodies as commodities that belong to the individual person and that may be sold by these individuals for a valuable consideration. This lets economics decide who will have access to transplantable organs and entails that market forces determine how organ shortages are dealt with. If the shortage is severe – so goes the theory – prices for organs will go up, sellers will appear in the market-place and the shortage will thus be alleviated.

Most countries have rejected this position for several reasons. *First*, they believe that people have such a close association with their bodies that to consider bodies and organs as property is tantamount to considering the people themselves as chattels. Hence they maintain that neither bodies nor body parts may be bought or sold. *Second*, they believe that if the ownership (and hence sale) of bodies or body parts were to be allowed, this would lead to a state of affairs where the rich would take advantage of the poor by offering such high prices for human organs that the poor would be unable to resist the enticement. The

Original publication details: Eike-Henner W. Kluge, "Organ Donation and Retrieval: Whose Body Is It Anyway?"
© 1999 by Eike-Henner W. Kluge.

Bioethics: An Anthology, Third Edition. Edited by Helga Kuhse, Udo Schüklenk, and Peter Singer.
© 2016 John Wiley & Sons, Inc. Published 2016 by John Wiley & Sons, Inc.

poor would therefore become the walking organ banks of the well-to-do. While this might alleviate the organ shortage in the case of affluent persons in need of organs, it would do nothing about the transplantation needs and the availability of organs for the poor.

In contrast, therefore, most countries have adopted the position that, while there is no ownership in human bodies, everyone has a right to decide what shall happen with her or his own body and that this right extends even beyond death. Beyond this, however, there is no general agreement. Some countries have instituted presumed consent legislation. That is to say, they have passed laws which mandate that, unless people have explicitly stipulated that they do not wish to be organ donors, their organs will be retrieved once they are dead. Other countries view organ donation as a supererogatory act that cannot reasonably be expected of all persons. Consequently they have passed laws which state that specific agreement to donation is a *sine qua non* for organ retrieval, and that this agreement must come either from the potential donor during her or his life time or, in the case of persons who have not made a decision in this matter, from those who are legally in possession of the body after the person is dead. These usually are the next of kin.

Unquestionably, the voluntary approach to organ donation can easily exacerbate the shortage of transplantable organs simply because potential donors (or their relatives) may be reluctant to agree to donation. This reluctance may be grounded in religious precepts which construe the removal of an organ as the sacrilegious mutilation of the body and hence consider it anathema. Alternatively, the refusal may be grounded in a psychological perspective that finds organ retrieval personally offensive on aesthetic grounds. Finally, the refusal to donate may be based on a mere misunderstanding about the process of retrieval itself and the nature of death. Specifically, it may be based on the assumption that death occurs only when there is a complete and irremediable cardiovascular collapse of the body which cannot be alleviated even by mechanical ventilation. This leads to the refusal to allow organ retrieval until after all such attempts have proved unsuccessful – which effectively guarantees that the relevant organs have also deteriorated beyond the point of usefulness for transplantation.

A further contribution to the shortage of organs lies in the fact that many potential donors are simply unaware of the option of donation. Hence organs that otherwise might well be donated are never retrieved.

There is little that can be done about a refusal to donate which finds its basis in religious conviction, short of changing the tenets of the relevant religion or prohibiting adherence to the religion itself. Neither of these is morally acceptable. With due alteration of details, similar considerations apply to refusals to donate that are based on personal aesthetics.

On the other hand, organ shortages that are grounded in misinformation or in ignorance of the option of donation can be alleviated by properly focused and conducted educational campaigns. Physicians can be encouraged to raise the subject of donation with their patients, to educate them about the benefits of donation and to explain to them the nature of death. Further, transplant societies can maximize the chance of retrieving donated organs by establishing organ donor registers which list everyone who has agreed to being a donor. On the death of such a person, it would be known immediately whether that person had agreed to donation.

Furthermore, it has been suggested that all jurisdictions adopt presumed consent legislation. In this way, it is hoped, the supply of organs will be increased because refusal to donate would have to be explicitly expressed.

However, there is a readily available supply of organs wich does not require the establishment of registers or changes in the current laws. Access to this supply does not require a change in anything – except in the way in which the various transplant societies work.

More precisely, in many countries that have consent legislation, the law states that the consent of a competent person is "full" and "binding" authority for the removal of that person's organs after death for the purposes of transplantation. In legal terms, the word "full" means that if someone has given consent, then this consent is sufficient and no one else needs to be asked for permission, while the term "binding" means that others may not overrule the consent of the donor and substitute their own wishes. Such consent is usually signified by an organ donor card or an organ donor sticker on the person's driver's licence.

Almost without exception, the organ retrieval protocols of most transplant societies are out of step with these provisions. Almost invariably, they state that the consent of the next of kin is required for organ retrieval *even when there is a donor card or sticker*. They further state that if the next of kin refuse the donation, the organs will not be retrieved.

In countries which have consent legislation that recognizes the individual's right to donate, these protocols clearly violate the law. In the great scheme of things, that may not be too important. However, what *is* important is that, because of these protocols, many organs that could be retrieved and used to save lives are never recovered. In other words, because of these protocols, the current organ shortage is greater than it needs to be, people are on waiting lists when they do not have to be, and people are dying while waiting for a suitable organ.

These are preventable deaths. They are therefore tragic. They are all the more tragic because they have ramifications far beyond the immediate sphere of the donor and the prospective recipient: they have implications for the availability of health care in general. Every organ that is not retrieved represents increased health-care costs for society. Health-care resources are finite: What is given to the one is taken away from the other. Therefore the impact of this non-retrieval affects not only the person who could have received the organ but everyone in the health-care system as a whole.

These protocols also have serious ethical implications for the ethics of informed consent. What the transplant societies are in effect saying with their guidelines is that the informed donor consent will not be considered binding if the donor is no longer capable of enforcing her or his wishes. Such an attitude sends the message that organ donation really doesn't mean anything: that the wishes of others really carry the day. If that practice were to be adopted in other areas of health care, informed consent would become meaningless. In fact, it would become a farce. It is surprising that, under the circumstances, anyone bothers to donate organs at all!

The transplant societies have argued that to retrieve organs against the wishes of the next of kin runs the danger of being perceived as ghouls, and that the negative publicity that would surround such actions might well result in a drop in organ donation. That is why they have proposed the establishment of a donor register, and that the law be changed in all jurisdictions in favour of presumed consent.

Unquestionably, the establishment of organ donor registers would be useful. So would the proposed change in legislation. Unfortunately, however, neither of these comes to grips with the real issue; and more important, neither of them would change the situation.

A register is useful only if the donors who are registered actually have their organs retrieved upon death. There is nothing inherent in a register to ensure that this would take place.

As to the proposed consent legislation, it would still leave the possibility that the next of kin might say *no* to organ retrieval even though the donor him- or herself had not said *no*. Therefore unless, under presumed consent legislation, the next of kin were *not asked for their consent*, the number of organ retrievals would not go up. The same number of next of kin who now refuse consent would also refuse their consent under the new legislation. The only way to avoid this would be not to ask the next of kin (or to ignore what they might say) and simply go on the assumption that, if the person had not wanted her or his organs retrieved, he or she would have said so. Therefore these proposed laws would work *only if the transplant societies acted the way they are supposed to act even under the current laws*. There is considerable justification for doubting that this would be the case.

The crux of the matter is really this: do people have the right to decide what shall be done with their body after they are dead? In particular, do they have the right to donate their organs in order to save lives? The answer may vary from society to society. However, once such a right is recognized, the ethics of informed consent entails that the donor's decision should not be overruled − or ignored − simply because others are uncomfortable with that decision. Not only does that violate the autonomous decision of the donor, it also costs lives. If others − e.g., the next of kin − are uncomfortable with the donor's decision, what is called for is not a refusal to follow the donor's last bequest but appropriate education and counselling in the ethics of donation and informed consent.

Always following the wishes of organ donors would not do away with the current shortage of organs. However, this shortage would not be so great if the donated organs were in fact retrieved, if the wishes of donors were followed – and if the ethics of informed consent were taken seriously. When every organ is a life, can one be less than ethical?

Note

1 Personal communication with various transplant organizations in Canada, US and Europe.

47

The Case for Allowing Kidney Sales

*Janet Radcliffe-Richards, A. S. Daar, R. D. Guttmann,
R. Hoffenberg, I. Kennedy, M. Lock, R. A. Sells, N. Tilney,
and for the International Forum for Transplant Ethics*

When the practice of buying kidneys from live vendors first came to light some years ago, it aroused such horror that all professional associations denounced it[1,2] and nearly all countries have now made it illegal.[3,4] Such political and professional unanimity may seem to leave no room for further debate, but we nevertheless think it important to reopen the discussion.

The well-known shortage of kidneys for transplantation causes much suffering and death. Dialysis is a wretched experience for most patients, and is anyway rationed in most places and simply unavailable to the majority of patients in most developing countries.[5] Since most potential kidney vendors will never become unpaid donors, either during life or posthumously, the prohibition of sales must be presumed to exclude kidneys that would otherwise be available. It is therefore essential to make sure that there is adequate justification for the resulting harm.

Most people will recognise in themselves the feelings of outrage and disgust that led to an outright ban on kidney sales, and such feelings typically have a force that seems to their possessors to need no further justification. Nevertheless, if we are to deny treatment to the suffering and dying we need better reasons than our own feelings of disgust.

In this paper we outline our reasons for thinking that the arguments commonly offered for prohibiting organ sales do not work, and therefore that the debate should be reopened.[6,7] Here we consider only the selling of kidneys by living vendors, but our arguments have wider implications.

The commonest objection to kidney selling is expressed on behalf of the vendors: the exploited poor, who need to be protected against the greedy rich. However, the vendors are themselves anxious to sell,[8] and see this practice as the best option open to them. The worse we think the selling of a kidney, therefore, the worse should seem the position of the vendors when that option is removed. Unless this appearance is illusory, the prohibition of sales does even more harm than first seemed, in harming vendors as well as recipients. To this argument it is replied that the vendors' apparent choice is not genuine. It is said that they are likely to be too uneducated to understand the risks, and that this precludes informed consent. It is also claimed that, since they are coerced by their economic circumstances, their consent cannot count as genuine.[9]

Although both these arguments appeal to the importance of autonomous choice, they are quite different. The first claim is that the vendors are not

Original publication details: Janet Radcliffe-Richards et al., "The Case for Allowing Kidney Sales," pp. 1950–2 from *The Lancet* 351: 9120 (June 27, 1998). Reprinted with permission from Elsevier.

competent to make a genuine choice within a given range of options. The second, by contrast, is that poverty has so restricted the range of options that organ selling has become the best, and therefore, in effect, that the range is too small. Once this distinction is drawn, it can be seen that neither argument works as a justification of prohibition.[7]

If our ground for concern is that the range of choices is too small, we cannot improve matters by removing the best option that poverty has left, and making the range smaller still. To do so is to make subsequent choices, by this criterion, even less autonomous. The only way to improve matters is to lessen the poverty until organ selling no longer seems the best option; and if that could be achieved, prohibition would be irrelevant because nobody would want to sell.

The other line of argument may seem more promising, since ignorance does preclude informed consent. However, the likely ignorance of the subjects is not a reason for banning altogether a procedure for which consent is required. In other contexts, the value we place on autonomy leads us to insist on information and counselling, and that is what it should suggest in the case of organ selling as well. It may be said that this approach is impracticable, because the educational level of potential vendors is too limited to make explanation feasible, or because no system could reliably counteract the misinformation of nefarious middlemen and profiteering clinics. But, even if we accepted that no possible vendor could be competent to consent, that would justify only putting the decision in the hands of competent guardians. To justify total prohibition it would also be necessary to show that organ selling must always be against the interests of potential vendors, and it is most unlikely that this would be done.

The risk involved in nephrectomy is not in itself high, and most people regard it as acceptable for living related donors.[10] Since the procedure is, in principle, the same for vendors as for unpaid donors, any systematic difference between the worthwhileness of the risk for vendors and donors presumably lies on the other side of the calculation, in the expected benefit. Nevertheless the exchange of money cannot in itself turn an acceptable risk into an unacceptable one from the vendor's point of view. It depends entirely on what the money is wanted for.

In general, furthermore, the poorer a potential vendor, the more likely it is that the sale of a kidney will be worth whatever risk there is. If the rich are free to engage in dangerous sports for pleasure, or dangerous jobs for high pay, it is difficult to see why the poor who take the lesser risk of kidney selling for greater rewards – perhaps saving relatives' lives,[11] or extricating themselves from poverty and debt – should be thought so misguided as to need saving from themselves.

It will be said that this does not take account of the reality of the vendors' circumstances: that risks are likely to be greater than for unpaid donors because poverty is detrimental to health, and vendors are often not given proper care. They may also be underpaid or cheated, or may waste their money through inexperience. However, once again, these arguments apply far more strongly to many other activities by which the poor try to earn money, and which we do not forbid. The best way to address such problems would be by regulation and perhaps a central purchasing system, to provide screening, counselling, reliable payment, insurance, and financial advice.[12]

To this it will be replied that no system of screening and control could be complete, and that both vendors and recipients would always be at risk of exploitation and poor treatment. But all the evidence we have shows that there is much more scope for exploitation and abuse when a supply of desperately wanted goods is made illegal. It is, furthermore, not clear why it should be thought harder to police a legal trade than the present complete ban.

Furthermore, even if vendors and recipients would always be at risk of exploitation, that does not alter the fact that, if they choose this option, all alternatives must seem worse to them. Trying to end exploitation by prohibition is rather like ending slum dwelling by bulldozing slums: it ends the evil in that form, but only by making things worse for the victims. If we want to protect the exploited, we can do it only by removing the poverty that makes them vulnerable, or, failing that, by controlling the trade.

Another familiar objection is that it is unfair for the rich to have privileges not available to the poor. This argument, however, is irrelevant to the issue of organ selling as such. If organ selling is wrong for this reason, so are all benefits available to the rich, including all private medicine, and, for that matter, all public provision of medicine in rich countries (including transplantation of donated organs) that is unavailable in poor ones. Furthermore, all purchasing could be done by a central organisation responsible for fair distribution.[12]

It is frequently asserted that organ donation must be altruistic to be acceptable,[13] and that this rules out payment. However, there are two problems with this claim. First, altruism does not distinguish donors from vendors. If a father who saves his daughter's life by giving her a kidney is altruistic, it is difficult to see why his selling a kidney to pay for some other operation to save her life should be thought less so. Second, nobody believes in general that unless some useful action is altruistic it is better to forbid it altogether.

It is said that the practice would undermine confidence in the medical profession, because of the association of doctors with money-making practices. That, however, would be a reason for objecting to all private practice; and in this case the objection could easily be met by the separation of purchasing and treatment. There could, for instance, be independent trusts[12] to fix charges and handle accounts, as well as to ensure fair play and high standards. It is alleged that allowing the trade would lessen the supply of donated cadaveric kidneys.[14] But, although some possible donors might decide to sell instead, their organs would be available, so there would be no loss in the total. And in the meantime, many people will agree to sell who would not otherwise donate.

It is said that in parts of the world where women and children are essentially chattels there would be a danger of their being coerced into becoming vendors. This argument, however, would work as strongly against unpaid living kidney donation, and even more strongly against many far more harmful practices which do not attract calls for their prohibition. Again, regulation would provide the most reliable means of protection.

It is said that selling kidneys would set us on a slippery slope to selling vital organs such as hearts. But that argument would apply equally to the case of the unpaid kidney donation, and nobody is afraid that that will result in the donation of hearts. It is entirely feasible to have laws and professional practices that allow the giving or selling only of non-vital organs. Another objection is that allowing organ sales is impossible because it would outrage public opinion. But this claim is about western public opinion: in many potential vendor communities, organ selling is more acceptable than cadaveric donation, and this argument amounts to a claim that other people should follow western cultural preferences rather than their own. There is, anyway, evidence that the western public is far less opposed to the idea than are medical and political professionals.[15]

It must be stressed that we are not arguing for the positive conclusion that organ sales must always be acceptable, let alone that there should be an unfettered market. Our claim is only that none of the familiar arguments against organ selling works, and this allows for the possibility that better arguments may yet be found.

Nevertheless, we claim that the burden of proof remains against the defenders of prohibition, and that, until good arguments appear, the presumption must be that the trade should be regulated rather than banned altogether. Furthermore, even when there are good objections at particular times or in particular places, that should be regarded as a reason for trying to remove the objections, rather than as an excuse for permanent prohibition.

The weakness of the familiar arguments suggests that they are attempts to justify the deep feelings of repugnance which are the real driving force of prohibition, and feelings of repugnance among the rich and healthy, no matter how strongly felt, cannot justify removing the only hope of the destitute and dying. This is why we conclude that the issue should be considered again, and with scrupulous impartiality.

References

1 British Transplantation Society Working Party, Guidelines on living organ donation. *BMJ* 293 (1986), pp. 257–258.

2 The Council of the Transplantation Society, Organ sales. *Lancet* 2 (1985), pp. 715–716.

3   World Health Organization. A report on developments under the auspices of WHO (1987–1991). Geneva: WHO, 1992: 12–28.

4   PJ Hauptman and KJ O'Connor, Procurement and allocation of solid organs for transplantation. *N Engl J Med* 336 (1997), pp. 422–431.

5   RS Barsoum. Ethical problems in dialysis and transplantation: Africa. In: CM Kjellstrand, JB Dossetor, eds. Ethical problems in dialysis and transplantation: Netherlands: Kluwer Academic Publishers, 1992: 169–82.

6   J Radcliffe-Richards, Nephrarious goings on: kidney sales and moral arguments. *J Med Philosoph. Netherlands: Kluwer Academic Publishers,* 21 (1996), pp. 375–416.

7   J Radcliffe-Richards, From him that hath not. In: CM Kjellstrand, JB Dossetor, eds. Ethical problems in dialysis and transplantation. Netherlands: Kluwer Academic Publishers, 1992: 53–60.

8   MK Mani. The argument against the unrelated live donor, ibid. 164.

9   RA Sells, The case against buying organs and a futures market in transplants. *Trans Proc* 24 (1992), pp. 2198–2202.

10   AD Daar, W Land, TM Yahya, K Schneewind, T Gutmann, A Jakobsen, Living-donor renal transplantation: evidence-based justification for an ethical option. *Trans Reviews* (in press) 1997.

11   JB Dossetor, V Manickavel, Commercialisation: the buying and selling of kidneys. In: CM Kjellstrand, JB Dossetor, eds. Ethical problems in dialysis and transplantation. Netherlands: Kluwer Academic Publishers, 1992: 61–71.

12   RA Sells, Some ethical issues in organ retrieval 1982–1992. *Trans Proc* 24 (1992), pp. 2401–2403.

13   R Sheil, Policy statement from the ethics committee of the Transplantation Society. *Trans Soc Bull* 3 (1995), p. 3.

14   JS Altshuler and MJ Evanisko. *JAMA* 267 (1992), p. 2037.

15   RD Guttmann and A Guttmann, Organ transplantation: duty reconsidered. *Trans Proc* 24 (1992), pp. 2179–2180.

48

Ethical Issues in the Supply and Demand of Human Kidneys

Debra Satz

Societies sometimes ban the sale of goods whose supply they actually wish to support or encourage.[1] Examples include bans on markets in votes, children, and human organs. In the United States sales of organs such as kidneys are currently illegal, and those needing transplants must rely on altruistic donation. From an economic perspective, an organ ban appears inefficient, as it seems likely that payments to donors would elicit greater supply, thereby reducing chronic shortages. From a libertarian perspective, a ban on organ sales is an illegitimate infringement on personal liberty; allowing people to sell their own body parts is merely a way of recognizing their legitimate sphere of control.[2] Nonlibertarian proponents of a market in human organs also argue that a ban on sales is morally dubious because lives would be saved by the increased supply.

The idea of establishing a kidney market is now attracting unprecedented support among those involved in transplantation, as well as among economists and medical ethicists. This chapter examines the values at stake. But I also raise a distinct consideration that is relevant to these markets: the link between markets and motives. Unlike the cases of child labor, bonded labor, sex, and surrogacy, we have an interest in motivating people to act in ways that increase the supply of transplant organs.

Brief Background: The Status Quo Systems of Kidney Procurement

Despite the prima facie case for organ markets just noted, kidney selling is currently illegal in every developed society in the world.[3] The United Nations and the European Union have instructed their member countries to prohibit the sale of body parts. The World Health Organization has interpreted the Universal Declaration of Human Rights as prohibiting the sale of organs. Indeed most of the globe's countries have enacted legal bans of such sales, although states differ dramatically in their enforcement capacity, and a black market thrives in many countries.

In the United States people can donate their kidneys after death or while they are alive only out of altruism. The Uniform Anatomical Gift Act, drafted in 1984 (the same year the National Organ Transplantation Act was enacted), made it illegal for anyone to receive any payment, or "valuable consideration," for providing an organ. Instead those who need kidneys must rely

Original publication details: Debra Satz, "Ethical Issues in the Supply and Demand of Human Kidneys," pp. 189–206 from *Why Some Things Should Not Be for Sale: The Moral Limits of Markets*, New York: Oxford University Press, 2010, ch. 9, based on an article from *Proceedings of the Aristotelian Society*. Reprinted by courtesy of the Editor of *Proceedings of the Aristotelian Society*. © 2010.

Bioethics: An Anthology, Third Edition. Edited by Helga Kuhse, Udo Schüklenk, and Peter Singer.

largely on individual or social exhortation to induce people to donate. The result is that most live donations come from close relatives or intimates, with parents entrusted to make decisions about whether a child can serve as a donor for a sibling or relative. Individuals have a right to donate their kidneys to loved ones, but not a right to sell them.

Cadaver organs in the United States come from two main groups: those who explicitly consented to have their organs used after their death, whether through a living will or indicating a wish to be a donor on a driver's license, and those who are *presumed* to have consented. More than fifteen states rely on presumed consent laws, whereby someone who undergoes a mandatory autopsy (often in the context of a homicide) is presumed to have consented to the use of some of his organs unless he explicitly objected to such donations prior to his death.[4] (In the United States presumed consent laws are limited to bodies under the authority of the coroner or medical examiner.)

Individuals also have the right *not* to donate their organs; *no* society makes kidney donation mandatory. Current U.S. law protects living persons from having their organs taken from them without their consent, even in cases in which another person's life is at stake.[5] If exhortation fails to secure an organ, the person needing the donation has no (legal) recourse but instead must wait his turn on the transplant list.[6] Currently there are long queues for obtaining a kidney. In the United States alone there were more than fifty thousand Americans on the waiting list for a kidney in 2003. That same year there were twelve thousand donors.[7] This means that thirty-eight thousand people were carried over onto the 2004 waiting list, along with the year's new additions to that list. Many people wait years before an organ becomes available. Several thousand people die each year in the United States alone while waiting for an organ transplant.[8] Some of these people would not have died had an organ been available for them at the time they needed it most.[9]

A number of European societies rely on an opt-out system of organ procurement rather than the opt-in system used in the United States. In many nations – including Austria, Belgium, Denmark, Finland, France, Italy, Luxemburg, Norway, Singapore, and Spain – all individuals are presumed to consent to allow their organs to be used after their death for the benefit of others. In an opt-out system the default position is that every individual's organs are available on her demise, although each individual is permitted to rebut the presumption (to opt out), usually signaled by an explicit notation on a driver's license.[10]

Moving toward an opt-out baseline allocation system could be a justified social policy if it saved lives, but it does not appear to solve the shortage of organs needed for transplant. Shortages remain in many European countries, including in those that rely on opt-out allocation systems.[11] In fact some studies suggest that the choice of opt-out systems over opt-in systems often makes little difference to the ultimate numbers of organs procured.[12] This result might seem counterintuitive, but there are three reasons why changing the default starting point might not increase the yield of organs. First, many countries with opt-out systems give relatives a right of refusal with respect to cadaveric donations, even when the deceased indicated support for such donations. And relatives frequently choose to forgo donation for religious or personal reasons. Second, many procured organs are simply not suitable for transplantation; the deceased may have been very old or very sick or not found in time for his organs to be useful after death.[13] And the ability to effectively procure an organ, to safely and quickly remove it and deliver it for transplantation, seems to depend crucially on institutional factors.[14] Third, given burgeoning rates of obesity and diabetes and longer life spans, the numbers of people needing kidney transplants continues to grow at a faster rate than do increases in the supply.

Anti-Market Considerations

As we have seen, the free market has considerable appeal: freedom of contract is taken to promote liberty; competitive markets are supposed to pay each input what it deserves (its marginal product); and markets tend to be extremely efficient mechanisms for the production and distribution of goods. Given the shortages in available kidneys and the strong interests at stake, it is not surprising that when a kidney was offered for sale on eBay the bidding reached $5.8 million before being shut down by the administrators of the site because the sale would violate U.S. law.[15]

Despite such considerations, I think there are reasons to be wary of jumping on the growing bandwagon for a market in human kidneys. Some of these reasons turn on nonideal features in a nonideal world and can be addressed through regulation; some of these reasons would hold in any realistic world.

Does a Market Ban Necessarily Decrease the Supply of Available Organs?

In his famous study *The Gift Relationship*, Richard Titmuss argued that a purely altruistic system for procuring blood is superior to a system that relies on a combination of altruistic donation plus a market.[16] Comparing the American and British systems of procuring blood, he demonstrated that a system of donated blood (the British system) is superior in quality to a system that also uses purchased blood (the American system), in part because blood sellers have a reason to conceal their illnesses, whereas altruistic blood donors do not. Furthermore Titmuss claimed that offering financial incentives for blood leads those in need of money to supply too frequently, endangering their own health. According to Titmuss, an altruistic system is not only more ethical, but it also produces a blood supply of higher quality.

Titmuss also argued, to the surprise of many economists, that a system that relied only on altruistic donation might be more *efficient* than a market system for blood. He claimed that, with respect to blood, the introduction of markets "represses the expression of altruism [and] erodes the sense of community."[17] If blood is treated as a commodity with an associated price tag, some people who would have donated when doing so bestowed the "gift of life" now decline to donate. Therefore blood supply would not necessarily be increased by the addition of a market; indeed Titmuss hypothesized that the net result of introducing a market for blood in England would be *less* blood of inferior quality.

This might seem surprising. Insofar as we are simply adding a new choice (i.e., selling blood) to a set of existing options, why should any of the existing options (i.e., donating blood), or their attractiveness to altruistic individuals, change?[18] Why should policies that appeal to self-interest also lead people to act in a less public-spirited way?

Consider the following real-life experiment, which illustrates the market effect that Titmuss conjectured on motivation. Faced with parents who habitually arrived late to pick up their children at the end of the day, six Haifa day care centers imposed a fine for such parental lateness. They hoped that the fines would give these parents a self-interested reason to arrive on time. The parents responded to the fine by *doubling* the amount of time they were late.[19] Even when the fine was revoked three months later the enhanced lateness continued. One plausible interpretation of this result is that the fine undermined the parents' sense that they were morally obligated not to take advantage of the day care workers; instead they now saw their lateness as a commodity that could be purchased.

This result has been replicated using carefully designed experiments. The experimental economist Bruno Frey and others have examined circumstances where *intrinsic motivation* is partially destroyed when price incentives are introduced.[20] An action is intrinsically motivated when it is performed simply because of the satisfaction the agent derives from performing the action. Whereas conventional economic analysis assumes that offers for monetary compensation will increase the willingness to accept otherwise unwanted projects, Frey found that support for building a noxious nuclear waste facility in a neighborhood actually *decreased* when monetary compensation to host it was offered. His study suggests that in cases where individuals are civically minded, using price incentives will not increase but can actually decrease levels of support for civic actions. For an intrinsically motivated agent, performing an act for money is simply not the same act when it is performed for free.[21] The presence of monetary incentives can crowd out a person's intrinsic reasons for performing the given action, changing the attractiveness of the options he faces. For example, in the nuclear waste example, citizens may feel bribed by the offer of money. In the case of timely day care pickup, altruistic concern for the teachers may be replaced by self-interested calculation about the worth of avoiding the fine.

This kind of crowding-out altruism result is not inevitable; the market can also be harnessed in a socially beneficial and more *altruistic* direction. A study of the introduction of a market wherein people purchased access to express carpool lanes in San Diego found that the program's initiation correlated with increased overall traffic in the express lanes, decreased traffic in the main lanes, and a significant *increase* in carpooling levels. (Carpoolers have access to the express lanes but do not have to pay for this access.) The author hypothesizes that the most likely explanation for the increase in carpoolers is that new drivers were attracted to carpooling by a *relative* monetary benefit: they felt better about getting for free what others pay for.[22]

If these case studies are illustrative, markets can change social norms. And if introducing a market does affect intrinsic motivations, we cannot a priori predict in which direction the net change of behavior will go. In the nuclear waste example we get less prosocial behavior, but the reverse is true in the carpooling example. Of course, kidney markets and blood markets are different from markets in access to faster commuting. Donations of organs and blood often involve questions of life and death, not simply convenience, and so it may well be that different motivations are invoked in those performing altruistic actions, motivations that are more likely to be vulnerable to crowding out.

Would the introduction of a kidney market actually serve to reduce supply by crowding out those with altruistic motivations? Even if kidney markets drove out altruists, it is still possible that the net supply of kidneys would be increased. Maybe there are more potential extrinsically motivated donors than donors who are only, or primarily, intrinsically motivated. Furthermore if the amount of organs procured through a market remained inadequate, increasing the price of organs would likely lead to more nonaltruistic donors. In Friedrich Dürrenmatt's splendid tragedy, *The Visit of the Old Lady*, an incredibly rich woman who had been wronged in her youth by her lover now offers the residents of her hometown $1 million to kill him. At first the offer is angrily rejected by the citizens as deeply immoral, but the woman induces them to raise their consumption and take on debts. Finally as they accommodate themselves to their new level of comfort, they decide to kill the lover who refused to accept paternity for her child so many years ago. Perhaps in the cases Frey and others examined the monetary rewards were simply insufficient to motivate people or offered before people had a chance to get used to the idea.[23]

It is also important to consider whether, if there are crowding-out effects on people with altruistic motivations, it is the case that *all* extrinsic rewards for giving up a kidney – including rewards to one's heirs after one's death, lifetime medical benefits, and payment of funeral costs – would have the same crowding-out effects as cash.[24]

Perhaps legalizing kidney sales decreases altruistic donation and at the same time increases the net supply of organs, at least if the price is right.[25] Whether or not it does so is an especially relevant consideration if a person's support for or opposition to organ markets rests solely on the effects of such markets on supply. Because the positive case for organ markets does largely rest on such grounds, it is clearly relevant to whether that case is a good one; moral motivations may be more fragile than we often assume. But whether the introduction of markets increases or decreases supply may not be decisive for some opponents of kidney markets; some people believe that kidney selling is wrong even if it increases supply.

Vulnerability

For some a kidney sale is objectionable because it is a paradigmatic *desperate exchange*, an exchange no one would ever make unless faced with no reasonable alternative. A kidney is, in the words of one organ market critic, the "organ of last resort."[26] Many people object to organ markets precisely because they believe that these markets would allow others to exploit the desperation of the poor. This objection to desperate exchanges is often associated with a paternalistic concern that sellers would actually be harmed by the sale of their organs, but that given their desperation they would sell their organs if it were legal.

A defender of organ markets might argue that the worries about exploitation could be addressed through regulation: by eliminating organ brokers who capture much of the price of the organ; by allowing open competition that is precluded by the black market; and by enforcing the terms of contracts. To address this concern, it might also be argued that organ donation should be legal only in contexts in which people are not likely to be desperately poor.[27]

Weak Agency

Whereas ideal markets involve fully informed partici-pants, we have seen in this book that many markets do not, and in fact cannot, function on that basis. This is sometimes because market transactions involve conse-quences that can be known only in the future. Kidney transplants involve surgical operations and, like all sur-gical operations, entail risks. In a careful study of India's kidney sellers, 86 percent of the participants in the study reported a marked deterioration in their health following their nephrectomy.[28] Although one kidney is capable of cleansing the blood if it is functioning well, the removal of a kidney leaves the seller vulnerable to future problems if the remaining kidney becomes damaged or if its filtering capability declines. (In fact the decrease in filtering capacity is a normal byproduct of aging.) Needless to say, the poor in the developing world who sell their kidneys have no health insurance and no claim on an additional kidney if their remaining one fails to function properly. Moreover, although most studies of kidney transplants have reported few adverse effects for the donors, these studies have been overwhelmingly conducted in wealthy countries; we simply do not know whether people in poor countries do as well with only one kidney as those in rich countries. Health risks are likely to be greater in places where people have little access to clean water or ade-quate nutrition and often are engaged in difficult manual labor.

Two other findings in the study of Indian kidney sellers relate to concerns with weak agency. First, an overwhelming majority of those interviewed (79 per-cent) said that they regretted their decision and would not recommend that others sell a kidney. Second, a majority of sellers interviewed (71 percent) were mar-ried women. Given the weak position of women in Indian society, the voluntary nature of the sales is questionable. The most common explanation offered by wives as to why they and not their husbands sold their organs were that the husbands were the family's income source (30 percent) or were ill (28 percent). Of course, as the authors of the study point out, most of the interviews of women were conducted in the presence of their husbands or other family members, so they may have been reluctant to admit to being pressured to donate.

Weak agency is a serious problem for those who wish to base their defense of the market in organs on the right of a person to make her own decisions with respect to her body parts, and this is especially true when the weak agency is connected to significant harm. The fact that most organ sellers would not recommend the practice suggests that potential sellers would be unlikely to sell a kidney if they were better informed about the outcomes of their sale.[29] Perhaps it is difficult to imagine what it means to lose a kidney before one actually experiences the loss. When we couple the information problems with the lack of benefit, the case for allowing a kidney market is thereby weakened.[30]

A defender of organ markets might reply that the appropriate response to the diminished agency of sell-ers is simply to make sure they are better informed about the likely consequences of their transactions. For example, organ sellers could be required to take classes dealing with the risks of live organ donation and to demonstrate that they understand the likely conse-quences of giving up a kidney. However, given the horrific poverty that many sellers face, and perhaps their lack of education, it is unclear to what extent they will refrain from undertaking the transaction simply because of the risks. Additionally, in poorer countries regulatory institutions are weak and underfunded.

Note, however, that the argument from weak agency – lack of information about how a seller will feel in the future about her kidney sale – might lead us to discourage altruistic organ donations as well as paid donations. That is, weak agency doesn't really sin-gle out what is problematic about the kidney *market*.[31] If the potential health risks for donors are substantial, then perhaps all such transfers from living donors should be banned. (And it is doubtful whether altru-istic donation is really made from the vantage point of full information and in the context of a range of choices. Family members are often under enormous pressure to donate and, as we have seen, parents are free to donate the organs of their own children.)

It is also important to consider just how substantial the potential harms are to organ donors and sellers. Currently we allow people to engage in risky occupa-tions (e.g., work in nuclear reactor plants); we do not prohibit markets enabling people to engage in risky behaviors such as cigarette smoking and skydiving; and we rely on financial incentives in military recruitment, which also exposes individuals to grave risks. So, to the extent that the argument from weak agency is compelling because it is predictive of harm, it is important to consider whether or not the potential harms are worse than from other sales that we currently permit.[32]

Equal Status Considerations

Current black markets in kidneys certainly reflect the different market situations of buyer and seller. Most sellers are extremely poor; most buyers are at least comparatively wealthy. It has been keenly noted that international organ markets transfer organs from poor to rich, third world to first world, female to male, and nonwhite to white. Indeed the fact that there is increasing pressure to allow kidneys to be bought and sold itself arguably reflects the fact that those who seek to purchase them tend to have the cash to be able to do so.[33] Contrast this with the situation of poor people whose health needs currently go unmet. Despite the fact that urgent health needs are shared by millions (billions?) of desperately poor people, poor people have little cash. Therefore their health needs tend to get far less attention than the health needs of the comparatively wealthy.

A system that relied on a kidney market of individual buyers and sellers for procurement and distribution would have the consequence that poor people would disproportionately be the organ sellers of the world and rich people the likely recipients.[34] By contrast, a procurement system that relies on donation is much more likely to have suppliers that come from all classes of people. Indeed Titmuss found just such a contrast between the American and British systems of blood donation.[35]

In his haunting novel *Never Let Me Go*, Kazuo Ishiguro imagines a world in which human clones are created to serve as organ donors for others.[36] Before these created humans are middle-aged, they start to donate their vital organs. At the end of the novel these purposely created humans "complete," that is, give up the last vital organs they have for transplantation into others, and then die. Along these lines critics of proposed organ markets have charged that such markets will effectively turn desperately poor people into "spare parts" for the rich. In her response to the argument that such organ markets

nevertheless transfer money to the poor, Organs Watch founder Nancy Scheper-Hughes caustically quips, "Perhaps we should look for better ways of helping the destitute than dismantling them."[37]

There is surely something disturbing about the picture of poor people supplying the rich with vital organs, just as the world Ishiguro portrays, where some are created to supply others with needed organs, is unsettling. Still, it is important to realize that there are many services that the poor of this world already provide for the rich that are not reciprocally provided by the rich for the poor. Few, if any, wealthy people take hazardous jobs in mines or work in nuclear power plants or are employed cleaning other people's latrines. Societies justify such tasks by pointing out that they are socially necessary and that what is important is that those who perform these tasks are justly compensated under conditions that meet health and safety standards. Given that, the inequality between suppliers doesn't pick out what is especially objectionable about a kidney market.

At the same time I think the critics raise the legitimate concern that kidney markets might actually *worsen* existing inequalities based on class. Such markets could expand inequality's scope by including body parts in the scope of things that money gives a person access to. There are people who have little or no money currently waiting on kidney transplant lists. To a large extent the selection of the person who receives a kidney for transplant is independent of his ability to pay. By contrast, a kidney market might mean that kidneys go to the highest bidders. But shouldn't kidneys be allocated on the basis of need, length of time waiting, and medical suitability and not on the basis of ability to pay?

Theoretically, of course, a legalized organ market could be regulated to ensure that rich and poor have access to kidneys, with the government providing funding for the organ purchases of poor buyers. Through subsidy and insurance the government *could* seek to make the demand for kidneys independent of the wealth of the buyer. Additionally the government might devote itself to finding donors for poorer patients.[38] From an egalitarian viewpoint, these regulations are desirable. Indeed the government might create a monopsony in which it was the *only* legal buyer of organs. And it could buy these organs using a future market, in which people are paid for their organs only after their death as a way of staving off coercive ploys. However, even if a government took such measures, it remains difficult for any government with limited resources and other priorities to make kidney allocation via a market completely independent of the wealth of the donor. Establishing a maximum price for kidneys under a monopsony might recreate the shortages that the kidney market was designed to overcome, especially if the availability of subsidized kidneys created a moral hazard problem.[39]

The Integrity of the Body

Three of the concerns that I have detailed thus far – weak agency, vulnerability, and the possibility that poor people will become suppliers of organ parts for the rich – can be dealt with through regulating the kidney market rather than blocking it. The concern about whether or not markets will increase supply is different: markets may decrease altruistic donation of organs under any realistic background social conditions, even in the context of regulation.

There is an additional consideration about kidney markets, a consideration that came out in my discussions of bonded and child labor: the way that adding a choice to a choice set changes the other choices that are available to the agent. I want to consider the ways that the existence of kidney markets might make some poor people worse off than they would otherwise be. Although this consideration isn't decisive – the banning of kidney markets makes others in desperate need of a kidney worse off than they would otherwise be – I think it has been missing from the current enthusiasm for organ markets and needs to be addressed. This consideration prompts us to think about the ways that a person's internal resources can differ from their external resources, a point that will resonate with specific egalitarian approaches.

The idea I want to explore here is that even if restrictions on kidney sales are beneficial from the point of view of an individual seller, they may be harmful to others. This is because allowing such markets as a widespread practice, as a pattern of repeated and regular exchanges backed up by laws, has effects on the nature of the choices that are available to people. While proponents of kidney markets usually focus on individual transactions within given environments, the introduction of markets can change environments (including, as we have seen, by possibly altering motivations). Consider that where the practice of kidney selling is widespread, kidneys are viewed as potential collateral and moneylenders acquire incentives to seek out additional borrowers as well as to change the terms of loans. The anthropologist Lawrence Cohen found that in areas of India where kidney selling was relatively common, creditors placed additional pressures on those who owed them money.[40] Cohen notes, "In the Tamil countryside with its kidney belts, debt is primary. ... Operable *women are vehicles for debt collateral.*"[41]

Cohen's finding suggests that if kidney selling became widespread, a poor person who did *not* want to sell her kidney might find it harder to obtain loans.[42] Ceteris paribus, the credit market allocates loans to people who can provide better collateral. If a kidney market exists, the total amount of collateral rises, which means that those without spare kidneys or those that refuse to sell them, will get fewer loans than before, assuming that the supply of loanable funds is more or less fixed. In other words, these people are made worse off by the kidney market. If this is so, then although allowing a market in kidneys expands a single individual's set of choices, if adopted in the aggregate it may reduce or change the available choices open to others, and those others will be worse off. They will have less effective choices insofar as they will no longer be able to find reasonable loan rates without mortgaging their organs. Once we see the effects of a kidney market on those who are not party to the transactions, we can no longer say that such markets have no harmful consequences.

Of course this argument is true of other linked markets; many markets generate pecuniary externalities. Recall that a pecuniary externality is an effect of production or transactions on outside parties through prices and not through direct resource allocations. For example, the introduction of a market in second homes in a rural community may price some first-time buyers out of the housing market in that community. But people who find kidney markets troubling do not necessarily find markets in second homes troubling. So my point about the effect of a kidney market on other people's choice sets does not settle the issue of whether that market should be blocked. Instead it leads us to ask, Should people have to pay a cost for their unwillingness to sell their organs? And if not, why not?

If we view kidneys as resources analogous to other resources we have, whether money or apples, it is unclear why we should not have to part with that resource if we wish to secure credit. But many people resist this analogy. They seem to tacitly believe, following Ronald Dworkin, that we have good reason to draw a "prophylactic line" around the body, a line "that comes close to making [it] inviolate, that is, making body parts not part of social resources at all."[43] I concur that there is something to this line of thought, and indeed that a horror at the thought of the conscription of our bodies by others may lie behind the repugnance people feel toward kidney markets, but my endorsement of it as a reason to block kidney markets is a bit tentative because it does not take into account the person who may be dying for lack of a kidney. Nevertheless it is worth stressing that whether or not this line of argument is ultimately successful, it offers a different perspective on kidney markets from one that focuses on the fact that a trade entered into out of desperation is also a trade that is likely to be exploitive, overreaching, or otherwise extremely unfair.[44] That is, this objection holds even if we think that the terms of trade are fair and that the choice made by the seller is not one of desperation.

Policy

I've analyzed the discomfort people feel with kidney markets in terms of vulnerability, weak agency, harmful outcomes, inequality, and motivations, looking at the case for curtailing such markets based on these considerations under both existing and more ideal circumstances. Many problems with kidney markets arise precisely because such markets are not likely to be ideal markets, but rather markets in which there are widespread market failures: weak agency, significant pockets of monopoly power, and human desperation leading to exploitation and inadequate pricing. Much of the repugnance that people feel toward kidney markets arises from the potential for harm stemming from the circumstances in which sellers are found: poverty, lack of clean water and basic health care, and

grueling labor. Market regulation may go some way to mitigating the problems along the dimensions of weak agency, although it is unlikely to make the problem of desperate world poverty go away. It is also possible that any potential harms from giving up a kidney can be addressed by mandating appropriate follow-up care, ensuring access to a replacement organ if needed, and perhaps banning the international trade of kidneys. But again, in parts of the world this may be difficult to enforce. One way of mitigating the possibility of harmful outcomes for sellers would be to have purchased organs taken only after the seller's death – a kind of futures market in organs.

Even with the ban on kidney markets and even with little follow-up or no care, people who are desperate are likely to resort to the black market. If the state is too weak to enforce the ban or not particularly inclined to do so, a black market in organs will thrive, as it does in parts of India, Pakistan, and Brazil. According to many observers, the sale of organs on the black market has reached alarming proportions in the third world, especially as advanced medical technology spreads. Regulating a legalized kidney market rather than relying on a black market would arguably go some way in redressing the worries about exploitation and one-sided terms of sale. If properly regulated, an organ market might be structured to discourage sales from extremely poor donors.

But this is where the argument from pecuniary externalities becomes relevant. Allowing the desperately poor to sell their organs as a social practice will have an effect on the choices that are open to those who do not want to participate in such a market. Some may think that it is inappropriate to make people pay a cost for exercising their choice not to sell their kidney. This issue also needs to be considered in policy design.

The problem of inequality, of turning poor people into "spare parts" for the rich, can also be addressed, at least in part, by regulation. Instead of relying on a competitive market we might create a monopsony, with the state the only legal buyer, and distribute on the basis of medical need. We might provide for the state to purchase organs for poor recipients. Nonetheless if there is a market there is likely to be greater stratification by wealth in organ donors and recipients than is currently the case. This may be significant for many reasons, not

Table 48.1 Evaluating alternative methods of organ allocation

Market/Allocation	Weak agency	Vulnerability	Individual harm	Harmful social inequality
Competitive market in supply and demand	Yes, although could be mitigated by informed consent	Yes	Yes: harm to very poor seller; externalities to other poor	Yes
Competitive market in supply only; government monopsony	Yes: see above	Yes	Yes: see above	No
Futures markets	No	No, unless this gives people an incentive to hasten the death of future donors	No	No
Matching-in kind exchanges	Possible: see above	No	No	No
Altruistic donation	Possible: see above	No	No	No

least of which is that it might "repress the expression of altruism and erode the sense of community."

Reflecting on the values at stake in different kinds of markets helps us to see why kidney markets are different from apple markets. Some of the values that I have discussed are internal to the functioning of markets: perfect information is assumed by the efficiency theorems of welfare economics; if the introduction of a market actually serves to decrease supply, then there is no social cost to banning it. Some of these values are external to the functioning of markets – in matters of life and death urgent needs should trump ability to pay – but widely shared. Some of these external values are more controversial: the list of goods that no one should have to pay a price for refusing to sell.

I want to conclude by briefly considering how a number of recent proposals for kidney markets, some of which are now being debated among policymakers, fare along the dimensions I have set out: vulnerability, weak agency, harmful individual outcomes, and harmful social inequality. The proposals I consider are (1) competitive markets governing supply and demand, in other words, treating kidneys like apples; (2) competitive markets governing supply only and distributing either on the basis of need or supplementing market distribution with subsidized distribution to the poor; (3) competitive futures markets with organs given up only after death; and (4) matching-in kind exchanges, where a patient with a willing donor who has an incompatible blood type can trade with another such incompatible patient-donor pair.[45]

A *yes* in table 48.1 indicates a problem along a dimension; a *no* indicates a relatively low (but not necessarily unproblematic) score.[46] As can be seen from this schematic, a pure competitive market in kidneys appears to be the most problematic, scoring fairly high on all parameters. By contrast, a market in apples would not normally score high along all these dimensions. Given the imperfect information, the potential for harmful outcomes, and the inequality in access to urgently needed goods (kidneys), I think we should view this market as morally unacceptable.

On my view, the greater the extent to which the concerns raised along the various dimensions can be addressed, the more acceptable is the market. Even for those who worry about the pecuniary effects of such markets – changing the terms of trade for those who do not want to participate in such markets – the question is whether mechanisms can be found that would prevent kidney sales from entering into other kinds of contracts, for example, as loan collateral or as a means of eligibility for social services.

And if these considerations cannot be adequately addressed, whether through information dissemination, regulation, income transfer, or some other means, other possibilities need to be considered, including increased exhortation to donate. I do not want to lose sight of the fact that in addition to the potential for harm to the seller from a kidney market, there is also the potential to extend the life of a person who would otherwise die. Much more could be done to encourage the altruistic donation of organs. Meanwhile, given the desperation on both the buyer and seller sides of the equation, the

search for solutions to the shortage of transplantable organs is likely to be with us for a long time to come.[47]

Notes

1   Thanks to Caleb Perl and Jose Campos for research assistance. Thanks also to Joe Shapiro, whose undergraduate honors thesis at Stanford, "The Ethics and Efficacy of Banning Human Kidney Sales," prompted me to think harder about this topic. I was the co-advisor of his thesis with Ken Arrow. Thanks to Ben Hippen for comments on a longer version of this chapter. Thanks also to the audience at the Aristotelian Society, the editor of the Society's proceedings, David Harris, and to Annabelle Lever, Eric Maskin, and Josh Cohen for written comments.

2   This libertarian view confronts serious questions about the scope of control a person has over her body. For example, does a person have the right to sell all of her organs, even if it means her death? Does my right to use my body as I wish mean that I can walk naked into my office? More to the point, do rights to bodily autonomy and integrity entail rights to *sell* one's body or body parts? Cécile Fabre has recently argued that, under many circumstances, justice requires conferring on the sick a right to confiscate the superfluous body parts of healthy individuals. See Fabre, *Whose Body Is It Anyway: Justice and the Integrity of the Person* (Oxford: Oxford University Press, 2006). Her argument depends on a close analogy between body parts and external resources and perhaps an overly optimistic view about the state's ability to fairly enforce the organ distribution policy.

3   Among undeveloped nations only Iran presently has a legalized kidney market.

4   Michelle Goodwin, *Black Markets: The Supply and Demand of Body Parts* (Cambridge: Cambridge University Press, 2006), 119–22.

5   In *McFall v. Shimp*, 10 Pa. D&C.3d 90 (Ch. Ct. 1978) a man (McFall) who would surely die without a bone marrow transplant, sought an injunction to require his cousin (Shimp) to donate bone marrow, a procedure that would have posed little risk but considerable pain. The court refused to grant the injunction, and the man subsequently died. In *Curran v. Bosze*, 566 N.E.2d 1319 (Ill. 1990) the Illinois Supreme Court refused to grant a noncustodial parent's request that his own twin three-year-old children be compelled to undergo blood testing and possible bone marrow harvesting to save the life of their twelve-year-old half-brother. (The half-brother died while the case was still being decided.)

6   Or perhaps I should say *lists*, since in the United States there is a national list as well as lists at regional transplant centers.

7   Goodwin, *Black Markets*, 40. Goodwin also importantly notes that there are racial disparities in how long people have to wait for a kidney, as well as racial differences in rates of organ donation. African Americans, for example, wait longer on lists and also donate organs less frequently than whites.

8   This figure also includes those who die while waiting for a heart to become available for transplant.

9   See Living Legacy Registry, Donation Statistics, at http://livinglegacy.org.

10 Some object that opt-out systems do not really allow for individual consent because many people do not have adequate information about their society's default position on cadaver organs. According to critics, opt-out systems are really systems of organ conscription. Those who would not have wished to donate their organs after their death, if they had properly reflected on this while they were alive, are forcibly drafted into donation: their actual consent is sidestepped. But *even if this were true*, that is, even if most people comply with such systems only out of ignorance, the critics' argument is insufficient to rebut those who favor such systems, since an analogous charge could be brought against opt-in systems. In opt-in systems there are likely to be people who have never thought about whether or not their organs should be available for others upon their death, yet would have ex ante preferred that they were. In opt-in donation systems, such people are simply presumed to have consented to nondonation and thus are forcibly drafted into nondonation; their consent to nondonation, in other words, is also sidestepped. Different attitudes about the respective degrees of coerciveness of opt-out and opt-in systems undoubtedly reflect different views about the extent to which an individual has strong ownership claims over her body parts, even after her death. The different default starting positions reflect, at least in part, different attitudes and preferences about social claims on cadaver organs. But these attitudes and preferences are themselves reciprocally influenced by framing effects and starting points. That is, *whichever* default position we choose for organ donation, opt in or opt out, may change the likelihood of certain choices over others. Initial

allocations, expectations, and laws about a person's organs form a starting point that affects her individual preferences and judgments. Because every society must have some donation or nondonation starting point, every society faces the question of deciding how this starting point should be determined.

11 See the data collected by Spain's Organización Nacional de Trasplantes, at http://ont.es. See also Newsletter *Transplant: International Figures on Organ Donation and Transplantation*, vol. 10, no 1. Madrid: Fundación Renal, 2005.

12 Remco Coppen et al., "Opting-out Systems: No Guarantee for Higher Donation Rates," *Transplant International*, 18 (2005): 1275–9.

13 Those who receive their kidneys from live donors tend to fare better than those who receive their kidneys from cadavers. See Editorial, "Renal Transplantation from Living Donors," *British Medical Journal* 318 (1999): 409–10; P. I. Terasaki, J. M. Cecka, D. W. Gjertson, and S. Takemoto, "High Survival Rates of Kidney Transplants from Spousal and Living Unrelated Donors," *New England Journal of Medicine*, 333 (1995): 333–6.

14 See Kieran Healy, *Last Best Gifts: Altruism and the Market for Human Blood and Organs* (Chicago: University of Chicago Press, 2006).

15 Cited in Paul Seabright, *The Company of Strangers: A Natural History of Economic Life* (Princeton: Princeton University Press, 2004), 151–2.

16 Richard Titmuss, *The Gift Relationship: From Human Blood to Social Policy* (New York: Random House, 1971).

17 Titmuss, *Gift Relationship*, 314.

18 Arrow, "Gifts and Exchanges," *Philosophy and Public Affairs*, 1 (1972): 343–62.

19 See Uri Gneezy and Aldo Rustichini, "A Fine Is a Price," *Journal of Legal Studies*, 29 (1) (Jan. 2000): 1–18.

20 Bruno Frey and Felix Oberholzer-Gee, "The Cost of Price Incentives: An Empirical Analysis of Motivation Crowding Out," *American Economic Review*, 87 (4) (Sept. 1997): 746–55.

21 See Elizabeth Anderson, *Value in Ethics and Economics* (Cambridge, MA: Harvard University Press, 1993).

22 Lior Jacob Strahilevitz, "How Changes in Property Regimes Influence Social Norms: Commodifying California's Carpool Lanes," *Indiana Law Journal*, 75 (2000): 1231–96.

23 Uri Gneezy and Aldo Rustichini, "Pay Enough or Don't Pay at All," *Quarterly Journal of Economics*, 115 (3) (2000): 791–810. Frey discusses the Dürrenmatt play in Bruno S. Frey, Felix Oberholzer-Gee, and Reiner Eichenberger, "The Old Lady Visits Your Backyard: A

Tale of Morals and Markets," *Journal of Political Economy*, 104 (6) (1996): 1297–1313.

24 Thanks to Ben Hippen for the point that not all extrinsic rewards need have the same consequences for altruistic donation.

25 A. J. Ghods, S. Savaj, and P. Khosravani, "Adverse Effects of a Controlled Living Unrelated Donor Renal Transplant Program on Living Related and Cadaveric Kidney Transplantation," *Transplantation Proceedings*, 32 (2000): 541.

26 Nancy Scheper-Hughes, "Keeping an Eye on the Global Traffic in Human Organs," *The Lancet*, 361 (2003): 1645–8, at 1645.

27 If we are concerned about desperation, banning kidney markets itself does nothing to rectify the desperate conditions that prompt such sales. If our concern with kidney markets is the desperation that is prompting the sale, it does no good to close off the sale but leave the circumstances that yielded the desperation in place. In fact, given the desperation, sellers and buyers may still resort to a black market, with a host of attendant abuses even more exploitive, overreaching, or unfair than a legalized market would be.

28 Madhav Goyal et al., "Economic and Health Consequences of Selling a Kidney in India," *Journal of the American Medical Association*, 288 (2002): 1589–93.

29 Indebtedness is a fact of life in many of the areas where kidney selling is widespread. The Goyal study found that 96 percent of sellers interviewed sold a kidney to pay off a debt; 74 percent were still in debt at the time of the survey, six years later. In fact, this study of 305 kidney sellers in Chennai, India, found that after selling a kidney family income actually declined. Many sellers experienced pain and were unable to work. Participants were also paid little for their organs, and often substantially less than they were promised. So even when they were able to stave off the moneylenders for a few years, they were soon in debt again.

30 Goyal et al., "Economic and Health Consequences," report that although people sell their kidneys to get out of debt, sellers are frequently in debt again within several years of the sale.

31 In the case of altruistic donation, our concerns about sellers' agency is presumably mitigated by the fact that the suppliers of kidneys are likely to come from many economic groups and not simply from the desperately poor, who also tend to be uneducated.

32 Recent studies have found that donating a kidney does not damage donors' health or reduce their life span, and they are less likely to develop kidney failure than the general population. See H. N. Ibrahim et al.,

"Long-Term Consequences of Kidney Donation," *New England Journal of Medicine*, 360 (5) (2009): 459–69. Of course, as I have stressed, the results of kidney donation in the developed world may not tell us very much about kidney donation in the undeveloped world. For one thing, donors in the United States, where this study was undertaken, are very carefully screened for health risks.

33 Joe Shapiro makes this observation as a framing background for his discussion of the morality of kidney markets. See "The Ethics and Efficacy of Banning Human Kidney Sales," Undergraduate thesis, Stanford University.

34 Christian Williams, "Note. Combating the Problems of Human Rights Abuses and Inadequate Organ Supply through Presumed Donative Consent," *Case Western Reserve Journal of International Law* 26 (1994): 315.

35 Titmuss, *Gift Relationship*. Goodwin, *Black Markets*, draws attention to racial disparities in who gives and who gets an organ.

36 Kazuo Ishiguro, *Never Let Me Go* (London: Faber& Faber, 2005). Recently, an article in the *New York Times* by Andrew Pollack raised concerns about the sale of plasma by poor Mexicans to centers run by pharmaceutical companies at the U.S. and Mexico border. See "Is Money Tainting the Plasma Supply?" Dec. 6, 2010, Sunday Business section, p. 1.

37 Nancy Scheper-Hughes, quoted in Michael Finkel, "Complications," *New York Times Magazine*, May 27, 2001, 32. The term *transplant tourism* refers to wealthy individuals or their brokers from the developed world flying halfway around the world to less developed countries searching for organ sellers.

38 See Shapiro, "Ethics and Efficacy," 120.

39 To what extent would the availability of kidneys through a market indemnify individuals against the effects of bad health choices? Thanks to Annabelle Lever for pressing this point.

40 Lawrence Cohen, "Where It Hurts: Indian Material for an Ethics of Organ Transplantation," *Zyogon*, 38 (3) (2003): 663–88.

41 Cohen, "Where It Hurts, 673.

42 I have made an analogous argument about child labor: the availability of child labor decreases the price of unskilled adult labor and thereby makes it harder for families to refrain from putting their children to work.

43 Ronald Dworkin, "Comment on Narveson: In Defense of Equality," *Social Philosophy and Policy*, 1 (1983): 24–40, at 39.

44 Michael Walzer, *Spheres of Justice* (New York: Basic Books, 1983), 102.

45 Alvin E. Roth, Tayfun Sonmez, and M. Utka Unver, "Pairwise Kidney Exchange," *Journal of Economic Theory*, 125 (2) (2005): 151–88.

46 The idea for this chart comes from Ravi Kanbur, "On Obnoxious Markets," in Steve Cullenberg and Prasanta Pattanaik (eds.), *Globalization, Culture and the Limits of the Market* (New Delhi: Oxford University Press, 2004).

47 An earlier version of this chapter appeared as Debra Satz, "The Moral Limits of Markets: The Case of Human Kidneys," *Proceedings of the Aristotelian Society*, 108, part 3 (2008).

49

The Survival Lottery

John Harris

Let us suppose that organ transplant procedures have been perfected; in such circumstances if two dying patients could be saved by organ transplants then, if surgeons have the requisite organs in stock and no other needy patients, but nevertheless allow their patients to die, we would be inclined to say, and be justified in saying, that the patients died because the doctors refused to save them. But if there are no spare organs in stock and none otherwise available, the doctors have no choice, they cannot save their patients and so must let them die. In this case we would be disinclined to say that the doctors are in any sense the cause of their patients' deaths. But let us further suppose that the two dying patients, Y and Z, are not happy about being left to die. They might argue that it is not strictly true that there are no organs which could be used to save them. Y needs a new heart and Z new lungs. They point out that if just one healthy person were to be killed his organs could be removed and both of them be saved. We and the doctors would probably be alike in thinking that such a step, while technically possible, would be out of the question. We would not say that the doctors were killing their patients if they refused to prey upon the healthy to save the sick. And because this sort of surgical Robin Hoodery is out of the question we can tell Y and Z that they cannot be saved, and that when they die they will have died of natural causes and not

of the neglect of their doctors. Y and Z do not however agree, they insist that if the doctors fail to kill a healthy man and use his organs to save them, then the doctors will be responsible for their deaths.

Many philosophers have for various reasons believed that we must not kill even if by doing so we could save life. They believe that there is a moral difference between killing and letting die. On this view, to kill A so that Y and Z might live is ruled out because we have a strict obligation not to kill but a duty of some lesser kind to save life. A. H. Clough's dictum 'Thou shalt not kill but need'st not strive officiously to keep alive' expresses bluntly this point of view. The dying Y and Z may be excused for not being much impressed by Clough's dictum. They agree that it is wrong to kill the innocent and are prepared to agree to an absolute prohibition against so doing. They do not agree, however, that A is more innocent than they are. Y and Z might go on to point out that the currently acknowledged right of the innocent not to be killed, even where their deaths might give life to others, is just a decision to prefer the lives of the fortunate to those of the unfortunate. A is innocent in the sense that he has done nothing to deserve death, but Y and Z are also innocent in this sense. Why should they be the ones to die simply because they are so unlucky as to have diseased organs. Why, they might argue, should their living or dying be left to chance when in so

Original publication details: John Harris, "The Survival Lottery," pp. 81–7 from *Philosophy* 50 (1975). © Royal Institute of Philosophy, published by Cambridge University Press. Reproduced with permission.

Bioethics: An Anthology, Third Edition. Edited by Helga Kuhse, Udo Schüklenk, and Peter Singer.

many other areas of human life we believe that we have an obligation to ensure the survival of the maximum number of lives possible.

Y and Z argue that if a doctor refuses to treat a patient, with the result that the patient dies, he has killed that patient as sure as shooting, and that in exactly the same way, if the doctors refuse Y and Z the transplants that they need, then their refusal will kill Y and Z, again as sure as shooting. The doctors, and indeed the society which supports their inaction, cannot defend themselves by arguing that they are neither expected, nor required by law or convention, to kill so that lives may be saved (indeed, quite the reverse) since this is just an appeal to custom or authority. A man who does his own moral thinking must decide whether, in these circumstances, he ought to save two lives at the cost of one, or one life at the cost of two. The fact that so called 'third parties' have never before been brought into such calculations, have never before been thought of as being involved, is not an argument against their now becoming so. There are, of course, good arguments against allowing doctors simply to haul passers-by off the street whenever they have a couple of patients in need of new organs. And the harmful side-effects of such a practice in terms of terror and distress to the victims, the witnesses and society generally, would give us further reason for dismissing the idea. Y and Z realize this and have a proposal, which they will shortly produce, which would largely meet objections to placing such power in the hands of doctors and eliminate at least some of the harmful side-effects.

In the unlikely event of their feeling obliged to reply to the reproaches of Y and Z, the doctors might offer the following argument: they might maintain that a man is only responsible for the death of someone whose life he might have saved, if, in all the circumstances of the case, he ought to have saved the man by the means available. This is why a doctor might be a murderer if he simply refused or neglected to treat a patient who would die without treatment, but not if he could only save the patient by doing something he ought in no circumstances to do – kill the innocent. Y and Z readily agree that a man ought not to do what he ought not to do, but they point out that if the doctors, and for that matter society at large, ought on balance to kill one man if two can thereby be saved, then failure to do so will involve responsibility for the consequent deaths.

The fact that Y's and Z's proposal involves killing the innocent cannot be a reason for refusing to consider their proposal, for this would just be a refusal to face the question at issue and so avoid having to make a decision as to what ought to be done in circumstances like these. It is Y's and Z's claim that failure to adopt their plan will also involve killing the innocent, rather more of the innocent than the proposed alternative.

To back up this last point, to remove the arbitrariness of permitting doctors to select their donors from among the chance passers-by outside hospitals, and the tremendous power this would place in doctors' hands, to mitigate worries about side-effects and lastly to appease those who wonder why poor old A should be singled out for sacrifice, Y and Z put forward the following scheme: they propose that everyone be given a sort of lottery number. Whenever doctors have two or more dying patients who could be saved by transplants, and no suitable organs have come to hand through 'natural' deaths, they can ask a central computer to supply a suitable donor. The computer will then pick the number of a suitable donor at random and he will be killed so that the lives of two or more others may be saved. No doubt if the scheme were ever to be implemented a suitable euphemism for 'killed' would be employed. Perhaps we would begin to talk about citizens being called upon to 'give life' to others. With the refinement of transplant procedures such a scheme could offer the chance of saving large numbers of lives that are now lost. Indeed, even taking into account the loss of the lives of donors, the numbers of untimely deaths each year might be dramatically reduced, so much so that everyone's chance of living to a ripe old age might be increased. If this were to be the consequence of the adoption of such a scheme, and it might well be, it could not be dismissed lightly. It might of course be objected that it is likely that more old people will need transplants to prolong their lives than will the young, and so the scheme would inevitably lead to a society dominated by the old. But if such a society is thought objectionable, there is no reason to suppose that a programme could not be designed for the computer that would ensure the maintenance of whatever is considered to be an optimum age distribution throughout the population.

Suppose that inter-planetary travel revealed a world of people like ourselves, but who organized their society according to this scheme. No one was considered to have an absolute right to life or freedom from interference, but everything was always done to ensure that as many people as possible would enjoy long and happy lives. In such a world a man who attempted to escape when his number was up or who resisted on the grounds that no one had a right to take his life might well be regarded as a murderer. We might or might not prefer to live in such a world, but the morality of its inhabitants would surely be one that we could respect. It would not be obviously more barbaric or cruel or immoral than our own.

Y and Z are willing to concede one exception to the universal application of their scheme. They realize that it would be unfair to allow people who have brought their misfortune on themselves to benefit from the lottery. There would clearly be something unjust about killing the abstemious B so that W (whose heavy smoking has given him lung cancer) and X (whose drinking has destroyed his liver) should be preserved to over-indulge again.

What objections could be made to the lottery scheme? A first straw to clutch at would be the desire for security. Under such a scheme we would never know when we would hear *them* knocking at the door. Every post might bring a sentence of death, every sound in the night might be the sound of boots on the stairs. But, as we have seen, the chances of actually being called upon to make the ultimate sacrifice might be slimmer than is the present risk of being killed on the roads, and most of us do not lie trembling a-bed, appalled at the prospect of being dispatched on the morrow. The truth is that lives might well be more secure under such a scheme.

If we respect individuality and see every human being as unique in his own way, we might want to reject a society in which it appeared that individuals were seen merely as interchangeable units in a structure, the value of which lies in its having as many healthy units as possible. But of course Y and Z would want to know why A's individuality was more worthy of respect than theirs.

Another plausible objection is the natural reluctance to play God with men's lives, the feeling that it is wrong to make any attempt to re-allot the life opportunities that fate has determined, that the deaths of Y and Z would be 'natural', whereas the death of

anyone killed to save them would have been perpetrated by men. But if we are able to change things, then to elect not to do so is also to determine what will happen in the world.

Neither does the alleged moral difference between killing and letting die afford a respectable way of rejecting the claims of Y and Z. For if we really want to counter proponents of the lottery, if we really want to answer Y and Z and not just put them off, we cannot do so by saying that the lottery involves killing and object to it for that reason, because to do so would, as we have seen, just beg the question as to whether the failure to save as many people as possible might not also amount to killing.

To opt for the society which Y and Z propose would be then to adopt a society in which saintliness would be mandatory. Each of us would have to recognize a binding obligation to give up his own life for others when called upon to do so. In such a society anyone who reneged upon this duty would be a murderer. The most promising objection to such a society, and indeed to any principle which required us to kill A in order to save Y and Z, is, I suspect, that we are committed to the right of self-defence. If I can kill A to save Y and Z then he can kill me to save P and Q, and it is only if I am prepared to agree to this that I will opt for the lottery or be prepared to agree to a man's being killed if doing so would save the lives of more than one other man. Of course there is something paradoxical about basing objections to the lottery scheme on the right of self-defence since, *ex hypothesi*, each person would have a better chance of living to a ripe old age if the lottery scheme were to be implemented. None the less, the feeling that no man should be required to lay down his life for others makes many people shy away from such a scheme, even though it might be rational to accept it on prudential grounds, and perhaps even mandatory on utilitarian grounds. Again, Y and Z would reply that the right of self-defence must extend to them as much as to anyone else; and while it is true that they can only live if another man is killed, they would claim that it is also true that if they are left to die, then someone who lives on does so over their dead bodies.

It might be argued that the institution of the survival lottery has not gone far to mitigate the harmful side-effects in terms of terror and distress to victims, witnesses and society generally, that would be occasioned by doctors simply snatching passers-by off the streets and disorganizing them for the benefit of the unfortunate. Donors would after all still have to be procured, and this process, however it was carried out, would still be likely to prove distressing to all concerned. The lottery scheme would eliminate the arbitrariness of leaving the life and death decisions to the doctors, and remove the possibility of such terrible power falling into the hands of any individuals, but the terror and distress would remain. The effect of having to apprehend presumably unwilling victims would give us pause. Perhaps only a long period of education or propaganda could remove our abhorrence. What this abhorrence reveals about the rights and wrongs of the situation is, however, more difficult to assess. We might be inclined to say that only monsters could ignore the promptings of conscience so far as to operate the lottery scheme. But the promptings of conscience are not necessarily the most reliable guide. In the present case Y and Z would argue that such promptings are mere squeamishness, an over-nice self-indulgence that costs lives. Death, Y and Z would remind us, is a distressing experience whenever and to whomever it occurs, so the less it occurs the better. Fewer victims and witnesses will be distressed as part of the side-effects of the lottery scheme than would suffer as part of the side-effects of not instituting it.

Lastly, a more limited objection might be made, not to the idea of killing to save lives, but to the involvement of 'third parties'. Why, so the objection goes, should we not give X's heart to Y or Y's lungs to X, the same number of lives being thereby preserved and no one else's life set at risk? Y's and Z's reply to this objection differs from their previous line of argument. To amend their plan so that the involvement of so called 'third parties' is ruled out would, Y and Z claim, violate their right to equal concern and respect with the rest of society. They argue that such a proposal would amount to treating the unfortunate who need new organs as a class within society whose lives are considered to be of less value than those of its more fortunate members. What possible justification could there be for singling out one group of people whom we would be justified in using as donors but not another? The idea in the mind of those who would propose such a step must be something like the following: since Y and Z cannot survive, since they are going to die in any event, there is no harm in putting their names into the lottery, for the chances of their dying cannot thereby be increased and will in fact almost certainly be reduced. But this is just to ignore everything that Y and Z have been saying. For if their lottery scheme is adopted they are not going to die anyway – their chances of dying are no greater and no less than those of any other participant in the lottery whose number may come up. This ground for confining selection of donors to the unfortunate therefore disappears. Any other ground must discriminate against Y and Z as members of a class whose lives are less worthy of respect than those of the rest of society.

It might more plausibly be argued that the dying who cannot themselves be saved by transplants, or by any other means at all, should be the priority selection group for the computer programme. But how far off must death be for a man to be classified as 'dying'? Those so classified might argue that their last few days or weeks of life are as valuable to them (if not more valuable) than the possibly longer span remaining to others. The problem of narrowing down the class of possible donors without discriminating unfairly against some sub-class of society is, I suspect, insoluble.

Such is the case for the survival lottery. Utilitarians ought to be in favour of it, and absolutists cannot object to it on the ground that it involves killing the innocent, for it is Y's and Z's case that any alternative must also involve killing the innocent. If the absolutist wishes to maintain his objection he must point to some morally relevant difference between positive and negative killing. This challenge opens the door to a large topic with a whole library of literature, but Y and Z are dying and do not have time to explore it exhaustively. In their own case the most likely candidate for some feature which might make this moral difference is the malevolent intent of Y and Z themselves. An absolutist might well argue that while no one intends the deaths of Y and Z, no one necessarily wishes them dead, or aims at their demise for any reason, they do mean to kill A (or have him killed). But Y and Z can reply that the death of A is no part of their plan, they merely wish to use a couple of his organs, and if he cannot live without them…*tant pis*! None would be more delighted than Y and Z if artificial organs would do as well, and so render the lottery scheme otiose.

One form of absolutist argument perhaps remains. This involves taking an Orwellian stand on some principle of common decency. The argument would then be that even to enter into the sort of 'macabre' calculations that Y and Z propose displays a blunted sensibility, a corrupted and vitiated mind. Forms of this argument have recently been advanced by Noam Chomsky (*American Power and the New Mandarins*) and Stuart Hampshire (*Morality and Pessimism*). The indefatigable Y and Z would of course deny that their calculations are in any sense 'macabre', and would present them as the most humane course available in the circumstances. Moreover they would claim that the Orwellian stand on decency is the product of a closed mind, and not susceptible to rational argument. Any reasoned defence of such a principle must appeal to notions like respect for human life. Hampshire's argument in fact does, and these Y and Z could make conformable to their own position.

Can Y and Z be answered? Perhaps only by relying on moral intuition, on the insistence that we do feel there is something wrong with the survival lottery and our confidence that this feeling is prompted by some morally relevant difference between our bringing about the death of A and our bringing about the deaths of Y and Z. Whether we could retain this confidence in our intuitions if we were to be confronted by a society in which the survival lottery operated, was accepted by all, and was seen to save many lives that would otherwise have been lost, it would be interesting to know.

There would, of course, be great practical difficulties in the way of implementing the lottery. In so many cases it would be agonizingly difficult to decide whether or not a person had brought his misfortune on himself. There are numerous ways in which a person may contribute to his predicament, and the task of deciding how far, or how decisively, a person is himself responsible for his fate would be formidable. And in those cases where we can be confident that a person is innocent of responsibility for his predicament, can we acquire this confidence in time to save him? The lottery scheme would be a powerful weapon in the hands of someone willing and able to misuse it. Could we ever feel certain that the lottery was safe from unscrupulous computer programmers? Perhaps we should be thankful that such practical difficulties make the survival lottery an unlikely consequence of the perfection of transplants. Or perhaps we should be appalled.

It may be that we would want to tell Y and Z that the difficulties and dangers of their scheme would be too great a price to pay for its benefits. It is as well to be clear, however, that there is also a high, perhaps an even higher, price to be paid for the rejection of the scheme. That price is the lives of Y and Z and many like them, and we delude ourselves if we suppose that the reason why we reject their plan is that we accept the sixth commandment.[1]

Note

1 Thanks are due to Ronald Dworkin, Jonathan Glover, M. J. Inwood and Anne Seller for helpful comments.

Part VII

Experimentation with Human Participants

Introduction

Medical research involving humans differs substantially from medical treatment. While medical treatment focuses on the healthcare needs of individual patients, medical research is a scientific enterprise. It seeks to gain a better understanding of biological processes in humans and aims to develop new drugs and other treatments, for future therapeutic use. Another way of putting this is to say that medical therapy is directed at the welfare of particular, identifiable patients, whereas medical research on humans seeks to improve the health and well-being of patients as a whole.

One of the central ethical issues in experimentation on humans is that human individuals are subjected to sometimes invasive and even risky procedures, for the sake of others. This has led some people to suggest that research should be conducted not on humans, but on nonhuman animals, human cells, and by way of computer modelling. Scientists argue that at least some experimentation on human beings is necessary; the knowledge gained by experimenting on nonhuman animals, cells, and so on does not always tell us how complex human organisms will respond to biomedical interventions. (We shall set the ethical issues raised by animal experimentation to one side for now, since these are dealt with in Part VIII, "Experimentation with Animals.")

Today, it is widely agreed that at least some research on autonomous human beings is morally permissible, provided the research subjects have given their informed consent. This leaves unanswered the question of whether, and if so when, experimentation may be performed on those who cannot consent – for example, human infants, the mentally disabled, and human embryos. Some of the central issues regarding research on embryos are discussed below, but issues relevant to research on mentally disabled people and young children are not explored in this selection.

Human Participants

The assumption that consent is crucial to the moral permissibility of research on autonomous human research participants has not always prevailed. At the end of World War II, for example, the world became aware of monstrous examples of medical research conducted in the name of medical science by German and Japanese doctors, on unconsenting subjects, in utter disregard of their interests or rights. Following these revelations, and the subsequent trial and conviction of German doctors at Nuremberg, the now famous Nuremberg Code was set up, the first principle of which states that "The voluntary consent of the human subject is absolutely essential …"

It was, however, not only in Germany and Japan that doctors subjected people to experimentation without their consent. Healthcare professionals in many other nations – including the United States – have engaged in practices that ignored the rights or

Bioethics: An Anthology, Third Edition. Edited by Helga Kuhse, Udo Schüklenk, and Peter Singer.
© 2016 John Wiley & Sons, Inc. Published 2016 by John Wiley & Sons, Inc.

interests of their research subjects. Some 20 years after the end of World War II, Henry K. Beecher published an article entitled "Ethics and Clinical Research" in the *New England Journal of Medicine* providing evidence that hundreds of patients in the United States had been unaware of the risks of the research they participated in, and that hundreds more did not even know they were participating in research. We include Beecher's landmark article in this anthology.

Since the publication of Beecher's data in the mid-1960s, various international, national and professional statements and regulations on human experimentation have been issued, and many countries have set up research ethics committees in attempts to regulate and oversee research.

Equipoise

It is widely accepted that randomized clinical trials, to be morally sound, require equipoise, that is, uncertainty as to the merits of each arm of the trial. If there was strong evidence that one treatment was superior to the other, it would be ethically unacceptable for a doctor to assign patients to a randomization process that might lead to them receiving inferior treatment. There are, however, different ways of understanding the concept of equipoise, and the notion of "uncertainty" that is central to it. In his article "Equipoise and the Ethics of Clinical Research," Benjamin Freedman argues that the common understanding of equipoise as uncertainty in the *researcher* as to the superiority of treatments is problematic. While individual investigators may well have views about the efficacy of treatments, these views are, in the absence of validated knowledge, mere hunches. Equipoise should therefore be understood as uncertainty in the *expert medical community*.

Freedman notes that understanding equipoise as uncertainty in the expert medical community will entail that researchers will, from time to time, find themselves in situations where they conduct trials believing that one treatment is superior to another. But this should not, he argues, be ethically troublesome: provided patients are fully informed, they are free to decide whether to opt for treatment in accordance with the nonvalidated judgment of their clinician, or whether they want to be part of the trial.

In "The Patient and the Public Good" Samuel Hellman argues that the traditional role of the doctor is incompatible with Benjamin's revisionist understanding of equipoise. The doctor's duty is, Hellman holds, first and foremost to each individual patient; and when the focus is on particular patients, rather than on groups of patients, there is rarely a state of equipoise. This is so because individual patients judge alternative treatments and outcomes differently. This important fact is, however, obscured by randomly assigning patients to different arms of a trial.

Hellman accepts that randomized clinical trials are important in furthering the public good but, he holds, doctors cannot do both – act for the public good *and* for the good of each individual patient. Rather than jeopardize the doctor/patient relationship, randomized clinical trials should be based not on equipoise within the expert medical community, but on equipoise for each individual *patient*. While this would make already cumbersome clinical trials even more cumbersome, this consequence is, Hellman argues, preferable to the undermining of the doctor's traditional role.

Duty to participate in research

Clinical research relies not only on researchers, it also depends on research participants. Sometimes they are patients, but by no means always. Some research poses significant risks to research participants, for instance phase 1 clinical trials that are designed to establish whether or not a particular drug is safe to take. The question arises whether we have a moral obligation to participate in clinical research. John Harris answers this question in the affirmative. He thinks that our traditional approach to the issue got it all wrong. Research participation is not a supererogatory individual act but actually is morally incumbent on us. In "Scientific Research Is a Moral Duty" he makes his case for our moral obligation to participate in clinical research. Harris argues that it is based on our obligation to assist others in need, as well as on fairness-related considerations. He thinks it is unfair to be a free rider on other research participants' risk-taking. Given that we all benefit to some extent from clinical research, and so from others' risk-taking, it is incumbent on us to volunteer for participation, too.

Sandra Shapshay and Kenneth Pimple concede in their article "Participation in Research Is an Imperfect Moral Duty: A Response to John Harris" that we have a moral general obligation to benefit others, including by means of participation in research. However, they argue that this obligation is merely an imperfect obligation, that is, an obligation not requiring us to participate in particular research projects. Kantian imperfect duties permit duty bearers to sometimes ignore what it is owed. On other occasions, imperfect duties permit us to act in benevolent ways toward others while still choosing not to participate in clinical research.

International research

Particularly pressing and difficult ethical issues are raised by internationally sponsored trials in developing countries, where very different social and economic circumstances separate researchers from research subjects. The debate over the administration of the drug AZT to pregnant HIV-positive women and their infants after birth provides a good example of this.

Millions of women in developing countries are HIV positive and may pass the virus on to their children during pregnancy and birth. Administration of an antiretroviral drug during pregnancy, at birth, and to the infants after birth in a regime known as ACTG 076 can substantially reduce HIV infections in infants. Soon after the regime's effectiveness had been established, it became the standard treatment for HIV-positive pregnant women in the United States, but its potential remains largely unrealized in developing countries because of the drug's exorbitant cost. This led to a decision to conduct a number of trials of less expensive treatment regimes in a number of developing countries, where the new drug regimes were tested not against the proven ACTG 076 treatment, but against a placebo. In a placebo trial, one group of research subjects receive a substance known to be ineffective, in order to give a basis of comparison with the other group, who are receiving the drug to be tested. The availability of an effective treatment regime in the US meant that it would be unethical to do such a trial in that developed country. Does the absence of an effective treatment in developing countries mean that it is ethical to do trials there that would not be ethical in developed countries?

In "Unethical Trials of Interventions to Reduce Perinatal Transmission of the Human Immunodeficiency Virus in Developing Countries," Peter Lurie and Sidney M. Wolfe argue that the application of a lower ethical standard to research in developing countries is morally wrong and involves a gross violation of human rights. While attempts have been made to defend research protocols using placebo groups in developing countries by arguing that the research subjects are no worse off than they would have been (given that no effective treatment is available in these countries for the prevention of HIV infection from pregnant women to their children), Lurie and Wolfe charge that the adoption of such a standard will create an incentive to use those who have the least access to healthcare as subjects in research.

Ugandan healthcare workers Danstan Bagenda and Philippa Musoke-Mudido disagree. They argue, in "We're Trying to Help Our Sickest People, Not Exploit Them," that it is somewhat presumptuous for critics from developed countries to think that they can lay down ethical research standards for others when these critics are unfamiliar with local conditions.

Leah Belsky and Henry S. Richardson note in their article on "Medical Researchers' Ancillary Clinical Care Responsibilities" that research participants are not patients, or at least they are not the investigators' patients. They ask what is ethically owed to these research participants by the investigators of the trial. Belsky and Richardson disagree with researchers who hold the view that they have no special responsibilities to trial participants. They note that trial participants are often patients who entrust the researchers with confidential clinical information that these researchers are ethically obliged to act upon. As a consequence, researchers have certain ancillary care obligations toward their trial participants. These obligations are a result of trial participants entrusting their health – partially or completely – for the duration of the trial to the investigators.

Human Embryos – Stem Cells

Every day people die of common degenerative diseases, or suffer because of medicine's present inability to repair or replace damaged tissues. Human stem cell research could lead to the development of treatments for many diseases and debilitating conditions, from Parkinson's disease, diabetes, heart disease, and paraplegia to the probably more distant possibility of growing new teeth. Embryonic stem cell research raises, however, an array of controversial ethical issues because embryonic stem cells are derived from human embryos (which are destroyed in the process). While stem cells can also be obtained from adult tissues and some other sources, the dominant scientific opinion is that embryonic stem cells hold greater promise, and that for the foreseeable future, research on embryonic stem cells, as well as on adult stem cells, is necessary to provide maximum potential benefit.

A frequent objection to embryonic stem cell research is that it involves the destruction of human embryos; embryos are seen as either actual or potential persons, who have a "right to life," or are deserving of respect, incompatible with their use in research. At the heart of the ethical debate over stem cell research is thus the question whether it is morally permissible to destroy human embryos to benefit others. This raises questions not only about the moral status of human embryos, but also related questions about such issues as instrumentalization and moral complicity in the destruction of embryos. (For a discussion of the controversial issues relating to the moral status of embryos and fetuses, see Part I of the anthology.)

Former United States President George W. Bush, in "President Discusses Stem Cell Research," explains why he issued a ban on government funding for destructive embryonic stem cell research. He permitted continuing research on existing embryonic stem cell lines but he prohibited the destruction of any further embryos for stem cell research purposes. The embryos that would have been utilized for this purpose would have been surplus IVF embryos. Such embryos are typically frozen and eventually discarded once a successful pregnancy has occurred. The controversial nature of this decision is probably best exemplified by the decision of President Barack Obama, President Bush's successor, to reverse this decision in his first executive order as President of the United States.

Jeff McMahan takes President Bush to task in his essay "Killing Embryos for Stem Cell Research." He argues that much of the opposition to embryonic stem cell research erroneously assumes that the destruction of an embryo is akin to killing someone like you or me, when really it merely amounts to preventing someone like you or me from coming into existence.

Human Participants

50

Ethics and Clinical Research

Henry K. Beecher

Human experimentation since World War II has created some difficult problems with the increasing employment of patients as experimental subjects when it must be apparent that they would not have been available if they had been truly aware of the uses that would be made of them. Evidence is at hand that many of the patients in the examples to follow never had the risk satisfactorily explained to them, and it seems obvious that further hundreds have not known that they were the subjects of an experiment although grave consequences have been suffered as a direct result of experiments described here. There is a belief prevalent in some sophisticated circles that attention to these matters would "block progress." But, according to Pope Pius XII,[1] "science is not the highest value to which all other orders of values…should be subordinated."

I am aware that these are troubling charges. They have grown out of troubling practices. They can be documented, as I propose to do, by examples from leading medical schools, university hospitals, private hospitals, governmental military departments (the Army, the Navy and the Air Force), governmental institutes (the National Institutes of Health), Veterans Administration hospitals and industry. The basis for the charges is broad.

I should like to affirm that American medicine is sound, and most progress in it soundly attained. There

is, however, a reason for concern in certain areas, and I believe the type of activities to be mentioned will do great harm to medicine unless soon corrected. It will certainly be charged that any mention of these matters does a disservice to medicine, but not one so great, I believe, as a continuation of the practices to be cited.

Experimentation in man takes place in several areas: in self-experimentation; in patient volunteers and normal subjects; in therapy; and in the different areas of *experimentation on a patient not for his benefit but for that, at least in theory, of patients in general*. The present study is limited to this last category.

Reasons for Urgency of Study

Ethical errors are increasing not only in numbers but in variety – for example, in the recently added problems arising in transplantation of organs.

There are a number of reasons why serious attention to the general problem is urgent.

Of transcendent importance is the enormous and continuing increase in available funds, as shown in table 50.1.

Since World War II the annual expenditure for research (in large part in man) in the Massachusetts General Hospital has increased a remarkable 17-fold.

Original publication details: Henry K. Beecher, "Ethics and Clinical Research," pp. 1354–60 from *New England Journal of Medicine* 274: 24 (June 1966). Copyright © 1996 Massachusetts Medical Society. Reprinted with permission from Massachusetts Medical Society.

Table 50.1 Money available for research each year

Massachusetts	General Hospital	National Institutes of Health*
1945	$ 500,000†	$ 701,800
1955	2,222,816	36,063,200
1965	8,384,342	436,600,000

*National Institutes of Health figures based upon decade averages, excluding funds for construction, kindly supplied by Dr John Sherman, of National Institutes of Health.
†Approximation, supplied by Mr David C. Crockett, of Massachusetts General Hospital.

At the National Institutes of Health, the increase has been a gigantic 624-fold. This "national" rate of increase is over 36 times that of the Massachusetts General Hospital. These data, rough as they are, illustrate vast opportunities and concomitantly expanded responsibilities.

Taking into account the sound and increasing emphasis of recent years that experimentation in man must precede general application of new procedures in therapy, plus the great sums of money available, there is reason to fear that these requirements and these resources may be greater than the supply of responsible investigators. All this heightens the problems under discussion.

Medical schools and university hospitals are increasingly dominated by investigators. Every young man knows that he will never be promoted to a tenure post, to a professorship in a major medical school, unless he has proved himself as an investigator. If the ready availability of money for conducting research is added to this fact, one can see how great the pressures are on ambitious young physicians.

Implementation of the recommendations of the President's Commission on Heart Disease, Cancer and Stroke means that further astronomical sums of money will become available for research in man.

In addition to the foregoing three practical points there are others that Sir Robert Plat[2] has pointed out: a general awakening of social conscience; greater power for good or harm in new remedies, new operations and new investigative procedures than was formerly the case; new methods of preventive treatment with their advantages and dangers that are now applied to communities as a whole as well as to individuals, with multiplication of the possibilities for injury;

medical science has shown how valuable human experimentation can be in solving problems of disease and its treatment; one can therefore anticipate an increase in experimentation; and the newly developed concept of clinical research as a profession (for example, clinical pharmacology) – and this, of course, can lead to unfortunate separation between the interests of science and the interests of the patient.

Frequency of Unethical or Questionably Ethical Procedures

Nearly everyone agrees that ethical violations do occur. The practical question is, how often? A preliminary examination of the matter was based on 17 examples, which were easily increased to 50. These 50 studies contained references to 186 further likely examples, on the average 3.7 leads per study; they at times overlapped from paper to paper, but this figure indicates how conveniently one can proceed in a search for such material. The data are suggestive of widespread problems, but there is need for another kind of information, which was obtained by examination of 100 consecutive human studies published in 1964, in an excellent journal; 12 of these seemed to be unethical. If only one quarter of them is truly unethical, this still indicates the existence of a serious situation. Pappworth,[3] in England, has collected, he says, more than 500 papers based upon unethical experimentation. It is evident from such observations that unethical or questionably ethical procedures are not uncommon.

The Problem of Consent

All so-called codes are based on the bland assumption that meaningful or informed consent is readily available for the asking. As pointed out elsewhere,[4] this is very often not the case. Consent in any fully informed sense may not be obtainable. Nevertheless, except, possibly, in the most trivial situations, it remains a goal toward which one must strive for sociologic, ethical and clear-cut legal reasons. There is no choice in the matter.

If suitably approached, patients will accede, on the basis of trust, to about any request their physician may make. At the same time, every experienced clinician investigator knows that patients will often submit to inconvenience and some discomfort, if they do not last very long, but the usual patient will never agree to jeopardize seriously his health or his life for the sake of "science."

In only 2 of the 50 examples originally compiled for this study was consent mentioned. Actually, it should be emphasized in all cases for obvious moral and legal reasons, but it would be unrealistic to place much dependence on it. In any precise sense statements regarding consent are meaningless unless one knows how fully the patient was informed of all risks, and, if these are not known, that fact should also be made clear. A far more dependable safeguard than consent is the presence of a truly *responsible* investigator.

Examples of Unethical or Questionably Ethical Studies

These examples are not cited for the condemnation of individuals; they are recorded to call attention to a variety of ethical problems found in experimental medicine, for it is hoped that calling attention to them will help to correct abuses present. During ten years of study of these matters it has become apparent that thoughtlessness and carelessness, not a willful disregard of the patient's rights, account for most of the cases encountered. Nonetheless, it is evident that, in many of the examples presented, the investigators have risked the health or the life of their subjects. No attempt has been made to present the "worst" possible examples; rather, the aim has been to show the variety of problems encountered.

References to the examples presented are not given, for there is no intention of pointing to individuals, but, rather, a wish to call attention to widespread practices. All, however, are documented to the satisfaction of the editors of the *Journal*.

Known effective treatment withheld

Example 1. It is known that rheumatic fever can usually be prevented by adequate treatment of streptococcal respiratory infections by the parenteral administration of penicillin. Nevertheless, definitive treatment was withheld, and placebos were given to a group of 109 men in service, while benzathine penicillin G was given to others.

The therapy that each patient received was determined automatically by his military serial number arranged so that more men received penicillin than received placebo. In the small group of patients studied 2 cases of acute rheumatic fever and 1 of acute nephritis developed in the control patients, whereas these complications did not occur among those who received the benzathine penicillin G.

Example 2. The sulfonamides were for many years the only antibacterial drugs effective in shortening the duration of acute streptococcal pharyngitis and in reducing its suppurative complications. The investigators in this study undertook to determine if the occurrence of the serious nonsuppurative complications, rheumatic fever and acute glomerulonephritis, would be reduced by this treatment. This study was made despite the general experience that certain antibiotics, including penicillin, will prevent the development of rheumatic fever.

The subjects were a large group of hospital patients; a control group of approximately the same size, also with exudative Group A streptococcus, was included. The latter group received only nonspecific therapy (no sulfadiazine). The total group denied the effective penicillin comprised over 500 men.

Rheumatic fever was diagnosed in 5.4 per cent of those treated with sulfadiazine. In the control group rheumatic fever developed in 4.2 per cent.

In reference to this study a medical officer stated in writing that the subjects were not informed, did not consent and were not aware that they had been involved in an experiment, and yet admittedly 25 acquired rheumatic fever. According to this same medical officer *more than 70* who had had known definitive treatment withheld were on the wards with rheumatic fever when he was there.

Example 3. This involved a study of the relapse rate in typhoid fever treated in two ways. In an earlier study by the present investigators chloramphenicol had been recognized as an effective treatment for typhoid fever, being attended by half the mortality that was experienced when this agent was not used. Others had made the same observations, indicating that to withhold this effective remedy can be a life-or-death decision. The present study was carried out to determine the relapse rate under the two methods of treatment; of 408 charity patients 251 were treated with chloramphenicol, of whom 20, or 7.97 per cent, died. Symptomatic treatment was given, but chloramphenicol was withheld in 157, of whom 36, or 22.9 per cent, died. According to the data presented, 23 patients died in the course of this study who would not have been expected to succumb if they had received specific therapy.

Study of therapy

Example 4. TriA (triacetyloleandomycin) was originally introduced for the treatment of infection with gram-positive organisms. Spotty evidence of hepatic dysfunction emerged, especially in children, and so the present study was undertaken on 50 patients, including mental defectives or juvenile delinquents who were inmates of a children's center. No disease other than acne was present; the drug was given for treatment of this. The ages of the subjects ranged from 13 to 39 years. "By the time half the patients had received the drug for four weeks, the high incidence of significant hepatic dysfunction...led to the discontinuation of administration to the remainder of the group at three weeks." (However, only two weeks after the start of the administration of the drug, 54 per cent of the patients showed abnormal excretion of bromsulfalein.) Eight patients with marked hepatic dysfunction were transferred to the hospital "for more intensive study." Liver biopsy was carried out in these 8 patients and repeated in 4 of them. Liver damage was evident. Four of these hospitalized patients, after their liver-function tests returned to normal limits, received a "challenge" dose of the drug. Within two days hepatic dysfunction was evident in 3 of the 4 patients. In 1 patient a second challenge dose was given after the first challenge and again led to evidence of abnormal liver function. Flocculation tests remained abnormal is some patients as long as five weeks after discontinuance of the drug.

Physiologic studies

Example 5. In this controlled, double-blind study of the hematologic toxicity of chloramphenicol, it was recognized that chloramphenicol is "well known as a cause of aplastic anemia" and that there is a "prolonged morbidity and high mortality of aplastic anemia" and that "chloramphenicol-induced aplastic anemia can be related to dose." The aim of the study was "further definition of the toxicology of the drug."

Forty-one randomly chosen patients were given either 2 or 6 gm. of chloramphenicol per day; 12 control patients were used. "Toxic bone-marrow depression, predominantly affecting erythropoiesis, developed in 2 of 20 patients given 2.0 gm. and in 18 of 21 given 6 gm. of chloramphenicol daily." The smaller dose is recommended for routine use.

Example 6. In a study of the effect of thymectomy on the survival of skin homografts 18 children, three and a half months to eighteen years of age, about to undergo surgery for congenital heart disease, were selected. Eleven were to have total thymectomy as part of the operation, and 7 were to serve as controls. As part of the experiment, full-thickness skin homografts from an unrelated adult donor were sutured to the chest wall in each case. (Total thymectomy is occasionally, although not usually part of the primary cardiovascular surgery involved, and whereas it may not greatly add to the hazards of the necessary operation, its eventual effects in children are not known.) This work was proposed as part of a long-range study of "the growth and development of these children over the years." No difference in the survival of the skin homograft was observed in the 2 groups.

Example 7. This study of cyclopropane anesthesia and cardiac arrhythmias consisted of 31 patients. The average duration of the study was three hours, ranging from two to four and a half hours. "Minor surgical procedures" were carried out in all but 1 subject. Moderate to deep anesthesia, with endotracheal intubation and controlled respiration, was used. Carbon dioxide was injected into the closed respiratory system until cardiac arrhythmias appeared. Toxic levels of carbon dioxide were achieved and maintained for considerable periods. During the cyclopropane anesthesia a variety of pathologic cardiac arrhythmias occurred. When the carbon dioxide tension was elevated above normal, ventricular extrasystoles were more numerous than when the carbon dioxide tension was normal, ventricular arrhythmias being continuous in 1 subject for ninety minutes. (This can lead to fatal fibrillation.)

Example 8. Since the minimum blood-flow requirements of the cerebral circulation are not accurately known, this study was carried out to determine "cerebral hemodynamic and metabolic changes...before and during acute reductions in arterial pressure induced by drug administration and/or postural adjustments." Forty-four patients whose ages varied from the second to the tenth decade were involved. They included normotensive subjects, those with essential hypertension and finally a group with malignant hypertension. Fifteen had abnormal electrocardiograms. Few details about the reasons for hospitalization are given.

Signs of cerebral circulatory insufficiency, which were easily recognized, included confusion and in some cases a nonresponsive state. By alternation in the tilt of the patient "the clinical state of the subject could be changed in a matter of seconds from one of alertness to confusion, and for the remainder of the flow, the subject was maintained in the latter state." The femoral arteries were cannulated in all subjects, and the internal jugular veins in 14.

The mean arterial pressure fell in 37 subjects from 109 to 48 mm. of mercury, with signs of cerebral ischemia. "With the onset of collapse, cardiac output and right ventricular pressures decreased sharply."

Since signs of cerebral insufficiency developed without evidence of coronary insufficiency the authors concluded that "the brain may be more sensitive to acute hypotension than is the heart."

Example 9. This is a study of the adverse circulatory responses elicited by intra-abdominal maneuvers:

When the peritoneal cavity was entered, a deliberate series of maneuvers was carried out [in 68 patients] to ascertain the effective stimuli and the areas responsible for development of the expected circulatory changes. Accordingly, the surgeon rubbed localized areas of the parietal and visceral peritoneum with a small ball sponge as discretely as possible. Traction on the mesenteries, pressure in the area of the celiac plexus, traction on the gallbladder and stomach, and occlusion of the portal and caval veins were the other stimuli applied.

Thirty-four of the patients were 60 years of age or older; 11 were 70 or older. In 44 patients the hypotension produced by the deliberate stimulation was "moderate to marked." The maximum fall produced by manipulation was from 200 systolic, 105 diastolic, to 42 systolic, 20 diastolic; the average fall in mean pressure in 26 patients was 53 mm. of mercury.

Of the 50 patients studied, 17 showed either atrioventricular dissociation with nodal rhythm or nodal rhythm alone. A decrease in the amplitude of the T wave and elevation or depression of the ST segment were noted in 25 cases in association with manipulation and hypotension or, at other times, in the course of anesthesia and operation. In only 1 case was the change pronounced enough to suggest myocardial ischemia. No case of myocardial infarction was noted in the group studied although routine electrocardiograms were not taken after operation to detect silent infarcts. Two cases in which electrocardiograms were taken after operation showed T-wave and ST-segment changes that had not been present before.

These authors refer to a similar study in which more alarming electrocardiographic changes were observed. Four patients in the series sustained silent myocardial infarctions; most of their patients were undergoing gallbladder surgery because of associated heart disease. It can be added further that, in the 34 patients referred to above as being 60 years of age or older, some doubtless had heart disease that could have made risky the maneuvers carried out. In any event, this possibility might have been a deterrent.

Example 10. Starling's law – "that the heart output per beat is directly proportional to the diastolic filling" – was studied in 30 adult patients with atrial fibrillation and mitral stenosis sufficiently severe to require valvulotomy. "Continuous alterations of the length of a segment of left ventricular muscle were recorded simultaneously in 13 of these patients by means of a mercury-filled resistance gauge sutured to the surface of the left ventricle." Pressures in the left ventricle were determined by direct puncture simultaneously with the segment length in 13 patients and without the segment length in an additional 13 patients. Four similar unanesthetized patients were studied through catheterization of the left side of the heart transeptally. In all 30 patients arterial pressure was measured through the catheterized brachial artery.

Example 11. To study the sequence of ventricular contraction in human bundle-branch block, simultaneous catheterization of both ventricles was performed in 22 subjects; catheterization of the right side of the heart was carried out in the usual manner; the left side was catheterized transbronchially. Extrasystoles were produced by tapping on the epicardium in subjects with normal myocardium while they were undergoing thoracotomy. Simultaneous pressures were measured in both ventricles through needle puncture in this group.

The purpose of this study was to gain increased insight into the physiology involved.

Example 12. This investigation was carried out to examine the possible effect of vagal stimulation on cardiac arrest. The authors had in recent years transected the homolateral vagus nerve immediately below the origin of the recurrent laryngeal nerve as palliation against cough and pain in bronchogenic carcinoma. Having been impressed with the number of reports of cardiac arrest that seemed to follow vagal stimulation, they tested the effects of intrathoracic vagal stimulation during 30 of their surgical procedures, concluding, from these observations in patients under satisfactory anesthesia, that cardiac irregularities and cardiac arrest due to vagovagal reflex were less common than had previously been supposed.

Example 13. This study presented a technic for determining portal circulation time and hepatic blood flow. It involved the transcutaneous injection of the spleen and catheterization of the hepatic vein. This was carried out in 43 subjects, of whom 14 were normal; 16 had cirrhosis (varying degrees), 9 acute hepatitis, and 4 hemolytic anemia.

No mention is made of what information was divulged to the subjects, some of whom were seriously ill. This study consisted in the development of a technic, not of therapy, in the 14 normal subjects.

Studies to improve the understanding of disease

Example 14. In this study of the syndrome of impending hepatic coma in patients with cirrhosis of the liver certain nitrogenous substances were administered to 9 patients with chronic alcoholism and advanced cirrhosis: ammonium chloride, diammonium citrate, urea or dietary protein. In all patients a reaction that included mental disturbances, a "flapping tremor" and electroencephalographic changes developed. Similar signs had occurred in only 1 of the patients before these substances were administered:

> The first sign noted was usually clouding of the consciousness. Three patients had a second or a third course

of administration of a nitrogenous substance with the same results. It was concluded that marked resemblance between this reaction and impending hepatic coma, implied that the administration of these [nitrogenous] substances to patients with cirrhosis may be hazardous.

Example 15. The relation of the effects of ingested ammonia to liver disease was investigated in 11 normal subjects, 6 with acute virus hepatitis, 26 with cirrhosis, and 8 miscellaneous patients. Ten of these patients had neurologic changes associated with either hepatitis or cirrhosis.

The hepatic and renal veins were cannulated. Ammonium chloride was administered by mouth. After this, a tremor that lasted for three days developed in 1 patient. When ammonium chloride was ingested by 4 cirrhotic patients with tremor and mental confusion the symptoms were exaggerated during the test. The same thing was true of a fifth patient in another group.

Example 16. This study was directed toward determining the period of infectivity of infectious hepatitis. Artificial induction of hepatitis was carried out in an institution for mentally defective children in which a mild form of hepatitis was endemic. The parents gave consent for the intramuscular injection or oral administration of the virus, but nothing is said regarding what was told them concerning the appreciable hazards involved.

A resolution adopted by the World Medical Association states explicitly: "Under no circumstances is a doctor permitted to do anything which would weaken the physical or mental resistance of a human being except from strictly therapeutic or prophylactic indications imposed in the interest of the patient." There is no right to risk an injury to 1 person for the benefit of others.

Example 17. Live cancer cells were injected into 22 human subjects as part of a study of immunity to cancer. According to a recent review, the subjects (hospitalized patients) were "merely told they would be receiving 'some cells'" – "the word cancer was entirely omitted."

Example 18. Melanoma was transplanted from a daughter to her volunteering and informed mother, "in the hope of gaining a little better understanding of cancer immunity and in the hope that the production of tumor antibodies might be helpful in the treatment of the cancer patient." Since the daughter died on the day after the transplantation of the tumor into her mother, the hope expressed seems to have been more theoretical than practical, and the daughter's condition was described as "terminal" at the time the mother volunteered to be a recipient. The primary implant was widely excised on the twenty-fourth day after it had been placed in the mother. She died from metastatic melanoma on the four hundred and fifty-first day after transplantation. The evidence that this patient died of diffuse melanoma that metastasized from a small piece of transplanted tumor was considered conclusive.

Technical study of disease

Example 19. During bronchoscopy a special needle was inserted through a bronchus into the left atrium of the heart. This was done in an unspecified number of subjects, both with cardiac disease and with normal hearts.

The technic was a new approach whose hazards were at the beginning quite unknown. The subjects with normal hearts were used, not for their possible benefit but for that of patients in general.

Example 20. The percutaneous method of catheterization of the left side of the heart has, it is reported, led to 8 deaths (1.09 per cent death rate) and other serious accidents in 732 cases. There was, therefore, need for another method, the transbronchial approach, which was carried out in the present study in more than 500 cases, with no deaths.

Granted that a delicate problem arises regarding how much should be discussed with the patients involved in the use of a new method, nevertheless, where the method is employed in a given patient for *his* benefit, the ethical problems are far less than when this potentially extremely dangerous method is used "in 15 patients with normal hearts, undergoing bronchoscopy for other reasons." Nothing was said about what was told any of the subjects, and nothing was said about the granting of permission, which was certainly indicated in the 15 normal subjects used.

Example 21. This was a study of the effect of exercise on cardiac output and pulmonary-artery pressure in 8 "normal" persons (that is, patients whose diseases were not related to the cardiovascular system), in 8 with congestive heart failure severe enough to have recently required complete bed rest, in 6 with hypertension, in 2 with aortic insufficiency, in 7 with mitral stenosis and in 5 with pulmonary emphysema.

Intracardiac catheterization was carried out, and the catheter then inserted into the right or left main branch of the pulmonary artery. The brachial artery was usually catheterized; sometimes, the radial or femoral arteries were catheterized. The subjects exercised in a supine position by pushing their feet against weighted pedals. "The ability of these patients to carry on sustained work was severely limited by weakness and dyspnea." Several were in severe failure. This was not a therapeutic attempt but rather a physiologic study.

Bizarre study

Example 22. There is a question whether ureteral reflux can occur in the normal bladder. With this in mind, vesicoureterography was carried out on 26 normal babies less than forty-eight hours old. The infants were exposed to x-rays while the bladder was filling and during voiding. Multiple spot films were made to record the presence or absence of ureteral reflux. None was found in this group, and fortunately no infection followed the catheterization. What the results of the extensive x-ray exposure may be, no one can yet say.

Comment on Death Rates

In the foregoing examples a number of procedures, some with their own demonstrated death rates, were carried out. The following data were provided by 3 distinguished investigators in the field and represent widely held views.

Cardiac catheterization: right side of the heart, about 1 death per 1000 cases; left side, 5 deaths per 1000 cases. "Probably considerably higher in some places, depending on the portal of entry." (One investigator had 15 deaths in his first 150 cases.) It is possible that catheterization of a hepatic vein or the renal vein would have a lower death rate than that of catheterization of the right side of the heart, for, if it is properly carried out, only the atrium is entered *en route* to the liver or the kidney, not the right ventricle, which can lead to serious cardiac irregularities. There is always the possibility, however, that the ventricle will be entered inadvertently. This occurs in at least half the cases, according to one expert – "but if properly done is too transient to be of importance."

Liver biopsy: the death rate here is estimated at 2 to 3 per 1000, depending in considerable part on the condition of the subject.

Anesthesia: the anesthesia death rate can be placed in general at about 1 death per 2000 cases. The hazard is doubtless higher when certain practices such as deliberate evocation of ventricular extrasystoles under cyclopropane are involved.

Publication

In the view of the British Medical Research Council[5] it is not enough to ensure that all investigation is carried out in an ethical manner: it must be made unmistakably clear in the publications that the proprieties have been observed. This implies editorial responsibility in addition to the investigator's. The question rises, then, about valuable data that have been improperly obtained. It is my view that such material should not be published. There is a practical aspect to the matter: failure to obtain publication would discourage unethical experimentation. How many would carry out such experimentation if they *knew* its results would never be published? Even though suppression of such data (by not publishing it) would constitute a loss to medicine, in a specific localized sense, this loss, it seems, would be less important than the far-reaching moral loss to medicine if the data thus obtained were to be published. Admittedly, there is room for debate. Others believe that such data, because of their intrinsic value, obtained at a cost of great risk or damage to the subjects, should not be wasted but should be published with stern editorial comment. This would have to be done with exceptional skill, to avoid an odor of hypocrisy.

Summary and Conclusions

The ethical approach to experimentation in man has several components: two are more important than the others, the first being informed consent. The difficulty of obtaining this is discussed in detail. But it is absolutely essential to *strive* for it for moral, sociologic and legal reasons. The statement that consent has been obtained has little meaning unless the subject or his guardian is capable of understanding what is to be undertaken and unless all hazards are made clear. If these are not known this, too, should be stated. In such a situation the subject at least knows that he is to be a participant in an experiment. Secondly, there is the more reliable safeguard provided by the presence of an intelligent, informed, conscientious, compassionate, responsible investigator.

Ordinary patients will not knowingly risk their health or their life for the sake of "science." Every experienced clinician investigator knows this. When such risks are taken and a considerable number of patients are involved, it may be assumed that informed consent has not been obtained in all cases.

The gain anticipated from an experiment must be commensurate with the risk involved.

An experiment is ethical or not at its inception; it does not become ethical *post hoc* – ends do not justify means. There is no ethical distinction between ends and means.

In the publication of experimental results it must be made unmistakably clear that the proprieties have been observed. It is debatable whether data obtained unethically should be published even with stern editorial comment.

References

1 Pope Pius XII. Address Presented at First International Congress on Histopathology of Nervous System, Rome. September 14, 1952.

2 Platt (Sir Robert). *Doctor and Patient: Ethics, Morals, Government* (London: Nutheld Provincial Hospitals Trust, 1963), pp. 62 and 63.

3 Pappworth, M. H., Personal communication.

4 Beecher, H. K., Consent in clinical experimentation: myth and reality. *Journal of the American Medical Association*, 195: 34 (1966).

5 Great Britain. Medical Research Council. *Memorandum*. 1953.

51

Equipoise and the Ethics of Clinical Research

Benjamin Freedman

There is widespread agreement that ethics requires that each clinical trial begin with an honest null hypothesis.[1,2] In the simplest model, testing a new treatment B on a defined patient population P for which the current accepted treatment is A, it is necessary that the clinical investigator be in a state of genuine uncertainty regarding the comparative merits of treatments A and B for population P. If a physician knows that these treatments are not equivalent, ethics requires that the superior treatment be recommended. Following Fried, I call this state of uncertainty about the relative merits of A and B "equipoise."[3]

Equipoise is an ethically necessary condition in all cases of clinical research. In trials with several arms, equipoise must exist between all arms of the trial; otherwise the trial design should be modified to exclude the inferior treatment. If equipoise is disturbed during the course of a trial, the trial may need to be terminated and all subjects previously enrolled (as well as other patients within the relevant population) may have to be offered the superior treatment. It has been rigorously argued that a trial with a placebo is ethical only in investigating conditions for which there is no known treatment;[2] this argument reflects a special application of the requirement for equipoise. Although equipoise has commonly been discussed in the special context of the ethics of randomized clinical trials,[4,5] it is important to recognize it as an ethical condition of all controlled clinical trials, whether or not they are randomized, placebo-controlled, or blinded.

The recent increase in attention to the ethics of research with human subjects has highlighted problems associated with equipoise. Yet, as I shall attempt to show, contemporary literature, if anything, minimizes those difficulties. Moreover, there is evidence that concern on the part of investigators about failure to satisfy the requirements for equipoise can doom a trial as a result of the consequent failure to enroll a sufficient number of subjects.

The solutions that have been offered to date fail to resolve these problems in a way that would permit clinical trials to proceed. This paper argues that these problems are predicated on a faulty concept of equipoise itself. An alternative understanding of equipoise as an ethical requirement of clinical trials is proposed, and its implications are explored.

Many of the problems raised by the requirement for equipoise are familiar. Shaw and Chalmers have written that a clinician who "knows, or has good reason to believe," that one arm of the trial is superior may not ethically participate.[6] But the reasoning or preliminary results that prompt the trial (and that may themselves be ethically mandatory)[7] may jolt the investigator (if not his or her colleagues) out of equipoise before

Original publication details: Benjamin Freedman, "Equipoise and the Ethics of Clinical Research," pp. 141–5 from *New England Journal of Medicine* 317: 3 (July 1987). Copyright © 1987 Massachusetts Medical Society. Reprinted with permission from Massachusetts Medical Society.

the trial begins. Even if the investigator is undecided between A and B in terms of gross measures such as mortality and morbidity, equipoise may be disturbed because evident differences in the quality of life (as in the case of two surgical approaches) tip the balance.[3–5,8] In either case, in saying "we do not know" whether A or B is better, the investigator may create a false impression in prospective subjects, who hear him or her as saying "no evidence leans either way," when the investigator means "no controlled study has yet had results that reach statistical significance."

Late in the study – when P values are between 0.05 and 0.06 – the moral issue of equipoise is most readily apparent,[9,10] but the same problem arises when the earliest comparative results are analyzed.[11] Within the closed statistical universe of the clinical trial, each result that demonstrates a difference between the arms of the trial contributes exactly as much to the statistical conclusion that a difference exists as does any other. The contribution of the last pair of cases in the trial is no greater than that of the first. If, therefore, equipoise is a condition that reflects equivalent evidence for alternative hypotheses, it is jeopardized by the first pair of cases as much as by the last. The investigator who is concerned about the ethics of recruitment after the penultimate pair must logically be concerned after the first pair as well.

Finally, these issues are more than a philosopher's nightmare. Considerable interest has been generated by a paper in which Taylor et al.[12] describe the termination of a trial of alternative treatments for breast cancer. The trial foundered on the problem of patient recruitment, and the investigators trace much of the difficulty in enrolling patients to the fact that the investigators were not in a state of equipoise regarding the arms of the trial. With the increase in concern about the ethics of research and with the increasing presence of this topic in the curricula of medical and graduate schools, instances of the type that Taylor and her colleagues describe are likely to become more common. The requirement for equipoise thus poses a practical threat to clinical research.

Responses to the Problems of Equipoise

The problems described above apply to a broad class of clinical trials, at all stages of their development. Their resolution will need to be similarly comprehensive.

However, the solutions that have so far been proposed address a portion of the difficulties, at best, and cannot be considered fully satisfactory.

Chalmers' approach to problems at the onset of a trial is to recommend that randomization begin with the very first subject.[11] If there are no preliminary, uncontrolled data in support of the experimental treatment B, equipoise regarding treatments A and B for the patient population P is not disturbed. There are several difficulties with this approach. Practically speaking, it is often necessary to establish details of administration, dosage, and so on, before a controlled trial begins, by means of uncontrolled trials in human subjects. In addition, as I have argued above, equipoise from the investigator's point of view is likely to be disturbed when the hypothesis is being formulated and a protocol is being prepared. It is then, before any subjects have been enrolled, that the information that the investigator has assembled makes the experimental treatment appear to be a reasonable gamble. Apart from these problems, initial randomization will not, as Chalmers recognizes, address disturbances of equipoise that occur in the course of a trial.

Data-monitoring committees have been proposed as a solution to problems arising in the course of the trial.[13] Such committees, operating independently of the investigators, are the only bodies with information concerning the trial's ongoing results. Since this knowledge is not available to the investigators, their equipoise is not disturbed. Although committees are useful in keeping the conduct of a trial free of bias, they cannot resolve the investigators' ethical difficulties. A clinician is not merely obliged to treat a patient on the basis of the information that he or she currently has, but is also required to discover information that would be relevant to treatment decisions. If interim results would disturb equipoise, the investigators are obliged to gather and use that information. Their agreement to remain in ignorance of preliminary results would, by definition, be an unethical agreement, just as a failure to call up the laboratory to find out a patient's test results is unethical. Moreover, the use of a monitoring committee does not solve problems of equipoise that arise before and at the beginning of a trial.

Recognizing the broad problems with equipoise, three authors have proposed radical solutions. All three think that there is an irresolvable conflict between the requirement that a patient be offered the best treatment known (the principle underlying the requirement for equipoise) and the conduct of clinical trials; they therefore suggest that the "best treatment" requirement be weakened.

Schafer has argued that the concept of equipoise, and the associated notion of the best medical treatment, depends on the judgment of patients rather than of clinical investigators.[14] Although the equipoise of an investigator may be disturbed if he or she favors B over A, the ultimate choice of treatment is the patient's. Because the patient's values may restore equipoise, Schafer argues, it is ethical for the investigator to proceed with a trial when the patient consents. Schafer's strategy is directed toward trials that test treatments with known and divergent side effects and will probably not be useful in trials conducted to test efficacy or unknown side effects. This approach, moreover, confuses the ethics of competent medical practice with those of consent. If we assume that the investigator is a competent clinician, by saying that the investigator is out of equipoise, we have by Schafer's account said that in the investigator's professional judgment one treatment is therapeutically inferior – for that patient, in that condition, given the quality of life that can be achieved. Even if a patient would consent to an inferior treatment, it seems to me a violation of competent medical practice, and hence of ethics, to make the offer. Of course, complex issues may arise when a patient refuses what the physician considers the best treatment and demands instead an inferior treatment. Without settling that problem, however, we can reject Schafer's position. For Schafer claims that in order to continue to conduct clinical trials, it is ethical for the physician to offer (not merely accede to) inferior treatment.

Meier suggests that "most of us would be quite willing to forgo a modest expected gain in the general interest of learning something of value."[15] He argues that we accept risks in everyday life to achieve a variety of benefits, including convenience and economy. In the same way, Meier states, it is acceptable to enroll subjects in clinical trials even though they may not receive the best treatment throughout the course of the trial. Schafer suggests an essentially similar approach.[5,14] According to this view, continued progress in medical knowledge through clinical trials requires an explicit abandonment of the doctor's fully patient-centered ethic.

These proposals seem to be frank counsels of desperation. They resolve the ethical problems of equipoise by abandoning the need for equipoise. In any event, would their approach allow clinical trials to be conducted? I think this may fairly be doubted. Although many people are presumably altruistic enough to forgo the best medical treatment in the interest of the progress of science, many are not. The numbers and proportions required to sustain the statistical validity of trial results suggest that, in the absence of overwhelming altruism, the enrollment of satisfactory numbers of patients will not be possible. In particular, very ill patients, toward whom many of the most important clinical trials are directed, may be disinclined to be altruistic. Finally, as the study by Taylor et al.[12] reminds us, the problems of equipoise trouble investigators as well as patients. Even if patients are prepared to dispense with the best treatment, their physicians, for reasons of ethics and professionalism, may well not be willing to do so.

Marquis has suggested a third approach. "Perhaps what is needed is an ethics that will justify the conscription of subjects for medical research," he has written. "Nothing less seems to justify present practice."[4] Yet, although conscription might enable us to continue present practice, it would scarcely justify it. Moreover, the conscription of physician investigators, as well as subjects, would be necessary, because, as has been repeatedly argued, the problems of equipoise are as disturbing to clinicians as they are to subjects. Is any less radical and more plausible approach possible?

Theoretical Equipoise versus Clinical Equipoise

The problems of equipoise examined above arise from a particular understanding of that concept, which I will term "theoretical equipoise." It is an understanding that is both conceptually odd and ethically irrelevant. Theoretical equipoise exists when, overall, the evidence on behalf of two alternative treatment regimens is exactly balanced. This evidence may be derived from a variety of sources, including data from the literature, uncontrolled experience, considerations of basic science and fundamental physiologic processes, and perhaps a "gut feeling" or "instinct" resulting from (or superimposed on) other considerations. The problems examined above arise from the principle that if theoretical equipoise is disturbed, the physician has, in Schafer's words, a "treatment preference" – let us say, favoring experimental treatment B. A trial testing A against B requires that some patients be enrolled in violation of this treatment preference.

Theoretical equipoise is overwhelmingly fragile; that is, it is disturbed by a slight accretion of evidence favoring one arm of the trial. In Chalmers' view, equipoise is disturbed when the odds that A will be more successful than B are anything other than 50 percent. It is therefore necessary to randomize treatment assignments beginning with the very first patient, lest equipoise be disturbed. We may say that theoretical equipoise is balanced on a knife's edge.

Theoretical equipoise is most appropriate to one-dimensional hypotheses and causes us to think in those terms. The null hypothesis must be sufficiently simple and "clean" to be finely balanced: Will A or B be superior in reducing mortality or shrinking tumors or lowering fevers in population P? Clinical choice is commonly more complex. The choice of A or B depends on some combination of effectiveness, consistency, minimal or relievable side effects, and other factors. On close examination, for example, it sometimes appears that even trials that purport to test a single hypothesis in fact involve a more complicated, portmanteau measure – e.g., the "therapeutic index" of A versus B. The formulation of the conditions of theoretical equipoise for such complex, multidimensional clinical hypotheses is tantamount to the formulation of a rigorous calculus of apples and oranges.

Theoretical equipoise is also highly sensitive to the vagaries of the investigator's attention and perception. Because of its fragility, theoretical equipoise is disturbed as soon as the investigator perceives a difference between the alternatives – whether or not any genuine difference exists. Prescott writes, for example, "It will be common at some stage in most trials for the survival curves to show visually different survivals," short of significance but "sufficient to raise ethical difficulties for the participants."[16] A visual difference, however, is purely an artifact of the research methods employed: when and by what means data are assembled and analyzed and what scale is adopted for the graphic presentation of data. Similarly, it is common for researchers to employ interval scales for phenomena that are recognized to be continuous by nature – e.g., five-point scales of pain or stages of tumor progression. These interval scales, which represent an arbitrary distortion of the available evidence to simplify research, may magnify the differences actually found, with a resulting disturbance of theoretical equipoise.

Finally, as described by several authors, theoretical equipoise is personal and idiosyncratic. It is disturbed when the clinician has, in Schafer's words, what "might even be labeled a bias or a hunch," a preference of a "merely intuitive nature."[14] The investigator who ignores such a hunch, by failing to advise the patient that because of it the investigator prefers B to A or by recommending A (or a chance of random assignment to A) to the patient, has violated the requirement for equipoise and its companion requirement to recommend the best medical treatment.

The problems with this concept of equipoise should be evident. To understand the alternative, preferable interpretation of equipoise, we need to recall the basic reason for conducting clinical trials: there is a current or imminent conflict in the clinical community over what treatment is preferred for patients in a defined population P. The standard treatment is A, but some evidence suggests that B will be superior (because of its effectiveness or its reduction of undesirable side effects, or for some other reason). (In the rare case when the first evidence of a novel therapy's superiority would be entirely convincing to the clinical community, equipoise is already disturbed.) Or there is a split in the clinical community, with some clinicians favoring A and others favoring B. Each side recognizes that the opposing side has evidence to support its position, yet each still thinks that overall its own view is correct. There exists (or, in the case of a novel therapy, there may soon exist) an honest, professional disagreement among expert clinicians about the preferred treatment. A clinical trial is instituted with the aim of resolving this dispute.

At this point, a state of "clinical equipoise" exists. There is no consensus within the expert clinical community about the comparative merits of the alternatives to be tested. We may state the formal conditions under which such a trial would be ethical as follows: at the start of the trial, there must be a state of clinical equipoise regarding the merits of the regimens to be tested, and the trial must be designed in such a way as to make it reasonable to expect that, if it is successfully concluded, clinical equipoise will be disturbed. In other words, the results of a successful clinical trial should be convincing enough to resolve the dispute among clinicians.

A state of clinical equipoise is consistent with a decided treatment preference on the part of the investigators. They must simply recognize that their less-favored treatment is preferred by colleagues whom they consider to be responsible and competent. Even if the interim results favor the preference of the investigators, treatment B, clinical equipoise persists as long as those results are too weak to influence the judgment of the community of clinicians, because of limited sample size, unresolved possibilities of side effects, or other factors. (This judgment can necessarily be made only by those who know the interim results – whether a data-monitoring committee or the investigators.)

At the point when the accumulated evidence in favor of B is so strong that the committee or investigators believe no open-minded clinician informed of the results would still favor A, clinical equipoise has been disturbed. This may occur well short of the original schedule for the termination of the trial, for unexpected reasons. (Therapeutic effects or side effects may be much stronger than anticipated, for example, or a definable subgroup within population P may be recognized for which the results demonstrably disturb clinical equipoise.) Because of the arbitrary character of human judgment and persuasion, some ethical problems regarding the termination of a trial will remain. Clinical equipoise will confine these problems to unusual or extreme cases, however, and will allow us to cast persistent problems in the proper terms. For example, in the face of a strong established trend, must we continue the trial because of others' blind fealty to an arbitrary statistical bench mark?

Clearly, clinical equipoise is a far weaker – and more common – condition than theoretical equipoise. Is it ethical to conduct a trial on the basis of clinical equipoise, when theoretical equipoise is disturbed? Or, as Schafer and others have argued, is doing so a violation of the physician's obligation to provide patients with the best medical treatment?[4,5,14] Let us assume that the investigators have a decided preference for B but wish

to conduct a trial on the grounds that clinical (not theoretical) equipoise exists. The ethics committee asks the investigators whether, if they or members of their families were within population P, they would not want to be treated with their preference, B? An affirmative answer is often thought to be fatal to the prospects for such a trial, yet the investigators answer in the affirmative. Would a trial satisfying this weaker form of equipoise be ethical?

I believe that it clearly is ethical. As Fried has emphasized,[3] competent (hence, ethical) medicine is social rather than individual in nature. Progress in medicine relies on progressive consensus within the medical and research communities. The ethics of medical practice grants no ethical or normative meaning to a treatment preference, however powerful, that is based on a hunch or on anything less than evidence publicly presented and convincing to the clinical community. Persons are licensed as physicians after they demonstrate the acquisition of this professionally validated knowledge, not after they reveal a superior capacity for guessing. Normative judgments of their behavior – e.g., malpractice actions – rely on a comparison with what is done by the community of medical practitioners. Failure to follow a "treatment preference" not shared by this community and not based on information that would convince it could not be the basis for an allegation of legal or ethical malpractice. As Fried states:"[T]he conception of what is good medicine is the product of a professional consensus." By definition, in a state of clinical equipoise, "good medicine" finds the choice between A and B indifferent.

In contrast to theoretical equipoise, clinical equipoise is robust. The ethical difficulties at the beginning and end of a trial are therefore largely alleviated. There remain difficulties about consent, but these too may be diminished. Instead of emphasizing the lack of evidence favoring one arm over another that is required by theoretical equipoise, clinical equipoise places the emphasis in informing the patient on the honest disagreement among expert clinicians. The fact that the investigator has a "treatment preference," if he or she does, could be disclosed; indeed, if the preference is a decided one, and based on something more than a hunch, it could be ethically mandatory to disclose it. At the same time, it would be emphasized that this preference is not shared by others. It is likely to be a matter of chance that the patient is being seen by a clinician with a preference for B over A, rather than by an equally competent clinician with the opposite preference.

Clinical equipoise does not depend on concealing relevant information from researchers and subjects, as does the use of independent data-monitoring committees. Rather, it allows investigators, in informing subjects, to distinguish appropriately among validated knowledge accepted by the clinical community, data on treatments that are promising but are not (or, for novel therapies, would not be) generally convincing, and mere hunches. Should informed patients decline to participate because they have chosen a specific clinician and trust his or her judgment – over and above the consensus in the professional community – that is no more than the patients' right. We do not conscript patients to serve as subjects in clinical trials.

The Implications of Clinical Equipoise

The theory of clinical equipoise has been formulated as an alternative to some current views on the ethics of human research. At the same time, it corresponds closely to a preanalytic concept held by many in the research and regulatory communities. Clinical equipoise serves, then, as a rational formulation of the approach of many toward research ethics; it does not so much change things as explain why they are the way they are.

Nevertheless, the precision afforded by the theory of clinical equipoise does help to clarify or reformulate some aspects of research ethics: I will mention only two.

First, there is a recurrent debate about the ethical propriety of conducting clinical trials of discredited treatments, such as Laetrile.[17] Often, substantial political pressure to conduct such tests is brought to bear by adherents of quack therapies. The theory of clinical equipoise suggests that, when there is no support for a treatment regimen within the expert clinical community, the first ethical requirement of a trial – clinical equipoise – is lacking and it would therefore be unethical to conduct such a trial.

Second, Feinstein has criticized the tendency of clinical investigators to narrow excessively the conditions and hypotheses of a trial in order to ensure the validity of its results.[18] This "fastidious" approach purchases scientific manageability at the expense of an inability to apply the results to the "messy" conditions of clinical practice. The theory of clinical equipoise adds some strength to this criticism. Overly "fastidious" trials, designed to resolve some theoretical question, fail to satisfy the second ethical requirement of clinical research, since the special conditions of the trial will render it useless for influencing clinical decisions, even if it is successfully completed.

The most important result of the concept of clinical equipoise, however, might be to relieve the current crisis of confidence in the ethics of clinical trials. Equipoise, properly understood, remains an ethical condition for clinical trials. It is consistent with much current practice. Clinicians and philosophers alike have been premature in calling for desperate measures to resolve problems of equipoise.

Acknowledgement

I am indebted to Robert J. Levine, MD, and to Harold Merskey, DM, for their valuable suggestions.

References

1   Levine, R. J. *Ethics and Regulation of Clinical Research.* 2nd edn (Baltimore, MD: Urban & Schwarzenberg, 1986).

2   Levine, R. J. The use of placebos in randomized clinical trials. *IRB: A Review of Human Subjects Research* (1985); 7(2): 1–4.

3   Fried, C. *Medical Experimentation: Personal Integrity and Social Policy* (Amsterdam: North-Holland Publishing, 1974).

4   Marquis, D. Leaving therapy to chance. *Hastings Center Report* (1983); 13(4): 40–7.

5   Schafer, A. The ethics of the randomized clinical trial. *New England Journal of Medicine* (1982); 307: 719–24.

6   Shaw, L. W. and Chalmers T. C. Ethics in cooperative clinical trials. *New England Journal of Medicine* (1970); 169: 487–95.

7   Hollenberg, N. K., Dzau, V. J. and Williams, G. H. Are uncontrolled clinical studies ever justified? *New England Journal of Medicine* (1980); 303: 1067.

8   Levine, R. J. and Lebacqz, K. Some ethical considerations in clinical trials. *Clinical Pharmacology and Therapeutics* (1979); 25: 728–41.

9   Klimt, C. R. and Canner, P. L. Terminating a long-term clinical trial. *Clinical Pharmacology and Therapeutics* (1979); 25: 641–6.

10 Veatch, R. M. Longitudinal studies, sequential designs and grant renewals: what to do with preliminary data. *IRB: A Review of Human Subjects Research* (1979); 1(4): 1–3.

11 Chalmers, T. The ethics of randomization as a decision-making technique and the problem of informed consent. In: T. L. Beauchamp and L. Walters (eds), *Contemporary Issues in Bioethics* (Encino, CA.: Dickenson, 1978), pp. 426–9.

12 Taylor, K. M., Margolese, R. C. and Soskolne, C. L. Physicians' reasons for not entering eligible patients in a randomized clinical trial of surgery for breast cancer. *New England Journal of Medicine* (1984); 310: 1363–7.

13 Chalmers, T. C. Invited remarks. *Clinical and Pharmacological Therapy* (1979); 25: 649–50.

14 Schafer, A. The randomized clinical trial: for whose benefit? *IRB: A Review of Human Subjects Research* (1985); 7(2): 4–6.

15 Meier, P. Terminating a trial – the ethical problem. *Clinical Pharmacology and Therapeutics* (1979); 25: 633–40.

16 Prescott, R. J. Feedback of data to participants during clinical trials. In: H. J. Tagnon and M. J. Staquet (eds), *Controversies in Cancer: Design of Trials and Treatment* (New York: Masson, 1979), pp. 55–61.

17 Cowan, D. H. The ethics of clinical trials of ineffective therapy. *IRB: A Review of Human Subjects Research* (1981); 3(5): 10–11.

18 Feinstein, A. R. An additional basic science for clinical medicine. II. The limitations of randomized trials. *Annals of Internal Medicine* (1983); 99: 544–50.

52

The Patient and the Public Good

Samuel Hellman

These are extraordinary times in medicine. There is both a revolution in the biology relevant to medicine and a revolution in the delivery of health care. We must translate laboratory discoveries into clinical practice, and we must do so in an increasingly cost-conscious environment. Faced with this challenge, physicians appear willing to modify the traditional doctor–patient relationship. The tension between clinical research and patient care is not new, but it has increased in intensity as we try to incorporate the new biology into patient care in a cost-effective way. It has been argued that research must take precedence if we are to use the advances in biology properly and if we are to efficiently allocate health care resources. Not only will clinical investigation have to assess the medical value of the new discoveries, but it will have to determine whether the advance is worth the cost. The emphasis on controlling costs takes us farther from the traditional physician role to where, in many managed care arrangements, the physician must both take care of the patient and husband the limited resources of the group, either for use for other patients or to provide profit for the plan and the physician. How can this be done in the context of the traditional doctor–patient relationship?

As a part of the doctor–patient relationship, physicians fashion a treatment plan to the needs of each patient. As the physician learns more about each patient and the details of his or her illness, the opportunities for crafting individual patient care increase. The advances in molecular medicine will allow us to know a great deal more about the disease state in each individual patient. Already current advances in oncology offer opportunities to characterize individual patients and their tumours with molecular and genetic information, distinguishing them from others, even within current staging classifications. Molecular medicine will provide many tools for this individualization of the extent, type and virulence of the disease as well as for characterization of the host in whom the disease is resident. Each constellation of signs, symptoms, disease extent, past medical history, concomitant illness, and molecular markers of disease proclivities will affect the desirability of specific plans of management. This same phenomenon will be true in most diseases other than cancer. Because clinical investigation requires collecting patients into groups, whereas medical practice tailors treatment to individuals, these distinctions will make the role of the clinical investigator doing randomized trials more difficult.

Although it relies on altruism and informed consent, the primary ethical basis for doing randomized trials has been developed by Benjamin Freedman of McGill University, who promulgates the concept of 'clinical equipoise'. This state exists when there is genuine uncertainty, within the expert medical

Original publication details: Samuel Hellman, "The Patient and the Public Good," pp. 400–2 from *Nature Medicine* 1: 5 (1995). Reprinted by permission from Macmillan Publishers Ltd.

community with regard to the alternatives applied in a trial. Most important, the concept applies to the views of the medical community as a whole but not necessarily to the individual physician-investigator for an individual patient. Patient-centered care implicit in the current relationship between doctor and patient requires that patients are seen as individuals rather than as members of a group with similar characteristics. Trials require combining patients into categories while the tenets of patient-centered care stress personal consideration. A related conflict is emerging as managed care is used to control health costs. Can one provide individual care and at the same time be responsible for controlling costs? Peter Toon from St. Bartholomew's Hospital in London argues that the individual physician, in particular the gatekeeper in a managed care setting, can fulfill responsibilities to an individual patient and to the husbanding of scarce public resources, both within the doctor–patient relationship.[1] I disagree!

The lessons of clinical investigation can illuminate the difficulties in containing health care costs in the context of individual patient care. To demonstrate the frequent incompatibility of randomized clinical trials and patient-centered care let us consider a patient with breast cancer who might be considered a candidate for a randomized clinical trial of therapeutic alternatives directed at either local or systemic disease. The considerations can be separated into three groups: (1) the tumour, (2) the patient, and (3) the physician.

The Tumour

In order to get sufficient numbers of patients into the trial most studies consolidate patients into what are hoped to be relatively homogeneous groups. This is necessary if there are to be sufficient patients in each arm of a study for statistical analysis. For example, all stage one patients might be randomized. Stage one breast cancer includes tumours of all sizes less than two centimeters that have not spread to lymph nodes. However, there are data that indicate that two centimeters is an arbitrary cut-off in a continuum in which patients with smaller tumours do better than those having larger tumours even within stage one. Breast tumours can now be subjected to a variety of tests

that appear to offer some prognostic significance. These include ploidy, proliferative activity, the relative expression of a variety of oncogenes, tumour suppressor genes, growth factors and their receptors, as well as tumour vascularity, nuclear and cytologic grade and histological characteristics. Already these are proving to be both of prognostic importance and a useful guide to therapy. Although some of these factors may be confounding variables, it is possible to develop a profile for each patient's tumour. As the number of useful molecular markers increases, so will the ability to characterize each tumour. This emphasizes the individuality of each patient's lesion and suggests that it may not be possible to assure equipoise among medical experts for each tumour although they may feel comfortable in doing so for patients with stage one tumours as a group. Further, even if it is possible for the medical experts, the physician caring for the patient may feel quite differently about each patient within the group depending on such prognostic indicators.

Women and Breast Cancer

There are anatomic differences in patients that might affect the potential benefit of treatment. Past medical history and current health status will be different for each person. Molecular medicine will further quantify the status of important host organ function. Some pre-existing conditions may proscribe a patient from the trial, but, in almost all studies, patients are included with a spectrum of health states that affect the physician's view of which arm of the study may be more appropriate for the individual patient. As medical advances allow for greater knowledge of the individual they will also serve as a guide to the most desirable therapy.

There are also differences in attitudes, wishes and emotional states of individual patients. For example, how does a patient feel about breast preservation? Does her body image require the presence of the breast or alternatively is she fearful of occult disease lurking within the breast and would she prefer that it be removed? How do the burdens of daily radiation treatment affect her life? Similarly, how does she feel about reconstructive surgery? What are the patient's social circumstances? Do these affect her choice of treatments?

The Physician

There are also many differences among physicians. How enthusiastic is the physician for an answer to the trial? What is his or her view of the severity of the disease? Is the physician risk-prone or risk-averse with regard to the treatment of suspected micrometastatic disease? What is the effect of previous education and training on the physician? What about differing community standards? What has the physician learned in following prior patients in the trial? All of these will affect the physician's view of the trial. What should the physician do with his or her *a priori* opinions? One of the founders of controlled trials, Sir Bradford Hill says, "If the doctor...thinks even in the absence of any evidence that for the patient's benefit he ought to give one treatment rather than the other, then that patient should not be admitted to the trial. Only if, in his state of ignorance, he believes the treatment given to be a matter of indifference can he accept a random distribution of patients to the different groups."[2]

Patient-Centered Care

This example highlights the conflict between the ethical basis of trials and the requirements of patient-centered care. Freedman's notion that clinical equipoise "is satisfied if there is genuine uncertainty within the expert medical community – not necessarily on the part of the individual investigator – about the preferred treatment"[3] is in conflict with the view of many investigators. Michael Baum, a leading British surgical oncologist, in discussing breast cancer trials states:[4] "To mount national trials there has to be first of all a professional equipoise where roughly equal numbers of the profession favour either the standard treatment or the novel treatment. For a physician to enter a patient into the trial a personal equipoise must exist." This balance must exist for each patient and the patient's preferences must be considered. This is very difficult to do when treatment is determined by random assignment.

Patient-centered care requires much more than a consensus of the medical community. We must learn about the particular patient and her disease and she must be an active participant in deciding on the best course of action. This is not 'clinical equipoise'. Only rarely is a balance between alternative therapies ever reached for an individual patient. Even when it is, it may be a different balance than that reached for another patient and grouping them together may obfuscate rather than clarify. Individual patients may have different views as to the utility of different functional or cosmetic end results. McNeil and colleagues in Boston demonstrated that loss of the larynx was viewed differently when comparing firefighters with management executives and within each group there was great heterogeneity, emphasizing the range of values individual patients place on different clinical alternatives.

The Public Good and Physician Responsibility

But what of the public good? This brings us to some of the vexing questions facing medicine today. Inherent in all proposed health care reform is control of the rising costs of medical care due in large measure to the advances in diagnosis and treatment that result from technical and scientific innovation. Many of these have potential benefit but at a considerable cost. There are powerful pressures to control the rate of rise of medical expenditures by limiting the use of such techniques. There is no problem when the procedure is of no value. The bind comes with those procedures that offer possible benefit but are very expensive. Charles Fried, of the Harvard Law School, in discussing what he calls the "economic model" worries that the obligation of personal care inherent in the relationship between physician and patient would be replaced by "the physician as agent of an efficient health-care delivery system." Although physicians should participate as medical experts in judgments as to the allocation of limited resources, the issues of societal cost should not enter into a doctor's decision when caring for an individual patient. Similarly, the patient cared for by the clinical investigator must believe that the physician will not compromise her care to perform the experiment.

Questions of the public good are a responsibility of society as a whole. Physicians should participate in public discussions and decision-making about the allocation of health care resources but in a different way. The physician can participate as a citizen, expressing views about the distribution of scarce societal resources and the value of the various health outcomes. Physicians may also participate in the public discussion of health care issues as experts, providing information about the efficacy of various treatments, but the physician ought not to be given the responsibility of making important societal decisions in the context of individual patient relationships. Not only does this involve the transference of an important public policy choice to small group of individuals, but, more important, it requires the physician to base treatment recommendations for an individual patient on general public policy grounds, which will compromise the character of the doctor–patient relationship.

Today financial imperatives appear to dominate medical care considerations. Simply stated, the view is that during these revolutionary times economics must pre-empt the niceties of the personal nature of the doctor–patient relationship. Most desirable are those arrangements that satisfy both but, it is suggested, we cannot afford to lose either the randomized clinical trial as a method of acquiring new knowledge or the cost–benefit analysis applied to the individual patient needed for expenditure control, at least until satisfactory alternatives are found. While however altruistically intended, I believe this notion is misguided. We lose much more than we gain if we damage the primacy of individual patient care, for this is based on the inalienable rights of human beings. These are not rights to health care but rather rights in health care. The patient is not entitled to any medical treatment, no matter how expensive, rather the patient is entitled to be treated in a particular manner by his or her physician. Society can make choices in which it balances the needs of some individuals against the needs of others. Based on this balancing, society can determine the level of health care coverage available and physicians must work within these limits. However, the ethical requirements of the doctor–patient relationship, as we now understand it, preclude the doctor from doing society's work of balancing patient and societal needs. The relationship established between the doctor and the patient is one of trust and loyalty. In fact, respect for the value of such relationships explains why maintaining the ability to choose one's doctor figured so centrally in the recent health care debate in the United States.

The doctor–patient relationship requires the fidelity of the doctor to the patient. We must not let the current transformation of health care compromise this ideal. The patient comes to the doctor in a vulnerable state – made so by illness, fear and lack of knowledge. In order to treat a vulnerable person with concern and respect, one must look out for that person's interests. Therefore the doctor treats the patient with the appropriate respect for both the patient's vulnerability and her autonomy by becoming an agent for the patient. Moreover, it is because the patient knows that the doctor is her doctor that the patient is able to relieve herself of some of the anxiety caused by illness. If the patient is unable to repose this trust in her physician (because she knows that the physician is busy balancing this patient's needs against community needs) she will lose her ally and friend and the doctor will have lost an important instrument to relieve suffering and minister to patients.

If we are to serve the individual patient and society, we must first agree on certain principles and then, within the constraints imposed by them, develop techniques to achieve our goals. There are two such principles that, if agreed upon, will allow enhancement of the public good in the context of patient-centered care. First, individual patients should not be used as a means to achieve even a societally desired end, if in so doing the individual right to personal medical care is compromised. Second, there are two roles for the physician, and they must not be confused. As an agent of society the physician must consider the greater good and be involved in the development of guidelines, directives, and limitations on practice. At the same time, we must fight against unreasonable limits on medical care. This is very important as we consider the best use of restricted resources. Once such regulations are promulgated by society, we as physicians are obligated to adhere to them. On the other hand, within those limits we are expected to act in the best interests of each patient. The responsibilities of physicians to society as a whole must be separated from our obligation to individual patients. These two different responsibilities must be undertaken in different settings with clear understanding by the physician, the patient and society as to which role is being played. Although clinical investigation and limiting health care expenditures are essential, we should not allow them to change the traditional relationship of the physician to the patient. For clinical investigation this means limiting the use of the randomized clinical trial and requiring that when it is used an individual equipoise exists for each patient. It also means separating the role of personal physician from that of the clinical investigator. These two roles residing in the same physician create conflicting goals, which have the potential to undermine the primacy of the patient. Randomized trials are already cumbersome and administratively burdened. These restrictions will make randomized trials even more difficult to perform. This does not suggest a return to non-scientific subjective methods of research but emphasizes the need to search for alternatives to random allocation that recognize the individual variables in each clinical

circumstance. For the physician concerned with controlling health care expenditures this means insulating the doctor from considering societal costs when advising or treating any individual patient. While decisions about the efficient use of resources may provide limits on management options, concern about health plan expense should not enter into an individual patient management decision.

Medicine in its essence deals with a relationship between an individual doctor and a particular patient. Clinical investigation and controlling health expenditures concern society as a whole. The physician may engage in both but it would be a most unfortunate unintended consequence if altruistic concerns for the public good undermined the assurance of optimal personal treatment promulgated in patient-centered care. Revolutionary times require greater diligence in assuring the primacy of the patient in the relationship with the caring physician.

References

1   Toon, P. D. Justice for gatekeepers, *Lancet*, 343, 585–7 (1994).
2   Hill, A. B. Medical ethics and controlled trials. *British Medical Journal*, 1, 1043–9 (1963).
3   Freedman, B. Equipoise and the ethics of clinical research. *New England Journal of Medicine*, 317, 141–5 (1987).

4   Baum, M., Zikha, K. and Houghton, J. Ethics of clinical research: Lessons for the future. *British Medical Journal*, 299, 251–3 (1989).

53

Scientific Research Is a Moral Duty

John Harris

Science is under attack. In Europe, America, and Australasia in particular, scientists are objects of suspicion and are on the defensive.[i]

"Frankenstein science"[5] is a phrase never far from the lips of those who take exception to some aspect of science or indeed some supposed abuse by scientists. We should not, however, forget the powerful obligation there is to undertake, support, and participate in scientific research, particularly biomedical research, and the powerful moral imperative that underpins these obligations. Now it is more imperative than ever to articulate and explain these obligations and to do so is the subject and the object of this paper.

Let me present the question in its starkest form: is there a moral obligation to undertake, support and even to participate in serious scientific research? If there is, does that obligation require not only that beneficial research be undertaken but also that "we", as individuals and "we" as societies be willing to support and even participate in research where necessary?

Thus far the overwhelming answer given to this question has been "no", and research has almost universally been treated with suspicion and even hostility by the vast majority of all those concerned with the ethics and regulation of research. The so called "precautionary approach"[6] sums up this attitude, requiring dangers to be considered more likely and more serious than benefits, and assuming that no sane person would or should participate in research unless they had a pressing personal reason for so doing, or unless they were motivated by a totally impersonal altruism. International agreements and protocols – for example, the *Declaration of Helsinki*[7] and the *CIOMS Guidelines*[8] – have been directed principally at protecting individuals from the dangers of participation in research and ensuring that, where they participate, their full informed consent is assured. The overwhelming presumption has been and remains that participation in research is a supererogatory, and probably a reckless, act not an obligation.

Suspicion of doctors and of medical research is well founded. In the modern era it stems from the aftermath of the Nazi atrocities and from the original Helsinki declaration prompted, although rather belatedly, by the Nazi doctors' trial at Nuremberg.[9,10] More recently it has been fuelled by further examples of extreme medical arrogance and paternalism. The Tuskegee Study of Untreated Syphilis,[11] for example, in which 412 poor African/American men were deliberately left untreated from 1932–1972 so that the natural history of syphilis could be determined.[12] Even when it became known that penicillin was effective against syphilis they were left untreated. More recently in the UK a major scandal caught the

Original publication details: John Harris, "Scientific Research Is a Moral Duty," pp. 242–8 from *Journal of Medical Ethics* 31: 4 (2005). Reproduced with permission from BMJ Publishing Group.

public imagination and reflected serious medical malpractice; it involved the unauthorised and deceitful post-mortem removal and retention of organs and tissue from children.[13] (For a commentary on some of the major issues concerning this case see my paper "Law and regulation of retained organs: the ethical issues".[14])

These and many other cases seem to provide ample justification for the presumption of suspicion of, and even hostility to, medical research. Vigilance against wrongdoing is, however, one thing; the inability to identify wrongdoing with the result that the good is frustrated and harm caused is quite another.

This paper challenges and seeks to reverse the presumption against medical research.

When we ask whether there is a moral obligation to support and even to participate in serious scientific research we need first to be clear that we are talking of research directed toward preventing serious harm or providing significant benefits to humankind. In all cases the degree of harm or benefit must justify the degree of burden on research subjects, individuals, or society. This balance will be explored below. Of course the research must also be serious in the sense that the project is well designed and with reasonable prospect of leading to important knowledge that will benefit persons in the future.[ii]

Two separate but complementary lines of argument underpin a powerful obligation to pursue, support, and participate in scientific research.

Do No Harm

The first is one of the most powerful obligations that we have, the obligation not to harm others. Where our actions will, or may probably prevent serious harm then if we can reasonably (given the balance of risk and burden to ourselves and benefit to others) we clearly should act because to fail to do so is to accept responsibility for the harm that then occurs. (I set out arguments for and the basis of this duty in *Violence and Responsibility*.[15]) This is the strong side of a somewhat weaker, but still powerful duty of beneficence, our basic moral obligation to help other people in need. This is sometimes called "the rule of rescue".[16] Most, if not all diseases create needs, in those who are affected, and in their relatives, friends, and carers and

indeed in society. Because medical research is a necessary component of relieving that need in many circumstances, furthering medical research becomes a moral obligation. This obligation is not limited to actual physical participation in research projects, but also involves supporting research in other ways, for instance economically, at the personal, corporate, and societal levels and indeed politically.

Fairness

Second, the obligation also flows from an appeal to basic fairness. This is sometimes expressed as an appeal to the unfairness of being a "free rider". We all benefit from the existence of the social practice of medical research. Many of us would not be here if infant mortality had not been brought under control, or antibiotics had not been invented. Most of us will continue to benefit from these and other medical advances (and indeed other advances such as clean drinking water and sanitation). Since we accept these benefits, we have an obligation in justice to contribute to the social practice which produces them. We may argue that since we could not opt out of advances that were made prior to our becoming capable of autonomous decision making we are not obliged to contribute. It may, however, still be unfair to accept their benefits and implies also that we will forgo the fruits of any future advances.[17] Few, however, are willing to do so, and even fewer are really willing to forgo benefits that have been created through the sacrifices of others when their own hour of need arises!

It should be clear how what I am claiming relates to the principle which is sometimes called the "principle of fairness" developed by Herbert Hart and later used by John Rawls.[18,19] That principle may be interpreted as saying "those who have submitted to … restrictions have a right to similar acquiescence on the part of those who have benefited from their submission".[20] Here I am not suggesting an *enforceable* obligation to participate based on fairness although such an enforceable obligation would, as we shall see, certainly in some circumstances be justified by the argument of this paper. Nor am I proposing any *right* possessed by those who participate, to similar acquiescence on the part of those who benefit. Being a free rider *is*, however, unfair and people always have a moral reason not to act unfairly. This moral reason is probably enough to justify an enforceable obligation but we do not have to use compulsion as a strategy of first resort. It is surely powerful enough, however, to rebut some of the presumptions against an obligation to support and participate in research.

There may be specific facts about me and my circumstances that absolve me from the obligation to be a research subject in a given situation. This could be the case if I have just participated in other burdensome experiments and there are other potential research subjects who have not done so, or if participation would create excessive burdens for me that it would not create for other potential participants. This does not show that the general obligation we have identified does not exist, just that it, like most other or perhaps all moral obligations, can be overridden by other moral considerations in specific circumstances.[iii]

The Moral Imperative for Research

We all benefit from living in a society, and, indeed, in a world in which serious scientific research is carried out and which utilises the benefits of past research. It is both of benefit to patients and research subjects and in their interests to be in a society which pursues and actively accepts the benefits of research and where research and its fruits are given a high priority. We all also benefit from the knowledge that research is ongoing into diseases or conditions from which we do not currently suffer but to which we may succumb. It makes us feel more secure and gives us hope for the future, for ourselves and our descendants, and for others for whom we care. If this is right, then I have a strong general interest that there be research, and in all well founded research; not excluding but not exclusively, research on me and on my condition or on conditions which are likely to affect me and mine. All such research is also of clear benefit to me. A narrow interpretation of the requirement that research be of benefit to the subject of the research is therefore perverse.[21]

Moreover, almost everyone now living, certainly everyone born in high income industrialised societies, has benefited from the fruits of past research. We all benefit – for example, either from having been vaccinated against diseases such as polio, smallpox, and others or because others have been vaccinated we benefit from the so called "herd" immunity; or we benefit (as in the case of smallpox) from the fact that the disease has actually been eradicated. To take another obvious example, almost at random, we all benefit from the knowledge of connections between diet, exercise, and heart disease. This knowledge enables us to adopt preventive strategies and gives us ways of calculating our level of personal risk.

In view of these considerations there is a clear moral obligation to participate in medical research in certain specific circumstances. This moral obligation is, as we have seen, straightforwardly derivable from either of two of the most basic moral obligations we have as persons.

This entails that there are circumstances where an adult, competent person ought to participate in research, even if participating is not in his or her best interests narrowly defined. If I am asked to give a blood sample for a worthwhile research project, or if I am asked if tissue removed during an operation may be retained for research or therapeutic use, I may have to think in the following way: in the case of giving the blood sample I may say to myself: "I hate needles and the sight of my own blood!" Equally with retained tissue or organs I may feel that since I understand little of the future uses for my tissue it would be safer to say "no".

In each case we will suppose that the disease being investigated is not one that I or anyone I know is likely ever to get, so giving this blood sample or allowing the use of excised tissue is not in my best interests narrowly conceived. In this situation doing what is best, all things considered, therefore seems to entail not doing what is best for myself, not pursuing my own best interests. However, this is not really so. Some of my main interests have not been identified and taken into account in this hypothetical train of thought. One of these is my interest in taking myself seriously as a reflective moral agent, and my interest in being taken seriously by others. Identifying my moral obligations, and acting on them is not contrary to my interests, but is an integral part of what makes me a moral agent.[iv]

More importantly, however, as we have seen, I do have a powerful interest in living in a society and indeed in a world in which scientific research is vigorously pursued and is given a high priority.

Do Universal Moral Principles Deny This Claim?

A number of the most influential international protocols on science research seem to contradict the claims
so far made and we must now examine these more
closely.[22] One of the most widely cited principles is
contained in a crucial paragraph of the World Medical
Association's *Declaration of Helsinki*, adopted by the
52nd General Assembly, in Edinburgh, Scotland, in
October 2000.

> In medical research on human subjects, considerations
> related to the wellbeing of the human subject should
> take precedence over the interests of science and society.
> (WMA,[7] para 5)

This paragraph is widely cited in support of restrictions on scientific research and is interpreted as
requiring that all human subject research is in the
narrowly conceived interests of the research subjects
themselves. This article of faith has become almost
unchallengeable.

We need first to examine more closely the idea of
what is or is not in someone's interests. (Here the
argument echoes that of my paper, "Ethical genetic
research".[3]) In this paper I shall neither follow nor
consider what other commentators have made of this
idea but attempt a rigorous analysis of the meaning
of the concepts involved. We should note at the outset that what is or is not in a particular individual's
interests is an objective matter. While subjects have a
special role to play in determining this, we know that
human beings are apt to act against their own interests. Indeed the idea of respect for persons which
underpins this guideline has two clear and sometimes
incompatible elements, namely, concern for welfare
and respect for autonomy. Because people often have
self harming preferences (smoking, drug abuse, self-
less altruism, etc) they are sometimes bad judges of
their interests.

The interests of the subject *cannot* be paramount
nor can they automatically take precedence over
other interests of comparable moral significance. Such
a claim involves a straightforward mistake: being or
becoming a research subject is not the sort of thing
that could conceivably augment either someone's

moral claims or, for that matter, her rights. *All* people
are morally important and, with respect to one
another, each has a claim to equal consideration. No
one has a claim to overriding consideration. To say
that the interests of the subject must take precedence
over those of others, if it means anything, must be
understood as a way of reasserting that a researcher's
narrowly conceived professional interests must not
have primacy over the human rights of research subjects. (The researcher may also have specific contractual
duties to them.) As a general remark about the obligations of the research community, the health care system,
society or indeed of the world community, it is not,
however, sustainable.

This is not of course to say that human rights are
vulnerable to the interests of society whenever these
can be demonstrated to be greater. On the contrary, it
is to say that the rights and interests of research subjects are just the rights and interests of persons and
must be balanced against comparable rights and
interests of other persons. In the case of medical
research the contrast is not between vulnerable individuals on the one hand and an abstract entity such as
"society" on the other, but rather between two different groups of vulnerable individuals. The rights and
interests of research subjects are surely not served by
privileging them at the expense of the rights and
interests of those who will benefit from research.
Both these groups are potentially vulnerable, neither
is obviously prima facie more vulnerable or deserving of special protection.

It is important to emphasise that the point here
is not that there is some general incoherence in the
idea of sometimes privileging the rights and interests of particularly vulnerable groups in order to
guarantee to them the equal protection that they
need and to which they are entitled. Rather I am
suggesting two things. The first is that all people
have equal rights and entitlement to equal consideration of interests. The second is that any derogation from a principle as fundamental as that of
equality must be justified by especially powerful
considerations.

Finally, although what is or is not in someone's
interests is an objective matter about which the subject her (or him) self may be mistaken, it is usually
the best policy to let people define and determine

"their own interests". While it is if course possible that people will misunderstand their own interests and even act against them, it is surely more likely that people will understand their own interests best. It is also more respectful of research subjects for us to assume that this is the case unless there are powerful reasons for not so doing – for example, in cases of research on young children, mental patients, and others whom it is reasonable to assume may not be adequately competent.

Is There an Enforceable Obligation to Participate in Research?

It is widely recognised that there is clearly sometimes an obligation to make sacrifices for the community or an entitlement of the community to go so far as to deny autonomy and even violate bodily integrity in the public interest and this obligation is recognised in a number of ways.[23]

There are a perhaps surprisingly large number of cases where we accept substantial degrees of compulsion or coercion in the interests of those coerced and in the public interest. Numerous examples can be given: limiting access to dangerous or addictive drugs or substances; control of road traffic, including compulsory wearing of car seat belts; vaccination as a requirement – for example, for school attendance or travel; screening or diagnostic tests for pregnant mothers or for newborns; genetic profiling for those suspected of crimes; quarantine for some serious communicable diseases; compulsory military service; detention under mental health acts; safety guidelines for certain professional activities of HIV positive people, and compulsory attendance for jury service at criminal trials. Some societies make voting compulsory, taxation is omnipresent, universal education for children, requiring as it does compulsory attendance in school, is another obvious example. All these involve some denial of autonomy, some imposition of public standards even where compliance is not based on the competent consent of individuals. These are, however, clearly exceptional cases where overriding moral considerations take precedence over autonomy. Might medical research be another such case?

Mandatory Contribution to Public Goods

The examples cited above demonstrate a wide range of what we might term "mandatory contribution to public goods".[v] I will take one of these as a model for how we might think about participation in science research. (For use of this principle in a different context see my paper, "Organ procurement – dead interests, living needs".[24] Taxation is of course the clearest and commonest example.)

All British citizens between 18 and 70[vi] are liable for jury service.

They may be called, and unless excused by the court, must serve. This may involve a minimum of 10 days but sometimes months of daily confinement in a jury box or room, whether they consent or not. However, although all are liable for service only some are actually called. If someone is called and fails to appear they may be fined. Most people will never be called but some must be if the system of justice is not to break down. Participation in, or facilitation of, this public good is mandatory. There are many senses in which participation in vaccine or drug trials involve features relevantly analogous to jury service. Both involve inconvenience and the giving up of certain amounts of time. Both are important public goods. It is this latter feature that is particularly important. Although jury service (or compulsory attendance as a witness) is an integral part of "due process", helping to safeguard the liberty and rights of citizens, the same is also true of science research. Disease and infirmity have profound effects on liberty and while putting life threatening criminals out of circulation or protecting the innocent from wrongful imprisonment is a minor (numerically speaking) product of due process, life saving is a major product of science research. If compulsion is justifiable in the case of due process the same or indeed more powerful arguments would surely justify it in the case of science research.

Of course "compulsion" covers a wide range of possible measures. Compulsion may simply mean that something is legally required, without there being any legal penalties for non-compliance. Such legal requirement may of course also be supported by various penalties or incentives, from public disapproval and criticism, fines or loss of tax breaks on the one hand, to imprisonment or forcible attendance or participation further along the spectrum. To say that it would be legitimate to make science research compulsory is not to say that any particular methods of compulsion are necessarily justified or justifiable. While it seems clear that mandatory participation in important public goods is not only justifiable but also widely accepted as justifiable in most societies, as the examples above demonstrate, my own view is that voluntary means are always best and that any form of compulsion should be a last resort to be used only when consensual means had failed or where the need for a particular research activity was urgent and of overwhelming importance. If the arguments of this paper are persuasive, compulsion should not be necessary and we may expect a climate more receptive to both the needs and the benefits of science. However, to point out that compulsion may be justifiable in some circumstances in the case of science research establishes that a fortiori less stringent means are justifiable in those circumstances.

I hope it is clear that I am not here advocating mandatory participation in research, merely arguing that it is in principle justifiable, and may in certain circumstances become justified in fact. There is a difference between ethics and public policy. To say that something is ethical and therefore justifiable is not the same as either saying it is justified in any particular set of circumstances, nor is it to recommend it nor yet to propose it as a policy for either immediate nor yet for eventual implementation. I believe that consensual participation is always preferable and that persuasion by a combination of evidence and rational argument is always the most appropriate way of achieving social and moral goals. This paper is an attempt to do precisely this. I believe, for example, that conscription into the armed forces is justifiable, but I am not recommending, still less advocating its reintroduction into the UK at this time. The distinction between ethical argument and policy proposal is crucial but is almost always ignored, particularly by the press and news media that report on these matters. In this paper I am intending to do ethics; this is not a policy proposal although it contains one policy proposal, which we will come to in due course.

If I am right in thinking that medical research is a public good, that may *in extremis* justify compulsory participation, then a number of things may be said to follow:

- It should not simply be assumed that people would not wish to act in the public interest, at least where the costs and risks involved are minimal. In the absence of specific evidence to the contrary, if any assumptions are made, they should be that people are public spirited and would wish to participate. (I talk here of minimal risk in the sloppy fashion usual in such contexts. "Risk" is, however, ambiguous between "degree of danger" and "probability of occurrence of danger". Risk may of course be minimal in either or both of these senses.)

- It may be reasonable to presume that people would not consent (unless misinformed or coerced) to do things contrary to their own and to the public interest. The reverse is true when (as with vaccine trials) participation is in both personal and public interest.

- If it is right to claim that there is a general obligation to act in the public interest, then there is less reason to challenge consent and little reason to regard participation as actually or potentially exploitative. We do not usually say: "are you quite sure you want to" when people fulfil their moral and civic obligations. We do not usually insist on informed consent in such cases, we are usually content that they *merely* consent or simply acquiesce. When, for example, I am called for jury service no one says: "only attend if you fully understand the role of trial by jury, due process, etc in our constitution and the civil liberties that fair trials guarantee".

If these suggestions are broadly acceptable and an obligation to participate in research is established, this may well become one of the ways in which research comes to be funded in the future.

We must weigh carefully and compassionately what it is reasonable to put to potential participants in a trial for their free and unfettered consideration. Provided, however, potential research subjects are given full information, and are free to participate or not as they choose, then the only remaining question is whether it is reasonable to permit people freely to choose to participate, given the risks and the sorts of likely gains. Is it reasonable to ask people to run whatever degree of risk is involved, to put up with the inconvenience and intrusion of the study, and so on in all the circumstances of the case? These circumstances will include both the benefits to them personally of participating in the study and the benefits that will flow from the study to other persons, persons who are of course equally entitled to our concern, respect, and protection. (If they are.) Putting the question in this way makes it clear that the standards of care and levels of protection to be accorded to research subjects who have full information must be, to a certain extent, study relative.

It is crucial that the powerful moral reasons for conducting science research are not drowned by the powerful reasons we have for protecting research subjects. There is a balance to be struck here, but it is not a balance that must always and inevitably be loaded in favour of the protection of research subjects. They are entitled to our concern, respect, and protection to be sure, but they are no more entitled to it than are, say, the people whom, for example, HIV/AIDS or other major diseases are threatening and killing on a daily basis.[vii]

It is surely unethical to stand by and watch three million people die this year of AIDS[viii] alone and avoid taking steps to prevent this level of loss, steps, which will not put lives at risk and which are taken only with the fully informed consent of those who participate.

Fully informed consent is the best guarantor of the interests of research subjects. While not foolproof, residual dangers must be balanced against the dangers of not conducting the trial or the research, which include the massive loss of life that possibly preventable diseases cause. These residual dangers include the difficulties of constructing suitable consent protocols and supervising their administration in rural and isolated communities and in populations which may have low levels of formal education.

An interesting limiting case is that in which the risks to research subjects are significant and the burdens onerous but where the benefits to other people are equally significant and large. In such a case the research is both urgent and moral but conscription would almost certainly not be appropriate because of the unfairness of conscripting any particular individual to bear such burdens in the public interest. That is not of course to say that individuals should not be willing to bear such burdens nor is it to say that it is not their moral duty so to do. In fact the history of science research is full of examples of people willing to bear significant risks in such circumstances, very often these have been the researchers themselves. (For one prominent example, that of Barry Marshall's work, in which he swallowed Heliobacter pylori bacteria, thereby poisoning himself, to test a bacterial explanation for peptic ulcers.[26])

Benefit Sharing

I have so far said nothing about the public/private divide in research funding and about the fact that much of the research we have referred to has been carried out in the private sector for profit. This has inevitably led both to a concentration on what the comedian Tom Lehrer memorably called "diseases of the rich" and on diseases and conditions where, for whatever reason, a maximum return on investment is to be expected. In this paper there is room simply to note that the duty to participate in research is not a duty to enable industry to profit from moral commitment or basic decency, and that fairness and benefit sharing as well as the widest and fairest possible availability of the products of research is, as we have seen, an essential part of the moral force of the arguments for the obligation to pursue research. Benefit sharing must therefore be part of any mechanisms for implementing the arguments of this paper.

A New Principle of Research Ethics

A new principle of research ethics suggests itself as an appropriate addition to the *Declaration of Helsinki*:

> Biomedical research involving human subjects cannot legitimately be neglected, and is therefore both permissible and mandatory, where the importance of the objective is great and the risks to and the possibility of exploitation of fully informed and consenting subjects is small.

For an earlier version of this principle applied in the context of genetics see my paper, "Ethical genetic research on human subjects".[3]

Thus while fully informed consent and the continuing provision to research subjects of relevant information does not eliminate all possibility of exploitation, it does reduce it to the point at which it could no longer be ethical to neglect the claims and the interests of those who may benefit from the research. It should be noted that it is fully informed consent, and the concern and respect for the individual that it signals, which severs all connection with the Nazi experiments and the concerns of Nuremberg, and which rebuts spurious comparisons with the Tuskegee study. It is this recognition of the obligation to show equal concern and respect for all persons, which is the defining characteristic of justice.[27] The recognition that the obligation to do justice applies not only to research subjects but also to those who will benefit from the research must constitute an advance in thinking about international standards of research ethics.

On Whom Does the Obligation to Participate in Research Fall?

The Declaration of Helsinki (paragraph 19) states:

> Medical research is only justified if there is a reasonable likelihood that the populations in which the research is carried out stand to benefit from the results of the research. (WMA,[7] para 19)

Me and My Kind

It is sometimes claimed that where consent is problematic or, as perhaps with genetic research on archival material, where the sources of the material are either dead or cannot be traced, that research may be legitimate if it is for the benefit of the health needs of the subjects or of people with similar or related disorders. See, for example, the CIOMS guidelines (CIOMS,[8] guideline 6: p 22). The suggestion that research which is not directly beneficial to the patient be confined to research that will benefit the category of patients to

which the subject belongs seems not only untenable but also offensive. What arguments sustain the idea that the most appropriate reference group is that of fellow sufferers from a particular disease, Alzheimer's, for example? Surely any moral obligation I have to accept risk or harm for the benefit of others is not plausibly confined to those others who are narrowly like me. This is surely close to claiming that research should be confined to others who are "black like me" or "English like me" or "God fearing like me"? The most appropriate category is surely "a person like me". (I make a distinction between humans and persons which is not particularly pertinent in this context but which explains my choice of terminology.[28, 29])

Children and the Incompetent

What, however, about children?[1] Do they have an obligation to participate in research and if they have, is a parent justified in taking it into account in making decisions for the child?

If children are moral agents, and most of them, except very young infants are, then they have both obligations and rights; and it will be difficult to find any obligations that are more basic than the obligation to help others in need. There is therefore little doubt that children share the obligation argued for in this paper, to participate in medical research. A parent or guardian is accordingly obliged to take this obligation into account when deciding on behalf of her child and is justified in assuming that the person they are making decisions for is or would wish to be, a moral person who wants to or is in any event obliged to discharge his or her moral duties. If anything is presumed about what children would have wished to do in such circumstances the presumption should surely be that they would have wished to behave decently and would not have wished to be free riders. If we simply consult their best interests (absent the possibility of a valid consent) then again, as this paper has shown, participation in research is, other things being equal, in their best interests. Because of the primacy of autonomy in the structure of this argument we should, however, be cautious about enrolling those who cannot consent in research and should never force resisting incompetent individuals to participate. It also follows from principles of justice and fairness that those who are not competent to consent should not be exploited as prime candidates for research. We should always therefore prefer autonomous candidates and only use those who cannot consent when such individuals are essential for the particular research contemplated and where competent individuals cannot, because of the nature of the research, be used – for example, because the research is into an illness which only affects children or those with a particular condition which affects competence. In those extreme cases in which we might contemplate mandatory participation the same will hold. The incompetent should only be used where competent individuals cannot be research subjects because of the nature of the research itself.

Inducements to Participate in Research

Before concluding, a word needs to be said about inducements to research. Most research ethics protocols and guidelines are antipathetic to inducements. The CIOMS guidelines – for example, state that if inducements to subjects are offered "[t]he payments should not be so large, however, or the medical services so extensive as to induce prospective subjects to consent to participate in the research against their better judgment (undue inducement)" (CIOMS,[8] guideline 7).

However, the gloss the CIOMS document offers on this guideline is perhaps confused. It states: "Someone without access to medical care may or may not be unduly influenced to participate in research simply to receive such care" (CIOMS,[8] pp 28ff). The nub of the problem is the question what is it that makes inducement *undue*? If inducement is undue when it undermines "better judgment", then it cannot simply be the level of the inducement nor the fact that it is the inducement that makes the difference between participation and non-participation that undermines better judgment. If this were so, all jobs with attractive remuneration packages would constitute "undue" interference with the liberties of subjects and anyone who used their better judgment to decide whether a total remuneration package plus job was attractive would have been unduly influenced.[ix]

Surely, it is only if things are very different that influence becomes undue. If, for example, it were true that no sane person would participate in the study and only incentives would induce them to disregard "better judgment" or "rationality", or if the study were somehow immoral, or participation was grossly undignified and so on, would there be a legitimate presumption of undue influence.

Grant a number of assumptions: that research is well founded scientifically; that it has important objectives which will advance knowledge; that the subjects are at minimal risk, and that the inconvenience and so on, of participation is not onerous. Then surely it is not only in everyone's best interests that *some* people participate but also in the interests of those who do. *Better judgment* surely will not indicate that any particular person should not participate. Of course someone consulting personal interest and convenience might not participate: "it's too much trouble, not worth the effort, rather inconvenient" and so on. However, removing the force of *these sorts of objections* with incentives is not undermining *better judgment* any more than is making employment attractive.[30-32]

Of course inducements may be undue in a different sense. If, for example, a research subject were a drug addict and she were to be offered the drug of her choice to participate, or subjects were blackmailed into participating in research, then in such cases we might regard the inducements as undue. It is important, however, to note that here the influence or inducement is undue, not because it is improper to offer incentives to participate, nor because participation is against the best interests of the subject, nor because the inducements are coercive in the sense that they are irresistible, but rather because the *type of incentive* offered is illegitimate or against the public interest or immoral in itself.

If I offer you a million dollars to do something involving minimal risk and inconvenience, something that is good in itself, is in your interests, and will benefit mankind, my offer may be irresistible but it will not be coercive. If, however, I threaten you with torture unless you do the same thing, my act will be coercive even if you were going to do it whether or not I threatened you. I should be punished for my threat or blackmail or criminal offer of illegal substances, but surely you should none the less do the deed and your freedom to do it should not be curtailed because of my wrongdoing in attempting to force your hand in a particular way. The wrong is not that I attempted to force your hand but resides rather in the wrongness of the methods that I chose. This is the distinction between undue inducement and inducements which are undue. "Undue inducement" is the improper offering of inducements, improper because no inducements should be offered. It is this that it referred to in the various international protocols we have been examining and which is almost always wrongly understood and applied. "Inducements which are undue", refer to the nature of the inducement, not to the fact of it being offered at all. This is an important but much neglected distinction. Here it is the nature of the inducement that is undue rather than the fact of inducements of some sorts (even irresistible sorts) being offered.

We can see that offering incentives, perhaps in the form of direct payment or tax concessions to people to participate in research, or, for example, to make archive samples available for research would not be unethical. We tend to forget that law and morality are methods of encouraging and indeed enforcing morality. Approval and inducements are others. All are acceptable if the conduct they promote is ethical and worthwhile. Where science research is both of these, encouragement and, as we have seen, enforcement are justifiable.

Conclusion

There is then a moral obligation to participate in medical research in certain contexts.[x]

This will obviously include minimally invasive and minimally risky procedures such as participation in biobanks, provided safeguards against wrongful use are in place. The argument concerning the obligation to participate in research should be compelling for anyone who believes there is a moral obligation to help others, and/or a moral obligation to be just and do one's share. Little can be said to those whose morality is so impoverished that they do not accept either of these two obligations.

Furthermore we are justified in assuming that a person would want to discharge his or her moral obligations in cases where we have no knowledge about their actual preferences. This is a way of recognising them as moral agents. To do otherwise would be to impute moral turpitude as a default. Parents making decisions for their children are therefore fully justified in assuming that their child will wish to do that which is right, and not do that which is wrong.

Acknowledgement

The author acknowledges the stimulus and support of the European Project (EU-RECA) sponsored by the European Commission, in the preparation of this paper. (DG-Research as part of the Science and Society research programme – 6th framework.)

Notes

i   In this paper I use arguments developed for a paper I wrote with my colleague Søren Holm. See our paper "Should we presume moral turpitude in our children?";[1] my chapter "Research on human subjects, exploitation and global principles of ethics"; and my paper "Ethical genetic research".[3] Recently these themes have been taken up by Martyn Evans. See his paper "Should patients be allowed to veto their participation in clinical research,"[4]

ii Here the argument is restricted to research projects that are not merely aimed at producing knowledge. Unless an increase in knowledge is a good in itself (a question I will not discuss here) some realistic hope of concrete benefits to persons in the future is necessary for the validity of our arguments.

iii It is perhaps also worth pointing out that there is a separate question about whether this moral obligation should be enforced on those who do not discharge it voluntarily. This is not a question I will discuss here.

iv I owe this formulation of the interest I have in being a moral agent to Søren Holm.

v   I use this term in a non-technical sense.

vi Those over 65 may be excused if they wish.

vii Of course the historical explanation of the *Declaration of Helsinki* and its concerns lies in the Nuremberg trials and the legacy of Nazi atrocities. We are, however, I believe, in real danger of allowing fear of repeating one set of atrocities to lead us into committing other new atrocities.

viii Figures are for 2003, with an estimated five million people newly acquiring HIV in that same year.[25]

ix The CIOMS gloss on their own guidelines creates a kind of Catch 22 which is surely unreasonable and unwarranted. Wherever the best proven diagnostic and therapeutic methods are guaranteed by a study in a context or for a population who would not normally expect to receive them, this guideline would be broken. The CIOMS guideline four therefore surely contradicts and violates not only the *Declaration of Helsinki* but also its own later guideline 14.

x This obligation has been partly endorsed by the Hugo Ethics Committee in its *Statement on Human Genomic databases*.[33] However, like so many statements by august ethics committees the Hugo statement contains not a single argument to sustain its proposals or conclusions. This paper and those referred to in references 1, 2, 3, and 4 provide the missing arguments. For a critique of the operation of national and international ethics committees see the introduction to my book, *Bioethics*.[34]

References

1 Harris J, Holm S. Should we presume moral turpitude in our children? Small children and consent to medical research. *Theor Med* 2003;24:121–9.

2 Harris J. Research on human subjects, exploitation and global principles of ethics. In: Lewis ADE, Freeman M, eds. *Current legal issue 3: law and medicine*. Oxford: Oxford University Press, 2000:379–99.

3 Harris J. Ethical genetic research. *Jurimetrics* 1999; 40:77–93.

4 Evans HM. Should patients be allowed to veto their participation in clinical research? *J Med Ethics* 2004;30:198–203.

5 Williams C, Kitzinger J, Henderson L. Envisaging the embryo in stem cell research: rhetorical strategies and media reporting of the ethical debates. *Sociol Health Illn* 2003;5:783–814.

6 Harris J, Holm S. Extended lifespan and the paradox of precaution. *J Med Philos* 2002;27:355–68.

7 World Medical Association. *Declaration of Helsinki*. Adopted by the 52nd General Assembly, Edinburgh, Scotland Oct 2000: note of clarification of para 29 added by the WMA General Assembly, Washington, 2002.

8 Council for International Organisations of Medical Sciences (CIOMS). *Guidelines*. Geneva: CIOMS, 2002.

9 Caplan AL, ed. *When medicine went mad*. Totowa: Hu mana Press, 1992.

10 Glover J. *Humanity: a moral history of the twentieth century*. London: Jonathan Cape, 1999, part 6.

11 Angell M. The ethics of clinical research in the Third World. *N Engl J Med* 1997;337:847.

12 Anon. Twenty years after: the legacy of the Tuskegee syphilis study. *Hastings Cent Rep* 1992;22:29–40.

13 *The Royal Liverpool Children's Inquiry Report*. London: The Stationery Office, London, 2001.

14 Harris J. Law and regulation of retained organs: the ethical issues. *Legal Studies* 2002;22:527–49.

15 Harris J. *Violence and responsibility*. London: Routledge & Kegan Paul, 1980.

16 Barry B. *Justice as impartiality*. Oxford: Clarendon Press, 1995:228.

17 Jonas H. Philosophical reflections on experimenting with human subjects. In: Freund PA, ed. *Experimentation with human subjects*. London: Allen and Unwin, 1972.

18 Hart HLA. Are there any natural rights? *Oxford Review No 4*, 1967;Feb.

19 Rawls J. *A theory of justice*. Cambridge: Harvard University Press, 1972.

20 Nozick R. *Anarchy, state and Utopia*. Oxford: Basil Blackwell, 1974:90.

21 Harris J. The ethics of clinical research with cognitively impaired subjects. *Ital J Neurol Sci* 1997;18:9–15.

22 Harris J, Holm S. Why should doctors take risks? Professional responsibility and the assumption of risk. *J R Soc Med* 1997;90:625–9.

23 Harris J. Ethical issues in geriatric medicine. In: Tallis RC, Fillett HM, eds. *Textbook of geriatric medicine and gerontology* [6th ed]. London: Churchill Livingstone, 2002.

24 Harris J. Organ procurement – dead interests, living needs. *J Med Ethics* 2003;29:130–5.

25 Joint United Nations Programme on HIV/AIDS. http://www.cdc.gov/hiv/stats.htm (accessed 3 Apr 2004).

26 Marshall B. [See now http://www.nobelprize.org/nobel_prizes/medicine/laureates/2005/marshall-bio.html.]

27 Dworkin R. *Taking rights seriously*. London: Duckworth, 1977.

28 Harris J. *The value of life*. London: Routledge and Kegan Paul, 1985, ch 1.

29 Harris J. The concept of the person and the value of life. *Kennedy Inst Ethics J* 1999;9:293–308.

30 Wilkinson M, Moore A. Inducements Revisited. *Bioethics* 1997;11:114–130.

31 McNeill P. Paying people to participate in research: why not? *Bioethics* 1997;11:390–7.

32 Harris J. *Wonderwoman and Superman: the ethics of human biotechnology.* Oxford: Oxford University Press, 1992, ch 6.

33 Hugo Ethics Committee. *Statement on human genomic databases,* http://www.hugo-international.org/img/genomic_2002.pdf.

34 Harris J, ed. *Bioethics: Oxford readings in philosophy series.* Oxford: Oxford University Press, 2001:1–25.

54

Participation in Biomedical Research Is an Imperfect Moral Duty

A Response to John Harris

Sandra Shapshay and Kenneth D. Pimple

In his paper "Scientific research is a moral duty" [chapter 53 in this volume], John Harris[1] intends to encourage individuals to volunteer as subjects in biomedical research by arguing that supporting biomedical research is a moral obligation, both for individuals and society. Although we agree that biomedical research is an important social good, we find Harris's arguments for the thesis that individuals have a moral duty to participate in serious scientific research to be unconvincing.

Most of Harris's arguments concern the moral duty of individuals, on which we will focus our attention. In our view, the moral duty of a society to support biomedical research is better approached separately.

The bulk of this paper will concern Harris's substantive arguments in making his case that those of us who have benefited from modern medical science – virtually all of us living in industrialised nations – have a moral obligation to volunteer as research subjects, but first we wish to touch briefly on his rhetorical strategy.

In our judgement, Harris makes a serious rhetorical mistake by engaging in hyperbole. For example,

Harris cites paragraph A.5 of the World Medical Association's *Ethical principles for medical research involving human subjects*,[2] commonly referred to as the Declaration of Helsinki.

> In medical research on human subjects, considerations related to the well-being of the human subject should take precedence over the interests of science and society.

According to Harris, "this paragraph is widely cited in support of restrictions on scientific research and is interpreted as requiring that all human subject research is in the narrowly conceived interests of the research subjects themselves. This article of faith has become almost unchallengeable" (p 243).

Unfortunately, Harris does not offer a single citation to support this claim. We know of no instance in which this paragraph has been so narrowly construed, and we suggest that such a construal conflates research with therapy, which is obviously contrary to the purpose of the Declaration. Indeed, Harris's later interpretation of this paragraph accords closely with our own, and, in our belief, with the majority opinion:

Original publication details: Sandra Shapshay and Kenneth D. Pimple, "Participation in Research Is an Imperfect Moral Duty: A Response to John Harris," pp. 414–17 from *Journal of Medical Ethics* 33 (2007). Reproduced with permission from BMJ Publishing Group.

"To say that the interests of the subject must take precedence over those of others ... must be understood as a way of reasserting that a researcher's narrowly conceived professional interest must not have primacy over the human rights of research subjects" (p 244).

Harris also hyperbolises in his first sentence, stating: "Science is under attack", and admonishes us to remember "the powerful moral obligation there is to undertake, support, and participate in scientific research, particularly biomedical research, and the powerful moral imperative that underpins these obligations" (p 242). But by the end of his article, he qualifies the moral duty to participate in biomedical research nearly out of existence.

Here, our aim is to show that Harris's arguments succeed only in showing that such participation and support is one moral good among many, but that there is no moral duty to support and/or participate in biomedical research per se, except, perhaps, in rare emergency situations. We will show this by focusing on the two major ethical principles that Harris employs: the principles of beneficence and fairness. We will detail why each ethical principle yields only a weaker discretionary obligation to help others in need and to reciprocate for sacrifices that others have made for the public good.

The Principle of Beneficence

Harris claims polemically that "the overwhelming presumption has been and remains that participation in research is a supererogatory, and probably a reckless, act, not an obligation" (p 242). This presumption should be abandoned, he argues, based on the "rule of rescue":

> Where our actions will, or may probably prevent serious harm then if we can reasonably (given the balance of risk and burden to ourselves and benefit to others) we clearly should act because to fail to do so is to accept responsibility for the harm that then occurs. (p 242)

He calls this rule "the stronger side" of the principle of beneficence, the duty to help others in need.[i]

On this basis of the rule of rescue, Harris argues that if our actions can prevent some harm, and we can reasonably perform those actions, then we ought so to act. This understanding of the principle is reminiscent of Singer's[3] famous statement: "If it is in our power to prevent something bad from happening, without thereby sacrificing anything of comparable moral importance, we ought, morally, to do it." Singer supports this obligation through the pond case: Imagine you are the only adult in view when you see a toddler drowning in a shallow pond. Clearly, you should rescue the child even if your clothes will be drenched.

However, the rule of rescue in the case of biomedical research would have to be derived from a rather different case: 50 agents surround the pond and 20 toddlers are in distress: one child is drowning, another is lost, a third is being attacked by a dog, etc, and neither you nor any of the other agents is uniquely situated to help any particular child. In this more analogous case, it would be strange to argue that every agent is obliged to save the drowning child, especially at the cost of the other 19 children. Clearly, each agent may justifiably choose which child to help.[ii]

Harris's application of the rule of rescue can be schematised as follows:

1. If our actions can prevent serious harm, and we can reasonably perform those actions, then we ought to act so.
2. Many diseases cause serious harm.
3. Medical research is a necessary component of preventing or relieving those harms.
4. Therefore, if we can take reasonable steps to further medical research (by volunteering as a research participant), we have an obligation to do so.

We accept premises 2 and 3 as true statements. However, premise 1 requires further specification: we should determine whether our moral duty to prevent serious harm when we reasonably can means that we have a duty

a. to prevent any and all serious harm whenever we reasonably can; or
b. to prevent only the most serious harm when we reasonably can; or
c. to prevent some subset of serious harm of our own choice when we reasonably can.

It seems that in order for Harris's argument to be valid, he must call on (a), the most general and stringent formulation. If our duty were only to prevent (b) the most serious harm, or if our duty were to prevent (c) some subset of serious harm of our own choice, it is not clear why the serious harms caused by disease in particular should necessarily entail a claim on us for our help. With the less general formulations of the rule of rescue, one might justifiably decide to prevent other forms of serious harm, say, political persecution, or illiteracy. It is only if we are duty-bound to prevent any and all serious harms when we reasonably can that we are obliged to prevent disease in particular. Without the most general formulation, we would be quite justified in working to prevent harm to at-risk youth instead of participating in biomedical research, even if we were reasonably capable of so participating.

But the most general formulation of the rule of rescue, "that we ought to prevent any and all serious harm, when we reasonably can", is implausible largely because it is over-demanding. Otherwise put, this form of the rule of rescue amounts to the act utilitarian injunction, always to act so as to minimise harm or bad states of affairs (the negative construal of the principle of utility). Bernard Williams[4] has forcefully criticised act utilitarianism on the grounds that it "makes integrity as a value more or less unintelligible" because it enjoins the agent to factor his or her own deepest commitments and projects in life equally alongside all the other factors in the utility calculus. As there are, as a matter of fact, so many opportunities to minimise harm, one is duty-bound to devote most of one's time and resources to preventing poverty, hunger, war and any number of other serious harms, rather than to other less useful projects.

A person who consistently acts on this formulation of the rule of rescue would become nothing more than "a channel between the input of everyone's projects, including his own, and an output of optimific decision". This principle thus reduces him to a harm-minimising conduit and destroys his personal integrity – the union of his actions with his own deepest convictions and projects in life. With Williams,[4] we argue, the most general formulation of the rule of rescue is profoundly alienating.

It might be argued that the qualifier "when we reasonably can" salvages individual integrity; it can hardly be considered "reasonable" to expect everyone to abandon all of their personal goals to minimise all serious harm. If this is what Harris intends, however, he is in fact endorsing a weaker formulation of the principle of beneficence, (c) above: where we reasonably can, we ought to prevent some subset of serious harm, of our own choice. If we do adopt this weaker formulation, we are left without a duty to participate in biomedical research per se. Rather, we are left with an imperfect duty to choose from all possible harms those which we will strive to prevent.

A Kantian imperfect duty is a duty to adopt certain ends – one's own perfection and the happiness of others. Accordingly, one may not totally neglect the happiness of others or the perfection of oneself, but one has a good deal of latitude in what one does to achieve these ends. According to Kant scholar Thomas Hill,

> imperfect duties allow us to do what we please on some occasions … [f]or example, though we have an imperfect duty of beneficence we may sometimes pass over an opportunity to make others happy simply because we would rather do something else.[5]

Despite some controversy concerning just how much latitude Kantian imperfect duties allow,[6] on reading (c) of Harris's principle, one may surely discharge one's imperfect obligation to prevent harm to others by volunteering at an animal shelter, or by donating money to Oxfam, or by participating in medical research – but one cannot be said to have a duty to do the latter, in particular.

Perhaps Harris's argument could be saved by use of version (b) of the rule of rescue – namely, "we have an obligation to prevent the most serious harm, when we reasonably can." By this formulation, one would be obliged to address only the most serious harms one reasonably could. Surely, the most significant harms facing people in the world today are not those which must be addressed through biomedical research. Citing statistics from the United Nations Development Report of 2002, Thomas Pogge[7] writes,

> poverty is far and away the most important factor in explaining health deficits. Because they are poor, 815 million persons are malnourished, 1.1 billion lack access to safe water, 2.4 billion lack access to basic sanitation, more than 880 million lack access to health services, and approximately 1 billion have no adequate shelter.

This staggering amount of suffering is due to preventable poverty, not due to disease.

Furthermore, Pogge argues that much poverty is due to global institutions (lending and trade practices) that exploit poor nations. Citizens of democratic, industrialised nations are thus materially implicated in the poverty-related harms caused in part by global institutions. It stands to reason that we have much more of an obligation to rectify the injustice that our own democratically elected governments have caused than to try to alleviate disease-related suffering in which we are not materially implicated. If we accept formulation (b) of the rule of rescue, we ought rather to work to change unjust institutions that foster poverty rather than participate in biomedical research.

We have analysed the rule of rescue following Harris's lead, but a similar analysis could be done along any of a number of dimensions:

- Are we obliged to rescue only persons in our own household, or those in our physical presence, or those we know to exist, or any potential persons (those untold billions not yet born)?
- Are we obliged to prevent only obvious and imminent harms, or likely harms, or potential but unlikely harms?
- Are we required to take action only if it will assure the prevention of harm, or if it is likely to prevent harm, or if it might possibly prevent harm?

We believe that the conclusion would be the same no matter which of these dimensions were pursued: the more extreme and stringent a formulation, the less reasonable it is to construe it as a perfect moral obligation.

Essentially, the main problem with Harris's overall argument so far is that he sets up a false dilemma: either participation in research is supererogatory or it is a positive and perfect moral obligation. However, there is a third possibility: The rule of rescue may constitute an "imperfect obligation", meaning that we must make others' happiness our end, and act in good faith to help some others some of the time, but we may justifiably use our own discretion as to whom, how and how much to help.[iii] Thus, we can say that participation in research per se is not morally obligatory, but neither is it supererogatory; it is one

way in which people may choose to discharge their imperfect obligation to help others.

The Principle of Fairness

The second principle which Harris invokes to show that we have a positive moral obligation to support/participate in biomedical research, is the principle of fairness developed by H L A Hart[8] and John Rawls[9]. As Harris puts it, as all of us (at least all members of industrialised countries[iv]) benefit from the existence of medical research, and we all accept these benefits (eg, through vaccines, public sanitation, personal medical services, etc), "we have an obligation in justice to contribute to the social practice which produces them."[1] In other words, if one accepts the benefits of biomedical research, then one ought to support the endeavour which makes those benefits possible in the first place; otherwise one would be acting unfairly as a "free rider".

Although this line of argument is far more promising than the previous one, it does not stand up to close scrutiny. Let us begin with a literal free-rider scenario. For the sake of argument, assume that the Berlin S-Bahn system runs more efficiently when all riders pay for and stamp their own tickets, with minimal enforcement. On the basis of this added efficiency, every resident of Berlin enjoys more generous public services. Hans, who is wealthy, decides that he will derive maximal personal benefit if he does not pay to ride – he enjoys all of the advantages of others' cooperation, but does not pay the price. Clearly Hans's action is unfair, and he has a perfect duty not to act unfairly in this way.

Harris implicitly draws a parallel between the classic free rider and the individual who benefits from but who does not personally participate in biomedical research. But there are two significant differences between these situations. The first difference concerns one's freedom to choose to use the benefit. In the case of Hans, he is certainly free not to ride the S-Bahn if he does not want to pay. He could walk or bike instead. But the beneficiary of biomedical research is not similarly free not to enjoy the fruits of the research. In our modern industrialised societies, as a child one does not choose to be immunised or brought up with modern sanitation. An adult could certainly decline further enjoyment of such benefits, but, as the benefits of biomedical research are ubiquitous in modern society, this would require one to move to the wilderness or what's left of it.

This disanalogy is morally significant because, if one does not truly choose to accept the benefits of such research, it is hard to see how one is thereby responsible for supporting the institutions that bestow those benefits, whereas Hans, our free rider, must explicitly choose to ride the S-Bahn and is thus responsible for playing fair by paying the fare.

Furthermore, the people who are harmed by Hans's free riding are the same people who would benefit from his cooperation. This is not likely to be the case with participation in medical research, where, due to the lag between trials and interventions, one generally benefits from past participation and is likely to benefit those in the future, not present participants in research.[v] Even if I owe a duty of reciprocity to those living people who participated in medical research, or to the descendants of those who participated in the past, if I have benefited from vaccinations, am I obliged to participate in vaccination research? What about mental health research? The list can be extended indefinitely. As in the case of beneficence, the more comprehensively a moral duty is construed, the less credible it is.

To the extent that we are obliged to discharge our debts for benefits "in kind", we can find ourselves with directly conflicting moral obligations. If not for the service of Allied military men and women, we would be living under a Nazi dictatorship; therefore, we have a moral obligation to enlist in the military. But if not for the sacrifices of conscientious objectors and war protesters, governments would be less constrained in choosing when to go to war; therefore, we should resist military operations.

There are many ways in which we ought to refrain from "free riding", but we cannot reasonably be expected to do them all. Harris might reply that those who have many other obligations imposed on them by the principle of fairness can only reasonably be expected to reciprocate – namely, biomedical research when it is easy for them to do so. He cites two examples of obligatory

participation in biomedical research when doing so seems not to be in one's best interest, narrowly construed:

> If I am asked to give a blood sample for a worthwhile research project, or if I am asked if tissue removed during an operation may be retained for research or therapeutic use [I should accede].[1]

This is what the duty to participate in biomedical research boils down to for Harris: when participation requires nothing more than a minor inconvenience, you should. We find it difficult to disagree with this extraordinarily modest conclusion, which is akin to asserting that telling the truth is a moral duty as long as it is convenient to do so.

But at this point, Harris implicitly concedes that the obligation to participate in biomedical research is only part of a discretionary duty to help others. In the cases Harris mentions, the demands are quite trivial. Insofar as the demand of participating is greater, in terms of time, hardship or risk, a person is justified in spending his or her time, money and effort in discharging her imperfect obligations in another way.

Conclusions

We have argued, contra Harris, that any duty to participate in biomedical research must be understood as part of a more general imperfect duty to promote the welfare of others. Any candid attempt to persuade people to volunteer as research participants should acknowledge this, emphasising that such participation helps to sustain a moral good.

While Harris does not succeed in proving the point he set out to prove, his line of reasoning supports what we believe is an important conclusion: we have a general obligation to support just institutions insofar as we benefit from them. The principle of fairness better supports a societal obligation to promote research in a way that protects subjects and distributes the fruits of research fairly. But, as individuals faced with multiple worthy collective enterprises, and finite lives, we must each decide how to discharge our duty to do our fair share, rather than being browbeaten into choosing one tactic over another.

Acknowledgments

We acknowledge the support of Indiana University, the Poynter Center for the Study of Ethics and American Institutions and the Indiana University Center for Bioethics. We would also like to thank an anonymous reader for the *Journal of Medical Ethics* for constructive criticism.

Notes

i   This section of Harris's article is confused. It is headed "Do no harm" and cites "the duty not to harm others", which we would call "non-maleficence". We agree that the obligation of non-maleficence is stronger than the obligation of beneficence, but the rule of rescue falls more happily under beneficence (which involves taking positive actions to do good) than non-maleficence (which involves avoiding or refraining from actions that cause harm).

ii   We are indebted to an anonymous reviewer for bringing this significant disanalogy to our attention.

iii   We are arguing that the rule of rescue may be seen as an imperfect duty when an agent is not uniquely situated to do the rescuing.

iv   Except, of course, in the US, where approximately 46 million people do not have reliable access to healthcare. By Harris's account, the principle of fairness would compel Britons more strongly than Americans to support biomedical research because in the US such research is not a truly public good.

v   We gained an appreciation of this salient point from an anonymous reviewer.

References

1   Harris J. Scientific research is a moral duty. *J Med Ethics* 2005;31:242–8.

2   World Medical Association. *Declaration of Helsinki: ethical principles for medical research involving human subjects*, 2004.

3   Singer P. Famine, affluence, and morality. *Philos Public Aff* 1972;1:229–43.

4   Williams B. A critique of utilitarianism. In: Smart JJC, Williams B, eds. *Utilitarianism, for and against.* Cambridge: Cambridge University Press, 1990:82–117.

5   Hill TE. *Dignity and practical reason in Kant's moral theory.* Ithaca: Cornell University Press, 1992.

6   Baron M. *Kantian ethics almost without apology.* Ithaca: Cornell University Press, 1995.

7   Pogge T. Responsibilities for poverty-related ill health. *Ethics Int Aff* 2002;16:71–9.

8   Hart HLA. Are there any natural rights? *Oxford Review* No. 4 1967.

9   Rawls J. *A theory of justice.* Cambridge: Harvard University Press, 1971.

55

Unethical Trials of Interventions to Reduce Perinatal Transmission of the Human Immunodeficiency Virus in Developing Countries

Peter Lurie and Sidney M. Wolfe

It has been almost three years since the Journal[1] published the results of AIDS Clinical Trials Group (ACTG) Study 076, the first randomized, controlled trial in which an intervention was proved to reduce the incidence of human immunodeficiency virus (HIV) infection. The antiretroviral drug zidovudine, administered orally to HIV-positive pregnant women in the United States and France, administered intravenously during labor, and subsequently administered to the newborn infants, reduced the incidence of HIV infection by two thirds.[2] The regimen can save the life of one of every seven infants born to HIV-infected women.

Because of these findings, the study was terminated at the first interim analysis and, within two months after the results had been announced, the Public Health Service had convened a meeting and concluded that the ACTG 076 regimen should be recommended for all HIV-positive pregnant women without substantial prior exposure to zidovudine and should be considered for other HIV-positive pregnant women on a case-by-case basis.[3] The standard of care for HIV-positive pregnant women thus became the ACTG 076 regimen.

In the United States, three recent studies of clinical practice report that the use of the ACTG 076 regimen is associated with decreases of 50 percent or more in perinatal HIV transmission.[4-6] But in developing countries, especially in Asia and sub-Saharan Africa, where it is projected that by the year 2000, 6 million pregnant women will be infected with HIV,[7] the potential of the ACTG 076 regimen remains unrealized primarily because of the drug's exorbitant cost in most countries.

Clearly, a regimen that is less expensive than ACTG 076 but as effective is desirable, in both developing and industrialized countries. But there has been uncertainty about what research design to use in the search for a less expensive regimen. In June 1994, the World Health Organization (WHO) convened a group in Geneva to assess the agenda for research on perinatal HIV transmission in the wake of ACTG 076.

Original publication details: Peter Lurie and Sidney M. Wolfe, "Unethical Trials of Interventions to Reduce Perinatal Transmission of the Human Immunodeficiency Virus in Developing Countries," pp. 853–6 from *New England Journal of Medicine* 337: 12 (September 1997). Copyright © 1997 Massachusetts Medical Society. Reprinted with permission from Massachusetts Medical Society.

The group, which included no ethicists, concluded, "Placebo-controlled trials offer the best option for a rapid and scientifically valid assessment of alternative antiretroviral drug regimens to prevent [perinatal] transmission of HIV."[8] This unpublished document has been widely cited as justification for subsequent trials in developing countries. In our view, most of these trials are unethical and will lead to hundreds of preventable HIV infections in infants.

Primarily on the basis of documents obtained from the Centers for Disease Control and Prevention (CDC), we have identified 18 randomized, controlled trials of interventions to prevent perinatal HIV transmission that either began to enroll patients after the ACTG 076 study was completed or have not yet begun to enroll patients. The studies are designed to evaluate a variety of interventions: antiretroviral drugs such as zidovudine (usually in regimens that are less expensive or complex than the ACTG 076 regimen), vitamin A and its derivatives, intrapartum vaginal washing, and HIV immune globulin, a form of immunotherapy. These trials involve a total of more than 17,000 women.

In the two studies being performed in the United States, the patients in all the study groups have unrestricted access to zidovudine or other antiretroviral drugs. In 15 of the 16 trials in developing countries, however, some or all of the patients are not provided with antiretroviral drugs. Nine of the 15 studies being conducted outside the United States are funded by the US government through the CDC or the National Institutes of Health (NIH), 5 are funded by other governments, and 1 is funded by the United Nations AIDS Program. The studies are being conducted in Côte d'Ivoire, Uganda, Tanzania, South Africa, Malawi, Thailand, Ethiopia, Burkina Faso, Zimbabwe, Kenya, and the Dominican Republic. These 15 studies clearly violate recent guidelines designed specifically to address ethical issues pertaining to studies in developing countries. According to these guidelines, "The ethical standards applied should be no less exacting than they would be in the case of research carried out in [the sponsoring] country."[9] In addition, US regulations governing studies performed with federal funds domestically or abroad specify that research procedures must "not unnecessarily expose subjects to risk."[10]

The 16th study is noteworthy both as a model of an ethically conducted study attempting to identify less expensive antiretroviral regimens and as an indication of how strong the placebo-controlled trial orthodoxy is. In 1994, Marc Lallemant, a researcher at the Harvard School of Public Health, applied for NIH funding for an equivalency study in Thailand in which three shorter zidovudine regimens were to be compared with a regimen similar to that used in the ACTG 076 study. An equivalency study is typically conducted when a particular regimen has already been proved effective and one is interested in determining whether a second regimen is about as effective but less toxic or expensive.[11] The NIH study section repeatedly put pressure on Lallemant and the Harvard School of Public Health to conduct a placebo-controlled trial instead, prompting the director of Harvard's human subjects committee to reply, "The conduct of a placebo-controlled trial for [zidovudine] in pregnant women in Thailand would be unethical and unacceptable, since an active-controlled trial is feasible."[12] The NIH eventually relented, and the study is now under way. Since the nine studies of antiretroviral drugs have attracted the most attention, we focus on them in this article.

Asking the Wrong Research Question

There are numerous areas of agreement between those conducting or defending these placebo-controlled studies in developing countries and those opposing such trials. The two sides agree that perinatal HIV transmission is a grave problem meriting concerted international attention; that the ACTG 076 trial was a major breakthrough in perinatal HIV prevention; that there is a role for research on this topic in developing countries; that identifying less expensive, similarly effective interventions would be of enormous benefit, given the limited resources for medical care in most developing countries; and that randomized studies can help identify such interventions.

The sole point of disagreement is the best comparison group to use in assessing the effectiveness of less-expensive interventions once an effective intervention has been identified. The researchers conducting the placebo-controlled trials assert that such trials represent the only appropriate research design, implying that they answer the question, "Is the shorter regimen better than nothing?" We take the more optimistic view that, given the findings of ACTG 076 and other clinical information, researchers are quite capable of designing a shorter antiretroviral regimen that is approximately as effective as the ACTG 076 regimen. The proposal for the Harvard study in Thailand states the research question clearly: "Can we reduce the duration of prophylactic [zidovudine] treatment without increasing the risk of perinatal transmission of HIV, that is, without compromising the demonstrated efficacy of the standard ACTG 076 [zidovudine] regimen?"[13] We believe that such equivalency studies of alternative antiretroviral regimens will provide even more useful results than placebo-controlled trials, without the deaths of hundreds of newborns that are inevitable if placebo groups are used.

At a recent congressional hearing on research ethics, NIH director Harold Varmus was asked how the Department of Health and Human Services could be funding both a placebo-controlled trial (through the CDC) and a non–placebo-controlled equivalency study (through the NIH) in Thailand. Dr. Varmus conceded that placebo-controlled studies are "not the only way to achieve results."[14] If the research can be satisfactorily conducted in more than one way, why not select the approach that minimizes loss of life?

Inadequate Analysis of Data from ACTG 076 and Other Sources

The NIH, CDC, WHO, and the researchers conducting the studies we consider unethical argue that differences in the duration and route of administration of antiretroviral agents in the shorter regimens, as compared with the ACTG 076 regimen, justify the use of a placebo group.[15-18] Given that ACTG 076 was a well-conducted, randomized, controlled trial, it is disturbing that the rich data available from the study were not adequately used by the group assembled by WHO in June 1994, which recommended placebo-controlled trials after ACTG 076, or by the investigators of the 15 studies we consider unethical.

In fact, the ACTG 076 investigators conducted a subgroup analysis to identify an appropriate period for prepartum administration of zidovudine. The approximate median duration of prepartum treatment was 12 weeks. In a comparison of treatment for 12 weeks or less (average, 7) with treatment for more than 12 weeks (average, 17), there was no univariate association between the duration of treatment and its effect in reducing perinatal HIV transmission (P = 0.99) (Gelber R: personal communication). This analysis is somewhat limited by the number of infected infants and its post hoc nature. However, when combined with information such as the fact that in non-breast-feeding populations an estimated 65 percent of cases of perinatal HIV infection are transmitted during delivery and 95 percent of the remaining cases are transmitted within two months of delivery,[19] the analysis suggests that the shorter regimens may be equally effective. This finding should have been explored in later studies by randomly assigning women to longer or shorter treatment regimens.

What about the argument that the use of the oral route for intrapartum administration of zidovudine in the present trials (as opposed to the intravenous route in ACTG 076) justifies the use of a placebo? In its protocols for its two studies in Thailand and Côte d'Ivoire, the CDC acknowledged that previous "pharmacokinetic modelling data suggest that [zidovudine] serum levels obtained with this [oral] dose will be similar to levels obtained with an intravenous infusion."[20]

Thus, on the basis of the ACTG 076 data, knowledge about the timing of perinatal transmission, and pharmacokinetic data, the researchers should have had every reason to believe that well-designed shorter regimens would be more effective than placebo. These findings seriously disturb the equipoise (uncertainty over the likely study result) necessary to justify a placebo-controlled trial on ethical grounds.[21]

Defining Placebo as the Standard of Care in Developing Countries

Some officials and researchers have defended the use of placebo-controlled studies in developing countries by arguing that the subjects are treated at least according to the standard of care in these countries, which consists of unproven regimens or no treatment at all. This assertion reveals a fundamental misunderstanding of the concept of the standard of care. In developing countries, the standard of care (in this case, not providing zidovudine to HIV-positive pregnant women) is not based on a consideration of alternative treatments or previous clinical data, but is instead an economically determined policy of governments that cannot afford the prices set by drug companies. We agree with the Council for International Organizations of Medical Sciences that researchers working in developing countries have an ethical responsibility to provide treatment that conforms to the standard of care in the sponsoring country, when possible.[9] An exception would be a standard of care that required an exorbitant expenditure, such as the cost of building a coronary care unit. Since zidovudine is usually made available free of charge by the manufacturer for use in clinical trials, excessive cost is not a factor in this case. Acceptance of a standard of care that does not conform to the standard in the sponsoring country results in a double standard in research. Such a double standard, which permits research designs that are unacceptable in the sponsoring country, creates an incentive to use as research subjects those with the least access to health care.

What are the potential implications of accepting such a double standard? Researchers might inject live malaria parasites into HIV-positive subjects in China in order to study the effect on the progression of HIV infection, even though the study protocol had been rejected in the United States and Mexico. Or researchers might randomly assign malnourished San (Bushmen) to receive vitamin-fortified or standard bread. One might also justify trials of HIV vaccines in which the subjects were not provided with condoms or state-of-the-art counseling about safe sex by arguing that they are not customarily provided in the developing countries in question. These are not simply hypothetical worst-case scenarios; the first two studies have already been performed,[22,23] and the third has been proposed and criticized.[24]

Annas and Grodin recently commented on the characterization and justification of placebos as a standard of care: " 'Nothing' is a description of what happens; 'standard of care' is a normative standard of effective medical treatment, whether or not it is provided to a particular community."[25]

Justifying Placebo-Controlled Trials by Claiming They Are More Rapid

Researchers have also sought to justify placebo-controlled trials by arguing that they require fewer subjects than equivalency studies and can therefore be completed more rapidly. Because equivalency studies are simply concerned with excluding alternative interventions that fall below some preestablished level of efficacy (as opposed to establishing which intervention is superior), it is customary to use one-sided statistical testing in such studies.[11] The numbers of women needed for a placebo-controlled trial and an equivalency study are similar.[26] In a placebo-controlled trial of a short course of zidovudine, with rates of perinatal HIV transmission of 25 percent in the placebo group and 15 percent in the zidovudine group, an alpha level of 0.05 (two-sided), and a beta level of 0.2, 500 subjects would be needed. An equivalency study with a transmission rate of 10 percent in the group receiving the ACTG 076 regimen, a difference in efficacy of 6 percent (above the 10 percent), an alpha level of 0.05 (one-sided), and a beta level of 0.2 would require 620 subjects (McCarthy W: personal communication).

Toward a Single International Standard of Ethical Research

Researchers assume greater ethical responsibilities when they enroll subjects in clinical studies, a precept acknowledged by Varmus recently when he insisted that all subjects in an NIH-sponsored needle-exchange trial be offered hepatitis B vaccine.[27] Residents of impoverished, postcolonial countries, the majority of whom are people of color, must be protected from potential exploitation in research. Otherwise, the abominable state of health care in these countries can be used to justify studies that could never pass ethical muster in the sponsoring country.

With the increasing globalization of trade, government research dollars becoming scarce, and more attention being paid to the hazards posed by "emerging infections" to the residents of industrialized countries, it is likely that studies in developing countries will increase. It is time to develop standards of research that preclude the kinds of double standards evident in these trials. In an editorial published nine years ago in the Journal, Marcia Angell stated, "Human subjects in any part of the world should be protected by an irreducible set of ethical standards."[28] Tragically, for the hundreds of infants who have needlessly contracted HIV infection in the perinatal-transmission studies that have already been completed, any such protection will have come too late.

References

1 Connor EM, Sperling RS, Gelber R, et al. Reduction of maternal–infant transmission of human immunodeficiency virus type 1 with zidovudine treatment. N Engl J Med 1994;331:1173–80.

2 Sperling RS, Shapiro DE, Coombs RW, et al. Maternal viral load, zidovudine treatment, and the risk of transmission of human immunodeficiency virus type 1 from mother to infant. N Engl J Med 1996;335:1621–9.

3 Recommendations of the US Public Health Service Task Force on the use of zidovudine to reduce perinatal transmission of human immunodeficiency virus. MMWR Morb Mortal Wkly Rep 1994;43(RR-11): 1–20.

4 Fiscus SA, Adimora AA, Schoenbach VJ, et al. Perinatal HIV infection and the effect of zidovudine therapy on transmission in rural and urban counties. JAMA 1996;275:1483–8.

5 Cooper E, Diaz C, Pitt J, et al. Impact of ACTG 076: use of zidovudine during pregnancy and changes in the rate of HIV vertical transmission. In: Program and abstracts of the Third Conference on Retroviruses and Opportunistic Infections, Washington, DC, January 28–February 1, 1996. Washington, DC: Infectious Diseases Society of America, 1996:57.

6 Simonds RJ, Nesheim S, Matheson P, et al. Declining mother to child HIV transmission following perinatal ZDV recommendations. Presented at the 11th International Conference on AIDS, Vancouver, Canada, July 7–12, 1996, abstract.

7 Scarlatti G. Paediatric HIV infection. Lancet 1996;348: 863–8.

8 Recommendations from the meeting on mother-to-infant transmission of HIV by use of antiretrovirals, Geneva, World Health Organization, June 23–25, 1994.

9 World Health Organization. International ethical guidelines for biomedical research involving human subjects. Geneva: Council for International Organizations of Medical Sciences, 1993.

10 45 CFR 46.111(a)(1).

11 Testing equivalence of two binomial proportions. In: Machin D, Campbell MJ. Statistical tables for the design of clinical trials. Oxford, England: Blackwell Scientific, 1987:35–53.

12 Brennan TA. Letter to Gilbert Meier, NIH Division of Research Ethics, December 28, 1994.

13 Lallemant M, Vithayasai V. A short ZDV course to prevent perinatal HIV in Thailand. Boston: Harvard School of Public Health, April 28, 1995.

14 Varmus H. Testimony before the Subcommittee on Human Resources, Committee on Government Reform and Oversight, US House of Representatives, May 8, 1997.

15 Draft talking points: responding to Public Citizen press conference. Press release of the National Institutes of Health, April 22, 1997.

16 Questions and answers: CDC studies of AZT to prevent mother-to-child HIV transmission in developing countries. Press release of the Centers for Disease Control and Prevention, Atlanta. (Undated document.)

17 Questions and answers on the UNAIDS sponsored trials for the prevention of mother-to-child transmission: background brief to assist in responding to issues raised by the public and the media. Press release of the United Nations AIDS Program. (Undated document.)

18 Halsey NA, Meinert CL, Ruff AJ, et al. Letter to Harold Varmus, Director of National Institutes of Health. Baltimore: Johns Hopkins University, May 6, 1997.

19 Wiktor SZ, Ehounou E. A randomized placebo-controlled intervention study to evaluate the safety and effectiveness of oral zidovudine administered in late pregnancy to reduce the incidence of mother-to-child transmission of HIV-1 in Abidjan, Côte d'Ivoire. Atlanta: Centers for Disease Control and Prevention. (Undated document.)

20 Rouzioux C, Costagliola D, Burgard M, et al. Timing of mother-to-child HIV-1 transmission depends on maternal status. AIDS 1993;7:Suppl 2:S49–S52.

21 Freedman B. Equipoise and the ethics of clinical research. N Engl J Med 1987;317:141–5.

22 Heimlich HJ, Chen XP, Xiao BQ, et al. CD4 response in HIV-positive patients treated with malaria therapy. Presented at the 11th International Conference on AIDS, Vancouver, BC, July 7–12, 1996, abstract.

23 Bishop WB, Laubscher I, Labadarios D, Rehder P, Louw ME, Fellingham SA. Effect of vitamin-enriched bread on the vitamin status of an isolated rural community – a controlled clinical trial. S Afr Med J 1996;86:Suppl:458–62.

24 Lurie P, Bishaw M, Chesney MA, et al. Ethical, behavioral, and social aspects of HIV vaccine trials in developing countries. JAMA 1994;271:295–301.

25 Annas G, Grodin M. An apology is not enough. Boston Globe. May 18, 1997:C1–C2.

26 Freedman B, Weijer C, Glass KC. Placebo orthodoxy in clinical research. I. Empirical and methodological myths. J Law Med Ethics 1996;24:243–51.

27 Varmus H. Comments at the meeting of the Advisory Committee to the Director of the National Institutes of Health, December 12, 1996.

28 Angell M. Ethical imperialism? Ethics in international collaborative clinical research. N Engl J Med 1988; 319:1081–3.

56

We're Trying to Help Our Sickest People, Not Exploit Them

Danstan Bagenda and Philippa Musoke-Mudido

Every day, like the beat of a drum heard throughout Africa, 1,000 more infants here are infected with HIV, the virus that causes AIDS. At Old Mulago Hospital, we are trying to educate people about AIDS, as well as study new therapies to prevent the disease's rampant spread. Recently, some of these studies have been attacked, with comparisons made to the notorious Tuskegee experiment in which black men in the United States were denied treatment for syphilis. Tuskegee? Is this really what is happening here in our mother–child clinic?

Our country lies in the heart of Africa, along the Great Rift Valley and Lake Victoria. It is one of those hardest hit by the AIDS epidemic. A few years ago, visitors here in the capital were greeted by the macabre sight of empty coffins for sale – piled in pyramids from adult to baby size – along the main road. These grim reminders have since been removed by city authorities, but the AIDS epidemic is omnipresent. In this city of 1 million, about one out of every six adults is infected with HIV. Hospitals and clinics like ours, which provide free medical care and therefore serve the poorest communities, are stretched beyond their resources.

At the Mulago Hospital, where more than 20,000 women deliver each year, we are trying to find effective therapies to stop transmission of HIV from pregnant women to their babies. About one in five babies becomes infected with HIV during pregnancy and delivery. If the mother breast-feeds her baby, there is an additional 15- to 25-percent chance that the baby will later become infected. There is no available treatment for the disease in Uganda. After careful consideration among researchers from developing and developed countries, the World Health Organization (WHO) recommended in 1994 that the best way to find safe and effective treatment for sufferers in countries in the developing world is to conduct studies in which new treatments, better tailored to the local population, are compared with placebos (inactive pills).

Women who enroll in our studies undergo intensive education and individual counseling. They are given a comprehensive consent form, written in the local language, which they are encouraged to take home and discuss with their families. It describes the potential risks of participating in the study and their chances of receiving a placebo. Only when they and their counselors are satisfied that all questions have been answered are they asked to sign the form. Our careful attention to these measures has consistently met the standards of national and international ethical review committees.

Bioethics: An Anthology, Third Edition. Edited by Helga Kuhse, Udo Schüklenk, and Peter Singer.
© 2016 John Wiley & Sons, Inc. Published 2016 by John Wiley & Sons, Inc.

Results from a clinical trial in the United States and France, known as the ACTG 076 protocol, showed as long ago as 1994 that, if a mother takes zidovudine (AZT) daily from the middle of her pregnancy until delivery, receives intravenous AZT during delivery, gives her infant oral AZT for the first six weeks of life and does not breast-feed, the transmission of HIV from mother to child can be reduced by two-thirds. The ACTG 076 protocol immediately became the recommended therapy in the United States. But it is not possible to simply transplant this protocol to Uganda for three main reasons: At a cost of between $800 and $1,000 per person, it is far too expensive; it requires treatment to begin in the middle of a pregnancy; and it means mothers must abstain from breast-feeding.

Some critics in the United States have asserted that we should compare new therapies with the ACTG 076 protocol rather than with a placebo. But, in Uganda, the government health expenditure is $3 per person per year, and the average citizen makes less than $1 per day. We think it is unethical to impose expensive treatment protocols that could never be used here. The situations are not parallel. In America, for instance, antibiotics are often over-prescribed; but here in Uganda we have difficulty even obtaining many needed antibiotics – to treat common complaints like ear infections. It is also naive to assume that what works for Americans will work for the rest of the world. Differences in nutrition, economics, societal norms and culture, and the frequency of tropical diseases make such extrapolations dangerously ethno-centric and wrong.

Many pregnant women here never show up for prenatal care and, of those who do, 70 percent make their first visit after the 30th week of pregnancy – too late for the US treatment protocol. Should we make a study available only to the minority of women who come early for care and tell the others, sorry, you came too late? We need to find treatments that will reach the most women possible – ones that can be given late in pregnancy or during labor.

There is also a huge gap between the United States and Uganda in breast-feeding practices. Should we apply the ACTG 076 protocol and tell women in the clinic not to breast-feed and instead give their babies infant formula? Access to clean water is a formidable challenge here, and we still remember the shocking epidemics of infant diarrhea and mortality in the early 1970s, when multinational companies shamelessly marketed formula in Africa. Despite the known risks of transmitting HIV through breast milk, the Ugandan Ministry of Health, UNICEF and WHO still encourage African women to breast-feed, as the nutritional benefits outweigh the risks of HIV transmission.

There are other factors we need to take into account. Every day, we treat both mothers and infants for malaria and iron deficiency. Both diseases contribute to anemia, which is also a major side effect of AZT. We are worried that AZT will exacerbate anemia in women and infants here. If we are to find out whether the new treatments are safe, the best way is to compare them with a placebo. How could we evaluate the safety of a new treatment if we compared it with the treatment used in America – one that has its own side effects? Could we really tell Ugandans that we had evaluated a new therapy for side effects using the best possible methods?

The AIDS epidemic has touched all our lives. Each of the 90 staff members in the mother–child health clinic has lost a family member, a loved one or a close friend. There is no dividing line between patients with HIV and those of us who care for them. A few years ago, we all chipped in money when a staff member needed to pay for the burial of a loved one, but recently we realized that we were all giving and receiving the same.

The ethical issues in our studies are complicated, but they have been given careful thought by the local community, ethicists, physicians and activists. Those who can speak with credibility for AIDS patients in Africa are those who live among and know the people here or have some basic cross-cultural sensitivity. We are suspicious of those who claim to speak for our people, yet have never worked with them. Callous accusations may help sell newspapers and journals, but they demean the people here and the horrible tragedy that we live daily.

In the next several months, we expect to see results from our study and others like it in Ivory Coast, South Africa, Tanzania and Thailand. We hope they will help bring appropriate and safe therapies to the people of the developing world. That hope is the driving force that brings us back to our work in the clinic after each of the all-too-frequent burials.

57

Medical Researchers' Ancillary Clinical Care Responsibilities

Leah Belsky and Henry S. Richardson

Researchers testing a new treatment for tuberculosis in a developing country discover some patients have HIV infection. Do they have a responsibility to provide antiretroviral drugs? In general, when do researchers have a responsibility to provide clinical care to participants that is not stipulated in the trial's protocol? This question arises regularly, especially in developing countries, yet (with rare exceptions[1]) existing literature and guidelines on research ethics do not consider ancillary clinical care. We propose an ethical framework that will help delineate researchers' responsibilities.

What Is Ancillary Care?

Ancillary care is that which is not required to make a study scientifically valid, to ensure a trial's safety, or to redress research injuries. Thus, stabilising patients to enrol them in a research protocol, monitoring drug interactions, or treating adverse reactions to experimental drugs are not ancillary care. By contrast, following up on diagnoses found by protocol tests or treating ailments that are unrelated to the study's aims would be ancillary care.

Two Extreme Views

When asked how much ancillary care they should provide to participants, the first reaction of many clinical researchers, especially those working in developing countries, is that they must provide whatever ancillary care their participants need. From an ethical perspective, this response makes sense. Research participants in trials in the developing world are typically desperately poor and ill, and everyone arguably has a duty to rescue those in need, at least when they can do so at minimal cost to themselves.[2,3] Yet this response fails to acknowledge that the goal of research is to generate knowledge not care for patients.[4,5] When researchers consider that offering ancillary care this broadly may drain limited human and financial resources and confound study results, they tend to retreat from this position.

Some researchers veer to the opposite extreme. "We may be doctors," they note, "but these are our research participants, not our patients, so we owe them nothing beyond what is needed to complete the study safely and successfully – that is, we owe them no ancillary care." But this extreme position is ethically questionable. Consider the case of researchers studying

Original publication details: Leah Belsky and Henry S. Richardson, "Medical Researchers' Ancillary Clinical Care Responsibilities," pp. 1494–6 from *British Medical Journal* 328 (June, 19, 2004). Reproduced with permission from BMJ Publishing Group.

Bioethics: An Anthology, Third Edition. Edited by Helga Kuhse, Udo Schüklenk, and Peter Singer.

a rare disease. It is ethically unacceptable to say to a participant, "We are going to monitor the toxicity and effectiveness of this experimental drug, and we will make sure it does not kill you, but we are not going to provide any palliative care for your condition." Closely monitoring a participant's disease without being willing to treat it in any way amounts to treating him or her as a mere means to the end of research.

A Better Model

We propose a model of the researcher–participant relationship that lies between these two views. It rests the special responsibilities of researchers on the idea that the relationship involves a partial and limited entrustment of participants' health to researchers.[6]

When participants join research trials, they implicitly or explicitly give researchers permission to access confidential medical information, to perform procedures and treatments, or to take samples. With this permission, researchers have discretionary power over how to respond to any collected medical information and potential diagnostic insights. Because researchers' responses to these needs will greatly affect participants' health and wellbeing, participants are vulnerable to the researchers. Participants thus tacitly entrust aspects of their health to researchers through the permission they give when joining a study.

The participants' entrustment is limited and partial. The permission entrusts only specific aspects of their health to researchers, not their health in general. Furthermore, how far researchers must go in caring for entrusted aspects of health will differ from case to case. In order to identify the depth and breadth of researchers' ancillary care responsibilities, we distinguish between the scope of entrustment (what is entrusted) and the strength of the duty of care.

What Do Participants Entrust to Researchers?

In the partial entrustment model, the scope of entrustment depends on the study. The research protocol, which specifies the information, interventions,

tests, and sample required, will determine what permission needs to be obtained. A protocol that collects only a single magnetic resonance image from each participant yields a limited scope of entrustment, pertaining mainly to the researchers' collection and use of the image. A study involving an extended inpatient stay, by contrast, will yield a far broader scope of entrustment.

Although the scope of this partial entrustment will vary, it is possible to generalise. Since a participant typically gives permission for a disease under study to be monitored, the scope of entrustment typically includes caring, as needed, for that disease. Since participants' permission is needed for doing tests or collecting confidential medical information, the scope of entrustment typically includes following up on any clinically relevant information or diagnoses generated.

How Strong Is the Entrustment Responsibility?

Researchers do not automatically have a responsibility to provide complete care for all aspects of health that fall within the scope of entrustment. Rather, the responsibility to provide ancillary care depends on the strength of the underlying, relationship based duty of care. This is influenced by at least four factors:

- Participants' vulnerability
- Participants' uncompensated risks or burdens
- Depth (intensity and duration) of the researcher–participant relationship[7]
- Participants' dependence on the researchers.

These four factors can vary independently.

The vulnerability of participants is assessed by looking at how much their wellbeing would be affected by researchers exercising their discretion – this is the vulnerability resulting from the participants' consent to participate. Participants' pre-existing vulnerabilities, such as those caused by illness, oppression, or poverty must also be taken

Hypothetical case: trial of antimicrobials for sexually transmitted diseases in a developing country

While performing clinical examinations on female patients to check for sexually transmitted diseases or side effects of the antimicrobial drug, researchers are likely to discover many women with vaginal candidiasis.[8] More than half are likely to be suffering from the results of poor dental care and hygiene. What care should be provided for these problems?

Vaginal candidiasis

This is clearly within the scope of entrustment because the diagnosis results from examinations essential to the research. The underlying duty of care also seems strong because untreated candidiasis will greatly affect their wellbeing and treating it is relatively cheap and easy

Decision: Researchers ought to treat vaginal candidiasis

Dental problems

These are not within the scope of entrustment. If we assume that the poor dental hygiene is apparent on casual observation, its diagnosis would not result from exercising the permission participants granted on entering the study. The question of strength thus does not arise.

Decision: Dental care falls outside the scope of ancillary care responsibilities

Hypothetical case: HIV treatment in tuberculosis treatment trial

The trial calls for screening out patients who are HIV positive and dropping participants who seroconvert during the trial. The local standard of care for HIV and AIDS includes only palliative care. Do the researchers have a responsibility to help provide antiretroviral drugs to people they find to be HIV positive?

People screened out because they are HIV positive

Such people are within the scope of entrustment because the study calls for checking HIV status; but the strength of the duty of care is questionable. Although vulnerability and dependence are high (since HIV infection is deadly and other sources of antiretroviral drugs do not exist), engagement and gratitude are weak because these are not yet research participants.

Decision: Researchers probably do not have a responsibility to provide drugs

Participants dropped mid-trial because they seroconvert

Treatment is within the scope of entrustment because the study design calls for monitoring HIV status, and the strength of the duty of care is high. Vulnerability and dependence remain high and with enrolled participants engagement and gratitude are greater.

Decision: Researchers probably have a responsibility to provide antiretroviral drugs

into account. The researchers' debt of gratitude to participants depends on whether participants have accepted uncompensated risks and burdens or offered researchers a hard to come by scientific opportunity. The depth of the relationship between a researcher and participant will vary from study to study because different protocols demand interactions of varying intensity, duration, and longevity. Researchers have a stronger moral responsibility to engage with the full range of participants' needs when the relationship is deeper. Finally, dependence matters because it may indicate that the research team is in a unique position to help participants. Participants may become dependent on researchers because they are impoverished, lack insurance, or have an otherwise untreatable disease and join a trial because it is their last hope. In each case, these strength factors need to be judged against the competition for limited financial and human resources and the danger of confounding study results. These considerations generate a decision tree, which can be used to determine when researchers have a responsibility to provide ancillary care (see figure 57.1). The boxes give hypothetical examples.

Conclusion

Researchers and ethics committees should attempt to anticipate the ancillary care responsibilities that will arise in a given protocol. Funding to cover researchers' ancillary care responsibilities must be included in research budgets. Many major research sponsors have been hesitant to fund medical care that is not necessary for the

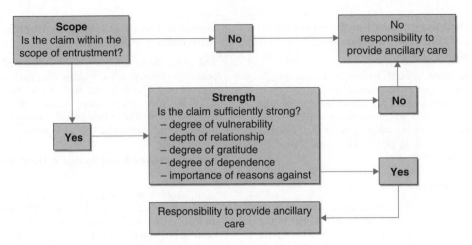

Figure 57.1   Diagram for assessing researchers' responsibility for ancillary care.

scientific success of a trial. Our hope is that the partial entrustment framework will encourage ethics committees, researchers, and sponsors to regard fulfilling ancillary care responsibilities as an essential part of ethical research.

Summary points

- Researchers need ethical guidance regarding their responsibilities for providing ancillary care to participants
- An ethically acceptable approach would recognise a partial entrustment of participants' health to researchers
- The scope of this entrustment is determined by the permission researchers need to do the study safely and validly
- Whether ancillary care should be provided then depends on the strength of the duty of care
- The strength of the duty of care depends on participants' vulnerability, dependence, and uncompensated risks or burdens and the depth of the researcher–participant relationship

---

Acknowledgments

We thank Ezekiel Emanuel, Christine Grady, Frank Miller, Leif Wenar, and David Wendler, and audiences at the Parasitology and International Programs Branch at NIAID, led by Lee Hall; the Department of Clinical Bioethics; the 3rd Africa Conference on Ethical Aspects of Clinical Research in Developing Countries, Kampala, Uganda; the Kennedy Institute of Ethics, Georgetown University; and the Latin American Conference on Ethical Aspects of International Collaborative Research. Kawango Agot, Kirana Bhatt, Stephen Chanock, Steven Holland, Samia Hurst, Matti Parri, Beyene Petros, Donald Rosenstein, Catherine Slack, and Douglas Wassenaar provided useful written comments and criticisms. LB and HSR attended the rounds of clinical researchers at the National Institutes of Health and interviewed them about ancillary care issues. In addition, they observed and met clinical researchers in Argentina and Uganda.

Note

HSR owns shares in various publicly traded pharmaceutical companies.

References

1 Nuffield Council on Bioethics. *The ethics of research related to healthcare in developing countries.* London, 2002: 97.

2 McIntyre A. Guilty bystanders? On the legitimacy of duty to rescue statutes. *Philos Public Aff* 1994; 23:157–91.

3 Scanlon TM. *What we owe to each other.* Cambridge: Harvard University Press, 1998:224–8.

4 Miller FG, Rosenstein DL, DeRenzo EG. Professional integrity in clinical research. *JAMA* 1998;280:1449–54.

5 Katz J. Human experimentation and human rights. *St Louis Univ Law J* 1993;38:7–54.

6 Richardson HS, Belsky L. The ancillary-care responsibilities of medical researchers. *Hastings Cent Rep* 2004;34:25–33.

7 Pellegrino ED. Nonabandonment: an old obligation revisited. *Ann Intern Med* 1995;122:337–78.

8 Fitzgerald DW, Behets F M-T. Women's health and human rights in HIV prevention research. *Lancet* 2003;361:68–9.

Human Embryos – Stem Cells

58

President Discusses Stem Cell Research

George W. Bush

THE PRESIDENT: Good evening. I appreciate you giving me a few minutes of your time tonight so I can discuss with you a complex and difficult issue, an issue that is one of the most profound of our time.

The issue of research involving stem cells derived from human embryos is increasingly the subject of a national debate and dinner table discussions. The issue is confronted every day in laboratories as scientists ponder the ethical ramifications of their work. It is agonized over by parents and many couples as they try to have children, or to save children already born.

The issue is debated within the church, with people of different faiths, even many of the same faith coming to different conclusions. Many people are finding that the more they know about stem cell research, the less certain they are about the right ethical and moral conclusions.

My administration must decide whether to allow federal funds, your tax dollars, to be used for scientific research on stem cells derived from human embryos. A large number of these embryos already exist. They are the product of a process called in vitro fertilization, which helps so many couples conceive children. When doctors match sperm and egg to create life outside the womb, they usually produce more embryos than are planted in the mother. Once a couple successfully has children, or if they are unsuccessful, the additional embryos remain frozen in laboratories.

Some will not survive during long storage; others are destroyed. A number have been donated to science and used to create privately funded stem cell lines. And a few have been implanted in an adoptive mother and born, and are today healthy children.

Based on preliminary work that has been privately funded, scientists believe further research using stem cells offers great promise that could help improve the lives of those who suffer from many terrible diseases – from juvenile diabetes to Alzheimer's, from Parkinson's to spinal cord injuries. And while scientists admit they are not yet certain, they believe stem cells derived from embryos have unique potential.

You should also know that stem cells can be derived from sources other than embryos – from adult cells, from umbilical cords that are discarded after babies are born, from human placenta. And many scientists feel research on these type of stem cells is also promising. Many patients suffering from a range of diseases are already being helped with treatments developed from adult stem cells.

However, most scientists, at least today, believe that research on embryonic stem cells offer the most promise because these cells have the potential to develop in all of the tissues in the body.

Original publication details: George W. Bush, "President Discusses Stem Cell Research," Office of the Press Secretary, White House, August 9, 2001.

Bioethics: An Anthology, Third Edition. Edited by Helga Kuhse, Udo Schüklenk, and Peter Singer.

Scientists further believe that rapid progress in this research will come only with federal funds. Federal dollars help attract the best and brightest scientists. They ensure new discoveries are widely shared at the largest number of research facilities and that the research is directed toward the greatest public good.

The United States has a long and proud record of leading the world toward advances in science and medicine that improve human life. And the United States has a long and proud record of upholding the highest standards of ethics as we expand the limits of science and knowledge. Research on embryonic stem cells raises profound ethical questions, because extracting the stem cell destroys the embryo, and thus destroys its potential for life. Like a snowflake, each of these embryos is unique, with the unique genetic potential of an individual human being.

As I thought through this issue, I kept returning to two fundamental questions: First, are these frozen embryos human life, and therefore, something precious to be protected? And second, if they're going to be destroyed anyway, shouldn't they be used for a greater good, for research that has the potential to save and improve other lives?

I've asked those questions and others of scientists, scholars, bioethicists, religious leaders, doctors, researchers, members of Congress, my Cabinet, and my friends. I have read heartfelt letters from many Americans. I have given this issue a great deal of thought, prayer and considerable reflection. And I have found widespread disagreement.

On the first issue, are these embryos human life – well, one researcher told me he believes this five-day-old cluster of cells is not an embryo, not yet an individual, but a pre-embryo. He argued that it has the potential for life, but it is not a life because it cannot develop on its own.

An ethicist dismissed that as a callous attempt at rationalization. Make no mistake, he told me, that cluster of cells is the same way you and I, and all the rest of us, started our lives. One goes with a heavy heart if we use these, he said, because we are dealing with the seeds of the next generation.

And to the other crucial question, if these are going to be destroyed anyway, why not use them for good purpose – I also found different answers. Many argue these embryos are byproducts of a process that helps create life, and we should allow couples to donate them to science so they can be used for good purpose instead of wasting their potential. Others will argue there's no such thing as excess life, and the fact that a living being is going to die does not justify experimenting on it or exploiting it as a natural resource.

At its core, this issue forces us to confront fundamental questions about the beginnings of life and the ends of science. It lies at a difficult moral intersection, juxtaposing the need to protect life in all its phases with the prospect of saving and improving life in all its stages.

As the discoveries of modern science create tremendous hope, they also lay vast ethical mine fields. As the genius of science extends the horizons of what we can do, we increasingly confront complex questions about what we should do. We have arrived at that brave new world that seemed so distant in 1932, when Aldous Huxley wrote about human beings created in test tubes in what he called a "hatchery."

In recent weeks, we learned that scientists have created human embryos in test tubes solely to experiment on them. This is deeply troubling, and a warning sign that should prompt all of us to think through these issues very carefully.

Embryonic stem cell research is at the leading edge of a series of moral hazards. The initial stem cell researcher was at first reluctant to begin his research, fearing it might be used for human cloning. Scientists have already cloned a sheep. Researchers are telling us the next step could be to clone human beings to create individual designer stem cells, essentially to grow another you, to be available in case you need another heart or lung or liver.

I strongly oppose human cloning, as do most Americans. We recoil at the idea of growing human beings for spare body parts, or creating life for our convenience. And while we must devote enormous energy to conquering disease, it is equally important that we pay attention to the moral concerns raised by the new frontier of human embryo stem cell research. Even the most noble ends do not justify any means.

My position on these issues is shaped by deeply held beliefs. I'm a strong supporter of science and technology, and believe they have the potential for incredible good – to improve lives, to save life, to conquer disease. Research offers hope that millions of our loved ones may be cured of a disease and rid of their suffering. I have friends whose children suffer from juvenile diabetes. Nancy Reagan has written me about President Reagan's struggle with Alzheimer's. My own family has confronted the tragedy of childhood leukemia. And, like all Americans, I have great hope for cures.

I also believe human life is a sacred gift from our Creator. I worry about a culture that devalues life, and believe as your President I have an important obligation to foster and encourage respect for life in America and throughout the world. And while we're all hopeful about the potential of this research, no one can be certain that the science will live up to the hope it has generated.

Eight years ago, scientists believed fetal tissue research offered great hope for cures and treatments — yet, the progress to date has not lived up to its initial expectations. Embryonic stem cell research offers both great promise and great peril. So I have decided we must proceed with great care.

As a result of private research, more than 60 genetically diverse stem cell lines already exist. They were created from embryos that have already been destroyed, and they have the ability to regenerate themselves indefinitely, creating ongoing opportunities for research. I have concluded that we should allow federal funds to be used for research on these existing stem cell lines, where the life and death decision has already been made.

Leading scientists tell me research on these 60 lines has great promise that could lead to breakthrough therapies and cures. This allows us to explore the promise and potential of stem cell research without crossing a fundamental moral line, by providing taxpayer funding that would sanction or encourage further destruction of human embryos that have at least the potential for life.

I also believe that great scientific progress can be made through aggressive federal funding of research on umbilical cord placenta, adult and animal stem cells which do not involve the same moral dilemma. This year, your government will spend $250 million on this important research.

I will also name a President's council to monitor stem cell research, to recommend appropriate guidelines and regulations, and to consider all of the medical and ethical ramifications of biomedical innovation. This council will consist of leading scientists, doctors, ethicists, lawyers, theologians and others, and will be chaired by Dr. Leon Kass, a leading biomedical ethicist from the University of Chicago.

This council will keep us apprised of new developments and give our nation a forum to continue to discuss and evaluate these important issues. As we go forward, I hope we will always be guided by both intellect and heart, by both our capabilities and our conscience.

I have made this decision with great care, and I pray it is the right one.

Thank you for listening. Good night, and God bless America.

59

Killing Embryos for Stem Cell Research

Jeff McMahan

1 Two Assumptions

Those who object to human embryonic stem cell (hESC) research believe that it is seriously morally objectionable to kill embryos, and most believe that it is also objectionable to allow them to die or to create them solely for certain instrumental purposes. Thus, when it was announced in August 2006 that researchers had discovered a way to harvest embryonic stem cells (hESCs) from embryos created for reproductive purposes without destroying the embryos – a way that would allow the embryos to live and be implanted – one might have expected that everyone who had previously opposed the research would have welcomed the prospect of having the medical benefits of hESC research without having to harm any embryos. But the general reaction to the announcement by those who had been opponents was to reiterate their opposition. In some respects this is baffling, though it may simply reflect the belief that the new technique is merely a Trojan horse, and that going forward with hESC research in any form will inevitably result in the deliberate destruction of embryos.

This belief is not entirely unwarranted. Much of the therapeutic promise of hESC research lies in the prospect of our being able to clone an embryo from a particular individual, derive stem cells from it, and use those stem cells to grow tissue or even an organ that would be an exact genetic match of that to be restored or replaced, thereby obviating problems of immunologic rejection. Even if the cloned embryo could survive the process whereby the stem cells would be derived, it would not have been created for reproductive purposes, and there would be no obvious way of enabling it to survive, especially if its source were male. There are, moreover, a great many people who support therapeutic cloning but are opposed to reproductive cloning. For these people, there would be a positive reason to destroy the cloned embryo after deriving stem cells from it. So, all things considered, the opponents of hESC research are probably right to be skeptical of the suggestion that this research can be pursued in a way that will avoid the killing of embryos. (Of course, a surviving embryo from which stem cells had been obtained would not have to be killed even if it were not going to be enabled to develop biologically. It could instead be indefinitely frozen. But if we assume that the embryo is the kind of entity for which things can be better or worse, it seems that to be killed would be no worse for the embryo than to be frozen with no prospect of ever being enabled to live and develop.)

Those who believe that the killing of human embryos is wrong typically support their view by

Original publication details: Jeff McMahan, "Killing Embryos for Stem Cell Research," pp. 170–89 from *Metaphilosophy* 38: 2/3 (2007). Reproduced with permission from John Wiley & Sons.

Bioethics: An Anthology, Third Edition. Edited by Helga Kuhse, Udo Schüklenk, and Peter Singer.

claiming that embryos are innocent human beings, and that innocent human beings must be protected, not harmed or destroyed or used solely as a means of benefiting others. This is what President George W. Bush claims to believe, perhaps after conferring with the same Higher Power whom he claimed to have consulted about invading Iraq and who advised him to go ahead.[1] (The identity of this Higher Power is, however, not altogether certain. Cynics suspect that it is really a group of voters known as the "religious right.")

Some reasons for believing that embryos are innocent human beings whom it is wrong to kill are religious in character. There are, however, two assumptions that I believe capture the essence of the religious concern but are also compatible with secular morality. I will focus my discussion on these. They are:

1. The embryo is the earliest stage in the existence of someone like you or me. That is, we were once embryos.
2. We have the same moral status at all times at which we exist. We mattered just as much when we were embryos as we do now.

I believe that both of these assumptions are false. For the most part, my challenges to the second assumption will be intuitive; for example, my argument in sections 2 and 3 is that our practices suggest that we really do not believe that embryos have the same status as children and adults. But even apart from its conflict with certain intuitions, the second assumption seems incompatible with the claim that many of the moral reasons why we have to treat an individual in certain ways and not treat that individual in other ways are given by that individual's intrinsic *nature*. If you were once an embryo, your nature was very different then from what it is now. It is reasonable to think that your moral status was correspondingly different, so that it may have been permissible to treat you then in ways that would be impermissible now. It seems implausible to suppose that radical changes in an individual's nature can never affect that individual's basic moral status.

If you were never an embryo, however, the question of what your status was as an embryo cannot arise. My main aim in this essay is to offer reasons for thinking that we were never embryos. I will focus on embryos at a very early stage in their development. The best time to

intervene to derive stem cells by the traditional method that involves killing the embryo is a little less than a week after conception, when the embryo – or, technically, blastocyst – is five or six days old. I will therefore consider whether it is plausible to suppose that we were once six-day-old embryos.

2 Assisted Conception

First, however, I will examine two grounds for skepticism about the two assumptions that commonly underlie people's opposition to hESC research. In each case the claim is that the conjunction of these two assumptions is incompatible with some other common and well-supported belief. One of these claims is, I think, weaker than one might initially suppose. The other is quite strong. I will begin with the weaker of the two.

As a society, we have come to accept assisted conception, even though it involves the creation of more embryos than will be implanted. It is now a socially accepted practice to create a number of embryos in vitro, select one or more for implantation, and either allow the remainder to die, to kill them, or, more commonly, to freeze them indefinitely so that they continue to exist in a state in which they are neither alive nor dead.

Some claim that if, as our second assumption asserts, an embryo has the same moral status that you and I have now, so that it is wrong to kill it for its stem cells, then it should also be wrong deliberately to create embryos in the knowledge that many of them will never be implanted.

But the matter is not so simple. It can be argued, for example, that while assisted conception involves creating embryos in the knowledge that each will have a relatively small chance of survival, the same is true, though to a somewhat lesser degree, of natural conception. An embryo created through natural conception has only about a 30 percent chance of surviving to birth. But no one suggests that natural conception is, for this reason, wrong, or that it *would* be wrong if the probability of survival were significantly lower than it is.

Still, even if each embryo's probability of survival were no lower in assisted conception than in natural conception, that would not show that the treatment of embryos in the process of assisted conception would be as benign as it is in natural conception. Naturally conceived embryos that are spontaneously aborted can very seldom be saved; their deaths are an unavoidable side effect of the procreative process. But in assisted conception, embryos that could in principle be saved are often allowed to die without any effort being made to save them. Moreover, the procedure could be done in such a way that embryos would be created and implanted only one at a time. Performed in this way, the procedure would be significantly less efficient and less successful, but if embryos have a high moral status, perhaps we should accept these costs in order to avoid creating embryos when we know that many of those created will never be implanted.

So, given the assumption that a human embryo has the same moral status that you and I have, there are reasons for thinking that assisted conception is morally objectionable on grounds that do not apply to natural conception. But this is not sufficient to show that those who oppose hESC research by appealing to the status of the embryo are thereby committed to opposing assisted conception as well, even as it is currently practiced. For there are also reasons for thinking that even if assisted conception involves treating some embryos in a morally objectionable way, hESC research treats embryos in a significantly more objectionable way. This seems true, in any case, of the current technique for deriving stem cells, which has involved the killing of embryos and in its projected applications would require both the creation and the subsequent killing of embryos. Both killing the embryo for its cells and creating and then killing it treat it merely as a means. In assisted conception, by contrast, nothing bad is intended for any embryo, no embryo is used merely as a means, and each embryo created gets some chance at life.

Indeed, it might be argued that assisted conception is not bad, or worse, for any embryo. For it is not intrinsically bad to be caused to exist in a nonconscious state for only a brief period, and to exist in this state is certainly not worse than never to exist at all. That an individual's life will be brief is not, in general, a reason not to cause that individual to exist. Yet, while this is true, it does not show that assisted conception is unobjectionable. For the same claims can be made about

causing an embryo to exist and then killing it in the process of deriving stem cells from it.

Suppose that the course of action that involves causing an embryo to exist and killing it to get stem cells is wrong. The alternative to this course of action, considered as a unit, is not to cause the embryo to exist at all. For embryos created for the purpose of hESC research would otherwise not be created at all. And, as I noted, it would not, in such a case, have been better for the embryo never to exist. In part, this is just a matter of logic. If the embryo had never existed, that could not have been better *for it*, as there can be no one for whom never existing can be either better or worse. But there is also a substantive claim here that is often expressed by saying that having been caused to exist was not worse for an individual than never existing. This is the claim that the life is worth living.

So what makes the course of action that involves both causing an embryo to exist and then killing it wrong (assuming for the moment that it *is* wrong) is that it involves killing. Causing the embryo to exist is objectionable as a component of the unit only because it is done in order to make the killing possible. So it is in fact morally irrelevant that the course of action consisting of causing the embryo to exist and then killing it is not bad for the embryo or worse for it than never existing. For the relevant comparison is between killing the embryo and allowing or enabling it to continue to exist. And while it is not worse for the embryo to exist and be killed than never to exist, it *is* worse for it to be killed than to be allowed or enabled to continue to live.

Similarly, the relevant comparison for evaluating assisted conception is not between causing embryos to exist for a brief period and not causing them to exist at all. It is instead between, on the one hand, killing the supernumerary embryos, allowing them to die, or freezing them indefinitely and, on the other, enabling them to continue to exist. And if killing an embryo is worse for it than allowing or enabling it to continue to exist, then allowing it die, or freezing it and allowing it to die only later, is also worse for it than enabling it to continue to exist – though, assuming that the distinction between killing and letting die has moral significance, allowing the embryo to die may be *less* morally objectionable than killing it.

This could, of course, be a morally significant difference between hESC research and assisted conception, if the former requires the killing of the embryo, while the latter does not. Indeed, if supernumerary embryos can be kept frozen for as long as we ourselves survive, they need never even be allowed to die. It is, however, hard to see how being frozen at time t, remaining indefinitely cryogenically preserved, and then dying without experiencing consciousness upon thawing could be better than simply being allowed to die at t. Being frozen is better than being allowed to die only because it leaves open the possibility of being restored to life. But if being frozen but never implanted is no better for an embryo than simply being allowed to die, then the practice of freezing supernumerary embryos produced in the process of assisted conception accomplishes rather little that is of moral significance. For the vast majority of embryos that are frozen cannot, though for contingent reasons, be enabled to develop into adult persons and thus will have to be allowed to die at some point. Freezing them simply defers their deaths without extending their lives, while shifting the responsibility for allowing them to die to our successors. (It is for this reason that it was deceptive and manipulative posturing for Bush to surrounded himself with babies developed from supernumerary embryos when he announced his veto of legislation that would have made such embryos available for stem cell research. For even with the most aggressive harvesting of embryonic stem cells that scientists could possibly desire, the remaining supply of frozen embryos available for implantation would still greatly exceed any possible level of demand.)

Still, despite the foregoing dialectical to and fro, our general social acceptance of procedures of assisted conception that involve the creation of supernumerary embryos does pose a challenge to those who argue that hESC research is wrong because embryos have the same moral status that you and I have. For if embryos really did have this status, it seems that our acceptance of assisted conception, as currently practiced, would be misplaced – even if assisted conception does not require killing embryos and does not use them merely as means. For once an embryo exists, if it would be seriously wrong to kill it, it should also be seriously objectionable to allow it to die – or to freeze it, which, as I have argued, amounts to the same thing in virtually all cases. (For the sake of brevity, I will henceforth write as if freezing an embryo were tantamount to allowing it to die, despite the fact that freezing leaves open a remote possibility of a restoration to an active living state.) Of course, if there is a special objection to using an embryo merely as a means, and if the distinction between killing and letting die has significance in this sort of case, then there are significant reasons for thinking that assisted conception, as currently practiced, is *less* morally objectionable than hESC research – though these reasons may be offset to a considerable extent by the vastly greater importance of the goals of hESC research, which aims to prevent or cure a range of deadly and debilitating diseases, while assisted conception aims primarily to enable people to have children that are genetically their own rather than having to settle for adoption. But if we really believed that embryos have the same moral status that we – cognitively normal adult human beings – have, it seems unlikely that we would be morally comfortable treating them the way we do in assisted conception, creating conditions in which vast numbers of them have to be frozen and thus, ultimately, allowed to die.

It is difficult to test our intuitions by devising a thought experiment in which the freezers at fertility clinics are full not of many thousands of embryos but of many thousands of adult human persons, and in which more frozen persons are being added to the stocks as a byproduct of people's efforts to have their own biological offspring rather than adopting already existing children. For the situation of embryos frozen in the process of assisted conception is in important respects sui generis. In the case of the many thousands of embryos that are frozen, the only feasible alternative to their being in this state is for them never to have existed. It is, relative to this alternative, not worse for them to be in their frozen state. They have not, moreover, had experiences in the past that might make it seem more urgent to restore them to life, and they are not specially related to other people in ways other than the purely biological. It is, for obvious reasons, difficult to formulate a science-fiction scenario in which parallel conditions apply to frozen adult persons.

I think, nevertheless, that we can learn something important from simply imagining discovering a vast number of frozen persons. Imagine, for example, a country with a despotic government that has for decades been sealed off from the rest of the world, in the way Cambodia was in the late 1970s. Over these decades many thousands of people, both real and imagined opponents of the regime, have been killed. For some reason, if any of these people had a single child between the ages of three and five, that child was cryogenically preserved in a state intermediate between life and death. The government has now been overthrown, and its secret laboratories have been opened to scrutiny. Many thousands of frozen children are discovered, though none has living parents, siblings, or friends. How much, if anything, ought strangers to sacrifice in order to restore these children to life? Suppose that the burden of restoring a child to life would be roughly comparable to the burden of pregnancy – for example, each child would have to be connected to the circulatory system of another person for nine months, as in Judith Jarvis Thomson's well-known "famous violinist" example (Thomson 1971 [see chapter 3 in this volume]). I think that many people would believe that we – all of us together – ought to try to devise ways to save these children that would divide the burdens equally among us. And I suspect that some people – *comparatively* few but in absolute terms a significant number – would feel it morally incumbent on themselves to volunteer to become connected to a child in order to save its life. This would be in sharp contrast to the conspicuous failure of even the most ardent "pro-life" activists to give frozen embryos a chance at life by offering the use of their bodies for fetal gestation.

The facts are that we as a society have accepted a practice of assisted conception that creates as a byproduct a vast and growing number of frozen embryos, yet very few if any of us are willing to make a significant sacrifice to restore any of them to life. We do not, as a society, demand the abolition of the practice, and our government does not restrict it in the way that it restricts hESC research; nor do we make any effort to enable the embryos we have created to live. Instead we freeze them in order to pass the burden of allowing them to die to others. The contrast between this behavior and our likely reaction to the hypothetical case of the frozen children suggests that, whatever people may profess on their bumper stickers, very few really believe that embryos have the same moral status as older children and adults. Some opponents of hESC research do, of course, extend their opposition to assisted conception as well, at least as it is currently practiced; but they seem to be a minority among the opponents of hESC research. For the majority, acceptance of assisted conception as practiced casts doubt on their commitment to the second of the two assumptions stated earlier.

3   Monozygotic Twinning

The first of our two assumptions – that we were once six-day-old embryos – is often challenged by appealing to the possibility of monozygotic twinning (that is, twinning that results from the division of a single embryo rather than from the simultaneous fertilization of more than one egg). Many people have argued that until the possibility of twinning has passed, at around two weeks after conception, the embryo cannot be a single or unique human being. As recently as 2004, for example, Alexander McCall Smith, a well-known novelist who is also a law professor, wrote:

> At an early point in its development, the embryo can divide into twins or remain a single individual. This is important because one might say that before that stage has been reached, we do not have an identifiable individual. It is only when the embryo can no longer divide in this way that we can say that a distinct individual has come into existence, or started. We cannot therefore say that there is a separate person there, if we're going to use the language of personhood, because we do not know whether there is going to be a separate person or two persons. (McCall Smith 2004, disc 1, track 7)

Although this argument is common, especially among defenders of hESC research, I think it is mistaken. That an entity can undergo division is no reason to think it is not a unique individual. It is no reason to think that an ameba is not an individual ameba, that it can divide, or that any other cell is not a unique individual object because it can undergo fission. Yet even though the possibility of twinning does not show that the first of our assumptions is wrong, it does suggest that the two assumptions cannot both be true.

Suppose that when fertilization results in the existence of a single-celled human zygote, a new human being – one of us – thereby begins to exist. What the phenomenon of twinning shows is that some of us begin to exist at a different time and in a different way. Monozygotic twins, on this view, begin to exist not at conception but when an embryo divides.

Consider again the ameba. When an ameba divides, the original ameba ceases to exist and is replaced by two qualitatively identical daughter amebas. Similarly, when an embryo divides to form twins, if the division is symmetrical, the original embryo also *ceases to exist*. The original embryo cannot be identical with *both* twins, since one thing cannot be numerically identical with two things that are not identical with each other. And if the division is symmetrical, the original embryo cannot be one twin but not the other, for there is nothing about one twin to identify it as the original embryo that is not also true of the other.

Of course, when the division that leads to twinning is asymmetrical – as it might be if a single totipotent cell (that is, a cell with the potential to develop into a mature human organism) were extracted from an early embryo and allowed to develop into a twin – the original embryo would survive. In that case, one twin would begin to exist at a different time and in a different way from the other.

But let us focus on cases in which the division is symmetrical, for these are the cases that challenge the idea that we were embryos. If the embryo is someone like you or me and if it matters in the way you and I do (the two assumptions), then when symmetrical twinning occurs and an embryo ceases to exist, this should be *tragic*. For it is the ceasing to exist of someone who matters. According to the two assumptions, therefore, there is a serious moral reason to try to prevent monozygotic twinning from occurring. Or at least we should try to ensure that all instances of twinning involve asymmetrical division, so that no one ceases to exist. But these suggestions are absurd, and I know of no one who believes either.

If the two assumptions stated in section 1 that seem to underlie most opposition to hESC research together imply both that accepted procedures for assisted conception are seriously objectionable and that monozygotic twinning is a terrible misfortune for an embryo and ought if possible to be prevented, then there is reason to believe that those assumptions

cannot both be true. As I noted earlier, I believe that neither is; but I will devote most of my space here to showing that the first assumption – that we were once embryos – is indefensible.

4 Are Six-Day-Old Embryos Human Organisms?

Many people who believe that we were once embryos attempt to defend that view by claiming (1) that an embryo is a human organism in the earliest stage of its life and (2) that we are essentially human organisms. I believe, however, that the first of these claims is contentious and that the second is false. I will begin with the first. Although I do not think that it can be shown to be false that a six-day-old embryo is a human organism, I think that there is room for reasonable doubt about this. I will try to show what is at issue here.

There are two interpretations of what happens in the first fortnight after conception. The first treats the embryo as a human organism; the second does not. I will sketch them both and state the case for thinking that the second is more plausible.

According to the first interpretation, the successive cell divisions that follow the process of conception are events in the history of a single entity composed of various cells. This entity begins as one cell – the zygote – and continues to exist, as two cells, then four, and so on.

Yet it is unclear what makes all the various cells, considered synchronically or diachronically, parts of a single individual. They are all contiguous within a single extracellular membrane (the zona pellucida), but that alone does not make them a single entity any more than placing a number of marbles in a sack turns them into a single entity.

To consider whether the cells within the membrane of the early human embryo constitute a human organism, it is necessary to be clear about what a human organism is. I accept the familiar idea that a living human organism is an entity with human genes that is composed of various living parts that function together in an integrated way to sustain a single life, and that is not itself a part of another living biological entity.[2] (The last clause is necessary in order to exclude the implication that living human cells or organs are themselves human organisms.)

According to the second interpretation of the events in the first two weeks following conception, the cells that compose an embryo during this period do not yet serve sufficiently different functions to allow us to say that they are coordinated in the service of a single life. While each cell is itself alive, they are not together involved in processes that are constitutive of a further, higher-order life. During the first couple of weeks after conception, all that exists is a collection of qualitatively almost identical cells living within a single membrane. They are like marbles in a sack.

On this interpretation, the single-celled zygote is a single living entity, though not itself a human organism. When it divides, nothing but its constituent matter continues to exist. The zygote itself ceases to exist, as an ameba does when it divides, though in doing so it gives rise to two daughter cells. When they in turn divide, they too cease to exist. There is no individual that persists through these transformations. Only when there is sufficiently significant cell differentiation, so that different cells begin to serve different though coordinated functions that are identifiable as the regulative and self-preservative processes of a higher-order individual of which the cells are parts, do the cells together constitute a human organism. Only then is there a new and further life that is constituted by the integrated processes carried out by the various groups of differently functioning cells. Since significant cell differentiation is clearly identifiable at around two weeks after conception, it seems reasonable to treat that as the time at which a human organism begins to exist. For those who persist in thinking that a unique human individual cannot exist until after the possibility of twinning has passed, it is perhaps significant that the time at which significant cell differentiation begins to occur coincides rather closely with the time at which twinning ceases to be possible.

This second interpretation may be disputed on the ground that the cells that compose the embryo are coordinated very early on, certainly before six days after conception.[3] There must, after all, be communication and coordination among them prior to significant differentiation, if only in order to ensure that different cell lines develop in different directions. Embryonic development would not get very far if all the cells decided, all at once, to specialize as skin cells.

This forceful objection helps to reveal what I think is fundamentally at issue in the dispute between proponents of these two different interpretations of what happens during the first two weeks after conception. Cellular specialization and intercellular coordination are matters of degree. Whether the cells within the zona pellucida constitute a human organism depends on whether they are differentiated and coordinated to a high enough degree to warrant the claim that their interactions constitute a higher-order life. But there is no objectively determinate degree of differentiation and coordination that is necessary and sufficient for the presence of a higher-order life. When we know all the facts about the various cells within the zona pellucida and their functions, we know all the basic facts there are to know. While there is no doubt a threshold along the spectrum of degrees of coordination beyond which it is undeniable that a collection of cells are functioning together to sustain a higher-order life, there may be, prior to that threshold, no objective fact about whether the cells together constitute an organism. Whether there is a human organism present may simply be underdetermined by the facts.

The question of when the level of differentiation and coordination becomes sufficient for the presence of a human organism is not a biological or scientific question but a metaphysical question. How we ought to answer it is a matter of overall coherence among our beliefs and concepts. Our answer should, for example, cohere with our beliefs about the end of life. If the minimal degree of cellular coordination that is present only a day or so after conception is sufficient for the existence of a living human organism, then it seems that we ought not to believe that brain death is the biological death of a human organism. For brain death is compatible with residual functioning among cells, tissues, and even organs that is far more extensive and highly coordinated than that found among the cells in a two-day-old or six-day-old embryo. Indeed, the level of coordination among the still-living parts of a brain-dead human organism that is given certain minimal forms of external support (such as mechanical ventilation) is immeasurably higher than that found among the cells in an early embryo, which is also dependent on life support from the maternal body. Thus, even most of those who reject brain death as the criterion of the biological death of a human organism, and embrace instead a criterion that is directly concerned with internally regulated integration among the organism's parts, would regard a once-living human organism as dead if it had no more coordination among its still-living parts than is present among the cells in a six-day-old embryo. This is one coherence-based reason for denying that such an embryo is a living human organism rather than a collection of cells that are each inner-directed along a path toward the formation of an organism.

Still, it may be best at this point to regard the question of when a human organism begins to exist as an open question. There is a strong case for the view that after about two weeks following conception there is sufficient differentiation and coordination among the cells in the zona pellucida to claim that together they constitute a higher-order life, the life of an organism. It is possible that before that point there is sufficient coordination to warrant the claim that the cells already constitute an organism. The best answer may well depend on facts about the cells and their relations with one another of which we are as yet unaware.

5   We Are Not Human Organisms

No doubt it is odd to suppose that whether you existed at six days after conception depends on the degree to which a set of embryonic cells were coordinated with one another. Many people will be dismissive of that idea and will accept as sturdy common sense that a human organism begins to exist at conception. Suppose this is right and two-day-old and six-day-old embryos are human organisms. Still, it follows that *we* were embryos only if we are essentially human organisms. I will argue that we are not.

Whether we are organisms is not a scientific question. There is no experiment that can be done to determine whether or not we are organisms, just as there is no experiment that could tell us whether a statue and the lump of bronze of which it is composed are one and the same thing or distinct substances. These are both metaphysical questions and must be settled by philosophical argument.

There are two arguments that I believe show that we cannot be human organisms. I will rehearse them only briefly here, as I have presented and developed each in more detail elsewhere (McMahan 2002, 31–39). The first appeals to a thought experiment, long familiar to students of philosophy, involving brain transplantation. (The thought experiment is actually more convincing if it involves transplantation only of the cerebrum and not of the entire brain. But for simplicity of exposition I will follow tradition and make it the entire brain.) Suppose that you and your identical twin are both involved in a terrible accident. Your brain is undamaged, but the rest of your body is so badly injured as to be moribund. Your identical twin's brain has been destroyed, but the rest of his or her body is undamaged. Exploiting new techniques that enable the proper neural connections to be made between your brain and your twin's body, your surgeons remove your twin's dead brain and transplant your perfectly functional brain in its place. Most of us believe that the person who then wakes up in that body is you. But if you were a human organism, you would now be the dead organism from which your brain was extracted, and the person who wakes up after the surgery would be your twin, now nicely equipped with a new brain.

Some people object to this argument because it depends on an example that is purely hypothetical. They think that we ought not to trust our intuitions about unrealistic cases. My second argument is not vulnerable to this objection, as it appeals to an actual phenomenon: dicephalus. Dicephalic twinning is a radically incomplete form of conjoined twinning in which two heads, each with its own brain and its own separate mental life, sit atop a single body. In some cases, there is very little duplication of organs below the neck; there is one circulatory system, one metabolic system, one reproductive system, and one immune system. In these cases, there are two persons but only one human organism. The two twins cannot both be the organism, because that would imply that they are not distinct individuals but one and the same person. Each twin's relation to the organism is the same; therefore there can be no reason to suppose that one of them is the organism while the other is not. It seems, therefore, that *neither* of them is identical with the organism. If dicephalic twins are essentially the same kind of thing that we are, then we are not organisms either.

But even if dicephalic twins were asymmetrically related to the organism as a whole, so that one twin had a much stronger claim to *be* the organism than the other, that could be sufficient to show that the other twin was clearly *not* the organism. But in that case there would be at least one person who was not identical to an organism. Unless that twin were essentially a different kind of entity from the rest of us, it would follow that we are not essentially organisms either.

There are in fact cases of highly asymmetric conjoined twins. In the phenomenon known as "craniopagus parasiticus," one conjoined twin is fully developed but the other, which is joined to the first at the head, has failed to develop a body and is thus, as the name suggests, a second head that draws life support from an organism to which it is attached but over which it exercises no control. There are only eleven recorded cases of this phenomenon, but two have occurred in the twenty-first century. In one case in Egypt, the second head was surgically removed, but the remaining twin died a little more than a year later from an infection of the brain. A BBC report comments that the "second head could smile and blink," but "whether it was capable of independent thought is unclear."[4] Whatever was true in this actual case, it seems possible that there could be a case in which the brain in the parasitic head would be fully developed and separate, thus forming a separate center of self-conscious, rational thought.

That this is possible is suggested by the series of experiments by Robert J. White in which various animals' heads were kept alive and fully conscious after being severed from the body, and by cases of high spinal cord transection. In such cases, the brain remains fully conscious if supplied with oxygenated blood even though it is otherwise actually or effectively unconnected with an organism. If there were a case of craniopagus parasiticus in which the parasitic head contained a fully developed brain, this would be a clear instance of a single organism supporting the existence of two distinct persons. Even if we were to claim that the person whose brain controlled the organism was identical with that organism, the person resident in the second head could not plausibly be identified with any organism. This again supports the view that individuals of the sort that you and I are cannot be essentially human organisms.

It might be objected to this argument that just as one of White's severed heads is itself a human organism shorn of most of its nonessential parts, so the parasitic head in craniopagus parasiticus is also a distinct organism. But both these claims are false. A severed but living head with an external blood supply is not an organism but a surviving part, rather like an organ salvaged from a now-dead organism and kept alive pending transplantation. Similarly, a parasitic head is no more an organism than my head is.

If, however, we are not human organisms, then even if a human organism begins to exist at conception, it does not follow that we began to exist at that point. If you are not identical with the organism that supports your existence, it is possible that you began to exist in association with it at some point after it began to exist, whether that was at conception or a couple of weeks later.

6   We Are Not Souls

Most Americans actually reject – if not consciously, then at least by implication – the view that we are essentially human organisms. They believe that we are something rather more exalted and spiritual than that. They believe that we are souls, or at least that each of us is an organism that is essentially informed by a soul. If, as most believe, the soul is created at conception, then embryos are souls in miniature. One of us – that is, an entity of our essential kind – is present from conception on, and this is entirely independent of what his or her cells might be doing.

The idea that we are souls faces an embarrassing array of questions to which it is difficult to provide answers that are supported by reasons and argument rather than mere conjecture. What is the nature of the soul? What reason is there to suppose that the soul, so conceived, exists? Do nonhuman animals have souls as well, and if not how can one detect the presence of the soul in an embryo while being confident of its absence in a dog? Assuming that souls do not come in degrees, so that the possession of a soul is all-or-nothing, when in the course of evolution did our ancestors begin to be endowed with souls? Was there a detectable difference between the parent that lacked a soul and the child who had one? If the soul can survive the death of the human organism and retain its full psychological capacities in a disembodied state, why are one's psychological capacities or states affected at all by what happens to one's brain? What happens to the soul of an embryo that divides and is replaced by two new embryos? What happens to the soul when the tissues connecting a person's cerebral hemispheres are surgically severed, creating two separate centers of consciousness, each capable of experiences inaccessible to the other?

There is no space to press these questions here. I will instead describe the two most common and well-articulated conceptions of the soul in the history of western thought and suggest that neither is compatible with the view that the soul is present at six days after conception.

The less familiar of these two conceptions among contemporary people is the conception associated with the Catholic Church, according to which a human being is a human organism informed by a rational soul. The soul is, it is said, the form of the body, and the rational soul, which distinguishes human beings from animals, is the way in which the matter of the organism is organized so that it has the capacity for rationality. Hence the tendency among Catholic theorists to refer to the soul as the "organizing principle."

The obvious problem for this view is that a six-day-old embryo does not seem to have the capacity for rationality. Its matter is not organized that way. Partly for this reason, some writers in the Catholic tradition have argued for the view known as "delayed hominization," according to which the early embryo is not a human being, which it develops into only later in pregnancy. Some contemporary Catholic philosophers have argued, however, that the early embryo does indeed have the "basic natural capacity" for rationality, though that capacity does not become "immediately exercisable" until later (George and Gómez-Lobo 2002, 260–61). What this really amounts to, I think, is the familiar claim that a normal embryo has the potential to develop the capacity for rationality, with special emphasis on the claim that the embryo's potential involves an intrinsic inner-directedness toward the development of rationality. But even if all embryos have this inner-directed or intrinsic potential, that seems insufficient for the truth of the claim that their constituent matter is organized in such a way as to have the capacity for rationality, which is what the Aristotelian-Thomist conception of form requires in order for them to have rational souls. Nor do I think it is true that all human embryos are inner-directed toward the development of rationality. I will not pursue these issues here, though I discuss some of them at length elsewhere (McMahan 2008).

The soul as understood in Catholic doctrine is really neither physical nor nonphysical. It is not a thing at all but is instead the form or organizing principle of the body. Most people, however, believe that the soul is a substance, that it is nonphysical, that it is the subject of consciousness, and that it can continue to exist and remain actively conscious in the absence of a body – which explains how we can survive in a disembodied state after death.

Because the soul, on this conception, is nonphysical, it is hard to make sense of its existing in the absence of mental properties. For this reason, Descartes, who developed this conception of the soul with greater rigor and detail than anyone else, thought that the soul must be continuously conscious. Consciousness is its defining property. If there is no consciousness – or even, to be more liberal than Descartes would allow, any capacity for consciousness – there can be no soul. But very few people, if any, seriously believe that a six-day-old embryo is conscious. If this is right and a six-day-old embryo has neither consciousness nor even the capacity for consciousness, then the soul cannot be present at that point; therefore, if we are Cartesian souls, we cannot have been present at that point; therefore we were never six-day-old embryos.

To make sense of the idea that we existed as early embryos, one has to accept that we are essentially either human organisms or souls and that the early embryo either is a human organism or has a soul. There really is no other kind of thing that we could be that is present only a few days after conception. I have argued, however, that the early embryo may not be a human organism at all, and that in any case we are not essentially human organisms. And I have argued that even if we are, or have, souls, the two dominant conceptions of the soul, together with the facts about the nature of the embryo, exclude the possibility that the soul is present in the early embryo. I also believe, though I have not argued for this here, that there is no reason to suppose that souls of any sort exist. I think, therefore, that it is a mistake to think that we were ever early embryos. In other words, the first of the two assumptions stated in section 1 is false.

If we were never early embryos, the main reason for thinking that it is seriously wrong to kill or otherwise use early embryos for hESC research collapses. To kill an early embryo is not to kill someone like you or me. It is to prevent one of us from coming into existence.

7   When We Begin to Exist

If we are neither human organisms nor souls, what kind of thing are we essentially, and when do things of our sort begin to exist? What I believe to be the best answer may emerge if you imagine yourself in the very early stages of progressive dementia. How long will you survive? You will be there as long as long as your brain continues to generate consciousness, and indeed as long as your brain retains the capacity to generate consciousness. As long as there is a subject of experiences present, or if it is possible to revive a subject of experiences in your body, then *someone* is present, and who might that be if not you?

But what if your brain altogether and irreversibly loses the capacity for consciousness? What remains? Suppose the organism that many people take to be you remains alive. If I am right that you are not and never were an organism, then that living organism cannot be you. It is hard to identify anything else that might be you. I think we should conclude that you ceased to exist along with the capacity for consciousness. That suggests that you are essentially an entity with the capacity for consciousness – a mind.

A human organism is conscious only by virtue of having a conscious part. We are that part. We are that which is nonderivatively the subject of consciousness. The label I use to describe what we essentially are is "embodied mind."

We coexist with our organisms throughout our lives, but our organisms begin to exist and are alive before we arrive on the scene, and they usually survive us, sometimes even remaining alive after we have ceased to be, as occurs, in my view, in persistent vegetative state. We begin to exist when the fetal brain develops the capacity for consciousness, which happens sometime between twenty-two and twenty-eight weeks after conception, when synapses develop among the neurons in the cerebral cortex. Only after the development of the capacity for consciousness is there anyone who can be harmed, or wronged, by being killed.

8   Potential

Even if I am right that we were never six-day-old embryos and that the main objection to killing embryos has no force, there remain two possible reasons for thinking that killing early embryos is wrong. Neither offers as strong an objection to killing early embryos as there would be if to kill an embryo were to kill someone whose moral status was the same as yours and mine. But each supports an objection serious enough to be worthy of discussion.

One appeals to potential. Unlike the Catholic view discussed in section 6, according to which the intrinsic potential for rationality *makes* an embryo a human being, this argument concedes that the embryo is not the same kind of thing that you and I are but claims that it has the potential to become one of us, and that this makes it a kind of thing that it is seriously wrong to kill, or to use as a mere means.

Although I claim that we are essentially embodied minds and are only contingently persons (that is, beings with psychological capacities of a certain level of complexity and sophistication), I also think that at those times when we are persons our moral status is conspicuously high. Some of those who object to the killing of embryos do so on the ground that although embryos are not persons, they have the potential to become persons. The problem with this suggestion, however, is that the sense in which embryos have the potential to become persons is not the sense in which potential might be a basis of moral status.

A little more than fifty years ago there existed a sperm and egg pair from which I eventually developed.

We say that that pair of cells had the potential to become me; yet I never existed as those two things. I am one thing and cannot ever have been identical with each of two distinct entities. The potential that the sperm and egg together possessed was merely the potential to give rise to the later existence of an entity – me – to which neither would be identical. That kind of potential is not a basis for a high, intrinsic moral status. Neither that sperm nor that egg would have been wronged by being killed. It would have been permissible to kill either or both, or to use either as a mere means.

The potential of an early embryo is like that: it is not the potential to *be* a person, in the sense that presupposes that the embryo would be one and the same thing as the later person. It is, rather, only the potential to give rise to the existence of a person who would be an individual numerically distinct from the embryo. An early embryo's potential, therefore, provides no more reason not to kill the embryo than there is not to kill any particular sperm and egg pair. (This is true unless we identify a different way in which the potential might be valuable. If the potential were valuable not as a basis of moral status but because it was important to have more persons in the world, then the value of the embryo's potential might be greater than that of a sperm and egg pair because the embryo's potential would have a higher probability of being realized.)

9 Intrinsic Value

Some philosophers argue that even if early human embryos do not have the same moral status that you and I have, they nevertheless have a special sort of value. They may not have interests or rights or be worthy of the sort of respect that is owed to rational beings, but they have a certain sanctity that prohibits our treating them in certain ways (Dworkin 1993; Steinbock 2006).

It is difficult to demonstrate that such a claim is false, though it is also difficult to explain on what basis, other than its potential, an early human embryo could have a special value that an animal, or even an animal embryo, lacks. But let us assume, for the sake of argument, that an early embryo does indeed have a special sort of value or sanctity. Just how important a value is this?

If we consider the social practices of our society, it is hard to avoid the conclusion that few people really think that early embryos have significant intrinsic value. As I noted earlier, even most of those who oppose the killing of embryos for hESC research tend not to protest strenuously at the inevitability of eventually killing the many thousands of embryos created and frozen as a byproduct of the practice of assisted conception, or allowing them to die. And even those who oppose assisted conception on the ground that it creates embryos that must eventually be killed, or be allowed to die, do not campaign for research on ways of preventing the vast number of deaths among early embryos that are occurring all the time all over the world through spontaneous abortion. Approximately two-thirds of all human embryos conceived die naturally before birth, and a high proportion of these deaths occur prior to implantation – that is, within the first couple of weeks after conception. If early embryos had significant intrinsic value, there would surely be serious reason to attempt to prevent these many deaths. But even the most vocal champions of early embryos have so far evinced little concern.

I think, therefore, that appeals to the early embryo's potential or to its intrinsic value support only a feeble case against the killing of embryos if it is true, as I have argued, that we were never early embryos. The conclusion I draw is that there is no serious moral objection to killing an early embryo. To kill an early embryo is morally comparable to killing both a sperm and an egg that would otherwise have fused to form a zygote. Indeed, on this view, there is not even any significant moral reason to prefer the new technique for acquiring hESCs that allows the embryo to live to the older technique that involves killing the embryo at five or six days.

Acknowledgments

I am very grateful for comments on this essay to Laura Grabel, Lori Gruen, and, especially, Alfonso Gómez-Lobo.

Notes

1 "President Discusses Stem Cell Research," 9 August
   2001 [see chapter 58 in this volume].
2 This definition of a human organism implies that a
   zygote is not a human organism, even though it is
   genetically human and is an organism. The definition has
   this implication because it stipulates that at least some of
   a human organism's parts must be living, whereas the
   parts of a zygote are not thought to be separately alive.
   Those who believe that zygotes are human organisms
   could amend the definition by deleting the adjective
   "living."

3 I am much indebted to Alphonso Gómez-Lobo for
   pressing me on this, and for providing me with evidence of
   various forms and degrees of intercellular coordination
   that are manifest shortly after fertilization. He has persuaded
   me that, at a minimum, I should be more agnostic about
   the time at which a human organism begins to exist than
   I was in McMahan 2002, in which I argued for the second
   of the two interpretations discussed here.
4 See http://news.bbc.co.uk/2/hi/health/4285235.stm
   and http://news.bbc.co.uk/1/hi/world/4848164.stm
   (both accessed on 22 October 2006).

References

Dworkin, Ronald. 1993. *Life's Dominion*. New York: Knopf.

George, Robert P., and Alfonso Gómez-Lobo. 2002. "Statement of Professor George (Joined by Dr. Gómez-Lobo)." In *Human Cloning and Human Dignity: An Ethical Inquiry*, report by the President's Council on Bioethics, 258–66, available at https://bioethicsarchive.georgetown.edu/pcbe/reports/cloningreport/.

McCall Smith, Alexander. 2004. *Creating Humans: Ethical Questions Where Reproduction and Science Collide*. Prince Frederick, Md.: Recorded Books.

McMahan, Jeff. 2002. *The Ethics of Killing: Problems at the Margins of Life*. New York: Oxford University Press.

McMahan, Jeff. 2008. "Challenges to Human Equality." *Journal of Ethics*, 12: 81–104.

Steinbock, Bonnie. 2006. "The Morality of Killing Human Embryos." *Journal of Law, Medicine, and Ethics* 34, no. 1 (Spring): 26–34.

Thomson, Judith Jarvis. 1971. "A Defense of Abortion." *Philosophy and Public Affairs* 1, no. 1 (Fall): 47–66.

Part VIII

Experimentation with Animals

Introduction

The seventeenth-century French philosopher René Descartes thought that nonhuman animals, including mammals and vertebrates, were insensitive automata, lacking consciousness. Today, this view has largely been discarded. Physiological studies and behavioral observations leave little doubt that at least all mammals and birds, and probably all vertebrates, have conscious experiences. They can experience pain, suffering and discomfort, and their lives can go better or worse for them. If this were not the case, animal experimentation would raise few ethical issues. The ethical debate over whether, and if so when, nonhuman animals – mice, rabbits, cats, dogs, rhesus monkeys and chimpanzees, for example – can justifiably be used in medical and biomedical research is premised on the belief that animals can experience distressing mental states.

Some people object to all experimentation on nonhuman animals. Many others – often persuaded by the view that experimentation can bring great benefits to humans (and sometimes to animals) – hold that nonhuman animals may at least sometimes justifiably be used in research. The readings in this Part VIII of the anthology focus on the second position, and on the kinds of argument that might be advanced for and against it. This position is typically held in conjunction with the view that distressing or dangerous research is more easily justified when conducted on animals than when conducted on humans.

The view that nonhuman animals deserve lesser consideration than humans is sometimes defended by appeal to religious teachings – for example, that the God of Judaism and Christianity has given humans dominion over animals, and that only humans but not "brutes" have immortal souls, or are made in the image of God. Religious appeals, however, address only a limited audience. They will be unpersuasive to those who subscribe to a different religion or to no religion at all.

Not all defenses of a substantive moral divide between humans and nonhuman rely on religious premises. The philosophy of the eighteenth-century German philosopher Immanuel Kant ("Duties towards Animals"), for example, centers on rationality and the capacity for autonomous action, which he regarded as the most ethically significant characteristics of humans. Rational beings, capable of autonomous action, are, according to Kant, ends in themselves; nonrational animals, on the other hand, "are there merely as means to an end." This does not entail that rational agents may inflict needless cruelty on animals. Being cruel to animals, Kant thought, will be bad for our relations with other humans, "for he who is cruel to animals becomes hard also in his dealings with men." In other words, we should refrain from inflicting needless suffering on an animal, not because it is bad for the animal, but rather because it is bad for humans.

In a footnote to *An Introduction to the Principles of Morals and Legislation*, the nineteenth-century British philosopher and reformer Jeremy Bentham urged – as one would expect from the founding father of English

Bioethics: An Anthology, Third Edition. Edited by Helga Kuhse, Udo Schüklenk, and Peter Singer.
© 2016 John Wiley & Sons, Inc. Published 2016 by John Wiley & Sons, Inc.

utilitarianism – that humans and animals have an important morally relevant characteristic in common: the capacity for pain and pleasure. Referring to animals, Bentham writes: "The question is not, Can they *reason?* Nor, Can they *talk?* but, Can they *suffer?*" According to Bentham, sentience or the capacity to experience pleasure and pain entitles a being to moral consideration. Animals matter morally because they are sentient. Bentham thought it wrong to inflict unnecessary pain and suffering on animals, not because our doing so harms humans, but because it harms the animals themselves.

Peter Singer's essay "All Animals Are Equal," first published in 1974, contains the key ideas of his 1975 book *Animal Liberation*, sometimes credited with triggering the modern animal rights movement. Most people support the idea that all humans are equal, but are not clear about the basis for this belief. Singer suggests that the only sound basis for it is the principle of equal consideration of interests. He questions, however, the almost universal assumption that this principle applies to humans only. The principle of the equal consideration of interests demands, he argues, that "the interests of every being affected by an action are to be taken into account and given the same weight as the like interests of any other being." This applies no matter what the species of the being. To give preference to the interests of members of the species *Homo sapiens*, simply because that is our species, is as morally objectionable as giving preference to those of our own race or sex.

The claim that "speciesism" is on the same moral plane as racism or sexism may be denied by those who hold that humans deserve special moral consideration on account of their superior mental capacities. For Kant, this meant rationality and autonomy. For Sir William Paton in his "Commentary from a Vivisecting Professor of Pharmacology" – part of "Vivisection, Morals and Medicine: An Exchange" – the crucial capacity is the ability to accumulate experiences, and "to build on the past and to look to the future." But as both R. G. Frey ("Morals and Medicine") and Singer argue, any such attempt to make the boundary of the species *Homo sapiens* coincide with something of clear moral significance runs into the problem that many humans – infants, the permanently comatose, and humans with severe mental disabilities – have

capacities far below those possessed by many nonhuman animals. Why, then, not experiment on these diminished humans, rather than on healthy animals? The answer that these diminished humans could not give their consent to such experimentation will not do, since as Frey points out, the inability of animals to give their informed consent has not stopped scientists from using them in research.

Neither Frey nor Singer puts his argument against animal experimentation in absolutist terms. But, Singer argues, experimentation ought to be drastically reduced. In many areas of scientific research nonhuman animals are simply regarded as items of laboratory equipment, "to be used and expended as desired" for purposes that are not sufficiently significant to justify the suffering caused to them. This objection to some research leaves unaffected research that does promise to have highly significant results. Would saving the lives of thousands justify experimentation on a single animal? But why, asks Singer, assume, as the hypothetical question does, that the saving of thousands of lives requires experimentation on a nonhuman animal? As Singer puts it:

> The way to reply to this purely hypothetical question is to pose another: would the experimenter be prepared to perform his experiment on an orphaned human infant, if that were the only way to save many lives? … If the experimenter is not prepared to use an orphaned human infant, then his readiness to use nonhumans is simple discrimination, since adult apes, cats, mice, and other mammals are more aware of what is happening to them, more self-directing and, so far as we can tell, at least as sensitive to pain, as any human infant.

It might be objected, of course, that most human infants, in distinction from all or most animals, have the potential to grow into persons. But that objection, Singer holds, still fails to provide us with a reason why we should use a nonhuman animal rather than humans with severe and irreversible brain damage, in research.

If this is correct, it would leave scientists engaged in genuinely important research with a dilemma. Frey, in his response to Paton, imagines a scientist doing serious work on blindness that needs to use animal retinas. The scientist could, Frey suggests, either blind rabbits or blind severely intellectually disabled humans. If it is deemed too distasteful to do these kinds of experiment on humans, then animals with similar or superior capacities ought to be excluded as well. On the other hand, if experimentation on animals were regarded as both necessary and justifiable, this would also – other things being equal – justify experimentation on some humans. Would scientists who defend experimentation on animals in a nonspeciesist manner be willing to face that implication of their argument?

60

Duties towards Animals

Immanuel Kant

Baumgarten speaks of duties towards beings which are beneath us and beings which are above us. But so far as animals are concerned, we have no direct duties. Animals are not self-conscious and are there merely as a means to an end. That end is man. We can ask, 'Why do animals exist?' But to ask, 'Why does man exist?' is a meaningless question. Our duties towards animals are merely indirect duties towards humanity. Animal nature has analogies to human nature, and by doing our duties to animals in respect of manifestations which correspond to manifestations of human nature, we indirectly do our duty towards humanity. Thus, if a dog has served his master long and faithfully, his service, on the analogy of human service, deserves reward, and when the dog has grown too old to serve, his master ought to keep him until he dies. Such action helps to support us in our duties towards human beings, where they are bounden duties. If then any acts of animals are analogous to human acts and spring from the same principles, we have duties towards the animals because thus we cultivate the corresponding duties towards human beings. If a man shoots his dog because the animal is no longer capable of service, he does not fail in his duty to the dog, for the dog cannot judge, but his act is inhuman and damages in himself that humanity which it is his duty to show towards mankind. If he is not to stifle his human feelings, he must practise

kindness towards animals, for he who is cruel to animals becomes hard also in his dealings with men. We can judge the heart of a man by his treatment of animals. Hogarth depicts this in his engravings ('The Stages of Cruelty', 1757). He shows how cruelty grows and develops. He shows the child's cruelty to animals, pinching the tail of a dog or a cat; he then depicts the grown man in his cart running over a child; and lastly, the culmination of cruelty in murder. He thus brings home to us in a terrible fashion the rewards of cruelty, and this should be an impressive lesson to children. The more we come in contact with animals and observe their behaviour, the more we love them, for we see how great is their care for their young. It is then difficult for us to be cruel in thought even to a wolf. Leibniz used a tiny worm for purposes of observation, and then carefully replaced it with its leaf on the tree so that it should not come to harm through any act of his. He would have been sorry – a natural feeling for a humane man – to destroy such a creature for no reason. Tender feelings towards dumb animals develop humane feelings towards mankind. In England butchers and doctors do not sit on a jury because they are accustomed to the sight of death and hardened. Vivisectionists, who use living animals for their experiments, certainly act cruelly, although their aim is praiseworthy, and they can justify their cruelty, since animals must be

Original publication details: Immanuel Kant, "Duties towards Animals," pp. 239–41 from *Lectures on Ethics*, trans. Louis Infield, London: Methuen, 1930. Copyright 1930 Methuen, reproduced by permission of Taylor & Francis Books UK.

regarded as man's instruments; but any such cruelty for sport cannot be justified. A master who turns out his ass or his dog because the animal can no longer earn its keep manifests a small mind. The Greeks' ideas in this respect were high-minded, as can be seen from the fable of the ass and the bell of ingratitude. Our duties towards animals, then, are indirect duties towards mankind.

61

A Utilitarian View

Jeremy Bentham

What other agents then are there, which, at the same time that they are under the influence of man's direction, are susceptible of happiness? They are of two sorts: 1. Other human beings who are styled persons. 2. Other animals, which, on account of their interests having been neglected by the insensibility of the ancient jurists, stand degraded into the class of *things*.[1]

Note

1 Under the Gentoo and Mahometan religions, the interests of the rest of the animal creation seem to have met with some attention. Why have they not, universally, with as much as those of human creatures, allowance made for the difference in point of sensibility? Because the laws that are have been the work of mutual fear; a sentiment which the less rational animals have not had the same means as man has of turning to account. Why *ought* they not? No reason can be given. If the being eaten were all, there is very good reason why we should be suffered to eat such of them as we like to eat: we are the better for it, and they are never the worse. They have none of those long-protracted anticipations of future misery which we have. The death they suffer in our hands commonly is, and always may be, a speedier, and by that means a less painful one, than that which would await them in the inevitable course of nature. If the being killed were all, there is very good reason why we should be suffered to kill such as molest us: we should be the worse for their living, and they are never the worse for being dead. But is there any reason why we should be suffered to torment them? Not any that I can see. Are there any why we should *not* be suffered to torment them? Yes, several. The day has been, I grieve to say in many places it is not yet past, in which the greater part of the species, under the denomination of slaves, have been treated by the law exactly upon the same footing as, in England for example, the inferior races of animals are still. The day *may* come, when the rest of the animal creation may acquire those rights which never could have been withholden from them but by the hand of tyranny. The French have already discovered that the blackness of the skin is no reason why a human being should be abandoned without redress to the caprice of a tormentor. It may come one day to be recognized, that the number of the legs, the villosity of the skin, or the termination of the *os sacrum*, are reasons equally insufficient for abandoning a sensitive being to the same fate. What else is it that should trace the insuperable line? Is it the faculty of reason, or, perhaps, the faculty of discourse? But a full-grown horse or dog is beyond comparison a more rational, as well as a more conversable animal, than an infant of a day, or a week, or even a month, old. But suppose the case were otherwise, what would it avail? The question is not, Can they *reason?* nor, Can they *talk?* but, Can they *suffer?*

Original publication details: Jeremy Bentham, "A Utilitarian View," section XVIII, IV from *An Introduction to the Principles of Morals and Legislation*, First published c.1820.

62

All Animals Are Equal

Peter Singer[1]

In recent years a number of oppressed groups have campaigned vigorously for equality. The classic instance is the Black Liberation movement, which demands an end to the prejudice and discrimination that has made blacks second-class citizens. The immediate appeal of the black liberation movement and its initial, if limited, success made it a model for other oppressed groups to follow. We became familiar with liberation movements for Spanish-Americans, gay people, and a variety of other minorities. When a majority group – women – began their campaign, some thought we had come to the end of the road. Discrimination on the basis of sex, it has been said, is the last universally accepted form of discrimination, practiced without secrecy or pretense even in those liberal circles that have long prided themselves on their freedom from prejudice against racial minorities.

One should always be wary of talking of "the last remaining form of discrimination". If we have learnt anything from the liberation movements, we should have learnt how difficult it is to be aware of latent prejudice in our attitudes to particular groups until this prejudice is forcefully pointed out.

A liberation movement demands an expansion of our moral horizons and an extension or reinterpretation of the basic moral principle of equality. Practices that were previously regarded as natural and inevitable come to be seen as the result of an unjustifiable prejudice. Who can say with confidence that all his or her attitudes and practices are beyond criticism? If we wish to avoid being numbered amongst the oppressors, we must be prepared to rethink even our most fundamental attitudes. We need to consider them from the point of view of those most disadvantaged by our attitudes, and the practices that follow from these attitudes. If we can make this unaccustomed mental switch we may discover a pattern in our attitudes and practices that consistently operates so as to benefit one group – usually the one to which we ourselves belong – at the expense of another. In this way we may come to see that there is a case for a new liberation movement. My aim is to advocate that we make this mental switch in respect of our attitudes and practices towards a very large group of beings: members of species other than our own – or, as we popularly though misleadingly call them, animals. In other words, I am urging that we extend to other species the basic principle of equality that most of us recognize should be extended to all members of our own species.

All this may sound a little far-fetched, more like a parody of other liberation movements than a serious objective. In fact, in the past the idea of "The Rights of Animals" really has been used to parody the case for women's rights. When Mary Wollstonecraft, a forerunner of later feminists, published her *Vindication of the Rights*

Original publication details: Peter Singer, "All Animals are Equal," pp. 103–16 from *Philosophic Exchange* 1: 5 (1974). Center for Philosophic Exchange, State University of New York, Brockford, NY, 1974.

Bioethics: An Anthology, Third Edition. Edited by Helga Kuhse, Udo Schüklenk, and Peter Singer.

of Women in 1792, her ideas were widely regarded as absurd, and they were satirized in an anonymous publication entitled *A Vindication of the Rights of Brutes*. The author of this satire (actually Thomas Taylor, a distinguished Cambridge philosopher) tried to refute Wollstonecraft's reasonings by showing that they could be carried one stage further. If sound when applied to women, why should the arguments not be applied to dogs, cats and horses? They seemed to hold equally well for these "brutes"; yet to hold that brutes had rights was manifestly absurd; therefore the reasoning by which this conclusion had been reached must be unsound, and if unsound when applied to brutes, it must also be unsound when applied to women, since the very same arguments had been used in each case.

One way in which we might reply to this argument is by saying that the case for equality between men and women cannot validly be extended to nonhuman animals. Women have a right to vote, for instance, because they are just as capable of making rational decisions as men are; dogs, on the other hand, are incapable of understanding the significance of voting, so they cannot have the right to vote. There are many other obvious ways in which men and women resemble each other closely, while humans and other animals differ greatly. So, it might be said, men and women are similar beings, and should have equal rights, while humans and nonhumans are different and should not have equal rights.

The thought behind this reply to Taylor's analogy is correct up to a point, but it does not go far enough. There *are* important differences between humans and other animals, and these differences must give rise to *some* differences in the rights that each have. Recognizing this obvious fact, however, is no barrier to the case for extending the basic principle of equality to nonhuman animals. The differences that exist between men and women are equally undeniable, and the supporters of Women's Liberation are aware that these differences may give rise to different rights. Many feminists hold that women have the right to an abortion on request. It does not follow that since these same people are campaigning for equality between men and women they must support the right of men to have abortions too. Since a man cannot have an abortion, it is meaningless to talk of his right to have one. Since a pig can't vote, it is meaningless to talk of

its right to vote. There is no reason why either Women's Liberation or Animal Liberation should get involved in such nonsense. The extension of the basic principle of equality from one group to another does not imply that we must treat both groups in exactly the same way, or grant exactly the same rights to both groups. Whether we should do so will depend on the nature of the members of the two groups. The basic principle of equality, I shall argue, is equality of consideration; and equal consideration for different beings may lead to different treatment and different rights.

So there is a different way of replying to Taylor's attempt to parody Wollstonecraft's arguments, a way which does not deny the differences between humans and nonhumans, but goes more deeply into the question of equality, and concludes by finding nothing absurd in the idea that the basic principle of equality applies to so-called "brutes". I believe that we reach this conclusion if we examine the basis on which our opposition to discrimination on grounds of race or sex ultimately rests. We will then see that we would be on shaky ground if we were to demand equality for blacks, women, and other groups of oppressed humans while denying equal consideration to nonhumans.

When we say that all human beings, whatever their race, creed or sex, are equal, what is it that we are asserting? Those who wish to defend a hierarchical, inegalitarian society have often pointed out that, by whatever test we choose, it simply is not true that all humans are equal. Like it or not, we must face the fact that humans come in different shapes and sizes; they come with differing moral capacities, differing intellectual abilities, differing amounts of benevolent feeling and sensitivity to the needs of others, differing abilities to communicate effectively, and differing capacities to experience pleasure and pain. In short, if the demand for equality were based on the actual equality of all human beings, we would have to stop demanding equality. It would be an unjustifiable demand.

Still, one might cling to the view that the demand for equality among human beings is based on the actual equality of the different races and sexes. Although humans differ as individuals in various ways, there are no differences between the races and sexes *as such*. From the mere fact that a person is black, or a woman, we cannot infer anything else about that person. This, it may be said, is what is wrong with racism and sexism. The white racist claims that whites are superior to blacks, but this is false – although there are differences between individuals, some blacks are superior to some whites in all of the capacities and abilities that could conceivably be relevant. The opponent of sexism would say the same: a person's sex is no guide to his or her abilities, and this is why it is unjustifiable to discriminate on the basis of sex.

This is a possible line of objection to racial and sexual discrimination. It is not, however, the way that someone really concerned about equality would choose, because taking this line could, in some circumstances, force one to accept a most inegalitarian society. The fact that humans differ as individuals, rather than as races or sexes, is a valid reply to someone who defends a hierarchical society like, say, South Africa, in which all whites are superior in status to all blacks. The existence of individual variations that cut across the lines of race or sex, however, provides us with no defence at all against a more sophisticated opponent of equality, one who proposes that, say, the interests of those with ratings above 100. Would a hierarchical society of this sort really be so much better than one based on race or sex? I think not. But if we tie the moral principle of equality to the factual equality of the different races or sexes, taken as a whole, our opposition to racism and sexism does not provide us with any basis for objecting to this kind of inegalitarianism.

There is a second important reason why we ought not to base our opposition to racism and sexism on any kind of factual equality, even the limited kind that asserts that variations in capacities and abilities are spread evenly between the different races and sexes: we can have no absolute guarantee that these abilities and capacities really are distributed evenly, without regard to race or sex, among human beings. So far as actual abilities are concerned, there do seem to be certain measurable differences between both races and sexes. These differences do not, of course, appear in each case, but only when averages are taken. More important still, we do not yet know how much of these differences is really due to the different genetic endowments of the various races and sexes, and how much is due to environmental differences that are the result of past and continuing discrimination. Perhaps all of the important differences will eventually prove to be environmental rather than genetic. Anyone opposed to racism and sexism will certainly hope that this will be so, for it will make the task of ending discrimination a lot easier; nevertheless it would be dangerous to rest the case against racism and sexism on the belief that all significant differences are environmental in origin. The opponent of, say, racism who takes this line will be unable to avoid conceding that if differences in ability did after all prove to have some genetic connection with race, racism would in some way be defensible.

It would be folly for the opponent of racism to stake his whole case on a dogmatic commitment to one particular outcome of a difficult scientific issue which is still a long way from being settled. While attempts to prove that differences in certain selected abilities between races and sexes are primarily genetic in origin have certainly not been conclusive, the same must be said of attempts to prove that these differences are largely the result of environment. At this stage of the investigation we cannot be certain which view is correct, however much we may hope it is the latter.

Fortunately, there is no need to pin the case for equality to one particular outcome of this scientific investigation. The appropriate response to those who claim to have found evidence of genetically-based differences in ability between the races or sexes is not to stick to the belief that the genetic explanation must be wrong, whatever evidence to the contrary may turn up: instead we should make it quite clear that the claim to equality does not depend on intelligence, moral capacity, physical strength, or similar matters of fact. Equality is a moral ideal, not a simple assertion of fact. There is no logically compelling reason for assuming that a factual difference in ability between two people justifies any difference in the amount of consideration we give to satisfying their needs and interests. The principle of the equality of human beings is not a description of an alleged actual equality among humans: it is a prescription of how we should treat humans.

Jeremy Bentham incorporated the essential basis of moral equality into his utilitarian system of ethics in the formula: "Each to count for one and none for more than one." In other words, the interests of every being affected by an action are to be taken into account and given the same weight as the like interests of any other being. A later utilitarian, Henry Sidgwick, put the point in this way: "The good of any one individual is of no more importance, from the point of view (if I may say so) of the Universe, than the good of any other."[2] More recently, the leading figures in contemporary moral philosophy have shown a great deal of agreement in specifying as a fundamental presupposition of their moral theories some similar requirement which operates so as to give everyone's interests equal consideration – although they cannot agree on how this requirement is best formulated.[3]

It is an implication of this principle of equality that our concern for others ought not to depend on what they are like, or what abilities they possess – although precisely what this concern requires us to do may vary according to the characteristics of those affected by what we do. It is on this basis that the case against racism and the case against sexism must both ultimately rest; and it is in accordance with this principle that speciesism is also to be condemned. If possessing a higher degree of intelligence does not entitle one human to use another for his own ends, how can it entitle humans to exploit non-humans?

Many philosophers have proposed the principle of equal consideration of interests, in some form or other, as a basic moral principle; but, as we shall see in more detail shortly, not many of them have recognized that this principle applies to members of other species as well as to our own. Bentham was one of the few who did realize this. In a forward-looking passage, written at a time when black slaves in the British dominions were still being treated much as we now treat nonhuman animals, Bentham wrote:

The day *may* come when the rest of the animal creation may acquire those rights which never could have been withholden from them but by the hand of tyranny. The French have already discovered that the blackness of the skin is no reason why a human being should be abandoned without redress to the caprice of a tormentor. It may one day come to be recognized that the number of the legs, the villosity of the skin, or the termination of the *os sacrum*, are reasons equally insufficient for abandoning a sensitive being to the same fate. What else is it that should trace the insuperable line? Is it the faculty of reason, or perhaps the faculty of discourse? But a full-grown horse or dog is beyond comparison a more

rational, as well as a more conversable animal, than an infant of a day, or a week, or even a month, old. But suppose they were otherwise, what would it avail? The question is not, Can they *reason*? nor, Can they *talk*? but, *Can they suffer*?[4]

In this passage Bentham points to the capacity for suffering as the vital characteristic that gives a being the right to equal consideration. The capacity for suffering – or more strictly, for suffering and/or enjoyment or happiness – is not just another characteristic like the capacity for language, or for higher mathematics. Bentham is not saying that those who try to mark "the insuperable line" that determines whether the interests of a being should be considered happen to have selected the wrong characteristic. The capacity for suffering and enjoying things is a prerequisite for having interests at all, a condition that must be satisfied before we can speak of interests in any meaningful way. It would be nonsense to say that it was not in the interests of a stone to be kicked along the road by a schoolboy. A stone does not have interests because it cannot suffer. Nothing that we can do to it could possibly make any difference to its welfare. A mouse, on the other hand, does have an interest in not being tormented, because it will suffer if it is.

If a being suffers, there can be no moral justification for refusing to take that suffering into consideration. No matter what the nature of the being, the principle of equality requires that its suffering be counted equally with the like suffering – in so far as rough comparisons can be made – of any other being. If a being is not capable of suffering, or of experiencing enjoyment or happiness, there is nothing to be taken into account. This is why the limit of sentience (using the term as a convenient, if not strictly accurate, shorthand for the capacity to suffer or experience enjoyment or happiness) is the only defensible boundary of concern for the interests of others. To mark this boundary by some characteristic like intelligence or rationality would be to mark it in an arbitrary way. Why not choose some other characteristic, like skin color?

The racist violates the principle of equality by giving greater weight to the interests of members of his own race, when there is a clash between their interests and the interests of those of another race.

Similarly the speciesist allows the interests of his own species to override the greater interests of members of other species.[5] The pattern is the same in each case. Most human beings are speciesists. I shall now very briefly describe some of the practices that show this.

For the great majority of human beings, especially in urban, industrialized societies, the most direct form of contact with members of other species is at meal-times: we eat them. In doing so we treat them purely as means to our ends. We regard their life and well-being as subordinate to our taste for a particular kind of dish. I say "taste" deliberately – this is purely a matter of pleasing our palate. There can be no defence of eating flesh in terms of satisfying nutritional needs, since it has been established beyond doubt that we could satisfy our need for protein and other essential nutrients far more efficiently with a diet that replaced animal flesh by soy beans, or products derived from soy beans, and other high-protein vegetable products.[6]

It is not merely the act of killing that indicates what we are ready to do to other species in order to gratify our tastes. The suffering we inflict on the animals while they are alive is perhaps an even clearer indication of our speciesism than the fact that we are prepared to kill them.[7] In order to have meat on the table at a price that people can afford, our society tolerates methods of meat production that confine sentient animals in cramped, unsuitable conditions for the entire durations of their lives. Animals are treated like machines that convert fodder into flesh, and any innovation that results in a higher "conversion ratio" is liable to be adopted. As one authority on the subject has said, "cruelty is acknowledged only when profit-ability ceases."[8] So hens are crowded four or five to a cage with a floor area of twenty inches by eighteen inches, or around the size of a single page of the *New York Times*. The cages have wire floors, since this reduces cleaning costs, though wire is unsuitable for the hens' feet; the floors slope, since this makes the eggs roll down for easy collection, although this makes it difficult for the hens to rest comfortably. In these conditions all the birds' natural instincts are thwarted: they cannot stretch their wings fully, walk freely, dust-bathe, scratch the ground, or build a nest. Although they have never known other conditions, observers have noticed that the birds vainly try to perform these actions. Frustrated at their inability to do so, they often develop what farmers call "vices", and peck each other to death. To prevent this, the beaks of young birds are often cut off.

This kind of treatment is not limited to poultry. Pigs are now also being reared in cages inside sheds. These animals are comparable to dogs in intelligence, and need a varied, stimulating environment if they are not to suffer from stress and boredom. Anyone who kept a dog in the way in which pigs are frequently kept would be liable to prosecution, in England at least, but, because our interest in exploiting pigs is greater than our interest in exploiting dogs, we object to cruelty to dogs while consuming the produce of cruelty to pigs. Of the other animals, the condition of veal calves is perhaps worst of all, since these animals are so closely confined that they cannot even turn around or get up and lie down freely. In this way they do not develop unpalatable muscle. They are also made anaemic and kept short of roughage, to keep their flesh pale, since white veal fetches a higher price; as a result they develop a craving for iron and rough-age, and have been observed to gnaw wood off the sides of their stalls, and lick greedily at any rusty hinge that is within reach.

Since, as I have said, none of these practices cater for anything more than our pleasures of taste, our practice of rearing and killing other animals in order to eat them is a clear instance of the sacrifice of the most important interests of other beings in order to satisfy trivial interests of our own. To avoid speciesism we must stop this practice, and each of us has a moral obligation to cease supporting the practice. Our custom is all the support that the meat industry needs. The decision to cease giving it that support may be difficult, but it is no more difficult than it would have been for a white Southerner to go against the traditions of his society and free his slaves; if we do not change our dietary habits, how can we censure those slaveholders who would not change their own way of living?

The same form of discrimination may be observed in the widespread practice of experimenting on other species in order to see if certain substances are safe for human beings, or to test some psychological theory about the effect of severe punishment on learning, or to try out various new compounds just in case something turns up. People sometimes think that all this experimentation is for vital medical purposes, and so will reduce suffering overall. This comfortable belief is very wide of the mark. Drug companies test new shampoos and cosmetics that they are intending to put on the market by dropping them into the eyes of rabbits, held open by metal clips, in order to observe what damage results. Food additives, like artificial colorings and preservatives, are tested by what is known as the "LD_{50}" – a test designed to find the level of consumption at which 50 per cent of a group of animals will die. In the process, nearly all of the animals are made very sick before some finally die, and others pull through. If the substance is relatively harmless, as it often is, huge doses have to be force-fed to the animals, until in some cases sheer volume or concentration of the substance causes death.

Much of this pointless cruelty goes on in the universities. In many areas of science, nonhuman animals are regarded as an item of laboratory equipment, to be used and expended as desired. In psychology laboratories experimenters devise endless variations and repetitions of experiments that were of little value in the first place. To quote just one example, from the experimenter's own account in a psychology journal: at the University of Pennsylvania, Perrin S. Cohen hung six dogs in hammocks with electrodes taped to their hind feet. Electric shock of varying intensity was then administered through the electrodes. If the dog learnt to press its head against a panel on the left, the shock was turned off, but otherwise it remained on indefinitely. Three of the dogs, however, were required to wait periods varying from 2 to 7 seconds while being shocked before making the response that turned off the current. If they failed to wait, they received further shocks. Each dog was given from 26 to 46 "sessions" in the hammock, each session consisting of 80 "trials" or shocks, administered at intervals of one minute. The experimenter reported that the dogs, who were unable to move in the hammock, barked or bobbed their heads when the current was applied. The reported findings of the experiment were that there was a delay in the dogs' responses that increased proportionally to the time the dogs were required to endure the shock, but a gradual increase in the intensity of the shock had no systematic effect in the timing of the response. The experiment was funded by the National Institutes of Health and the United States Public Health Service.[9]

In this example, and countless cases like it, the possible benefits to mankind are either nonexistent or fantastically remote; while the certain losses to members of other species are very real. This is, again, a clear indication of speciesism.

In the past, argument about vivisection has often missed this point, because it has been put in absolutist terms: would the abolitionist be prepared to let thousands die if they could be saved by experimenting on a single animal? The way to reply to this purely hypothetical question is to pose another: would the experimenter be prepared to perform his experiment on an orphaned human infant, if that were the only way to save many lives? (I say "orphan" to avoid the complication of parental feelings, although in doing so I am being overfair to the experimenter, since the non-human subjects of experiments are not orphans.) If the experimenter is not prepared to use an orphaned human infant, then his readiness to use nonhumans is simple discrimination, since adult apes, cats, mice, and other mammals are more aware of what is happening to them, more self-directing and, so far as we can tell, at least as sensitive to pain, as any human infant. There seems to be no relevant characteristic that human infants possess that adult mammals do not have to the same or a higher degree. (Someone might try to argue that what makes it wrong to experiment on a human infant is that the infant will, in time and if left alone, develop into more than the non-human, but one would then, to be consistent, have to oppose abortion, since the fetus has the same potential as the infant – indeed, even contraception and abstinence might be wrong on this ground, since the egg and sperm, considered jointly, also have the same potential. In any case, this argument still gives us no reason for selecting a nonhuman, rather than a human with severe and irreversible brain damage, as the subject for our experiments.)

The experimenter, then, shows a bias in favor of his own species whenever he carries out an experiment on a nonhuman for a purpose that he would not think justified him in using a human being at an equal or lower level of sentience, awareness, ability to be self-directing, etc. No one familiar with the kind of results yielded by most experiments on animals can have the slightest doubt that if this bias were eliminated the number of experiments performed would be a minute fraction of the number performed today.

Experimenting on animals and eating their flesh are perhaps the two major forms of speciesism in our society. By comparison, the third and last form of speciesism is so minor as to be insignificant, but it is perhaps of some special interest to those for whom this paper was written. I am referring to speciesism in contemporary philosophy.

Philosophy ought to question the basic assumptions of the age. Thinking through, critically and carefully, what most people take for granted is, I believe, the chief task of philosophy, and it is this task that makes philosophy a worthwhile activity. Regrettably, philosophy does not always live up to its historic role. Philosophers are human beings and they are subject to all the preconceptions of the society to which they belong. Sometimes they succeed in breaking free of the prevailing ideology: more often they become its most sophisticated defenders. So, in this case, philosophy as practiced in the universities today does not challenge anyone's preconceptions about our relations with other species. By their writings, those philosophers who tackle problems that touch upon the issue reveal that they make the same unquestioned assumptions as most other humans, and what they say tends to confirm the reader in his or her comfortable speciesist habits.

I could illustrate this claim by referring to the writings of philosophers in various fields – for instance, the attempts that have been made by those interested in rights to draw the boundary of the sphere of rights so that it runs parallel to the biological boundaries of the species *Homo sapiens*, including infants and even mental defectives, but excluding those other beings of equal or greater capacity who are so useful to us at mealtimes and in our laboratories. I think it would be a more appropriate conclusion to this paper, however, if I concentrated on the problem with which we have been centrally concerned, the problem of equality.

It is significant that the problem of equality, in moral and political philosophy, is invariably formulated in terms of human equality. The effect of this is that the question of the equality of other animals does not confront the philosopher or student as an issue in itself – and this is already an indication of the failure of philosophy to challenge accepted beliefs. Still, philosophers have found it difficult to discuss the issue of human equality without raising, in a paragraph or

two, the question of the status of other animals. The reason for this, which should be apparent from what I have said already, is that, if humans are to be regarded as equal to one another, we need some sense of "equal" that does not require any actual, descriptive equality of capacities, talents or other qualities. If equality is to be related to any actual characteristics of humans, these characteristics must be some lowest common denominator, pitched so low that no human lacks them – but then the philosopher comes up against the catch that any such set of characteristics which covers *all* humans will not be possessed *only by humans*. In other words, it turns out that, in the only sense in which we can truly say, as an assertion of fact, that all humans are equal, at least some members of other species are also equal – equal, that is, to each other and to humans. If, on the other hand, we regard the statement "All humans are equal" in some nonfactual way, perhaps as a prescription, then, as I have already argued, it is even more difficult to exclude nonhumans from the sphere of equality.

This result is not what the egalitarian philosopher originally intended to assert. Instead of accepting the radical outcome to which their own reasonings naturally point, however, most philosophers try to reconcile their beliefs in human equality and animal inequality by arguments that can only be described as devious.

As a first example, I take William Frankena's well-known article "The Concept of Social Justice."[10] Frankena opposes the idea of basing justice on merit, because he sees that this could lead to highly inegalitarian results. Instead he proposes the principle that:

> all men are to be treated as equals, not because they are equal, in any respect but simply because they are human. They are human because they have emotions and desires, and are able to think, and hence are capable of enjoying a good life in a sense in which other animals are not.

But what is this capacity to enjoy the good life which all humans have, but no other animals? Other animals have emotions and desires, and appear to be capable of enjoying a good life. We may doubt that they can think – although the behavior of some apes, dolphins and even dogs suggests that some of them can – but what is the relevance of thinking? Frankena goes on to admit that by "the good life" he means "not so much the morally good life as the happy or satisfactory life," so thought would appear to be unnecessary for enjoying the good life; in fact to emphasize the need for thought would make difficulties for the egalitarian since only some people are capable of leading intellectually satisfying lives or morally good lives. This makes it difficult to see what Frankena's principle of equality has to do with simply being *human*. Surely every sentient being is capable of leading a life that is happier or less miserable than some alternative life, and hence has a claim to be taken into account. In this respect the distinction between humans and nonhumans is not a sharp division, but rather a continuum along which we move gradually, and with overlaps between the species, from simple capacities for enjoyment and satisfaction, or pain and suffering, to more complex ones.

Faced with a situation in which they see a need for some basis for the moral gulf that is commonly thought to separate humans and animals, but can find no concrete difference that will do the job without undermining the equality of humans, philosophers tend to waffle. They resort to high-sounding phrases like "the intrinsic dignity of the human individual".[11] They talk of the "intrinsic worth of all men" as if men (humans?) had some worth that other beings did not,[12] or they say that humans, and only humans, are "ends in themselves," while "everything other than a person can only have value for a person."[13]

This idea of a distinctive human dignity and worth has a long history; it can be traced back directly to the Renaissance humanists, for instance to Pico della Mirandola's *Oration on the Dignity of Man*. Pico and other humanists based their estimate of human dignity on the idea that man possessed the central, pivotal position in the "Great Chain of Being" that led from the lowliest forms of matter to God himself; this view of the universe, in turn, goes back to both classical and Judeo-Christian doctrines. Contemporary philosophers have cast off these metaphysical and religious shackles and freely invoke the dignity of mankind without needing to justify the idea at all. Why should we not attribute "intrinsic dignity" or "intrinsic worth" to ourselves? Fellow-humans are unlikely to reject the accolades we so generously bestow on them, and those to whom we deny the honor are unable to object. Indeed, when one thinks only of humans, it can be

very liberal, very progressive, to talk of the dignity of all human beings. In so doing, we implicitly condemn slavery, racism, and other violations of human rights. We admit that we ourselves are in some fundamental sense on a par with the poorest, most ignorant members of our own species. It is only when we think of humans as no more than a small subgroup of all the beings that inhabit our planet that we may realize that in elevating our own species we are at the same time lowering the relative status of all other species.

The truth is that the appeal to the intrinsic dignity of human beings appears to solve the egalitarian's problems only as long as it goes unchallenged. Once we ask *why* it should be that all humans – including infants, mental defectives, psychopaths, Hitler, Stalin and the rest – have some kind of dignity or worth that no elephant, pig, or chimpanzee can ever achieve, we see that this question is as difficult to answer as our original request for some relevant fact that justifies the inequality of humans and other animals. In fact, these two questions are really one: talk of intrinsic dignity or moral worth only takes the problem back one step, because any satisfactory defence of the claim that all and only humans have intrinsic dignity would need to refer to some relevant capacities or characteristics that all and only humans possess. Philosophers frequently introduce ideas of dignity, respect and worth at the point at which other reasons appear to be lacking, but this is hardly good enough. Fine phrases are the last resource of those who have run out of arguments.

In case there are those who still think it may be possible to find some relevant characteristic that distinguishes all humans from all members of other species, I shall refer again, before I conclude, to the existence of some humans who quite clearly are below the level of awareness, self-consciousness, intelligence, and sentience of many nonhumans. I am thinking of humans with severe and irreparable brain damage, and also of infant humans. To avoid the complication of the relevance of a being's potential, however, I shall henceforth concentrate on permanently retarded humans.

Philosophers who set out to find a characteristic that will distinguish humans from other animals rarely take the course of abandoning these groups of humans by lumping them in with the other animals. It is easy to see why they do not. To take this line without rethinking our attitudes to other animals would entail that we have the right to perform painful experiments on retarded humans for trivial reasons; similarly it would follow that we had the right to rear and kill these humans for food. To most philosophers these consequences are as unacceptable as the view that we should stop treating non-humans in this way.

Of course, when discussing the problem of equality it is possible to ignore the problem of mental defectives, or brush it aside as if somehow insignificant.[14] This is the easiest way out. What else remains? My final example of speciesism in contemporary philosophy has been selected to show what happens when a writer is prepared to face the question of human equality and animal inequality without ignoring the existence of mental defectives, and without resorting to obscurantist mumbo-jumbo. Stanley Benn's clear and honest article "Egalitarianism and Equal Consideration of Interests"[15] fits this description.

Benn, after noting the usual "evident human inequalities" argues, correctly I think, for equality of consideration as the only possible basis for egalitarianism. Yet Benn, like other writers, is thinking only of "equal consideration of human interests". Benn is quite open in his defence of this restriction of equal consideration:

> not to possess human shape *is* a disqualifying condition. However faithful or intelligent a dog may be, it would be a monstrous sentimentality to attribute to him interests that could be weighed in an equal balance with those of human beings…if, for instance, one had to decide between feeding a hungry baby or a hungry dog, anyone who chose the dog would generally be reckoned morally defective, unable to recognize a fundamental inequality of claims.
>
> This is what distinguishes our attitude to animals from our attitude to imbeciles. It would be odd to say that we ought to respect equally the dignity or personality of the imbecile and of the rational man… but there is nothing odd about saying that we should respect their interests equally, that is, that we should give to the interests of each the same serious consideration as claims to considerations necessary for some standard of well-being that we can recognize and endorse.

Benn's statement of the basis of the consideration we should have for imbeciles seems to me correct, but why should there be any fundamental inequality of claims between a dog and a human imbecile? Benn sees that, if equal consideration depended on rationality, no reason could be given against using imbeciles for research purposes, as we now use dogs and guinea pigs. This will not do: "But of course we do distinguish imbeciles from animals in this regard," he says. That the common distinction is justifiable is something Benn does not question; his problem is how it is to be justified. The answer he gives is this:

> we respect the interests of men and give them priority over dogs not *insofar* as they are rational, but because rationality is the human norm. We say it is *unfair* to exploit the deficiencies of the imbecile who falls short of the norm, just as it would be unfair, and not just ordinarily dishonest, to steal from a blind man. If we do not think in this way about dogs, it is because we do not see the irrationality of the dog as a deficiency or a handicap, but as normal for the species. The characteristics, therefore, that distinguish the normal man from the normal dog make it intelligible for us to talk of other men having interests and capacities, and therefore claims, of precisely the same kind as we make on our own behalf. But although these characteristics may provide the point of the distinction between men and other species, they are not in fact the qualifying conditions for membership, or the distinguishing criteria of the class of morally considerable persons; and this is precisely because a man does not become a member of a different species, with its own standards of normality, by reason of not possessing these characteristics.

The final sentence of this passage gives the argument away. An imbecile, Benn concedes, may have no characteristics superior to those of a dog; nevertheless this does not make the imbecile a member of "a different species" as the dog is. *Therefore* it would be "unfair" to use the imbecile for medical research as we use the dog. But why? That the imbecile is not rational is just the way things have worked out, and the same is true of the dog – neither is any more responsible for their mental level. If it is unfair to take advantage of an isolated defect, why is it fair to take advantage of a more general limitation? I find it hard to see anything in this argument except a defence of preferring the interests of members of our own species because they are members of our own species. To those who think there might be more to it, I suggest the following mental exercise. Assume that it has been proven that there is a difference in the average, or normal, intelligence quotient for two different races, say whites and blacks. Then substitute the term "white" for every occurrence of "men" and "black" for every occurrence of "dog" in the passage quoted; and substitute "high IQ" for "rationality" and when Benn talks of "imbeciles" replace this term by "dumb whites" – that is, whites who fall well below the normal white IQ score. Finally, change "species" to "race." Now reread the passage. It has become a defence of a rigid, no-exceptions division between whites and blacks, based on IQ scores, *not withstanding an admitted overlap* between whites and blacks in

this respect. The revised passage is, of course, outrageous, and this is not only because we have made fictitious assumptions in our substitutions. The point is that in the original passage Benn was defending a rigid division in the amount of consideration due to members of different species, despite admitted cases of overlap. If the original did not, at first reading, strike us as being as outrageous as the revised version does, this is largely because, although we are not racists ourselves, most of us are speciesists. Like the other articles, Benn's stands as a warning of the ease with which the best minds can fall victim to a prevailing ideology.

Notes

1 Passages of this article appeared in a review of *Animals, Men and Morals*, edited by S. and R. Godlovitch and J. Harris (London: Gollancz and Taplinger, 1972) in the *New York Review of Books*, April 5, 1973. The whole direction of my thinking on this subject I owe to talks with a number of friends in Oxford in 1970–1, especially Richard Keshen, Stanley Godlovitch, and, above all, Roslind Godlovitch.

2 *The Methods of Ethics*, 7th edn, p. 382.

3 For example, R. M. Hare, *Freedom and Reason* (Oxford, 1963) and J. Rawls, *A Theory of Justice* (Harvard, 1972); for a brief account of the essential agreement on this issue between these and other positions, see R. M. Hare, "Rules of War and Moral Reasoning," *Philosophy and Public Affairs*, I, no. 2 (1972).

4 *Introduction to the Principles of Morals and Legislation*, ch. XVII.

5 I owe the term "speciesism" to Dr Richard Ryder.

6 In order to produce 1 lb of protein in the form of beef or veal, we must feed 21 lb of protein to the animal. Other forms of livestock are slightly less inefficient, but the average ratio in the US is still 1:8. It has been estimated that the amount of protein lost to humans in this way is equivalent to 90% of the annual world protein deficit. For a brief account, see Frances Moore Lappe, *Diet for a Small Planet* (New York: Friends of the Earth/Ballantine, 1971), pp. 4–11.

7 Although one might think that killing a being is obviously the ultimate wrong one can do to it, I think that the infliction of suffering is a clearer indication of speciesism because it might be argued that at least part of what is wrong with killing a human is that most humans are conscious of their existence over time, and have

desires and purposes that extend into the future – see, for instance, M. Tooley, "Abortion and Infanticide", *Philosophy and Public Affairs*, 2, no. 1 (1972). Of course, if one took this view one would have to hold – as Tooley does – that killing a human infant or mental defective is not in itself wrong, and is less serious than killing certain higher mammals that probably do have a sense of their own existence over time.

8 Ruth Harrison, *Animal Machines* (London: Stuart, 1964). This book provides an eye-opening account of intensive farming methods for those unfamiliar with the subject.

9 *Journal of the Experimental Analysis of Behavior*, 13, no. 1 (1970). Any recent volume of this journal, or of other journals in the field, like the *Journal of Comparative and Physiological Psychology*, will contain reports of equally cruel and trivial experiments. For a fuller account, see Richard Ryder, "Experiments on Animals" in *Animals, Men and Morals*.

10 In R. Brandt (ed.), *Social Justice* (Englewood Cliffs, NJ: Prentice-Hall, 1962); the passage quoted appears on p. 19.

11 Frankena in Brandt, *Social Justice*, p. 23.

12 H. A. Bedau, "Egalitarianism and the Idea of Equality" in *Nomos IX: Equality*, ed. J. R. Pennock and J. W. Chapman (New York, 1967).

13 G. Vlastos, "Justice and Equality" in Brandt, *Social Justice*, p. 48.

14 For example, Bernard Williams, "The Idea of Equality", in *Philosophy, Politics and Society* (second series), ed. P. Laslett and W. Runciman (Oxford: Blackwell, 1962), p. 118; J. Rawls, *A Theory of Justice*, pp. 509–10.

15 *Nomos IX: Equality*; the passages quoted are on pp. 62ff.

63

Vivisection, Morals and Medicine
An Exchange

R. G. Frey and Sir William Paton

Note

The following debate occurred in the Journal of Medical Ethics.

If one wishes to accept that some painful animal experimentation can be justified on grounds that benefit is conferred, one is faced with a difficult moral dilemma argues the first author, a philosopher. Either one needs to be able to say why human lives of any quality however low should be inviolable from painful experimentation when animal lives are not; or one should accept that sufficient benefit can justify certain painful experiments on human beings of sufficiently low quality of life. Alternatively, one can reject the original premise and accept antivivisectionism.

Original publication details: R. G. Frey and Sir William Paton, "Vivisection, Morals and Medicine: An Exchange," pp. 94–7 and 102–4 from *Journal of Medical Ethics* 9 (1983). Reproduced with permission from BMJ Publishing Group.

Morals and Medicine

R. G. Frey

I am not an antivivisectionist, and I am not in part for the same reason most people are not, namely, that vivisection can be justified by the benefits it confers. I do not believe it is widely realized, however, to what those who employ this reason are committed. Since many medical people also employ it to justify animal experiments, I think some discussion of the most important of these commitments is in order here. That members of the medical profession will almost certainly find this commitment repugnant in the extreme is perhaps reason enough for making sure that they are aware of it and of why they are in need of some means of avoiding it. (In order to stress this commitment, I am going only to sketch some matters and to avoid some others which, in a fuller treatment of vivisection, would have to be explored. My remarks are non-technical and will be familiar to those knowledgeable of recent controversies involving utilitarianism and the taking of life and of the work on vivisection of Peter Singer, one of the utilitarians involved in these controversies.)

I

Most people are not antivivisectionists, I suspect, because they think that some benefit or range of benefits can justify experiments, including painful ones, on animals. Increasingly, there are some things such people do not think; for example, that they are committed (i) to regarding simply anything – another floor polish, another eye shadow, for which animals have suffered – as a benefit, (ii) to approving of simply any experiment whatever on animals, in the hallowed name of research, (iii) to forgoing criticism of certain experiments as trivial or unnecessary or a (mere) PhD exercise, (iv) to halting the search for alternatives to the use of animals or to refraining from criticism of scientists who, before commencing experiments, conduct at best a perfunctory search for such alternatives, (v) to approving of (extravagant) wastage, as when twenty rabbits are used where five will do, and (vi) to refraining, in the case of some painful experiments, from a long, hard look at whether even *this* projected benefit is really important and substantial enough to warrant the infliction of *this* degree of pain.

Who benefits? Sometimes animals do, and sometimes both humans and animals do; but, not infrequently, indeed, perhaps typically, the experiments are carried out on animals with an eye to human benefit.

Some antivivisectionists appear to reject this appeal to benefit. I have in mind especially those who have, as it were, a two-stage position, who begin by objecting to painful animal experiments and eventually move on to objecting to animal experiments per se. Among other reasons for this move, two are noteworthy here. First, vivisectionists may well seek to reduce and eliminate the pain involved in an experiment, for example by redesigning it, by dropping parts of it, by adopting different methods for carrying it out, by the use of drugs and pain-killers (and by fostering new developments in drugs, pain-killers, and genetic engineering), by painlessly disposing of the animals before they come to feel post-operative pain, and so on. The point, of course, is not that the vivisectionist must or will inevitably succeed in his, or her, aim but rather that, if he did, or to the extent that he does, the argument from pain would, or does, cease to apply. Thus, giving up painful experiments may well not be the only or the only effective way of dealing with the pain they involve. So it is tempting to shift to a condemnation of animal experiments per se, which at once reduces the manoeuvrings of the vivisectionist over pain to nothing. Second, and, to a great many antivivisectionists, possibly even more importantly, the pain argument has nothing to say to the countless millions of painless and relatively painless animal experiments performed each year throughout the world; and these, I should have thought, vastly outnumber the painful ones. So, in order to encompass them in one's antivivisectionism, it is once again tempting to shift to a condemnation of animal experiments per se.

The above in no way denies, of course, that the antivivisectionist may want to deal first with painful experiments, before turning to look at any others; but turn he will, if those I have talked to are representative. For, in the end, *it is the use of animals as experimental subjects at all*, not just or possibly even primarily their use as subjects of painful experiments, that I have found lies at the bottom of their antivivisectionism.

To the vivisectionist, the antivivisectionist would appear to think that *no* benefit is important and substantial enough to justify painful animal experiments and, eventually, that *no* benefit is important and substantial enough to justify animal experiments. And this position, the vivisectionist will think, is very unlikely to recommend itself to many people. It is obvious why. Would your view of Salk vaccine simply be turned on its head, if it came to light that it was tested on monkeys or that some monkeys suffered pain (perhaps even intense pain) in the course of testing it or that it is made by cultivating strains of a virus in monkey tissue?

It would be silly to pretend that all animal experiments are of vast, stupendous importance; it would be equally silly, however, to deny that benefit has accrued to us (and sometimes to animals) through animal experimentation. (Often, the problem is that a series of experiments, at different times, by different people, enable still someone else to build upon those experiments to yield a benefit; for this reason, it is not always easy to tell of a particular experiment what its ultimate significance will be.) If informed, concerned people

do not want animal research carried out without guidelines as to animal welfare, since animals are not merely another piece of equipment, to be manipulated however one will, neither do they want our laboratories closed down until, assuming such a time comes, all experiments can be carried out on bacteria, or, more generally, on non-animal subjects.

II

I believe this vivisectionist I have sketched represents what a great many people think about animal experimentation and antivivisectionism. To be sure, it represents what they think only in its most general outline; but even this much shows the central role the appeal to benefit plays in their thinking.

Now there is a feature of this appeal which, though perfectly straightforward, is nevertheless not widely appreciated, a feature which has implications for the medical profession. Michael W Fox, a long-serving member of the animal welfare movement, comes out against antivivisectionism.[1] 'Some antivivisectionists would have no research done on animals. This is a limited and unrealistic view since in many cases it is the only way to test a new vaccine or drug which could save many lives – human and animal. Often the drugs being tested will treat or alleviate disease in both animal and human.' Fox might have posed a sterner test for himself and vivisectionists generally if he had drawn the example so that the vaccine benefited only humans but was tested, and tested painfully, only on animals; but this is by the way. The important point is Fox's entirely false presumption that the only alternative to not testing the vaccine and reaping the benefit is to test it upon animals; it could, of course, be tested upon human beings. There is absolutely nothing about the appeal to benefit which precludes this; so far as this appeal is concerned, if securing the benefit licenses (painful) experiments on animals, it equally licenses (painful) experiments on humans, since the benefit may be secured by either means. Moreover, we must not forget that we have already a powerful reason *for* human experiments: we typically experiment upon animals with an eye towards benefiting humans, and it seems only sensible, if we want to find out the effect of some substance upon humans, that we test it upon humans.

This is especially true, as doubts increasingly arise about whether extrapolations from the animal to the human case are not very prone to error and to the effects of in-built differences between animals and humans. (The saccharin controversy is sometimes cited as a case in point.) In some cases, such extrapolations may be positively dangerous; I have in mind cases where a substance has far less marked or severe effects in animals than in humans. (I have heard thalidomide, and what testing was done with it, cited in this connection.)

What I am saying, then, is that someone who relies upon the appeal to benefit to justify (painful) experiments on animals needs one more shot in his locker, if he is to prevent the appeal from justifying (painful) experiments upon humans. Specifically, he needs some reason which demarcates humans from animals, and which shows why we are not justified in doing to humans what we in our laboratories do to animals.

A great many things could be said at this point (the claim that animals do not feel pain is hardly one of them, since, whatever else may be said about this claim, the experiments in question could be painless), but I do not have space for even a few of them. I propose to leap, therefore, to what I think would be widely held, upon reflection, to be the reason to allow the appeal to benefit in the case of animals but to disallow it in the case of humans. Quite simply, human life, it will be said, is more valuable than animal life. Not only is this something which is widely thought, but it is also something which even such a fervent defender of animal liberation as the philosopher Peter Singer accepts.[2]

What is the source of this greater value? To some, it may be traced to their religious beliefs; but to the ever increasing numbers of non-believers, which I presume include some medical people as well as others, this appeal to religion is unavailable. I am not myself religious, and I cannot in good faith maintain that humans have souls but animals do not, that humans have been granted dominion over the beasts of the earth, that human life is sacred or sanctified whereas animal life is either not similarly blessed or blessed to a far less extent, and so on. So, what is left? One might try to appeal to some non-religiously grounded principle of respect or reverence for life; but, prima facie, such a principle does not cede human life greater value than animal life but rather enjoins us to revere life or living things per se. Accordingly, a person who adopts the appeal to benefit and who accepts a respect or reverence-for-life view still has no reason for thinking the benefit may only be secured through animal and never through human experiments.

Ultimately, though many twists and turns of argument have to be disposed of first, I think the non-religious person who thinks that human life is more valuable than animal life will find himself forced back upon our complex make-up to find the source of that value. What I mean is this. If we ask ourselves what makes our lives valuable, I think we shall want to give as answers such things as the pleasures of friendship, eating and drinking, listening to music, participating in sports, obtaining satisfaction through our job, reading, enjoying a beautiful summer's day, getting married and sharing experiences with someone, sex, watching and helping our children to grow up, solving quite difficult practical and intellectual problems in pursuit of some goal we highly prize, and so on. Within this mixed bag, there are some activities we may well share with animals; but our make-up is complex, and there are dimensions to us which there are not to animals. When we think in these terms, of dimensions to us which there are not to animals, we are quite naturally led to cede our lives more value *because of the many more possibilities for enrichment they contain.*

To think in this way is very common; it is, I believe, the way many non-religious people find greater value in human life. It should be obvious, however, that those who think this way must eventually confront an undeniable fact: not all human lives have the same enrichment or scope for enrichment. (There are babies, of course, but most people seem happy to regard them as leading lives which have the relevant potentialities for enrichment.) Some people lead lives of a quality we would not wish upon even our worst enemies, and some of these lives have not the scope for enrichment of ordinary human lives. If we regard the irreversibly comatose as living human lives of the lowest quality, we must nevertheless face the fact that many humans lead lives of a radically lower quality than ordinary human lives. We can all think of numerous such cases, cases where the lives lack enrichment and where the scope, the potentialities for enrichment are severely truncated or absent, as with spina bifida children or the very, very severely mentally enfeebled.

If we confront the fact that not all human life has the same quality, either in terms of the same enrichment or the same scope for enrichment, and if we are thinking of the value of life in these terms, then we seem compelled to conclude that not all human life has the same value. And, with this conclusion, the way is open for redrawing Fox's vaccine example in a way that makes it far less apparent that we should test the vaccine on animals. For, as opposed to testing it on quite ordinary and healthy animals, with a reasonably high quality of life, the alternative is to test it on humans whose quality of life is so low *either* as to be exceeded by the quality of life of the healthy animals *or* as to approach their quality of life. On the former alternative, and it is as well to bear in mind that a great many experiments are performed upon healthy, vigorous animals, we would have a reason to test the vaccine on the humans in question; on the latter alternative, we would again find ourselves in need of a reason for thinking it justified to test the vaccine on animals but not on humans.

III

Where, then, are we? If we are not to test the vaccine on humans, then we require some reason which justifies testing it on animals but not on humans. If we purport to find that reason in the greater value of human life, then we must reckon with the fact that the value of human life is bound up with and varies according to its quality; and this opens the way either for some animals to have a higher quality of life than some humans or for some humans to have so low a quality of life as to approach that of some animals. Either way, it is no longer clear that we should test the vaccine on animals.

So, in order to make this clear, what is needed, in effect, is some reason for thinking that a human life, no matter how truncated its scope for enrichment, no matter how low its quality, is more valuable than an animal life, no matter what its degree of enrichment, no matter how high its quality. (Bear in mind that those who have this need are those who, for whatever reason, are not religious and so cannot escape the need that way.) I myself have and know of nothing with which to satisfy this need; that is, I have and know of nothing which enables me to say, *a priori*, that a human life of any quality, however low, is more valuable than an animal life of any quality, however high. Perhaps some readers think that they can satisfy this need; certainly, I am receptive to suggestions.

In the absence of something with which to meet the above need, we cannot, with the appeal to benefit, justify (painful) animal experiments without justifying (painful) human experiments. We seem to have, then, two directions in which we may move. On the one hand, we may take the fact that we cannot justify animal experiments without justifying human experiments as a good reason to re-examine our whole practice of (painful) animal experiments. The case for antivivisectionism, I think, is far stronger than most people allow: so far as I can see, the only way to avoid it, if you are attracted by the appeal to benefit and are not religious, is *either* to have in your possession some means of conceding human life of any quality greater value than animal life of any quality *or* to condone experiments on humans whose quality of life is exceeded by or equal to that of animals. If you are as I am and find yourself without a means of the required sort, then the choice before you is either antivivisectionism or condoning human experiments. On the other hand, we may take the fact that we cannot justify animal experiments without justifying human experiments as a good reason to allow some human experiments. Put differently, if the choice before us is between antivivisectionism and allowing human experiments, can we bring ourselves to embrace antivivisectionism? For, consider: we find ourselves involved in this whole problem because we strongly believe that some benefit or range of benefits can justify (painful) animal experiments. If we choose antivivisectionism, we may very well lose the many benefits obtained through vivisection, and this, at times, even if we concede, as we must, that not every experiment leads to a Salk vaccine, may be a serious loss indeed. Certainly, it would have been a serious loss in the past, if we had had to forgo the benefits which accrued through (and which we presently enjoy as a result of) vivisection. Scientific research and technological innovation have completely altered the human condition, occasionally in rather frightening ways, but typically in ways for which most people are thankful, and very few people indeed would look in the face the benefits which medical research in particular has conferred upon us, benefits which on the whole have most certainly involved vivisections. If the appeal to benefit exerts its full attraction upon us, therefore, we may find ourselves unable to make the choice in favour of antivivisectionism, especially if that meant a good deal of serious research in serious affairs of health had either to be stopped until suitable, alternative experimental subjects were developed for a full range of experiments or, if nothing suitable for a full range of experiments were developed, to be stopped entirely.

Accordingly, we are left with human experiments. I think this is how I would choose, not with great glee and rejoicing, and with great reluctance; but if this is the price we must pay to hold the appeal to benefit and to enjoy the benefits which that appeal licenses, then we must, I think, pay it.

I am well aware that most people, including most medical people, will find my choice repugnant in the extreme, and it is easy to see how I can appear a monster in their eyes. But I am where I am, not because I begin a monster and end up choosing the monstrous, but because I cannot in good faith think of anything at all compelling that cedes human life of any quality greater value than animal life of any quality. It might be claimed by some that this shows in me the need for some religious beliefs, on the assumption that some religious belief or other will allow me to say that any human life is more valuable than any animal life. Apart from the fact that this appears a rather strange reason for taking on religious beliefs (for example, believing in the existence of God and of God's gifts to us in order to avoid having to allow experiments on humans), other questions about those beliefs, such as their correctness and the evidence for their truth, intrude. I may well find that I cannot persuade myself of the beliefs in question.

Is there nothing, then, that can now be cited which, even if we accept that we are committed to allowing human experiments, would nevertheless serve to bar them? I think all I can cite – I do not by this phraseology mean to undercut the force of what follows – are the likely side-effects of such experiments. Massive numbers of people would be outraged, society would be in an uproar, hospitals and research centres would come under fierce attack, the doctor–patient relationship might be irrevocably affected, and so on. (All of us will find it easy to carry on with the list.) Such considerations as these are very powerful, and they would have to be weighed very carefully, in deciding whether actually to perform the experiments. Perhaps their weight would be so great that we could not proceed with the experiments; certainly, that is possible.

But what I meant by saying that such important side-effects of human experiments are 'all I can cite' in the present context is this: it is an utterly contingent affair whether such side-effects occur, and their occurrence is not immune to attempts – by education, by explaining in detail and repeatedly why such experiments are being undertaken, by going through, yet again, our inability to show that human life is always more valuable than animal life, etc. – to eliminate them. It is this last fact especially, that such things as outrage and harm to the doctor–patient relationship can be affected by education, information, and careful explanation, that poses a danger to those who want actually to bar human experiments by appeal to side-effects. So, I do not play down the importance of side-effects in deciding whether actually to perform human experiments, I only caution that they do not provide a once-and-for-all bar to such experiments, unless they survive any and all attempts to mitigate and eliminate them.

References

1 Fox, M. *Returning to Eden: Animal Rights and Human Obligations* (New York: Viking Press, 1980), p. 116.

2 Singer, P. *Animal Liberation* (London: Jonathan Cape, 1976).

Commentary from a Vivisecting Professor of Pharmacology

Sir William Paton

It would be best to start by summarizing what (for this comment) I take to be the essential points of Dr Frey's interesting, and I believe novel, argument. (1) A major justification of animal experiment, commonly accepted, is the benefit that results. (2) This justification is rejected by some, initially on the grounds that the benefit does not justify the pain inflicted; but when it is noted that experiments may be painless, or that steps are taken to minimize the pain, the fundamental ground of rejection is revealed by a shift to the statement that the use of animals for these purposes is *absolutely* wrong. (3) Those who argue this way will accept the loss of the benefits. (4) But is it necessary to forgo these benefits? Why not, in order to retain them, be willing to use man for these experiments? (5) If it is said against this that man is more valuable than animals, in what way is this so? (6) Dr Frey does not believe in 'souls', nor does he accept the 'dominion' of man, and he can only identify 'capacity for enrichment' as a suitable defining characteristic of humanity. (7) He finds that this criterion does not separate man from animals; for instance, he concludes that some animals may possess *more* of this capacity than some humans (for example, the very, very severely mentally enfeebled or spina bifida children). (8) He therefore accepts (with great reluctance) that human experiment should be permissible, with due precaution, in order to obtain the benefits concerned. (9) While acknowledging that the side-effects of such experiment (society's outrage, damage to doctor–patient relations) might prevent particular experiments, their occurrence would be 'utterly contingent', and would not negate the general principle of permissibility.

It is not always clear whether Dr Frey himself holds the views expressed, or is doing no more than presenting them for discussion. In the latter spirit, anything which follows refers to what Dr Frey happens to be voicing, and not to whatever may be his actual opinions.

Before coming to the specific question of human experiment, two general points arise. The first concerns the method of argument. It is an old one: that of reviewing a section of experience (in this case, experience of other people's opinion; reports regrettably hearsay, about experimental work – thalidomide, saccharin, and experience of the life of animals and of handicapped humans); and then of abstracting from this experience particular propositions which then become the subject of the discourse. A single instance (the tree in the quad, or the visual experience of a red patch) has sometimes sufficed to create such a proposition. This is a blameless, indeed common activity. The problem comes with 're-entry' to the experiential world. The proposition may be combined with others to yield further propositions. One such result here is: 'It is not possible to say, *a priori*, that a human life of any quality, however low, is more valuable than an animal life of any quality, however high.' (Dr Frey does not put it so bluntly, but says only that nothing enables *him* to say this. I believe, however, that he is not merely wishing to report on his own psychological state, but wishes the proposition to be considered generally.) What *use* is this proposition? None that I can see. It explicitly assumes that there are scales of human and animal life, and explicitly compares the lower extreme of one with the upper extreme of the other; yet it gives no criterion as to where (or whether) the scales end. Even given these, and comparing (say) an anencephalic fetus with a favourite sheep-dog, over which people could make up their minds, all that has been done is to discuss extreme cases. What then? Few would accept that because a particular instance of animal life is more valuable than a particular instance of human life, therefore no human life is more valuable than animal life. The general proposition merely ends by regurgitating the sort of special case from which it originated.

This links with a second general point, the general philosophical mayhem created by continuity. The type of argument by which Dr Frey fails to find a 'dimension' by which humans differ from animals is one that can also be used to fail to distinguish between light and dark, sweet and sour, motion and immobility. Yet this does not prevent (for instance) the specification of a well-lit factory or an efficient dark-room, or the formulation of successful cooking recipes, or the measurement of velocity. The idea of continuity in the 'scale of creation' is an old and cogent one. It is true that individual species represent discrete steps, but within each species, variation is such as to blur the absolute demarcation in respect of any chosen character between neighbours. Dr Frey could have gone further, and added that no one has yet produced any logically rigorous principle of division at any point in the scale from the inanimate, through bacteria, protozoa, vegetables, insects and animals to man – whether reproduction, complexity, or evidence of responsiveness, purposiveness or sentience is considered. Even the leech will respond to morphine. But the recognition of continuity does not debar the drawing of *operational* divisions.

This brings us to the specific question of whether such operational distinctions can, or cannot, be drawn between humans and animals, particularly distinctions to which 'value' can be attached. Dr Frey's strongest candidate is 'self-enrichment', exemplified chiefly by a capacity for enjoyable experience. But he has to reject this as a discriminant between man and animal because he believes that a very, very severely mentally enfeebled person or a spina bifida child has less capacity for enrichment than a healthy animal. It is a comment on moral philosophy today that 'capacity for enrichment' should be advanced as the strongest index of value in

human activity. In such a context, one cannot expect that other indices, such as capacity for goodness, altruism, responsibility, or forgiveness, would be admissible. But one need not resort to these. There is one respect in which the human has come increasingly to distance himself from the animal – namely the capacity to accumulate his experience by the spoken and (especially) by the written and printed word. This means that successive generations build on their predecessors' achievements, not (as with a crystal, an anthill, or a coral reef) more and more of the same, but continually changing what they build. The scratches in the Lascaux caves lead to the Renaissance; Pythagorean harmonics in time grow up to the Bach fugue; Archimedes' method of exhaustion, transmuted in the seventeenth century to the calculus, becomes O-level mathematics for today's schoolboy. Man's mastery of the environment, initially little more than adequate for survival, is now so great as to arouse his deepest sense of responsibility and his deepest questions of meaning and purpose. Nor must this human capacity be linked only to the 'normal' human in perfect health. Human achievement owes much to the deformed, diseased, epileptic and insane; but perhaps only those familiar with the handicapped know that achievement is not restricted to geniuses, but can pervade all levels of personal and social relationships. (There is the medical point, too, that one must not assume a present handicap to be necessarily permanent: the cretin used to be a striking example of severe handicap, seemingly irreversible in 1890, but curable by 1900. Phenylketonuria provides a more recent example.)

If we accept that man can accumulate his experience (not only that of other men: he can and does accumulate his experience of animals) how does that affect the argument? It is not necessary to argue that an absolute distinction from the animal has been found. Indeed there is some evidence (though it remains inconclusive) for vestiges of a capacity to build a language and to frame abstract thought in the higher primates, although it is hard to see evidence of the use of these for progressive cumulation. But all that is needed is to recognize a quantitative distinction between man and animal sufficiently great to be accepted in practice as qualitative. That this is the case seems to me, whether or not the reasons are articulated, the general consensus. The capacity to accumulate, and thus to build on the past and to look to the future, is a quality, too, to which value can be attached, and a value which looks beyond personal enjoyment to the needs of other individuals. This constitutes an answer to the question (5) in my initial summary of Dr Frey's argument, and a rebuttal to (6) and (7), after which (8) and (9) lapse.

One might stop there, but Dr Frey's paper – from which an uninformed reader might suppose that no human experiment had hitherto taken place – calls for something more. One can now identify three approaches to such experiment: (a) The one argued above, which gives a greater value to the human than to the animal; this does not debar human experiment, but only introduces a coefficient to be applied to the choices to be made. (b) At the opposite extreme is an equation of human and animal value. This, too, fails to debar human experiment. The question becomes instead that of choosing animals or human beings for experiments, presumably simply by practical criteria such as scientific suitability (large animals such as man would need much larger apparatus), cost, and availability. The question of availability is interesting; it would entail consent on the part of a human subject. How does one obtain the consent of an animal? It is not possible for a human to speak for it, for that would deny the postulated human–animal equivalence. The question illustrates the crucial character of one's view of human and animal relationships. (c) In between, it seems, is Dr Frey's position, which appears to accept that there *are* different scales of value for human beings and animals, but argues that they overlap. Thus Beethoven is more valuable than a mouse, but the severely handicapped human is of less value than a healthy 'higher' animal. The implications of this are not worked out; but such a calculus would appear to legitimize the use especially of the diseased and mentally deficient. I doubt if this is what he intends.

More important, perhaps, is to make clear how much human experiment has been, and is being, done. I do not believe Dr Frey would have written as he has if he had adequately consulted the original medical literature, or medical scientists. Human experiment has a long and honourable, though still unwritten, history. Some is severely ad hoc: experiments on effects of acceleration on the human body, leading to ejector seats; or on oxygen poisoning, high pressure, carbon dioxide poisoning, and the 'bends', to make diving safer. Some is to help to improve medical understanding: the cardiologist first passing a cardiac catheter on himself; self-curarization; the paralysis of nerves by local anaesthesia, or nerve section, or vascular occlusion, to throw light on neurological problems. Much takes place in pharmacological work: early trials of metabolism, pilot studies on dose-level, analyses of mechanism of action. Unlike animal experiment no licence is needed, no annual return of the numbers of human experiments is needed, and no government office counts them. Thus it is not easy to estimate their number. But some indication is given by a single issue of just one monthly journal, the *British Journal of Clinical Pharmacology*, which contained 20 papers, covering 124 experiments on normal human subjects (both young and old) and 99 experiments on patients. Scale this up, and one may well doubt if there is scope for much more human experiment than is already conducted.

Dr Frey's argument raises yet other issues. One can well argue that, if no distinction can be drawn between man and animals, then neither can it be drawn between the animal and the vegetable world. So one could ask, as one contemplates the insectivorous plant *Drosera*, responsive to sun, rain, and the nutrients of the soil, and exquisitely sensitive to chemicals, and watches it close a leaf around and digest an insect caught on its hairs, 'Can anyone say that this plant is *less* enriched by its experience than a lion as it devours a buck, or a man enjoying his dinner?' But this merely emphasizes again the importance of one's view of man's relation to the rest of creation. But these are not the issues at the heart of the debate about animal experiment. In practice, I take the most important to be the assessment of the scientific value of an experiment, of the knowledge or benefit to be gained, and of the suffering (if any) involved, and the question of how to balance these. It is ultimately a moral problem, and a question of responsibility borne both by the scientist and by the rest of society in the characteristically human task of removing ignorance and minimizing suffering.

Response

R. G. Frey

Professor Paton would have us believe that man's capacity to accumulate his experience by the spoken, written and printed word confers greater value on his life; but this generalization does not help over the problem I posed.

A medical scientist engaged in serious work needs to perform experiments on retinas, experiments which in the end involve loss of sight and not in some accidental fashion; he may use the retinas of perfectly healthy rabbits or those of severely mentally enfeebled humans. To put the matter somewhat elliptically, the scientist can blind the rabbits or blind the humans. How is this choice to be made? Presumably, Professor Paton would point to the humans and maintain that they belong to a species that has the capacity to make significant advances on any number of fronts as a result of accumulated experience; but exactly how does this fact help with the case before us? These same mentally enfeebled humans belong to a species capable of producing Beethovens, Mozarts and Schuberts, but that in no way makes *them* composers or confers on *their* lives any value. So exactly how is the fact that our species has been capable of great wonders supposed to help out in the cases of those humans far removed from any such wonders? Professor Paton writes: 'Few would accept that because a particular instance of animal life is more valuable than a particular instance of human life, therefore no human life is more valuable than animal life.' Of course not; nor did I suggest anything so silly. But the people to be used by the scientist are not fully normal humans but seriously defective ones, who are still such – they have eyeballs – as to be suitable experimental subjects.

Clearly, Professor Paton has given us no reason for not carrying out the experiment upon the humans in question; for, to repeat, the mere fact that my species can produce a Beethoven does not per se make *my* life any more valuable than that of a mouse.

Professor Paton writes at one point about our having to obtain the consent of human subjects and of our having no means of obtaining consent from animals; but I should have thought he was unwise to make much of this. Animals may not be able to consent, but that does not appear to stop Professor Paton using them as experimental subjects; whereas, though it makes no sense to speak of obtaining the consent of the severely mentally enfeebled, I presume he would recoil from *their* use as subjects for blinding. Why? What makes him hesitate in their case but go ahead in the case of rabbits? My strong suspicion is that he intuitively accepts human life as more valuable than animal life, even when all the grandiose talk of our capacities and accomplishments is inapplicable, and it would be interesting to know how he justifies this intuition.

Professor Paton speaks of my use of hearsay, my failure to consult medical reports, my making it appear as if no human experiments have been performed; well, here is his chance to nail down his accusations. I can point to a number of instances where rabbits with good eyesight have knowingly been blinded in the course of experimental work; I ask him if he can point to a single instance where a human subject, with otherwise good or perfect eyesight, has knowingly been blinded by a medical experimenter. If he can, then let him name names; if he cannot, then he might justly be accused of having failed to take my point, which, as readers will know, is that we do not do to defective humans all that we presently do in our laboratories to quite healthy animals. My interest is in why we do not. If the justification is that we think human life of greater value than animal life, then we must be prepared to face the facts, at least on the grounds I suggested, that (i) not all human life is of the same value and (ii) some human life has a value so low as to be exceeded by some animal life.

Part IX

Public Health Issues

Introduction

Public health ethics is concerned with ethical issues in public or community health. Simply put: problematic individual behavior has the potential to affect very large numbers of other people very quickly. Michael Selgelid reminds us of this in the introduction to his article "Ethics and Infectious Disease." The Black Death killed about one third of Europe's population in the fourteenth century.

At the heart of many problems in public health ethics is the vexing question of what limitations on individual freedoms are ethically defensible when the greater good of society is at stake. John Stuart Mill famously argued in his 1859 essay *On Liberty* (an extract from which appears in Part X of this anthology) that "the only purpose for which power can be rightfully exercised over any member of a civilized community, against his will, is to prevent harm to others." Unfortunately, this does not help us a great deal, because the diseases we are concerned about in public health ethics invariably pose a threat to others. Michael Selgelid in his contribution lays out the territory of public health ethics. He explains the importance of looking at ethical issues in infectious diseases control, and provides a brief background discussion of the conflict between individual liberty and the greater good of society. He then proceeds to explain why some of the problems are also importantly problems of justice because they are inextricably linked to the living conditions of the world's poor and the world economic order that arguably gave rise to their plight.

Udo Schüklenk and Anita Kleinsmidt argue in "Rethinking Mandatory HIV-Testing during Pregnancy in Areas with High HIV Prevalence Rates" that we ought to consider the introduction of mandatory HIV testing of pregnant women presenting for antenatal care in areas where there are high rates of HIV. They think that an ethical case can be made for mandatory testing provided those found to be infected with HIV are guaranteed access to life-preserving HIV medication. Such a policy would reduce the number of HIV-infected newborns quite significantly while at the same time the survival of the pregnant infected women who carry them to term could be ensured. These authors note that experience from various jurisdictions shows that the more difficult it is made for pregnant women to avoid getting tested, the more women ultimately end up getting tested and clinically cared for. On the other hand, Russell Armstrong warns in "Mandatory HIV Testing in Pregnancy: Is There Ever a Time?" that while mandatory HIV testing could well be the ethical way forward under ideal circumstances, the reality on the ground mitigates strongly against its introduction. As a case in point he discusses South Africa. It has one of the highest HIV prevalence rates in the world, and yet, according to Armstrong, it is not one of those countries that ought to introduce mandatory HIV testing. His consequentialist argument specifically notes the lack of reliable access to testing and treatment as reasons to reject Schüklenk and Kleinsmidt's analysis.

Bioethics: An Anthology, Third Edition. Edited by Helga Kuhse, Udo Schüklenk, and Peter Singer.
© 2016 John Wiley & Sons, Inc. Published 2016 by John Wiley & Sons, Inc.

Multiple drug resistant infectious diseases such as some strains of tuberculosis constitute significant public health threats. Jerome Amir Singh and colleagues, in their article "XDR-TB in South Africa: No Time for Denial or Complacency," look at extensively drug-resistant and multi-drug-resistant tuberculosis in South Africa . They consider these strains a serious threat to public health. Their article proposes that South Africa ought to consider temporary detainment of infected people to protect public health. They conclude, "forced isolation and confinement of individuals infected with XDR-TB and selected MDR-TB may be an appropriate and proportionate response in defined situations, given the extreme risk posed by both strains and the fact that less severe measures may be insufficient to safeguard public interest."

64

Ethics and Infectious Disease

Michael J. Selgelid

I Distribution of Research Resources

The '10/90 divide' is a phenomenon whereby 'less than 10 percent of [medical] research funds are spent on the diseases that account for 90% of the global burden of disease … [D]iseases affecting large proportions of humanity are given comparatively little attention.'[1] Because medical research so often aims at the promotion of profits rather than solutions to the world's most urgent medical problems, a majority of funds focus on the wants of a minority of the world's population – those who are relatively wealthy. As a result, health care is often unavailable to those who need it most.

A situation analogous to the 10/90 divide in medical research apparently holds true for research in bioethics. A quick flip through most bioethics texts and journals (or a visit to any number of websites) reveals attention on abortion, euthanasia, assisted reproduction, genetics, and doctor-patient relationships. To a large extent the issues examined one way or another involve advanced technologies or expensive interventions available primarily in wealthy developed nations. 'Distribution of resources' is a common topic; but discussion here often (at least implicitly) concerns domestic allocation rather than issues of *international* justice. Greatly lacking, in

comparison, is discussion of ethical issues involving infectious disease and the (related) health care situation in the developing world. Infectious diseases (such as AIDS, tuberculosis, and a variety of other emerging and reemerging pathogens) and the health care situation in developing countries pose some of the most serious problems of our times, but they have received relatively little attention from medical ethicists. In what follows I will (1) argue that the topic of infectious disease should be recognized as one of *the* most important topics for the discipline of bioethics, (2) briefly illustrate that it has received comparatively little attention from bioethicists,[2] and (3) attempt to explain why it has not received the attention it warrants.

II The Ethical Importance of Infectious Disease

The lack of bioethics discussion of infectious disease is both odd and unfortunate. Given that infectious disease was traditionally a – if not *the* – primary focus of medicine, for example, one would expect this to be obvious territory for a discipline concerned with 'medical ethics.'[3] More specific reasons why this should be recognized as one of the most relevant and important topics for bioethics are the following:

Original publication details: Michael J. Selgelid: "Ethics and Infectious Disease," pp. 272–89 from *Bioethics* 19: 3 (2005). Reproduced with permission from John Wiley & Sons.

Bioethics: An Anthology, Third Edition. Edited by Helga Kuhse, Udo Schüklenk, and Peter Singer.

1   The historical and likely future consequences of infectious diseases are almost unrivalled,
2   Infectious diseases raise exceedingly difficult ethical questions of their own, and
3   The topic of infectious disease is closely connected to the topic of justice – which is a central concern of ethics.

1   Consequences

First, the paramount ethical importance of infectious diseases is illustrated by the fact that their consequences have been, and will likely continue to be, enormous. Epidemics have constituted some of the most catastrophic events in human history. The Black Death, for example, is famous for eliminating approximately one third of the European population between 1347 and 1350.[4] Another devastating epidemic occurred in 1918 when a nasty strain of influenza killed somewhere between 20 and 100 million people. According to the historian Alfred Crosby, the 1918 flu undoubtedly 'killed more humans than any other disease in a period of similar duration in the history of the world.'[5] Gina Kolata writes that the 1918 flu killed 'more Americans in a single year than died in battle in World War I, World War II, the Korean War, and the Vietnam War.'[6] (According to the *New York Times*, '[J]ust about everyone who has studied the disease says [that] a new pandemic is inevitable.')[7]

A third major killer, which has received high-profile attention in American newspapers recently, is smallpox. Smallpox allegedly killed more people in history than any other infectious disease. In the 20th Century alone it killed somewhere between 300 and 540 million people – or 'more than all the wars and epidemics [of that century] combined.'[8] Michael Oldstone claims that smallpox killed three times more people during the 20th Century than were killed by all the wars of that period.[9] Although the disease was declared eradicated by the World Health Organization (WHO) in 1980, fears about smallpox have resurfaced. It has recently come to light that the Soviet Union, until its fall in the early 1990s, manufactured and froze tens of tons of smallpox for military purposes. Many are worried that stocks of the Soviet supply may have fallen into the hands of 'rogue nations' or terrorists.

Experts claim that a smallpox bioterrorist attack could spark a catastrophic global epidemic now that the world population largely lacks immunity (because routine vaccination ended 20 or 30 years ago).[10] Modeling has shown that a smallpox attack could cause the devastation of (perhaps a series of) nuclear attack(s).

Smallpox aside, it is important to recognize that the enormous impact of infectious diseases is not just a matter of history. Infectious diseases are currently the world's largest 'killer[s] of children and young adults. They account for more than 13 million deaths a year – one in two deaths in developing countries.'[11] The rapidly growing HIV/AIDS epidemic perhaps provides the clearest illustration that infectious diseases continue to have the power of their past. AIDS is arguably 'the greatest health disaster in history.'[12] In 24 years, it has killed 20 million people (whereas the Black Death killed only 9 to 11 million people in Europe between 1346 and 1350).[13] HIV prevalence rates commonly exceed 30% (of adults) in sub-Saharan Africa, and similar scenarios may follow in parts of Asia and the former Soviet Union. As of 1999, anyway, only 5% of those infected could afford life-extending antiretroviral therapy.[14] In 2004, 3 million people died from AIDS, and 5 million people were newly infected with HIV. At the end of 2004, an estimated 39 million people were living with HIV.[15]

A related, but less well publicized, scenario involves the re-emergent spread of tuberculosis. Previously thought to be controlled, or at least considered controllable, TB was declared a global health emergency by the World Health Organization in 1993 and currently kills more people than ever before. 'Each year, 2 to 3 million people die from tuberculosis … despite the fact that the disease in its most common form is entirely preventable and treatable.'[16] One third of the world's population is infected with the latent form of the disease; and, a tenth of these are expected to develop active illness. 'It is estimated that between 2000 and 2020, nearly one billion people will be newly infected, 200 million people will get sick, and 35 million will die from TB - if control is not further strengthened.'[17] Of particular concern is the rise and spread of multi-drug resistant TB, resulting from the improper use of medication (in Russian prisons, for example).

The recent emergence and spread of SARS (Severe Acute Respiratory Syndrome) is, of course, the latest indicator that the impact of infectious diseases will continue to be severe. According to studies, the 'death rate from SARS may be … up to 55 percent in people 60 and older, and up to 13.2 percent in younger people … unless the numbers fall drastically, SARS would be among the infectious diseases with the highest death rates … By contrast, the influenza pandemic of 1918 … had an estimated mortality rate, overall, of 1 percent or less.'[18] In the meanwhile, there is no treatment, vaccine, or reliable diagnostic test for the SARS virus – which 'can survive on surfaces [such as doorknobs] for up to four days.'[19] Isolation, quarantine, travel advisories, travel restrictions, and related public health measures were put into effect; and the economic impact, alone, was staggering – '[j]ust a few weeks after SARS was identified, WHO [calculated] that the cost of the disease [was] already close to $30 billion.'[20]

It is now widely acknowledged that, in addition to posing global health and economic threats, AIDS and other infectious diseases threaten global security. Historical studies reveal that factors such as high infant mortality, low life expectancy, decreasing life expectancy, etc. – which are being severely affected in places like sub-Saharan Africa and the former Soviet Union – are among the most reliable indicators of major social upheaval. Given the serious historical and potential future consequences of infectious disease, it is no wonder that the CIA recently conducted (and published) a special investigation of *The Global Infectious Disease Threat and Its Implications for the United States.*[21] It is puzzling, on the other hand, that medical ethicists have not had more to say about infectious disease – compared to abortion, euthanasia, and genetics, for example, which have saturated the literature.

2 Difficult ethical questions

A second reason why infectious diseases warrant more of bioethics' attention is that they raise serious, difficult philosophical/ethical questions of their own. Obvious examples arise from the fact that infectious diseases can be contagious. Depending on the disease in question, infected individuals can threaten the health of other individuals or society as a whole. The public health measures required to protect other individuals and society from contagion (again, depending on the disease) might sometimes involve surveillance, mandatory testing, mandatory vaccination or treatment, notification of authorities or third parties, isolation (of individuals), quarantine (of entire regions), or travel restrictions. Because such public health care measures could infringe upon widely accepted basic human rights and liberties, we are here confronted with conflicting values.

An extremely difficult ethical question asks how, in situations of conflict, the utilitarian aim to promote the greater good in the way of public health should be balanced against libertarian aims to protect privacy and individual rights and liberties such as freedom of movement, and so on. Most philosophers, policy makers, and ordinary citizens would (upon reflection, I imagine) deny that *either* liberty or aggregate utility should *always* be given *absolute* priority over the other regardless of the degree (in terms of likelihood and severity) to which the other is threatened. So the challenge is to find a principled way of striking a balance between these presumably legitimate, but apparently conflicting, social aims in contexts involving diseases that are – to varying degrees[22] – contagious, deadly, or otherwise dangerous.[23] I will later say more about the difficulty of ethical issues raised by infectious disease.

3 Justice

Third, infectious disease should be recognized as a crucial topic for bioethics because the topic of infectious disease is closely connected to the topic of justice. Pathogens primarily prey upon the poor. Bad nutrition, dirty water, crowded living conditions, poor education, lack of access to basic medicines, disempowerment of women, and a complex host of other factors combine to make the populations of developing nations especially vulnerable to infectious diseases:

> Most deaths from infectious diseases occur in developing countries – the countries with the least money to spend on health care. In developing countries, about one third of the population – 1.3 billion people – live on incomes of less than $1 a day. Almost one in three children are malnourished. One in five are not immunized by their first birthday. And over one third of the world's population lack access to essential drugs.[24]

Today it is widely acknowledged that ailments called 'tropical diseases' are often not peculiar to tropical regions at all. To a large extent 'tropical diseases' are those that afflict poor developing countries, rather than necessarily tropical ones.[25] Sanitation, hygiene, vaccination, antibiotics, other drugs, and general improvements in living conditions have, in recent decades anyway, left privileged populations relatively sheltered from the scourges of the developing world.

Relationships between poverty and disease are well illustrated by the AIDS pandemic and the health care situation in Africa at the beginning of the 21st Century. Of the (roughly) 40 million people estimated to be living with HIV/AIDS in 2002, 28 million – or 70% – lived in sub-Saharan Africa.[26]

> [A]nd 95% [in 2001] live[d] in developing nations. Most of the infected people who live in these countries have no access to new or existing drugs for HIV/AIDS. But the problem of access to medications goes far beyond the HIV/AIDS pandemic: people in developing nations also cannot afford medications used to treat or prevent malaria, tuberculosis, cholera, dysentery, meningitis, and typhoid fever. The affordability problem also extends beyond a lack of access to new drugs designed to treat devastating, infectious diseases: 50% of people in developing nations do not have access to even basic medications, such as antibiotics, analgesics, broncho-dilators, decongestants, anti-inflammatory agents, anti-coagulants, or diuretics.[27]

The fact that those who are already worse-off in virtue of their poverty thus have their misfortunes compounded – as they are more likely to fall victim to disease – will strike most of us as an injustice in itself.[28] It seems especially unjust when the ailments that cause the already unfortunate to suffer and die are – sometimes easily and inexpensively – treatable or preventable with existing medications (that have often been developed at least partly through public funding). Egalitarians and utilitarians should agree on this point.

Poverty and (consequent) illness in many cases can also be attributed to what should be considered injustices even by staunch libertarians. As (one of) the wealthiest African nation(s), for example, South Africa should have been better able than its sub-Saharan neighbors to stave off AIDS. It has, however, famously failed to do so. This country has more HIV positive persons than any other country in the world; and, its (increasing) prevalence rate is estimated (from antenatal clinic data) to be almost 25% of adults.

> About 5 [million] South Africans are living with HIV and, at the current rate of infection, about half the country's teenagers under 15 can expect to contract it. By 2005 South Africa is likely to have about 1 [million] orphans.[29]

A recent Medical Research Council (MRC) report estimates that AIDS, which is already the leading cause of death in the country, will kill between four and seven million South Africans within a decade.[30]

This situation is not merely *unfortunate*. We here suffer social and political *injustice*. The facts that the current South African government (for mysterious reasons) consistently[31] but (apparently) illegitimately (1) challenged the causal link between HIV and AIDS (and perhaps even the very existence of HIV and AIDS), (2) challenged the safety and efficacy of antiretroviral therapy, (3) suppressed scientific research which cast doubt on its HIV/AIDS stance,[32] (4) failed to provide inexpensive (or, in some cases, free) antiretroviral treatment to reduce the risk of mother-to-child transmission of HIV, (5) refused to comply with court orders requiring it to do so, (6) forbid provision of prophylactic antiretroviral therapy to rape victims (some of which were *gang-raped babies*, less than a year old),[33] and (7) over-spent on the military (in an apparently scandalous fashion) while under-spending on health care are only a part of what I have in mind.

The current state of AIDS in South Africa – and the government's failure to effectively deal with the situation – should also be attributed to wrongs with longer histories. The etiology of the AIDS epidemic is extremely complex; its present state is the result of a wide variety of social, political, economic, and historical factors. The new South African government's failure to ameliorate the situation is at least partly forgivable – or, in any case, explainable – by virtue of the fact that it had so many other enormous tasks to accomplish in the aftermath of apartheid. In addition to overhauling the political apparatus of the country, provision of decent education, housing, sanitation, and water to those who were victims of systematic racial oppression for decades – i.e. the vast majority of the population – posed monumental challenges for the new South African government. The shambles in which apartheid left this country is thus at least partly to blame for the health care *status quo*.[34] The fact that urbanization, overcrowded living conditions, migrant working conditions, poor education, fatalistic behavior, prostitution, and other ravishes of poverty (including poor nutrition, widespread infection with worms, and lack of treatment for other STDs[35]) each contribute to the AIDS epidemic – and are each (at least partly) the result of exploitative racist colonial oppressive practices – corroborates the point that the South African AIDS epidemic should largely be blamed on social injustice.

Similar things can be said about other developing nations where health care is compromised because of impoverishment resulting from colonialization, oppression, exploitation, protectionist trade policies, domestic corruption, failure of democracy, and so on. According to Solomon R. Benatar, for example, the poverty and consequent poor health of many in the developing world should be attributed to (militarization and) exploitative global economic activities involving irresponsible business practices of multi-national corporations in particular. The result is a widening of the gap – in terms of both wealth and human rights protection – between the haves and have-nots.[36]

Pulitzer Prize-winning journalist Laurie Garrett provides an extreme example of the link between disease and injustice. In her recent book *Betrayal of Trust: The Collapse of Global Public Health*, she blames the famous 1995 Ebola (hemorrhagic fever) epidemic in Zaire (now the Democratic Republic of the Congo) on the corruption of the leader Mobutu who stole billions of dollars from public coffers, leaving public hospitals (which were primary *sources* of infection) in complete disarray and lacking the most basic supplies.

> Two things are clear: Ebola spread in Kikwit because the most basic, essential elements of public health were non-existent. And those exigencies were lacking in Kikwit – indeed, throughout Zaire – because Mobutu Sese Seko and his cronies had for three decades looted the national treasuries. Ebola haunted Zaire because of corruption and political repression … [Ebola's] emergence into human populations required the special assistance of

humanity's greatest vices: greed, corruption, arrogance, tyranny, and callousness. What unfolded in Zaire in 1995 was not so much the rain forest terror widely depicted then in popular media worldwide as an inevitable outcome of disgraceful disconcern – even disdain – for the health of the Zairois public.[37]

Garrett implicates American meddling in the affair, insofar as the U.S. government backed Mobutu and propped him into power. She insinuates CIA involvement with the murder of his predecessor Patrice Lumumba, unfavored because of supposedly socialist sympathies. In her earlier book *The Coming Plague: Newly Emerging Diseases in a World Out of Balance*, Garrett suggests that the AIDS epidemic in Africa was at least partly fueled by the fact that underequipped hospitals in places like Congo sometimes had no choice but to use the same unsterilized syringes over and over and over again.

III   Why the Neglect?

Based on what I have said so far, one would expect that infectious disease would already be a typical topic of dedicated discussion in a discipline called 'medical ethics.' One would expect that there would be books on ethics and infectious disease and that articles and sections specifically devoted to ethical aspects of infectious diseases would be regular fare in bioethics journals and anthologies. In reality, however, 'infectious disease' is hardly found even in indexes of standard bioethics texts; and I have never seen a book on this general topic. An October 2002 Google (internet) search of the phrase 'ethics and infectious disease' yielded only 11 entries.[38] Six of these referred to a single project (of Margaret Battin), and some of the others were false positives. In March 2005 a similar search yielded 35 entries[39] – while a search of 'ethics and genetics' led to 5,100 entries.

1   High tech medicine

Why, then, has the topic been neglected by bioethics? It is likely that part of the explanation relates to the origins of the discipline of medical ethics itself. Although the roots of bioethics extend twenty-five hundred years back to the world of Hippocrates, bio-ethics' birth as an autonomous discipline is a relatively recent phenomenon. Medical ethics really came into its own during the last four or five decades, largely as a result of advancements in biological science and technology. With revolutionary developments in medical technology came unprecedented moral and policy dilemmas, and hence an academic discipline was born.[40] If this rough sketch of the birth of bioethics captures much truth, then there should be less surprise that there has been a high-tech, wealthy-world slant to discussion within the discipline.

2   Optimism in medicine

A second probable reason why infectious disease has not received more attention of medical ethicists similarly relates to the timing of the birth of the discipline. The rise of bioethics coincided with a period of tremendous optimism in medicine. The development of antibiotics in the 1940's and the hugely successful Salk Polio vaccination program in the 1950's, and other developments such as the discovery of DDT, led the medical community to believe that infectious disease would soon be defeated through medical progress.[41] As early as

> 1948 U.S. Secretary of State George C. Marshall declared at the Washington, D.C., gathering of the Fourth International Congress on Tropical Medicine and Malaria that the conquest of all infectious diseases was imminent. Through a combination of enhanced crop yields to provide adequate food for humanity and scientific breakthroughs in microbe control, Marshall predicted, all the earth's microscopic scourges would be eliminated.[42]

In 1955 the World Health Organization decided to 'eliminate all malaria on the planet' via the eradication of mosquitoes with DDT. 'Few doubted that such a lofty goal was possible: nobody at the time could imagine a trend of worsening disease conditions; the arrow of history always pointed towards progress.'[43] 'By 1965, more than 25,000 different antibiotic products had been developed; physicians and scientists felt that bacterial diseases, and the microbes responsible, were no longer of great concern or of research interest.'[44] In 1967 U.S. Surgeon General William H. Stewart was so convinced of success that he told a

White House gathering of health officers 'that it was time to close the book on infectious diseases and shift all national attention (and dollars) to what he termed "the New Dimensions" of health: chronic diseases.'[45] 'In 1972, the Nobel laureate Macfarlane Burnet concluded that "the most likely forecast about the future of infectious disease is that it will be very dull."'[46] Fields such as bacteriology and parasitology appeared less important and subsequently fell out of vogue in the medical scientific community. The rise of medical ethics thus occurred at a time when it was popular – though perhaps hubristic – to think that infectious disease would no longer be a central concern of medicine. This presumably explains at least part of the neglect on the part of those concerned with medical ethics.

3   'The other'

AIDS, of course, has been on the scene for more than twenty years already – and thus overlaps with roughly half the lifespan of bioethics proper. And it has been clear for quite some time that malaria, TB, and other infectious diseases would not just disappear as planned. To the contrary, plenty of pathogens have developed more dangerous drug-resistant strains. And many morbid microbes – such as SARS and Ebola – have newly emerged during the last few decades.

A third reason why infectious diseases receive sparse discussion by academic ethicists is that they have likely been relegated as problems of 'the other.'[47] AIDS, for example, for a long time was, and perhaps still is, considered a problem for homosexuals, IV drug users, and poor black people in Africa. AIDS and other infectious diseases are, as has already been said, by far more prevalent in the developing world. Given that the vast majority of professional medical ethicists are straight, non-drug-injecting, relatively well-to-do whites who reside and work in wealthy developed nations, it should not be entirely unexpected that they have focused most on matters of more obvious central domestic concern, rather than problems of 'strangers' on the fringe of society and foreigners in faraway places. This third explanation involves both psychological and practical elements. Regarding the latter, (relatively conservative) university employers (and research funders) likely expect academic ethicists to focus most on pressing local issues rather than (radically) concentrating on international justice.[48] This has *explanatory* power, but I doubt it makes the failure of medical ethicists to further discuss one of world's most consequential topics *excusable*. Ethics and morality essentially involve elements of impartiality; and, *tenured* professors, in any case, have substantial freedom to choose their topics.

4   Complexity

A fourth explanation of neglect by bioethicists relates to the complexity of the issues in question.[49] Traditional topics in medical ethics already require difficult interdisciplinary study. Expertise in both ethics and science are required to do bioethics well. Though many scholars have expertise in the discipline of ethics and many scholars expertise in scientific and technological aspects of biology and medicine, it is rare to find both kinds of expertise embodied in single individuals. One result is the relatively weak reputation of medical ethics within philosophical circles. Philosophers commonly complain about a 'low level' of discussion in medical ethics. This is attributed to the fact that (1) contributors with philosophical mastery in ethics often fail to get the science right and are thus unrealistic while (2) contributors with scientific backgrounds too often lack sufficient training in rigorous philosophical argumentation to get the ethics right, and (3) too few contributors are skilled enough in both areas to generate a consistently high level of discussion.

I have been discussing the challenging nature of the interdis-ciplinarity of medical ethics scholarship because I believe this difficulty is greatly exacerbated with discussion of infectious disease and the health care situation in the developing world. In addition to grounding in ethics and science/medicine (the latter of which is itself complicated by entry into the realm of epidemiology and drug-resistant pathogen emergence), we here need a greater grip on complex social, political, historic, and economic dynamics in order to *explain* – and thus comment upon the justice of – the current global healthcare situation.[50] A similarly broadened understanding is needed to realistically assess – and base moral/policy prescriptions upon – *predictions of impact*. Exploring the issues I have in mind requires more *empirical* work than most (medical) ethicists are

likely to be trained for or accustomed to.[51] With regard to distribution of resource questions, confrontation with issues of international (rather than merely domestic) justice is an additional obvious way in which *theoretical* discussion is complicated.[52] The fact that infectious diseases do not respect international borders is just one of the ways in which the topic is inherently international. My fourth explanation, thus, is that questions concerning infectious disease and the healthcare situation in the developing world have been neglected by biomedical ethicists at least partly because of the *difficulty* of working on them.

5   Apparent ease

My fifth explanation, ironically, is that this area has been ignored because of a *misperception* that the questions raised are all-too-easy. The injustice of the situation, which has received substantial *media* attention at least, whereby AIDS medications are unavailable because they are unaffordable – at least partly because of prices set by profit-driven pharmaceutical companies – to populations in sub-Saharan Africa where they are by far needed most will strike many as a clear and blatant injustice. 'Of course this is wrong. Of course more should be done to make medication available to AIDS victims in Africa,' many might say, 'and you don't need to be a philosopher – or priest – to figure that out.' Questions about the justice of the health care situation in the developing world, where the innocent poor are sick and suffering, at first glance anyway, *appear* to lack the deep philosophical significance of questions upon which medical ethicists usually focus their attention.[53] Topics such as euthanasia and abortion, for example, raise what might look like deeper and more intellectually challenging issues: When is it morally permissible to kill another human being? What is a person? Upon what is the moral status of human beings based? What does quality of life consist in? Notice that emerging bioethical debates surrounding genetics and embryo/stem cell research often revolve around these same sorts of questions. In comparison with these more theoretical (or perhaps *metaphysical*) questions, the injustice of a situation where tens of millions of (relatively innocent) people will soon suffer and die because they are too poor to buy medications might look like a no-brainer.

6   Religious hijacking

My final explanation of why infectious disease has not received more attention from bioethicists refers to the fact that bioethicists have been kept so occupied by discussion of *religious objections* to things like abortion, euthanasia, cloning, stem cell research, and so on. Contrary to Paul Farmer,[54] my own belief is that most bioethicists *are* (at heart, anyway) genuinely concerned about issues of justice. Liberal-minded bioethicists presumably would have focused much more attention on the topic of infectious disease and the injustice of the health care situation in the developing world if they hadn't been kept so busy battling the illiberal policy agenda (regarding abortion, euthanasia, cloning, stem cell research, etc.) advocated by the church.[55] Debate in bioethics has thus, to a large extent, been hijacked by religion.

Conclusion

I have offered six explanations of why ethical issues associated with infectious disease (and the related health care situation in the developing world) have not been more prominent in medical ethics literature. I have suggested that this is the case roughly because (1) bioethics was born (as an autonomous discipline) with advances in medical technology and thus has largely focused on these, (2) bioethics' birth and initial development (as an autonomous discipline) came at a time when it was believed that infectious disease would be conquered by medicine, (3) infectious diseases are often seen as problems of others, (4) bioethical research on infectious disease in the developing world is especially difficult because it is so empirical and interdisciplinary, (5) ethical questions about infectious disease (in the developing world) might not *appear* to pose the kinds of deep philosophical questions that academic ethicists are interested in, and (6) bioethics debate has been hijacked by the church. These are just suggestions; and this list is not meant to be exhaustive. Rather than choosing between these alternative explanations, I believe that they each likely capture *parts* of the story we are after. In any case, as argued above, it would be entirely wrong to explain the lack of discussion of infectious diseases by denying their central importance and/or relevance to the discipline of bioethics.

Notes

A version of this paper was presented at the VI World Congress of Bioethics, Brasilia, Brazil, October 2002.

1   K. Lee, and A. Mills. Strengthening Governance for Global Health Research. *British Medical Journal* 2000; 321: 775–776, at http://www.bmj.com/cgi/content/full/321/7264/775.

2   Although I shall not in this article discuss this point at great length, others who have worked in this area, such as Margaret Battin and Solomon Benatar, have agreed that it is quite correct. A similar point is made by (especially Chapter 8 of) P. Farmer. 2003. *Pathologies of Power: Health, Human Rights, and the New War on the Poor.* Los Angeles. University of California Press.

3   I shall use the expressions 'bioethics', 'biomedical ethics', and 'medical ethics', interchangeably.

4   P. Ziegler. 1969. *The Black Death.* London. Penguin.

5   A.W. Crosby. 1989. *America's Forgotten Epidemic: The Influenza of 1918.* Cambridge, UK. Cambridge University Press: 203.

6   G. Kolata. 1999. *Flu.* London. Pan Books: xii.

7   B. Gewen. 'The Great Influenza' and 'Microbial Threats to Health': Virus Alert. *The New York Times* March 14, 2004, available at: http://www.nytimes.com/2004/03/14/books/review/14GEWENT.html.

8   J. Miller, S. Engelberg & W. Broad. 2001. *Germs: The Ultimate Weapon.* London. Simon and Schuster: 58.

9   M.B.A. Oldstone. 1998. *Viruses, Plagues, and History.* New York. Oxford University Press: 3.

10   For more on smallpox, see M.J. Selgelid. Smallpox Revisited? *American Journal of Bioethics* 2003; 3, 1; and M.J. Selgelid. Bioterrorism and Smallpox Planning: Information and Voluntary Vaccination. *Journal of Medical Ethics* 2004; 30, 6: 558–560; available at http://jme.bmjjournals.com/cgi/reprint/30/6/558, accessed 1 March 2005.

11   World Health Organization. 1999. *Removing Obstacles to Healthy Development: Report on Infectious Diseases.* Geneva: WHO. At http://apps.who.int/iris/handle/10665/65847.

12   C. Gilbert. AIDS Draws New Attention. *Milwaukee Journal Sentinel*, 15 April, 2002.

13 L. Garrett. 2000. *Betrayal of Trust: The Collapse of Global Public Health.* New York. Hyperion: 474.

14 Ibid., p. 473.

15 UNAIDS: AIDS Epidemic Update, 2004. Available at www.unaids.org.

16 L.B. Reichman and J.H. Tanne. 2002. *Timebomb: The Global Epidemic of Multi-Drug-Resistant Tuberculosis.* New York. McGraw Hill: x–xi. See also P. Farmer. 1999. *Infections and Inequalities: The Modern Plagues.* Berkeley, CA. University of California Press.

17 World Health Organization. Tuberculosis, Fact Sheet No. 104, revised April 2000, p. 1.

18 L.K. Altman. Death Rate from SARS is Revised Upward. *International Herald Tribune* May 8, 2003.

19 Ibid.

20 Kickbusch. A Wake-Up Call for Global Health. *International Herald Tribune* April 29, 2003.

21 One conclusion of the report is that we should perhaps worry most about new infectious diseases – more dangerous than AIDS – likely to emerge in the future.

22 I highlight variation in severity to suggest that there is likely no simple, obvious answer to this question. I should here point out the practical importance, in addition to theoretical difficulty, of this kind of question. It is now widely acknowledged, for example, that quarantine policy is outdated and in need of revision. Biodefense planning and the emergence of SARS provide the most recent illustrations of the immediate importance of this issue.

23 This topic, of course, has not been altogether ignored. For discussion in the context of AIDS see U. Schuklenk. 1998. AIDS: Individual and 'Public' Interests, in *A Companion to Bioethics*, P. Singer & H. Kuhse. eds. Oxford, UK. Blackwell: 343–354. For recent discussion of quarantine policy in light of the smallpox bioterrorist threat, see G.J. Annas. Bioterrorism, Public Health, and Civil Liberties. *The New England Journal of Medicine* 2002; 346: 1337–1342.

24 World Health Organization, *Removing Obstacles to Health Department.*

25 N.L. Stepan. 2001. *Picturing Tropical Nature.* Ithaca, NY. Cornell University Press; L. Garrett. 1994. *The Coming Plague: Newly Emerging Diseases in a World Out of Balance.* New York. Penguin.

26 Gilbert, AIDS Draws New Attention.

27 D.B. Resnik. Developing Drugs for the Developing World: An Economic, Legal, Moral, and Political Dilemma. *Developing World Bioethics* 2001; 1: 11.

28 Others, to the contrary, might claim that this situation is 'unfortunate' but not necessarily 'unfair' or 'unjust'.

29 Fighting Back. *The Economist* May 11–17, 2002, 27.

30 R. Dorrington, D. Bourne, D. Bradshaw, R. Laubscher & I.M. Timaeus. The Impact of HIV/AIDS on Adult Mortality in South Africa. Burden of Disease Research Unit, Medical Research Council of South Africa.

31 At the time of this writing the South African Government appears to finally be changing its stance on HIV/AIDS.

32 This seemed to occur with regard to the above-mentioned MRC Report, for example.

33 Note that points (4)–(6), at least, appear to conflict with the South African constitution by failing to respect what are recognized as human rights here. The same thing may be said about the failure to provide antiretrovirals to HIV-positive South Africans more generally speaking.

34 See D. Webb. 1997. *HIV and AIDS in Africa.* London. Pluto Press; A. Whiteside & C. Sunter. 2000. *AIDS: The Challenge for South Africa.* Cape Town. Human & Rousseau; H. Marais. 2000. *To the Edge: AIDS Review 2000.* Pretoria, South Africa. University of Pretoria, Centre for the Study of AIDS.

35 Increased risk of HIV infection results, for example, in the presence of other untreated STDs or when immune systems are weakened from poor nutrition or infection with worms.

36 S.R. Benatar. Global Disparities in Health and Human Rights: A Critical Commentary. *American Journal of Public Health* 1998; 88: 295–300.

37 Garrett, *Betrayal of Trust*, p. 59.

38 Search conducted on October 30, 2002 at www.google.com.

39 Many of these referred to a more recent work of Ronald Bayer. There have of course been books and anthology sections on ethical issues associated with AIDS in particular. And Internet searches of 'Ethics and AIDS', as was pointed out by Peter Singer in discussion, will yield more results – i.e. 408 results on 1 March 2005. The fact remains, however, that discussion of infectious diseases in general (which would likely inform discussion of particular diseases such as AIDS) is lacking. In my opinion even AIDS – with the exception of doctor–patient relationship issues (especially the 'duty to treat') and AIDS-related international research ethics (especially the debate over 'standards of care') – has not received adequate attention in mainstream bioethics literature, given the magnitude of the problem. On 1 March 2005, in any case, a Google search of 'ethics and tuberculosis' yielded only 42 results (though tuberculosis kills two or three million persons per year) and 'ethics and malaria' yielded zero (though malaria kills one million per year). On the same date, 'ethics and stem cells'

yielded 440 results – despite the newness of stem cell research (in comparison with AIDS).

40 The development of elaborate life-sustaining technologies made the question of euthanasia, for example, more urgent. I should note that – in addition to technological advance – the birth of bioethics was also importantly related to the civil rights movement of the 1960s. See H. Kuhse and P. Singer. 1998. What is Bioethics? A Historical Introduction, in *A Companion to Bioethics*, P. Singer and H. Kuhse eds. Oxford, UK. Blackwell: 3–11.

41 See Garrett, *The Coming Plague*, pp. 30–52, esp. pp. 30–31.

42 Ibid., pp. 30–31.

43 Ibid., p. 31. Not only did it fail, but this program was somewhat counter-productive. DDT-resistant mosquitoes returned in higher numbers than before; and misuse of medication promoted drug-resistant strains of malaria. By '1975 the worldwide incidence of malaria was about 2.5 times what it had been in 1961 … A new global iatrogenic form of malaria was emerging – "iatrogenic" meaning created as a result of medical treatment. In its well-meaning zeal to treat the world's malaria scourge, humanity had created a new epidemic' (p. 52).

44 Ibid., p. 36.

45 Ibid., p. 33.

46 Gewen, 'The Great Influenza'.

47 See H. Joffe. 1999. *Risk and the Other*. Cambridge, U.K. Cambridge University Press; & N.L. Stepan, *Picturing Tropical Nature*, for discussions of how AIDS and tropical diseases, respectively, are regularly understood and portrayed as problems of others.

48 Udo Schüklenk suggested this point in conversation.

49 This was (independently) suggested by Mary Tjiattas. Peter Singer concurred in conversation.

50 I do not mean to imply that other issues in bioethics do not require appreciation of social, political, historical, and economic phenomena. My point is one of degree: assessment of the health care situation in the developing world *often* requires substantially *more* contact with these other disciplines. Others who have worked in this area will agree.

51 For further illustration of what I here have in mind see M.J. Selgelid. Ethics, Economics, and AIDS in Africa. *Developing World Bioethics* 2004; 4, 1: 96–105.

52 See D. Moellendorf. 2002. *Cosmopolitan Justice*. Boulder, Colorado. Westview Press.

53 This objection was (independently) raised by Julian Savulescu in discussion.

54 In discussion.

55 James William Ley, philosophy Ph.D. student at the University of Sydney, encouraged explicit inclusion of this point.

65

Rethinking Mandatory HIV Testing during Pregnancy in Areas with High HIV Prevalence Rates

Ethical and Policy Issues

Udo Schüklenk and Anita Kleinsmidt

In 2005, between 36.7 and 45.3 million people were estimated to be HIV positive. Between 4.3 and 6.6 million persons were infected with HIV in that year alone, and approximately 3.1 million deaths were attributed to AIDS. About 35% of newborns born to HIV-infected women contract the virus from their mothers if efforts to prevent mother-to-child transmission are not in place. In 2004, for example, this mode of transmission resulted in up to 2.8 million HIV-infected children worldwide. More than 600 000 children were newly infected with HIV during 2005, and it is estimated that a similar number of children died of AIDS in the same year.[1]

A landmark 1994 multicenter trial conclusively demonstrated the efficacy of using antiretroviral therapy to reduce mother-to-child transmission of HIV,[2] showing a 67.5% relative reduction in mother-to-child transmission with the use of zidovudine. Since then, researchers have investigated the effects on mother-to-child HIV transmission of different drug regimens, shorter courses of drugs, breastfeeding, delivery by caesarian section, vitamin supplements, and treatment of newborns whose mothers did not receive antiretroviral therapy.

This intensity of research into ways of reducing vertical transmission of HIV has led to a focus of attention on the obstetric care of pregnant women in high-prevalence regions. Treatment is contingent upon the pregnant woman seeking antenatal care, being screened for HIV, and agreeing to medical intervention. The continuing high number of children with vertically acquired HIV attests to failures at various stages of this process. The scale of the problem demonstrates individual tragedies on an overwhelming scale and a threat to the public health of the communities in question.

Pregnant women who seek antenatal care are typically offered 1 of 2 types of HIV testing, referred to as *opt in* and *opt out*. With opt-in testing, the health worker offers the HIV test, and if the woman seeking antenatal care elects to have the test, it is accompanied by pretest counseling and voluntary first-person informed consent. In most developed countries, HIV testing of pregnant women is voluntary and requires informed consent and elaborate counseling procedures.[3] Whether opt-in testing should be applied in developing countries with substantially higher HIV prevalence rates has been called into

Original publication details: Udo Schüklenk and Anita Kleinsmidt, "Rethinking Mandatory HIV Testing during Pregnancy in Areas with High HIV Prevalence Rates: Ethical and Policy Issues," pp. 1179–83 from *American Journal of Public Health* 97: 7 (2007). Reproduced with permission from American Public Health Association.

question.[4] In most developing countries, antenatal clinics are short staffed and counselors overburdened.[5]

Opt-out testing involves the woman being told that HIV testing will be carried out along with other routine tests unless she refuses. Adoption of the opt-out approach to prenatal HIV testing has resulted in a marked increase in pregnant women agreeing to take the test.[6] In Canada, provinces using the opt-out approach show almost universal uptake, whereas testing rates in provinces using opt in are only 50% to 60%.[7] In Alabama, uptake increased from 75% to 88% after a switch from opt-in to opt-out testing.[8]

It is significant that making it more difficult to avoid testing translates into larger numbers of pregnant women finding out about their HIV status. In turn, they and their health care providers are able to make informed choices about appropriate courses of action. In Ivory Coast, fewer than 50% of pregnant women who test HIV positive return to receive treatment, which would lower rates of mother-to-child transmission.[9] An analysis of pregnant women in the United Kingdom who refused testing showed that these "refusers" were twice as likely to be infected with hepatitis B virus as those who agreed to be tested.[10]

A study conducted at the South African Johannesburg Hospital determined that the HIV seroprevalence rate among women who refused routine antenatal HIV screening was a staggering 44%. This rate was higher than the HIV prevalence in the general antenatal population at the hospital, which was 29.4%.[11] The women who refused HIV testing agreed to take part in this anonymous study if their HIV status was not disclosed to them. Women may have refused testing because they believed that they were not at risk or, conversely, that their fear of being at risk would be confirmed by the test. Other crucial factors may have been fear of the stigma associated with HIV/AIDS and the possibility of being shunned by one's community or worse (e.g., harassment, loss of livelihood, eviction, murder).[12]

Failure to undergo testing for HIV could also be related to external factors such as poverty and poor access to clinics (the testing model proposed here would apply to pregnant women who have access to antenatal clinics). In a meta-analysis of recent studies of HIV/AIDS-related stigma in developing countries, it was concluded that much-feared negative community

or partner responses are far less common than women assume.[5] Indian investigators concluded that actual stigma experienced by women with HIV infection is lower (reported by 26% of women) than the fear of being stigmatized (reported by 97%).[13] This suggests that many women are probably overly concerned about stigma and that, in reality, their likelihood of being stigmatized is substantially smaller than they think it is.

Confidential HIV tests as well as free or affordable drugs aimed at preventing mother-to-child transmission of HIV are accessible to an increasing number of pregnant women in developing countries. The price paid by HIV-infected newborns for their mothers' failure to undergo testing and treatment is very high; the average life expectancy of an HIV-infected newborn who does not receive state-of-the-art medical care is about 2 years.[14] During this time the newborn suffers from a range of life-threatening illnesses; the average HIV-infected newborn lives a short life of low quality.

In South Africa, where the HIV antenatal prevalence rate is approximately 30%, we estimated that a 25% increase in testing would result in an additional increase in HIV detection of 7.5%. Use of the ACTG076 regimen (antepartum and intrapartum zidovudine for the mother and 6 weeks of treatment for the newborn) would result in HIV being averted in 1.1% to 1.5% of all newborns. Given South Africa's 1 million births per year, 11 000 to 15 000 infections could be prevented (Mike Urban, National Health and Laboratory Services, Johannesburg, South Africa, written communication, September 2006).

Here we address an important ethical and policy issue, namely the obligations of pregnant women and authorities in reducing the number of infants born with HIV infection in high-prevalence countries where medications aimed at preventing mother-to-child transmission are available to individuals irrespective of their capacity to pay. Recent bioethical analyses diverge from the developed world consensus on this issue and argue that both compulsory testing and compulsory treatment could be defensible in a public health emergency such as that of AIDS.[15] The initial developed world consensus stemmed from the wide acceptance of arguments suggesting that women have an absolute right to control their own body and that only very few infections of newborns would occur as a consequence of some infected women's choice not to undergo testing.[16]

Botswana, a southern African country, has adopted the opt-out system of HIV testing for all patients who seek care at health care facilities, including pregnant women. One of the objectives of such programs is to reduce the number of infected newborns. Botswana and other countries with similar programs offer free (but voluntary) highly active antiretroviral therapy (HAART) to parents for as long as clinically indicated in an effort to ensure that children have surviving parents capable of looking after them. This is a direct response to the ever-growing number of AIDS orphans on the African continent. In a dramatic turnaround of the developed world status quo, Clark concluded his analysis of the problem by suggesting that "the prevention of perinatal HIV transmission in Botswana, because of the availability of antiretroviral therapy for infected mothers and their children, greatly outweighs the burdens of the possible violation of the pregnant woman's privacy."[15(p7)]

Our argument in favor of mandatory testing and treatment of HIV-infected pregnant women in areas with high HIV prevalence rates depends on a number of conditions being met: the women in question would have voluntarily chosen to carry the fetus to term; they would have had a reasonable alternative to this course of action (e.g., abortion at least until the point of fetal viability); and continuing voluntary treatment with HAART would be available to them. The confidentiality of the women's HIV status should ideally be maintained during as well as after their pregnancy. Delivery mechanisms should be developed that allow testing and treatment and ensure continuing confidentiality. However, ultimately the latter condition is not imperative.

Liability for Harm to an Unborn Child

Courts have often been confronted with the problem of conflict between the rights to autonomy, privacy, and freedom of movement of pregnant women and the prevention of harm to fetuses. The Canadian case of *Winnipeg Child and Family Services v DFG* concerned

a glue addict who had given birth to 2 children with abnormalities.[17] Upon her becoming pregnant for the fourth time, the child care services department applied for an order placing her in a treatment center to manage her withdrawal and monitor the pregnancy. The lower court granted the order "because the court should only step in when it is certain that the mother intends to proceed to give birth."[17]

The majority in the appeals court overturned the order on the basis that the fetus did not have legal status while in utero and that the pregnant mother could not therefore be forcibly held for treatment. An infant acquires rights only upon being born alive. The court also expressed concern that penalizing pregnant women might deter them from seeking antenatal care. Dissenting judges Sopinka and Major were in favor of the intervention to prevent harm to the fetus:

> this interference is always subject to the woman's right to end it by deciding to have an abortion. ... When a woman chooses to carry a fetus to term, she must accept some responsibility for its well-being and the state has an interest in trying to ensure the child's health.[17]

Canadian law does backdate fetal rights if the child is born alive. This means that a child born alive who suffered harm before birth can recover compensation for damages, even though the harm occurred at a time when he or she was not legally a person. In one instance, a mother who withheld her HIV status from medical staff and subsequently gave birth to an HIV-positive child was charged with criminal negligence causing bodily harm and failure to provide the necessities of life (i.e., proper care, protection, shelter, food).[18] In contrast, civil courts have ruled that a child cannot sue his or her mother for injuries incurred during pregnancy as a result of the mother's conduct (e.g., *Dobson v Dobson*,[19] a Canadian case in which a child sued his mother for the injuries he incurred as a consequence of her negligent driving while pregnant with him).

In Canada, child protection legislation has also been used to forcibly treat pregnant women in an effort to prevent harm to the fetus. In the United States, health and social services authorities obtain court orders for this purpose.[20] Given that a competent person is allowed to refuse even life-saving treatment, some courts appear to be giving recognition to the fetus as a separate patient, although technically, as mentioned, infants acquire rights only after being born alive. US social services agencies have removed children from the custody of a pregnant woman who has exposed a fetus to harm through substance abuse and brought charges of inter alia child abuse, neglect, reckless endangerment, and manslaughter.[21]

The United States has seen a wave of "fetal protectionism" in the form of laws criminalizing prenatal harm through abuse of alcohol and illegal drug use, as well as legislation allowing double homicide charges to be brought against someone who harms a pregnant woman and a child she wished to carry to term. In South Africa and Australia, legal personhood of the fetus can be backdated if the child is born alive and has a legal claim that arose while he or she was in utero. Although it is beyond the scope of this article to discuss wrongful life litigation and disability rights arguments against prenatal screening, we wish to point out that a number of legal systems are attempting to find a balance between discouraging prenatal harm and preserving the right to termination of pregnancy.

The Traditional versus the Current Debate

In this debate, it is worthwhile to recall strategies deployed in the abortion controversies and reflect on the question of how the current debates do and do not relate to those bitterly fought issues. Arguments by various authors have attempted to place the suggestion that compulsory testing should be introduced for women in high-prevalence areas in the same category as the view that abortion is always wrong.[22] The suggestion here is that the fetus's life is of greater importance than the woman's right to control her own body. This analysis overlooks the fact that the pro-test argument is not necessarily about fetal life but about that of the newborn itself. In the current controversy, it is logically possible to hold a pro-choice view in the abortion debates and a compulsory testing and treatment view.

The traditional debates on the issue of interfering with women's reproductive choices were squarely focused on the moral status of embryos and the question of whether or not abortion is morally acceptable. A variety of hotly contested marker events (i.e., stages in fetal development) were proposed after which abortion was argued to be unethical.[23] The abortion debates effectively address the question of whether fetuses have an overriding moral claim on women to carry them to term. There is at least 1 similarity between these debates and the current debate, namely the question of whether an abortion might be an acceptable solution for an HIV-infected pregnant woman trying to avoid giving birth to an infected newborn. This is comparable to traditional discussions about the moral acceptability of abortion in cases in which the newborn is at serious risk of an inheritable genetic illness.

That, however, is where the similarity ends. Although this is not the place to argue[24–26] our position on the abortion controversy, we consider it important to stress that, from a policy perspective and from an ethics perspective, logically it is perfectly feasible to hold a liberal point of view in the abortion controversy and to favor a restrictive point of view on the issue of mandatory HIV testing of pregnant women in areas with high HIV prevalence rates.

The current debate on this issue started in developed countries, most vigorously in the United States, after a 1994 study demonstrated that zidovudine, when given to infected pregnant women and newborns, would reduce perinatal transmission of the virus. After years of controversy, the scales seem to be tipping slowly toward the mandatory approach we advocate. Several US states advocate mandatory testing of newborns, and recently, additional states have moved toward introducing legislation making HIV testing of pregnant women mandatory.[22] The prevalence of HIV is several magnitudes lower in the United States than it is, for instance, in Botswana, yet even there liberal attitudes are beginning to be replaced by policies designed to achieve better (public) health outcomes.

Feminist activists in developed countries have argued against compulsory testing and treatment, criticizing a supposedly "maternal ideology [according to which] good mothers engage in acts of self-sacrifice and self-abnegation, always putting the interests of their children before their own."[22(p349)] It is unclear to us how HIV testing and acceptance of medication that not only reduces perinatal HIV transmission rates but also preserves mothers' lives can reasonably be considered self-sacrificial acts. The critics have also reconstructed the dispute as akin to the traditional conflict between fetal and maternal interests, that is, the fetus's supposed interests weighed against the pregnant woman's interest in maintaining control over her own body.

This argument is flawed in a crucial respect. What if we granted such women the right to have an abortion instead of undergoing testing? If pregnant women decide voluntarily not to have an abortion, the issue is no longer about fetal rights but clearly about an infant they want to bring to term. Moral obligations toward improving the newborn's chances of living a life worth living can be derived from the pregnant women's decision that the infant should come into being (i.e., the decision not to abort). The decision to simultaneously choose to carry the fetus to term and not, at the very least, reduce the fetus's chances of contracting HIV constitutes a case of harm to the subsequently born child. As has been argued persuasively by various authors from different philosophical traditions, choosing deliberately not to act to prevent harm when one could have acted without unreasonably high costs to oneself is comparable to similarly deliberate actions that actively produce the same amount of harm.[27, 28]

What is significant about both the conservative and the liberal view is that they lead to a conclusion many would consider counterintuitive, namely that pregnant women in countries with high HIV prevalence rates should undergo compulsory testing and, if HIV positive, they should possibly be compelled to take medication to reduce the risk of perinatal transmission. The conservative, or anti-choice view, arrives at this conclusion because it prioritizes the developing fetus above women's rights to privacy and control over their own bodies. The liberal, or pro-choice view, reaches the same conclusion through a very different route. Here the argument focuses entirely on the harm-to-others case. Abortion is considered morally neutral (or nearly neutral) for reasons that predominantly have to do with the developmental state of the fetus. This pro-choice rationale leads to a seemingly nonliberal conclusion whenever women decide autonomously to carry the fetus to term. In that case, all other things being equal, there is a high likelihood that a newborn will be born. Infected newborns, then, have been harmed by their mother's refusal to test for HIV and to take the necessary medication to reduce the likelihood of passing on the infection.

Defending Conditionality

We propose stringent conditions that must be met before the introduction of any mandatory testing and treatment programs. Our first condition: women must have made a voluntary decision to carry the fetus to term, and the option of abortion must be made available to them. Building on Thomson's classical analysis,[29] we agree that although women are not morally obliged to altruistically carry a fetus to term that they do not wish to carry to term, they are not entitled to injure or prejudice the future life of a fetus they wish to carry to term. As Colb pointed out, the latter is a qualitatively different proposition altogether.[30] However, if women are unable to access a reasonable alternative to carrying the fetus to term (i.e. abortion) and their decision to continue the pregnancy is rendered involuntary, it is less clear why they should accept obligations toward the fetus or the prospective newborn for that matter.

In cases in which women visit antenatal clinics too late to have an abortion (after the fetus is viable outside the pregnant women's body in its own right), it is arguable that mandatory testing and treatment are acceptable. Prior to viability, abortion, from a liberal perspective, could be argued to be morally cost neutral. After viability has been attained by the fetus, destroying it is morally questionable because its survival does not depend any longer on a pregnant woman's altruistic act of carrying it to term.

Our second essential condition is that women be provided with continuing access to essential life-extending AIDS drugs. This access would have to be voluntary, in that continuing mandatory HAART treatment would not be feasible in a coercive regulatory environment. There are several good reasons for this condition. Newborns' chances of survival are improved significantly if there is a parent available to care for them. Developing countries with high HIV prevalence rates are unable to cope with the existing number of AIDS orphans. Adding orphans to those already in existence is likely to increase the strain on such societies. In addition, women who are temporarily on HAART and then taken off such medication are likely to develop drug-resistant strains of HIV.[31] Approximately 25% of women who only have taken a HAART short course (e.g., nevirapine) develop drug-resistant HIV strains within a year. Should they give birth in a subsequent year, treatment would be substantially more difficult. Mothers are likely to die faster as a consequence of this problem. To expect such excessive altruism from them is unreasonable. It is also likely that some of these women would introduce drug-resistant strains of the virus into the wider community, making the fight against AIDS even more difficult to win.

Our final condition is that women's confidentiality should be maintained. Although there is some evidence that the concern displayed by many pregnant women about the probable negative reaction a positive test result would trigger from partners and their communities is exaggerated, there is also sufficient evidence to suggest that such concerns are legitimate and must be taken seriously. We propose a compromise solution. Health care providers should develop treatment strategies that enable practitioners to maintain the confidentiality of both the mother and the newborn. However, at the same time, we recognize that once women decide to carry on with their pregnancy, they must accept some of the negative consequences that flow from an HIV-positive test result, especially the difficulty of obtaining medical care for themselves and their newborns under conditions of strict confidentiality.

One could argue that, as opposed to advocating mandatory testing and treatment, we should aim to increase the number of women who voluntarily undergo testing and treatment. We should expand educational programs and persuade rather than force pregnant women to be tested and treated. We believe that although such programs are valuable, it is not good public health policy, given resource constraints in countries with high HIV prevalence rates, to divert resources away from testing and treating people toward activities related to health promotion and counseling.

In cases of conflicting needs and limited resources, preserving lives must take priority over counseling.

Our analysis cannot be extended directly to developed countries with low HIV prevalence rates. The ethical framework driving our model is consequentialist in nature. The negative effect of subjecting excessively large numbers of pregnant women at very low or low levels of risk to the stress of HIV testing arguably outweighs the beneficial effect of reducing the number of HIV-infected newborns by very few.

Conclusions

A strong prima facie case for the introduction of mandatory HIV testing of pregnant women, as well as for compulsory treatment of HIV-positive pregnant women, can be made. There remain concerns regarding the protection of women's privacy and their risk of becoming victims of various forms of stigmatization. Careful consideration of the issue leads us to propose pilot studies introducing mandatory testing and treatment programs at a number of sites in Botswana and South Africa, with a view toward establishing how such programs can best be implemented and a view toward investigating stigmatization that affects women giving birth within these programs. Such pilot programs should also enable us to answer the question of whether or not mandatory testing and treatment would have a deterrent effect sufficiently high to cancel out any public health benefits that could be derived.[32]

We are not suggesting that this strategy is a panacea for the continuing pandemic of perinatally transmitted HIV, given the lack of access to antenatal care faced by many women who reside in developing world countries.[33] However, whenever feasible, governments and other health care providers should consider mandatory testing and treatment regimes.

Acknowledgments

We thank the 3 anonymous reviewers for their tremendously helpful and detailed critical comments, most of which led to significant improvements in this article. An earlier version was critically read and commented on by Marge Berer, Peter Singer, and Mike Urban.

References

1   *AIDS Epidemic Update 2005*. Geneva, Switzerland: Joint United Nations Programme on HIV/AIDS; 2005.

2   Connor EM, Sealing RS, Gelber R, et al. Reduction of maternal infant transmission of human immuno-deficiency virus type 1 with zidovudine treatment. *N Engl J Med*. 1994;331: 1173–1180.

3   Gostin LO. *The AIDS Pandemic*. Chapel Hill, NC: University of North Carolina Press; 2004.

4   De Kock K, Mbori-Ngacha D, Marum E. Shadow on the continent: public health and HIV/AIDS in Africa in the 21st century. *Lancet*. 2002;360: 67–72.

5   Medley A, Garcia-Moreno C, McGill S, Maman SR. Barriers and outcomes of HIV serostatus disclosure among women in developing countries: implications for prevention of mother-to-child transmission programmes. *Bull World Health Organ*. 2004;82: 299–307.

6   Centers for Disease Control and Prevention. Advancing HIV prevention: new strategies for a changing epidemic. *MMWR Morb Mortal Wkly Rep*. 2003; 52:329.

7   Walmesley S. Opt in or opt out: what is optimal for prenatal screening for HIV infection? *Can Med Assoc J*. 2003;168:707–708.

8   Stringer EM, Stringer JS, Cliver SP, Goldenberg RL, Goepfert AR. Evaluation of a new testing policy for human immunodeficiency virus to improve screening rates. *Obstet Gynecol*. 2001; 98:1104–1108.

9   *AIDS Epidemic Update 2001*. Geneva, Switzerland: Joint United Nations Programme on HIV/AIDS; 2001.

10 Boxall E, Smith N. Antenatal screening for HIV: are those who refuse testing at higher risk than those who accept testing? *J Public Health (Oxf)*. 2004;26:285–287.

11 Mseleku M, Smith TH, Guidozzi F. HIV seropositivity in pregnant South African women who initially refuse routine antenatal HIV screening. *Br J Obstet Gynaecol*. 2005;112:370–371.

12 Bond V, Chase E, Aggleton P. Stigma, HIV/AIDS and the prevention of mother-to-child transmission in Zambia. *Eval Prog Plann*. 2002;25:347–356.

13 Thomas BE, Rehman F, Suryanarayanan D, et al. How stigmatizing is stigma in the life of people living with HIV: a study on HIV positive individuals from Chennai, South India. *AIDS Care*. 2005;17:795–801.

14 *The Impact of HIV/AIDS: A Population and Development Perspective*. New York, NY: United Nations Population Fund; 2003.

15 Clark PA. Mother-to-child transmission of HIV in Botswana: an ethical perspective on mandatory testing. *Developing World Bioeth*. 2006;6:1–12.

16 McGovern T. Mandatory HIV testing and treating of childbearing women: an unnatural, illegal and unsound approach. *Columbia Hum Rights Law Rev*. 1997;28:469–499.

17 *Winnipeg Child and Family Services v DFG*, 3 SCR 925 (1997).

18 Csete J. Vectors, vessels and victims. Available at: http://www.aidslaw.ca/site/wp-content/uploads/2013/04/Women+and+HIV+-+Rpt+-+Womens+Rights+-+ENG.pdf.

19 *Dobson (Litigation Guardian of) v Dobson*, 2 SCR 753 (1999).

20 Martin S, Coleman M. Judicial intervention in pregnancy. *McGill Law J*. 1995;40:13.

21 Toscano V. Misguided retribution: criminalization of pregnant women who take drugs. *Soc Leg Stud*. 2005;14: 359–386.

22 Zivi K. Contesting motherhood in the age of AIDS: maternal ideology in the debate over HIV testing. *Fem Stud*. 2005;31:347–374.

23 Gibson S. The problem of abortion: essentially contested concepts and moral autonomy. *Bioethics*. 2004;18: 221–233.

24 Tooley M. *Abortion and Infanticide*. Oxford, England: Oxford University Press; 1983.

25 Warren M. The moral significance of birth. In: Holmes HB, Purdy L, eds. *Feminist Perspectives in Medical Ethics*. Bloomington, Ind: Indiana University Press; 1992: 198–215.

26 Singer P. *Rethinking Life and Death*. Melbourne, Victoria, Australia: Text Publishing Co; 1994.

27 Glover J. *Causing Death and Saving Lives*. Harmondsworth, England: Penguin Books; 1977.

28 Rachels J. *The End of Life*. Oxford, England: Oxford University Press; 1986.

29 Thomson JJ. A defense of abortion. *Philos Public Aff*. 1971;1:47–66 [see chapter 3 in this volume].

30 Colb SF. Woman on trial for delivering cocaine to her unborn child. Available at: http://writ.lp.findlaw.com/colb/20040811.html. Accessed April 24, 2006.

31 Palmer S, Boltz V, Martinson N, et al. Persistence of nevirapine-resistant HIV-1 in women after single-dose nevirapine therapy for prevention of maternal-to-fetal HIV-1 transmission. *Proc Natl Acad Sci U S A*. 2006 May 2;103(18): 7094–7099.

32 Nakchbandi IA, Longenecker JC, Ricksecker MA, Latta RA, Healton C, Smith DG. A decision analysis of mandatory compared with voluntary HIV testing in pregnant women. *Ann Intern Med*. 1998;128:760–767.

33 Zanconato G, Msolomba R, Guarenti L, Franchi M. Antenatal care in developing countries: the need for a tailored model. *Semin Fetal Neonatal Med*. 2006;11:15–20.

66

Mandatory HIV Testing in Pregnancy

Is There Ever a Time?

Russell Armstrong

Despite recent advances in ways to prevent transmission of HIV from a mother to her child during pregnancy, infants continue to be born and become infected with HIV, particularly in southern Africa where HIV prevalence is high.[1] Encouraging pregnant mothers to learn their HIV status early in their pregnancy is the first in a series of strategies used to prevent mother-to-child transmission. This allows maternal health issues to be addressed proactively (whether or not to begin antiretroviral therapy, for example) and for preparations to be made for the administration of prophylactic treatment during delivery. A number of interventions are available that significantly reduce the transmission of HIV from a mother to her infant.[2] All require timely administration and careful follow-up to achieve maximum effectiveness. As the number of infected infants continues to rise, however, attention remains focused on the mother-to-be and how to ensure she makes the best decision for her and her future child. In high-prevalence settings, where there is some urgency to affect the rate of transmission, emphasis has shifted from voluntary HIV counselling and testing towards routine testing.[3] More recently, there have been discussions on mandatory testing.[4] Could mandatory testing ever be the right option in these settings, and how would we know it was the right step to take?

Considerations of mandatory HIV testing in any context raise strong legal and ethical concerns. Others have written about the benefits and harms of mandatory HIV testing in pregnancy. However, most of these discussions deal with the issue in the context of low HIV prevalence (less than 1%) where mandatory testing appears unnecessary and appropriate resources are available to provide adequate care and support to HIV-positive pregnant women.[5] In this discussion, some different assumptions are made. First, it is assumed that the HIV prevalence rate amongst the expectant mother group is 20% or greater, as it is in much of southern Africa.[6] Second, it is assumed that the overall burden of HIV across the population is also high, ranging from 15% to 40% of the adult population, as is the case in the southern African region.[7] Thirdly, it is assumed that those states experiencing an HIV epidemic of this magnitude are struggling not only to support the burden of morbidity and mortality of those infected, but also to deal with the wider impacts of the epidemic, including the large and growing number of orphaned children, both infected and uninfected, now being left in its wake. The question posed in this

Original publication details: Russell Armstrong, "Mandatory HIV Testing in Pregnancy: Is There Ever a Time?," pp. 1–10 from *Developing World Bioethics* 8: 1 (2008). Reproduced with permission from John Wiley & Sons.

discussion is as follows: if mandatory HIV testing of pregnant women cannot be justified under these conditions, can it ever be justified? The stakes in the discussion are high. On the one hand, it could be unethical to remove from play the one strategy that might be effective. On the other hand, nothing should be done to make the situation worse. What is certain is that as the number of HIV-infected women and children continues to rise in high-prevalence settings, so too does the sense of urgency that something definitive and effective must be done, and done soon.

The concept of mandatory testing explored in this paper is the following: as part of care and services offered during and after pregnancy, a mother-to-be is *required* to undergo an HIV test. The purpose of the test is to determine her HIV status and, if HIV-positive, to ensure that she has the option to receive counselling and treatment in line with current methods for protecting and promoting her own health while at the same time reducing the probability of HIV transmission to her infant during labour, delivery and post-partum care. (It is also assumed that post-test counselling would include options regarding termination of pregnancy in countries where this is available to women.) The nature of the test is explained to the individual before the test is performed. Results are communicated in private and post-test counselling and support are provided. Confidentiality is assured, including where exchange of information is required between healthcare providers in the course of appropriate post-test care. Where treatment is required, it is available in a supportive and accessible manner. The overall goal of this approach is reducing mother-to-child transmission of HIV as much as possible while improving quality of care to mother and child and minimizing any adverse effects to either. Mandatory testing is proposed in a situation where rates of uptake of other types of testing, voluntary or routine, remain low, an assumption examined later in this discussion. In short, the context for considering mandatory testing is one of last resort where other strategies have not shown significant reductions in the rate of mother-to-child transmission.

Mandatory HIV testing in any situation is the most problematic of any testing strategy. Even when performed according to a high standard of professionalism, as suggested above, it still involves very significant limitations of individual autonomy and deep incursions into the domain of individual privacy. In pregnancy, unless the health of the pregnant woman is considered to be of equal importance to the goal of preventing transmission to future children, mandatory HIV testing threatens to create a situation where her moral value is secondary to that of her yet-to-be-born child. The most serious objection to mandatory testing schemes is the denial of dignity. Some other overriding objective is substituted for that of an individual's freedom to exercise his or her autonomy in the pursuit of moral fulfilment. An individual becomes a means to some other end and is no longer respected or empowered as an end in his or herself. In the absence of the ability to freely consent to an HIV test, an individual loses full power to determine under what circumstances he or she chooses to learn this important life-altering fact. So too is lost a significant degree of control over future decisions regarding things like subsequent disclosure to others and choosing appropriate options for ongoing care, treatment and support.

For pregnant women, these conflicts occur at a time when there is additional vulnerability in their situation, when they need essential healthcare or other services to assist them in the safe management of their pregnancy. As Erin Nicholson notes:

> A woman who may already feel the most vulnerable in the medical care environment, may feel even less respect for and trust in a system that refuses to let her be in charge of the decision of whether or not to have an HIV test.[8]

The denial of the opportunity to consent to an HIV test, and to freely choose a course of action subsequent to the test that is in the best interest of the mother and child-to-be, is argued by many to have far-reaching negative consequences. These include the potential for psychological, social and even physical harms to newly diagnosed HIV-positive pregnant women, erosion of trust between pregnant women and healthcare providers that would jeopardize the development of effective caring relationships, and, most significantly, the possibility that the women who could most benefit from interventions aimed at preventing mother-to-child-transmission will avoid using healthcare services altogether.[9] Whether exhaustive or not, this list does raise significant challenges to those who would seek to justify mandatory testing strategies as an element of care and support for HIV-positive pregnant women, and as a tool in the prevention of mother-to-child transmission.

The magnitude of the objections to mandatory HIV testing notwithstanding, the fundamental ability of any individual to enjoy autonomy, bodily integrity and personal privacy is not unlimited. Compelling reasons must be put forward to impose limits. Overall, the benefit to be gained must be proportionate to the limitation imposed. Recall that the context for this discussion is a situation where other strategies involving lesser limits have not been successful. Peter A. Clark has called for mandatory testing of pregnant women in Botswana where prevalence rates in pregnant women are amongst the highest on the African continent, and where resources for managing the HIV epidemic are constrained.[10] According to Clark, despite efforts to improve rates of testing and treatment, through the use of routine offers of HIV testing, for example, the uptake of prevention strategies has not dramatically improved and, consequently, the rate of perinatal transmission of HIV has not declined. As a framework for an ethical analysis of mandatory testing, quoting Kelly,[11] Clark uses the concept of 'proportionate reason': 'Proportionate reason means that "according to a sound prudential estimate, the good to be obtained is of sufficient value to compensate for the evil that must be tolerated."'[12] There are three criteria for achieving 'a sound prudential estimate':

1. the means used will not cause more harm than necessary to achieve the value;
2. no less harmful way exists to protect the value;
3. the means used to achieve the value will not undermine it.[13]

These three criteria are very similar to three of the five Siracusa principles that deal with limitations on fundamental freedoms in the context of human rights:

  i. there must be a legitimate objective;
 ii. the restriction must be necessary to achieve the objective;

iii. no less restrictive or obtrusive means are available to achieve the objective.[14]

Both Clark's criteria and the Siracusa principles provide a way of organizing and addressing concerns regarding mandatory HIV testing in pregnancy.[15] This discussion primarily uses the language of human rights, but Clark's moral framework, with its poles of good and evil, reminds us of the wider ethical and philosophical implications. Health programs and health systems operate within legal and regulatory regimes that in turn function in relation to both national and international human rights frameworks. However, mandatory testing also has broader impacts on human dignity and moral order.

Some Preliminaries: Human Rights for Women in the Developing World

The plight of HIV-positive pregnant women in developing world settings, including southern Africa, is an extremely difficult one. Women become infected with HIV and become pregnant in the larger context of women's vulnerability that continues to be driven by poverty, violence, gender-related discrimination and a host of other social, economic and cultural factors that perpetuate these conditions of disadvantage. Within this context, the exercise of human rights and the ability to achieve liberty and personal freedom are significantly compromised by forces that are beyond much individual influence or control. With regards to HIV testing, the International Community of Women Living with HIV/AIDS has described these layers of disempowerment in compelling terms:

> VCT [voluntary counselling and testing], even at its most benign, assumes generally that all women – even those who have limited ability to negotiate, have been subjected to subordination all their lives, and may, as a result of their circumstances, have very limited self-esteem – are somehow going to be able to make a meaningful decision as to whether to be tested.[16]

Women's ability to exercise agency or to inhabit the full extent of their autonomy is significantly limited.

As Rebecca Cook notes, where we find burdens of disease, such as HIV, that disproportionately affect women, the situation may be pointing to a much larger and more complex problem:

> Women's poor physical and psychological health may represent a metaphor for the poor health of women's rights in the body politic and in influential community institutions, whether political, economic, religious or health care.[17]

Given these circumstances, any proposal which places additional limitations on women's autonomy, like mandatory HIV testing in pregnancy, must be carefully scrutinized. Rather than place either minor or major limitations on personal freedoms for the sake of some compelling moral good, like the birth of HIV-negative children, it may layer on just one more deprivation of liberty, discouraging and even alienating women from attempting to exercise moral agency at all. Without doubt, this is an outcome that we must seek to avoid. While it is a denial of rights, it is also a much deeper denial of moral value and human dignity.

From the perspective of human rights, at both the country and international levels, women's vulnerability in the developing world has not gone unnoticed. There are a number of international instruments now in force, for example, aimed at protecting women from further marginalization and providing them with positive means to emerge from the complex layers of vulnerability and disadvantage that currently exist. Fareda Banda has recently reviewed the legal and human rights instruments relevant to the southern African region.[18] These include the African Charter on Human and Peoples' Rights (hereafter the African Charter),[19] the Convention on the Elimination of All Forms of Discrimination against Women (CEDAW),[20] and, more recently, the Protocol to the African Charter on the Rights of Women in Africa (hereafter the Protocol on Women).[21] The Protocol on Women focuses the more general human rights protections in the African Charter on the specific circumstances of women and girls in Africa. It also takes as a source of inspiration the global protections for women and girls described in CEDAW. The Protocol sets out broad, aspirational guarantees for the fulfilment of the rights and freedom of women within the specific context of Africa. It defines as harmful to women (and girls) any actions 'which negatively affect the fundamental rights of women and girls, such as their right to life, health, dignity, education and physical integrity.'[22] Violence against women is defined as 'acts that undertake the imposition of arbitrary restrictions on or deprivation of fundamental freedoms in private or public life in peace time and during situations of armed conflict or of war.'[23] Through the Protocol, women are guaranteed full autonomy, including the right to life, integrity and security of the person. States who ratify the Protocol are obliged to enact legislation curbing all forms of discrimination, particularly those harmful practices that endanger the health and wellbeing of women. The promotion of access to health care services is required, including those involving childbirth and those involving termination of pregnancy when the physical or mental health of either the woman or the foetus is threatened.[24] For mandatory testing to succeed in this context, the balance of benefits and harms would need to fall on the side of enabling the health and well-being of women during pregnancy. Otherwise, according to the Protocol, it could be construed as both discrimination and, far worse, violence against women to the extent that it limits protected freedoms and imposes on them a limitation that is not imposed on others.

The Good to Be Obtained

In order to justify mandatory HIV testing in pregnancy in any setting, one must first show that the objective of mandatory testing is itself reasonable. Is the use of mandatory testing as a gateway to treatment and care for pregnant women and to effective prevention of transmission of HIV during pregnancy a reasonable objective? Few have argued that there is any legitimate objective for using mandatory testing, even in the context of the HIV epidemic in southern Africa.[25] Mandatory testing occurs most commonly in this region in relation to insurance, the military, blood and organ donation, and immigration. None of these uses of mandatory testing is unproblematic. In settings like Botswana, where mother-to-child transmission continues to occur but where there are effective though unused means to prevent it, the reasonable objective of any intervention must be to improve the health of pregnant women and to prevent HIV transmission to newly born children. Knowing one's HIV status is linked to making such choices both during and after pregnancy. Knowing one's status, however, does not necessarily cause the correct choices to be made. Increases in HIV testing rates amongst pregnant women do not necessarily increase the rate of uptake of prevention interventions.[26] Clark, in his argument, states: 'Scientific data has proven that mandatory testing of all pregnant women could save the lives of thousands of children.'[27] With respect, Clark appears confused. Science has shown that effective interventions exist but has not shown a causal link between mandatory testing and effective uptake of these interventions. For this reason, mandatory testing on its own may not be a reasonable objective if no plausible evidence exists that it would encourage greater use of interventions to improve maternal health and to prevent HIV-transmission during pregnancy.

For mandatory testing to achieve a reasonable objective, it must be linked to mandatory provision of treatment and care, since it is these aspects of the intervention that actually reduce the risk of HIV transmission. Making treatment mandatory, at least to the extent that it prevents HIV transmission during pregnancy, significantly extends the limitations on personal freedoms that would be imposed. It may still be justifiable, however, since treatment, if taken appropriately, has several known benefits. Treating HIV-positive women early in their pregnancy with antiretroviral therapy lowers viral load, for example. The lower the viral load, particularly during delivery, the lower the risk of HIV transmission to an infant.[28] In addition, the drug Nevirapine, administered to the mother during delivery and to the infant shortly after birth, has become widely used in Africa based on its effectiveness in resource-limited settings for reducing HIV transmission.[29] Thus there are benefits to treatment, and these can only reasonably be made available once the HIV status of a pregnant woman is known. Mandatory testing, coupled with mandatory provision of treatment and care is, on the surface, a reasonable objective where other less intrusive

strategies have failed, and where the burden of HIV is high and continues to grow. The objective brings with it, though, significant obligations for the state or entity seeking to impose such a requirement. It must be prepared to support the infrastructure needed to assure women that treatment is available and that there is appropriate monitoring and support. Few countries where such measures could be contemplated meet such stringent requirements. Problems range from access to testing, the infrastructure required to deliver care and support to pregnant women on treatment, the availability of treatment itself, and the overall state of perinatal health programs generally in these settings. Without guaranteed access to a high standard of medical care both during and after pregnancy, under mandatory testing HIV-positive pregnant women are left with the burden of knowing their HIV status but with no assistance or support to take appropriate measures to address their own health and the health of the soon-to-be-born child. Decoupled from the mandatory provision of treatment, mandatory testing limits freedoms with no corresponding benefit, neither a reasonable objective nor any other moral good is obtained, in a high-prevalence setting or otherwise.

The Means Used Will Not Cause More Harm

The test for harm resulting from the use of mandatory HIV testing in pregnancy is relatively straightforward in the first instance. The number of HIV-positive mothers treated and HIV infections prevented must be greater than those achieved using other less intrusive means. Additionally, the number of HIV-positive mothers tested and treated under mandatory requirements must be greater than those that seek to evade such requirements. Nakchbandi and colleagues have attempted to model the impact of mandatory testing on rates of detection and treatment using decision analysis.[30] With low-prevalence estimates, mandatory testing fails due to high rates of deterrence (i.e. women in need of treatment not coming forward) relative to the number of women and infants tested and treated and the number of HIV infections prevented. However, the analysis is very sensitive to both prevalence and deterrence rates. As the authors state:

> The prevalence of HIV infection among women of child-bearing age was also important in the model. At the current [low] prevalence, a voluntary policy is warranted. However, if the overall prevalence increases to 0.58% or more, the question of mandatory HIV testing policy should be revisited.[31]

The authors suggest that the conclusions of their analysis could change with a significant increase in the prevalence rate (consider that the prevalence rate in 2005 in Botswana was 33.5%, dramatically greater than the 0.58% threshold noted above). The authors also state that the actual deterrence rate under a mandatory HIV testing scheme is not known and should be studied. Modelling analyses have limits and do not necessarily reflect the realtime complexities of women living in situations where a range of influences beyond individual choice affects their decision whether or not to submit to mandatory testing. While there is not sufficient evidence in the model to justify mandatory testing in high-prevalence settings, there is nevertheless the suggestion that different assumptions need to be made in these settings and that these may lead to different conclusions.

In order to grasp the magnitude of other harms that may result from mandatory testing, one must first seek an insight into why pregnant women would choose not to know their HIV status and, subsequently, not to take advantage of ways to improve their own health and significantly reduce the risk of HIV infection in their newly born children. There is growing evidence to show that high rates of agreement to test can be achieved with appropriate education and support, particularly if women are informed that one objective of knowing their status is preventing transmission to future children.[32] The reasons for not wanting to test involve fear: fear of stigma and discrimination, fear of loss of confidentiality, privacy, employment and other benefits, and fear of violence and rejection within families and communities.[33] Clearly during pregnancy women do not arbitrarily choose both to not know their own health status and to put the health status of future children at risk.

There are motivating factors at play related to the wider social context in which these women and children live. Evidence does suggest that when women understand the potential benefits of testing and the opportunities available for prevention of transmission once HIV status is known, rates of intention to test increase. This may not extend to actual testing or to the use of prevention interventions during labour and delivery. What the evidence does say is that the context for testing is important and that the more supportive the context the higher the likelihood that pregnant women will make choices to improve their own health and protect the health of their future children.

It is difficult to see how mandatory testing would resolve these challenges. If it were to be imposed on pregnant women alone, there would be a significant danger of further stigmatizing and singling out an already vulnerable group. In resource-poor settings, it is hard not to view pregnancy itself as a condition of vulnerability. During pregnancy, women require the assistance of their families, their social networks and the health care system. HIV-infected women may have additional needs during pregnancy for HIV-related care. Physical and social environments may not always be supportive and may be fraught with risk. There is real danger that mandatory HIV testing as a condition of receiving assistance during pregnancy may act as a deterrent to the use of the health care system where treatment and prevention interventions are available. One study has shown, for example, that those seeking not to test or to evade testing may have a higher frequency of HIV infection than those agreeing to be tested.[34] Should this be the case amongst those avoiding mandatory testing requirements, the results could be disastrous, particularly in a high-prevalence setting.

The risks of imposing mandatory testing are significant, particularly in places where any intervention that increases the rate of transmission and the overall burden of disease would be both illogical and intolerable. It is equally wrong to impose a limitation on individuals and to do nothing to mitigate those risks that arise to the individual consequent on the limitations imposed. Are the risks so great, however, that they could never be mitigated or controlled? As Clark suggests, risks associated with stigma and discrimination could be addressed through laws and other interventions aimed at safeguarding and protecting the rights of all HIV-positive individuals, pregnant women included.[35] Mandatory testing could be introduced as part of a larger program to improve services and supports for women during pregnancy, including the mandatory provision of treatment and care. In order for a state to justify mandatory HIV testing during pregnancy, it must take significant steps to address and resolve issues of HIV-related stigma and discrimination, and women's vulnerability generally. It must also take steps to address other adverse conditions that surround pregnancy for women. While such steps are plausible, they may not always be immediately feasible. Fareda Banda has noted the ongoing gap between resounding promises to women about human rights protections and the reality that many women in the southern African setting have yet to see such protections realized in the context of their day-to-day struggles to survive.[36] Mandatory testing for pregnant women, given the implications it has for them in terms of access to needed services and supports at a time of compounded vulnerability, is not a limited intervention. It connects to a much broader array of barriers that persist despite the efforts of national and international bodies to articulate and enforce protections of fundamental rights and entitlements for women in these settings.

Means Used Will Achieve and Not Undermine the Objective

In order for mandatory HIV testing to meet this final test, it must be shown that it could truly achieve the objective of improving maternal health and preventing mother-to-child transmission. Mandatory HIV testing on its own is unlikely to improve the conditions under which pregnant women manage their pregnancy and give birth, particularly in high-prevalence resource-limited settings, unless it is accompanied by a number of other measures guaranteeing access to treatment and care, assuring confidentiality and privacy, and preventing as much as possible the negative impacts of stigma and discrimination. Mandatory testing in pregnancy is uncharted territory for many states that might seek to impose it.

Clark states that 'At present, there does not appear to be an alternative that is as effective as mandatory testing.'[37] Routine HIV testing in pregnancy was introduced in Botswana in 2004, and at the time Clark was writing, no preliminary results were available. New information indicates that routine HIV testing for pregnant women has led to an increase in both the number of women who know their status and the number of women accepting treatment and prophylaxis to avoid transmission.[38] Given the magnitude of the risks involved in mandatory testing schemes, particularly for women in pregnancy, more experience is required with routine HIV testing strategies before renewing calls for mandatory testing. Although routine testing itself raises concerns regarding the extent to which autonomy is limited, the limitations are not so severe as those involved in mandatory testing.

A Compromise: Treatment in the Absence of Testing

As ways continue to be investigated to improve rates of HIV testing for pregnant women, other strategies have been proposed. These involve providing prophylaxis to all women, or a subset of women, during labour and delivery and to their infants shortly after birth.[39] Providing Nevirapine to women who refuse an HIV test or whose status is unknown at the time of delivery is the most widely discussed option. It may also be cost-effective as the cost of providing Nevirapine to women who may not need it is less than the cost of treatment and care for HIV-infected children.[40] The biggest challenge to this approach is assuring compliance, particularly in the group that does not know their HIV status or has chosen not to know, and who may not be motivated to take treatment or to ensure that treatment is provided to the newly born infant.[41] Hankins has gone so far as to suggest that requiring an HIV test, whether voluntary or not, as a condition of accessing treatment during delivery, may itself have ethical problems in that it may force a woman to know something she does not want to know as a condition of safeguarding the health of her future child.[42] Although there are still challenges to overcome, providing prophylactic treatment independent of testing does represent a pragmatic compromise and one that could be implemented or at least tried within existing approaches to perinatal prevention without the need to introduce mandatory testing. Knowledge of HIV status is still critical to effective management of the health of the mother and her infant. However, in this approach, presumably, other opportunities for testing could be provided over the course of the mother's contacts with the health care system during post-partum care.

Is There Ever a Time?

This discussion has looked at mandatory HIV testing in pregnancy in a context of last resort, where other means to test and to treat appear not to be effective in significantly lowering the rate of mother-to-child transmission. As the analysis has unfolded, it has become clear that the challenges involved in encouraging more pregnant women to know their HIV status and, if HIV-positive, to take appropriate measures to protect their own health and the health of their soon-to-be-born child, are complex and far reaching. Mandatory testing in these settings remains problematic. The limits on individual autonomy and privacy can only be justified provided there are a number of other guarantees made at the time that mandatory testing is introduced. In many settings where mother-to-child transmission rates are highest, pregnant women still have poor access to testing and to appropriate care and support. Mandatory testing on its own will not address these gaps, and could make them worse. An argument for mandatory testing is unlikely to succeed while these other opportunities exist to improve the provision of care and services to HIV-positive pregnant women in high-prevalence resource-limited settings. There are still less obtrusive means to be tried.

It would be wrong to say that states struggling with high-prevalence should never consider intrusive measures like mandatory testing. The dilemma these states face is the need for swift, effective action in a situation where children continue to become infected with HIV at birth while unused means exist to prevent infection. As Clark notes: 'The very survival of

Botswana and other sub-Saharan countries, both socially and economically, will depend on drastic and innovative measures.'[43] This is indeed a significant moral challenge, but the anguish we feel cannot cloud our reason in devising legally and ethically acceptable strategies to address it. This argument has not shown that mandatory testing could never be used, but it has shown that even in high-prevalence countries with high rates of mother-to-child transmission other less problematic interventions, like routine HIV testing and providing prophylaxis to women whose HIV status is unknown at the time of delivery, have yet to be fully implemented.[44] In high-prevalence settings, these still count as 'bold and innovative' measures as, for the most part, they have yet to be tried across the southern African setting. Until this is done, one can only say that the time to consider mandatory testing has not yet come.

Michael Kirby has stated recently that 'We are in a new international situation that demands new thinking and a willingness, if necessary, to reconsider past approaches.'[45] In this respect, the full range of approaches to deal with HIV, including mandatory testing, must continue to be reviewed. According to Kirby: 'There is an equation that reflects the necessary adjustment of the content of human rights to the circumstance of the epidemic and its proper management.'[46] Part of the content of the equation for southern Africa must be a realization that many influences are affecting women's ability to choose in the context of prevention of HIV transmission during pregnancy, and that these influences are related to persistent conditions of poverty, inequality and disadvantage, something that the fulfilment of rights will address, not the opposite. The Protocol on Women promises access to health care services, including during pregnancy and after, but we must ask for how many this is currently a reality. These human rights instruments exist to protect impoverished, vulnerable women, even in the midst of extreme situations. While rights and freedoms can be limited in the context of preventing transmission of HIV, benefits must outweigh harms in the specific setting in which the limitation is proposed. For southern Africa, this means recognizing the much broader implications of further limits on already limited rights and entitlements and seeking, at all costs, to avoid this. Some have argued that such an approach is clouding the debate where there is extreme urgency to take measures to control the epidemic.[47] Gruskin and Loff have disagreed.[48] In their view, rights-based approaches to public health ensure that the strategies used are informed by evidence and openly debated: 'This approach protects against unproved and potentially counterproductive strategies, even those motivated by genuine despair in the face of overwhelming public health challenge.'[49] There is no doubt that the ongoing transmission of HIV from mothers to children, when effective interventions exist to prevent it, is a situation of genuine despair. The situation is not solely related to individual decisions around testing, however, and so long as this is the case, mandatory HIV testing of pregnant women is unlikely to substantially improve it.

Notes

1 Joint United Nations Programme on HIV/AIDS/ World Health Organization (UNAIDS/WHO). 2006. *Report on the Global AIDS Epidemic*. Geneva: UNAIDS/WHO. Available at: http://data.unaids.org/ pub/Report/2006/2006_gr_en.pdf.

2 E.J. Abrams. Prevention of Mother-to-Child Transmission of HIV – Successes, Controversies, *Critical Questions. AIDS Rev* 2004; 6: 131–143.

3 Centers for Disease Control and Prevention (CDC). Revised Recommendations for HIV Testing of Adults, Adolescents, and Pregnant Women in Health-Care Settings. *MMWR* 2006; 55(RR-14): 9–10.

4 P.A. Clark. Mother-to-Child Transmission of HIV in Botswana: An Ethical Perspective on Mandatory Testing. *Developing World Bioeth* 2006; 6: 1–12; and, U. Schüklenk and A. Kleinsmidt. Rethinking Mandatory HIV Testing during Pregnancy in Areas with High HIV Prevalence Rates: Ethical and Policy Issues. *Am J Public Health* 2007; 97: 1179–1183 [see chapter 65 in this volume].

5 See, for example, T.M. McGovern. Mandatory HIV Testing and Treating of Child-bearing Women: An Unnatural, Illegal, and Unsound Approach. *Columbia Human Rights Law Rev* 1997; 28: 469–499; and E. Nicholson. Mandatory HIV Testing of Pregnant Women: Public Health Policy Considerations and Alternatives. *Duke J Gend Law Policy* 2002; 9: 175–191.

6 UNAIDS/WHO, *Report on the Global AIDS Epidemic*, p. 509. HIV prevalence estimates amongst pregnant women in capital cities were as follows in 2005: Botswana, 33.5%; Lesotho, 27.3%; South Africa, 25.2%; Swaziland, 37.3%.

7 UNAIDS/WHO, *Report on the Global AIDS Epidemic*, p. 506. National HIV prevalence estimates were as follows in 2005: Botswana, 24.1%; Lesotho, 23.2%; South Africa, 18.8%; Swaziland, 33.4%.

8 Nicholson, Mandatory HIV Testing of Pregnant Women, p. 184.

9 Nicholson, Mandatory HIV Testing of Pregnant Women, pp. 184–186.

10 Clark, Mother-to-Child Transmission of HIV in Botswana.

11 G. Kelly. 1957. *Medico-Moral Problems*. St Louis, MO. The Catholic Hospital Association: 14.

12 Clark, Mother-to-Child Transmission of HIV in Botswana, p. 9.

13 Clark, Mother-to-Child Transmission of HIV in Botswana, p. 9.

14 As quoted in S. Gruskin and B. Loff. Do Human Rights Have a Role in Public Health Work? *Lancet* 2002; 360: 1880.

15 Other analysis frameworks are available based both on human rights and on the emerging concept of public health ethics. They too rely on key concepts of effectiveness, proportionality and least restrictive means. See, for example, S. Gruskin, A. Hendriks and K. Tomasevski. 1996. Human Rights and the Response to HIV/AIDS. In *AIDS in the World II*. J.H. Mann and D.J.M Torantola, eds. New York, NY: Oxford University Press: 326–340; and N.E. Kass. Public Health Ethics: From Foundations and Frameworks to Justice and Global Public Health. *J Law Med Ethics* 2004; 32: 232–242.

16 International Community of Women Living with HIV/AIDS (ICW). The International Community of Women Living with HIV/AIDS: Point of View. *Health Hum Rights* 2005; 8(2): 25–26: 26.

17 R. Cook. Gender, Health and Human Rights. *Health Hum Rights* 1995; 1: 350–366: 362.

18 F. Banda. Women, Law and Human Rights in Southern Africa. *J South Afr Stud* 2006; 32: 13–27.

19 Organization of African Unity (OAU). 1981 (entered into force in 1986). *African Charter on Human and Peoples' Rights*. Addis Ababa: OAU.

20 United Nations. Division for the Advancement of Women. 1979. *Convention on the Elimination of All Forms of Discrimination against Women*. New York, NY: United Nations. Available at: http://www.un.org/womenwatch/ daw/cedaw/cedaw.htm [Accessed 14 Aug 2007].

21 African Union (AU). 2003. *Protocol to the African Charter on the Rights of Women in Africa*. Addis Ababa: AU. Available:http://www.achpr.org/files/instruments/women-protocol/achpr_instr_proto_women_eng.pdf.

22 African Union, Protocol on Women, Article 1(g).

23 African Union, Protocol on Women, Article 1(j).

24 African Union, Protocol on Women. See Article 14.

25 K.M. De Cock, D. Mbori-Ngacha and E. Marum. Shadow on the Continent: Public Health and HIV/AIDS in African in the 21st Century. *Lancet* 2002; 360: 67–77.

26 I.M. Malonza et al. The Effect of HIV-1 Testing on Uptake of Perinatal HIV-1 Interventions: A Randomized Clinical Trial. *AIDS* 2003; 17: 113–118.

27 Clark, Mother-to-Child Transmission of HIV in Botswana, p. 9.

28 Abrams, Prevention of Mother-to-Child Transmission of HIV.

29 Abrams, Prevention of Mother-to-Child Transmission of HIV.

30 I. Nakchbandi et al. A Decision Analysis of Mandatory Compared with Voluntary HIV Testing in Pregnant Women. *Ann Intern Med* 1998; 128: 760–767.

31 Nakchbandi et al., A Decision Analysis, 765.

32 E.E. Ekanem and A. Gbadegesin. Voluntary Counselling and Testing (VCT) for Human Immunodeficiency Virus: A Study of Acceptability by Nigerian Women Attending Antenatal Clinics. *Afr J Reprod Health* 2004; 8: 91–100.

33 C. Hankins. Preventing Mother-to-Child Transmission in Developing Countries: Recent Development and Ethical Implications. *Reprod Health Matters* 2000; 8: 87–92; and A. Medley et al. Rates, Barriers and Outcomes of HIV Serostatus Disclosure among Women in Developing Countries: Implications for Prevention of Mother-to-Child Transmission Programmes. *Bull World Health Org* 2004; 82: 299–307.

34 M. Mseleku, T.H. Smith and F. Guidozzi. HIV Seroprevalence in South African Women Who Initially Refuse Routine Antenatal HIV Screening. *BJOG* 2005; 112: 370–371.

35 Clark, Mother-to-Child Transmission of HIV in Botswana.

36 Banda, Women, Law and Human Rights in Southern Africa.

37 Clark, Mother-to-Child Transmission of HIV in Botswana, p. 11.

38 T.L. Creek et al. Successful Introduction of Routine Opt-Out HIV Testing in Antenatal Care in Botswana. *J Acquir Immune Defic Syndr* 2007; 45: 102–107.

39 See, for example, T.T. Sint et al. Should Nevirapine Be Used to Prevent Mother-to-Child Transmission among Women of Unknown Sero-status? *Bull World Health Org* 2005; 83: 224–228; Hankins, Preventing Mother-to-Child Transmission in Developing Countries, p. 89; and Nicholson, Mandatory HIV Testing of Pregnant Women.

40 E. Marseille et al. Cost Effectiveness of Single-dose Nevirapine Regimen for Mothers and Babies to Decrease Vertical HIV-1 Transmission in sub-Saharan Africa. *Lancet* 1999; 354: 803–809.

41 F. Dabis and E.R. Ekpini. HIV-1/AIDS and Maternal and Child Health in Africa. *Lancet* 2002; 359: 2097–2104.

42 Hankins, Preventing Mother-to-Child Transmission in Developing Countries.

43 Clark, Mother-to-Child Transmission of HIV in Botswana, p. 3.

44 An alternative, as suggested by Schüklenk and Kleinsmidt, Rethinking Mandatory HIV Testing, is to conduct pilot studies in southern African settings of mandatory testing coupled with guaranteed access to care and treatment or to safe abortion.

45 M. Kirby. The Never-Ending Paradoxes of HIV/AIDS and Human Rights. *African Human Rights Law Journal* 2004; 4: 163–180.

46 Kirby, The Never-Ending Paradoxes, 180.

47 De Cock et al., Shadow on the Continent.

48 Gruskin and Loff, Do Human Rights Have a Role in Public Health Work?.

49 Gruskin and Loff, Do Human Rights Have a Role in Public Health Work?, 1880.

67

XDR–TB in South Africa

No Time for Denial or Complacency

Jerome Amir Singh, Ross Upshur, and Nesri Padayatchi

On September 1, 2006, the World Health Organization (WHO) announced that a deadly new strain of extensively drug-resistant tuberculosis (XDR–TB) had been detected in Tugela Ferry (Figure 67.1), a rural town in the South African province of KwaZulu-Natal (KZN),[1] the epicentre of South Africa's HIV/AIDS epidemic. Of the 544 patients studied in the area in 2005, 221 had multi-drug-resistant tuberculosis (MDR–TB), that is, *Mycobacterium tuberculosis* that is resistant to at least rifampicin and isoniazid. Of these 221 cases, 53 were identified as XDR–TB (see Table 67.1 and[2]), i.e., MDR–TB plus resistance to at least three of the six classes of second-line agents.[3] This reportedly represents almost one-sixth of all known XDR–TB cases reported worldwide.[4] Of the 53, 44 were tested for HIV and all were HIV infected.

The median survival from the time of sputum specimen collection was 16 days for 52 of the 53 infected individuals, including six health workers and those reportedly taking antiretrovirals.[2] Such a fatality rate for XDR–TB, especially within such a relatively short period of time, is unprecedented anywhere in the world.

The Threat to Regional and Global Health

South Africa is one of the world's fastest growing tourist destinations,[5] home to millions of migrant labourers from neighbouring countries, and its ports and roads service several other African countries. Seroprevalence rates for HIV in South Africa, and in adjoining nations such as Lesotho and Swaziland, are very high. Cumulatively, these factors make for a potentially explosive international health crisis.

The threat to regional and global public health is thus clear,[6] and further underlined by reports that XDR–TB is now considered endemic to KZN,[7] as it has been reported in at least 39 hospitals throughout the province[8] and in other parts of the country.[9–11] At least 30 new cases of XDR–TB are reportedly detected each month in KZN alone.[12]

Original publication details: Jerome Amir Singh, Ross Upshur, and Nesri Padayatchi, "XDR–TB in South Africa: No Time for Denial or Complacency," *PLoS Med* 4: 1 (2007): e50. doi:10.1371/journal.pmed.0040050. Copyright: © 2007 Singh et al.

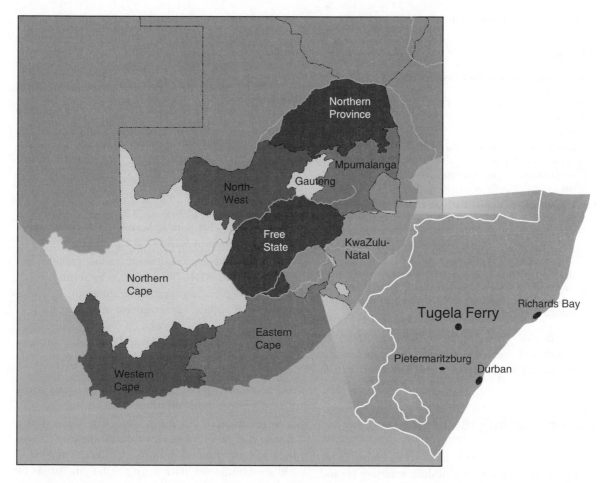

Figure 67.1 Map of South Africa showing Tugela Ferry in the province of KwaZulu-Natal, the epicentre of South Africa's HIV/AIDS epidemic

The True Extent of the Problem

Diagnosed cases of XDR–TB likely represent a small proportion of the true extent of the problem. The number of persons harbouring latent infections is unknown (and likely unknowable at present). Official statistics also likely underestimate the true prevalence of XDR–TB, as the current national TB guidelines prescribe the conditions under which *M. tuberculosis* susceptibility testing should be done.[13] These guidelines recommend susceptibility testing for those patients who have previously been treated for TB or fail to respond to treatment after two months of TB treatment, at which point there is a high treatment interruption rate. In addition, specialised laboratory facilities are required for such testing. Routine sputum culture and susceptibility testing of all patients suspected as having TB should form part of a multi-faceted approach to identifying and addressing TB drug resistance.

In recognition of the global threat posed by these factors, on September 9, 2006, WHO urged a response to the outbreak akin to recent global efforts to control severe acute respiratory syndrome (SARS) and bird flu.[14] The South African government's initial lethargic reaction to the crisis[15,16] and uncertainty amongst South African health professionals concerning the ethical, social, and human rights implications of effectively tackling

Table 67.1   Characteristics of patients in South Africa with XDR-TB

Characteristic	No. (%)
Tuberculosis (TB) characteristics ($n = 53$):	
Pulmonary TB alone	40 (75%)
Pulmonary and extrapulmonary TB	13 (25%)
Sputum-smear positive	42 (79%)
Sputum-smear negative	11 (21%)
Previous TB treatment ($n = 47$):	
No previous treatment	26 (55%)
Previous treatment: cure or completed treatment	14 (30%)
Treatment default or failure	7 (15%)
Previous admission in past 2 y ($n = 42$)	
Admission for any cause	28 (67%)
No previous admission	14 (33%)

Data from Gandhi NR, Moll A, Sturm AW, Pawinski R, Govender T, et al. (2006) Extensively drug-resistant tuberculosis as a cause of death in patients co-infected with tuberculosis and HIV in a rural area of South Africa. *Lancet* 368: 1575–1580. doi:10.1371/journal. pmed.0040050.t001

this outbreak[17,18] highlight the urgent need to address these issues lest doubt and inaction spawn a full-blown XDR-TB epidemic in South Africa and beyond.

Factors Fuelling the Outbreak

Several well-documented factors, including high treatment interruption rates of drug-sensitive TB and consequent low cure rates, together with the HIV epidemic, have contributed to the emergence of MDR-TB and XDR-TB in South Africa and merit urgent remediation. For instance, the development of drug resistance may result from inappropriate treatment regimens (e.g., choice of drugs, dosage, duration of treatment), programme factors (e.g., irregular drug supply, incompetent health personnel), and patient factors (e.g., poor adherence, mal-absorption). In fact, it could be said that the emergence of MDR-TB itself is evidence of the systematic failure of the global community to tackle a curable disease.

The factors that facilitate the spread of tuberculosis are well known and abundantly present in sub-Saharan Africa. Alongside inadequate healthcare system response, poverty and global inequity contribute to the worsening of the global TB situation.[19,20] According to South Africa's Medical Research Council, about half of adults in South Africa with active TB are cured each year, compared with 80% in countries with better resources. Moreover, nationally, about 15% of patients default on the first-line six-month treatment, while almost a third of patients default on second-line treatment.[21] This highlights the urgent need for the health system (which includes health-care workers) to reinforce the DOTS (directly observed treatment, short-course) and DOTS-plus strategy, to revise current adherence counselling and public information strategies, and to actively promote avoidance of a "victim blaming approach". The emergence of MDR-TB and XDR-TB is an indicator of the poor implementation of South Africa's TB Control Programme.

A neglected but significant factor fuelling the MDR-TB and XDR-TB outbreaks in South Africa[22] is the lack of infection control in institutions, including the lack of simple administrative measures such as triaging of patients, as well as more sophisticated expensive environmental control measures, such as negative pressure rooms and personal respiratory protection (respirators). Infection control must be addressed in order to reduce the nosocomial transmission of these infections.

In the modern era, tuberculosis is recognised as a disease that preys upon social disadvantage.[23,24] Thus, the inadvertent deterrent impact that health and social welfare policies are having on the hospitalisation of such patients needs to be explored. Currently, 10 million South Africans – almost one in four citizens – are beneficiaries of some form of social welfare.[25] With unemployment in South Africa conservatively estimated at about 27% of the population,[26] social welfare grants often constitute the sole or primary income of many households. While South Africa does not have a formal universal health-care system, those who require but who cannot afford to pay for hospitalisation are often treated free of charge in the public sector.[27] However, current government policy stipulates that those who are hospitalised at state expense lose their social welfare benefits for the duration of their hospitalisation.

Faced with the prospect of being deprived of their gainful employment and/or having their welfare benefits suspended for the duration of hospitalisation – which in the case of MDR-TB or XDR-TB could last 18–24 months – many MDR-TB patients opt not to stay in hospitals, where their treatment adherence and resistance profile could be closely monitored by health personnel. Instead, understandably, these highly infectious individuals fail to receive appropriate therapy and are likely to default on adherence. They mix broadly in society among non-infected individuals, typically utilise public transport, and seek or continue their gainful employment. In so doing, they pose a significant public health risk to their families, co-workers, local community, and the wider public they encounter.

Given the cost of trying to manage a MDR-TB or XDR-TB epidemic,[28] the South African government ought to rethink its policy of suspending welfare benefits to patients with MDR-TB or XDR-TB for the duration of their hospitalisation. Moreover, it ought to consider extending welfare benefits to those infected patients who are gainfully employed as an incentive to draw such patients into the health system so that their adherence to anti-TB medication and resistance profile can be monitored. Although these measures will undoubtedly have cost implications for the government and may not adequately compensate patients for their lost income, they would at least serve as some form of incentive and encouragement for infected individuals to enter and remain in the health system, although admittedly, their confinement could conceivably be indefinite or until they die. It would also be a partial realisation of the reciprocity principle, which we explore below.

Factors That Could Undermine Efforts to Tackle the Outbreak

Several factors threaten to stymie efforts to control the XDR-TB outbreak in South Africa. Drug resistance can only be detected if a patient presents to the health system, a health-care worker suspects TB, an appropriate specimen is taken, facilities exist for smear and cultures, and if laboratories are equipped to do drug susceptibility testing. Moreover, because most hospital beds in South Africa are occupied by patients infected with opportunistic infections associated with HIV/AIDS, there is little or no spare capacity to accommodate patients with MDR-TB and XDR-TB.

However, given the airborne transmission of TB and the grave threat that MDR-TB and XDR-TB pose immediately to such immunocompromised patients and, if the spread of XDR-TB is not abated, to global health, the government ought to reconsider its prioritisation of hospital resources. It seems that, at minimum, patients with XDR-TB requiring inpatient care should be housed in facilities independent both of patients with MDR-TB and patients who are immunocompromised. The containment of infectious patients with XDR-TB may arguably take precedence over any other patients not infected with highly infectious and deadly airborne diseases, including those with full-blown AIDS. This is an issue requiring urgent attention from the global community.

Is There a Role for Involuntary Detention?

The successful containment of TB, MDR-TB, and XDR-TB in South Africa and elsewhere carries human rights[29] and ethical implications. An important question that we must come to terms with is the extent to which judicially sanctioned restrictive measures should be employed to bring about control of what could develop into a lethal global pandemic.

As diagnosis of MDR-TB and XDR-TB can take several weeks, questions remain about what to do with patients suspected of being infected with MDR-TB or XDR-TB while awaiting susceptibility results. And once patients have been determined to be infected, there are questions about how long and how closely their clinical status should be monitored and under what conditions. Ideally, patients suspected of having TB should be isolated in an acute infectious diseases setting while awaiting anti-tuberculosis drug-susceptibility testing, and then triaged for further management based on these results. Current WHO guidelines recognise that this strategy is not feasible in resource-constrained environments. WHO recommends that persons with MDR-TB voluntarily refrain from mixing with the general public and from those susceptible to infection, while they are infectious and in ambulatory care.[30] The document is silent on what steps to take should such voluntary measures fail.

The emergence of XDR-TB indicates that the WHO strategy of allowing the patient to assume responsibility for mixing with the general public may be too permissive and more attention to strategies of infection control in the community is required. In general, from both an ethical and legal perspective, measures that rely on voluntary cooperation and are the least restrictive in terms of interfering with human rights are preferred. However, if such measures prove to be ineffective, then more restrictive measures may need to be contemplated. Such measures should be taken with due consideration for the possibility that they may increase disincentives to seek care. However, if due care is taken to provide for the rights and needs of those so detained and therapeutic goals are kept paramount, such measures could play an important role in containing XDR-TB before it spreads more generally in the population globally.

The use of involuntary detention may legitimately be countenanced as a means to assure isolation and prevent infected individuals possibly spreading infection to others. However, South African officials have raised human rights concerns in dealing with the country's XDR-TB and MDR-TB outbreaks,[18] although they have conceded that forcible treatment may be a viable option in tackling the outbreak.[31] Health workers and human rights advocates in South Africa and elsewhere must be reminded that although a country's Bill of Rights may bestow a range of human rights on individuals, these rights can usually be restricted if doing so is reasonable and justifiable. They should be made aware of any national laws and municipal by-laws that permit the provision of involuntary treatment and isolation measures in the interests of public health.

Moreover, the judiciary often has the authority to issue orders compelling involuntary confinement/ hospitalisation and treatment, even against the wishes of an affected party, if doing so is in the public interest. This option should only be invoked if non-coercive measures have failed. Such an approach has been endorsed by the European Court on Human Rights (ECHR) in *Enhorn v. Sweden*.[32] The applicant in this case was an HIV-infected man who had infected another party and disobeyed the instructions of public health officials to desist from irresponsible and risky behaviour. The man complained to the ECHR that the compulsory isolation orders and his involuntary detention in a hospital had been in breach of Article 5(1) of the European Convention for the Protection of Human Rights and Fundamental Freedoms. This article states that "Everyone has the right to liberty and security of the person. No one shall be deprived of his liberty save in the following cases and in accordance with a procedure prescribed by law". Section 5(1) (e) provides for the situation at hand: "the lawful detention of persons for the prevention of the spreading of infectious diseases".

The applicant argued that the substantive provisions of Article 5 were not made out in his case, given that the detention did not constitute a proportionate response to the need to prevent the spread of infectious disease. The court held that any such detention must be in compliance with both the principle of proportionality and the requirement that there be an "absence of arbitrariness" such that other less severe measures have been considered and found to be insufficient to safeguard the individual and the public. This would entail that the deprivation of liberty was necessary in all circumstances.[33]

Moreover, for detention to comply with principles of proportionality and freedom from arbitrariness, it must be established that the detained person is suffering from an infectious disease, that the spread of disease is dangerous to public safety, and that the detention of the infected person is the last resort measure in order to prevent disease spread. The court ruled that the institution of detention for infectious disease must be appropriate to the nature of the disease. Where these conditions are satisfied, deprivation of liberty is justified, both on grounds of public policy and in order to provide medical treatment to the affected party. In ruling in favour of the applicant the court found that the compulsory isolation of the applicant by Swedish authorities ought to have been considered only as a last resort in order to prevent him from spreading HIV after less severe measures had been considered and found to be insufficient to safeguard the public interest. We believe that the forced isolation and confinement of individuals infected with XDR-TB and selected MDR-TB may be an appropriate and proportionate response in defined situations, given the extreme risk posed by both strains and the fact that less severe measures may be insufficient to safeguard public interest. Patients with XDR-TB should also be quarantined separately from those with MDR-TB, as the latter is potentially curable.

Although the justness and effectiveness of forcibly confining and treating patients with TB[34,35] has been called into question,[36] such an approach has met with some degree of success in the US,[37] where it helped bring down TB infection rates in states such as New York in the 1990s.[38] We would not argue for forcible treatment of patients with MDR-TB or XDR-TB, simply restriction of mobility rights of such individuals.

Emulation of New York's aforementioned successful approach in controlling its TB outbreak could empower health officials in South Africa and elsewhere to act decisively in tackling emerging XDR-TB and MDR-TB outbreaks. The consequences of not educating health workers of the state's powers in such instances were highlighted on September 12, 2006, in Johannesburg, Africa's commercial and air transport hub, when health workers allowed a patient diagnosed with XDR-TB, who refused to be hospitalised, to discharge herself. Although this patient was eventually traced and forcibly hospitalised five days after her self-discharge,[39] it remains unknown how many people she may have infected in the months between her sputum sample being taken and her eventual diagnosis in September 2006, and before she was traced after her self-discharge.

Questions also remain about how authorities should deal with patients with MDR-TB whom treatment has failed to cure as well as patients with XDR-TB in whom cure is unlikely as few active drugs remain. While isolating such patients until they die – which in the case of the slightly less deadly MDR-TB could be years – has been described as "ethically questionable and impractical,"[21] this option may, of necessity, need to be countenanced. It is not, *a priori*, unethical to restrict the movement of those whose infection poses risks to public health. It is a matter of what types of safeguards are put in place to assure the legitimacy of such acts.

There are many such justifications emerging in the field of public health ethics that recognise that prevention of harm and protection of public health are legitimate ethical norms.[40-42] Human rights doctrine also recognises the limitation of many rights in a public health emergency, provided the measures employed are legitimate, non-arbitrary, publicly rendered, and necessary. In this regard, section 25 of the Siracusa Principles on the Limitation and Derogation of Provisions in the International Covenant on Civil and Political Rights holds: "Public health may be invoked as a ground for limiting certain rights in order to allow a state to take measures dealing with a serious threat to the health of the population or individual members of the population. These measures must be specifically aimed at preventing disease or injury or providing care for the sick and injured."[43] It must be assured that detained individuals have appropriate legal council, and given the uncertainty of the duration of restrictions required, duly constituted independent tribunals could be established to oversee the process. At issue from a human rights perspective is whether such prolonged isolation represents the least restrictive means to achieve this goal and the extent of the belief in the severity of the threat. We do not intend to resolve this issue presently, but believe it is worth tabling for broader debate.

The use of legally sanctioned restrictive measures for the control of XDR-TB should not obscure the fact that being infected is not a crime. A strong reciprocal obligation is borne by authorities so wishing to invoke these measures. Those who are isolated require humane and decent living conditions. In fact the restriction of their liberties is more for a collective good than for their own. Thus every effort must be made to ensure conditions of living that preserve dignity. Harris and Holm have argued that all people with a communicable disease have a duty not to infect others. They stress, however, that "[i]t is ... also a duty which we can expect people to discharge *only if they live in a community that does not leave them with all the burdens involved in discharging this duty*"[38] (italics ours). The task of global health is to help create these communities.

Conclusion

XDR-TB is a serious global health threat. It has the potential to derail the global efforts to contain HIV/AIDS, as broadly disseminated XDR-TB will prove to be a much more serious public health threat owing to its mode of transmission. The emergence of XDR-TB is also an uncomfortable reminder of the failure of health systems to control problems at a tractable scale. If, in the recent past, TB were to have been adequately managed when it was completely drug sensitive, we would not be in such a dire situation as is currently the case. This failure rests upon us all. We should begin to contemplate the response when we move to the predictable next phase: completely drug-resistant tuberculosis.

By December 1, 2006 – World AIDS Day – South Africa had reported more than 300 cases of XDR-TB[44] (based on the latest definition of XDR-TB, i.e., resistance to at least rifampicin and isoniazid, with resistance to one of the injectable drugs [kanamycin, amikacin, capreomycin] and one of the quinolones). Given the South African government's poor track record in dealing with the country's HIV/AIDS epidemic and what is at stake if it adopts a similar lethargic and denialist response to the country's XDR-TB outbreak, the international community must be vigilant in monitoring the government's response to this emerging crisis. Although recent initiatives of the government[45,46] and the Medical Research Council of South Africa[28,47] are encouraging, these will hopefully not inspire complacency amongst officials.

While it is encouraging that the South African government invited the WHO to an October 2006 meeting on the emerging crisis,[48] it is worth noting that neither party raised the human rights and ethical dimensions of controlling the outbreak. Containing XDR-TB and selected MDR-TB will require an interdisciplinary approach[49] and the synergistic cooperation of all organs of the state, including, in particular, the judiciary, as well as various government departments. Moreover, the government should urgently consider devising strategies to control the disease amongst particularly high-risk groups such as prisoners and migrant labourers, which might necessitate the involvement of prisoner advocacy groups and neighbouring countries, respectively.

If WHO is sincere in calling for the XDR-TB outbreak in South Africa to be treated in the same light as SARS and bird flu, then global efforts to develop rapid diagnostic tests and novel treatment regimens must be stepped up. In addition to drug development, the appropriateness of using these technologies in countries with TB/HIV epidemics needs to be explored. The determination of XDR-TB requires specialised laboratories and quality assurance, particularly when testing for resistance to second-line antituberculosis agents. Moreover, while the diagnosis of MDR-TB may take weeks or months, new technologies, including liquid culture and PCR probes, can reduce this time. Efforts must be stepped up to sponsor and equip poor countries to address these challenges. Depending on how successfully the South African government controls the outbreak, as in the case of SARS, infection monitoring at hospitals, border posts, and airports may become necessary.

Given the ethical and legal implications of these measures, the experience of countries that were affected by SARS[50] could prove valuable in guiding South Africa to deal with its XDR-TB outbreak. Admittedly though, more is known of XDR-TB than was the case with SARS when it first emerged. In the meantime, South Africa must urgently reduce crowding in hospitals where patients with TB are being treated to reduce the risk of the infection spreading, drastically expand its surveillance of the disease, and rethink its current counselling, treatment, reporting, and tracing strategies. It must also devise measures to reduce contact between patients with TB and those suspected or confirmed with MDR-TB and XDR-TB in the weeks or months it takes to diagnose the latter two infections. It must also devise appropriate infection-prevention strategies for health workers treating such patients.

All reasonable attempts must be made to accommodate the interests of infected patients in a sensitive and humane manner, although, if necessary, the government must adopt a more robust approach towards uncooperative patients with MDR-TB and XDR-TB, which might necessitate favouring the interests of the wider public over that of the patient. Although such an approach might interfere with the patient's right to autonomy and will undoubtedly have human rights implications, such measures are reasonable and justifiable, and must be seen in a utilitarian perspective. Ultimately in such crises, the interests of public health must prevail over the rights of the individual.

References

1 South African Press Association (2006 September 1) New deadly TB strain detected in SA. Available: http://www.iol.co.za/news/south-africa/new-deadly-tb-strain-detected-in-sa-1.292028#.VYVW0PlVhBc.

2 Gandhi N, Moll A, Pawinski R, Zeller K, Lalloo U, et al. (2006) Favorable outcomes of integration of TB and HIV treatment in a rural South Africa: The Sizonqoba study [abstract]. 16th International AIDS Conference; 2006 13–18 August; Toronto, Canada. Abstract MOPE0181.

3 Centers for Disease Control and Prevention (2006) Emergence of Mycobacterium tuberculosis with extensive resistance to second-line drugs worldwide, 2000–2004. *MMWR Morb Mortal Wkly Rep* 55: 301–305. Available: http://www.medicalnewstoday.com/medicalnews.php?newsid=40511. Accessed 23 December 2006.

4 WHO (2006 September 5) Emergence of XDR-TB. WHO concern over extensive drug resistant TB strains that are virtually untreatable. Available: http://www.who.int/mediacentre/news/notes/2006/np23/en/index.html. Accessed 23 December 2006.

5 Pressly D (2006 September 11) Foreign tourists boost SA coffers.

6 Editorial (2006) XDR-TB – a global threat. *Lancet* 368: 964.

7 Zulu X (2006 September 11) Super TB "now endemic in KZN". Available: http://www.iol.co.za/news/south-africa/super-tb-now-endemic-in-kzn-1.293133#.VYVSpflVhBc.

8 Staff reporter (2006 November 30). Report: Drug-resistant TB at 39 KZN hospitals. *Mail and Guardian.* Available: http://mg.co.za/article/2006-11-30-report-drugresistant-tb-at-39-kzn-hospitals.

9 Smith C, Clarke L (2006 September 10) Prospect of TB epidemic sets medics trembling. Available: http://www.iol.co.za/news/south-africa/prospect-of-tb-epidemic-sets-medics-trembling-1.293002#.VYVYYPlVhBc.

10 McGregor S (2006 September 11) New TB strain could fuel South Africa AIDS toll. Available: http://www.iol.co.za/news/south-africa/new-tb-strain-could-fuel-aids-toll-1.293202#.VYVd1flVhBc.

11 South African Press Association (2006 October 17) Extreme TB spreading across the nation – MRC. Available: http://www.iol.co.za/news/south-africa/extreme-tb-spreading-across-the-nation-mrc-1.297989#.VYVgd_lVhBc.

12 McGregor S (2006 November 27) Hospital struggles with deadly SA TB. *Mail and Guardian.* Available: http://mg.co.za/article/2006-11-27-hospital-struggles-with-deadly-tb.

13 Department of Health, Republic of South Africa (2000) *The South African Tuberculosis Control Programme Practical Guidelines.* Available: https://www.westerncape.gov.za/text/2003/tb_guidelines2000.pdf.

14 Reuters (2006 September 7) WHO urges South Africa to curb TB killer super-bug.

15 McGregor S (2006 September 17) State slammed for "delayed reaction" to TB. Available: http://www.iol.co.za/news/south-africa/state-slammed-for-delayed-reaction-to-tb-1.293975#.VYVjj_lVhBc.

16 Clark L, Smith C (2006 September 10) Extreme TB outbreak just "tip of the iceberg". Available: http://www.iol.co.za/news/south-africa/extreme-tb-outbreak-just-tip-of-the-iceberg-1.293026#.VYVkIPlVhBc.

17 South African Associated Press, South African Broadcasting Corporation (2006 September 8) Drug-resistant TB: Whose rights should prevail?

18 Agence France-Presse (2006 October 24) South Africa's anti-TB fight hamstrung by Constitution.

19 Verma G, Upshur RE, Rea E, Benatar SR (2004) Critical reflections on evidence, ethics and effectiveness in the management of tuberculosis: Public health and global perspectives. *BMC Med Ethics* 12: E2.

20 Yong Kim J, Shakow A, Mate K, Vanderwarker C, Gupta R, et al. (2005) Limited good and limited vision: Multidrug-resistant tuberculosis and global health policy. *Soc Sci Med* 61: 847–859.

21 Beresford B (2006 September 8) Call to isolate TB victims. *Mail and Guardian.*

22 Sacks LV, Pendle S, Orlovic D, Blumberg L, Constantinou C (1999) A comparison of outbreak- and nonoutbreak-related multidrug-resistant tuberculosis among human immunodeficiency virus-infected patients in a South African hospital. *Clin Infect Dis* 29: 96–101.

23 Benatar S (2005) Why tuberculosis persists as a global problem. *Int J Tuberc Lung Dis* 9: 235.

24 Benatar SR (2006) Extensively drug resistant tuberculosis: Problem will get worse in South Africa unless poverty is alleviated. *BMJ* 333: 705.

25 SouthAfrica.info (2005 September 12) Spreading the social security net.

26 Statistics South Africa (September 2005) P0210 – Labour Force Survey (LFS). Available: www.statssa.gov.za/publications/P0210/P0210September2005.pdf.

27 Singh JA, Govender M, Reddy N (2005) South Africa a decade after apartheid: Realising health through human rights. *Georgetown Journal of Poverty Law and Policy* 7: 355–388.

28 Medical Research Council of South Africa (2006) Managing multidrug-resistant TB: Legal implications. Available: http://www.mrc.ac.za/policybriefs/managingTB.pdf. Accessed 23 December 2006.

29 WHO (2001) A human rights approach to TB: Stop TB guidelines for social mobilization. Available: http://whqlibdoc.who.int/hq/2001/WHO_CDS_STB_2001.9.pdf. Accessed 23 December 2006.

30 WHO (2006) *Guidelines for the Programmatic Management of Drug-Resistant Tuberculosis*. Available: http://whqlibdoc. who.int/publications/2006/9241546956_eng.pdf. Accessed 23 December 2006.

31 De Lange D (2006 October 25) Patients "could be quarantined". Available: http://www.news24.com/South Africa/News/Patients-could-be-quarantined-20061024.

32 European Court of Human Rights (2005) *Enhorn v. Sweden*. ECHR 56529/00.

33 Martin R (2006) The exercise of public health powers in cases of infectious disease: Human rights implications. *Enhorn v. Sweden*. *Med Law Rev* 14: 132–143.

34 Connecticut Department of Public Health (2006) Tuberculosis quarantine laws.

35 Public Health Institute (2003) TB control and the law. Frequently asked questions on civil commitment.

36 Coker R (2001) Just coercion? Detention of nonadherent tuberculosis patients. *Ann NY Acad Sci* 953: 216–223.

37 William J, Burman WJ, Cohn DL, Rietmeijer CA, Judson FN, et al. (1997) Short-term incarceration for the management of noncompliance with tuberculosis treatment. *Chest* 112: 57–62.

38 Harris J, Holm S (1995) Is there a moral obligation not to infect others? *BMJ* 311: 1215–1217.

39 News24 (2006 September 13) Woman with killer TB found. Available: http://www.news24.com/SouthAfrica/News/Woman-with-killer-TB-found-20060913.

40 Kass N (2001) An ethics framework for public health. *Am J Public Health* 91: 1776.

41 Childress JF, Faden R, Gaare RD, Gostin LO, Kahn J, et al. (2002) Public health ethics: Mapping the terrain. *J Law Med Ethics* 30: 170–178.

42 Uphsur R (2002) Principles for the justification of public health intervention. *Can J Public Health* 93: 101–103.

43 United Nations, Economic and Social Council, U.N. Sub-Commission on Prevention of Discrimination and Protection of Minorities (1984) Siracusa principles on the limitation and derogation of provisions in the International Covenant on Civil and Political Rights, Annex. Available:http://www1.umn.edu/humanrts/instree/siracusaprinciples.html.

44 News24 (2006 November 23) 300+ cases of killer TB in SA. Available:http://www.news24.com/SciTech/News/300-cases-of-killer-TB-in-SA-20061123.

45 Department of Health, Republic of South Africa (2006) TB crisis management plan.

46 Dlamini N (2006 September 5) Department addresses extremely drug resistant TB in KZN. Available: http://allafrica.com/stories/200609051470.html. Accessed 23 December 2006.

47 Dlamini N, Dube S (2006 September 7) Action plan developed to combat drug resistant TB.

48 South Africa Press Association/Agence France-Presse (2006 October 12) South Africa invites WHO experts for killer TB talks. Available:http://www.iol.co.za/news/south-africa/sa-invites-who-experts-for-killer-tb-talks-1.297401#.VYVsSflVhBc.

49 Lienhardt C, Rustomjee R (2006) Improving tuberculosis control: An interdisciplinary approach. *Lancet* 367: 949–950.

50 Working group of the University of Toronto Joint Centre for Bioethics (2003) Ethics and SARS: Learning lessons from the Toronto experience. Available: http://www.yorku.ca/igreene/sars.html. Accessed 18 September, 2006.

Part X

Ethical Issues in the Practice of Healthcare

Introduction

In the Hippocratic tradition, it has long been assumed that the first responsibility of doctors is toward the health and well-being of each individual patient, rather than to patients as a whole, or to society at large. Another traditional assumption among physicians was that they are entitled to be paternalistic toward their patients. This means that doctors may sometimes – in seeking to protect the physical health and well-being of patients – ignore their wishes, and deceive them about the state of their health. Today, however, it is widely assumed that respect for patient autonomy, rather than medical paternalism, ought to be the cornerstone of the doctor/patient relationship. It is also commonly accepted that the duties and responsibilities of doctors extend beyond those they owe to their individual patients. But, as the articles in the present Part X of the anthology illustrate, the contemporary emphasis on autonomy and patient consent raises some complex ethical issues.

Confidentiality

One of the pledges in the Hippocratic Oath reads: "What I may see or hear in the course of treatment or even outside of the treatment in regard to the life of men, which on no account must spread abroad, I will keep to myself …"

Traditional Western medicine has taken the principle of confidentiality very seriously. But is the principle still relevant today? Patients are often treated by a number of doctors and a range of other healthcare professionals, in large hospitals. Pathology companies perform a myriad of tests that may reveal sensitive information. Records are stored and transmitted electronically, with large numbers of people having access. Record-keeping, the involvement of different healthcare specialists, and good communication between them are essential for the effective delivery of healthcare. While patients are the prime beneficiaries of these contemporary arrangements, Mark Siegler argues that they spell the end of confidentiality in the traditional sense. His view is encapsulated in the title of his essay: "Confidentiality: A Decrepit Concept." Rather than invest energy in vainly trying to preserve confidentiality as a whole, Siegler suggests that patients and doctors would be better served if attention were directed toward determining which aspects of the principle are worthy of preservation, and which we can and should do without.

As Siegler notes, there are two reasons for treating medical information as confidential: First, confidentiality might be defended as a corollary of the value of respecting the patient's autonomy and privacy. Secondly, confidentiality might be seen as an important element in the provision of good healthcare. If patients did not trust their doctors and feared disclosure of sensitive medical information to third parties, some would be unlikely to confide in their doctors, thus jeopardizing both diagnosis and treatment. After suggesting that these two functions of confidentiality are as important today as they have been in the past, Siegler proceeds to sketch a number of ways in which "the confidentiality problem" might be solved.

While it has sometimes been argued that the doctor's duty to respect patient confidentiality is absolute, this duty can clash with equally or even more compelling duties such as the obligation to protect the life and health of others. In "The Duty to Warn and Clinical Ethics: Legal and Ethical Aspects of Confidentiality and HIV/AIDS," Christian Säfken and Andreas Frewer discuss the tragic 1976 case involving Tatiana Tarasoff which established that there are circumstances in which the duty to warn a person at risk of being murdered overrides the physician's – or in this case, the psychotherapist's – duty to keep information given in a clinical setting confidential.

The Tarasoff case occurred before the spread of HIV/AIDS, which, when it first became a major public health issue, was an incurable and fatal disease, sexually transmitted by people who may have no visible symptoms. The prevalence of HIV/AIDS led to a sharper focus on the dilemma of confidentiality versus the duty to warn. As Säfken and Andreas Frewer indicate, there have been different judicial responses to this situation, with some courts and legislatures giving priority to the duty of confidentiality, or at least to the right of the healthcare professionals to maintain confidentiality, and others giving priority to the duty to warn those at risk of serious harm. Säfken and Frewer are clear about which side of this dispute they think is right.

Truth-Telling

Another set of moral problems in healthcare relates to the issue of truth-telling. As we have already noted, in the Hippocratic medical tradition, it used to be regarded as proper for doctors to act paternalistically, if they considered it to be in the best interests of the patient. In line with this thinking, doctors are seen as justified in withholding the truth from patients, or lying to them, if – in the doctor's view – a patient would be harmed by knowing the truth. The questioning of medical paternalism, and the movement for greater patient autonomy that began in the twentieth century, has led to the widespread rejection of the view that doctors

can lie to their patients. But, as with the notion of confidentiality, the question arises whether, and if so when, the principle that doctors should not deliberately deceive patients may be broken.

Not many philosophers have claimed that it is always wrong to lie. Immanuel Kant is the most notable exception. In his essay "On a Supposed Right to Lie from Altruistic Motives" he defends the principle that we must never lie, even if our doing so could prevent the death of an innocent human being. For Kant, "To be *truthful* … is … a sacred unconditional command of reason, and not to be limited by any expediency." Joseph Collins, in his essay "Should Doctors Tell the Truth?" written in 1927, takes a very different view. He argues that many patients do not want to know the truth, and would be harmed by being given bad news. They would often enjoy life less, and sometimes even die earlier than they would have if they had been shielded from the truth. Rather than burden patients with this kind of information, there is, Collins argues, merit in cultivating "lying as a fine art."

Roger Higgs ("On Telling Patients the Truth") accepts that the temptation to withhold bad news from patients can be strong. But, he argues, truth is important for trust in the doctor–patient relationship, and is a prerequisite for respect for patient autonomy – for how can patients decide on their treatment if they do not know the truth about their diagnosis and prognosis? While some writers draw a moral distinction between lying and other forms of deliberately withholding or masking the truth, Higgs follows the philosopher Sissela Bok in holding that any statement or omission that is intended to mislead amounts to lying, even if the statement itself is not false. While not ruling out the possibility that there might be occasions when lying is justified, such occasions would, Higgs concludes, be rare. Higgs's position thus lies somewhere between those of Kant and Collins.

Informed Consent and Patient Autonomy

The idea that autonomy or self-determination is valuable is not new. It has been defended by many philosophers on the grounds that without autonomy, liberty or self-determination we are not our own persons, deciding on how we shall live, but rather the creatures of others who directly or indirectly impose their will on us. John Stuart Mill, in his essay "On Liberty," an excerpt of which we include here, provides a forceful and eloquent defense of liberty, and rejects the idea that the state should restrict individual liberty for the good of those whose liberty is restricted. In a famous sentence, he writes: "the only purpose for which power can be rightfully exercised over any member of a civilized community, against his will, is to prevent harm to others. His own good, either physical or moral, is not a sufficient warrant."

Nevertheless, as Tom Beauchamp describes in "Informed Consent: Its History, Meaning, and Present Challenges," it was only in second half of the twentieth century that courts began to hold that competent patients have a right not to be treated without their informed consent. US Justice Benjamin Cardozo had articulated the general idea already in 1914 when he stated that "Every human being of adult years and sound mind has a right to determine what shall be done with his own body …" (*Schloendorff v. New York Hospital*, 1914), but it was not until the 1970s that informed consent became part of more mainstream legal thinking, and subsequently found its way into medical practice.

For a patient's consent to a procedure to be valid, "informed consent," it is widely held that at least the following five conditions must be met. The patient must

1   be competent or of "sound mind";
2   be adequately informed;
3   substantially understand the information;
4   make the decision free from coercion or undue influence;
5   intentionally authorize the medical procedure or treatment plan.

If all five conditions are fully observed, we would have what Beauchamp argues is the essence of informed consent as it should be understood: an autonomous authorization for treatment (or for participation in a research project). This is, however, a high standard, and it is not clear how much progress has been made in achieving it.

Part of the problem is that terms like "adequately" and "substantially" are vague. What does it mean for a patient to be "adequately informed"? How do we know whether a patient has "substantially understood" or is subject to "undue influence" – and what kind of influence is "due"? Beauchamp gives one example – a research project involving the Havasupai Indians of the Grand Canyon – where it seems clear that there was no substantial understanding of the purposes for which biological samples would be used.

Should we assume that people from different cultural backgrounds – whether indigenous people like the Havasupai, or people from East Asia, or the Middle East, or parts of Europe – share our view of the importance of informed consent, patients' rights, and autonomy? Some have claimed that the current emphasis in healthcare ethics on autonomy is part of a distinctively North American elevation of the individual over the community. Most other societies around the world, so the criticism goes, place the family, the community, or society above the rights or interests of the individual. This is often understood as supporting the argument that ethics is relative and that what is right in one society may be wrong in another. Ruth Macklin discusses this question in "The Doctor–Patient Relationship in Different Cultures." Drawing on a rich array of examples from different parts of the world, Macklin shows that arguments in support of cultural relativism are often confused and simplistic. Cultures are not monolithic, and different members of them may take different views, so the differences between cultures are not as sharp as many assume. Even if they were, however, Macklin argues, it would not necessarily show that it was right for a doctor to tell the patient the truth in North America, and wrong for the doctor to do that in another country.

Carl Elliott's "Amputees by Choice" deals with people with what, to most of us, seems a bizarre desire. If someone asks a doctor to amputate a healthy arm or leg, would it ever be appropriate for the doctor to accede to such a request? How far does patient autonomy stretch in these circumstances? Or is the very fact of making such a request sufficient to show that the patient, or would-be patient, is not of sound mind, and that therefore questions of autonomy do not apply?

Elliott writes that he was initially revolted by the idea of amputating healthy limbs as a form of treatment, but his opinion changed after he began talking to people who wanted to have a limb amputated, and understood their condition better. Moreover, if their requests or amputation are rejected on the grounds that the conditions of informed consent are not satisfied, or that doctors should not remove healthy tissue, Elliott's account suggests that many other similarly situated patients and a range of accepted surgical procedures would have to be rejected as well. Surgeons already suck fat from people's thighs, lengthen penises, reduce or increase the size of breasts, redesign labia and split tongues. Why, then, not amputate a limb, particularly if the aim is to alleviate the intense suffering of a patient?

Arguably, if the only thing that will stop me being miserable is the amputation of a healthy limb, then the desire to have that limb amputated is rational. What might be considered irrational, in this situation, is the fact that the presence of a healthy limb is making me miserable. In situations of the kind that Julian Savulescu discusses in his article "Rational Desires and the Limitation of Life-Sustaining Treatment," however, we may consider a patient's desire to be irrational. It may, for instance, be inconsistent with other stronger or more enduring desires that the patient has. This leads to a broader problem for the notion of informed consent: should we do what a patient desires even if the patient's desire is not rational? Savulescu answers that question in the negative. To defend that answer, we need to be able to distinguish between rational and irrational desires, and then to evaluate whether a specific desire in a particular context is or is not rational. While not downplaying the difficulties inherent in this task, Savulescu argues that it is one we cannot avoid if we are to respect patient autonomy. As Savulescu himself notes, however, such a policy is open to paternalistic abuse. Because of this it might be

preferable to have a policy that accepts a competent patient's choices as a matter of course. But in that case the justification does not lie, Savulescu suggests, with respect for patient autonomy, but elsewhere. Presumably the justification he has in mind is the desirability of avoiding the harms that can flow from excessive paternalism.

Shlomo Cohen is also concerned with avoiding harms; but the harms that he discusses in "The Nocebo Effect of Informed Consent" are those that flow, not from excessive paternalism, but from taking the need for fully informed consent too far. The "nocebo effect" that he is referring to is the opposite of the well-known placebo effect. Telling patients that the drug you are prescribing for them will make them feel better is likely to make them feel better, even if the drug has no active ingredients. Similarly, telling patients that the drug you are prescribing for them can, as a side-effect, cause headaches means that they are more likely to experience headaches than if they had been given the same drug without the warning.

How far must we go, then, in warning patients of all the possible – and possibly dire – side-effects of a drug that is overwhelmingly likely to do them a lot of good, and which very rarely has undesirable side-effects (unless patients are told that they may experience specific undesirable side-effects). Here Cohen's conclusions about the full implementation of informed consent are similar to those of Joseph Collins on the obligation to tell the truth. Providing the information required for informed consent is a form of truth-telling that can clash with what has often been seen as the strictest principle of medical ethics: "First, do no harm." When it does, then just as Collins argued that "do no harm" should sometimes prevail over the obligation to tell the truth, so Cohen argues that "do no harm" should sometimes prevail over the requirement for full information that is taken to be part of "informed consent."

Confidentiality

68

Confidentiality in Medicine

A Decrepit Concept

Mark Siegler

Medical confidentiality, as it has traditionally been understood by patients and doctors, no longer exists. This ancient medical principle, which has been included in every physician's oath and code of ethics since Hippocratic times, has become old, worn-out, and useless; it is a decrepit concept. Efforts to preserve it appear doomed to failure and often give rise to more problems than solutions. Psychiatrists have tacitly acknowledged the impossibility of ensuring the confidentiality of medical records by choosing to establish a separate, more secret record. The following case illustrates how the confidentiality principle is compromised systematically in the course of routine medical care.

A patient of mine with mild chronic obstructive pulmonary disease was transferred from the surgical intensive-care unit to a surgical nursing floor two days after an elective cholecystectomy. On the day of transfer, the patient saw a respiratory therapist writing in his medical chart (the therapist was recording the results of an arterial blood gas analysis) and became concerned about the confidentiality of his hospital records. The patient threatened to leave the hospital prematurely unless I could guarantee that the confidentiality of his hospital record would be respected.

This patient's complaint prompted me to enumerate the number of persons who had both access to his hospital record and a reason to examine it. I was amazed to learn that at least 25 and possibly as many as 100 health professionals and administrative personnel at our university hospital had access to the patient's record and that all of them had a legitimate need, indeed a professional responsibility, to open and use that chart. These persons included 6 attending physicians (the primary physician, the surgeon, the pulmonary consultant, and others); 12 house officers (medical, surgical, intensive-care unit, and "covering" house staff); 20 nursing personnel (on three shifts); 6 respiratory therapists; 3 nutritionists; 2 clinical pharmacists; 15 students (from medicine, nursing, respiratory therapy, and clinical pharmacy); 4 unit secretaries; 4 hospital financial officers; and 4 chart reviewers (utilization review, quality assurance review, tissue review, and insurance auditor). It is of interest that this patient's problem was straightforward, and he therefore did not require many other technical and support services that the modern hospital provides. For example, he did not need multiple consultants and fellows, such specialized procedures as dialysis, or social workers, chaplains, physical therapists, occupational therapists, and the like.

Upon completing my survey I reported to the patient that I estimated that at least 75 health professionals and hospital personnel had access to his medical

Original publication details: Mark Siegler, "Confidentiality in Medicine: A Decrepit Concept," pp. 1518–21 from *New England Journal of Medicine* 307: 24 (December 1982). Copyright © 1982 Massachusetts Medical Society. Reprinted with permission from Massachusetts Medical Society.

Bioethics: An Anthology, Third Edition. Edited by Helga Kuhse, Udo Schüklenk, and Peter Singer.

record. I suggested to the patient that these people were all involved in providing or supporting his health-care services. They were, I assured him, working for him. Despite my reassurances the patient was obviously distressed and retorted, "I always believed that medical confidentiality was part of a doctor's code of ethics. Perhaps you should tell me just what you people mean by 'confidentiality'!"

Two Aspects of Medical Confidentiality

Confidentiality and third-party interests

Previous discussions of medical confidentiality usually have focused on the tension between a physician's responsibility to keep information divulged by patients secret and a physician's legal and moral duty, on occasion, to reveal such confidences to third parties, such as families, employers, public-health authorities, or police authorities. In all these instances, the central question relates to the stringency of the physician's obligation to maintain patient confidentiality when the health, well-being, and safety of identifiable others or of society in general would be threatened by a failure to reveal information about the patient. The tension in such cases is between the good of the patient and the good of others.

Confidentiality and the patient's interest

As the example above illustrates, further challenges to confidentiality arise because the patient's personal interest in maintaining confidentiality comes into conflict with his personal interest in receiving the best possible health care. Modern high-technology health care is available principally in hospitals (often, teaching hospitals), requires many trained and specialized workers (a "health-care team"), and is very costly. The existence of such teams means that information that previously had been held in confidence by an individual physician will now necessarily be disseminated to many members of the team. Furthermore, since health-care teams are expensive and few patients can afford to pay such costs directly, it becomes essential to grant access to the patient's medical record to persons

who are responsible for obtaining third-party payment. These persons include chart reviewers, financial officers, insurance auditors, and quality-of-care assessors. Finally, as medicine expands from a narrow, disease-based model to a model that encompasses psychological, social, and economic problems, not only will the size of the health-care team and medical costs increase, but more sensitive information (such as one's personal habits and financial condition) will now be included in the medical record and will no longer be confidential.

The point I wish to establish is that hospital medicine, the rise of health-care teams, the existence of third-party insurance programs, and the expanding limits of medicine all appear to be responses to the wishes of people for better and more comprehensive medical care. But each of these developments necessarily modifies our traditional understanding of medical confidentiality.

The Role of Confidentiality in Medicine

Confidentiality serves a dual purpose in medicine. In the first place, it acknowledges respect for the patient's sense of individuality and privacy. The patient's most personal physical and psychological secrets are kept confidential in order to decrease a sense of shame and vulnerability. Secondly, confidentiality is important in improving the patient's health care – a basic goal of medicine. The promise of confidentiality permits people to trust (i.e., have confidence) that information revealed to a physician in the course of a medical encounter will not be disseminated further. In this way patients are encouraged to communicate honestly and forthrightly with their doctors. This bond of trust between patient and doctor is vitally important both in the diagnostic process (which relies on an accurate history) and subsequently in the treatment phase, which often depends as much on the patient's trust in the physician as its does on medications and surgery. These two important functions of confidentiality are as important now as they were in the past. They will not be supplanted entirely either by improvements in medical technology or by recent changes in relations between some patients and doctors toward a rights-based, consumerist model.

Possible Solutions to the Confidentiality Problem

First of all, in all nonbureaucratic, noninstitutional medical encounters – that is, in the millions of doctor–patient encounters that take place in physicians' offices, where more privacy can be preserved – meticulous care should be taken to guarantee that patients' medical and personal information will be kept confidential.

Secondly, in such settings as hospitals or large-scale group practices, where many persons have opportunities to examine the medical record, we should aim to provide access only to those who have "a need to know." This could be accomplished through such administrative changes as dividing the entire record into several sections – for example, a medical and financial section – and permitting only health professionals access to the medical information.

The approach favored by many psychiatrists – that of keeping a psychiatric record separate from the general medical record – is an understandable strategy but one that is not entirely satisfactory and that should not be generalized. The keeping of separate psychiatric records implies that psychiatry and medicine are different undertakings and thus drives deeper the wedge between them and between physical and psychological illness. Furthermore, it is often vitally important for internists or surgeons to know that a patient is being seen by a psychiatrist or is taking a particular medication. When separate records are kept, this information may not be available. Finally, if generalized, the practice of keeping a separate psychiatric record could lead to the unacceptable consequence of having a separate record for each type of medical problem.

Patients should be informed about what is meant by "medical confidentiality." We should establish the distinction between information about the patient that generally will be kept confidential regardless of the interest of third parties and information that will be exchanged among members of the health-care team in order to provide care for the patient. Patients should be made aware of the large number of persons in the modern hospital who require access to the medical record in order to serve the patient's medical and financial interests.

Finally, at some point most patients should have an opportunity to review their medical record and to make informed choices about whether their entire record is to be available to everyone or whether certain portions of the record are privileged and should be accessible only to their principal physician or to others designated explicitly by the patient. This approach would rely on traditional informed-consent procedural standards and might permit the patient to balance the personal value of medical confidentiality against the personal value of high-technology, team health care. There is no reason that the same procedure should not be used with psychiatric records instead of the arbitrary system now employed, in which everything related to psychiatry is kept secret.

Afterthought: Confidentiality and Indiscretion

There is one additional aspect of confidentiality that is rarely included in discussions of the subject. I am referring here to the wanton, often inadvertent, but avoidable exchanges of confidential information that occur frequently in hospital rooms, elevators, cafeterias, doctors' offices, and at cocktail parties. Of course, as more people have access to medical information about the patient the potential for this irresponsible abuse of confidentiality increases geometrically.

Such mundane breaches of confidentiality are probably of greater concern to most patients than the broader issue of whether their medical records may be entered into a computerized data bank or whether a respiratory therapist is reviewing the results of an arterial blood gas determination. Somehow, privacy is violated and a sense of shame is heightened when intimate secrets are revealed to people one knows or is close to – friends, neighbors, acquaintances, or hospital roommates – rather than when they are disclosed to an anonymous bureaucrat sitting at a computer terminal in a distant city or to a health professional who is acting in an official capacity.

I suspect that the principles of medical confidentiality, particularly those reflected in most medical codes of ethics, were designed principally to prevent just this sort of embarrassing personal indiscretion rather than to maintain (for social, political, or economic reasons) the absolute secrecy of doctor–patient communications. In this regard, it is worth noting that Percival's Code of Medical Ethics (1803) includes the following admonition: "Patients should be interrogated concerning their complaint in a tone of voice which cannot be over-heard." We in the medical profession frequently neglect these simple courtesies.

Conclusion

The principle of medical confidentiality described in medical codes of ethics and still believed in by patients no longer exists. In this respect, it is a decrepit concept. Rather than perpetuate the myth of confidentiality and invest energy vainly to preserve it, the public and the profession would be better served if they devoted their attention to determining which aspects of the original principle of confidentiality are worth retaining. Efforts could then be directed to salvaging those.

69

The Duty to Warn and Clinical Ethics
Legal and Ethical Aspects of Confidentiality and HIV/AIDS

Christian Säfken and Andreas Frewer

Introduction

Confidentiality is a principal corollary to medical treatment. It is founded on two main principles: first, there is the physician-patient relationship; only a patient who fully relies upon the physicians' confidentiality will reveal personal and intimate details about his state of health. The second is keeping the patient's secrets, which is essential for public confidence in the medical profession and an efficient health care system.

There are, however, difficult cases in which physicians contemplate exceptions to confidentiality. They arise in situations where medical secrecy puts the physical integrity or the life of others at risk. Such situations raise special ethical and legal concerns. Prime examples for lifting medical confidentiality are mental diseases and HIV/AIDS cases, although some venereal diseases such as Hepatitis B trigger the same level of concerns.

Leading Cases and Legislation Concerning Reckless HIV Infections

In many countries, courts have ruled that knowingly infecting someone with HIV constitutes a criminal offense. It satisfies the elements of fraud, assault, or grievous bodily harm. In addition to criminal prosecution, knowingly transmitting HIV may also create civil liability. In an early decision on HIV infection, a German court stated in 1988: "An HIV infected person who knows about his transmission and who has sexual intercourse with someone else without using protective means is liable to prosecution because of dangerous bodily injury" (German Federal Supreme Court; Nov. 4, 1988; BGHSt 36, 1; No. 1 StR 262/88).

In 2004, a Swiss court elaborated on the grounds for a prison sentence of three and a half years by reference to the severe implications resulting from HIV transmissions:

> The infection with HIV is already objective grievous (perilous) bodily harm. … After an unknown, relatively long time period, the infection with the HIV virus leads with a high probability in many affected persons to an outbreak of the immune deficiency AIDS and, subsequently, with a high probability to death. Therefore, infection with HIV is perilous, and because of that it is a serious bodily harm … (Swiss Federal Court; *X. v. The Public Prosecutors' Department of the Canton of Zurich*; Oct. 27, 2004; No. 131 IV 1; 6S.176/2004)

A similar rationale evolved in many common law countries, such as Canada:

Original publication details: Christian Säfken and Andreas Frewer, "The Duty to Warn and Clinical Ethics: Legal and Ethical Aspects of Confidentiality and HIV/AIDS," pp. 313–326 from *HEC Forum* 19: 4 (2007). With kind permission from Springer Science+Business Media.

Where public health endeavours fail to provide adequate protection to individuals, the … criminal law can be effective. … Persons knowing that they are HIV positive who engage in sexual intercourse without advising their partner of the disease may be found to fulfil the traditional requirements of fraud namely dishonesty and deprivation. That fraud may vitiate a partner's consent to engage in sexual intercourse. … In summary, an individual who knows he is HIV-positive and has unprotected sexual intercourse without disclosing this condition to his partner may be found guilty of contravening the provisions of s. 265 of the Criminal Code [assault]. (Supreme Court of Canada; *R. v. Cuerrier*; Dec. 3, 1998; 2 S.C.R. 371; No. 25738; see also 7, p. 450)

In a comparable 1995 case, a New Zealand court ruled that a man who transmitted HIV to two women was guilty of committing grievous bodily harm (New Zealand Court of Appeal; *R v Mwai* [1995] 3 NZLR 149). In 1997, a court in Cyprus sentenced a man to fifteen months in prison for knowingly infecting a woman with HIV (Bennet, Draper, and Frith, 2000, p. 9).

There have been similar judgments in Great Britain. In 2001, a court in Scotland, where the law is different from England and Wales, sentenced a man to five years because of "reckless behaviour and transmitting HIV" to a woman (High Court of Justiciary Glasgow; *Her Majesty's Advocate against Stephen Robert Kelly*; Feb. 20, 2001). In 2005, a London court sentenced a man to four and a half years in prison for infecting a woman with HIV. The conduct was assessed as causing grievous bodily harm (Court of Appeal, Criminal Division; *R v Dica* [2005] EWCA Crim 2304) and resulted in the first case in England and Wales in 137 years with a conviction for deliberately transmitting a disease (Weait, 2005, pp. 121ff).

While these jurisdictions solved HIV cases with existing tools, some member states of the United States adopted new legislation (Chalmers, 2004, pp. 448f). These statutes punish those who deliberately or recklessly transmit HIV to unsuspecting victims. A good example is a bill passed by the California Senate in 1998. Under the statute, anyone aware of his or her own HIV infection, who donates blood, body organs, or other tissue, semen or breast milk to any medical center, semen or milk bank, is punishable by law (s. 1621.5 California Health and Safety Code). Also, any

person who exposes another to HIV by engaging in unprotected sexual activity when the infected person knows at the time of the unprotected sex of the infection, has not disclosed his or her HIV positive status, and acts with the specific intent to infect the other person with HIV, can be sentenced to imprisonment for three, five, or eight years (s. 120291 California Health and Safety Code). Similar acts exist in several other states, including Iowa (s. 709C.1 Iowa Code) and Virginia (§ 18.2-67.4:1 Code of Virginia).

The Allowance to Warn

The legal situation becomes more complicated when a physician is involved. Maintaining medical confidentiality is not only a moral duty of physicians. The legal systems of most countries protect medical confidentiality in their civil and criminal law. In some countries, physicians' rules of professional ethics function as important sources of medical law on the protection of confidentiality in the physician-patient relationship (e.g., AMA, 2006–2007, s. E-5.05; Bradley, Bradley and Boyle, 2002, § 9).

Violating confidentiality obligations can lead to civil and penal liability and, in some cases, an infringing physician may even be banned from the medical profession. A person known to have an infection with HIV often faces continuous questions, fear, or even discrimination from society. To grapple with these issues, most jurisdictions have special HIV confidentiality acts, such as § 2782 New York Public Health Law, or general data protection statutes, see also German *Bundesdatenschutzgesetz* = Federal Data Protection Act (BGBl. I 2006, p. 1970).

Most legal systems provide either statutes or precedent for the breach of confidentiality in certain instances. For example, some public agencies register infectious diseases or even electronic public health records (Carney, 2001, pp. 138ff). In the event that personal safety, physical inviolability, or the life of a person are at risk, a physician may inform other persons who are able to avert the danger. In Germany and Switzerland, both civil law systems, the exception is known as "state of emergency as justification" (§ 34 German Penal Code, Art. 34 s. 2 Swiss Penal Code). Similar principles govern common law systems, for example "justifying necessity" or "use of force for the protection of other persons" (see, e.g., 2C New Jersey Code of Criminal Justice s. 3–5; 18 Pennsylvania Consolidated Statutes § 506). In relation to physicians, this concept is often called "privilege to disclose" (Muhammed, 2006, p. 42).

An HIV infected patient, like any other person, is morally and legally required not to injure or harm others. Therefore, unprotected sexual intercourse with noninfected partners can lead to prosecution. At the same time, HIV infected persons have a duty to alert their partners of potential harm. The failure to warn or to use appropriate protection means a high risk of a viral transmission and a danger to health or even life. A physician, who notices a patient being careless about an HIV infection and the health of a partner, benefits from the principle of "justifying necessity", which enables him to inform third parties. It depends on the circumstances of the specific case whether the physician must inform the sexual partner, a public health authority, the police or someone else (Felthous, 2006, p. 339).

Is There a Duty to Warn?

While there is no doubt that a physician is allowed to break confidentiality if there is danger for third persons, there is a controversial debate whether the physician has a legal and moral duty to do so. Some authors believe that if the life and health of others are at risk, physicians are not only allowed to break confidentiality, but have a moral duty to warn. Others believe that every person has an obligation to protect himself by using protective means in sexual intercourse with others or, in the case of drug addiction, avoid sharing needles with others. A legal duty to warn has also been characterized as discriminating against HIV infected patients (Bennet, Draper and Frith, 2000, pp. 12ff). While this concept may work on people who are not bound by close relationships to each other, it obviously fails in cases of partnerships and families. For physicians the situation is even worse if they treat not only HIV infected persons but also their family members or close friends.

There are some interesting cases in the last decades dealing with medical confidentiality and danger for third parties in different legal systems. They are also helpful for the understanding of ethical implications on the subject.

The Tarasoff Case

The leading case concerning the duty to warn is as interesting as tragic. In 1969, Prosenjit Poddar, a student at the University of California, fell in love with Tatiana Tarasoff, another student of the university. After a short relationship with her, he fell into depression and consulted a psychotherapist because he had fantasies of killing her. He even purchased a gun. The psychotherapist counselled a colleague and informed the campus police. After interviewing Poddar, the campus police decided there was no actual danger. Neither Tarasoff nor her parents received any warning. Two months later, Poddar stabbed Tarasoff to death.

The parents of Tarasoff sued the campus police, the health service, and the Regents of the University of California, because neither they nor their daughter were informed of the danger. The trial court dismissed the case because it lacked a cause of action. Before Tarasoff, there was no duty for physicians to inform others.

The plaintiffs then filed an appeal. In 1974, an appellate court ruled in its first Tarasoff-decision that the campus police were liable because they failed to warn the victim (Supreme Court of California, *Tarasoff v. the Regents of the University of California*, 529 P.2d 533 (Cal. 1974), also known as *Tarasoff I*). In March 1975, the court granted a rehearing and changed the first decision. This rather unusual procedure was possibly provoked by a public discussion about the role of the police, but the second judgment, *Tarasoff II*, gives no reason for the rehearing. The second judgment released the police from all liability and focused on the therapist's duty to warn the victim. The court ruled:

> When a therapist determines, or pursuant to the standards of his profession should determine, that his patient presents a serious danger of violence to another, he incurs an obligation to use reasonable care to protect the intended victim against such danger. The discharge of this duty may require the therapist to take one or more of various steps, depending upon the nature of the

case. Thus, it may call for him to warn the intended victim or others likely to apprise the victim of the danger, to notify the police, or to take whatever other steps are reasonably necessary under the circumstances. (Supreme Court of California; *Tarasoff v. the Regents of the University of California*; 551 P.2d 334 (Cal. 1976); see also Buckner and Firestone, 2000)

Interestingly, the court established a "duty to warn" in *Tarasoff I*, yet replaced it in *Tarasoff II* with the term "duty to protect" (Herbert and Young, 2002, p. 275). The first phrase is more accurate because the lack of a warning hit the mark on the matter in dispute. Also, physicians cannot protect third parties at all times from dangerous patients, but a warning will enable others to protect themselves.

The conflict between the patient's right of confidentiality and the protection of body and life of others is resolved by the court with a renowned dictum: "The protective privilege ends where the public peril begins" (*Tarasoff II*, see above). Both *Tarasoff* decisions had consequences for legislation. Arizona, California, Colorado, Delaware, Idaho, Indiana, Kentucky, Louisiana, Maryland, Massachusetts, Michigan, Minnesota, Mississippi, Missouri, Montana, Nebraska, New Hampshire, New Jersey, Ohio, Oklahoma, Pennsylvania, South Carolina, Tennessee, Utah, Vermont, Washington, and Wisconsin adopted "*Tarasoff* statutes" which stipulate a duty to warn potential victims of mentally ill patients. Nine states and the District of Columbia have statutes that allow a breach of confidentiality, while thirteen other states have no statutory law or court decision dealing with the topic (Herbert and Young, 2002, pp. 277ff and references therein; see also Chenneville, 2000, p. 662 and Felthous, 2006, pp. 341f).

As an example of *Tarasoff* legislation, the Maryland statute demands a mental health care provider either to seek civil commitment of a violent patient, formulate a diagnostic impression and establish and undertake a documented treatment plan calculated to eliminate the possibility that the patient will carry out the threat, or inform the appropriate law enforcement agency and, if feasible, the specified victim or victims of the nature of the threat, the identity of the patient making the threat, and the identity of the specified victim or victims (§ 5–609, Maryland Courts and

Judicial Proceedings). When a physician warns a potential victim under such legislation, she is not liable for any further occurrences. Some other states allow a physician to choose civil commitment, but do not impose a duty. This suggests that *Tarasoff* is more about warning than protecting (Herbert and Young, 2002, p. 275).

The Reisner Case

While *Tarasoff* dealt with mentally ill persons and the duty of therapists, the 1990s brought HIV cases to court. It was again the University of California where another serious incident took place. In 1985 a surgeon operated on Jennifer Lawson, a twelve-year-old girl. During the operation she received a blood transmission. The day after the operation, the physician discovered the blood was contaminated with HIV antibodies. Although the same physician continued to treat Jennifer for the next several years, he never warned her or her parents of the infection. Some years later, Jennifer had an intimate relationship with Daniel Reisner. In 1990 Jennifer was diagnosed with AIDS, and informed Daniel immediately, who was HIV positive. Shortly after the test, Jennifer died.

Daniel Reisner sued the physician for damages. The court, citing the *Tarasoff II* decision, concluded that the surgeon had a duty to warn his patient or at least her parents. Because of the physician's negligence they could not prevent the plaintiff from infection. The difference between *Tarasoff* and *Reisner* is the fact that the physician did not know the identity of the person in danger. The court found this irrelevant and said:

> California law already imposes a duty to third persons and the only arguably "new" issue in this case is whether that duty is the same when the third person's identity is unknown to the physician and not readily ascertainable. … the duty involved in this case – a duty to warn a contagious patient to take steps to protect others – has nothing to do with a physician's decision about how to treat his patient or with a physician's potential liability for the unauthorized disclosure of AIDS test results. … Once the physician warns the patient of the risk to others and advises the patient how to prevent the spread of the disease, the physician has fulfilled his duty – and no more (but no less) is required. (Court of Appeal of California;

Reisner v. the Regents of University of California; Jan. 26, 1995; 31 Cal. App. 4th 1195, 37 Cal. Rptr. 2d 518 (Cal. App.Dist.2 1995); see also Buckner and Firestone, 2000)

The Garcia Case

Another HIV case in which a third party was involved took place in Texas. Adalberto Balderas, a hemophiliac man, received blood products from a hospital during the 1980s. The hospital later realized that some of the blood products they used were contaminated with HIV, and that there was a possibility Balderas was infected. Even though his health status was checked a few times in the following years, he was not informed of his possible infection. In 1987 Balderas met Linda Garcia; they married one year later. In December 1989, he became ill and tested positive for HIV. Garcia avoided HIV testing because she was afraid of the result. The couple then sued the hospital, but Balderas died in 1993 and his estate voluntarily dismissed the claims made on his behalf. The trial court decided the hospital had no duty to notify Garcia of a possible HIV infection from Balderas because the Texas Communicable Disease Prevention and Control Act (§ 81.101ff, Texas Health and Safety Code) at that time generally prohibited the release or disclosure of a possible HIV status.

This decision was reversed by the Texas Court of Appeals in 1996. The appellate court found the Communicable Disease Prevention and Control Act unapplicable because the hospital did not test the patient. The information of his possible HIV status resulted from the information of the blood bank. The court cited *Tarasoff II* and ascertained that

> health care professionals who discover some disease or medical condition with their services or products have likely caused to a particular recipient and endanger a readily identifiable third party, owe a duty to reasonably warn the third party to the extent that such warning may be given without any duty of confidentiality to the recipient of services or products. (Texas Court of Appeals; *Garcia v. Santa Rosa Health Care Corporation*; 925 S.W.2d 376 (Tex. App. 1996))

Although it was not clear if Garcia was infected with HIV, the court decided she could claim damages: the fear and anguish of a possible transmission fulfilled a valid cause of action. In a recent case, a New Jersey court followed this ruling (Appellate Division of the Superior Court of New Jersey; *C.W. v. The Cooper Health System*; Aug. 10, 2006; No. A-6100-04T2, 2006; Health Law Reporter 2006, 989; WL 2286377).

The Frankfurt Case

In Germany, a civil law system, there was no new legislation adopted to handle HIV cases. But in 1999, an interesting case was decided by the Frankfurt Appellate Court. A woman demanded compensation of material and immaterial damages in the amount of 100,000 German marks because her physician knew of her partner's HIV infection and did not inform her. The physician, who treated the whole family, claimed medical confidentiality. After the trial court dismissed the case, the plaintiff sought to appeal. Unfortunately, she did not have not enough money to pay the court and attorney fees, so she applied for legal aid. In the legal aid procedure, the court summarized the case and the plaintiff's chance of success.

The court took the opportunity to allege the legal situation and many details of the case. It reasoned that the physician had a special responsibility to the infected woman because she was also his patient. This established a duty to protect the plaintiff's health and avoid danger. This "special responsibility" in German law is comparable to the "special relationship" demanded in *Tarasoff*. The court held the physician should have known that the physical inviolability of the plaintiff was of higher value than the secrecy of the HIV infection of her partner. The physician should have realized that his patient "did not give the impression of a person who is dealing responsibly with his disease" (Appellate Court of Frankfurt; Jul. 8, 1999; No. 8 U 67/99; NStZ 2001, p. 150). The court judged this as a grave error in treatment. However, the court refused to grant legal aid because the claim lacked causality: the woman did not submit evidence that her infection originated from her partner and not from a different source.

There are currently no decisions of the federal high courts concerning the duty to warn, so this holding led to a controversial debate about the responsibility of physicians for the life and safety of third parties in both medical and legal journals which has not yet come to an end (Frewer and Säfken, 2003, pp. 18ff and references therein). Until there is a leading decision from the Federal Supreme Court on this issue, or a statute from the German parliament, the issue of whether there exists a duty to warn will remain open under German Law.

From an English law point of view, the question is whether the physician is not only civilly, but also criminally liable, for reckless transmission of HIV to a third party (Chalmers, 2004, pp. 786f). This is indeed an interesting question under common and civil criminal law.

Anti-Tarasoff Jurisdiction

Not all states follow the *Tarasoff* legislation, and some state courts refuse to establish a duty to forewarn. In 1995, the Supreme Court of Virginia did not impose a duty to warn. A psychiatrist treated a patient for 17 years and knew he was violent against women who rejected him. The psychiatrist also knew his patient recently threatened another woman, who was so afraid of him that she left her home in fear. After the patient was hospitalized, the woman returned to her home. Some days later, the angry and depressed patient was allowed to leave the hospital, but the woman was not warned. The patient went to her home, killed first her and then himself (Felthous, 2006, pp. 345f). The court found the *Tarasoff* decision "unpersuasive" and ruled that a physician–patient relationship alone is not enough to establish a "special relation" with a "higher degree of control over the patient than exists in an ordinary doctor-patient or hospital-patient relationship" (Supreme Court of Virginia; *Nasser v. Parker*, 455 S.E.2d 502 (Va. 1995)).

In 1995, the District Court for the District of Columbia refused to grant damages in a case in which a plaintiff sued a hospital that failed to disclosure the HIV status of his wife. The District possesses not only one of the highest HIV infection rates of the United States, but also strict confidentiality statutes regarding HIV and AIDS. The court found that the confidentiality statutes prohibited reporting (District of Columbia Court of Appeals; *N.O.L. v. District of Columbia*; 674 A.2d 498 (D.C. 1995)). This jurisdiction is, even with regard to antidiscrimination issues, irreproducible.

How Should the Physician Decide?

When a clinical practitioner has to decide whether he has to warn third persons of a potentially dangerous patient, the details of the case, as well as the legal situation, may be unclear. But it is crucial for physicians and hospitals to react fast, professionally and in accordance with the legal framework. Understandably, physicians are unclear about what they should do if patients are infected with HIV and do not care about the health and life of others. This results from the high value of confidentiality in the relationship between physicians and patients. Another crucial aspect is the fact of uncertainty: who can be sure that the patient is really a danger for others? Even if the physician concludes that her patient may infect another person with HIV, whom exactly shall she warn?

The physician has to balance the reasons for and against breaking confidentiality. These include the probability of danger for other persons, often called foreseeability of harm, and the gravity of a possible injury, as well as the interest of the patient in keeping his personal secrets. The first question a physician has to answer is whether a patient is a possible threat to other persons. Some authors argue that actions for a breach of confidentiality should not be allowed because consensual sex between adults is a legal act. Following this argument, sexually transmitting HIV would not create a duty to warn (Chenneville, 2000, p. 663). But as shown above, knowingly infecting someone else with HIV is criminal in most common and civil law systems. For many reasons, patients are not willing to inform their partners and others about their HIV infection. Therefore, it is important that the physician informs an HIV infected patient about his or her obligation to inform sexual and needle-sharing partners about the infection. Communication between the physician and patient is essential. If the physician receives the impression that the patient will not inform his or her partner, intervention becomes necessary (for details on a decision-making model see Chenneville, 2000, pp. 663ff).

If there is the probability of an imminent intent or, in some cases, an act of gross negligence, the physician has to determine, in a second step, if the patient is capable of inflicting serious harm against another person. In balancing the health and life of third parties against confidentiality between physician and patient, the physician will likely conclude that health and life are higher values than keeping personal secrets. Therefore, potential victims should be warned. Depending on the legal situation, the physician may also face registration duties to public agencies, and in some states only these agencies may inform third parties (Bradley, Bradley, and Boyle, 2002, p. 4; Muhammad, 2006, p. 43).

Organizations of health care professionals have responded to this matter and adopted recommendations for their members. For example, the German Medical Association states in the Professional Code for German Physicians: "Physicians are allowed to disclose [personal data], if they are released from professional secrecy or if the disclosure is necessary to conserve legally protected interests of higher value" (Bundesärztekammer, 2011, § 9 s. 2). Interestingly, the code only speaks of an allowance, not a duty to warn, even though the protection of legal interests of higher value demands a duty to forewarn. Contrary to the German Medical Association, the Council on Ethical and Judicial Affairs of the American Medical Association has approved a Code of Medical Ethics in which physicians who treat HIV infected patients who may be endangering a third party are explicitly advised to

1. attempt to persuade the infected patient to cease endangering the third party;
2. if persuasion fails, notify authorities; and
3. if the authorities take no action, notify the endangered third party (AMA, 2006–2007, § 2.23).

But how can a physician estimate a higher or lower probability of dangerousness? In *Tarasoff*, the defendants, assisted by an amicus curiae brief of the American Psychological Association, brought forward the argument that therapists are not able precisely to predict violent behavior. The court replied to this objection:

> We recognize the difficulty that a therapist encounters in attempting to forecast whether a patient presents a serious danger of violence. Obviously, we do not require that the therapist, in making that determination, render a perfect performance; the therapist need only exercise "that reasonable degree of skill, knowledge, and care ordinarily possessed and exercised by members of [that professional specialty] under similar circumstances."
> (*Tarasoff II*, see above)

Furthermore, the problem of *Tarasoff* was not a false prediction of the patient's violence by the therapist, but reluctance to inform the victim about it.

Breaching the confidentiality is always a serious step in the physician-patient relationship. The physician has to bring to mind all legal statutes and ethical guidelines that exist in his state to make a decision. In cases of doubt, it may be useful to contact a clinical ethics committee (Neitzke and Frewer, 2005, pp. 167ff; Rogers and Draper, 2003, pp. 220ff) and the facilities' attorney. Whether the consultation will lead to a disclosure of the HIV status or not, it is in both cases crucial to document the reasons behind the decision. In a possible lawsuit, proper documentation can prove strong evidence to avert liability.

Clinical Ethics Committees and Confidentiality

In an unpublished survey, members of clinical ethics committees from different professions were anonymously questioned about medical confidentiality and the duty to warn. Although the survey is not quantitatively representative, it reveals some interesting tendencies. More than 90 percent fully agree with the statement that confidentiality is a "founding pillar" of clinical practice, while one finds it at least "rather appropriate". More than 70 percent believe confidentiality to be "hard and fast" for physicians and the nursing staff. Two members believe confidentiality to be "widely binding", while only one finds it "rather binding". In contrast, more than 90 percent are not acquainted with *Tarasoff*, while only one person knows the case to a large extent. Furthermore, the German Central Ethics Commission mentions the problem in its "Comment on the Protection of Ethical Principles in Medicine and its Neighboring Disciplines", but provides no advice how to solve it (Zentrale Ethikkommission, 2006, pp. A1703ff).

These facts are alarming. They demonstrate insufficient knowledge about basic principles in jurisdiction regarding exceptions of confidentiality at members of clinical ethic committees – those, who should support clinical practitioners. In consequence, more professional training and continuing ethical and legal education is needed. Also, the importance of interdisciplinary cooperation cannot be underestimated.

Conclusion

The duty to warn is an imperfect instrument for imperfect cases. Unfortunately there are patients who lack either the capacity or the will to behave responsibly toward others. In these cases, it can be difficult for the physician to know if she has an allowance or even a duty to warn third parties. The legal concept of a duty to warn contains some problems: (1) It may affect the physician-patient relationship in general, and it is a violation of patient autonomy; (2) it may prevent patients from agreeing to voluntary HIV testing; (3) it leads to difficult moral and legal questions, e.g., how to warn persons in danger (Felthous, 2006, p. 341; Buckner and Firestone, 2000) and there is uncertainty of a duty to warn victims who may already know the danger (Felthous, 2006, p. 346). In contrast, the positive effect of a duty to warn is overwhelming: persons become aware of their risk to HIV infection, or may be identified as undiagnosed but infected. In this case, their treatment can begin early so they do not unknowingly infect others (Kaldjian, 2003, p. 413). In spite of all insufficiencies, the duty to warn is a useful tool to protect the personal safety, health, and life of various persons.

References

American Medical Association (AMA), Council on Ethical and Judicial Affairs (2006–2007). *Code of medical ethics. Current opinions with annotations.* Chicago: American Medical Association.

Bennett, R., Draper, H. and Frith, L. (2000). Ignorance is bliss? HIV and moral duties and legal duties to forewarn. *Journal of Medical Ethics*, 26, 9–15.

Bradley, T., Bradley, H., and Boyle, B. (2002). Legal issues associated with disclosure of patient's HIV+ status to third parties. *The Nexus*, Summer, 4–5.

Buckner, F. and Firestone, M. (2000). "Where the public peril begins": 25 years after *Tarasoff. Journal of Legal Medicine*, 21, 187–222.

Bundesärztekammer (German Medical Association) (2011). *(Muster-)Berufsordnung für die deutschen Ärztinnen und Ärzte* (Professional Code for German Physicians). http://www.bundesaerztekammer.de/recht/berufsrecht/muster-berufsordnung-aerzte/muster-berufsordnung.

Carney, B.M. (2001). Breaches of confidentiality and the electronic community health record: challenges for healthcare organizations and the community. *HEC Forum*, 13 (2), 138–147.

Chalmers, J. (2002). The criminalization of HIV transmission. *Sexually Transmitted Infections*, 78, 448–451.

Chalmers, J. (2004). Criminalization of HIV transmission: can doctors be liable for the onward transmission of HIV? *International Journal of STD and AIDS*, 15, 782–787.

Chenneville, T. (2000). HIV, confidentiality, and duty to protect: a decisionmaking model. *Professional Psychology: Research and Practice*, 31 (6), 661–670.

Felthous, A.R. (2006). Warning a potential victim of a person's dangerousness: clinician's duty or victim's right? *Journal of the American Academy of Psychiatry and the Law*, 34, 338–348.

Frewer, A. and Säfken, C. (2003). Ärztliche Schweigepflicht und die Gefährdung Dritter. Medizinethische und juristische Probleme der neueren Rechtsprechung. *Ethik in der Medizin*, 1, 15–24.

Herbert, P.B. and Young, K.A. (2002). Tarasoff at twenty-five. *Journal of the American Academy of Psychiatry and the Law*, 30, 275–281.

Kaldjian, L.C. (2003). HIV testing and partner notification: physicians' ethical responsibilities in a persistent epidemic. *Advanced Studies in Medicine*, 7, 413–414.

Muhammad, A. (2006). Mandatory HIV notification: bioethical concerns vs. public health concerns, health and medical dilemmas. *Journal of American Science*, 2 (1), 42–45.

Neitzke, G. and Frewer, A. (2005). Beratung in Krisensituationen und Klinische Ethik-Komitees. Zum Umgang mit moralischen Problemen in der Patientenversorgung. In: Andreas Frewer/Rolf Winau (ed.). *Ethische Probleme in Lebenskrisen. Grundkurs Ethik in der Medizin Band 3* Erlangen and Jena: Palm und Enke Verlag, 167–176.

Rogers, W.A. and Draper, H. (2003). Confidentiality and the ethics of medical ethics. *Journal of Medical Ethics*, 29, 220–224.

Weait, M. (2005). Criminal law and the sexual transmission of HIV: R v Dica. *Modern Law Review*, 68 (1), 121–134.

Zentrale Ethikkommission (Central Ethics Commission) (2006). Ethikberatung in der klinischen Medizin: Stellungnahme der Zentralen Kommission zur Wahrung ethischer Grundsätze in der Medizin und ihren Grenzgebieten. *Deutsches Ärzteblatt*, 103 (24), A1703–A1707.

Truth-Telling

70

On a Supposed Right to Lie from Altruistic Motives

Immanuel Kant

In the work called *France*, for the year 1797, Part VI., No. 1, on Political Reactions, by *Benjamin Constant*, the following passage occurs, p. 123: –

"The moral principle that it is one's duty to speak the truth, if it were taken singly and unconditionally, would make all society impossible. We have the proof of this in the very direct consequences which have been drawn from this principle by a German philosopher, who goes so far as to affirm that to tell a falsehood to a murderer who asked us whether our friend, of whom he was in pursuit, had not taken refuge in our house, would be a crime."

The French philosopher opposes this principle in the following manner, p. 124: – "It is a duty to tell the truth. The notion of duty is inseparable from the notion of right. A duty is what in one being corresponds to the right of another. Where there are no rights there are no duties. To tell the truth then is a duty, but only towards him who has a right to the truth. But no man has a right to a truth that injures others." The πρῶτον ψεῦδος here lies in the statement that "*To tell the truth is a duty, but only towards him who has a right to the truth.*"

It is to be remarked, first, that the expression "to have a right to the truth" is unmeaning. We should rather say, a man has a right to his own *truthfulness* (*veracitas*), that is, to subjective truth in his own person.

For to have a right objectively to truth would mean that, as in *meum* and *tuum* generally, it depends on his *will* whether a given statement shall be true or false, which would produce a singular logic.

Now, the *first* question is whether a man – in cases where he cannot avoid answering Yes or No – has the *right* to be untruthful. The *second* question is whether, in order to prevent a misdeed that threatens him or some one else, he is not actually bound to be untruthful in a certain statement to which an unjust compulsion forces him.

Truth in utterances that cannot be avoided is the formal duty of a man to everyone, however great the disadvantage that may arise from it to him or any other; and although by making a false statement I do no wrong to him who unjustly compels me to speak, yet I do wrong to men in general in the most essential point of duty, so that it may be called a lie (though not in the jurist's sense), that is, so far as in me lies I cause that declarations in general find no credit, and hence that all rights founded on contract should lose their force; and this is a wrong which is done to mankind.

If, then, we define a lie merely as an intentionally false declaration towards another man, we need not add that it must injure another; as the jurists think proper to put in their definition (*mendacium est falsiloquium in praejudicium alterius*). For it always injures

Original publication details: Immanuel Kant, "On a Supposed Right to Lie from Altruistic Motives," pp. 361–3 from *Critique of Practical Reason and Other Works on the Theory of Ethics*, 6th edition, trans. T. K. Abbott, London, 1909. This essay was first published in a Berlin periodical in 1797.

another; if not another individual, yet mankind generally, since it vitiates the source of justice. This benevolent lie *may*, however, by *accident* (*casus*) become punishable even by civil laws; and that which escapes liability to punishment only by accident may be condemned as a wrong even by external laws. For instance, if you have *by a lie* hindered a man who is even now planning a murder, you are legally responsible for all the consequences. But if you have strictly adhered to the truth, public justice can find no fault with you, be the unforeseen consequence what it may. It is possible that whilst you have honestly answered Yes to the murderer's question, whether his intended victim is in the house, the latter may have gone out unobserved, and so not have come in the way of the murderer, and the deed therefore have not been done; whereas, if you lied and said he was not in the house, and he had really gone out (though unknown to you), so that the murderer met him as he went, and executed his purpose on him, then you might with justice be accused as the cause of his death. For, if you had spoken the truth as well as you knew it, perhaps the murderer while seeking for his enemy in the house might have been caught by neighbours coming up and the deed been prevented. Whoever then *tells a lie*, however good his intentions may be, must answer for the consequences of it, even before the civil tribunal, and must pay the penalty for them, however unforeseen they may have been; because truthfulness is a duty that must be regarded as the basis of all duties founded on contract, the laws of which would be rendered uncertain and useless if even the least exception to them were admitted.

To be *truthful* (honest) in all declarations is therefore a sacred unconditional command of reason, and not to be limited by any expediency.

71

Should Doctors Tell the Truth?

Joseph Collins

This is not a homily on lying. It is a presentation of one of the most difficult questions that confront the physician. Should doctors tell patients the truth? Were I on the witness stand and obliged to answer the question with "yes" or "no," I should answer in the negative and appeal to the judge for permission to qualify my answer. The substance of this article is what that qualification would be.

Though few are willing to make the test, it is widely held that, if the truth were more generally told, it would make for world-welfare and human betterment. We shall probably never know. To tell the whole truth is often to perpetrate a cruelty of which many are incapable. This is particularly true of physicians. Those of them who are not compassionate by nature are made so by experience. They come to realize that they owe their fellow-men justice, and graciousness, and benignity, and it becomes one of the real satisfactions of life to discharge that obligation. To do so successfully they must frequently withhold the truth from their patients, which is tantamount to telling them a lie. Moreover, the physician soon learns that the art of medicine consists largely in skillfully mixing falsehood and truth in order to provide the patient with an amalgam which will make the metal of life wear and keep men from being poor shrunken things, full of melancholy and indisposition, unpleasing to themselves and to those who love them. I propose therefore to deal with the question from a pragmatic, not a moral standpoint.

"Now you may tell me the truth," is one of the things patients have frequently said to me. Four types of individuals have said it: those who honestly and courageously want to know so that they may make as ready as possible to face the wages of sin while there is still time; those who do not want to know, and who if they were told would be injured by it; those who are wholly incapable of receiving the truth. Finally, those whose health is neither seriously disordered nor threatened. It may seem an exaggeration to say that in forty years of contact with the sick, the patients I have met who are in the first category could be counted on the fingers of one hand. The vast majority who demand the truth really belong in the fourth category, but there are sufficient in the second – with whom my concern chiefly is – to justify considering their case.

One of the astonishing things about patients is that the more serious the disease, the more silent they are about its portents and manifestations. The man who is constantly seeking assurance that the vague abdominal pains indicative of hyperacidity are not symptoms of cancer often buries family and friends, some of whom have welcomed death as an escape from his burdensome iterations. On the other hand, there is the man whose first warning of serious disease is lumbago

Original publication details: Joseph Collins, "Should Doctors Tell the Truth?," pp. 320–6 from *Harper's Monthly Magazine* 155 (August 1927). Copyright © 1927 Harper's Magazine. All rights reserved. Reproduced from the August issue by special permission.

who cannot be persuaded to consult a physician until the disease, of which the lumbago is only a symptom, has so far progressed that it is beyond surgery. The seriousness of disease may be said to stand in direct relation to the reticence of its possessor. The more silent the patient, the more serious the disorder.

The patient with a note-book, or the one who is eager to tell his story in great detail, is rarely very ill. They are forever asking, "Am I going to get well?" and though they crave assistance they are often unable to accept it. On the other hand, patients with organic disease are very chary about asking point blank either the nature or the outcome of their ailment. They sense its gravity, and the last thing in the world they wish to know is the truth about it; and to learn it would be the worst thing that could happen to them.

This was borne in upon me early in my professional life. I was summoned one night to assuage the pain of a man who informed me that he had been for some time under treatment for rheumatism – that cloak for so many diagnostic errors. His "rheumatism" was due to a disease of the spinal cord called locomotor ataxia. When he was told that he should submit himself to treatment wholly different from that which he had been receiving, the import of which any intelligent layman would have divined, he asked neither the nature nor the probable outcome of the disease. He did as he was counselled. He is now approaching seventy and, though not active in business, it still engrosses him.

Had he been told that he had a disease which was then universally believed to be progressive, apprehension would have depressed him so heavily that he would not have been able to offer the resistance to its encroachment which has stood him in such good stead. He was told the truth only in part. That is, he was told his "rheumatism" was "different"; that it was dependent upon an organism quite unlike the one that causes ordinary rheumatism; that we have preparations of mercury and arsenic which kill the parasite responsible for this disease, and that if he would submit himself to their use, his life would not be materially shortened, or his efficiency seriously impaired.

Many experiences show that patients do not want the truth about their maladies, and that it is prejudicial to their well-being to know it, but none that I know is more apposite than that of a lawyer, noted for his urbanity and resourcefulness in Court. When he entered my consulting room, he greeted me with a bonhomie that bespoke intimacy but I had met him only twice – once on the golf links many years before, and once in Court where I was appearing as expert witness, prejudicial to his case.

He apologized for engaging my attention with such a triviality, but he had had pain in one shoulder and arm for the past few months, and though he was perfectly well – and had been assured of it by physicians in Paris, London, and Brooklyn – this pain was annoying and he had made up his mind to get rid of it. That I should not get a wrong slant on his condition, he submitted a number of laboratory reports furnished him by an osteopath to show that secretions and excretions susceptible of chemical examinations were quite normal. His determination seemed to be to prevent me from taking a view of his health which might lead me to counsel his retirement. He was quite sure that anything like a thorough examination was unnecessary but he submitted to it. It revealed intense and extensive disease of the kidneys. The pain in the network of nerves of the left upper-arm was a manifestation of the resulting autointoxication.

I felt it incumbent upon me to tell him that his condition was such that he should make a radical change in his mode of life. I told him if he would stop work, spend the winter in Honolulu, go on a diet suitable to a child of three years, and give up exercise, he could look forward confidently to a recovery that would permit of a life of usefulness and activity in his profession. He assured me he could not believe that one who felt no worse than he did should have to make such a radical change in his mode of life. He impressed upon me that I should realize he was the kind of person who had to know the truth. His affairs were so diversified and his commitments so important that he *must* know. Completely taken in, I explained to him the relationship between the pain from which he sought relief and the disease, the degeneration that was going on in the excretory mechanisms of his body, how these were struggling to repair themselves, the procedure of recovery and how it could be facilitated. The light of life began to flicker from the fear that my words engendered, and within two months it sputtered and died out. He was the last person in the world to whom the truth should have been told. Had

I lied to him, and then intrigued with his family and friends, he might be alive today.

The longer I practice medicine the more I am convinced that every physician should cultivate lying as a fine art. But there are many varieties of lying. Some are most prejudicial to the physician's usefulness. Such are: pretending to recognize the disease and understand its nature when one is really ignorant; asserting that one has effected the cure which nature has accomplished, or claiming that one can effect cure of a disease which is universally held to be beyond the power of nature or medical skill; pronouncing disease incurable which one cannot rightfully declare to be beyond cessation or relief.

There are other lies, however, which contribute enormously to the success of the physician's mission of mercy and salvation. There are a great number of instances in support of this but none more convincing than that of a man of fifty who, after twenty-five years of devotion to painting, decided that penury and old age were incompatible for him. Some of his friends had forsaken art for advertising. He followed their lead and in five years he was ready to gather the first ripe fruit of his labor. When he attempted to do so he was so immobilized by pain and rigidity that he had to forgo work. One of those many persons who assume responsibility lightly assured him that if he would put himself in the hands of a certain osteopath he would soon be quite fit. The assurance was without foundation. He then consulted a physician who without examining him proceeded to treat him for what is considered a minor ailment.

Within two months his appearance gave such concern to his family that he was persuaded to go to a hospital, where the disease was quickly detected, and he was at once submitted to surgery. When he had recovered from the operation, learning that I was in the country of his adoption, he asked to see me. He had not been able, he said, to get satisfactory information from the surgeon or the physician; all that he could gather from them was that he would have to have supplementary X-ray or radium treatment. What he desired was to get back to his business which was on the verge of success, and he wanted assurance that he could soon do so.

He got it. And more than that, he got elaborate explanation of what surgical intervention had accomplished, but not a word of what it had failed to accomplish. A year of activity was vouchsafed him, and during that time he put his business in such shape that its eventual sale provided a modest competency for his family. It was not until the last few weeks that he knew the nature of his malady. Months of apprehension had been spared him by the deception, and he had been the better able to do his work, for he was buoyed by the hope that his health was not beyond recovery. Had he been told the truth, black despair would have been thrown over the world in which he moved, and he would have carried on with corresponding ineffectiveness.

The more extensive our field of observation and the more intimate our contact with human activity, the more we realize the finiteness of the human mind. Every follower of Hippocrates will agree that "judgment is difficult and experience fallacious." A disease may have only a fatal ending, but one does not know; one may know that certain diseases, such as general paresis, invariably cause death, but one does not know that tomorrow it may no longer be true. The victim may be reprieved by accidental or studied discovery or by the intervention of something that still must be called divine grace.

A few years ago physicians were agreed that diabetes occurring in children was incurable; recently they held that the disease known as pernicious anemia always ended fatally; but now, armed with an extract from the pancreas and the liver, they go out to attack these diseases with the kind of confidence that David had when he saw the Philistine approach.

We have had enough experience to justify the hope that soon we shall be able to induce a little devil who is manageable to cast out a big devil who is wholly out of hand – to cure general paresis by inoculating the victim with malaria, and to shape the course of some varieties of sleeping sickness by the same means.

I am thankful for many valuable lessons learned from my early teachers. One of them was an ophthalmologist of great distinction. I worked for three years in his clinic. He was the most brutally frank doctor I have known. He could say to a woman, without the slightest show of emotion, that she was developing a cataract and would eventually be blind. I asked a colleague, who was a co-worker in the clinic at that time and who has since become an eminent specialist, if all these patients developed complete opacity of the crystalline lens.

"Not one half of them," said he. "In many instances the process is so slow that the patient dies before the cataract arrives; in others it ceases to progress. It is time enough for the patient to know he has cataract when he knows for himself that he is going blind. Then I can always explain it to him in such a way that he does not have days of apprehension and nights of sleeplessness for months while awaiting operation. I have made it a practice not to tell a patient he has cataract."

"Yes, but what do you tell them when they say they have been to Doctor Smith who tells them they have cataract and they have come to you for denial or corroboration?"

"I say to them, 'You have a beginning cloudiness of the lens of one eye. I have seen many cases in which the opacity progressed no farther than it has in your case; I have seen others which did not reach blindness in twenty years. I shall change your glasses, and I think you will find that your vision will be improved.'"

And then he added, "In my experience there are two things patients cannot stand being told: that they have cataract or cancer."

There is far less reason for telling them of the former than the latter. The hope for victims of the latter is bound up wholly in early detection and surgical interference. That is one of the most cogent reasons for bi-yearly thorough physical examination after the age of forty-five. Should we ever feel the need of a new law in this country, the one I suggest would exact such examination. The physician who detects malignant disease in its early stages is never justified in telling the patient the real nature of the disease. In fact, he does not know himself until he gets the pathologist's report. Should that indicate grave malignancy no possible good can flow from sharing that knowledge with the patient.

It is frequently to a patient's great advantage to know the truth in part, for it offers him the reason for making a radical change in his mode of life, sometimes a burdensome change. But not once in a hundred instances is a physician justified in telling a patient point blank that he has epilepsy, or the family that he has dementia præcox, until after he has been under observation a long time, unless these are so obvious that even a layman can make the diagnosis. We do not know the real significance of either disease, or from what they flow – we know that so many of them terminate in dementia that the outlook for all of them is bad. But we also know that many cases so diagnosticated end in complete recovery; and that knowledge justifies us in withholding from a patient the name and nature of his disorder until we are beyond all shadow of doubt.

Patients who are seriously ill are greedy for assurance even when it is offered half-heartedly. But those who have ailments which give the physician no real concern often cannot accept assurance. Not infrequently I have been unable to convince patients with nervous indigestion that their fears and concern were without foundation, and yet, years later when they developed organic disease, and I became really concerned about them, they assured me that I was taking their ailments too seriously.

There was a young professor whose acquaintance I made while at a German university. When he returned he took a position as professor in one of the well-known colleges for women. After several years he consulted me for the relief of symptoms which are oftentimes associated with gastric ulcer. It required no elaborate investigation to show that in this instance the symptoms were indicative of an imbalance of his nervous system. He refused to be assured and took umbrage that he was not given a more thorough examination each time that he visited me. Finally he told me that he would no longer attempt to conceal from me that he understood fully my reasons for making light of the matter. It was to throw him off the track, as it were. No good was to be accomplished from trying to deceive him; he realized the gravity of the situation and he was man enough to confront it. He would not show the white feather, and he was entitled to know the truth.

But the more it was proffered him, the greater was his resistance to it. He gave up his work and convinced his family and friends that he was seriously ill. They came to see me in relays; they also refused to accept the truth. They could understand why I told the patient the matter was not serious, but to them I could tell the facts. It was their right to know, and I could depend upon them to keep the knowledge from the patient and to work harmoniously with me.

My failure with my patient's friends was as great as with the patient himself. Fully convinced his back was to the wall, he refused to be looked upon as a lunatic or a hypochondriac and he decided to seek other counsel. He went from specialist to naturopath, from electrotherapist to Christian Scientist, from sanatorium to watering place and, had there been gland doctors and chiropractors in those days, he would have included them as well. Finally, he migrated to the mountains of Tennessee, and wooed nature. Soon I heard of him as the head of a school which was being run on novel pedagogic lines; character-building and health were the chief aims for his pupils; scholastic education was incidental. He began writing and lecturing about his work and his accomplishments, and soon achieved considerable notoriety. I saw him occasionally when he came north and sometimes referred to his long siege of ill-health and how happily it had terminated. He always made light of it, and declared that in one way it had been a very good thing: had it not been for that illness he would never have found himself, never have initiated the work which was giving him repute, happiness, and competency.

One summer I asked him to join me for a canoe trip down the Allegash River. Some of the "carrys" in those days were rather stiff. After one of them I saw that my friend was semi-prostrated and flustered. On questioning him, I learned that he had several times before experienced disagreeable sensations in the chest and in the head after hard manual labor, such as chopping trees or prying out rocks. He protested against examination but finally yielded. I reminded myself how different it was fifteen years before when he clamored for examination and seemed to get both pleasure and satisfaction from it, particularly when it was elaborate and protracted. He had organic disease of the heart, both of the valve-mechanism and of the muscle. His tenure of life depended largely on the way he lived. To counsel him successfully it was necessary to tell him that his heart had become somewhat damaged. He would not have it. "When I was really ill you made light of it, and I could not get you interested. But now, when I am well, you want me to live the life of a dodo. I won't do it. My heart is quite all right, a little upset no doubt by the fare we have had for the past two weeks, but as soon as I get back to normal I shall be as fit as you are, perhaps more so."

We returned to New York and I persuaded him to see a specialist, who was no more successful in impressing him with the necessity of careful living than I was. In despair, I wrote to his wife. She who had been so solicitous, so apprehensive, and so deaf to assurance during the illness that was of no consequence wrote, "I am touched by your affectionate interest, but Jerome seems so well that I have not the heart to begin nagging him again, and it fills me with terror lest he should once more become introspective and self-solicitous. I am afraid if I do what you say that it might start him off again on the old tack, and the memory of those two years frightens me still."

He died about four years later without the benefit of physician.

No one can stand the whole truth about himself; why should we think he can tolerate it about his health, and even though he could, who knows the truth? Physicians have opinions based upon their own and others' experience. They should be chary of expressing those opinions to sick persons until they have studied their psychology and are familiar with their personality. Even then it should always be an opinion, not a sentence. Doctors should be detectives and counsellors, not juries and judges.

Though often it seems a cruelty, the family of the patient to whom the truth is not and should not be told are entitled to the facts or what the physician believes to be the facts. At times, they must conspire with him to keep the truth from the patient, who will learn it too soon no matter what skill they display in deception. On the other hand, it is frequently to the patient's great advantage that the family should not know the depth of the physician's concern, lest their unconcealable apprehension be conveyed to the patient and then transformed into the medium in which disease waxes strong – fear. Now and then the good doctor keeps his own counsel. It does not profit the family of the man whose coronary arteries are under suspicion to be told that he has angina pectoris. If the patient can be induced to live decorously, the physician has discharged his obligation.

I recall so many instances when the truth served me badly that I find it difficult to select the best example. On reflection, I have decided to cite the case of a young man who consulted me shortly after his marriage.

He was sane in judgment, cheerful in disposition, full of the desire to attract those who attracted him. Anything touching on the morbid or "unnatural" was obviously repellent to him. His youth had been a pleasant one, surrounded by affection, culture, understanding, and wealth. When he graduated he had not made up his mind what he wanted to do in the world. After a year of loafing and traveling he decided to become an engineer. He matriculated at one of the technical schools, and his work there was satisfactory to himself and to his professors.

He astonished his intimates shortly after obtaining a promising post by marrying a woman a few years older than himself who was known to some of them as a devotee of bohemian life that did not tally with the position in society to which she was entitled by family and wealth. She had been a favorite with men but she had a reputation of not being the "marrying kind."

My friend fell violently in love with her, and her resistance went down before it. His former haunts knew him no more, and I did not see him for several months. Then, late one evening, he telephoned to say that it was of the greatest importance to him to consult me. He arrived in a state of repressed excitement. He wanted it distinctly understood that he came to me as a client, not as a friend. I knew, of course, that he had married. This, he confessed, had proved a complete failure, and now his wife had gone away and with another woman, one whom he had met constantly at her home during his brief and tempestuous courtship.

I attempted to explain to him that she had probably acted on impulse; that the squabbles of early matrimony which often appeared to be tragedies, were adjustable and, fortunately, nearly always adjusted.

"Yes," said he, "but you don't understand. There hasn't been any row. My wife told me shortly after marrying me that she had made a mistake, and she has told me so many times since. I thought at first it was caprice. Perhaps I should still have thought so were it not for this letter." He then handed me a letter. I did not have to read between the lines to get the full significance of its content. It set forth briefly, concretely, and explicitly her reasons for leaving. Life without her former friend was intolerable, and she did not propose to attempt it longer.

He knew there were such persons in the world, but what he wanted to know from me was, Could they not, if properly and prudently handled, be brought to feel and love like those the world calls normal? Was it not possible that her conduct and confession were the result of a temporary derangement and that indulgent handling of her would make her see things in the right light? She had not alienated his love even though she had forfeited his respect; and he did not attempt to conceal from me that if the tangle could not be straightened out he felt that his life had been a failure.

I told him the truth about this enigmatic gesture of nature, that the victims of this strange abnormality are often of great brilliancy and charm, and most companionable; that it is not a disease and, therefore, cannot be cured.

In this instance, basing my opinion upon what his wife had told him both in speech and in writing, I was bound to believe that she was one of the strange sisterhood, and that it was her birthright as well as her misfortune. Such being the case, I could only advise what I thought might be best for their mutual and individual happiness. I suggested that divorce offered the safest way out for both. He replied that he felt competent to decide that for himself; all that he sought from me was enlightenment about her unnatural infatuation. This I had only too frankly given him.

Two days later his body with a pistol wound in the right temple was found in a field above Weehawken.

That day I regretted that I had not lied to him. It is a day that has had frequent anniversaries.

72

On Telling Patients the Truth

Roger Higgs

That honesty should be an important issue for debate in medical circles may seem bizarre. Nurses and doctors are usually thought of as model citizens. Outside the immediate field of health care, when a passport is to be signed, a reference given, or a special allowance made by a government welfare agency, a nurse's or doctor's signature is considered a good warrant, and false certification treated as a serious breach of professional conduct. Yet at the focus of medical activity or skill, at the bedside or in the clinic, when patient meets professional there is often doubt. Is the truth being told?

Many who are unfamiliar with illness and its treatment may well be forgiven for wondering if this doubt has not been exaggerated. It is as if laundry-men were to discuss the merits of clean clothes, or fishmongers of refrigeration. But those with experience, either as patients or professionals, will immediately recognize the situation. Although openness is increasingly practised, there is still uncertainty in the minds of many doctors or nurses faced with communicating bad news; as for instance when a test shows up an unexpected and probably incurable cancer, or when meeting the gaze of a severely ill child, or answering the questions of a mother in mid-pregnancy whose unborn child is discovered to be badly handicapped. What should be said? There can be few who have not, on occasions such as these, told less than the truth.

Certainly the issue is a regular preoccupation of nurses and doctors in training. Why destroy hope? Why create anxiety, or something worse? Isn't it 'First, do no harm'?[1]

The concerns of the patient are very different. For many, fear of the unknown is the worst disease of all, and yet direct information seems so hard to obtain. The ward round goes past quickly, unintelligible words are muttered – was I supposed to hear and understand? In the surgery the general practitioner signs his prescription pad and clearly it's time to be gone. Everybody is too busy saving lives to give explanations. It may come as a shock to learn that it is policy, not just pressure of work, that prevents a patient learning the truth about himself. If truth is the first casualty, trust must be the second. 'Of course they wouldn't say, especially if things were bad,' said the elderly woman just back from out-patients, 'they've got that Oath, haven't they?' She had learned to expect from doctors, at the best, silence; at the worst, deception. It was part of the system, an essential ingredient, as old as Hippocrates. However honest a citizen, it was somehow part of the doctor's job not to tell the truth to his patient...

It is easier to decide what to do when the ultimate outcome is clear. It may be much more difficult to know what to say when the future is less certain, such as in the first episode of what is probably multiple

Original publication details: Roger Higgs, "On Telling Patients the Truth," pp. 186–202 and 232–3 from Michael Lockwood (ed.), *Moral Dilemmas in Modern Medicine*, Oxford: Oxford University Press, 1985. By permission of Oxford University Press.

Bioethics: An Anthology, Third Edition. Edited by Helga Kuhse, Udo Schüklenk, and Peter Singer.

sclerosis, or when a patient is about to undergo a mutilating operation. But even in work outside hospital, where such dramatic problems arise less commonly, whether to tell the truth and how much to tell can still be a regular issue. How much should this patient know about the side effects of his drugs? An elderly man sits weeping in an old people's home, and the healthy but exhausted daughter wants the doctor to tell her father that she's medically unfit to have him back. The single mother wants a certificate to say that she is unwell so that she can stay at home to look after her sick child. A colleague is often drunk on duty, and is making mistakes. A husband with venereal disease wants his wife to be treated without her knowledge. An outraged father demands to know if his teenage daughter has been put on the pill. A mother comes in with a child to have a boil lanced. 'Please tell him it won't hurt.' A former student writes from abroad needing to complete his professional experience and asks for a reference for a job he didn't do.[2] Whether the issue is large or small, the truth is at stake. What should the response be?

Discussion of the apparently more dramatic situations may provide a good starting-point. Recently a small group of medical students, new to clinical experience, were hotly debating what a patient with cancer should be told. One student maintained strongly that the less said to the patient the better. Others disagreed. When asked whether there was any group of patients they could agree should never be told the truth about a life-threatening illness, the students chose children, and agreed that they would not speak openly to children under six. When asked to try to remember what life was like when they were six, one student replied that he remembered how his mother had died when he was that age. Suddenly the student who had advocated non-disclosure became animated. 'That's extraordinary. My mother died when I was six too. My father said she'd gone away for a time, but would come back soon. One day he said she was coming home again. My younger sister and I were very excited. We waited at the window upstairs until we saw his car drive up. He got out and helped a woman out of the car. Then we saw. It wasn't mum. I suppose I never forgave him – or her, really.'[3]

It is hard to know with whom to sympathize in this sad tale. But its stark simplicity serves to highlight some essential points. First, somehow more clearly than in the examples involving patients, not telling the truth is seen for what it really is. It is, of course, quite possible, and very common in clinical practice, for doctors (or nurses) to engage in deliberate deceit without actually *saying* anything they believe to be false. But, given the special responsibilities of the doctor, and the relationship of trust that exists between him and his patient, one could hardly argue that this was morally any different from telling outright lies. Surely it is the *intention* that is all important. We may be silent, tactful, or reserved, but, if we intend to deceive, what we are doing is tantamount to lying. The debate in ward or surgery is suddenly stood on its head. The question is no longer 'Should we tell the truth?' but 'What justification is there for telling a lie?' This relates to the second important point, that medical ethics are part of general morality, and not a separate field of their own with their own rules. Unless there are special justifications, health-care professionals are working within the same moral constraints as lay people. A lie is a lie wherever told and whoever tells it.

But do doctors have a special dispensation from the usual principles that guide the conduct of our society? It is widely felt that on occasion they do, and such a dispensation is as necessary to all doctors as freedom from the charge of assault is to a surgeon. But, if it is impossible to look after ill patients and always be open and truthful, how can we balance this against the clear need for truthfulness on all other occasions? If deception is like a medicine to be given in certain doses in certain cases, what guidance exists about its administration?

My elderly patient reflected the widely held view that truth-telling, or perhaps withholding, was part of the tradition of medicine enshrined in its oaths and codes. Although the writer of the 'Decorum' in the Hippocratic corpus advises physicians of the danger of telling patients about the nature of their illness '… for many patients through this cause have taken a turn for the worse',[4] the Oath itself is completely silent on this issue. This extraordinary omission is continued through all the more modern codes and declarations. The first mention of veracity as a principle is to be found in the American Medical Association's 'Principles of Ethics' of 1980, which states that the physician should 'deal honestly with patients and colleagues and strive to expose those physicians deficient in character or competence, or who engage in fraud and deception'.[5] Despite the difficulties of the latter injunction, which seems in some way to divert attention from the basic need for honest communication with the patient, here at last is a clear statement. This declaration signally fails, however, to provide the guidance that we might perhaps have expected for the professional facing his or her individual dilemma.

The reticence of these earlier codes is shared, with some important exceptions, by medical writing elsewhere. Until recently most of what had been usefully said could be summed up by the articles of medical writers such as Thomas Percival, Worthington Hooker, Richard Cabot, and Joseph Collins, which show a wide scatter of view points but do at least confront the problems directly.[6] There is, however, one widely quoted statement by Lawrence Henderson, writing in the *New England Journal of Medicine* in 1955.[7] 'It is meaningless to speak of telling the truth, the whole truth and nothing but the truth to a patient… because it is…a sheer impossibility…Since telling the truth is impossible, there can be no sharp distinction between what is true and what is false.'…

But we must not allow ourselves to be confused, as Henderson was, and as so many others have been, by a failure to distinguish between truth, the abstract concept, of which we shall always have an imperfect grasp, and *telling* the truth, where the intention is all important. Whether or not we can ever fully grasp or express the whole picture, whether we know ultimately what the truth really is, we must speak truthfully, and intend to convey what we understand, or we shall lie. In Sissela Bok's words, 'The moral question of whether you are lying or not is not *settled* by establishing the truth or falsity of what you say. In order to settle the question, we must know whether you *intend your statement to mislead*.'[8]

Most modern thinkers in the field of medical ethics would hold that truthfulness is indeed a central principle of conduct, but that it is capable of coming into conflict with other principles, to which it must occasionally give way. On the other hand, the principle of veracity often receives support from other principles. For instance, it is hard to see how a patient can have autonomy, can make a free choice about matters concerning himself, without some measure of understanding of the facts as they influence the case; and that implies, under normal circumstances, some open, honest discussion with his advisers.[9] Equally, consent is a nonsense if it is not in some sense informed…

Once the central position of honesty has been established, we still need to examine whether doctors and nurses really do have, as has been suggested, special exemption from being truthful because of the nature of their work, and if so under what circumstances…It may finally be decided that in a crisis there is no acceptable alternative, as when life is ebbing and truthfulness would bring certain disaster. Alternatively, the moral issue may appear so trivial as not to be worth considering (as, for example, when a doctor is called out at night by a patient who apologizes by saying, 'I hope you don't mind me calling you at this time, doctor', and the doctor replies, 'No, not at all.'). However…occasions of these two types are few, fewer than those in which deliberate deceit would generally be regarded as acceptable in current medical practice, and should regularly be debated 'in public' if abuses are to be avoided.[10] To this end it is necessary now to examine critically the arguments commonly used to defend lying to patients.

First comes the argument that it is enormously difficult to put across a technical subject to those with little technical knowledge and understanding, in a situation where so little is predictable. A patient has bowel cancer. With surgery it might be cured, or it might recur. Can the patient understand the effects of treatment? The symptom she is now getting might be due to cancer, there might be secondaries, and they in turn might be suppressible for a long time, or not at all. What future symptoms might occur, how long will she live, how will she die – all these are desperately important questions for the patient, but even for her doctor the answers can only be informed guesses, in an area where uncertainty is so hard to bear.

Yet to say we do not know anything is a lie. As doctors we know a great deal, and *can* make informed guesses or offer likelihoods. The whole truth may be impossible to attain, but truthfulness is not. 'I do not know' can be a major piece of honesty. To deprive the patient of honest communication because we cannot know everything is, as we have seen, not only confused thinking but immoral. Thus deprived, the patient cannot plan, he cannot choose. If choice is the crux of morality, it may also, as we have argued elsewhere, be central to health. If he cannot choose, the patient cannot ever be considered to be fully restored to health.[11]

This argument also raises another human failing – to confuse the difficult with the unimportant. Passing information to people who have more restricted background, whether through lack of experience or of understanding, can be extremely difficult and time-consuming, but this is no reason why it should be shunned. Quite the reverse. Like the difficult passages in a piece of music, these tasks should be practised, studied, and techniques developed so that communication is efficient and effective. For the purposes of informed consent, the patient must be given the information he needs, as a reasonable person, to make a reasoned choice.

The second argument for telling lies to patients is that no patient likes hearing depressing or frightening news. That is certainly true. There must be few who do. But in other walks of life no professional would normally consider it his or her duty to suppress information simply in order to preserve happiness. No accountant, foreseeing bankruptcy in his client's affairs, would chat cheerfully about the Budget or a temporarily reassuring credit account. Yet such suppression of information occurs daily in wards or surgeries throughout the country. Is this what patients themselves want?

In order to find out, a number of studies have been conducted over the past thirty years.[12] In most studies there is a significant minority of patients, perhaps about a fifth, who, if given information, deny having been told. Sometimes this must be pure forgetfulness, sometimes it relates to the lack of skill of the informer, but sometimes with bad or unwelcome news there is an element of what is (perhaps not quite correctly) called 'denial'. The observer feels that at one level the news has been taken in, but at another its validity or reality has not been accepted. This process has been recognized as a buffer for the mind against the shock of unacceptable news, and often seems to be part of a process leading to its ultimate acceptance.[13] But once this group has been allowed for, most surveys find that, of those who have had or who could have had a diagnosis made of, say, cancer, between two-thirds and three-quarters of those questioned were either glad to have been told, or declared that they would wish to know. Indeed, surveys reveal that most *doctors* would themselves wish to be told the truth, even though (according to earlier studies at least) most of those same doctors said they would not speak openly to their patients – a curious double standard! Thus these surveys have unearthed, at least for the present, a common misunderstanding between doctors and patients, a general preference for openness among patients, and a significant but small group whose wish not to be informed must surely be respected. We return once more to the skill needed to detect such differences in the individual case, and the need for training in such skills.

Why doctors have for so long misunderstood their patients' wishes is perhaps related to the task itself. Doctors don't want to give bad news, just as patients don't want it in abstract, but doctors have the choice of withholding the information, and in so doing protecting themselves from the pain of telling and from the blame of being the bearer of bad news. In addition it has been suggested that doctors are particularly fearful of death and illness. Montaigne suggested that men have to think about death and be prepared to accept it, and one would think that doctors would get used to death. Yet perhaps this very familiarity has created an obsession that amounts to fear. Just as the police seem over-concerned with violence, and firemen with fire, perhaps doctors have met death in their professional training only as the enemy, never as something to come to terms with, or even as a natural force to be respected and, when the time is ripe, accepted or even welcomed.

Undeniably, doctors and nurses like helping people and derive much satisfaction from the feeling that the patient is being benefited. This basic feeling has been elevated to major status in medical practice. The principle of beneficence – to work for the patient's good – and the related principle of non-maleficence – 'first do no harm' – are usually quoted as the central guiding virtues in medicine. They are expanded in the codes, and underlie the appeal of utilitarian arguments in the context of health care. 'When you are thinking of telling a lie,' Richard Cabot quotes a teacher of his as saying, 'ask yourself whether it is simply and solely for the patient's benefit that you are going to tell it. If you are sure that you are acting for his good and not for your own profit, you can go ahead with a clear conscience.'[14] But who should decide what is 'for the patient's benefit'? Why should it be the doctor? Increasingly society is uneasy with such a paternalistic style. In most other walks of life the competent individual is himself assumed to be the best judge of his own interests. Whatever may be thought of this assumption in the field of politics or law, to make one's own decisions on matters that are central to one's own life or welfare and do not directly concern others would normally be held to be a basic *right*; and hardly one to be taken away simply on the grounds of illness, whether actual or merely potential.

Thus if beneficence is assumed to be the key principle, which many now have come to doubt, it can easily ride roughshod over autonomy and natural justice. A lie denies a person the chance of participating in choices concerning his own health, including that of whether to be a 'patient' at all. Paternalism may be justifiable in the short term, and to 'kid' someone, to treat him as a child because he is ill, and perhaps dying, may be very tempting. Yet true respect for that person (adult or child) can only be shown by allowing him allowable choices, by granting him whatever control is left, as weakness gradually undermines his hold on life. If respect is important then at the very least there must be no acceptable or effective alternative to lying in a particular situation if the lie is to be justified…

However, a third argument for lying can be advanced, namely, that truthfulness can actually do harm. 'What you don't know can't hurt you' is a phrase in common parlance (though it hardly fits with concepts of presymptomatic screening for preventable disease!). However, it is undeniable that blunt and unfeeling communication of unpleasant truths can cause acute distress, and sometimes long-term disability. The fear that professionals often have of upsetting people, of causing a scene, of making fools of themselves by letting unpleasant emotions flourish, seems to have elevated this argument beyond its natural limits. It is not unusual to find that the fear of creating harm will deter a surgical team from discussing a diagnosis gently with a patient, but not deter it from performing radical and mutilating surgery. Harm is a very personal concept. Most medical schools have, circulating in the refectory, a story about a patient

who was informed that he had cancer and then leapt to his death. The intended moral for the medical student is, keep your mouth shut and do no harm. But that may not be the correct lesson to be learned from such cases (which I believe, in any case, to be less numerous than is commonly supposed). The style of telling could have been brutal, with no follow-up or support. It may have been the suggested treatment, not the basic illness, that led the patient to resort to such a desperate measure. Suicide in illness is remarkably rare, but, though tragic, could be seen as a logical response to an overwhelming challenge. No mention is usually made of suicide rates in other circumstances, or the isolation felt by ill and warded patients, or the feelings of anger uncovered when someone takes such precipitate and forbidden action against himself. What these cases do, surely, is argue, not for no telling, but for better telling, for sensitivity and care in determining how much the patient wants to know, explaining carefully in ways the patient can understand, and providing full support and 'after-care' as in other treatments.

But even if it is accepted that the short-term effect of telling the truth may sometimes be considerable psychological disturbance, in the long term the balance seems definitely to swing the other way. The effects of lying are dramatically illustrated in 'A Case of Obstructed Death?'[15] False information prevented a woman from returning to healthy living after a cancer operation, and robbed her of six months of active life. Also, the long-term effect of lies on the family and, perhaps most importantly, on society, is incalculable. If trust is gradually corroded, if the 'wells are poisoned', progress is hard. Mistrust creates lack of communication and increased fear, and this generation has seen just such a fearful myth created around cancer.[16] Just how much harm has been done by this 'demonizing' of cancer, preventing people coming to their doctors, or alternatively creating unnecessary attendances on doctors, will probably never be known.

There are doubtless many other reasons why doctors lie to their patients; but these can hardly be used to justify lies, even if we should acknowledge them in passing. Knowledge is power, and certainly doctors, though usually probably for reasons of work-load rather than anything more sinister, like to remain 'in control'. Health professionals may, like others, wish to protect themselves from confrontation, and may find it easier to coerce or manipulate than to gain permission. There may be a desire to avoid any pressure for change. And there is the constant problem of lack of time. But, in any assessment, the key issues remain. Not telling the truth normally involves telling lies, and doctors and nurses have no *carte blanche* to lie…

If the importance of open communication with the patient is accepted, we need to know when to say what. If a patient is going for investigations, it may be possible at that time, before details are known, to have a discussion about whether he would like to know the details. A minor 'contract' can be made. 'I promise to tell you what I know, if you ask me.' Once that time is past, however, it requires skill and sensitivity to assess what a patient wants to know. Allowing the time and opportunity for the patient to ask questions is the most important thing, but one must realize that the patient's apparent question may conceal the one he really wants answered. 'Do I have cancer?' may contain the more important questions 'How or when will I die?' 'Will there be pain?' The doctor will not necessarily be helping by giving an extended pathology lesson. The informer may need to know more: 'I don't want to avoid your question, and I promise to answer as truthfully as I can, but first…' It has been pointed out that in many cases the terminal patient will tell the doctor, not vice versa, if the right opportunities are created and the style and timing is appropriate. Then it is a question of not telling but listening to the truth.[17]

If in spite of all this there still seems to be a need to tell lies, we must be able to justify them. That the person is a child, or 'not very bright', will not do. Given the two ends of the spectrum of crisis and triviality, the vast middle range of communication requires honesty, so that autonomy and choice can be maintained. If lies are to be told, there really must be no acceptable alternative. The analogy with force may again be helpful here: perhaps using the same style of thinking as is used in the Mental Health Act, to test whether we are justified in removing someone's liberty against their will, may help us to see the gravity of what we are doing when we consider deception. It also suggests that the decision should be shared, in confidence, and be subject to debate, so that any alternative which may not initially have been seen may be considered. And it does not end there. If we break an important moral principle, that principle still retains its force, and its 'shadow' has to be acknowledged. As professionals we shall have to ensure that we follow up, that we work through the broken trust or the disillusionment that the lie will bring to the patient, just as we would follow up and work through bad news, a major operation, or a psychiatric 'sectioning'. This follow-up may also be called for in our relationship with our colleagues if there has been major disagreement about what should be done.

In summary, there are *some* circumstances in which the health professions are probably exempted from society's general requirement for truthfulness. But not telling the truth is usually the same as telling a lie, and a lie requires strong justification. Lying must be a last resort, and we should act as if we were to be called upon to defend the decision in public debate, even if our duty of confidentiality does not allow this in practice. We should always aim to respect the other important principles governing interactions with patients, especially the preservation of the patient's autonomy. When all is said and done, many arguments for individual cases of lying do not hold water. Whether or not knowing the truth is essential to the patient's health, telling the truth is essential to the health of the doctor–patient relationship.

Notes

1 *Primum non nocere* – this is a Latinization of a statement which is not directly Hippocratic, but may be derived from the *Epidemics* Book 1 Chapter II: 'As to diseases, make a habit of two things – to help, or at least do no harm.' *Hippocrates*, 4 vols (London: William Heinemann, 1923–31), vol. I, trans. W. H. S. Jones.

2 Cases collected by the author in his own practice.

3 Case collected by the author.

4 Quoted in Reiser, Dyck, and Curran (eds), *Ethics in Medicine, Historical Perspectives and Contemporary Concerns* (Cambridge, MA: MIT Press, 1977).

5 American Medical Association, 'Text of the American Medical Association New Principles of Medical Ethics', *American Medical News* (August 1–8 1980), 9.

6   To be found in Reiser et al., *Ethics in Medicine*.

7   Lawrence Henderson, 'Physician and Patient as a Social System', *New England Journal of Medicine*, 212 (1935).

8   Sissela Bok, *Lying: Moral Choice in Public and Private Life* (London: Quartet, 1980).

9   Alastair Campbell and Roger Higgs, *In That Case* (London: Darton, Longman and Todd, 1982).

10 John Rawls, *A Theory of Justice* (Cambridge, MA: Harvard University Press, Belknap Press, 1971).

11 See Campbell and Higgs, *In That Case*.

12 Summarized well in Robert Veatch, 'Truth-telling I' in *Encyclopaedia of Bioethics*, ed. Warren T. Reich (New York: Free Press, 1978).

13 The five stages of reacting to bad news, or news of dying, are described in *On Death and Dying* by Elizabeth Kubler-Ross (London: Tavistock, 1970). Not everyone agrees with her model. For another view see a very stimulating article 'Therapeutic Uses of Truth' by Michael Simpson in E. Wilkes (ed.), *The Dying Patient* (Lancaster: MTP Press, 1982). 'In my model there are only two stages – the stage when you believe in the Kubler-Ross five and the stage when you do not.'

14 Quoted in Richard Cabot, 'The Use of Truth and Falsehood in Medicine; an experimental study', *American Magazine*, 5 (1903), 344–9.

15 Roger Higgs, 'Truth at the Last – A Case of Obstructed Death?' *Journal of Medical Ethics*, 8 (1982), 48–50, and Roger Higgs, 'Obstructed Death Revisited', *Journal of Medical Ethics*, 8 (1982), 154–6.

16 Susan Sontag, *Illness as Metaphor* (New York: Farrar, Straus and Giroux, 1978).

17 Cicely Saunders, 'Telling Patients', *District Nursing* (now *Queens Nursing Journal*) (September 1963), 149–50, 154.

Informed Consent and Patient Autonomy

73

On Liberty

John Stuart Mill

The object of this essay is to assert one very simple principle, as entitled to govern absolutely the dealings of society with the individual in the way of compulsion and control, whether the means used be physical force in the form of legal penalties, or the moral coercion of public opinion. That principle is, that the sole end for which mankind are warranted, individually or collectively, in interfering with the liberty of action of any of their number, is self-protection. That the only purpose for which power can be rightfully exercised over any member of a civilized community, against his will, is to prevent harm to others. His own good, either physical or moral, is not a sufficient warrant. He cannot rightfully be compelled to do or forbear because it will be better for him to do so, because it will make him happier, because, in the opinions of others, to do so would be wise, or even right. These are good reasons for remonstrating with him, or reasoning with him, or persuading him, or entreating him, but not for compelling him, or visiting him with any evil in case he do otherwise. To justify that, the conduct from which it is desired to deter him must be calculated to produce evil to someone else. The only part of the conduct of anyone, for which he is amenable to society, is that which concerns others. In the part which merely concerns himself, his independence is, of right, absolute. Over himself, over his own body and mind, the individual is sovereign.

It is perhaps hardly necessary to say that this doctrine is meant to apply only to human beings in the maturity of their faculties. We are not speaking of children, or of young persons below the age which the law may fix as that of manhood or womanhood. Those who are still in a state to require being taken care of by others, must be protected against their own actions as well as against external injury. For the same reason, we may leave out of consideration those backward states of society in which the race itself may be considered as in its nonage. The early difficulties in the way of spontaneous progress are so great, and there is seldom any choice of means for overcoming them; and a ruler full of the spirit of improvement is warranted in the use of any expedients that will attain an end, perhaps otherwise unattainable. Despotism is a legitimate mode of government in dealing with barbarians, provided the end be their improvement, and the means justified by actually effecting that end. Liberty, as a principle, has no application to any state of things anterior to the time when mankind have become capable of being improved by free and equal discussion. Until then, there is nothing for them but implicit obedience to an Akbar or a Charlemagne, if they are so fortunate as to find one. But as soon as mankind have attained the capacity of being guided to their own improvement by conviction or persuasion (a period long since reached in all nations with whom we need here concern ourselves), compulsion,

Original publication details: John Stuart Mill, "On Liberty," first published in 1859.

Bioethics: An Anthology, Third Edition. Edited by Helga Kuhse, Udo Schüklenk, and Peter Singer.

either in the direct form or in that of pains and penalties for non-compliance, is no longer admissible as a means to their own good, and justifiable only for the security of others.

It is proper to state that I forgo any advantage which could be derived to my argument from the idea of abstract right, as a thing independent of utility. I regard utility as the ultimate appeal on all ethical questions; but it must be utility in the largest sense, grounded on the permanent interests of a man as a progressive being. Those interests, I contend, authorized the subjection of individual spontaneity to external control, only in respect to those actions of each which concern the interest of other people. If anyone does an act hurtful to others, there is a *prima facie* case for punishing him, by law, or, where legal penalties are not safely applicable, by general disapprobation. There are also many positive acts for the benefit of others, which he may rightfully be compelled to perform: such as to give evidence in a court of justice; to bear his fair share in the common defense, or in any other joint work necessary to the interest of the society of which he enjoys the protection; and to perform certain acts of individual beneficence, such as saving a fellow-creature's life, or interposing to protect the defenseless against ill usage, things which whenever it is obviously a man's duty to do, he may rightfully be made responsible to society for not doing. A person may cause evil to others not only by his actions but by his inaction, and in either case he is justly accountable to them for the injury. The latter case, it is true, requires a much more cautious exercise of compulsion than the former. To make anyone answerable for doing evil to others is the rule; to make him answerable for not preventing evil is, comparatively speaking, the exception. Yet there are many cases clear enough and grave enough to justify that exception. In all things which regard the external relations of the individual, he is *de jure* amenable to those whose interests are concerned, and, if need be, to society as their protector. There are often good reasons for not holding him to the responsibility; but these reasons must arise from the special expediencies of the case: either because it is a kind of case in which he is on the whole likely to act better, when left to his own discretion, than when controlled in any way in which society have it in their power to control him; or because the attempt to exercise control would produce other evils, greater than those which it would prevent. When such reasons as these preclude the enforcement of responsibility, the conscience of the agent himself should step into the vacant judgment seat, and protect those interests of others which have no external protection; judging himself all the more rigidly, because the case does not admit of his being made accountable to the judgment of his fellow-creatures.

But there is a sphere of action in which society, as distinguished from the individual, has, if any, only an indirect interest; comprehending all that portion of a person's life and conduct which affects only himself, or if it also affects others, only with their free, voluntary, and undeceived consent and participation. When I say only himself, I mean directly, and in the first instance; for whatever affects himself, may affect others through himself; and the objection which may be grounded on this contingency, will receive consideration in the sequel. This, then, is the appropriate region of human liberty. It comprises, *first*, the inward domain of consciousness; demanding liberty of conscience in the most comprehensive sense; liberty of thought and feeling; absolute freedom of opinion and sentiment on all subjects, practical or speculative, scientific, moral, or theological. The liberty of expressing and publishing opinions may seem to fall under a different principle, since it belongs to that part of the conduct of an individual which concerns other people; but, being almost of as much importance as the liberty of thought itself, and resting in great part on the same reasons, is practically inseparable from it. *Secondly*, the principle requires liberty of tastes and pursuits; of framing the plan of our life to suit our own character; of doing as we like, subject to such consequences as may follow: without impediment from our fellow-creatures, so long as what we do does not harm them, even though they should think our conduct foolish, perverse, or wrong. *Thirdly*, from this liberty of each individual, follows the liberty, within the same limits, of combination among individuals; freedom to unite, for any purpose not involving harm to others: the persons combining being supposed to be of full age, and not forced or deceived.

No society in which these liberties are not, on the whole, respected, is free, whatever may be its form of government; and none is completely free in which they do not exist absolute and unqualified. The only freedom which deserves the name, is that of pursuing our own good in our own way, so long as we do not attempt to deprive others of theirs, or impede their efforts to obtain it. Each is the proper guardian of his own health, whether bodily, or mental and spiritual. Mankind are greater gainers by suffering each other to live as seems good to themselves, than by compelling each to live as seems good to the rest.

From *Schloendorff v. New York Hospital*

Justice Benjamin N. Cardozo

Every human being of adult years and sound mind has a right to determine what shall be done with his own body; and a surgeon who performs an operation without his patient's consent commits an assault, for which he is liable in damages. (*Pratt* v. *Davis*, 224 III. 300; *Mohr* v. *Williams*, 95 Minn. 261.) This is true except in cases of emergency where the patient is unconscious and where it is necessary to operate before consent can be obtained.

Original publication details: Justice Benjamin N. Cardozo, Judgment from *Schloendorff* v. *New York Hospital* (1914), p. 526 from Jay Katz (ed.), *Experimentation with Human Beings: The Authority of the Investigator, Subject, Professions, and State in the Human Experimentation Process*, New York: Russell Sage Foundation, 1972. Reproduced with permission of Russell Sage Foundation.

Bioethics: An Anthology, Third Edition. Edited by Helga Kuhse, Udo Schüklenk, and Peter Singer.
© 2016 John Wiley & Sons, Inc. Published 2016 by John Wiley & Sons, Inc.

Informed Consent

Its History, Meaning, and Present Challenges

Tom L. Beauchamp

The practice of obtaining informed consent has its history in, and gains its meaning from, medicine and biomedical research. Discussions of disclosure and justified nondisclosure have played a significant role throughout the history of medical ethics, but the term "informed consent" emerged only in the 1950s. Serious discussion of the meaning and ethics of informed consent began in medicine, research, law, and philosophy only around 1972. In the mid-1970s medical and research ethics gradually moved from a narrow focus on the physician's or the researcher's obligation to disclose information to an emphasis on the quality of a patient's or subject's understanding of information and right to authorize or refuse a biomedical intervention. This shift was the real beginning of a meaningful notion of informed consent. However, it may be doubted that this notion has ever been put into real-world contexts of practice. Put another way, the bulk of consents given still today may not be sufficiently informed to qualify as *informed* consents.

I first discuss the early history of informed consent, including its critical landmarks. I argue that its arrival was sudden and impressive, but the path thereafter to high-quality consents has been rocky. I then explore two different meanings of "informed consent" at work in literature on the subject. The most established meaning derives from institutional and regulatory rules, although I give reasons to think that this meaning is morally suspicious. Finally, in the third part I discuss several contemporary challenges to informed consent that suggest we still have unresolved problems about whether, when, and how to obtain informed consents.

The Historical Foundations of Informed Consent

Classic documents in the history of medicine such as the Hippocratic writings (fifth to fourth century BC) and Thomas Percival's *Medical Ethics* (1803)[1] present an extremely disappointing history from the perspective of the right to give informed consent. The central concern in these writings was how to avoid making disclosures that might harm or upset patients. Physician ethics was traditionally a nondisclosure ethics with virtually no appreciation of a patient's right to consent. The doctrine of informed consent was imposed on medicine through nonmedical forms of authority such as judges in courts and government officials in regulatory agencies.

During the 1950s and 1960s the duty to obtain consent in a few medical fields, such as surgery, evolved through the courts into an explicit duty to disclose

Original publication details: Tom L. Beauchamp, "Informed Consent: Its History, Meaning, and Present Challenges," pp. 515–23 from *Cambridge Quarterly of Health Care Ethics* 20: 4 (2011). © Royal Institute of Philosophy, published by Cambridge University Press. Reproduced with permission from Cambridge University Press and T. Beauchamp.

certain forms of information and to obtain consent in both practice and research. This development needed a new term, and so the word "informed" was tacked onto the word "consent," creating the expression "informed consent." This expression appeared publicly for the first time in the landmark decision in *Salgo v. Leland Stanford, Jr. University Board of Trustees* (1957).[2] The *Salgo* court said – prophetically, but probably incorrectly – that the duty to disclose the risks and alternatives of treatment was not a new duty, only a logical extension of the already-established duty to disclose the treatment's nature and consequences. In fact, *Salgo* not only introduced new elements into the law but initiated the history of informed consent. The *Salgo* court was not merely interested in whether a recognizable consent had been given. The court latched tenaciously onto the problem of whether the consent was itself *adequately informed*.

This development initiated a series of court cases that step-by-step added requirements into the doctrine of informed consent. For 15 years after *Salgo*, these changes came slowly and incrementally in courts of law. Then, suddenly, in 1972 there came down three court decisions in three separate state courts in the United States that would solidify the place of informed consent and advance to prominence the importance of its moral demands. The three landmark cases were *Canterbury v. Spence*, *Cobbs v. Grant*, and *Wilkinson v. Vesey*.[3] *Canterbury* had a particularly massive influence in demanding a more patient-oriented standard of disclosure. Judge Spottswood Robinson held that "[t]he patient's right of self-decision shapes the boundaries of the duty to reveal. That right can be effectively exercised only if the patient possesses enough information to enable an intelligent choice."[4] Informed consent would never thereafter lose its place as a significant legal doctrine, but it would soon be considerably expanded through discussions of the ethical demands of consent in both medicine and research.

Numerous articles in the medical literature on issues of consent were soon published, largely on the significance of the precedent cases. Doctors were fearful, and their articles functioned to alert physicians to informed consent as a worrisome new legal development with the potential to increase malpractice risk. A study done in the mid-1960s, conducted by a lawyer-surgeon team, showed that *consent forms* were not yet a ubiquitous

feature even of the practice of surgery – let alone elsewhere in medicine.[5] This would change rapidly after the 1972 court decisions. During the years between 1972 and 1978, there was a dramatic solidification of the view that both physicians and biomedical researchers have a moral and legal duty to obtain consent for certain procedures. These developments prompted an explosion of largely negative commentary on informed consent in the medical literature of the mid-1970s. Physicians saw the demands of informed consent as impossible to fulfill and, at least in some cases, inconsistent with good patient care.[6]

We might ask why informed consent became so important and the focus of so much attention in case law, ethics, and biomedicine in the next few years. The most likely explanation is that law, ethics, medicine, and research were all affected by issues of individual liberty and social equality in the wider society. These issues were made dramatic by an increasingly technological and impersonal medical care. Informed consent was swept along with this tide of social concerns, which broadly propelled the new bioethics throughout the 1970s. As it happened, the arrival of informed consent and the birth of bioethics occurred at exactly the same time.

These developments, as thus far traced, tell us little about physicians' and researchers' actual consent practices or opinions, or about how informed consent was viewed or experienced by patients and subjects. The empirical evidence on this subject during the late 1970s and early 1980s is mixed. Perhaps the best and most interesting data on the subject are the findings of a national survey conducted by Louis Harris and Associates for a U.S. President's Commission on bioethics in 1982. Almost all of the physicians surveyed indicated that they obtained written consent from their patients before inpatient surgery or the administration of general anesthesia. Approximately 85 percent said they usually obtain consent – written or oral – for minor office surgery, setting of fractures, local anesthesia, invasive diagnostic procedures, and radiation therapy. Only blood tests and prescriptions appear to have proceeded frequently without some form of patient consent.[7]

This survey indicates that the explosion of interest in informed consent in the 1970s had an enormously powerful impact on medical practice by the early 1980s.

However, evidence from the Harris survey and other sources also questions the quality and meaningfulness of this consent-related activity. The overwhelming impression from the available empirical literature and from reported clinical experience is that the process of soliciting informed consent often fell far short of a show of respect for the decisional authority of patients. As the authors of one empirical study of physician-patient interactions put it, "[D]espite the doctrine of informed consent, it is the physician, and not the patient, who, in effect, makes the treatment decision."[8]

To conclude this section, the history of informed consent indicates that medicine quickly experienced widespread changes under the influence of legal requirements of informed consent, setting in motion an evolving process in our understanding of informed consent and the moral demands involved in obtaining it. The 1970s framers of the rules wanted genuine informed consent, but that goal has been more difficult to achieve than was the impressive body of rules, court decisions, and books on informed consent that soon followed the early history. Practice has been slow to conform to abstract theory.

The Concept of Informed Consent

Accordingly, the claim that a signed consent form is evidence of an informed consent cannot always be taken at face value. Before we can legitimately infer that what is called an informed consent is truly an informed consent, we need to know what to look for. If one uses overly demanding criteria of informed consent – such as full disclosure and complete understanding – then an informed consent can hardly ever be obtained. Conversely, if underdemanding criteria such as a signed consent form are used, an informed consent becomes too easy to obtain, and the term loses its moral significance. Although a physician's or a research investigator's truthful disclosure to a patient has often been declared the essence of informed consent in legal and medical literature, mere disclosure is seldom evidence of an informed consent.

The question "What is an informed consent?" is complicated because at least two common, entrenched, and irreducibly different meanings of "informed consent" have been at work in its history. In the first

sense, an informed consent is an *autonomous authorization* by individual patients or subjects. A person gives an informed consent in this first sense if and only if the person, with substantial understanding and in substantial absence of control by others, intentionally authorizes a health professional to do something. Here informed consent is fundamentally a matter of autonomous or self-determining choice.

In the second sense, informed consent is analyzable in terms of *institutional and policy rules of consent* that collectively form the social practice of informed consent in institutional contexts. Here "informed consent" refers only to a legally or institutionally effective approval given by a patient or subject. An approval is therefore "effective" or "valid" if it conforms to the rules that govern specific institutions. In this sense, unlike the first, conditions and requirements of informed consent are relative to the social and institutional context and need not be truly autonomous authorizations. Informed consent in the second sense has been the mainstream conception in the regulatory rules of U.S. federal agencies as well as in healthcare institutions, and this situation is not likely to change.[9]

However, literature in bioethics has increasingly maintained, as I would, that any justifiable analysis of informed consent must be rooted in autonomous choice by patients and subjects, because otherwise there is no truly informed consent. The first sense captures the morally best standard, because the whole point of the practice of informed consent is to protect and enable meaningful choice. Although living up to this standard has proved to be difficult in contexts of practice, informed consent as autonomous authorization arguably provides a model standard for fashioning institutional and policy requirements of informed consent. That is, truly autonomous choice can and should serve as the benchmark against which the moral adequacy of prevailing rules and practices are to be evaluated.

Current Challenges to Informed Consent

I turn next to some of the challenges we face today in the theory and practice of informed consent, with an emphasis on challenges in practice.

The limits of the law in biomedical ethics

A first challenge is how to understand the way the law should shape our understanding of informed consent. I maintained previously that the law has been more influential historically than any other field of thought in the United States. The doctrine of informed consent *is* the legal doctrine, and informed consent has often been treated as synonymous with this legal doctrine, which is centered almost entirely on *disclosure* and on *liability for injury*. This basis is unduly narrow for thinking about both research and medical practice, which is to say that the law is ill-equipped to help us in our thinking about informed consent beyond the restricted limits within which the law operates. Those limits can and often have misled us about our responsibilities to patients and subjects. American legal scholar and psychiatrist Jay Katz was appropriately unrelenting, throughout his career, in criticizing court decisions and the legal model. He regarded the declarations of courts as filled with overly optimistic and often morally empty and evasive rhetoric. The problem, in his view, is that the law has little to do with fostering morally required forms of communication in the clinic and in the research environment.[10]

The theory of liability under which a case is tried in American law determines the duty that must be fulfilled. In classic informed consent cases, negligence is the reigning theory of liability. This approach is itself a misleading and uninformative basis for thinking about informed consent in contexts of clinical practice and research. Negligence may be good for understanding what has gone wrong in some cases, but this rationale provides an inadequate framework for determining what we ought to be doing in soliciting consent or in waiving consent in institutions.

In the end, legal standards are not of major assistance in formulating a conception of informed consent for medicine and research. These standards do as much to distract us from an appropriate model as to contribute to the model, because they focus on illegal rather than unethical treatment. The heart of issues about informed consent is moral, not legal.[11]

The quality of consent

In discussing both meaningful choice and the limits of law, I have noted that problems about the quality and adequacy of consent probably cannot be resolved unless conventional disclosure rules are refocused so that we look instead at the quality of understanding in a consent as well as the rights of patients and their needs for information. This approach centers attention on the need for effective communication and genuine understanding by patients and subjects. Without a proper climate of exchange in the consent context, a request from a professional that the patient or subject ask for information is as likely to result in silence as to elicit the desired result of a meaningful informational exchange and consent. However, it is not clear how much progress has been made on this front in the last 20 years, and it is a good guess that relatively little educating and communication that conform to this model occur at present in either clinical practice or research. Achieving informed consent under the first of the two senses of informed consent discussed previously is still the principal challenge that we confront.

Problems of broad consent

A third set of challenges derives from contemporary concerns about broad consent. In Europe there is currently an active discussion of broad consent in settings in which obtaining consent is difficult or in which risk is extremely low. Although it is not as active, this topic haunts U.S. discussions as well. There has been a pervasive view in U.S. bioethics that if we must get consent, then it should be an *adequately informed* consent and that a broad consent is not an adequately informed consent. However, this view is now under pressure. I will approach the problem primarily through questions of the banking of biological samples.

The banking of samples   Certain advances in science have made efficiently promoting scientific advances while protecting the rights of donors ever more problematic. Samples collected for future – not merely present – research may not be adequately described in a protocol or consent form when sample collection occurs. How shall we understand what constitutes an adequately informed consent under these circumstances? The content of the consent will be roughly dictated by current and anticipated future uses of the samples. In giving consent, research subjects should be assured that sensitive personal information and data will be protected in a way that will not cause stigma or harm their dignity, will not violate privacy and confidentiality, and will not lead to discriminatory treatment.[12]

This challenge cannot be met merely by internal protections when obtaining consent. Biological samples and data from samples are often obtained from external sources such as industry, government, universities, or nonprofits. Here it must be ascertained whether samples were collected under valid consent policies. Surplus biological material that is often described as waste raises similar concerns. The use of a sample for purposes other than those specifically stated in the consent process is a violation of the trust that bonds the subject–investigator relationship and the original consent situation. If an investigator seeks to use a sample for purposes not originally stated in an informed consent form, the subject likely would have to be re-contacted and re-consented. However, there are exceptions to this rule – for example, when only minor departures are made from the original protocol and consent form and (in some cases) when samples cannot be linked with a donor. However, there seems to be only a narrow range of such valid exceptions. Even making samples anonymous is not a valid exception, because it may well violate the investigator–subject trust relationship.

These are just some of the problems that need to be addressed about the notion of broad consent. I will not try to resolve these issues here. However, I will follow up the challenges thus far noted with analysis of a case in which broad consent was used with disastrous consequences. This case beautifully exemplifies how morally complicated the informed consent process can be.

The Havasupai Indians and diabetes research This case involves research conducted at the Arizona State University using as research subjects the Havasupai Indians of the Grand Canyon. Matters did not go well both because a broad consent was used by investigators when it was inappropriate and because university committee review of the research was ineffective. The case starts in 1990, when members of the fast-disappearing Havasupai tribe gave DNA samples to university researchers at Arizona State with the goal

of providing genetic information about the tribe's rate of diabetes. Dating from the 1960s, the Havasupai had experienced a surprisingly high incidence of type 2 diabetes, which led to amputations and had forced many tribal members to leave their village in the Grand Canyon for dialysis.

The tribe's diabetes was examined in the research, but the blood samples that had been donated were then put to additional uses in genetics research, and here the trouble began. One use of the samples was to study mental illness (one professor had a special interest in schizophrenia). Another use was to study the tribe's geographical origins, which cast doubt on cherished tribal views about their historical origins. Approximately two dozen scholarly articles were published on the basis of research on the samples. Some of this research was judged by the Havasupai to be offensive, insulting, and provocative. For example, one study reported a high degree of inbreeding in the tribe.

A geneticist responsible for some of the research reported that she had obtained an adequate informed consent for wide-ranging genetic studies and defended her actions as late as 2009 as ethically justified. The problem was the use of broad consent. From 1990 to 1994, about 100 members of the tribe signed a broad consent that said the research was to "study the causes of behavioral/medical disorders." The consent form was intentionally confined to clear, simply written, basic information, because English is a second language for many Havasupai, and few of the tribe's remaining 650 members had graduated from high school. From the researchers' perspective, tribe members had consented to collecting the blood and to its use in genetic research well beyond the research on their particular disease. The Havasupai, however, adamantly deny that they gave permission for any non-diabetes research or that they were given an adequate understanding of the risks of the research before they agreed to participate.[13]

This case presents paradigmatic problems of human rights and informed consent. One reading of the case is that it is essentially about researchers' responsibility to communicate what might happen with the samples. The case also raises classic questions of whether scientists had taken advantage of a vulnerable population, and in this respect the case raises questions about exploitation that preys on ignorance.

Both the researchers and the review committee at the university overlooked the serious risks involved. One scholarly article eventually published by investigators theorized that the tribe's ancestors had crossed the frozen Bering Sea to arrive in North America. This directly contradicted the tribe's traditional stories and cosmology, which have quasi-religious significance for the Havasupai. Their history has it that they originated in the Grand Canyon and that the tribe had been assigned to be the canyon's guardian. To be told that the tribe was instead of Asian origin and that this was learned from studies on their blood, which has a special significance to the Havasupai, is to them disorienting and abhorrent. The account also introduced legal alarm. The Havasupai had argued that their origin in the canyon was the legal basis of their entitlement to the land, which is otherwise U.S. federal land.

Finally, in retrospect, there were significant risks for the university in the conduct of this research and in allowing a broad consent. In the end the university's Board of Regents agreed to pay $700,000 to 41 of the tribe's members, while acknowledging that the payment was to "remedy the wrong that was done." The university spent $1.7 million fighting lawsuits by tribe members. The university had worked for years to establish good relationships with Native American tribes in Arizona. The reservoir of trust that had been established was seriously threatened by this case.[14]

This tragic case apparently happened with virtually no appreciation, during the course of ethics review, that obtaining a broad consent, under the circumstances, was an ethically dubious practice.

The regulation of consent and the research-treatment distinction

A fourth type of challenge to informed consent requirements comes in how we should alter the ways in which consent is regulated.

I start with a basic distinction in bioethics, viz., that between clinical research and medical practice. This distinction has dominated how we think about biomedical ethics, including informed consent. Since the early 1970s it has been thought that research is risky, whereas accepted practice is aimed at the best interests of the patient. This belief is probably traceable to the history of abuses of subjects in biomedical research,

and so there arose in the 1970s the assumption that research using human subjects is dangerous, exists for the benefit of future patients, and is aimed at scientific knowledge, not benefit for immediate subjects.

Accordingly, it has been thought that the need for consent is more pervasive and the threshold of an adequate informed consent higher in research than in medical practice. But do we have good reasons to warrant this sharp distinction between research and practice – and the different levels of consent requirements that co-travel with it? And should the distinction between research and practice make any difference to requirements of informed consent? Perhaps today patients are underprotected, and research subjects overprotected, by our moral arrangements for consent. This matter will likely receive close inspection in upcoming years, and it presents an important challenge to current consent practices.

One central question will be whether we should have a moral system in which there is an intense, close ethical review of consent forms in research protocols and no close parallel attention given to consent forms in medical practice. One dimension of the problem is whether we should have government regulatory systems for research, but no comparable systems for the regulation of practice. In America, the vast differences in our systems rest on doctors' desires to not be regulated in the practice of medicine. But from the perspective of genuine informed consent, the U.S. system sometimes seems irrational, especially if there are dangers and risks in medical practice comparable to those in research. If so, then is it time for us to have comparable oversight systems in both research and practice?

Conclusion

I have been critical of various practices in the obtaining of and the failure to obtain informed consents. However, before we too sternly condemn defects in the judgments and practices of the past, we should remember that the history of informed consent is still unfolding and that current failures may be no less apparent to future generations than are the failures that I have found in the past and the present. Clearly we still face unresolved and critical moral challenges.

Notes

1 Percival T. *Medical Ethics; or a Code of Institutes and Precepts, Adapted to the Professional Conduct of Physicians and Surgeons*. Manchester: S. Russell; 1803.

2 *Salgo v. Leland Stanford Jr. University Board of Trustees*, 317 P.2d 170 (1957).

3 *Canterbury v. Spence*, 464 F.2d 772 (D.C. Cir. 1972); *Cobbs v. Grant*, 104 Cal. Rptr. 505, 502 P.2d 1 (1972); *Wilkinson v. Vesey*, 295 A.2d 676 (R.I. 1972).

4 See *Canterbury v. Spence*, at 786.

5 Hershey N, Bushkoff SH. *Informed Consent Study*. Pittsburgh: Aspen Systems Corporation; 1969:4.

6 National Library of Medicine, 272 citations on informed consent in the period from January 1970 to April 1974, in Medical Literature Analysis and Retrieval System (MEDLARS), NLM Literature Search No. 74–16 (1974); Kaufmann CL. Informed consent and patient decision making: Two decades of research. *Social Science and Medicine* 1983;17:1657–64.

7 Louis Harris and Associates. Views of informed consent and decisionmaking: Parallel surveys of physicians and the public. In: President's Commission for the Study of Ethical Problems in Medicine and Biomedical and Behavioral Research. *Making Health Care Decisions*. Washington: U.S. Government Printing Office; 1982: vol. 2:302.

8 Siminoff LA, Fetting JH. Factors affecting treatment decisions for a life-threatening illness: The case of medical treatment for breast cancer. *Social Science and Medicine* 1992;32:813–8, at 817.

9 Faden RR, Beauchamp TL. *A History and Theory of Informed Consent*. New York: Oxford University Press; 1986:276–87.

10 Katz J. *The Silent World of Doctor and Patient*. New York: Free Press; 1984.

11 For an example of how the legal doctrine is still today used by prominent authors in bioethics as a foundational starting point for theory and practice, see Appelbaum PS, Lidz CW, Klitzman R. Voluntariness of consent to research: A conceptual model. *Hastings Center Report* 2009;39(1):30–9.

12 Buchanan A. An ethical framework for biological samples policy. In: National Bioethics Advisory Commission. *Research Involving Human Biological Materials: Ethical Issues and Policy Guidance,* vol. II: *Commissioned Papers*. Rockville: National Bioethics Advisory Commission; January 2000; Pentz RD, Billot L, Wendler D. Research on stored biological samples: Views of African American and White American cancer patients. *American Journal of Medical Genetics*. 2006 Mar 7; available at http://onlinelibrary.wiley.com/doi/10.1002/ajmg.a.31154/full (accessed 14 Sept 2010).

13 Harmon A. Indian tribe wins fight to limit research of its DNA. *New York Times*. 2010 Apr 21; available at http://www.nytimes.com/2010/04/22/us/22dna.html; Harmon A. Havasupai case highlights risks in DNA research. *New York Times*. 2010 Apr 22; available at http://www.nytimes.com/2010/04/22/us/22dnaside.html (last accessed 14 Sept 2010).

14 Harmon A. Where'd you go with my DNA? *New York Times*. 2010 Apr 25; available at http://www.nytimes.com/2010/04/25/weekinreview/25harmon.html (accessed 14 Sept 2010). Also see Harmon, Indian tribe wins fight to limit research of its DNA; Harmon, Havasupai case highlights risks in DNA research.

76

The Doctor–Patient Relationship in Different Cultures

Ruth Macklin

When bioethicists from the United States call for recognition of the rights of patients, are they simply expressing their unique American adherence to individualism? The familiar charge of "ethical imperialism" is leveled against proposals that patients in other countries, where individualism is not a prominent value, should nevertheless be granted a similar right to informed consent. While it is true that the doctrine of informed consent focuses on the rights of individual patients, it is not rooted solely in the cultural value of individualism. Rather, it stems from a value many cultures recognize, especially those that aspire to democracy and a just social order: the notion that powerful agents, be they from governmental or nongovernmental organizations, may not invade the personal lives, and especially the bodies, of ordinary citizens.

The prominent American sociologist Renée Fox accurately describes the early focus of American bioethics: "From the outset, the conceptual framework of bioethics has accorded paramount status to the value-complex of individualism, underscoring the principles of individual rights, autonomy, self-determination, and their legal expression in the jurisprudential notion of privacy."[1] Critics of mainstream bioethics within the United States and abroad have complained about the narrow focus on autonomy and the concept of individual rights. Such critics

argue that much – if not most – of the world embraces a value system that places the family, the community, or the society as a whole above that of the individual person. But we need to ask: What follows from value systems that accord the individual a lower priority than the group? It hardly follows that individual patients should not be granted a right to full participation in medical decisions. Nor does it follow that individual doctors need not be obligated to disclose information or obtain their patients' voluntary, informed consent. It surely does not follow that the needs of society or the community for organs, bone marrow, or blood should permit those bodily parts or products to be taken from individuals without their permission. What might follow, however, is that patients' families may be fuller participants in decision-making than the patient autonomy model ordinarily requires.

Perhaps we need to be reminded just why American bioethics began with such a vigorous defense of autonomy. It is because patients traditionally had few, if any, rights of self-determination: Doctors neither informed patients nor obtained their consent for treatment or for research. In a country founded on conceptions of liberty and freedom, it was at least odd that the self-determination Americans so highly prized in other areas of life was largely absent from the sphere of medical practice. An evolution took

Original publication details: Ruth Macklin, "The Doctor–Patient Relationship in Different Cultures," pp. 86–107 from *Against Relativism: Cultural Diversity and the Search of Ethical Universals in Medicine*, © 1999 by Oxford University Press, Inc. By permission of Oxford University Press, USA.

place in the United States over a period of many years, from an early court ruling in 1914 that required surgeons to obtain the consent of patients through a series of informed consent cases in the 1950s and 1970s. By the time bioethics became an international field of study, paternalistic medicine had been largely transformed in the United States and patients' rights had been solidly established. The same developments are occurring today in the many developing countries where bioethics has more recently become a topic of interest and study. Although most of these countries lack the tradition of individualism that marks North American culture, the legal guarantee of certain rights of the individual has in the past few decades been one of the goals of social and political reformers.

Cross-cultural misunderstandings can affect the way people in one country perceive a situation in another. Participating in a workshop in the Philippines,[2] I encountered an example of a common cross-cultural misunderstanding about informed consent. The discussion focused on the ethical principle of respect for persons and its role in justifying the need to inform patients and obtain their permission to carry out therapeutic or research procedures. A Filipino physician in the audience objected that informed consent may be needed in the United States, where people do not trust their doctors, but, he said, in the Philippines patients place great trust in their physicians. Doctors do not need to protect themselves against lawsuits by having patients sign a consent form.

Throughout the world (and even at times in the United States), people confuse informed consent with the informed consent document. The Filipino physician misunderstood two things: first, the ethical basis for informed consent; and second, the difference between the *process* of informing and obtaining permission and the piece of paper (the documentation) attesting that the process took place. The ethical judgment that patients should be full participants in their treatment decisions is the ethical justification for the doctrine of informed consent. It is not the protection of the doctor, as the Filipino physician believed, that serves as an ethical basis for the practice. Although it is true that the number of medical malpractice lawsuits in the United States far exceeds that in other countries, especially in the developing world, that phenomenon bears little relation to whether patients lack trust in their doctors.

"Physicians Treat Patients Badly"

"Physicians treat patients badly" was a constant theme in virtually all of the developing countries I visited. Unfortunately, many of the shortcomings in the physician—patient relationship that are all too common in many countries continue to exist in the United States, as well. A major difference is that patients in this country are more aware of their legal and moral rights and are consequently more assertive. An Egyptian physician said that in Egypt there is no process by which consent is obtained in clinical practice. She complained that there is no physician—patient communication, in part because doctors do not have the time. Patients are not told about complications, about medical errors, or anything that transpires in the course of treatment. Patients can get no information whatsoever from doctors about their diagnosis, prognosis, or proposed treatment. Before surgical procedures, papers are signed. But those papers say nothing at all. Patients who ask questions are viewed by the doctors as "impolite," and in any case doctors do not like to answer questions posed by patients.

This Egyptian physician did not seek to defend the customary practices of doctors in her country or to argue that they were reflections of cultural values in Egypt. On the contrary, she was attempting in her work to introduce reforms into medical practice in order to bring about better treatment of patients. When I asked what possible remedies there could be for all these ethical shortcomings, she replied by describing two broad strategies. The first is to document abuses – violations of patients' rights, failures to obtain proper informed consent, and the like; the second is to mount a campaign by lobbying, bringing these issues before the public, and putting cases into court. I asked whether these steps are likely to be effective, and she replied that they can succeed in raising consciousness and awareness and further that people have received some compensation when their cases have reached the courts. Gathering cases and making them public can be used to mount campaigns. By this means reforms might be accomplished. The Egyptian physician's criticism of practices in her own country and the specific reforms she sought to introduce show that, however different in other ways the culture of Egypt may be from that of Western nations, the ethical ideal that requires physicians to treat their patients with respect is widely acknowledged, if not always honored.

A colleague in Mexico gave a similar account of the lack of recognition of patients' rights in her country.[3] One example was a story told to her by the doorman of her building. His wife was in labor and went to the public hospital. She remained in labor for 2 days, during which time neither the woman nor her husband were told anything about her condition. Eventually she gave birth and was discharged from the hospital while the baby had to remain there for a while longer. Still the couple was told nothing. My colleague expressed her outrage at this situation, blaming the doctors in public hospitals for their unwillingness to disclose information to patients, much less to obtain properly informed consent.

While I agreed that this was an outrage, I noted that things were not so very different years ago in the United States. It is a mere 40 years since the concept of informed consent to treatment was introduced into the legal domain and probably only about 25 years since the practice of obtaining informed consent took root. Still, my Mexican colleague insisted, there are cultural differences. As an example, she cited the pervasive corruption in Latin America as a difference between that region and the North. "What, no corruption in the United States or in Europe?" was my surprised reaction. Of course there is, but we have a much lower tolerance for official corruption, we make strenuous efforts to root it out, and we probably succeed more often in punishing instances that are discovered.

In India I heard more stories about how doctors treat patients badly. One physician described the efforts he and others have been making to inform and enlist the public in opposing unethical medical practices.[4] He recounted a long list of horrors: incompetent doctors practicing poorly or negligently; untrained and unlicensed doctors practicing medicine; physicians overcharging patients; and more. The array of unethical behavior ranged from genuine malpractice to arrogance and indifference to patients. I asked about legal recourse, and here the situation is just as bleak. There exists a body called the Medical Council of India, which is supposed to be responsible for monitoring and dealing with the standard of care delivered by physicians. But this is a peer review system in which

doctors protect other doctors. When cases of blatant malpractice are brought before this council, they fail to find the physician at fault. As a result, nothing is done to remedy instances of actual malpractice or the behavior of incompetent physicians. Patients can, in principle, bring suits against doctors. However, doctors win most of the cases brought to court in spite of their having committed actual malpractice, and judicial appeals take many years.

A different group of doctors repeated the same list of horror stories that I had heard from the first Indian physician, and more. When they mentioned the "kickback" system, I naively though they were referring only to money paid to the referring doctor by the surgeon or specialist to whom the referral was made. But they meant much more by "kickbacks," including demands by the referring doctor that the surgeon perform unnecessary procedures, charge the patient for them, and then give a percentage of the take to the referring doctor. Surgeons and other specialists who rely on referrals for their practice have to play the game or else they are not sent a single patient. Thus even doctors who begin by being ethical and idealistic end up getting caught up in a system in which they must play or fail to make a living.

All these accounts of bad behavior of physicians toward patients have little to do with cultural differences or with ethical relativism. They simply remind us that arrogance, corruption, greed, and indifference are universal character flaws that can be found in human beings throughout the world, wherever they live and whatever their profession. The chief difference between these countries and the United States lies not in a divergence in the cultural acceptance of such behavior by physicians but, rather, in the existence of laws and other forms of social control to root out and punish doctors who violate universally acknowledged ethical norms and standards of good clinical practice. The efforts of the Egyptian physician and the Indian doctors to bring about reforms in their countries are evidence of a widespread cross-cultural identification of the same ethical values that ought to govern the doctor–patient relationship everywhere. Respect for persons – in this case, individual patients – was the principle invoked implicitly or explicitly by people from Latin America, Asia, and North Africa in my visits to those regions.

Similarities and Differences

Even in those parts of the world where the cultural traditions differ radically from those in the West, certain values in the doctor–patient relationship are overarching. I participated in a meeting in Nigeria that included several non-English speaking tribal chiefs and native healers. One chief was asked for his views about helping a woman to have an abortion. (Abortion is illegal in Nigeria as in many other countries, but legal prohibitions have never succeeded anywhere in eliminating requests for or performance of the procedure.) Suppose a woman came to him, a traditional healer, asking for an abortion. What would he do? His reply was translated from his native tongue as follows: "If a client comes to me, as a professional, I will help the woman because I have the knowledge to do so." He added, however, that "the community would not be happy."

Here was a medical person – a traditional healer – referring to his "professional" obligation to his patient. He invoked precisely the same consideration most Western physicians would appeal to as a reason why they should help a woman to have an abortion despite the community's disapproval of abortion. Although the cultures may differ in significant ways, the obligations of healers to those who come to them for help remain a cultural universal, one that exists in virtually all societies.

Not every customary practice is properly termed a *tradition*. Values inherent in a social institution such as medical practice may be a reflection of a value in the culture at large, or they may be specific to that particular institution. Lack of recognition and respect for the decision-making autonomy of patients has been a feature of Western medicine throughout most of history and even today remains prominent in other parts of the world. There is a difference, however, between the professional norm in which doctors decide for their patients and a cultural norm that gives family members complete control of another's freedom of decision and action.

Similarly, not every set of norms deserves to be called a *culture*. Although phrases like "the culture of Western medicine" are tossed around, medicine is not a culture in the genuine sense of the term, as anthropologists define it. To refer to "the culture of medicine" is to speak metaphorically rather than anthropologically. As one commentator observes: "Used metaphorically, *culture* is everywhere these days.... Today the press is full of stories about the 'culture' of the Defense Department, the Central Intelligence Agency..., Congress..., and any large corporation that happens to be in the news. GQ even describes opera as being characterized by 'the culture of booing.'"[5]

Rural areas in many parts of the world still maintain many features of traditional culture in the true sense of the term. Women's health advocates in Mexico reported that in some areas the husband or mother-in-law of a woman decides whether she may visit a physician or whether she may use a method of birth control.[6] This behavior prevails today in rural areas and among indigenous groups and is sanctioned by certain beliefs and values regarding women. For example, women are believed incapable of making their own decisions; or, even if they are capable, they must remain subordinate to men; or the role of women is to reproduce and therefore they should not be permitted to choose to control their own fertility. Control by husbands and mothers-in-law of a woman's fertility is based on the traditional culture and has little to do with the social institution of medicine. Although these sorts of beliefs and values have deep cultural roots they, too, may change over time, as women's health advocates work at the grass-roots level and expose women in rural and indigenous communities to the ideas of the global women's movement. Defenders of traditional culture condemn these activists in Mexico and elsewhere as intrusive purveyors of Western feminism who seek to destroy traditional cultural values.

Interestingly, some women's health advocates worry about the effect of introducing values such as autonomy and independence to the women they work with. One social scientist used the example of women with whom they work in a traditional Mexican setting. These women have to ask permission from their mothers-in-law to visit a physician. A mother-in-law may question that decision or refuse to grant permission. The woman then asks the researcher for help. This poses a problem for the researcher: Can the researcher provide some assistance without causing the research subject further psychological damage or harm to her interests? The woman might actually be expelled from her home if the mother-in-law finds out she has gone to a physician without her permission.

While it is no doubt true that some customary practices are rooted in cultural traditions, others may simply have been passed down from one generation to the next as ways of behaving that no one questioned or sought to change. The medical profession has a long history of customary practices, but few qualify as "cultural" traditions. The custom of physicians withholding information from patients and talking, instead, to family members is probably a good example. Everyone from Western anthropologists to physicians in non-Western cultures remark on the difference between the nature of communications between doctors and patients in North America and other parts of the world as if this represents a deep-seated difference in cultural traditions. These commentators probably do not realize, or may have forgotten, that it is only a few decades since physicians in the United States began disclosing diagnoses of fatal illnesses directly to patients. One may call these norms of truth-telling a "tradition," but that would be to distort the more prevalent meaning of "tradition." That meaning is related to the concerns of the ethical relativist – that different societies have distinct and possibly incommensurate ethical values stemming from their cultural diversity.

One commentator suggests that cross-cultural differences in the physician–patient relationship are attributable to different systems of biomedical ethics. Diego Gracia, a professor of public health and history of science in Spain, distinguishes between Mediterranean biomedical ethics and the Anglo-American variety. Gracia notes that patients in Southern European nations are generally less concerned with matters related to informed consent and respect for autonomy than with trust in their physician. Mediterranean bioethics emphasizes virtues rather than rights. Accordingly, the virtue of trustworthiness is more crucial to patients than the right to information.[7]

But Gracia also points to a recent trend in Mediterranean countries, a trend that once again shows the evolution of the physician–patient relationship and the introduction of new ethical values. Gracia notes that, in all Mediterranean countries, respect for patients' autonomy and the right of patients to participate in medical decisions have grown extensively in the last decades. Coming some decades after the patients' rights

movement began in the United States, this new trend in the Mediterranean countries also includes complaints about health care workers' failure to provide information and for nonconsensual touching.

This phenomenon is one of historical evolution of the doctor–patient relationship rather than a cross-cultural difference between individualistic American culture and the more communitarian or virtue-based value systems in other countries. If the "culture" of medicine has evolved in this way first in the United States and shortly thereafter in some European countries, it is reasonable to suppose that the wider culture – society as a whole – may undergo other changes. No country today is so isolated from the rest of the world that it can remain aloof from and immune to cross-cultural influences.

Conceptions of Autonomy: East and West

A Japanese physician, Noritoshi Tanida, describes sharp differences between features of Japanese and Western culture related to the role of the individual.[8] Tanida says that tradition has left little room for the individual or for individualism in Japan; yet he acknowledges that, since the opening of Japan to the West about 130 years ago, Western individualism was introduced into the country. Nevertheless, most Japanese are much less individualistic than are Westerners, a feature that is evident in the decision-making process. In general, Tanida notes, there is no open discussion or clear responsibility, but rather a process of mutual dependency. As a result, the person most affected by a decision may not be informed of what is happening and is not always a part of the decision-making process. The clearest example of this, Tanida holds, is concealing the truth from cancer patients in the practice of clinical medicine.

Another East Asian, Ruiping Fan, puts forth an even stronger view of the difference between East and West with regard to the individual's role in medical decision-making.[9] Fan argues that the Western concept of autonomy, which demands self-determination on the part of the individual, is incommensurable with the East Asian principle of autonomy, which requires family determination. In contending that these two notions of autonomy are incommensurable, Fan insists that there is no shared abstract content between the Western and Eastern principles of autonomy; the two are separate and distinct.

One conclusion that can be drawn from the contrast between East and West is that there simply is no universal ethic regarding disclosure of information, informed consent, and decision-making in medical practice. Not only do these practices differ as a matter of fact in different societies, but they are incompatible. This conclusion is obviously true for the descriptive thesis of ethical relativism: Truth-telling, informed consent, and decision-making about medical treatment vary in different cultures. Furthermore, if we accept Fan's account, a conceptual variation exists as well; autonomy means something different in East Asia from what it signifies in the West.

The East Asian principle of autonomy holds that "Every agent should be able to make his or her decisions and actions harmoniously in cooperation with other relevant persons."[10] Thus, when patients and family are in harmony, they decide together. That situation probably prevails most of the time in Western medical practice as well. However, it is the family who has the final authority to make clinical decisions in accordance with the East Asian principle. According to Ruiping Fan, if a patient requests or refuses a treatment while a relevant family member disagrees with that decision, the doctor should not simply follow the patient's wish but should urge the patient and the family to negotiate and come to an agreement before the physician will act. It is the family that constitutes the autonomous social unit, and the physician may not act contrary to their decision.

This example of cultural diversity raises the enduring question of normative ethical relativism: Has Western bioethics arrived at the ethically right position with regard to respecting the individual autonomy of the patient? Is the practice in other cultures of deferring to the patient's family, or leaving the decision in the hands of the physician, right in those cultures although it would be wrong in the United States?

The emphasis on autonomy, at least in the early days of bioethics in the United States, was never intended to cut patients off from their families by insisting on an obsessive focus on the patient. Rather, it was intended to counteract the predominant mode of paternalism on the part of the medical profession. In fact, there was little discussion of where the family entered in and no presumption that a family-centered approach to sick patients was somehow a violation of the patient's autonomy. Most patients want and need the support of their families whether or not they seek to be autonomous agents regarding their own care. Respect for autonomy is perfectly consistent with recognition of the important role that families play when a loved one is ill. Autonomy has fallen into such disfavor among some ethicists in the United States that the pendulum has begun to swing in the direction of families, with urgings to "take families seriously"[11] and even to consider the interests of family members equal to those of the competent patient.[12]

Fan says that some people may deny that what he refers to as the "East Asian principle of autonomy" can even be characterized as a principle of autonomy. He nevertheless defends his use of the term, noting that the word for autonomy in the Chinese language is often used not only for individuals, but also for units like a family or a community. The same is true in the English language: In its political sense, *autonomy* means "self-rule" and can therefore apply to communities, countries, and, as in Mexico, universities.

Fan demonstrates that the East Asian principle of autonomy has significant implications for truth-telling, informed consent, and advance directives in the East Asian clinical setting. If a physician directly informs a patient about a diagnosis of a terminal disease instead of first telling a member of the family, that would be extremely rude and inappropriate. Interestingly, however, while East Asian custom allows the family to choose a treatment on behalf of a competent patient, the family may not readily refuse a treatment on behalf of a competent patient. This is evidently because of the underlying assumption that a treatment recommended by a physician will be beneficial to the patient, whereas it is at least questionable whether a withholding or withdrawing of treatment is in the interests of a competent patient.

So when it comes to actually making medical decisions, who should decide? Should it be patients themselves in the West, in accordance with the principle of autonomy as "self-determination," and families of patients in the East, in accordance with the "family-determination-oriented" principle? There is little doubt at this point that in the United States the patient with decisional capacity holds the moral and legal right to decide, with very rare exceptions. Those exceptions include some cases in which a pregnant woman's refusal of an intervention is deemed harmful to the life or health of the fetus (forced cesarean sections are the clearest example of this) and the situation in which physicians judge a treatment to be "medically futile" and take the decision-making out of the patient's hands. But these exceptions are contested by those who contend that pregnant women should have all the rights of other competent patients and that a physician's assessment that a treatment is "medically futile" should not replace the patient's wish for the treatment, which may have psychological value.

So we are left with ethical relativism. As Ruiping Fan puts it: "Which principle is more true: the Western principle of autonomy or the East Asian principle of autonomy? Who should give up their own principle and turn to the principle held by the other side?"[13] Fan's own solution is to adopt the procedural principle of freedom, allowing both Western and East Asian people to follow their respective and incommensurable principles of autonomy. Interestingly, Fan's solution appeals to a higher principle, that of freedom or liberty. He acknowledges as much and articulates the principle of freedom commonly associated with Western philosophical and political thought: "Every group of people as well as every single individual has freedom to act as they see appropriate, insofar as their action does not harm other people."[14] That sounds remarkably like something John Stuart Mill might have written.

Application of this principle appears to grant to an individual patient the right to reject the cultural custom of family autonomy in favor of individual decision-making. But would it really? If East Asian patients insisted on their freedom to act as they deem appropriate, doing so might damage family harmony, so perhaps other people would be harmed after all. Ruiping Fan does not raise the explicit question of what individual patients or physicians might do, but refers only to "Western and East Asian people" being free to follow their respective principles of autonomy. It leaves ambiguous the status of the individual patient in East Asia and possibly also the role of a family in the West that seeks to follow the family-determination notion of autonomy.

Is this a relativist solution? Fan says no, it is not to surrender to ethical relativism, "but to secure the most reasonable in a peaceful way in this pluralist world."[15] This reply embraces tolerance and is a practical accommodation to cross-cultural diversity. If not a surrender to relativism, how can we characterize Fan's position? Fan himself describes this type of thought as a "transcendental argument for a content-less principle that ought to be employed in a secular pluralist society."[16] This merely replaces the puzzling with the obscure. Philosophy should seek to explain and clarify, not to obfuscate and muddy. We have to do better.

Truth-Telling

In the Western world the custom of withholding information from patients goes back at least as far as Hippocrates. Hippocrates admonished physicians to perform their duties

> calmly and adroitly, concealing most things from the patient while you are attending to him. Give necessary orders with cheerfulness and sincerity, turning his attention away from what is being done to him; sometimes reprove sharply and emphatically, and sometimes comfort with solicitude and attention, revealing nothing of the patient's future or present condition.[17]

Does this ancient practice represent a tradition of some cultural group? If so, which one? Ancient Greek tradition, carried down through the Greco-Roman empire? That would not have been a likely influence on Asian medical practice. If it is part of any "culture" at all, it is that of the medical profession (speaking metaphorically), renowned throughout the ages for its paternalism. Medical paternalism remains the rule rather than the exception in Asia and Latin America, and it persists to a somewhat lesser extent in some parts of Western Europe, as well.

The shift in attitude toward disclosing the diagnosis to cancer patients began to occur in the United States in the late 1960s, a millennial moment since the time of Hippocrates. Although often portrayed as a cultural tradition, one in which many countries diverge from the preeminence accorded to the individual in the United States, nondisclosure by physicians to patients appears rather to have been a nearly universal customary practice dictated by medical professionals throughout the world.

But things change. Attitudes and practices of physicians in the United States have undergone a striking reversal in the past three decades. A study conducted in 1961 revealed that 90% of physicians did not inform their patients of the diagnosis of cancer.[18] When that study was redone in 1977, it revealed that 98% of doctors usually informed patients of the diagnosis of cancer.[19] It is entirely possible that such changes will begin to occur in other countries as well. Evidence suggests that this has already begun to happen.

These changes do not require us to impugn the motives of physicians who have thought it best not to tell patients they have cancer, nor is it to condemn the benevolence that undergirds medical paternalism in general. Now, as in the past, most justifications for withholding information from patients have rested implicitly or explicitly on an appeal to the principle of beneficence. If the behavior of doctors in the United States has changed in the past three decades or so, it is not because the principle of beneficence no longer serves as a justification or that physicians no longer act from benevolent motives. It is simply that the competing ethical principle of respect for autonomy has taken priority over the principle of beneficence in motivating and justifying physicians' behavior. Once it became evident that patients wished to know their diagnoses (or already knew they had cancer in spite of families and physicians conspiring to keep the news from them), and once physicians came to realize that disclosing a diagnosis of cancer did not typically cast the patient into a deep depression and very rarely, if ever, led to documented cases of patients committing suicide, then benevolent paternalism could no longer be sustained on ethical grounds.

From the earliest moments of modern bioethics, some people worried about the alleged requirement always to "tell the truth." In response to the claim that patients have "a right to know" their diagnosis and prognosis, challengers replied: what about "the right not to know?" Of course, there is no inconsistency here. People have a right to receive information, if they want it, and also the right to refuse to receive that information. That is precisely what "respect for persons" supports: respect for the wishes and values of the individual patient.

This is the point at which the philosophical distinction between ultimate moral principles and specific rules of conduct becomes critical. "Respect for persons" is a fundamental, or ultimate, ethical principle. The imperative "tell patients the truth about their condition" is a specific rule of conduct. Moreover, respecting a particular patient's wish not to know is perfectly consistent with the general obligation to disclose to patients their diagnosis. This also demonstrates the distinction between ethical universals and moral absolutes. "Always tell patients the truth about their condition" would be the moral absolute in this case, clearly a different imperative from one that mandates respect for the wishes of patients.

On this analysis, the answer to the question of how the case of truth telling to patients fits into the debates over ethical relativism is simple (relatively speaking). No universal ethical mandate exists to tell patients the truth about their terminal illness. Nor is it the case that telling the patients the truth is right in some countries or cultures and wrong in others. Moreover, to contend that the principle of autonomy mandates disclosure misinterprets how that ethical principle should be applied. Respect for autonomy means, among other things, acting in a way that respects the values of individuals. Individuals' values often mirror the predominant values of their country or culture, but they do not always do so. When they do, we must be sensitive to those values and respectful of the people who hold them.

A lingering problem, however, is that doctors often do not know or do not take the time or trouble to find out the patient's values. They take the family's word for whether the patient "can handle" the information. Or they simply honor the family's wish not to tell the patient. Here is where the practice in the United States is most likely to diverge from that in other countries. Because respect for the patient's autonomy has become entrenched in American medical practice, most physicians will probably not automatically comply with the family's wish not to reveal a diagnosis of cancer or other fatal or terminal illness.

It is clear from published reports in the medical and bioethical literature that doctors in other countries do readily honor a family's request not to tell the patient a diagnosis of cancer or other terminal illness. I believe that behavior is as much a reflection of the still dominant paternalism of physicians as it is an expression of a cultural value. When respect for autonomy is not recognized as an ethical principle in medical practice, physicians see no need to find out whether a patient wants to know the diagnosis of cancer or terminal illness. Medicine has always been paternalistic and hierarchical. In some ways, the culture of medicine remains paternalistic in the United States, as anyone can attest who has heard physicians urge the omission of "scary" items from consent forms.

A medical oncologist from Italy, who had practiced for a while in the United States, reported what she had learned in medical school.[20] The Italian Deontology Code, written by the Italian Medical Association, included the following statement: "A serious or lethal prognosis can be hidden from the patient, but not from the family."[21] That was in the late 1970s. The Deontology Code was revised in 1989, with this statement: "The physician has the duty to provide the patient – according to his cultural level and abilities to understand – the most serene information about the diagnosis, the prognosis and the therapeutic perspectives and their conse-quences....Each question asked by the patient has to be accepted and answered clearly." The code goes on to grant to physicians the well-known "therapeutic privilege" of withholding information if disclosure would be harmful to the patient, and in that case the information must be communicated to the family. But the revised code still represents a sharp reversal from the presumption of nondisclosure in the code of a mere decade earlier.

The Italian oncologist who wrote about this shift stated her belief that ethics is connected to cultural values and varies in different societies. She rejected a belief in "absolute values" in favor of respecting the pluralism of different cultures. This was by way of background to her contention that "the Italian society is not prepared for the American way." She explained further, saying that even today Italians believe that patients will never acquire enough knowledge to enable them to understand what physicians tell them and therefore to participate in their own care. Italians still believe that protecting an ill family member from painful information prevents the sick person from suffering alone, from isolation, and is essential for keeping the family together.

Is it reasonable to expect that these attitudes will gradually be transformed, just as similar attitudes were in the United States several decades ago? The Italian oncologist waffled a bit on this point. On the one hand, she stated her belief that "Italians should not borrow the American way." On the other hand, she urged Italians to learn from Americans and "try to find a better Italian way." As examples of changes taking place within the medical profession, she noted courses in bioethics in universities and medical meet-ings on truth-telling and communicating with patients. In the end, she reached the conclusion that "the only way to respect both Italian ethical principles and the patient's autonomy and dignity is to let the patient know that there are no barriers to communi-cation and to the truth."[22] What is most peculiar is the reference to "Italian ethical principles." Withholding information from patients is not a function of ethnic traditions but rather of how the medical profession has historically conducted its practice in most places in the world. It is also a class phenomenon, since doctors are typically better educated than most of their patients and question the ability of patients to fully understand what they have been told.

A mere 5 years after its 1989 revision, the Italian code of medical ethics was revised once again. The revision reflected the "constantly changing relation-ship between the medical profession and society, and between physicians and patients."[23] In the newly revised code, the "Italian way" has come very close to the "American way." Article three of the new code adds to the physician's obligation expressed in the 1989 code "to respect the dignity of the human being" the additional obligation to respect the patient's freedom of choice. Article four of the new code adds the physi-cian's obligation to respect the rights of the individual, and extensive revisions of the doctrine of informed consent are in conformity with other modern codes of ethics. The code mandates respect for the decisional autonomy of the patient, even in cases in which the life of the patient is threatened.[24]

Equally striking are revisions on the topic of confi-dentiality. Whereas the earlier Italian code permitted doctors to conceal the truth from the patient and disclose it to the next of kin, the new code essentially prohibits nondisclosure to the patient and disclosure to a third party. Two exceptions to this rule are, first, when the patient specifically authorizes disclosure to others and, second, when there is potential for harm to a third party.[25] It would be absurd to conclude that "Italian ethical principles" have changed in this brief interlude between the 1989 code and the more recent revisions. Instead, as the authors of an article describing the new code observe, "from a paternalistic attitude in which the physician, for the good of the patient, felt authorised and justified to set aside the personal requests of the patient and even to violate his wishes, a therapeutic alliance has evolved, in which the two partners together try to decide on the clinical choices that best promote the patient's wellbeing."[26]

Changes are also occurring in Asia, a region of the world often cited as adhering to family and group values almost to the exclusion of recognizing the importance of the individual. A Japanese physician observes that the concept of informed consent has recently been recognized in his country, yet he acknowledges that most Japanese physicians withhold information about diagnosis and prognosis from their patients who have cancer.[27] It is reasonable to wonder whether "informed consent" means the same thing in Japan as it does in the West. One report notes that the Bioethics Council of the Japanese Medical Association introduced the idea of "Japanese informed consent," which was to be carried out in accordance with the prevailing medical paternalism in that country.[28] A survey in Japan showed that 67% of physicians would disclose the diagnosis to patients with early cancer, but only 16% would tell those with advanced cancer. Studies from other countries show that many patients do want to be informed of a diagnosis of cancer, but a discrepancy exists between patients' preferences and physicians' attitudes.[29]

A physician speaking at an international conference about truth-telling in Japanese medicine[30] described a number of cultural features that help to explain physicians' reluctance to disclose a bad prognosis. That reluctance stems from patients' unwillingness to receive such information, which in turn is based on deeper cultural roots. Patients want to have an "edited" version of the truth. They enter a tacit conspiracy with their family and the physician to avoid a difficult subject. This results in the family taking over all responsibility and decisions for the patient's illness. Although many patients will guess and come to know the truth eventually, they still will not ask directly. This

behavior is rooted in the Japanese ethos in which silent endurance is a virtue. The aim is to make dying easier, not to invoke a dogma of telling patients the truth. Patients want to die as calmly and peacefully as possible, and that goal is more readily achieved if they remain ignorant of their prognosis. Relatives assume the burden of making an intuitive judgment of whether the patient wants to know the diagnosis and can handle it. Not to accept one's death gallantly is worse than death itself. Physicians, patients, and families all want to avoid a "disgraceful upset" that conveying bad new could produce. The physician who explained all this echoed what others discussing medicine in Japan have said: Despite powerful influences from Western countries, Japan is not totally Westernized, yet the Japanese do not want to stick to their old traditions completely. The physician ended by saying that the Japanese people must achieve a new type of death education, with more ethical emphasis, closer to the Western style of dealing with death.

But let us assume that a cultural gap does exist between North American practices of disclosing bad news to patients and different customs in other parts of the world. What should we conclude about whether one cultural practice is "right" and the other "wrong"? How does this example fit into the debates over ethical relativism?

The answer depends entirely on how the question is framed and how the situation is described. Consider the following alternative descriptions.

1 Doctors and patients in the United States believe that patients should be told the truth about a diagnosis of terminal illness. Doctors and patients in other countries believe that doctors should tell the family but not the patient. The ethical principle of "respect for autonomy" mandates that doctors treat patients as autonomous individuals and so must inform them about their illness. The truth-telling practice in the United States conforms to this principle and is ethically right, whereas the nondisclosure practice in other countries violates this practice and is ethically wrong.

2 Autonomy is the predominant value in North American culture. Doctors and patients in the United States adhere to an autonomy model of disclosure in medical practice. Family-centered values

are more prominent than individual autonomy in other cultures. Doctors and patients in these cultures adhere to a family-centered practice of disclosure of terminal illness. Therefore, it is right to disclose to a patient a diagnosis of terminal cancer in the United States and wrong to make that same disclosure in the other countries.

3　Autonomy is the predominant value in North American culture, but disclosure of terminal illness by doctors to patients is nevertheless a fairly recent practice. The US population comprises many recent immigrants, and some cultural groups adhere to family-centered values from their country of origin, especially in specific matters such as disclosure of terminal illness. Family-centered values predominate in other countries, but practices such as disclosure of a diagnosis of terminal illness have begun to change in those places. "Respect for persons" requires that in any country or culture, doctors should discuss with their patients whether they want to receive information and make decisions about their medical care or whether they want the physician to discuss these matters only with the family.

The third description is obviously the "right" answer. What is wrong with the other two descriptions shows what is frequently amiss in debates over ethical relativism. Description 1 has two main flaws. The first is the common failing of distorting or misusing the principle of respect for autonomy. The principle does not require inflicting unwanted information on people; rather, it requires first finding out how much and what kind of information they want to know and then

respecting that expressed wish. When the principle of autonomy is interpreted in that way, nothing automatically follows regarding whether patients should be told the truth about their diagnosis. The second flaw is the assumption that all people in a country or culture have the same attitudes and beliefs toward the values that predominate in that culture. In a Los Angeles study of senior citizens' attitudes toward disclosure of terminal illness, in no ethnic group did 100% of its members favor disclosure or nondisclosure to the patient. Forty-seven percent of Korean-Americans believed that a patient with metastatic cancer should be told the truth about the diagnosis, 65% of Mexican-Americans held that belief, 87% of European-Americans believed patients should be told the truth, and 89% of African-Americans held that belief. If physicians automatically withheld the diagnosis from Korean-Americans because the majority of people in that ethnic group did not want to be told, they would be making a mistake almost 50% of the time.[31]

Description 2 is flawed for one of the same reasons that description 1 is flawed: It presupposes that all people in a country or culture have the same attitudes and beliefs toward the values that predominate in that culture. That assumption is clearly false, as the Los Angeles study just cited demonstrates. In a multicultural society such as the United States, ethical relativism poses an array of problems not likely to arise in countries that enjoy a common cultural heritage (if any such countries still remain). "Multiculturalism is good," its proponents contend.[32] Whether or not that is true, it surely causes difficulties for doctors and patients.

Notes

1　Renée C. Fox, "The Evolution of American Bioethics: A Sociological Perspective," in George Weisz (ed.), *Social Science Perspectives on Medical Ethics* (Philadelphia: University of Pennsylvania Press, 1990), p. 206.

2　The workshop, part of my Ford Foundation project, took place in Davao, Mindanao, in December 1995.

3　This interview took place in February 1996 during my second Ford Foundation project.

4　This interview took place in April 1994 in Bombay.

5　Christopher Clausen, "Welcome to Postculturalism," *The Key Reporter*, Vol. 62, No. 1 (1996), p. 2.

6　This meeting took place during my Ford Foundation visit to Mexico in February 1993.

7　Diego Gracia, "The Intellectual Basis of Bioethics in Southern European Countries," *Bioethics*, Vol. 7, No. 2/3 (1993), pp. 100–101.

8　Noritoshi Tanida, "Bioethics Is Subordinate to Morality in Japan," *Bioethics*, Vol. 10 (1996), pp. 202–211.

9　Ruiping Fan, "Self-Determination vs. Family-Determination: Two Incommensurable Principles of Autonomy," *Bioethics*, Vol. 11 (1997), pp. 309–322.

10　Fan, p. 316.

11 James Lindemann Nelson, "Taking Families Seriously," *Hastings Center Report*, Vol. 22 (1992), pp. 6–12.

12 John Hardwig, "What About the Family?" *Hastings Center Report*, Vol. 20 (1990), pp. 5–10.

13 Fan, p. 322.

14 Fan, p. 322.

15 Fan, p. 322.

16 Fan quotes this phrase from H. Tristram Engelhardt, Jr., *The Foundations of Bioethics*, 2nd edition (New York: Oxford University Press, 1996).

17 Citation from President's Commission for the Study of Ethical Problems in Medicine and Biomedical and Behavioral Research, *Making Health Care Decisions* (Washington, DC: Government Printing Office, 1982), Vol. 1, p. 32.

18 D. Oken, "What To Tell Cancer Patients: A Study of Medical Attitudes," *Journal of the American Medical Association*, Vol. 175 (1961), pp. 1120–1128.

19 Dennis H. Novack, Robin Plumer, Raymond L. Smith, Herbert Ochitill, Gary R. Morrow, and John M. Bennett, "Changes in Physicians' Attitudes Toward Telling the Cancer Patient," *Journal of the American Medical Association*, Vol. 341 (1979), pp. 897–900.

20 Antonella Surbone, "Truth-Telling to the Patient," *Journal of the American Medical Association*, Vol. 268 (1992), pp. 1661–1662.

21 Surbone, p. 1661.

22 Surbone, p. 1662.

23 Vittorio Fineschi, Emanuela Turillazzi, and Cecilia Cateni, "The New Italian Code of Medical Ethics," *Journal of Medical Ethics*, Vol. 23 (1997), p. 238.

24 Fineschi, Turillazzi, and Cateni, pp. 241–242.

25 Fineschi, Turillazzi, and Cateni, p. 243.

26 Fineschi, Turillazzi, and Cateni, p. 241.

27 Atsushi Asai, "Should Physicians Tell Patients the Truth?" *Western Journal of Medicine*, Vol. 163 (1995), pp. 36–39.

28 Tanida, p. 208.

29 Asai, p. 36.

30 Shin Ohara, "Truth-Telling and We-Consciousness in Japan: Some Biomedical Reflections on Japanese Civil Religion," unpublished paper presented at the conference, "Ethics Codes in Medicine and Biotechnology," Freiburg, Germany, October 12–15, 1997.

31 Leslie J. Blackhall, Sheila T. Murphy, Gelya Frank, Vicki Michel, and Stanley Azen, "Ethnicity and Attitudes Toward Patient Autonomy," *Journal of the American Medical Association*, Vol. 274, No. 10 (1995), pp. 820–825.

32 Blaine J. Fowers and Frank C. Richardson, "Why Is Multiculturalism Good?" *American Psychologist*, Vol. 51, No. 6 (1996), pp. 609–621.

77

Amputees by Choice

Carl Elliott

I get glimpses of the horror of normalcy.
Arturo Binewski in *Geek Love*

In January 2000 British newspapers began running articles about Robert Smith, a surgeon at Falkirk and District Royal Infirmary, in Scotland. Smith had amputated the legs of two patients at their request, and he was planning to carry out a third amputation when the trust that runs his hospital stopped him. These patients were not physically sick. Their legs did not need to be amputated for any medical reason. Nor were they incompetent, according to the psychiatrists who examined them. They simply wanted to have their legs cut off. In fact, both the men whose limbs Smith amputated have declared in public interviews how much happier they are, now that they have finally had their legs removed.[1]

Healthy people seeking amputations are not nearly as rare as one might think. In May 1998 a seventy-nine-year-old man from New York traveled to Mexico and paid $10,000 for a black-market leg amputation; he died of gangrene in a motel. In October 1999 a mentally competent man in Milwaukee severed his arm with a homemade guillotine, and then threatened to sever it again if surgeons reattached it. That same month a legal investigator for the California state bar, after being refused a hospital amputation, tied off her

legs with tourniquets and began to pack them in ice, hoping that gangrene would set in, necessitating an amputation. She passed out and ultimately gave up. Now she says she will probably have to lie under a train, or shoot her legs off with a shotgun.[2]

For the first time that I am aware of, we are seeing clusters of people seeking voluntary amputations of healthy limbs and performing amputations on themselves. The cases I have identified are merely those that have made the newspapers. On the Internet there are enough people interested in becoming amputees to support a minor industry. One discussion listserv has over 3,200 subscribers.

"It was the most satisfying operation I have ever performed," Smith told a news conference in February 2000. "I have no doubt that what I was doing was the correct thing for those patients."[3] Although it took him eighteen months to work up the courage to do the first amputation, Smith eventually decided that there was no humane alternative. Psychotherapy "doesn't make a scrap of difference in these people," psychiatrist Russell Reid, of Hillingdon Hospital in London, said in a BBC documentary on the subject, called "Complete Obsession."[4] "You can talk till the

Original publication details: Carl Elliott, "Amputees by Choice," pp. 208–10, 210–15, 219–23, 227–31, 234–6, 323–6 from *Better Than Well: American Medicine Meets the American Dream*, New York and London: W. W. Norton, 2003. Copyright © 2003 by Carl Elliott. Used by permission of W. W. Norton & Company, Inc.

Bioethics: An Anthology, Third Edition. Edited by Helga Kuhse, Udo Schüklenk, and Peter Singer.
© 2016 John Wiley & Sons, Inc. Published 2016 by John Wiley & Sons, Inc.

cows come home; it doesn't make any difference. They're still going to want their amputation, and I know that for a fact." Both Smith and Reid pointed out that these people may unintentionally harm or even kill themselves trying to amputate their own limbs. As retired psychiatrist Richard Fox observed in the BBC program, "Let's face it, this is a potentially fatal condition."

Yet the psychiatrists and the surgeon were all baffled by the desire for amputation. Why would anyone want an arm or a leg cut off? Where does this sort of desire come from? Smith has said that the request initially struck him as "absolutely, utterly weird." "It seemed very strange," Reid told the BBC interviewer. "To be honest, I couldn't quite understand it."

In 1977, mental health professionals published the first modern case histories of what Johns Hopkins University psychologist John Money termed "apotemnophilia" – an attraction to the idea of being an amputee.[5] Money distinguished apotemnophilia from "acrotomophilia," a sexual attraction to amputees. The suffix -*philia* is important here. It places these conditions in the group of psychosexual disorders called paraphilias, often referred to outside medicine as perversions. Fetishes are fairly common sorts of paraphilias. In the same way that some people are turned on by, say, shoes or animals, others are turned on by amputees. Not by blood or mutilation – pain is not usually what they are looking for. The apotemnophile's desire is to be an amputee, whereas the acrotomophile's desire is turned toward those who happen to be amputees. In the *Bulletin of the Menninger Clinic* that same year, another group of researchers described a patient who would have qualified as both an apotemnophile and an acrotomophile: a twenty-eight-year-old man who was sexually attracted to female amputees, and who intensely wished to be handicapped himself.[6] [...]

Reviewing the medical literature, it is easy to conclude that apotemnophilia and acrotomophilia are extremely rare. Fewer than half a dozen articles have been published on apotemnophilia, most of them in arcane journals.[7] Most psychiatrists and psychologists I have spoken with – even those who specialize in paraphilias – have never heard of apotemnophilia. On the Internet, however, it is an entirely different story.

Acrotomophiles are known on the Web as "devotees," and apotemnophiles are known as "wannabes." "Pretenders" are people who are not disabled but use crutches, wheelchairs, or braces, often in public, in order to feel disabled. Various Web sites sell photographs and videos of amputees, display stories and memoirs, recommend books and movies, and provide chat rooms, meeting points, and electronic bulletin boards. Much of this material caters to devotees, who seem to be far greater in number than wannabes. It is unclear just how many people out there actually want to become amputees, but there exist numerous wannabe and devotee listservs and Web sites.

Like Robert Smith, I have been struck by the way wannabes use the language of identity and selfhood in describing their desire to lose a limb. "I have always felt I should be an amputee." "I felt, this is who I was." "It is a desire to see myself, be myself, as I 'know' or 'feel' myself to be." This kind of language has persuaded many clinicians that apotemnophilia has been misnamed – that it is not a problem of sexual desire, as the -philia suggests, but a problem of body image. What true apotemnophiles share, Smith said in the BBC documentary, is the feeling "that their body is incomplete with their normal complement of four limbs." Smith has elsewhere speculated that apotemnophilia is not a psychiatric disorder but a neuropsychological one, with biological roots.[8] Perhaps it has less to do with desire than with being stuck in the wrong body.

Yet what exactly does it mean to be stuck in the wrong body? Even people who use more conventional enhancement technologies often use the language of self and identity to explain why they want these interventions: a woman who says she is "not herself" unless she is on Prozac; a bodybuilder who says he took anabolic steroids because he wants to look on the outside the way he feels on the inside; a transsexual who describes her experience as "being trapped in the wrong body." The image is striking, and more than a little odd. In each case the true self is the one produced by medical science.

Some people are inclined to think of this language as a literal description. Maybe some people really do feel as if they have found their true selves on Prozac. Maybe they really did feel incomplete without cosmetic surgery. Yet it may be better to think of these descriptions not as literally true but as expressions of an ambivalent moral ideal – a struggle between the impulse toward self-improvement and the impulse to be true to oneself. Not that I can see no difference between a middle-aged man rubbing Rogaine on his head every morning and a man whose discomfort in his own body is so all-consuming that he begins to think of suicide. But we shouldn't be surprised when any of these people, healthy or sick, use phrases like "becoming myself" and "I was incomplete" and "the way I really am" to describe what they feel, because the language of identity and selfhood surrounds us. This is simply the language we use now to describe the way we live.

Perhaps the question to be answered is not only why people who want to be amputees use the language of identity to describe what they feel, but also what exactly they are using it to describe. One point of contention among clinicians is whether apotemnophilia is, as John Money thought, really a paraphilia. "I think that John Money confused the apotemnophiles and the acrotomophiles," Robert Smith wrote to me from Scotland. "The devotees I think are paraphilic, but not the apotemnophiles." The question here is whether we should view apotemnophilia as a problem of sexual desire – a variety of the same genre of conditions that includes pedophilia, voyeurism, and exhibitionism. Smith, in agreement with many of the wannabes I have spoken with, believes that apotemnophilia is closer to gender-identity disorder, the diagnosis given to people who wish to live as the opposite sex. Like these people, who are uncomfortable with their identities and want to change sex, apotemnophiles are uncomfortable with their identities and want to be amputees.

But deciding what counts as apotemnophilia is part of the problem in explaining it. Some wannabes are also devotees. Others who identify themselves as wannabes are drawn to extreme body modification. There seems to be some overlap between people who want finger and toe amputations and those who seek piercing, scarring, branding, genital mutilation, and such. Some wannabes, Robert Smith suggests, want amputation as a way to gain sympathy from others. And finally, there are "true" apotemnophiles, whose desire for amputation is less about sex than about

identity. "My left foot was not part of me," says one amputee, who had wished for amputation since the age of eight. "I didn't understand why, but I knew I didn't want my leg."[9] Another says, "My body image has always been as a woman who has lost both her legs."[10] A woman in her early forties wrote to me, "I will never feel truly whole with legs." Her view of herself has always been as a double amputee, with stumps of five or six inches.

Many devotees and wannabes describe what Lee Nattress, an adjunct professor of social work at Loma Linda University, in California, calls a "life-changing" experience with an amputee as a child. "When I was three years old, I met a young man who was completely missing all four of his fingers on his right hand," writes a twenty-one-year-old woman who says she is planning to have both her arms amputated. "Ever since that time, I have been fascinated by all amputees, especially women amputees who were missing parts of their arms and wore hook prostheses." Hers is not an unusual story. Most wannabes trace their desire to become amputees back to before the age of six or seven, and some will say that they cannot remember a time when they didn't have the desire. Nattress, who surveyed fifty people with acrotomophilia (he prefers the term "amelotasis") for a 1996 doctoral dissertation, says that much the same is true for devotees. Three quarters of the devotees he surveyed were aware of their attraction by the age of fifteen, and about a quarter wanted to become amputees themselves.[11]

Many of the news reports about the case at the Falkirk and District Royal Infirmary identified Smith's patients as having extreme cases of body dysmorphic disorder. Like people with anorexia nervosa, who believe themselves to be overweight even as they become emaciated, people with body dysmorphic disorder are preoccupied with what they see as a physical defect: thinning hair, nose shape, facial asymmetry, the size of their breasts or buttocks. They are often anxious and obsessive, constantly checking themselves in mirrors and shop windows, or trying to disguise or hide the defect. They are often convinced that others find them ugly. Sometimes they seek out cosmetic surgery, but frequently they are unhappy with the results and ask for more surgery. Sometimes they redirect their obsession to another part of the body.[12] But none of this really describes most of the people who are looking for amputations – who, typically, are not convinced they are ugly, do not imagine that other people see them as defective, and are usually focused exclusively on amputation (rather than on, say, a receding hairline or bad skin). Amputee wannabes more often see their limbs as normal, but as a kind of surplus. Their desires frequently come with chillingly precise specifications: for instance, an above-the-knee amputation of the right leg.

Like many conditions, it is not clear whether the desire to be an amputee is new, or whether it is merely taking a new shape in response to changing cultural conditions. The psychiatrist Douglas Price has unearthed and translated a 1785 text by the French surgeon and anatomist Jean-Joseph Sue that describes an Englishman who may have been both a wannabe and a devotee. The Englishman was in love with a woman who was an amputee, and wanted to become an amputee himself. He offered 100 guineas to a French surgeon to amputate his healthy leg. The surgeon refused, protesting that he did not have the proper equipment. But he changed his mind when the Englishman produced a gun, and then he proceeded to amputate the Englishman's leg under threat of death. Later he received a letter in the mail, along with payment for the amputation. "You have made me the happiest of all men," explained the Englishman, "by taking away from me a limb which put an invincible obstacle to my happiness."[13]

When John Money designated apotemnophilia a "paraphilia," he placed it in a long and distinguished lineage of psychosexual disorders. The grand old man of psychosexual pathology, Richard von Krafft-Ebing, cataloged an astonishing range of paraphilias in his 1906 classic *Psychopathia Sexualis*, from necrophilia and bestiality to fetishes for aprons, handkerchiefs, and kid gloves. Some of his cases involve an attraction to what he called "bodily defects." One was a twenty-eight-year-old engineer who had been excited by the sight of women's disfigured feet since the age of seventeen. Another had pretended to be lame since early childhood, limping around on two brooms instead of crutches. The philosopher René Descartes, Krafft-Ebing noted, was partial to cross-eyed women.[14]

Yet the term "sexual fetish" could be a misleading way to describe the fantasies of wannabes and devotees, if what is on the Web is any indication (and, of course, it might well not be). Many of these fantasies seem almost presexual. This is not to suggest that there is any shortage of amputee pornography on the Internet. *Penthouse* has published in its letters section many of what it terms "monopede mania" letters, purportedly from devotees, and *Hustler* has published an article on amputee fetishism. But many other amputee Web sites have an air of thoroughly wholesome middle-American hero worship, and perhaps for precisely that reason they are especially disconcerting, like a funeral parlor in a shopping mall. Some show disabled men and women attempting nearly impossible feats – running marathons, climbing mountains, creating art with prostheses. It is as if the fantasy of being an amputee is inseparable from the idea of achievement – or, as one of my correspondents put it, from an "attraction to amputees as role models." "I've summed it up this way," John Money said, a little cruelly, in a 1975 interview: "Look, Ma, no hands, no feet, and I still can do it."[15] One woman, then a forty-two-year-old student and housewife whose history Money presented in a 1990 research paper, said one of the appeals of being an amputee was "coping heroically."[16] A man told Money that his fantasy was that of "compensating or overcompensating, achieving, going out and doing things that one would say is unexpected."[17] One of my wannabe correspondents wrote that what attracted him to being an amputee was not heroic achievement so much as "finding new ways of doing old tasks, finding new challenges in working things out and perhaps a bit of being able to do things that are not always expected of amputees." [...]

But how should the shared desire [of wannabes] be characterized? Some argue that the desire to have a limb amputated is no different in principle from the desires motivating other enhancement technologies, like cosmetic surgery. In the same way that a person might want to have healthy tissue removed through breast-reduction surgery, so an amputee wannabe wants to have healthy tissue removed through amputation. Cosmetic surgery is certainly not prohibited by law, and the courts have even allowed healthy organs and other tissue to be removed for medical purposes deemed worthwhile, such as the transplantation of a kidney, bone marrow, or a liver lobe from a healthy donor into a needy recipient. (Courts have allowed such transplantations even when the donor is a child or a mentally impaired adult.)[18] But others believe that the desire to have a limb amputated qualifies, at least in some cases, as a psychiatric illness, for which surgery is a potentially effective treatment. On purely pragmatic grounds, this second strategy may be the best way for wannabes to get surgeons to cooperate with them – to have the desire for amputation recognized as a mental disorder, codified in the forthcoming *DSM-V*, reported on in respected medical journals, and legitimated with diagnostic instruments, reimbursement codes, and specialty clinics.

Some clinicians do not like to admit it, but even wannabes who describe the desire for amputation as a wish for completeness will often admit that there is a sexual undertone to the desire. "For me having one leg improves my own sexual image," one of my correspondents wrote. "It feels 'right,' the way I should always have been and for some reason in line with what I think my body ought to have been like." When I asked one wannabe (who also happens to be a psychologist) if he experiences the wish to lose a limb as a matter of sex or a matter of identity, he disputed the very premise of the question. "You live sexuality," he told me. "I am a sexual being twenty-four hours a day." Even ordinary sexual desire is bound up with identity, as I was reminded by Michael First, a psychiatrist at Columbia University, who was an editor of the fourth edition of the American Psychiatric Association's *Diagnostic and Statistical Manual*. First is undertaking a study that will help determine whether apotemnophilia should be included in the fifth edition of the *DSM*. "Think of the fact that, in general, people tend to be more sexually attracted to members of their own racial group," he pointed out. What you are attracted to (or not attracted to) is part of who you are.

It is clear that for many wannabes, the sexual aspect of the desire is much less ambiguous than many wannabes and clinicians have publicly admitted. A man described seventeen years ago in the *American Journal of Psychotherapy* said that he first became aware of his attraction to amputees when he was eight years old. That was in the 1920s, when the fashion was for children to wear short pants. He remembered several boys who had wooden legs. "I became extremely

aroused by it," he said. "Because such boys were not troubled by their mutilation and cheerfully, and with a certain ease, took part in all the street games, including football, I never felt any pity towards them." At first he nourished his desire by seeking out people with wooden legs, but as he grew older, the desire became self-sustaining. "It has been precisely in these last years that the desire has gotten stronger, so strong that I can no longer control it but am completely controlled by it." By the time he finally saw a psychotherapist, he was consumed by the desire. Isolated and lonely, he spent some of his time hobbling around his house on crutches, pretending to be an amputee, fantasizing about photographs of war victims. He was convinced that his happiness depended on getting an amputation. He desperately wanted his body to match his self-image: "Just as a transsexual is not happy with his own body but longs to have the body of another sex, in the same way I am not happy with my present body, but long for a peg-leg."[19]

The comparison of limb amputation to sex-reassignment surgery comes up repeatedly in discussions of apotemnophilia, among patients and among clinicians. "Transsexuals want healthy parts of their body removed in order to adjust to their idealized body image, and so I think that was the connection for me," psychiatrist Russell Reid stated in the BBC documentary "Complete Obsession." "I saw that people wanted to have their limbs off with equally as much degree of obsession and need and urgency."[20] The comparison is not hard to grasp. When I spoke with Michael First, he told me that his group was considering calling it "amputee identity disorder," a name with obvious parallels to the gender-identity disorder that is the diagnosis given to prospective transsexuals. The parallel extends to amputee pretenders, who, like cross-dressers, act out their fantasies by impersonating what they imagine themselves to be.

But gender-identity disorder is far more complicated than the "trapped in the wrong body" summary would suggest. For some patients seeking sex-reassignment surgery, the wish to live as a member of the opposite sex is itself a sexual desire. Ray Blanchard, a psychologist at the University of Toronto's Center for Addiction and Mental Health, has studied men being evaluated for sex-reassignment surgery. He has found an intriguing difference between two groups: men who are homosexual and men who are heterosexual, bisexual, or asexual. The "woman trapped in a man's body" tag fit the homosexual group relatively well. As a rule, these men had no sexual fantasies about being a woman; only a small percentage say they are sexually excited by cross-dressing, for example. Their main sexual attraction is to other men.[21]

Not so for the men in the other group: almost all are excited by fantasies of being a woman. Three-quarters of them are sexually excited by cross-dressing. Blanchard coined the term "autogynephilia" – "the propensity to be sexually aroused by the thought or image of oneself as a woman" – as a way of designating this group. Note the suffix -philia. Blanchard thought that a man might be sexually excited by the fantasy of being a woman in more or less the same way that people with paraphilias are sexually excited by fantasies of wigs, shoes, handkerchiefs, or amputees. But here sexual desire is all about sexual identity – the sexual fantasy is not about someone or something else, but about yourself. Anne Lawrence, a transsexual physician and a champion of Blanchard's work, calls this group "men trapped in men's bodies."[22]

If sexual desire, even paraphilic sexual desire, can be directed toward one's own identity, then perhaps it is a mistake to try to distinguish pure apotemnophilia from the kind that is contaminated with sexual desire. Reading Blanchard's work, I was reminded of a story that Peter Kramer tells in his introduction to *Listening to Prozac*. Kramer describes a middle-aged architect named Sam who came to him with a prolonged depression set off by business troubles and the deaths of his parents. Sam was charming, unconventional, and a sexual nonconformist. He was having marital trouble. One of the conflicts in his marriage was his insistence that his wife watch hard-core pornographic videos with him, although she had little taste for them. Kramer prescribed Prozac for Sam's depression, and it worked. But one of the unexpected side-effects was that Sam lost his desire for hard-core porn. Not the desire for sex: his libido was undiminished. Only the desire for pornography went away.[23]

Antidepressants like Prozac have long been used to treat compulsive desires, and some clinicians are also starting to use them for patients with paraphilias and sexual compulsions.[24] Can an antidepressant selectively knock out an aberrant or unwanted sexual desire, while leaving ordinary sexual desire intact? Even more interesting, though, is the way in which Sam came to view his desire. Before treatment he had thought of his taste for porn simply as part of who he was – an independent, sexually liberated guy. Once it was gone, however, it seemed as if it had been a biologically driven obsession. "The style he had nurtured and defended for years now seemed not a part of him but an illness," Kramer writes. "What he had touted as independence of spirit was a biological tic." Does this suggest that erotic desire is simply a matter of biology? Not necessarily. What it suggests is that an identity can be built around a desire. The person you have become may be a consequence of the things you desire. This may be as true for wannabes as it was for Sam, especially if their desires have been with them for as long as they can remember. [...]

Even if we assume that the obsessive desire for amputation is evidence of a psychiatric disorder, it is unclear why such a desire should be growing more common just now. Why do certain psychopathologies arise, seemingly out of nowhere, in certain societies and during certain historical periods, and then disappear just as suddenly? Why did young men in late-nineteenth-century France begin lapsing into fugue states, wandering the continent with no memory of their past, coming to themselves months later in Moscow or Algiers with no idea how they got there? What was it about America in the 1970s and 1980s that made it possible for thousands of Americans and their therapists to come to believe that two, ten, even dozens of personalities could be living in the same head? One does not have to imagine a cunning cult leader to envision alarming numbers of desperate people asking to have their limbs removed. One has only to imagine the right set of historical and cultural conditions.

So, at any rate, suggests the philosopher and historian of science Ian Hacking, who has attempted to explain just how "transient mental illnesses" such as the fugue state and multiple-personality disorder arise.[25] A transient mental illness is by no means an imaginary mental illness, though in what ways it is real (or "real," as the social constructionists would have it) is a matter for philosophical debate. A transient mental illness is a mental illness that is limited to a certain time and place. It finds an "ecological niche," as Hacking puts it. In the same way that the idea of an ecological niche helps to explain why the polar bear is adapted to the Arctic ecosystem, or the chigger to the South Carolina woods, Hacking's ecological niches help to explain the conditions that made it possible for multiple-personality disorder to flourish in late-twentieth-century America and the fugue state to flourish in nineteenth-century Bordeaux. If the niche disappears, the mental illness disappears along with it.

Hacking does not intend to rule out other kinds of causal mechanisms, such as traumatic events in child-hood and neurobiological processes. His point is that a single causal mechanism isn't sufficient to explain psychiatric disorders, especially those contained within the boundaries of particular cultural contexts or historical periods. Even schizophrenia, which looks very much like a brain disease, has changed its form, outlines, and presentation from one culture or historical period to the next. The concept of a niche is a way to make sense of these changes. Hacking asks: What makes it possible, in a particular time and place, for this to be a way to be mad?

Hacking's books *Rewriting the Soul* and *Mad Travelers* are about "dissociative" disorders, or what used to be called hysteria. He has argued, I think very persuasively, that psychiatrists and other clinicians helped to create the epidemics of fugue in nineteenth-century Europe and multiple-personality disorder in late-twentieth-century America simply by the way they viewed the disorders – by the kinds of questions they asked patients, the treatments they used, the diagnostic categories available to them at the time, and the way these patients fit within those categories. He points out, for example, that the multiple-personality-disorder epidemic rode on the shoulders of a perceived epidemic of child abuse, which began to emerge in the 1960s and which was thought to be part of the cause of multiple-personality disorder. Multiple personalities were a result of child-hood trauma; child abuse is a form of trauma. It seemed to make sense that, if there were an epidemic of child abuse, we would see more and more multiples.

Sociologists have made us familiar with the idea of "medicalization," which refers to the way that a society manages deviant behavior by bringing it under the medical umbrella.[26] A stock example of medicalization is the way that homosexuality was classified by the American Psychiatric Association as a psychiatric disorder until the 1970s. Many enhance-ment technologies become popular only when they are conceptualized as treatments for medicalized conditions, such as Ritalin and Adderall for Attention Deficit Disorder (medicalized distractibility) or Paxil and Nardil for social phobia (medicalized shyness). Many technologies (including some of those used to treat medicalized conditions) are also used as "normalizing" procedures. Normalizing procedures bring a deviant behavior, characteristic, or personality type back within a range considered normal, or at least aesthetically acceptable. Cosmetic facial surgery for children with Down's syndrome is a normalizing procedure, in that it is performed not for medical reasons but to make the child look more like an ordinary child. Both "normalization" and "medicali-zation" are related to the processes that Hacking describes, but Hacking is onto something slightly different. By "transient mental illnesses" he does not have in mind new descriptions of old conditions so much as conditions that look new in themselves.[27]

Crucial to the way that transient mental illnesses arise is what Hacking calls "looping effects," by which he means the way a classification affects the thing being classified. Unlike objects, people are conscious of the way they are classified, and they alter their behavior and self-conceptions in response to their classification. Look at the concept of "genius," Hacking says, and the way it affected the behavior of people in the Romantic period who thought of themselves as geniuses. Look also at the way in which their behavior in turn affected the concept of genius. This is a looping effect: the concept changes the object, and the object changes the concept. To take a more contemporary example, think about the way that the concept of a "gay man" has changed in recent decades, and the way this concept has looped back to change the way that gay men behave. Looping effects apply to mental disorders too. In the 1970s, Hacking argues, therapists started asking patients they thought might be multiples if they had been abused as children, and patients in therapy began remembering episodes of abuse (some of which may not have actually occurred). These memories reinforced the diagnosis of multiple-personality disorder, and once they were categorized as multiples, some patients began behaving as multiples are expected to behave. Not intentionally, of course, but the category "multiple-personality disorder" gave them, as Hacking provocatively puts it, a new way to be mad.

I am simplifying a very complex and subtle argument, but the basic idea should be clear. By regarding a phenomenon as a psychiatric diagnosis – treating it, reifying it in psychiatric diagnostic manuals, developing instruments to measure it, inventing scales to rate its severity, establishing ways to reimburse the costs of its treatment, encouraging pharmaceutical companies to search for effective drugs, directing patients to support groups, writing about possible causes in journals – psychiatrists may be unwittingly colluding with broader cultural forces to contribute to the spread of a mental disorder.

Suppose doctors started amputating the limbs of wannabes. Would that contribute to the spread of the desire? Could we be faced with an epidemic of people wanting their limbs cut off? Most people would say, Clearly not. Most people do not want their limbs cut off. It is a horrible thought. The fact that others are getting their limbs cut off is no more likely to make these people want to lose their own limbs than state executions are to make people want to be executed. And if by some strange chance more people did ask to have their limbs amputated, that would be simply because more people with the desire were encouraged to "come out" rather than suffer in silence.

I'm not so sure. Clinicians and patients alike often suggest that apotemnophilia is like gender-identity disorder, and that amputation is like sex-reassignment surgery. Let us suppose they are right. Fifty years ago the suggestion that tens of thousands of people would someday want their genitals surgically altered so that they could change their sex would have been ludicrous. But it has happened. The question is, Why? One answer would have it that this is an ancient condition, that there have always been people who fall outside the traditional sex classifications, but that only during the past forty years or so have we developed the surgical and endocrinological tools to fix the problem.

But it is possible to imagine another story, that our cultural and historical conditions have not just revealed transsexuals but created them. That is, once "transsexual" and "gender-identity disorder" and "sex-reassignment surgery" became common linguistic currency, more people began conceptualizing and interpreting their experience in these terms. They began to make sense of their lives in a way that hadn't been available to them before, and to some degree they actually became the kinds of people described by these terms.

I don't want to take a stand on whether either of these accounts is right. It may be that neither is. It may be that there are elements of truth in both. But let us suppose that there is some truth to the idea that sex-reassignment surgery and diagnoses of gender-identity disorder have helped to create the growing number of cases we are seeing. Would this mean that there is no biological basis for gender-identity disorder? No. Would it mean that the term is a sham? No. Would it mean that these people are faking their dissatisfaction with their sex? Again, no. What it would mean is that certain social and structural conditions – diagnostic categories, medical clinics, reimbursement schedules, a common language to describe the experience, and, recently, a large body of academic work and transgender activism – have made this way of interpreting an experience not only possible but more likely. [...]

I will confess that my opinions about amputation as a treatment have shifted since I began talking to wannabes. My initial thoughts were not unlike those of a magazine editor I approached about writing a piece on the topic, who replied, "Thanks. This is definitely the most revolting query I've seen for quite some time." Yet there is a simple, relentless logic to these people's requests for amputation. "I am suffering," they tell me. "I have nowhere else to turn." They realize that life as an amputee will not be easy. They understand the problems they will have with mobility, with work, with their social lives; they realize they will have to make countless adjustments just to get through the day. They are willing to pay their own way. Their bodies belong to them, they tell me. The choice should be theirs. What is worse: to live without a leg or to live with an obsession that controls your life? For at least some of them, the choice is clear – which is why they are talking about chain saws and shotguns and railroad tracks.

And to be honest, haven't surgeons made the human body fair game? You can pay a surgeon to suck fat from your thighs, lengthen your penis, augment your breasts, redesign your labia, even (if you are a performance artist) implant silicone horns in your forehead or split your tongue like a lizard's. Why not amputate a limb? At least Robert Smith's motivation was to relieve his patients' suffering.

It is exactly this history, however, that makes me worry about a surgical "cure" for apotemnophilia. Psychiatry and surgery have had an extraordinary and very often destructive collaboration over the past seventy-five years or so: clitoridectomy for excessive masturbation, cosmetic surgery as a treatment for an "inferiority complex," intersex surgery for infants born with ambiguous genitalia, and – most notorious – the frontal lobotomy. It is a collaboration with few unequivocal successes. Yet surgery continues to avoid the kind of ethical and regulatory oversight that has become routine for most areas of medicine. If the proposed cure for apotemnophilia were a new drug, it would have to go through a rigorous process of regulatory oversight. Investigators would be required to design controlled clinical trials, develop strict eligibility criteria, recruit subjects, get the trials approved by the Institutional Review Board, collect vast amounts of data showing that the drug was safe and effective, and then submit their findings to the US Food and Drug Administration. But this kind of oversight is not required for new, unorthodox surgical procedures. (Nor, for that matter, is it required for new psychotherapies.) New surgical procedures are treated not like experimental procedures but like "innovative therapies," for which ethical oversight is much less uniform.

The fact is that nobody really understands apotemnophilia. Nobody understands the pathophysiology; nobody knows whether there is an alternative to surgery; and nobody has any reliable data on how well surgery might work. Many people seeking amputations are desperate and vulnerable to exploitation. "I am in a constant state of inner rage," one wannabe wrote to me. "I am willing to take that risk of death to achieve the needed amputation. My life inside is just too hard to continue as is." These people need help, but, when the therapy in question is irreversible and disabling, it is not at all clear what that help should be. Many wannabes are convinced that amputation is the only possible solution to their problems, yet they have never seen a psychiatrist or a psychologist, have never tried medication, have never read a scientific paper about their problems. More than a few of them have never even spoken face to face with another human being about their desires. All they have is the Internet, and their own troubled lives, and the place where those two things intersect. "I used to pretend as a child that my body was 'normal' which, to me, meant short, rounded thighs," one wannabe wrote to me in an e-mail message. "As a psychology major, I have analyzed and reanalyzed, and re-reanalyzed just why I want this. I have no clear idea."

Editors' Note

Various passages have been deleted. Readers interested in following up specific issues may want to consider the original publication.

Notes

1   P. Taylor, "'My Left Foot Was Not Part of Me,'" *The Guardian*, February 6, 2000, 14; Tracey Lawson, "Therapist Praises Doctor's Bravery," *The Scotsman*, February 1, 2000; Clare Dyer, "Surgeon Amputated Healthy Legs," *British Medical Journal* 320 (February 5, 2000): 332.

2   J. H. Burnett, "Southside Man Uses Homemade Guillotine to Sever Arm," *Milwaukee Journal Sentinel*, October 7, 1999; Stephen McGinty and Sue Leonard, "Secret World of Would-Be Amputees," *Sunday Times*, February 6, 2000; Michelle Williams, "Murder Trial Opens for Fetish M.D.," *Associated Press*, September 29, 1999.

3   Cherry Norton, "Disturbed Patients Have Healthy Limbs Amputated," *The Independent*, February 1, 2000.

4   BBC2 Horizon, "Complete Obsession," Transcript of television documentary, screened in United Kingdom Feb 17, 2000; http://www.bbc.co.uk/science/horizon/1999/obsession.shtml. More recently, the Australian radio program "Soundprint" broadcast a documentary on amputee wannabes, availableon-line at: http://soundprint.org/radio/display_show/ID/87/name/Wannabes.

5   J. Money, R. Jobaris, and G. Furth, "Apotemnophilia: Two Cases of Self-Demand Amputation as a Paraphilia," *Journal of Sex Research* 13:2 (May 1977): 114–25.

6 P. L. Wakefield, A. Frank, R. W. Meyers, "The Hobbyist: A Euphemism for Self-mutilation and Fetishism," *Bulletin of the Menninger Clinic* 41 (1977): 539–52.

7 W. Everaerd, "A Case of Apotemnophilia: a Handicap as a Sexual Preference," *American Journal of Psychotherapy* 37:2 (April 1983): 285–93; J. Money, "Paraphilia in Females: Fixation on Amputation and Lameness: Two Personal Accounts," *Journal of Psychology and Human Sexuality* 3:2 (1990): 165–72; R. L. Bruno, "Devotees, Pretenders and Wannabes: Two Cases of Factitious Disability Disorder," *Sexuality and Disability* 15:4 (Winter 1997): 243–60; Wakefield, Frank, and Meyers, "The Hobbyist." On acrotomophilia, see Grant Riddle, *Amputees and Devotees* (New York: Irvington Publishers, 1989).

8 Keren Fisher, Robert Smith, "More Work Is Needed to Explain Why Patients Ask for Amputation of Healthy Limbs," letter, *British Medical Journal* 320 (April 22, 2000): 1147. Smith and Gregg Furth also recently published a book titled *Amputee Identity Disorder: Information, Questions, Answers, and Recommendations About Self-Demand Amputation* (Portland, Ore.: 1st Books Library, 2000).

9 Taylor, "'My Left Foot Was Not Part of Me.'"

10 Helen Rumbelow and Gillian Harris, "Craving That Drives People to Disability," *The Times* (London), February 1, 2000.

11 L. E. Nattress, "Amelotasis: A Descriptive Study." Unpublished doctoral dissertation, Walden University, 1996.

12 Katherine A. Phillips, *The Broken Mirror: Understanding and Treating Body Dysmorphic Disorder* (New York: Oxford University Press, 1996). Phillips is a psychiatrist at Brown University who has also published extensively on body dysmorphic disorder in the medical literature. The patients she describes generally do not much resemble amputee wannabes, but she does briefly mention a man who asked a surgeon to remove his nose (p. 289).

13 J-J Sue, *Anecdotes Historiques, Littéraires et Critiques, sur la Médecine, la Chirurgie, & la Pharmacie* (Paris: Chez la Bocher, 1785). I am indebted to Dr. Price, who wrote to me about this text and generously sent me his translation, along with other materials on amputation.

14 Richard von Krafft-Ebing, *Psychopathia Sexualis* (New York: Putnam, 1906; originally published in 1898), 234–38.

15 B. Taylor, "Amputee Fetishism: An Exclusive Journal Interview with Dr. John Money of Johns Hopkins," *Maryland State Medical Journal* (March 1976): 35–38.

16 John Money, "Paraphilia in Females: Fixation on Amputation and Lameness, Two Personal Accounts," *Journal of Psychology and Human Sexuality* 3:2 (1990): 165–72.

17 Money, Jobaris, and Furth, "Apotemnophilia."

18 Josephine Johnston has written about the legal aspects of healthy limb amputation for her master's dissertation at the University of Otago. She and I have also written about the issue in a forthcoming article in *Clinical Medicine*. For a comprehensive review of moral and legal aspects of organ and tissue donation by children, see Robert Crouch, "The Child as Tissue and Organ Donor" (Master's Dissertation, McGill University, Department of Philosophy, 1996); also R. Crouch and C. Elliott, "Moral Agency and the Family: The Case of Living Related Organ Transplantation," *Cambridge Quarterly of Healthcare Ethics* 8:3 (1999), 257–87. See also Sally Sheldon and Stephen Wilkinson, "Female Genital Mutilation and Cosmetic Surgery: Regulating Non-Therapeutic Body Modification," *Bioethics* 12:4 (1998): 263–85.

19 Everaerd, "A Case of Apotemnophilia," 286–87.

20 BBC2 Horizon, "Complete Obsession."

21 R. Blanchard, "The Concept of Autogynephilia and the Typology of Male Gender Dysphoria," *Journal of Nervous and Mental Disease* 177:10 (October 1989): 616–23; R. Blanchard, "Clinical Observations and Systematic Studies of Autogynephilia," *Journal of Sex and Marital Therapy* 17:4 (Winter 1991): 235–51; R. Blanchard, "Nonmonotonic Relation of Autogynephilia and Heterosexual Attraction," *Journal of Abnormal Psychology* 101:2 (May 1992): 271–76.

22 See Anne Lawrence's Web site at: http://www.annelawrence.com. Blanchard has also found that a subset of autogynephiles is sexually aroused by the thought of themselves not as complete women, but as having a mixture of male and female sex characteristics. He calls this group "partial autogynephiles." See R. Blanchard, "The She-Male Phenomenon and the Concept of Partial Autogynephilia," *Journal of Sex and Marital Therapy* 19:1 (Spring 1993): 69–76.

23 Peter D. Kramer, *Listening to Prozac* (London: Fourth Estate, 1993), ix–xi.

24 M. P. Kafka and J. Hennen, "Psychostimulant Augmentation during Treatment with Selective Serotonin Reuptake Inhibitors in Men with Paraphilias and Paraphilia-Related Disorders: A Case Series," *Journal of Clinical Psychiatry* 61:9 (September, 2000): 664–70; A. Abouesh and A. Clayton, "Compulsive Voyeurism and Exhibitionism: A Clinical Response to Paroxetine," *Archives of Sexual Behavior*

28:1 (February, 1999): 23–30; V. B. Galli, N. J. Raute, B.
J. McConville, S. L. McElroy, "An Adolescent Male
with Multiple Paraphilias Successfully Treated with
Fluoxetine," *Journal of Child and Adolescent
Psychopharmacology* 8:3 (1998): 195–97; R. Balon,
"Pharmacological Treatment of Paraphilias with a
Focus on Antidepressants," *Journal of Sex and Marital
Therapy* 24:4 (October–December, 1998): 241–54;
M. P. Kafka, "Sertraline Pharmacotherapy for
Paraphilias and Paraphilia-Related Disorders: An
Open Trial," *Annals of Clinical Psychiatry* 6:3
(September 1994): 189–95.

25 See especially Ian Hacking, *Mad Travelers: Reflections
on the Reality of Transient Mental Illness* (Charlottesville:
University Press of Virginia, 1998) and Ian Hacking,
*Rewriting the Soul: Multiple Personality and the Sciences
of Memory* (Princeton, N.J.: Princeton University
Press, 1995).

26 Ivan Illich, *Limits to Medicine* (London: Marion Boyars,
2002); Peter Conrad and Joseph W. Schneider, *Deviance
and Medicalization: From Badness to Sickness* (Philadelphia,
Pa.: Temple University Press, 1992); Allan V. Horwitz,
Creating Mental Illness (Chicago: University of Chicago
Press, 2002).

27 What looks like an entirely new condition may on closer
examination turn out to be a new variation on previously
existing conditions. Hacking suggests, for instance, that
some of the young men characterized as having fugue
states would, in the terms of today, be characterized as
having epilepsy or traumatic head injuries.

78

Rational Desires and the Limitation of Life-Sustaining Treatment

Julian Savulescu[1]

That suicide may often be consistent with interest and with our duty to ourselves, no one can question, who allows that age, sickness or misfortune may render life a burden, and make it worse even than annihilation. I believe that no man ever threw away life, while it was worth keeping. For such is our natural horror of death, that small motives will never be able to reconcile us to it.[2]

Two hundred years after Hume wrote these words, society has begun to accept that continued life can be worse than "annihilation" and that it is not necessary, nor even desirable, to prolong all lives as long as is biologically possible. "Quality of life", we now realize, is important too. "Living wills", "advance directives", "respect for autonomy", "shared decision-making" and "the right to die" help to ensure, we hope, that the days are over when a person is compelled to live a life which has become a burden.

But there is naive optimism in Hume's second belief "that no man ever threw away life, while it was worth keeping". There are good reasons to believe that normal people, when evaluating whether it is worth living in a disabled state in the future, will undervalue that existence, even in terms of what they judge is best. I will examine the evidence for this claim and look at the implications for the limitation of life-sustaining treatment of formerly competent but now incompetent patients, and, more briefly towards the end, of competent patients.

It has been argued that life-sustaining treatment ought to be limited when such treatment limitation shows respect for a patient's autonomy or promotes a patient's best interests. I will examine what constitutes autonomy and, more briefly, best interests. My point is that being autonomous involves making a certain kind of judgement about how one would like one's life to go over time. It involves making some quite complex evaluations. Which of a person's desires are expressions of her autonomy may not be transparent to casual observation. Indeed, some expressed desires actually prevent a person achieving what she judges to be best for herself. We need to look more carefully and critically at a person's desire to die before we can say that the satisfaction of it shows respect for her autonomy.

Questions of treatment limitation can be considered from many perspectives: that of the patient, his family or society. I will consider only the patient perspective. I use the term "treatment limitation" to cover all cases of withdrawal, with-holding or other limitation of treatment. Within the following sets, I use the terms interchangeably: "preference" and "desire", "autonomy" and "autonomous desire" as a desire which is a reflection of a person's autonomy.

Original publication details: Julian Savulescu, "Rational Desires and the Limitation of Life-Sustaining Treatment," pp. 191–222 from *Bioethics* 8: 3 (1994). Reproduced with permission from John Wiley & Sons.

The President's Commission Report

The President's Commission Report argues that treatment of incompetent patients ought to be limited if the patient in question would now desire to have treatment limited, if he were competent. This, it is said, shows respect for the patient's former autonomy. If there is no evidence concerning what the patient would desire, treatment can be limited if it is not in the best interests of the patient.

> [D]ecisionmaking for incapacitated patients should be guided by the principle of substituted judgement which promotes the underlying values of self-determination and well-being better than the best interests standard does.[3]

This is based on the guiding principle of the Commission that "a competent patient's self-determination is and should be given greater weight than other people's views of that individual's well-being."[4]

How are we to determine what a person "would now desire"? It has been claimed that a patient's past preference on a related issue or an advance directive constitute sufficient evidence for what a patient would now desire. I will argue that this sense of "what a patient would now desire" is insufficient to determine whether life-sustaining treatment should be limited. It reflects a superficial understanding of what constitutes autonomy. In order to respect former autonomy, we must ask not, "What would the patient now desire if she were competent?" but rather, "What would she now rationally desire if she were competent?" I will argue that self-determination is reflected by a person's own rational hypothetical desire.

Part I. What Is Autonomy?

The word, "autonomy", comes from the Greek: *autos* (self) and *nomos* (rule or law).[5] Autonomy is self-government or self-determination.[6] "Self-determination" entails forming a plan for how one's life is to go through time, choosing a course according to what one judges is best for oneself. Autonomous choice fundamentally involves evaluation. It is not mere desiring; rather, it is the weighing and evaluation of alternatives by a person, and the selection of that alternative which best suits that person's judgement for how she wants her life to go.

Self-determination thus entails forming desires for how one's life is to go through time. These desires constitute what has been called a "life-plan". As Robert Young puts it, "[t]he term 'plan' here is intended to refer merely to whatever it is that a person broadly wants to do in and with his or her life – thus covering career, life-style, dominant pursuits and the like."[7]

Consider the simple case of a person, P, faced with only two options: A and B. Imagine that A is suffering from a painful cancer of the knee and B is having one leg amputated. For P's preference for, say, A over B to be a reflection of his autonomy, it must be the result of an evaluation which judges that A is better for P than B. I will argue that being self-determining entails that this evaluation must involve at least three elements: (1) knowledge of relevant, available information concerning each of the states of affairs A and B, (2) no relevant, correctable errors of logic in evaluating that information, and (3) vivid imagination by P of what each state of affairs would be like for P. Call those desires which satisfy these three conditions, rational desires. That is,

> P rationally desires some state of affairs, that q, iff (if and only if) P desires that q while in possession of all relevant, available information, without making relevant, correctable error of logic and vividly imagining what each state of affairs would be like for P.[8]

I will argue that:

> One necessary condition for a desire to be an expression of a person's autonomy is that it is a rational desire or that it satisfies a rational desire.

An argument for rational desiring

The paradigm of P autonomously choosing between A and B entails that, having appreciated the nature of A and B, P judges that one is better for her, fits better her "life-plan", than the other. Why is appreciation of the nature of A and B important? It will not do when imagining what A is like, to imagine some state of affairs which is more like B, or some other state of affairs. If P were to choose A under these circumstances, what P would really want is B, or something else entirely.

To appreciate A and B as they are, P must know what each is like. P must have relevant, available information. If the cancer will cease to be painful after a certain stage, or if amputation means that P can still get around with an artificial leg, it is relevant for P to know these facts.

In processing this information, it is important not to make any errors of logic. P is trying to decide whether to have the amputation. Suppose that P is provided with information and reasons in the following way.

1. There is a risk of dying from anaesthesia. (true)
2. I will require an anaesthetic if I am to have an amputation. (true)
   Therefore, if I have an amputation, I will die. (false)

Logic is important so that P can utilize available facts properly. False beliefs which arise from correctable errors of logic corrupt P's appreciation of the nature of the options, and so reduce the autonomy of his choice.

Not all false beliefs corrupt P's appreciation of the alternatives in a way that matters. If P falsely believes that the anaesthetic will be a gas, when it will be an intravenous infusion with the same risks and benefits, then this false belief is irrelevant to her evaluation of the anaesthetic.[9]

What if P desires to not use all the information available or to commit errors of logic? What if P wants only to know whether an operation will cause pain or not? P does not want to know what its likely benefits are. Should these be presented to her?

The default answer is that such a person should be compelled to confront available information and any errors of logic. It is only then that she can be self-determining and get what she really wants.

However, there is one exception. Some people really do not want to know all the facts. They might not want to know the risk of death which an operation entails. That desire ought to be respected *if it has been evaluated in the right way*. Has the person stood back and imagined the possible implications of such a stance? If she has, then this desire may inherit autonomy from the parent evaluation. If, however, such a reaction is driven only by fear or dread, then it is not an expression of autonomy.

In addition to the provision and logical evaluation of information, the evaluative sense of the concept of

self-determination requires that alternative states of affairs be "vividly imagined". What constitutes "vivid imagination"?

The concept of choice entails that at least two alternatives are available. But it is necessary to distinguish between subjectively and objectively available alternatives. Two objective alternatives may exist with only one subjective alternative.

Consider the converse of Locke's case.[10] A person in a room is led to believe that the room is locked, when in fact one door is open. This person has two objective alternatives (leave or stay) but only one subjective alternative (stay).

It is only after a person has presented herself with subjective alternatives that she can choose the one which she judges is best. One cannot logically be self-determining if one believes that the path one sets upon is the only path available. As far as demonstrating that a choice is autonomous, it is not enough to show that objective choices exist. There must be some evidence that subjective choice exists.[11]

In order to be self-determining, then, it is necessary to present at least two alternatives to oneself. However, being autonomous requires more than this. Imagine that P wants to do A. P believes that he could also do B. However, it is A that P wants to do, and P does not think about B. In one sense, it can be said that P has *chosen* to do A, but is doing A an expression of P's *self-determination*? Self-determination is an active process of actually determining the path of one's life. In order to judge what is best for himself, P must think and imagine what it would be like for her if A and B obtained, and what the consequences, at least in the short term, of each of these would be for her. Thus, not only must P know what A and B are like, but she must also imagine what A and B would be like *for her*. I call this vivid imagination.

Depression is one condition which may reduce one's capacity to be autonomous. The depressive loses the ability to "live life". At the level of decision-making, this manifests itself as an inability to present alternatives in the vivid colours of reality. Once depression has lifted, some describe the experience as being one where a "veil" descended on their life. Such people may be cognizant of facts, but they are unable to engage in the process of vivid imagination which brings meaning to our choices.[12]

Two objections to vivid imagination

1 Uncertainty and the unknown   It might be argued that my requirement for vivid imagination is too strong. We do not require that our choices be made with knowledge of what the outcome will be. Such knowledge may not be available. The paradigm case is that of explorers such as Captain Cook or Columbus. These men could not have vividly imagined the outcome of their explorations, but surely their decision to explore the unknown could have been autonomous?[13]

I am not suggesting that one must vividly imagine what an alternative is like before one can autonomously choose that alternative; I am only suggesting that one must imagine it *as far as is possible*. These explorers were faced with many different courses of action. The results of some of these were clearly imaginable (like staying at home and reading a book), while the results of others were largely unpredictable (like exploring the Pacific). One can autonomously choose to explore the unknown. However, one must gather as many facts as possible about the unknown, if one is to choose to explore it autonomously.

We are in some ways like these explorers. There are various courses of action open to us, and various outcomes are possible with each course of action. Under conditions of uncertainty, we must present to ourselves a "reasonable range of alternatives" for each course of action entertained. A "reasonable range of alternatives" is that range defined by P's rational beliefs about what courses of action are open to P (and their probabilities of producing various outcomes).[14] P's beliefs are rational if they are based on an appreciation of all relevant facts available at the time to P, evaluated by P without any errors of logic being committed. We must vividly imagine these alternatives, as far as is possible.

Contrast this with an example of non-autonomously choosing the unknown. Imagine that John is considering setting out to explore an uncharted part of the interior of Africa. Although this area has not been mapped, it is known from natives who have been there that it is infested with tsetse flies. These flies cause a fatal sleeping sickness. John knows this fact, but does not vividly imagine what it would be like to be in a dense jungle infested with tsetse flies. It is not that he wants to die. He is merely a person who can't be bothered thinking carefully about the consequences of his actions. John's desire to explore the interior of Africa without appropriate precautions frustrates what he really wants: to chart the interior of Africa and stay alive.

2 Impulsiveness and choosing to ignore available facts   It might be objected that we are in many ways like John. We often choose impulsively and choose to ignore available facts, yet we do not believe that the impulsiveness of our choice precludes it from being autonomous.[15] If this is so, then vivid imagination of the alternatives is not necessary.

It is true that a person can autonomously choose to lead an impulsive life. What matters is whether she evaluates the impulsive life, whether she imagines in broad and general strokes, what it is to live an impulsive life, and what other lives are like. She can only then *autonomously* choose to live the impulsive life.

The impulsive explorer comes in two versions. In one version, at some prior point she stands back from her life and evaluates it as the best overall for her. She sees people living their lives like accountants, or crude short-sighted utilitarians, scrutinizing the value of every possible option. She decides that spontaneity is more important. This impulsive explorer is autonomous. Autonomy of choice can be inherited if the parent choice was autonomous.

In the second version, the impulsive explorer never stands back and engages in vivid imagination of the alternatives. She never evaluates her life. She is not self-determining.

Two senses of rational desiring

A rational desire can be described in an actual (non-counterfactual) sense: (1) as a desire which *does* satisfy or *has* satisfied the three evaluative conditions, or in a hypothetical (counterfactual) sense: (2) as a desire which *would* satisfy the three conditions. I favour the actual (non-counterfactual) reading.

Consider the happy follower. This person is happy simply being one of the herd. She passively does as others do, lets her friends and family decide for her, leads the most unoriginal of existences. This person can be autonomous, if she has chosen her life for a reason. Such a person may find choice burdensome, or realize that she is a bad chooser. Or perhaps she enjoys the pleasure others feel in choosing for her. If she stands back and evaluates her life as good for one of these reasons, she may be autonomous in being a follower. But if there has been no such reflection, no such deliberate choice, no such conscious planning, then her life is the paradigm of lack of autonomy.

It may be true of this latter person that, *if* she had confronted her life, she would have endorsed it. However, it is necessary for self-determination that she *determine* her life, that she *actually* chooses a certain life according to what she judges best, not that she would have chosen that life under certain ideal conditions.

It might be objected that few people have rational desires. Clearly, we hardly ever go through the process of collecting information, logically evaluating it and vividly imagining the alternatives in a formal, overt and organized way. Evaluation is often fractured over time, and in the background of our minds. Yet I believe that we do engage in this kind of evaluation. We do form considered judgements about what is best for ourselves.

Autonomy as a dispositional concept

It is important to recognize that to be autonomous it is not necessary that we are *always* evaluating states of affairs rationally, in the way I have described. Firstly, as I have shown, a desire can inherit autonomy if it springs from an overall plan or desire which is itself rational and autonomous.

However, there is a second way in which we are often autonomous at a certain time in the absence of having a rational desire at that time. Autonomy is a dispositional concept.[16] When we say that P is autonomous, we mean that P has a disposition to behave (under certain conditions[17]) in a certain way. That is, P is autonomous if P *would* behave in way A if circumstances C were present. More specifically, P is autonomous if, under certain conditions, P would bring about what she rationally evaluates to be best for herself. That is, P would act, and perhaps also form other desires, so as to realize her rational desires for how she would like her life to go. Thus, while it is necessary that a person rationally evaluate states of affairs *at some point* in order to be autonomous, it is not true that she is only autonomous when she is actually rationally desiring some end.

Being autonomous thus requires both: (1) forming a rational desire for what is best for ourselves, and (2) having a disposition to realize our rational desires, that is, having a disposition (or tendency) to bring about what we judge to be best for ourselves.

The account of rational desiring I have provided is like some accounts of valuing.[18] However, valuing is a dispositional concept.[19] (I still value freedom when I am anaesthetized, yet I may have no desires at that time. So values must not necessarily be actual desires.) The relationship between valuing and rational desiring can be put this way:

P values that q iff P would rationally desire that q in C.

"To value" is the dispositional verb to which the corresponding occurrent or episodic verb is "to rationally desire". Valuing captures the dispositional sense of being autonomous.

Ulysses and the Sirens: an example of obstructive desire

I have argued that a rational desire is a desire formed under conditions of awareness of available information, evaluated without error of logic and after engaging in a process of vivid imagination. Call a desire which does not satisfy these three conditions, a non-rational desire. Some non-rational desires frustrate the satisfaction of our rational desires, that is, obstruct the expression of our autonomy. Call these irrational or obstructive desires.

An example of obstructive desire is seen in the case of Ulysses and the Sirens. Ulysses was to pass "the Island of the Sirens, whose beautiful voices enchanted all who sailed near. [They]…had girls' faces but birds' feet and feathers…[and] sat and sang in a meadows among the heaped bones of sailors they had drawn to their death," so irresistible was their song. Ulysses desired to hear this unusual song, but also wanted to avoid the usual fate of sailors who succumbed to this desire. So he contrived to plug his men's ears with beeswax and instructed them to bind him to the mast of his ship. He told them: "if I beg you to release me, you must tighten and add to my bonds." As he passed the island, "the Sirens sang so sweetly, promising him foreknowledge of all future happenings on earth." Ulysses shouted to his men to release him. However, his men obeyed his previous orders and only lashed him tighter. They passed safely.[20]

Before sailing to the Island of the Sirens, Ulysses made a considered evaluation of what he judged was best. His order that he would remain shackled was an expression of his autonomy. In the grip of the Sirens' song, Ulysses' strongest desire was that his men release him. This may have been his only desire. But it was an irrational desire. Moreover, this desire obstructed the expression of his autonomy.

We see in this case how it is necessary to frustrate some of a person's desires if we are to respect his autonomy.

One objection

How, it might be objected, can Ulysses' desire to be released obstruct his autonomy when he has no other desire at the time of hearing the Sirens?

Ulysses did rationally desire to live and he will rationally desire to live, but he now irrationally desires to move closer to the Island. This last desire entails dying.[21] His past and future rational desires are reflections of a settled disposition to stay alive. Ulysses has this disposition at the time of hearing the Sirens, though it fails to issue in a present desire. It is out of respect for autonomy in its dispositional sense that we believe Ulysses ought to be lashed tighter to the mast.[22] It is out of respect for Ulysses' values that we restrain him.

Part II. "No Man Ever Threw Away Life, While It Was Worth Keeping"

It is difficult for a person to evaluate future states in which she suffers a significant physical disability. In such cases, there are several hurdles to forming a desire which expresses our autonomy. Obstructive desires often arise. I will now review the evidence for these claims.

Consider the following case.

Mrs X was a woman in her mid-forties with severe diabetes, and many complications of that disease, including severe vascular disease. She was admitted to hospital with pain in her foot. The circulation of blood to her foot was so poor that it required amputation. The necessity of amputation was explained to her. She, however, refused to have an amputation. She did not want to be bed- or wheelchair-bound and dependent on her husband, she said. It was carefully explained to her that most amputees were able to walk independently on an artificial leg. She did not believe that she would be able to walk on a prosthesis. She would, she said, rather die. Amputees were brought in to the ward to show that it was possible to independently ambulate with an artificial leg. Other attempts were made to dispel any false belief about amputation. She, however, remained unmoved. She was discharged home. Sometime later, she was rushed to hospital. Gangrene had developed in her foot. She was in septic shock. She became delirious. It became obvious that she would die without amputation. On death's door, the medical staff cajoled her into "consenting" to an above knee amputation, though it appeared clear to all that this was not what she had wanted and that she was at the time incompetent to consent to operation. Her amputation went well (from a medical point of view), her infection cleared and she went to a rehabilitation hospital. When one of her doctors saw her a year later, she had had a second amputation. Remarkably, she was walking on bilateral prostheses. He asked her how she was going with the amputations. "Fine," she remarked to his astonishment. "But you never even wanted the first amputation." "Yes," she replied, "but that was because I never believed that *I* would be able to walk with an amputation. It was being stuck in a wheelchair that I dreaded. But now I can get around by myself and it's not so bad."

Why did this woman refuse amputation?

The problem was not merely one of lack of information, although information could have been more effectively presented. Let us assume that all the facts had been made available. Mrs X had at least one relevantly false belief: that *she* would not be independent after an amputation. This belief was not supported by the information available to her. However, she made a second evaluative error: she failed to vividly imagine what life as an amputee would be like for her.[23]

Before I address why these evaluative errors might have occurred, I will show that in some respects

Mrs X is not an unusual case. Many people ultimately adapt to disability following life-threatening illness.

Adaptation to disability

People suffering painful or disabling illnesses often adapt to a significant decrement in function. Following a large review of the medical literature, De Haes and Van Knippenberg conclude:

It is commonly assumed that cancer and cancer treatment have a severe, negative impact on the QOL [quality of life] of patients…However, no differences were found with respect to most QOL indicators: satisfaction with family, friends, work, income, values, activities, community, local government, health, the overall quality of life; psychological functioning; anxiety, depression, positive well-being, general mental well-being; daily activities; and work satisfaction. Interestingly, survived cancer patients have reported more satisfaction with care from their partner and others than have healthy controls.[24]

There were no differences between normal and mastectomy, chemotherapy or melanoma patients over a wide range of subjective indicators of quality of life. Cancer patients judged their situation more positively and more like "normals" than patients with skin disease.[25] Patients with chronic renal failure on dialysis subjectively rank their life quality only 6% below the average of the normal population.[26] Kidney transplant recipients rank their subjective quality of life more highly than the general population rates theirs.[27] Brickman, Coates and Janoff-Bulman found that recent lottery winners were no happier than control groups. Paraplegics were less happy, though still above the midpoint of the scale.[28]

Some victims of personal tragedy even derive something positive from their experience. One polio victim remarked:

Far away from the hospital experience, I can evaluate what I have learned…I know my awareness of people has deepened and increased, that those who are close to me can want me to turn all my heart and mind and attention to their problems. I could not have learned *that* dashing all over the tennis court.[29]

Interviews with women with breast cancer revealed similar experiences:

I have much more enjoyment of each day, each moment. I am not so worried about what is or isn't or what I wish I had. All those things you get so entangled with don't seem to be part of my life right now.

You take a long look at your life and realize that many things you thought were important before are totally insignificant…What you do is put things in perspective. You find out things like relationships are really the most important things you have – the people you know and your family – everything is just way down the line. It's very strange that it takes something serious to make you realize that.[30]

Taylor concludes:

victims of life-threatening attacks, illness, and natural disaster sometimes seem from their accounts…to have benefited from it…Studies of chronic illness or conditions, such as cancer, diabetes, severe burns, cystic fibrosis, or hemophilia, and investigations of coping with the loss of a child or a spouse reveal that most people experiencing such events are able to say that their lives are as good as or better than they were before the events.[31]

It is possible to portray an overly rosy picture of serious illness. Many people do not find meaning in their illness. But many at least appear to adapt.[32]

Hurdles to evaluation: loss aversion and contrast

If it is true that many people, like Mrs X, will ultimately adapt to their disability, is there any reason to believe that they will, like Mrs X, fail to rationally evaluate those states of disability? The psychological coding mechanisms of *contrast* and *loss aversion* tend to prevent rational evaluation.

Maintenance of a state and frequent repetition of a stimulus result in adaptation. Exposure to repeated stimulation thus tends to produce a neutral subjective state, or null state. Contrasting states become the primary determinants of experience.[33] The principle of contrast states that the experience of a given stimulus or state is determined to a significant extent by its contrast to the null or present adapted state (size and rate of change of difference are important).

Consider an example. In one experiment, subjects were asked to describe the facial expression of a woman seen in a photograph. The face was "enigmatically une-motional". Before viewing this photograph, however, subjects were shown another photograph which expressed a strong emotion. The target face was judged by subjects to express a moderately intense *contrasting* emotion.[34] Tversky and Griffin have shown that perceived levels of happiness behave in a similar way.[35]

Thus, it is not the level of a person's function, but the change from whatever level she has adapted to which is important in determining a person's evaluation of that state. Although many paraplegics ultimately adapt to their level of function, becoming a paraplegic is a terrible event because one moves rapidly from a normal state to a paralysed state. One paraplegic stated in a television interview, "You probably think that I am unhappy but you are wrong. And I used to think that I knew what suffering was, but I was wrong."[36]

The phenomenon of *loss aversion* also distorts the evaluative experience. This is the psychological phenomenon where "losses loom larger than gains." The dread Mrs X had of dependency may be one example.

Consider another example. Participants in an experiment were indifferent between the following prospects: (1) equal chances to win $20 or lose $5, with a 0.5 chance to win or lose nothing and (2) equal chances to win $60 or lose $15, and a 0.5 chance to win or lose nothing. "Here, a chance to win $60 rather than $20 was needed to compensate for the risk of losing $15 rather than $5 − a ratio of 4:1 between matched differences of losses and gains."[37]

From experiments such as these, it has been concluded that "[w]hen left to their own devices…decision makers focus myopically at problems one at a time, and their choices appear to be dominated by the anticipated emotional consequences of individual losses."[38]

People often also focus on the present and near future, and discount the more distant future. They are biased to the present and near future.[39]

It would be expected, then, that people, prior to injury, will concentrate "myopically" on the loss of becoming disabled, and ignore the value of their adapted state. Kahneman and Varey conclude:

> In dealing with unfamiliar states, however, most people probably have a more accurate view of the utility of the transition than of the steady state. As a consequence,

adaptation will tend to be neglected or underestimated and differences between states correspondingly exaggerated.[40]

This is in agreement with Tversky and Griffin's conclusions:

> A common bias in the prediction of utility is a tendency to overweight one's present state or mood… A related source of error is the failure to anticipate our remarkable ability to adapt to new states…People generally have a reasonable idea of what it is like to lose money or to have a bad cold, but they probably do not have a clear notion of what it means to go bankrupt, or to lose a limb.[41]

The implication here is that people may have a good idea about treatment decisions relating to familiar problems, like having a cold, a sprained or broken limb. But, as treatment decisions pertain to more unfamiliar states, people will have more difficulty in imagining what these states will be like. The evidence is that, prior to experiencing them, they will systematically underrepresent their utility. The President's Commission appears to fail to appreciate the difficulty facing patients who make decisions concerning unfamiliar states:

> The Commission has found no reason for decisions about life-sustaining therapy to be considered differently from other treatment decisions. A decision to forego such treatment is awesome because it hastens death, but that does not change the elements of decision-making capacity and need not require greater abilities on the part of the patient.[42]

While the Commission is right that such decisions are not different to other decisions about unfamiliar states (such as those involving serious disability), they are different to the everyday health care decisions which people make about familiar health problems.

Mrs X failed to vividly imagine what it would be like to adapt to a disabled state. Loss aversion, contrast and discounting of the future prejudice appreciation of future life with disability. Importantly, false beliefs about dependency may persist even after presentation of evidence to the contrary. Kahneman and Miller describe the "well-documented" phenomenon of "the perseverance of discredited beliefs".[43] "The message…is that traces of an induced belief persist even when its evidential basis has been discredited."[44]

In conclusion, the process of vivid imagination so necessary for evaluation is no easy or straight-forward process to engage in. It involves not only the provision of much information, but the overcoming of several innate psychological hurdles.

Part III.   Limitations of Treatment of Incompetent Patients

Should Mrs X's leg have been amputated when she was incompetent?

The President's Commission Report argues that the limitation of treatment of formerly competent but now incompetent patients should attempt to achieve two goals: promotion of well-being and respect for autonomy.[45] Respect for self-determination becomes embodied in the notion of "substituted judgement". Substituted judgement attempts to arrive at a hypothetical or counter-factual preference – what the patient would prefer, were she competent now. Treatment is only to be in accordance with the best interests standard if we cannot form a substituted judgement.

How are we to determine what a patient would prefer?

Buchanan and Brock claim that there must be "sufficient evidence". Exactly what constitutes sufficient evidence is left somewhat unclear. They seem to equate it with the expression of a past preference for a related issue (including an advance directive). The manner in which they restrict the use of substituted judgement provides support for this contention. Substituted judgements do *not* represent "a surrogate exercise of the right of self-determination" if: (1) individuals "have not clearly expressed the relevant preferences prior to the onset of incompetence or because they have expressed relevant but contradictory preferences" and (2) patients have never been competent.[46]

Which desires will count as reflecting a patient's autonomy according to the President's Commission? Firstly, the principal (person making the directive) should be legally competent. Secondly, "[a] statute might require evidence that the person has the capacity to understand the choice embodied in the directive when it is executed." This capacity will be assessed in

lay terms by lay people. "Furthermore, the standard they are asked to attest to may be as low as that used in wills, unless specified differently." The principal should also understand the seriousness of the step being taken. The Commission recommends that the principal "have had a discussion with a health care professional about a directive's potential consequences".[47]

The loaded concept in these accounts is "competence". If competence to make a life and death choice means that the patient must be in possession of the available facts, without committing relevant errors of logic and vividly imagining the relevant states of affairs, then it is *ex hypothesi* true that a competent patient will make an autonomous choice.[48] However, the notions of competence and autonomy, although related, are generally though to be separate.[49] I will not address the notion of competence. It suffices to say that unless the notions of competent choice and autonomous choice are collapsed, it will be possible that a competent person will express a non-autonomous desire.

If this is right, it will not do to look only to a past competent preference if we wish to respect an incompetent patient's former autonomy. Some desires, even some competent desires, frustrate a person's autonomy. We need also to ask: was the desire obstructive?

Consider the case of Mrs X. She rationally desired to live independently (let us assume). Amputation and a prosthetic leg would have allowed her to live independently. Her false belief (that she would be dependent after an amputation) led her to desire to die. This desire prevented her from getting what she rationally desired (and valued). Her expressed desire to die was obstructive.

Moreover, it would be wrong to conclude from this expressed past desire that she would now, at the time of being incompetent, rationally desire to die if she were competent. She would now rationally desire to be treated.

False belief is not always present. But other evaluative failings are equally important. If Mrs X had failed to vividly imagine what it would be like to adapt to life with a prosthetic leg, her previous desire to die would have been irrational and quite possibly obstructive.

The important question, then, is: was Mrs X's past desire an expression of her *autonomy*? Buchanan and Brock claimed that "acting in accordance with a patient's prior preferences" shows "a respect for the patient's former autonomy".[50] This claim is not necessarily true. Some preferences, and even some preferences of competent persons, frustrate autonomy. In order to determine whether a desire is rational or obstructive requires considerable evaluation, and certainly more than that suggested by the President's Commission.

In order to form a substituted judgement, we must ask not what would the patient desire, but what *would* the patient *rationally desire*? A person's past rational desires give us a clue as to what this person's "life-plan" is, and so to what she would now rationally prefer.

In the case where a past desire to die now is obstructive, and it is clear that the patient would now *rationally* desire to live, then respect for autonomy requires that we treat the patient.

In many cases, it will not be possible to clarify whether a past desire was an expression of a person's autonomy. In health care, there is often a presumption of competence: a person is presumed to be competent until proven otherwise. What will *not* do is to presume that a competent person's desire is autonomous, in so far as treatment limitation decisions are concerned. There are too many factors operative which can interfere with the required evaluation.

Moreover, it is possible that some people have never rationally evaluated their lives and lack entirely a rational life plan. Without a plan, without making certain evaluations, a person cannot be autonomous.

What ought to be done, then, when it is not clear what the patient would now rationally desire or if the patient lacks the relevant rational desires?

The following principle is reasonable: in the case that a person has no relevant rational desires or as we become more unclear what the patient would now rationally desire, treatment should promote that patient's best interests.

These principles apply to advance directives. If there are reasons to believe that such a directive was not an expression of the patient's autonomy, then it is appropriate to disregard such a directive and assess the situation afresh.

Consider an example from The *Hastings Center Report*.[51] A 32-year-old, HIV-positive man presented with shortness of breath. He was diagnosed as having *Pneumocystis* pneumonia. Upon being told his diagnosis, the man produced a living will forbidding artificial ventilation "under any circumstances" and endowing his friend with Enduring Power of Attorney (or equivalent). The friend left. Upon commencement of antibiotic treatment, the patient had an unexpected anaphylactic reaction, rendering him incompetent. The doctor, who "believe[d] strongly in patient autonomy", was faced with a dilemma: the patient required immediate intubation or he would die. He was likely to require such intubation only until the anaphylaxis resolved. However, such intubation had been expressly forbidden by the patient. His proxy was not contactable. What should the doctor do?

This is a case where the meaning of the past desire is unclear. It is likely that the patient did not intend to forbid artificial ventilation in a case of drug-related anaphylaxis. Indeed, it is likely that he would rationally desire to be ventilated in these circumstances.

I am arguing for something stronger. I am arguing that there is still a case for artificial ventilation to be given even if the patient has expressly forbidden that "artificial ventilation in cases of anaphylaxis" be instituted *if* that desire was based on inadequate information, either about artificial ventilation or anaphylaxis and their consequences, or inadequate imagination or feeble reflection. I am claiming that such deficiencies may be common. It is necessary then to go beyond what people have said, or written, to how they have lived their lives, what they have thought important, what their goals and rational desires are, that is, to what they have rationally evaluated is the best life for themselves. It is important to know what they value.

When is limitation of treatment in a patient's best interests?

If we do not know what this person values or if she has no values, then she ought to be treated according to her best interests. But how are we to define interests?

The President's Commission defines "interests" in terms of "more objective, societally shared criteria" of "welfare". The following factors are important:

> the relief of suffering, the preservation or the restoration of functioning, and the quality as well as the extent of life sustained. An accurate assessment will encompass consideration of present desires, the opportunities of future satisfactions, and the possibility of developing or regaining the capacity for self-determination.[52]

This is all rather superficial. What precisely is meant by "quality of life"? More rigorous accounts are available. Derek Parfit has distinguished three theories of well-being: Hedonistic Theories, Desire-Fulfilment Theories and Objective List Theories.[53]

The classical doctrine of Hedonism describes only one valuable mental state – happiness or pleasure – and one negative mental state – unhappiness or pain. More recent accounts argue that there are many mental states aside from pleasure which are valuable.

Desire-Fulfilment Theories claim that a person's life goes well when her desires are satisfied.

The Objective List approach to well-being claims that certain activities are objectively good. Parfit argues that being morally good, engaging in rational activity, developing one's abilities, having children and being a good parent (and presumably engaging in other meaningful human relationships), gaining knowledge and being aware of "true" beauty are examples of such activities.[54]

Each of these theories has problems.[55] Parfit argues that, while each of these three elements (desire satisfaction, happiness, valuable activity) is necessary for a good life, no one in isolation is sufficient for a valuable life. What makes a life go well is to have all three together.[56] On this approach, an example of what is good for someone is to be engaged in fulfilling, meaningful human relationships, wanting to be so engaged and gaining pleasure from these relationships.

There are problems still with this account. However, the aim of this paper is to show when a person's interests ought to be invoked, and not how we should construe interests.

Two points are important. Firstly, the account makes clear that there is a difference between a person's (narrowly construed) medical interests. Restoring the hearing of a member of the deaf community may make him better off medically (from the point of view of his health), but, if it will alienate him from his community and he strongly desires not to have the operation, the operation may not be in his overall best interests.

Secondly, one item missing from Parfit's list of objectively valuable activities is that activity which is an expression of a person's autonomy. Promoting a person's interests is thus interconnected with respecting her autonomy.[57] However, even if autonomous

activity is valuable, the account makes clear that autonomous activity is only *a part* of what makes a person's life go well. A person's interests ought not be equated with satisfaction of autonomous desires. A person can autonomously choose a way of life which makes her life go less well overall than it could. Satisfaction of autonomous desire is not the only good in life.

Consider an example. A Jehovah's Witness refuses a blood transfusion and suffers serious brain damage which fundamentally impairs her ability to get what she wants, to carry on social relations, etc. She has made her life go badly. If her choice is to be justified, it will have to be in terms of her autonomy, not in terms of her interests.

When should treatment be limited in a person's best interests? On this account, life would be not worth living when it fell below a certain threshold where a person could no longer engage in a reasonable spectrum of valuable activity, could no longer gain happiness from that life and no longer satisfy her desires to engage in worthwhile activity.

There are lives which are so bad. A life with late stage Huntington's Chorea is one example. However, from empirical studies of patients with paraplegia, it appears that such people are able to lead fulfilling lives.[58]

Limitation of Treatment of Competent Patients

> An advance directive does not, however, provide self-determination in the sense of active moral agency by the patient on his or her behalf…[A]lthough self-determination is involved when a patient establishes a way to project his or her wishes into a time of anticipated incapacity, it is a sense of self-determination lacking in one important attribute: active, contemporaneous personal choice. Hence a decision not to follow an advance directive may sometimes be justified when it is not acceptable to disregard a competent patient's contemporaneous choice. Such a decision would most often rest on a finding that the patient did not adequately envision and consider the particular situation within which the actual medical decision must be made.[59]

The point made here by the President's Commission is that an advance directive which was formed by a person who failed to adequately envision the situation at hand does not provide self-determination. It can be disregarded *because it is not an instance of active, contemporaneous choice*. Implied, then, is that (competent) active, contemporaneous choice ought to be respected, *even when* that choice is the result of evaluation which does not adequately envision the situation at hand. I will argue that we ought not to respect all competent contemporaneous choices. Consider an example.

J is a man in a situation very like that of Mrs X. He, however, has no false beliefs. He believes that he will be able to walk independently on an artificial leg. He finds this abhorrent. An attempt is made to bring in amputees to talk to him about their lives. He refuses to see them. He has made his decision, he says, and we do not have the right to interfere.

J's wife subsequently reveals that J was involved in a car accident 10 years ago. As a result, J was critically ill. At the time, it was clear that if he was treated, he would be left a paraplegic. J desired to die. However, his doctors treated him against his will. He was left a paraplegic. Initially, J was depressed and continued to want to die, but gradually he adapted. He came to find life very fulfilling, participating in the "Para-Olympics". Some years later, a new surgical technique involving the use of a "nerve growth factor" was developed for conditions of spinal injury. After being operated on, J was able to regain the use of his legs. J's wife claims that he is now deliberately suppressing this information. He is an attention-seeker, she claims, and always tries to make his situation look as bad as possible to manipulate the sympathy of others. "He pulled the same stunt last time," she says. "He doesn't really want to die. He just wants you all running around after him, like I do every day."

A person's evaluation of what is best for himself can change. A person can judge that p is best now, but later judge that not-p is best.[60] But imagine that J's wife can give us good reasons why she believes that J would now rationally desire to live, that J values life as a paraplegic more than death. (His past behaviour provides valuable clues.) J's desire to die is then obstructive.[61]

What ought to be done when a competent person's desire obstructs the expressions of his autonomy?

If a person's expressed desire is obstructive, steps should be taken to facilitate the expression of his rational desires. Exactly how this can be done is a matter for psychological investigation.

In some cases, it will not be possible to set the conditions which will facilitate autonomous choice. A young trauma victim, rushed to hospital, may refuse to have some urgent, life-saving operation, like having a bleeding spleen removed. She may not believe that, if her spleen is removed, she will completely recover. Or she might claim to "not like operations". There may not be time to present enough information in a way that promotes adequate evaluation. It is reasonably to operate on this young person if there is a reasonable expectation that, with appropriate information and reflection, she would consent. In some cases, we ought to satisfy a person's rational, hypothetical desire (her values), rather than her actual desire. If we wish to respect autonomy, it is more important to respect a person's values than satisfy an obstructive actual desire.

The situation becomes more complicated when an obviously obstructive desire is resistant to change, even after considerable counselling and provision of information. My own feeling is that, if we wish to respect autonomy, such desires ought to be overridden. This is contentious.

Another difficult situation arises when we suspect, but do not know, that an expressed desire is obstructive. Or we may believe that this person has never formed a rational life-plan, that she has failed entirely to rationally evaluate *anything*. Such a person is not autonomous. One possible solution is to treat her according to her interests.

It might be objected that such a policy is liable to paternalistic abuse. We may, in these cases, abide by competent persons' desires *as a matter of policy*. But the justification for this lies not necessarily with respect for this patient's autonomy, but elsewhere.

Two Objections

1.   Respect only articulated desires?

It might be agreed that in cases like that of Ulysses, where a person has expressed two conflicting desires, the desire which better promotes autonomy ought to be respected. However, it might be argued that if a competent person, like J, expresses a desire to die, and there is *no contrary desire articulated*, then that desire ought to be presumed to be autonomous.

There are two reasons why we ought not to respect only articulated desires.

Firstly, being autonomous does not entail that one has a rational desire at the moment. Being autonomous does entail having a certain disposition, but this disposition will not always be "momentarily actualized", as Ryle put it,[62] in the form of a desire. Assume that, when I am deeply asleep, I have no desires. *A fortiori*, at that time I do not desire my freedom. But if I were awoken by the gunshots of a revolution, I *would* desire my freedom. When I am asleep, I still value my freedom, but I do not at that time rationally desire it.

The less my valuing of, say, freedom manifests itself in an actual desire, the less chance there is for someone to witness my desiring freedom. I may still value freedom, but few may ever have heard me *articulate* that value.

Secondly, some of a person's desires are *never* articulated. Some rational desires remain unarticulated. Is this claim plausible?

What determines whether a person articulates her desires or not? A lot depends on what sort of person she is: is she the kind of person who articulates her thoughts and beliefs to others? Is she the sort of person who thinks in terms of words, sentences and "propositions"? Or is she a person who does not verbalize in her own mind her experiences? Moreover, articulation of desire has nothing necessarily to do with whether the desire is rational or not. There is no reason to believe that rational desires will necessarily be articulated. There is no reason to believe that all people who value freedom will have articulated this value at some point in time.

A related objection can be levelled at articulated desires: how do we *know* that Mrs X *rationally desired* living independently?[63] Why wasn't *this* desire obstructive? The answer turns on how we can come to know whether the three evaluative conditions were satisfied. There is not space to address this important issue. I suspect that the answer is, in part, in the realm of the psychologist. However, we *can* know that some of a person's desires are rational. Ulysses' men, confronted with two conflicting desires, knew what he judged was best, what he rationally desired. It was clear, without him *fully articulating* it, what Ulysses' *plan* was. Though his instructions were brief, his intentions were clear. Our plans may not be so clear, but they are,

I believe, intelligible. And they are often intelligible to a greater extent than we articulate them.

It is of course possible that Mrs X has not rationally evaluated her life at any stage. I think this unlikely, but, if so, she ought to be treated according to her interests.

2. Autonomy and false beliefs

> Every creature that lives and moves shall be food for you…But you must not eat the flesh with life, which is the blood, still in it. (Gen. 9:3–5)
>
>   Abstain from…fornication, from anything that has been strangled and from blood. (Acts 15:19–21)

Jehovah's Witnesses interpret these passages as forbidding blood transfusion.

A Jehovah's Witness (JW) is involved in a car accident. He requires a blood transfusion if he is to live. He refuses to have the blood transfusion. He would prefer to die. Should his desire be respected?

I have argued that Mrs X's false belief distorts her appreciation of treatment options available to her. It precludes her choice to die from being autonomous. However, not giving blood to JW is said to respect his autonomy. Yet JW (let us assume) holds a false belief: if he receives a blood transfusion, he'll go to Hell. Why is the refusal of treatment of JW an expression of his autonomy, and that of Mrs X not? Aren't they both under a misapprehension as to a matter of relevant fact? Why does "If I have an amputation, I'll be confined to a wheelchair" make Mrs X's refusal non-autonomous, whereas "If I get blood, I'll be confined to Hell" doesn't make the Witness' refusal non-autonomous?[64]

a. Instrumental irrationality   JW may be instrumentally irrational, that is, mistaken about the appropriate means to his ends. Assume that the Bible only forbids the consumption of animal blood. Assume also that JW rationally desires (in the narrow sense in which I have defined it) to live in accordance with the dictates of the Bible. JW mistakenly believes that the Bible forbids blood transfusion, when the Bible is only referring to certain dietary practices. His desire not to receive blood is the result of false belief about what the Bible says. His desire will cause him to die. It is thus an obstructive desire. It prevents him achieving what he judges is best: *living* in accordance with the Bible. His *instrumental* irrationality frustrates his autonomy. This kind of JW is like Mrs X.[65]

b. Instrumentally valuable false beliefs   A person can rationally (in both my sense and a broader sense) choose to hold false beliefs. Knowing that I must fight courageously in battle to survive, I might form the false belief that I am the incarnation of a great Hindu Warrior. Or I may be dying of some disease. In order to put on a brave face for my family, I cause myself to believe that death will not be the end. Indeed, a person can rationally cause himself to act irrationally.[66] Desire based on false belief is often instrumentally irrational; however, it is not *necessarily* instrumentally irrational.

If it is the case that JW's false belief serves some useful purpose, then this provides some reason to hold this belief. For instance, the belief that Witnesses have in bodily purity sets them apart from other sects. If holding this false belief is necessary for their identity as members of this discrete sect, and being a member confers great advantages not easily found elsewhere (feelings of solidarity, uniqueness, camaraderie, loyalty, etc.), then each person would have a reason to hold the false belief.

As I argued before, autonomy can be inherited from a parent evaluation. If JW autonomously chose to be a member of this sect, having appreciated what it entails, including the risk of death from blood loss, and holding this false belief is *necessary* if one is to be a member of this sect, then holding this false belief is an expression of his autonomy.

To what degree the false belief is necessary in either of these two senses is an open question.

c. Descriptive and non-descriptive beliefs   One can have beliefs about descriptive and non-descriptive statements or claims. Descriptive statements are pure statements of fact. Non-descriptive statements are not pure statements of fact, but may in part be "expressions of attitudes, prescriptions or something else non-descriptive".[67] A belief about a descriptive statement is meant to describe the way the world is. Examples might be "I believe that the cat is on the mat" or "I believe that Rome is further north than Athens." Beliefs about descriptive statements are verifiable by

empirical investigation of the world. That is, my belief is false if the cat is *not* on the mat, and so on.

I will call beliefs about descriptive statements, descriptive beliefs. One way to interpret religious belief is as descriptive belief, that is, as representing the way the world is. This would include the belief that there *is* a place, Heaven and another, Hell, there *is* a being, God, and so on. On this interpretation, JW is expressing a descriptive belief: if he gets a blood transfusion, he will actually go to Hell, which is supposed to be a place of fire and eternal torment, inhabited by beings with horns on their heads and tails, holding small pitch-forks.

As far as being an empirical hypothesis about the way the world is, there is no good reason to believe that such descriptions of the world represent true propositions. Available evidence suggests that there is no Hell of any description. If held in this descriptive manner, religious belief distorts one's grasp on the nature of the world. In this case, the JW's belief would be like that of Mrs X; his desire to die would not be autonomous.

Compare the following statements: (1) I ought to hand in the money I found. (2) The painting is beautiful. (3) God exists.

(1) represents a moral statement. There is division about whether moral statements are descriptive or non-descriptive. I will not enter that debate. A non-descriptive account of (1) is that the statement expresses in part some attitude on the part of the speaker. The meaning of the statement is not fixed by properties of actions, the world or other descriptive criteria.[68]

It seems to me that if non-descriptivism is a coherent account of the meaning of moral statements, then it may also be a coherent account of other statements. I have in mind statements like (2). It is possible to agree on all the facts concerning a painting: what colours it employs, the type of brush strokes, the subject, the quality of the canvas, and so on, and yet disagree about whether it is beautiful. The expression that something is beautiful is, at least in part, the expression of a certain attitude.

But, if this is right, it is possible that religious statements, although ostensibly purporting to report some property or fact about the world, may be non-descriptive statements.[69] Statements "reporting" religious fact may be like statements "reporting" aesthetic fact. (3) may be like (2). Statement (3) may represent, not a mere statement of fact or the description of a property, but an expression of an attitude, a commitment to a way of life, an adherence to an ideal. On this reading, religion is a construct which gives meaning to people's lives, rather than an empirical statement about the nature of the world. JW's belief, B, that if he receives blood, he'll go to Hell, can thus be viewed as a belief about a non-descriptive statement. The following statements all represent a similar attitude or commitment about which we can have beliefs: "If I receive blood, it will be very bad," "If I receive the blood, I'll go to Hell," "I ought not to receive the blood."

Since non-descriptive statements do not describe properties of the world, they cannot be assessed for their truth or falsehood by empirical examination of the world or of the people in it.

Just as there is no property of descriptive criterion of a painting that will establish that the painting is beautiful, so too there is no property of the world that will establish that God exists. To say to JW that B is false is like saying to a small clique of painters that their paintings are ugly. They might reply, "But we think that they are beautiful." There is no fact of the matter which will settle that the paintings are "truly beautiful". Beauty is in the eye of the beholder, at least for the non-descriptivist.

Nor is there any necessary irrationality or failure of rational evaluation in dying for a non-descriptive construct. It is no more non-autonomous to die for one's religion than it is to die for one's country.

There is, then, not one kind of Jehovah's Witness, but many. Some are irrational and non-autonomous, while others are as autonomous as the next man, or woman. What respect for autonomy requires depends on how a particular Witness holds his belief.

Conclusion

The President's Commission, along with many contemporary bioethicists, accepts that treatment of previously competent but now incompetent patients can be limited if that is what the patient would desire, if she were now competent. If this hypothetical desire cannot be determined, then treatment can be limited if it is not in the patient's best interests. On this approach, a past preference on a related issue or an advance directive constitutes sufficient evidence of what a patient would now desire, if she were competent.

I have distinguished between desiring and rational desiring. One necessary condition for a desire to be fully autonomous is that it is a rational desire or that it satisfies a rational desire. A person rationally desires a state of affairs if that person desires that state of affairs while being in possession of all available relevant facts, without committing relevant error of logic, and vividly imagining what a reasonable range of states of affairs associated with each course of action would be like for him or her.

Not all desires are expressions of a person's autonomy. Some competent, expressed desires obstruct one's autonomy. In evaluating a life of suffering and disability, there are several psychological mechanisms which tend to prevent adequate evaluation of those states. The process of vivid imagination so necessary for rational evaluation is no easy or straightforward process to engage in. When deciding whether to live or die, there are many hurdles to forming a desire which is an expression of our autonomy.

In relation to limitation of treatment of incompetent patients, I conclude: (1) If past desires (including those expressed in advance directives) are to be full expressions of a person's former autonomy, they must have been formed by a person who was in possession of all relevant, available information, who did not commit relevant logical errors and who was vividly acquainted with the lives on offer. (2) In the realm of decisions about states of significant disability, it ought not to be presumed that past competent desires (including advance directives) were necessarily autonomous. (3) Past competent desires (including advance directives) ought to be evaluated to examine whether they were the expression of a person's autonomy. (4) In order to respect a now incompetent patient's former autonomy, it is not enough to know what a patient would now desire if she were competent. We must know what she would rationally desire. (5) Treatment of an incompetent person ought to be limited if limitation is what she would rationally desire. Evidence of what a patient would now rationally desire is what she did rationally desire. (6) If it is clear that allowing a patient to die is a violation of his former autonomy (as reflected by what he or she rationally desired), then he or she ought not to be allowed to die. This may entail acting contrary to an expressed past preference (including an advance directive), if that preference was irrational (obstructive). (7) As our degree of belief that a past expressed desire (including an advance directive) was not autonomous increases, and we are not confident that we know what the patient would now rationally desire, treatment should promote an incompetent patient's best interests.

My arguments have implications for the limitation of treatment of competent patients. My conclusions in this regard are: (1) Care providers ought to ensure that the conditions under which a patient can choose autonomously are secured. This includes provision of information, purging of errors of logic and facilitation of imagination of options on offer. (2) When it is clear that a competent desire is obstructive, and what the person would rationally desire can be confidently estimated, then it is best if we wish to respect autonomy to override the obstructive desire in favour of what the patient would rationally desire. (3) Cases where an obstructive desire persists, or where a person has failed to rationally evaluate the relevant states of affairs, or it is unclear whether the expressed desire is obstructive are complex. If we elect to obey a competent desire, we must recognize that we may not be respecting, and may even be frustrating, this patient's autonomy.

Notes

1 Thanks to two anonymous referees who reviewed an earlier draft. Their detailed comments greatly improved the paper. I am also indebted to Helga Kuhse, Justin Oakley, Cora Singer, Robert Young, Professor R. M. Hare, Hilary Madder and, most of all, to Peter Singer, for their pains and the many invaluable comments which they gave me. This paper was written with the support of a National Health and Medical Research Council of Australia Medical Scholarship.

2 David Hume, "Of Suicide", in P. Singer (ed), *Applied Ethics* (Oxford: Oxford University Press, 1986), p. 26.

3 President's Commission for the Study of Ethical Problems in Medicine and Biomedical and Behavioral Research, *Deciding to Forgo Life-Sustaining Treatment: A Report on the Ethical, Medical and Legal Issues in Treatment Decisions* (March 1983), p. 136.

4 Ibid., p. 27.

5 G. Dworkin, *The Theory and Practice of Autonomy* (Cambridge: Cambridge University Press, 1988), p. 12.

6 R. Young, *Personal Autonomy: Beyond Negative and Positive Liberty* (London: Croom Helm, 1986), p. 8.

7 Ibid., p. 8. The term "life-plan" is used on p. 78.

8 This account is like Brandt's account of rational desires (*A Theory of the Good and the Right* (Oxford: Clarendon Press, 1979), pp. 111ff). One important difference is that Brandt's is a counterfactual account. Young also appeals to a similar notion of rational desire (*Personal Autonomy*, p. 10 and pp. 43–5).

9 I assume she does not have an intrinsic distaste for intravenous infusions.

10 In Locke's case, the person believes the door is open when in fact it is locked (J. Locke, *An Essay concerning Human Understanding*, ed. A. S. Pringle-Pattinson (Oxford: Clarendon Press, 1924), Book II, Chapter xxi, sec. 10).

11 Kahneman and Varey note: "A basic tenet of psychological analysis is that the contents of subjective experience are coded and interpreted representations of objects and events. An objective description of stimuli is not adequate to predict experience because coding and interpretation can cause identical physical stimuli to be treated as identical." (D. Kahneman and C. Varey, "Notes on the psychology of utility", in J. Elster and J. E. Roemer, *Interpersonal Comparisons of Well-Being* (Cambridge: Cambridge University Press, 1991), p. 141.)

12 If the reader does not accept the preceding argument, then his or her favoured account of autonomous desiring should be inserted.

13 This formulation of the objection is Robert Young's.

14 I will not discuss the more complex problem of which of all the possible courses of action open to an agent ought to be entertained for a choice to be autonomous.

15 This formulation of the objection is again Robert Young's. Dan Brock puts the problem in the form of "impetuous Adam". (See D. Brock, "Paternalism and Autonomy", *Ethics*, 98 (April 1988), 550–65.) My response is similar to that of Feinberg (*Harm to Self* (New York: Oxford University Press, 1986), p. 109).

16 Professor Hare convinced me of this (personal communication). I use "dispositional concept" in Ryle's sense (G. Ryle, *The Concept of Mind* (Harmondsworth: Penguin, 1963), pp. 43, 113–20). Young also argues that autonomy has an important dispositional sense (*Personal Autonomy*, p. 8).

17 I will not discuss these in detail. Examples might be that the person is not asleep, not under anaesthesia, not in the grip of psychotic illness, not under the influence of certain drugs, not being coerced by others, etc.

18 See, for example, G. Watson, "Free Agency", *Journal of Philosophy*, 72 (1975) and D. Gauthier, *Morals by Agreement* (Oxford: Clarendon Press, 1986).

19 P desires that q iff P would desire that q under conditions C. See: M. Smith, "Valuing: Desiring or Believing?" in D. Charles and D. Lennon (eds), *Reduction, Explanation and Realism* (Oxford University Press, 1995).

20 R. Graves, *The Greek Myths*, vol. 2 (Harmondsworth: Penguin, 1960), p. 361.

21 One editor asked whether Ulysses knows that he will die at the time he commands his men to move closer to the Island. If he does, his desire is more clearly irrational. But let us assume that he does not know this at the time. Let us assume that the Sirens' song removes this belief or makes it inaccessible. It might be objected that Ulysses is not then irrational because he does not know that he will die in moving closer to the Sirens. However, Ulysses' desire is still irrational because it has not been made by vividly imagining the relevant alternatives. The Sirens' song causes Ulysses' mind to be dominated by one alternative.

22 I thank Professor Hare for this objection and for drawing to my attention this crucial distinction between disposition and desire.

23 I will not address the relationship between these two errors. It may be that the false belief caused the failure of imagination *or* that the failure in imagination caused the false belief. Her *dread* of amputation may have prevented her believing she would walk.

24 J. C. J. M. De Haes and F. C. E. Van Knippenberg, "Quality of life of cancer patients: a review of the literature" in N. K. Aaronson and J. Beckmann (eds), *The Quality of Life of Cancer Patients* (New York: Raven Press, 1987), p. 170. These results represent the cumulation of a series of studies – see De Haes and Van Knippenberg for specific references.

25 Ibid. for specific references.

26 P. Menzel, *Strong Medicine* (Oxford: Oxford University Press, 1990), p. 82. Menzel also shows that these patients will prefer to shorten their lives by 50% to be cured of their disease, p. 81. These findings together may suggest that these patients value normality more than normal people do.

27 Ibid., p. 82, n. 11.

28 P. Brickman, D. Coates, and R. Janoff-Bulman, "Lottery winners and accident victims: is happiness relative?" *Journal of Personality and Social Psychology*, 36(8) (1978),

917–27 as quoted in D. Kahneman and C. Varey, "Notes on the psychology of utility", in J. Elster and J. E. Roemer, *Interpersonal Comparisons of Well-Being* (Cambridge: Cambridge University Press, 1991).

29 From Heinrich and Kriefel cited in E. Goffman, *Stigma: Notes on the Management of Spoiled Identity* (Englewood Cliffs, NJ: Prentice-Hall, 1963) as cited in S. E. Taylor, *Positive Illusions* (Basic Books, 1989), p. 161.

30 All quotations are from S. E. Taylor, "Adjustment to threatening events: A theory of cognitive adaptation", *American Psychologist*, 38 (1983), 1161–73 as quoted in Taylor, *Positive Illusions*, pp. 195–6.

31 Ibid, p. 166. She quotes from several different sources (see text for full references).

32 Kahneman and Varey ("Psychology of Utility", pp. 136–7) argue that adaptation is a normal phenomenon.

33 Ibid. pp. 136–7.

34 J. A. Russell, and B. Fehr, "Relativity in the perception of emotion in facial expressions", *Journal of Experimental Psychology: General*, 116(3) (1987), 223–37, as quoted in Kahneman and Varey, "Psychology of Utility", p. 139.

35 For more recent experiments illustrating the significance of contrast effects, see A. Tversky and D. Griffin, "Endowment and contrast in judgements of well-being" in F. Strack, M. Argyle and N. Schwarz (eds), *Subjective Well-Being* (Oxford: Pergamon, 1991), pp. 101–18.

36 Kahneman and Varey, "Psychology of Utility", p. 144.

37 Ibid., p. 149.

38 Ibid., p. 149.

39 See D. Parfit, *Reasons and Persons* (Oxford: Clarendon Press, 1984), Part III for a discussion of the rationality of this bias. I am not arguing that these attitudes or psychological responses *necessarily* preclude autonomy. I am not arguing that one cannot be autonomously loss or risk-averse, or "live for the moment". But, to be autonomous and hold these attitudes and biases, they must at some point have been evaluated in the right way and endorsed. Most people have not evaluated their biases.

40 "Psychology of Utility", p. 144.

41 "Endorsement", pp. 113–14.

42 President's Commission, p. 45.

43 D. Kahneman and D. T. Miller, "Norm Theory: Comparing Reality to Its Alternatives", *Psychological Review*, 93(2), (1986), 136–53. The quote is on p. 148.

44 Ibid., p. 148.

45 President's Commission, p. 132.

46 A. Buchanan and D. Brock, "Deciding for Others", *Milbank Quarterly*, 64(Suppl. 2), (1986), 17–94.

47 President's Commission, p. 149.

48 I here assume that a desire's being rational is *sufficient* for

its being autonomous. This is an oversimplification. Other necessary conditions must be satisfied for a desire to be autonomous.

49 T. L. Beauchamp and J. F. Childress, *Principles of Biomedical Ethics* (New York: Oxford University Press, 1989), p. 83. Beauchamp and Childress describe a competent person as one who possesses certain abilities or capacities, pp. 79–85. They claim that it "seems a plausible hypothesis that an autonomous person is necessarily a competent person", p. 83. The more relevant question for me is: is a competent person *necessarily* autonomous?

50 Buchanan and Brock, "Deciding for Others", p. 70.

51 L. M. Silverman, et al., "Whether No Means No", *Hastings Center Report*, (May–June 1992), 26–7.

52 President's Commission, p. 135.

53 See D. Parfit, *Reasons and Persons*, pp. 493–502 and J. Griffin, *Well-Being* (Oxford: Clarendon Press, 1986).

54 Parfit, *Reasons and Persons*, p. 499.

55 See Parfit (*Reasons and Persons*) and Griffin (*Well-Being*).

56 Parfit, *Reasons and Persons*, p. 502.

57 A point forcefully made by Robert Young.

58 Clearly not all paraplegics later find life worth living. There is some uncertainty about whether *this* person's life will be worth living as a paraplegic. This issue is dealt with in my "Treatment Limitation Decisions under Uncertainty: the Value of Subsequent Euthanasia", *Bioethics*, 8(1), (Jan. 1994).

59 President's Commission, p. 137.

60 Better than vivid imagination is actual experience. Still, there are factors which can interfere with rational evaluation based on experience. We may focus on only one aspect of that experience or unjustifiably generalize from one aspect, and so on.

61 Third party evaluations of what a patient values raise problems. There is a suggestion of antipathy between J and his wife. She may want him to be punished. We must keep clear that our aim is to determine what the patient values. Third party evaluations constitute just one line of evidence.

62 *Concept of Mind*, p. 84.

63 Another related question is: if one can rationally desire death, then one must have vividly imagined what death is like. Is this possible? Imagination of what being dead is like ought only to occur to the extent that it can occur. One way in which being dead can be imagined is as the absence of certain states of affairs.

64 This objection is Peter Singer's.

65 The importance of the instrumentality, and the example given, was raised by one referee.

66 See Derek Parfit's "Could It Be Rational to Cause Oneself to Act Irrationally?" in *Reasons and Persons*, pp. 12–13.

67 R. M. Hare, *Moral Thinking* (Oxford: Clarendon Press, 1981), p. 208.

68 Ibid., p. 70.

69 Professor Hare gives a detailed non-descriptivist interpretation of religious statements in "The Simple Believer", "Appendix: Theology and Falsification" and "Religion and Morals" in his *Essays on Religion and Education* (Oxford: Clarendon Press, 1992). I thank Professor Hare for very valuable discussion on these points.

79

The Nocebo Effect of Informed Consent

Shlomo Cohen

The placebo effect is a well-documented phenomenon, whereby people experience improvement of symptoms in response to an intervention which is biologically inert with respect to their condition yet which they believe is helpful.[1] The mirror-phenomenon to the placebo effect is the nocebo effect, where the expectation of a negative outcome precipitates the corresponding symptom or leads to its exacerbation.[2] While much literature in medical ethics has dealt with the placebo effect, virtually nothing in philosophy has been written specifically on the ethics of the nocebo effect. (The search for 'nocebo' in the Philosopher's Index yields a striking *zero* result.)[3] The use of placebo in clinical practice raises moral concerns since it often involves a kind of deception which, as such, clashes with the principle of respect owed to patient autonomy. The well-known moral dilemma with regard to the placebo effect is therefore in cases where the positive effects on patient well-being may outweigh the harm to patient autonomy. The ethical problem with regard to producing the nocebo effect is obvious: the nocebo is in and of itself painful, stressful, or otherwise noxious to the patient. The relevant parallel dilemma is when the harmfulness of the nocebo effect may outweigh the good in proper disclosure of medical information to the patient, and where the duty to inform may therefore be suspended. This is of special importance with respect to the clinical practice of informed consent, where the very disclosure of potential side effects or complications can bring them about through a nocebo effect. I shall refer to this as the dilemma of the nocebo effect of informed consent (NEIC). While this was acknowledged as a problem mainly for the methodology of clinical trials,[4] the *moral* dilemma of the NEIC has gone unnoticed in medical ethics. (This dilemma arises in both clinical research and clinical practice, but has different characteristics in each. The ethical analysis in this paper concentrates on clinical practice.) The first task of this paper is the very articulation of this important yet unrecognized dilemma. Next, it will proceed to discuss its main ethical features.

The dilemma stemming from the potential for the NEIC is arguably more acute than the parallel dilemma with respect to the placebo effect, since the prevention of harm takes precedence over the enhancement of well-being, as indeed the supreme principle of clinical medicine reminds us. Contemporary views in medical ethics often hold that the principle of respect for patient autonomy trumps the principle of furthering patient well-being (paternalism is looked down upon); however, the balance of reasons may not point in the same direction when respect for autonomy is pitted against the stricter duty not to harm – as in nocebo cases.

Original publication details: Shlomo Cohen, "The Nocebo Effect of Informed Consent," pp. 147–54 from *Bioethics* 2014; 28: 147–154.
Reproduced with permission from John Wiley & Sons.

The uniqueness of this dilemma should be clarified more precisely. The dilemma of the NEIC is more pernicious than the different, well-known dilemma regarding the nondisclosure of bad news to a patient about his condition, when this can be especially detrimental psychologically. Such is the case where, for instance, the caregiver decides to postpone the bad news about the patient's exact diagnosis while the patient is suffering from depression, is therefore especially vulnerable, and the additional bad news may increase significantly his suicidal tendencies. The problem of the NEIC raises a special moral concern, since, in contrast to the above example, the caregiver is not called to refrain from reporting actual reality to the patient, but to refrain from describing hypothetical harmful possibilities (of potential side effects or other complications) – a description which could in and of itself be causal in turning them from mere potentialities to actualities. The causality of harm by the caregiver is therefore of a different magnitude altogether; his moral responsibility and the cautiousness he is required to exercise are hence of a correspondingly higher magnitude. The moral dilemma is thus distinct and unique, and a different balance of reasons is arguably called for.

After this basic articulation of the dilemma, let us proceed to examine it in more detail.

I

While the point of this paper is a philosophical one, a review of relevant biological evidence is mandatory background. The nocebo effects of negative expectations (secondary to suggestion) are well documented.[5] Examples abound. When healthy subjects are made to believe falsely that electric current is being transmitted through their heads, more than two thirds experience a headache.[6] Similarly, one quarter of patients with food allergies develop allergic symptoms when injected with saline that is described to them as an allergen.[7] The nocebo effect of verbal suggestion was shown to be strong enough to reverse the placebo effect achieved by conditioning via pre-treatment with a potent analgesic.[8] The nocebo effect demonstrates its greatest power, however, by the ability of verbal suggestion to completely *reverse the biological effect* of an agent, as in turning the analgesic effect of nitrous oxide into a hyperalgesic one.[9]

The potential nocebo effect of verbal suggestion is no less relevant when the suggestion is part of the informed consent procedure. Before turning to discuss the ethical implications, let us review an example. The outcome of mentioning potential side effects in the consent form was examined in a trial of aspirin or sulfinpyrazone in the treatment of unstable angina.[10] The consent form in two of the participating centers but not in the third included the mention of 'occasional gastrointestinal irritation' as a potential side effect. As a result, significantly more patients in the first two centers suffered from subjective gastrointestinal symptoms; with a striking sixfold increase ($P < 0.001$) in the relative number of patients who consequently discontinued their participation in the study. (There was no difference between the groups in the number of patients experiencing objective gastrointestinal complications or non-gastrointestinal symptoms.) The disclosure of information regarding potential adverse effects was instrumental in causing them. Just as this is seen in clinical trials, it is also pertinent to the therapeutic setting.

The special cautiousness that the caregiver is called upon to exercise due to her potential causal role in generating noxious symptoms in the patient is accentuated by the fact that the nocebo effect can cause actual clinical deterioration. This was illustrated in patients with Parkinson's disease who had electrodes implanted into the subthalamic nuclei of their brains for 'deep brain stimulation' therapy. When the patients were tested for best motor performance, the false suggestion that the stimulator was turned off had similar negative effects on the velocity of hand movement – a nocebo effect – as when the stimulator was indeed turned off.[11] The traditional understanding of the difference between placebo/nocebo effects and real medical intervention was that while the latter works on the target tissue or organ, the former works 'just psychologically.' (This provided the basis for rejection of placebo treatment on the grounds of deception.) This dichotomy (as opposed to a mere distinction) is in the process of deconstruction by accumulating scientific research, and at any event is untenable in its simple form. This is not the place to review the evidence for the *objective biological effects* of placebos,[12] but, to continue with the Parkinson example, PET scanning (a form of functional brain imaging) showed increased dopamine release in the striatum of parkinsonian patients in response to suggestion of motor improvement,[13] which is precisely the biological response that real anti-Parkinson medications are designed to achieve. For obvious ethical reasons, research on patients designed to create nocebo effects in order to unravel their neurobiology is much more difficult to conduct, and so evidence is scarcer, but there is reason to believe that just as the placebo effect can at times mimic the actual physiologic action of real treatments, so does the nocebo effect. A possible example is the finding that proglumide – an antagonist of the pain mediator cholecystokinin – blocks the nocebo effect of pain suggestion,[14] in parallel to the finding that naloxone – which antagonizes endogenous opioids – blocks the placebo effect of suggestion of pain relief.[15] The important conclusion from all of this is the following. The emerging robustness of the nocebo effect and the potential objective harmful effects of nocebos – whether behavioral or physiological – underscore the significant moral liability of the caregiver when creating a nocebo effect in the patient and the gravity of the moral responsibility to prevent it.

The idea of the potential for harm in the mere disclosing of potential harms has often been criticized in recent decades as a rationalization used to justify the outdated paternalistic approach in medicine.[16] It may be the case, however, that that criticism is to an extent a form of rationalization *itself*, which in a parallel manner helps support the opposite, patient-centered, approach dominating current medical ethics. Much more importantly, the developing scientific understanding of the power of the nocebo was simply not available until a generation ago. Tom Beauchamp and James Childress, in their authoritative discussion of informed consent and specifically of intentional nondisclosure, make no mention of the nocebo phenomenon and – no doubt, partially as a consequence of this neglect – opine that: 'empirical evidence indicates more often than not that physician-hypothesized negative effects [of information disclosure] … do not materialize.'[17] One suspects that the paradigm of nocebo that ethicists (as everyone else) had in mind was something rather exotic, maybe along the lines of 'tribal phenomena,' such as 'voodoo death.' Although voodoo death may be a physiologic nocebo phenomenon in its own right,[18] it is surely of

anecdotal importance and prevalence compared with the robust evidence of the variety of nocebo effects, as discussed here. (On a larger scale, the central importance of top-down modulation of sensory experience in general was much less scientifically established a generation ago.)

Let us conclude: the traditional ethical problem regarding disclosure of information to the patient is raised in conditions of an existing or impending harm, and the dilemma involves the justification for the physician's adding psychological harm to the patient by *reporting* on it (i.e. disclosing the diagnosis or prognosis). In the dilemma of the NEIC, the harm in point does *not* exist; rather, as the evidence presented here suggests, the physician risks *creating* it by merely mentioning its potentiality. Moreover, this harm can be biologically real and cannot be dismissed as 'merely psychological.' This raises a different, new moral dilemma, which demands a search for a new moral balance between respect for autonomy and paternalistic nonmaleficence, and which ethicists are called upon to investigate.

II

Since the 1970s or so, the view that accords prominence to the principle of respect for patient autonomy has risen to dominance in medical ethics.[19] After the Belmont Report of 1979, the *locus classicus* with respect to informed consent, it became somewhat of a truism that informed consent is justified by that principle of autonomy. In their classic work, *Principles of Biomedical Ethics*, Beauchamp and Childress argue accordingly that 'the primary function and justification of informed consent is to enable and protect individual autonomous choice.'[20] In particular, the prominence of the autonomy paradigm tended to downplay the seriousness of perusal that considerations of nondisclosure merit.

Opposition to the above view has intensified in recent years, and has involved both a reevaluation of our understanding of informed consent and a more nuanced understanding of patient autonomy (these two factors are often connected). The relevant criticism may either reduce (even deny) the dependence of informed consent on respect for autonomy, or argue that even if autonomy is central, it should be understood in more complex ways, which, specifically, may diminish the duty to disclose medical information. I will review the basic relevant points, and then discuss considerations specific to the NEIC.

Despite the centrality of the notion of informed consent in medical ethics, the attempt to elucidate its philosophical foundation and rationale has led to persistent difficulties. As Onora O'Neill puts it, 'informed consent has been supported by poor arguments and lumbered with exaggerated claims.'[21] The idea that the duty to procure informed consent is founded on respect for autonomous choice – as common wisdom in medical ethics has it – runs into the following intractable problem:

> if an account makes autonomy sufficiently demanding that actions which meet it are worthy of respect for their own sake, then the account will be too demanding to allow the vast majority of the choices that patients make about their healthcare … to count as autonomous. However, if the account is sufficiently lax as to allow the ordinary choices of patients … to meet it, then we will no longer have reason to think of such choices as worthy of respect.[22]

The list of the myriad irrationalities that people ordinarily exhibit in decision-making defies repetition, and this contradicts the presumption that the practice of obtaining informed consent, in its common universal form, rests on a duty to respect people's autonomous choice. This author has sharpened this dilemma by showing that the question of the nature of the connection between the information and the consent gives rise to a dilemma analogous to the Gettier problem in the concept of knowledge, and that this puts in great doubt the explanation of informed consent by respect for autonomous choice.[23] Following her diagnosis and exposition of the problem with informed consent, O'Neill argues that its ethical point is indeed more elementary than respect for autonomous choice: it is to provide reasonable assurance that a patient has not been deceived or coerced.[24] This necessitates the provision of some essential information (along with the liberty of the patient to request more information at any time), but the question of what should be disclosed – which nowhere has a precise answer – gets some degree of freedom from the straightjacket of the lofty articulations of autonomous decision making; the caregiver is consequently allowed more leeway in judging the limits of disclosure, in ways that preserve trust. Specifically, consideration of the harmfulness of the NEIC can then be legitimately assessed.

It would be impossible to provide here a comprehensive review of the criticisms of the justification of informed consent by respect for autonomous choice; the above, however, as well as other criticisms have led to alternative justifications. Alongside O'Neill's solution, others justify informed consent by: caring for patient well-being – and then respect for autonomy is relegated to an instrumental value, alongside other considerations of beneficence;[25] by respect for spontaneous free choice, where considerations of decisional rationality become marginal (this is the libertarian position, to which certain conceptions of 'procedural autonomy' come close); or by respect for a sphere of privacy, specifically in decisions that concern one's body.[26] Whatever the precise alternative justification, as long as it is not autonomous choice *per se*, we would be allowed to relax the almost reflexive reasoning against nondisclosure, as exemplified by the categorical statement in the AMA's Code of Medical Ethics that 'Withholding medical information from patients without their knowledge or consent is ethically unacceptable.'[27] Rather, the criticism provides enhanced legitimacy to factor potential harms – notably, the NEIC – into our considerations of information nondisclosure.

Another venue through which certain relaxation of the moral injunction against nondisclosure is justified involves more nuanced interpretations of the meaning of autonomous choice itself. This author has introduced the concept of 'ironic autonomy' to describe cases where a manipulation, such as nondisclosure of information, which would otherwise compromise patient autonomy, is in a given context necessary to *uphold* her autonomy. This characterizes situations where the nondisclosure is in complete consistency with the patient's considered preferences and *necessary* for their achievement, as the patient cannot effect the self-ignorance necessary to advance her goal. Ironic autonomy describes the status of the patient in certain non-deceptive placebo interventions, allowing nondisclosure while preserving autonomy via an ironic process.[28] This confers moral legitimacy to nondisclosure within a restricted domain. This legitimacy is in conditions that do not involve harm to the patient; a fortiori nondisclosure will be justified in situations that involve harm to patients, such as the NEIC.

A related yet different view was advanced by Bennett Foddy, who also claims that placebo treatments preserve patient autonomy when used judiciously, but argues that this happens despite their being deceptive.[29] Deception is wrong when it injures the victim's autonomy. But this is so only if, by camouflaging reality, it prevents her from making reasoned choices, thus thwarting her self-government. The judicious use of placebo, however, takes place only when no other acceptable treatment is available, and therefore no restriction of the patient's choice range takes place. Nor does it prevent objecting to the treatment on grounds of preferring one's symptoms to the side effects, since placebo treatment has no side effects. In addition, the concealment does not injure autonomy by coercing the physician's decision on the unsuspecting patient, since the placebo is not really treatment, and in this respect not different from the beneficial effect of the physician's reassuring smile; but it would be absurd to object to physicians smiling to patients on account that it coerces patients into a therapeutic set of mind, without informed consent.

The conclusion, again, is that nondisclosure does not automatically injure patient autonomy. Beauchamp and Childress acknowledge that 'the meaning of informed consent … is better analyzed in terms of autonomous authorization, which has nothing to do with disclosure specifically.'[30] Our important insight is that respect for autonomy is not identical with full disclosure not only because 'full disclosure' is often impossible, and possibly meaningless, but also because autonomy can indeed be preserved in situations where its meaning and phenomenology are more nuanced – indeed, even ironic.

Since we can find ourselves in ironic situations where respect for autonomy involves nondisclosure, and since the disclosure of nondisclosure (to gain patient permission) would ordinarily defeat its purpose, determining the obligation to disclose must sometimes refer to the idea of the reasonable person and his interests in knowing. At this point, however, even those who argue that 'medical information should never be permanently withheld from the patient' admit that 'little is known of the extent to which disclosure of alarming medical information may ultimately harm patients.'[31] Research into the nocebo effect is of course supremely relevant in this regard, and it must receive the close scrutiny that ethicists have so far neglected to give it. In view of the mounting evidence in this field, however, the conclusion that physicians should 'think out loud' with patients[32] sounds at best premature and possibly outright reckless; words indeed can maim.[33] While it has been reported that most patients welcome accurate information, that this can reduce rather than augment anxiety levels and enhance healing and patient satisfaction,[34] the relevant data refers to knowing one's diagnosis, treatment and prognosis; it does not tell us to what extent patients want to know (let alone are better off knowing) details about certain side effects of treatments. In the absence of clear data, some caution is morally reasonable. To be sure, O'Neill's principle of 'extendable information' must always be operative: whenever extra information is requested, it ought to be provided. We should remember, at the same time, that, as Foddy emphasized, the reliance of the duty to disclose on the principle of patient autonomy makes sense to the extent that the information is important for self-government, i.e. for patients' ability to make optimal life decisions based on their individual needs and personal values. This, however, is much less the case with knowing certain side effects (see discussion below), as compared with knowing the diagnosis, prognosis, or basic treatment alternatives. The nocebo effect is hence a special kind of case, whose harmful potential caregivers must consider very cautiously in the practice of obtaining informed consent.

Can the advised caution be reconciled with the concern for patient autonomy by a prior pact between doctor and patient? It is not clear when and if discussing the nocebo effect with patients will help reduce the negative impact of disclosure (in some cases it might exacerbate the relevant unconscious processes and have the opposite effect). But even if the more optimistic possibility is indeed the rule – in which case discussing the nocebo effect should of course be a requirement – it is highly doubtful that this could eliminate the phenomenon and make nondisclosure unnecessary: some evidence in placebo research suggests that overt placebo also works.[35] It stands to reason that this is at least as true with the nocebo, if not truer (for it is simpler to scare patients than to reassure them).

Medical ethicists have tended to think that respect for autonomous choice is the justification for seeking informed consent and to understand the meaning of such choice in rather rigid ways. These assumptions, we saw, must be qualified. The conclusion that non-disclosure is essentially wrong is therefore in need of similar qualification and balancing. This sharpens the difficulty in the dilemmas that the NEIC cases often pose. The next section will review practical considerations in dealing with these dilemmas.

III

The various arguments for the relaxation of the rigid conception of informed consent as grounded in autonomous choice do not mean that considerations of autonomy are not important – they obviously are. These arguments allow us, however, to think more freely and fruitfully on the optimal *balance* between respect for autonomy and care for patient well-being in the practice of informed consent.

Some authors see balancing as secondary in importance, and rather endorse an order of priority with autonomy at the top.[36] The uncompromising primacy of respect for autonomy, specifically with respect to the placebo, is expressed in the opposition by the AMA's Code of Medical Ethics to the deceptive use of placebos in clinical practice. While it is a truism that *ceteris paribus* deception is morally bad, the great majority of moral thinkers agree that deception (and even straightforward lying) is sometimes justified in order to prevent harm to innocent persons. (Augustine and Kant are the luminary exceptions.) This view characterizes the consequentialist perspective almost by definition, but is common also among Kantians.[37] A deontologist such as W. D. Ross views veracity as (only) *prima facie* obligating,[38] and Sissela Bok's seminal work on the ethics of lying similarly determines 'the principle of veracity' as (only) a *presumption* in favor of truthfulness.[39] Virtue ethicists too find the goodness in truthfulness to be qualified in various ways[40] and, as Bernard Williams in his masterpiece *Truth and Truthfulness*, argues: to know when *not* to say the truth 'is part of what it is for someone's disposition of Sincerity to be correctly shaped.'[41]

In light of all this, one should not find it surprising that the view that the value of truthfulness always trumps the benefits of placebo treatment has been reexamined and contested recently.[42] But if indeed deception can sometimes be ethically justified in placebo treatment, then *a fortiori* the prevention of the nocebo effect can be justified too. This follows from two important reasons. (1) The nature of the manipulation of the patient is significantly milder in the nocebo case: while ethical objection to placebo treatment is based on the fact that it involves (when it does) a deceptive message, the problem presented by the NEIC stems from the element of nondisclosure of information; and it is widely agreed that *ceteris paribus* nondisclosure is the least morally problematic of all kinds of deceptive manipulation.[43] (2) The prevention of harm is *ceteris paribus* of greater moral weight compared with improving well-being.

Moral dilemmas force us to assess the relative claims of opposing moral duties. In medical ethics, one of the most oft discussed is the dilemma between respect for patients' autonomy and care for their well-being. This dilemma has usually been recognized as one between autonomy and paternalistic beneficence, while the parallel dilemma between autonomy and nonmaleficence has received far less attention (Beauchamp and Childress, for example, dedicate a 20 page discussion to the former, while the latter can only be gleaned from between the lines).[44] The dilemma of the NEIC brings this important but relatively neglected topic to front stage. Miller and Colloca have recently sounded an important seminal call to rethink the traditional separateness of two duties: risk-benefit assessment of treatments before they are recommended to patients and the obligation to obtain informed consent, arguing that information disclosure can by itself produce or shape the risks and benefits. They also rightly claim that this calls for a reevaluation of the dominant, autonomy-based justification of informed consent.[45] The present articulation of the NEIC and its analysis support this perspective, provide it with ethical substance, and focus attention specifically on assessing the strength of the duty not to harm, as pitted against the duty to respect patient autonomy – both integral to the obligation to obtain informed consent.

With any serious moral dilemma, it is often the details of the case that tip the balance of reasons in favor of one argument or the other. In the case of the

NEIC, we should assess the nature and degree of manipulation in nondisclosure and its effect on autonomy versus the chances and magnitude of the harm it can prevent. Particular cases will present important idiosyncratic details, which will influence our consideration; here, we can do no more than review some preliminary general considerations. The advancement of empirical research on nocebos (and related subjects) will enable more precise distinctions to be made and thus enrich our tools for decision making.

It would seem that the most obvious first consideration ought to be the level of harm to the patient: the greater the harm of the nocebo effect, the weaker the obligation to disclose. But it is unlikely in fact that this should make a difference, since just as it is worse to cause greater harm via the NEIC, it is equally worse to hide a more serious potential harm from the patient. Since these opposing considerations increase simultaneously, they seem to cancel each other out. (The one exception would be if recognizing a side effect were important for seeking immediate medical evaluation – then disclosure would be mandatory.) What we can say instead is that nondisclosure should be directly related to the degree of sensitivity of the particular side effect or complication to suggestion. For example, not all symptoms of Parkinson's disease are equally sensitive to suggestion: while bradykinesia is sensitive, tremor and rigidity apparently are not.[46] The more the potential side effect is sensitive to suggestion, the more caution should be applied in disclosing it. In contrast, the rarer a side effect or complication, the lesser is the duty to disclose it (this is true in general and is not unique to the NEIC). With the dilemma of the NEIC in mind, therefore, the duty to disclose should be directly correlated to the ratio between the probability of a specific side effect to occur after suggestion and the rarity of its occurrence as a result of the real drug or intervention. For example, in a study on the efficacy of placebo versus anti-hypertensive drugs for the treatment of stage 1 and stage 2 hypertension, at least as many subjects (proportionally) had to discontinue treatment due to adverse drug effects in the placebo group (i.e. a nocebo effect) as in the treatment group.[47] This shows an unacceptably high ratio between the prevalence of suggestion-induced symptoms and symptoms due to real drugs. (The interpretation of those results is more complicated, in fact, but that discussion does not change the conclusion and thus is irrelevant here.) Since side effects reduce compliance to treatment, and since hypertension is responsible for much mortality (and in patients with other conditions, such as cardiac or pulmonary insufficiency, even low-level hypertension may be dangerous), it is very clear why doctors must recognize the serious moral dilemma they potentially face when disclosing information about side effects to patients.

The more a specific nocebo effect is empirically validated, the more weight it should get in our ethical calculation. If or when we have well defined cases where evidence of the creation of specific nocebo effects is robust and compelling, we may have no choice but to begin thinking of the full disclosure of information in those cases as if coupled with a real and actual harm (say, painful electrocution of the patient), and think whether this kind of treatment of the patient is indeed the necessary price for the respect owed to her autonomy.

The above considerations concerning the nature of the intervention should be supplemented with consideration of the nature of the patient. The need for personal tailoring of informed consent is underdeveloped in medical ethics. Here, however, I am not speaking of tailoring the amount, timing or character of disclosure to the values and interests of the individual patient – an important thing in itself – but of fitting the level of disclosure to the personality type of the patient and its susceptibility to nocebo effects. This seems to be recognized as a moral concern virtually nowhere in the informed consent literature, at least not in any systematic manner. It was found, for example, that, among patients with temporomandibular disorder, those suffering from somatization disorder or tendency (high values on the Somatization Scale) are three times more susceptible to suffer pain secondary to placebo examination and treatment.[48] A tendency to anxiety or depression is similarly correlated with heightened nocebo effects.[49] In contrast, optimists are more likely to experience placebo effects,[50] and it is conceivable (though needs empirical validation) that they are reciprocally less likely to experience nocebo effects. Empirical data of this sort can be valuable for caregivers in assessing the amount of suffering they are likely to cause to different patients, and thus guide their moral judgment regarding the dilemma of the NEIC.

It might be argued that suffering more pain is not a dangerous side effect, and so cannot offset the duty to disclose; but (aside from the fact that ongoing pain can lead to sedentariness or depression, and these can form positive feedback cycles with pain, and indeed set off lethal cascades of pathologies) we surely ought not to be dismissive toward the gravity of causing real suffering to patients. Respect for autonomy ought not to fall into the moral trap of relying on the fact that 'every person has enough resilience to endure the agony of others,' as the Duke de La Rochefoucauld put it, with typical wit. It might be argued further that the gravity of the problem of the NEIC is mitigated by the fact that, on the one hand, the nocebo effect usually does not involve serious medical complications, and on the other hand, when the adverse symptoms are not medically very consequential, the duty to obtain informed consent is less rigorous to begin with. While there is some truth in this observation, we must think of the duty to obtain informed consent as spanning a wide range of practices, from the most formal to much less formal patterns of information sharing. Seen in this light, the potential for the dilemma of the NEIC to arise in various medical settings is substantial and merits our close attention, both conceptually and practically. And there are no doubt cases where serious repercussions of the NEIC may be seen in settings where the most explicit informed consent is needed. An example discussed above that may illustrate this is that the medical benefit from implantation of electrodes in the brain (of parkinsonian patients) is susceptible to nocebo effects.[51]

Beyond questions of *non*disclosure, the responsibility to prevent the NEIC refers also to the question of *how* to disclose information, invoking the issue of framing. The way any message is framed affects the way it is accepted and hence its effects, and this well-known truth obviously holds with respect to medical information as well. For example, when information on side effects of drugs (in information leaflets) used less ominous frequency adverbs – 'seldom' instead of 'sometimes' – patients experienced fewer side effects.[52] In such cases of framing, it is often not clear whether the reformulations that are meant to manipulate amount to deception at all. In the example just mentioned, it seems that the change of adverbs is *not* deceptive, as the study also showed that the precise

meaning of those frequency words is ill-defined in the population (with near-total overlap in the ranges of frequencies people stated as defining those two adverbs); hence substituting the one for the other does not create a change of meaning that constitutes an untruth. If or when the framing amounts to deception, then the dilemma of the NEIC may arise; when it does not, then there is no dilemma: the potential for the NEIC creates a straightforward moral duty to use the formulation that causes fewer side effects. Similar cases of framing that do not amount to deception are the stating of treatment outcomes as the probability of survival versus the complementary probability of dying,[53] the more rather than less frequent use of professional terms as opposed to vernacular terms, or vice versa, and so on.

The danger of hurting the trust between doctor and patient is often rightly invoked when discussing placebo treatment. But in cases such as these, it is hard to see how the framing manipulation which does not amount to deception injures trust. An important element of the trust of the patient in the doctor is surely that the latter will not harm him; and this should be the dominant consideration in these cases. The extent to which patients perceive marginally deceptive framing effects as injuring trust and how this should be optimally calculated against the loss of trust in harming the patient through nocebo effects are important questions which need empirical examination. (Most of the literature on nocebos as well as on informed consent deals with the research setting. In the therapeutic setting, however, the patient is not recruited for the potential benefit of humanity, but rather stands to benefit *individually*; the weight of the reasons that can legitimately counterbalance the required respect for autonomy is therefore greater.)

The duty to disclose information to patients is a basic duty in medical ethics. Its precise interpretation in practice is less than straightforward, however, and encompasses questions such as: the scope of that which ought to be disclosed (physicians' levels of competence, various institutional policies, genetic information, minor medical mistakes, etc.), the obligation to disclose uncertain diagnoses and other uncertain medical assessments, the conditions under which nondisclosure amounts to deception, and more. This paper is an attempt to shed light on another, important question: the optimal balance between disclosure and nonmaleficence, which assumes an especially critical form in the dilemma of the NEIC. Further research into the nocebo effect coupled with philosophical attention to the problem of the NEIC can help determine how best to minimize harm to patients, while treating them with due respect.

Notes

1   D.D. Price, D.G. Finniss and F. Benedetti. A Comprehensive Review of the Placebo Effect: Recent Advances and Current Thought. *Annu Rev Psychol* 2008; 59: 565–590; D.G. Finniss et al. Biological, Clinical, and Ethical Advances of Placebo Effects. *Lancet* 2010; 375: 686–695.

2   R. Hahn. 1997. The Nocebo Phenomenon: Scope and Foundations. In *The Placebo Effect: An Interdisciplinary Exploration.* A. Harrington, ed. Cambridge, MA: Harvard University Press: 56–76; F. Benedetti et al. When Words Are Painful: Unraveling the Mechanisms of the Nocebo Effect. *Neuroscience* 2007; 147: 260–271.

3   Accessed 20 Sep 2011.

4   R.J. Levine. The Apparent Incompatibility between Informed Consent and Placebo-Controlled Clinical Trials. *Clin Pharmacol Ther* 1987; 42: 247–249.

5   A. Barsky et al. Nonspecific Medication Side Effects and the Nocebo Phenomenon. *JAMA* 2002; 287: 622–627; F. Benedetti et al. Conscious Expectation and Unconscious Conditioning in Analgesic, Motor and Hormonal Placebo/Nocebo Responses. *J Neurosci* 2003; 23: 4315–4323.

6   A. Schweiger and A. Parducci. Nocebo: The Psychologic Induction of Pain. *Pavlovian Journal of Biological Science* 1981; 16: 140–143.

7   D.L. Jewett, G. Fein and M.H. Greenberg. A Double-Blind Study of Symptom Provocation to Determine Food Sensitivity. *N Engl J Med* 1990; 323: 429–433.

8   Benedetti et al. 2003, Conscious Expectation and Unconscious Conditioning.

9   S.F. Dworkin et al. Cognitive Reversal of Expected Nitrous Oxide Analgesia for Acute Pain. *Anesth Anal* 1983; 62: 1073–1077.

10   M.G. Myers, J.A. Cairns and J. Singer. The Consent Form as a Possible Cause of Side Effects. *Clin Pharmacol Ther* 1987; 42: 250–253.

11   Benedetti et al. 2003, Conscious Expectation and Unconscious Conditioning.

12   F. Benedetti. Mechanisms of Placebo and Placebo-Related Effects across Diseases and Treatments. *Annual Review of Pharmacology and Toxicology* 2008; 48: 33–60; B.S. Oken. Placebo Effects: Clinical Aspects and Neurobiology. *Brain* 2008; 131: 2812–2823.

13   R. De la Fuente-Fernández et al. Expectation and Dopamine Release: Mechanism of the Placebo Effect in Parkinson's Disease. *Science* 2001; 293: 1164–1166.

14   Benedetti et al. 2007, When Words Are Painful.

15   J.D. Levine, N.C. Gordon and H.L. Fields. The Mechanisms of Placebo Analgesia. *Lancet* 1978; 2: 654–657.

16   S. Bok. 1978. *Lying: Moral Choice in Public and Private Life.* New York: Vintage; H. Waitzkin. 1991. *The Politics of Medical Encounters: How Patients and Doctors Deal with Social Problems.* New Haven, CT: Yale University Press; R. Buckman and Y. Kason. 1992. *How to Break Bad News: A Guide for Health Professionals.* Baltimore, MD: Johns Hopkins University Press.

17   T. Beauchamp and J. Childress. 1994. *Principles of Biomedical Ethics* (4th edn). New York: Oxford University Press: 151.

18   E. Sternberg. Walter B. Cannon and 'Voodoo' Death: A Perspective from 60 Years On. *Am J Public Health* 2002; 92: 1564–1566.

19   D. Callahan. Can the Moral Commons Survive Autonomy? *Hastings Cent Rep* 1996; 26: 41–42.

20   Beauchamp and Childress, *Principles of Biomedical Ethics*, p. 142.

21   O. O'Neil. Some Limits of Informed Consent. *J Med Ethics* 2003; 29: 4–7: 4.

22   J. Wilson. Is Respect for Autonomy Defensible? *J Med Ethics* 2007; 33: 353–356: 354.

23   S. Cohen. The Gettier Problem in Informed Consent. *J Med Ethics* 2011; 37: 642–645.

24   O. O'Neil. 2002. *Autonomy and Trust in Bioethics.* Cambridge: Cambridge University Press.

25   J. Varelius. The Value of Autonomy in Medical Ethics. *Med HealthC Philos* 2006; 9: 377–388.

26   Cohen, The Gettier Problem in Informed Consent.

27   American Medical Association. 2006. *AMA's Code of Medical Ethics,* E-8.082. http://www.ama-assn.org/ama/pub/physician-resources/medical-ethics/code-medical-ethics/opinion8082.page [Accessed 1 Oct 2011].

28   S. Cohen and H. Shapiro. 'Comparable Placebo Treatment' and the Ethics of Deception. *J Med Philos* 2013 Dec; 38(6): 696–709. doi:10.1093/jmp/jht052.

29   B. Foddy. A Duty to Deceive: Placebos in Clinical Practice. *Am J Bioeth* 2009; 9(12): 4–12.

30   Beauchamp and Childress, *Principles of Biomedical Ethics*, p. 145.

31   N. Bostick et al. Report of the American Medical Association Council on Ethical and Judicial Affairs: Withholding Information from Patients: Rethinking the Propriety of 'Therapeutic Privilege'. *J Clin Ethics* 2006; 17: 302–306: 303.

32   H. Brody. 1992. *The Healer's Power*. New Haven, CT.: Yale University Press: 116.

33   B. Lown. 1999. *The Lost Art of Healing*. New York: Ballantine Books.

34   K. Brown and A. Jameton. 1995. Information Disclosure. In *The Encyclopedia of Bioethics*. W.T. Reich, ed. New York: Macmillan, 1221–1232.

35   L.C. Park and L. Covi. Non-blind Placebo Trial: An Exploration of Neurotic Patients' Responses to Placebo When Its Inert Content Is Disclosed. *Archives of General Psychiatry* 1965; 12: 336–345; T.J. Kaptchuk et al. Placebos without Deception: A Randomized Controlled Trial in Irritable Bowel Syndrome. *PLoS One* 2010; 5(12): e15591.

36   R. Gillon. Ethics Needs Principles – Four Can Encompass the Rest – and Respect for Autonomy Should Be 'First among Equals'. *J Med Ethics* 2003; 29: 307–312.

37   C. Korsgaard. 1996. Two Arguments against Lying. In Korsgaard, *Creating the Kingdom of Ends*. Cambridge: Cambridge University Press: 335–362.

38   W.D. Ross. 2002. *The Right and the Good*. P. Stratton-Lake, ed. Oxford: Oxford University Press.

39   Bok, *Lying*.

40   A. Baier. 1990. Why Honesty Is a Hard Virtue? In *Identity, Character, and Morality*. O. Flanagan and A. Oksenberg Rorty, eds. Cambridge MA: MIT Press.

41   B. Williams. 2002. *Truth and Truthfulness*. Princeton: Princeton University Press: 114.

42   P. Lichtenberg, U. Heresco-Levy and U. Nitzan. The Ethics of the Placebo in Clinical Practice. *J Med Ethics* 2004; 30: 551–554; Foddy, A Duty to Deceive; F. Miller and L. Colloca. The Legitimacy of Placebo Treatments in Clinical Practice: Evidence and Ethics. *Am J Bioeth* 2009; 9(12): 39–47: Cohen and Shapiro, 'Comparable Placebo Treatment' and the Ethics of Deception.

43   R. Chisholm and T. Feehan. The Intent to Deceive. *J Philos* 1977; 74: 143–159.

44   Beauchamp and Childress, *Principles of Biomedical Ethics*.

45   F. Miller and L. Colloca. The Placebo Phenomenon and Medical Ethics: Rethinking the Relationship between Informed Consent and Risk-Benefit Assessment. *Theor Med Bioeth* 2011; 32: 229–243.

46   Benedetti et al., When Words Are Painful.

47   R.A. Preston et al. Placebo-Associated Blood Pressure Response and Adverse Effects in the Treatment of Hypertension. *Arch Intern Med* 2000; 160: 1449–1454.

48   L. Wilson et al. Somatization and Pain Dispersion in Chronic Temporomandibular Disorder Pain. *Pain* 1994; 57: 55–61.

49   Barsky et al., Nonspecific Medication Side Effects and the Nocebo Phenomenon.

50   A.L. Geers et al. Reconsidering the Role of Personality in Placebo Effects: Dispositional Optimism, Situational Expectations, and the Placebo Response. *J Psychosom Res* 2005; 58: 121–127.

51   Benedetti et al., Conscious Expectation and Unconscious Conditioning.

52   H. Pander Maat and R. Klaassen. Side Effects of Side Effect Information in Drug Information Leaflets. *J Tech Writ Comm* 1994; 24: 389–404.

53   B.J. McNeil et al. On the Elicitation of Preferences for Alternative Therapies. *N Engl J Med* 1982; 306: 1259–1262.

Part XI

Special Issues Facing Nurses

Introduction

Modern nursing came into being in England in the middle of the nineteenth century, following the revolutionary reforms introduced by Florence Nightingale. During the second half of the nineteenth century, medicine learned more than ever before about the transmission of disease, its treatment, cure, and prevention. It became a discipline that would increasingly benefit patients, and doctors needed assistants – nurses – to aid them in their work.

Nursing came to be seen as a reputable occupation for women and then, as now, most nursing was carried out by women. Medicine, on the other hand, was the exclusive domain of men. Nursing began at a time of hierarchical social organization and authoritarian lines of command, and when women were assumed to be subordinate to men. These historical conditions have played an important role in shaping the relationship between nursing and medicine, and nurses and doctors.

Until the 1960s nurses largely saw themselves as the assistants of doctors, and obedience was seen as one of the cardinal virtues of the nurse. One of many nurses and nurse educators to express this view was Sarah Dock in 1917, writing from Paducah, Kentucky ("The Relation of the Nurse to the Doctor and the Doctor to the Nurse"): "In my estimation, obedience is the first law and the very cornerstone of good nursing … The first and most helpful criticism I ever received from a doctor was when he told me that I was supposed to be simply an intelligent machine for the purpose of carrying out his orders."

Although critical voices began to be heard, it was not until the 1960s and 1970s that better-educated and more assertive nurses were seriously questioning their role. The 1965 *International Code of Nursing Ethics* still stated: "The nurse is under an obligation to carry out the physician's orders intelligently and loyally," but the 1973 International Council of Nurses' *Code for Nurses* signaled a change. It held that the "primary responsibility" of nurses was to patients – "to those people who require nursing care" – and instead of reminding nurses that they were under an obligation to carry out doctors' orders, it merely admonished them to sustain "a cooperative relationship with co-workers in nursing and other fields." In other words, nurses were now seeing themselves as professionals, whose primary responsibility was to patients rather than to doctors.

This change in role perception suggests that nurses have a professional obligation to question and oppose medical orders that are contrary to the rights or interests of patients, and to take positive steps to act as "patient advocates." Many contemporary nurses, deeply dissatisfied with their past subservient role, have welcomed this change as recognition of their professional skills and the contribution they can make to good patient care. Contrary voices argue, however, that whatever is true of some other areas of healthcare,

Bioethics: An Anthology, Third Edition. Edited by Helga Kuhse, Udo Schüklenk, and Peter Singer.
© 2016 John Wiley & Sons, Inc. Published 2016 by John Wiley & Sons, Inc.

nurses working in contemporary hospitals must retain their traditional role. Significant departures from that subservient role would seriously threaten the delivery of healthcare, and thus be to the detriment of patients as a whole.

Lisa Newton ("In Defense of the Traditional Nurse") denies that such a change to the traditional nursing role would benefit hospital patients. Newton's three-pronged defense of the traditional nurse is based on the nature of (hospital) bureaucracies, the nature of medicine, and the needs of patients. She holds that hospitals are bureaucratic institutions that rely for efficient functioning on adherence to procedures and on avoidance of initiative by those who have been charged with certain tasks. While this is true of all bureaucratic institutions, strict adherence to these rules becomes critically important when the focus is on hospitals. A patient's life and health will depend on the quick and reliable response of members of the healthcare team to the directions of the doctor, who is trained in the field of medicine. The doctor is thus, Newton writes, the only one who knows how to deal with serious medical situations that arise without warning.

After arguing against the claims that that the adoption of a subservient role is incompatible with the value of nurse autonomy and the aspirations of feminism, Newton concludes that the traditional nursing role is "crucial to health care in the hospital context; its subservient status, required for its remaining features, is neither in itself demeaning nor a barrier to its assumption by men or women."

Even if one accepts that there are some specific areas and situations in hospital medicine where a doctor's professional expertise and a nurse's unquestioning swift response will benefit patients most, can this principle be applied to all areas of hospital care?

Sarah Breier's answer ("Patient Autonomy and Medical Paternity: Can Nurses Help Doctors to Listen to Patients?") would be "no." Focusing on end-of-life care, she draws a distinction between medical expertise and ethical judgment and suggests that while doctors have expertise in medicine, they have no particular expertise in ethics. In fact, medicine's traditional focus on saving life, on the aggressive treatment of disease and the restoration and maintenance of functioning may lead to medical paternalism and the "medicalization of

death," where life is maintained without the consent of competent but vulnerable patients.

For Breier, respect for patient autonomy should occupy a prominent place in healthcare and, she argues, nurses are uniquely placed to act as patient advocates for dying patients. In distinction from doctors, nurses are constantly and intimately involved in the day-to-day care of individual patients and are thus well positioned to listen to patients and to act as their advocates in making end-of-life decisions.

Good patient care requires, the author concludes, that the particular expertise and skills of both nurses and doctors be recognized, as "This will surely improve the ability of doctors and nurses to complement each other in the decision-making process, ultimately for the benefit and holistic well-being of patients and their families."

The adoption of an advocacy role is an expansion of the traditional role of nurses as it adds a layer of professional and ethical obligations and responsibilities to their more conventional nursing duties. Questions have, however, been raised about the limits of the advocacy role of nurses. As Carol Pavlish et al. note ("Health and Human Rights Advocacy: Perspectives from a Rwandan Refugee Camp") there is no clear understanding of the term "advocacy," and the literature has paid scant attention to what advocacy might amount to when the focus goes beyond individual patient care. In different parts of the world, nurses work not only within widely differing healthcare settings, but also in countries with diverse social structures, economies, and power relationships. This diversity in healthcare settings invites consideration of a possibly wider, or different, understanding of advocacy.

A well-documented connection exists between poverty, human rights abuses, and ill-health. This means, Pavlish et al. write, that social injustices and abuses are, or should be, of concern to nurses – a stance seemingly also taken by the 2006 *ICN Code of Ethics for Nurses* when it states that nurses should "promote an environment in which human rights, values, customs and spiritual beliefs of the individual, family and community are respected."

Drawing on the results of an ethnographic human rights study in Rwanda, the authors reach the conclusion that social injustices and abuses become part of nurses' professional concerns for the well-being of patients and people in general. Violence against women, for example, not only harms women themselves, but also their children and the community at large. In short, nurses should adopt the role of "social advocate," that is, take "responsibility for creating health-conducive conditions that emphasize the principles of justice, equity, non-discrimination, transparency, fairness, and collaboration."

The small research study by Pavlish et al. does not allow for context-free generalizations. If correct, their reasoning would, however, entail that nurses should at least sometimes, and perhaps frequently, act as social advocates.

But should individual nurses take on social advocacy as a *professional* role, or would it be too much to demand that possibly ill-equipped nurses take even risky action in attempts to right health-related social wrongs?

The Relation of the Nurse to the Doctor and the Doctor to the Nurse

Sarah E. Dock

In my estimation obedience is the first law and the very cornerstone of good nursing. And here is the first stumbling block for the beginner. No matter how gifted she may be, she will never become a reliable nurse until she can obey without question. The first and most helpful criticism I ever received from a doctor was when he told me that I was supposed to be simply an intelligent machine for the purpose of carrying out his orders.

Original publication details: Sarah E. Dock, "The Relation of the Nurse to the Doctor and the Doctor to the Nurse," p. 394 (extract) from *The American Journal of Nursing* 17: 5 (1917).

In Defense of the Traditional Nurse

Lisa H. Newton

When a truth is accepted by everyone as so obvious that it blots out all its alternatives and leaves no respectable perspectives from which to examine it, it becomes the natural prey of philosophers, whose essential activity is to question accepted opinion. A case in point may be the ideal of the "autonomous professional" for nursing. The consensus that this ideal and image are appropriate for the profession is becoming monolithic and may profit from the presence of a full-blooded alternative ideal to replace the cardboard stereotypes it routinely condemns. That alternative, I suggest, is the traditional ideal of the skilled and gentle caregiver, whose role in health care requires submission to authority as an essential component. We can see the faults of this traditional ideal very clearly now, but we may perhaps also be able to see virtues that went unnoticed in the battle to displace it. It is my contention that the image and ideal of the traditional nurse contain virtues that can be found nowhere else in the health care professions, that perhaps make an irreplaceable contribution to the care of patients, and that should not be lost in the transition to a new definition of the profession of nursing.

A word should be said about what this article is, and what it is not. It is an essay in philosophical analysis, starting from familiar ideas, beliefs, and concepts, examining their relationships and implications and

reaching tentative conclusions about the logical defensibility of the structures discovered. It is not the product of research in the traditional sense. Its factual premises – for example, that the "traditional" nursing role has been criticized by those who prefer an "autonomous professional" role – are modest by any standard, and in any event may be taken as hypothetical by all who may be disposed to disagree with them. It is not a polemic against any writer or writers in particular, but a critique of lines of reasoning that are turning up with increasing frequency in diverse contexts. Its arguments derive no force whatsoever from any writings in which they may be found elsewhere.

Role Components

The first task of any philosophical inquiry is to determine its terminology and establish the meanings of its key terms for its own purposes. To take the first term: a *role* is a norm-governed pattern of action undertaken in accordance with social expectations. The term is originally derived from the drama, where it signifies a part played by an actor in a play. In current usage, any ordinary job or profession (physician, housewife, teacher, postal worker) will do as an example of a social role; the term's dramatic origin is nonetheless

Original publication details: Lisa H. Newton, "In Defense of the Traditional Nurse," pp. 348–54 from *Nursing Outlook* 29: 6 (1981). Copyright Elsevier 1981.

worth remembering, as a key to the limits of the concept.

Image and ideal are simply the descriptive and prescriptive aspects of a social role. The *image* of a social role is that role as it is understood to be in fact, both by the occupants of the role and by those with whom the occupant interacts. It describes the character the occupant plays, the acts, attitudes, and expectations normally associated with the role. The *ideal* of a role is a conception of what that role could or should be – that is, a conception of the norms that should govern its work. It is necessary to distinguish between the private and public aspects of image and ideal.

Since role occupants and general public need not agree either on the description of the present operations of the role or on the prescription for its future development, the private image, or self-image of the role occupant, is therefore distinct from the public image or general impression of the role maintained in the popular media and mind. The private ideal, or aspiration of the role occupant, is distinct from the public ideal or normative direction set for the role by the larger society. Thus, four role components emerge, from the public and private, descriptive and prescriptive, aspects of a social role. They may be difficult to disentangle in some cases, but they are surely distinct in theory, and potentially in conflict in fact.

Transitional Roles

In these terms alone we have the materials for the problematic tensions within transitional social roles. Stable social roles should exhibit no significant disparities among images and ideals: what the public generally gets is about what it thinks it should get; what the job turns out to require is generally in accord with the role occupant's aspirations; and public and role occupant, beyond a certain base level of "they-don't-know-how-hard-we-work" grumbling, are in general agreement on what the role is all about. On the other hand, transitional roles tend to exhibit strong discrepancies among the four elements of the role during the transition; at least the components will make the transition at different times, and there may also be profound disagreement on the direction that the transition should take.

The move from a general discussion of roles in society to a specific discussion of the nursing profession is made difficult by the fact that correct English demands the use of a personal pronoun. How shall we refer to the nurse? It is claimed that consistent reference to a professional as "he" reinforces the stereotype of male monopoly in the professions, save for the profession of nursing, where consistent reference to the professional as "she" reinforces the stereotype of subservience. Though we ought never to reinforce sex and dominance stereotypes, the effort to write in gender-neutral terms involves the use of circumlocutions and "he/she" usages that quickly becomes wearisome to reader and writer alike. Referring to most other professions, I would simply use the universal pronouns "he" and "him", and ignore the ridiculous accusations of sexism. But against a background of a virtually all-female profession, whose literature until the last decade universally referred to its professionals as "she", the consistent use of "he" to refer to a nurse calls attention to itself and distracts attention from the argument.

A further problem with gender-neutral terminology in the discussion of this issue in particular is that it appears to render the issue irrelevant. The whole question of autonomy for the nurse in professional work arises because nurses have been, and are, by and large, women, and the place of the profession in the health care system is strongly influenced by the place of women in society. To talk about nurses as if they were, or might as well be, men is to make the very existence of a problem a mystery. There are, therefore, good reasons beyond custom to continue using the pronoun "she" to refer to the nurse. I doubt that such use will suggest to anyone who might read this essay that it is not appropriate for men to become nurses; presumably we are beyond making that error at this time.

Barriers to Autonomy

The first contention of my argument is that the issue of autonomy in the nursing profession lends itself to misformulation. A common formulation of the issue, for example, locates it in a discrepancy between public image and private image. On this account, the public is asserted to believe that nurses are ill-educated, unintelligent, incapable of assuming responsibility, and hence properly excluded from professional status and responsibility. In fact they are now prepared to be truly autonomous professionals through an excellent education, including a thorough theoretical grounding in all aspects of their profession. Granted, the public image of the nurse has many favorable aspects – the nurse is credited with great manual skill, often saintly dedication to service to others, and, at least below the supervisory level, a warm heart and gentle manners. But the educational and intellectual deficiencies that the public mistakenly perceives outweigh the "positive" qualities when it comes to deciding how the nurse shall be treated, and are called upon to justify not only her traditionally inferior status and low wages, but also the refusal to allow nursing to fill genuine needs in the health care system by assuming tasks that nurses are uniquely qualified to handle. For the sake of the quality of health care as well as for the sake of the interests of the nurse, the public must be educated through a massive educational campaign to the full capabilities of the contemporary nurse; the image must be brought into line with the facts. On this account, then, the issue of nurse autonomy is diagnosed as a public relations problem: the private ideal of nursing is asserted to be that of the autonomous professional and the private image is asserted to have undergone a transition from an older subservient role to a new professional one but the public image of the nurse ideal is significantly not mentioned in this analysis.

An alternative account of the issue of professional autonomy in nursing locates it in a discrepancy between private ideal and private image. Again, the private ideal is that of the autonomous professional. But the actual performance of the role is entirely slavish, because of the way the system works – with its tight budgets, insane schedules, workloads bordering on reckless endangerment for the seriously ill, bureaucratic red tape, confusion, and arrogance. Under these conditions, the nurse is permanently barred from fulfilling her professional ideal, from bringing the reality of the nurse's condition into line with the self-concept she brought to the job. On this account, then, the nurse really is not an autonomous professional, and total reform of the power structure of the health care industry will be necessary in order to allow her to become one.

A third formulation locates the issue of autonomy in a struggle between the private ideal and an altogether undesirable public ideal: on this account, the public does not want the nurse to be an autonomous professional, because her present subservient status serves the power needs of the physicians; because her unprofessional remuneration serves the monetary needs of the entrepreneurs and callous municipalities that run the hospitals; and because the low value accorded her opinions on patient care protects both physicians and bureaucrats from being forced to account to the patient for the treatment he receives. On this account, the nurse needs primarily to gather allies to defeat the powerful interest groups that impose the traditional ideal for their own unworthy purposes, and to replace that degrading and dangerous prescription with one more appropriate to the contemporary nurse.

These three accounts, logically independent, have crucial elements of content in common. Above all, they agree on the objectives to be pursued: full professional independence, responsibility, recognition, and remuneration for the professional nurse. And, as corollary to these objectives, they agree on the necessity of banishing for ever from the hospitals and from the public mind that inaccurate and demeaning stereotype of the nurse as the Lady with the Bedpan: an image of submissive service, comforting to have around and skillful enough at her little tasks, but too scatterbrained and emotional for responsibility.

In none of the interpretations above is any real weight given to a public ideal of nursing, to the nursing role as the public thinks it ought to be played. Where public prescription shows up at all, it is seen as a vicious and false demand imposed by power alone, thoroughly illegitimate and to be destroyed as quickly as possible. The possibility that there may be real value in the traditional role of the nurse, and that the public may have good reasons to want to retain it, simply does not receive any serious consideration on any account. It is precisely that possibility that I take up in the next section.

Defending the "Traditional Nurse"

As Aristotle taught us, the way to discover the peculiar virtues of any thing is to look to the work that it accomplishes in the larger context of its environment. The first task, then, is to isolate those factors of need or demand in the nursing environment that require the nurse's work if they are to be met. I shall concentrate, as above, on the hospital environment, since most nurses are employed in hospitals.

The work context of the hospital nurse actually spans two societal practices or institutions: the hospital as a bureaucracy and medicine as a field of scientific endeavor and service. Although there is enormous room for variation in both hospital bureaucracies and medicine, and they may therefore interact with an infinite number of possible results, the most general facts about both institutions allow us to sketch the major demands they make on those whose function lies within them.

To take the hospital bureaucracy first: its very nature demands that workers perform the tasks assigned to them, report properly to the proper superior, avoid initiative, and adhere to set procedures. These requirements are common to all bureaucracies, but dramatically increase in urgency when the tasks are supposed to be protective of life itself and where the subject matter is inherently unpredictable and emergency prone. Since there is often no time to re-examine the usefulness of a procedure in a particular case, and since the stakes are too high to permit a gamble, the institution's effectiveness, not to mention its legal position, may depend on unquestioning adherence to procedure.

Assuming that the sort of hospital under discussion is one in which the practice of medicine by qualified physicians is the focal activity, rather than, say, a convalescent hospital, further contextual requirements emerge. Among the prominent features of the practice of medicine are the following: it depends on esoteric knowledge which takes time to acquire and which is rapidly advancing; and, because each patient's illness is unique, it is uncertain. Thus, when a serious medical situation arises without warning, only physicians will know how to deal with it (if their licensure has any point), and they will not always be able to explain or justify their actions to nonphysicians, even those who are required to assist them in patient care.

If the two contexts of medicine and the hospital are superimposed, three common points can be seen. Both are devoted to the saving of life and health; the atmosphere in which that purpose is carried out is inevitably tense and urgent; and, if the purpose is to be accomplished in that atmosphere, all participating activities and agents must be completely subordinated to the medical judgments of the physicians. In short, those other than physicians, involved in medical procedures in a hospital context, have no right to insert their own needs, judgments, or personalities into the situation. The last thing we need at that point is another autonomous professional on the job, whether a nurse or anyone else.

Patient Needs: The Prime Concern

From the general characteristics of hospitals and medicine, that negative conclusion for nursing follows. But the institutions are not, after all, the focus of the endeavor. If there is any conflict between the needs of the patient and the needs of the institutions established to serve him, his needs take precedence and constitute the most important requirements of the nursing environment. What are these needs?

First, because the patient is sick and disabled, he needs specialized care that only qualified personnel can administer, beyond the time that the physician is with him. Second, and perhaps most obviously to the patient, he is likely to be unable to perform simple tasks such as walking unaided, dressing himself, and attending to his bodily functions. He will need assistance in these tasks, and is likely to find this need humiliating; his entire self-concept as an independent human being may be threatened. Thus, the patient has serious emotional needs brought on by the hospital situation itself, regardless of his disability. He is scared, depressed, disappointed, and possibly, in reaction to all of these, very angry. He needs reassurance, comfort, someone to talk to. The person he really needs, who would be capable of taking care of all these problems, is obviously his mother, and the first job of the nurse is to be a mother surrogate.

That conclusion, it should be noted, is inherent in the word "nurse" itself: it is derived ultimately from the Latin *nutrire*, "to nourish or suckle," the first meaning of "nurse" as a noun is still, according to *Webster's New Twentieth Century Unabridged Dictionary* "one who suckles a child not her own." From the outset, then, the function of the nurse is identical with that of the mother, to be exercised when the mother is unavailable. And the meanings proceed in logical order from there: the second definitions given for both noun and verb involve caring for children, especially young children, and the third, caring for those who are childlike in their dependence – the sick, the injured, the very old, and the handicapped. For all those groups – infants, children, and helpless adults – it is appropriate to bring children's caretakers, surrogate mothers, nurses, into the situation to minister to them. It is especially appropriate to do so, for the sake of the psychological economies realized by the patient: the sense of self, at least for the Western adult, hangs on the self-perception of independence. Since disability requires the relinquishing of this self-perception, the patient must either discover conditions excusing his dependence somewhere in his self-concept, or invent new ones, and the latter task is extremely difficult. Hence the usefulness of the maternal image association: it was, within the patient's understanding of himself, "all right" to be tended by mother; if the nurse is (at some level) mother, it is "all right" to reassume that familiar role and to be tended by her.

Limits on the "Mother" Role

The nurse's assumption of the role of mother is therefore justified etymologically and historically but most importantly by reference to the psychological demands of and on the patient. Yet the maternal role cannot be imported into the hospital care situation without significant modification – specifically, with respect to the power and authority inherent in the role of mother. Such maternal authority, includes the right and duty to assume control over children's lives and make all decisions for them; but the hospital patient most definitely does not lose adult status even if he is sick enough to want to. The ethical legitimacy as well as the therapeutic success of his treatment depend on his voluntary and active cooperation in it and on his deferring to some forms of power and authority – the hospital rules and the physician's

sapiential authority, for example. But these very partial, conditional, restraints are nowhere near the threat to patient autonomy that the real presence of mother would be; maternal authority, total, diffuse, and unlimited, would be incompatible with the retention of moral freedom. And it is just this sort of total authority that the patient is most tempted to attribute to the nurse, who already embodies the nurturant component of the maternal role. To prevent serious threats to patient autonomy, then, the role of nurse must be from the outset, as essentially as it is nurturant, unavailable for such attribution of authority. Not only must the role of nurse not include authority; it must be incompatible with authority: essentially, a subservient role.

The nurse role, as required by the patient's situation, is the nurturant component of the maternal role and excludes elements of power and authority. A further advantage of this combination of maternal nurturance and subordinate status is that, just as it permits the patient to be cared for like a baby without threatening his autonomy, it also permits him to unburden himself to a sympathetic listener of his doubts and resentments, about physicians and hospitals in general, and his in particular, without threatening the course of his treatment. His resentments are natural, but they lead to a situation of conflict, between the desire to rebel against treatment and bring it to a halt (to reassert control over his life), and the desire that the treatment should continue (to obtain its benefits). The nurse's function speaks well to this condition: like her maternal model, the nurse is available for the patient to talk to (the physician is too busy to talk), sympathetic, understanding, and supportive; but, in her subordinate position, the nurse can do absolutely nothing to change his course of treatment. Since she has no more control over the environment than he has, he can let off steam in perfect safety, knowing that he cannot do himself any damage.

The norms for the nurse's role so far derived from the patient's perspective also tally, it might be noted, with the restrictions on the role that arise from the needs of hospitals and medicine. The patient does not need another autonomous professional at his bedside, any more than the physician can use one or the hospital bureaucracy contain one. The conclusion so far, then, is that, in the hospital environment, the traditional (nurturant and subordinate) role of the nurse seems more adapted to the nurse function than the new autonomous role.

Provider of Humanistic Care

So far, we have defined the hospital nurse's function in terms of the specific needs of the hospital, the physician, and the patient. Yet there is another level of function that needs to be addressed. If we consider the multifaceted demands that the patient's family, friends, and community make on the hospital once the patient is admitted, it becomes clear that this concerned group cannot be served exclusively by attending to the medical aspect of care, necessary though that is. Nor is it sufficient for the hospital-as-institution to keep accurate and careful records, maintain absolute cleanliness, and establish procedures that protect the patient's safety, even though this is important. Neither bureaucracy nor medical professional can handle the human needs of the human beings involved in the process.

The general public entering the hospital as patient or visitor encounters and reacts to that health care system as an indivisible whole, as if under a single heading of "what the hospital is like." It is at this level that we can make sense of the traditional claim that the nurse represents the "human" as opposed to "mechanical" or "coldly professional" aspect of health care, for there is clearly something terribly missing in the combined medical and bureaucratic approach to the "case": they fail to address the patient's fear for himself and the family's fear for him, their grief over the separation, even if temporary, their concern for the financial burden, and a host of other emotional components of hospitalization.

The same failing appears throughout the hospital experience, most poignantly obvious, perhaps, when the medical procedures are unavailing and the patient dies. When this occurs, the physician must determine the cause and time of death and the advisability of an autopsy, while the bureaucracy must record the death and remove the body; but surely this is not enough. The death of a human being is a rending of the fabric of human community, a sad and fearful time; it is appropriately a time of bitter regret, anger, and weeping. The patient's family, caught up in the institutional

context of the hospital, cannot assume alone the burden of *discovering and expressing the emotions* appropriate to the occasion; such expression, essential for their own regeneration after their loss, must originate somehow within the hospital context itself. The hospital system must, somehow, be able to share pain and grief as well as it makes medical judgments and keeps records.

The traditional nurse's role addresses itself directly to these human needs. Its derivation from the maternal role classifies it as feminine and permits ready assumption of all attributes culturally typed as "feminine" tenderness, warmth, sympathy, and a tendency to engage much more readily in the expression of feeling than in the rendering of judgment. Through the nurse, the hospital can be concerned, welcoming, caring, and grief-stricken; it can break through the cold barriers of efficiency essential to its other functions and share human feeling.

The nurse therefore provides the in-hospital health care system with human capabilities that would otherwise be unavailable to it and hence unavailable to the community in dealing with it. Such a conclusion is unattractive to the supporters of the autonomous role for the nurse, because the tasks of making objective judgments and of expressing emotion are inherently incompatible; and since the nurse shows grief and sympathy on behalf of the system, she is excluded from decision-making and defined as subordinate.

However unappealing such a conclusion may be, it is clear that, without the nurse role in this function, the hospital becomes a moral monstrosity, coolly and mechanically dispensing and disposing of human life and death, with no acknowledgement at all of the individual life, value, projects, and relationships of the persons with whom it deals. Only the nurse makes the system morally tolerable. People in pain deserve sympathy, as the dead deserve to be grieved for; it is unthinkable that the very societal institution to which we generally consign the suffering and the dying should be incapable of sustaining sympathy and grief. Yet its capability hangs on the presence of nurses willing to assume the affective functions of the traditional nursing role, and the current attempt to banish that role, to introduce instead an autonomous professional role for the nurse, threatens to send the last hope for a human presence in the hospital off at the same time.

The Feminist Perspective

From this conclusion it would seem to follow automatically that the role of the traditional nurse should be retained. It might be argued, however, that the value of autonomy is such that any non-autonomous role ought to be abolished, no matter what its value to the current institutional structure.

Those who aimed to abolish black slavery in the United States have provided a precedent for this argument. They never denied the slave's economic usefulness; they simply denied that it could be right to enslave any person and insisted that the nation find some other way to get the work done, no matter what the cost. On a totally different level, the feminists of our own generation have proposed that the traditional housewife and mother role for the woman, which confined women to domestic life and made them subordinate to men, has been very useful for everyone except the women trapped in it. All the feminists have claimed is that the profit of others is not a sufficient reason to retain a role that demeans its occupant. As they see it, the "traditional nurse" role is analogous to the roles of slave and housewife – it is derived directly, in fact, as we have seen, from the "mother" part of the latter role – exploitative of its occupants and hence immoral by its very nature and worthy of abolition.

But the analogy does not hold. A distinction must be made between an autonomous person – one who, over the course of adult life, is self-determining in all major choices and a significant number of minor ones, and hence can be said to have chosen, and to be responsible for, his own life – and an autonomous *role* – a role so structured that its occupant is self-determining in all major and most minor role-related choices. An autonomous person can certainly take on a subordinate role without losing his personal autonomy. For example, we can find examples of slaves (in the ancient world at least) and housewives who have claimed to have, and shown every sign of having, complete personal integrity and autonomy with their freely chosen roles.

Furthermore, slave and housewife are a very special type of role, known as "life-roles." They are to be played 24 hours a day, for an indefinite period of time; there is no customary or foreseeable respite from them. Depending on circumstances, there may be

de facto escapes from these roles, permitting their occupants to set up separate personal identities (some of the literature from the history of American slavery suggests this possibility), but the role definitions do not contemplate part-time occupancy. Such life-roles are few in number; most roles are the part-time "occupational roles," the jobs that we do eight hours a day and have little to do with the structuring of the rest of the twenty-four. An autonomous person can, it would seem, easily take up a subordinate role of this type and play it well without threat to personal autonomy. And if there is excellent reason to choose such a role – if, for example, an enterprise of tremendous importance derives an essential component of its moral worth from that role – it would seem to be altogether rational and praiseworthy to do so. The role of "traditional nurse" would certainly fall within this category.

But, even if the traditional nurse role is not inherently demeaning, it might be argued further, it should be abolished as harmful to the society because it preserves the sex stereotypes that we are trying to overcome. "Nurse" is a purely feminine role, historically derived from "mother", embodying feminine attributes of emotionality, tenderness, and nurturance, and it is subordinate – thus reinforcing the link between femininity and subordinate status. The nurse role should be available to men, too, to help break down this unfavorable stereotype.

This objection to the traditional role embodies the very fallacy it aims to combat. The falsehood we know as sexism is not the belief that some roles are autonomous, calling for objectivity in judgment, suppression of emotion, and independent initiative in action, but discouraging independent judgment and action and requiring obedience to superiors; the falsehood is the assumption that only men are eligible for the first class and only women are eligible for the second class.

One of the most damaging mistakes of our cultural heritage is the assumption that warmth, gentleness, and loving care, such as are expected of the nurse, are simply impossible for the male of the species, and that men who show emotion, let alone those who are ever known to weep, are weaklings, "sissies," and a disgrace to the human race. I suspect that this assumption has done more harm to the culture than its more publicized partner, the assumption that women are (or should be) incapable of objective judgment or executive function. Women will survive without leadership roles, but it is not clear that a society can retain its humanity if all those eligible for leadership are forbidden, by virtue of that eligibility, to take account of the human side of human beings: their altruism, heroism, compassion, and grief, their fear and weakness, and their ability to love and care for others.

In the words of the current feminist movement, men must be liberated as surely as women. And one of the best avenues to such liberation would be the encouragement of male participation in the health care system, or other systems of the society, in roles like the traditional nursing role, which permit, even require, the expressive side of the personality to develop, giving it a function in the enterprise and restoring it to recognition and respectability.

Conclusions

In conclusion, then, the traditional nurse role is crucial to health care in the hospital context; its subordinate status, required for its remaining features, is neither in itself demeaning nor a barrier to its assumption by men or women. It is probably not a role that everyone would enjoy. But there are certainly many who are suited to it, and should be willing to undertake the job.

One of the puzzling features of the recent controversy is the apparent unwillingness of some of the current crop of nursing school graduates to take on the assignment for which they have ostensibly been prepared, at least until such time as it shall be redefined to accord more closely with their notion of professional. These frustrated nurses who do not want the traditional nursing role, yet wish to employ their skills in the health care system in some way, will clearly have to do something else. The health care industry is presently in the process of very rapid expansion and diversification, and has created significant markets for those with a nurse's training and the capacity, and desire, for autonomous roles. Moreover, the nurse in a position which does not have the "nurse" label does not need to combat the "traditional nurse" image and is ordinarily accorded greater freedom of action. For this reason alone it would appear that those nurses intent on occupying autonomous roles and tired of fighting stereotypes that they find degrading and unworthy of their abilities should seek out occupational niches that do not bear the label, and the stigma, of "nurse."

I conclude, therefore: that much of the difficulty in obtaining public acceptance of the new "autonomous professional" image of the nurse may be due, not to public ignorance, but to the opposition of a vague but persistent public ideal of nursing; that the ideal is a worthy one, well-founded in the hospital context in which it evolved; and that the role of traditional nurse, for which that ideal sets the standard, should therefore be maintained and held open for any who would have the desire, and the personal and professional qualifications, to assume it. Perhaps the current crop of nursing school graduates do not desire it, but there is ample room in the health care system for the sort of "autonomous professional" they wish to be, apart from the hospital nursing role. Wherever we must go to fill this role, it is worth going there, for the traditional nurse is the major force remaining for humanity in a system that will turn into a mechanical monster without her.

82

Patient Autonomy and Medical Paternity
Can Nurses Help Doctors to Listen to Patients?

Sarah Breier

Nurses are increasingly faced with situations in practice regarding the prolongation of life and withdrawal of treatment. They play a central role in the care of dying people, yet they may find themselves disempowered by medical paternalism or ill-equipped in the decision-making process in end-of-life situations. This article is concerned with the ethical relationships between patient autonomy and medical paternalism in end-of-life care for an advanced cancer patient. The nurse's role as the patient's advocate is explored, as are the differences between nursing and medicine when confronted with the notion of patient autonomy. The impetus for this discussion stems from a clinical encounter described in the following scenario.

Scenario

Mr X was admitted to the oncology ward with a primary diagnosis of multiple myeloma for which he received a bone marrow transplant. This was complicated by stage 4 graft versus host disease (GVHD) and cytomegalovirus infection. Mr X's response to aggressive chemotherapy was poor and he suffered intractable nausea, vomiting, diarrhoea, rectal bleeding and extreme abdominal pain for over three months after the transplant. He was then

diagnosed with sepsis secondary to ischaemia of the bowel and was found to be gancyclovir resistant. During this time Mr X became progressively weak yet remained lucid and, despite aggressive treatment, continued to deteriorate. He spoke with nursing and medical staff about his wish for cessation of the treatment. His children were supportive of his wishes and conveyed these to the medical staff. They requested their father to be transferred home with hospice care or to a palliative care setting. The medical team rejected this request, explaining that there were still other treatments they wanted to try that may alleviate the GVHD. Mr X and his family reluctantly complied, yet the patient did not respond to the other treatments and was rendered severely ill owing to the drugs' side-effects and catheter sepsis. Both the patient and his family became frustrated and angry. Their request for palliation was finally granted a week later when Mr X deteriorated suddenly and returned home with full hospice support. He died peacefully, surrounded by his family, a mere 24 hours later. After his passing, Mr X's family stated at a follow-up bereavement visit by home hospice staff that they felt angry and cheated over their father's prolonged suffering in hospital and could not understand why the doctors did not listen to him.

Original publication details: Sarah Breier, "Patient Autonomy and Medical Paternity: Can Nurses Help Doctors to Listen to Patients?," pp. 510–21 from *Nursing Ethics* 8: 6 (2001). Reproduced with permission from Sage and S. Breier.

Introduction

Nurses are directly involved with patients such as Mr X on a day to day basis and, while clinical decision making has been seen traditionally as the responsibility of the doctor, the consequences of those decisions fall largely on the nurses who are caring for such patients. Although there is an obligation to carry out the doctor's orders when decisions are medically orientated, there is no evidence that doctors are any more qualified in ethical decision making than nurses.[1] Others argue that there is no reason why doctors should have a monopoly over ethical decision making.[2] Nurses have a professional obligation to act in the best interests of their patients[3] and if they are to take part in the analysis of ethical issues they need to be well versed in the practical philosophies underpinning the ethical debates on end-of-life care in order to contribute effectively. Consideration of the ethical principle of autonomy forms the basis of this article.

Futility and the End of Life

Defining medical futility is significant in the efforts of clinicians and ethicists who seek to identify the limits of patient autonomy. In general, the nursing literature has not contained much discussion about nursing's role in facilitating respect for patients' preferences at the end of life. For example, although an extensive amount of medical research has been carried out on the utilization and efficacy of advance directives, there has been little nursing research on any aspect of advance directives, with some important exceptions.[4–6] This raises the question of who should be involved in making the decision that the patient's condition is medically futile. Given nursing's greater degree of presence at the bedside and a key role in patient communication, more discussion and enquiry are needed in this area.

Futile treatment at the end of life is not a new predicament. In its original encounter it was experienced most often by patients as undesired care.[7] Efforts to extend the education of health care professionals about a patient's right to be self-determining and the securing of legal protection for this right have done much (primarily in the USA) to mitigate this problem.

Similarly, the high-profile ethical debate of physician-assisted suicide has done much to fuel efforts to improve end-of-life care.[8] Nurse advocates who inform and alert their health professional colleagues to thorough consideration of the patient good beyond mere physical well-being have also been helpful.

It is first necessary to recognize the two different consequences of beneficial health care: improved physical well-being and improved overall well-being.[7] Although medicine suggests the physical benefits of treatment interventions, only the patient or those who know the patient best can determine if such medical care is improving and enhancing the patient's overall well-being. This latter determinant is a subjective measurement. Using these distinctions, medical care can be classified as follows: (1) not futile: beneficial to both physical and overall well-being; (2) futile: nonbeneficial to either physical or overall well-being; (3) futile from the clinician's perspective: considered valuable by the patient, or by his or her proxy, but not clinically indicated; and (4) futile from the patient's perspective: clinically indicated but not considered valuable by the patient, or by his or her proxy. It is the last point that is the focus of this discussion. Despite this component being partially resolved by an increased emphasis on patient autonomy in recent years,[7] plenty of anecdotal evidence abounds to the contrary. This assumption leads us to a compelling question: Are health care providers obligated to comply with patients' wishes? or, more candidly: Are nurses obligated to comply with doctors' wishes and ignore patients' wishes and sanction further aggressive treatment by their provision of such treatment?

Autonomy Analysed

Western health care systems have long considered autonomy as an important ethical principle in directing clinical decisions. Patient autonomy has been promoted significantly in declaring the moral and legal right of competent individuals to make decisions about the course of their dying, in improving methods for the expression of their preferences, and in better understanding of the family's role and experience in decision making.[4] Highly publicized court cases, including the Karen Quinlan,

Nancy Cruzan (USA) and Tony Bland (UK) cases, have brought professional and public recognition to the question of the patient's voice in medical decision making about aggressive treatment in terminal conditions.

It is useful here to undertake a brief analysis of the predominant discourse within this argument. The term autonomy has its foundations in the Greek words *auto* (self) and *nomos* (rule, legislation, or determination). The term *autonomia* originally described Greek city-states that were independent of external control, whereby citizens set their own governing laws rather than being subjected to laws imposed by an outside source. Gillon[9] defines autonomy in its most literal sense as being 'self-rule' or the capacity to think, decide and act on the basis of such thought and decision, unhindered and independently without fear of reprisal. Rubin[10] explains that self-rule, or autonomy, contrasts with other-rule, or heteronomy. Rather than being ruled by another, autonomous individuals develop and act on their own life plan.

Encumbrance with one's right to choose one's own goals and ends, or the imposition of another's rule instead, subjects an autonomous individual to a heteronomous life. When doctors attempt to substitute their judgement for that of their patients, they are attempting to substitute autonomy with heteronomy.[10] Within the clinical context, this is traditionally the disparity between patient autonomy and medical paternalism. The 'overriding' of a patient's autonomous preferences, decisions, or actions out of a concern for the patient's welfare constitutes medical paternalism. Conversely, the principle of patient autonomy necessitates the empowering of patients through the provision of information. It is often in connection with the choices that patients wish to make about controlling the end of their lives that doctors find patient autonomy most problematic.[11]

Patients who are confronted with the autonomy/paternalism dichotomy, are often unable to verbalize their needs or wants to their doctors, either because they are intimidated by the doctors' perceived power, or because the doctors lack the time to listen to their concerns.[12] Nurses, however, as patients' advocates, are ideally positioned to assist the patients and their families to clarify their needs and desires.[13]

Nurses' Role in Futile Treatment Decisions

Once cure of illness and/or restoration to 'health' are no longer realistic, the decision to modify the treatment plan so that either stabilized functioning or a comfortable dignified death results is indispensable.[7] In an ideal world, the patient, the family, and the health care team are in agreement about the goal for continued treatment or what constitutes continued treatment. Unfortunately, however, this is often not the case. The opening scenario alludes to an all too common situation whereby clinicians are allowed to decide upon futility, that is, to subordinate patient autonomy to physician autonomy or, as described by Nuland,[14] to the paternalism of doctors. Ideally, the decision either to proceed with or to withdraw aggressive treatment should be one of negotiation between all parties.[7] Others maintain that the parties should try to reach an understanding of treatment expectations as early as possible, before the patient reaches the terminal stage.[15] Such expectations include, but are not limited to, what care would be deemed futile, and what care falls within acceptable limits for the patient, the family, the doctor and the institution. It is by reaching this understanding via negotiation that nurses can play a critical role in effecting a just outcome. Nurses are in a unique position to initiate discussions regarding patients' preferences for treatment and quality of life.[16] The intent of such nurse-driven negotiation is to ensure that everyone works together to secure the best possible outcome for the patient, not that any one person or party asserts their assumed authority.

Historically, nurses have situated patients and their values at the centre of care.[7] The futility debate accentuates the pressing need for professionals to introduce into ethical discourse and clinical treatment decisions a sense of who the patient is and the values that underlie the patient's (and/or the proxy's) demands for treatment or refusal of treatment. Equally pressing is the need for an honest evaluation of the variables influencing both patient and doctor determination of when a given treatment justifies the risk of suffering and the allocation of both scarce and costly resources. Nurses are well placed to bring the realities of patient autonomy to the ethical discourse, as well as contributing significantly to the burden/benefit discussion that should always be present in such scenarios.

Patient Knows Best

Much of the bioethics literature in general, particularly the futility literature, presupposes that, in conflicts between patients and doctors, patients are more authoritative in evaluative matters that have direct consequences for their lives and bodies and doctors are more authoritative in exacting technological matters. Following this general assumption, many contributors to the futility literature have suggested that patients are in the foremost position to decide on therapeutic goals and to determine whether or not they are worth achieving.[17–22]

Correspondingly, they are in a prime position to evaluate, interpret and contemplate available medical information and to make evaluative judgements about whether a particular treatment modality is appropriate and worth trying.[10] This is generally accepted as true because only patients know how much risk they are willing to take and can judge particular benefits.[23] More importantly, patients alone live with the outcome of medical interventions. From this perspective they are consequently best situated to recognize when treatments are futile for them, that is, are not worth trying. At the very least, they should be significantly involved in making such determinations. However, it occurs seldom that patients are considered to be sufficiently authoritative to make judgements about the probability of a treatment's success in achieving their desired goal.[10]

Doctor Knows Best

A basic assumption is that when it comes to data collection and its interpretation and evaluation of relevance for a given patient, doctors are the more expert. On that account, many have argued that doctors are in the best position to detect authoritatively when treatment goals can or can not be accomplished.[24–28] It is also argued that doctors possess the knowledge,

expertise and authority to recognize when they are confronted with either physiologically viable or futile treatments. Accordingly, it is ultimately the doctor's responsibility to review the clinical facts and to recognize when treatment modalities will be futile in accomplishing specified goals.[10,29] The obvious disparity between the 'patient knows best' and the 'doctor knows best' arguments essentially forms what is the autonomy/paternalism dichotomy.

Us and Them: Do Doctors and Nurses Consider Patient Autonomy Differently?

In an ethnographic study by Robertson,[30] nurses and doctors viewed patient autonomy differently. Although they were reported to share a commitment to the liberal and utilitarian concepts of the principle of autonomy, nurses emphasized patient autonomy while doctors were more likely to emphasize beneficence via treatment provision. The key professional goals of nurses were daily care and helping patients to live as normally and independently as possible. These goals were sought through ongoing relationships whose sustenance necessitated the demonstration of character virtues. The most important goals of doctors were systematic problem solving, improving organ function, and research. For doctors the priority was the technological imperative, essentially the improvement of organ function.[30] An exception to this assumption is the recent efforts of the medical profession to move away from the biomedical model to a more holistic model, as, for example, in Pellegrino's ethics of caring.[31]

Much anecdotal evidence exists about the differences in caring priorities in addition to those research findings noted above. Robertson[30] explains that this emphasis of nurses regarding patient autonomy is secondary to the fact that nurses' most salient professional goal (patient normality and independence) is defined by patients' abilities. This relationship is established through the daily and nightly care of the ever-present nurse rather than via the episodic consultative nature of typical patient–doctor contact.

Assuming the role of patient advocate when conflict develops between patients and doctors means taking the 'middle ground' and uncovering what it is that truly underpins the patient's (and/or the proxy's) requests as well as the factors that give rise to doctors' professional discomfort about these requests. Patient advocacy also means uncovering the factors that make health professionals uncomfortable about those demands for treatment.[32] Unfortunately there is not always a satisfactory resolution of the conflict until these factors are identified.[7] Nurses, however, can intervene and provide much needed clarity in the identification of such conflict variables. This kind of intervention is enhanced by nurses gaining skills in mediation.

It is essential for nurses to develop the necessary communication skills, including interpersonal competence and group process adeptness. Related to this, the American Nurses Association code of ethics[33] and standards of clinical nursing practice[34] obligate nurses to be patient advocates. Similarly, in the UK[3] as well as in Australia,[35] nurses share a responsibility to inform the public and to contribute to public debate on ethical issues. Skills development in effective interpersonal communication in problem-solving groups should therefore feature strongly at unit or ward ongoing education level, if not within all nursing curricula.

To assume successfully the role of mediator, nurses must know the patient and their proxies, otherwise their effect as advocates is futile in itself. Central to nurses' contribution to the interdisciplinary team is the nurse–patient relationship. It is this relationship that empowers nurses to speak with authority regarding the effects of the illness on the patient. As Taylor[7] explains, it is a triple assessment of the current health state, the influence of this state on the person, and the influence on the person's ability to achieve meaningful life goals, that distinguishes nursing from medicine. By virtue of this assessment, nurses are able to discuss futility from the patient's perspective and elucidate why some patients (and/or their proxies) are requesting the withdrawal of treatment that doctors consider appropriate. This discussion may also open up opportunities for suggesting strategies for clarifying unrealistic expectations of both treatment provider and treatment recipient. In order to fulfil this mediating role effectively, nurses must also be both reactive and sensitive to professional and societal factors that promote conflict. For example, bias and discrimination

can always influence clinical decision making.[7] More problematic may be the need to separate surrogate suffering from patient suffering to guarantee that treatment decisions such as its provision or withdrawal are based on the interests of the patient rather than on those of the surrogate, especially when the surrogate is the primary caregiver.

End-of-Life Care and Autonomy

The unanimous efforts to improve end-of-life care that are now burgeoning in the USA are focused on better provision of palliative care. These efforts are reflected in the recent progress of institutional futility policies: the 'Last acts: care and caring at the end of life' initiative of the Robert Wood Johnson Foundation, and the EPEC project ('Education for physicians on end-of-life care') of the American Medical Association. Similarly, in the UK a recent British Medical Association publication[36] demonstrates a raised awareness in the complexity of end-of-life care. Finucane,[37] however, exposes the shortfall of end-of-life care by claiming that some dying patients do suffer unnecessarily because doctors lack the skills, temperament, or motivation to provide good palliative care:

> This is a serious failure. An ardent focus on technical aspects of symptom control, however, could distract broader efforts to improve care of those near death. Symptom control is often not the most difficult aspect of management. In caring for a severely, progressively ill patient, what may be the most difficult is moving through the transition from gravely ill to fighting death to terminally ill and seeking peace, shifting the goals of treatment from cure or longer survival to preservation of comfort and dignity.[37]

Elisabeth Kübler-Ross[38] wrote that 'death is still a fearful, frightening happening and the fear of death is a universal fear even if we think we have mastered it on several levels'. Most readers may agree that this is still the case, with many doctors espousing much of that fear. This fear is not helped by the fact that the majority of medical curricula, regardless of their geographical margins, offer little education for would-be-doctors on end-of-life care or the actual process of dying itself.[39] Nurses, on the contrary, deal regularly with the realities of the active process of dying. These realities – be they physiological or the complex personal, spiritual and emotional actualities – are not new to the majority of nurses, especially those working in clinical environments such as oncology, palliative and hospice care, critical care, emergency departments and geriatric care facilities, to name just a few. Nurses are also 'there', that is, on the ward, at the bedside, 24 hours a day, providing continuous care rather than the segmented consultative care that is so characteristic of the practice of hospital medicine. Yet it is not only the doctor who may be unprepared to deal with 'death' but also the patient who is in a state of dying. This may be the greatest difficulty that nurses deal with in empowering patients' right to self-determination in futile treatment decisions.

As Fox and colleagues[40] claim, dying patients who receive hospice care and their families are more satisfied with the care than those who are cared for elsewhere. This reflects the skill, compassion and dedication of the people working in the hospice environment, predominantly nurses. The doctor's central task in caring for seriously ill persons who are near to death is to accompany and guide these patients, who generally do not want to die, through the critical transition of being ill to dying. Several of the following tasks are therefore important: giving the best estimate of prognosis; identifying situations where palliative care may supplant the desire for aggressive treatment; and at times giving permission for a patient or loved one to agree to forgo treatment.[40]

A patient–doctor relationship based on continuing communication, truth telling and an awareness of the experience of the patient and loved ones is paramount to good care of the dying. However, the establishment of such a relationship may require encouragement of the nurse to step in and 'get the ball rolling'. The foundation for such a relationship is to understand and respect a patient's desire for all aggressive treatment to stop, even if this goes against the doctor's commitment to fight the disease and preserve life at all cost. Encouragement, support, fidelity, virtue and realism remain the cornerstones of good care for the dying.[40] Yet even with these considerations and with impeccable technical expertise in symptom management, patients, doctors, nurses and family members are likely to continue to struggle with the decisions that must be made as patients enter the active stage of life's final outcome.

Avoiding a Medicalized Death

The care of people who are dying has been greatly affected by the process of 'medicalization' of contemporary society.[41] It is often problematic for doctors to shift their care from restorative intervention and aggressive management of disease and focus it on a pattern of care where primacy is granted to the quality of life. Within hospitals this transition to palliative care is a frequent area of tension between medical and nursing staff.[42,43] In a study by Singer and colleagues[44] on patient perspectives on quality of life, participants were afraid of 'lingering' and 'being kept alive' after they could no longer enjoy their lives. Quality of life concerns seemed to fuel this fear; many were terrified of becoming a 'vegetable' or living in a coma. These participants adamantly denounced 'being kept alive by a machine'. They wanted to be 'allowed to die naturally' or 'in peace'. Ufema[45] directly encouraged nurses to ask patients what they want, claiming that people know what is best for themselves, right up to the moment they die. Such claims do not fit comfortably within the technological imperative of medical treatment, yet the above study identifies five domains of quality end-of-life care from the patient perspective that challenge such an imperative: to receive adequate pain and symptom control; to avoid inappropriate prolongation of dying; to achieve a sense of control; to relieve the burden; and to strengthen relationships with loved ones.[44] Two of these domains require further exploration in the context of this discussion.

Achieving a Sense of Control

In the above study, participants were adamant that they wanted to retain control of their end-of-life care decisions while they were capable of doing so, and that they wanted the proxy of their choice to retain control of doing so if they became incapable. One of the participants said, 'That's my life. Nobody has any right to tell me that.'[44] This essentially captures the true voice of autonomy. This true voice is, however, often not heard or, as in the case of Mr X, is either ignored or silenced from dwindling energy levels secondary to the disease process and the crippling side-effects of aggressive treatment. This silencing of the true voice is characteristic of the disempowering nature of medical paternity in certain clinical situations.[14]

Avoiding Inappropriate Prolongation of Dying

The inappropriate prolongation of dying has been described by some as the deliberate medicalization of death[46,47] and the failure to palliate rather than continue fighting the disease at all costs.[48] Caring for terminally ill patients in a system by system or organ by organ approach, as is typical in tertiary settings, fragments the process of dying into a series of medical events. By 'demedicalizing' death[49] via the holistic nature of care that renders nursing different from medicine,[50] such inappropriate prolongation of dying may be successfully challenged.

How Can We Determine a Patient's Quality of Life?

Despite efforts to develop measurements for and indicators of quality of life[51] none of us can claim legitimately to know truly and authoritatively what another's quality of life is. The quality of one's life, based on rational decisions, can be measured only by the individual's own value system.[52] As nurses we may be in a position to make observations and assumptions about patients' semblance but, unless we are living in their body and mind, and in their intrinsic world of experience, we cannot claim to know how they perceive or value the quality of their existence. Essentially, a patient's personhood is that of the patient. Consequently, only patients themselves are in a position to impart reliable and meaningful information about their own quality of life. Moreover, recent studies have documented the outright disqualification of health care providers and family members to know accurately how patients actually assess their own quality of life.[53–56] Despite the dilemmas inherent in the quality of life debate, the inclination to provide only those treatments that will preserve, restore or ameliorate quality of life reverberates throughout contemporary discussions on medical futility.

Delivery System Differences

More than death itself, what seems frightening is the very real prospect of losing control over one's own dying process.[57] As Salem[49] explains, the reaction to this exorbitant sway of medicine from caring to curing has been nourished since the 1970s by virtue of patients' empowerment or, more generally, the liberal individualism that has extended vigorously into the medical system. In response, advance directives, health care proxies, durable power of attorney for health care and other devices founded on the right to forgo medical treatment aim to protect patients from doctors, medicine and hospital institutional imperatives.

This, however, is essentially the US view that emanates from the consequences of what can simply be defined as a 'capitalized/privatized' health care delivery system. The situation in other developed countries, especially those that espouse a health care delivery system that is commonly referred to as socialized medicine[58–60] and/or universal health care,[61,62] is very different. In the UK and Australia for example, the litigious nature of health care is something that is seen as almost exclusively 'American', possibly resulting from the capitalized/privatized nature of health services provision. This model of health care delivery can only raise patient (or more aptly 'consumer') awareness, rights, ownership and control. In this case it could be argued that the elusive trait of medicine's power is so deeply embedded in a socialized system of health care delivery that it goes unnoticed. Essentially, the point here is that medical paternity is alive and well, as is patient ignorance of their rights as recipients of health care to say 'no'.

Conclusion

By challenging the judgements that doctors can make in order to restrict patient access to desired treatment raises obvious concerns about protecting autonomous patients from unwanted and unnecessary medical paternalism. This is reflected in the opening scenario, where access to palliative management was requested by the patient and the family, yet not granted by the medical team until the last moment. From the position of patient autonomy, we may even ask not which value judgements doctors should be entitled to make or whether they should make them, but when (i.e. under what circumstances) they should be sanctioned to supplant their own values or their sense of appropriateness for those of their patients.

To claim that patients have autonomy is to argue that they have the capacity and right to decide for themselves the values and rules that will govern their existence. This claim works because it provides a justification for limiting the power that doctors can exercise over patients, specifically the power to judge and make decisions without their knowledge, understanding or consent. If doctors exercised such power over patients, they would violate the capacity and right of patients to self-determination. Ultimately, granting doctors unilateral decision-making power on the basis of medical dominance would substitute a system of medical paternity for patient autonomy. Nurses can situate themselves realistically within this ever-present dichotomy and

in effect are in a position to challenge such a process. By assuming the role of patient advocate plus embracing their own professional power via professional development within this area of clinical ethics, nurses can make a significant and worthwhile contribution to ensuring that patients' true wishes are respected, or at least heard.

Respect for patient autonomy should occupy a prominent place in the moral commitments of all health professionals. Understanding the differences between nurses' and doctors' views on patient autonomy, the role of the nurse as patient advocate, and the need for doctors to heighten their awareness for more established therapeutic communication in end-of-life situations, can give everyone valuable insight into each other's strengths and weaknesses as ethical decision makers. This will surely improve the ability of doctors and nurses to complement each other in the decision-making process, ultimately for the benefit and holistic well-being of patients and their families.

References

1 McCormack PB. Quality of life and the right to die: an ethical dilemma. *J Adv Nurs* 1998; 28: 63–69.

2 Goodhall L. Tube feeding dilemmas: can artificial nutrition and hydration be legally or ethically withheld or withdrawn? *J Adv Nurs* 1997; 25: 217–22.

3 United Kingdom Central Council for Nursing, Midwifery and Health Visiting. *Code of professional conduct.* London: UKCC, 1992.

4 Tilden VP. Ethics perspectives on end of life care. *Nurs Outlook* 1999; 47: 162–67.

5 Ott BB, Hardy TL. Readability of advance directive documents. *IMAGE J Nurs Sch* 1997; 29: 53–57.

6 Nolan T, Bruder M. Patients' attitudes toward advance directives and end-of-life treatment decisions. *Nurs Outlook* 1997; 45: 204–208.

7 Taylor C. Medical futility and nursing. *IMAGE J Nurs Sch* 1995; 27: 301–306.

8 Brody H. Kevorkian and assisted death in the USA: the ethical debate drags on but fuels efforts to improve end of life care. *BMJ* 1999; 319: 953–54.

9 Gillon R. *Philosophical medical ethics.* Chichester: Wiley, 1992.

10 Rubin S. *When doctors say no: the battleground of medical futility.* Bloomington, IN: Indiana University Press, 1998.

11 British Medical Association. *Medical ethics today: its practice and philosophy.* London: BMJ Publishing Group, 1998.

12 Corley MC, Selig P, Ferguson C. Critical care nurse participation in ethical and work decisions. *Crit Care Nurse* 1993; 13: 120–28.

13 Baggs JC. Collaborative interdisciplinary bioethical decision making in intensive care units. *Nurs Outlook* 1993; 41: 108–11.

14 Nuland SB. *How we die – reflections on life's final chapter.* New York: Vintage Books, 1995.

15 Charatan F. AMA issues guidelines on end of life care [News]. *BMJ* 1999; 318: 690.

16 Hiltunen EF, Puopolo AL, Marks GK, *et al.* The nurse's role in end of life treatment discussions: preliminary report from the SUPPORT project. *J Cardiovasc Nurs* 1995; 9: 68–77.

17 Brennan TA. Silent decisions: limits of consent and the terminally ill patient. *Law Med Health Care* 1988; 16: 204–209.

18 Imbus SH, Zawacki BE. Autonomy for burned patients when survival is unprecedented. *N Engl J Med* 1977; 297: 308–11.

19 Lantos JD, Singer PA, Walker RM, *et al.* The illusion of futility in clinical practice. *Am J Med* 1989; 87: 81–84.

20 Tomlinson TL, Brody H. Ethics and communication in do-not-resuscitate orders. *N Engl J Med* 1988; 318: 43–46.

21 Truog RT, Allan SB, Frader J. The problem with futility. *N Engl J Med* 1992; 326: 1560–64.

22 Younger SJ. Who defines futility? *JAMA* 1988; 260: 2094–95.

23 Jonsen AR. Do no harm. *Ann Intern Med* 1978; 88: 827–32.

24 Brett AS, McCulloch LB. When patients request specific interventions: defining the limits of physicians' obligations. *N Engl J Med* 1986; 15: 1347–51.

25 Marsh FH, Staver A. Physician authority for unilateral DNR orders. *J Legal Med* 1991; 12: 115–65.

26 Paris JJ, Crone RK, Reardon FE. Physicians' refusal of requested treatment: the case of Baby L. *N Engl J Med* 1990; 322: 1012–15.

27 Pellegrino ED. Withholding and withdrawing treatments: ethics at the bedside. *Clin Neurosurg* 1989; 35: 164–84.

28 Schneiderman LJ, Jecker NS, Jonsen AR. Medical futility: its meaning and ethical implications. *Ann Intern Med* 1990; 112: 949–54.

29 Quinn C, Smith M. *The professional commitment: issues and ethics in nursing.* Philadelphia, PA: Saunders, 1987.

30 Robertson DW. Ethical theory, ethnography, and differences between doctors and nurses in approaches to patient care. *J Med Ethics* 1996; 22: 292–99.

31 Pellegrino DE, Thomasma DC. *The virtues in medical practice.* New York: Oxford University Press, 1993.

32 McConnell EA. Medical devices and medical futility: when is enough enough? *Nursing* 1997; 27: HN1–HN4.

33 American Nurses Association. *Code for nurses with interpretive statements.* Kansas City, KA: ANA, 1985.

34 American Nurses Association Task Force on Nursing Standards Practice. *Standards of clinical nursing practice.* Kansas City, KA: ANA, 1991.

35 Royal College of Nursing Australia. *Ethics in nursing practice* [Position statement]. Canberra: RCNA, 1999.

36 British Medical Association. *Withholding or withdrawing life-prolonging treatment: guidance for decision making.* London: BMJ Books, 1999.

37 Finucane TE. How gravely ill becomes dying: a key to end-of-life care. *JAMA* 1999; 282: 1670–72.

38 Kübler-Ross E. *On death and dying.* New York: Macmillan, 1969.

39 Field M, Cassel C eds. *Approaching death: improving care at the end of life.* Washington, DC: National Academic Press, 1997: 6.

40 Fox E, Landrum-McNiff K, Zhong Z, *et al.* Evaluation of prognostic criteria for determining hospice eligibility in patients with advanced lung, heart, or liver disease. *JAMA* 1999; 282: 1638–45.

41 Illich I. *Limits to medicine: medical nemesis – the expropriation of health.* London: Penguin, 1990.

42 Field D. *Nursing the dying.* London: Routledge, 1989.

43 Walby S, Greenwell J, Mackay L, Soothill, K. *Medicine and nursing: professions in a changing health service.* London: Sage, 1994.

44 Singer A, Martin DK, Kelner M. Quality end-of-life care: patient perspectives. *JAMA* 1999; 281: 163–68.

45 Ufema J. Reflections on death and dying. *Nursing* 1999; 29(6): 56–59.

46 McCue JD. The naturalness of dying. *JAMA* 1995; 273: 1039–43.

47 Madan TN. Dying with dignity. *Soc Sci Med* 1992; 35: 425–32.

48 O'Connell LJ. Changing the culture of dying. A new awakening of spirituality in America heightens sensitivity to needs of dying persons. *Health Prog* 1996; 77: 16–20.

49 Salem T. Physician-assisted suicide: promoting autonomy – or medicalizing suicide? *Hastings Cent Rep* 1999; 29(3): 30–36.

50 James V, Field D. Who has the power? Some problems and issues affecting the nursing care of dying patients. *Eur J Cancer Care* 1996; 5: 73–80.

51 Pearlman RA, Jonsen AR. The use of quality of life considerations in medical decision making. *J Am Geriatr Soc* 1985; 33: 344–52.

52 Jonsen AR, Siegler M, Winsdale WJ. *Clinical ethics*, second edition. New York: Macmillan, 1986.

53 Danis M, Patrick DL, Southerland LI, *et al.* Patients' and families' preferences for medical intensive care. *JAMA* 1988; 260: 797–802.

54 Pearlman RA, Uhlmann RF, Jecker NS. Spousal understanding of patient quality of life: implications for surrogate decision making. *J Clin Ethics* 1992; 3: 114–20.

55 Schneiderman LJ, Kaplan RM, Pearlman RA, Teetzel H. Do physicians' own preferences for life-sustaining treatment influence their perceptions of patients' preferences? *J Clin Ethics* 1993; 4: 28–33.

56 Uhlmann RF, Pearlman RA, Cain KC. Physicians' and spouses' predictions of elderly patients' resuscitation preferences. *J Gerontol* 1988; 43: M115–21.

57 Callahan D. *What kind of life: the limits of medical progress.* Washington, DC: Georgetown University Press, 1990.

58 Parker RG. Drifting toward socialized medicine [Abstract]. *Tex Med* 1999; 95: 9.

59 Holm S. 'Socialized medicine', resource allocation and two-tiered health care: the Danish experience. *J Med Philos* 1995; 20: 631–37.

60 Himmelstein DU and Woolhandler S. Socialized medicine: a solution to the cost crisis in health care in the United States. *Int J Health Serv* 1986; 16: 339–54.

61 Frenkel M. Financing universal health care coverage for America's children. *J Health Care Finance* 1998; 24: 84–86.

62 Schramm CJ. Government, private health insurance, and the goal of universal health care coverage. *Inquiry* 1992; 29: 263–68.

83

Health and Human Rights Advocacy
Perspectives from a Rwandan Refugee Camp

Carol Pavlish, Anita Ho, and Ann-Marie Rounkle

Introduction

Even though human rights concepts permeated ancient governing structures and conduct codes and were officially formalized in 1948 through the Universal Declaration of Human Rights, the struggle to realize rights continues for many individuals and groups. The International Council of Nurses' (ICN)[1] Code of Ethics asserts that nurses should 'promote an environment in which the human rights, values, customs and spiritual beliefs of the individual, family and community are respected' (p.2). With this statement, ICN acknowledges that context is a primary mediator of people's ability to realize their health and human rights. National nursing organizations are also placing more emphasis on nurses' role as social advocate for conditions that favor human rights. For example, in 2001 nurses in the USA were charged with becoming 'aware … of broader health concerns such as world hunger, environmental pollution, lack of access to health care … violation of human rights, and inequitable distribution of nursing and health care resources' (p.13).[2] More recently, the American Nurses Association (ANA) released a position statement on ethics and human rights that clearly links people's living and social conditions to health, human rights, and nursing ethics. ANA stated, 'Emerging approaches to human rights place their emphasis on relational principles of inclusiveness and the need for changes in social structures that create or sustain unequal treatment of human beings' (p.5).[3] Additionally, the Canadian Nurses Association (2008) asserted that nurses are ethically bound to individually and collectively challenge the social inequities that impact people's health and well-being.[4] These nursing organizations call nurses to action in creating conditions that promote human rights. However, human rights-based advocacy is not clearly defined and, therefore, difficult to enact. This article applies the results of an ethnographic human rights research study in a Rwandan refugee camp to argue for developing a rights-based advocacy role for nurses. We first examine current literature on human rights and advocacy and then present our research findings on human rights facilitators, which provide valuable lessons about human rights advocacy. We conclude by encouraging nurses to adopt social advocacy roles that support sociopolitical agendas for health equity and create opportunities for all persons to achieve their human right to health-positive living situations.

Original publication details: Carol Pavlish, Anita Ho, and Ann-Marie Rounkle, "Health and Human Rights Advocacy: Perspectives from a Rwandan Refugee Camp," pp. 538–49 from *Nursing Ethics* 19: 4 (2012).
Copyright © 2012 by SAGE Publications. Reprinted by Permission of SAGE.

Bioethics: An Anthology, Third Edition. Edited by Helga Kuhse, Udo Schüklenk, and Peter Singer.
© 2016 John Wiley & Sons, Inc. Published 2016 by John Wiley & Sons, Inc.

Background

Human rights

In the philosophical and legal literature, human rights pertain primarily to governmental and institutional management of certain behaviors such as discrimination, and are often described as moral, legal, and political standards.[5,6] Human rights are often categorized according to first and second generation. Presented in the United Nations Universal Declaration of Human Rights[7] and more recently specified in the International Covenant on Civil and Political Rights,[8] first generation rights impose certain obligations on governments to refrain themselves and their citizens from activities that violate human dignity and security. Examples include freedom from degrading treatment and arbitrary detention as well as freedom of speech and religion. Enumerated in the International Covenant on Economic, Social and Cultural Rights,[9] second generation rights aim to achieve certain social outcomes and obligate governments to provide citizens with access to education, adequate living standard, and health care. Many regional human rights documents, such as the African Charter on Human and Peoples' Rights[10] and the Rwanda Constitution[11] explicitly endorse similar first and second generation rights.

However, some scholars criticize the traditional view of human rights as entitlements as too narrow. Portraying human rights as sites of struggle around and sometimes between power and justice, Yamin asserted that actualizing rights requires more than moral and legal statements.[12] Claiming and actualizing rights require social actors to negotiate from varying power stances within hierarchal and often unjust social structures. For example, operating at society's margins and distant from political decision-makers, vulnerable populations often struggle within competitive and sometimes contentious social spaces to realize their rights to a health-adequate standard of living.[13]

The persistent, strong link between poverty and ill-health reveals deep intersections between human rights, social justice, and people's health.[14,15] Furthermore, the World Health Organization[16] contended that human rights violations have serious health consequences. For example, violence against women leads not only to physical injury but also psychological and spiritual harm.[17,18] Violence against women also has a profound impact on community development and perpetuates poverty by reducing women's mobility, access to information, and capacity to work.[19] Moreover, harm to women negatively impacts children's health outcomes and school attendance.[19] For example, intimate partner violence tends to promote violent and delinquent behaviors, which increases healthcare costs for entire families.[20]

When human rights are respected in health policy and programs, vulnerability to ill health is reduced.[16] Advancing a human rights-based approach to health, Yamin claimed that health has special importance in nearly every society.[12] Whether concerned with preserving people's opportunities, achieving capabilities, or protecting well-being, health is 'produced, experienced, and understood in the social, political, historical, and economic contexts in which we live' (p.47).[12] As such, a rights-based approach to health is more than providing a set of goods and services; it also links health protection to non-discrimination, democracy, and accountability. Introducing human rights into discussions of population health as partially contextual allows structural inequalities to become part of the health experience of individuals and populations.

Advocacy

The nursing profession was among the first professions to define nurses' role in terms of advocacy.[21] Frequently associated with Carper's ethical pattern of knowing, advocacy is grounded within the moral foundation of nursing, which seeks to promote what is good and right for people's health.[22] Historically, nurse advocacy has been most closely associated with supporting individual patients' autonomy[21] and protecting their right to self-determination.[23,24] The current advocacy literature also emphasizes patient autonomy. For example, in a concept analysis of nurse advocacy, three attributes surfaced: valuing patients' right to self-determination, informing patients so they are prepared to make decisions, and interceding for patients with others, such as family members and physicians, so patients' wishes are honored.[25] Similarly, in an international systematic literature review of 89 studies, authors found nurse advocacy activities included informing patients, assisting with patient decision making, and protecting patient's rights and safety.[26] However, authors noted the lack of consistency in advocacy definitions and activities and concluded that how nurses view advocacy influences what they do in the name of advocacy. In a literature review on nurses' descriptions of their advocacy role, two primary themes emerged. First, the emotional connection between nurses and their patients was significant to nurses' advocacy activities. Second, nurses often emphasized the degree to which values and goals of care were shared among healthcare team members. These relationships were key components in nurses' ethical deliberations about their advocacy activities.[24]

Several authors noted that advocacy, despite its centrality to nursing, lacks clear definition in the nursing literature and requires further study.[27,28] Moreover, nurses around the world work within their particular social structures, economic realities, and system power hierarchies. As a result, nurses tend to actualize advocacy out of their own definitions and sense of ethical obligations rather than a clearly-developed professional role. Furthermore, some authors also noted that nurse advocacy has primarily been studied from nurses' or other healthcare providers' perspectives.[26] Rarely has advocacy been studied from patient, family, or community perspectives. Also, scant attention to advocacy beyond what one can do for individual patients is evident.[22] Therefore, in an effort to contribute to research on nurse advocacy, we apply findings from our human rights research to develop deeper and more expansive understandings about the meaning of health and human rights advocacy that extends beyond the individual patient to attend to systemic issues. We first describe the context in which this research occurred, and then present the findings on human rights facilitators.

Human Rights Research

The 1994 Rwanda genocide contributed to persistent border conflicts with the Democratic Republic of Congo. As a result, many Congolese residents fled the fighting and settled in refugee camps in Rwanda. Having experienced and witnessed many forms of violence and deprivation, Congolese refugees seem particularly suited to offer insights about the meaning of human rights and the health impact of human rights violations. The refugee camp where this study occurred receives essential goods and services from the United Nations High Commissioner for Refugees (UNHCR) and two international non-governmental organizations (NGO). Researchers collaborated with one of the NGOs to plan and implement this ethnographic study. The research was designed to investigate community beliefs and practices regarding human rights. After receiving ethics approval from the Universities of California Los Angeles and British Columbia, researchers collected data during six focus groups with camp residents and 20 in-depth interviews with East African key informants who were either in leadership positions within the camp or lived outside the camp but worked in the field of health or human rights. For example, camp residents included a section chief, clan leader, and woman's representative. Non-resident key informants included Rwanda political leaders, healthcare professionals, and security officials. All focus groups were conducted through a Rwandan language interpreter; most key informant interviews were conducted in English although some were interpreted. All interview sessions and five focus groups were recorded; one women-only focus group refused permission to record the session. Careful notes were taken by both researchers at all sessions. Researchers then imported all data into Atlas.ti data management system for coding and sorting. Five categories of data emerged: human rights descriptors, violations, structures, facilitators, and barriers. Further data analysis with second-level coding uncovered patterns within each category including human rights facilitators. Specific findings on human rights descriptors, violations, and structures were previously reported.[29] To deepen understanding about health and human rights advocacy, this article details findings on human rights facilitators.

Findings

When asked about their definition of human rights, refugee informants primarily discussed their experiences of human rights violations, offering numerous examples of discrimination, marginalization, sexual violence, and exploitation. Noting concerns ranging from involuntary repatriation to forced marriage, some refugees cited violations to their self-determination rights. Describing violations to their rights to security and protection from harm, many female informants were particularly distressed about intimate partner violence, heightened risk of sexual violence and exploitation for girls and women, and discriminatory social practices. In the face of persistent poverty, informants of both genders used their daily experiences to illustrate inadequate opportunities to realize fundamental human rights. For example, youth lamented lack of access to education opportunities beyond primary levels. Both men and women described lack of job and income opportunities. Prevailing sentiment among these refugees of ethnic violence included that rights protection belongs to 'every human being regardless of the differences between us, either skin color, regions, or other differences.' Providing this important protection were human rights facilitators. Four patterns of facilitators were identified in the data.

Sensitization campaigns

The lack of community awareness about human rights was frequently cited as the cause of human rights violations. As a result, the Gender-based Violence Program (GBV) received numerous commendations from many research participants. Spreading awareness, performing daily surveillance, and providing an abuse reporting mechanism were the GBV initiatives that earned the greatest recognition in advancing human rights perspectives throughout the community. Commenting on the role of spreading awareness, one female focus group participant stated:

> GBV has been very important because it held campaigns which awaken young girls not to be involved in sexual exploitation, and those who have become prematurely pregnant have been advised not to go back for sexual exploitation. GBV taught [young girls] ways to prevent themselves from participating in any sexual act.

Another female focus group member noted, 'Back in 2000, a woman was obliged to have sex when she

didn't want to, but now there is a change thanks to the GBV project, and there is mutual agreement about what to do.' Changing long-standing community perceptions about gender roles and relationships is difficult; however, the GBV program is apparently making progress. A male key informant asserted that 'girls used to be raped by boys, so that was a violation of their rights. But with GBV there is an improvement because it does not occur often now.'

Acknowledging the importance of surveillance, one focus group respondent explained that 'GBV workers go every morning to see what has taken place in all blocks to examine the security that's going on in the blocks. They don't just wait for an issue to happen. And they always try to follow up on what is going on in the camp.' Prevention is the ideal of any sensitization program, and many research participants praised the surveillance program for their significant role in preventing human rights abuses.

The GBV program also advances human rights by teaching community members how to report abuses. For example, one focus group member offered:

> GBV sensitizes us to know our rights and also teaches us to know what we should report and when we should report and where we should report. This is a very good thing, but it's only the beginning. We have a long journey because women are still being beaten at home and they don't report it.

As noted by this participant, possessing awareness about human rights is not enough; a smooth mechanism for reporting and intervening are important adjuncts. Sensitization campaigns for prevention and GBV specialists for surveillance and follow up seemed particularly significant in facilitating human rights by protecting people – especially women and girls – from human rights abuses. One male key informant with a Rwandan NGO indicated that sensitization programs that are specifically geared toward men are also critically important.

Collaboration and participation

Agencies that serve camp residents were acknowledged for their human rights work such as supplying food, offering health care services, providing protection, or offering primary education opportunities. Carving a life for themselves and family members in a refugee camp was often described as 'very difficult.' Most participants acknowledged that their situations would certainly worsen without the services of outside agencies. Many participants asserted that coordination among outside agencies and 'partnerships' with community residents were the most effective approaches for agencies to implement human rights strategies, suggesting that advocacy should not take a top-down approach. For example, one focus group participant explained, 'Many stakeholders are involved in protecting our rights, and we need to work together to solve human rights problems.' Another focus group participant asserted that when all agencies work together to mobilize camp leaders to hold themselves and other community members accountable for human rights, 'more protection [for human rights] results.'

Many female focus group participants expressed preference for being involved in decisions about human rights. For example, one group member stated, 'If we are put together and talk about human rights we can identify some cases to help them [agencies and leaders] to monitor and come up with some solutions.' Partnerships and participatory approaches were lauded as the preferred method to construct human rights campaigns and to address human rights abuses. Key informants from Rwandan NGOs echoed the significance of collaborative human rights planning with community members.

Protection: human rights safeguards

According to several focus group participants, jobs, education, and income generation initiatives empowered vulnerable populations to protect their own human rights. These human development opportunities seemed to act as a buffer against human rights abuses. For example, women who were educated about their human rights and the process for reporting human rights abuses seemed to express more power against those persons who could potentially abuse them. As one key informant observed, when young girls are offered ways to reduce the risk of being sexually exploited, they tended to strengthen their stance against sexual exploitation. Another inform-

ant suggested that women and girls who have the opportunity to generate income gain a stronger voice against potential human rights abuses especially since they can resist sexual exploitation and forced early marriage. By providing information, offering education, supplying income generation activities, and furnishing jobs, aid agencies advocate for and offer vulnerable persons the opportunities to develop more power and status in their relationships and in their community, which safeguarded them from human rights abuses. One female focus group participant stated, 'Agencies intervene to protect us, to facilitate us to get access to education so we can generate our own income so men and young boys don't attract us with their money.' Another focus group member suggested, 'Most of the people here in camp who earn money are men and boys, so when agencies help women to make their own income, they will not be [encouraged] by men or young boys for sexual exploitation.'

Good governance and accountability

Research participants identified three community structures for insuring fair and just treatment: the traditional family court system, camp leaders, and camp police. As detailed by a male focus group participant:

> When there is a problem or an issue between people, the one whose rights are violated can go to the traditional family court in the camp, the kind of system where families gather their problems and try to solve them at the family level. When it [family court] does not satisfy them, they can consult their leaders, the representatives of the camp who can become involved in that problem. When it is a very crucial issue, such as trying to kill a person, the police become involved.

Different types of disputes were usually processed at each level. For example, family court often heard spousal dispute cases. Because traditional social norms were the primary framework for decisions made at the family court level, women's rights were sometimes violated. However, participants emphasized that interaction and collaboration between all three governing levels contributed to better governance and accountability. For example, describing instances of wife beatings, a male focus group participant indicated that 'If there is no punishment, we don't take it as a serious thing, as a problem.' This required moving issues of women's rights beyond the family level and into the enforcement level. Collaboration between family and police governing units was more likely to safeguard women's health and human rights. As a key informant, a police officer described weekly meetings whereby human rights violations were discussed with the camp leadership. The police emphasized that they 'prevent beatings and domestic violence' by sensitizing clan and camp leaders to the issue of violence against women. Asked whether men generally accept these messages, the police officer said, 'No. But we take measures against people who will not practice that. So we punish one so that he will be an example to others.' Implementing sensitization and enforcement, this police officer explained his approach to prevention of human rights abuses against women.

Additionally, special advocacy groups such as camp condifas (women's advocates) become involved in human rights decision making and governance. Illustrating the process of collaborative and interactive governance, one condifa as key informant explained:

> I carry out a home-based visit and when that doesn't work [to settle the issue], I invite people who are implicated to the committee of the camp which is made up of 28 condifas. I invite people to talk altogether. Four condifas work as a team to solve small cases and for the big cases, they go to the full committee [all condifas]. And if there is a problem that is beyond our expectation, we call old men and women leaders to solve it, and they are always helpful.

Participants emphasized that when decisions are made within one governing body, women's rights may not be observed. For example, rape used to be considered only at the family level; however, with the availability of condifas and a GBV advocacy program, rape is now brought to the family and enforcement levels with greater attention toward holding perpetrators accountable for their actions. The collaborative and interactive efforts between these governing bodies were the essential elements of good governance and accountability, which facilitated the enforcement of people's rights.

Discussion

Overall, despite refugees' limited or absent awareness of human rights documents, significant confluence existed between their rights-perspectives and the UN Declaration of Human Rights.[7] These included: *security rights* against crimes such as murder, assault, theft, and rape; *liberty rights* to freedoms of speech and movement; and *social rights* to human health and development opportunities. However, despite prevalent confluence in overall human rights perspectives, questions about who is obligated to insure which rights and to what extent they are responsible were evident. Currently, many human rights organizations assume an indirect advocacy role by monitoring state governments' obligations to refrain from first generation rights violations. However, most participants in our research emphasized the protective value of second generation rights. Even though rights to development opportunities are recognized by both the United Nations and African Union, the extent to which governments and aid agencies mainstream human rights and adopt a rights-based approach to offering health and development services is controversial.[29] Participants in our study wondered who should be held accountable when host governments, international agencies, and non-governmental organizations lack resources and cannot provide access to essential goods and health and education services. The question about the degree to which state governments and international organizations are obligated to dedicate resources to fulfill second generation rights remains unanswered.

International law and human rights documents frequently consider first and second generations as indivisible and mutually reinforcing,[31] implying that human dignity and security cannot be protected without guaranteeing access to health and other development opportunities. Such indivisibility is clearly illustrated when considering the UN-sanctioned, first generation *political rights* and *equality rights* that respectively protect the liberty to participate in public decision making and guarantee nondiscrimination. These laws formally treat everyone the same; however, when 'those who are poor have no word,' or when women who are less educated 'are dominated' at meetings, political and equality rights are not actualized. In essence, equal access to second generation rights strongly influenced opportunities to realize first generation rights. Despite human rights organizations' focus on advancing first generation rights, respondents in this study emphasized the importance of second generation rights. Many participants claimed that if their second generation rights were guaranteed, they would be in a stronger position to advocate for and protect themselves against first generation rights abuses.

Refugee informants' reference to both first and second generation rights in their descriptions of human rights violations is informative for nurses and other health care providers. Having fled the terror of a violent, militia-led invasion of their homeland, refugee participants emphasized first generation rights when incorporating security and protection as a vital component of their human rights definition. This emphasis echoes the security rights as presented in the UN Declaration and the African Charter on Human and Peoples' Rights and substantiates the importance of the United Nations Responsibility to Protect (R2P) doctrine.[32,33] R2P established governments' responsibilities to protect their own populations and an obligation for the international community to act when these governments fail to protect their people from genocide, massive human rights abuses, and other security catastrophes.

However, informants in our study and various international bodies recognize that human security is not simply about military defense of political or national boundaries. The Commission on Human Security, for example, identified the primary objective of human security as safeguarding the essence of human lives from critical pervasive threats *while promoting sustainable human flourishing*.[34] Correlating this definition, all refugee informants emphasized that essential human rights included protection from not only state or militia-based harm but also from the pervasive and interconnected threats of poverty, hunger, illness, discrimination, and stagnation – all of which influence human health and well-being. Participants in our study indicated that women were especially vulnerable to poverty. Sexual exploitation and forced early marriages were specifically cited. The extreme poverty experienced by refugee and internally displaced families often create conditions that lead families to subject their daughters to the coercion, abduction, imprisonment, rape, and physical violence associated with forced marriage. This health-harming practice perpetrated against young and adolescent girls remains a major human rights violation.[35] From this second generation human rights perspective, the meaning of health expands beyond biology and individual lifestyles to include struggles for voice and power within family and sociopolitical relationships.

Refugees' perspectives on human rights facilitators and system issues provide a strong foundation for nurse advocacy. Nurses can be important spokespersons to support vulnerable populations such as refugee women and girls as they struggle for equal access to health, education, and development opportunities. Participants in our study asserted that creating these opportunities were not only empowering but also protective. Research participants supported a dual role of advocacy – protecting not only individual rights but also advancing policies and practices that create contextual and systemic conditions to support patients to realize their own rights. Unfortunately, in the nursing literature, advocacy is most often viewed at the individual rather than population or societal level.[36] Emphasis on the individual view of advocacy constrains the potential for nurse advocacy. As a result, nurses might view advocacy primarily in terms of individual and family care and, therefore, miss important opportunities to influence social and political agendas that advocate for people's right to health-enabling opportunities and healthy living situations.[13,22] Chiding all health care professionals to extend their bioethics agenda beyond dyadic relationships between healthcare providers and patients, Daniels claimed that bioethics has been 'myopic, not seeing and not addressing the context in which these relationships operate' (p.23).[37] Assuming that inequitable baselines are neutral, Daniels continued by asserting that little attention has been paid to resolving health inequities and systemic issues fueling such injustices. Nurse advocates must thus respond to Daniels' call for a broader bioethics platform by recognizing the social determinants of health that contribute to or exacerbate health inequalities, and pursuing equity in opportunities and fairness across groups in resource distribution.

Participants in our study indicated that a partnered approach to spreading human rights awareness and working toward equity in opportunities within the context of transparent and accountable governance were key elements of advocacy.

Drawing on an ecological perspective of health, Kalipeni and Oppong asserted that refugee health is best understood in terms of contextually-based political ecology, which offers a framework for analyzing context and multidimensional structural relationships.[38] Context refers to the political, economic, historical, environmental, and social factors that influence health; structural relationships emphasize interacting systems of domination and oppression.[39] Contextual factors interact within systems of power and oppression to create social arrangements that marginalize and increase vulnerability of some populations.[40] As groups are pushed further from powerful forces with less opportunity to participate and engage in decisions that impact their lives, risk of human rights violations increases and consequently, population health may suffer. Similarly, participants in this study indicated that unilateral and unresponsive governance increased their risk for human rights violations and, consequently, health problems. Therefore, the health and human rights advocacy role of healthcare professionals becomes increasingly important. Nurse advocates benefit from ecological analyses of people's health concerns whereby multi-level and mutually reinforcing structural barriers become more apparent. In this circumstance, human rights can be conceptualized as tools that 'allow people to live lives of dignity, to be free and equal citizens, to exercise meaningful choices, and to pursue life plans' (p.46).[12] For example, the human right to an adequate living standard can be a useful instrument in strengthening a claim when advocating for social conditions that result in healthy outcomes. According to research participants in our study, incorporating an ecological analysis of people's health concerns whereby multi-level and mutually reinforcing structural barriers become more apparent is beneficial to their health.

Recognizing the important contribution of sensitization, participation, interactive and collaborative governance, and safeguards in advancing human rights, refugee participants offer nurses important

lessons on social advocacy. When advocating for health improvements, nurses should focus on using the language of human rights to promote social change for health-positive living conditions. Human rights advocacy that changes policies and practices toward greater equity improves health as well as the conditions that influence health.[22,41] When healthcare providers collaborate and support vulnerable populations toward second-generation rights realization, health improvements will occur.[12]

These ideas resonate with Gadow's view of nursing advocacy as existentially finding meaning in partnership with others.[42] Gadow provides a philosophical foundation for research that engages community members in public discussion of interactions between health and human rights. The emphasis on partnership encourages nurses to recognize the most marginalized members of society as rights bearers rather than passive aid recipients. Several participants in our study emphasized the importance of having resources and opportunities so they could advocate for their own rights and also suggested that being involved in decisions about human rights was beneficial. Partnership-based nursing advocacy requires members of the profession to refrain from paternalistic approaches to advocacy that may reinforce power hierarchy. This approach demands nurses and allies to acknowledge the importance of community knowledge – those who are experiencing human rights violations and resource deprivation are often the most knowledgeable in how systemic factors continue to create barriers for their flourishing. Partnership-based care that encourages nurses to collaborate with community members and local advocacy groups in searching for and promoting community-based solutions that are culturally sensitive and sustainable is thus important.

Nurses in their professional advocacy role are in a key position to strengthen the reciprocal relationship between health and human rights – but only if they adopt a rights-based approach to health that recognizes people's needs as human rights. Fowler suggested that a nurse advocacy model founded on acknowledging human differences but emphasizing commonality in human needs and rights is our most 'demanding interpretation' of advocacy (p.98) and binds nurses in a moral obligation to support human rights.[43] Participants in our study offered a nurse advocacy model that helps to define nurses' moral obligation to 'support' human rights. These participants suggested that nurses should be accountable for partnering with vulnerable populations and patients to create conditions of empowerment, equity, and fairness in relationships – personal as well as political – so vulnerable groups have the opportunity to realize, protect, and promote their own human rights as much as possible. Falling short of this obligation to create appropriate conditions for human rights jeopardizes the health of vulnerable populations and weakens the advocacy role of nurses.

Limitations

Despite a wide variety of participants in this research study, the small number of respondents may not represent community viewpoints, and, therefore, precludes generalization of these findings to other post-conflict settings. Additionally, all focus groups and some key informant interviews were conducted through a language interpreter. Some meaning may have been altered or lost through translation.

Conclusion

Unfortunately, and all too often, human rights perspectives are debated outside of the daily human experience, and as a result, reactive and reductive strategies often fail to curb insidious violations. While much attention currently focuses on protection against violent human rights incursions, many refugees, who feel they are 'prisoners with few opportunities,' summon the international nursing community to place greater visibility on human rights within a daily-experience framework and more recognition of second generation rights. Nurses, international health organizations, and human rights activists must consider this call toward a more integrated and rights-based approach to health and development. Community voices combined with documents like the African Charter and the UN Declaration of Human Rights could serve as cogent frameworks for public health programs and human development opportunities as well as a significant foundation for community and interdisciplinary collaboration. Only by acknowledging local contexts can sustainable progress toward more equitable and just distribution of health and development opportunities occur.

The Nightingale and Wald legacies of collaborating within systems to advance human rights and improve the social and economic conditions of vulnerable populations require resurrection in this time of expanding global health disparities.[13,36] Nurse advocacy at all levels requires a contextual view of health. Widening advocacy to include an assessment of human rights obstacles that interfere with health increases the probability of addressing root causes of ill health such as human rights violations.

As health advocates, nurses can also be important advocates for human rights. Advocacy is generally associated with nurses' attention to vulnerable populations that exist within a structural context that often creates and reinforces vulnerability. Advocacy stems from the nursing profession's obligation to society to practice with the intent of improving health at all levels of society. When nurses recognize the critical intersections between health and human rights, then nurses also accept responsibility for human rights advocacy. As noted by the International Council of Nurses, health is a human right, and, therefore, nurses must take responsibility for creating health-conducive conditions that emphasize the principles of justice, equity, nondiscrimination, transparency, fairness, and collaboration.[44]

References

1   International Council of Nurses. *Code of ethics*. Geneva: International Council of Nurses. http://www.icn.ch/images/stories/documents/about/icncode_english.pdf (2006, accessed January 2012).

2   American Nurses Association. *Code of ethics for nurses* (2001).

3   American Nurses Association. *Position Statement: the nurse's role in ethics and human rights: protecting and promoting individual worth, dignity, and human rights in practice settings.*

http://gm6.nursingworld.org/MainMenuCategories/Policy-Advocacy/Positions-and-Resolutions/ANAPositionStatements/Position-Statements-Alphabetically/Nursess-Role-in-Ethics-and-Human-Rights.pdf (2010, accessed June 2011).

4   Canadian Nurses Association. *Code of ethics for registered nurses*. Available from: https://www.cna-aiic.ca/~/media/cna/page-content/pdf-fr/code-of-ethics-for-registered-nurses.pdf?la=en (2008).

5   Nickel JW. *Making sense of human rights*. Oxford: Blackwell, 2007.

6   Pogge T. The international significance of human rights. *J Ethics* 2000; 4: 45–69.

7   United Nations. *Universal declaration of human rights*. New York: United Nations. http://www.un.org/en/documents/udhr/ (1948).

8   United Nations. *International covenant on civil and political rights*. New York: United Nations. http://www.ohchr.org/en/professionalinterest/pages/ccpr.aspx (1966).

9   United Nations. *International covenant on economic, social and cultural rights*. New York: United Nations. http://www.ohchr.org/EN/ProfessionalInterest/Pages/CESCR.aspx (1966).

10 Organization of African Unity. *African charter on human and peoples' rights*. http://www.hrcr.org/docs/Banjul/afrhr.html (1981, accessed February 2009).

11 Republic of Rwanda. *The constitution of the Republic of Rwanda*. http://www.wipo.int/wipolex/en/details.jsp?id=7505 (2003).

12 Yamin A. Will we take suffering seriously? Reflections on what applying a human rights framework to health means and why we should care. *Health Hum Rights* 2008; 10(1): 45–63.

13 Harrison E and Falco S. Health disparity and the nurse advocate: reaching out to alleviate suffering. *ANS Adv Nurs Sci* 2005; 28(3): 252–264.

14 Crigger N. Towards a viable and just global nursing ethics. *Nurs Ethics* 2008; 18(3): 17–27.

15 Fox A and Meier B. Health as freedom: addressing social determinants of global health inequities through the human right to development. *Bioeth* 2009; 23(2): 112–122.

16 World Health Organization. *25 questions and answers on health and human rights*. Health and Human Rights series, 1. http://www.who.int/hhr/NEW37871OMSOK.pdf (2002, accessed January 2009).

17 Campbell J, Baty M, Ghandour R, Stockman J, Francisco L and Wagman J. The intersection of intimate partner violence against women and HIV/AIDS: a review. *Int J Inj Contr Saf Promot* 2008; 15(4): 221–231.

18 Nussbaum M. Women's bodies: violence, security, capabilities. *Journal of Human Development* 2005; 6(2): 167–183.

19 Krantz G. Violence against women: a global public health issue. *Epidemiol Community Health* 2002; 56: 242–243.

20 Morrison A and Orlando M. *The costs and impacts of gender-based violence in developing countries: methodological considerations and new evidence*. http://siteresources.worldbank.org/INTGENDER/Resources/costsandimpactsofgbv.pdf (2004, accessed February 2009).

21 Gilkey M, Earp J and French E. What is patient advocacy? In: Earp J, French E and Gilkey M (eds) *Patient advocacy for health care quality: strategies for achieving patient-centered care*. Sudbury, MA: Jones & Bartlett, 2008.

22 Spenceley S, Reutter L and Allen M. The road less traveled: nursing advocacy at the policy level. *Policy Polit Nurs Pract* 2006; 7(3): 180–194.

23 Hanks R. Barriers to nursing advocacy: a concept analysis. *Nurs Forum* 2007; 42(4): 171–177.

24 MacDonald H. Relational ethics and advocacy in nursing: literature review. *J Adv Nurs* 2007; 57(2): 119–126.

25 Baldwin M. Patient advocacy: a concept analysis. *Nurs Stand* 2003; 17: 33–39.

26 Vaartio H and Leino-Kilpi H. Nursing advocacy: a review of the empirical research 1990–2003. *Int J Nurs Stud* 2005; 42(6): 705–714.

27 Hanks R. The lived experience of nursing advocacy. *Nurs Ethics* 2008; 15(4): 468–477.

28 Zomorodi M and Foley BJ. The nature of advocacy vs. paternalism in nursing: clarifying the 'thin line'. *J Adv Nurs* 2009; 65(8): 1746–1752.

29 Pavlish C and Ho A. Pathway to social justice: research on human rights and gender-based violence in a Rwandan refugee camp. *Adv Nurs Sci* 2009; 32(2): 144–157.

30 Gruskin S, Mills E and Tarantola D. History, principles, and practice of health and human rights. *Lancet* 2007; 370: 449–455.

31 Uvin P. *Human rights and development*. Bloomfield, CT: Kumarian, 2004.

32 International Commission on Intervention and State Sovereignty. *Responsibility to protect*. Ottawa: International Development Research Centre. http://www.responsibilitytoprotect.org/ICISS%20Report.pdf (2001, accessed August 2011).

33 Pace WR and Deller N. Preventing future genocides: an international responsibility to protect. *World Order* 2005; 36: 15–32.

34 Commission on Human Security. *Human security now.* http://reliefweb.int/sites/reliefweb.int/files/resources/91BAEEDBA50C6907C1256D19006A9353-chs-security-may03.pdf (2003).

35 United Nations High Commissioner for Refugees. *Handbook for the protection of women and girls.* http://www.unhcr.org/protect/PROTECTION/47cfae612.html (2008, accessed August 2011).

36 Falk-Rafael A. Speaking truth to power: nursing's legacy and moral imperative. *ANS Adv Nurs Sci* 2005; 28(3): 212–223.

37 Daniels N. Equity and population health: towards a broader bioethics agenda. *Hastings Cent Rep* 2006; 36(4): 22–35.

38 Kalipeni E and Oppong J. The refugee crisis in Africa and implications for health and disease: a political ecology approach. *Social Science & Medicine* 1998; 46: 1637–1653.

39 Farmer P. *Pathologies of power: health, human rights, and the new war on the poor.* Berkeley, CA: University of California Press, 2003.

40 Vasas E. Examining the margins: a concept analysis of marginalization. *ANS Adv Nurs Sci* 2005; 28: 194–202.

41 Pavlish C and Pharris M. *Community-based collaborative action research: a nursing approach.* Sudbury, MA: Jones & Bartlett, 2012.

42 Gadow S. Body and self: a dialectic. *Journal of Medicine & Philosophy* 1980; 5: 172–185.

43 Fowler M. Social advocacy: ethical issues in critical care. *Heart and Lung* 1989; 18(1): 97–99.

44 International Council of Nurses. *ICN on health and human rights* (2009). See http://www.icn.ch/what-we-do/ethics-and-human-rights/ethics-and-human-rights-1704.html.

Part XII

Neuroethics

Introduction

Neuroethics is a relatively new area of inquiry within bioethics. Significant research at the intersection of neuroscience and ethics began only around the turn of the century. Neuroethics asks questions such as whether or not we should permit healthy people to use cognition-enhancing drugs, whether psychopaths can be held morally responsible for their actions, and whether we should consider developing or using drugs designed to improve us as moral agents. Jonathan Moreno in "Neuroethics: An Agenda for Neuroscience and Society" argues that the objectives of ethical inquiries should not be limited to asking specific questions, for instance about moral responsibility for our actions, because that would mean losing sight of the long-term societal implications of neuroscientific findings. He notes, quite rightly, that many of the questions that are being asked in neuroethics today, for instance those pertaining to the problem of free will and moral responsibility, have been debated by philosophers in years gone by.

Sally Adee's "How Electrical Brain Stimulation Can Change the Way We Think" describes vividly how her self-experiment with tDCS went. In tDCS, basically, low-voltage electric currents are sent through your brain by means of a 'thinking cap' attached to your skull. She discovered that her fear of failure and self-doubt disappeared and so permitted her, right when she needed to perform a difficult task, to do so

in a much more focused way. Adee wonders what the ethical implications of such a technology are. Do we remain as morally responsible if a technology removes any doubts that we might have during our action about what we are doing? Might we become more ethical in our choices because in some ways we think more clearly about the issues at hand?

Neil Levy provides an overview of the ethical debates on questions such as these in his article "Neuroethics: Ethics and the Sciences of the Mind." He is specifically interested in memory modification and enhancement possibilities brought about by recent findings in the neurosciences. Would it be a good idea to provide a memory-suppressing drug to people suffering from post-traumatic stress disorder? Should such medication be provided to soldiers returning from active duty? Levy thinks that currently existing drugs offer effects sufficiently subtle as to make strong condemnations of memory-suppressing drugs sound unreasonably alarmist.

Adam Kolber describes in "Freedom of Memory Today" a real-life case in which an anesthesiologist used a memory-suppressing drug on a cancer patient without the patient's consent. He tried to "fix" the accidental disclosure of a grave diagnosis by a colleague. Kolber thinks that we ought to consider today how we regulate the use of such drugs by healthcare professionals. In the example described in Kolber's

Bioethics: An Anthology, Third Edition. Edited by Helga Kuhse, Udo Schüklenk, and Peter Singer.
© 2016 John Wiley & Sons, Inc. Published 2016 by John Wiley & Sons, Inc.

article the patient did not consent to having her memory erased, and it prevented her from considering potential legal action.

Neil Levy also turns his attention to drugs shown to have memory and attention-enhancing capacity. Philosophers or bioethicists such as Michael Sandel and Carl Elliott have argued that such drugs would likely increase the risk of some or many of our actions becoming inauthentic. Levy rejects this line of reasoning. He suspects that these kinds of arguments are triggered by the fact that the success of cognitive enhancement would constitute a "violation of implicit dualism."

Henry Greely et al. in "Towards Responsible Use of Cognitive-Enhancing Drugs by the Healthy" show that performance-enhancing drugs are widely used on college campuses across the United States. They argue that memory- and attention-enhancing drugs should be made available to mentally competent adults. Greely et al. address in their article three concerns that are typically mentioned when the wider availability of these kinds of drugs is discussed: safety, freedom from coercion to enhance, and fairness in terms of affordable access to these drugs. Essentially they aim for societal policies that permit the maximization of benefits and the minimization of harms.

Julian Savulescu and Anders Sandberg in "Engineering Love" wonder whether we should try to assist people to live in lifelong loving relationships. They suspect that it isn't within our biological nature to live – happily – in relationships lasting much longer than 10 or 15 years. Given that loving relationships contribute significantly to our well-being, they suggest that we should use all available tools in our drug armament that could make our lives better, in this case to promote or enable loving lifelong relationships.

84

Neuroethics
An Agenda for Neuroscience and Society

Jonathan D. Moreno

Announcing the arrival of neuroethics, the Charles W. Dana Foundation and Stanford University sponsored a highly publicized conference, in which I participated, on May 13–14 2002 in San Francisco. The multidisciplinary sessions included talks by leading scientists on various aspects of neuroscience, with reactions from philosophers, law professors, bioethicists and science educators.

Some participants wondered about an analogy with the 1975 Asilomar conference on the potential hazards of recombinant DNA technology. Unlike Asilomar, however, there is currently no widespread public clamour for self-restraint on the part of the relevant scientific community. If anything, there is a broad-based fascination with the prospects of neuroscience-based innovation, especially as awareness of the ravages of neurological diseases has grown, and as ageing baby boomers hope that science will help them extend their own mental acuity. In addition, early recombinant DNA technology was not nearly as steeped in commercial opportunities as current neuroscience, which operates in the middle of the lucrative environment that is created by modern psychopharmacology.

Free Will and Mind–Body Reductionism

In the context of this new interest on neuroethics, there are long-standing issues on the control or alteration of mind and brain that are sure to surface again. There is no better example than free will and determinism, a potential philosophical quagmire that has, since the ancient Greeks, inspired some of the most imaginative intellectual footwork. Does our growing knowledge about the origins and physical basis of mental states, let alone the possibility of controlling them with some specificity, threaten the liberal ideals of freedom and personal responsibility? In short, is neuroscience on the road to showing, once and for all, that mental states reduce to brain states, and even to brain states that could be subject to direct manipulation?

Consider the following results that exemplify what some may find disturbing information that is provided by the new brain science. Using evidence from functional imaging data, investigators found that social judgments about trustworthiness seem to be based on facial representations that involve the extrastriate

Original publication details: Jonathan D. Moreno, "Neuroethics: An Agenda for Neuroscience and Society," pp. 149–53 from *Nature Reviews* 4 (February 2003). Reprinted by permission from Macmillan Publishers Ltd.

visual cortices in the fusiform and superior temporal gyri. Perceptual processing is then linked to social judgments, drawing on the amygdala and regions of the prefrontal and somatosensory cortices.[1] Similarly, researchers from Stanford University have obtained evidence that the fusiform region is involved in the preferential response to faces of one's own race.[2] What implications do such data have for the notion of free will?

There are several different concerns here that should not be conflated. First, is the mental reducible to the physical? Second, if the mental is reducible to the physical, does that imply that there is no freedom of the will? Third, if the mental can be controlled by physical manipulation, does this imply that there is no freedom of the will?

Even if the mental is reducible to the physical, it does not follow that free will is an illusion, nor does it follow that cases in which the mental is manipulated cannot be distinguished from cases in which it is not. However, the challenges involved in drawing such distinctions might be formidable.

Let us begin with the problem of mind–body reductionism, one that is vexed with imprecise language, including the notion of reduction itself. Probably the most widely admired contemporary treatment of this and related issues is that from Patricia Churchland. Well before the current enthusiasm for neuroethics, Churchland published her landmark work *Neurophilosophy*[3] in 1989. Churchland canvassed the various meanings of reduction and traced the epistemological debates behind them, noting that the underlying question is which theory of the mind is reducible to which theory of the brain, or vice versa. There is, as she points out, no received view of the interconnections between mental states and behaviour, but the idea that there could be such a theory is neither implausible nor necessarily offensive. As I shall note shortly, philosophers have been living with this possibility for a long time while managing to preserve useful ideas like freedom of the will.

The view that there is something offensive about intertheoretic reduction seems to rest on the view that there is something inherently objectionable about the idea that nonphysical brain states can be explained in terms of neuronal states. Dualists and non-dualists have raised such objections, but they do not seem to

be persuasive. For example, the view that the mental and the physical are two distinct substances has a hard time explaining their interaction.

A more subtle position to take is that mental properties are distinct from physical properties, so that mental experience can, at most, be said to emerge from the physical. Here, a great burden is placed on the idea of emergence, which seems to rule out a comprehensive neurobiological theory. Yet various difficulties infect 'emergentist' views, including that, in at least some cases, they run aground on the intentional fallacy – thoughts about objects are mistaken for the properties of the objects themselves.

Another set of objections to intertheoretic reduction argue that the logic of nonphysical description is distinct from the logic of physical description – that the relations between the sentences used to describe one domain are different from those that are used to describe another. Here, again, the objections appeal to folk psychology – the commonsense means, at our disposal, to explain behaviour with reference to beliefs, desires, expectations, goals and so on. But if not all cognitive activity operates like language (as is the case for some models of information storage or seemingly intelligent animal communication), then sentential relations need not be the ultimate appeal, and it remains an empirical question whether folk psychology could be improved to the point of radical transformation by neuroscientific insights.

Meanwhile, according to Churchland, we are left with a more or less serviceable theory of the mental – folk psychology. Scientific discoveries in the neurosciences (proceeding, perhaps, from the kinds of examples that I will consider shortly) might require gradual improvements in folk psychology. These improvements, she observes, could proceed so gradually that folk psychology will be seen as having been replaced by, rather than reduced to, a theory of the brain.

Suppose that the reductionist debate continues indefinitely. As the hypothesized ongoing refinement of folk psychology by improved neuroscientific understanding takes place, history gives us reason to believe that the idea of free will will be left standing. To the fledgling student, the issue of freedom and causation has long seemed an enticing and hopeless quandary – the Scylla and Charybdis of psychology.

But the most notable thinkers have been unruffled by the matter, often taking a middle-ground position known as 'soft determinism', the view that we are capable of entering into the chain of causes of our thoughts and actions. That is, although my individual psychology and experience shape my preferences, they do not do so in detail, and I am capable of inserting more or less original choices into the chain of causes. So, even knowing the whole of a person's reinforcement history would not be sufficient to predict all of their behaviours. Recent analytic philosophers have gone so far as to call free will and determinism a pseudo-problem – one that subsists only in the linguistic expressions that are available to us.

It is worth recalling in an overview like this paper that the most important precursor of modern neuroscience was William James, the Harvard-trained physician who spent much of his career reflecting on the implications of psychology for philosophy. James' typically vigorous take on the question of free will was to assert what he called 'the will to believe' – that free will could be established by the act of determining to believe in it. What refutation to such a declaration is possible? If either option is equally plausible, he argued, one might as well reach for the more attractive of the two. James' approach is perhaps more compelling in the context of his remarkable *The Principles of Psychology*,[4] published in 1890, in which he developed nearly all of what was then known about the brain and nervous system into a coherent psychological theory.

The implications of this information for moral development were of particular importance for James. In this respect, he followed a long line that started with Aristotle. As the original soft determinist, Aristotle argued that subjects are partly responsible for the kind of person they become by, for example, choosing those with whom they associate, a choice that in turn influences their own moral character. James continued a tradition that Aristotle started in the analysis of habit formation. James applied the early lessons of neurophysiology to admonitions about launching strongly and repeatedly on any new behaviour to establish a pattern in neural material that will increase the likelihood that the behaviour will be repeated, gradually with less effort. Within a few years, and influenced by these ideas, John Dewey designed an educational system that was intended to bolster the habits of inquisitiveness and problem-solving skills, the beginning of the 'progressive' education movement in which the development of learning habits are viewed as more important than absorbing factual content.

All of this discussion is by way of pointing out that the ground has long been prepared for anticipated transformations in folk psychology by previous generations of thinkers who observed such changes in their own lifetimes and who seem to have expected them to continue. This is not to say that the process has been or will be without stress, both at the level of theory and at the level of social practices. In the rest of this article, I will allude to examples of these stress points and their implications, proceeding roughly from the more immediate to the science fictional. However farfetched, the most speculative implications are appropriate areas for the ethics of neuroscience. The point of such a discourse is not merely to assess the implications of brain science in topics of more immediate concern, such as changing ideas about legal responsibility, but also to consider the social consequences over the longer term.

Reductionism Redux

The legal system is at the frontier of formal social responses to advances in scientific understanding of human behaviour. Numerous law courts have already begun to assess defense strategies involving medications that were alleged to compromise the defendants' *mens rea* – the state of mind required for culpability. A number of such cases have involved people who were undergoing treatment with fluoxetine (Prozac). In these cases, the law courts have focused on expert testimony concerning the causal role of the medication in committing a crime.[5]

As the legal system is inclined to look to the scientific community for guidance in establishing culpability when psychoactive medication is implicated (therefore participating importantly in the modification of folk psychology), it will also do so in cases of traumatic brain injury. Such cases, involving lesions of the prefrontal region, have been observed as leaving the patient with adequate moral reasoning, but without the capacity to act upon an appropriate conclusion.[6] Improved imaging and diagnostic techniques, particularly if damage to the ventromedial sector can be identified,[6] show promise for identifying similar cases that stem from non-traumatic disorders. So, a more subtle approach to offenders whose behaviour can be correlated with trauma in certain neural systems seems inevitable.

A reasoned respect for the law depends in part on the extent to which findings of culpability are consistent with the best available evidence for self-determination. As Damasio[6] notes, a criminal who is evidently brain damaged has the moral status of a patient whose condition could be brought under a medical rubric. But emerging data indicate that the traditional category of 'criminal insanity' might not necessarily apply to a person who is capable of understanding, but not appreciating, the difference between right and wrong. To use Damasio's terms, cases in which understanding is a function of the reasoning/decision-making system and appreciation is a function of the emotion/feeling system.[6] It seems inevitable that further categories will have to be developed to capture more precise senses of culpability, as has already started to happen in cases that involve psychoactive drugs.

A far different and more speculative problem with the law arises from the possibility that subjects could deliberately forget actions for which they should be held culpable, but for which the evidence is circumstantial. Work by Levy and Anderson suggests that people who have been abused by their parents are able to intentionally repress those memories.[7] Clearly, in these cases, there is a powerful psychological impetus to forget trauma at the hands of those on whom one is dependent. It would be interesting to know if the same mechanism can be used to forget selected events or actions, even without the same emotional drive, and also if physiological indicators like the galvanic skin response can be inhibited. Psychologically sophisticated offenders would be handed a new tool to evade prosecution.

Personal Identity

Closely related to these issues about free will are concerns about personal identity. The past few years have already witnessed a vigorous debate about the implications of Prozac and other selective serotonin reuptake inhibitors. These psychopharmacological interventions seem to last longer, and perhaps be more pervasive in their effects on the human personality, than more familiar mind-altering substances with fewer side effects. However, the ethical issues that are raised in connection with the newer psychoactive drugs might not be different from assertions that these or any other alterations of mentation or conduct are 'artificial' and therefore suspect. To make such assertions stick, a background theory of the 'natural' is required, a challenging job in itself. In any case, the decision to use a drug that modifies one's personality may be a free choice, at least in the sense of soft determinism, and therefore an expression of authentic personality.

This view applies as long as the effect of medications ends as they leave the system, and there can be a return to baseline and to the individual choice about continuing using them or not. A more ethically challenging scenario runs as follows: suppose that we have the ability to permanently alter the brainstem nuclei that release serotonin, among other neurotransmitters. In primates, it has been found that the greater the number of a subtype of serotonin receptors, the less aggressive and more social is the animals behaviour.[8] Suppose further that neuronal deficiency can be determined in at least some extremely hostile subjects. For those who have trouble controlling their hostile behaviour, drug therapy would no longer be needed if the number of crucial neurons were increased to the normal range. Old-fashioned psycho-surgery, classically in the form of a prefrontal lobotomy, deforms normal structure. Would this newer form of psychosurgery be acceptable if it were seen as helping the brain attain the physiological standard?

New brain tissue grafts are only one sort of medical intervention that is suggested from information about the relationship between neurons and behaviour. Another study leads to the intersection of neuroscience with genetics and prenatal diagnosis. Investigators at the University of Wisconsin reported that members of a group of men who were both abused as children and had an alteration in the gene responsible for producing monoamine oxidase A (MAOA), were nine times more likely to commit criminal or anti-social acts than control subjects.[9] If this or other neurotransmitters are roughly associated with socially offensive behaviour, even under less extreme environmental insults, they could be brought into the controversy over preimplantation genetic diagnosis. Prospective parents might therefore test embryos for the MAOA marker before implantation to avoid giving birth to a child with this particular potential for criminality.

Researchers from Harvard and Beth Israel (Boston) Medical Center are pursuing a more general approach to disorders of brain development.[9] The group reports that they have already identified some of the genetic alterations that result in brains that are too small, abnormally patterned, or show evidence of abnormal location of cortical cells. Specifically, they report that the cerebral cortex of transgenic mice with an alteration in the *β-catenin* gene showed gyri and sulci, which are commonly not found in the brains of lower animals. This group theorizes that β-catenin regulated the proliferation of progenitor cells that lead to a thickened cortical sheet, as is present in human beings.[9]

Although it is far to early to assess the relation of the β-catenin regulator to intelligence, results like these may lead us to think about developing diagnostic tests for disorders such as mental retardation or epilepsy. Suppose that this kind of work were to eventually lead to the control of at least some of the mechanisms that control the functional performance of the brain. One can only imagine the pressure to bring to fruition one of the great science-fiction scenarios: genetic engineering that not only corrects for the presence of genes that code for conditions recognized as patent disorders, but actually seeks to enhance mental capacity.

Examples like this suggest that neuroethical debates are unlikely to appear completely separate from more familiar bioethical issues that arise in genetics and reproduction. An example of a controversy that, in retrospect, could have been brought under the ambit of neuroethics, was the use of fetal tissue for implantation into the brains of sufferers from Parkinson's disease and other neurological disorders. In the late 1980s, claims of success made by surgeons in Mexico and Sweden stimulated a debate about the acceptability of using fetal brain tissue in this way. Unfortunately, the early hopes for the procedure have not been realized, but the incident foreshadowed the current dispute about embryonic stem cells.

Impaired Consent

We can add to this list of previous neuroethics issues, experiments with persons whose decision-making capacity, and hence their ability to give valid consent, is impaired. This is a surprisingly old problem to which governments in Europe and the United States tried to regulate as long ago as 1900. Patients in medical institutions, including the mentally ill, have long been the preferred research subjects because they are confined and can be monitored. Historically, experiments involving asylum inmates have not always been confined to conditions from which they suffered. Often they were 'animals of necessity' for experiments that required human models. Gradually the law, policy and public outcry have made persons with mental disorders less desirable subjects.[11]

The opportunity to diagnose and treat dementias, led by research on Alzheimer's disease, has renewed attention to the ethics of research on people with impaired or absent decision-making ability. Imaging techniques, sometimes combined with agents intended to provoke neurological processes, have created enormous pressures on the old consensus. Some agreement has crystallized around the proposition that it is possible to devise protection for those with decisional impairments that are consistent with low-risk experimental procedures or for those that, while of higher risk, carry some potential benefit to the patient. However, several stumbling blocks remain. One is the uncertainty of who would authorize such research to be carried out if the patient cannot, a particularly serious issue for incapacitated adults. Many of the lessons that can be learned from basic research with impaired brains, as well as innovative translations of neuroscientific discoveries to clinical medicine, turn on the social question of who would give permission on behalf of those who cannot give it by themselves.[12]

A different sort of quandary sits on the border between research and therapy. Early detection of lesions associated with Alzheimer's disease might only be the leading edge of diagnostic tools for neurological disorders in the preclinical state, disorders for which there are no effective therapies. In this case the capacity of the patient at the time of testing is not in doubt. A number of those at risk from Alzheimer's disease might request brain imaging. Some clinicians will view testing for risk status as appropriate, arguing that it will facilitate long-term planning, whereas others will urge that any such detection should only take place as part of a clinical trial until a medical intervention is available. Some consensus will be required concerning appropriate counselling in such cases.

In these circumstances, we can learn from history. When pre-symptomatic diagnosis for Huntington's disease became available, some expected a rush to testing. But in the absence of an adequate intervention, many have opted against knowing their genetically determined destiny. If ignorance is not exactly bliss, neither is knowledge in the absence of a solution.

Manipulations; Natural and Not

Some neuroscientific discoveries, once they become more widely appreciated, are likely to become objects of popular imagination. Magnetic resonance imaging (MRI) studies conducted by colleagues at Emory University indicate that women who undertook cooperative acts during the Prisoner's Dilemma trials experienced activation of dopamine-rich neurons.[13] The Prisoner's Dilemma is a means to analyze cooperation in which two players win when both cooperate, but if only one of them cooperates, the defector wins more. Businesses that value socially cooperative employees might be interested in using these measures of proclivity on prospective workers as a hiring screen, even though they might not add anything to psychological testing and letters of reference from previous employers. On the other hand, firms interested in more competitive types of employees might use a pre-employment MRI to ferret out those who experience less pleasure from cooperation. It would be interesting to know whether these scans will be received as unacceptably invasive or just part of the job search routine.

A different sort of competitive advantage might be sought by ardent lovers with just enough neuroscientific knowledge to be dangerous. Investigators recently reported that thin, slow cortical fibres are associated with the pleasure that comes from a loving touch.[14] These fibres connect to the somatosensory system and are present at birth, whereas the thicker fibres that rapidly convey sensation develop somewhat later. This

Swedish and Canadian team theorizes that an infant is therefore capable of experiencing the emotional effect of parental touching before the tactile sensation itself.[14] Considering the profound psychological depth of these feelings, unscrupulous Lotharios may someday find techniques for thin-fibre stimulation to be important parts of their arsenal.

Aristotle's taxonomic biology, built around the classification of flora and fauna into genus and species, helped give credence to his metaphysical doctrine of natural kinds. Since then, the idea of species mixing has been taken as 'unnatural'. Natural-law philosophy draws the moral implications from this doctrine, with bestiality as a prime example of a crime against nature based on the essential distinctness of natural kinds. When a presidential commission on ethics set out early rules for genetic engineering in the 1980s, the species barrier was cited as one to be respected.

To paraphrase Justice O'Connor's famous remark on the trimester scheme for the regulation of abortion, the species barrier is a standard at war with itself. A pincer movement has been established by the results of comparative genome projects on one side, and the need for animal models with telescoped life spans for critical medical research on the other. Both undermine the commitment to the view that each species has its own unique essence.

Studies that aim to produce genetically altered rodents with human neurons are an interesting example, and might someday test public tolerance of species mixing. Researchers have identified one among presumably many genes linked to human speech. But this particular gene, *FOXP2*, is especially important because it appears to have conferred tremendous evolutionary advantage around 200,000 years ago, when modern humans appeared.[15] To test this claim, the creation of a genetically modified mouse with the *FOXP2* alteration seems to be the obvious next step. Interesting changes in physiology and behaviour would presumably not include a talking mouse, as one of the investigators joked to the media, but at what point, if any, would the public find the presence of human neural tissue in mice to be an intolerable breach of the species barrier? It may only be fortuitous that the creation of mice that are transgenic for the Huntington's disease gene has not already aroused public anxiety about species mixing.

Once again, there are historic analogies to be drawn. Initial discomfort with porcine heart valves and other animal–human tissue grafts have given way to routine, in spite of continuing concern about the introduction of animal viruses into humans. Neural tissue, however, may push up against what Leon Kass, the chairman of the President's Council on Bioethics, calls 'the wisdom of repugnance,' especially if more than a tiny proportion of neurons is involved. A mouse with a brain that was entirely constructed from human neurons would surely provide remarkable research opportunities, as well as probably prompting a global debate.

Mind Wars

During the 1940s and 1950s, the bulk of psychological research funding was provided by national security agencies that were interested in gaining an advantage during the cold war. Many of the scandals associated with this research, such as the CIA and army experiments with LSD and other hallucinogens, has become part of our cultural legacy.[16] They have also spawned a legion of conspiracy theorists prepared to entertain any rumored 'mind-control' technology without being inhibited by scientific implausibility. However, national security agencies continue to be interested in the benefits that could be conferred by scientific breakthroughs, as shown by the current attempt of the United States government to control the publication of data deemed related to national security that has been obtained through research supported by federal grants or contracts. Paranoia and naivete about these matters are not the only alternatives.

One favourite worry of conspiracy theorists is that of long-range surveillance by state authorities. The introduction of increasingly sophisticated imaging technologies, such as functional MRI will probably give such fears a field day. Perhaps these fears would not be without merit. If devices based on these principles could be small and sensitive enough to detect high blood flow in neural systems associated with violence, they would be of great interest for use in airports and other sensitive public spaces. People who activate these alarms could be stopped and interviewed, or simply closely monitored while in the facility through the already ubiquitous video surveillance system. The civil liberties issues at stake here hardly require elaboration.

The potential military applications of neuroscientific developments are rarely mentioned in the literature. Daniel L. Schacter provides an exception; in *The Seven Sins of Memory*[17] he gives an example related to the gene that codes for the N-methyl-D-aspartate (NMDA) receptor. As this gene is linked to synaptic plasticity, mice with extra copies of a subtype of NMDA receptors showed superior learning skills. Schacter notes that if NMDA proves to have the memory-improving properties that the early work indicates, it might not only lead to a useful therapy for people with memory disorders, but might also be useful in those with normal memories. Again, we face the question of whether such genetic intervention in brain processes is acceptable, and under what conditions.

Particularly striking is Schacter's report of an observation by neurobiologist Tim Tully. A pacifist, Tully acknowledges that memory-enhancing medications would be very attractive in the heat of combat, when complex information about, say, a target-rich bombing mission, must be apprehended by fighter pilots in a short amount of time and many details stored. Schacter's allusion to the national security angle of the fruits of neuroscience, brief as it is, is nonetheless one of the few such references in this literature.

One need not, of course, adopt Tully's view of the matter. As is the case for researchers in other fields, the post-9/11 environment should prompt a discussion about the moral responsibilities of neuroscientists that includes the aims and implications of their work, with particular attention to the agendas of various funding sources. In other words, they will need to join the ranks of atomic physicists and geneticists in fighting a moral crucible. If the neurosciences are indeed poised for their own great leap forward, such will be the burdens of success.

Is Neuroethics New?

The frequent references made in this paper both to important historic figures in philosophy and science, and to the longstanding issues and debates, have perhaps tipped the reader to my view that neuroethics is in some ways old wine in a new bottle. There is no reason for surprise here, but some reason for comfort. Ethical problems seem to never be completely new; there are always precursors and therefore analogies to be drawn. And there are prior conceptual schemes to be considered and revised or reformed. If there is an appearance of novelty as ethical issues come to widespread awareness, it is mainly because of peculiar aspects of a particular case that oblige a new analytical approach. In the early days of bioethics, many issues attracted attention because of new technological capabilities, such as the implications of life-extending modalities for the definition of clinical death. With its access to improving technologies,

particularly functional imaging, current work in the neurosciences provides rich ground for such cases. Many of those engaged in these efforts will find themselves the subjects of the sort of public attention that was previously experienced by their colleagues in nuclear physics and genetics. Neuroscientists will increasingly be challenged to explain the significance of their work in moral as well as scientific terms.

Acknowledgment

I express my gratitude to Paul Lombard.

References

1   Winston, J. S., Strange, B. A., Doherty, J. and Dolan, R. J. Automatic and intentional brain responses during evaluation of trustworthiness of faces. *Nature Neurosci.* 5, 277–283 (2002).

2   Golby, A. J., Gabrieli, J. D. E., Chiao, J. Y. and Eberhardt J. L. Differential responses in the fusiform region to same-race and other-race faces. *Nature Neurosci.* 4, 845–850 (2001).

3   Churchland, P. *Neurophilosophy: Toward a Unified Science of the Mind-Brain* (MIT Press, Cambridge, Mass., 1989).

4   James, W. *The Principles of Psychology* (Henry Holt, New York, 1890).

5   Guillan vs State, S. E. 2d. WL 31553982 Ga. App. 2002.

6   Damasio, A. *Descartes' Error: Emotion, Reason, and the Human Brain* (HarperCollins, New York, 1994).

7   Levy, B. J. and Anderson, M. C. Inhibitory processes and the control of memory retrieval. *Trends Cogn. Sci.* 6, 299–305 (2002).

8   Balaban, E., Alper, J. S. and Kasamon, Y. L. Mean genes and the biology of aggression: a critical review of recent animal and human research. *J. Neurogenet.* 11, 1–43 (1996).

9   Caspi, A. *et al.* Role of genotype in the cycle of violence in maltreated children. *Science* 297, 851–854 (2002).

10 Chenn, A. and Walsh, C. A. Regulation of cerebral cortical size by control of cell cycle exit in neural precursors. *Science* 297, 365–369 (2002).

11 Moreno, J. D. Regulation of research in the decisionally impaired: history and gaps in the current regulatory system. *J. Health Care Law Policy* 1, 1–21 (1998).

12 National Bioethics Advisory Commission. *Research Involving Persons with Mental Disorders That May Affect Decisionmaking Capacity* (National Bioethics Advisory Commission, Rockville, Md, 1999).

13 Rilling, J. K. *et al.* A neural basis for social cooperation. *Neuron* 35, 395–405 (2002).

14 Olausson, H. *et al.* Unmyelinated tactile afferents signal touch and project to insular cortex. *Nature Neurosci.* 5, 900–904 (2002).

15 Editorial. In search of language genes. *Nature Neurosci.* 4, 1049 (2002).

16 Moreno, J. D. *Undue Risk: Secret State Experiments on Humans* (Routledge, New York, 2001).

17 Schacter, D. L. *The Seven Sins of Memory: How the Mind Forgets and Remembers* (Houghton Mifflin, Boston, Mass., 2001).

85

How Electrical Brain Stimulation Can Change the Way We Think

Sally Adee

Have you ever wanted to take a vacation from your own head? You could do it easily enough with liberal applications of alcohol or hallucinogens, but that's not the kind of vacation I'm talking about. What if you could take a very specific vacation only from the stuff that makes it painful to be you: the sneering inner monologue that insists you're not capable enough or smart enough or pretty enough, or whatever hideous narrative rides you. Now that would be a vacation. You'd still be you, but you'd be able to navigate the world without the emotional baggage that now drags on your every decision. Can you imagine what that would feel like?

Late last year, I got the chance to find out, in the course of investigating a story for *New Scientist* about how researchers are using neurofeedback and electrical brain stimulation to accelerate learning. What I found was that electricity might be the most powerful drug I've ever used in my life.

It used to be just plain old chemistry that had neuroscientists gnawing their fingernails about the ethics of brain enhancement. As Adderall, Ritalin, and other cognitive enhancing drugs gain widespread acceptance as tools to improve your everyday focus, even the stigma of obtaining them through less-than-legal channels appears to be disappearing. People will overlook a lot of moral gray areas in the quest to juice their brain power.

But until recently, you were out of luck if you wanted to do that without taking drugs that might be addictive, habit-forming, or associated with unfortunate behavioral side effects. Over the past few years, however, it's become increasingly clear that applying an electrical current to your head confers similar benefits.

US military researchers have had great success using "transcranial direct current stimulation" (tDCS) – in which they hook you up to what's essentially a 9-volt battery and let the current flow through your brain. After a few years of lab testing, they've found that tDCS can more than double the rate at which people learn a wide range of tasks, such as object recognition, math skills, and marksmanship.

We don't yet have a commercially available "thinking cap," but we will soon. So the research community has begun to ask: What are the ethics of battery-operated cognitive enhancement? Recently, a group of Oxford neuroscientists released a cautionary statement about the ethics of brain boosting; then the UK's Royal Society released a report that questioned the use of tDCS for military applications. Is brain boosting a fair addition to the cognitive enhancement arms race? Will it create a Morlock/Eloi–like social divide, where the rich can afford to be smarter and everyone else will be left behind? Will Tiger Moms force their lazy kids to strap on a zappity helmet during piano practice?

Original publication details: Sally Adee, "How Electrical Brain Stimulation Can Change the Way We Think," *The Week*, March 30, 2012.

After trying it myself, I have different questions. To make you understand, I am going to tell you how it felt. The experience wasn't simply about the easy pleasure of undeserved expertise. For me, it was a near-spiritual experience. When a nice neuroscientist named Michael Weisend put the electrodes on me, what defined the experience was not feeling smarter or learning faster: The thing that made the earth drop out from under my feet was that for the first time in my life, everything in my head finally shut up.

The experiment I underwent was accelerated marksmanship training, using a training simulation that the military uses. I spent a few hours learning how to shoot a modified M4 close-range assault rifle, first without tDCS and then with. Without it I was terrible, and when you're terrible at something, all you can do is obsess about how terrible you are. And how much you want to stop doing the thing you are terrible at.

Then this happened:

The 20 minutes I spent hitting targets while electricity coursed through my brain were far from transcendent. I only remember feeling like I'd just had an excellent cup of coffee, but without the caffeine jitters. I felt clear-headed and like myself, just sharper. Calmer. Without fear and without doubt. From there on, I just spent the time waiting for a problem to appear so that I could solve it.

It was only when they turned off the current that I grasped what had just happened. Relieved of the minefield of self-doubt that constitutes my basic personality, I was a hell of a shot. And I can't tell you how stunning it was to suddenly understand just how much of a drag that inner cacophony is on my ability to navigate life and basic tasks.

It's possibly the world's biggest cliché that we're our own worst enemies. In yoga, they tell you that you need to learn to get out of your own way. Practices like yoga are meant to help you exhume the person you are without all the geologic layers of narrative and cross talk that are constantly chattering in your brain. I think eventually they just become background noise. We stop hearing them consciously, but believe me, we listen to them just the same.

My brain without self-doubt was a revelation. There was suddenly this incredible silence in my head; I've experienced something close to it during two-hour Iyengar yoga classes, or at the end of a 10k [run], but the fragile peace in my head would be shattered almost the second I set foot outside the calm of the studio. I had certainly never experienced instant Zen in the frustrating middle of something I was terrible at.

What had happened inside my skull? One theory is that the mild electrical shock may depolarize the neuronal membranes in the part of the brain associated with object recognition, making the cells more excitable and responsive to inputs. Like many other neuroscientists working with tDCS, Weisend thinks this accelerates the formation of new neural pathways during the time that someone practices a skill, making it easier to get into the "zone." The method he was using on me boosted the speed with which wannabe snipers could detect a threat by a factor of 2.3.

Another possibility is that the electrodes somehow reduce activity in the prefrontal cortex – the area of the brain used in critical thought, says psychologist Mihaly Csikszentmihalyi of Claremont Graduate University in California. And critical thought, some neuroscientists believe, is muted during periods of intense Zen-like concentration. It sounds counterintuitive, but silencing self-critical thoughts might allow more automatic processes to take hold, which would in turn produce that effortless feeling of flow.

With the electrodes on, my constant self-criticism virtually disappeared, I hit every one of the targets, and there were no unpleasant side effects afterwards. The bewitching silence of the tDCS lasted, gradually diminishing over a period of about three days. The inevitable return of self-doubt and inattention was disheartening, to say the least.

I hope you can sympathize with me when I tell you that the thing I wanted most acutely for the weeks following my experience was to go back and strap on those electrodes. I also started to have a lot of questions. Who was I apart from the angry bitter gnomes that populate my mind and drive me to failure because I'm too scared to try? And where did those voices come from? Some of them are personal history, like the caustically dismissive 7th grade science teacher who advised me to become a waitress. Some of them are societal, like the hateful lady-mag voices that bully me every time I look in a mirror. An invisible narrative informs all my waking decisions in ways I can't even keep track of.

What would a world look like in which we all wore little tDCS headbands that would keep us in a primed, confident state, free of all doubts and fears? I'd wear one at all times and have two in my backpack ready in case something happened to the first one.

I think the ethical questions we should be asking about tDCS are much more subtle than the ones we've been asking about cognitive enhancement. Because how you define "cognitive enhancement" frames the debate about its ethics.

If you told me tDCS would allow someone to study twice as fast for the bar exam, I might be a little leery because now I have visions of rich daddies paying for Junior's thinking cap. Neuroscientists like Roy Hamilton have termed this kind of application "cosmetic neuroscience," which implies a kind of "First World problem" – frivolity.

But now think of a different application – could school-age girls use the zappy cap while studying math to drown out the voices that tell them they can't do math because they're girls? How many studies have found a link between invasive stereotypes and poor test performance?

And then, finally, the main question: What role do doubt and fear play in our lives if their eradication actually causes so many improvements? Do we make more ethical decisions when we listen to our inner voices of self-doubt or when we're freed from them? If we all wore these caps, would the world be a better place?

And if tDCS headwear were to become widespread, would the same 20 minutes with a 2 milliamp current always deliver the same effects, or would you need to up your dose like you do with some other drugs?

Because, to steal a great point from an online commenter, pretty soon, a 9-volt battery may no longer be enough.

86

Neuroethics
Ethics and the Sciences of the Mind

Neil Levy

The spectacular growth of applied ethics over the past several decades has been spurred, in important part, by the growth in medical knowledge and associated technologies. As our powers over life and death have expanded, so have the potential for these powers to be misused; accordingly, high quality ethical reflection on the nature and limits of these powers has come to seem necessary. As a consequence, a whole new sub-discipline was born, called bioethics. More recently, we have seen an equally dramatic expansion in our knowledge of the workings of the mind/brain. Our increasing powers over the mind have led to a similar demand for ethical reflection, and thus the birth of another new subfield of applied ethics: *neuroethics*. Neuroethics is to the sciences of the mind as bioethics is to the medical sciences.

In one central respect, however, neuroethics is significantly different to bioethics in its scope and ambitions. Whereas bioethics could be described as applying the tools of philosophers to a new set of issues, neuroethics is as much concerned with the nature of the tools it uses as with the problems to which it seeks to apply them. Since the tools of philosophers are cognitive, and the sciences of the mind are concerned with the nature of cognition (broadly understood), the sciences of the mind are concerned with our tools: with their nature, their strengths and weaknesses and with their reliability.

Hence the neuroethicist is adrift on Neurath's boat to an even greater extent than most philosophers: she must address first-order ethical issues using tools whose very reliability is one of her concerns

Given the dual focus of neuroethics, on first-order ethical questions arising from the sciences of the mind, and on the tools the neuroethicist uses in addressing these questions, neuroethics might be said to have two distinct branches. Roskies calls these two branches the *ethics of neuroscience* and the *neuroscience of ethics*. The ethics of neuroscience is concerned with first-order ethical issues; the neuroscience of ethics with normative ethics, meta-ethics and moral psychology insofar as these branches of philosophy are illuminated by the sciences of the mind.

The Ethics of Neuroscience

The sciences of the mind offer us a range of apparently unprecedented powers to intervene in the mind of human beings, some actual, some just over the horizon, and some very distant (it is a matter of lively dispute which technologies are distant and which imminent). These powers arouse a great deal of unease in many people, prompting philosophers to reflect upon the permissibility of their use. These actual or potential powers include the ability to

Original publication details: Neil Levy, "Neuroethics: Ethics and the Sciences of the Mind," pp. 69–74 (extract) from *Philosophy Compass* 4: 10 (2009), pp. 69–81. Reproduced with permission from John Wiley & Sons.

enhance cognition, to *modify memories and emotions*, and to *control or insert beliefs*.[1] Each of these has been the focus of sustained ethical reflection. For reasons of space, I shall consider only the first two topics (see Levy, *Neuroethics* for discussions of the ability to control or insert beliefs).

Memory Modification and Enhancement

Existing techniques to modify memories are relatively crude and weak. These techniques have been developed with therapeutic goals in mind: either to slow the progress of dementia, in the case of techniques that might improve memory, or to treat post-traumatic stress disorder (PTSD) in the case of techniques aimed at weakening specific memories.

Post-traumatic stress disorder is a relatively common, very debilitating psychiatric illness. It is especially common in emergency services personnel and soldiers (Kessler et al.). Since it is burdensome for sufferers and for their families, the treatment of PTSD is prima facie laudable. Obviously, the best way to deal with the problem is to prevent its occurrence, by preventing exposure to potentially traumatic events. Given, however, that the jobs of emergency services personnel and perhaps soldiers are indispensable, the next best option is to prevent PTSD from arising as a result of such exposure.

There is now a promising technique in development which might serve to prevent PTSD. Post-traumatic stress disorder is apparently caused by the over-consolidation of traumatic memories, as a result of the misfiring of a mechanism designed to ensure effective recall of survival-relevant events. Since endogenous epinephrine plays a crucial role in the over-consolidation cycle, Pitman et al. hypothesized that the development of the syndrome could be prevented by blocking the effect of the stress hormone on the amygdala. Clinical trials using the beta-blocker Propranolol (widely used for the treatment of hypertension) have yielded promising results. Subjects administered Propranolol after involvement in auto accidents were less likely to develop PTSD than controls (Pitman and Delahanty; Vaiva et al.).

Obviously the prevention of PTSD is a laudable goal, yet the research outlined above has been surprisingly controversial. Much of the worry has focused on the potential for abuse of a successful treatment for PTSD. It is plausible to think that painful memories are often both instrumentally valuable and intrinsically significant. Painful memories ought sometimes to be treasured by us, not eliminated: the person who erases, or even just significantly dampens, the memory of the death of a beloved child does not improve her life thereby; instead she strips it of elements central to its meaning. But it might be that developing the kind of emotional maturity needed to appreciate this fact takes time and exposure to pain. Thus, a culture in which drugs are available that have these kinds of effects might be much less conducive to the development of the requisite maturity. The availability of these drugs might therefore contribute to what many people fear is an increasing shallowness characteristic of Western culture. Moreover, Leon Kass, formerly the head of the President's Council of Bioethics, worries that Propranolol might be used to facilitate wrongdoing. For most of us, even for most habitual criminals, the sting of conscience is a genuine and aversive phenomenon. Kass worries that Propranolol might effectively erase that sting, providing a 'morning-after pill for just about anything that produces regret, remorse, pain, or guilt' (Baard).

The worries just sketched focus on the *misuse* of Propranolol and its probable successors; their proponents accept that preventing PTSD is a valuable goal, but worry about the availability of a particular means to that goal. Others have questioned the desirability of treating PTSD at all. Ethicists have worried that treating or preventing PTSD might deny access to the meaning of traumatic events (Hurley; Evers) or deny people access to opportunities for personal growth (Warnick).

Some of these worries are relatively easily dispensed with, especially insofar as they seem to suggest – falsely – that PTSD is, on balance, a good thing for the sufferer (see Levy and Clarke for discussion). Others are worth taking seriously. One question we must ask ourselves whenever we discuss new technologies and their possible problems is the extent to which the problem is genuinely new. Will Propranolol really give us greater powers to dampen the emotional powers of memories than, say, alcohol? Given that the latter has high costs beyond the effects on the emotional life of the subject via memory dampening, perhaps the availability of the former is, on balance, a good thing, allowing people to pursue emotional oblivion at a lower cost; on the other hand, the lower cost might encourage greater use of Propranolol than of alcohol to this end. This question is largely an empirical one; philosophers have no special expertise when it comes to predictions about such matters as to whether people are more likely to use Propranolol than alcohol.

It is probable, however, that some of the anxiety surrounding the use of Propranolol comes from an exaggerated sense of how effective it is likely to be. It has, for instance, the potential to cut us from the emotional significance of events only if it is relatively powerful: if it does not simply prevent *over*-consolidation of memories, but also the normal degree of consolidation. Given that Propranolol has been taken by many thousands of people over an extended period of time, it seems unlikely that its effects will be dramatic. Propranolol has some, relatively subtle, effects on cognition: subjects exhibit a conservative bias on certain memory tasks, compared to controls (Corwin et al.; Callaway et al.). But these effects simply seem too subtle to give cause for alarm.

While much of the debate in the recent neuroethical literature has focused on the use of memory dampeners, far more scientific attention has been focused on means to *improve* memory. The reason is not far to seek: far more people are affected by dementia than by PTSD, and aging populations ensure that these numbers will only rise. Though to my knowledge no one has objected to the use of medication to treat dementia – it is difficult to see how progressive memory loss could be conducive to any human good – many ethicists have expressed concerns about 'off label' use of such medication, to enhance memory beyond normal. Related concerns have focused on cognitive enhancers – psychopharmaceuticals used to enhance human intelligence beyond its normal limits – more generally.

When considering these kinds of issues, it is necessary to deal separately with questions about the potential unforeseen harms of cognitive or memory enhancers and the more general question: is cognitive

enhancement permissible in principle? The former is, once again, largely an empirical question. However, there are certainly some philosophical questions here. For instance, the claim that improvements in some aspects of memory or cognition are likely to come at the cost of deterioration in other aspects, because our memory systems are the product of evolution and therefore likely to be optimal (Glannon 108), seem to me to rest on an implausibly strong adaptationism: evolution is a satisficing process, not an optimising process. Similarly, philosophical expertise (amongst others kinds) is needed to assess the oft-repeated claim that widespread availability of enhancements will cause or exacerbate inequality.

Here I will set aside these important questions, in order to focus on in principle objections to enhancements. Some philosophers have suggested that we ought to reject all such enhancements because they promote attitudes that are incompatible with the virtues, with authenticity or with an attitude to the world which is obligatory. For Michael Sandel, the use of enhancements is incompatible with the gratitude we ought to feel toward the unforced products of nature. Carl Elliott worries that enhancement, especially *affective* enhancement, runs the risk of inauthenticity, as we lose contact with the emotional significance of events, while Carol Freedman worries that the use of such enhancements risks mechanizing ourselves inappropriately. I do not think that any of these concerns are significant enough to warrant serious disquiet regarding the development of cognitive or affective enhancements.

Sandel's concern is to my mind the weakest. It is simply false that there is any interesting sense in which human powers and achievements are currently a gift for which we ought to feel grateful but would no longer be such a gift were cognitive enhancement to become widespread. Our phenotypic traits have never been an unforced gift from nature. Phenotypic traits are always the product of the interaction of the genome (and other developmental resources) and the environment, and *homo sapiens* is a niche constructing animal, an animal who shapes the environment that shapes it in turn (Sterelny). We are deeply and essentially cultural animals; deeply and essentially because it is not just our social organization, but our intrinsic capacities and traits that are shaped by our culture. There is simply no sense in which our current capacities and traits are a gift of nature; at least, there is no sense in which they would not equally be a gift of nature were they also the product of cognitive enhancing pharmaceuticals.

Concerns about authenticity are almost as easily dismissed. As David DeGrazia has pointed out, Elliott's claim that we ought to be true to ourselves, in some sense incompatible with using psychopharmaceuticals, entails the notion of a pregiven self. Deep and persistent changes in an agent's traits or dispositions can be inauthentic only if there is an underlying self apart from these merely accidental properties, with which our traits ought to harmonize. But the self is a creation: we are always in the process of remaking ourselves. There is no essence to which we are required to conform, on pain of inauthenticity. Freedman's worry about inappropriate mechanism of the self is harder to dismiss. We should recognize, first, that there is a sense in which we *are* machines, or, more exactly, built out of machines; our minds emerge from or are realized by myriad mechanisms, each of which is itself mindless. But it certainly doesn't follow from the fact that we are built out of machines that it is appropriate to treat us as machines; we, unlike the machines out of which we are built, are *not* mindless. Human beings live in the space of reasons: it is this fact that motivates Freedman's concern. If we respond to ourselves or to others as though our emotions and thoughts are merely mechanical reactions, we do not show the proper respect due to agents. Worse, Freedman worries, treat ourselves mechanically and we might actually threaten our status as rational beings.

Still, we must be careful not to overdraw the worry. It does not seem objectionable to treat oneself mechanically, on occasion and to some extent. Some effective treatments for mild depression that do not involve psychopharmaceuticals, such as sun lamps for the treatment of Seasonal Affective Disorder, or the use of exercise to lift mood, are equally mechanistic. They do not give us *reasons* to be happier; they *cause* our mood to improve. Intuitively, these means are acceptable (whether they lift someone out of depression or elevate mood above the normal level). Why should any greater suspicion fall upon psychopharmaceuticals?

By way of transition to a consideration of the neuroscience of ethics, it is worth reflecting further on this question. Given that in many ways the enhancements in question seem to be relevantly similar to existing techniques of increasing cognitive ability – from ensuring adequate nutrition to choosing better schools – why is the use of psychopharmaceuticals, transcranial magnetic stimulation, or what have you so widely regarded with suspicion? It might be that these intuitions have causes that do not reflect good reasons. Jonathan Haidt has argued that very often the reasons people offer for their moral judgments have nothing to do with their actual causes. Together with Thalia Wheatley, moreover, he has shown that the causes of moral judgments can be morally irrelevant. For instance, invoking a disgust response in subjects intensifies their judgments of moral wrongness: it can even cause subjects to judge an entirely innocuous action to be morally wrong (Wheatley and Haidt). It is therefore possible that the causes motivating the judgment that cognitive enhancement is distinctively wrong are morally irrelevant: since a feeling of unease is capable of being mistaken for or generating a moral intuition, evidence that cognitive enhancement would generate such a feeling of unease due to morally irrelevant factors is evidence that the intuition ought to be discounted.

There are, I suggest, good reasons to suggest that the negative response to cognitive enhancement is produced via a morally irrelevant route. The feeling of unease may well be a response to the fact that cognitive enhancement is a violation of implicit dualism. There is evidence that dualism is the cognitive default (Bering; Bering and Bjorklund). Moreover, reaction time studies suggest that it is a default that is not *replaced* by physicalist convictions but merely *displaced*: that is, we continue to have dualist intuitions which we must effortfully override in order to express a physicalist judgment. Now, there is an obvious sense in which cognitive enhancement is a violation of implicit dualism: it produces alterations in the mind via its physical substrate, which ought to be impossible if dualism is true. Hence it is likely that contemplating the mere possibility of such alterations produces a feeling of unease in us, which is easily mistaken for a moral intuition.

Note

1   There is an ongoing debate whether it is possible to draw a treatment/enhancement distinction that is capable of doing the work that bioethicists typically demand of it (usually distinguishing between permissible and impermissible interventions). Rather than enter into this debate, I use 'enhancement' here simply to refer to interventions that elevate functioning above the statistically normal level. For an argument that no interesting treatment/enhancement distinction is defensible, see Levy, *Neuroethics*.

References

Baard, E. 'The Guilt-Free Soldier'. *Village Voice* January 2003. At http://www.villagevoice.com/2003-01-21/news/the-guilt-free-soldier/1.

Bering, J. M. 'Intuitive Conceptions of Dead Agents' Minds: The Natural Foundations of Afterlife Beliefs as Phenomenological Boundary'. *Journal of Cognition and Culture* 2 (2002): 263–308.

Bering, J. M. and D. F. Bjorklund. 'The Natural Emergence of Reasoning about the Afterlife as a Developmental Regularity'. *Developmental Psychology* 40 (2004): 217–33.

Callaway, E., et al. 'Propranolol and Response Bias: An Extension of Findings Reported by Corwin et al.'. *Biological Psychiatry* 30 (1991): 739–42.

Corwin, J., et al. 'Disorders of Decision in Affective Disease: An Effect of β-Adrenergic Dysfunction?'. *Biological Psychiatry* 27 (1990): 813–33.

DeGrazia. 'Prozac, Enhancement, and Self-Creation'. *Hastings Center Report* 30 (2000): 34–40.

Elliott, C. 'The Tyranny of Happiness: Ethics and Cosmetic Psychopharmacology'. *Enhancing Human Traits: Ethical and Social Implications*. Ed. Erik Parens. Washington, DC: Georgetown University Press, 1998. 177–88.

Evers, K. 'Perspectives on Memory Manipulation: Using Beta-Blockers to Cure Post-Traumatic Stress Disorder'. *Cambridge Quarterly of HealthCare Ethics* 16 (2007): 138–46.

Freedman, C. 'Aspirin for the Mind? Some Ethical Worries about Psychopharmacology'. *Enhancing Human Traits: Ethical and Social Implications*. Ed. Erik Parens. Washington, DC: Georgetown University Press, 1998. 135–50.

Glannon, W. *Bioethics on the Brain*. Oxford: Oxford University Press, 2007.

Haidt, J. 'The Emotional Dog and Its Rational Tail: A Social Intuitionist Approach to Moral Judgment'. *Psychological Review* 108 (2001): 814–34.

Hurley, E. A. 'The Moral Costs of Prophylactic Propranolol'. *AJOB* 7.9 (2007): 35–6.

Kessler, R. C., et al. 'Posttraumatic Stress Disorder in the National Comorbidity Survey'. *Archives of General Psychiatry* 52 (1996): 1048–60.

Levy, N. *Neuroethics*. Cambridge: Cambridge University Press, 2007.

Levy, N. and S. Clarke. 'Neuroethics and Psychiatry'. *Current Opinion in Psychiatry* 21 (2008): 568–571.

Pitman, R. K. and D. L. Delahanty. 'Conceptually Driven Pharmacologic Approaches to Acute Trauma'. *CNS Spectrum* 10 (2005): 99–106.

Pitman, R. K., et al. 'Pilot Study of Secondary Prevention of Posttraumatic Stress Disorder with Propanolol'. *Biological Psychiatry* 51 (2002): 189–92.

Roskies, A. 'Neuroethics for the New Millennium'. *Neuron* 35 (2002): 21–3.

Sandel, M. *The Case against Perfection: Ethics in the Age of Genetic Engineering*. Cambridge, MA: Belknap Press, 2007.

Sterelny, K. *Thought in a Hostile World: The Evolution of Human Cognition*. Oxford: Blackwell, 2003.

Vaiva, G., et al. 'Immediate Treatment with Propranolol Decreases Posttraumatic Stress Disorder Two Months after Trauma'. *Biol Psychiatry* 54 (2003): 947–9.

Warnick, J. E. 'Propranolol and Its Potential Inhibition of Positive Post-Traumatic Growth'. *AJOB* 7.9 (2007): 37–8.

Wheatley, T. and J. Haidt. 'Hypnotic Disgust Makes Moral Judgments More Severe'. *Psychological Science* 16 (2005): 780–4.

87

Freedom of Memory Today

Adam Kolber

We tend to think of our memories as our own in some deep, fundamental way. As we get better at manipulating memories, however, it becomes increasingly clear that our memories are not entirely our own and that we ought not have unfettered control over them. For example, suppose a witness to a horrific crime could eliminate upsetting memories of the incident. The victim might nevertheless have an obligation to the rest of society to preserve the memory in order to testify at a later judicial proceeding,[1] (pp. 1579–1583, 1589–1592). Similarly, while we generally do not have the right or even the ability to erase others' memories, there are cases where we do have the ability and arguably should have the right to do so, even without explicit consent. At least, this seems to be the view of a couple of doctors in a fascinating case involving what can fairly be described as memory *erasure*.

The case is not science fiction. In fact, the events occurred over a decade ago:[2] A young mother came to see Dr. Scott Haig, an orthopedic surgeon, for a bone biopsy. The patient agreed to receive local anesthesia, rather than the general anesthesia commonly given as part of the procedure. According to Haig, the patient "was adamant about not going under, but agreed to 'some sedation' if we thought it was necessary." Also, the patient agreed to have an anesthesiologist in the room "just in case".[2]

Haig removed the tissue sample and had it sent immediately to a pathologist at the hospital. The pathologist was not expected to make an on-the-spot diagnosis. Rather, Haig wanted to confirm that he had removed an adequate sample before closing up the patient's wound. The pathologist, who was working in another part of the hospital, contacted Haig through an intercom system in the operating room. The pathologist, not realizing that the patient was conscious, started discussing the sample in very grave terms. Before Haig could convey to the pathologist that the patient was able to hear every word being said (the intercom was only working in one direction), the pathologist revealed that the patient had a very serious form of cancer and said so without the delicacy he would have used if he thought the patient were awake.[2]

The patient, obviously distraught by the news, began shrieking, "Oh, my God. Oh, my God. My kids." In response, the anesthesiologist decided to inject the patient with an anesthetic called propofol. In addition to its anesthetic effects, propofol, nicknamed "milk of amnesia," frequently "erases" the patient's memory of events that precede injection

Original publication details: Adam Kolber, "Freedom of Memory Today," pp. 145–8 from *Neuroethics* 1 (2008).
With kind permission from Springer Science+Business Media.

by a few minutes. Here is what happened next, according to Haig:

> Ten minutes later Ellen [the patient] woke up, happy and even-keeled, not even knowing she'd been asleep. From the recovery room she was home in time for dinner. "The procedure went smoothly, but we'll have to wait for the final pathology reports," I said, which was not exactly the whole truth, but it let me get the oncology people cued up, a proper diagnosis, and Ellen herself emotionally prepared. I would give her the bad news at a more appropriate time.
>
> The ending was not quite happy; it was a recurrence of the cancer she'd had years before – fairly rare for that type of tumor. Ellen died of it about six years later. I confess I never told her about the incident with the intercom.
>
> Over a decade later, I'm still not sure that was right.[2]

The case raises a panoply of legal and ethical issues, and I will highlight a few of them. First, the anesthesiologist probably lacked the patient's informed consent to receive the injection. The patient agreed to receive general anesthesia if her doctors thought it was really "necessary," but she likely meant to authorize anesthesia for extreme pain arising from physical rather than emotional distress. This is not entirely clear, however, and the scope of the patient's consent might depend on precisely what the patient said in her discussion with her doctors.

There is an emergency exception to the informed consent doctrine, and perhaps the patient might have thrashed about in some clearly dangerous way if she were not sedated. Barring that possibility, however, it seems questionable to apply the emergency exception under circumstances that arguably contradict the patient's earlier request. Moreover, it is at least possible that the anesthesiologist could have sought the patient's consent in the brief moments prior to the injection. Assuming that the injection was outside the scope of consent, medical personnel could have been liable for failure to obtain informed consent under a theory of negligence or even tortious battery. Criminal liability for battery or poisoning seems unlikely, though not unimaginable.

Second, by erasing the patient's memory, the anesthesiologist not only eased the patient's emotional distress, he also erased some of the evidence that could have been used against him in a legal proceeding.

This raises questions about evidence tampering. At a minimum, the anesthesiologist might be deemed to have "spoliated evidence," meaning that fact finders in subsequent litigation would be entitled to presume that the spoliated evidence was adverse to the anesthesiologist. What's interesting and unusual in this case is that the same act which eases the patient's pain also eliminates evidence that could be used against the anesthesiologist. Of course, the facts in no way prove that the anesthesiologist sought to destroy evidence; he may well have acted from perceived medical necessity. On the other hand, if the destruction of information in the patient's memory were just an unfortunate side effect of the drug, the anesthesiologist could have revealed the events to the patient later in time (though he may have nevertheless feared legal liability even if he were confident that he acted appropriately under the circumstances).

Third, the case raises interesting questions about the valuation of memories. Suppose that the patient had a legally-cognizable claim against medical personnel for bringing about the circumstances that led to the memory erasure. How would we put a price on her lost memory? Did the propofol mitigate damages by preventing the patient from reliving a traumatic memory, or did it augment damages by causing an additional harm – an invasion of the patient's autonomy interests in her own memories? Perhaps it augmented some harms and mitigated others.[i]

Of course, the circumstances described here are very unusual. Propofol has a retrograde amnestic effect that stretches back just a few minutes, making the drug generally impractical for treating the emotional pain of recent traumatic events. In 2002 and 2003, however, the President's Council on Bioethics heard testimony on the use of pharmaceuticals to dampen at least the emotional intensity of somewhat older memories.[3] The discussion focused on the possible use of the drug propranolol (already approved by the Food and Drug Administration to treat hypertension) as a memory-dampening agent. A few preliminary studies suggest that propranolol may ease the emotional valence of memories formed several hours prior to consumption and make it less likely that trauma victims will develop post-traumatic stress disorder.[4,5]

If propranolol does affect the emotional valence of memory, the effects are probably modest. Moreover, it is unclear whether propranolol affects factual associations with memories. (Some experiments suggest that propranolol may reduce factual recall of events that occurred while under the influence of the drug,[6] and the Physicians' Desk Reference lists short-term memory loss as one of propranolol's side effects,[7] (p. 3423)). But even if propranolol fails as a memory-dampening agent, some more potent drug is likely to step into its place. In 2004, US veterans received benefits payments for post-traumatic stress disorder totaling $4.3 billion.[8] Not surprisingly, governments and other healthcare providers are quite interested in finding comparatively inexpensive pharmaceutical methods of easing or preventing the emotional distress associated with bad memories.[ii]

Propranolol has already been tested on human subjects who show up in the emergency room with physical and emotional trauma from assaults and car accidents. Some of these assaults and car accidents are likely to give rise to civil or criminal litigation. Even if propranolol ultimately has no noteworthy effects on memory, courts may still have to explore and address the scientific validity of claims made about propranolol. Attorneys seeking to impeach the testimony of a witness who participated in one of these studies are sure to ask, "Is it true that you participated in a Harvard Medical School research study investigating drugs that alter the intensity of memories?" We are thus confronted with legal and ethical issues related to memory dampening even before we have demonstrated the efficacy of proposed memory-dampening treatments.

In "Therapeutic forgetting: The legal and ethical implications of memory dampening",[1] I argued that the President's Council on Bioethics was too pessimistic in its assessment of the ethical issues raised by memory dampening.[10] While memory-dampening drugs may someday require thoughtful regulation, prohibition or even heavy-handed regulation is unlikely to be necessary. Pharmaceutical companies and memory researchers must decide today how to invest their limited budgets, and the President's Council may well scare some of them off. If researchers fear regulatory obstacles to the eventual marketing of memory-dampening drugs, they may divert their attention elsewhere.

Thus, the contours of our freedom of memory – our limited bundle of rights to control our memories and be free of outside control,[1] (p. 1622) – are worthy of some attention even before we have proven, practical methods of dampening traumatic memories. We need to decide how to handle rare cases that already arise, like that of Dr. Haig, that present core questions about the value of treating traumatic memories. We also need to decide how to handle questions related to memory dampening during periods of experimental investigation, when litigants make claims that cannot await the clear consensus of the scientific community. Finally, researchers must decide how much of their resources to invest in technologies that raise interesting and sometimes troubling neuroethical questions. If we tread too cautiously over novel neuroethical terrain, we will *de facto* limit our freedom of memory, for reasons of technology and not necessarily of good policy.

Notes

i We happen to live in a world where memory erasure is strange and peculiar. If it were more common, doctors might be sued for negligently *failing* to erase memories. Then, we would confront questions about the valuation of traumatic memories that could have been erased but were not due to a physician's failure to erase memories in a timely fashion.

ii There is even a growing field of "relaxation" dentistry that takes advantage of memory dampening techniques. According to an article in the *New York Times*, "[i]n the last five years, thousands of dentists have been trained to administer drugs to anxious patients using medications that doctors say create a mild amnesia for patients who are awake, but not necessarily alert, and may forget the whole experience or have only vague recollections".[9]

References

1 Kolber, A.J. 2006. Therapeutic forgetting: The legal and ethical implications of memory dampening. *Vanderbilt Law Review* 59: 1561–1626.

2 Haig, S. 2007. The ethics of erasing a bad memory. *Time* (online edition, Oct. 15, 2007), http://www.time.com/time/health/article/0,8599,1671492,00.html.

3 Remembering and Forgetting: Physiological and Pharmacological Aspects: Hearings before the President's Council on Bioethics (Oct. 17, 2002), http://biotech.law.lsu.edu/research/pbc/transcripts/oct02/session3.html; Remembering and Forgetting: Psychological Aspects: Hearings before the President's Council on Bioethics (Oct. 17, 2002), http://biotech.law.lsu.edu/research/pbc/transcripts/oct02/session4.html; Beyond Therapy: Better Memories? Hearings before the President's Council on Bioethics (Mar. 6, 2003), http://biotech.law.lsu.edu/research/pbc/transcripts/march03/session4.html.

4 Pitman, R.K. et al. 2002. Pilot study of secondary prevention of posttraumatic stress disorder with propranolol. *Biological Psychiatry* 51: 189–192.

5 Vaiva, G. et al. 2003. Immediate treatment with propranolol decreases posttraumatic stress disorder two months after trauma. *Biological Psychiatry* 54: 947–949.

6 Cahill, L., and J.L. McGaugh. 1995. A novel demonstration of enhanced memory associated with emotional arousal. *Consciousness & Cognition* 4: 410–421.

7 Physicians' Desk Reference. 2006.

8 Department of Veterans Affairs, Office of Inspector General. 2005. Review of state variances in VA disability compensation claims, Rep. No. 05–00765–137, http://www.va.gov/oig/52/reports/2005/VAOIG-05-00765-137.pdf.

9 Kershaw, S. 2008. My root canal? It's a blur. *New York Times*, Mar. 6, 2008, G1.

10 President's Council on Bioethics. 2003. *Beyond Therapy: Biotechnology and the Pursuit of Happiness*, http://biotech.law.lsu.edu/research/pbc/reports/beyondtherapy/beyond_therapy_final_report_pcbe.pdf.

88

Towards Responsible Use
of Cognitive-Enhancing Drugs by the Healthy

Henry Greely, Barbara Sahakian, John Harris, Ronald C. Kessler, Michael Gazzaniga, Philip Campbell, and Martha J. Farah

Today, on university campuses around the world, students are striking deals to buy and sell prescription drugs such as Adderall and Ritalin – not to get high, but to get higher grades, to provide an edge over their fellow students or to increase in some measurable way their capacity for learning. These transactions are crimes in the United States, punishable by prison.

Many people see such penalties as appropriate, and consider the use of such drugs to be cheating, unnatural or dangerous. Yet one survey[1] estimated that almost 7% of students in US universities have used prescription stimulants in this way, and that on some campuses, up to 25% of students had used them in the past year. These students are early adopters of a trend that is likely to grow, and indications suggest that they're not alone.[2]

In this article, we propose actions that will help society accept the benefits of enhancement, given appropriate research and evolved regulation. Prescription drugs are regulated as such not for their enhancing properties but primarily for considerations of safety and potential abuse. Still, cognitive enhancement has much to offer individuals and society, and a proper societal response will involve making enhancements available while managing their risks.

Paths to Enhancement

Many of the medications used to treat psychiatric and neurological conditions also improve the performance of the healthy. The drugs most commonly used for cognitive enhancement at present are stimulants, namely Ritalin (methyphenidate) and Adderall (mixed amphetamine salts), and are prescribed mainly for the treatment of attention deficit hyperactivity disorder (ADHD). Because of their effects on the catecholamine system, these drugs increase executive functions in patients and most healthy normal people, improving their abilities to focus their attention, manipulate information in working memory and flexibly control their responses.[3] These drugs are widely used therapeutically. With rates of ADHD in the range of 4–7% among US college students using DSM criteria,[4] and stimulant medication the standard therapy, there are plenty of these drugs on campus to divert to enhancement use.

Original publication details: Henry Greely and Colleagues, "Towards Responsible Use of Cognitive-Enhancing Drugs by the Healthy," pp. 702–5 from *Nature* 456 (December 11, 2008). Reprinted by permission from Macmillan Publishers Ltd.

A newer drug, modafinil (Provigil), has also shown enhancement potential. Modafinil is approved for the treatment of fatigue caused by narcolepsy, sleep apnoea and shift-work sleep disorder. It is currently prescribed off label for a wide range of neuropsychiatric and other medical conditions involving fatigue[5] as well as for healthy people who need to stay alert and awake when sleep deprived, such as physicians on night call.[6] In addition, laboratory studies have shown that modafinil enhances aspects of executive function in rested healthy adults, particularly inhibitory control.[7] Unlike Adderall and Ritalin, however, modafinil prescriptions are not common, and the drug is consequently rare on the college black market. But anecdotal evidence and a readers' survey both suggest that adults sometimes obtain modafinil from their physicians or online for enhancement purposes.[2]

A modest degree of memory enhancement is possible with the ADHD medications just mentioned as well as with medications developed for the treatment of Alzheimer's disease such as Aricept (donepezil), which raise levels of acetylcholine in the brain.[8] Several other compounds with different pharmacological actions are in early clinical trials, having shown positive effects on memory in healthy research subjects (see, for example, ref. 9). It is too early to know whether any of these new drugs will be proven safe and effective, but if one is it will surely be sought by healthy middle-aged and elderly people contending with normal age-related memory decline, as well as by people of all ages preparing for academic or licensure examinations.

Favouring Innovation

Human ingenuity has given us means of enhancing our brains through inventions such as written language, printing and the Internet. Most authors of this Commentary are teachers and strive to enhance the minds of their students, both by adding substantive information and by showing them new and better ways to process that information. And we are all aware of the abilities to enhance our brains with adequate exercise, nutrition and sleep. The drugs just reviewed, along with newer technologies such as brain stimulation and prosthetic brain chips, should be viewed in the same general category as education, good health habits, and information technology – ways that our uniquely innovative species tries to improve itself.

Of course, no two enhancements are equivalent in every way, and some of the differences have moral relevance. For example, the benefits of education require some effort at self-improvement whereas the benefits of sleep do not. Enhancing by nutrition involves changing what we ingest and is therefore invasive in a way that reading is not. The opportunity to benefit from Internet access is less equitably distributed than the opportunity to benefit from exercise. Cognitive-enhancing drugs require relatively little effort, are invasive and for the time being are not equitably distributed, but none of these provides reasonable grounds for prohibition. Drugs may seem distinctive among enhancements in that they bring about their effects by altering brain function, but in reality so does any intervention that enhances cognition. Recent research has identified beneficial neural changes engendered by exercise,[10] nutrition[11] and sleep,[12] as well as instruction[13] and reading.[14] In short, cognitive-enhancing drugs seem morally equivalent to other, more familiar, enhancements.

Many people have doubts about the moral status of enhancement drugs for reasons ranging from the pragmatic to the philosophical, including concerns about short-circuiting personal agency and undermining the value of human effort.[15] Kass,[16] for example, has written of the subtle but, in his view, important differences between human enhancement through biotechnology and through more traditional means. Such arguments have been persuasively rejected (for example, ref. 17). Three arguments against the use of cognitive enhancement by the healthy quickly bubble to the surface in most discussions: that it is cheating, that it is unnatural and that it amounts to drug abuse.

In the context of sports, pharmacological performance enhancement is indeed cheating. But, of course, it is cheating because it is against the rules. Any good set of rules would need to distinguish today's allowed cognitive enhancements, from private tutors to double espressos, from the newer methods, if they are to be banned.

As for an appeal to the 'natural', the lives of almost all living humans are deeply unnatural; our homes, our clothes and our food – to say nothing of the medical care we enjoy – bear little relation to our species''natural' state. Given the many cognitive-enhancing tools we accept already, from writing to laptop computers, why draw the line here and say, thus far but no further?

As for enhancers' status as drugs, drug abuse is a major social ill, and both medicinal and recreational drugs are regulated because of possible harms to the individual and society. But drugs are regulated on a scale that subjectively judges the potential for harm from the very dangerous (heroin) to the relatively harmless (caffeine). Given such regulation, the mere fact that cognitive enhancers are drugs is no reason to outlaw them.

Based on our considerations, we call for a presumption that mentally competent adults should be able to engage in cognitive enhancement using drugs.

Substantive Concerns and Policy Goals

All technologies have risks as well as benefits. Although we reject the arguments against enhancement just reviewed, we recognize at least three substantive ethical concerns.

The first concern is safety. Cognitive enhancements affect the most complex and important human organ, and the risk of unintended side effects is therefore both high and consequential. Although regulations governing medicinal drugs ensure that they are safe and effective for their therapeutic indications, there is no equivalent vetting for unregulated 'off label' uses, including enhancement uses. Furthermore, acceptable safety in this context depends on the potential benefit. For example, a drug that restored good cognitive functioning to people with severe dementia but caused serious adverse medical events might be deemed safe enough to prescribe, but these risks would be unacceptable for healthy individuals seeking enhancement.

Enhancement in children raises additional issues related to the long-term effects on the developing brain. Moreover, the possibility of raising cognitive abilities beyond their species-typical upper bound may engender new classes of side effects. Persistence of unwanted recollections, for example, has clearly negative effects on the psyche.[18]

An evidence-based approach is required to evaluate the risks and benefits of cognitive enhancement. At a minimum, an adequate policy should include mechanisms for the assessment of both risks and benefits for enhancement uses of drugs and devices, with special attention to long-term effects on development and to the possibility of new types of side effects unique to enhancement. But such considerations should not lead to an insistence on higher thresholds than those applied to medications.

We call for an evidence-based approach to the evaluation of the risks and benefits of cognitive enhancement.

The second concern is freedom, specifically freedom from coercion to enhance. Forcible medication is generally reserved for rare cases in which individuals are deemed threats to themselves or others. In contrast, cognitive enhancement in the form of education is required for almost all children at some substantial cost to their liberty, and employers are generally free to require employees to have certain educational credentials or to obtain them. Should schools and employers be allowed to require pharmaceutical enhancement as well? And if we answer 'no' to this question, could coercion occur indirectly, by the need to compete with enhanced classmates and colleagues?

Questions of coercion and autonomy are particularly acute for military personnel and for children. Soldiers in the United States and elsewhere have long been offered stimulant medications including amphetamine and modafinil to enhance alertness, and in the United States are legally required to take medications if ordered to for the sake of their military performance.[19] For similar reasons, namely the safety of the individual in question and others who depend on that individual in dangerous situations, one could imagine other occupations for which enhancement might be justifiably required. A hypothetical example is an extremely safe drug that enabled surgeons to save more patients. Would it be wrong to require this drug for risky operations?

Appropriate policy should prohibit coercion except in specific circumstances for specific occupations, justified by substantial gains in safety. It should also discourage indirect coercion. Employers, schools or governments should not generally require the use of cognitive enhancements. If particular enhancements are shown to be sufficiently safe and effective, this position might be revisited for those interventions.

Children once again represent a special case as they cannot make their own decisions. Comparisons between estimates of ADHD prevalence and prescription numbers have led some to suspect that children in certain school districts are taking enhancing drugs at the behest of achievement-oriented parents, or teachers seeking more orderly classrooms.[20] Governments may be willing to let competent adults take certain risks for the sake of enhancement while restricting the ability to take such risky decisions on behalf of children.

The third concern is fairness. Consider an examination that only a certain percentage can pass. It would seem unfair to allow some, but not all, students to use cognitive enhancements, akin to allowing some students taking a maths test to use a calculator while others must go without. (Mitigating such unfairness may raise issues of indirect coercion, as discussed above.) Of course, in some ways, this kind of unfairness already exists. Differences in education, including private tutoring, preparatory courses and other enriching experiences give some students an advantage over others.

Whether the cognitive enhancement is substantially unfair may depend on its availability, and on the nature of its effects. Does it actually improve learning or does it just temporarily boost exam performance? In the latter case it would prevent a valid measure of the competency of the examinee and would therefore be unfair. But if it were to enhance long-term learning, we may be more willing to accept enhancement. After all, unlike athletic competitions, in many cases cognitive enhancements are not zero-sum games. Cognitive enhancement, unlike enhancement for sports competitions, could lead to substantive improvements in the world.

Fairness in cognitive enhancements has a dimension beyond the individual. If cognitive enhancements are costly, they may become the province of the rich, adding to the educational advantages they already enjoy. One could mitigate this inequity by giving every exam-taker free access to cognitive enhancements, as some schools provide computers during exam week to all students. This would help level the playing field.

Policy governing the use of cognitive enhancement in competitive situations should avoid exacerbating socioeconomic inequalities, and should take into account the validity of enhanced test performance. In developing policy for this purpose, problems of enforcement must also be considered. In spite of stringent regulation, athletes continue to use, and be caught using, banned performance-enhancing drugs.

We call for enforceable policies concerning the use of cognitive-enhancing drugs to support fairness, protect individuals from coercion and minimize enhancement-related socioeconomic disparities.

Maximum Benefit, Minimum Harm

The new methods of cognitive enhancement are 'disruptive technologies' that could have a profound effect on human life in the twenty-first century. A laissez-faire approach to these methods will leave us at the mercy of powerful market forces that are bound to be unleashed by the promise of increased productivity and competitive advantage. The concerns about safety, freedom and fairness, just reviewed, may well seem less important than the attractions of enhancement, for sellers and users alike.

Motivated by some of the same considerations, Fukuyama[21] has proposed the formation of new laws and regulatory structures to protect against the harms of unrestrained biotechnological enhancement. In contrast, we suggest a policy that is neither laissez-faire nor primarily legislative. We propose to use a variety of scientific, professional, educational and social resources, in addition to legislation, to shape a rational, evidence-based policy informed by a wide array of relevant experts and stake-holders. Specifically, we propose four types of policy mechanism.

The first mechanism is an accelerated programme of research to build a knowledge base concerning the usage, benefits and associated risks of cognitive enhancements. Good policy is based on good information, and there is currently much we do not know about the short- and long-term benefits and risks of the cognitive-enhancement drugs currently being used, and about who is using them and why. For example, what are the patterns of use outside of the United States and outside of college communities? What are the risks of dependence when used for cognitive enhancement? What special risks arise with the enhancement of children's cognition? How big are the effects of currently available enhancers? Do they change 'cognitive style', as well as increasing how quickly and accurately we think? And given that most research so far has focused on simple laboratory tasks, how do they affect cognition in the real world? Do they increase the total knowledge and understanding that students take with them from a course? How do they affect various aspects of occupational performance?

We call for a programme of research into the use and impacts of cognitive-enhancing drugs by healthy individuals.

The second mechanism is the participation of relevant professional organizations in formulating guidelines for their members in relation to cognitive enhancement. Many different professions have a role in dispensing, using or working with people who use cognitive enhancers. By creating policy at the level of professional societies, it will be informed by the expertise of these professionals, and their commitment to the goals of their profession.

One group to which this recommendation applies is physicians, particularly in primary care, paediatrics and psychiatry, who are most likely to be asked for cognitive enhancers. These physicians are sometimes asked to prescribe for enhancement by patients who exaggerate or fabricate symptoms of ADHD, but they also receive frank requests, as when a patient says 'I know I don't meet diagnostic criteria for ADHD, but I sometimes have trouble concentrating and staying organized, and it would help me to have some Ritalin on hand for days when I really need to be on top of things at work.' Physicians who view medicine as devoted to healing will view such prescribing as inappropriate, whereas those who view medicine more broadly as helping patients live better or achieve their goals would be open to considering such a request.[22] There is certainly a precedent for this broader view in certain branches of medicine, including plastic surgery, dermatology, sports medicine and fertility medicine.

Because physicians are the gatekeepers to medications discussed here, society looks to them for guidance on the use of these medications and devices, and guidelines from other professional groups will need to take into account the gatekeepers' policies. For this reason, the responsibilities that physicians bear for the consequences of their decisions are particularly sensitive,

being effectively decisions for all of us. It would therefore be helpful if physicians as a profession gave serious consideration to the ethics of appropriate prescribing of cognitive enhancers, and consulted widely as to how to strike the balance of limits for patient benefit and protection in a liberal democracy. Examples of such limits in other areas of enhancement medicine include the psychological screening of candidates for cosmetic surgery or tubal ligation, and upper bounds on maternal age or number of embryos transferred in fertility treatments. These examples of limits may not be specified by law, but rather by professional standards.

Other professional groups to which this recommendation applies include educators and human-resource professionals. In different ways, each of these professions has responsibility for fostering and evaluating cognitive performance and for advising individuals who are seeking to improve their performance, and some responsibility also for protecting the interests of those in their charge. In contrast to physicians, these professionals have direct conflicts of interest that must be addressed in whatever guidelines they recommend: liberal use of cognitive enhancers would be expected to encourage classroom order and raise standardized measures of student achievement, both of which are in the interests of schools; it would also be expected to promote workplace productivity, which is in the interests of employers.

Educators, academic admissions officers and credentials evaluators are normally responsible for ensuring the validity and integrity of their examinations, and should be tasked with formulating policies concerning enhancement by test-takers. Laws pertaining to testing accommodations for people with disabilities provide a starting point for discussion of some of the key issues, such as how and when enhancements undermine the validity of a test result and the conditions under which enhancement should be disclosed by a test-taker.

The labour and professional organizations of individuals who are candidates for on-the-job cognitive enhancement make up our final category of organization that should formulate enhancement policy. From assembly line workers to surgeons, many different kinds of employee may benefit from enhancement and want access to it, yet they may also need protection from the pressure to enhance.

We call for physicians, educators, regulators and others to collaborate in developing policies that address the use of cognitive-enhancing drugs by healthy individuals.

The third mechanism is education to increase public understanding of cognitive enhancement. This would be provided by physicians, teachers, college health centres and employers, similar to the way that information about nutrition, recreational drugs and other public-health information is now disseminated. Ideally it would also involve discussions of different ways of enhancing cognition, including through adequate sleep, exercise and education, and an examination of the social values and pressures that make cognitive enhancement so attractive and even, seemingly, necessary.

We call for information to be broadly disseminated concerning the risks, benefits and alternatives to pharmaceutical cognitive enhancement.

The fourth mechanism is legislative. Fundamentally new laws or regulatory agencies are not needed. Instead, existing law should be brought into line with emerging social norms and information about safety. Drug law is one of the most controversial areas of law, and it would be naive to expect rapid or revolutionary change in the laws governing the use of controlled substances. Nevertheless, these laws should be adjusted to avoid making felons out of those who seek to use safe cognitive enhancements. And regulatory agencies should allow pharmaceutical companies to market cognitive-enhancing drugs to healthy adults provided they have supplied the necessary regulatory data for safety and efficacy.

We call for careful and limited legislative action to channel cognitive-enhancement technologies into useful paths.

Conclusion

Like all new technologies, cognitive enhancement can be used well or poorly. We should welcome new methods of improving our brain function. In a world in which human work-spans and lifespans are increasing, cognitive enhancement tools – including the pharmacological – will be increasingly useful for improved quality of life and extended work productivity, as well as to stave off normal and pathological age-related cognitive declines.[23] Safe and effective cognitive enhancers will benefit both the individual and society.

But it would also be foolish to ignore problems that such use of drugs could create or exacerbate. With this, as with other technologies, we need to think and work hard to maximize its benefits and minimize its harms.

Note

B.S. consults for a number of pharmaceutical companies and Cambridge Cognition, and holds shares in CeNeS. R.C.K. consults for and has received grants from a number of pharmaceutical companies.

References

1 McCabe, S. E., Knight, J. R., Teter, C. J. and Wechsler, H. *Addiction* 100: 96–106 (2005).

2 Maher, B. *Nature* 452: 674–675 (2008).

3 Sahakian, B. and Morein-Zamir, S. *Nature* 450: 1157–1159 (2007).

4 Weyandt, L. L and DuPaul, G. *J. Atten. Disord.* 10: 9–19 (2006).

5 Minzenberg, M. J. and Carter, C. S. *Neuropsychopharmacology* 33: 1477–1502 (2008).

6 Vastag, B. *J. Am. Med. Assoc.* 291: 167–170 (2004).

7 Turner, D. C. *et al. Psychopharmacology* 165: 260–269 (2003).

8 Grön, G., Kirstein, M., Thielscher, A., Riepe, M. W. and Spitzer, M. *Psychopharmacology* 182: 170–179 (2005).

9 Lynch, G. and Gall C. M. *Trends Neurosci.* 29: 554–562 (2006).

10 Hillman, C. H., Erikson, K. I. and Kramer, A. F. *Nature Rev. Neurosci.* 9: 58–65 (2008).

11 Almeida, S. S. *et al. Nutr. Neurosci.* 5: 311–320 (2002).

12 Boonstra, T. W., Stins, J. F., Daffertshofer, A. and Beek, P. J. *Cell. Mol. Life Sci.* 64: 934–946 (2007).

13 Draganski, B. *et al. Nature* 427: 311–312 (2004).

14 Schlaggar, B. L. and McCandliss, B. D. *Annu. Rev. Neurosci.* 30: 475–503 (2007).

15 Farah, M. J. *et al. Nature Rev. Neurosci.* 5: 421–425 (2004).

16 Kass, L. R. *et al. Beyond Therapy: Biotechnology and the Pursuit of Happiness* (President's Council on Bioethics, 2003); available at http://biotech.law.lsu.edu/research/pbc/reports/beyondtherapy/beyond_therapy_final_report_pcbe.pdf.

17 Harris, J. *Enhancing Evolution: The Ethical Case for Making Better People* (Princeton University Press, 2007).

18 Schacter, D. L. *Seven Sins of Memory* (Houghton Mifflin, 2002).

19 Moreno, J. D. *Mind Wars: Brain Research and National Defense* (Dana Press, 2006).

20 Diller, L. H. *Hastings Cent. Rep.* 26: 12–18 (1996).

21 Fukuyama, F. *Our Posthuman Future: Consequences of the Biotechnology Revolution* (Farrar, Straus & Giroux, 2002).

22 Chatterjee, A. *Neurology* 63: 968–974 (2004).

23 Beddington, J. *et al. Nature* 455: 1057–1060 (2008).

89

Engineering Love

Julian Savulescu and Anders Sandberg

It's easy to forget that we humans are animals too. After all, our relatively large cortices have enabled us to create advanced technology, megacities, nuclear weapons, art, philosophy – in short, a radically different environment to the African savannah we inhabited for most of our history. To top that, we have developed an extraordinarily complex medical system capable of doubling the human lifespan.

Yet in many ways we are stuck with the psychology and drives of our hunter-gatherer ancestors. We are not made for the world and institutions we have created for ourselves, including that of life-long marriage.

Throughout most of our history, people survived for a maximum of 35 years. Staying alive was a full-time job, and most pair-bonds ended with one partner dying. Given this lifespan, at least 50 per cent of mating alliances would have ended within 15 years. This figure is surprisingly close to the current global median duration of marriage, 11 years. It seems unlikely that natural selection equipped us to keep relationships lasting much more than a decade.

The fact is that in the US divorce has surpassed death as the major cause of marital break-up. This has significant consequences, especially for children. As law professor Katherine Spaht of Louisiana State University in Baton Rouge wrote in the *Notre Dame Law Review*: "In comparison with children of intact first marriages, children of divorce suffer in virtually every measure of well-being."

On the other side of the coin, stable, loving relationships are good for us, improving both parent and child welfare through the social support they provide. Most research confirms that successful marriages boost physical and emotional health, self-reported happiness and even longevity. So how can we make up the gap between the health-giving ideal of "till death do us part" and the heartbreaking reality and harms of widespread divorce? And do parents have a special responsibility to do so, given those harms?

One promising route is to consider the advances in neurobiology and see how we might use science. Some of the latest research suggests we could tweak the chemical systems involved to create a longer-lasting love.

Helen Fisher, an evolutionary psychologist at Rutgers University in New Brunswick, New Jersey, argues that human love is constructed on top of a set of basic brain systems for lust, romantic attraction and attachment that evolved in all mammals. Lust promotes mating with any appropriate partner, attraction makes us choose and prefer a particular partner, while attachment allows pairs to cooperate and stay together until parental duties are complete.

Original publication details: Julian Savulescu and Anders Sandberg, "Engineering Love"/"Love Machine: Engineering Lifelong Romance," pp. 28–9 from *New Scientist* 2864. © 2012 Reed Business Information – UK. All rights reserved. Distributed by Tribune Content Agency.

Bioethics: An Anthology, Third Edition. Edited by Helga Kuhse, Udo Schüklenk, and Peter Singer.
© 2016 John Wiley & Sons, Inc. Published 2016 by John Wiley & Sons, Inc.

Human love, of course, is complex. While there is no single "love centre" in the brain, neuroimaging studies of people experiencing romantic love have shown patterns of activation in areas linked to the hormones oxytocin and vasopressin, as well as the brain's reward centres. These findings fit with research into the mating habits of monogamous prairie voles (*Microtus ochrogaster*) and their cousins the polygamous montane voles (*Microtus montanus*).

The receptors for these hormones are distributed differently in monogamous and polygamous voles. Infusing oxytocin into the brains of female prairie voles and vasopressin into the brains of males encouraged pair-bonding activity such as spending time together exclusively and driving away sexual competitors, even in the absence of mating, while the hormones did not affect the non-monogamous montane voles.

In one striking experiment, researchers introduced a vasopressin receptor gene from the faithful prairie vole into the brain of its promiscuous cousin. The modified voles became monogamous (*Neuroscience*, vol 125, p 35).

This gene controls a part of the brain's reward centre. In humans, differences in this gene have been associated with changes in the stability of relationships and in partner satisfaction. If human and vole brains share similar wiring, as research suggests, we might be able to modify our mating behaviour biologically as well.

Tapping into the power of oxytocin could prove useful in other ways. Oxytocin is released during physical contact such as touching, massage or sex, and is involved in nursing behaviour, trust and "mind-reading" – our attempts to work out what our partners think and feel – as well as in counteracting stress and fear. Taking oxytocin in the form of a nasal spray would promote unstressed, trusting behaviours that might reduce the negative feedback in some relationships and help strengthen the positive sides. It could also be used alongside marital therapy to open up communication and encourage bonding.

What of testosterone, the hormone that helps to control sexual desire in men and women? People who have been given the hormone report an increase in sexual thoughts, activity and satisfaction – though not in romantic passion or attachment. But since levels of sexual interest in men and women diverge as a relationship continues, and since this disparity strongly affects its stability, synchronising levels of desire by altering levels of testosterone might help.

It also looks likely that the strong dopamine and oxytocin signals elicited during the early romantic phase of a relationship and during sex help to imprint details of the partner and create positive emotional associations to the relationship. So it may be possible to trigger this imprinting by giving the right drugs while someone is close to their partner.

The stick rather than the carrot in the maintenance of a pair bond is that love is linked to fear and the sadness of separation. This may be due to corticotropin releasing hormone. Carefully boosting it or, rather, the processes behind the "stick" effect, might be useful as a deterrent from straying.

So what of the future? We already modify sexual behaviour, for example, by offering paedophiles chemical castration to squash their sex drive. And given the growing knowledge of the cognitive neuroscience of love and its chemical underpinning, we should expect far more precise interventions to become available soon.

Whether we should do any of this is another matter. Love and relationships are among the most potent contributors to our collective well-being so there are strong moral reasons to make relationships better. But the use of neuroenhancements leads to many questions. Will they render relationships inauthentic, the product of pharmaceutical design? Could we become addicted to love? And could such drugs and chemicals be used to imprison people in bad relationships? So should we change our institutions or stick with modifying our behaviour using counselling and therapy instead?

On balance, no. We argue we need all the help we can get to liberate ourselves from evolution. It has not created us to be happy, but offers enough transient happiness to keep us alive and reproducing. Yet from our human perspective, happiness and flourishing are primary goals. In a conflict between human values and evolution we might well ignore what evolution promotes. "Love drugs" are not a silver bullet, but in a regulated, professional environment and with an informed public, they could help overcome some of biology's obstacles. Why not use all the strategies we can to give us the best chance of the best life?

Index

Note: page numbers in italics refer to figures or tables

Bioethics: An Anthology, Third Edition. Edited by Helga Kuhse, Udo Schüklenk, and Peter Singer.
© 2016 John Wiley & Sons, Inc. Published 2016 by John Wiley & Sons, Inc.